BARRON'S

GUIDE TO LAW SCHOOLS

19TH EDITION

Introduction by
Gary A. Munneke
Professor of Law
Pace University School of Law

© Copyright 2010, 2008, 2006, 2004, 2002, 2000, 1998, 1996, 1994, 1992, 1990, 1988, 1986, 1984,
1983, 1980, 1978, 1970, 1967 by Barron's Educational Series, Inc.

The model LSAT Exam contained in this book is reprinted from *Barron's
LSAT*, by Jerry Bobrow, rev. by Bernard V. Zandy, 2009. Chapter 9, "What Should I Expect in Law School?"
contained in this book is reprinted from *Barron's How to Succeed in Law School*,
by Gary A. Munneke, 2010.

All inquiries should be addressed to:
Barron's Educational Series, Inc.
250 Wireless Boulevard
Hauppauge, New York 11788
www.barronseduc.com

Every effort has been made to ensure the accuracy
of the information in this book. Because costs and
statistics change from year to year, prospective
students should contact the schools to verify this
information.

ISBN-13: 978-0-7641-4522-3
ISBN-10: 0-7641-4522-3

International Standard Serial Number 1062-2489

PRINTED IN THE UNITED STATES OF AMERICA
987654321

Contents

Abbreviations and Degrees

ABBREVIATIONS

AALL—American Association of Law Libraries

AALS—Association of American Law Schools

ABA—American Bar Association

ALAS—Auxiliary Loans to Assist Students

CCRAA—College Cost Reduction and Access Act

CLEO—Council on Legal Education Opportunity

CPPVE—Council for Private Postsecondary and Vocational Education

CRS—Candidate Referral Service

CSS—College Scholarship Service

CWSP—College Work-Study Program

FAFSA—Free Application for Federal Student Aid

FFS—Family Financial Statement

FWS—Federal Work Study Program

GAPSFAS—Graduate and Professional School Financial Aid Service

GBBE—Georgia Board of Bar Examiners

GPA—Grade Point Average

GSL—Guaranteed Student Loans

LSAT—Law School Admission Test

LSDAS—Law School Data Assembly Service

MBR—Massachusetts Board of Regents

MSA—Middle States Association

NALP—National Association for Law Placement

NCA—North Central Association of Colleges and Schools

NDSL—National Direct Student Loan

NEASC—New England Association of Schools and Colleges

NWCCU—Northwest Commission on Colleges and Universities

SAAC—Student Aid Application for California

SACS—Southern Association of Colleges and Schools

SBC—State Bar of California

WASC—Western Association of Schools and Colleges

UGPA—Undergraduate Grade Point Average

DEGREES

D.C.L.—Doctor of Civil Law

D.C.L.—Doctor of Comparative Law

J.D.—Doctor of Jurisprudence

J.D./M.B.A.—Juris Doctor/Master of Business Administration

J.M.—Master of Jurisprudence

J.S.D.—Doctor of the Science of Law

J.S.M.—Master of the Science of Law

LL.B.—Bachelor of Laws

LL.M.—Master of Laws

M.A.—Master of Arts

M.Acc.—Master of Accountancy

M.A.L.I.R.—Master of Arts in Labor and Industrial Relations

M.A.P.A.—Master of Arts in Public Administration

M.A.S.—Master of Accounting Science

M.B.A.—Master of Business Administration

M.B.T.—Master of Business Taxation

M.C.J.—Master of Criminal Justice

M.C.L.—Master of Comparative Law

M.C.P.—Master of City Planning

M.C.P.—Master of Community Planning

M.C.R.P.—Master of City and Regional Planning

M.D.—Doctor of Medicine

M.H.A.—Master of Health Administration

M.I.L.R.—Master of Industrial and Labor Relations

M.L.S.—Master of Legal Studies

M.L.S.—Master of Library Science

M.L. & T.—Master of Law and Taxation

M.M.—Master of Management

M.O.B.—Master of Organizational Behavior

M.P.A.—Master of Public Administration

M.P.H.—Master of Public Health

M.P.P.A.—Master of Public Policy Administration

M.P.P.M.—Master of Public and Private Management

M.R.P.—Master of Regional Planning

M.S.—Master of Science

M.S.L.—Master of Studies in Law

M.S.S.A.—Master of Science in Social Administration

M.S.W.—Master of Social Work

M.U.P.—Master of Urban Planning

M.U.R.P.—Master of Urban and Regional Planning

Ph.D.—Doctor of Philosophy

S.J.D.—Doctor of the Science of Law

PART I

Choosing a Law School

CHAPTER 1

Introduction to Law Schools

Legal problems are pervasive in modern society. Virtually every day, news stories track legal issues, from laws that affect the way we live, to notorious cases that intrigue and even disgust us. Dramatizations of legal disputes and high-profile prosecutions capture the imaginations of viewers in a cycle of never-ending pathos. We live, in short, in a world of law and lawyers.

It is easy to forget that law is an ancient and traditional profession. One can go back to Greek and Roman times to find records of a class of people who represented other citizens before judicial tribunals. Our American brand of legal representation emerged in the wake of the Norman Conquest of England in 1066, when Anglo-Saxon-speaking peasants needed a voice in the French-speaking Norman courts. For a thousand years, lawyers in the British Commonwealth of nations and in the United States have continued the tradition of standing up for the accused and injured, and guiding them through the arcane labyrinth of the judicial system.

Conflict is at the heart of legal problems. If we did not have disputes, we would not need a legal system. But we do. Over the centuries, various utopian theorists have sought to create societies where people got along, where conflict was eliminated, and where a system for resolving disputes was unnecessary. These efforts have been uniformly unsuccessful, and in the absence of utopia, lawyers and a legal system remain essential to civilized society.

Lawyers and the Rule of Law are the last bastion of order as an alternative to anarchy and chaos. The law is nothing less than a substitute for violence as a means of resolving disputes. In a world where terrorism, ethnic cleansing, genocide, drive-by shootings, and domestic violence are all too commonplace, lawyers provide access to a peaceful option for resolving problems. Ironically, the oft-quoted Shakespearean line, "The first thing we do, we'll kill all the lawyers," was spoken by a character, Jack the Butcher, who was an avowed anarchist determined to overthrow the King. Without lawyers, he reasoned, his aims were more easily attainable.

Critics of lawyers and the judicial system complain about a litany of injustices, procedural loopholes, outrageous damage awards, and disparate treatment of the rich and poor. Yet, even recognizing that the legal system has room for improvement, few people are willing to scrap an institution that keeps the barbarians, like Jack the Butcher, at bay.

No corner of the globe is immune from breakdowns in the Rule of Law, which simply put is societal reliance on the orderly and peaceful resolution of disputes, in contrast to violence and mayhem as the dominant form of problem solving. In December of 2007, President Pervez Musharraf of Pakistan suspended the nation's constitution, curtailed civil rights, arrested perceived opponents, and dismissed the Supreme Court when justices would not sign an oath of personal loyalty to him. Spearheaded by Pakistani lawyers, members of the legal profession throughout the world protested these flagrant departures from the Rule of Law.

Lawyers are sometimes accused of greed for charging exorbitant fees for their services. The truth is that lawyers are compensated well for their work, but lawyer incomes are not out of line with incomes for other professionals with comparable education and training.

Lawyers are encouraged to provide a portion of their legal work to persons who cannot afford the fees, and many, if not all, lawyers take this admonition seriously. Other lawyers volunteer their time in community service to legislative bodies, councils, boards, and commissions. This tradition of public service goes back to the earliest days of the profession. A small percentage of lawyers earn significantly more than the average $150,000 for all lawyers, and many, including most younger lawyers, earn less. News stories reporting that law graduates earn as much as $160,000, or more with bonuses, refer to the highest starting salaries, not the lower or even mid-range rates. The economic downturn of 2008–09 produced a decline in the income of lawyers in every segment of the profession, producing layoffs among both associates and partners in law firms. As the economy recovered in

2010, the situation is not as dire, but it is apparent that lawyers are subject to depredations of the economy, just like the rest of society.

As you read the ensuing chapters, keep in mind that you are not just choosing an advanced degree program that will land you a job and pay your bills; you are assuming a unique professional identity and following a long line of predecessors in service to society. In all likelihood, you will earn a good living as a lawyer, but more importantly, you will do some good for society along the way. You are choosing a career whose practitioners are proud of what they do and welcome recent law school graduates who bring enthusiasm, idealism, and energy to the practice of law.

by Gary A. Munneke, Professor of Law at Pace University School of Law, where he teaches Torts, Professional Responsibility and Law Practice Management. Prior to joining the Pace faculty in 1988, he served on the faculty of the Widener University School of Law, and as Assistant Dean at the University of Texas School of Law. Professor Munneke is the author of 20 books and numerous articles about current issues in the legal profession. His other books provide information about choosing law as a career (*Careers in Law* [2003] and *Opportunities in Law Careers* [2002], VGM Career Horizons, Lincolnwood, IL), what to do after you enter law school (*How to Succeed in Law School,* Barron's, NY, 2008), and what to do after you graduate from law school (*The Legal Career Guide: From Law Student to Lawyer* [2002], and *Nonlegal Careers for Lawyers* [2006], American Bar Association, Chicago). In addition, he has lectured extensively on these topics. Professor Munneke is Past Chair of the American Bar Association Law Practice Management Section and a former member of the ABA Board of Governors. He has served as President and Research Chair of the National Association for Law Placement as well as Chair of the ABA Standing Committee on Professional Utilizational and Career Development. Professor Munneke received his J.D. from the University of Texas Law School in 1973 and is licensed to practice law in Texas and Pennsylvania. He is a Fellow of the American Bar Foundation, and the College of Law Practice Management.

CHAPTER 2

Should I Go to Law School?

You picked up this book because you have given some thought to the question of going to law school, or else someone you know is thinking about going to law school. Each year, more than 40,000 students in the United States begin the long and arduous journey associated with law school. There was a time when large numbers of attorneys received their legal training by studying law books at home until they were knowledgeable enough to pass an oral examination to become a lawyer. Today, almost all lawyers attend a law school before taking a standardized written bar exam. The educational process takes three or four years, depending on whether the curriculum is full or part time, and whether it is obtained at one of the law schools approved by the American Bar Association, or a handful of other law schools approved in the state where they are located. Chapters 15–16 of this Guide provide detailed descriptions of these law schools, in order to help you decide which school is right for you. Chapter 7 offers a variety of thoughts on how to make this decision.

Law school is not for everyone. Some individuals cannot cope with the intellectual demands, while others find the psychological stress associated with the study and practice of law to be suffocating. Many bright and ambitious people do not succeed at law because they find other activities more rewarding and challenging. However, many college graduates will find law school to be the most stimulating experience of their lives.

There is a great deal of popular mythology about law school and the legal profession. This book attempts to get past much of the confusing rhetoric facing individuals contemplating a legal education. *Barron's Guide to Law Schools* is full of factual information about law schools and no nonsense advice on the application process, the LSAT, and the decision-making process. The rest of this chapter explains why the decision to go to law school is so complex and gives reasons why people make this important decision.

A COMPLEX DECISION

The process of choosing a law school is a complex one, and there are no easy answers along the way. Accordingly, this Guide should be viewed more as a road map to your destination than as the answer to all your questions. A road map may help you find your way, but it cannot replace the experience of getting there yourself.

This book focuses on the choices that each law school applicant must make during the admission process. As you are considering whether and where to attend law school, you will spend considerable energy weighing various options. The fact that you will feel confused (and at times overwhelmed) is normal. Regardless of your background, you cannot escape facing tough decisions that will affect the rest of your life. If you struggle with the choices, it is a sign that you appreciate the importance of the process.

The two basic problems (Which school is best for you? and Can you get admitted?) are the same for every applicant. Regardless of whether you have many choices or a single acceptance, so much rests on your decision that it is impossible not to feel the pressure. Most important decisions in life are fraught with stress; this is no exception.

The publisher and authors of this text have no ax to grind and no personal investment in whether you attend law school or not. Our aim is to provide objective information that will help you make an informed choice about a tough decision. We encourage you to listen to other voices who have opinions on this subject. There certainly is room for divergence of viewpoints on many of the subjects addressed here. One person will tell you that you have to be a lawyer, and the next person will tell you that nobody should be a lawyer. In the end, only you can decide on your best course of action. The best way to assure that your final decision will be the right one for you is to become fully informed on all the issues.

WHY GO TO LAW SCHOOL?

You might choose to go to law school for a number of different reasons. In fact, many lawyers were influenced by a variety of factors:

• They wanted the prestige, power, and panache that a degree in law provides;

• They wanted a professional career in which they could make enough money to establish and maintain a comfortable lifestyle;

• They wanted to change the world in order to make it a little better than it was when they arrived;

• They wanted to pursue a long family tradition;

• They wanted to do something different from anyone else in their family;

• They took an aptitude test during college and the career counselor said that they should become a lawyer; or

• They went to a prelaw association meeting as a favor to a roommate, got elected president, and couldn't back out (my personal reason for attending law school).

Everyone arrives at the law school door for different reasons. Some of these are more valid than others. Here are a few of the wrong reasons to go to law school:

• *Don't* go to law school because other people expect you to. Spouses, family, friends, and advisors seem perpetually willing to push their loved one, associate, or advisee in this direction. While these people almost always want what is best for you, their personal motives are inevitably more complex. Look at the source and weigh the advice accordingly. Ask yourself what these other people have to gain (or lose) if you go to law school. What will they contribute along the way to your success (or failure)? Can you listen to these voices and still make your own decision?

• *Don't* go to law school because of what you see on television or read in the newspapers about lawyers. Media coverage of high profile cases such as the David Goldman case, where an American father spent five years regaining custody from his former wife's new husband's family in Brazil, may present a skewed picture of what practicing law is all about. Popular television shows such as *Boston Legal* inevitably portray lawyers in a very different light than most lawyers experience in their daily lives. Lawyers are neither as rich, good-looking, and fast-talking, or as weasly, manipulative, and grasping as the stereotypes suggest. Most practicing lawyers will tell you that these images have little in common with their real lives. We smile bemusedly at the antics of the characters on popular television series, but in our hearts we know that they could never exist in the flesh.

If you want to discover how real-life lawyers work and live, ask them. Visit a law firm, or better yet, get a job in one. Look for lawyers outside the world of work; find out about lawyers in their neighborhoods and communities. Investigate how they live and play when they go home at night. You will probably discover that lawyers are a well-educated and intense (but diverse) lot, who give as much to the community as they do to their jobs.

• *Don't* go to law school because you can't figure out what to do with your life, or because you can't find anything else that interests you. Law school is not the place to go to find yourself. Legal education is no place to buy more time to make a decision because you just can't bear to face the real world.

Whatever other motives may influence your decision to attend law school, make certain that a major consideration is your genuine desire to study law. If you have doubts about whether you want to *study* law (as opposed to *practice* law), do something else for a year or two. Work in a law firm, or join the Peace Corps. If you find you can't get the idea of law school out of your mind, that should be a sign to you. If, on the other hand, you forget about it, forget about it.

These admonitions may fall on deaf ears, but at least you've been warned. Many people find law school to be the most interesting, intellectually stimulating, and challenging experience of their educational lives (despite its many aggravations); others hate it almost more than they can bear. If you find that you fit into the latter group and not the former, don't put yourself through the misery of sitting through three years or more of law school classes.

The question of whether to go to law school is sometimes confused with the question of which law school to choose. A person may thrive at one law school and wither at another. To the extent that the decision to attend law school is influenced by the choice of which law school to attend, applicants need to look closely at both sets of consideration. The issue of which law school to attend is covered in greater depth in Chapter 7, but for now it is sufficient to link these two areas of inquiry.

CHAPTER 3

Where Can I Find Information About Law School?

There is both a wealth and paucity of information about law schools. Books and guides of various sorts abound on the shelves of libraries and bookstores. A considerable amount of information is available in electronic formats. Information in the form of advice from well-meaning advisors is also easily accessible. If you are thinking about attending law school, the one thing you will find in abundance is advice. What is often in short supply is any way to tell whether the advice you get is good or not. This informational paradox was apparent to the developers of this Guide. The result is a Guide that is easy to use and understand, containing up-to-the-minute information about law schools.

In addition to the *Guide to Law Schools,* Barron's offers other excellent publications, two of which are excerpted in this book. They are *Barron's LSAT* by Jerry Bobrow and revised by Bernard V. Zandy, an in-depth preparation guide for the law school admission test, and *How to Succeed in Law School* by Professor Gary A. Munneke, which describes what law school will be like and what students need to do to maximize their performance and opportunities. A smaller version of the LSAT book, *Pass Key to the LSAT*, is also available. These books should provide you with enough information to tackle the law school challenge. Many readers, however, will want more. For those with the time, energy, and inclination, the following paragraphs discuss many other sources of information.

Web Sites

The Internet makes it easy to find information about law schools, legal education, and the practice of law (see Chart, page 9). Virtually all law schools provide web sites not only for their own students, but also for prospective students, alumni, and the public. These web sites are easily accessible to anyone with a computer and a browser. Most law schools, as well as Law Services, permit students to apply on line, and many applicants are more comfortable with the on line application format than the traditional mail-in option.

The problem with online research is that often there is too much information, rather than too little. Locating the specific information you want can require persistence. When looking at law school sites, you may be able to find in-depth profiles of faculty members, courses, activities, and services beyond the superficial treatment in catalogs and other marketing pieces published by the school. Remember, however, that many law schools are sophisticated enough to create their web sites as marketing tools, and like other promotional materials, they provide you with a picture of the institution that is carefully painted.

What everyone is looking for is unbiased comparative information, isn't it? Much of the information you need appears right here in *Barron's Guide to Law Schools*, in a format that is easy to use and understand. There are a number of electronic resources that contain interesting compilations of data and commentary that go beyond the scope of this book. By using Google, Bing, or some other search engine, you might be able to drill down through layers of information to discover facts that will help you in making your decision. No matter how much time you spend on the Internet, however, your final decision may come down to intangible factors, such as how you feel about a law school through dealing with representatives or visiting in person.

Prelaw Advisors

Most colleges and universities designate one or more professors as prelaw advisors. Students thinking about law school are routinely fun-

Web Site	Sponsor	Subject Matter
http://lsac.org	Law School Admissions Council	Provides information on preparing for law school, choosing a law school, taking the LSAT, applying to law school, and financing law school.
www.abanet.org/home.cfm	American Bar Association	A detailed website offering information on everything you always wanted to know about law and the legal profession
www.abanet.org/legaled/ home.html	ABA Section of Legal Education and Admissions to the Bar	
www.abanet.org/cpr/	ABA Center for Professional Responsibility	
www.abanet.org/lsd/home.html	ABA Law Student Division	
www.abanet.org/journal/ redesign/home.html	*ABA Journal*	
www.alm.com/	American Lawyer Media	An expansive online source for lawyers, law managers, and in-house counsels regarding news, trends, and market intelligence
www.americanlawyer.com/	*American Lawyer Magazine*	An online magazine that features articles on the legal community both nationally and internationally and discusses lawyers and their work
www.law.com/index.shtml	*Law.com* information services	Offers information regarding recent changes in the law and reports regional and local news
http://nalp.org/	National Association for Law Placement	A website designed to promote legal careers by posting opportunities
http://www.lawschool.com	*Lawschool.com*	Provides law school ranks, information on moot court, law review, and bar exam information on each US state
http://grad-schools.usnews. rankingsandreview.com/ best-graduate-schools/ top-law-schools/rankings	*U. S. News & World Report*	Provides annual law school ranks and an A–Z law school directory
http://jurist.law.pitt.edu/ admissions.htm	JURIST	Provides prelaw guidance and explains the ins and outs of law school
http://www.ilrg.com/	PublicLegal, a product of the Internet Legal Research Group (ILRG)	A comprehensive one-stop-shopping resource of information concerning law and the legal profession that offers a categorized index of more than 4000 links

neled to these professors and administrators for guidance. The question of prelaw school education is addressed in more depth in the next chapter: The comments here are aimed more at assessing the pros and cons of utilizing a prelaw advisor at school.

First of all, it is very difficult to make generalizations about the type of individuals who become prelaw advisors or the quality of advice they dispense. Prelaw advisors may come from almost any discipline, although it seems that a high percentage are political science professors. Many, but certainly not all, possess a law degree themselves, in addition to professional credentials in their teaching field. They may be young professors, barely out of school themselves, or wizened veterans who have been advising generations of prospective law students.

Prelaw advisors often come to the table with a distinct set of biases in favor of or against certain law schools, approaches to the application process, and the qualities that are needed to succeed in law school. Keep in mind, however, that the more definite the advisor is in his or her opinions, the more likely it is that there are differing points of view that make as much sense. Some prelaw advisors diligently collect information about law schools, such as law school catalogs or information about former students who have attended certain law schools. Other advisors may have little in the way of written materials, but willingly commit many hours to give to those who want to talk.

Whether or not you should take the advice of your prelaw advisor is a very personal question. Just as it is with doctors, dentists, psychologists, and other professionals, chemistry is important. You need to find someone with whom it is easy to carry on a conversation, someone whose opinion you value, and someone who strikes you as well-informed and objective. The same prelaw advisor might hit it off with one student and turn off another. For this reason, it makes sense to get in to talk to your prelaw advisor as early as you can during your college career. If you have already graduated from college, you may be able to contact the prelaw advisor at your college anyway. And if you are in grad school, you may be able to talk to the prelaw advisor there.

If you are not happy with the advice you get, or not comfortable talking to the advisor, you have an opportunity to find another person to fill this role. You may find that advice from a trusted faculty mentor, such as a club sponsor, academic advisor, or favorite teacher who may work just as well for you as the school's official prelaw advisor. While this mentor may not be as well-versed on law schools as the regular prelaw advisor, the benefit that you will derive from being able to speak openly and candidly can be invaluable.

Prelaw Associations

Many colleges and universities have a prelaw association or club committed to supporting prelaw students at those institutions. These student organizations may sponsor programs, collect information, and at universities affiliated with a law school, provide opportunities for direct contact with law school faculty and students.

Career Counselors

At some institutions, the office of career services provides information and advice about law schools and legal education. Because career counselors have training and experience in helping people to make career decisions, they may be able to assist you in ways that a faculty member could not. Some career services offices offer testing programs, which attempt to identify things like work values, personality types, and vocational interests. These tests are often validated by comparison to control groups of individuals from particular professions. Thus, you can determine whether your personality type or professional values are similar to the values or personality of other people who have chosen to go into law. Such tests can lay a trap for those who do not interpret the results with a critical eye. It is one thing to say that you are like other members of a group; it does not necessarily follow that you have to have those traits in order to be successful in a given field. In reality, successful lawyers are as diverse in terms of personality and values as the general population, and while it may be possible to identify characteristics common among typical lawyers, it is not uncommon to find lawyers who do not fit into the mold. For example, tests may tell you that you should be a trial lawyer, but if you hate trial work, the test results do not matter.

Other Advisors

It is not necessary to limit the universe of potential advisors to educational settings. Well-informed family members, work supervisors, friends, and business associates all may have qualities that make them good advisors for you. If you know a practicing lawyer personally, you can seek guidance from him or her. In fact, nowhere is it written that you can seek advice from only one person. You may want to take a sampling of opinions from various people and reach your own decisions.

Law School Career Days

One of the best ways to get information about law schools is to attend a law school career day. These events come in a variety of forms, from those sponsored by a single university, attended by as few as a single law school, to those sponsored by Law Services in major U.S. cities, sometimes attended by more than one hundred law schools. Law schools typically send representatives to these events, in areas where they hope to draw their students. Individual law schools may schedule a day of interviews through the career service office, or the prelaw advisor. Several colleges may join together to schedule panels or career fairs of law school representatives. The Law Services

CHECKLIST FOR CAMPUS VISIT

☐ Were the arrangements professionally and accurately made?

☐ Was it easy to get to the campus for your visit?
  ☐ Directions
  ☐ Traffic (for automobile visitors)
  ☐ Public transportation

☐ Were the law school staff who greeted you friendly and accommodating?

☐ Did you visit one or more class(es) during your visit?
  ☐ Did you enjoy the class?
  ☐ Did the students in the class seem to enjoy the class?
  ☐ Did the professor seem interesting?

☐ Did you attend a formal program on campus?
  ☐ Did speakers provide useful information about the law school?
  ☐ Did you gain insights into the application/ admission process?
  ☐ Did you have an opportunity to talk to faculty and students?

☐ Did you take a tour of the law school facilities?
  ☐ Were the facilities clean, attractive, and appealing?
  ☐ Did there appear to be enough space for the programs of the law school?

☐ Did the law school share space with other university activities?

☐ Did you check out the adequacy of parking, housing, food services?

☐ Were the facilities adequate to accommodate your physical disabilities?

☐ Were there places for students to study, meet in small groups, and talk?

☐ What kind of technology support does the law school provide?

☐ Did the people you encountered on the tour seem to be having a good time?

☐ Did you have a formal interview while you were on campus?

☐ Was the interview for information purposes only?

☐ Was the interview a part of the admission process?

☐ Were the interviewers faculty, staff, students, alumni, or a combination?

☐ Were the evaluation criteria used in the interview explained to you?

☐ Did you have a chance to make your case for admission?

annual law forums are regional fairs in major cities attended by a large number of American law schools (see page 14 for a listing of the fall 2010 fairs). Law school forums allow you to visit a number of law school representatives in person and in close proximity for easy comparison. The law schools usually bring catalogs, applications, and other literature for you to take, thus providing a quick way to receive materials.

Law School Visits

If you have narrowed the number of law schools to which you plan to apply to two or three, it may make sense for you to visit the schools in person. When you applied to undergraduate schools, you probably visited campuses before you made your final choice. What you learned about the setting, ambiance, and facilities undoubtedly contributed to your final decision. It is no different with the decision to attend law school. Some law schools encourage on-site visits through open houses on specific dates. Most law schools, however, are happy to arrange for a campus visit at any time. It makes sense to try to schedule your visit at a time when classes are in session in order to get a sense of what law school life is like at the school. You may be able to visit classes, talk to students and faculty, and meet with officials about such matters as applications and financial aid. See the checklist above to guide you on campus visits.

Interviews

Some law schools incorporate personal interviews into the application process. A few schools utilize interviews as a formal part of the selection process. Some other schools encourage, but do not require, applicants to interview with a representative of the law school as a means of gathering more data about the candidate. An interview is typically a one- or two-on-one process, not unlike a job interview, as distinguished from more informal visits with law school personnel in conjunction with law forums or campus visits. Find out if the schools to which you plan to apply provide for interviews. If they do, decide whether you want to avail yourself of this opportunity. Most applicants welcome the chance to sell themselves directly to the school.

Law-Related Jobs

Part of the information gathering process may include finding out more about what lawyers do. If you grew up in a family of one or more lawyers, you probably learned a great deal about the legal profession and the practice of law through contact with these family members. You probably learned more about lawyers than you realized at the time. The fact that you remain interested in a career in law suggests that something about the lifestyle of a lawyer appeals to you.

If you did not grow up in such a family, or if you did and you want to learn more, one of the best ways to find out whether you want to practice law is to work in a law firm or other legal organization. Even if you visited a law office as part of a career day in high school or college, nothing will give you a first-hand view of legal work better than a job in the law. You might be surprised at how many opportunities there are in the law firms, corporate law departments, government law departments, district attorney and public defender offices, and public service organizations. These organizations include, in addition to the legal staff, a support staff of people who have not attended law school, such as legal assistants, legal secretaries, and file clerks.

The jobs may be full time or part time, depending on the needs of the employer, and the pay may vary widely depending on the qualifications for the job and the marketplace for workers in the area. You may be able to find a job with a law firm or other employer for the summer, or as part of a school-sponsored internship. If you are already working for a company, you may be able to arrange for temporary assignments with the company's legal department, or to take on other law-related tasks.

The greatest number of opportunities in the legal marketplace is probably for permanent support staff positions. For paralegals or legal secretaries, training or experience in the field will be helpful; however, there are no state or national standards for these positions such as there would be for becoming a lawyer in the organization. Some firms try to hire highly intelligent and motivated people, who possess basic skills such as keyboarding, word processing, and other computer skills, and provide the training to these individuals themselves.

Over the past two decades, law firms have delegated more work to staff in order to devote themselves more fully to the practice of law. This phenomenon has been most pronounced in larger law firms, but has slowly filtered down to smaller organizations. Here are a few of the areas where prelaw students may find employment, which many continue throughout law school. The common though not exclusive undergraduate and graduate degree programs are listed in parentheses.

- General management (BBA, MBA)
- Librarian (MLS)
- Information Technology (computer sciences)
- Human Resources (BBA, MBA)
- Accounting, Finance (accounting, CPA)
- Paralegal work (paralegal studies, bachelor's degree)
- Investigation, security (criminal justice)
- Economic modeling, research (economics)
- Jury selection (psychology, social science)
- Marketing (BBA, MBA)
- Writing, editing (English, journalism)
- Translation (foreign languages)
- Secretarial (secretarial training or experience)

It is not uncommon for law students today to have spent two to three years, or more, working in a law firm or other organization, before coming to law school. Many law students continue these prelegal positions while they go to law school, either cutting back on their work hours to part-time status while they are in school, or continuing to work full time, but attending law school part time in the evening. One potential advantage of working in a law-related position before or during law school, is that there may be an increased probability of obtaining employment with that organization as a lawyer after graduation. Even more important, however, employment in a legal setting may help you to decide whether you want to work in law at all. You will see up close that the practice of law is very different from the images of legal work garnered from books, television, and second-hand anecdotal information.

LITERATURE AND THE MEDIA

Lawyers are portrayed in a variety of lights in literature and the media. Many of the images of lawyers in television and film, as well as in books and the news, are exaggerated, distorted, and stereotypical. It is very difficult to capture the essence of legal work through a literary or cinematic eye. Notwithstanding this limitation, the pervasiveness of media images of lawyers makes it inevitable that we are influenced by these images. Even lawyers themselves are sometimes influenced by their own media hype.

There are a number of excellent books and films on the legal profession, and regular viewing of court proceedings and discussion of legal issues on CNN, C-SPAN, and other news channels can be highly illuminating. Here are a few specific recommendations on books and films:

- *The Bramble Bush* by Carl Llewellyn, read by generations of law students.

- *The Paper Chase* by John Jay Osborne. The book (or the movie with John Houseman) presents a fictitious first year with the quintessential law professor who does intellectual battle with his less-than-equal student nemesis, Hart.

- *One L* by Scott Turow. Probably a more realistic picture of law school, this book is based on Turow's school notes about the first year of law school.

- *A Civil Action* by Jonathan Harr is a riveting account of the colossal battle between a brash, aggressive plaintiff lawyer and an icon of the Boston legal establishment in an environmental pollution case in the town of Woburn, Massachusetts—a true story.

- *Michael Clayton.* The sad story of a lawyer (George Clooney) who was passed over for partnership in a big law firm and carries out all the mundane grunt work and unseemly tasks for his more successful counterparts.

- *Inherit the Wind.* The book, the play, and the movie present a fictionalization of the Scopes Monkey Trial, in which a Tennessee science teacher was prosecuted for teaching evolution. The lawyers in the real case were three-time presidential candidate William Jennings Bryan and famed defense counsel Clarence Darrow.

- *A Few Good Men,* with Jack Nicholson and Tom Cruise, tells the story of military justice, after a commander's rigid discipline leads to a soldier's death. We all know that the villain doesn't usually break down on the stand in real life, but Jack makes us believe anyway.

- *Gideon's Trumpet* by Anthony Lewis. If ever you wanted a reason to become a lawyer, this is it: indigent man fights to the Supreme Court for the right to be represented by counsel.

- *To Kill a Mockingbird* by Harper Lee, or the movie with Gregory Peck. A classic in print or film: small town Southern lawyer stands for courage and dignity as he faces the challenges of practicing law, while standing up for truth, justice, and the American way of life.

- Anything by John Grisham. Sure, the plots are far-fetched, and the dialogue hardly Hemingway, but each one of Grisham's tales provides great imagery on different practice settings from personal injury practice (*The Rainmaker*), to elite corporate work (*The Firm*), to high profile criminal cases (*A Time to Kill*).

- *Kramer v. Kramer.* Dustin Hoffman and Meryl Streep fight for custody in a courtroom drama that demonstrates how justice isn't always easy to find in the courtroom.

- *Erin Brockovich.* A feisty paralegal played by Julia Roberts helps expose Pacific Gas & Electric pollution coverup. Based on a true story.

The list could go on and on, because lawyers, trials, and the stories of people who encounter the justice system provide such fertile soil for intriguing plotlines. Whether the source is books, movies, or TV (depictions of lawyers on the small screen are legion), it is possible to learn about the work of lawyers by watching how they are depicted in various media. What you learn may not dictate your choices about law school, but it may provide useful clues to help you answer your questions. See also Richard Burst, "The 25 Greatest Legal Movies," ABA Journal (August 2008).

A Variety of Sources

It should be apparent to you that in order for you to gather information about law schools, you need to evaluate information from a variety of sources in light of your own aspirations. The decision to attend law school may involve the outlay of one hundred thousand dollars, or more, in direct costs, and require you to forego other income for a period of three or four years. For this reason, the decision to go to law school should not be made lightly. This chapter has provided an overview of the primary sources of information available to help you make this decision. The rest is up to you.

Law School Forums in 2010*

If you're considering law school, come to a Law School Forum. Free admission. Registration is easy. Register at the forum or avoid the wait and register online at *www.LSAC.org*.

- talk with representatives of LSAC-member law schools from across the United States and Canada;
- obtain admission materials, catalogs, and financial aid information;
- view video programs about the law school admission process, legal education and careers, minority perspectives on legal education, and gay and lesbian issues;
- attend informational sessions on the law school admission process, financing a legal education, and issues of importance to minority applicants; and
- review LSAC publications, videos, software, and LSAT® preparation materials.

Miami, FL	September 11, 2010 Hyatt Regency Miami
Los Angeles, CA	September 25, 2010 Millennium Biltmore Hotel Los Angeles
New York, NY	October 1–2, 2010 Hilton New York
Boston, MA	October 16, 2010 Renaissance Boston Waterfront Hotel
Chicago, IL	October 30, 2010 Hyatt Regency McCormick Place
Atlanta, GA	November 6, 2010 Hyatt Regency Atlanta
Houston, TX	November 20, 2010 JW Marriott Houston

For further information contact: *LSACinfo@lsac.org*

*Check for updated dates and locations for 2010 and beyond, as they become available at *www.lsac.org*

CHAPTER 4

What Course of Prelaw Study Should I Take?

There is no standard prelaw curriculum. Law schools do not require any particular undergraduate degree, course of study, or particular courses in order to gain admission. Statistics on the entering class of every law school will demonstrate that students come from a wide variety of backgrounds. Perhaps the largest number of law students started out as political science majors, but other majors from the arts and social sciences are well represented, including history, English, psychology, and sociology. Law schools generally have a high concentration of business majors, including tax and accounting, general business, economics, criminal justice, and international relations. There are usually smaller but significant numbers from the hard sciences like physics, chemistry, and biology, or engineering. Other majors, such as journalism, environmental science, art, music, or drama, are likely to be found in a typical first-year class. Included in this group may be a variety of other professionals including doctors, psychologists, CPAs, professors, and even members of the clergy. You should not be surprised in your first year law school class to find yourself sitting between an anesthesiologist and a history professor. You may have obtained a graduate degree yourself, and wondered if there is room in law school for someone like you. The answer is yes.

Because law schools only require that you complete an undergraduate degree, every degree program is equal, at least in theory. In practice, law schools may find that they have had better success with graduates from certain degree programs at certain universities than others. Individual admissions committee members at different schools may have their own ideas about what kind of prelaw training will prepare students best for law school. Undergraduate advisors may channel prelaw students into certain majors that they perceive to have a nexus with law school. If your research discloses that certain concentrations or degree programs are likely to receive favorable treatment in the admissions process of schools where you plan to apply, you would be wise to pursue such a course of study.

Otherwise, the best advice for your prelegal education is to follow a curriculum that you enjoy. It is important for you to possess an interest independent of law school. There are two important reasons for this: First, chances are that you will do better in a subject area that you enjoy than you will in one that you hate. If you have to struggle each day to get up and go to class, it will undoubtedly be reflected in your grades, and a poor showing will adversely affect your chances to be admitted to law school. Second, if you do not get into law school or decide not to go to law school, you will have pursued a course of study that will help you in some alternative career path.

Much the same advice can be said about specific courses. Take courses that you like, that provide an intellectual challenge for you personally. Study under professors who are interesting and exciting, rather than those who put you to sleep. Take classes that make you want to learn, rather than those that fit into a convenient schedule or guarantee an "A."

There is no washout course for prelaw, like Organic Chemistry for premed majors. There is no one course that every law school applicant must complete. Yet, prelaw students continue to pose the question: What courses will help me most in law school? At the risk of negating the advice of take what you like, the following are this author's personal suggestions for courses that may help you to develop skills you can use in law school:

1. **Research and writing.** Any course that imposes a demanding regimen of critiqued writing based upon academic research will help you in law school. All law students are required to complete research and writing assignments during law school—

an activity that does not end with graduation, because much of lawyering involves research and writing. In addition, many law school exams are essay tests, which favor effective writers. The more writing experience you get, the better off you will be in law school. If your high school preparation for research and writing was poor, you may want to impose a remedial curriculum on yourself during college or graduate school. If your writing skills are strong, you can always do more to enhance them.

2. **Logic or reasoning.** Much of law school centers on legal analysis, which is fundamentally deductive logic. Learning about logic and reasoning can help to prepare you for the kind of thinking you will be required to do in law school.

3. **Legal history.** Although you will read historical cases in law school, law professors give scant attention to the roots of our legal system. A course that traces the development of the law, particularly Anglo-American jurisprudence, will provide you with a useful background throughout your legal career.

4. **Public speaking.** You will be required to speak when called on in class, and you will need to be able to make oral arguments throughout law school. Courses that polish your speaking ability and the skill of thinking on your feet will make the inevitable speaking requirements of law school more palatable. A course like this might be particularly valuable for someone who is not accustomed to, or afraid of, standing up and speaking publicly. Many high schools and colleges also sponsor extra-curricular programs in speech, drama, and debate, which provide preparation for oral advocacy in law school.

5. **Basic accounting.** Certain law school courses in the areas of contracts, business and tax, assume a fundamental understanding of financial and accounting terms and principles. Legal practitioners are constantly required to deal with their clients' money, as well as their own. Understanding the basics of accounting and business will prove invaluable.

6. **Speed reading.** You will probably be required to do more reading in law school than you ever have before. You will also be expected to understand the material in greater depth than in the past. Accordingly, the ability to pore over a great amount of reading with a high level of retention is important. Many universities offer such courses on either a credit or noncredit basis; if yours does not, consider taking such a course outside of school.

Here are a few other suggestions for course selection in undergraduate school:

• Do not be afraid of courses that are intellectually demanding; these classes will train your mind for the rigors of a legal education.

• Get a well-rounded education; take courses outside your major. Legal problems draw from the experience of humankind, and so lawyers inevitably must be renaissance people in order to understand these legal problems.

• Master technology; universities provide wired (or wireless) environments, and college students use computers in a variety of ways. This will not change.

• Do more than go to classes; get involved in extracurricular activities as well. Evidence of learning is found in more places than transcripts.

If it has been several years since you were in school, you may find yourself experiencing some uneasiness about returning to the world of education. Some of this malaise you should discount out of hand. You will find that your reacclimation to school comes quickly. You will also discover that life experiences gained since college give you valuable perspectives that you will use in the law. The discipline of managing life in the real world will undoubtedly help you to organize your time and maximize your performance in law school. If you have been out of school for a long time, or remain nervous about returning to school for any other reason, then take courses before you apply to law school. These might be undergraduate courses at a local community college or a university, or they might be graduate level courses offered through your employer. Such experiences may help to make the transition go more smoothly.

Although the bulk of this section has dealt with undergraduate education, it is worth noting that a significant number of law school entrants possess advanced degrees, including MBAs, CPAs, master's degrees in a variety of other fields, Ph.D.s, MDs, and other medical degrees. People who come to law school with professional degree certification usually fall into one of two groups: those who hope to build upon their prior training with a degree in law, and those who hope to make a complete career change because they are not satisfied with their chosen occupation. Both groups are well represented in law school. Graduate level training can be a useful credential for law school admission and an excellent preparation for the study of law. However, because the admission process typically focuses on undergraduate grades, A's in graduate school will not wipe out C's in college.

Finally, a word about *which* college. Law schools take into consideration the reputations of undergraduate institutions just as other graduate programs do. If you went to a school with an excellent reputation, or a highly regarded degree program, it will help you in the application process. Because law schools are able to compare the performance of admitted students with their undergraduate institutions, they may have evidence to show that students from a particular school or college perform above or below the average of admitted students. This may be because the undergraduate school recommends more or fewer of its better students to a particular law school. It may be that a larger number of applicants coming from a particular university (say a local one) means that admitted students fall within the full range of qualifications in the entering class. Whatever the reasons, your school does make a difference. If you think that law schools may not know enough about your prelegal schools or degree programs to be able to make an accurate assessment of these institutions, send informational material about the school or program with your application.

In the final analysis, your prelegal education can help you in a variety of ways to prepare for the rigors of law school. The absence of specific requirements gives you a great deal of freedom in choosing a path. Select one that builds the skills you will need in law school, that is simultaneously interesting and fulfilling on its own.

CHAPTER 5

How Do I Apply to Law School?

The law school application process that you will complete as an applicant is somewhat analogous to what you will be doing as a law student. You will research the issue, you will analyze the results of your research, and you will reach a conclusion.

The application process must be taken seriously and applicants should investigate all options available to them. Fortunately, there are many sources of information for prospective law students to use. See Chapter 3, particularly the schedule of Law School Forums for 2010.

GRADES

Unlike the LSAT, which represents a straightforward index of performance, grades represent a murky and sometimes unfathomable representation of law school applicants' capabilities. Rather than a single test that compares all test takers to all other exam takers at discrete points in time, grades represent hundreds of tests, papers, projects, objective and subjective assessments, and other considerations accumulated over a period of years. Grading standards vary by institution, and even within schools, colleges, and departments within institutions. Grades are affected by myriad variables, from time available to devote to schoolwork, test taking, and writing skills, to personal commitment to learning, health, and lifestyle. Grades can cover a four-year undergraduate curriculum, a degree earned over an extended number of years, graduate and professional school attendance, and even non-degree course work. Grades may represent a candidate's performance over the past four or five years, or educational accomplishments that may be decades old.

The illusiveness of attaching meaning to grades can be as confusing to applicants as it is to the law schools, which vary from school to school as to how they treat grades. Some basic considerations are worth noting. Law schools *do* look at grades, and a dismal academic performance may preclude admission to any law school. You may be able to cite chapter and verse to explain why your grades do not represent your ability to do law school work. In fact, grades may not reflect as much about your innate intellect as they do about your ability to withstand the demands of a legal education. Grades reflect some level of discipline, commitment, and skill in mastering a course of instruction over an extended period of time, in addition to substantive knowledge.

Law Services will take your transcripts and produce a report to the law schools to which you apply summarizing your undergraduate grades. Relying on information from hundreds of institutions, Law Services attempts to give the law schools information that they can interpret with some degree of reliability. Thus, your report will include an undergraduate grade point average (UGPA) that may differ from your actual GPA at the school from which you graduated. This is because the UGPA reported to the law schools includes all the undergraduate courses you took from all the universities you attended. So, if you attended summer school at a university in your hometown, the grades from summer may be recorded as a "Pass" by your home university, but they will be recorded with actual grades by Law Services. If your college uses a different grading system—for instance, reporting all grades on a 100-point scale instead of a 4.0 scale—Law Services will convert the grades to a standard 4.0 scale.

If your school's grading system is different from the norm, you should be prepared to explain to the law schools considering your application what your GPA means. If your actual GPA includes anomalies, such as one terrible semester when you had health problems or changed majors, you should explain candidly, without being apologetic, about what happened. If your grades have shown improvement over the course of time, be sure to point out the improvement. If you have participated in special programs or received academic awards that may not be apparent on standard reports, describe what these honors mean.

Graduate School Grades

One area that surprises many applicants is the way that law schools treat graduate education. As a rule, graduate level grades are not included in the calculation of your undergraduate GPA. This is because undergraduate and graduate schools are not the same. Graduate school often requires the same kind of competitive application process that it takes to get into law school, so acceptance into a graduate program merely says that an applicant possesses the requisite qualifications that the law school is considering. Graduate level grades are often considerably higher than undergraduate grades, and may not reflect the same range of performance as undergraduate grades. Although law schools do not incorporate graduate school grades into the UGPA, admissions committees typically are very interested in post-baccalaureate educational experiences. Thus, if you have attended graduate or professional school, do not hesitate to mention these experiences.

In the final analysis, law schools want to know how well you have done in school in the past, because they believe that your past performance gives some indication of how you will do in law school. Despite the fact that interpretation of academic performance is challenging, law schools do learn valuable information about you. Combined with the LSAT, the UGPA provides a strong indicator of future success in law school.

THE LSAT

Each applicant to law school is required to take the Law School Admission Test (LSAT). The LSAT is administered four times per year, typically June, October, December, and February. (See page 32 for 2010–11 test dates.) For most law schools, the LSAT is one of the most important factors in making admission decisions, as it is a common denominator for every applicant

In determining whether a particular application is appropriate, law school representatives will release median numbers. Applicants should know that a median means the middle score in a series. At any given school, there are students with numbers above and below the median undergraduate GPA and LSAT scores. Some schools may also release average scores, which represent the sum of the scores divided by the number of students. Applicants should also be aware that the LSAT and GPA medians are not the same for the total applicant pool, admitted students, and enrolled students. The admitted pool is higher than the total pool, because schools admit the best applicants, but the enrolled pool is lower than the admitted pool, because some good students choose to go to other schools.

To see how this might work in practice, let's take a look at three law schools and six students. Assume that School A is a highly competitive, elite school; School B is a mid-range state school; and School C is a less competitive, new private school. Chart A illustrates where the median UGPA and LSAT scores fall:

Chart A
GPA and LSAT Medians for Three Hypothetical Law Schools

LSAT	UGPA	SCHOOL A LSAT	SCHOOL A GPA	SCHOOL B LSAT	SCHOOL B GPA	SCHOOL C LSAT	SCHOOL C GPA
175–180	3.9–4.0						
170–174	3.7–3.8	172	3.8				
165–169	3.5–3.6				3.6		
160–164	3.3–3.4						
155–159	3.1–3.2			158			
150–154	2.9–3.0						3.0
145–149	2.7–2.8					148	
140–144	2.6–2.7						
Below 140	2.5–2.6						
	Below 2.5						

Now let's look at the six students, each with different UGPA and LSAT scores, some higher or lower on one, and others high or low on both:

Chart B
LSAT and GPA Scores for Six Hypothetical Students

LSAT	UGPA	Student 1	Student 2	Student 3	Student 4	Student 5	Student 6
175–180	3.9–4.0		3.9				
170–174	3.7–3.8	174			170		
165–169	3.5–3.6	3.5				3.6	
160–164	3.3–3.4			162/3.4			
155–159	3.1–3.2						
150–154	2.9–3.0		150				
145–149	2.7–2.8						
140–144	2.6–2.7					144	
Below 140	2.5–2.6				2.2		140/2.5
	Below 2.5						

With the caveat that medians can be deceiving and that the number of students competing for seats may affect who is selected from the applicant pool, these charts show, in general terms, how each of six students will fare at three schools described.

- Student 1 will easily get into Schools B and C, but is marginal at A, where her LSAT is in the ballpark, but her GPA is a little low. If School A looks at a variety of factors, such as where she went to school, her major, her GPA improvement over four years, and her extracurricular activities, she may have a chance. If they rely on a formula, she may be in trouble.
- Although student 2 has excellent grades, his LSAT is probably too low for School A. Although he is a little below the median for the LSAT at B, if the rest of the application is strong, he has a reasonably good chance. School C will be glad to get him.
- Student 3 with solid LSAT and GPA scores is also out of the picture at School A but a pretty sure bet at B. School C will offer scholarship money.
- Student 4 has really great LSAT and a disastrous GPA. For this student, School B is likely to be very nervous but may want to look behind the numbers; even School A may be curious to see if there is some reason for the low GPA, but this is a long shot. This is an ideal candidate for School C with great potential and a significant risk of failure (if whatever happened in undergraduate school happens again in law school). All three schools will want to see what Student 4 has done to turn his life around.
- Student 5 has a solid GPA, but a weak LSAT. Neither A nor B will give her much of a shot, but School C will find the good grades appealing, and depending on the overall applicant pool, the LSAT is not dramatically below the school's median LSAT. Depending on other factors, she has a fair chance of admission at School C.
- Student 6 is out of bounds at all three schools. His LSAT is a big risk factor. There is a relationship between LSAT score and bar passage, so any school is going to expect a strong academic record to offset the weak LSAT. Even retaking the LSAT is not likely to help. Student 6 may want to look at admission to a law school not approved by the American Bar Association, or acceptance in a summer trial admission program.

It would appear to be a rather simple matter to compare law schools based on their medians if that were the only criteria used in admission. However, an applicant's undergraduate career typically plays an equally important role in the decision process. A student's academic record must be analyzed very carefully. Factors such as school(s) attended, classes taken, major, minor, number of hours worked while in school, as well as grade progression are all important factors. Therefore, applicants should acknowledge particular strengths in their academic performance, and point out events such as a change of major that may have had a significant impact on the progression of grades.

FACTORS TO CONSIDER

Choosing a law school is a complex process that requires a great deal of thought. The preceding chapters have given you a sense of the considerations that will go into your decision. It is worth noting that all the charts and lists will not answer the intangible questions about which law school is best for you. Where will you be most comfortable? Where are you most likely to be successful? What law school is most likely to further your long-term career aspirations? Where will you be happiest in your personal life?

The answers to these questions are not easy, and in fact may not lend themselves to clear answers at all; but they do bring into play subjective feelings that are very important. Gut feeling, instinct, intuition, prescience, whatever you want to call it, plays a role. All your logical analysis may tell you to go to school X, but your heart tells you to go to school Y. What do you do?

For many applicants, a visit to campus can help to clarify the decision. Taking the time to meet the admissions staff, faculty, students, and even alumni may help you to confirm or clarify your feelings. Imagining yourself in the environment and culture of a particular law school may provide insights that do not appear in any of your charts or logical analyses. Sometimes, as it is in your personal life, your heart is your best guide. If you feel good about one particular law school and kind of creepy about another, go with the one that makes you feel good. In the end, assuming you have choices, you will involve some combination of objective evaluation and subjective guesswork to reach a decision. As long as you have done your homework, and invested your time and energy into the process, your decision will probably be the best one for you.

What you want to avoid is not doing your homework, procrastinating until you foreclose desirable outcomes, delude yourself into thinking that one choice is right for you when in your heart of hearts you know it isn't, and listening to friends, family, and advisors who are pushing their own agendas for you. If you can avoid these pitfalls, you are more likely to end up in a law school that works for you. And if you hate your law school, you can consider transferring after the first year, or getting out of law school altogether.

At this point, the key is to complete the application process in a timely fashion, and to present the best possible case to the law schools you have chosen. If you do this, you can maximize the options that are open to you and the likelihood of making a sound decision.

The number of law schools remaining after this cursory review is probably still too large a number for you to consider applying to all, not only because of the time associated with filling out the applications, but also because of the fees associated with each one. Therefore, look closely at the schools that meet your needs, based on the preliminary information you have gathered. How well do you match up with the profile of these law schools' most recent incoming class? What are the medians of the schools in which you are interested and how do your numerical predictors match up with their numbers?

It may appear that applicants are judged only on the numbers; to the extent that strong or weak scores affect your admissibility, this is true. However, most law schools consider many other aspects of the application as discussed earlier. Applicants must recognize that the LSAT and GPA are the most common factors to each applicant, thus placing everyone at a starting point or on a level playing field. Other factors then become important, such as major, undergraduate institution, advanced degrees, leadership roles in community or within extracurricular activities, letters of recommendation, and the personal essay.

Most applicants submit anywhere from seven to nine applications to various law schools. Applying to one law school is probably unwise; likewise, applying to 100 law schools is not necessary and is very expensive.

It might make sense to use a technique that is common among college applicants: to identify a dream school, one of stronger possibilities, and one safe school. The dream school might be one where you are on the low side of the admission criteria, but you think you have some chance for admission. (If you have no chance of being admitted to a school, don't bother.) The strong schools would include institutions where your credentials are competitive with other applicants, but because of the competition for seats, admission is no guarantee. The safe school is one where your credentials are such that you have a very high likelihood of being admitted.

Some students may find that their credentials are not strong enough to use this approach;

other students may have a limited number of choices because of geographic limitations. Many applicants live and/or work in a city where there is only one law school, and they have to gain admission to that school or forego law school altogether. However, if you are in a position where you have options, do not fail to reach for the sky, as long as you keep a safety net if you fall.

DIVERSITY IN THE ADMISSIONS PROCESS

Law schools seek to enroll a diverse student body. In part, this reflects a desire to create opportunities for all Americans to obtain professional education and to gain a degree of upward economic and social mobility. This model has worked for over two centuries in the United States, where generations of children of immigrants have sought and achieved the American Dream as lawyers. And immigrant parents, aspiring to a better life for their children than they experienced themselves, have pushed their children to pursue a career in the law. Today, however, there is another reason to foster diversity: demographers report that by the year 2050, Caucasians of Western European backgrounds will constitute less than 50 percent of the population of the United States. At the current rates of graduation, however, only about 10 percent of lawyers will come from ethnically diverse backgrounds. This gap leads many leaders in the legal profession to support efforts to increase the representation of diverse lawyers in this country.

The American Bar Association Standards for the Approval of Law Schools call upon all approved law schools to seek diversity in the student body and faculty of the institution. This policy has created a considerable amount of controversy because there are not enough seats for everyone who wants to go to law school to be admitted to law school, and some of those denied admission believed that they were more qualified than students admitted under so-called affirmative action plans. Lawsuits going all the way to the U.S. Supreme Court have produced holdings that have forced law schools to rethink admission criteria and procedures.

A short version of what the Supreme Court said is that it is not inappropriate for law schools and other educational institutions to seek to enroll a diverse student body, as long as the criteria for achieving such diversity are narrowly tailored. Thus, schools could not create quotas for minority students, or give minority applicants "bonus" points in admission formu-

las. Law schools may employ a race-conscious admissions program in order to attain their diversity goals. What this means is that law schools can look at a variety of factors, including those which might be useful in identifying qualified diversity applicants, but if the criteria go too far and create de facto quotas, they are subject to challenge and are likely to be struck down.

FILLING OUT THE APPLICATION

Once you have identified the schools you will be applying to, you must complete the applications in a timely manner. Applicants must read the instructions for each school carefully. Complete all questions that are not identified as optional and provide explanations where necessary. Any questions labeled "optional" may be left blank. (See the sample application provided on page 23.)

Applications may be completed by utilizing school specific on-line applications or the LSAC web site (*www./lsac.org*). All ABA-approved law schools are included in the LSAC's fully searchable database and easy-to-use application forms. Most applications at many schools are processed through the LSAC site. Most law schools also allow you to apply on-line through their web sites. See individual school profiles for web site addresses. If you do not have access to the Internet, contact the schools where you want to apply to obtain a printed application form. Remember to make copies of each application that is submitted.

The Personal Statement

Because most law schools in the country do not interview candidates for admission, your personal statement is the only place in which you are able to sell yourself to the law school. This may be the only opportunity that the admissions committee has to get to know the person behind the application. It is an opportunity for you to respond to questions you think the committee members may have when they review your application and academic record. It is the place to express who you are and what is important to you. You may wish to emphasize any personal or professional experiences and how they have contributed to your growth and/or personal development. Examples of items that applicants might consider including are:

- a description of work experience and extracurricular activities;

(go to page 30)

APPLICATION FOR ADMISSION

APPLICATION AS:
☐ First-year student: Fall term 20____

☐ Reactivation

☐ Transfer student: _____ term 20 ____

☐ Visiting student: _____ term 20 ____

☐ Twenty credit student: _____ term 20 ____
(Only for students with foreign law degrees who wish to qualify for bar exam)

PACE LAW SCHOOL
P A C E   U N I V E R S I T Y

Office of Admissions
78 North Broadway
White Plains, NY 10603
Telephone: 914.422.4210
Fax: 914.989.8714
Email: admissions@law.pace.edu

Application to enter: (check only one)*

☐ Three-year, Full-Time Day   ☐ Four-year, Part-Time Day**   ☐ Four-year, Part-Time Evening

Application Review Status: (check only one)

☐ Rolling Admission (Priority Deadline: March 1, 2011)

☐ Early Decision – Signature Required (Deadline: November 2, 2010)
"I have read and agreed to the Early Decision Process requirements described in the Application Instructions"

Signature of Applicant _____

Please type or print in ink: ☐ Ms./ ☐ Mr. (optional)

1. Name _____
           Last   First   Middle

    If we will be receiving documents under any other name, please indicate name: _____

2. Social Security # ☐☐☐ – ☐☐ – ☐☐☐☐   LSAC Account # _____

3. Are you at least 18 years of age? ☐ Yes ☐ No Date of Birth ___/___/___ optional

4. Present Mailing Address _____
                              Number and Street   City   State Zip Code Country

    Date when current address no longer applies _____
                                                 MM/DD/YY

    Home Telephone (____)_____ Business/Cell Telephone (____)_____
                    Area Code/Number   Circle One   Area Code/Number

    E-mail _____
           (Required for Admissions Staff to communicate application status with applicant)

5. Permanent Address _____
                        Number and Street   City   State Zip Code Country

    Home Telephone (____)_____
                    Area Code/Number

6. Citizenship: Are you a U.S. citizen? ☐ Yes ☐ No   Are you a permanent resident of the U.S.? ☐ Yes ☐ No

7. If any member of your family has attended Pace Law School, please list his/her name, date of graduation and relationship.
    _____

    List the name, address, and telephone number of a person through whom you can be reached.

    _____
    Name   Address   Telephone Number

* If the program you have checked is closed at the time your application is processed, do you wish to be considered for the alternate division?   ☐ Yes   ☐ No

** Applicants who have selected the part-time, day division must submit a one-page, type-written statement describing their need to attend in the part-time division.

8. Please complete the following summary of your academic history in chronological sequence. This section must be completed. If additional space is required please attach an addendum.

	Name of Institution	College Code Number (See LSAT/ LSDAS registration materials.)	Location of school attended	Dates of attendance	Degree or expected degree	Date awarded or expected	Major field of study
Secondary School(s)							
College(s) and/or Universities							
Graduate and/or Law Schools							

SAMPLE

9. Describe in a typed addendum your participation in any or all extracurricular or community activities. Indicate your involvement and contribution to each activity. We are primarily concerned with those experiences that demonstrate your leadership, communication, and creative thinking abilities as well as your initiative.

10. List any academic honors, awards, prizes or other recognition you have received._____
    _____

11. As an undergraduate, were you employed during the academic year?

    No. of hours per week: Fr. Year_____ Soph. Year_____ Jr. Year_____ Sr. Year_____

    Position(s) held: _____

12. Please state your last four positions (paid or volunteer) of full- or part-time employment, including summer employment. You may, in addition to or in place of the following, submit a current résumé.

From	To	Position held	Name and address of employer	Reason for leaving

ANSWER ALL OF THE FOLLOWING QUESTIONS.
If your answer to any of questions 13-22 is yes, please explain fully on a supplemental sheet.

13. Have you ever applied for admission to this law school?
    ☐ Yes   ☐ No
    If so, in what year and with what result?_____

14. Have you ever been enrolled (registered) in another law school including a Conditional Admissions Program?
    ☐ Yes   ☐ No   Dates of Attendance ____/____/____ to ____/____/____
    School Name _____

    ☐ I am ☐ I am not eligible to return to the above school.
    If not eligible, briefly state the reason(s) why you are ineligible on a supplementary sheet.

15. Has your college, university, graduate or professional school course been interrupted for one or more terms for any reason? (Interruptions between the end of one degree program and the beginning of another need not be explained.).
    ☐ Yes   ☐ No

16. Have you ever been placed on probation or dismissed from any college, university, graduate, or professional educational institution for academic reasons or otherwise?   ☐ Yes   ☐ No

17. Have you ever been placed on academic and/or disciplinary probation for actions arising from allegations of academic dishonesty, plagiarism or cheating during your college, university, graduate or professional coursework?
    ☐ Yes   ☐ No

18. Are there any disciplinary charges pending against you?   ☐ Yes   ☐ No

19. Have you ever been convicted of a crime other than a minor traffic violation?   ☐ Yes   ☐ No
    If so, describe the nature of the charge and sentence/punishment on a supplemental sheet.

20. Are there any criminal charges pending against you?   ☐ Yes   ☐ No

21. Have you ever been disciplined, reprimanded, suspended or discharged from any job for conduct involving dishonesty, fraud, misrepresentation, deceit or any violation of Federal or State laws or regulations?   ☐ Yes   ☐ No

22. Have you ever resigned or quit a job when you were under investigation or inquiry for conduct which could have been considered as involving dishonesty, fraud, misrepresentation, deceit or violation of Federal or State laws or regulations, or after receiving notice or being advised of possible investigation, inquiry or disciplinary action for such conduct?   ☐ Yes   ☐ No

Note: Admission to law school does not mean that you will meet the character and fitness requirements for admission to the bar of any state. If you are concerned as to whether an event in your life will affect your eligibility for a license to practice law you should discuss the matter with the Board of Bar Examiners in the state(s) where you plan to practice.

23. Please indicate when you took (or plan to take) the Law School Admissions Test.

    Date(s)_____ Score(s)_____

24. Ethnic Status (Optional)

☐ African-American   ☐ Chicano/Mexican   ☐ American Indian/Alaskan Native (Native American)   ☐ Hispanic
☐ Asian/Pacific Islander   ☐ Puerto Rican   ☐ Caucasian/White (non-Hispanic)   ☐ Other : _____

25. Two appraisals must be submitted on your behalf. Please list the names and titles of those persons from whom you have requested an appraisal. *Please Print Clearly.*

a. _____   b. _____

_____   _____

26. **Personal Statement:** On a separate sheet of paper, please complete the required statement as described in the instructions to applicants. The statement must be **typed and double-spaced.**

27. **Please complete.** Information regarding the status of my application may be released to the following individual. If this section is left blank, information will not be released to anyone except the applicant. Final decisions are not released over the telephone to anyone.

_____   _____
Name   *Relationship*

28. How did you first learn of Pace Law School? ☐ Web ☐ Advertisement ☐ Colleague (Please specify source)_____

29. Did you meet a representative of Pace Law School? ☐ Yes ☐ No

If yes, indicate where:_____

LSAC-Sponsored Law Forum at:

☐ New York   ☐ Boston   ☐ Texas   ☐ Washington, D.C.   ☐ Atlanta   ☐ Chicago   ☐ Los Angeles

☐ San Francisco   ☐ College/Law School Fair at: _____

30. If you are interested in information concerning a specific area of law, indicate below the area of interest:

☐ Environmental Law   ☐ Intellectual Property   ☐ Women's Justice   ☐ Criminal Law   ☐ Land Use/Real Estate
☐ Joint Degree Offerings   ☐ International Law   ☐ Public Interest Law   ☐ Experiential Learning
☐ Business/Securities/Commercial Law   ☐ Other _____

Please be sure that all of the Instructions to Applicants have been followed. An application will be considered only after it has been completed in full and the Office of Admissions has received all required documents.

I understand that, if I am admitted to the Law School and register as a student, the School will retain this application and all supporting materials and may make them available to state bar character committees, and I consent to such disclosure.

I certify that the information provided by me in this application is true and complete. From time of application through enrollment, I shall promptly advise the Law School Office of Admissions **in writing** of any change in any of the facts indicated in this application. I understand that matriculation and attendance at any other law school (from time of application through enrollment) would render any offer of admission from Pace Law School void.

I understand that falsification of this application and supporting materials will be grounds for its denial, or if I am accepted, for dismissal from the Law School. I further agree and authorize Pace Law School to publish, for public relations purposes, any photographs in which I appear.

I understand that my admission to Pace Law School is a privilege and not a right and I agree that my admission, if granted, my registration and continuance on the rolls and graduation are subject to all policies, rules, regulations and procedures set forth in the current viewbooks, catalogs, and other publications and notices of Pace University and as they may be amended and further subject to the right of the authorities of Pace Law School to require my withdrawal for scholastic, disciplinary or other reasons, under circumstances deemed sufficient by them.

_____   _____
Signature of Applicant   *Date*

APPRAISAL FOR ADMISSION

PACE LAW SCHOOL
PACE UNIVERSITY

TO THE APPLICANT: WE REQUIRE THAT YOU UTILIZE THE LSDAS LETTER OF RECOMMENDATION SERVICE. THIS FORM MAY BE USED FOR ANY ADDITIONAL LETTERS.

Please complete the first part of this form. Deliver or mail it to the person who will write your recommendation. If you waive your right of access to this letter, you must provide the recommender with a non-transparent envelope into which the completed recommendation should be placed. The recommender then signs the sealed recommendation in a continuous movement across the flap and envelope. It is to be returned to you and mailed to Pace with your application materials.

Name of Applicant _____ College _____

Address_____ SS# _____

Person Submitting Appraisal (print or type)

Title _____ Institution _____

I understand that federal legislation provides me with a right of access to this recommendation which may be waived, and that no school or person can require me to waive this right. (Check and sign one of the following statements.)

☐ I do NOT waive my right of access to this recommendation and authorize the person named above to provide a candid evaluation and all relevant information to Pace Law School. _____

Signature

☐ I hereby waive my right of access to this recommendation and authorize the person named above to provide a candid evaluation and all relevant information to Pace Law School. _____

Signature

SAMPLE

TO THOSE PROVIDING APPRAISALS:

The applicant named above has applied for admission to Pace Law School. The Admissions Committee would appreciate your frank appraisal of this applicant's intellectual qualities and potential for achievement. We have frequently found letters of recommendation to be helpful in selecting the best candidates from a large group of well-qualified applicants.

Each applicant to the Law School is given the opportunity to waive his or her right under the Family Educational Rights and Privacy Act of 1974 to inspect this form or any letter of appraisal you may submit in connection with the application. If the applicant has agreed to the waiver, as indicated by his or her signature on the appropriate line above, your appraisal will be kept confidential from the applicant as well as from the public. If the applicant has not agreed, your appraisal will be kept confidential from the public, but may be made available to the applicant if and when the applicant becomes a registered student and so requests.

Please return this form directly to the applicant. Your prompt response will be greatly appreciated by both the applicant and the Law School. We are grateful for your help.

PLEASE (✔) each line at the appropriate point on the scale to show the applicant's rating on the characteristic concerned.

CHARACTERISTIC	No basis for judgment	Below Average (lowest 40%)	Average (middle 20%)	Very Good (next 15%)	Unusual (next highest 15%)	Outstanding (highest 10%)
Intelligence, Analytical Powers, etc.						
Independence of Thought, Originality, etc.						
Effectiveness of Communication — Oral						
Written						
Judgment and Maturity						
Industry, Persistence — In scholastic activities						
In non-scholastic activities						
Leadership Ability						
Integrity						
Honesty						

Applicant's Last Name	First	Middle

We would be grateful for your candid assessment of this applicant's intellectual qualities and potential for achievement. If you have known the applicant in an academic capacity, it would be helpful if you could draw qualitative comparisons between the applicant and other students you have taught. Please describe specific accomplishments that demonstrate this candidate's strengths and weaknesses.

A.

SAMPLE

B. I do not know the applicant well enough to write the assessment requested. ☐ Check if true

How long and in what connection have you known the applicant?

_____

Would you give us your considered judgment of the applicant with respect to his or her admission to law school as follows:

☐ I do not recommend.   ☐ I recommend with enthusiasm.
☐ I recommend routinely.   ☐ I recommend most enthusiastically.

_____

Signature   Institution (College or Business)

_____

Name and Title (please print or type)   Date

_____

Address

- an explanation of distinct trends or discrepancies among grades;

- a description of substantial time commitments while attending school;

- verification that standardized tests have underpredicted academic performance in the past (prior test scores should be provided);

- cultural, ethnic, educational, or other factors that might cause the LSAT score or GPA to be an inaccurate measure of potential for law study.

In addition, you may wish to mention the fact that you are the first member of the family to graduate from college, or you may wish to explain hardships or handicaps that you have overcome in order to achieve your degree. Whereas test scores place all applicants in a standardized light, the personal statement focuses on the uniqueness of the applicant. If you can paint a favorable picture of yourself, you may be able to stand out among a group of similarly credentialed applicants.

In sum, the personal statement is a case that you have made for yourself to the admissions committee. Above all, it must be typed carefully and accurately. Correct spelling and grammar are essential. If you tell a great story poorly, you might as well not tell it at all.

Letters of Recommendation

Letters of recommendation can be very helpful to the admissions committee. For recent graduates (within two years), most schools prefer at least one faculty appraisal. Other applicants who would find it difficult to obtain faculty appraisals may request recommendations from individuals who can appraise their ability to perform in law school. Where an institution has a central file for appraisals that are duplicated as needed, or where a committee provides a composite appraisal, typically these alternative procedures are acceptable.

Applicants who have been out of school for a number of years should seek letters of recommendation from individuals who can speak to the applicant's character, leadership abilities, and analytical skills. The quality of the recommendation and content are more important than who writes the letter. It is generally better to use only enthusiastic recommendations; being cursed by faint praise is worse than no praise at all.

Letters of recommendation are additional pieces of evidence that support your case for admission. Many law schools utilize standard recommendation forms in lieu of or in addition to letters. If the school provides such forms, make sure that your references are complete, then return them.

Most law schools utilize Law Services to handle letters of recommendation. You simply have to arrange for your letters to be submitted through the LSDAS letter of recommendation service that serves all member schools. The service is included in your LSDAS registration subscription. Your letters will be copied and sent to law schools along with your LSDAS report, or as received. To use this service, follow the directions for submitting letters outlined in the LSAT/LSDAS Registration and Information Book. Be sure to fill out and give each letter writer a letter of recommendation form from the LSAT/LSDAS Registration and Information Book.

Although the convenience of Law Services for disseminating letters of recommendation is attractive, and most students use this service, it is worth noting that there may be times when a personalized letter is better than a generic one. You may have a contact who has special ties to a law school where you are applying, either to the school generally, or to the dean or a faculty member. If this is the case, a personalized letter on your behalf discussing your interest in this particular school may be worth the extra effort.

Occasionally, a student will get the idea that if one letter is good, then one hundred letters must be one hundred times better. Nothing could be further from the truth. A file containing a large number of letters of recommendation is likely to trigger the MEGO (My Eyes Glaze Over) phenomenon among admissions committee members and staff. It is much better to have a small number of really glowing personal recommendations than a sheaf of letters that bury the good recommendations in a sea of verbiage. Make sure that you know what your recommendations will say. An otherwise good application could easily be destroyed by an offhand negative comment. This seems to be so fundamental that it does not bear repeating, but anyone who has served on a law school Admissions Committee can recount applicants whose letters of reference did nothing to help their applications.

DEADLINES, DEADLINES, DEADLINES

All law schools specify deadlines for submission of the application materials to their institution. However, you should begin to explore your options in your junior year of college. This allows you enough time to narrow your choices, gather the appropriate information, and be prepared to submit timely applications in the fall of your senior year. Even if you later decide to work for a period of time after graduation, you keep your choices open by starting early.

First, determine when you are going to take the LSAT. (See the schedule of LSAT offerings for 2010–11; the dates for 2010–11 will be similar but not identical.) Registration materials are available through Law Services. Almost all ABA-approved law schools require the use of the Law School Data Assembly Service (LSDAS), and, therefore, upon registration for the exam, you should register simultaneously for the service. This service analyzes your transcript (you must have one sent to Law Services from each undergraduate institution you have attended) and submits a report of your undergraduate record along with your LSAT score and an unofficial copy of your transcript to the law schools you have indicated. You can add schools to this list later if you choose. Complete your LDAS reports as early as possible. Most law schools will not treat your application as complete and act upon it unless all the required elements have been submitted. You can call law schools where you have applied to determine whether your application is complete, but do not reduce your chances of admission by ignoring something that can be easily fixed.

Send the transcript to Law Services once all your junior year courses have been completed. Typically, upward grade trends occur after the first year of college. Some law schools may even require fall grades in your senior year if a significant trend is noted.

The registration date for the LSAT should be made individually by each applicant. Since test preparation is essential, you should allow adequate time to properly prepare for the test. There are many commercial preparation courses, various books such as Barron's *How to Prepare for the LSAT,* as well as preparation materials through Law Services. (See also Chapters 12 and 13 of this Guide.)

You should be prepared the first time you sit for the exam; never enter the exam with the thought of it being a dry run. Since most law schools average repeated scores, multiple test scores can hurt your application. If you want to practice under exam conditions, you can take the GRE, MCAT, or other professional school exam. You must understand that the content of these exams differs from discipline to discipline, and that none will replicate the LSAT; however, the format of the tests is often very similar. If you want to "practice" a real

test, take the GRE or other professional school admission test, remember that you may be able to help your test-taking skills generally, but that each test measures different ability and knowledge.

THE WAITING PERIOD

When all the appropriate materials are filed with the admissions office, you begin a waiting period. The decision-making process takes time.

Once an application is received, the office of admissions opens a file on you, requests the LSDAS report, and, when all materials are received, reviews your application. The process may be held up if, for example, you have left blank questions on the application that were not marked "optional," or do not file a fee with the application, or do not sign the application form.

When you are notified that the file is complete and ready for review by the admissions committee, the process may take anywhere from two weeks to two months. Patience is essential; however, if you have not heard anything from a law school, do not hesitate to contact that school. You may be missing vital information, or your correspondence may have been delayed by the mail.

Every school employs a slightly different approach to making admissions decisions and notifying applicants of their acceptance. Many schools employ automatic acceptance and rejection categories for very high or low LSAT scores and GPAs. Most applicants fall somewhere in the middle, and their applications are reviewed more carefully by the admissions committee. Some schools may send out all acceptance letters at one time ("batch" admissions), while others notify applicants as decisions are made ("rolling" admissions). Although the notification process may begin prior to January 1 of the academic year preceding admission, most applicants will hear from law schools between February and April. Later decisions may occur for students who are included on a waiting list, from which they are drawn if other accepted students decide not to matriculate at the school. Waiting list decisions may be made as late as August.

A few schools offer conditional summer programs for students with marginal credentials. Typically, the final decision for these applicants is made on the basis of their performance in the summer courses. Although the experience of attending such programs is good preparation for law school itself, ABA standards do not permit schools to give law school credit for preadmission work.

The admissions office at the schools to which you apply will be able to explain the idiosyncrasies of their procedures, and keep you advised on the progress of your application. Don't call them every day, however, because excessive phone calls actually slow down the admissions process. Use common sense in deciding whether to call for assistance and information.

THE FINAL DECISION

Once the admissions committee reaches a final decision, you must begin your decision-making process. There are basically four scenarios you might find yourself facing: (1) you have multiple offers of admission; (2) you have one offer; (3) you are on one or more wait lists; or (4) you have no offers. The second scenario is simple, and the fourth represents a challenge in terms of deciding what to do next. The first and third situations raise the specter of having to make choices from competing offers. The first scenario, albeit the most enviable one,

of having to choose among more than one offer, can be maddening. The third scenario can be frustrating when you are wait listed for the school you really want to attend, but you have offers from one or more schools that are not your first choice. When faced with such a dilemma, you will simply have to make the best choice you can within the time frame involved. Most schools will require a deposit no earlier than April but as early as two weeks after your offer of admission is made.

Cost is always an issue, and you should recognize the need to submit the required financial aid forms in a timely manner. The submission of financial aid forms (Free Application for Federal Student Aid) does not have an impact on the admission decision. The filing of the appropriate forms should be completed at the time of application to the individual schools. If all the appropriate financial aid materials have been submitted, a law school should be able to provide you with a financial aid package at the time of acceptance, allowing you to make an educated decision. (See Chapter 8 of this Guide for more information on financial aid.)

by Gary A. Munneke, Professor of Law (see page 4), Angela D'Agostino, Assistant Dean for students, and Cathy Alexander, Director of Admissions, Pace University School of Law, White Plains, NY.

2010–2011 LSAT Dates and Registration Deadlines

Published Test Centers
(United States, Canada, and the Caribbean)

National Test Dates	Regular Registration Online, by Mail, by Telephone (receipt deadline)	Late Registration by Mail (receipt deadline)	Late Registration Online, by Telephone (receipt deadline)
Monday, June 7, 2010	May 4, 2010	May 5–11, 2010	May 4–15, 2010
Saturday, October 9, 2010 / Tuesday, October 12, 2010[1]	September 7, 2010	September 8–14, 2010	September 8–17, 2010
Saturday, December 11, 2010 / Monday, December 13, 2010[1]	November 9, 2010	November 10–16, 2010	November 10–19, 2010
Saturday, February 12, 2011 / Monday, February 14, 2011[1]	January 11, 2011	January 12–18, 2011	January 12–21, 2011

Other LSAT Options

National Test Dates	Test Center Change by Mail, Phone, Fax, Online (receipt deadline)	Nonpublished Test Centers— United States, Canada, and the Caribbean (receipt deadline)	LSAT Registration Refunds partial only (receipt deadline)
Monday, June 7, 2010	May 14, 2010 (mail, phone, fax) / May 16, 2010 (online)	April 30, 2010	May 14, 2010
Saturday, October 9, 2010 / Tuesday, October 12, 2010[1]	September 17, 2010 (mail, phone, fax) / September 19, 2010 (online)	September 3, 2010	September 17, 2010
Saturday, December 11, 2010 / Monday, December 13, 2010[1]	November 19, 2010 (mail, phone, fax) / November 21, 2010 (online)	November 5, 2010	November 19, 2010
Saturday, February 12, 2011 / Monday, February 14, 2011[1]	January 21, 2011 (mail, phone, fax) / January 23, 2011 (online)	January 7, 2011	January 21, 2011

LSAT Score Release Dates

National Test Dates	Score by E-mail For online account holders only. No additional charge.	Score Report Mailed Additional charges may apply.
Monday, June 7, 2010	June 28, 2010	July 6, 2010
Saturday, October 9, 2010 / Tuesday, October 12, 2010[1]	Nov. 1, 2010	Nov. 9, 2010
Saturday, December 11, 2010 / Monday, December 13, 2010[1]	Jan. 10, 2011	Jan. 18, 2011
Saturday, February 12, 2011 / Monday, February 14, 2011[1]	March 7, 2011	March 11, 2011

(All score release dates are approximate.)

- For Telephone Services: **215.968.1001** (for hours)
- For Online Services: ***www.LSAC.org*** *Registration closes midnight ET on deadline date.*

1 This test is for Saturday Sabbath observers only. For details, please see Saturday Sabbath Observers. This test is nondisclosed.

Test dates and times vary for some centers. Check your LSAT Admission Ticket to confirm the correct test date and time.

Scores by e-mail will take several hours from the beginning time to reach all test takers.

Please allow 5–7 days from this date for receipt of your score report.

Note *Walk-in registration on the day of the test is not permitted at any test center for any test administration.*

Registrants whose test registrations are received by mail during the late registration period and that are not accompanied by the late registration fee will be billed the fee, and a hold will be placed on their accounts.

Not every LSAT is *disclosed*. For a complete schedule of disclosed and nondisclosed LSAT administrations, please see Your Score Report and Test Disclosure. For all other info, including dates and info for test centers outside the United States, Canada, and the Carribean, contact *www.lsac.org*.

CHAPTER 6

What Are Your Chances of Law School Admission?

A PROFILE OF RECENT FIRST-YEAR LAW STUDENTS

The table in this section provides basic admissions statistics for the law schools that have been approved by the American Bar Association. All these schools offer the J.D. degree. The information has been compiled from the most recent available information received from schools. If you compare your own GPA and your LSAT score and percentile with those of students recently admitted, and if you note the number of students who applied and the number who were accepted, you will be able to get an idea of your chances of admission to any given law school.

Remember that your credentials may place you at the top of the applicant pool at one school, and at the bottom of the pool at another. Finding schools that will at least consider you is essential. If both your LSAT and GPA fall below the median for a school, your chances of being admitted are typically slim. Often applicants with lower LSATs have higher GPAs to offset their test scores, and vice versa. A school may be able to tell you whether there are realistic limits below which you will not be admitted. For example, a school may say that for the previous year it offered admission only to applicants who scored above 155 on the LSAT. If you have a 153, the likelihood of your being admitted to such a school would be nil. Conversely, if your scores are on the high side of a school's applicant pool, you are likely to be a strong candidate for that school (see the discussion on pages 19–21 for more information on this question). In any event, it is important for you to do your homework to get a sense of where you stand.

A blank cell on the chart means that information was not available.

The point has been made previously that timing is important. The earlier you take the LSAT, submit transcripts and other information to the LSDAS, and complete individual law school applications, the better your chances in the process. Since law schools make their decisions only on completed applications, if you are not in the pool, you are not in the game. Since many schools use a rolling admissions process—accepting candidates as soon as they decide to admit them, rather than sending out all offers of admission in a batch—the sooner you are in front of the admissions committee, the better. Even a negative decision can be helpful because a denial at one school might trigger your application at another.

LAW SCHOOL	ACADEMIC STATISTICS				ADMISSION STATISTICS		
	Median LSAT Percentile of Enrolled	Median LSAT Score of Enrolled	Lowest LSAT Percentile of Accepted	Median GPA (4.0 scale) of Enrolled	Total Applicants	Applicants Accepted	Applicants Enrolled
Albany Law School 80 New Scotland Avenue Albany, NY 12208 518-445-2326 Fax: 518-445-2369 admissions@albanylaw.edu	63	155		3.3	2215	972	255
American University (Washington College of Law) 4801 Massachusetts Avenue, N.W. Washington, DC 20016-8186 202-274-4101 Fax: 202-274-4107 wcladmit@wcl.american.edu	79	161	32	3.42	8864	2066	464
Appalachian School of Law P.O. Box 2825 Grundy, VA 24614 276-935-4349 Fax: 276-935-8496 npruitt@asl.edu	40	149	32	3.08	1630	630	
Arizona State University (Sandra Day O'Connor College of Law) 1100 S. McAllister Ave. - Box 877906 Tempe, AZ 85287-7906 480-965-1474 Fax: 480-727-7930 chitra.damania@asu.edu	84	161	26	3.6	2400	667	184
Atlanta's John Marshall Law School 1422 W. Peachtree St., NW Atlanta, GA 30309 404-872-3593 Fax: 404-873-3802 admissions@johnmarshall.edu		151	25	2.97	1789	712	211
Ave Maria School of Law 3475 Plymouth Road Ann Arbor, MI 48105 734-827-8063 Fax: 734-622-0123 info@avemarialaw.edu	46	151	16	3.15	1543	786	127
Barry University (School of Law) 6441 East Colonial Drive Orlando, FL 32807 321-206-5600 Fax: 321-206-5662 acruz@mail.barry.edu		150		3.3	1989	1117	253
Baylor University (School of Law) One Bear Place #97288 Waco, TX 76798-7288 254-710-1911 Fax: 254-710-2316 becky_beck@baylor.edu	81	160	71	3.62	3436	1146	186
Boston College (Law School) 885 Centre Street Newton, MA 02459 617-552-4351 Fax: 617-552-2917 bclawadm@bc.edu	93	166		3.53	7168	1431	264
Boston University (School of Law) 765 Commonwealth Avenue Boston, MA 02215 617-353-3100 Fax: 617-353-0578 bulawadm@bu.edu	91	166	44	3.7	7660	1801	271

LAW SCHOOL	ACADEMIC STATISTICS				ADMISSION STATISTICS		
	Median LSAT Percentile of Enrolled	Median LSAT Score of Enrolled	Lowest LSAT Percentile of Accepted	Median GPA (4.0 scale) of Enrolled	Total Applicants	Applicants Accepted	Applicants Enrolled
Brigham Young University (J. Reuben Clark Law School) 342 JRCB Brigham Young University Provo, UT 84602 801-422-4277 Fax: 801-422-0389 kucharg@law.byu.edu	89	163	26	3.74	733	216	147
Brooklyn Law School 250 Joralemon Street Brooklyn, NY 11201 718-780-7906 Fax: 718-780-0395 admitq@brooklaw.edu	86	163		3.46	5886	1652	496
California Western School of Law 225 Cedar Street San Diego, CA 92101-3046 619-525-1401 Fax: 619-615-1401 admissions@cwsl.edu	50	153	25	3.28	2922	1348	340
Campbell University (Norman Adrian Wiggins School of Law) 225 Hillsborough Street, Suite 401 Releigh, NC 24603 919-865-5988 Fax: 919-865-5886	71	156		3.37	1525	460	161
Capital University (Law School) 303 East Broad Street Columbus, OH 43215-3200 614-236-6500 Fax: 614-236-6972 admissions@law.capital.edu	58	153	18	3.2	1298	629	247
Case Western Reserve University (School of Law) 11075 East Boulevard Cleveland, OH 44100 216-368-3600 Fax: 216-368-1042 lawadmissions@case.edu		158		3.39	2330	832	248
Catholic University of America (Columbus School of Law) Cardinal Station Washington, DC 20064 202-319-5151 Fax: 202-319-6285 admissions@law.edu		158		3.33	3299	1078	268
Chapman University (School of Law) One University Drive Orange, CA 92866 714-628-2500 Fax: 714-628-2501 metten@chapman.edu	75	158	32	3.43	2957	891	181
Charleston School of Law P.O. Box 535 Charleston, SC 29402 843-377-2143 Fax: 843-329-0491 jbenfield@charlestonlaw.org	60	154		3.2	2062	895	241

LAW SCHOOL	ACADEMIC STATISTICS				ADMISSION STATISTICS		
	Median LSAT Percentile of Enrolled	Median LSAT Score of Enrolled	Lowest LSAT Percentile of Accepted	Median GPA (4.0 scale) of Enrolled	Total Applicants	Applicants Accepted	Applicants Enrolled
Charlotte School of Law 2145 Suttle Avenue Charlotte, NC 28208 704-971-8542 Fax: 704-971-8599 admissions@charlottelaw.edu	50	151	140	3.11	2120	1163	249
City University of New York (CUNY School of Law) 65-21 Main Street Flushing, NY 11367-1300 718-340-4210 Fax: 718-340-4435 mail.law.cuny.edu	56	153	36	3.31	3265	575	158
Cleveland State University (Cleveland-Marshall College of Law) 2121 Euclid Avenue LB138 Cleveland, OH 44115-2214 216-687-2304 Fax: 216-687-6881 christophe.lcak@law.csuohio.edu	60	156	11	3.44	1822	622	203
College of William & Mary (William & Mary Law School) P.O. Box 8795 Williamsburg, VA 23187-8795 757-221-3785 Fax: 757-221-3261 lawadm@wm.edu	92	165	20	3.66	8984	1109	213
Columbia University (School of Law) 435 West 116th Street New York, NY 10027 212-854-2670 Fax: 212-854-1109 admissions@law.columbia.edu	99	171	50	3.67	8020	1143	378
Cornell University (Law School) Myron Taylor Hall Ithaca, NY 14853-4901 607-255-5141 Fax: 607-255-7193 lawadmit@postoffice.law.cornell.edu	97	167		3.63	4207		206
Creighton University (School of Law) 2500 California Plaza Omaha, NE 68178 402-280-2586 Fax: 402-280-3161 lawadmit@creighton.edu	56	153	30	3.43	1366	771	178
De Paul University (College of Law) 25 East Jackson Boulevard Chicago, IL 60604 312-362-6831 Fax: 312-362-5280 lawinfo@depaul.edu	78	159	33	3.4	5068	1988	364
Drake University (Law School) 2507 University Avenue Des Moines, IA 50311 515-271-2782 Fax: 515-271-1990 lawadmit@drake.edu		155		3.42	1105	584	156

LAW SCHOOL	ACADEMIC STATISTICS				ADMISSION STATISTICS		
	Median LSAT Percentile of Enrolled	Median LSAT Score of Enrolled	Lowest LSAT Percentile of Accepted	Median GPA (4.0 scale) of Enrolled	Total Applicants	Applicants Accepted	Applicants Enrolled
Drexel University **(Earle Mack School of Law)** 3320 Market Street Philadelphia, PA 15282 215-895 1LAW Fax: 215-571-4769		160	25	3.42			156
Duke University **(Duke University School of Law)** Science Drive and Towerview Road, Box 90362 Durham, NC 27708-0362 919-613-7020 Fax: 919-613-7257 nash@law.duke.edu	96	168		3.72	4486		199
Duquesne University **(School of Law)** 900 Locust Street, Hanley Hall Pittsburgh, PA 15282 412-396-6296 Fax: 412-396-1073 campion@duq.edu	66	153		3.5			225
Elon University **(School of Law)** 201 North Greene Street Greensboro, NC 27401 336-279-9200 Fax: 336-279-8199 law@elon.edu		154		3.29	761	316	121
Emory University **(School of Law)** Gambrell Hall, 1301 Clifton Road, N.E. Atlanta, GA 30322 404-727-6801 Fax: 404-727-2477 erosenz@law.emory.edu		166		3.57	4588	1149	248
Faulkner University **(Thomas Goode Jones School of Law)** 5345 Atlanta Highway Montgomery, AL 36109 334-386-7210 Fax: 334-386-7223 law@faulkner.edu	40	149		3.08	747	405	150
Florida Agricultural and Mechanical University **(Florida A & M University College of Law)** 201 N. Beggs Avenue Orlando, FL 32801 407-254-3268 famulaw.admissions@famu.edu	50	146		3.07	1807	569	234
Florida Coastal **(School of Law)** 8787 Baypine Rd. Jacksonville, FL 32256 904-680-7710 Fax: 904-680-7776 admissions@fcsl.edu	50	151	25	3.17	4663	1725	566
Florida International University **(College of Law)** FIU College of Law, RDB 1055 Miami, FL 33199 (305) 348-8006 Fax: (305) 348-2965 miroa@fiu.edu		154	151	3.4	2443	632	250

LAW SCHOOL	ACADEMIC STATISTICS				ADMISSION STATISTICS		
	Median LSAT Percentile of Enrolled	Median LSAT Score of Enrolled	Lowest LSAT Percentile of Accepted	Median GPA (4.0 scale) of Enrolled	Total Applicants	Applicants Accepted	Applicants Enrolled
Florida State University (College of Law) 425 W. Jefferson St. Tallahassee, FL 32306-1601 850-644-3787 Fax: 850-644-7284 admissions@law.fsu.edu	81	160		3.53	3316	860	244
Fordham University (School of Law) 140 West 62nd Street New York, NY 10023 212-636-6810 Fax: 212-636-7984 lawadmissions@law.fordham.edu	93	165	62	3.56	6866	1493	483
Franklin Pierce Law Center 2 White Street Concord, NH 03301 603-228-9217 Fax: 603-228-1074 admissions@piercelaw.edu	53	152	17	3.35	1336	671	158
George Mason University (School of Law) 3301 Fairfax Drive Arlington, VA 22201 703-993-8010 Fax: 703-993-8088 aprice1@gmu.edu	89	163	44	3.72	6411	1300	246
George Washington University (Law School) 2000 H Street, N.W. Washington, DC 20052 202-994-7230 Fax: 202-994-3597 jd@law.gwu.edu	93	166	41	3.71	10311	2039	504
Georgetown University (Law Center) 600 New Jersey Avenue, N.W. Washington, DC 20001 202-662-9010 Fax: 202-662-9439 admis@law.georgetown.edu	98	170	56	3.68	11653	2645	590
Georgia State University (College of Law) P.O. Box 4037 Atlanta, GA 30302-4037 404-413-9200 Fax: 404-413-9203 cjgeorge@gsu.edu	80	159	43	3.45	2980	491	217
Golden Gate University (School of Law) 536 Mission Street San Francisco, CA 94105-2968 415-442-6630 lawadmit@ggu.edu	53	152	11	3.08	2747	1695	271
Gonzaga University (School of Law) Box 3528 Spokane, WA 99220-3528 509-313-5532 Fax: 509-313-3697 admissions@lawschool.gonzaga.edu		155		3.3	1513	649	188
Hamline University (School of Law) 1536 Hewitt Avenue St. Paul, MN 55104-1284 651-523-2461 Fax: 651-523-3064 lawadm@gw.hamline.edu	60	154	15	3.42	1506	744	207

LAW SCHOOL	ACADEMIC STATISTICS				ADMISSION STATISTICS		
	Median LSAT Percentile of Enrolled	Median LSAT Score of Enrolled	Lowest LSAT Percentile of Accepted	Median GPA (4.0 scale) of Enrolled	Total Applicants	Applicants Accepted	Applicants Enrolled
Harvard University **(Harvard Law School)** Cambridge, MA 02138 617-495-3179 *jdadmiss@law.harvard.edu*	99	173		3.81	7127	811	557
Hofstra University **(School of Law)** 121 Hofstra University Hempstead, NY 11549 516-463-5916 Fax: 516-463-6264 *lawadmissions@hofstra.edu*	71	157	8	3.3	5232	1991	386
Howard University 2900 Van Ness Street, N.W. Washington, DC 20008 202-806-8008 Fax: 202-806-8162 *admissions@law.howard.edu*	50	152		3.2			
Illinois Institute of Technology **(Chicago-Kent College of Law)** 565 West Adams Street Chicago, IL 60661 312-906-5020 Fax: 312-906-5274 *admit@kentlaw.edu*	87	162		3.6	3534	1212	319
Indiana University **(Maurer School of Law)** 211 S. Indiana Avenue Bloomington, IN 47405-7001 812-855-4765 Fax: 812-855-0555 *Lawadmis@indiana.edu*	91	164	17	3.7	2524	805	220
Indiana University-Purdue University **at Indianapolis** **(Indiana University School of** **Law-Indianapolis)** 530 West New York Street Indianapolis, IN 46202-3225 317-274-2459 Fax: 317-278-4780 *khmiller@iupui.edu*	67	156	15	3.5	1766	710	297
Inter American University of Puerto Rico **(School of Law)** P.O. Box 70351 San Juan, PR 00936-8351 787-751-1912, ext. 2013, 2526	64	139	2	3.37	1044	362	238
John Marshall Law School 315 South Plymouth Court Chicago, IL 60604 312-987-1406 Fax: 312-427-5136 *admission@jmls.edu*		154		3.3	3027	1322	385
Lewis and Clark College **(Lewis and Clark Law School)** 10015 Southwest Terwilliger Boulevard Portland, OR 97219 503-768-6613 Fax: 503-768-6793 *lawadmss@lclark.edu*		161	17	3.52	3181	1407	231
Liberty University **(School of Law)** 1971 University Blvd. Lynchburg, VA 24502 434-592-5300 Fax: 434-592-0202 *law@liberty.edu*		150		3.16			

LAW SCHOOL	ACADEMIC STATISTICS				ADMISSION STATISTICS		
	Median LSAT Percentile of Enrolled	Median LSAT Score of Enrolled	Lowest LSAT Percentile of Accepted	Median GPA (4.0 scale) of Enrolled	Total Applicants	Applicants Accepted	Applicants Enrolled
Louisiana State University (Paul M. Hebert Law Center) 202 Law Center, 1 East Campus Drive Baton Rouge, LA 70803 225-578-8646 Fax: 225-578-8647 lynell.cadray@law.lsu.edu	72	157	25	3.44	1407	422	235
Loyola Marymount University (Loyola Law School) 919 Albany Street Los Angeles, CA 90015 213-736-1074 Fax: 213-736-6523 admissions@lls.edu		161		3.44	4640	1433	418
Loyola University Chicago (School of Law) 25 East Pearson Street Chicago, IL 60611 312-915-7170 Fax: 312-915-7906 law-admissions@luc.edu	81	160	26	3.47	4295	1279	267
Loyola University of New Orleans (School of Law) 7214 St. Charles Avenue New Orleans, LA 70118 504-861-5575 Fax: 504-861-5772 ladmit@loyno.edu	56	153	23	3.27	1827	928	323
Marquette University (Law School) Office of Admissions, P.O. Box 1881 Milwaukee, WI 53201-1881 414-288-6767 Fax: 414-288-0676 law.admission@marquette.edu	73	157		3.39	2121	927	219
Mercer University (Walter F. George School of Law) 1021 Georgia Avenue Macon, GA 31207 478-301-2605 Fax: 478-301-2989 Sutton_me@law.mercer.edu		156		3.43	1605	600	161
Michigan State University (College of Law) 230 Law College Bldg. East Lansing, MI 48824-1300 517-432-0222 Fax: 517-432-0098	50	153	10	3.32	1937	929	393
Mississippi College (School of Law) 151 E. Griffith Street Jackson, MS 39201 601-925-7152 pevans@mc.edu	50	150		3.21	1153	603	196
New England Law/Boston 154 Stuart Street Boston, MA 02116 617-422-7210 Fax: 617-422-7201 admit@admin.nesl.edu	53	152	36	3.22	3163	1851	403
New York Law School 185 West Broadway New York, NY 10013-2960 212-431-2888 Fax: 212-966-1522 admissions@nyls.edu		154		3.3	4188	2246	736

LAW SCHOOL	ACADEMIC STATISTICS				ADMISSION STATISTICS		
	Median LSAT Percentile of Enrolled	Median LSAT Score of Enrolled	Lowest LSAT Percentile of Accepted	Median GPA (4.0 scale) of Enrolled	Total Applicants	Applicants Accepted	Applicants Enrolled
New York University (School of Law) 161 Avenue of the Americas, 5th Floor New York, NY 10013 212-998-6060 Fax: 212-995-4527 *law.moreinfo@nyu.edu*		171		3.72	7272	1644	450
North Carolina Central University (School of Law) 640 Nelson Street Durham, NC 27707 919-530-6333 Fax: 919-530-6339 *sbrownb@nccu.edu*		145	143	3.24	3089	531	204
Northeastern University (School of Law) 400 Huntington Avenue Boston, MA 02115 617-373-2395 Fax: 617-373-8865 *c.taubman@neu.edu*	84	161	23	3.4	3798	1280	214
Northern Illinois University (College of Law) Swen Parson Hall, Room 151 De Kalb, IL 60115-2890 815-753-8595 Fax: 815-753-5680 *lawadm@niu.edu*	60	154	17	3.23	1183	474	107
Northern Kentucky University (Salmon P. Chase College of Law) Louie B. Nunn Hall Highland Heights, KY 41099 859-572-5490 Fax: 859-572-6081 *brayg@nku.edu*		153		3.35	1225	526	194
Northwestern University (School of Law) 357 East Chicago Avenue Chicago, IL 60611 312-503-8465 Fax: 312-503-0178 *admissions@law.northwestern.edu*	98	170	20	3.72	5025	952	272
Nova Southeastern University (Shepard Broad Law Center) 3305 College Avenue Fort Lauderdale, FL 33314-7721 954-262-6117 Fax: 954-262-3844 *admission@nsu.law.nova.edu*	41	149	5	3.2	2543	1095	430
Ohio Northern University (Claude W. Pettit College of Law) 525 South Main Street Ada, OH 45810 419-772-2211 Fax: 419-772-3042	50	151	14	3.32	1260	423	130
Ohio State University (Michael E. Moritz College of Law) 55 West 12th Avenue, John Deaver Drinko Hall Columbus, OH 43210-1391 614-292-8810 Fax: 614-292-1383 *lawadmit@osu.edu*	80	161		3.5	2282	629	217

LAW SCHOOL	ACADEMIC STATISTICS				ADMISSION STATISTICS		
	Median LSAT Percentile of Enrolled	Median LSAT Score of Enrolled	Lowest LSAT Percentile of Accepted	Median GPA (4.0 scale) of Enrolled	Total Applicants	Applicants Accepted	Applicants Enrolled
Oklahoma City University (School of Law) 2501 North Blackwelder Avenue Oklahoma City, OK 73106-1493 405-208-5354 Fax: 405-208-5814 lawadmit@okcu.edu	44	150	15	3.2	1334	721	224
Pace University (School of Law) 78 North Broadway White Plains, NY 10603 914-422-4210 Fax: 914-989-8714 calexander@law.pace.edu	62	156	30	3.41	3048	1172	263
Pennsylvania State University (Dickinson School of Law) 100 Beam Building University Park, PA 16802-1910 814-867-1251 Fax: 717-241-3503 dsladmit@psu.edu		158		3.43			
Pepperdine University (School of Law) 24255 Pacific Coast Highway Malibu, CA 90263 310-506-4631 Fax: 310-506-7668	77	158		3.3	3450	909	273
Phoenix School of Law 4041 N. Central Ave. Suite 100 Phoenix, AZ 85012-3330 (602) 682-6800	57	153	15	3.27	724	261	91
Pontifical Catholic University of Puerto Rico (School of Law) 2250 Avenida las Americas suite 543 Ponce, PR 00717-9997 787-841-2000, ext. 1836 Fax: 787-840-4620	13			2.9			
Quinnipiac University (School of Law) 275 Mt. Carmel Avenue Hamden, CT 06518-1908 203-582-3400 Fax: 203-582-3339 ladm@quinnipiac.edu	71	157	36	3.31	2825	1167	160
Regent University (School of Law) 1000 Regent University Drive Virginia Beach, VA 23464-9800 757-352-4584 Fax: 757-352-4139 lawschool@regent.edu		152		3.37	786	368	162
Roger Williams University (School of Law) Ten Metacom Avenue Bristol, RI 02809-5171 401-254-4555 Fax: 401-254-4516 admissions@rwu.edu		152		3.3	1490	871	210
Rutgers University/Camden (School of Law) Fifth and Penn Streets Camden, NJ 08102 856-225-6102 Fax: 856-225-6537 admissions@camlaw.rutgers.edu	85	161	45	3.45	2173	657	235

LAW SCHOOL	ACADEMIC STATISTICS				ADMISSION STATISTICS		
	Median LSAT Percentile of Enrolled	Median LSAT Score of Enrolled	Lowest LSAT Percentile of Accepted	Median GPA (4.0 scale) of Enrolled	Total Applicants	Applicants Accepted	Applicants Enrolled
Rutgers University/Newark (School of Law) Center for Law and Justice, 123 Washington St. Newark, NJ 07102 973-353-5557/5554 Fax: 973-353-3459 *lawinfo@andromeda.rutgers.edu*	75	158		3.33	3519	930	263
Saint John's University (School of Law) 8000 Utopia Parkway Queens, NY 11439 718-990-6474 Fax: 718-990-2526 *lawinfo@stjohns.edu*	84	161		3.48	4036	1479	315
Saint Louis University (School of Law) 3700 Lindell Boulevard St. Louis, MO 63108 314-977-2800 Fax: 314-977-1464 *admissions@law.slu.edu*	68	156	17	3.41	2284	1160	331
Saint Mary's University (School of Law) One Camino Santa Maria San Antonio, TX 78228-8601 210-436-3523 Fax: 210-431-4202 *wwilson@stmarytx.edu*	60	154	18	3.21	1900	806	304
Saint Thomas University (School of Law) 16401 NW 37th Avenue Miami Gardens, FL 33054 305-623-2310 *fkhan@stu.edu*	40	149	11	3.08	2712	1235	228
Samford University (Cumberland School of Law) 800 Lakeshore Drive Birmingham, AL 35229 205-726-2702 Fax: 205-726-2057 *law.admissions@samford.edu*	56	155		3.31	980	506	178
Santa Clara University (School of Law) 500 El Camino Real Santa Clara, CA 95053 408-554-4800 Fax: 408-554-7897 *lawadmissions@scu.edu*	78	159	40	3.36	3717	1888	326
Seattle University (School of Law) 901 12th Avenue, Sullivan Hall, P.O. Box 222000 Seattle, WA 98122-4340 206-398-4200 Fax: 206-398-4058 *lawadmis@seattleu.edu*	71	157	17	3.35	2626	998	332
Seton Hall University (School of Law) One Newark Center Newark, NJ 07102-5210 973-642-8747 Fax: 973-642-8876 *admitme@shu.edu*	78	160	44	3.45	3378	1499	367

LAW SCHOOL	ACADEMIC STATISTICS				ADMISSION STATISTICS		
	Median LSAT Percentile of Enrolled	Median LSAT Score of Enrolled	Lowest LSAT Percentile of Accepted	Median GPA (4.0 scale) of Enrolled	Total Applicants	Applicants Accepted	Applicants Enrolled
South Texas College of Law 1303 San Jacinto Street Houston, TX 77002-7000 713-646-1810 Fax: 713-646-2906 *admissions@stcl.edu*		153		3.21	2330	1169	454
Southern Illinois University (School of Law) Lesar Law Building, Mail Code 6804 Carbondale, IL 62901 618-453-8858 Fax: 618-453-8921 *lawadmit@siu.edu*	56	153	96	3.25	753	362	137
Southern Methodist University (Dedman School of Law) Office of Admissions, P.O. Box 750110 Dallas, TX 75275-0110 214-768-2550 Fax: 214-768-2549 *lawadmit@smu.edu*	91	164		3.76	2790	604	254
Southern University and A & M College (Law Center) Post Office Box 9294 Baton Rouge, LA 70813-9294 225-771-5340 Fax: 225-771-2121 *vwilkerson@sulc.edu*		146		2.8	1002	249	177
Southwestern University (Law School) 3050 Wilshire Boulevard Los Angeles, CA 90010-1106 213-738-6717 Fax: 213-383-1688 *admissions@swlaw.edu*	3	154		3.29	3355	1140	352
Stanford University (Stanford Law School) Crown Quadrangle, 559 Nathan Abbott Way Stanford, CA 94305-8610 650-723-4985 Fax: 650-723-0838 *admissions@law.stanford.edu*		170		3.87	3994	364	170
State University of New York (University at Buffalo Law School) 309 O'Brian Hall Buffalo, NY 14260 716-645-2907 Fax: 716-645-6676 *lwiley@buffalo.edu*	72	157	26	3.52	2104	689	208
Stetson University (Stetson University College of Law) 1401 61st Street South Gulfport, FL 33707 727-562-7802 Fax: 727-343-0136 *zuppo@law.stetson.edu*		156		3.46	3466	1233	395
Suffolk University (Law School) 120 Tremont Street Boston, MA 02108-4977 617-573-8144 Fax: 617-523-1367	75	157		3.3	3261	1696	531
Syracuse University (College of Law) Office of Admissions and Financial Aid, Suite 340 Syracuse, NY 13244-1030 315-443-1962 Fax: 315-443-9568	60	154		3.29	2069		223

LAW SCHOOL	ACADEMIC STATISTICS				ADMISSION STATISTICS		
	Median LSAT Percentile of Enrolled	Median LSAT Score of Enrolled	Lowest LSAT Percentile of Accepted	Median GPA (4.0 scale) of Enrolled	Total Applicants	Applicants Accepted	Applicants Enrolled
Temple University (James E. Beasley School of Law) 1719 N. Broad Street Philadelphia, PA 19122 215-204-5949 Fax: 215-204-1185 *lawadmis@temple.edu*	84	161	20	3.35	5243	1544	323
Texas Southern University (Thurgood Marshall School of Law) 3100 Cleburne Avenue Houston, TX 77004 713-313-7114 Fax: 713-313-1049 *cgardner@tmslaw.tsu.edu*		147		2.91	2135	710	186
Texas Tech University (School of Law) 1802 Hartford Avenue Lubbock, TX 79409 806-742-3990, ext. 273 Fax: 806-742-4617 *donna.williams@ttu.edu*	67	156	15	3.43	1855	652	213
Texas Wesleyan University (School of Law) 1515 Commerce Street Fort Worth, TX 76102 817-212-4040 Fax: 817-212-4141 *lawadmissions@law.txwes.edu*	56	153	33	3.17	1977	873	233
Thomas Jefferson School of Law 2121 San Diego Avenue San Diego, CA 92110 619-297-9700 Fax: 619-294-4713 *info@tjsl.edu*		151	20	2.96	2932	1553	395
Thomas M. Cooley Law School 300 South Capitol Avenue Lansing, MI 48901 517-371-5140 Fax: 517-334-5718 *admissions@cooley.edu*		146	79	3.03	4978	3699	1580
Touro College (Jacob D. Fuchsberg Law Center) 225 Eastview Drive Central Islip, NY 11722 631-761-7010 Fax: 631-761-7019 *gjustice@tourolaw.edu*		149	15	3.04	2075	711	286
Tulane University (Law School) Weinmann Hall, 6329 Freret Street New Orleans, LA 70118 504-865-5930 Fax: 504-865-6710 *admissions@law.tulane.edu*	87	162	25	3.6	2990	890	282
University of Akron (School of Law) 302 Buchtel Common Akron, OH 44325-2901 330-972-7331 Fax: 330-258-2343 *lthorpe@uakron.edu*	56	153	15	3.39	1896	740	202
University of Alabama (School of Law) Box 870382 Tuscaloosa, AL 35487-0382 205-348-5440 Fax: 205-348-3917 *admissions@law.ua.edu*	91	164		3.63	1197	369	182

LAW SCHOOL	ACADEMIC STATISTICS				ADMISSION STATISTICS		
	Median LSAT Percentile of Enrolled	Median LSAT Score of Enrolled	Lowest LSAT Percentile of Accepted	Median GPA (4.0 scale) of Enrolled	Total Applicants	Applicants Accepted	Applicants Enrolled
University of Arizona (James E. Rogers College of Law) 120 E. Speedway P.O. Box 210176 Tucson, AZ 85721-0176 520-621-3477 Fax: 520-621-9140 *admissions@law.arizona.edu*	89	162		3.5	2589	455	153
University of Arkansas (School of Law) Robert A. Leflar Law Center, Waterman Hall Fayetteville, AR 72701 479-575-3102 Fax: 479-575-3937 *jkmiller@uark.edu*		155		3.49	1167	395	139
University of Arkansas at Little Rock (UALR William H. Bowen School of Law) 1201 McMath Avenue Little Rock, AR 72202-5142 501-324-9903 Fax: 501-324-9909 *lawadm@ualr.edu*	57	153	25	3.37	1571	402	161
University of Baltimore (School of Law) 1420 North Charles Street Baltimore, MD 21201-5779 410-837-4459 Fax: 410-837-4450 *lwadmiss@ubmail.ubalt.edu; jzavrotny@ubalt.edu*	61	153	23	3.23	2515	1102	384
University of California (Hastings College of the Law) 200 McAllister Street San Francisco, CA 94102 415-565-4623 Fax: 415-581-8946 *admiss@uchastings.edu*	88	163	33	3.57	5142	1364	401
University of California at Berkeley (School of Law) 215 Boalt Hall Berkeley, CA 94720 510-642-2274 Fax: 510-643-6222 *adissions@law.berkeley.edu*		167	35	3.79	6980	839	269
University of California at Davis (School of Law) Martin Luther King, Jr. Hall - 400 Mrak Hall Drive Davis, CA 95616-5201 530-752-6477 *admissions@lawucdavis.edu*	88	163	52	3.52	3320	1026	213
University of California at Los Angeles (UCLA School of Law) P.O. Box 951445 Los Angeles, CA 90095-1445 310-825-2080 Fax: 310-206-7227 *admissions@law.ucla.edu*	96	168	47	3.75	8255	1383	320
University of Chicago (Law School) 1111 East 60th Street Chicago, IL 60637 773-702-9484 Fax: 773-834-0942 *admissions@law.uchicago.edu*	98	171		3.76	4798	777	190

LAW SCHOOL	ACADEMIC STATISTICS				ADMISSION STATISTICS		
	Median LSAT Percentile of Enrolled	Median LSAT Score of Enrolled	Lowest LSAT Percentile of Accepted	Median GPA (4.0 scale) of Enrolled	Total Applicants	Applicants Accepted	Applicants Enrolled
University of Cincinnati (College of Law) P.O. Box 210040 Cincinnati, OH 45221-0040 513-556-6805 Fax: 513-556-2391 admissions@law.uc.edu	81	160	26	3.6	1322	666	138
University of Colorado (Law School) Campus Box 403, Wolf Law Building Boulder, CO 80309-0403 303-492-7203 Fax: 303-492-2542	89	163	40	3.68	3059	709	166
University of Connecticut (School of Law) 55 Elizabeth Street Hartford, CT 06105 860-570-5159 Fax: 860-570-5153 admissions@law.uconn.edu	90	161		3.38	3260	685	182
University of Dayton (School of Law) 300 College Park Dayton, OH 45469-2760 937-229-3555 Fax: 937-229-4194 lawinfo@notes.udayton.edu	48	151	13	3.16	2097	1214	202
University of Denver (Sturm College of Law) 2255 E. Evans Avenue Denver, CO 80208 303-871-6135 Fax: 303-871-6992 admissions@law.du.edu	78	159	33	3.51	2925	961	300
University of Detroit Mercy (School of Law) 651 East Jefferson Avenue Detroit, MI 48226 313-596-0264 Fax: 313-596-0280 udmlawao@udmercy.edu	44	150	15	3.16	1926	859	282
University of Florida (Fredric G. Levin College of Law) 141 Bruton-Geer Hall, P.O. Box 117622 Gainesville, FL 32611-7622 352-273-0890 Fax: 352-392-4087 madorno@law.ufl.edu		161		3.67	3421	780	308
University of Georgia (School of Law) Hirsch Hall, 225 Herty Drive Athens, GA 30602-6012 706-542-7060 Fax: 706-542-5556 ugajd@uga.edu	90	164	40	3.7	3074	857	241
University of Hawaii at Manoa (William S. Richardson School of Law) 2515 Dole Street Honolulu, HI 96822 808-956-7966 Fax: 808-956-3813 lawadm@hawaii.edu	74	156	23	3.45	1416	269	124

LAW SCHOOL	ACADEMIC STATISTICS				ADMISSION STATISTICS		
	Median LSAT Percentile of Enrolled	Median LSAT Score of Enrolled	Lowest LSAT Percentile of Accepted	Median GPA (4.0 scale) of Enrolled	Total Applicants	Applicants Accepted	Applicants Enrolled
University of Houston (Law Center) 100 Law Center Houston, TX 77204-6060 713-743-2280 Fax: 713-743-2194 lawadmissions@uh.edu	84	161	15	3.34	3652	903	256
University of Idaho (College of Law) P.O. Box 442321 Moscow, ID 83844-2321 208-885-2300 Fax: 208-885-5709 jfinney@uidaho.edu	61	155	15	3.29	743	355	114
University of Illinois (College of Law) 504 East Pennsylvania Avenue Champaign, IL 61820 217-244-6415 Fax: 217-244-1478 admissions@law.uiuc.edu	96	166	25	3.6	2520	761	173
University of Iowa (College of Law) 320 Melrose Avenue Iowa City, IA 52242 319-335-9095 Fax: 319-335-9646 law-admissions@uiowa.edu	84	161		3.61	1291	566	195
University of Kansas (School of Law) 205 Green Hall, 1535 W. 15th Street Lawrence, KS 66045 785-864-4378 Fax: 785-864-5054 admitlaw@ku.edu	71	157	15	3.5	1098	389	163
University of Kentucky (College of Law) 209 Law Building Lexington, KY 40506-0048 606-257-7938 Fax: (859) 323-1061 lawadmissions@email.uky.edu	82	160	30	3.63	1080	392	127
University of La Verne (College of Law) 320 East D Street Ontario, CA 91764 909-460-2001 Fax: 909-460-2082 lawadm@ulv.edu	49	151	33	3.3	1007	429	109
University of Louisville (Louis D. Brandeis School of Law) University of Louisville Belknap Campus-Wilson W. Wyatt Hall Louisville, KY 40292 502-852-6364 Fax: 502-852-8971 brandon.hamilton@louisville.edu		157	16	3.5	1255	465	141
University of Maine (School of Law) 246 Deering Avenue Portland, ME 04102 207-780-4341 Fax: 207-780-4239 mainelaw@usm.maine.edu	65	156	15	3.31	694	280	75

LAW SCHOOL	ACADEMIC STATISTICS				ADMISSION STATISTICS		
	Median LSAT Percentile of Enrolled	Median LSAT Score of Enrolled	Lowest LSAT Percentile of Accepted	Median GPA (4.0 scale) of Enrolled	Total Applicants	Applicants Accepted	Applicants Enrolled
University of Maryland (School of Law) 500 West Baltimore Street Baltimore, MD 21201 410-706-3492 Fax: 410-706-1793 admissions@law.umaryland.edu	84	160	20	3.59	3747	598	290
University of Memphis (Cecil C. Humphreys School of Law) 1 North Front Street Memphis, TN 38103-2189 901-678-5403 Fax: 901-678-0741 lawadmissions@.memphis.edu	68	156	23	3.37	941	313	149
University of Miami (School of Law) P.O. Box 248087, 1311 Miller Drive Coral Gables, FL 33124-8087 305-284-2523 Fax: 305-284-4400 admissions@law.miami.edu	75	157	25	3.46	4695	2409	530
University of Michigan (Law School) 625 South State Street Ann Arbor, MI 48109-1215 734-764-0537 Fax: 734-647-3218 law.jd.admissions@umich.edu	97	169		3.7	5414	1178	371
University of Minnesota (Law School) 229 19th Avenue S. Minneapolis, MN 55455 612-625-3487 Fax: 612-626-1874 jdadmissions@umn.edu	95	167		3.64	3594	911	215
University of Mississippi (L.Q.C. Lamar Hall) P.O. Box 1848 Lamar Law Center University, MS 38677 662-915-6910 Fax: 662-915-1289 bvinson@olemiss.edu	64	155	15	3.59	1572	482	173
University of Missouri-Columbia (School of Law) 103 Hulston Hall Columbia, MO 65211 573-882-6042 Fax: 573-882-9625 heckm@missouri.edu	75	158		3.47	914	400	147
University of Missouri-Kansas City (School of Law) 500 East 52nd Street Kansas City, MO 64110-2499 816-235-1644 Fax: 816-235-5276 brooks@umkc.edu	60	154	17	3.3	950	451	164
University of Montana (School of Law) Missoula, MT 59812 406-243-2698 Fax: 406-243-2576 heidi.fanslow@umontana.edu	60	154	9	3.41	458	172	85

LAW SCHOOL	ACADEMIC STATISTICS				ADMISSION STATISTICS		
	Median LSAT Percentile of Enrolled	Median LSAT Score of Enrolled	Lowest LSAT Percentile of Accepted	Median GPA (4.0 scale) of Enrolled	Total Applicants	Applicants Accepted	Applicants Enrolled
University of Nebraska-Lincoln (College of Law) P.O. Box 830902 Lincoln, NE 68583-0902 402-472-2161 Fax: 402-472-5185 lawadm@unl.edu	72	156	44	3.55	712	369	137
University of Nevada, Las Vegas (William S. Boyd School of Law) 4505 Maryland Parkway, Box 451003 Las Vegas, NV 89154-1003 702-895-2440 Fax: 702-895-2414 request@law.unlv.edu		158		3.48	1737	384	158
University of New Mexico (School of Law) MSC11-6070, 1 University of New Mexico Albuquerque, NM 87131-0001 505-277-0958 Fax: 505-277-9958 witherington@law.unm.edu		156		3.36	1200	264	112
University of North Carolina at Chapel Hill (School of Law) Campus Box 3380, Van Hecke-Wettach Hall Chapel Hill, NC 27599-3380 919-962-5109 Fax: 919-843-7939 law_admission@unc.edu	83	161	36	3.65	3286	609	241
University of North Dakota (School of Law) Box 9003 Grand Forks, ND 58202 701-777-2104 Fax: 701-777-2217 linda.kohoutek@thor.law.und.nodak.edu		151		3.57	382	153	69
University of Notre Dame (Notre Dame Law School) P.O. Box 780 Notre Dame, IN 46556-0780 574-631-6626 Fax: 574-631-5474 lawadmit@nd.edu		166		3.6	3178	810	186
University of Oklahoma (College of Law) Andrew M. Coats Hall, 300 Timberdell Road Norman, OK 73019 405-325-4728 Fax: 405-325-0502 rlucas@ou.edu	75	158	49	3.51	1137	355	199
University of Oregon (School of Law, William W. Knight Law Center) 1221 University of Oregon Eugene, OR 97403-1221 541-346-3846 Fax: 541-346-3984 admissions@law.uoregon.edu		159		3.34	2093	888	182
University of Pennsylvania (Law School) 3400 Chestnut Street Philadelphia, PA 19104-6204 215-898-7400 Fax: 215-898-9606 admissions@law.upenn.edu	98	170	50	3.82	6205	895	255

LAW SCHOOL	ACADEMIC STATISTICS				ADMISSION STATISTICS		
	Median LSAT Percentile of Enrolled	Median LSAT Score of Enrolled	Lowest LSAT Percentile of Accepted	Median GPA (4.0 scale) of Enrolled	Total Applicants	Applicants Accepted	Applicants Enrolled
University of Pittsburgh (School of Law) 3900 Forbes Avenue Pittsburgh, PA 15260 412-648-1413 Fax: 412-648-1318 Mccall@law.pitt.edu		159		3.4	2177	811	235
University of Puerto Rico (School of Law) P.O. Box 23349, UPR Station Rio Piedras, PR 00931-3349 787-999-9551 Fax: 787-999-9564 arosario-lebron@law.upr.edu	27	146	2	3.64	614	220	197
University of Richmond (School of Law) 28 Westhampton Way Richmond, VA 23173 804-289-8189 Fax: 804-287-6516 lawadmissions@richmond.edu	84	161	44	3.18	2036	584	150
University of Saint Thomas (School of Law) 1000 LaSalle Ave. Minneapolis, MN 55403 651-962-4895 Fax: 651-962-4876 lawschool@stthomas.edu	72	157	33	3.44	1551	785	174
University of San Diego (School of Law) 5998 Alcala Park San Diego, CA 92110 619-260-4528 Fax: 619-260-2218 jdinfo@sandiego.edu	84	161		3.28	4694		359
University of San Francisco (School of Law) 2130 Fulton Street San Francisco, CA 94117-1080 415-422-6586 Fax: 415-422-5442 lawadmissions@usfca.edu	78	159	15	3.28	3582	1300	250
University of South Carolina (School of Law) 701 South Main Street Columbia, SC 29208 803-777-6605 Fax: 803-777-7751 usclaw@law.sc.edu		158		3.46	1973	730	240
University of South Dakota (School of Law) 414 East Clark Street Vermillion, SD 57069-2390 605-677-5443 Fax: 605-677-5417 law.school@usd.edu	53	152	8	3.44	382	217	79
University of Southern California (Gould School of Law) Los Angeles, CA 90089-0071 213-740-2523 admissions@law.usc.edu	96	167		3.6	6024	1149	215

LAW SCHOOL	ACADEMIC STATISTICS				ADMISSION STATISTICS		
	Median LSAT Percentile of Enrolled	Median LSAT Score of Enrolled	Lowest LSAT Percentile of Accepted	Median GPA (4.0 scale) of Enrolled	Total Applicants	Applicants Accepted	Applicants Enrolled
University of Tennessee (College of Law) 1505 W. Cumberland Avenue Knoxville, TN 37996-1810 865-974-4131 Fax: 865-974-1572 lawadmit@utk.edu	81	160	26	3.55	1468	398	158
University of Texas at Austin (School of Law) 727 East Dean Keeton Street Austin, TX 78705 512-232-1200 Fax: 512-471-2765 admissions@law.utexas.edu	92	166	35	3.6	4789	1172	401
University of the District of Columbia (David A. Clarke School of Law) 4200 Connecticut Avenue, N.W. Washington, DC 20008 202-274-7341 Fax: 202-274-5583 vcanty@udc.edu; lawadmission@udc.edu	53	152	23	3	1601	336	123
University of the Pacific (McGeorge School of Law) 3200 Fifth Avenue Sacramento, CA 95817 916-739-7105 Fax: 916-739-7301 mcgeorge@pacific.edu	75	158	44	3.4	3042	1293	330
University of Toledo (College of Law) 2801 West Bancroft Street Toledo, OH 43606-3390 419-530-4131 Fax: 419-530-4345 law.utoledo.edu	64	155	44	3.35	869	522	182
University of Tulsa (College of Law) 3120 East Fourth Place Tulsa, OK 74104-2499 918-631-2406 Fax: 918-631-3630 april-fox@utulsa.edu	64	155	41	3.22	1304	659	140
University of Utah (S.J. Quinney College of Law) 332 South 1400 East Room 101 Salt Lake City, UT 84112 801-581-7479 Fax: 801-581-6897 aguilarr@law.utah.edu	82	160	17	3.6	1277	375	128
University of Virginia (School of Law) 580 Massie Road Charlottesville, VA 22903-1738 434-924-7351 Fax: 434-982-2128 lawadmit@virginia.edu	98	170	48	3.85	7880	1166	368
University of Washington (School of Law) Box 353020 Seattle, WA 98195-3020 206-543-4078 Fax: 206-543-5671 lawadm@u.washington.edu	89	163	49	3.66	2448	623	181
University of Wisconsin (Law School) 975 Bascom Mall Madison, WI 53706 608-262-5914 Fax: 608-263-3191 admissions@law.wisc.edu	86	162		3.6	2951	698	278

LAW SCHOOL	ACADEMIC STATISTICS				ADMISSION STATISTICS		
	Median LSAT Percentile of Enrolled	Median LSAT Score of Enrolled	Lowest LSAT Percentile of Accepted	Median GPA (4.0 scale) of Enrolled	Total Applicants	Applicants Accepted	Applicants Enrolled
University of Wyoming (College of Law) Dept. 3035, 1000 East University Avenue Laramie, WY 82071 307-766-6416 Fax: 307-766-6417 dburke@uwyo.edu	58	153	13	3.41	631	198	83
Valparaiso University (School of Law) Wesemann Hall, 656 S. Greenwich Street Valparaiso, IN 46383-6493 219-465-7821 Fax: 219-465-7808 law.admissions@valpo.edu		151		3.47	3248	810	214
Vanderbilt University (Law School) 131 21st Avenue South Nashville, TN 37203 615-322-6452 Fax: 615-322-1531 admissions@law.vanderbilt.edu	96	168		3.71	4851	1193	195
Vermont Law School P.O. Box 96, Chelsea Street South Royalton, VT 05068-0096 802-831-1239 Fax: 802-831-1174 admiss@vermontlaw.edu	64	155		3.32	884	590	233
Villanova University (School of Law) 299 N. Spring Mill Road Villanova, PA 19085 610-519-7010 Fax: 610-519-6291 admissions@law.villanova.edu	87	162	53	3.44	3254	1401	255
Wake Forest University (School of Law) P.O. Box 7206, Reynolda Station Winston-Salem, NC 27109 336-758-5437 Fax: 336-758-4632 admissions@law.wfu.edu	93	162	40	3.6	2775	908	154
Washburn University (School of Law) 1700 College Topeka, KS 66621 785-670-1185 Fax: 785-670-1120 admissions@washburnlaw.edu		154		3.31	957	453	159
Washington and Lee University (School of Law) Lewis Hall Lexington, VA 24450 540-458-8503 Fax: 540-458-8586 lawadm@wlu.edu	94	166	44	3.53	3416	873	135
Washington University in St. Louis (School of Law) Box 1120, One Brookings Drive St. Louis, MO 63130 314-935-4525 Fax: 314-935-8778 admiss@wulaw.wustl.edu		166	50	3.6	3770	954	222
Wayne State University (Law School) 471 West Palmer Street Detroit, MI 48202 313-577-3937 Fax: 313-993-8129 emjackson@wayne.edu	67	156	35	3.51	1510	568	185

LAW SCHOOL	ACADEMIC STATISTICS				ADMISSION STATISTICS		
	Median LSAT Percentile of Enrolled	Median LSAT Score of Enrolled	Lowest LSAT Percentile of Accepted	Median GPA (4.0 scale) of Enrolled	Total Applicants	Applicants Accepted	Applicants Enrolled
West Virginia University (College of Law) P.O. Box 6130 Morgantown, WV 26506 304-293-5304 Fax: 304-293-6891 *wvulaw.Admissions@mail.wvu.edu*	81	151	9	3.51	831	326	152
Western New England College (School of Law) 1215 Wilbraham Road Springfield, MA 01119 413-782-1406 Fax: 413-796-2067 *admissions@law.wnec.edu*	56	153	33	3.23	1696	914	181
Western State University (College of Law) 1111 North State College Blvd Fullerton, CA 92831 714-459-1101 Fax: 714-441-1748 *adm@wsulaw.edu*		151		3.16	1640	794	188
Whittier College (Whittier Law School) 3333 Harbor Blvd. Costa Mesa, CA 92626 714-444-4141, ext. 121 Fax: 714-444-0250 *info@law.whittier.edu*	61	154	23	3.1	3144	982	273
Widener University (Widener University School of Law) 4601 Concord Pike, P.O. Box 7474 Wilmington, DE 19803-0474 302-477-2162 Fax: 302-477-2224 *law.admissions@law.widener.edu*	52	152	15	3.12	2368	1074	383
Widener University (Widener University School of Law) 3800 Vartan Way, P.O. Box 69381 Harrisburg, PA 17106-9381 717-541-3903 Fax: 717-541-3999 *law.admissions@law.widener.edu*	44	150	15	3.2	908	624	183
Willamette University (College of Law) 245 Winter Street S.E. Salem, OR 97301 503-370-6282 Fax: 503-370-6087 *law-admission@willamette.edu*	60	154		3.22	1532	598	148
William Mitchell College of Law 875 Summit Avenue St. Paul, MN 55105-3076 651-290-6343 Fax: 651-290-6414 *admissions@wmitchell.edu*	68	156	24	3.4	1692	792	300
Yale University (Yale Law School) P.O. Box 208329 New Haven, CT 06520-8329 203-432-4995 *admissions.law@yale.edu*	99	173	80	3.91	3677	249	189
Yeshiva University (Benjamin N. Cardozo School of Law) 55 Fifth Avenue New York, NY 10003 212-790-0274 Fax: 212-790-0482 *lawinfo@yu.edu*	91	164		3.52	4815	1348	371

CHAPTER 7

Which Law School?

The decision as to which law school to attend can be even more complicated than the decision whether to attend law school. Beware of law school admissions and recruitment people. They want you—actually they want your seat deposit. Most of them are personable, well-informed, and genuine. They are, however, selling a product: their school. The best defense against the hard sell is comparison shopping. Listen to a number of different pitches before you make a choice. Check out the various claims and promises relying on your own independent investigation rather than on stock promotional materials. *Barron's Guide to Law Schools* is particularly suited to help you accomplish this objective (see Part III of this Guide for more information).

Beware of family, friends, and prelaw advisors, who push you to attend a particular law school. Utilize impartial advice, particularly guidance from professional counselors and advisors, in making your decision. Their experience and knowledge can be invaluable. But remember! Your prelaw advisor may like a certain school because she graduated from it. Your career counselor may have been particularly impressed by the speech he heard at an open house for a certain law school. Your lawyer friend may or may not be privy to accurate information. Sometimes, opinions masked by objectivity are far from objective. And most important of all, remember that no single school is right for everyone.

Beware of letting your procrastination make decisions for you. There are many critical dates in the law school admission process. Don't be foreclosed from applying to schools, seeking financial aid, or pursuing any alternative because you didn't do it in time. If you want to make the best choice, you should seek to maximize your options, and the best way to maximize your options is to stay on top of the process. Start early. Develop a tickler file to remind you in advance about critical dates. Most calendar programs for personal computers allow you to save important dates. Set aside sufficient time to meet deadlines and accomplish your objectives. Remember that the easiest decision is not always the best one.

Barron's Guide to Law Schools contains chapters on the LSAT (Chapters 12 and 13), the job outlook for graduates, including starting salaries (Chapter 10), financial aid (Chapter 8), and profiles of law schools themselves (Chapters 15 and 16).

The checklist on page 56 may help you to clarify your objectives and focus your research efforts as you think about law school. It lists the primary questions you should address as you evaluate law schools. If you can determine what choices are best for you, you not only will increase your chances of being accepted, but also improve the likelihood that law school will be a rewarding experience.

GEOGRAPHY

Geographical considerations inevitably come into play. A majority of law school graduates accept positions in the region where they went to law school. Those who do not stay in the same geographic area tend to return to the region where they grew up or where they have family. This is true not only for so-called local and regional law schools, but for national law schools as well. It is easier to find a job if you are physically located in the area where your job search occurs. Thus, if you know where you want to settle after graduation, you may want to consider limiting your applications to law schools in that geographic area.

Although most law school graduates settle in the largest metropolitan areas, both law schools and legal employment are found in a variety of settings. You may want to consider, as an alternative to pursuing a legal education at a school in a big city, attending school or working in a smaller city or town, a suburban area within a larger metropolitan population, or a rural area. You may have business, political, or personal ties to a community that would make it advantageous to target that place for postgraduate

CHECKLIST ON CHOOSING A LAW SCHOOL

Where geographically do you want to go to law school?

Family considerations
- ☐ Desire to be close to parents, relatives
- ☐ Sick or special needs relatives for whom you have responsibilities
- ☐ Contacts that will help you as a practicing lawyer
- ☐ Work in a family business
- ☐ Financial considerations (such as needing to live at home)
- ☐ Family ties to a particular law school

Personal considerations
- ☐ Significant other lives in area
- ☐ Significant other works in area
- ☐ Friends or social activities
- ☐ Support groups (church, social clubs, business relationships)
- ☐ Health care
- ☐ Contacts that will help you as a practicing lawyer

Current job
- ☐ Future job prospects
- ☐ Knowledge of local business and legal community
- ☐ Work experience
- ☐ Employment opportunities

Community setting
- ☐ Urban
- ☐ Suburban
- ☐ Rural
- ☐ Ethnic or religious community

Regional preferences
- ☐ Northeast
- ☐ Midwest
- ☐ Southeast
- ☐ Southwest
- ☐ West Coast
- ☐ Mountains

What areas of law practice interest you?
- ☐ Representing individuals with ordinary legal problems
- ☐ Representing corporations in national and international business transactions
- ☐ Representing government entities in carrying out the law
- ☐ Representing people of limited means
- ☐ Engaging in law reform and other public interest activities

What programs does the law school you are considering offer?
- ☐ General legal curriculum
- ☐ Curriculum built around the law of a particular state
- ☐ Specialized course offerings in particular fields of law
- ☐ Access to part time and summer jobs
- ☐ Internship and externship opportunities
- ☐ Clinical programs designed to prepare you to practice law
- ☐ Sponsorship of and access to extracurricular cultural or legal activities

What kind of law school can you afford?
- ☐ State or private institution
- ☐ Evening (part time) or day (full time) program
- ☐ Availability of financial aid, scholarships

Cost of living in the community where the law school is located
- ☐ Housing in the community
- ☐ Campus housing
- ☐ Transportation
- ☐ Food and entertainment

What sort of atmosphere do you want in your law school?

Size of student body
- ☐ Large (1,000+ students)
- ☐ Medium (600–1,000 students)
- ☐ Small (fewer than 600 students)

Competitiveness of students
- ☐ Cutthroat atmosphere
- ☐ Cooperative atmosphere

Physical plant
- ☐ General appearance
- ☐ Classrooms
- ☐ Faculty and administrative offices
- ☐ Student space
- ☐ Technology support
- ☐ Parking and access to transportation

Library resources
- ☐ Available volumes
- ☐ Professional support
- ☐ Study space

Student services
- ☐ General attitude of students toward the institution
- ☐ Student government (Student Bar Association)
- ☐ Law reviews
- ☐ Moot court and other competitions
- ☐ Active student organizations
- ☐ Academic support
- ☐ Personal and crisis counseling

Educational approach
- ☐ Like *The Paper Chase*
- ☐ Indifferent to students
- ☐ Positive atmosphere for students
- ☐ Intellectually stimulating
- ☐ Focus on bar preparation

University community
- ☐ Part of a large university
- ☐ Part of a small university or liberal arts college
- ☐ Part of an urban university
- ☐ Law school is/is not situated on main university campus
- ☐ Independent law school not connected to university

Special Programs, concentration
- ☐ Areas of practice represented by curricular concentrations
- ☐ Graduate law programs
- ☐ Special centers and research projects

Which schools will accept you?
- ☐ LSAT Scores
- ☐ Undergraduate GPA
- ☐ Special considerations (such as ethnicity)
- ☐ Work, education, life experiences
- ☐ Other factors that make you unique
- ☐ Recommendations
- ☐ Opportunity for personal interview
- ☐ Timing of your application
- ☐ Availability of pre-law school preparatory program

employment. You or your family may have ties to a university or law school that would lead you to go to school there.

COURSE CONCENTRATION

You may want to give thought to what substantive areas of practice interest you. Although many entering law students do not have a clue about what areas of law they wish to pursue, sometime during the tenure of their legal education, they will have to make those choices. Other law students know before they begin law school that they are interested in a particular type of practice, and may choose a law school because of its curricular concentration in that field. Although the first year curriculum and many core upper-level electives are common in most law schools, different law schools will have different upper-level course offerings and concentrations. You should look carefully at law school web sites and catalogs, and talk to school representatives about these differences as part of the decision-making process. In addition, discuss law schools with alumni, or lawyers who may be in a position to compare different schools in a state or metropolitan area with more than one law school.

COST

What kind of school can you afford? State law schools are usually less expensive for residents than for nonresidents, or than private schools. Among private schools, tuition may differ considerably depending on the prestige of the institution and other considerations. Schools also differ considerably as to the amount of financial aid and scholarship funds that are available to incoming students. You may be able to get substantial financial assistance from a school that is less competitive academically than you could expect from a more prestigious institution. Additionally, schools with part-time or evening programs provide an opportunity for students to attend law school while continuing to work full time.

INSTITUTIONAL CULTURE

You should look carefully for information about the school's institutional culture. Although it is hard to discern sometimes, every school has a unique personality. Its geographic location and student body demographic makeup will affect the school's atmosphere. The background of the faculty members will, too. Do most of them have experience practicing law? Or did most come directly into teaching from postgraduate appellate clerkships? What is the size of the student body, the faculty, and average classes? In some ways, a larger law school may seem more vibrant and diverse, while a smaller law school will feel more intimate and supportive. Look at the competitiveness of the institution. Do you want to see how you fare in the most highly charged competitive environment? Do you want to be a big fish in a little pond? Will you be happy just to get accepted? Take a look at the physical plant, the library, and other resources available to the law school. Consider what benefits accrue to the law school from affiliation with its parent university. Think about the history of the university and the law school, and how the institutional roots have molded the law school culture today. Ask about the educational philosophy of the institution, whether it is highly theoretical, or practical and skills-oriented. Find out whether the curriculum focuses on the law of a particular jurisdiction, or is concentrated in some other way.

STUDENT LIFE

Observe whether current students are satisfied with services, such as financial aid and career services. Consider the availability of cocurricular and extracurricular groups, such as law review, moot court, law school student government, and other student organizations.

LIKELIHOOD OF ADMISSION

Finally, look at which law schools will accept you. If your LSAT and GPA are both very strong, you will have significantly more opportunities than people with less impressive credentials. If either your LSAT or GPA is less stellar, the number of law schools interested in you will inevitably drop. You may need to demonstrate your aptitude through other activities and experiences. If your LSAT and GPA are both low, you may find it challenging to find a single law school that will accept you (see pages 20–22). A few law schools offer programs that permit applicants to compete for slots during the summer prior to admission.

Some law schools may be located in a geographic area that does not draw as many applications as more populous ones. Some states accredit law schools not approved by the

American Bar Association (ABA). Graduates of non-ABA-approved schools usually can only take the bar in the state in which the school is accredited. These schools usually have fewer and less competitive applications, and for some people this may be the only way to go to law school. Before committing to a law school not approved by the ABA you should look carefully at all the factors described in the last paragraph (see also Chapter 16).

U.S. NEWS AND OTHER RANKINGS

Each year *U.S. News and World Report* produces a ranking of law schools that is relied on extensively by many law school applicants and their advisors. The rankings, based on both statistical data and surveys of lawyers, judges and legal educators, have a tendency to imbue a degree of certainty into the process of evaluating law schools that does not exist in reality. Other similar surveys, reported by different publications, fall into the same trap. They all presume that a single set of measurable criteria will work for all applicants. This is simply not the case.

The American Bar Association has circulated a statement warning students against the uncritical use of law school rankings (see box below). This position is supported by the Law School Admissions Council and most law school deans and admissions officers.

Rating of Law Schools

No rating of law schools beyond the simple statement of their accreditation status is attempted or advocated by the American Bar Association. Qualities that make one kind of school good for one student may not be as important to another. The American Bar Association and its Section of Legal Education and Admissions to the Bar have issued disclaimers of any law school rating system. Prospective law students should consider a variety of factors in making their choice among approved schools.

If you look at a ranking system such as *U.S. News,* do so with a skeptical eye. Remember that reputations in legal education are established over decades. Recognize that different schools are "best" for different people. And accept the fact that all ABA-approved law schools go through the same rigorous accreditation process. The process involves both quality standards and regular inspection of ABA-approved institutions. Thus, qualitative differences among law school educational programs are negligible, although the credentials of students who attend different schools may vary according to the relative prestige of those schools.

Rather than looking at a rough-tiered ranking of schools that means very little in terms of the quality of legal education you will receive, it makes more sense to rank specific factors that do have a relationship to the quality of education, to the experience that individual students will encounter in different schools, and to the potential to achieve the career choice most suited to the individual.

The following list includes a number of factors you can use to compare law schools. The information relevant to these factors is easily accessible in the school profiles included in this Guide, beginning on page 216. Some of the factors may require you to search law school websites or consult other information sources. You might even call law schools with specific questions. The key, however, is to collect the same data from all the schools you are considering.

You may want to develop tables or charts comparing the schools on your list to see how well they do in the areas that are important to you. Remember: this list is just a guide; you may find some of the factors less germane to your personal evaluation of schools, and you may also think of other comparisons that are not included in the list. The message, however, is that you should rank schools on specific criteria that will have meaning to your choice of law school to attend, and ultimately to your success in the legal profession. You might be surprised what you learn.

- Student qualifications for enrolled students
  - LSAT
    - Median
    - Highest and lowest quartiles
  - Undergraduate GPA
    - Median
    - Highest and lowest quartiles
- Average age of students
  - Full-time students
  - Part-time students
- Diversity percentages
  - African Americans
  - Latinos
  - Asian Americans
  - Native Americans
  - GLBT students
  - Other significant religious, ethnic, political groups

- Women
- Foreign lawyers/law students
- Cost of tuition
- Location
  - Urban
  - Suburban
  - Rural
  - State Capital
  - Cost of Living
- Availability of part-time enrollment option
- Financial aid
  - Percentage of students on full academic scholarship
  - Percentage of students on partial academic scholarship
  - Percentage of students on full need-based scholarship
  - Percentage of students on partial need-based scholarship
  - Percentage of students with college work study, co-op, or other work-based financial aid
  - Percentage of students with student loans
  - Average loan indebtedness for students at graduation
- Organization of curriculum
  - Law school religious or political affiliation
  - First year courses
    - Number of hours required
    - Number of courses required
    - Grading system/mandatory curve
  - Legal research/writing program
    - Full-time, adjunct, or student teachers
    - Upper-level writing opportunities (seminars, drafting courses)
  - Availability of clinical programs
    - Practice areas
    - Number of students served
  - Professional skills courses
  - Specialized programs
    - Substantive concentrations
    - Certificate programs
    - Joint degree programs
    - LLM programs
    - Internships (Local, Abroad)
    - Externships
  - Availability of independent research opportunities with faculty members
  - Availability of opportunities to serve as a faculty research assistant
- Library
  - Number of library volumes
  - Number of study spaces in the library
- Commitment to innovative technology?
  - IT support
  - Laptop requirement
  - Wired or wireless classrooms
  - Connectivity or computers in the library

- Class size
  - First year class?
    - Average number of students in first year sections
    - Number of small enrollment classes
  - Graduates
  - Attrition
- Faculty
  - Student-to-faculty ratio
  - Credentials
  - Expertise in specialized fields
  - Scholarship
  - Community and bar activities
  - Accessibility to students
  - Percentage of tenured faculty
  - Percentage of diversity faculty
- Career patterns
  - Percentage of employed graduates
  - Percentage of graduates practicing law
    - Large Firms
    - Small Firms
    - Corporate Legal
    - Government
    - Judicial clerkships
    - Legal services, public interest
    - Nonlegal jobs
  - Student employment
    - Summer after first year
    - Summer after second year
    - Part-time legal employment
    - Full-time employment for part-time students
    - Nonlegal employment
  - Geographic distribution of graduates
- Bar passage
  - Percentage compared to state average where most graduates take the exam
  - First time percentage
  - Ultimate percentage (graduates who eventually pass a bar exam)
- Campus
  - Part of larger university campus or standalone
  - Transportation
  - Parking
  - Housing
  - Safety, security
- Student activities
  - Law reviews
  - Moot court programs
  - Student government
  - Political, religious, ethnic, public interest organizations
- Services
  - Career Services
    - Career counseling
    - Career library and resources
    - Career programs
    - Campus interviews (Number of firms, Cities represented)

- Job listings and contacts with firms not coming to campus
- Part-time job listings
- Assistance for alumni
- Government employment
- Public interest employment
○ Health insurance and services
○ Counseling services
○ Child care
○ Recreational facilities
○ Students with disabilities

All of these factors are quantifiable, and as such permit you to compare schools to each other. Thus, if you are considering ten schools, you only have to look at the comparative data for those schools, but rather than saying that one school is in Tier 2 while another is in Tier 3, you can actually rank the schools based on factors that are important to you. This approach may be a little more labor intensive, but it is much more likely to produce an outcome that is tailored to your needs, priorities, and expectations.

CHAPTER 8

Is Financial Aid Available?

Unless you are independently wealthy, you are probably having some concerns about financing your legal education. The important thing to keep in mind is that funds are available to help you. The bulk of the assistance for law school students takes the form of student loans. There is very little money available for outright grants. Most law school students and their families are willing to take on a heavy debt load as an investment in the future.

There are certain concepts relative to financial aid that all applicants should know. All programs that are federally funded or sponsored have very strict requirements as to eligibility. Law school financial aid offices process the loan applications in accordance with these rules and regulations. They have very little leeway except in the awarding of institutional funds.

Federal Methodology (FM) Federal Methodology is the federally mandated method of determining financial need.

Need Based Need-based loans require a demonstration of need based on FM.

Merit Based Merit-based aid does not require a showing of need.

Base Year Base year is the prior calendar year and is used to calculate need under FM.

Independent Student Law school students are deemed to be independent due to their professional student status.

Budget The budget is set by the financial aid office each year. FM allows only *required* student expenses. These expenses are: tuition, fees, books, living expenses including room and board, transportation costs, an allowance for personal expenses, health insurance, and miscellaneous expenses. Required student expenses will not cover, in most cases, car payments, credit card monthly payments, alimony, or mortgage payments.

Financial Need Financial need is the difference between expected family contribution and the total cost of attendance.

Packaging Policy Packaging policy is set by each law school and delineates the priorities for awarding financial aid.

CAMPUS-BASED PROGRAMS

Certain financial aid programs are referred to as campus-based. First in this category of aid would be scholarships and grants funded entirely by the law school. At most law schools the amount of money available for this form of aid is small. Since the money comes from the institution, the institution sets the requirements for receiving the aid. In most cases these awards will require a showing of need. Occasionally, a law school will have some merit-based aid.

Carl D. Perkins Loans are another form of campus-based aid. Each year the institution receives an allocation from the federal government for this program. It is basically a loan program administered by the institution in that the institution lends the money to the student and the institution is responsible for collecting the loans from the recipients. Perkins loans carry the lowest interest rate and at most schools are reserved for the neediest students. There is a cumulative limit of $40,000 on all Perkins loans, both graduate and undergraduate.

Another type of campus-based aid is the Federal Work Study (FWS) program. Again, the institution receives a yearly allocation from the federal government to fund this program. FWS is a need-based program and may be reserved for the neediest students. The financial aid award will indicate that the law student is eligible to receive a certain amount of money under the FWS program. This money can be earned either by working on campus or off campus. On-campus jobs take the form of working in the library or other law school offices or as research assistants for faculty members. Off-campus jobs can only be with nonprofit or governmental entities. Some examples would be work at a public defender's office, as a law clerk for a judge, or for a state or federal agency. FWS funds do not have to be repaid.

FEDERAL LOAN PROGRAMS

Other federal loan programs are available through the U.S. Department of Education. These loans were formally administered under the auspices of banks, credit unions, savings and loan associations, and other private lenders. The Stafford Student Loan is a relatively low-interest federal loan available to law school students. There are two types of Stafford loans: the Federal Family Education Loan Program (provided by private lenders) and the Federal Direct Student Loan Program (provided by the U.S. government directly to students). Stafford loans are insured by state guarantee agencies and must be approved by that agency. Subsidized Stafford loans require demonstration of financial need. Law school students can borrow a maximum of $20,500 per academic year under this program but may not exceed $138,500 in total Stafford loans for law school.

OTHER LOAN PROGRAMS

Other loan programs are available to law school students but do not receive federal interest subsidies. These loan programs do not require demonstration of financial need and carry the highest interest rates. An applicant may also have to show a good credit rating or creditworthiness.

The Access Group has developed a loan program specifically designed to fit the needs of law school students. Under this program the student can apply for federally subsidized and unsubsidized Stafford loans as well as a private loan from The Access Group. This private loan is the Law Access Loan (LAL). Students with good credit can borrow up to the total cost of attendance.

There are other private loan programs available. Law Loans is one such program. Your financial aid office will have information on these programs.

OUTSIDE FUNDING

Various foundations and business and professional organizations offer assistance in financing your education. Some programs are geared for minority and disadvantaged students such as the Council on Legal Education Opportunity, the Earl Warren Legal Training Program, the ABA Legal Opportunity Scholarship and the Mexican American Legal Defense Education Fund. The financial aid office can give you complete information on these other programs. As funds for most of these programs are limited, you should apply early.

Another source of outside funding comes from various state and county bar associations that award scholarships. The amounts and requirements will vary, but this possibility should not be overlooked.

Some states also offer grants to needy graduate students. Contact your local state guarantee agency to explore this option. Your financial aid office (both graduate and undergraduate) can supply you with their names and addresses.

Money is available to finance your legal education. But at what cost? The interest rate increases as you move from the Perkins loan (lowest interest) to the Stafford and the private loans. Borrowing decisions should be carefully made as these loans ultimately have to be repaid.

APPLICATION PROCESS

All law schools require that the financial information necessary to determine financial need be submitted to a national processing center. Most schools use the Free Application for Federal Student Aid (FAFSA). See *http://www. fafsa.ed.gov/.*

The FAFSA should be filed online as early as possible, and in any event prior to the FAFSA Priority Deadline, which was February 15 in 2008. Processing time for the FAFSA is approximately four to six weeks. Read the forms carefully and answer all required parts. After the FAFSA has been analyzed, a report will be sent to the schools you have designated.

When the law school financial aid office receives your report generated by the FAFSA, it will review your file in accordance with its packaging policy. This means that the expected student contribution will be subtracted from the school budget to arrive at financial need.

Some schools' packaging policies will require that the first level of need be met by the Stafford loan. If there is any remaining need, you may be eligible for Perkins loan funds and Federal Work Study. After the financial aid office determines your level of eligibility for aid, you will receive notification. This may be four to six weeks or longer after the receipt of the FAFSA report.

The loan applications must be completed, signed, and returned to the lender. If a credit report is required, it is done at this time. If the lender/guarantee agency approves your loan, the check will be disbursed. The approval process can take up to six weeks. For most loans the interest starts to accrue when the check is disbursed. In most cases the check will be made co-payable to the student and the law school. When the check arrives, you will be asked to endorse it, and then the school will endorse it and credit it to your account. If the amount credited is more than is owed, the school will process a refund check for you.

DEFERMENT

It is possible to defer repayment on student loans you received as an undergraduate as long as you are a full-time student. You should request deferment forms from your lender. Take these forms to the registrar at your law school. Federal regulations require that you be a matriculated student so these forms will not be signed and sent to your lender until after the semester starts.

It is important to file deferment forms and to know if they have to be filed annually with your lender. If you are not granted a deferment, don't make payments on your undergraduate loans, and are declared in default, you run the risk of being denied loans for your legal education.

REPAYMENT AND CONSOLIDATION

While the money is available to finance your legal education, ultimately it must be repaid. You will have to start making payments six to nine months after graduation. There are several different ways to repay a Federal Direct Loan.

A Standard Repayment Plan has a fixed monthly repayment amount for a fixed period of time, usually 10 years.

An Extended Repayment Plan has a lower fixed monthly payment amount, and loan repayment can be extended beyond the usual 10 years.

A Graduated Repayment Plan usually begins with lower monthly payments, and payment amounts increase at specified times. Payments may be for the usual 10-year period, or they may be extended beyond 10 years.

An Income-contingent Repayment Plan for Direct Stafford loans sets annual repayment amounts based on the borrower's income after leaving school. The loan is repaid over an extended period of time, not to exceed 25 years.

College Cost Reduction and Access Act was enacted in September 2007, creating a new loan forgiveness option for borrowers who hold public service jobs. To qualify for the public service loan forgiveness, a borrower must:

• Make 120 qualifying monthly payments on an elegibile Federal Direct Loan on or after October 1, 2007.
• Be employed in a public service job as defined in the CCRAA during the time he or she makes the qualifying monthly payments.
• Be employed in a public service job as defined in the CCRAA at the time the Secretary of Education forgives the loan.
• Make qualifying payments under one (or a combination of) the following:
  ○ Income contingent repayment plan
  ○ Income-based repayment plan
  ○ Standard repayment play with a 10-year repayment period
  ○ One of the other Direct Loan repayment plans under which the borrower paid a monthly amount that is not less than what the borrower would pay under a 10-year repayment plan.

To find out more information, please visit *http://www.nasfaa.org/PDFs/2007/FAQPublic.pdf.*

by Angela D'Agostino and Cathy Alexander, adapted from the original article by Christine A. Koterba, Director of Financial Aid, Widener University School of Law.

CHAPTER 9

What Should I Expect in Law School?

[Barron's *How to Succeed in Law School* provides an in-depth look at legal education from the student's point of view, particularly the critical first year. The premise of the book is that being intelligent is not enough; the successful law student needs to know how to play the game. The portion of the book reprinted below provides an overview of the first year; other chapters deal with classroom preparation, studying, test taking, and a variety of other key elements in law school success. Readers who successfully gain admission to law school should read *How to Succeed in Law School** as the next step in their preparation for a career in law. Ed.]

THE LAW SCHOOL CALENDAR

No two people are the same. A key to your success in law school will be your ability to channel the skills you already have into a new educational program, while building new skills that will serve you in the future as a lawyer. It may help you to understand what is happening during the first year of law school by looking at the law school calendar. Although every law school is slightly different from all the others, in many respects they are all much the same. Virtually every law school in the United States models its curriculum, particularly in the first year, after the socratic system promulgated at Harvard Law School in the 1870s. Although legal education has evolved in the past century, the general comment in this chapter will be substantially descriptive of your law school.

Orientation

Law school starts with orientation. Orientation is designed to introduce you to the law school community (and some would say to lull you into a false sense of security about the upcoming ten months). The first step is check-in. Check-in is run by the Admissions Office, and you will be greeted by the smiling countenance of the admissions officer who recruited you or dealt with you during the admissions process. The Admissions Office will want to make sure that you have paid your tuition, that your financial aid is in order, and that your registration is complete. Depending on how check-in is organized, you may or may not have to wait in a long line. If the line is long, it generally portends three to four years of the same thing.

After checking in, and grabbing a cup of hot coffee, you will proceed to an auditorium where you will be subjected to a series of speeches you will not remember. You will hear from the dean, some associate deans, assistant deans, the financial aid officer, placement director, student bar president, law review editor, moot court board chair, head of security, and other administrators and students too numerous to name. They will all tell you how glad they are to see you, how talented you all are, and how their doors will always be open. You will never see most of them again. While most schools have abandoned the tactic, a few of them may still use the old "Look to the right of you; look to the left of you; one of you won't be here next August." The truth is, 90–95 percent of those who enter law school eventually will graduate.

After this convocation, you may be given a tour of the facilities, including the law library, by engaging upperclass students just dying to tell you what law school is "really like." You also may be solicited by various student organizations; they will all be around and still anxious for your membership after the first year.

One of your first lessons in law school will be to separate the wheat from the chaff. Find out where the assignments are posted. Find out how you can sign up for a locker. Learn to recognize The Dean by sight. (There are many deans, but only one Dean.)

*by Professor Gary A. Munneke, Pace Univ. School of Law

At many schools, class assignments for the first day are posted prior to orientation. An assignment sheet for each class will also tell you what books to buy for the course so you can go to the law school bookstore and pick up your books before the crowds arrive. Don't wait until school has started to obtain your books and start reading.

ORIENTATION CHECKLIST

___Admissions
   ___College transcripts (if needed)
   ___Identification
___Financial aid (if applicable)
___Registrar—class schedule
___Bursar—bring checkbook if not prepaid
___Course assignments
___Bookstore
___Parking Sticker
___Locker
___ID photo
___Law school tour
___Find out who is "The Dean"
___Nearby food
___Library carrel (if available)

First Classes

Unlike classes in undergraduate school, the first classes in law school are generally real classes. The professor may simply walk in and call on a student for the first case. She may give a short speech on what will be expected of you in her course before turning to the cases. Or she may provide a background lecture for most of the first hour. It is likely that the professor will not simply say, "Hello, I'm Professor Jones. Your assignment for Tuesday will be to read the first 30 pages in the book. I'll see you Tuesday." During the first class, the professor may present certain special rules such as the maximum number of class cuts you are allowed, the number of times you may be unprepared before being dropped from the course, what the final exam will be like, what her office hours will be, what outside materials (hornbooks, treatises, etc.) you should read. Such information is important to know.

Such works as *One L* and *The Paper Chase* probably have instilled a sense of fear in the minds of many beginning law students. In reality, not all law professors are as intimidating as Professor Kingsfield, although the terror and alienation described there are very accurate.

You will find yourself in a lecture hall with roughly one hundred more or less equally frightened souls. Your sense of anonymity and privacy will be invaded by the seemingly all-knowing professor armed with a seating chart and an uncanny ability to identify the least prepared student in the class to discuss the case at hand.

During the first week of classes, you will learn the ground rules. Let there be no doubt about it: This is the lions versus the Christians, and regardless of your religious affiliation, you and your classmates are the Christians.

Also, during the first week, you will be introduced to the subject matter to be covered in each course, the professor's unique philosophy of legal education, a new language called legalese, and those ponderous, pictureless tomes called casebooks.

You will also begin to get acquainted with your fellow law students. You may meet a few individuals whom you come to know as real people. Most of your classmates will fall into one of two groups: the nameless faces who fill the classroom and the ones who, by virtue of having been called on or volunteered to speak in class, are identified by name (as in "Mr. Simon, who sits in the first row in Torts"). Custom dictates that you use last names to identify students (as in "Ms. Miller" or "Mr. Musser") and you refer to the teacher as "Professor" or "Dean" as appropriate.

You may encounter some upperclass students who offer with a certain patronizing smugness to teach you the tricks of the trade. A healthy sense of skepticism about the value or motives of such advice is a good sign that you will eventually become a successful lawyer.

Routine

After the first week of classes, you will begin to establish a pattern in each course, and a timetable for your entire life. The reading will average between 10 and 30 pages per night, per class. You may find that the progress in some of the classes is painfully slow, with the professor covering only a portion of the assigned reading each time. Some classes may move along at an almost military clip of three to four cases per class, no matter what. During the first few weeks, you will find yourself spending an inordinate amount of time briefing cases, attempting to fathom the classroom discussion, and wondering secretly if someone in the admissions office hadn't screwed up by sending you an acceptance letter. You will wonder with increasing frequency whether you screwed up in deciding to come to law school. During this phase of school, you may wonder why everyone else in the class but you seems to know what is going on.

When I was in law school, there was a guy named Holtzman, and although Holtzman was only three or four years older than most of the rest of us, it seemed that in every class he had some personal experience relating to the case. If the case involved shoes, he had been in the shoe business; if the case involved clothes, he had been in the clothing business; if the case involved doctors, he had been in the medical business.

Other students will amaze you with their seeming ability to converse freely with the professor in legalese, whereas you find yourself stuck at the *Bonjour Jean* stage. But you will derive hope from the fact that some students' comments will seem totally inane to you, reassuring you that you must be smarter than *someone* in the class. And you will find a wicked satisfaction in seeing a handful of students whose hands are always in the air given their comeuppance by the professor. In every class, there will be at least one individual who, no matter how bloodied by the fray, will keep coming back for more. A pack psychology will come to dominate the class and seek to drive out the weak or the deviant. By mid-semester, the fear of embarrassment in front of the class will inhibit all but the most fearless souls from making rash statements. This mentality is typified by graffito on a bathroom stall at one law school: "After the sixth week of class, if you don't know who the class jerk is, it's you."

These pressures to conform may dissuade some students from ever participating in class discussions unless specifically required to do so by the professor. By laughing at a fellow student, you help to create an environment where one day others may laugh at you.

As the semester wears on, the professor comes to be viewed not so much as a god, but as a common enemy. You learn that the classroom routine is a game the teacher always wins. You learn that the stupidest answers have some value, and you begin to recognize that even the most articulate students really don't know much more than you do. When you come to this realization, you will have reached another milestone in your law school journey.

The Wall

Somewhere between the tenth and twelfth week of classes you will hit the wall. It is during this period that some students actually drop out of school; virtually every student at least contemplates that possibility. By this time in the semester, your work is piling up, final exams are just around the corner, and you still don't have a clue what you need to know. At this point, when your psychological and physical resources are drained, you will wonder if you can possibly survive for two and a half or three and a half more years. It is critical when you hit the wall to press on. It may help during this period to talk to a sympathetic professor, mentor, or counselor. Family and loved ones, who up until now have been totally supportive, will seem to become part of the problem. Prelaw school friends may find that you have changed, and you may find yourself increasingly irritated that they never see the issue.

Panic

By about the thirteenth week of the semester, you will have no time to worry about such self-indulgent psychological concerns, because finals will be upon you. Some professors, in what is variously perceived as a last minute attempt to catch up with the syllabus or a final effort to break your backs, will increase the reading assignments to two or three times what they were at the beginning of the semester. A full-scale panic attack may threaten to debilitate you before the first test. Somehow, you will survive.

First Semester Finals

At last, final examinations will arrive. As a rule, law school exams average one hour of exam for each credit hour of class. The amount of material you will have to study will be immense. Whole parts of some courses may be incomprehensible when you go back to review them. When you walk out of these exams, your head will feel as if Evander Holyfield had used it as a punching bag. You will have no idea how well you did, but if you thought the test was easy, you probably missed something really big.

Semester Break

Semester break is the time when you regroup. Immediately after your last exam, your impulse will be to engage in the most hedonistic activity possible. Many will actually succumb to this impulse. Next, you will sleep for two days. Then, you will engage in mindless activity such as watching soap operas or football games, reading trashy novels, attending holiday parties, or vegging out with your family. If you are an evening student, you may not have the luxury of all of this R & R. However, to the extent possible, you should try to get away from both school and work for a while.

Toward the end of semester break, you will begin to think about law school again. You may do some reading for class. You may reflect about how you will avoid making the same mistakes you did the first semester. You will rush madly to clear up loose ends in your personal life, in order to give yourself time to devote your full attention to law school.

Renewed Hope

The second semester is better in some ways, and worse in others. It is better in that you know the ropes. You have a better picture of what to expect. You have a clearer idea of what it will take to succeed. On the other hand, the workload will pick up even more. The professors will take off at the same pace they ended the previous semester. In addition, at many schools a required moot court problem will swallow the bulk of your free time.

The January Blues

During January (and sometimes February or March) first semester grades will be posted. The wait for grades may be agonizing. The actual knowledge of your grades may be worse. Most students are disappointed in some or all of their marks. You learn how fast the track really is. Unfortunately, many students do not handle this experience well. They go into a depression from which they do not escape until after the bar exam. Although there is no grade for it, your grade point average may depend on your ability to bounce back psychologically and to learn from this experience.

Falling Behind

In all but the warmest climates, the arrival of spring will bring the last great temptation of the school year. When the flowers begin to bloom and warm winds touch the land, sitting in a law school classroom will not be your first choice of activities. Spring break may help but chances are good that you will fall behind in your reading and studying. If you are not careful, you could find yourself in the proverbial hot water.

The Mad Rush

As March dissolves into April, you will once again find yourself staring at final exams. If you have been diligent, you will simply experience anxiety about finishing the year on a high note; if you find yourself hopelessly behind your

schedule, you will be working feverishly to catch up. The last two weeks of school will pass quickly, and your first year will be almost over.

Finals Again

Final exams in the spring will probably not seem as daunting. The experience will be the same as in the fall, but this time you will be more prepared for it mentally. The amount of work you cover in these exams will be more prodigious than in the fall. But the skills you have developed during the course of the year will make the load seem more manageable. This time, when finals are over, you will just go home, have dinner with friends, and go on about your business.

Over a period of 36 weeks, more or less, you will have been transformed from an ordinary person into a budding lawyer. Whether you want it or not, like it or not, or need it or not, you will never be the same again. The process is in some ways like marine boot camp, taking apart whatever you were before you arrived and rebuilding it into a new person. Whatever other criticisms of law school one might make, it certainly cannot be said that the program does not work.

LAW SCHOOL COURSES

The curricula at most American law schools are comparable. In fact, the first year law school curriculum has not changed appreciably in the past one hundred years. At the same time, there are minor variations in course offerings from school to school, reflecting differences in educational philosophy and institutional tradition.

Most law school courses are offered as 2-, 3-, or 4-semester-hour courses. Full-time first year students take five or six courses for a total of 15-16 credit hours; part-time students generally take one or two fewer courses and 10-11 hours. At some schools, grades are based on an entire year's work for 4- to 6-hour courses. You will study some, if not all, of the following courses during the first year of law school. Some schools will defer certain courses until the second year or not require them at all.

Torts

The word tort comes from an old French term meaning wrong. Torts as a law school subject area refers to a series of legal actions and remedies against wrongdoers for injuries sustained.

Torts fall into three broad groups: *intentional torts* where an actor intends conduct that causes injury to another; *negligence torts* where an actor owing a duty to act with reasonable care toward another breaches that duty and causes injury resulting in damages; and *strict liability torts* where an actor causes injury to another without fault or intent but is held liable for policy reasons. You will study a number of distinct tort actions, including assault, battery, false imprisonment, and intentional infliction of emotional distress; negligence actions; misrepresentation; defamation; products liability; and privacy.

Property

The Property course deals with the rights associated with the ownership of property. In the beginning of the course you will probably discuss the origins of property rights in Anglo-American law. You will study such tantalizing questions as who owns the rights to the meteorite: the farmer in whose field it fell or the guy walking down the road who saw it fall? Some of us are still trying to figure that one out. A small portion of the course is devoted to the law of personal property, but the bulk of the year will involve issues relating to real property, or land. In the first semester, you will devote considerable time to basic concepts such as estates in land, transferability of land, and title. Some time during the year you will learn about future interests, those medieval devices for controlling the ownership of land beyond the life of the owner. In the second semester, you will deal with more modern concepts such as easements, zoning, and land use planning.

Contracts

Contracts involves the study of the body of law governing the making and breaking of agreements. You will learn what it takes to create a binding contract with another party. You will spend considerable time discussing what happens when one of the parties breaks its promises, or breaches the contract. You will learn about liquidated damages, specific performance, express and implied warranties, and unilateral contracts. Much of the course will deal with the development of contracts in the commercial setting, including the "battle of forms" and substitution of statutory law in the form of the Uniform Commercial Code for the common law in many situations.

Civil Procedure

Civil Procedure refers to the rules by which the civil courts operate. Most Civ Pro instructors utilize the Federal Rules of Civil Procedure in teaching their courses. Some of the course may touch upon historical material, such as the evolution of the English forms of action into the rules of procedure of today. Most of your time will be spent looking at such concepts as jurisdiction (including subject matter, personal, and diversity), standing, discovery, pleading, appeal, summary judgments, and numerous other provisions of the Rules. A substantial part of the course will address the Erie problem. The case of *Erie Railroad v. Tompkins* held that the federal courts, while applying federal procedural rules, must apply the substantive common law of the state. The ripples from this seemingly simple rule have extended far beyond the original case and have engrossed generations of judges, law professors, legal writers, and students (perhaps *engrossed* is too strong a word for the student response).

Constitutional Law

Many law schools require Constitutional Law during the first year. As the name suggests, Con Law deals with the enforcement of rights and duties established under the United States Constitution. Because there are so many constitutional issues, no two professors will emphasize exactly the same topics. You will look at some fundamental problems such as jurisdiction and standing, separation of powers, the commerce clause, and the privileges and immunities clause. You will deal with cases arising under the first, fifth, and fourteenth amendments as well as others. Perhaps most importantly, you will study the decision-making process in the United States Supreme Court from Chief Justice Marshall's power grab of judicial review in *Marbury v. Madison* to Chief Justice Rehnquist's reshaping the direction of the court in the 1980s.

Criminal Law

Criminal Law is the law of crimes. For a good portion of this course, you will grapple with concepts such as intent, *mens rea,* and lesser included offenses. You will learn the basic elements of crimes you have known about all your life, and a few you have never heard of before. You will study such issues as the right to trial by jury, double jeopardy, the state's burden of proof, and conspiracy.

Professional Responsibility

Although most law schools offer Professional Responsibility during the last year of law school, some require it during the second year, and a few the first. Professional Responsibility deals with the ethical obligations of the lawyer in representing clients. A few of the subjects you will cover in this course are: lawyer/client confidentiality, conflicts of interest, legal fees, advertising and solicitation of business, fitness to practice law, lawyer discipline, and candor to the tribunal. In a broader sense, however, professional responsibility addresses the role of the legal profession in society. What is a lawyer anyway? Are there limits on his or her conduct? Is law a business, a profession, or both? What is the role of the Bar Association? Can one be a good lawyer and a good person at the same time?

Legal Writing

At every law school, there is a course known by a variety of names, but with a general aim of teaching you how to conduct legal research, draft legal briefs and memoranda, prepare and make oral arguments, and gain an understanding of a legal system. These courses are often much maligned by first-year students, but revered by lawyers who come to know the value of the skills they learned in that course. Legal Writing frequently requires a time commitment out of proportion with the amount of credit received. An important consideration during the course of the school year will be your ability to allocate time to Legal Writing in accordance with its relative importance and credit weight, and not to set aside work in other classes for research, writing, and advocacy projects.

THE PROFESSORS

Law students develop a special relationship with their first year teachers. It is not uncommon to experience a love/hate relationship with these professors. Later in law school you will wonder how you placed some of these individuals on such high pedestals. During the first semester of law school they will be like gods—not necessarily in their perfection of appearance, but in their seeming knowledge and omnipotence.

Many of those who become law teachers attained their positions by having done very well academically in law school. Additionally, many of them enter the profession after having served as judicial clerks for the United States Supreme Court or other prestigious tribunals. Increasingly, today, law teachers have some experience in the practice of law. They come from large law firms, corporations, and government agencies. All of them have made an affirmative decision to pursue a career in education, rather than one in a traditional area of law practice. Professors who worked in large law firms or possess more than a few years of experience probably have taken a considerable cut in pay to enter the teaching field. Although law professors as a group have a higher median income than the average of all lawyers, they probably could make more money doing something else.

THE STUDENTS

Classmates

Your classmates can be allies as well as foes during your struggle to master the first year of law school. They can help you to cope in a number of different ways. First, they can help you with assignments. If you happen to miss a class, you need to find someone whose notes you can review. If your own notes have gaps, you may be able to fill them with the help of someone else. If reading assignments or case citations are unclear, you should identify one or more people to call. Even though law school is a competitive environment, most students are willing to help out in this way, as long as their generosity is not abused.

You may study with one of more other students from time to time. Informal small group discussions are common even among students who do not organize formal study groups. In law school, a great amount of learning takes place outside the classroom, and to the extent that your out-of-class conversations are discussions begun during class, the learning process will continue.

If you have ever been to the zoo, you may recall watching a pride of lions or other large cats. The young ones will tussle and play endlessly. Sometimes Mom or Dad will play too, letting the kittens attack and snarl and slap. You know that the older cat can send the kittens flying with a flick of the paw, but they play along until they get bored. You know that the kittens are learning skills they will need as adults in the wild, and the big cats are helping in the process. You also know that the kittens learn from their mock battles with each other just as they do from Mom and Dad. In law school, the professors take on the role of the big cats, and you as kittens should learn from them. However, you should remember that you learn from the rest of the litter as well.

Your classmates can provide an outlet from the pressures of law school. Whether it involves coffee in the morning, eating lunch or dinner, exercising or working out, or partying, you need to socialize from time to time. Those of you who are married to people unconnected with the legal profession, and those who have jobs in nonlegal settings may find it less difficult to break away from law school psychologically. On the other hand, it may be more difficult to find the time to get to know your classmates socially. If you don't want your families and coworkers to despise you because you talk about law all the time, you should try to make some time to get to know your fellow law students in a social setting.

There is an insidious downside to developing relationships with your classmates. Several caveats are in order. Law school is very competitive. Some students will help no one. Some students will promise help, but fail to deliver. Some will take far more than they give. Always remember that the admissions committee did not pick the first year class on the basis of integrity. Although you will meet some of the most honest and honorable people you could hope to know, you may also encounter others who would stoop to any depth to get ahead, and use any means to reach a desired end. Most of you will conclude that you are unwilling to lie, cheat, and steal in order to succeed in law school. Do not be so naive as to believe that everyone feels the same. Beware of the snakes in the grass, and pick your friends carefully.

Your classmates can exert considerable pressure not to succeed. A collective striving for mediocrity may seem to be the norm. Those who study too much, talk too often in class, or don't get into the law school social scene may be branded as outsiders. You have had to deal with similar peer pressure since grade school. The point here is that the pressure to conform does not end in law school. You may have seen the gopher game at the boardwalk or midway. In this game, the gopher pops his head out of one of the number of round holes while the player, wielding a mallet, tries to knock him back into the hole again. If you imagine that the class is the midway player ready to knock down any gopher who has the audacity to stick his head up above the crowd, you get the picture.

One way the group may push you toward mediocrity is by encouraging you to socialize. Although occasional social activity is benefi-

cial, too much can be the kiss of death. When study sessions deteriorate into bull sessions like you had when you were a freshman in college, when quick lunches extend into afternoon shopping trips, when an occasional class party becomes an evening ritual, then you will know you have exceeded the bounds of moderation.

Some semblance of self-discipline in the area of time management is absolutely essential. You must decide how much time you are willing to devote to personal and social activities, and live with that decision.

Socializing with other students can take on a more serious note: emotional involvement through love and dependency. Guess what? Law students fall in love. They fall in love with each other and with nonlaw students. It would be futile to say: "Don't fall in love." However, if you do, you will find yourself in turmoil. When you fall in love, your lover tends to become (at least during early stages of infatuation) all-important in your life. Unfortunately, so does law school. Justice Holmes once remarked that the law is a jealous mistress. This conflict appears in the play *Phantom of the Opera*. Christine, the heroine, is torn between her physical relationship with the Vicomte de Chegny and her passion to excel in her career represented by her relationship with the Phantom. It is interesting to note that the author of the book, Gaston Leroux, was himself a lawyer and may have understood the conflict in terms of the law.

A second dangerous emotional involvement is to buy into someone else's problems to the detriment of your own studies. Law students are not immune from the vagaries of life. Some of your friends will have serious problems while they are in school. The stress of law school may compound their anxiety. Some may turn to you to serve as an emotional crutch. In fact, some students are like magnets for those with problems. Lest your friend's difficulties drag you down, the best thing you can do is to get them to go to someone who can really help.

Upperclass Students

When you arrive at law school, you will find a place already populated by students who have gone before you. These upperclass students will be ready and willing to regale you with tales of their own experiences in the first year, to give you the inside scoop on all the profs, and to share the definitive answers on what you need to do to get ahead. Some of them will want you to join their organizations, come to their parties, or buy their old books. They may seem like the smug but grizzled veterans joined in the field by some new recruits in the standard war movie: "Don't worry, kid; I'll show you what you need to do to get out of this place alive." Of course, in the movies, the guy who says that always seems to get killed.

The lesson to learn is to take everything you hear with a grain of salt. You will find out information that is useful. Every law school has a grapevine, and the news, if not always accurate, is at least entertaining. Some of your sources may prove better than others. So use what you can and discard the rest.

Consider the motivation of the upperclass student who offers advice. Is this someone who just likes being a big shot? Someone who needs reaffirmation for his or her own decisions in law school (even if those choices have produced a record of mediocrity)? Someone who would like to ask you out? (Yes, this goes on in law school like everywhere else!) Someone who wants to sell you something (bar reviews, books, bar association memberships)? You do not have to shun all these people, just remember that they want something in return for their information. (In the words of Hannibal Lecter from *The Silence of the Lambs,* "Quid pro quo, Clarice.")

While casual advice should be approached with skepticism, it might be valuable to look for an upperclass mentor. Such a person might well be someone who has similar interests, career aspirations, problems, or background. For example, a first year student with young children at home might encounter an upperclass student who has gone through the same experience and survived. A mentor might be someone you happen to meet and become friendly with during the course of the year. Some schools even offer programs that assign upperclass mentors to first year students. However it occurs that a true mentoring relationship develops, take advantage of it.

A mentor can help to guide you through the law school maze, talk to you when you are down, share your joy when you are flush with success, and set an example for you to follow. Mentoring relationships are built upon a foundation of common interest, molded by walls of trust, and covered by a protective roof of the experience of the mentor for the student. Mentoring relationships are common in the legal profession, not only in law school but in practice as well. To the extent that you find a good mentor, you will discover that the law school experience is a more palatable one.

THE LAW SCHOOL CULTURE

Rules and Procedures

Law school culture is unique, created in part by the intense experience of those involved, and in part by the insular setting of the law school itself. Because most law students did not attend undergraduate school at the university where they attend law school, they tend to have limited interaction with the university community generally. The law school on many campuses is set apart on the edge of campus or on a separate campus altogether. Some law schools are not connected with an undergraduate university at all. There are advantages and disadvantages to attending an independent law school. Such a school can devote all its resources to the law students, but may lack the rich culture of a university setting.

There may be other differences about the physical location or layout of the law building(s) that make the law school environment unique. Does the law school share its campus with undergrads or graduate students? Does the law school share space with other departments? Are law school facilities located in one building or several? The presence or absence of a nonlegal academic community affects not only the type and extent of extracurricular programs and activities, but also the sense of the law school as an insular institution.

In one sense, every law school is different, but in another sense, every law school is the same. Regardless of the idiosyncrasies of different law schools, the process of legal education is similar everywhere.

In this environment, a distinct law school culture has evolved. Law schools have their own student government (the Student Bar Association or SBA), activities, social events, intramurals, and newspapers. Some law schools even have their own yearbooks. At many law schools, the students put on an annual comedy show, generally making fun of the faculty in a singular effort to even the score for a year's worth of abuse.

Within the law school culture, there are several common elements worth noting: First, rules and procedures take on a distinctly legal flavor. Announcements and information may be posted by the registrar, the Dean's Office, or teachers. You will be deemed to know what is in these notices by virtue of the doctrine of constructive notice. The upshot of this concept is that you have to watch out for announcements that pertain to you. The first example of constructive notice during your law school tenure will be the posting of class assignments on a wall or bulletin board prior to the beginning of classes. You will find very little hand-holding by law school teachers and administrators. Students who graduated from small intimate colleges may find this somewhat of a shock.

A second concept that permeates the rules and procedures is the notion of due process. Lawyers, more than those who are not trained in the law, tend to be aware of individual rights to hearings, representation, confrontation of accusers, and appeal. Most law schools operate under some code of conduct for dealing with academic dishonesty, as well as a code of academic standards to cover issues involving academic performance. Both sets of rules tend to focus heavily on due process and protection of the individual.

Another aspect of the law school culture is that it is a small world. The largest law school in the country has around 2,000 students; at most law schools the enrollment is no more than several hundred. The small size of the student body, combined with the nature of the educational process, means that students know much more about each other, law school affairs, and their professors than they did in all but the smallest undergraduate schools. Unlike your high school or college acquaintances, you will tend to maintain contact with many of your law school classmates throughout your career. At every law school there is a student grapevine, laden with information about everything from what courses to take, which firms to interview, to who is sleeping with whom. The old adage, "Believe a tenth of what you hear and half of what you see," is apropos.

Socializing and Breaks

You will find an abundance of opportunities for escape from law school studies in the form of parties and school-sponsored social events. During the year, there will be several receptions, mixers, and even a dance or two sponsored by the SBA. Many student organizations offer periodic social events for their members. And informal groups of students organize their own parties as a break from the grind of law school or meet at a local bar for drinks after class.

In fact, if you are interested, you can find a party almost every night. Unfortunately, partying leads you down a certain path of self-destruction in law school. Everyone needs an occasional break from study; however, the occasional break can easily become a regular habit. The party scene can become an escape

from law school pressures generally, and may shift your values away from learning.

If you were a party animal in college, it may be difficult to break out of old patterns. Unfortunately, most of us cannot get by with the same antics we did in undergraduate school. In law school one all-nighter will not save a semester of neglect.

Law school provides abundant breaks between and during semesters. You will probably have two weeks or more between the end of first semester exams and the start of spring semester classes. Most schools provide a spring break midway through the second semester. And, of course, summers are open.

Students usually use breaks during the year either to get away for a vacation or to get ahead in their work. Sometimes you may not have a choice. If you decide to vacation, leave your guilt at home. If you take your books with you, plan and make time to study. If you have no time to study, do not make a pretense of it by surrounding yourself with symbols of law school while doing nothing to further your cause.

Summer vacation is another matter. Here are 12 to 14 weeks that you can utilize in a variety of different ways. How you choose to spend your summer vacation will have an impact, one way or the other, on your legal education.

A large percentage of law students work for legal employers during the summer. Although it is harder for them to find positions, many first year students take this option, even if they have to work for free. For some students, it is necessary to work in high paying nonlegal jobs in order to earn enough to come back to school the next year.

Many students go to summer school, at their institution or abroad. You may find, however, that you are so burned out that you simply want to relax. And some students do just that after the first year. If you want to travel, this might be the time to do it, before you take your first job.

Competition

A final note about the law school culture is that it is competitive. Entrance to law school was competitive; law school itself is competitive; and law practice by its nature is competitive. Your relationships with other students will be colored by competition. Ironically, many students try to deny the competitive nature of the process. They will say to each other that grades don't matter. They will ostracize fellow students who appear too competitive. They may deny to other students that they study as much as they do. On the other hand, competitiveness can go too far. In all likelihood, before you graduate from law school, you will hear about at least one cheating incident at your school. You will see other examples, such as library books being misshelved by unscrupulous students. If you should be tempted, it's not worth it. In the 1988 presidential campaign, a law school indiscretion may have cost one candidate the nomination for the presidency of the United States.

Excerpted from *How to Succeed in Law School,* by Gary A. Munneke, Barron's Educational Series, Inc. 2008, 2001, 1994, 1989.

CHAPTER 10

What Are the Career Opportunities in Law?

Although it may seem quite early to begin to think about employment after law school, many prelaw students ask themselves whether they will find employment after investing thousands of dollars in a legal education. Some students understand that the choice of law schools has an impact on the career choices they ultimately make. The school's reputation, geographic location, substantive curriculum, and many other factors go into determining what opportunities are most likely to be available to its graduates. For instance, law schools in the Washington, DC area typically have more graduates go to work for the federal government than law schools in other areas. Law schools with specialty programs may have a disproportionate number of graduates pursue careers in the specialty field.

First year law students are often surprised to discover that after spending considerable time and energy making a career choice to go to law school, they are now called upon to make additional career choices about what to do with their law degree. Law is practiced in many different ways and many different settings. Some legally trained individuals never practice law at all, but use their legal training in a variety of other fields.

A career counselor at your law school will be able to help you make decisions about your legal career. Although career services for law students may vary from school to school, most law schools employ full-time professionals who possess either a counseling or law degree (or both) to work with law students in developing career plans. Law professors may be able to help, not only with advising, but also with information about contacts and recommendations. The chart beginning on page 76 provides an overview of the career services of the law schools included in this guide. For a more extensive discussion of the career opportunities for law graduates and the career planning process, see Gary A. Munneke and Ellen Wayne, *The Legal Career Gude: From Law Student to Lawyer*, American Bar Association (2008). You cannot begin too early to start reflecting on career issues.

WORK DURING LAW SCHOOL

Many law students work in legal or law-related jobs while they are in law school. Still others will work in nonlegal jobs that lead them to legal jobs in the area of business where they were working, or into a totally alternative career. Many law students work in law firms, corporate law departments, or government law offices. These positions may be full-time or part-time, and they may be summer jobs, work during the school year, or permanent positions.

Many larger firms, government agencies, and corporate legal departments offer summer internship or clerkship programs as part of a formal recruiting process. These positions tend to be highly competitive, and hiring for them may be heavily influenced by academic performance in law school and the prestige of the law school attended. Many of the organizations that sponsor these summer programs use them as a tool to help make permanent hiring decisions. It is worth noting, however, that these organizations represent only a small percentage of the legal job market.

Even in law firms and other employers that do not regularly recruit on campus for summer clerks or permanent associates, it is common for students who work in these organizations during law school to accept positions there when they graduate. If they do not ultimately stay with the organization where they have worked, the experience they gain is still very likely to impress other employers with whom they apply. This kind of hands-on training is an excellent counterbalance to the more esoteric experience of law school.

Types of Employment

Law school graduates accept jobs in a variety of settings. The largest numbers go to work in private law firms. These firms provide legal services to clients for profit. The owners of the firms may be individual lawyers, practitioners, organizations of several hundred partners, or anything in between. In addition to the partners/owners, law firms also employ salaried junior lawyers or associates. Some of these associates may eventually become partners in the firm; some may remain as permanent associates or staff attorneys; and some may leave the firm to find other employment or start their own practices. The percentage of lawyers in private practice has decreased from around 80 percent in 1950 to around 60 percent today.

Between 2008–2009, as the U.S. economy deteriorated, law firms faced economic challenges as well. Although some practice areas like bankruptcy and collections grew, other areas of practice, including corporate law declined. As clients faced uncertain times, there was less legal work to go around and fewer resources available to pay lawyers for their services. The popular legal press was filled with stories of law firms that closed their doors, of reduced partner compensation, of cuts in associate salaries, and the rescinding of job offers already made. Some firms even gave newly-hired lawyers a sabbatical at reduced pay because there just was not enough work to keep them busy.

The upshot of the economic downturn is that job opportunities for law school graduates in 2008 and 2009 were not as good as they had been in prior years. The good news is that the legal job market has always been very resilient, and as the economy recovers, work for lawyers will expand, and job opportunities will increase. It is further good news that a law degree is a very versatile education, which means that law graduates can and do find work in a variety of different settings (See Gary A. Munneke, William D. Henslee and Ellen Wayne, *Nonlegal Careers for Lawyers*, American Bar Association, 2007). Historically, as the legal job market constricts, law graduates and lawyers consider using their legal skills in organizations outside the practice of law, and this recession is no exception.

Many lawyers go into other lines of work outside the practice of law altogether, having never gone into law, or having left the practice at some time during their careers. Some of these people may simply want a law degree to supplement other qualifications they have. Others may become enticed by personal dreams or business deals along the way. Some, unfortunately, discover after going to law school and practicing law that they are not happy with the career choices they have made and leave the practice of law for greener pastures. The ranks of these legal expatriates are filled with entrepreneurs, athletes, writers, correspondents, inventors, entertainers, restaurateurs, and even a prominent wine critic. A list of well-known personalities who are also lawyers would surprise most people.

The National Association for Law Placement keeps employment statistics for American law schools (See http://www.nalp.org). An annual employment and salary survey is taken of each graduating class about nine months after graduation; because many legal employers do not make hiring decisions until after bar exam results are released; the reporting delay produces a more accurate picture than a survey at the time of graduation. Nevertheless, the classes of 2008 and 2009 reflect the national economic downturn.

The breakdown for private practice shows that 55.9 percent of the law school graduates in 2009 entered private practice, down from a high of 64.3 percent some fifteen years earlier. A very small percentage of law students actually open their own law offices, a practice euphemistically referred to as "hanging out a shingle." More law graduates go to work in law offices of less than 100 lawyers than accept positions in large offices. The judicial cohort is made up of judicial clerks rather than judges and courts administrators for obvious reasons. The largest area of government practice for recent graduates is work in a prosecutor's office. Another area, often listed as a separate category, is the military, which recruits lawyers for the judge advocate general corps for the service branches, as well as individuals who have completed law school before fulfilling other military obligations. Very few law school graduates go into teaching, particularly law school teaching, directly out of law school, but an appreciable number pursue advanced degrees both in law and other fields.

As you contemplate law school and subsequent career paths, you can take comfort in knowing that your chances of finding employment are good. Of those whose employment status was known, 88.3 percent were employed, down from 90.7 percent two years earlier. In addition, 25 percent of those who had jobs

(go to page 101)

THE JOB OUTLOOK

	Albany Law School	American University (Washington College of Law)	Appalachian School of Law	Arizona State University (Sandra Day O'Connor College of Law)	Atlanta's John Marshall Law School	Ave Maria School of Law	Barry University (School of Law)
AVERAGE STARTING SALARY	$40,000–$175,000	$48,000–$135,000	$26,000–$68,000	$37,000–$16,000		$46,300–$60,000	
PLACEMENT RECORD — Percentage Breakdown of Type of Employer							
OTHER		27	5			6	58
ACADEMIC	2	2		3	3	2	3
MILITARY	1		3	1			
PUBLIC INTEREST	6	7	7	9	3	3	7
BUSINESS/INDUSTRY	18	18	12	10	13	24	16
GOVERNMENT	16	13	19	17	11	14	15
JUDICIAL CLERKSHIPS	9	11	8	7		17	1
PRIVATE PRACTICE 51–100 ATTORNEYS	9	2		5		5	
PRIVATE PRACTICE 26–50 ATTORNEYS	3	3	6	6		2	
PRIVATE PRACTICE 11–25 ATTORNEYS	8	4	3	2		8	
PRIVATE PRACTICE 2–10 ATTORNEYS	28	13	34	25	70	19	
PLACEMENT WITHIN 6 TO 9 MONTHS	97%	99%	64%	99%	94%	74%	
CAREER SERVICES — Services							
ALUMNI PLACEMENT	●	●	●	●	●	●	●
INTERNSHIPS	●	●	●	●	●	●	●
PART-TIME/SUMMER EMPLOYMENT	●	●	●	●	●	●	
ALUMNI CONTACTS	●	●	●	●	●	●	
LAW, CORPORATE, AND GOVERNMENT CONTACT	●	●	●	●	●	●	
JOB INTERVIEWS ARRANGEMENT	●	●	●	●	●	●	
EMPLOYMENT PLANNING	●	●	●	●	●	●	
INTERVIEW COUNSELING	●	●	●	●	●	●	
RESUME PREPARATION	●	●	●	●	●	●	
SOLO PRACTICE ADVICE	●	●	●	●	●	●	
JOB OPENINGS INFORMATION	●	●	●	●	●	●	
EMPLOYMENT COUNSELING	●	●	●	●	●	●	●
FACILITIES							
UNIVERSITY PLACEMENT OFFICE					●		●
LAW PLACEMENT OFFICE	●	●	●	●		●	

SCHOOL

Albany Law School
80 New Scotland Avenue
Albany, NY 12208
518-445-2326
Fax: 518-445-2369
admissions@albanylaw.edu

American University (Washington College of Law)
4801 Massachusetts Avenue, N.W.
Washington, DC 20016-8186
202-274-4101
Fax: 202-274-4107
wcladmit@wcl.american.edu

Appalachian School of Law
P.O. Box 2825
Grundy, VA 24614
276-935-4349
Fax: 276-935-8496
npruitt@asl.edu

Arizona State University (Sandra Day O'Connor College of Law)
1100 S. McAllister Ave. - Box 877906
Tempe, AZ 85287-7906
480-965-1474
Fax: 480-727-7930
chitra.damania@asu.edu

Atlanta's John Marshall Law School
1422 W. Peachtree St., NW
Atlanta, GA 30309
404-872-3593
Fax: 404-873-3802
admissions@johnmarshall.edu

Ave Maria School of Law
3475 Plymouth Road
Ann Arbor, MI 48105
734-827-8063
Fax: 734-622-0123
info@avemarialaw.edu

Barry University (School of Law)
6441 East Colonial Drive
Orlando, FL 32807
321-206-5600
Fax: 321-206-5662
acruz@mail.barry.edu

School	Salary Range												% Employed
Baylor University (School of Law) One Bear Place #97288 Waco, TX 76798-7288 254-710-1911 Fax: 254-710-2316 becky_beck@baylor.edu	$51,000–$93,122	17	2	1	1	10	12	10	3	8	11	25	98%
Boston College (Law School) 885 Centre Street Newton, MA 02459 617-552-4351 Fax: 617-552-2917 bclawadm@bc.edu	$26,400–$160,000		4		3	5	7	53	6	2	2	8	97%
Boston University (School of Law) 765 Commonwealth Avenue Boston, MA 02215 617-353-3100 Fax: 617-353-0578 bulawadm@bu.edu	$48,000–$160,000	58	7		3			6	4	2	2	3	100%
Brigham Young University (J. Reuben Clark Law School) 342 JRCB Brigham Young University Provo, UT 84602 801-422-4277 Fax: 801-422-0389 kucharg@law.byu.edu	$31,000–$195,000	30	1	5	1	13	8	16	5	2	7	13	96%
Brooklyn Law School 250 Joralemon Street Brooklyn, NY 11201 718-780-7906 Fax: 718-780-0395 admitq@brooklaw.edu	$35,000–$170,000	3	1	3	6	12	15	6	2	4	3	19	92%
California Western School of Law 225 Cedar Street San Diego, CA 92101-3046 619-525-1401 Fax: 619-615-1401 admissions@cwsl.edu	$50,000–$200,000	7	1	2	7	13	12	5	3	6	3	41	91%
Campbell University (Norman Adrian Wiggins School of Law) 225 Hillsborough Street, Suite 401 Raleigh, NC 24603 919-865-5988 Fax: 919-865-5886	$54,500–$63,500				5	9	12	5	14	8	9	59	94%
Capital University (Law School) 303 East Broad Street Columbus, OH 43215-3200 614-236-6500 Fax: 614-236-6972 admissions@law.capital.edu	$39,781–$75,724	10	4	1	6	20	20	3	2	2	6	26	95%
Case Western Reserve University (School of Law) 11075 East Boulevard Cleveland, OH 44106 216-368-3600 Fax: 216-368-1042 lawadmissions@case.edu	$32,000–$150,000		2	3	8	20	9	6	3	10	9	24	98%

Career Services

School	Facilities: Law Placement Office	University Placement Office	Employment Counseling	Job Openings Information	Solo Practice Advice	Resume Preparation	Interview Counseling	Employment Planning	Job Interviews Arrangement	Law, Corporate, and Government Contact	Alumni Contacts	Part-Time/Summer Employment	Internships	Alumni Placement
Catholic University of America (Columbus School of Law)	•		•	•	•	•	•	•	•	•	•	•	•	•
Chapman University (School of Law)	•		•	•	•	•	•	•	•	•	•	•	•	•
Charleston School of Law	•		•	•	•	•	•	•	•	•	•	•	•	•
Charlotte School of Law	•		•	•	•	•	•	•	•	•	•	•	•	•
City University of New York (CUNY School of Law)	•		•	•	•	•	•	•	•	•	•	•	•	•
Cleveland State University (Cleveland-Marshall College of Law)	•		•	•	•	•	•	•	•	•	•	•	•	•
College of William & Mary (William & Mary Law School)	•		•	•	•	•	•	•	•	•	•	•	•	•

Placement Record

School	Placement Within 6 to 9 Months	Private Practice 2-10 Attorneys	Private Practice 11-25 Attorneys	Private Practice 26-50 Attorneys	Private Practice 51-100 Attorneys	Judicial Clerkships	Government	Business/Industry	Public Interest	Military	Academic	Other	Average Starting Salary
Catholic University of America (Columbus School of Law)	93%	42				12	27	13	2		2		$28,000-$135,000
Chapman University (School of Law)	97%	29	3	4	2	3	8	8	1	2	20	19	$27,040-$160,000
Charleston School of Law	67%					31	14	7	4		1	43	$39,000-$74,000
Charlotte School of Law													
City University of New York (CUNY School of Law)	92%	27	4	5	1	11	19	11	27		4		$41,000-$55,000
Cleveland State University (Cleveland-Marshall College of Law)	90%	23	2	2	2	5	10	23	3	2	3	19	$36,000-$120,000
College of William & Mary (William & Mary Law School)	97%	12	2	2	6	14	8	7	4	7			$33,700-$225,000

School Contact Information

Catholic University of America (Columbus School of Law)
Cardinal Station
Washington, DC 20064
202-319-5151
Fax: 202-319-6285
admissions@law.edu

Chapman University (School of Law)
One University Drive
Orange, CA 92866
714-628-2500
Fax: 714-628-2501
melten@chapman.edu

Charleston School of Law
P.O. Box 535
Charleston, SC 29402
843-377-2143
Fax: 843-329-0491
jbenfield@charlestonlaw.org

Charlotte School of Law
2145 Suttle Avenue
Charlotte, NC 28208
704-971-8599
Fax: 704-971-8542
admissions@charlottelaw.edu

City University of New York (CUNY School of Law)
65-21 Main Street
Flushing, NY 11367-1300
718-340-4210
Fax: 718-340-4435
mail.law.cuny.edu

Cleveland State University (Cleveland-Marshall College of Law)
2121 Euclid Avenue LB138
Cleveland, OH 44115-2214
216-687-2304
Fax: 216-687-6881
christophe.lcak@law.csuohio.edu

College of William & Mary (William & Mary Law School)
P.O. Box 8795
Williamsburg, VA 23187-8795
757-221-3785
Fax: 757-221-3261
lawadm@wm.edu

Columbia University (School of Law) 435 West 116th Street New York, NY 10027 212-854-2670 Fax: 212-854-1109 *admissions@law.columbia.edu*	•		•	•		•	•	•	•	•	•	•	•	•	99%					14	4	2	3			77	$35,000-$175,000
Cornell University (Law School) Myron Taylor Hall Ithaca, NY 14853-4901 607-255-5141 Fax: 607-255-7193 *lawadmit@postoffice.law.cornell.edu*	•		•	•	•	•	•	•	•	•	•	•	•	•	99%		2	2	5	14	1		3			73	$46,000-$145,000
Creighton University (School of Law) 2500 California Plaza Omaha, NE 68178 402-280-2586 Fax: 402-280-3161 *lawadmit@creighton.edu*	•		•	•	•	•	•	•	•	•	•	•	•	•	93%	22	2	9	5	5	21	21	2	2		9	$25,000-$190,000
De Paul University (College of Law) 25 East Jackson Boulevard Chicago, IL 60604 312-362-6831 Fax: 312-362-5280 *lawinfo@depaul.edu*	•	•	•	•	•	•	•	•	•	•	•	•	•	•	94%	46	16	8	6	3	11	21	4	1	2	24	$26,000-$256,000
Drake University (Law School) 2507 University Avenue Des Moines, IA 50311 515-271-2782 Fax: 515-271-1990 *lawadmit@drake.edu*	•		•	•	•	•	•	•	•	•	•	•	•	•	97%	25	5	3	6	9	10	20	6	2	2		$37,500-$110,000
Drexel University (Earle Mack School of Law) 3320 Market Street Philadelphia, PA 15282 215-895 1LAW Fax: 215-571-4769																			25	40	10	15	10				$70,360
Duke University (Duke University School of Law) Science Drive and Towerview Road, Box 90362 Durham, NC 27708-0362 919-613-7020 Fax: 919-613-7257 *nash@law.duke.edu*	•		•	•	•	•	•	•	•	•	•	•	•	•	100%					16		1			4		$42,000-$135,000
Duquesne University (School of Law) 900 Locust Street, Hanley Hall Pittsburgh, PA 15282 412-396-6296 Fax: 412-396-1073 *campion@duq.edu*	•		•	•	•	•	•	•	•	•	•	•	•	•	89%					12	11	17	8		2	50	$30,000-$125,000
Elon University (School of Law) 201 North Greene Street Greensboro, NC 27401 336-279-9200 Fax: 336-279-8199 *law@elon.edu*	•		•	•	•	•	•	•	•	•	•	•	•	•													

	Emory University (School of Law)	Faulkner University (Thomas Goode Jones School of Law)	Florida Agricultural and Mechanical University (Florida A & M University College of Law)	Florida Coastal (School of Law)	Florida International University (College of Law)	Florida State University (College of Law)
PLACEMENT RECORD						
AVERAGE STARTING SALARY	$52,000–$145,000		$35,000–$110,000	$35,000–$80,000	$42,000–$110,000	$31,800–$160,000
OTHER	52		12			9
ACADEMIC						1
MILITARY			2			3
PUBLIC INTEREST	2		8		14	9
BUSINESS/INDUSTRY	11		8	18	8	10
GOVERNMENT	9		22	18		23
JUDICIAL CLERKSHIPS	9		2		1	2
PRIVATE PRACTICE 51–100 ATTORNEYS	2				9	4
PRIVATE PRACTICE 26–50 ATTORNEYS	6				6	5
PRIVATE PRACTICE 11–25 ATTORNEYS	4		5		3	5
PRIVATE PRACTICE 2–10 ATTORNEYS	9		30	63	52	26
PLACEMENT WITHIN 6 TO 9 MONTHS	95%		90%	90%	86%	98%
CAREER SERVICES — Services						
ALUMNI PLACEMENT	●	●	●	●	●	●
INTERNSHIPS	●	●	●	●	●	●
PART-TIME/SUMMER EMPLOYMENT	●	●	●	●	●	●
ALUMNI CONTACTS	●	●	●	●	●	●
LAW, CORPORATE, AND GOVERNMENT CONTACT	●	●	●	●	●	●
JOB INTERVIEWS ARRANGEMENT	●	●	●	●	●	●
EMPLOYMENT PLANNING	●	●	●	●	●	●
INTERVIEW COUNSELING	●	●	●	●	●	●
RESUME PREPARATION	●	●	●	●	●	●
SOLO PRACTICE ADVICE	●	●	●	●	●	●
JOB OPENINGS INFORMATION	●	●	●	●	●	●
EMPLOYMENT COUNSELING	●	●	●	●	●	●
Facilities						
UNIVERSITY PLACEMENT OFFICE						●
LAW PLACEMENT OFFICE	●	●	●	●		●

School contact information

Emory University (School of Law)
Gambrell Hall, 1301 Clifton Road, N.E.
Atlanta, GA 30322
404-727-6801
Fax: 404-727-2477
erosenz@law.emory.edu

Faulkner University (Thomas Goode Jones School of Law)
5345 Atlanta Highway
Montgomery, AL 36109
334-386-7210
Fax: 334-386-7223
law@faulkner.edu

Florida Agricultural and Mechanical University (Florida A & M University College of Law)
201 N. Beggs Avenue
Orlando, FL 32801
407-254-3268
famu.law.admissions@famu.edu

Florida Coastal (School of Law)
8787 Baypine Rd.
Jacksonville, FL 32256
904-680-7710
Fax 904-680-7776
admissions@fcsl.edu

Florida International University (College of Law)
FIU College of Law, RDB 1055
Miami, FL 33199
(305) 348-8006
Fax: (305) 348-2965
miroa@fiu.edu

Florida State University (College of Law)
425 W. Jefferson St.
Tallahassee, FL 32306-1601
850-644-3787
Fax 850-644-7284
admissions@law.fsu.edu

School	Salary Range												%
Fordham University (School of Law) 140 West 62nd Street New York, NY 10023 212-636-6810 Fax: 212-636-7984 lawadmissions@law.fordham.edu	$60,000–$140,000	52	2		3	6	11	4	3	4	8	7	99%
Franklin Pierce Law Center 2 White Street Concord, NH 03301 603-228-9217 Fax: 603-228-1074 admissions@piercelaw.edu	$37,200–$135,000	15	1	1	4	14	12	10	8	6	8	19	96%
George Mason University (School of Law) 3301 Fairfax Drive Arlington, VA 22201 703-993-8010 Fax: 703-993-8088 aprice1@gmu.edu	$32,500–$240,000	23	5	2	8	10	15	13	1	1	4	17	99%
George Washington University (Law School) 2000 H Street, N.W. Washington, DC 20052 202-994-7230 Fax: 202-994-3597 jd@law.gwu.edu	$90,000–$135,000	62	1		4	9	11	10					95%
Georgetown University (Law Center) 600 New Jersey Avenue, N.W. Washington, DC 20001 202-662-9010 Fax: 202-662-9439 admis@law.georgetown.edu	$50,000–$160,000			2	5	5	6	8	3	1	1	2	97%
Georgia State University (College of Law) P.O. Box 4037 Atlanta, GA 30302-4037 404-413-9200 Fax: 404-413-9203 cjgeorge@gsu.edu	$38,000–$160,000	17	4	2	6	18	8	4	2	3	8	23	98%
Golden Gate University (School of Law) 536 Mission Street San Francisco, CA 94105-2968 415-442-6630 lawadmit@ggu.edu	$30,000–$200,000	3	6		4	28	17	1	8	1	6	26	82%
Gonzaga University (School of Law) Box 3528 Spokane, WA 99220-3528 509-313-5532 Fax: 509-313-3697 admissions@lawschool.gonzaga.edu	$62,000–$70,000	20	2	2	6	13	15	8	1	7	5	21	94%
Hamline University (School of Law) 1536 Hewitt Avenue St. Paul, MN 55104-1284 651-523-2461 Fax: 651-523-3064 lawadm@gw.hamline.edu	$36,500–$240,000	5	1	1	7	27	8	15	5	1	2	28	93%

School	PLACEMENT RECORD — Placement Within 6 to 9 Months	Private Practice 2–10 Attorneys	Private Practice 11–25 Attorneys	Private Practice 26–50 Attorneys	Private Practice 51–100 Attorneys	Judicial Clerkships	Government	Business/Industry	Public Interest	Military	Academic	Other	Average Starting Salary	CAREER SERVICES — Law Placement Office	University Placement Office	Employment Counseling	Job Openings Information	Solo Practice Advice	Resume Preparation	Interview Counseling	Employment Planning	Job Interviews Arrangement	Law, Corporate, and Government Contact	Alumni Contacts	Part-Time/Summer Employment	Internships	Alumni Placement
Harvard University (Harvard Law School), Cambridge, MA 02138, 617-495-3179, jdadmiss@law.harvard.edu	99%					29	3	3	4		1	60		•		•	•	•	•	•	•	•	•	•	•	•	•
Hofstra University (School of Law), 121 Hofstra University, Hempstead, NY 11549, 516-463-5916, Fax: 516-463-6264, lawadmissions@hofstra.edu	98%	29	9	7	4	6	13	12	2		2	12	$35,000–$125,000	•		•	•	•	•	•	•	•	•	•	•	•	•
Howard University, 2900 Van Ness Street, N.W., Washington, DC 20008, 202-806-8008, Fax: 202-806-8162, admissions@law.howard.edu	94%	5	1	3	3	16	30	19	3		1	19	$30,000–$150,000	•		•	•	•	•	•	•	•	•	•	•	•	•
Illinois Institute of Technology (Chicago-Kent College of Law), 565 West Adams Street, Chicago, IL 60661, 312-906-5020, Fax: 312-906-5274, admit@kentlaw.edu	97%	22	9	3	3	5	15	19	3		1		$30,000–$145,000	•		•	•	•	•	•	•	•	•	•	•	•	•
Indiana University (Maurer School of Law), 211 S. Indiana Avenue, Bloomington, IN 47405-7001, 812-855-4765, Fax: 812-855-0555, Lawadmis@indiana.edu	96%	8	6	5	3	11	17	17	6		4	23	$38,000–$165,000	•		•	•	•	•	•	•	•	•	•	•	•	•
Indiana University-Purdue University at Indianapolis (Indiana University School of Law-Indianapolis), 530 West New York Street, Indianapolis, IN 46202-3225, 317-274-2459, Fax: 317-278-4780, khmiller@iupui.edu	94%					1	17	20	2	1	2	54	$43,000–$160,000	•		•	•	•	•	•	•	•	•	•	•	•	•
Inter American University of Puerto Rico (School of Law), P.O. Box 70351, San Juan, PR 00936-8351, 787-751-1912, ext. 2013, 2526	91%	10	10	10	7	9	23	21	1		3		$28,000–$68,000		•	•	•	•	•	•	•	•	•	•	•	•	•

School	Salary Range												%
John Marshall Law School 315 South Plymouth Court Chicago, IL 60604 312-987-1406 Fax: 312-427-5136 admission@jmls.edu	$78,500	7	3	2	2	23	13	2	5	4	6	33	89%
Lewis and Clark College **(Lewis and Clark Law School)** 10015 Southwest Terwilliger Boulevard Portland, OR 97219 503-768-6613 Fax: 503-768-6793 lawadmss@lclark.edu	$67,834		2		11	20	17	6	2	2	6	34	96%
Liberty University **(School of Law)** 1971 University Blvd. Lynchburg, VA 24502 434-592-5300 Fax: 434-592-0202 law@liberty.edu													
Louisiana State University **(Paul M. Hebert Law Center)** 202 Law Center, 1 East Campus Drive Baton Rouge, LA 70803 225-578-8646 Fax: 225-578-8647 lynell.cadray@law.lsu.edu	$27,500- $160,000				1	3	9	21	6	11	16	26	92%
Loyola Marymount University **(Loyola Law School)** 919 Albany Street Los Angeles, CA 90015 213-736-1074 Fax: 213-736-6523 admissions@lls.edu	$60,000- $125,000	59	2		9	21	8	3					97%
Loyola University Chicago **(School of Law)** 25 East Pearson Street Chicago, IL 60611 312-915-7170 Fax: 312-915-7906 law-admissions@luc.edu	$47,167- $115,077		1		4	17	12	3	7	4	11	39	88%
Loyola University of New Orleans **(School of Law)** 7214 St. Charles Avenue New Orleans, LA 70118 504-861-5575 Fax: 504-861-5772 ladmit@loyno.edu		62	1		4	11	12	10					87%
Marquette University **(Law School)** Office of Admissions, P.O. Box 1881 Milwaukee, WI 53201-1881 414-288-6767 Fax: 414-288-0676 law.admission@marquette.edu	$32,000- $170,000	14	3	1	5	14	9	4	2	3	11	32	93%
Mercer University **(Walter F. George School of Law)** 1021 Georgia Avenue Macon, GA 31207 478-301-2605 Fax: 478-301-2989 Sutton_me@law.mercer.edu	$33,000- $145,000	16	4	4	3	5	14	8	4	6	13	23	88%

PLACEMENT RECORD — Percentage Breakdown of Type of Employer

School	Average Starting Salary	Placement within 6 to 9 months	Private Practice 2–10 Attorneys	Private Practice 11–25 Attorneys	Private Practice 26–50 Attorneys	Private Practice 51–100 Attorneys	Judicial Clerkships	Government	Business/Industry	Public Interest	Military	Academic	Other
Michigan State University (College of Law)	$35,000–$145,000	92%	29	9	5	6	5	12	18	5	2	2	9
Mississippi College (School of Law)	$45,770–$95,333	87%	30	4	4	11	8	11	13	5		1	
New England Law/Boston	$30,000–$160,000	90%	27	4	2	1	11	14	27	4	1	2	10
New York Law School	$25,000–$16,000	91%			43		4	14	23	6		4	6
New York University (School of Law)	$57,354–$160,000	98%				75	11	2	2	9		1	
North Carolina Central University (School of Law)		83%					6	22	6	7		1	58
Northeastern University (School of Law)	$36,000–$160,000	94%	9	6	4	2	13	8	26	16		3	13

CAREER SERVICES & FACILITIES

For all seven schools listed, the following **Services** are marked (•): Alumni Placement, Internships, Part-Time/Summer Employment, Alumni Contacts, Law/Corporate and Government Contact, Job Interviews Arrangement, Employment Planning, Interview Counseling, Resume Preparation, Solo Practice Advice, Job Openings Information, Employment Counseling.

Under **Facilities**: Law Placement Office (•) for all seven schools; University Placement Office (not marked).

School contact information

Michigan State University (College of Law)
230 Law College Bldg.
East Lansing, MI 48824-1300
517-432-0222
Fax: 517-432-0098

Mississippi College (School of Law)
151 E. Griffith Street
Jackson, MS 39201
601-925-7152
pevans@mc.edu

New England Law/Boston
154 Stuart Street
Boston, MA 02116
617-422-7210
Fax: 617-422-7201
admit@admin.nesl.edu

New York Law School
185 West Broadway
New York, NY 10013-2960
212-431-2888
Fax: 212-966-1522
admissions@nyls.edu

New York University (School of Law)
161 Avenue of the Americas, 5th Floor
New York, NY 10013
212-998-6060
Fax: 212-995-4527
law.moreinfo@nyu.edu

North Carolina Central University (School of Law)
640 Nelson Street
Durham, NC 27707
919-530-6333
Fax: 919-530-6339
sbrownb@nccu.edu

Northeastern University (School of Law)
400 Huntington Avenue
Boston, MA 02115
617-373-2395
Fax: 617-373-8865
c.taubman@neu.edu

School (Contact)	Salary Range												%
Northern Illinois University (College of Law), Swen Parson Hall, Room 151, De Kalb, IL 60115-2890, 815-753-8595, Fax: 815-753-5680, lawadmit@niu.edu	$42,000–$52,000		2	4	5	13	15	2		2	8	42	90%
Northern Kentucky University (Salmon P. Chase College of Law), Louie B. Nunn Hall, Highland Heights, KY 41099, 859-572-5490, Fax: 859-572-6081, brayg@nku.edu	$28,000–$140,000	13	1	1	7	21	10	8	3	2	2	31	93%
Northwestern University (School of Law), 357 East Chicago Avenue, Chicago, IL 60611, 312-503-8465, Fax: 312-503-0178, admissions@law.northwestern.edu	$45,000–$160,000		2		5	5	2	12	74				99%
Nova Southeastern University (Shepard Broad Law Center), 3305 College Avenue, Fort Lauderdale, FL 33314-7721, 954-262-6117, Fax: 954-262-3844, admission@nsu.law.nova.edu	$39,000–$123,000	21	2		6	12	17	3	2	4	8	24	82%
Ohio Northern University (Claude W. Pettit College of Law), 525 South Main Street, Ada, OH 45810, 419-772-2211, Fax: 419-772-3042	$30,000–$110,000	8		3	3	14	15	6	8		6	58	94%
Ohio State University (Michael E. Moritz College of Law), 55 West 12th Avenue, John Deaver Drinko Hall, Columbus, OH 43210-1391, 614-292-8810, Fax: 614-292-1383, lawadmit@osu.edu	$42,500–$90,000		4		3	14	15	12		2	22	52	
Oklahoma City University (School of Law), 2501 North Blackwelder Avenue, Oklahoma City, OK 73106-1493, 405-208-5354, Fax: 405-208-5814, lawadmit@okcu.edu	$22,000–$120,000	19	3	2	6	14	13	5	2	3	6	55	83%
Pace University (School of Law), 78 North Broadway, White Plains, NY 10603, 914-422-4210, Fax: 914-989-8714, calexander@law.pace.edu	$46,000–$160,000	7	7		7	17	17		2			20	92%
Pennsylvania State University (Dickinson School of Law), 100 Beam Building, University Park, PA 16802-1910, 814-867-1251, Fax: 717-241-3503, dsladmit@psu.edu	$36,369–$118,750	21	2		3	14	12	14	6	4	5	18	92%

PLACEMENT RECORD / CAREER SERVICES

School	Average Starting Salary	Placement Within 6 to 9 Months	Private Practice 2-10 Attorneys	Private Practice 11-25 Attorneys	Private Practice 26-50 Attorneys	Private Practice 51-100 Attorneys	Judicial Clerkships	Government	Business/Industry	Public Interest	Military	Academic	Other
Pepperdine University (School of Law) 24255 Pacific Coast Highway, Malibu, CA 90263, 310-506-4631, Fax: 310-506-7668		95%											
Phoenix School of Law 4041 N. Central Ave. Suite 100, Phoenix, AZ 85012-3330, (602) 682-6800													
Pontifical Catholic University of Puerto Rico (School of Law) 2250 Avenida las Americas suite 543, Ponce, PR 00717-9997, 787-841-2000, ext. 1836, Fax: 787-840-4620	$14,000–$24,000											50	50
Quinnipiac University (School of Law) 275 Mt. Carmel Avenue, Hamden, CT 06518-1908, 203-582-3400, Fax: 203-582-3339, ladm@quinnipiac.edu	$20,000–$253,000	95%	15	5	1	3	11	23	28	2		1	11
Regent University (School of Law) 1000 Regent University Drive, Virginia Beach, VA 23464-9800, 757-352-4584, Fax: 757-352-4139, lawschool@regent.edu	$49,439–$115,000	91%	34	2	4	1	11	14	11	9	6	5	5
Roger Williams University (School of Law) Ten Metacom Avenue, Bristol, RI 02809-5171, 401-254-4555, Fax: 401-254-4516, admissions@rwu.edu	$28,000–$250,000	86%	23	3	2	1	13	6	21	8	7	1	15
Rutgers University/Camden (School of Law) Fifth and Penn Streets, Camden, NJ 08102, 856-225-6102, Fax: 856-225-6637, admissions@camlaw.rutgers.edu	$45,000–$110,000	92%	5	9	12	15	40	6	9	2	1		1

CAREER SERVICES — Services & Facilities

School	Alumni Placement	Internships	Part-Time/Summer Employment	Alumni Contacts	Law, Corporate, and Government Contact	Job Interviews Arrangement	Employment Planning	Interview Counseling	Resume Preparation	Solo Practice Advice	Job Openings Information	Employment Counseling	University Placement Office	Law Placement Office
Pepperdine University	•	•	•		•	•	•	•	•	•	•	•		
Phoenix School of Law	•	•	•	•	•	•	•	•	•	•	•	•		•
Pontifical Catholic University of Puerto Rico				•	•						•			•
Quinnipiac University	•	•	•	•	•	•	•	•	•	•	•	•		•
Regent University	•	•	•	•	•	•	•	•	•	•	•	•		•
Roger Williams University	•	•	•	•	•	•	•	•	•	•	•	•		•
Rutgers University/Camden	•	•	•	•	•	•	•	•	•	•	•	•		•

School	Salary												Placement
Rutgers University/Newark (School of Law) Center for Law and Justice, 123 Washington St. Newark, NJ 07102 973-353-5557/5554 Fax: 973-353-3459 lawinfo@andromeda.rutgers.edu	$35,000–$192,000		2	2	3	13	5	28	11	11	11	11	98%
Saint John's University (School of Law) 8000 Utopia Parkway Queens, NY 11439 718-990-6474 Fax: 718-990-2526 lawinfo@stjohns.edu	$42,000–$16,000	25	3		3	15	17	4	5	6	5	17	96%
Saint Louis University (School of Law) 3700 Lindell Boulevard St. Louis, MO 63108 314-977-2800 Fax: 314-977-1464 admissions@law.slu.edu	$58,500	10			11	17	7	3	5	5	14	28	89%
Saint Mary's University (School of Law) One Camino Santa Maria San Antonio, TX 78228-8601 210-436-3523 Fax: 210-431-4202 wwilson@stmarytx.edu	$60,000–$70,000		2	2	2	11	16	5	1	1	1	40	89%
Saint Thomas University (School of Law) 16401 NW 37th Avenue Miami Gardens, FL 33054 305-623-2310 fkhan@stu.edu	$38,000–$40,000	10	1		8	22	13	2	3	2	9	33	74%
Samford University (Cumberland School of Law) 800 Lakeshore Drive Birmingham, AL 35229 205-726-2702 Fax: 205-726-2057 law.admissions@samford.edu	$30,000–$175,000		2	1		11	10	3	8	6	12	26	94%
Santa Clara University (School of Law) 500 El Camino Real Santa Clara, CA 95053 408-554-4800 Fax: 408-554-7897 lawadmissions@scu.edu	$38,000–$145,000	32	1		3	27	9	1	4	4	4	15	90%
Seattle University (School of Law) 901 12th Avenue, Sullivan Hall, P.O. Box 222000 Seattle, WA 98122-4340 206-398-4200 Fax: 206-398-4058 lawadmis@seattleu.edu	$44,500–$130,000	9	1		5	31	12	6	2	3	3	26	94%
Seton Hall University (School of Law) One Newark Center Newark, NJ 07102-5210 973-642-8747 Fax: 973-642-8876 admitme@shu.edu	$55,000–$75,000		1		3	15	5	35	8	5	10	18	97%

	South Texas College of Law	Southern Illinois University (School of Law)	Southern Methodist University (Dedman School of Law)	Southern University and A & M College (Law Center)	Southwestern University (Law School)	Stanford University (Stanford Law School)	State University of New York (University at Buffalo Law School)
AVERAGE STARTING SALARY	$70,000–$135,000	$35,000–$60,000	$62,400–$160,000		$52,000–$140,000		$22,000–$165,000
PLACEMENT RECORD — Percentage Breakdown of Type of Employer							
OTHER	16	8	38	14	10	61	5
ACADEMIC	1	3	2	5	1	1	4
MILITARY	1	2	1				3
PUBLIC INTEREST	2	7	1	2	4	6	7
BUSINESS/INDUSTRY	17	14	16	6	15	5	11
GOVERNMENT	11	24	6	10	14	4	8
JUDICIAL CLERKSHIPS	3	2	4	21	5	23	5
PRIVATE PRACTICE 51–100 ATTORNEYS	2	2	7	5	10	6	
PRIVATE PRACTICE 26–50 ATTORNEYS	2		12	3	7		9
PRIVATE PRACTICE 11–25 ATTORNEYS	7	7	8	2	8		5
PRIVATE PRACTICE 2–10 ATTORNEYS	38	29	29	24	26		24
PLACEMENT WITHIN 6 TO 9 MONTHS	80%	80%	99%	26%	97%	99%	96%
CAREER SERVICES — Services							
ALUMNI PLACEMENT	•	•	•	•	•	•	•
INTERNSHIPS	•	•	•	•	•	•	•
PART-TIME/SUMMER EMPLOYMENT	•	•	•	•	•	•	•
ALUMNI CONTACTS	•	•	•	•	•	•	•
LAW, CORPORATE, AND GOVERNMENT CONTACT	•	•	•	•	•	•	•
JOB INTERVIEWS ARRANGEMENT	•	•	•	•	•	•	•
EMPLOYMENT PLANNING	•	•	•	•	•	•	•
INTERVIEW COUNSELING	•	•	•	•	•	•	•
RESUME PREPARATION	•	•	•	•	•	•	•
SOLO PRACTICE ADVICE	•				•	•	•
JOB OPENINGS INFORMATION	•	•	•	•	•	•	•
EMPLOYMENT COUNSELING	•	•	•	•	•	•	•
Facilities							
UNIVERSITY PLACEMENT OFFICE							•
LAW PLACEMENT OFFICE	•	•	•	•		•	•

School addresses:

South Texas College of Law
1303 San Jacinto Street
Houston, TX 77002-7000
713-646-1810
Fax: 713-646-2906
admissions@stcl.edu

Southern Illinois University (School of Law)
Lesar Law Building, Mail Code 6804
Carbondale, IL 62901
618-453-8921
Fax: 618-453-8858
lawadmit@siu.edu

Southern Methodist University (Dedman School of Law)
Office of Admissions, P.O. Box 750110
Dallas, TX 75275-0110
214-768-2550
Fax: 214-768-2549
lawadmit@smu.edu

Southern University and A & M College (Law Center)
Post Office Box 9294
Baton Rouge, LA 70813-9294
225-771-5340
Fax: 225-771-2121
vwilkerson@sulc.edu

Southwestern University (Law School)
3050 Wilshire Boulevard
Los Angeles, CA 90010-1106
213-738-6717
Fax: 213-383-1688
admissions@swlaw.edu

Stanford University (Stanford Law School)
Crown Quadrangle, 559 Nathan Abbott Way
Stanford, CA 94305-8610
650-723-4985
Fax: 650-723-0838
admissions@law.stanford.edu

State University of New York (University at Buffalo Law School)
309 O'Brian Hall
Buffalo, NY 14260
716-645-2907
Fax: 716-645-6676

School	Data columns											%	Salary range
Stetson University (Stetson University College of Law) 1401 61st Street South Gulfport, FL 33707 727-562-7802 Fax: 727-343-0136 zuppo@law.stetson.edu	11	1	2	7	13	21	5	4	7	12	18	96%	$42,000–$110,000
Suffolk University (Law School) 120 Tremont Street Boston, MA 02108-4977 617-573-8144 Fax: 617-523-1367	1	3	1	2	28	13	11	11	3	5	20	86%	$44,000–$95,000
Syracuse University (College of Law) Office of Admissions and Financial Aid, Suite 340 Syracuse, NY 13244-1030 315-443-1962 Fax: 315-443-9568	10	3	2	4	16	13	15	6	5	6	20	90%	$36,700–$113,000
Temple University (James E. Beasley School of Law) 1719 N. Broad Street Philadelphia, PA 19122 215-204-5949 Fax: 215-204-1185 lawadmis@temple.edu	4	2		7	17	14	9	4	4	8	13	93%	$30,000–$160,000
Texas Southern University (Thurgood Marshall School of Law) 3100 Cleburne Avenue Houston, TX 77004 713-313-7114 Fax: 713-313-1049 cgardner@tmslaw.tsu.edu				2	4	7					88	72%	$47,000
Texas Tech University (School of Law) 1802 Hartford Avenue Lubbock, TX 79409 806-742-3990, ext. 273 Fax: 806-742-4617 donna.williams@ttu.edu		1	4	3	17	17	5	2	12	15	49	92%	$25,000–$160,000
Texas Wesleyan University (School of Law) 1515 Commerce Street Fort Worth, TX 76102 817-212-4040 Fax: 817-212-4141 lawadmissions@law.txwes.edu	4	1		1	29	11	2	2	6	11	34	85%	$28,800–$200,000
Thomas Jefferson School of Law 2121 San Diego Avenue San Diego, CA 92110 619-297-9700 Fax: 619-294-4713 info@tjsl.edu	27	3	1	3	2	8	6	1	2	5	24	86%	$44,500–$95,000
Thomas M. Cooley Law School 300 South Capitol Avenue Lansing, MI 48901 517-371-5140 Fax: 517-334-5718 admissions@cooley.edu		2		6	20	17	8	1	1	3	20	82%	$14,560–$135,000
Touro College (Jacob D. Fuchsberg Law Center) 225 Eastview Drive Central Islip, NY 11722 631-761-7010 Fax: 631-761-7019 gjustice@tourolaw.edu	2	3		5	23	21	2	2	5	6	31	78%	$40,000–$63,000

PLACEMENT RECORD / CAREER SERVICES

School	Avg. Starting Salary	Other	Academic	Military	Public Interest	Business/Industry	Government	Judicial Clerkships	Pvt. Practice 51-100	Pvt. Practice 26-50	Pvt. Practice 11-25	Pvt. Practice 2-10	Placement Within 6 to 9 Months
Tulane University (Law School) — Weinmann Hall, 6329 Freret Street, New Orleans, LA 70118; 504-865-5930; Fax: 504-865-6710; admissions@law.tulane.edu	$35,000–$140,000	59	1		6	5	9	10					95%
University of Akron (School of Law) — 302 Buchtel Common, Akron, OH 44325-2901; 330-972-7331; Fax: 330-258-2343; lthorpe@uakron.edu	$30,000–$156,000	14	1		5	23	19	5	4	5	4	29	82%
University of Alabama (School of Law) — Box 870382, Tuscaloosa, AL 35487-0382; 205-348-5440; Fax: 205-348-3917; admissions@law.ua.edu	$23,000–$105,000		4	8	5	9	9	17	7	11	9	16	99%
University of Arizona (James E. Rogers College of Law) — 120 E. Speedway P.O. Box 210176, Tucson, AZ 85721-0176; 520-621-3477; Fax: 520-621-9140; admissions@law.arizona.edu	$43,326–$79,622	5	1	2	5	10	17	22	15	12	8	3	94%
University of Arkansas (School of Law) — Robert A. Leflar Law Center, Waterman Hall, Fayetteville, AR 72701; 479-575-3102; Fax: 479-575-3937; jkmiller@uark.edu		14	1		5	17	11	3	1	5	7	36	95%
University of Arkansas at Little Rock (UALR William H. Bowen School of Law) — 1201 McMath Avenue, Little Rock, AR 72202-5142; 501-324-9903; Fax: 501-324-9909; lawadm@ualr.edu	$40,000–$65,000	11	5		4	14	13	13	2	2	11	26	95%
University of Baltimore (School of Law) — 1420 North Charles Street, Baltimore, MD 21201-5779; 410-837-4450; Fax: 410-837-4459; lwadmiss@ubmail.ubalt.edu; jzavrotny@ubalt.edu	$27,500–$145,000	10	3	1	5	18	13	23	2	3	3	18	94%

CAREER SERVICES — Services / Facilities

School	Alumni Placement	Internships	Part-Time/Summer Employment	Alumni Contacts	Law, Corporate, and Government Contact	Job Interviews Arrangement	Employment Planning	Interview Counseling	Resume Preparation	Solo Practice Advice	Job Openings Information	Employment Counseling	University Placement Office	Law Placement Office
Tulane University	•	•	•	•	•	•	•	•	•	•	•	•		•
University of Akron	•	•	•	•	•	•	•	•	•	•	•	•	•	•
University of Alabama	•	•	•	•	•	•	•	•	•	•	•	•		•
University of Arizona	•	•	•	•	•	•	•	•	•	•	•	•		•
University of Arkansas	•	•	•	•	•	•	•	•	•	•	•		•	•
University of Arkansas at Little Rock	•	•	•	•	•	•	•	•	•	•	•	•		•
University of Baltimore	•	•	•	•	•	•	•	•	•	•	•	•		•

School												%	Salary Range
University of California (Hastings College of the Law) 200 McAllister Street San Francisco, CA 94102 415-565-4623 Fax: 415-581-8946 admiss@uchastings.edu	45	2		4	9	8	4	4	4	6	14	94%	$26,000-$150,000
University of California at Berkeley (School of Law) 215 Boalt Hall Berkeley, CA 94720 510-642-2274 Fax: 510-643-6222 adissions@law.berkeley.edu	70			10	2	6	12					99%	$30,000-$180,000
University of California at Davis (School of Law) Martin Luther King, Jr. Hall - 400 Mrak Hall Drive Davis, CA 95616-5201 530-752-6477 Fax: 530-752-6477 admissions@lawdavis.edu	1	1		13	8	7	11	5	3	10	15	98%	$30,000-$125,000
University of California at Los Angeles (UCLA School of Law) P.O. Box 951445 Los Angeles, CA 90095-1445 310-825-2080 Fax: 310-206-7227 admissions@law.ucla.edu	49	2	1	9	7	7	9	3	2	4	5	99%	$32,000-$168,000
University of Chicago (Law School) 1111 East 60th Street Chicago, IL 60637 773-702-9484 Fax: 773-834-0942 admissions@law.uchicago.edu	82			1	3	2	13					100%	$50,000-$165,000
University of Cincinnati (College of Law) P.O. Box 210040 Cincinnati, OH 45221-0040 513-556-6805 Fax: 513-556-2391 admissions@law.uc.edu	50	5	3	13	13	9	6	5	4	4	15	95%	$22,800-$160,000
University of Colorado (Law School) Campus Box 403, Wolf Law Building Boulder, CO 80309-0403 303-492-7203 Fax: 303-492-2542	14	4	4	7	6	11	26	8	3	6	13	88%	$44,440-$93,460
University of Connecticut (School of Law) 55 Elizabeth Street Hartford, CT 06105 860-570-5159 Fax: 860-570-5153 admissions@law.uconn.edu	7	2	1	2	14	10	13	8	4	4		92%	$31,200-$180,000
University of Dayton (School of Law) 300 College Park Dayton, OH 45469-2760 937-229-3555 Fax: 937-229-4194 lawinfo@notes.udayton.edu	6	3	2	4	11	11	9	4	8	4	37	97%	$22,500-$125,000

PLACEMENT RECORD / CAREER SERVICES

	University of Denver (Sturm College of Law)	University of Detroit Mercy (School of Law)	University of Florida (Fredric G. Levin College of Law)	University of Georgia (School of Law)	University of Hawaii at Manoa (William S. Richardson School of Law)	University of Houston (Law Center)	University of Idaho (College of Law)
AVERAGE STARTING SALARY	$31,080–$150,000	$64,448	$55,000–$92,500	$33,000–$125,000	$32,000–$160,000	$20,000–$350,000	$33,000–$160,000
PLACEMENT RECORD — Percentage Breakdown of Type of Employer							
OTHER	3	57	24			23	2
ACADEMIC	1	5	3	1		2	2
MILITARY							2
PUBLIC INTEREST	4	5	5	6		4	8
BUSINESS/INDUSTRY	17	22	8	7	12	21	6
GOVERNMENT	14	5	13	11	15	10	19
JUDICIAL CLERKSHIPS	10	4	5	17	36	4	24
PRIVATE PRACTICE 51–100 ATTORNEYS		5	58	8	1	1	
PRIVATE PRACTICE 26–50 ATTORNEYS		8		7	2	2	
PRIVATE PRACTICE 11–25 ATTORNEYS		9	9	8	10		12
PRIVATE PRACTICE 2–10 ATTORNEYS			21	13	18		18
PLACEMENT WITHIN 6 TO 9 MONTHS	88%		87%	99%	100%	96%	89%
CAREER SERVICES — Services							
ALUMNI PLACEMENT	•	•	•	•	•	•	•
INTERNSHIPS	•	•	•	•	•	•	•
PART-TIME/SUMMER EMPLOYMENT	•	•	•	•	•	•	•
ALUMNI CONTACTS	•	•	•	•	•	•	•
LAW, CORPORATE, AND GOVERNMENT CONTACT	•	•	•	•	•	•	•
JOB INTERVIEWS ARRANGEMENT	•	•	•	•	•	•	•
EMPLOYMENT PLANNING	•	•	•	•	•	•	•
INTERVIEW COUNSELING	•	•	•	•	•	•	•
RESUME PREPARATION	•	•	•	•	•	•	•
SOLO PRACTICE ADVICE	•	•	•	•	•	•	•
JOB OPENINGS INFORMATION	•	•	•	•	•	•	•
EMPLOYMENT COUNSELING	•	•	•	•		•	•
Facilities							
UNIVERSITY PLACEMENT OFFICE							
LAW PLACEMENT OFFICE	•	•	•	•	•	•	•

School contact information

- **University of Denver (Sturm College of Law)**, 2255 E. Evans Avenue, Denver, CO 80208, 303-871-6135, Fax: 303-871-6992, admissions@law.du.edu
- **University of Detroit Mercy (School of Law)**, 651 East Jefferson Avenue, Detroit, MI 48226, 313-596-0264, Fax: 313-596-0280, udmlawao@udmercy.edu
- **University of Florida (Fredric G. Levin College of Law)**, 141 Bruton-Geer Hall, P.O. Box 117622, Gainesville, FL 32611-7622, 352-273-0890, Fax: 352-392-4087, madomo@law.ufl.edu
- **University of Georgia (School of Law)**, Hirsch Hall, 225 Herty Drive, Athens, GA 30602-6012, 706-542-7060, Fax: 706-542-5556, ugajd@uga.edu
- **University of Hawaii at Manoa (William S. Richardson School of Law)**, 2515 Dole Street, Honolulu, HI 96822, 808-956-7966, Fax: 808-956-3813, lawadm@hawaii.edu
- **University of Houston (Law Center)**, 100 Law Center, Houston, TX 77204-6060, 713-743-2280, Fax: 713-743-2194, lawadmissions@uh.edu
- **University of Idaho (College of Law)**, P.O. Box 442321, Moscow, ID 83844-2321, 208-885-2300, Fax: 208-885-5709, jfinney@uidaho.edu

School	Contact												%	Salary Range
University of Illinois (College of Law)	504 East Pennsylvania Avenue, Champaign, IL 61820 · 217-244-6415 · Fax 217-244-1478 · admissions@law.uiuc.edu	35	3		1	12	9	6	3	1	7	10	98%	
University of Iowa (College of Law)	320 Melrose Avenue, Iowa City, IA 52242 · 319-335-9095 · Fax: 319-335-9646 · law-admissions@uiowa.edu	26	3		3	14	17	12	6	5	4	10	99%	$30,000-$165,000
University of Kansas (School of Law)	205 Green Hall, 1535 W. 15th Street, Lawrence, KS 66045 · 785-864-4378 · Fax: 785-864-5054 · admitlaw@ku.edu	16	1		4	15	18	7	4	4	9	22	94%	$24,000-$160,000
University of Kentucky (College of Law)	209 Law Building, Lexington, KY 40506-0048 · 606-257-7938 · Fax: (859) 323-1061 · lawadmissions@email.uky.edu		1		9	11	10	18	12	3	9	27	99%	$24,000-$120,000
University of La Verne (College of Law)	320 East D Street, Ontario, CA 91764 · 909-460-2001 · Fax: 909-460-2082 · lawadm@ulv.edu					14	11		14	14	5	48		
University of Louisville (Louis D. Brandeis School of Law)	University of Louisville Belknap Campus–Wilson W. Wyatt Hall, Louisville, KY 40292 · 502-852-6364 · Fax: 502-852-8971 · brandon.hamilton@louisville.edu	3	3			15	17	5	9	9	15	28	97%	$37,000-$103,000
University of Maine (School of Law)	246 Deering Avenue, Portland, ME 04102 · 207-780-4341 · Fax: 207-780-4239 · mainelaw@usm.maine.edu		1	2	5	18	15	15	9	9	9	19	90%	$39,000-$52,000
University of Maryland (School of Law)	500 West Baltimore Street, Baltimore, MD 21201 · 410-706-3492 · Fax: 410-706-1793 · admissions@law.umaryland.edu	19	5		5	10	13	25	2	4	3	12	98%	$61,498-$150,000
University of Memphis (Cecil C. Humphreys School of Law)	1 North Front Street, Memphis, TN 38103-2189 · 901-678-5403 · Fax: 901-678-0741 · lawadmissions@.memphis.edu	6	2		4	11	9	5	2	6	6	39	95%	$25,000-$100,000

Guide to Law Schools

	University of Miami (School of Law)	University of Michigan (Law School)	University of Minnesota (Law School)	University of Mississippi (L.Q.C. Lamar Hall)	University of Missouri-Columbia (School of Law)	University of Missouri-Kansas City (School of Law)	University of Montana (School of Law)
FACILITIES							
Law Placement Office	●	●	●	●	●	●	●
University Placement Office	●				●		
CAREER SERVICES							
Employment Counseling	●	●	●	●	●		●
Job Openings Information	●	●	●	●	●	●	●
Solo Practice Advice	●	●	●	●	●	●	●
Resume Preparation	●	●	●	●	●	●	●
Interview Counseling	●	●	●	●	●	●	●
Employment Planning	●	●	●	●	●	●	●
Job Interviews Arrangement	●	●	●	●	●	●	●
Law, Corporate, and Government Contact	●	●	●	●	●	●	●
Alumni Contacts	●	●	●	●	●	●	●
Part-Time/Summer Employment	●	●	●	●	●	●	●
Internships	●	●	●	●	●	●	●
Alumni Placement	●	●	●	●	●	●	●
PLACEMENT RECORD							
Placement Within 6 to 9 Months	96%	100%	98%	93%	88%	56%	90%
Private Practice 2-10 Attorneys	48			28	15	22	39
Private Practice 11-25 Attorneys	14			5	6	4	
Private Practice 26-50 Attorneys	7			7	1	2	
Private Practice 51-100 Attorneys	7			8	3		
Judicial Clerkships	4	14	17	18	13	11	24
Government	13	3	9	10	14	16	10
Business/Industry	7	5	6	6	12	6	9
Public Interest	6	5	4	4	5	5	
Military			2	2		8	
Academic	2	2		2	2	1	1
Other	2	73		11	30	15	3
Average Starting Salary	$37,500-$200,000	$30,000-$190,000	$30,000-$160,000	$28,000-$100,000	$30,000-$160,000	$30,000-$115,000	$33,750

School contact information:

University of Miami (School of Law)
P.O. Box 248087, 1311 Miller Drive
Coral Gables, FL 33124-8087
305-284-2523
Fax: 305-284-4400
admissions@law.miami.edu

University of Michigan (Law School)
625 South State Street
Ann Arbor, MI 48109-1215
734-764-0537
Fax: 734-647-3218
law.jd.admissions@umich.edu

University of Minnesota (Law School)
229 19th Avenue S.
Minneapolis, MN 55455
612-625-3487
Fax: 612-626-1874
jdadmissions@umn.edu

University of Mississippi (L.Q.C. Lamar Hall)
P.O. Box 1848 Lamar Law Center
University, MS 38677
662-915-6910
Fax: 662-915-1289
bvinson@olemiss.edu

University of Missouri-Columbia (School of Law)
103 Hulston Hall
Columbia, MO 65211
573-882-6042
Fax: 573-882-9625
heckm@missouri.edu

University of Missouri-Kansas City (School of Law)
500 East 52nd Street
Kansas City, MO 64110-2499
816-235-1644
Fax: 816-235-5276
brooks@umkc.edu

University of Montana (School of Law)
Missoula, MT 59812
406-243-2698
Fax: 406-243-2576

School	Salary Range	Col1	Col2	Col3	Col4	Col5	Col6	Col7	Col8	Col9	Col10	Col11	%
University of Nebraska-Lincoln (College of Law) P.O. Box 830902 Lincoln, NE 68583-0902 402-472-2161 Fax: 402-472-5185 lawadm@unl.edu	$24,000-$115,000	41	4	3	4	15	23	11					93%
University of Nevada, Las Vegas (William S. Boyd School of Law) 4505 Maryland Parkway, Box 451003 Las Vegas, NV 89154-1003 702-895-2440 Fax: 702-895-2414 request@law.unlv.edu	$56,000-$87,500	16	2	2	4	12	8	16	6	3	3	27	94%
University of New Mexico (School of Law) MSC11-6070, 1 University of New Mexico Albuquerque, NM 87131-0001 505-277-0958 Fax: 505-277-9958 witherington@law.unm.edu	$12,000-$120,000	1	5	5	12	6	17	9	5	5	6	29	96%
University of North Carolina at Chapel Hill (School of Law) Campus Box 3380, Van Hecke-Wettach Hall Chapel Hill, NC 27599-3380 919-962-5109 law_admission@unc.edu	$34,000-$145,000	30	2	1	9	5	12	13	3	4	5	15	89%
University of North Dakota (School of Law) Box 9003 Grand Forks, ND 58202 701-777-2104 Fax: 701-777-2217 linda.kohoutek@thor.law.und.nodak.edu	$24,000-$90,000	1		3	8	7	14	15	7	2	9	34	91%
University of Notre Dame (Notre Dame Law School) P.O. Box 780 Notre Dame, IN 46556-0780 574-631-6626 Fax: 574-631-5474 lawadmit@nd.edu		61	1		7	6	12	14					99%
University of Oklahoma (College of Law) Andrew M. Coats Hall, 300 Timberdell Road Norman, OK 73019 405-325-4728 Fax: 405-325-0502 rlucas@ou.edu	$30,000-$175,000	12	3	2	2	15	18	3	10	4	2	29	95%
University of Oregon (School of Law, William W. Knight Law Center) 1221 University of Oregon Eugene, OR 97403-1221 541-346-3846 admissions@law.uoregon.edu	$24,000-$120,000	45	4	1	11	11	16	14					90%
University of Pennsylvania (Law School) 3400 Chestnut Street Philadelphia, PA 19104-6204 215-898-7400 Fax: 215-898-9606 admissions@law.upenn.edu	$45,500-$160,000	76			3	4	16						100%

Career Services & Placement Record

SCHOOL	LAW PLACEMENT OFFICE	UNIVERSITY PLACEMENT OFFICE	EMPLOYMENT COUNSELING	JOB OPENINGS INFORMATION	SOLO PRACTICE ADVICE	RESUME PREPARATION	INTERVIEW COUNSELING	EMPLOYMENT PLANNING	JOB INTERVIEWS ARRANGEMENT	LAW, CORPORATE, AND GOVERNMENT CONTACT	ALUMNI CONTACTS	PART-TIME/SUMMER EMPLOYMENT	INTERNSHIPS	ALUMNI PLACEMENT	PLACEMENT WITHIN 6 TO 9 MONTHS	PRIVATE PRACTICE 2-10 ATTORNEYS	PRIVATE PRACTICE 11-25 ATTORNEYS	PRIVATE PRACTICE 26-50 ATTORNEYS	PRIVATE PRACTICE 51-100 ATTORNEYS	JUDICIAL CLERKSHIPS	GOVERNMENT	BUSINESS/INDUSTRY	PUBLIC INTEREST	MILITARY	ACADEMIC	OTHER	AVERAGE STARTING SALARY
University of Pittsburgh (School of Law), 3900 Forbes Avenue, Pittsburgh, PA 15260, 412-648-1413, Fax: 412-648-1318, hlcall@law.pitt.edu	•		•	•	•	•	•	•	•	•	•	•	•	•	94%	22	4	2	4	7	10	17	4	2	1	28	$40,000-$145,000
University of Puerto Rico (School of Law), P.O. Box 23349, UPR Station, Rio Piedras, PR 00931-3349, 787-999-9551, Fax: 787-999-9554, arosario-lebron@law.upr.edu	•		•	•		•	•	•	•	•	•	•	•	•	81%	15	3	22		18	17	20			5		$24,000-$50,999
University of Richmond (School of Law), 28 Westhampton Way, Richmond, VA 23173, 804-289-8189, Fax: 804-287-6516, lawadmissions@richmond.edu	•	•	•	•	•	•	•	•	•	•	•	•	•	•	88%	11	9	4	2	18	20	8	3	2	1	25	$40,000-$165,000
University of Saint Thomas (School of Law), 1000 LaSalle Ave., Minneapolis, MN 55403, 651-962-4895, Fax: 651-962-4876, lawschool@stthomas.edu			•	•	•	•	•	•	•	•	•	•	•	•	87%	20	4	3	3	14	10	21	6	2	2	15	
University of San Diego (School of Law), 5998 Alcala Park, San Diego, CA 92110, 619-260-4528, Fax: 619-260-2218, jdinfo@sandiego.edu	•		•	•	•	•	•	•	•	•	•	•	•	•	97%	38	14	10	11	2	13	17	5	1	2	4	$35,000-$160,000
University of San Francisco (School of Law), 2130 Fulton Street, San Francisco, CA 94117-1080, 415-422-6586, Fax: 415-422-5442, lawadmissions@usfca.edu	•		•	•	•	•	•	•	•	•	•	•	•	•	92%	42	8	6	8	4	12	12	14			21	$38,000-$135,000
University of South Carolina (School of Law), 701 South Main Street, Columbia, SC 29208, 803-777-6605, Fax: 803-777-7751, usclaw@law.sc.edu	•		•	•	•	•	•	•	•	•	•	•	•	•	95%	19	10	5	3	15	11	9	7	1	1	13	$34,000-$160,000

School / Contact	Salary												Empl. %
University of South Dakota (School of Law) 414 East Clark Street, Vermillion, SD 57069-2390, 605-677-5443, Fax: 605-677-5417, law.school@usd.edu	$41,271–$55,000	2	4		8	14	22	18		4	6	22	96%
University of Southern California (Gould School of Law) Los Angeles, CA 90089-0071, 213-740-2523, admissions@law.usc.edu	$135,000–$165,000	50	2		3	9	8	7	3	4	4	9	96%
University of Tennessee (College of Law) 1505 W. Cumberland Avenue, Knoxville, TN 37996-1810, 865-974-4131, Fax: 865-974-1572, lawadmit@utk.edu	$40,000–$145,000		2	2	4	6	14	13	22	3	5	29	97%
University of Texas at Austin (School of Law) 727 East Dean Keeton Street, Austin, TX 78705, 512-232-1200, Fax: 512-471-2765, admissions@law.utexas.edu	$37,333–$118,519	44	1	2	5	7	10	13	3	5	4	6	99%
University of the District of Columbia (David A. Clarke School of Law) 4200 Connecticut Avenue, N.W., Washington, DC 20008, 202-274-7341, Fax: 202-274-5583, vcanty@udc.edu; lawadmission@udc.edu	$37,000–$66,000	4	5	2	14	17	21	10				29	85%
University of the Pacific (McGeorge School of Law) 3200 Fifth Avenue, Sacramento, CA 95817, 916-739-7105, Fax: 916-739-7301, mcgeorge@pacific.edu	$25,000–$135,000	1	3		9	8	25	2	2	5	3	50	98%
University of Toledo (College of Law) 2801 West Bancroft Street, Toledo, OH 43606-3390, 419-530-4131, Fax: 419-530-4345, law.utoledo.edu	$32,000–$100,000	11	5	3	8	13	22	4	3	2	13	23	95%
University of Tulsa (College of Law) 3120 East Fourth Place, Tulsa, OK 74104-2499, 918-631-2406, Fax: 918-631-3630, april-fox@utulsa.edu	$50,794	8	3	1	5	21	10	1	2	5	8	33	93%
University of Utah (S.J. Quinney College of Law) 332 South 1400 East Room 101, Salt Lake City, UT 84112, 801-581-7479, Fax: 801-581-6897, aguilar@law.utah.edu	$25,215–$215,000	20	3	2	5	7	13	10				25	98%
University of Virginia (School of Law) 580 Massie Road, Charlottesville, VA 22903-1738, 434-924-7351, Fax: 434-982-2128, lawadmit@virginia.edu	$27,000–$180,000	70			4	1	4	14					99%

School	Avg. Starting Salary	Other	Academic	Military	Public Interest	Business/Industry	Government	Judicial Clerkships	PP 51-100	PP 26-50	PP 11-25	PP 2-10	Placement within 6 to 9 months	Alumni Placement	Internships	Part-Time/Summer Employment	Alumni Contacts	Law, Corporate, and Government Contact	Job Interviews Arrangement	Employment Planning	Interview Counseling	Resume Preparation	Solo Practice Advice	Job Openings Information	Employment Counseling	University Placement Office	Law Placement Office
University of Washington (School of Law) Box 353020, Seattle, WA 98195-3020; 206-543-4078; Fax: 206-543-5671; lawadm@u.washington.edu	$48,150-$119,298	3	1		7	8	13	16	2	7	2	9	98%	●	●	●	●	●	●	●	●	●	●	●	●		●
University of Wisconsin (Law School) 975 Bascom Mall, Madison, WI 53706; 608-262-5914; Fax: 608-263-3191; admissions@law.wisc.edu	$42,250-$120,033	28	2	2	7	12	12	6	3	2	6	17	96%	●	●	●	●	●	●	●	●	●	●	●	●		●
University of Wyoming (College of Law) Dept. 3035, 1000 East University Avenue, Laramie, WY 82071; 307-766-6416; Fax: 307-766-6417; dburke@uwyo.edu	$30,000-$120,000	7	2	5	7	15	12	14		2		32	83%	●	●	●	●	●	●	●	●	●	●	●	●	●	●
Valparaiso University (School of Law) Wesemann Hall, 656 S. Greenwich Street, Valparaiso, IN 46383-6493; 219-465-7821; Fax: 219-465-7808; law.admissions@valpo.edu	$35,000-$140,000	56	1		4	14	16	7			5		88%	●	●	●	●	●	●	●	●	●	●	●	●		●
Vanderbilt University (Law School) 131 21st Avenue South, Nashville, TN 37203; 615-322-6452; Fax: 615-322-1531; admissions@law.vanderbilt.edu	$52,000-$165,000	59			3	3	6	15	3	2		4	99%	●	●	●	●	●	●	●	●	●	●	●	●		●
Vermont Law School P.O. Box 96, Chelsea Street, South Royalton, VT 05068-0096; 802-831-1239; Fax: 802-831-1174; admiss@vermontlaw.edu	$30,000-$160,000	6	1	1	15	19	15	15	4	4	6	15	96%	●	●	●	●	●	●	●	●	●	●	●	●		●
Villanova University (School of Law) 299 N. Spring Mill Road, Villanova, PA 19085; 610-519-7010; Fax: 610-519-6291; admiss@law.villanova.edu	$28,000-$145,000	26	1	2	6	17	4	15	4	8	6	11	95%	●	●	●	●	●	●	●	●	●	●	●	●		●

School	Data columns											%	Salary Range
Wake Forest University (School of Law) P.O. Box 7206, Reynolda Station, Winston-Salem, NC 27109, 336-758-5437, Fax: 336-758-4632, admissions@law.wfu.edu	3	4		6	6	9	9	1				96%	$73,000–$145,000
Washburn University (School of Law) 1700 College, Topeka, KS 66621, 785-670-1185, Fax: 785-670-1120, admissions@washburnlaw.edu	1	1	2	9	13	21	9	1	1	3	28	97%	$38,000–$105,000
Washington and Lee University (School of Law) Lewis Hall, Lexington, VA 24450, 540-458-8503, Fax: 540-458-8586, lawadm@wlu.edu	37	1		6	7	9	20	6	5	3	6	91%	$12,000–$160,000
Washington University in St. Louis (School of Law) Box 1120, One Brookings Drive, St. Louis, MO 63130, 314-935-4525, Fax: 314-935-8778, admiss@wulaw.wustl.edu	30	1	1	5	5	16	9	9	12	8	4	99%	$30,000–$125,000
Wayne State University (Law School) 471 West Palmer Street, Detroit, MI 48202, 313-577-3937, Fax: 313-993-8129, emjackson@wayne.edu	9	2		3	13	4	3	3	9	7	35	88%	$24,000–$125,000
West Virginia University (College of Law) P.O. Box 6130, Morgantown, WV 26506, 304-293-5304, Fax: 304-293-6891, wvulaw.Admissions@mail.wvu.edu			2	1	5	8	18	10	7	14	37	88%	$45,000–$110,000
Western New England College (School of Law) 1215 Wilbraham Road, Springfield, MA 01119, 413-782-1406, Fax: 413-796-2067, admissions@law.wnec.edu		2		8	17	10	16		9	9	21	87%	$20,000–$120,000
Western State University (College of Law) 1111 North State College Blvd, Fullerton, CA 92831, 714-459-1101, Fax: 714-441-1748, adm@vsulaw.edu	1	4	1	1	13	6		4	3	13	46	69%	$30,000–$105,000
Whittier College (Whittier Law School) 3333 Harbor Blvd., Costa Mesa, CA 92626, 714-444-4141, ext. 121, Fax: 714-444-0250, info@law.whittier.edu	3	5	1	5	27	9	9	2	2	3	43	90%	$26,400–$110,000

Schools

Widener University (Widener University School of Law)
4601 Concord Pike, P.O. Box 7474
Wilmington, DE 19803-0474
302-477-2162
Fax: 302-477-2224
law.admissions@law.widener.edu

Widener University (Widener University School of Law)
3800 Vartan Way, P.O. Box 69381
Harrisburg, PA 17106-9381
717-541-3903
Fax: 717-541-3999
law.admissions@law.widener.edu

Willamette University (College of Law)
245 Winter Street S.E.
Salem, OR 97301
503-370-6282
Fax: 503-370-6087
law-admission@willamette.edu

William Mitchell College of Law
875 Summit Avenue
St. Paul, MN 55105-3076
651-290-6343
Fax: 651-290-6414
admissions@wmitchell.edu

Yale University (Yale Law School)
P.O. Box 208329
New Haven, CT 06520-8329
203-432-4995
admissions.law@yale.edu

Yeshiva University (Benjamin N. Cardozo School of Law)
55 Fifth Avenue
New York, NY 10003
212-790-0274
Fax: 212-790-0482
lawinfo@yu.edu

Placement Record

	Widener (DE)	Widener (PA)	Willamette	William Mitchell	Yale	Yeshiva (Cardozo)
Average Starting Salary	$28,000-$160,000	$35,000-$135,000	$19,760-$178,500	$20,000-$200,000	$30,000-$160,000	$35,000-$160,000
Placement within 6 to 9 months	93%	97%	94%	97%	97%	94%
Private Practice 2-10 Attorneys	24	30	28	25	42	19
Private Practice 11-25 Attorneys	5	3	3	9	10	
Private Practice 26-50 Attorneys	2	3	5	3	7	7
Private Practice 51-100 Attorneys	4			9	7	7
Judicial Clerkships	23	14	6	10	42	5
Government	7	21	17	6	2	8
Business/Industry	21	17	19	24	4	19
Public Interest	3	6	6	3	7	10
Military	1	1	1			
Academic	2	2	1	1	3	
Other	8	3	14	7		58

Percentage Breakdown of Type of Employer.

Placement Services

Services	Widener (DE)	Widener (PA)	Willamette	William Mitchell	Yale	Yeshiva (Cardozo)
Alumni Placement	•	•	•	•	•	•
Internships	•	•	•	•	•	•
Part-Time/Summer Employment	•	•	•	•	•	•
Alumni Contacts	•	•	•	•	•	•
Law, Corporate, and Government Contact	•	•	•	•	•	•
Job Interviews Arrangement	•	•	•	•	•	•
Employment Planning	•	•	•	•	•	•
Interview Counseling	•	•	•	•	•	•
Resume Preparation	•	•	•	•	•	•
Solo Practice Advice	•	•	•		•	
Job Openings Information					•	
Employment Counseling	•	•	•	•	•	•

Facilities:

	Widener (DE)	Widener (PA)	Willamette	William Mitchell	Yale	Yeshiva (Cardozo)
University Placement Office						
Law Placement Office	•	•	•	•	•	•

reported that they did not need a law degree to do the work they were handling. The remainder were unemployed or enrolled in advanced degree programs at the time of the NALP survey, approximately nine months after graduation. These numbers have remained fairly consistent over the period of thirty-five years during which NALP has surveyed law school graduates. Not surprisingly, the employment picture is slightly better in years when the general economy is strong and slightly worse in years with recession. The NALP survey does support the observation that the legal job market is fairly stable and predictable. Competition for the most prestigious and desirable jobs can be fierce, although most people who want jobs as lawyers will eventually get them.

Employment in the Profession as a Whole

According NALP, law graduates go into positions in the percentages not too different from the makeup of the legal profession as a whole. Based upon a 2010 lawyer population of more than 1.1 million lawyers, there are between 650,000 and 700,000 private practitioners in the United States. Roughly 40 percent (more than 250,000) of these lawyers work as solo practitioners. The next largest group of lawyers practice in small firms of two to five lawyers, followed by lawyers in firms of over one hundred lawyers, and the rest work in medium-sized firms of six to ninety-nine lawyers.

The most dramatic change in the makeup of law firms since 1980 has been the growth of large law firms. Before 1980, only a handful of law firms employed more than one hundred lawyers, but by 2010, hundreds of firms included several hundred lawyers, and the largest firms were over 3,000 lawyers. The percentage of private practitioners who work in large firms has grown over the course of the last two decades from less than 5 percent to over 20 percent of the practicing bar. Although the recession has produced some retrenchment among larger firms, the overall trend in this segment of the market during the last three decades has been growth. In addition, there are large law firms outside the United States even larger than the largest domestic firms. In a globalized economy, U.S. and foreign firms are often competing for the same business.

It is worth noting that the largest law firm in the United States is small compared to business entities in many other fields. There is no big five of law firms like there is in accounting, and there is no legal equivalent of Microsoft or Toyota.

Most lawyers will engage in the private practice of law at some point during their careers, but if six out of ten lawyers work in private practice, the remaining four are employed in a variety of different endeavors. Corporations (including both in-house counsel and other corporate positions), and government service in federal, state, and local agencies represent the largest of these groups. Government service also includes work as prosecutors and public defenders in the criminal justice system, judicial administration, and law enforcement.

Other lawyers work for political action or public interest organizations, serve in legislatures as representatives, or aides, and participate in political parties, campaigns, non-government organizations (NGOs), and other related activities. Such lawyers may draft legislation, organize campaigns, direct public policy initiatives, or exercise other forms of public service.

Geographic Locations

Lawyers work almost everywhere. More lawyers are concentrated in the largest population centers because of the high volume of legal and commercial activity that occurs in those areas. Lawyers are also concentrated in the seats of government, from Washington, DC, to state capitals, to county seats throughout the United States. Even in rural areas, lawyers can be found with offices close to the clients they serve. An increasing number of U.S. lawyers work outside the boundaries of the United States. With the increasing internationalization of business, lawyers have become a new kind of export.

The NALP statistics for the employment of law school graduates parallel the demographic patterns for lawyers as a whole. More legal jobs are found in the largest cities, but law graduates are dispersed to a wide variety of smaller places throughout the country as well. There is some location of first employment, suggesting that people either choose their law school because of the geographic area or become attached to the area while they are in law school.

Another factor influencing where lawyers practice is the bar exam administered by each state. The bar exam represents a hurdle to entry into the practice of law because for most legal positions, it is necessary to pass the bar exam in the state where the lawyer will be working prior to beginning to serve clients. The majority of law graduates take only one bar exam, and are thus limited to the jurisdiction where they become licensed. A smaller number of graduates take the bar exam in two states, often states in close geographical proximity with overlapping economies, such as New York and New Jersey. Because of scheduling practicalities, it is almost impossible to sit for more than two bar exams at once, and as a result, very few lawyers are initially licensed in more than one or two states.

If graduates find employment in a jurisdiction where they do not pass the bar exam, they will lose those jobs. If they take the exam before they have a job, they will be limited in their job search to positions where they become licensed. Applicants to law school should be aware of these jurisdictional requirements and investigate the possibilities as appropriate.

Salaries

Lawyers' salaries are reported by various bar associations and consultant surveys, as well as by the U.S. Bureau of Labor Statistics and NALP. All of these surveys seem to show that there is a wide range of income among lawyers. Some lawyers, particularly in the rural areas, may not have enough business to sustain a full-time practice. Lawyers in certain metropolitan areas with high lawyer populations may find competition for clients to be intense. Some of these lawyers may discover that even after years of practice they do not make a good living practicing law. On the other end of the spectrum are lawyers whose income is in the seven figure range.

Different surveys show discrepancies in reported results that may reflect more on their sampling techniques than actual differences, but most seem to point to an average income for all lawyers of between $100,000 and $150,000. These figures include not only law firm partners, but also semi-retired senior lawyers and employed lawyers.

The range of salaries for recent law school graduates is from as high as $160,000 in some large firms to as low as $30,000 in some rural areas, with a median of over $70,000. Some evidence suggests that the highest salaries and perhaps the medium-range salaries have declined and may not return to their pre-recession levels, but the lowest salaries remain fairly stable.

Diversity

Before 1960, the legal profession was overwhelmingly Caucasian and male. Since that time, law schools have systematically recruited women and minority applicants. The percentage of law students from diverse ethnic, racial, and cultural backgrounds increased substantially, although not as much as critics have suggested they should. In an increasingly diverse society, larger numbers of diverse lawyers are needed to serve the needs of these populations. With respect to women, the numbers have swelled to over 50% at many law schools, and as these women graduate and enter the ranks of practitioners, the gender gap in the profession as a whole narrows. Some evidence points to a "glass ceiling" in the legal profession, suggesting that even if women are initially hired in equal numbers as men, over time more women make alternative career choices, leaving fewer women at the top ranks of the firms where they work. Certainly, many women have assumed partnership and leadership roles in law firms, but gains have been slow enough that women's legal groups keep a close eye on progress.

CHAPTER 11

What Trends Are Affecting the Practice of Law?

Like other businesses and professions, the practice of law has changed dramatically in recent years. A revolution in technology has swept the business world. Computers have altered the way law is practiced in countless ways, including how lawyers relate to their clients. Technology has even altered the dynamics of how lawyers relate to each other in organizations.

During the first half of the twentieth century, most lawyers practiced alone. Since World War II, however, more and more lawyers have gone to work in ever-larger law firms. In these firms, partners hired junior lawyers—associates—to assist them in the delivery of legal services. The development of these large law firms paralleled the growth of corporations, which fueled an increase in the need for legal services, and for large firms.

During the same period of time the demographics of the U.S. population were also changing. More and more people were living in large cities or metropolitan areas. Waves of immigrants were producing an increasingly diverse society. Global conflict and worldwide interdependency became the norm. As a new world order emerged, the number of lawyers in the United States grew dramatically. As legal problems multiplied, so did the competition among service providers. Many lawyers were particularly ill-prepared for the dramatic changes in the practice of law that occurred during the twentieth century. Evolution is a good word to use to describe these developments, because they produced a kind of economic Darwinism, in which the fittest adapt and survive, and the less competitive individuals and forms of practice become extinct.

As someone who is thinking about going to law school, you should understand that this evolution is continuing and is likely to continue for the foreseeable future. You should recognize that the changes that have transformed other segments of business and industry have had an impact on the practice of law as well. You should know that some people will succeed in these times and some will not. Law, far from being a refuge from a competitive workplace, is subject to risks like most other fields of endeavor.

What you can do to improve the likelihood that you will be successful in this environment is seek to understand the changes that have occurred and that are likely to take place in the future. Of course, it is impossible to predict the future, but sensitivity to trends and insightful analysis of events can help you to adapt. Several areas are worth watching:

GLOBALIZATION

Electronic communication, air transportation, and global migration have produced a world that is inevitably interconnected. It is possible to know the local news almost anywhere in the world. The distribution of products and services transcends international boundaries, producing at the same time tremendous variety in the marketplace and increased homogeneity in availability. English has increasingly become the default language of world commerce. Stock markets in Asia, wars in Africa, and mergers in Europe all have an impact on business in America. Lawyers increasingly will be called upon to represent clients who have interests outside the United States, or who come from outside the United States and need a lawyer's assistance here. Lawyers themselves will face competition from foreign law firms, and even from organizations that provide law-related services, which would be viewed as unauthorized practice of law in the United States. Even lawyers who represent American companies and individuals exclusively are likely to have dealings with foreign companies, individuals, and governments because their clients have dealings with foreigners and non-U.S. entities.

TECHNOLOGY

The information revolution has transformed the way law is practiced. Today, most lawyers have a computer on their desktop with access to the Internet, legal databases, and software applications. Technology allows lawyers and law firms to practice more efficiently. These new resources also place additional demands on practitioners, particularly older lawyers, who grew up in an era when the most advanced technology needed to practice law was an Underwood typewriter. Technological advancements force lawyers to find new ways to ply their services, and to communicate with clients who are increasingly wired and connected themselves. As legal information and forms become increasingly available on the Internet and other electronic formats, the role of the lawyer shifts to one of information provider, interpreter, and advisor.

Over the course of the last two decades of the twentieth century, computers and other technology transformed the practice of law, as was the case with other forms of business. Lawyers today regularly utilize a variety of technologies to communicate with clients and other parties, to file documents with the courts, to conduct research using the Internet, to prepare documents for clients, to support litigation, and to manage cases and files. Increasingly, law firms provide sophisticated web sites, some with interactive service delivery and client portals. Some firms are experimenting with outsourcing work to other countries where it can be performed more economically. Virtually all law firms recognize that technological change will continue to impact the practice of law in the near future.

DEMOGRAPHICS

The study of demographics—where people live and work—is important to any consideration of the marketplace for legal services because they determine where and what kinds of legal services are needed to serve the population. Over time, the population changes, which has an impact on the need for legal services. This section highlights the demographic changes that are likely to affect the way you practice law if you become a lawyer.

- One demographic trend that seems to be gaining momentum with the young professionals is the re-urbanization of inner cities abandoned by flight to the suburbs a half century before. In almost every major city, and many smaller ones, the number of people who both live and work in the city center is on the rise. In many cities, older buildings that were used for a variety of purposes have been renovated and refurbished as residences. At the same time, developers have begun new high-rise construction of both moderate and luxury housing. The evidence points to young professionals seeking the vibrant and diverse cultural life that cities can offer, and eschewing the hour-each-way commute their parents endured.

- A second demographic trend that has had a significant impact on lawyers is the entrance of large numbers of women into the workforce. Before the 1960s, only a handful of women entered the legal profession, and law firms were often an exclusively male domain. Over the past three decades, the legal profession has experienced a dramatic increase in the number of women lawyers. Today, half of all law students are women, and the percentage of women in the profession continue to increase. This change not only produces more opportunities for women in the practice of law, but it also puts pressure on law firms and other organizations that employ lawyers to assure that these opportunities are meaningful ones.

- More women lawyers have produced more two-career families where both spouses either choose to work or have to work in order to sustain a desired lifestyle. When one or both of the people in such a family is a lawyer, there can be a variety of interesting problems, from conflicts of interest between the two lawyers' firms, to employment in different cities, to questions about allocating responsibility for child care and housework.

- Since divorce hits one out of two American families, single parents are often forced to raise children without a partner. The problem of single parenting impacts not only the lawyers but also the support staff in law firms. The upheaval can be disruptive to organizations that are trying to provide quality legal services to clients. For law firms, most of which are very small organizations compared to nonlegal businesses, it can be difficult to accommodate the needs of employees in our complex society.

- Baby Boomers who went to law school between 1965 and 1985 will be retiring over the next two decades. This will produce an array of opportunities in politics, senior management in organizations, and other leadership roles in society. Preliminary research suggests that the Boomers will live longer, remain more active, and require more services than past generations of retirees. This observation is not so much about what will happen to the aging Boomer, but about the legal and other impacts that this will produce for the next generation of lawyers.

• A final demographic shift involves recent waves of migration into the United States. The issue of migration from Mexico, Central and South America has become a political football, but these are not the only new arrivals. The number of Asians, both from the Far East (China/Japan/Korea) and from the Indian subcontinent (India/Pakistan/Bangladesh) continues to rise. Immigrants from Africa, the Middle East, the former Soviet Bloc countries, and the Caribbean all continue to make America, if not a melting pot, at least an alphabet soup. Immigrants have a variety of legal needs, but often come from cultures where suspicion of government, lawyers, and the legal system makes them reticent to seek legal assistance. Immigrants often face language and social barriers in their adopted home as well. One thing is clear: the legal work serving these populations will continue to grow commensurate with the growth of the immigrant population.

LIFESTYLES

Many young lawyers must face fundamental lifestyle issues, enhanced in part by the great variety of choices available to them:

• How many hours a week do you and your spouse/partner want to put into the practice of law? Forty? Sixty? Eighty? One hundred?

• Do you want to have children or not?

• If so, when?

• Who will stay at home with young children and for how long?

• What kind of childcare and early education will children receive?

• What kind of geographical setting is most compatible with your interests, hobbies, and professional needs?

• The beach? The mountains? The big city? A rural county seat?

• Where do you see yourself in ten or twenty years as your practice matures?

• And family? Do you want the people you grew up with to be close at hand, or will you be satisfied to see them once or twice a year?

• Is the type of law that you hope to practice likely to be available in the geographic locale where you would like to live?

The answers to these questions are intimately wrapped up in the life choices you will be required to make in the coming years. One negative aspect of the practice of law is that the hours can be long and the work demanding. In the past, young lawyers were often forced to make sacrifices to meet the workloads imposed by their employers. It remains to be seen whether today's neophyte lawyers will press for reforms, and whether, if they do, law firms will respond. It is certain, however, that these lifestyle issues are not going away any time soon.

CHANGE

One common thread that cuts through all the trends described above is change. The world is changing in unprecedented ways, and will continue to change throughout the professional lives of those students entering law school in the coming years. The changes that we are experiencing are profound; they are transforming. Author Tom Peters, at a 1999 conference on the future of the legal profession, said that humankind may be in the midst of the biggest revolution in the way people live since we came in off the savannahs to live in permanent villages—a 10,000-year sea change. Other observers might not go as far as Peters does, but virtually everyone who has thought about the future believes that we are in the midst of something really big.

It should come as no surprise that the legal profession is undergoing dramatic change in the way legal services are delivered. Just as the industrial base of America has shifted to Third World countries, and the medical profession has endured the rise of managed care, lawyers face an increasingly competitive environment and pressures to deliver better services more economically. Although the number of law school graduates continues to climb, more and more lawyers opt to work in settings outside of private practice (i.e., law firms). An increasing number of graduates accept positions in corporations, government service, private associations, accounting or professional services firms, banks, group legal services, private associations, and a variety of other organizations. Other lawyers start out in law firms, but move to some other type of organization, often one that has been a client of the firm. Some lawyers may abandon the law completely, but the vast majority of them continue to utilize their legal skills and "practice law" in a new environment.

Someone contemplating a career in law should appreciate the fact that the opportunities for lawyers are changing as the world around them changes. All this change creates tremendous challenges and risks, but it also generates unusual opportunities. It will be important for you to stay attuned to how society and the practice of law continue to evolve in order to maximize your opportunities and achieve your goals in the coming years.

These are not simple questions, and there are no easy answers. But both lawyers and applicants to law school will have to face these issues at some time or other. It makes sense to think now about how lifestyle questions will affect the career choices that you make as a lawyer, and try to make decisions that are consistent with your long-term personal needs.

SUBSTANTIVE PRACTICE AREAS

People often ask what are the growing practice areas in the law? There is probably no consensus answer to this question, and many pundits have attempted to predict substantive trends in the law—many with great imprecision. Understanding the risks inherent in such predictions, this author will offer insights into a number of practice areas that are likely to experience growth in the coming decade:

- **Bankruptcy.** With the recession of 2008-09, both individuals and companies faced financial challenges, which frequently led to restructuring, refinancing, or in worst cases bankruptcy. Lawyers working with clients in this area often provide "workout" services extending for years after the financial crisis.

- **Transnational business.** The growing international interdependence of countries, particularly in the delivery of goods and services, will continue to produce a high level of complex legal work. Lawyers from this country and others around the world will be involved in solving the legal problems that these commercial transactions create. From the European community to the Pacific Rim, from the former Eastern bloc to Central and South America, American lawyers will find opportunities in all these areas.

- **Intellectual property law.** The growth in certain specialized businesses, particularly in the health care and computer technology industries, will require lawyers who have technological or scientific backgrounds to assist clients in protecting the new technologies they develop. While patent law and copyright law are not new, continued innovations, particularly those triggered by the Internet, and growing technological sophistication, have created an increase in demand for lawyers to help clients secure patents and to help clients protect their intellectual property.

- **Health care.** In the United States there have been dramatic changes in the way health care services are delivered. The availability of medical treatment, risks associated with scientific advancement, and issues involving death and dying all present health care issues. Decisions about treatment are no longer limited to the patient and provider, but often involve a hospital and/or other corporate employer, and an insurance company or HMO. With a population that is graying demographically, health care issues can be expected to increase during the early part of the twenty-first century.

- **Elder law.** In addition to health care, older citizens have a variety of other issues that they must confront, from increased leisure associated with retirement to legal issues like estate planning, to a variety of other unique problems. An increasing number of lawyers are defining their practice in terms of these clients under the heading of Elder Law. The number of Americans age 55 and older continues to grow.

- **Environmental law.** Global warming and other environmental issues are protracted; resources are limited. It is inevitable that a world population of six billion will have to confront issues like global warming, extinction of animal species, resource allocation, and sustainable development. Lawyers involved in this process are likely to have their hands full for the foreseeable future. The oil spill caused by an explosion of a British Petroleum oil rig in the Gulf of Mexico caused an unprecedented environmental disaster in 2010.

- **Communications and technology.** The Internet, satellite communications, cable, and other legal problems associated with computers and electronic technology will continue to evolve in the near future. Many of the concepts of common law from copyright to theft must be redefined in the electronic environment.

- **Leisure law.** Sports and entertainment law, travel law, and related subject areas will experience a period of growth in the coming years, as people have more and more free time. Even those who work long hours will be seeking leisure opportunities during their vacation periods. Many workers will be retiring earlier and looking for leisure activities to fill their time. Although this is a fairly small field of practice today, it is likely to grow in the coming decades.

- **Preventive law.** Estate planning, business planning, tax planning, and other areas where lawyers can advise individuals and businesses on how to avoid legal problems, rather than trying to help once things have fallen apart, will experience considerable growth. This will be not only because lawyers will be seeking these markets, but also because a more sophisticated client base will seek to have this kind of legal help more readily available.

- **Mediation and other forms of alternative dispute resolution.** More and more legal cases will be resolved without going to court, through mediation and alternative dispute resolution processes. Lawyers will be involved in these practice areas as well, because their legal skills of negotiation, persuasion, analysis, and organization will work well to help clients solve problems in a variety of different ways.

- **Employment law.** The proliferation of state and federal law governing the workplace has created a growing practice in employment law. Practice settings in private firms range from small and large law firms devoted exclusively to this area of practice to more general practice firms in which fewer than all of the lawyers specialize in this area. With the growth in business generally, and with large corporate

mergers, there will continue to be a need for lawyers to advise clients on employee matters, such as ERISA and pension benefits, to train clients and their employees on prevention (e.g., harassment training) and to litigate or mediate employee complaints and claims arising under the many laws in this area.

Although the areas of practice described above represent fields where growth can be inferred from a variety of factual indicia, many other specialized or "boutique" practice areas will blossom in the coming years. Because virtually every form of human endeavor has legal implications, it follows that very little in life can be conducted outside the law. This means that there is a substantive practice area for almost anything you can imagine, and if you can imagine it, you can bet that somewhere there is a lawyer practicing in that field. Lawyers today are increasingly becoming specialists, who concentrate their practice in a narrow field of expertise. The general practitioner is a dying breed in law, just as in medicine. And as in medicine, the more complex society becomes, the more specialties emerge.

CONCLUSION

For someone about to enter law school, it should be clear that choosing to become a lawyer is just the beginning of a long path of career choices. Not only will law school graduates have to choose from a variety of practice settings, they will have to decide among an almost infinite array of substantive fields within the law. On top of all this, they will have to be astute enough to understand that the underpinnings of their decisions will be undergoing continual change.

The element of change will be a factor in every facet of life, whether you decide to attend law school or not, but if you do elect to go to law school, do not imagine that you will be immune from the forces that are transforming the rest of the world. If you remember that society and the practice of law are both changing, and continually reflect upon how these changes will affect you, you will improve your chances of achieving success professionally and personally.

Adapted from Gary A. Munneke, *Careers in Law,* VGM Professional Careers Series, 1992, pages 9-12, 15-17. Reprinted by permission.

PART II

Taking the LSAT

CHAPTER 12

The LSAT and the Admissions Process

The Law School Admission Test (LSAT) is required for all law school applicants. Although law school admissions committees consider a variety of criteria, there is little doubt that the LSAT plays a significant role in the selection process.

Preparation for the LSAT is the rule rather than the exception. This section is an introduction to the LSAT preparation process.

ANSWERS TO SOME COMMONLY ASKED QUESTIONS

What does the LSAT measure?

The LSAT is designed to measure a range of mental abilities related to the study of law; therefore, it is used by most law schools to evaluate their applicants.

Will any special knowledge of the law raise my score on the LSAT?

The LSAT is designed so that candidates from a particular academic background are given no advantage. The questions measure reading comprehension, logical reasoning, and analytical reasoning, drawing from a variety of verbal and analytical material.

Does a high score on the LSAT predict success in law school or in the practice of law?

Success on the LSAT demonstrates your ability to read with understanding and to reason clearly under pressure; surely these strengths are important to both the study and the practice of law, as is the ability to write well, measured by the LSAT Writing Sample. To say that success on the LSAT *predicts* success in law school may overstate the case, however, because success in law school also involves skills that are not measured by the LSAT.

When is the LSAT administered?

The regular administration of the test occurs nationwide four times each year, around the beginning of the fall, winter, spring, and summer seasons. Except for the summer month, the test is usually administered on a Saturday morning from 8:30 A.M. to about 1:00 P.M. For the past few years, the *summer exam* has been given on a Monday afternoon. Dates are announced annually by the Law School Admission Council (LSAC) in Newtown, PA.

What if I cannot take the test on a Saturday?

Some special arrangements are possible: Check the Law School Admission Services (LSAS) General Information Booklet in your registration packet. Those who must take the exam at a time when the regular administration occurs on Saturday, but who cannot participate on Saturday for religious reasons, may arrange for a special Monday administration.

How early should I register?

Regular registration closes about one month before the exam date. Late registration is available up to three weeks prior to the exam date. There is an additional fee for late registration.

Is walk-in registration available?

For security reasons, walk-in registration is no longer permitted. Be sure to read very carefully the General Information Booklet section on "registering to take the LSAT."

What is the LSDAS?

The LSDAS (Law School Data Assembly Service) compiles a report about each subscribing applicant. The report contains LSAT results, a summary of the applicant's academic work, and copies of college transcripts. A report is sent to each law school that the applicant designates. Thus, if you register for the LSDAS, you will not need to mail a separate transcript to each of your prospective law schools. REMINDER: You should review information regarding the Candidate Referral Service in your *LSAT & LSDAS Information Book*.

How is the LSAT used?

Your LSAT score is one common denominator by which a law school compares you to other applicants. Other factors also determine your acceptance to law school: a law school may consider your personal qualities, grade-point average, extracurricular achievements, and letters of recommendation. Requirements for admission vary widely from school to school, so you are wise to contact the law school of your choice for specific information.

How do I obtain registration forms and registration information?

The registration form covering both the LSAT and the LSDAS is available in the LSAT & LSDAS REGISTRATION/INFORMATION BOOK. Copies of the packet are available at the admissions offices of most law schools and the testing offices at most undergraduate universities and colleges. You may also obtain the book and more information by writing to Law Services, Box 2000, 662 Penn Street, Newtown, PA 18940-0998; by Internet using *www.LSAC.org*; by fax at (215) 968-1119; by e-mail at *Lsacinfor@LSAC.org* or by telephone at (215) 968-1001.

What is the structure of the LSAT?

The LSAT contains five 35-minute multiple-choice sections followed by a 35-minute Writing Sample. The Writing Sample does not count as part of your LSAT score. The common question types that do count toward your score are Logical Reasoning (two sections), Analytical Reasoning (one section), and Reading Comprehension (one section). In addition to these four sections, one experimental or pretest section will appear. This experimental or pretest section, which will probably be a repeat of one of the common question types, will not count in your score.

How is the LSAT scored?

The score for the objective portion of the test ranges from 120 to 180, and there is no penalty for wrong answers. The Writing Sample is unscored, but copies are sent to the law schools of your choice for evaluation.

What about question structure and value?

All LSAT questions, apart from the Writing Sample, are multiple-choice with five choices. All questions within a section are of equal value, regardless of difficulty.

Should I guess?

There is no penalty for guessing on the LSAT. Therefore, before you move on to the next question, at least take a guess. You should fill in guess answers for those you have left blank or did not get to, before time is called for that section. If you can eliminate one or more choices as incorrect, your chances for a correct guess increase.

How often can I take the LSAT?

You may take the LSAT more than once if you wish. But keep in mind that any report sent to you or to law schools will contain scores for any exams taken over the past few years, along with an average score for those exams. The law school receiving your scores will decide which score is the best estimate of your ability; many law schools rely on the average score as a figure. Normally, you may not take the test more than three times in a two-year period.

Is it at all possible to cancel my LSAT score?

You may cancel your score only within nine calendar days after taking the test.

How early should I arrive at the test center, and what should I bring?

Arrive at the test center 20 to 30 minutes before the time designated on your admission ticket. Bring three or four sharpened No. 2

pencils, an eraser, and a noiseless watch (no alarm, calculator, or beeping), as well as your LSAT Admission Ticket and proper identification as described in the LSAT & LSDAS Registration/Information Booklet.

Can I prepare for the LSAT?

Yes. Reading skills and test-taking strategies should be the focus of your preparation for the test as a whole. Success on the more specialized analytical sections of the test depends on your thorough familiarity with the types of problems you are likely to encounter and the reasoning process involved. For maximum preparation, work through this book and practice the strategies and techniques outlined in each section.

BASIC FORMAT OF THE LSAT AND SCORING

THE *ORDER* OF THE FOLLOWING MULTIPLE-CHOICE SECTIONS *WILL* VARY. The Experimental Section is not necessarily the last section.

	Section	Number of Questions	Minutes
I.	Logical Reasoning	24-26	35
II.	Analytical Reasoning	22-24 (4 sets)	35
III.	Reading Comprehension	26-28 (4 passages)	35
IV.	Logical Reasoning	24-26	35
V.	Experimental Section	varies	35
	Writing Sample	1 essay	35
TOTALS		118-132 questions (only 96-104 count toward your score)	210 minutes or 3 hours 30 minutes

NOTE: For your convenience, this Barron's text labels each section of this Model Test (e.g., Reading Comprehension, Logical Reasoning, etc.). In contrast, sections of the actual LSAT exam are not usually labeled.

The LSAT is scored on a 120 to 180 scale.

The following simple chart will give you a very general approximation of the LSAT scoring system. It shows the approximate percentage of right answers necessary on the LSAT to be in a certain score range.

Approximate % of right answers	Approximate Score Range
Between 75% and 100%	160-180
Between 50% and 75%	145-159
Between 25% and 50%	130-144
Between 0% and 25%	120-129

Note that this chart is meant to give you an *approximate* score range.

A Closer Look at the Timing—What It Really Means

Although the LSAT is comprised of five 35-minute multiple-choice sections and a 35-minute unscored essay, it is important to understand the timing breakdown and what it means. The test is actually broken down as follows:

105 min. { Section I 35 minutes
          Section II 35 minutes
          Section III 35 minutes
          Short break—usually 10-15 minutes
70 min. { Section IV 35 minutes
         Section V 35 minutes
         Very, very short break—usually 1 or 2 minutes
35 min. { Writing Sample (Essay)—35 minutes

Notice that you are given three multiple-choice sections with no breaks in between. When they say "stop" at the end of 35 minutes they will immediately say something like, "Turn to the next section, make sure that you are in the right section, ready, begin." So, in essence, you are working three sections back to back to back. This means that when you practice you should be sure to practice testing for 1 hour and 45 minutes without a break.

After the short break, when you may get up, get a drink, and go to the restroom, you are back for two more back-to-back multiple-choice sections.

For the final 35-minute writing sample you will be given scratch paper to do your pre-writing or outlining.

Keep in mind that there will be some time taken before the exam and after the exam for clerical-type paperwork—distributing and picking up paperwork, filling out test forms, and so on.

Important Reminders

- At least half of your test will contain Logical Reasoning questions; prepare accordingly. Make sure that you are good at Logical Reasoning!
- The experimental or pretest section will usually repeat other sections and can appear in different places on the exam. At the time of the exam, you will not know which section is experimental. Take the test as if all of the sections count.
- Scoring will be from 120-180. This is the score, and the percentile rank that goes with it is what the law schools look at and are referring to in their discussions.
- All questions in a section are of equal value, so do not get stuck on any one question. The scores are determined by totaling all of your right answers on the test and then scaling.
- Answer all the easy questions first; then come back and answer the tougher questions. Don't be afraid to skip a question, but always at least take a guess.
- There is NO PENALTY for guessing, so at least take a guess before you move to the next question.

- The 35-minute Writing Sample will not be scored, but copies will be forwarded to the law schools to which you apply. Scratch paper will be provided for the Writing Sample only.
- Keep in mind that regardless of the format of your exam, two sections of Logical Reasoning, one section of Analytical Reasoning, and one section of Reading Comprehension always count toward your score.

SOME WORDS TO THE WISE

Ask a Few Questions

Before you actually start your study plan there are four basic questions that you should ask the law schools to which you are applying:

1. Considering my GPA and other qualifications, what score do you think I need to get into your law school?
2. When do you need to get my score reports? Or, When should I take the test to meet your deadlines?
3. What do you do if I take the LSAT more than once? Remember that when the law school receives your score report it will see a score for each time you've taken the test *and* an average of the scores. It is up to the law schools and their governing bodies as to what score(s) they will consider. Try to do your best on the first try and take the LSAT only once, if possible.
4. What do you do with my Writing Sample? Is it used as a tiebreaker? Do you score it yourself? Is it just another piece of the process?

Knowing the answers to most of these questions before you start your study will help you understand what is expected and will help you get mentally ready for the task ahead.

Excerpted from *Barron's LSAT,* by Jerry Bobrow, Ph.D., rev. by Bernard V. Zandy, Barron's Educational Series, Inc., 2009.

CHAPTER 13

A Model LSAT

This chapter contains a full-length Model Test. It is geared to the format of the LSAT and it is complete with answers and explanations. It is equivalent to the LSAT in question structure, number of questions, level of difficulty, and time allotments. (The questions used are not taken directly from the LSAT, as those questions are copyrighted and may not be reproduced.)

The Model Test should be taken under strict test conditions. The test ends with a 35-minute Writing Sample, which is not scored.

Section	Description	Number of Questions	Time Allowed
I	Logical Reasoning	26	35 minutes
II	Reading Comprehension	28	35 minutes
III	Analytical Reasoning	23	35 minutes
IV	Logical Reasoning	26	35 minutes
V	Reading Comprehension	28	35 minutes
	Writing Sample		35 minutes
TOTALS:		131	3 hours 30 minutes

Now please turn to the next page, remove your answer sheets, and begin the Model Test.

1   1   1   1   1

SECTION I
TIME — 35 MINUTES
26 QUESTIONS

Directions: In this section you will be given brief statements or passages and will be required to evaluate the reasoning involved. In some instances, more than one choice will appear to be a possible answer. You are to choose the *best* answer. Use common sense and reasonableness in making your selection; then mark the proper space on the answer sheet.

Questions 1–2

Professor: Probability is a curiously unstable concept. Semantically speaking, it is an assumption, a pure artifice, a concept that may or may not be true, but nevertheless facilitates a logical process. It is not a hypothesis because, by its very nature, it cannot be proved. Suppose we flip a coin that has a distinguishable head and tail. In our ignorance of the coming result we say that the coin has one chance in two of falling heads up, or that the probability of a head turning up is one-to-two. Here it must be understood that the one-to-two is not "true" but is merely a species of the genus probability.

1. The professor assumes that

    (A) nothing about our coin influences its fall in favor of either side or that all influences are counterbalanced by equal and opposite influences
    (B) probability can be dealt with or without the use of logic
    (C) an assumption must be plausible
    (D) the probability of the coin's landing on an edge is counterbalanced by the probability of its not landing on an edge
    (E) probability can be precisely calculated

2. The last sentence implies that

    (A) probability is not absolute
    (B) one-to-two is merely a guess
    (C) one-to-two is a worthless ratio
    (D) truth is not important
    (E) genus is a category of species

3. Self-confidence is a big factor in success. The person who thinks he can, will master most of the things he attempts. The person who thinks he can't, may not try.

    The author of these statements would agree that

    (A) nothing is impossible
    (B) no task is too large
    (C) success relies on effort
    (D) self-confidence is of utmost importance
    (E) trying is half the battle

GO ON TO THE NEXT PAGE ➤

4. People who risk riding on roller coasters are more likely to take risks in other areas of their lives than those who avoid roller coasters. So roller coaster riders are more likely than others to be successful in situations in which taking risks can result in benefit to them.

If the above comments are true, they most strongly support which one of the following statements?

(A) No roller coaster riders avoid taking risks in other areas of their lives, but some may take more risks than others.

(B) Risk taking in life decisions is important not only because of the possible financial gain but because of the psychological benefits produced.

(C) Some people who are not roller coaster riders may take more risks in other areas of their lives than do roller coaster riders.

(D) Mountain climbing is riskier than riding on roller coasters, so people who climb mountains will be more successful in other areas of their lives than are roller coaster riders.

(E) Risk taking in one type of activity indicates a likelihood of risk taking in other types of activities.

5. *Anthropologist:* For many years, anthropologists believed that the longevity of the men of the island of Zobu was the result of their active lives and their eating only fish from the lagoon and fruits and vegetables grown on the island. However, recent studies of the inhabitants of nearby Luku, where the way of life and diet are virtually identical with Zobu's, have revealed that the men there rarely survive beyond early middle age.

If the information in this paragraph is correct, it best supports which one of the following ?

(A) There are important differences in the lagoons of the two islands of which scientists are unaware.

(B) The inhabitants of Luku and Zobu probably have many ancestors in common.

(C) The longevity of the natives of Zobu is not due simply to their diet and way of life.

(D) Some, though not all, of the residents of Luku live as long as some of the residents of Zobu.

(E) Since longevity depends on so many different factors, it is useless to compare longevity in one area with that in another.

GO ON TO THE NEXT PAGE ➤

1   1   1   1   1

Questions 6–7

Because college-educated men and women as a group earn more than those without college educations, and because in Eastern Europe and Latin America, 105 women are enrolled in colleges for every 100 men, the total earnings of college women in these areas should be equal to, if not greater than, the earnings of college men. But college women in Eastern Europe and in Latin America earn only 65 percent of what college men in these countries earn.

6. Which one of the following, if true, is most useful in explaining this discrepancy?

 (A) The earning power of both men and women rises sharply in accord with their level of education.
 (B) In some countries of Western Europe, the earning power of college-educated women is higher than that of men in Eastern Europe and Latin America.
 (C) In Eastern Europe, more men than women who enter college fail to complete their educations.
 (D) The largest percentage of women in Eastern European and Latin American universities study to become teachers; the largest percentage of men study engineering.
 (E) In Eastern Europe and Latin America, about 60 percent of the total workforce is college educated.

7. Which one of the following is a faulty assumption based on the statistics of the passage?

 (A) The passage assumes that all of the college women enter the workforce.
 (B) The passage assumes conditions in Eastern Europe and in Latin America are the same.
 (C) The passage assumes that men and women should be paid equally.
 (D) The passage assumes that college-educated women outnumber women who have not attended college in Eastern Europe and Latin America.
 (E) The passage assumes that all college-educated workers will be paid more than workers who do not have college educations.

GO ON TO THE NEXT PAGE ➤

8. *Economist:* When consumers are in a buying mood, and the cost of money is low, a shrewd retailer with a popular product will reduce prices of items that are selling slowly and will make up for any loss by raising prices on the product or products that are popular.

In which one of the following situations are these recommendations observed?

(A) At Easter, John's Markets offered one dozen eggs at half their usual price and hams and turkeys at a 40 percent discount, but because of heavy rains, they raised the price of many green vegetables.

(B) This Christmas, Arrow Clothiers is offering six-month interest-free charge accounts to any customers who purchase $50 or more of merchandise from their stock of discontinued summer wear and the fashionable new op-art neck wear.

(C) Since interest rates have reached a yearly low, the price of tax-free bonds is near an all-time high. Discount Brokerage has launched a campaign to sell off all of its holding in precious metals mutual funds that are now at their lowest price in years.

(D) Angus Jewelry is offering special savings for customers who make purchases in May. With graduations coming soon, they are offering engraved gold Swiss watches, as well as lower prices on heart-shaped jewelry items that were featured on Valentine's Day.

(E) Travel agents in Orlando are capitalizing on the lowered air-fares to lure tourists by offering special rates on hotel accommodations and discounted admission tickets to two of the large theme parks in the area.

9. While some cities impose tough, clear restrictions on demolitions of older buildings, our city has no protection for cultural landmarks. Designation as a landmark by the Cultural Heritage Commission can delay a demolition for only one year. This delay can be avoided easily by an owner's demonstrating an economic hardship. Developers who simply ignore designations and tear down buildings receive only small fines. Therefore, ...

Which one of the following best completes the passage above?

(A) the number of buildings protected by Cultural Heritage Commission designation must be increased

(B) developers must be encouraged to help preserve our older buildings

(C) the designation as landmark must be changed to delay demolition for more than one year

(D) developers who ignore designations to protect buildings must be subject to higher fines

(E) if our older buildings are to be saved, we need clearer and more rigorously enforced laws

10. Michael claimed that the large dent in the fender of the company-owned vehicle he had borrowed was caused by the careless act of another motorist, who backed into the car when it was parked in a public garage. Yet Michael's own car has several similar dents in its fenders, all of which he acknowledges as having been caused by his own careless driving. Therefore, Michael's contention that the dent in the formerly undented company-owned vehicle was caused by the careless act of another person is NOT true.

    The reasoning in this argument is vulnerable because it

    (A) fails to recognize that Michael could be lying about the dents in his own vehicle
    (B) fails to recognize that the motorist who backed into him simply did not see him
    (C) fails to acknowledge that many such accidents occur in parking garages
    (D) presumes, without justification, that because Michael has caused similar dents to his own car, he caused the dent in the company car
    (E) fails to take into consideration that Michael was recently named Employee of the Month

Questions 11–12

Sixty percent of the American people, according to the latest polls, now believe that inflation is the nation's most important problem. This problem of inflation is closely related to rising prices. The inflation rate has been 10 percent or more most of this year. Undoubtedly, our gluttonous appetite for high-priced foreign oil has been a major factor. We have been shipping billions of dollars overseas, more than foreigners can spend or invest here. Dollars are selling cheaply and this has forced the value of the dollar down. Government programs now being inaugurated to slow this trend are at best weak, but deserve our support, as they appear to be the best our government can produce. Hopefully, they won't fail as they have in the past.

11. The author of this passage implies that

    (A) inflation cannot be stopped or slowed, because of a weak government
    (B) the fear of inflation is not only unwarranted, but also detrimental
    (C) 40 percent of non-Americans believe inflation is not the most important problem
    (D) foreign oil is the sole reason for the sudden increase in inflation
    (E) the present programs will probably not slow inflation

12. Which one of the following contradicts something in the preceding passage?

    (A) Foreign oil is actually underpriced.
    (B) The inflation rate has not risen for most of this year.
    (C) Overseas investors are few and far between.
    (D) Our government is trying a new approach to end inflation.
    (E) The weakness of the programs stems from lack of support.

13. Sales of new homes in Arizona fell almost 20 percent in the month of February, compared to last year. Analysts attribute the decline to several factors. Record rainfalls kept both builders and buyers indoors for most of the month. The rise in the interest rates have brought mortgage rates to a ten-month high. Both the sales of new homes and housing starts have reached new lows. With every indication that mortgage rates will remain high for the rest of the year, Arizona home-builders foresee a very grim year ahead.

Which one of the following would add support to the conclusion of this passage?

(A) Last year's sales increased in the second half of the year, despite some increase in interest rates.
(B) Last year's sales were accelerated by good weather in January and February.
(C) Widespread advertising and incentives to attract buyers this February were ineffective.
(D) Rain in Arizona usually ends late in February.
(E) Home sales and building starts throughout the country are about the same this year as last year.

14. No one reads *Weight-Off* magazine unless he or she is fat. Everyone reads *Weight-Off* magazine unless he or she eats chocolate.

Which one of the following is inconsistent with the above?

(A) No one is fat and only some people eat chocolate.
(B) Some people are fat and no one eats chocolate.
(C) Everyone is fat.
(D) No one is fat and no one reads *Weight-Off*.
(E) No one who is fat eats chocolate.

15. *Jerry:* Every meal my wife cooks is fantastic.

Dave: I disagree. Most of my wife's meals are fantastic, too.

Dave's response shows that he understood Jerry to mean that

(A) Dave's wife does not cook fantastic meals
(B) only Jerry's wife cooks fantastic meals
(C) every one of Jerry's wife's meals is fantastic
(D) not every one of Jerry's wife's meals is fantastic
(E) no one cooks fantastic meals all the time

1   1   1   1   1 ➤

Questions 16–17

Commentators and politicians are given to enlisting the rest of America as allies, sprinkling such phrases as "Americans believe" or "Americans will simply not put up with" into their pronouncements on whatever issue currently claims their attentions. They cite polls showing 60 or 80 or 90 percent support for their views. There may (or may not) have been such polls, but even if the polls are real, their finer points will not be reported because they usually contradict the speaker's point. The alleged 80 percent support for a balanced budget amendment, for example, plummets to less than 30 percent if the pollster so much as mentions an entitlement program like social security. People do have opinions, but they are rarely so specific or so unequivocal as your news broadcaster or your senator would lead you to believe.

16. The argument of this passage would be less convincing if it could be shown that

    (A) In a recent poll, 80 percent of the Americans responding supported a balanced budget amendment.
    (B) Most polls used by television commentators are conducted by telephone calls lasting less than 35 seconds.
    (C) Far more Americans are indifferent to or badly informed about current affairs than are well informed.
    (D) The polls' predictions of who will be elected president have been correct about every presidential election since Truman defeated Dewey.
    (E) Many polls are based on samples that do not accurately represent the demographics of an area.

17. The argument of this passage proceeds by using all of the following EXCEPT:

    (A) supporting a general point with a specific example
    (B) questioning the honesty of politicians and commentators
    (C) reinterpreting evidence presented as supporting a position being rejected
    (D) pointing out inherent inconsistencies in the claims of the politicians and commentators
    (E) exposing the limitations of arguments based on statistics

18. The most often heard complaint about flights on Scorpio Airlines is that there is insufficient room in the cabin of the plane to accommodate all of the passengers' carry-on baggage. The number of passengers who carry on all of their luggage rather than checking it at the ticket counter has increased so much that on more than half of the flights on Scorpio Airlines passengers have difficulty finding space for their bags in the cabin of the plane. The company is considering ways to alleviate this problem.

    All of the following are plausible ways of dealing with the problem EXCEPT:

    (A) reducing the allowable size of carry-on luggage
    (B) charging passengers who carry on more than one bag a fee
    (C) increasing the fares of flights on lightly traveled routes
    (D) reducing the seating capacity of the cabins to provide more space for luggage
    (E) offering a price reduction to ticket buyers who check their bags

GO ON TO THE NEXT PAGE ➤

19. *X:* "We discover new knowledge by the syllogistic process when we say, for example, 'All men are mortal; Socrates is a man; therefore Socrates is mortal.'"

Y: "Yes, but the fact is that if all men are mortal we cannot tell whether Socrates is a man until we have determined his mortality—in other words, until we find him dead. Of course, it's a great convenience to assume that Socrates is a man because he looks like one, but that's just a deduction. If we examine its formulation—'Objects that resemble men in most respects are men; Socrates resembles men in most respects; therefore Socrates is a man'—it's obvious that if he is a man, he resembles men in *all* necessary respects. So it's obvious we're right back where we started."

X: "Yes, we must know all the characteristics of men, and that Socrates has all of them, before we can be sure."

Which one of the following best expresses X's concluding observation?

(A) In deductive thinking we are simply reminding ourselves of the implications of our generalizations.

(B) It is often too convenient to arrive at conclusions simply by deduction instead of induction.

(C) Socrates' mortality is not the issue; the issue is critical thinking.

(D) Socrates' characteristics do not necessarily define his mortality.

(E) The key to the syllogistic process is using theoretical, rather than practical, issues of logic.

20. It takes a good telescope to see the moons of Neptune. I can't see the moons of Neptune with my telescope. Therefore, I do not have a good telescope.

Which one of the following most closely parallels the logic of this statement?

(A) It takes two to tango. You are doing the tango. Therefore, you have a partner.

(B) If you have a surfboard, you can surf. You do not have a surfboard. Therefore, you cannot surf.

(C) You need gin and vermouth to make a martini. You do not have any gin. Therefore, you cannot make a martini.

(D) If you know the area of a circle, you can find its circumference. You cannot figure out the circumference. Therefore, you do not know the area.

(E) You can write a letter to your friend with a pencil. You do not have a pencil. Therefore, you cannot write the letter.

Questions 21–22

Over 90 percent of our waking life depends on habits which for the most part we are unconscious of, from brushing our teeth in the morning to the time and manner in which we go to sleep at night. Habits are tools which serve the important function of relieving the conscious mind for more important activities. Habits are stored patterns of behavior which are found to serve the needs of the individual who has them and are formed from what once was conscious behavior which over years of repetition can become an automatic behavior pattern of the unconscious mind.

21. It can be inferred that the author bases his beliefs on

    (A) the testimony of a controlled group of students
    (B) biblical passages referring to the unconscious state
    (C) an intense psychological research
    (D) extensive psychological research
    (E) recent findings of clinical psychologists

22. The last sentence implies that

    (A) all repetitious patterns become unconscious behavior
    (B) conscious behavior eventually becomes habit
    (C) the unconscious mind causes repetitive behavior
    (D) automatic behavior patterns of the conscious mind are not possible
    (E) habits can be good or bad

Questions 23–24

It should be emphasized that only one person in a thousand who is bitten by a disease-carrying mosquito develops symptoms that require hospitalization, according to Dr. Reeves. But it is a potentially serious disease that requires close collaboration by citizens and local government to prevent it from reaching epidemic proportions.

Citizens should fill or drain puddles where mosquitoes breed. They should repair leaking swamp coolers and be sure swimming pools have a good circulating system. Make sure drain gutters aren't clogged and holding rainwater. Keep barrels and other water-storage containers tightly covered. Use good window screens.

23. Which one of the following statements, if true, would most strengthen the advice given in the second paragraph above?

    (A) Leaking swamp coolers are the primary cause of mosquito infestation.
    (B) It is possible to completely eliminate mosquitoes from a neighborhood.
    (C) No one can completely protect herself from being bitten by a mosquito.
    (D) Tightly covered water containers do not ensure the purity of the water in all cases.
    (E) Window screens seldom need to be replaced.

24. What additional information would strengthen the clarity of the second sentence above?

    (A) The names of some local governments that have fought against disease.
    (B) The name of the disease under discussion.
    (C) The names of those bitten by disease-carrying mosquitoes.
    (D) The full name of Dr. Reeves.
    (E) A description of the symptoms that a bitten person might develop.

GO ON TO THE NEXT PAGE ➤

25. That which is rare is always more valuable than that which is abundant. And so we are continually frustrated in our attempts to teach young people how to use time wisely; they have too much of it to appreciate its value.

Which one of the following statements, if true, would most weaken the argument above?

(A) Appreciation is not the same as obedience.
(B) Teaching something as abstract as the appreciation of time is difficult.
(C) Currency that is based on rare metals is more valuable than currency that is not.
(D) Many young people possess an intuitive knowledge of what time is, a knowledge they lose around middle age.
(E) The leisure time of people aged 18–24 has decreased significantly over the last 10 years.

26. Many theorists now believe that people cannot learn to write if they are constantly worrying about whether their prose is correct or not. When a would-be writer worries about correctness, his ability to be fluent is frozen.

With which one of the following statements would the author of the above passage probably agree?

(A) Writing theorists are probably wrong.
(B) Writing prose is different from writing poetry.
(C) Literacy is a function of relaxation.
(D) Fear blocks action.
(E) Most good writers are careless.

STOP

IF YOU FINISH BEFORE TIME IS CALLED, YOU MAY CHECK YOUR WORK ON THIS SECTION ONLY.
DO NOT WORK ON ANY OTHER SECTION IN THE TEST.

2   **2**   **2**   **2**   **2**

SECTION II
TIME — 35 MINUTES
28 QUESTIONS

<u>Directions:</u> Read the passages and answer the questions following each passage by blackening the appropriate space on the answer sheet. You may refer back to the passages when answering the questions. Answer all questions on the basis of what is stated or implied.

The Sixth Amendment's right to the "assistance of counsel" has been the subject of considerable litigation
line in twentieth-century American courts.
(5) The emphasis has traditionally centered on the degree to which a criminal defendant can demand the assistance of counsel in various courts and at different hierarchical stages of the criminal
(10) proceeding. Although past courts have alluded to the idea that a defendant has a converse right to proceed without counsel, the issue had not been squarely addressed by the United States Supreme
(15) Court until late in its 1974–75 term. At that time, the Court held that within the Sixth Amendment rests an implied right of self-representation.
   As early as 1964, Justice Hugo Black
(20) wrote that "the Sixth Amendment withholds from federal courts, in all criminal proceedings, the power and authority to deprive an accused of his life or liberty unless he has or waives
(25) the assistance of counsel." However, recognizing that the Sixth Amendment does not require representation by counsel, it is quite another thing to say that the defendant has a constitutional
(30) right to reject professional assistance and proceed on his own. Notwithstanding such a logical and legal fallacy, the Court has, by way of opinion, spoken of a Sixth Amendment "correlative right"
(35) to dispense with a lawyer's help. Many lower federal courts have seized upon this and supported their holdings on it, in whole or in part.
   The basic motivation behind this
(40) proffered right of self-representation is that "respect for individual autonomy

requires that (the defendant) be allowed to go to jail under his own banner if he so desires" and that he should not be
(45) forced to accept counsel in whom he has no confidence. Courts have ruled that neither due process nor progressive standards of criminal justice require that the defendant be represented at trial
(50) by counsel. The Supreme Court, in its 1975 decision, held that a defendant in a state criminal trial has a constitutional right to waive counsel and carry on his own case *in propria persona.* In raising
(55) this obscure privilege to a constitutional level, the Court stated that, so long as the defendant is made aware of the dangers and disadvantages of self-representation, his lack of technical
(60) legal knowledge will not deprive him of the right to defend himself personally.
   The Court conceded that the long line of right to counsel cases have alluded
(65) to the idea that the assistance of counsel is a prerequisite to the realization of a fair trial. However, the Court noted that the presence of counsel is of minor significance when a stubborn,
(70) self-reliant defendant prohibits the lawyer from employing his knowledge and skills. This line of reasoning is concluded with the observation that "the defendant and not his lawyer or the state,
(75) will bear the personal consequences of a conviction." The logical extension of this premise brings the Court to its decision that, recognizing the traditional American respect for the individual,
(80) the defendant "must be free personally to decide whether in his particular case counsel is to his advantage."

GO ON TO THE NEXT PAGE ➤

2   **2**   **2**   **2**   **2**

1. According to the passage, the chief purpose of the Sixth Amendment is to

   (A) assure a defendant the assistance of counsel in capital cases
   (B) assure a defendant the assistance of counsel in civil cases
   (C) assure a defendant the assistance of counsel in criminal cases
   (D) allow a defendant to represent himself in a criminal trial
   (E) allow a defendant to represent himself in a civil trial

2. The "logical and legal fallacy" referred to in line 32 is probably

   (A) the ability to waive a right does not automatically give rise to a replacement of that right
   (B) the right to reject implies a correlative right to refuse to reject
   (C) the right to dispense with a lawyer's help
   (D) the right to legal assistance
   (E) the defendant who chooses to go to jail is free to do so

3. From the passage, the phrase *"in propria persona"* in line 54 means

   (A) in his own person
   (B) by an appropriate person
   (C) in place of another person
   (D) improperly
   (E) by using a stand-in

4. In allowing a defendant to refuse counsel, the Supreme Court may have reasoned all of the following EXCEPT:

   (A) A defendant who objected to a court-appointed attorney would prevent the lawyer from defending him effectively.
   (B) The assistance of counsel is necessary to the realization of a fair trial.
   (C) In the event of an unfavorable verdict, the defendant will suffer the consequences.
   (D) American tradition recognizes the individual's freedom to make decisions that will affect him.
   (E) It is possible that a defendant might defend himself more effectively than a court-appointed lawyer.

5. A defendant who is acting as counsel in his own defense must be

   (A) given additional legal assistance
   (B) allowed to give up his own defense if he chooses to do so before the trial has concluded
   (C) warned of the disadvantages of self-representation
   (D) assisted by the judge in areas where the defendant's lack of knowledge of technical legal terms is deficient
   (E) tried before a jury

6. All of the following are objections that might be raised to self-representation EXCEPT:

   (A) By accepting the right to self-representation, a defendant must waive his right to assistance of counsel.
   (B) A defendant determined to convict himself can do so more easily.
   (C) If the right to self-representation is not asserted before the trial begins, it is lost.
   (D) Self-representation has a tradition in American law that dates back to the colonial period.
   (E) A self-representation defendant may be unruly or disruptive.

GO ON TO THE NEXT PAGE ➤

2　　**2**　　**2**　　**2**　　**2**

African art could have been observed and collected by Europeans no earlier than the second half of the fifteenth
line century. Before that time Europe knew
(5) of Africa only through the writing of classical authors such as Pliny and Herodotus and the reports of a few Arabic travelers. Unfortunately, until the latter years of the nineteenth century
(10) Europe was little interested in the arts of Africa except as curiosities and souvenirs of exotic peoples. Indeed, with the growth of the slave trade, colonial exploitation, and Christian missionizing
(15) the arts were presented as evidence of the low state of heathen savagery of the African, justifying both exploitation and missionary zeal. Even with the early growth of the discipline of anthropology
(20) the assumption was that Africa was a continent of savages, low on the scale of evolutionary development, and that these savages, because they were "preliterate," could, by definition, have no history and
(25) no government worth notice.

In recent years the development of critical studies of oral traditions, of accounts by Islamic travelers of the great Sudanese kingdoms, of the descriptions
(30) of the coast by early European travelers, and—above all—of the concept of cultural relativism, has led to a far more realistic assessment of the African, his culture, history, and arts.

(35) Cultural relativism is, in essence, the attitude whereby cultures other than one's own are viewed in *their* terms and on *their* merits. As an alternative to the prejudgment of missionaries
(40) and colonials it allows us to view the cultures and arts of the African without the necessity of judging his beliefs and actions against a Judeo-Christian moralistic base, or his art against a
(45) Greco-Renaissance yardstick.

Curiously, the "discovery" and enthusiasm for African art early in this century was not based on an objective, scientific assessment but rather resulted
(50) from an excess of romantic rebellion at the end of the last century against the Classical and Naturalist roots of western art. Unfortunately this uncritical adulation swept aside many rational
(55) concerns to focus upon African sculpture as if it were the product of a romantic, rebellious, *fin de siècle,* European movement. Obviously, African art is neither anti-classical nor anti-
(60) naturalistic: to be either it would have had to have had its roots in Classicism or in Naturalism, both European in origin. Nor was the concept of rebellion a part of the heritage of art in sub-Saharan
(65) Africa; rather, as we shall see, it was an art conservative in impulse and stable in concept.

We may admire these sculptures from a purely twentieth-century aesthetic,
(70) but if we so limit our admiration we will most certainly fail to understand them in the context of their appearance as documents of African thought and action.

(75) In sharp contrast to the arts of the recent past in the Western world, by far the greatest part, in fact nearly all of the art of the history of the world, including traditional Africa, was positive in its
(80) orientation; that is, it conformed in style and meaning to the expectations—the norms—of its patrons and audience. Those norms were shared by nearly all members of the society; thus, the
(85) arts were conservative and conformist. However, it must be stressed that they were not merely passive reflections, for they contributed actively to the sense of well-being of the parent culture. Indeed,
(90) the perishable nature of wood—the dominant medium for sculpture— ensured that each generation reaffirmed its faith by re-creating its arts.

GO ON TO THE NEXT PAGE ➤

7. According to the passage, before the latter part of the nineteenth century, Europeans viewed African art as

   (A) simple and direct
   (B) odd but beautifully crafted
   (C) savage and of little value
   (D) ugly and of grotesque proportions
   (E) warlike and lacking in beauty

8. According to the passage, which one of the following contributed to the initial dismissal of African art by Europeans?

   (A) Europeans valued color and sophisticated techniques, both of which were absent in African arts.
   (B) It was easier to justify exploitation of Africans if their art was dismissed as heathen.
   (C) Europeans were made uncomfortable by the Africans' tendency to depict coarse acts and vulgar positions.
   (D) It was important to reject African art because it was dangerous to a stable European society.
   (E) It was believed that an influx of African art could seriously disrupt the market for European art.

9. According to the passage, all of the following contributed to a change in the European view of African art EXCEPT:

   (A) the writings of Pliny
   (B) cultural relativism
   (C) Islamic travel accounts
   (D) descriptions by early European travelers
   (E) studies of oral traditions

10. Which one of the following most accurately represents the concept of cultural relativism as defined in the passage?

    (A) The words "good" and "bad" are irrelevant when judging between works of art.
    (B) One cannot enjoy a work of art without a complete understanding of the culture from which it came.
    (C) The best art will always be art that is positive in its orientation.
    (D) If an artist goes outside his own tradition in creating a work of art, that work of art will be inferior.
    (E) To determine the success of a work of art, it should be judged against the values of its own culture.

11. According to the passage, the early twentieth-century European view of African art was inadequate because it

    (A) was based on a limited number of objects available to the Western world
    (B) was a result of a romantic rebellion against traditions in Western art
    (C) did not take into account the importance of oral traditions
    (D) was dependent on classical rather than naturalistic standards
    (E) was dictated by the judgments of Christian missionaries

12. Which one of the following best describes the author's point about the relationship between twentieth-century Western art and African art?

(A) African art and twentieth-century Western art both have their roots in a desire to escape tradition and rediscover man's primitive state.

(B) The techniques used in African sculpture are remarkably similar to the techniques used in twentieth-century Western sculpture.

(C) It isn't possible to enjoy African art if we judge it by twentieth-century European aesthetic standards.

(D) Compared to twentieth-century Western art, African art is conservative and conformist, in that it is in keeping with the expectations of its society.

(E) Because it was produced by artists unschooled in technique, African art does not display the sophistication and ingenuity of twentieth-century Western art.

13. According to the author, the use of wood in African art is especially significant because

(A) it is a simpler, more available medium than marble

(B) unlike the hardness of stone, its relative softness allows intricate carvings representing African beliefs

(C) it represents a rebellion from the media used in Western sculpture and a return to African roots

(D) it is unique to primitive cultures uncorrupted by the Western world.

(E) its impermanence ensures that each generation creates new art reaffirming the beliefs of the culture

14. In this passage, one of the principal methods the author uses to develop his subject is

(A) discussion and explanation of reactions to African art in the Western world

(B) examination and analysis of several specific African works of art

(C) criticism and refutation of Western traditions such as Classicism and Naturalism

(D) description and explanation of African religious and social beliefs

(E) discussion and analysis of the aesthetic principles at the foundation of African art

GO ON TO THE NEXT PAGE ➤

In the competitive model—the economy of many sellers each with a small share of the total market—the
line restraint on the private exercise of
(5) economic power was provided by other firms on the same side of the market. It was the eagerness of competitors to sell, not the complaints of buyers, that saved the latter from spoliation.
(10) It was assumed, no doubt accurately, that the nineteenth-century textile manufacturer who overcharged for his product would promptly lose his market to another manufacturer who did not.
(15) If all manufacturers found themselves in a position where they could exploit a strong demand, and mark up their prices accordingly, there would soon be an inflow of new competitors. The resulting
(20) increase in supply would bring prices and profits back to normal.

As with the seller who was tempted to use his economic power against the customer, so with the buyer who was
(25) tempted to use it against his labor or suppliers. The man who paid less than the prevailing wage would lose his labor force to those who paid the worker his full (marginal) contribution to the
(30) earnings of the firm. In all cases the incentive to socially desirable behavior was provided by the competitor. It was to the same side of the market—the restraint of sellers by other sellers and of
(35) buyers by other buyers, in other words to competition—that economists came to look for the self-regulatory mechanisms of the economy.

They also came to look to competition
(40) exclusively and in formal theory still do. The notion that there might be another regulatory mechanism in the economy

had been almost completely excluded from economic thought. Thus, with the
(45) widespread disappearance of competition in its classical form and its replacement by the small group of firms if not in overt, at least in conventional or tacit, collusion, it was easy to suppose that
(50) since competition had disappeared, all effective restraint on private power had disappeared. Indeed, this conclusion was all but inevitable if no search was made for other restraints, and so complete was
(55) the preoccupation with competition that none was made.

In fact, new restraints on private power did appear to replace competition. They were nurtured by the same process
(60) of concentration which impaired or destroyed competition. But they appeared not on the same side of the market but on the opposite side, not with competitors but with customers or
(65) suppliers. It will be convenient to have a name for this counterpart of competition and I shall call it countervailing power.

To begin with a broad and somewhat
(70) too dogmatically stated proposition, private economic power is held in check by the countervailing power of those who are subject to it. The first begets the second. The long trend toward
(75) concentration of industrial enterprise in the hands of a relatively few firms has brought into existence not only strong sellers, as economists have supposed, but also strong buyers, a fact they have
(80) failed to see. The two develop together, not in precise step, but in such manner that there can be no doubt that the one is in response to the other.

GO ON TO THE NEXT PAGE ➤

2 **2** **2**

15. Which one of the following would be the best title for this passage?

    (A) Capitalism and the Competitive Model
    (B) Competition and the Concept of "Countervailing Power"
    (C) Problems in American Capitalism
    (D) The Importance of Economic Regulatory Mechanisms
    (E) The Failure of the Classic Competition Model

16. In the classic competition model, when competitive manufacturers marked up prices because of strong demand, a return to normal was provided by

    (A) new manufacturers entering the market
    (B) refusal to buy on the part of customers
    (C) governmental intervention in the form of regulation
    (D) repositioning of the labor force
    (E) failure of weaker manufacturers

17. In the classic competition model, the incentive for manufacturers to behave in a socially desirable way toward workers was provided by

    (A) competition for the labor supply
    (B) competition for the customer
    (C) imbalance between supply and demand
    (D) self-regulation among competitors
    (E) humanistic economic theory

18. According to the author, which one of the following statements is true?

    (A) The classic model of competition was inadequate because it ignored the role of labor and rewarded individual greed.
    (B) The classic model of competition provided self-regulation prior to, but not after, the Industrial Revolution.
    (C) The classic model of competition was undermined by the "restraint of sellers by other sellers and of buyers by other buyers."
    (D) The classic model of competition was replaced by concentration of industrial enterprise and collusion among manufacturers.
    (E) The classic model of competition was destroyed by the growth of "countervailing power."

19. Examples of "countervailing power" in the regulation of the economic power of manufacturers could include all of the following EXCEPT:

    (A) organized customer boycotts
    (B) cooperative buying organizations
    (C) large retail chains
    (D) retailers developing their own sources of supply
    (E) organizations that network manufacturers

GO ON TO THE NEXT PAGE ➤

2   **2**   **2**   **2**   **2**

20. According to the author, a weakness of economic thought has been

   (A) a preoccupation with competition

   (B) a failure to recognize the need for reasonable government regulation

   (C) a belief in the "trickle-down" theory

   (D) a failure to recognize concentration of industrial enterprise

   (E) a bias toward unregulated capitalism

21. Which one of the following best describes the structure of this passage?

   (A) The first three paragraphs describe the strengths of economic competition and the fourth and fifth paragraphs describe its weaknesses.

   (B) The first paragraph presents the historical perspective on competition, the second and third present examples of its effect on the economy, and the fourth and fifth paragraphs set forth the idea of "countervailing power."

   (C) The first two paragraphs describe how competition is thought to work, the third paragraph provides a transition, and the fourth and fifth paragraphs describe "countervailing power."

   (D) The first three paragraphs describe the classic model of competition, while the fourth and fifth paragraphs describe "countervailing power."

   (E) The first three paragraphs present a view of competition in opposition to the author's, while the fourth and fifth paragraphs present the author's view.

Passage A

Antoine-Laurent Lavoisier (1743–1794) can justly be called the father of modern chemistry, not because of earth-shaking discoveries or experiments but
(5) because he introduced a new approach to the understanding of chemical reactions. Some of his conclusions were later called into question or improved upon, but his relentless pursuit of knowledge
(10) and logical reasoning led to hundreds of experiments, all of which challenged the preconceived scientific notions of his day.

Lavoisier at twenty-five was elected
(15) to France's Academy of Sciences, in large part because of his work in geology, not chemistry. In 1775, he was appointed to the Royal Gunpowder and Saltpeter Administration, and
(20) in his laboratory he produced better gunpowder, in part by focusing on the purity of its ingredients and improved methods of granulating the powder.

An important aspect of Lavoisier's
(25) work was his determination of the weights of reagents and products, including gaseous components, involved in chemical reactions. He believed that matter, identified by weight, would
(30) always be conserved through these reactions. Lavoisier's methods led to, among other things, his definitive proof that water was made up of oxygen and hydrogen.

(35) His methods also led him to challenge the phlogistic theory of combustion, which initially had been proposed by the German alchemist Johann Joachim Becher in the late 1600s and which
(40) was still widely accepted well into the eighteenth century. According to that theory, something called "phlogiston," named by Georg Ernst Stahl, existed in all materials and was released
(45) during combustion, the resulting ash being the remaining material, but "dephlogisticated." Since phlogiston wasn't—according to its proponents—a material substance, it was unweighable
(50) and without color or odor. Also according to the theory, acids produced by combustion were elementary substances, not the products of a chemical reaction. Lavoisier, through
(55) his experiments, came to recognize that

GO ON TO THE NEXT PAGE ➤

a chemical reaction with oxygen, not a vague principle called phlogiston, caused combustion.

(60) At first, Lavoisier referred to oxygen as "air in its purest form," but he later called it oxygen, from the Greek words *oxus*, meaning sharp, acidic, and *ginomai*, meaning to become or cause to be. He believed that oxygen caused the (65) acids produced by combustion. Later, however, Sir Humphry Davy, Louis Joseph Gay-Lussac, and Louis-Jacques Thenard showed in their experiments with hydrochloric acid, chlorine, and (70) hydrocyanic acid that acid could be produced without oxygen.

But Lavoisier, even though some of his ideas were later proved wrong, succeeded in turning away from (75) alchemy and the theory of phlogiston. In the words of Justus von Liebig, Lavoisier's immortal glory "consists in this—that he infused into the body of the science a new spirit."

Passage B

(80) Among the definitions of *theory* is "the analysis of a set of facts in their relation to one another." That definition doesn't take us very far, however, because almost any set of facts can be (85) analyzed in a dozen or more ways. In science, theories are set forth and later discarded, or modified, all the time.

For example, in the seventeenth century, heat was erroneously explained (90) through theories of combustion. Johann Joachim Becher and Georg Ernst Stahl introduced the theory that phlogiston, present in all matter, was released during combustion. It was thought to be the (95) source of heat. Phlogiston couldn't be weighed and, in fact, wasn't considered a material at all but rather a principle. Such notable scientists as Joseph Priestley (1733–1804), who conducted extensive (100) research on the nature and property of gases, interpreted his results in terms of phlogiston. Priestley's experiments isolated and characterized eight gases, including oxygen, which he described as (105) "dephlogisticated air."

Antoine Lavoisier, a French scientist who rightly explained combustion in terms of oxygen and not the principle of phlogiston, introduced another (110) theory of heat. In his *Reflexions sur le*

phlogistique (1783), he argued that the phlogiston theory was inconsistent with his experimental results. Ironically, however, Lavoisier proposed a (115) substance called *caloric* (which he considered an "element"—one of 33 substances that couldn't be broken down into simpler entities) as the source of heat. Like phlogiston, caloric couldn't (120) be weighed, and Lavoisier called it "a subtle fluid." The quantity of caloric, according to Lavoisier, was constant throughout the universe and flowed from warmer to colder bodies.

(125) Not surprisingly, observable facts could be explained by the caloric theory. For instance, a hot bowl of soup cools at room temperature. Why? Because caloric slowly flows from regions dense (130) with it (the hot soup) to regions less dense with it (the cooler air in the room). Another example is that air expands when heated. According to the caloric theory, this would be because caloric (135) is absorbed by air molecules, thereby increasing the volume of the air.

Ultimately, the caloric theory as posited by Lavoisier was discarded. The calorists' principle of the conservation (140) of heat was replaced by a principle of conservation of energy.

Modern thermodynamics defines heat not as a result of a "subtle fluid" but as a result of the kinetic energy of molecules.

22. Which of the following characterizes the main difference between Passage A and Passage B?

(A) Passage A praises Antoine Lavoisier, whereas Passage B discredits him.
(B) The focus in Passage A is on a scientist's work, while the focus in Passage B is on a particular theory.
(C) Passage A explains the phlogiston theory, whereas Passage B does not.
(D) In Passage A, the emphasis is on chemical reactions, while in Passage B the emphasis is on the scientific method.
(E) The author of Passage A is objective toward science, while the author of Passage B is skeptical.

2   2   2   2   2

23. The author of Passage B uses the term "ironically" in line 113 to

(A) emphasize how fallible scientists can be in interpreting their own results and the results of their predecessors
(B) undermine Lavoisier's designation as the "father of modern chemistry"
(C) note that while Lavoisier proved that phlogiston didn't exist, he introduced another nonexistent substance
(D) suggest the absurdity of scientific debates
(E) lighten the tone of the passage as a whole

24. According to Passage A, among Lavoisier's accomplishments was

(A) proving the chemical composition of water
(B) explaining the cause of heat
(C) changing the composition of gunpowder
(D) identifying caloric as a fluid
(E) isolating and characterizing eight gases

25. Which of the following best illustrates that facts can be explained by more than one theory (paragraph 1 of Passage B)?

(A) Hydrochloric acid cannot be produced without oxygen.
(B) The agent of combustion is weightless and odorless.
(C) Boiling water will cool at room temperature.
(D) Combustion results in ash made up of "dephlogisticated" material.
(E) Acids produced by combustion are elementary substances.

26. The author of Passage B would most likely agree with which of the following statements?

(A) Alchemy contributed nothing to science.
(B) Joseph Priestley was not as important as Antoine Lavoisier in the study of gases.
(C) Thermodynamics is an inexact science.
(D) A theory is a possible, but not necessarily the only, explanation of facts.
(E) The scientific method is seriously flawed and cannot be counted on to prove a fact.

27. According to information in Passage A and Passage B, Lavoisier believed that

(A) matter was not destroyed during a chemical reaction
(B) the acids produced during combustion were elementary substances
(C) molecular movement was responsible for the production of heat
(D) matter was converted to energy in chemical reactions
(E) a fluid called "caloric" caused combustion

28. In Passage B, Joseph Priestley is used as an example of

(A) a scientist who relied heavily on alchemy
(B) the importance of an open exchange of ideas between scientists
(C) a scientist who made a major discovery, as distinguished from Lavoisier
(D) a precursor to Lavoisier's experiments with gases
(E) the persistence of the phlogistic theory well into the eighteenth century

STOP

IF YOU FINISH BEFORE TIME IS CALLED, YOU MAY CHECK YOUR WORK ON THIS SECTION ONLY.
DO NOT WORK ON ANY OTHER SECTION IN THE TEST.

3   **3**   **3**   **3**   **3**

SECTION III
TIME — 35 MINUTES
23 QUESTIONS

<u>Directions:</u> In this section you will be given groups of questions based on different sets of conditions. Drawing a simple diagram may be helpful in answering some of the questions. You are to choose the best answer and mark the corresponding space on your answer sheet.

<u>Questions 1–6</u>

There are five flagpoles lined up next to each other in a straight row in front of a school. Each flagpole flies one flag (red, white, or blue) and one pennant (green, white, or blue). The following are conditions that affect the placement of flags and pennants on the poles:

On a given flagpole, the pennant and the flag cannot be the same color.

Two adjacent flagpoles cannot fly the same color flags.

Two adjacent flagpoles cannot fly the same color pennants.

No more than two of any color flag or pennant may fly at one time.

1. If the 2nd and 5th pennants are blue, the 2nd and 5th flags are red, and the 3rd flag is white, then which one of the following must be true?

   (A) Two of the flags are white.
   (B) Two of the pennants are white.
   (C) The 4th pennant is green.
   (D) If the 1st pennant is green, then the 1st flag is blue.
   (E) If the 1st flag is white, then the 1st pennant is green.

2. If the 1st flag is red and the 2nd pennant is blue, then which one of the following is NOT necessarily true?

   (A) The 2nd flag is white.
   (B) If the 5th flag is red, then the 3rd flag is blue.
   (C) If the 4th pennant is green, then the 1st pennant is white.
   (D) If the 1st and 5th flags are the same color, then the 3rd flag is blue.
   (E) If the 4th pennant is green and the 5th pennant is white, then the 1st and 3rd pennants are different colors.

3. If the 1st and 3rd flags are white and the 2nd and 4th pennants are blue, then which one of the following is false?

   (A) The 4th flag is red.
   (B) The 1st pennant is green.
   (C) The 3rd pennant is not red.
   (D) The 5th pennant is green.
   (E) There is one blue flag.

GO ON TO THE NEXT PAGE ➤

3   **3**   **3**   **3**   **3**

4. If the 1st and 4th flags are blue, and the 3rd pennant is white, then which one of the following must be true?

   (A) If the 1st pennant is green, then the 5th pennant is white.
   (B) If the 5th pennant is white, then the 1st pennant is green.
   (C) The 2nd flag is red.
   (D) The 5th flag is red.
   (E) The 1st pennant is green.

5. If the 2nd flag is red and the 3rd flag is white, and the 4th pennant is blue, then which one of the following must be true?

   (A) If the 5th flag is white, then two of the pennants are blue.
   (B) If the 1st flag is white, then the 2nd flag is white.
   (C) If the 1st pennant is blue, then the 5th pennant is green.
   (D) If the 1st pennant is green, then the 5th flag is not blue.
   (E) If the 1st and 5th flags are the same color, then the 1st and 5th pennants are not the same color.

6. If the 1st flag and the 2nd pennant are the same color, the 2nd flag and the 3rd pennant are the same color, the 3rd flag and the 4th pennant are the same color, and the 4th flag and the 5th pennant are the same color, then which one of the following must be true?

   (A) The 1st pennant is white.
   (B) The 2nd flag is not white.
   (C) The 5th flag is red.
   (D) The 3rd pennant is blue.
   (E) The 4th flag is white.

Questions 7–13

In the Norfolk Library returned book section there are ten books standing next to each other on a shelf. There are two math books, two science books, three English books, and three poetry books. The books are arranged as follows:

There is a math book on one end and an English book on the other end.

The two math books are never next to each other.

The two science books are always next to each other.

The three English books are always next to each other.

7. If the 8th book is a math book, then which one of the following must be true?

   (A) The 5th book is a science book.
   (B) The 7th book is an English book.
   (C) The 6th book is not a poetry book.
   (D) The 4th book is next to an English book.
   (E) The 9th book is a science book.

8. If the 9th book is an English book and the 5th and 6th books are poetry books, then which one of the following must be true?

   (A) There is a math book next to a poetry book.
   (B) The 2nd book is a science book.
   (C) The 3 poetry books are all next to one another.
   (D) The 7th book is a math book.
   (E) The 4th book is not a poetry book.

3   **3**   **3**   **3**   **3**

9. If the 1st book is a math book and the 7th book is a science book, then which one of the following could be false?

(A) Both math books are next to poetry books.
(B) All three poetry books are next to each other.
(C) The 2nd book is a poetry book.
(D) The 10th book is an English book.
(E) The 6th book is a science book.

10. If the 4th book is a math book and the 5th book is a science book, then which one of the following must be true?

(A) An English book is next to a science book.
(B) If the 7th book is a poetry book, then the 3rd book is an English book.
(C) If the 8th book is an English book, then the 2nd book is a poetry book.
(D) If the 10th book is a math book, then a poetry book is next to an English book.
(E) The three poetry books are next to each other.

11. If no two poetry books are next to each other, then which one of the following must be true?

(A) A science book is next to a math book.
(B) The 7th book is a poetry book.
(C) The 8th book is an English book.
(D) An English book is next to a science book.
(E) A poetry book is next to an English book.

12. If a science book is next to an English book, but not next to a poetry book, then which one of the following must be true?

(A) The 7th book is a poetry book.
(B) The 3rd book is an English book or a math book.
(C) The 5th or the 6th book is a math book.
(D) The three poetry books are not next to each other.
(E) The 7th or the 10th book is a math book.

13. If the 7th and 8th books are poetry books, how many different arrangements are there for the ten books?

(A) one
(B) two
(C) three
(D) four
(E) five

GO ON TO THE NEXT PAGE ➤

3   **3**   **3**   **3**   **3**

Questions 14–18

State College offers the following courses for first-year students: languages (French, German, Italian), sciences (biology, chemistry, physics), and mathematics (algebra, statistics, trigonometry). Each student must enroll in exactly five of the courses, subject to the following conditions:

 Not more than two math classes may be taken.
 If physics is taken, then algebra cannot be taken.
 If algebra is taken, then Italian must be taken.
 Chemistry may be taken only if both trigonometry and French are taken.
 If both German and biology are taken, then statistics cannot be taken.
 Exactly one language must be taken.

14. Which one of the following could be a list of the five courses taken by a first-year student at State College?

 (A) algebra, trigonometry, French, Italian, physics
 (B) statistics, trigonometry, Italian, biology, physics
 (C) algebra, statistics, French, Italian, chemistry
 (D) algebra, statistics, trigonometry, French, chemistry
 (E) statistics, trigonometry, German, biology, physics

15. If a first-year student at State College takes statistics, which one of the following pairs of courses may also be taken?

 (A) Italian, chemistry
 (B) algebra, German
 (C) German, chemistry
 (D) algebra, French
 (E) chemistry, physics

16. Which one of the following could be a list of three of the courses taken by a first-year student at State College?

 (A) algebra, French, biology
 (B) algebra, Italian, physics
 (C) statistics, German, chemistry
 (D) statistics, chemistry, physics
 (E) trigonometry, German, chemistry

17. Other than the language course, which one of the following could be a list of the courses taken by a first-year student at State College?

 (A) algebra, statistics, biology, chemistry
 (B) algebra, biology, chemistry, physics
 (C) algebra, statistics, trigonometry, physics
 (D) trigonometry, biology, chemistry, physics
 (E) statistics, biology, chemistry, physics

18. If a first-year student at State College takes Italian, which one of the following pairs of courses must also be taken?

 (A) German, biology
 (B) biology, physics
 (C) statistics, chemistry
 (D) biology, chemistry
 (E) algebra, French

GO ON TO THE NEXT PAGE ➤

3   **3**   **3**   **3**   **3**

Questions 19–23

Seven track and field coaches, A, B, C, D, E, F, and G, are each assigned to coach exactly one of four activities—sprints, distance, jumpers, and throwers. Coaching assignments are made subject to the following conditions:

Each sport is coached by one or two of the seven coaches.

B coaches jumpers.

Neither E nor F is a distance coach.

If C coaches sprints, F and G coach throwers.

If D coaches distance or throwers, A and G do not coach either distance or throwers.

19. If C and E coach sprints, which one of the following must be true?

    (A) Distance has two coaches.
    (B) G coaches jumping.
    (C) A coaches jumping or throwing.
    (D) D coaches jumping.
    (E) Jumping has one coach.

20. If G coaches jumping and A coaches distance, which one of the following must be true?

    (A) D coaches sprints.
    (B) F coaches throwing.
    (C) E coaches sprints.
    (D) C coaches distance.
    (E) F coaches sprints.

21. If D coaches throwing, which one of the following CANNOT be true?

    (A) G coaches sprints.
    (B) A coaches jumping.
    (C) E coaches sprints.
    (D) F coaches throwing.
    (E) C coaches jumping.

22. If G is the only throwing coach, which one of the following could be true?

    (A) D coaches distance.
    (B) If F coaches sprints, D coaches sprints.
    (C) A coaches jumping.
    (D) If F coaches jumping, D coaches jumping.
    (E) C and D coach the same sport.

23. If A does not coach sprints and D coaches distance, which one of the following CANNOT be true?

    (A) C coaches distance.
    (B) E coaches throwing.
    (C) G coaches jumping.
    (D) F coaches sprints.
    (E) E coaches sprints.

STOP

IF YOU FINISH BEFORE TIME IS CALLED, YOU MAY CHECK YOUR WORK ON THIS SECTION ONLY.
DO NOT WORK ON ANY OTHER SECTION IN THE TEST.

4   4   4   4   4

SECTION IV
TIME — 35 MINUTES
26 QUESTIONS

<u>Directions:</u> In this section you will be given brief statements or passages and will be required to evaluate the reasoning involved. In some instances, more than one choice will appear to be a possible answer. You are to choose the *best* answer. Use common sense and reasonableness in making your selection; then mark the proper space on the answer sheet.

Questions 1–2

The spate of bills in the legislature dealing with utility regulation shows that our lawmakers recognize a good political issue when they see one. Among the least worthy is a proposal to establish a new "Consumers Utility Board" to fight proposed increases in gas and electric rates.

It is hardly a novel idea that consumers need representation when rates are set for utilities which operate as monopolies in their communities. That's exactly why we have a state Public Utilities Commission.

Supporters of the proposed consumer board point out that utility companies have the benefit of lawyers and accountants on their payrolls to argue the case for rate increases before the PUC. That's true. Well, the PUC has the benefit of a $40 million annual budget and a staff of 900—all paid at taxpayer expense—to find fault with these rate proposals if there is fault to be found.

1. Which one of the following is the best example to offer in support of this argument against a Consumers Utility Board?

   (A) the percentage of taxpayer dollars supporting the PUC
   (B) the number of lawyers working for the Consumers Utility Board
   (C) the number of concerned consumers
   (D) a PUC readjustment of rates downward
   (E) the voting record of lawmakers supporting the board

2. Which one of the following would most seriously weaken the above argument?

   (A) Private firms are taking an increasing share of the energy business.
   (B) Water rates are also increasing.
   (C) The PUC budget will be cut slightly, along with other state agencies.
   (D) Half of the PUC lawyers and accountants are also retained by utilities.
   (E) More tax money goes to education than to the PUC.

GO ON TO THE NEXT PAGE ➤

3. Most of those who enjoy music play a musical instrument; therefore, if Maria enjoys music, she probably plays a musical instrument.

Which one of the following most closely parallels the reasoning in the statement above?

(A) The majority of those who voted for Smith in the last election oppose abortion; therefore, if the residents of University City all voted for Smith, they probably oppose abortion.

(B) If you appreciate portrait painting you are probably a painter yourself; therefore, your own experience is probably the cause of your appreciation.

(C) Most of those who join the army are male; therefore, if Jones did not join the army, Jones is probably female.

(D) Over 50 percent of the high-school students polled admitted hating homework; therefore, a majority of high-school students do not like homework.

(E) If most workers drive to work, and Sam drives to work, then Sam must be a worker.

4. *Mayor:* There must be no official or unofficial meeting of two or more members of the City Council that is not open to the public or a matter of public record. Though certain subjects can only be discussed in private, the danger of elected officials pursuing a private agenda, rather than what most benefits the public, is a serious concern in an age when politicians are too often willing to promote their private interests behind closed doors.

On which one of the following grounds is this argument especially subject to criticism?

(A) It treats popular opinion as if it were conclusive evidence.

(B) It misleadingly generalizes from the actions of a few to the actions of an entire group.

(C) It concedes the point that effectively undermines its argument.

(D) It uses an ambiguous term without making clear which meaning of the term applies here.

(E) It reaches a conclusion based on limited evidence chosen only because that evidence supports the argument.

GO ON TO THE NEXT PAGE ➤

5. "Good personnel relations of an organization depend upon mutual confidence, trust, and goodwill. The basis of confidence is understanding. Most troubles start with people who do not understand each other. When the organization's intentions or motives are misunderstood, or when reasons for actions, practices, or policies are misconstrued, complete cooperation from individuals is not forthcoming. If management expects full cooperation from employees, it has a responsibility of sharing with them the information which is the foundation of proper understanding, confidence, and trust. Personnel management has long since outgrown the days when it was the vogue to 'treat them rough and tell them nothing.' Up-to-date personnel management provides all possible information about the activities, aims, and purposes of the organization. It seems altogether creditable that a desire should exist among employees for such information which the best-intentioned executive might think would not interest them and which the worst-intentioned would think was none of their business."

The above paragraph implies that one of the causes of the difficulty that an organization might have with its personnel relations is that its employees

(A) have not expressed interest in the activities, aims, and purposes of the organization
(B) do not believe in the good faith of the organization
(C) have not been able to give full cooperation to the organization
(D) do not recommend improvements in the practices and policies of the organization
(E) can afford little time to establish good relations with their organization

6. Of all psychiatric disorders, depression is the most common; yet, research on its causes and cures is still far from complete. As a matter of fact, very few facilities offer assistance to those suffering from this disorder.

The author would probably agree that

(A) depression needs further study
(B) further research will make possible further assistance to those suffering from depression
(C) most facilities are staffed by psychiatrists whose specialty is not depression
(D) those suffering from depression need to know its causes and cures
(E) depression and ignorance go hand in hand

7. *Editorial:* The politicians who wish to see the schools run like businesses will have some trouble establishing a standard of accountability. In the business world, profits provide a clear standard, measurable in numbers. But in public education, standards are culturally derived, and differ very widely among age, ethnic, and political groups. We can evaluate a school's record keeping or its facilities, but there is no way to use the standards of quality control that are used to judge the profitability of a business and apply them to the academic performance of students throughout a public school system.

To which one of the following is the writer of this passage objecting?

(A) the assumption that a school and a business are analogous
(B) the belief that profitability is a universal standard
(C) the assumption that schools, like businesses, can show a financial profit
(D) the belief that school vouchers are undemocratic
(E) the assumption that record keeping and facilities are adequate gauges of business success

GO ON TO THE NEXT PAGE ➤

8. *Ivan:* What the Church says is true because the Church is an authority.
   Mike: What grounds do you have for holding that the Church is a genuine authority?
   Ivan: The authority of the Church is implied in the Bible.
   Mike: And why do you hold that the Bible is true?
   Ivan: Because the Church holds that it is true.

   Which one of the following is the best description of the reasoning involved in the argument presented in the foregoing dialogue?

   (A) deductive
   (B) inductive
   (C) vague
   (D) pointed
   (E) circular

9. *Mary:* All Italians are great lovers.
   Kathy: That is not so. I have met some Spaniards who were magnificent lovers.

   Kathy's reply to Mary indicates that she has misunderstood Mary's remark to mean that

   (A) every great lover is an Italian
   (B) Italians are best at the art of love
   (C) Spaniards are inferior to Italians
   (D) Italians are more likely to be great lovers than are Spaniards
   (E) there is a relationship between nationality and love

Questions 10–11

Mr. Dimple: Mrs. Wilson's qualifications are ideal for the position. She is intelligent, forceful, determined, and trustworthy. I suggest we hire her immediately.

10. Which one of the following, if true, would most weaken Mr. Dimple's statement?

    (A) Mrs. Wilson is not interested in being hired.
    (B) There are two other applicants whose qualifications are identical to Mrs. Wilson's.
    (C) Mrs. Wilson is currently working for a rival company.
    (D) Mr. Dimple is not speaking directly to the hiring committee.
    (E) Mrs. Wilson is older than many of the other applicants.

11. Which one of the following, if true, offers the strongest support of Mr. Dimple's statement?

    (A) All the members of the hiring committee have agreed that intelligence, trustworthiness, determination, and forcefulness are important qualifications for the job.
    (B) Mr. Dimple holds exclusive responsibility for hiring new employees.
    (C) Mr. Dimple has known Mrs. Wilson longer than he has known any of the other applicants.
    (D) Mrs. Wilson is a member of Mr. Dimple's family.
    (E) Mrs. Dimple is intelligent, forceful, determined, and trustworthy.

GO ON TO THE NEXT PAGE ➤

12. All of the candidates for the spring track team must have participated in fall cross-country and winter track. Some runners, however, find cross-country tedious, and refuse to run in the fall. Thus, some winter track runners who would like to be members of the spring track teams are not permitted to try out.

In which one of the following is the reasoning most like that of this passage?

(A) Mice become aggressive if confined in close quarters for an extended period of time, or if they are deprived of protein-rich foods. Therefore, highly aggressive mice have been closely confined and denied high-protein foods.

(B) Roses grown in full sun are less susceptible to mildew than roses grown in partial shade. Roses grown in partial shade are also more susceptible to black spot. Thus, roses should be grown in full sun.

(C) To qualify for the June primary, a candidate for office must reside in the district for six months and gather 500 signatures of district residents who support the candidate. Thus, a longtime district resident would not qualify for the June primary if she gathered only 300 signatures.

(D) A convenience store sells three chocolate bars for a dollar, and a large soft drink for 50 cents. A competitor sells four chocolate bars for a dollar, and a medium-size soft drink for 50 cents. Therefore, neither of the two stores offers more for the same price.

(E) The City Council has passed an ordinance that allows cyclists to use the city bike paths only if they are over 12 years old and are wearing bicycle helmets. Thus, parents with children under 12 will be unable to cycle with their families on the city bike paths unless they wear helmets.

13. When a dental hygienist cleans your teeth, you may not see much evidence that she is supervised by a dentist. Hygienists often work pretty much on their own, even though they are employed by dentists. Then why can't hygienists practice independently, perhaps saving patients a lot of money in the process? The patients would not have to pay the steep profit that many dentists make on the hygienists' labors.

Which one of the following statements weakens the argument above?

(A) Some patients might get their teeth cleaned more often if it costs less.

(B) Some dentists do not employ dental hygienists.

(C) Hygienists must be certified by state examinations.

(D) A dentist should be on hand to inspect a hygienist's work to make sure the patient has no problems that the hygienist is unable to detect.

(E) In some states, there are more female hygienists than male.

14. There are those of us who, determined to be happy, are discouraged repeatedly by social and economic forces that cause us nothing but trouble. And there are those of us who are blessed with health and wealth and still grumble and complain about almost everything.

To which one of the following points can the author be leading?

(A) Happiness is both a state of mind and a state of affairs.

(B) Both personal and public conditions can make happiness difficult to attain.

(C) Happiness may be influenced by economic forces and by health considerations.

(D) No one can be truly happy.

(E) Exterior forces and personal views determine happiness.

GO ON TO THE NEXT PAGE ➤

15. "Keep true, never be ashamed of doing right; decide on what you think is right and stick to it."—*George Eliot*

    If one were to follow Eliot's advice, one

    (A) would never change one's mind
    (B) would do what is right
    (C) might never know what is right
    (D) would never be tempted to do wrong
    (E) would not discriminate between right and wrong

16. To paraphrase Oliver Wendell Holmes, taxes keep us civilized. Just look around you, at well-paved superhighways, air-conditioned schools, and modernized prisons, and you cannot help but agree with Holmes.

    Which one of the following is the strongest criticism of the statement above?

    (A) The author never actually met Holmes.
    (B) The author does not acknowledge those of us who do not live near highways, schools, and prisons.
    (C) The author does not assure us that he has been in a modernized prison.
    (D) The author does not offer a biographical sketch of Holmes.
    (E) The author does not define "civilized."

Questions 17–18

Information that is published is part of the public record. But information that a reporter collects, and sources that he contacts, must be protected in order for our free press to function free of fear.

17. The above argument is most severely weakened by which one of the following statements?

    (A) Public information is usually reliable.
    (B) Undocumented evidence may be used to convict an innocent person.
    (C) Members of the press act ethically in most cases.
    (D) The sources that a reporter contacts are usually willing to divulge their identity.
    (E) Our press has never been altogether free.

18. Which one of the following statements is consistent with the argument above?

    (A) Privileged information has long been an important and necessary aspect of investigative reporting.
    (B) Not all the information a reporter collects becomes part of the public record.
    (C) Tape-recorded information is not always reliable.
    (D) The victim of a crime must be protected at all costs.
    (E) The perpetrator of a crime must be protected at all costs.

GO ON TO THE NEXT PAGE ➤

Questions 19–21

A federal court ruling that San Diego County can't sue the government for the cost of medical care of illegal aliens is based upon a legal technicality that ducks the larger moral question. But the U.S. Supreme Court's refusal to review this decision has closed the last avenue of legal appeal.

The medical expenses of indigent citizens or legally resident aliens are covered by state and federal assistance programs. The question of who is to pay when an undocumented alien falls ill remains unresolved, however, leaving California counties to bear this unfair and growing burden.

19. The author implies that

(A) the U.S. Supreme Court has refused to review the federal court ruling
(B) the burden of medical expenses for aliens is growing
(C) the larger moral question involves no legal technicalities
(D) San Diego should find another avenue of appeal
(E) the federal government is dodging the moral issue

20. Which one of the following arguments, if true, would most seriously weaken the argument above?

(A) There are many cases of undocumented aliens being denied medical aid at state hospitals.
(B) A private philanthropic organization has funded medical aid programs that have so far provided adequate assistance to illegal aliens nationwide.
(C) Illegal aliens do not wish federal or state aid, because those accepting aid risk detection of their illegal status and deportation.
(D) Undocumented aliens stay in California only a short time before moving east.
(E) Judges on the Supreme Court have pledged privately to assist illegal aliens with a favorable ruling once immigration laws are strengthened.

21. Which one of the following changes in the above passage could strengthen the author's argument?

(A) adding interviews with illegal aliens
(B) a description of the stages that led to a rejection by the Supreme Court
(C) a clarification with numbers of the rate at which the burden of medical expenses is growing
(D) the naming of those state and federal assistance programs that aid indigent citizens
(E) the naming of those California counties that do not participate in medical aid to illegal aliens

22. *Historian:* History is strewn with the wreckage of experiments in communal living, often organized around farms and inspired by religious or philosophical ideals. To the more noble failures can now be added Mao Tse-tung's notorious Chinese communes. The current rulers of China, still undoing the mistakes of the late Chairman, are quietly allowing their agricultural communes to . . . .

Which one of the following is the most logical completion of the passage above?

(A) evolve
(B) increase
(C) recycle
(D) disintegrate
(E) organize

23. *Sal:* Herb is my financial planner.
Keith: I'm sure he's good; he's my cousin.

Which one of the following facts is Keith ignoring in his response?

(A) Financial planning is a professional, not a personal, matter.
(B) Sal is probably flattering Keith.
(C) Professional competence is not necessarily a family trait.
(D) "Good" is a term with many meanings.
(E) Sal's financial planner is no one's cousin.

4   4   4   4   4

24. Many very effective prescription drugs are available to patients on a "one time only" basis. Suspicious of drug abuse, physicians will not renew a prescription for a medicine that has worked effectively for a patient. This practice denies a patient her right to health.

Which one of the following is a basic assumption made by the author?

(A) A new type of medicine is likely to be more expensive.
(B) Physicians are not concerned with a patient's health.
(C) Most of the patients who need prescription renewals are female.
(D) Most physicians prescribe inadequate amounts of medicine.
(E) Patients are liable to suffer the same ailment repeatedly.

Questions 25–26

Forty years ago, hardly anybody thought about going to court to sue somebody. A person could bump a pedestrian with his Chrysler Airflow, and the victim would say something like "No harm done" and walk away. Ipso facto. No filing of codicils, taking of depositions, or polling the jury. Attorneys need not apply.

25. Which one of the following sentences most logically continues the above passage?

(A) The Chrysler Airflow is no longer the harmless machine it used to be.
(B) Fortunately, this is still the case.
(C) Unfortunately, times have changed.
(D) New legislation affecting the necessity for codicils is a sign of the times.
(E) But now, as we know, law schools are full of eager young people.

26. Which one of the following details, if true, would most strengthen the above statement?

(A) There were fewer courthouses then than now.
(B) The marked increase in pedestrian accidents is a relatively recent occurrence.
(C) Most citizens of 40 years ago were not familiar with their legal rights.
(D) The number of lawsuits filed during World War II was extremely low.
(E) Most young attorneys were in the armed forces 40 years ago.

STOP

IF YOU FINISH BEFORE TIME IS CALLED, YOU MAY CHECK YOUR WORK ON THIS SECTION ONLY.
DO NOT WORK ON ANY OTHER SECTION IN THE TEST.

5 **5** **5** **5** **5**

SECTION V
TIME — 35 MINUTES
28 QUESTIONS

Directions: Read the passages and answer the questions following each passage by blackening the appropriate space on the answer sheet. You may refer back to the passages when answering the questions. Answer all questions on the basis of what is stated or implied.

In the negotiation of tax treaties, developing nations, as a group, share two objectives somewhat at odds with those of developed-nation treaty
(5) partners. One such goal, attracting foreign investment, is in the broader context of foreign policy objectives. In the narrower realm of tax policy a common developing-country objective
(10) is to maximize the public capture of revenues from foreign investment activities.
  Unfortunately for potential Third World treaty partners, this latter goal can
(15) conflict directly with the desires of both First World governments and individual investors. The preference of First World authorities for restricted source-based taxation is due to considerations
(20) of administrative feasibility. Such restrictions, though formally reciprocal, only produce equitable revenue effects when investment flows between treaty partners are relatively equal. However,
(25) when investment flows primarily in one direction, as it generally does from industrial to developing countries, the seemingly reciprocal source-based restrictions produce revenue sacrifices
(30) primarily by the state receiving most of the foreign investment and producing most of the income—namely, the developing country partner. The benefit is captured either by the taxpayer in the
(35) form of reduced excess credits, or by the treasury of the residence (First World) state as the taxpayer's domestically creditable foreign tax liabilities decrease.

The potential public revenue gain
(40) to the residence state further bolsters the industrial nations' preference for restrictions on source-based taxation—at the direct expense of the treaty partner's revenue goals.
(45)   The facilitation of foreign investment by tax treaties, whereas potentially serving the tax-policy goal of maximizing public revenue, also (or even instead) may serve broader
(50) economic objectives of developing countries. Foreign investments may be seen as essential sources of technical and managerial knowledge, capital, jobs, and foreign exchange. As such, the
(55) significance of foreign investments as an immediate source of public revenue could pale next to their longer-term "ripple effect" on development. In the negotiation of tax treaties, then, a
(60) developing country might be expected to ignore revenue goals and accept substantial limitations on source-based taxation, at least insofar as such limitations could be expected to
(65) encourage investment.
  Frequently, however, Third World nations take a considerably more aggressive approach, seeking treaty terms that, in effect, provide subsidies to
(70) private investors at the expense of First World treaty partners. The United States traditionally has followed a strict policy of "capital export neutrality," providing no tax incentives for investment in the
(75) Third World through either the Internal Revenue Code or tax treaty provisions.

GO ON TO THE NEXT PAGE ➤

5 **5** **5** **5**

1. Normally, a developing country will negotiate a tax treaty for the purpose of

    (A) attracting foreign workers
    (B) decreasing tax revenues
    (C) attracting international investment and reducing tax revenues
    (D) attracting foreign investment and increasing tax revenues
    (E) decreasing dependence on special interest local investors

2. We can infer that a reciprocal source-based taxation treaty between a First World and a developing nation will produce

    (A) greater revenues for the First World nation
    (B) greater revenues for the developing nation
    (C) equal revenues for each country
    (D) no revenues for either country
    (E) losses to the economy of the First World nation

3. In negotiated treaties with developing countries, a First World country is likely to prefer

    (A) unrestricted source-based taxation
    (B) reciprocal restricted source-based taxation
    (C) nonreciprocal source-based taxation
    (D) equal investment flow between the partners
    (E) limited investment flow between the partners

4. In a treaty with a developing country that generates an excess of foreign tax credits, all of the following are likely EXCEPT:

    (A) the treaty will require some reduction of at-source taxation
    (B) the treaty will discourage private investors
    (C) the treaty will not produce what is perceived as the optimal revenue-producing balance
    (D) the treaty will require some expansion of at-source taxation
    (E) the excess of tax credits will be larger if the source country reserves more taxing jurisdiction

5. According to the passage, all of the following are potential advantages of foreign investment to developing countries EXCEPT:

    (A) increased managerial expertise
    (B) increased capital
    (C) increased availability of new materials
    (D) increased foreign exchange
    (E) increased employment

6. A developing country that did not insist upon immediate higher public revenues might be expected to

    (A) deter foreign investment
    (B) increase foreign investment
    (C) avoid the "ripple effect"
    (D) decrease employment
    (E) decrease the availability of raw materials

GO ON TO THE NEXT PAGE ➤

5 **5** **5** **5** **5**

The following paired passages discuss twentieth-century Mexican artists' interpretations of the pre-Columbian world.

Passage A

The pre-Columbian past is everywhere evident in Mexico. Material remains are abundant. Indigenous
line peoples comprise a great majority of
(5) the population. Twentieth-century artists have been cognizant of this past, with [Diego] Rivera at the forefront of those who champion it and José Clemente Orozco equally forceful in
(10) denouncing it. But, regardless of their attitudes toward this past, Mexican artists have not been able to ignore it. All muralists used various aspects of the pre-Columbian world in their
(15) mural programs. Rivera presented it as an ideal world in his National Palace murals, and the conquest as a heroic struggle against all odds. David Alfaro Siqueiros developed a thematic program
(20) in his murals at Chillán, Chile, and in Mexico City, in which Cuauhtemoc personifies the successful fight against the oppressor, symbolized by the centaur—half man, half beast. To
(25) Orozco, this world was inhabited by inhospitable gods, who appear to have more in common with the vengeful god in the Judaic tradition than with the pre-Columbian world. He, of course,
(30) overwhelms the opposition with a massive satyrical [sic] brush, as he on occasion did in his murals. In fact, it is when this part of his personality was allowed to go unchecked that we have
(35) caricature rather than painting.
At any rate, whatever the attitudes toward their pre-Columbian past— *negative* or *positive*—all used a European pictorial language. Even the
(40) techniques are European. The muralists' use of fresco and the thematic and formal programs fit into a European . . . tradition that was initiated in Florence during the fifteenth century by Masaccio
(45) and others. The content is Mexican, the expression is Mexican, the language is European.

Passage B

It must be kept in mind that Mexico was a colonized nation from the
(50) sixteenth to the nineteenth centuries and, despite the 1810 War of Independence that freed Mexico politically from Spain, the colonized mentality of the ruling classes maintained a position of
(55) imitation vis-à-vis European culture and a contempt for indigenous culture.
In Mexico, as in Latin America generally, nationalism has been one of the greatest forces impelling change.
(60) It has been deeply entwined with a necessary sense of dignity, pride, and affirmation. To counter engendered feelings of inferiority, intellectuals have reconstructed the past, and in so doing
(65) have created a mythology of ancient utopias. The Mexican painter who epitomized this tendency was Diego Rivera who, within a framework of Marxism, dialectically compared the
(70) positive and negative forces operating in a historical period, with an emphasis on the positive. In his vast epic of Mexican history on the staircase of the Palacio Nacional, Mexico City, he created a
(75) golden age, where Quetzalcoatl is the prophet. Cultural reaffirmation alone, however, is not the full substance of Rivera's mural. Mexico's Indian population also composed the largest and
(80) most exploited class of the country, the rural base on which the entire economic structure rested. To revitalize this class, to set before it, in a mural, not only its ancient tradition idealized but also its
(85) power to reconstruct the present and control the future, was to continue the work that the military phase of the revolution had started. This is the true significance of Rivera's murals, which
(90) rest on a twin construct of nationalism and indigenism.
Nationalism and indigenism were also elements in the work of both Siqueiros and Orozco, but serving
(95) different purposes. Siqueiros's 1944 mural *Cuauhtémoc Against the Myth* used the Aztec emperor as a symbol of the possibility of a struggle against seemingly overwhelming forces. On

GO ON TO THE NEXT PAGE ➤

(100) the surface, Orozco disdained the use of nationalism, partly because of his scorn for romanticized visions of Indian life "fit to flatter the tourist" and partly because of a middle-class snobbery

(105) directed at "hateful and degenerate types of the lower classes" that caused him to eschew the painting of "Indian sandals and dirty clothes." Nevertheless, his treatment of the positive aspects

(110) of the human condition often present Quetzalcoatl and the revolutionary heroes Hidalgo and Zapata in heroic and grandiose terms.

7. Which one of the following is the best description of the subject of both passages?

(A) The reaction to colonialism by twentieth-century Mexican muralists
(B) The techniques dominating the work of Mexican muralists
(C) Pre-Columbian mysticism in the works of the muralists
(D) The differences among the three main Mexican muralists
(E) Pre-Columbian influence on three Mexican muralists

8. From information in both Passage A and Passage B, which one of the following can be inferred?

(A) Diego Rivera most successfully captured pre-Columbian history in his murals.
(B) The three major muralists rejected European painting techniques.
(C) Of the three major muralists, Orozco's attitude toward the pre-Columbian past was the most ambivalent.
(D) Siqueiros primarily produced murals depicting life during the period of colonialism.
(E) Only Rivera used his art for political purposes.

9. Which one of the following statements illustrates a contrast between Passage A and Passage B?

(A) Passage A mentions the technique used by the muralists, whereas Passage B does not.
(B) Passage B praises the work of Rivera, Orozco, and Siqueiros, whereas Passage A is neutral toward Siqueiros.
(C) Passage A places the works of the muralists in historical context, whereas Passage B places them in a sociopolitical context.
(D) Passage B describes the public's reaction to the works of the muralists, whereas Passage A does not.
(E) Passage A identifies Rivera as the most important of the Mexican muralists, whereas Passage B makes no judgment.

10. According to Passage A and Passage B, all of the following characterize Orozco EXCEPT:

(A) his tendency to use caricature in his works
(B) his portrayal of the gods as unfriendly
(C) his snobbery toward the lower-class Indian population
(D) his romanticized picture of the indigenous population
(E) his use of satire

11. The term "cultural reaffirmation" (line 76) in Passage B refers to which one of the following?

(A) The use of indigenous art and culture in the muralists' works
(B) Antagonism toward European domination of art
(C) The public's interest in and acceptance of pre-Columbian art
(D) The insistence on a nationalistic spirit in modern Mexican art
(E) Attempts by the muralists to glorify the accomplishments of pre-Columbian artists

GO ON TO THE NEXT PAGE ➤

5   **5**

12. According to Passage B, Diego Rivera's primary political intention in his mural of Mexican history was to

(A) show his feelings about Karl Marx
(B) depict the heroic battles of the revolution
(C) energize the Indian population and direct it to the future
(D) create an artistic language for modern Mexico
(E) preserve pre-Columbian symbolism and mythology

13. According to both passages, all of the following are mentioned or implied as characterizing the Mexican muralists EXCEPT:

(A) the use of Mexican subject matter
(B) disdain for European art
(C) recognition of the indigenous population
(D) appreciation for pre-Columbian works of art
(E) reference to Mexican heroes

War and change—political and economic foremost, but social and cultural not far behind—have been
line linked in America from the beginning.
(5) War was the necessary factor in the birth of the new American republic, as it has been in the birth of every political state known to us in history. War, chiefly the Civil War, in U.S.
(10) history has been a vital force in the rise of industrial capitalism, in the change of America from a predominantly agrarian and pastoral country to one chiefly manufacturing in nature. War,
(15) in focusing the mind of a country, stimulates inventions, discoveries, and fresh adaptations. Despite its manifest illth*, war, by the simple fact of the intellectual and social changes it
(20) instigates, yields results which are tonics to advancement.

By all odds, the most important war in U.S. history, the war that released the greatest number and diversity of changes
(25) in American life, was the Great War, the war that began in Europe in August 1914 and engulfed the United States in April 1917. Great changes in America were immediate.
(30) In large measure these changes reflected a release from the sense of isolation, insularity, and exceptionalism that had suffused so much of the American mind during the nineteenth
(35) century. The early Puritans had seen their new land as a "city upon a hill" with the eyes of the world on it. It was not proper for the New World to go to the Old for its edification; what
(40) was proper was for the Old World, grown feeble and hidebound, to come to America for inspiration. A great deal of that state of mind entered into what Tocqueville called the "American
(45) Religion," a religion compounded of Puritanism and ecstatic nationalism.

*illth = ill effects (word coined by the author earlier in the full selection)

GO ON TO THE NEXT PAGE ➤

What we think of today as modernity—in manners and morals as well as ideas and mechanical things—
(50) came into full-blown existence in Europe in the final part of the nineteenth century, its centers such cities as London, Paris, and Vienna. In contrast America was a "closed" society, one
(55) steeped in conventionality and also in a struggle for identity. This was how many Europeans saw America and it was emphatically how certain somewhat more sophisticated Americans
(60) saw themselves. The grand tour was a veritable obligation of better-off, ambitious, and educated Americans— the tour being, of course, of Europe.
     Possibly the passage of American
(65) values, ideas, and styles from "closed" to "open," from the isolated to the cosmopolitan society, would have taken place, albeit more slowly, had there been no transatlantic war of 1914–1918. We
(70) can't be sure. What we do know is that the war, and America's entrance into it, gave dynamic impact to the processes of secularization, individualization, and other kinds of social-psychological
(75) change which so drastically changed this country from the America of the turn of the century to the America of the 1920s.

14. In the passage the author makes all of the following points about war EXCEPT:

   (A) war increases the pace of changes that might occur anyway
   (B) war stimulates new inventions and discoveries
   (C) war causes social and intellectual changes
   (D) war in a capitalistic society is inevitable
   (E) war sometimes stimulates a closed society toward greater openness

15. If true, which of the following best illustrates the author's point about the effects of war on American society?

   (A) During World War II, the Germans developed a variety of lethal nerve gas to use in the field.
   (B) The development of radioactive isotopes used in treating cancer grew out of research to build the atomic bomb used in World War II.
   (C) The American influenza epidemic of 1919 in all likelihood was a result of the return of infected soldiers from the battlefields of World War I.
   (D) After the Civil War and the abolition of slavery in the South, racial intolerance across America grew in bitterness.
   (E) A significant drain on America's material resources was a result of relaxed immigration policies occurring after World War II.

16. According to the author, World War I was the most important war in U.S. history because it

   (A) ended the notion of a war to end all wars
   (B) resulted in a weakened Germany that in turn led to Hitler's appeal
   (C) changed America from a dominantly agrarian country to a manufacturing country
   (D) led to more changes and a wider diversity of changes than any other American war
   (E) made Americans more aware of advances made in European centers such as London, Paris, and Vienna

GO ON TO THE NEXT PAGE ➤

5 **5** **5** **5** **5**

17. The main purpose of paragraph 3 is to

   (A) characterize the American mind in the nineteenth century
   (B) define Tocqueville's concept of American religion
   (C) indicate the main cause of America's entrance into World War I
   (D) contrast Civil War America with World War I America
   (E) indicate the areas of America's strength at the start of World War I

18. According to the author, which one of the following contributed to America's insularity before World War I?

   (A) The inability of all but the most wealthy, educated Americans to travel abroad
   (B) The nationalistic view that the New World (America) shouldn't turn to the Old World (Europe) for ideas
   (C) The emphasis on agrarian pursuits as opposed to belief in industry and technology
   (D) The puritanical idea that traveling widely in the world exposed one to sin and corruption
   (E) The superiority of the New World (America) to a feeble, decadent Old World (Europe)

19. Which one of the following best describes the main subject of this passage?

   (A) a comparison of wars in America
   (B) the benefits of war to society
   (C) the importance of World War I to changes in America
   (D) the contrast between the New World (America) and the Old World (Europe)
   (E) secularization and individualization in American society

20. The relationship of paragraph 1 to the rest of the passage is best described by which one of the following?

   (A) It presents a popular view that is proved inadequate by the rest of the passage.
   (B) It introduces a philosophical question that is then answered in the rest of the passage.
   (C) It outlines the contents of each of the other four paragraphs in the passage.
   (D) It sets up the first of four examples developed in the rest of the passage.
   (E) It presents a general idea that introduces the specific topic developed in the rest of the passage.

21. According to information in the passage, all of the following inferences can be made EXCEPT:

   (A) Well-to-do nineteenth-century American parents would be more likely to send their son to Europe than to California.
   (B) European "ecstatic nationalism" would be greater after World War I than before it.
   (C) Religious influence in the daily workings of American society would be less evident in 1920 than 1900.
   (D) A census in America 20 years after the Civil War would indicate more manufacturing operations than before the war.
   (E) In the nineteenth century, avant garde movements in art and literature would be more likely to originate in Europe than in the United States.

The theory of natural selection cites the fact that every organism produces more gametes and/or organisms than *line* can possibly survive. If every gamete
(5) produced by a given species united in fertilization and developed into offspring, the world would become so overcrowded in a short period of time that there would be no room for
(10) successive generations. This does not happen. There is a balance that is maintained in the reproduction of all species and therefore natural populations remain fairly stable, unless
(15) upset by a change in conditions. In the struggle for existence, some organisms die and the more hardy survive.

The differences that exist between organisms of the same species, making
(20) one more fit to survive than another, can be explained in terms of variations. Variations exist in every species and in every trait in members of a species. Therefore some organisms can compete
(25) more successfully than others for the available food or space in which to grow, or they can elude their enemies better. These variations are said to add survival value to an organism.
(30) Survival value traits are passed on to the offspring by those individuals that live long enough to reproduce. As time goes on, these special adaptations for survival are perpetuated and new species evolve
(35) from a common ancestral species. The environment is the selecting agent in natural selection because it determines which variations are satisfactory for survival and which are not.
(40) The major weakness in Darwin's theory of natural selection is that he did not explain the source, or genetic basis, for variations. He did not distinguish between variations that are hereditary
(45) and those that are nonhereditary, making the assumption that all variations that have survival value are passed on to the progeny. Like Jean Baptiste Lamarck, Darwin believed
(50) in the inheritance of even acquired characteristics.

Hugo De Vries (1845–1935), a Dutch botanist, explained variations in terms of mutations. His study of 50,000 plants
(55) belonging to the evening primrose species enabled him to identify changes in the plants that were passed on from parent to offspring. In 1901 De Vries offered his mutation theory to explain
(60) organic evolution. Today, we know that mutations are changes in genes that can come about spontaneously or can be induced by some mutagenic agent. Spontaneous mutation rates are very
(65) low, and mutations alone do not affect major changes in the frequencies of alleles, which are alternative forms of genes that occupy a given place on a chromosone.
(70) An important cause of variation within species is genetic recombination that results from sexual reproduction. The genes of two individuals are sorted out and recombined into a new
(75) combination, producing new traits—and thus variation.

Gene flow is also responsible for the development of variations. It is the movement of new genes into a
(80) population. Gene flow often acts against the effects of natural selection. Genetic drift is a change in a gene pool that takes place in a population as a result of chance. If a mutation occurs in a
(85) gene of one person, and that person does not reproduce, the gene is lost to the population. Sometimes a small population breaks off from a larger one. Within that population is a mutant gene,
(90) and because the mating within the small population is very close, the frequencies of the mutant gene will increase. In the Amish population, for example, where there is little or no outbreeding,
(95) an increase in the homozygosity of the genes in the gene pool is evinced in the high frequencies of genetic dwarfism and polydactyly (six fingers). The isolated smaller population has a
(100) different gene frequency than the larger population from which it came. This is known as the "founder principle."

GO ON TO THE NEXT PAGE ➤

5   **5**

Genetic drift and the random mutations that increase or decrease as the result
(105) of genetic drift are known as non-Darwinian evolution.

Another cause of variation is speciation, or the forming of new species from a species already in
(110) existence. This can happen when a population becomes geographically divided and part of the original species continues life in a new habitat. The separated populations cannot interbreed.
(115) Over evolutionary time, different environments present different selective pressures, and the change in gene pools will eventually produce new species.

22. The passage supports which one of the following statements?

(A) Spontaneous mutations cause the most significant evolutionary changes.

(B) Darwin's theory of evolution depends on rejecting the idea that acquired characteristics can be inherited.

(C) Variations among individual members of a species occur only when new genes move into an established population of that species.

(D) It is possible for a survival value trait to be eliminated from a species.

(E) New species are generally the result of genetic recombination.

23. Which one of the following, if true, would support the idea that acquired characteristics can be inherited?

(A) A spontaneous mutation causes some members of a rodent population to develop webbed feet. This segment of the population becomes isolated and is unable to breed with the original group. An exceptionally high frequency of webbed feet occurs in the successive generations of the isolated segment.

(B) A gene from a virus is experimentally transmitted to a fruit fly, making it vulnerable to carbon dioxide poison. This vulnerability is then passed on to the fruit fly's offspring.

(C) Antelopes raised in captivity are released into the wild. They run significantly more slowly than the wild antelope. After a year, the released antelopes' speed equals that of the wild antelopes.

(D) A population of long-haired dogs is shaved and bred with a population of hairless dogs. Their offspring include more hairless than long-haired pups.

(E) Fourteen different species of finches live on the Galapagos Islands. It is determined that all descended from a single species of finch found on mainland Peru.

GO ON TO THE NEXT PAGE ➤

24. The passage provides explanations for each of the following EXCEPT:

    (A) genetic drift
    (B) the founder principle
    (C) survival value
    (D) speciation
    (E) homozygosity

25. Random mutations are known as non-Darwinian evolution because they

    (A) are not necessarily related to the survival value of an organism
    (B) are more infrequent than spontaneous mutations
    (C) tend to refute Darwin's theories about the formation of species
    (D) occur only in small populations that have been isolated
    (E) were first described by Hugo De Vries, not Charles Darwin

26. The founder principle

    (A) accounts for genetic dwarfism
    (B) supports the importance of "weeding out" non-adaptive organisms
    (C) explains the concept of homozygosity
    (D) relates to gene frequencies in isolated populations
    (E) refutes Darwin's theory of natural selection

27. Based on the passage, which one of the following can be inferred about Charles Darwin?

    (A) Darwin did not believe the theory of genetic inheritance.
    (B) Darwin did not believe that genetic theories were relevant to evolution.
    (C) Darwin's work was more concerned with the survival value of traits than with the mechanics of how they were inherited.
    (D) Darwin's theories did not include a recognition that variation within members of a species was crucial to evolution.
    (E) Darwin was more interested in traits that were acquired and passed on than he was in genetically inherited traits.

28. In the passage, the author's primary concern is to

    (A) address briefly the history of evolutionary theory
    (B) provide a brief overview of the concept of variation
    (C) expose the weakness inherent in Darwin's evolutionary theory
    (D) differentiate between genetic and evolutionary theories
    (E) describe one of the ways in which nonadaptive traits can be inherited

STOP

IF YOU FINISH BEFORE TIME IS CALLED, YOU MAY CHECK YOUR WORK ON THIS SECTION ONLY.
DO NOT WORK ON ANY OTHER SECTION IN THE TEST.

Writing Sample

Directions: You have 35 minutes to write an essay in response to a given topic. Take a few minutes to plan your work before you begin writing. DO NOT WRITE ON A TOPIC OF YOUR OWN CHOICE. ESSAYS THAT DO NOT ADDRESS THE GIVEN TOPIC ARE UNACCEPTABLE.

The quality of your writing is more important than the length of your response or the content. Pay attention to organization, appropriate diction, and correct usage. You will not be expected to display any specialized knowledge in your response, nor will you be expected to write a "perfect" essay; law schools understand that you are writing under a time constraint, and will allow for the minor lapses in writing ability that might occur under this circumstance.

Only the lined area on your response sheets will be reproduced for the law schools, so do not write outside this space. Make sure your handwriting is legible.

Scratch Paper
Do not write your essay in this space

Sample Topic

Read the following descriptions of Thomas and Peters, candidates for the position of head coach of the Ventura Vultures professional football team. *Then, in the space provided, write an argument for appointing one candidate over the other.* Use the information in this description and assume that the two general policies below equally guide the Vultures' decision on the appointment:

- The head coach should possess the ability to work with players and coaching staff toward achieving a championship season.
- The head coach should successfully manage the behind-the-scenes activities of recruiting, analyzing scouting reports, and handling the media and fans in order to enhance the public relations and image of the team.

THOMAS has been General Manager of the Vultures for the past ten years. A physical education major with a master's in psychology, he knows the player personnel as well as anyone, including the coaching staff. His on-target assessment of player skills and weaknesses has been instrumental in building a more balanced team over the past decade through his skillful trading and recruitment of college athletes. As the chief managing officer, he has also enhanced the team's image by his careful press relationship and understated approach when negotiations with star players reached an impasse. He rarely alienates players, coaches, press, or fans with his even-handed (though sometimes unemotional) attitude, and the Vultures' owners feel fortunate that they were able to entice him away from his high-school coaching position, which he left 10 years ago. He has never played either pro or college ball.

PETERS is presently a wide receiver and defensive end for the Vultures. A one-time star, Peters has played both offense and defense for the Vultures since their inception in the league 14 years ago, a remarkable feat equaled by few in the game. He was elected captain of the team the past five years because of his charisma, although he occasionally angers management and fellow players with his strong comments about his philosophy of the game. His only experience in the front office was leading a player charity benefit for the Vultures, which raised more than $2,000,000 for abused Ventura County children. Although a high school dropout, Peters is a self-made man who firmly believes the key to life is having a strong educational background, even though he sometimes feels uncomfortable around college-educated athletes. The Vulture owners believe Peters may provide the emotional charge the team needs at its helm to win its first championship.

Scratch Paper
Do not write your essay in this space

Answer Key

Section I: Logical Reasoning

1. A	6. D	11. E	16. D	21. D	26. D
2. A	7. A	12. D	17. D	22. B	
3. D	8. B	13. C	18. C	23. B	
4. E	9. E	14. A	19. A	24. B	
5. C	10. D	15. B	20. D	25. E	

Section II: Reading Comprehension

1. C	6. D	11. B	16. A	21. C	26. D
2. A	7. C	12. D	17. A	22. B	27. A
3. A	8. B	13. E	18. D	23. C	28. E
4. B	9. A	14. A	19. E	24. A	
5. C	10. E	15. B	20. A	25. C	

Section III: Analytical Reasoning

1. E	5. A	9. B	13. B	17. D	21. E
2. C	6. C	10. C	14. B	18. B	22. B
3. D	7. D	11. E	15. E	19. D	23. C
4. B	8. A	12. C	16. D	20. A	

Section IV: Logical Reasoning

1. D	6. B	11. A	16. E	21. C	26. D
2. D	7. A	12. C	17. B	22. D	
3. A	8. E	13. D	18. A	23. C	
4. C	9. A	14. D	19. E	24. E	
5. B	10. B	15. B	20. B	25. C	

Section V: Reading Comprehension

1. D	6. B	11. A	16. D	21. B	26. D
2. A	7. E	12. C	17. A	22. D	27. C
3. B	8. C	13. B	18. B	23. B	28. B
4. D	9. A	14. D	19. C	24. E	
5. C	10. D	15. B	20. E	25. A	

MODEL TEST ANALYSIS

Doing model exams and understanding the explanations afterward are, of course, important in acquainting you with typical LSAT question types and successful approaches to the questions. However, another benefit of carefully analyzing these model tests is to understand the kinds of errors you are making and thus work to minimize them. For instance, if a very high percentage of your incorrect answers is due to "careless error" or "misread problem," then perhaps you are working much too fast and should slow your pace accordingly. If your incorrect answers are due primarily to "lack of knowledge," then a careful rereading and reworking of the appropriate question-type chapter may be in order. Or, if you find that you aren't completing a large number of questions because of lack of time, you may need to either increase your speed or learn to use the "one-check, two-check" technique more effectively.

This kind of analysis of the model tests will enable you to identify your particular weaknesses and thus remedy them.

Model Test Analysis

Section	Total Number of Questions	Number Correct	Number Incorrect	Number Unanswered*
I. Logical Reasoning	26			
II. Reading Comprehension	28			
III. Analytical Reasoning	23			
IV. Logical Reasoning	26			
V. Reading Comprehension	28			
Writing Sample				
TOTALS:	131			

*At this stage in your preparation, you should not be leaving any blank answer spaces. At least fill in a guess, as there is no penalty for a wrong answer.

NOTE: Refer to page 113 for instructions on obtaining your approximate score range.

Reasons for Incorrect Answers

You may wish to evaluate the explanations before completing this chart.

Section	Total Number Incorrect	Lack of Knowledge	Misread Problem	Careless Error	Unanswered or Wrong Guess
I. Logical Reasoning					
II. Reading Comprehension					
III. Analytical Reasoning					
IV. Logical Reasoning					
V. Reading Comprehension					
TOTALS:					

Explanation of Answers

Section I

1. **A** The author must assume that "nothing about our coin influences its fall in favor of either side or that all influences are counterbalanced by equal and opposite influences"; otherwise "our ignorance of the coming result" is untrue. Also, he mentions that the chances are one out of two that the coin will fall heads up; this could not be correct if the coin had been weighted or tampered with.

2. **A** (A) is implied by the author's statement that one-to-two is not "true." (B), (C), (D), and (E) are not implied and would not follow from the passage.

3. **D** The author is actually pointing out that self-confidence is of most importance. (C) and (E) focus on behavior, while the author is focusing on mental attitude.

4. **E** Only choice (E) is supported by these comments. The comments suggest that riding on roller coasters is taking a risk and that this risk translates to a proclivity to taking other risks in life. The passage doesn't suggest, however, that *no* roller coaster riders avoid taking risks elswhere (A), nor does it have any bearing on the importance of taking risks (B). Choice (C) is a difficult one to eliminate because the passage certainly doesn't rule out this possibility (the passage says "than other," not "than *all* others")—but it doesn't directly support it, either. The comments have nothing to do with varying levels or types of risk taking (D).

5. **C** If the diet and way of life of the men of the two islands are alike, but the life expectancies are very different, the cause of the difference is probably something other than diet and the way of life. Some of the other answers are reasonable inferences, but they do not follow so clearly from the paragraph as (C).

6. **D** None of the other four choices offer information that explains the discrepancy. If the women in college are preparing for a profession that pays less (teaching) than the profession the men will enter (engineering), the discrepancy is explained.

7. **A** To conclude that the women should earn as much as or more than the men, the passage must assume that all of the men and all of the women, or at least an equal number, enter the workforce. It also assumes that all of them, or at least an equal number, graduate from college, though the passage says only "are enrolled."

8. **B** The six-month interest-free charge is the money at a low cost; the stock of discontinued summer wear is the slow selling product, and the fashionable new neck wear is the popular product. None of the other choices covers all three conditions.

9. **E** Though all of the choices are plausible, (E) deals with all three of the problems mentioned in the paragraph. Each of the other choices deals only with one.

10. **D** Although Michael may be lying, there is no factual evidence to that effect. Michael is truthful and readily admits to the previous dents to his own vehicle (A). (B) and (C) reinforce Michael's contention that the dents were caused by someone else. Even (E) reflects positively on Michael's character, though it is not mentioned in the original set of conditions.

11. **E** The author states that the present programs are at best weak and hopefully won't fail as they have in the past.

12. **D** The statement that "Hopefully, they won't fail as they have in the past" tells us that our government is not trying a new approach to end inflation. (A) is close, but the passage states that foreign oil is "high-priced," not "overpriced." "High-priced" tells us the relative cost, not the actual comparative value.

13. **C** The conclusion is the prediction of a grim year for home-builders. Choices (A), (B), (D), and (E) do not point to continued bad sales, but (C), revealing that sales fell even with advertising and incentives, supports the prediction of a bad year ahead.

14. **A** Three possibilities exist:
(a) You read *Weight-Off* magazine, are fat, and do not eat chocolate.
(b) You are fat, eat chocolate, but do not read *Weight-Off* magazine.
(c) You eat chocolate, are not fat, and do not read *Weight-Off* magazine.

Thus, (A) is inconsistent by (a) and (b). (B) is not inconsistent if (b) and (c) are void of people. (C) is not inconsistent if (c) is void of people. (D) and (E) are not inconsistent by (c) and (a).

15. **B** Dave felt that Jerry implied that no one except Jerry's wife cooks fantastic meals.

16. **D** Only (D) offers an instance of success in the polls. (A) simply repeats a point of the passage without including the qualification that comes later. Choices (B), (C), and (E) would support rather than undermine the viewpoint of the passage.

17. **D** The passage does not point out inherent inconsistencies. It does support a point with a specific example (the two figures on the balanced budget poll), question the honesty of politicians (the phrase "or may not"), reinterprets the 80 percent support figure, and shows how statistics can be used to mislead.

18. **C** Decreasing the fares on lightly traveled routes might attract some passengers away from the overcrowded, more popular flights, but increasing the fares would not help to solve the luggage problem. The four other suggestions are plausible ways of dealing with the lack of space.

19. **A** X's new realization is expressed in his final sentence: "We must know all the characteristics of men, and that Socrates has all of them, before we can be sure." The "characteristics of men" are what is implied by the generalization "man," in "Socrates is a man." Therefore, deductive thinking is simply reminding ourselves of the particular specifics implied by generalizations.

20. **D** Symbolically, A is necessary to have B (a good telescope to see moons of Neptune). You do not have B (can't see moons with my telescope). Therefore, you cannot have A (a good telescope). (D) is the only choice that follows this line of reasoning. Symbolically, A is necessary to have B (knowing area of circle to find circumference). You do not have B (can't figure out circumference). Therefore, you cannot have A (area of circle).

21. **D** Extensive psychological research would most likely give the information that the author discusses. (E) limits the research to clinical psychologists and to recent findings.

22. **B** "Conscious behavior eventually becomes habit" is indirectly stated in the last sentence. (A) is a close answer, but that absolute word "all" is inconsistent with the words "can become" in the last sentence. This does not imply that they *must* become unconscious behavior.

23. **B** The given advice would be strengthened by the assurance that such measures are effective. Each of the other choices either weakens the advice, or addresses only a portion of the paragraph.

24. **B** The disease under discussion is termed "it," and thus its identity is unclear. The other choices either are not applicable to the second sentence or refer to terms that require no further definition.

25. **E** (E) weakens the argument that young people have abundant time. The other choices are only tangentially relevant to the argument.

26. **D** The passage says that worrying about writing unfortunately keeps one from writing at all; (D) summarizes this viewpoint. (B) and (C) are irrelevant notions; (A) contradicts the author's implied support for writing theorists; and (E) is an unreasonable, unsupported conclusion.

Section II

Passage 1

1. **C** The chief purpose of the Sixth Amendment was to ensure the assistance of counsel in criminal cases. The guarantee to the right of self-representation was not the chief purpose of the amendment although the amendment has been used to support it.

2. **A** The phrase refers to the end of the second paragraph. The author regards the waiving of the right to counsel as a choice, which should not be seen as a guarantee of the right of self-representation.

3. **A** The phrase "*in propria persona*" means "in his own person," "by himself," or "by herself."

4. **B** If the Court had believed a fair trial was impossible without the assistance of counsel, it would not have allowed self-representation.

5. **C** The passage emphasizes the importance of warning a defendant of the risks of self-representation.

6. **D** Though true, the tradition of self-representation is not a valid objection to the practice. In fact, it might be cited as an argument in favor of self-representing defendants.

Passage 2

7. **C** The passage states that African arts were curiosities and were presented as evidence of the "low state of heathen savagery of the African." The implication of lines 18–25 is that the arts, like the government and history, were not worth notice. (D) and (E) are incorrect; nothing is implied concerning the proportions or the subjects of African art. (A) and (B) both suggest a positive reaction to the art; this reaction is not supported by the passage.

8. **B** See lines 12–18. (C), whether true or not, is not supported by the passage. (D) is incorrect; Africa wasn't a threat to European society. In fact, Africans were exploited or made objects of missionary zeal. (A) and (E) are clearly irrelevant or incorrect.

9. **A** The writings of Pliny are cited as one of the early sources of knowledge about Africa—not one of the factors contributing to a change in the European view. See lines 26–34 for support of (B), (C), (D), and (E).

10. **E** Lines 35–38 make it clear that cultural relativism refers to viewing a culture in its own terms and on its own merits rather than judging it by the standards of one's own culture. (E) most clearly defines this point of view in relation to art. (A) is incorrect; the passage does not suggest that value judgments about works of art cannot be made, as long as the works are judged against the values of their own culture. (B) and (C) are irrelevant to the idea of cultural relativism. (D) is also irrelevant, and its judgment is not supported by any statements in the passage.

11. **B** See lines 46–53. The author states that when the attitude toward African art did change, it changed as a result of an "excess of romantic rebellion" against Classicism and Naturalism, not as a result of an objective assessment. No point is made in the passage about the availability of African art (A). (C) is unclear, and (D) is clearly inaccurate. The judgments of missionaries (E) were irrelevant to the twentieth-century European assessment of African art.

12. **D** See lines 75–85. One of the author's main points is that African art was very much in tune with its audience, unlike modern European art, which represented a rebellion against European traditions. (A) is the opposite of the point the author makes about African art. (B) and (E) are irrelevant and not supported by information in the passage. (C) is incorrect because although the author says we cannot have full understanding of African art if we judge it by twentieth-century Western aesthetic standards, we can still "admire" the works in a limited way. See lines 68–74.

13. **E** See lines 89–93. The author states that the works of art, while conservative and conformist, were not "passive reflections" of the culture; the perishable nature of wood ensured that every generation reaffirmed its faith. No comparison between wood and stone is made (with the exception of the implied comparison of impermanence and permanence). Therefore, (A) and (B) are incorrect. Also, no point is made about Western art or the Western world (C), (D).

14. **A** Throughout the passage the author talks about European or Western reactions to African art, from the earliest knowledge of Africa in Europe until the twentieth-century reassessment of African art. No specific works are analyzed (B), nor is any information included about African religious and social beliefs (D) or African aesthetic principles (E).

Passage 3

15. **B** (B) is the best choice because the passage first describes the classic model of competition and then introduces what the author refers to as the concept of "countervailing power." Although the ideas in (D) and (E) are both present in the passage, these titles are too restrictive. (A) is incomplete, and (C) is clearly wrong, in that the passage doesn't specifically address "American capitalism."

16. **A** (A) is directly from the passage (lines 17–21). Although (B) and (C) might occur, these are not part of the classic competition model described by the author. (E) would certainly not provide a return to normal prices; although it might offer a change in *supply*, it would not alter *demand*. Answer (D) is simply unclear.

17. **A** (A) is the best choice. See lines 26–32. (D) and (E) are clearly wrong. (C) is unclear. The second-best answer is (B), since the behavior of manufacturers is ultimately related to competition for the customer. However, (A) is the more specific answer provided by the passage.

18. **D** (D) is the best choice. See lines 44–52. (A) is incorrect because the classic model of competition does *not* ignore the role of labor (lines 26–30). Also, although the author might agree that greed undermined the classic model, this is not an issue addressed in the passage. (B) is incorrect because the author does not relate change in self-regulation of competition to any particular event, nor does he place it in a specific time frame. (C) is clearly the opposite of the point made in the passage. The restraint of "sellers by other sellers and buyers by other buyers" is part of the classic model of competition. (E) is incorrect because, according to the author, "countervailing power" did not destroy competition but grew as a result of a change in the classic model, i.e., the reduction of the number of competitors and resulting concentration of power among a small group of firms.

19. **E** Organizations that network manufacturers would not provide a customer- or supplier-generated restraint on them, which is the way the author defines "countervailing power." All of the other choices are possible wielders of "countervailing power."

20. **A** In lines 32–44 and lines 52–56, the author makes it clear that economists have almost exclusively focused on the classic model of competition in considering restraints on manufacturers. (B) is incorrect because the author does not discuss government regulation or the lack of it as part of economic theory. Similarly, (C) is incorrect; the "trickle-down" theory (i.e., that what is good for those at the top will ultimately benefit those at the bottom) is also not mentioned in the passage. (D) is contradicted in the passage; according to the author, economists did recognize the trend toward concentration (lines 44–52, 73–80). Finally, although the author might agree with (E), the passage suggests that economists have been preoccupied with the classic model of competition (including its built-in restraints) rather than biased toward "unregulated" capitalism. The preoccupation with the classic models led them to ignore other types of restraint in the economy.

21. **C** The passage sets up the classic model of competition in paragraphs 1 and 2. Paragraph 3 is a shift in the discussion to the idea that there might be a restraining mechanism exclusive of the competitive model that economists haven't recognized. Paragraphs 4 and 5 describe this restraining mechanism. The second-best answer is (D); however, paragraph 3 does provide a transition, which makes (C) the better choice.

Passage 4

22. **B** Although Passage B includes Lavoisier, its focus is on the caloric theory of heat, while Passage A covers other aspects of the scientist, not just one theory. Passage B, while showing how Lavoisier's theory of heat was later disproved, does not "discredit" him (A). (E) is also inaccurate; while showing how theories can be supplanted by new theories, the author's tone toward science is not skeptical.

23. **C** The use of the term follows the statement that Lavoisier disproved the theory of phlogiston, a nonexistent substance (or "flammability principle"). It is ironic that he then posits another substance, caloric, that cannot be weighed or measured.

24. **A** In lines 31–34, the passage states that Lavoisier's methods led to his proof that oxygen and hydrogen made up water, and therefore (A) is the best answer. Lavoisier's caloric theory was incorrect in explaining heat (B) and (D), and it was Priestley (mentioned in Passage B), not Lavoisier, who isolated eight gases (E). Although Passage A says that Lavoisier produced better gunpowder, there is no indication that he changed its composition (C).

25. **C** (C) is the best example of the author's point in the first paragraph. In lines 127–136, two specific examples are given of how observable facts can be explained by Lavoisier's caloric theory, a theory that was later proved wrong. None of the other choices are observable facts explained by the caloric theory.

26. **D** The best answer is (D), a point the author makes in the first paragraph. The passage doesn't imply either that alchemy "contributed nothing to science" (A) or that thermodynamics is an inexact science (C). Although (E) may seem like a possible answer, the author doesn't criticize the scientific method but merely suggests that theories can be disproved or modified in time.

27. **A** (A) is the best answer (lines 28–31). Although Lavoisier did believe in a fluid called caloric, he thought it caused heat, not combustion (E). (B) was part of the phlogiston theory, not Lavoisier's theory, and (C) and (D) are related to theories after Lavoisier.

28. **E** Passage B refers to Priestley as an important eighteenth century scientist who firmly believed in the phlogiston theory, making (E) the best answer.

Section III

Answers 1–6

UPPER-case letters denote colors given in the problem, and lower-case letters denote deduced colors.

1. **E**

1	2	3	4	5	
b/w	R	W	b	R	(flag)
w/g	B	g	w	B	(pennant)

The 3rd pennant cannot be blue or white, so therefore it is green. The 4th flag cannot be white or red, so it must be blue. The 4th pennant cannot be green or blue, so it must be white. The 1st flag cannot be red, so it is either blue or white. The 1st pennant cannot be blue, so it must be green or white.

2. **C**

1	2	3	4	5	
R	w	r/b			(flag)
g/w	B	g/w			(pennant)

(A) is clearly true. If the 5th flag is red, then the 3rd flag cannot be, since the 1st flag is red and we can have only two of any one color. Thus, (B) is true. If the 4th pennant is green, then the 3rd pennant must be white. But that does not determine the color of the 1st pennant. Thus, (C) is not necessarily true. (D) is the same as (A) and is also true. If the 4th pennant is green, this implies that the 3rd pennant must be white. If the 5th pennant is white, then the 1st pennant cannot be. Therefore, (E) is true.

3. **D** Here is what you start with:

	1	2	3	4	5
Flag		W		W	
Pennant		B		B	

The 2nd and 4th flags cannot be white because they are adjacent to white flags and they cannot be blue because they would be the same colors as the pennants on the same flagpoles. Therefore, they must be red (A).

	1	2	3	4	5
Flag		W	R	W	R
Pennant		B		B	

For the same reasons, the 1st and 3rd pennants cannot be white or blue, so they must be green (B) and (C).

	1	2	3	4	5
Flag		W	R	W	R
Pennant	G	B	G	B	

Since no more than two flags or pennants of the same color can be flying at the same time, the 5th flagpole must have a blue flag and a white pennant (E). The 5th pennant could not be green because there are already two green pennants flying (D). (D) is therefore false.

	1	2	3	4	5
Flag		W	R	W	R	B
Pennant	G	B	G	B	W

4. **B**

1	2	3	4	5	
B	w	r	B		(flag)
	W	g			(pennant)

Statement (B) is true since the 1st pennant cannot be blue or white. Statement (A) is false since the 5th pennant could be blue or white. Statement (C) is false since it is white. Statements (D) and (E) are false since they could be white.

5. **A**

1	2	3	4	5	
	R	W	r		(flag)
	g	B			(pennant)

If the 5th flag is white, then the 5th pennant must be green. Thus, the 1st and 2nd pennants cannot be green and cannot be the same color, so one of them is blue. Therefore, (A) is true. All the other statements are false.

6. **C**

1	2	3	4	5	
W	B	W	B	r	(flag)
g	W	B	W	B	(pennant)

1	2	3	4	5	
B	W	B	W	r	(flag)
g	B	W	B	W	(pennant)

Since blue and white are the two common colors between flags and pennants, the above are the only two arrangements possible. In both cases, the 5th flag is red and the 1st pennant is green.

Answers 7–13

7. **D**

1	2	3	4	5	6	7	8	9	10
E	E	E					M		M

If the 8th book is a math book, then the three English books must be in positions 1, 2, and 3, since they cannot be in positions 8, 9, and 10. Thus, the other math book is in position 10. The 4th book must be next to the English book in position 3.

8. **A**

1	2	3	4	5	6	7	8	9	10
M			P	P			E	E	E

If the 9th book is an English book, then so are the 8th and 10th books. Thus there is a math book in position 1. The science books must be in positions 2 and 3 *or* 3 and 4. This leaves only positions 4 and 7 for the other math book. Thus (A) is always true. (C) could be true, but does not have to be true. The 3rd poetry book could be in position 2.

9. **B**

1	2	3	4	5	6	7	8	9	10
M					S	S	E	E	E

If the 1st book is a math book, then the 8th, 9th, and 10th books must be the English books. If the 7th book is a science book, so must be the 6th book. This means that the other math book must be either the 3rd, the 4th, or the 5th book. The remainder of the books are poetry books, including the 2nd book.

10. **C**

1	2	3	4	5	6	7	8	9	10
M	P	P	M	S	S	P	E	E	E

or

1	2	3	4	5	6	7	8	9	10
E	E	E	M	S	S	P	P	P	M

If the 4th book is a math book and the 5th book is a science book, then the 6th book is also a science book. This leaves two possible arrangements for the remaining books, as shown above. Statement (C) is the only correct one.

11. **E**

1	2	3	4	5	6	7	8	9	10
E	E	E	P					P	M

or

1	2	3	4	5	6	7	8	9	10
M	P					P	E	E	E

The poetry books must be in positions 4 and 9 *or* 2 and 7, depending on whether the math book is in position 1 or 10. See diagrams above. For example, let us assume that the math book is the 10th book. In order for no two poetry books to be next to each other, the 4th and 9th books must be poetry books, with the 3rd poetry book in either position 6 or 7, depending on the positions of the science books. The same argument holds if the 1st book is a math book.

12. **C**

1	2	3	4	5	6	7	8	9	10
E	E	E	S	S	M	P	P	P	M

and

1	2	3	4	5	6	7	8	9	10
M	P	P	P	M	S	S	E	E	E

These are the two possible arrangements. We see that (A) is false, (B) could be false, (D) is false, and (E) could be false. Only (C) is always true.

13. **B**

1	2	3	4	5	6	7	8	9	10
E	E	E	M	S	S	P	P	P	M

and

1	2	3	4	5	6	7	8	9	10
E	E	E	S	S	M	P	P	P	M

These are the only two possible combinations; thus, (B) is the correct answer.

Answers 14–18

The initial conditions can be summarized as follows:

Total = 5
Languages   F, G, I
Sciences   B, C, P
Math   A, S, T
Math ≤ 2
P̶A̶
A → I
C → (only if T and F)
(G and B) → S̶
Languages = 1

14. **B** (A) and (C) are incorrect since only one language may be taken. (D) is incorrect because if algebra is taken, Italian must be taken. And (E) is incorrect because statistics cannot be taken if both German and biology are taken.

15. **E** Chemistry may be taken only if French is taken. If French is taken, then Italian cannot be taken, since only one language may be taken. (A) is incorrect. If algebra is taken, Italian must be taken, and thus German cannot be taken, making (B) the wrong choice. Chemistry may be taken only if French is taken, and therefore German cannot be taken, so (C) won't work. If algebra is taken, Italian must be taken and thus French cannot be taken, making (D) incorrect.

16. **D** If algebra is taken, Italian must be taken. If Italian is taken, then French cannot be taken, so (A) is the wrong choice. (B) is also the wrong choice since physics cannot be taken with algebra. And (C) and (E) won't work because if chemistry is taken, French must also be taken, and therefore German cannot be taken.

17. **D** Neither (A), (B), nor (E) will work because if chemistry is taken, trigonometry must be taken. (C) is incorrect since a maximum of two math classes may be taken, and if physics is taken, algebra cannot be taken.

18. **B** Both (A) and (E) won't work because a second language may not be taken. And (C) and (D) won't work because if chemistry is taken, French must be taken, and that would be a second language. Since Italian is taken, French is not, thus chemistry is not taken either. One math class must be eliminated, since all three cannot be taken. This leaves both biology and physics that must be taken.

Answers 19–23

From the information given, you could have constructed the following display:

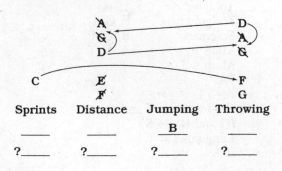

Sprints	Distance	Jumping	Throwing
		B	
?_____	?_____	?_____	?_____

19. **D** If C and E are both sprint coaches, then from the original conditions, F and G coach throwers. Since G coaches throwers, D cannot coach distance, so D must coach jumping.

Sprints	Distance	Jumping	Throwing
C		B	F
? E	?_____	? D	? G

20. **A** If G coaches jumping and A coaches distance we have:

Sprints	Distance	Jumping	Throwing
	A	B	
?_____	?_____	? G	?_____

If D coaches distance or throwing, A must coach sprints or jumping. Since A coaches distance, D cannot coach distance or throwing. This means D must coach sprints. The other choices are possible, but not necessarily true.

Sprints	Distance	Jumping	Throwing
D	A	B	
?_____	?_____	? G	?_____

21. **E** If D coaches throwing, A and G cannot coach distance or throwing. This leaves only C to be the distance coach. So C CANNOT coach jumping.

Sprints	Distance	Jumping	Throwing
	~~E~~		
	~~F~~		
	C	B	D
?_____	?_____	?_____	?_____
	~~A~~		~~A~~
	~~G~~		~~G~~

22. **B** If G is the only throwing coach, we have the following:

E
F̶

Sprints	Distance	Jumping	Throwing
		B	G
?____	?____	?____	?_X_

If D coaches distance or throwers, G must coach sprints or jumping. Since G coaches throwing, D does not coach distance or throwers. Thus, A and C must coach distance giving the following arrangement:

E
F̶

Sprints	Distance	Jumping	Throwing
	A	B	G
?____	?_C_	?____	?_X_
	D̶		D̶

Choice (A) is incorrect since D doesn't coach distance.
Choice (C) is incorrect since A coaches distance.
Choice (D) is incorrect since, if F coaches jumping, D and E must coach sprints.
Choice (E) is incorrect since C and D coach different sports.

23. **C** If D coaches distance, A and G do not coach distance or throwing.

E
F̶

Sprints	Distance	Jumping	Throwing
A̶	D	B	
?____	?____	?____	?____
	A̶		A̶
	G̶		G̶

Since A does not coach sprints, then A must coach jumping. So A and B coach jumping; therefore, G CANNOT coach jumping.

E
F̶

Sprints	Distance	Jumping	Throwing
A̶	D	B	
?____	?____	?_A_	?____
	A̶		A̶
	G̶		G̶

Section IV

1. **D** This choice provides the most direct evidence of the effectiveness of the PUC consumer action. Each of the other choices is only tangentially related to the argument.

2. **D** This choice most seriously weakens the author's contention that the PUC acts in the public interest. (C) is a weaker choice, especially because "slightly" softens the statement.

3. **A** This choice parallels both the reasoning and the structure of the original. The original reasoning may be summarized as follows: most $X \to Y$; therefore $X \to Y$ (probably).

4. **C** By conceding that certain subjects can only be discussed in private, the argument self-destructs. Several of the other choices are tempting, but none is as much to the point as choice (C).

5. **B** Since good personnel relations of an organization, according to the passage, rely upon "mutual confidence, trust and goodwill," one of the causes of personnel difficulties would most certainly be the employees' not believing in the good faith of the organization.

6. **B** In the second sentence, the author implies that the lack of facilities is related to the lack of research mentioned in the first sentence. In any case, the passage reveals the author's concern with both research and assistance, and therefore agrees more fully with (B) than with (A), which mentions research only.

7. **A** The "But" that begins the third sentence marks a contrast between the business world and the schools. The writer's point is that they are not alike and therefore cannot be run using the same standards of judgment.

8. **E** The correct answer is "circular." The argument that what the Church says is true is ultimately based upon this same assertion.

9. **A** Kathy believes Mary to have meant that only Italians are great lovers. Therefore, Kathy takes issue with this and points out in her reply that there are non-Italians who are great lovers. (A), if replaced for Mary's statement, would make Kathy's reply a reasonable one.

10. **B** Only (B) addresses Dimple's assumption that Mrs. Wilson is the only applicant whose qualifications are ideal. Other choices are irrelevant to the argument, although some may be relevant to the implied situation.

11. **A** Only (A) addresses the substance of Dimple's argument.

12. **C** The passage offers a pattern in which failure to meet one of two specific requirements results in a failure to qualify for something. In (C), the fall and winter track seasons become the residence requirement and the collecting of signatures. Failure to complete both leads to disqualification (for the spring team, for the June primary).

13. **D** The author of the argument avoids the issue of quality. The statement that stresses the incompleteness of the pro-hygienist position weakens it. (B) and (E) are irrelevant.

14. **D** The passage describes two types of obstacles to happiness: exterior forces and personal attitude. Both these factors are mentioned in (A), (B), (C), and (E). (D) requires the assumption that the two categories discussed by the author are the only categories.

15. **B** (A) may be eliminated because changing one's mind need not involve issues of right and wrong (in the moral sense that Eliot implies). (C) and (E) may be eliminated because they refute the underlying assumption of Eliot's words, that one can tell what is right. The passage does not address the issue of temptation (D).

16. **E** Without an implied or explicit definition of "civilized," the relevance of the examples is vague, at best. (A) and (D) are irrelevant considerations, and (B) and (C), although possibly relevant, do not address the most apparent weakness of the passage.

17. **B** (A) and (C) strengthen the argument. Although (D) and (E) partially weaken certain aspects of the argument, only (B) introduces a situation which suggests that freedom of the press may have harmful consequences.

18. **A** (B) and (C) are irrelevant to the argument. (D) and (E) contradict the implied assertion that a free press must be protected at all costs. Only (A) offers a statement both favorable to the concept of a free press and directly relevant to the subject discussed: the use of privileged information.

19. **E** By stating that "a legal technicality . . . ducks the . . . moral question," the author is implying that the federal government, which benefits from the technicality, is associated with dodging the issue. (A) and (B) restate explicit information; (C) is implausible; and (D) contradicts information in the passage.

20. **B** Private medical aid would render the author's argument unnecessary. (C), a choice worth considering, is not the best one because the author's focus is less on the aliens' needs than on the monetary burden borne by the counties.

21. **C** By documenting the rate at which the medical expense burden grows, the author could strengthen the argument that the situation he describes is indeed a burden.

22. **D** The passage talks about communes as failures. Therefore, the most logical completion must be a negative term consistent with failure. The only negative choice is (D).

23. **C** By linking Herb's ability with his "cousinhood," Herb is assuming that the latter determines the former; therefore, he is ignoring (C). (B) is irrelevant. (A) is too vague to be the best answer. (D) is inapplicable, because Keith uses "good" in a context that makes its meaning clear. Finally, (E) refers to contradictory information.

24. **E** In order to argue for the value of renewable prescriptions, the author must first assume that more medicine may be necessary, or, in other words, that the patient may suffer a relapse. Without the possibility of relapse, a call for more medicine that has already effected a cure ("worked effectively") is illogical.

25. **C** The passage consistently implies a difference between the past and the present, and (C) makes this contrast explicit. (B) contradicts the implication of the passage, while (A) and (D) narrow the focus unnecessarily, and (E) is irrelevant.

26. **D** This fact would strengthen the merely impressionistic evidence that lawsuits were less prevalent 40 years ago. It is the only choice dealing directly with the implied subject of the passage—lawsuits.

Section V

Passage 1

1. **D** According to the first paragraph, a developing country hopes to attract foreign investment and increase its revenues from taxation ("maximize the public capture of revenues").

2. **A** Unless the investment flow is equal in each direction, the First World nation from which the greater revenue is likely to come is more likely to benefit.

3. **B** According to the second paragraph, reciprocal source-based taxation produces revenue sacrifices by the state receiving most of the foreign investment, that is, the developing country.

4. **D** Excess foreign tax credits are a disincentive to private investors. If the at-source taxation is reduced, there will be fewer excess foreign credits.

5. **C** The passage makes no reference to the availability of raw materials. The four other options are cited.

6. **B** A country that reduced its revenue expectations would be expected to increase foreign investment.

Passage 2

7. **E** Both passages show how the pre-Columbian past affected Mexico's most prominent muralists. Answers (A) through (D), although perhaps true, are too narrow to define the subject of the passages.

8. **C** According to Passage A, Orozco denounced the pre-Columbian past (see lines 8–10, 24–29) and according to Passage B, he treated "the positive aspects of the human condition" in the person of Quetzalcoatl (lines 108–113). This suggests ambivalence. Although Passage B states that Rivera "epitomized" the creation of a mythology of ancient Mexico, it does not imply that he "most successfully" captured history in his murals (A). (B) and (D) are simply inaccurate. (E), which may seem a good answer, is not implied; although Passage B makes it clear that Rivera did use his art for political purposes (e.g., "within a Marxist framework" to inspire the indigenous population to "reconstruct the present and control the future"), it does not imply that the other muralists did not have political purposes.

9. **A** Passage A, in the last paragraph, states that the muralists' "pictorial language" and techniques—for example, the use of fresco—fit into the European tradition. Passage B makes no references to techniques. (B) through (E) are inaccurate.

10. **D** Orozco scorned romanticized visions of Indian life (lines 103–104). (A) through (E) are all mentioned in either Passage A or Passage B (and sometimes both). Note the word *except* in the question.

11. **A** To counter the "colonized mentality" of Mexico, the muralists reaffirmed their national heritage by turning to pre-Columbian history and art. This does not indicate, however, that they were antagonistic to Europe's role in art history (B), nor does it indicate the public's reaction (C). (D) and (E), which may seem possible answers, are not as accurate as (A). "Insistence" on a nationalistic spirit (D) is not mentioned, nor do the muralists "glorify" pre-Columbian artists, although they may glorify pre-Columbian deeds.

12. **C** See lines 82–88. Although (A), (B), (D), and (E) may be interests of Rivera, the passage makes it clear that revitalizing the Indian population was one of his primary "political" intentions.

13. **B** Neither passage indicates that the muralists disdained European art; in fact, Passage A states that the muralists used traditional European techniques. Both passages include or imply (A), (C), (D), and (E).

Passage 3

14. **D** The author says that war and change have been inevitably linked in America, and that war has been a vital force in the rise of capitalism, but he does not say that war is inevitable. All of the other answers are supported by the passage: (A)—lines 64–77; (B)—lines 14–17; (C)—lines 18–20; (E)—lines 64–69.

15. **B** See lines 13–17. Radioactive isotopes used in treating cancer are an example of a positive advance caused by preparations for war. On the other hand, lethal nerve gases (A), in addition to being a German and not an American development, did not lead to positive peacetime uses. (C), (D), and (E), while possibly effects of wars that have changed America, did not "yield results which are tonics to advancement."

16. **D** See lines 23–28. (C) is incorrect; the author states that this is a result of the Civil War. (E) is a statement supported by the passage, but is not the primary reason for World War I's importance. (A) and (B) are not supported by information in the passage.

17. **A** In this paragraph the author paints a picture of, and indicates some of the reasons for, the "isolation, insularity, and exceptionalism" of America before World War I. The paragraph does define "American Religion" (B), but this is too limited an answer to describe the paragraph's main point. (C) and (E) are not covered in this paragraph. There is no contrast drawn between Civil War America and World War I America (D).

18. **B** See lines 35–46. (A) is incorrect; the grand tour is cited as an example that sophisticated Americans saw a trip to Europe as necessary to overcome insularity and complete an education. No social comment is made about its availability only to the rich. (D) is also incorrect; Puritanism is cited in paragraph four, but not in the context indicated in this answer, i.e., the sin and corruption of the world. (E) might seem correct at first, but the passage does not state that America was in fact superior to Europe; it comments on the view that Americans had of their country. (C) is irrelevant; this point is not made in relation to America's insularity.

19. **C** After the first paragraph introduces the idea of war as a force of change, the passage is devoted to the importance of World War I in changing American society. (B) is incorrect; paragraph one concerns some of the benefits of war, but this is not the main topic of the passage; it is an underlying idea. (A) is also incorrect; the passage mentions the Civil War briefly but is mostly concerned with World War I. (D) and (E) are points touched on in the passage, but neither is the main subject.

20. **E** War as a force for change (the topic of paragraph one) is a general idea that introduces the passage's main subject of World War I. It is not a "popular view" that is refuted in the passage (A), nor does the passage ask a question (B). The first paragraph doesn't outline the contents of the passage (C), nor does it set up the first of four examples (D).

21. **B** "Ecstatic nationalism" is part of what Tocqueville called "American Religion." It would not increase in Europe after World War I. (A) can be inferred because Europe was seen as a necessity in a young man's education. (California would have been considered the Wild West.) The inference in (C) is supported by lines 70–77; (D), by lines 9–14; (E), by lines 47–56.

Passage 4

22. **D** In lines 81–87, the passage describes genetic drift, a change in the gene pool that occurs by chance. If an organism with a survival trait gene doesn't reproduce, the gene is lost. (A) is incorrect; the passage does not indicate which mutations are most "significant." (B) is contrary to fact; see lines 48–51. (C) is contradicted by several examples in the passage of the ways variations occur, and genetic recombination (E) is not cited as the cause of the formation of new species.

23. **B** The vulnerability to carbon dioxide was a trait from a gene that was transmitted to the fruit fly by an outside agent; it is therefore an acquired characteristic. That the fruit fly's offspring exhibit the same vulnerability supports the theory that acquired characteristics can be inherited. In (A), the webbed feet are not an acquired characteristic but a result of mutation and were perpetuated by inbreeding. (C) has no relevance to the question of inheritance, and in (D), the shaving of the dogs has nothing to do with the number of hairless offspring; genetic inheritance (dominant and recessive genes) account for that. (E) does not address the issue of how characteristics were transmitted.

24. **E** (A), (B), (C), and (D) are all explained (however briefly) in the passage. Although (E) is mentioned in line 95, it is not defined or explained.

25. **A** By definition, random mutations occur by chance and are therefore not necessarily related to any survival trait. Darwin's theory states that natural selection accounts for the perpetuation of traits. (B) is incorrect; although spontaneous mutations are said to be infrequent, the frequency of random mutations is not addressed. That random mutations occur doesn't refute or replace Darwin's evolutionary concept; it is simply another possibility for explaining the inheritance of certain traits (C). Both (D) and (E) are factually incorrect.

26. **D** The founder principle (lines 101–102) is that a smaller, isolated population has a gene frequency different from the larger population from which it came. (A) is incorrect because although the passage states that more genetic dwarfism occurs in the Amish population as a result of the founder principle, it does not state that the founder principle explains all genetic dwarfism. The principle doesn't refute the theory of natural selection (E), nor does it explain homozygosity (C), although the term is related. (B) is incorrect; nothing intrinsic in the principle supports the importance of "weeding out" non-adaptative organisms.

27. **C** Darwin was more concerned with why certain traits were passed on (survival of the fittest) than with the mechanics of inheritance. (A) and (B) are incorrect; the passage doesn't imply that Darwin had any opinion about genetics. (In fact, the concept of the gene was developed after Darwin's work.) (D) is incorrect because Darwin recognized that variation among members of a species was central to the idea of natural selection. Although the passage states that he believed acquired characteristics could be inherited, it does not imply that he felt acquired traits were more important than hereditary ones (E).

28. **B** Most of the passage deals briefly with how variation occurs, not with the history of a theory (A) or the differences between genetic and evolutionary theories (D). (C) may seem to be a good answer because the author mentions that Darwin's failure to address the source of variations is "a major weakness." "Expose," however, is too strong a word; the passage is focused not on Darwin's weakness but rather on brief explanations of variation. (E) is a minor, not the primary, concern of the passage.

ANALYZING YOUR LSAT SCORE: A BROAD RANGE SCORE APPROXIMATOR

The chart that follows is designed to give you a *general approximation* of the number of questions you need to get right to fall into a general score range and percentile rank on your LSAT. It should help you see if you are in the "ballpark" of the score you need. This range approximator is *not* designed to give you an exact score or to predict your LSAT score. The actual LSAT will have questions that are similar to the ones encountered in this book, but some questions may be either easier or more difficult. The variance in difficulty levels and testing conditions can affect your score range.

Obtaining Your Approximate Score Range

Although the LSAT uses a very precise formula to convert raw scores to scaled scores, for the purpose of this broad range approximation simply total the number of questions you answered correctly. Next, divide the total number of correct answers by the total number of questions on the sample test. This will give you the percent correct. Now look at the following chart to see the approximate percent you need to get right to get into your score range. Remember, on the actual test one of the sections is experimental and, therefore, doesn't count toward your score.

On the actual LSAT, the percent of correct answers to get certain scores will vary slightly from test to test, depending on the number of problems and level of difficulty of that particular exam.

An average score is approximately 151.

If you are not in the range that you wish to achieve, check the approximate percent of correct answers that you need to achieve that range. Carefully analyze the types of errors you are making and continue practicing and analyzing. Remember, in trying to approximate a score range, you must take the complete sample test under strict time and test conditions.

Approximate Scaled Score Range	Approx. % of Correct Answers Necessary	Approx. Score Percentile for Test-takers (Est. % below)
171–180	95 and up	99–99.9%
161–170	80–94%	88–98%
151–160	65–79%	53–85%
141–150	45–64%	17–48%
131–140	30–44%	3–15%
121–130	20–29%	0–2%

PART III

Profiles of Law Schools

CHAPTER 14

Overview of ABA-Approved Law Schools

At the time this book was researched, there were 197 law schools approved by the American Bar Association (including the U.S. Army Judge Advocate General's School, which is not profiled here). At press time, three additional schools were given ABA approval: Charlotte School of Law, Drexel University College of Law, and Elon University School of Law. Contact these institutions directly for more information. The ABA is the largest organization of lawyers in the world, and its members come from every state in the United States. Because the ABA is a voluntary bar association, its members are not required to join in order to practice law, although nearly 40 percent of all American lawyers are currently members.

The power to grant individuals a license to practice law resides in the highest court of each state; thus, every jurisdiction administers its own bar examination, character and fitness inquiry, and licensing procedures for admission to the bar. The states also administer the disciplinary process for sanctioning lawyers who violate ethics rules of professional conduct. Because each state adopts its own rules establishing who is eligible to take the bar examination, some states require all candidates to be graduates of ABA-approved law schools, while others do not (see Chapter 16 for a discussion of non-ABA-approved law schools).

Authority to approve the right of educational institutions to grant degrees has been delegated by Congress to the U.S. Department of Education, which in turn delegates the responsibility for approving degree programs to designated accrediting agencies. In the case of law schools, the agency that has been given this power is the American Bar Association. Within the ABA, accreditation matters are handled by the Accreditation Committee of the Section of Legal Education and Admissions to the Bar with the support of a Consultant on Legal Education. The standards of approval themselves are promulgated by the ABA's governing body,

the House of Delegates, upon recommendation of the Section of Legal Education. The Accreditation Committee is charged with the inspection and evaluation of law schools and law school programs, not only when a school or program is started, but also periodically during the life of the institution. The purpose of the accreditation process is to assure that every law school in the United States meets a common set of quality standards, and that every degree awarded confers the same benefit on recipients as comparable degrees at other ABA-approved law schools.

The imprimatur of the ABA carries great weight with state bar admission authorities, and every state allows graduates of any ABA law school to sit for the bar exam. From an applicant's standpoint, graduating from an ABA-approved law school is like a stamp of approval, a ticket to seek admission to practice law anywhere in the country. From the point of view of a law student, ABA approval is a guarantee that certain basic educational requirements have been met, and that the education they receive will be comparable to the education at any other ABA-approved law school. Additional information on the accreditation process and law schools generally may be obtained by writing the ABA Section of Legal Education and Admissions to the Bar, 750 North Lake Shore Drive, Chicago, IL 60611 (*www.abanet.org/le*).

This does not mean that law schools are all the same. As this Guide demonstrates, law schools come in many shapes and sizes. Some are more difficult to get into than others. Some offer special programs that set them apart from other schools. Some serve special audiences that others do not. Some are rated more highly than others. Neither the ABA nor this Guide attempts to rank law schools. The ABA certifies that approved schools meet minimum standards, but encourages them to seek to exceed those standards. Barron's *Guide to Law Schools* provides a wealth of information to help applicants make the difficult decision about which law school is best for them. Implicit in this approach is the notion that different schools are right for different people, and that no single school is best for everyone.

The ranking of law schools by some publications may provide interesting reading, and may reflect the relative prestige of law schools as filtered through the eyes of the publication's editors, but the uncritical use of such rankings without looking at the facts and figures behind them can distort the process of selecting a law school. The real question should be: What are the top ten schools for you personally? The question is not: What are the top ten schools for some faceless editor at some magazine or publishing house?

The following table provides information about the tuition, programs, and academic community at the schools that have been approved by the American Bar Association. This is designed to provide a quick overview of the schools, and should be used in conjunction with the detailed profiles of the individual schools that can be found in Chapter 15.

Most of the information on these charts should be self-explanatory. If you are uncertain about the significance of any item, consult the profile of the school for additional information or explanation.

In several sections of the table, a check ($\checkmark$) indicates "yes" and a blank indicates "no." For example, under Calendar, the possibilities are Fall, Winter, Spring, and Summer. At any given school, you can begin your law studies only at those times indicated by a check.

Since most law schools operate on a semester basis, information about credits and required courses is given in terms of semester hours. If a school operates on the quarter system, the abbreviation *qh* is added.

Similarly, tuition is generally given for a full year. When part-time tuition is given per credit, this refers to semester courses unless the abbreviation *qh* is used.

Where a category does not apply to a school or when information was not available, the cell is left blank.

INSTITUTION	Profile Page	Fee	Deadline	Deadline Financial Aid	In State Full Time (Part Time)	Out of State Full Time (Part Time)	Fall	Winter	Spring	Summer	Day	Evening	Credits for JD	Required Credits for Courses	Transferable Summer Courses	Joint Degree	Graduate Law Degree	Enrolled Full Time (Part Time)	Average Age First Year	% Women	% Minority	Attrition Rate %	Faculty Full Time (Part Time)	Volumes	Microforms
Albany Law School 80 New Scotland Avenue Albany, NY 12208 518-445-2326 Fax: 518-445-2369 admissions@albanylaw.edu	208	$60	Feb 15	rolling	$38,900 ($29,175)	$38,900 ($29,175)	4				4	4	87	42	4	4	4	726 (45)	23	44	27	1	49 (48)	292,198	2,020,246
American University (Washington College of Law) 4801 Massachusetts Avenue, N.W. Washington, DC 20016-8186 202-274-4101 Fax: 202-274-4107 wcladmit@wcl.american.edu	210	$65	March 1	March 1	$36,464 ($22,838)	$36,464 ($22,838)	4				4	4	86	32	4	4	4	1250 (233)	24	57	32	5	101 (180)	592,065	92,643
Appalachian School of Law P.O. Box 2825 Grundy, VA 24614 276-935-4349 Fax: 276-935-8496 npruitt@asl.edu	212	$60	June 1	July 1	$26,500 ($990/hr)	$26,500 ($990/hr)	4				4		90	69		4	4	340	26	35	6		20 (4)	128,552	104,163
Arizona State University (Sandra Day O'Connor College of Law) 1100 S. McAllister Ave. - Box 877906 Tempe, AZ 85287-7906 480-965-1474 Fax: 480-727-7930 chitra.damania@asu.edu	214	$50	Feb 1	rolling	$18,378	$31,572	4				4	4	88	39	4	4	4	576	26	43	21	4	57 (37)	275,773	142,341
Atlanta's John Marshall Law School 1422 W. Peachtree St., NW Atlanta, GA 30309 404-872-3593 Fax: 404-873-3802 admissions@johnmarshall.edu	216	$50	open	open	$15,360 ($9,216)	$15,360 ($9,216)	4				4	4	88	63	4	4	4	345 (195)	24	51	32	8	35 (21)	96,000	711,151
Ave Maria School of Law 3475 Plymouth Road Ann Arbor, MI 48105 734-827-8063 Fax: 734-622-0123 info@avemarialaw.edu	218	$50	April 1	June 1	$31,862	$31,862	4				4	4	90	60	4	4	4	331 (1)	25	35	17	4	28 (10)	117,104	5,319
Barry University (School of Law) 6441 East Colonial Drive Orlando, FL 32807 321-206-5600 Fax: 321-206-5662 acruz@mail.barry.edu	220	$50	April 1	June	$31,700 ($23,920)	$31,700 ($23,920)	4		4		4	4	90	53 to 55	4	4	4	609 (152)	25	44	18	3	24 (54)	200,000	92,839
Baylor University (School of Law) One Bear Place #97288 Waco, TX 76798-7288 254-710-1911 Fax: 254-710-2316 becky_beck@baylor.edu	222	$40	March 1	Feb 15	$36,750	$36,750	4		4	4	4		126	78		4	4	465	23	47	20	4	27 (29)	241,927	127,451

INSTITUTION	Profile Page	APPLICATIONS Fee	Deadline	Deadline Financial Aid	TUITION In State Full Time (Part Time)	Out of State Full Time (Part Time)	CALENDAR Fall	Winter	Spring	Summer	PROGRAMS Day	Evening	Credits for JD	Required Credits for Courses	Transferable Summer Courses	Joint Degree	Graduate Law Degree	ENROLLED Full Time (Part Time)	Average Age First Year	STUDENT BODY % Women	% Minority	Attrition Rate %	FACULTY Full Time (Part Time)	LIBRARY Volumes	Microforms
Boston College (Law School) 885 Centre Street, Newton, MA 02459, 617-552-4351, Fax: 617-552-2917, bclawadm@bc.edu	224	$75	March 1	March 15	$39,340	$39,340	4				4		85	36		4	4	814 (5)	24	42	23	2	66 (35)	481,235	231,805
Boston University (School of Law) 765 Commonwealth Avenue, Boston, MA 02215, 617-353-3100, Fax: 617-353-0578, bulawadm@bu.edu	226	$75	March 1	March 1	$38,816	$38,816	4				4	4	84	33		4	4	807	24	50	23	4	56 (19)	659,182	321,809
Brigham Young University (J. Reuben Clark Law School) 342 JRCB Brigham Young University, Provo, UT 84602, 801-422-4277, Fax: 801-422-0389, kucharg@law.byu.edu	228	$50	March 1	June 1	$9,980	$19,960	4			4	4	4	90 sem.	36	4	4	4	458 (2)	25	34	17	1	39 (38)	523,234	157,007
Brooklyn Law School 250 Joralemon Street, Brooklyn, NY 11201, 718-780-7906, Fax: 718-780-0395, admitq@brooklaw.edu	230	$65	April 1	April 30	$43,664 ($32,748)	$43,664 ($32,748)	4		4		4	4	86	31	4	4	4	1286 (181)	25	49	26	7	75 (121)	580,994	1,600,012
California Western School of Law 225 Cedar Street, San Diego, CA 92101-3046, 619-525-1401, Fax: 619-615-1401, admissions@cwsl.edu	232	$55	April 1	April 1	$38,400 ($27,000)	$38,400 ($27,000)	4			4	4	4	89 sem.	43	4	4	4	791 (101)	27	55	28	18	52 (87)	345,342	161,909
Campbell University (Norman Adrian Wiggins School of Law) 225 Hillsborough Street, Suite 401, Raleigh, NC 24603, 919-865-5988, Fax: 919-865-5886	234	$50	April 1	open	$30,450	$30,450	4				4	4	90	67		4	4	402	26	50	11	9	25 (40)	106,265	87,368
Capital University (Law School) 303 East Broad Street, Columbus, OH 43215-3200, 614-236-6500, Fax: 614-236-6972, admissions@law.capital.edu	236	$40	May 1	April 1	$29,275 ($19,525)	$29,275 ($19,525)	4			4	4	4	89	46	4	4	4	460 (216)	27	44	12	11	37 (63)	258,223	55,144
Case Western Reserve University (School of Law) 11075 East Boulevard, Cleveland, OH 44106, 216-368-3600, Fax: 216-368-1042, lawadmissions@case.edu	238	$40	April 1	May 1	$34,700 ($1,446/hr)	$34,700 ($1,446/hr)	4			4	4		88	39	4	4	4	678 (24)	25	42	18		56 (73)	307,071	104,733

#	School / Contact	App Fee	Deadline 1	Deadline 2	Tuition 1	Tuition 2									Enrollment							Library A	Library B
240	**Catholic University of America (Columbus School of Law)** — Cardinal Station, Washington, DC 20064; 202-319-5151; Fax: 202-319-6285; *admissions@law.edu*	$65	March 12	July 15	$37,850 ($555/hr)	$37,850 ($555/hr)	4		4	4	84	33	4	4	4	588 (318)	26	51	18	10	91 (87)	203,232	199,613
242	**Chapman University (School of Law)** — One University Drive, Orange, CA 92866; 714-628-2500; Fax: 714-628-2501; *metten@chapman.edu*	$65	April 15	March 2	$37,950 ($30,240)	$37,950 ($30,240)	4		4	4	88	51-52	4	4	4	510 (37)	25	48	22	10	52 (40)	303,429	206,609
244	**Charleston School of Law** — P.O. Box 535, Charleston, SC 29402; 843-377-2143; Fax: 843-329-0491; *jbenfield@charlestonlaw.org*	$50	March 1	April 1	$34,568 ($27,774)	$34,568 ($27,774)	4		4	4	88	63	4	4	4	459 (200)	23	44	10	3	32 (33)	26,267	99,339
246	**Charlotte School of Law** — 2145 Suttle Avenue, Charlotte, NC 28208; 704-971-8542; Fax: 704-971-8599; *admissions@charlottelaw.edu*	$50	open		$31,754 ($25,404)	$31,754 ($25,404)	4	4	4	4	90	60	4	4	4	380 (101)	28	50	11	10	22 (27)	196,308	
248	**City University of New York (CUNY School of Law)** — 65-21 Main Street, Flushing, NY 11367-1300; 718-340-4210; Fax: 718-340-4435; *mail.law.cuny.edu*	$40	May 1	May 3	$10,240	$17,020	4		4	4	91	60	4	4	4	406 (7)	26	50	31	1	37 (11)	284,829	1,063,674
250	**Cleveland State University (Cleveland-Marshall College of Law)** — 2121 Euclid Avenue LB138, Cleveland, OH 44115-2214; 216-687-2304; Fax: 216-687-6881; *christophe.lck@law.csuohio.edu*	$50	March 1	May 1	$16,764 ($12,895)	$22,995 ($17,689)	4		4	4	90	41	4	4	4	482 (157)	26	41	15	17	43 (34)	538,989	234,094
252	**College of William & Mary (William & Mary Law School)** — P.O. Box 8795, Williamsburg, VA 23187-8795; 757-221-3785; Fax: 757-221-3261; *lawadm@wm.edu*			Feb 15	$21,946	$32,146	4		4	4	86	34	4	4	4	626	24	49	16	1	35 (70)	406,000	929,860
254	**Columbia University (School of Law)** — 435 West 116th Street, New York, NY 10027; 212-854-2670; Fax: 212-854-1109; *admissions@law.columbia.edu*				$40,000	$40,000	4		4	4	83	35	4	4	4	1260	24	45	30		98 (69)	1,092,534	235,424
256	**Cornell University (Law School)** — Myron Taylor Hall, Ithaca, NY 14853-4901; 607-255-5141; Fax: 607-255-7193; *lawadmit@postoffice.law.cornell.edu*	$80	Feb 1	March 15	$48,950 ($48,950)	$48,950	4		4	4	84	36	4	4	4	622	23	52	30		53 (60)	670,000	5,500

Column groups: APPLICATIONS (Fee, Deadline, Deadline Financial Aid); TUITION — In State / Out of State (Full Time (Part Time)); CALENDAR (Fall, Winter, Spring, Summer); PROGRAMS (Day, Evening, Credits for JD, Required Credits for Courses, Transferable Summer Courses, Joint Degree, Graduate Law Degree); ENROLLED (Full Time (Part Time)); STUDENT BODY (Average Age First Year, % Women, % Minority, Attrition Rate %); FACULTY (Full Time (Part Time)); LIBRARY (Volumes, Microforms).

Institution	Profile Page	Fee	Deadline	Deadline Financial Aid	In State Full Time (Part Time)	Out of State Full Time (Part Time)	Fall	Winter	Spring	Summer	Day	Evening	Credits for JD	Required Credits for Courses	Transferable Summer Courses	Joint Degree	Graduate Law Degree	Enrolled Full Time (Part Time)	Average Age First Year	% Women	% Minority	Attrition Rate %	Faculty Full Time (Part Time)	Volumes	Microforms
Creighton University (School of Law) 2500 California Plaza Omaha, NE 68178 402-280-2586 Fax: 402-280-3161 lawadmit@creighton.edu	258	$50	May 1	March 1	$28,988 ($966/hr)	$28,988 ($966/hr)	✓				✓	✓	94	57	✓	✓		471 (13)	23	42	11	6	31 (39)	384,395	175,086
De Paul University (College of Law) 25 East Jackson Boulevard Chicago, IL 60604 312-362-6831 Fax: 312-362-5280 lawinfo@depaul.edu	260	$60	March 1	March 1	$37,525 ($24,380)	$37,525 ($24,380)	✓			✓	✓	✓	86	40	✓	✓	✓	772 (255)	24	51	24	3	60 (66)	402,000	190,418
Drake University (Law School) 2507 University Avenue Des Moines, IA 50311 515-271-2782 Fax: 515-271-1990 lawadmit@drake.edu	262	$40	April 1	March 1	$30,750 ($950/hr)	$30,750 ($950/hr)	✓			✓	✓	✓	90	41	✓	✓	✓	451 (16)	25	45	13	4	38 (33)	330,000	117,967
Drexel University (Earle Mack School of Law) 3320 Market Street Philadelphia, PA 15282 215-895 1LAW Fax: 215-571-4769	264		open		$32,921	$32,921				✓	✓				✓	✓	✓	410	25				24 (25)	48,148	
Duke University (Duke University School of Law) Science Drive and Towerview Road, Box 90362 Durham, NC 27708-0362 919-613-7020 Fax: 919-613-7257 nash@law.duke.edu	266			March 15	$40,000	$40,000	✓			✓	✓		84	32	✓	✓	✓		25	46	23	1	55 (67)	622,400	78,067
Duquesne University (School of Law) 900 Locust Street, Hanley Hall Pittsburgh, PA 15282 412-396-6296 Fax: 412-396-1073 campion@duq.edu	268	$60	April 1	May 31	$30,206 ($23,214)	$30,206 ($23,214)					✓	✓	86	56		✓	✓	445 (255)	22	52	4	2	26 (34)	230,261	74,366
Elon University (School of Law) 201 North Greene Street Greensboro, NC 27401 336-279-9200 Fax: 336-279-8199 law@elon.edu	270	$50	July 31		$30,750		✓				✓	✓	90	49				315	23	45	12	6	21 (33)	169,180	91,000

Page	App Fee	Deadline 1	Deadline 2	Tuition 1	Tuition 2				%	%				Enrollment						Library vols
272	$70	March 1	April 1	$40,900	$40,900	4		4	90	47	4	4	4	715	23	48	31	2	64 (42)	308,364 / 107,514
274	$30	June 15		$30,500	$30,500	4		4	90	51	4	4	4	323 (18)		38	11		29	
276	$30		March 1	$9,036 ($6,627)	$28,302 ($20,755)	4	4	4	90	61	4	4	4	385 (228)	31	55	69	3	46 (11)	368,923 / 128,224
278	$50	open		$27,570 ($22,060)	$27,570 ($22,060)	4	4	4	87	56	4	4	4	1231 (164)	27	48	18	8	62 (45)	223,820 / 469,002
280	$20	May 1	Feb 1	$12,471 ($9,353)	$26,255 ($19,692)	4	4	4	90	31	4	4	4	300 (330)	26	48	54	5	32 (21)	213,410 / 123,491
282	$30	April 1	April 1	$12,263	$12,263	4	4	4	88	36	4	4	4	763	23	41	17	3	59 (29)	525,173 / 1,065,200
284	$70	June 30	May 15	$39,450	$39,450	4	4	4	83	39	4	4	4	1222 (391)	24	47	26	2	73 (117)	384,966 / 241,265
286	$55	April 1	open	$36,900	$36,900	4	4	4	85	39	4	4	4	437 (3)	27	40	12	8	25 (30)	307,364 / 663,822
288	$35	April 1	March 1	$20,556 ($16,721)	$34,220 ($27,945)	4	4	4	89	40	4	4	4	480 (217)	25	42	18	1	48 (139)	488,944 / 233,330

272 **Emory University (School of Law)**
Gambrell Hall, 1301 Clifton Road, N.E.
Atlanta, GA 30322
404-727-6801
Fax: 404-727-2477
erosenz@law.emory.edu

274 **Faulkner University (Thomas Goode Jones School of Law)**
5345 Atlanta Highway
Montgomery, AL 36109
334-386-7210
Fax: 334-386-7223
law@faulkner.edu

276 **Florida Agricultural and Mechanical University (Florida A & M University College of Law)**
201 N. Beggs Avenue
Orlando, FL 32801
407-254-3268
famulaw.admissions@famu.edu

278 **Florida Coastal (School of Law)**
8787 Bayline Rd.
Jacksonville, FL 32256
904-680-7710
Fax: 904-680-7776
admissions@fcsl.edu

280 **Florida International University (College of Law)**
FIU College of Law, RDB 1055
Miami, FL 33199
(305) 348-8006
Fax: (305) 348-2965
miroa@fiu.edu

282 **Florida State University (College of Law)**
425 W. Jefferson St.
Tallahassee, FL 32306-1601
850-644-3787
Fax: 850-644-7284
admissions@law.fsu.edu

284 **Fordham University (School of Law)**
140 West 62nd Street
New York, NY 10023
212-636-6810
Fax: 212-636-7984
lawadmissions@law.fordham.edu

286 **Franklin Pierce Law Center**
2 White Street
Concord, NH 03301
603-228-9217
Fax: 603-228-1074
admissions@piercelaw.edu

288 **George Mason University (School of Law)**
3301 Fairfax Drive
Arlington, VA 22201
703-993-8010
Fax: 703-993-8088
aprice1@gmu.edu

INSTITUTION	Profile Page	APPLICATIONS Fee	APPLICATIONS Deadline	APPLICATIONS Deadline Financial Aid	TUITION In State Full Time (Part Time)	TUITION Out of State Full Time (Part Time)	CALENDAR Fall	CALENDAR Winter	CALENDAR Spring	CALENDAR Summer	PROGRAMS Day	PROGRAMS Evening	PROGRAMS Credits for JD	PROGRAMS Required Credits for Courses	PROGRAMS Transferable Summer Courses	PROGRAMS Joint Degree	PROGRAMS Graduate Law Degree	ENROLLED STUDENT BODY Full Time (Part Time)	ENROLLED STUDENT BODY Average Age First Year	ENROLLED STUDENT BODY % Women	ENROLLED STUDENT BODY % Minority	ENROLLED STUDENT BODY Attrition Rate %	FACULTY Full Time (Part Time)	LIBRARY Volumes	LIBRARY Microforms
George Washington University (Law School) 2000 H Street, N.W. Washington, DC 20052 202-994-7230 Fax: 202-994-3597 jd@law.gwu.edu	290	$80	March 1		$38,198 ($25,540)	$38,198 ($25,540)	4				4	4	84	34	4	4	4	1412 (250)	24	43		1	100 (288)	611,190	130,195
Georgetown University (Law Center) 600 New Jersey Avenue, N.W. Washington, DC 20001 202-662-9010 Fax: 202-662-9439 admis@law.georgetown.edu	292	$80	March 1	March 1	$43,750 ($31,900)	$43,750 ($31,900)	4				4	4	85	33	4	4	4	1548 (354)	24	43	24		152 (231)	593,978	591,932
Georgia State University (College of Law) P.O. Box 4037 Atlanta, GA 30302-4037 404-413-9200 Fax: 404-413-9203 cjgeorge@gsu.edu	294	$50	March 15	April 1	$10,296 ($429/hr)	$31,320 ($1,305/hr)	4				4	4	90	43	4	4	4	488 (185)	26	47	19	11	55 (50)	160,054	191,256
Golden Gate University (School of Law) 536 Mission Street San Francisco, CA 94105-2968 415-442-6630 lawadmit@ggu.edu	296	$60	April 1	rolling	$32,700 ($22,890)	$32,700 ($22,890)	4				4	4	88	57	4	4	4	538 (150)	26	56	34	27	41 (67)	377,000	238,000
Gonzaga University (School of Law) Box 3528 Spokane, WA 99220-3528 509-313-5532 Fax: 509-313-3697 admissions@lawschool.gonzaga.edu	298	$50	April 15	Feb 1	$31,320	$29,250	4				4	4	90	49	4	4	4	516 (10)	25	40	9	14	34 (42)	167,286	141,329
Hamline University (School of Law) 1536 Hewitt Avenue St. Paul, MN 55104-1284 651-523-2461 Fax: 651-523-3064 lawadm@gw.hamline.edu	300	$35	April 1	open	$31,600 ($22,752)	$31,600 ($22,757)	4				4	4	88	35	4	4	4	468 (182)	26	54	13	4	45 (84)	154,942	130,432
Harvard University (Harvard Law School) Cambridge, MA 02138 617-495-3179 jdadmiss@law.harvard.edu	302				$40,000	$40,000	4				4	4	82	30	4	4	4	1670	24	45	33	1	132 (71)	1,723,645	1,973,552
Hofstra University (School of Law) 121 Hofstra University Hempstead, NY 11549 516-463-5916 Fax: 516-463-6264 lawadmissions@hofstra.edu	304			April 1	$35,000 ($25,000)	$35,000 ($25,000)	4				4	4	87	39	4	4	4		24	47	26	11	40 (59)	550,765	1,823,120

Howard University (Howard University) 2900 Van Ness Street, N.W. Washington, DC 20008 202-806-8008 Fax: 202-806-8162 *admissions@law.howard.edu*	306			April 1	$12,950	$15,000	4		4		4	4	88	n/av	4	4	4	420	25	60	94	5	33 (23)	428,494	54,000
Illinois Institute of Technology (Chicago-Kent College of Law) 565 West Adams Street Chicago, IL 60661 312-906-5020 Fax: 312-906-5274 *admit@kentlaw.edu*	308	$60	March 1	April 15	$33,570 ($24,630)	$33,570 ($24,630)	4				4	4	87	42	4	4	4	751 (224)	24	48	19	10	73 (153)	550,789	145,312
Indiana University (Maurer School of Law) 211 S. Indiana Avenue Bloomington, IN 47405-7001 812-855-4765 Fax: 812-855-0555 *Lawadmis@indiana.edu*	310	$50	open	March 1	$24,000	$39,800	4			4			88	31	4	4	4	620 (2)	24	42	18	1	55 (34)	463,190	1,677,604
Indiana University-Purdue University at Indianapolis (Indiana University School of Law-Indianapolis) 530 West New York Street Indianapolis, IN 46202-3225 317-274-2459 Fax: 317-278-4780 *khmiller@iupui.edu*	312	$50	March 1	March 1	$17,563 ($13,465)	$37,878 ($29,040)	4				4	4	90	35	4	4	4	625 (319)	26	45	15	1	62 (73)	609,151	66,847
Inter American University of Puerto Rico (School of Law) P.O. Box 70351 San Juan, PR 00936-8351 787-751-1912, ext. 2013, 2526	314	$63	March 31	Aug 13	$12,900 ($9,890)	$12,900 ($9,890)	4				4	4	92	62		4		423 (406)	24	55	1	8	23 (31)	202,325	353,804
John Marshall Law School 315 South Plymouth Court Chicago, IL 60604 312-987-1406 Fax: 312-427-5136 *admission@jmls.edu*	316	$60	March 1	June 1	$36,664 ($25,324)	$36,664 ($22,500)	4		4		4	4	90	48	4	4	4	1139 (407)	23	46	16	9	73 (110)	409,154	158,195
Lewis and Clark College (Lewis and Clark Law School) 10015 Southwest Terwilliger Boulevard Portland, OR 97219 503-768-6613 Fax: 503-768-6793 *lawadmss@lclark.edu*	318	$50	March 1	March 1	$30,461 ($22,851)	$30,461 ($22,851)	4				4	4	88	28-35		4	4	521 (194)	26	51	24	4	55 (71)	220,765	311,765
Liberty University (School of Law) 1971 University Blvd. Lynchburg, VA 24502 434-592-5300 Fax: 434-592-0202 *law@liberty.edu*	320	$50	June 1	Rolling	$24,160	$24,160	4						90	69				170	26	35	15	10	19 (6)	94,815	155,383
Louisiana State University (Paul M. Hebert Law Center) 202 Law Center, 1 East Campus Drive Baton Rouge, LA 70803 225-578-8646 Fax: 225-578-8647 *lynell.cadray@law.lsu.edu*	322	$50	March 1	April 1	$14,470	$25,570	4				4		94	70	4	4	4	598	24	45	10	2	38 (50)	848,000	2,153,035

INSTITUTION	Profile Page	Fee	Deadline	Financial Aid Deadline	Tuition In State Full Time (Part Time)	Tuition Out of State Full Time (Part Time)	Fall	Day	Evening	Credits for JD	Required Credits for Courses	Transferable Summer Courses	Joint Degree	Graduate Law Degree	Enrolled Full Time (Part Time)	Average Age First Year	% Women	% Minority	Attrition Rate %	Faculty Full Time (Part Time)	Volumes	Microforms
Loyola Marymount University (Loyola Law School) 919 Albany Street, Los Angeles, CA 90015, 213-736-1074, Fax 213-736-6523, admissions@lls.edu	324	$65	Feb 1	March 14	$35,800 ($24,000)	$35,800 ($24,000)	4	4	4	87	41	4	4	4	1000 (290)	23	49			75 (59)	592,499	117,616
Loyola University Chicago (School of Law) 25 East Pearson Street, Chicago, IL 60611, 312-915-7170, Fax 312-915-7906, law-admissions@luc.edu	326	$50	April 1	March 1	$36,290 ($27,240)	$36,290 ($27,240)	4	4	4	86	34	4	4	4	652 (188)	24	52	16	1	48 (113)	398,495	220,923
Loyola University of New Orleans (School of Law) 7214 St. Charles Avenue, New Orleans, LA 70118, 504-861-5575, Fax 504-861-5772, ladmit@loyno.edu	328	$40	March 1	June 1	$34,317 ($23,247)	$34,317 ($23,247)	4	4	4	90	53	4	4	4	726 (156)	25	49	28	3	50 (57)	404,868	178,132
Marquette University (Law School) Office of Admissions, P.O. Box 1881, Milwaukee, WI 53201-1881, 414-288-6767, Fax 414-288-0676, law.admission@marquette.edu	330	$50	April 1	March 1	$32,410 ($10,360)	$32,410 ($10,360)	4	4	4	90	38	4	4	4	565 (180)	25	44	15	9	48 (71)	362,586	163,520
Mercer University (Walter F. George School of Law) 1021 Georgia Avenue, Macon, GA 31207, 478-301-2605, Fax 478-301-2989, Sutton_me@law.mercer.edu	332	$50	March 15	April 1	$34,130	$34,130	4	4		91	59	4	4	4	443	23	43	18	4	32 (39)	195,673	147,045
Michigan State University (College of Law) 230 Law College Bldg., East Lansing, MI 48824-1300, 517-432-0222, Fax 517-432-0098	334	$60	March 1	April 1	$29,899 ($24,744)	$29,899 ($24,744)	4	4	4	88	44	4	4	4	696 (310)	23	42	13	5	38 (41)	133,882	152,890
Mississippi College (School of Law) 151 E. Griffith Street, Jackson, MS 39201, 601-925-7152, pevans@mc.edu	336	$50	June 1		$23,720	$23,720	4	4	4	90	36	4	4		528 (9)	26	41	9	7	22 (42)	346,941	217,570
New England Law/Boston 154 Stuart Street, Boston, MA 02116, 617-422-7210, Fax 617-422-7201, admit@admin.nesl.edu	338	$65	March 15	April 8	$38,500 ($28,880)	$38,500 ($28,880)	4	4	4	86	43	4	4	4	735 (357)	26	55	13	17	35 (68)	320,682	857,787

School	No.	Fee	Deadline	Deadline	Tuition	Tuition																	
New York Law School 185 West Broadway New York, NY 10013-2960 212-431-2888 Fax: 212-966-1522 admissions@nyls.edu	340	$65	April 1	April 15	$44,800 ($34,500)	$44,800 ($34,500)	4		4	4	86	38	4	4	4	1408 (448)	25	50	20	11	75 (123)	534,789	175,305
New York University **(School of Law)** 161 Avenue of the Americas, 5th Floor New York, NY 10013 212-998-6060 Fax: 212-995-4527 law.moreinfo@nyu.edu	342	$75	Feb 1	April 15	$44,820	$44,820	4		4	4	83	38 to 42	4	4	4	1427	24	44	23	–	125 (70)	1,098,972	146,070
North Carolina Central University **(School of Law)** 640 Nelson Street Durham, NC 27707 919-530-6333 Fax: 919-530-6339 sbrownb@nccu.edu	344	$40	March 31	June 30	$5,916 ($3,640)	$18,654 ($15,530)	4		4	4	88	59	4	4	4	480 (121)	23	61	55	13	29 (20)	388,660	1,074,887
Northeastern University **(School of Law)** 400 Huntington Avenue Boston, MA 02115 617-373-2395 Fax: 617-373-8665 c.taubman@neu.edu	346	$75	March 1	Feb 15	$39,750	$39,750	4		4	4	87	37	4	4	4	602 (2)	25	60	23	1	36 (45)	335,453	201,355
Northern Illinois University **(College of Law)** Swen Parson Hall, Room 151 De Kalb, IL 60115-2890 815-753-8595 Fax: 815-753-5680 lawadm@niu.edu	348	$50	May 15	March 1	$12,504	$25,008	4		4	4	90	43	4	4	4	298 (11)	25	46	25	10	24 (14)	262,244	98,075
Northern Kentucky University **(Salmon P. Chase College of Law)** Louie B. Nunn Hall Highland Heights, KY 41099 859-572-5490 Fax: 859-572-6081 brayg@nku.edu	350	$40	June 1	March 1	$14,742 ($11,340)	$32,162 ($24,740)	4		4	4	90	48	4	4	4	372 (233)	27	47	10	6	29 (14)	335,312	173,343
Northwestern University **(School of Law)** 357 East Chicago Avenue Chicago, IL 60611 312-503-8465 Fax: 312-503-0178 admissions@law.northwestern.edu	352	$100	Feb 15	Feb 1	$47,472	$47,472	4	4	4	4	83	29	4	4	4	814	26	47	36	1	88 (64)	779,880	88,914
Nova Southeastern University **(Shepard Broad Law Center)** 3305 College Avenue Fort Lauderdale, FL 33314-7721 954-262-6117 Fax: 954-262-3844 admission@nsu.nova.edu	354	$50	April 1	March 1	$31,172 ($23,378)	$31,172 ($23,378)	4		4	4	90	57	4	4	4	903 (189)	26	53	30	14	58 (50)	330,000	145,222
Ohio Northern University **(Claude W. Pettit College of Law)** 525 South Main Street Ada, OH 45810 419-772-2211 Fax: 419-772-3042	356		open	April 3	$22,000	$22,000	4	4	4	4	87	45	4	4	4	300	25	45	11	3	18 (7)	222,422	115,944

INSTITUTION	Profile Page	APPLICATIONS Fee	Deadline	Deadline Financial Aid	TUITION In State Full Time (Part Time)	Out of State Full Time (Part Time)	CALENDAR Fall	Winter	Spring	Summer	PROGRAMS Day	Evening	Credits for JD	Required Credits for Courses	Transferable Summer Courses	Joint Degree	Graduate Law Degree	ENROLLED STUDENT BODY Full Time (Part Time)	Average Age First Year	% Women	% Minority	Attrition Rate %	FACULTY Full Time (Part Time)	LIBRARY Volumes	Microforms
Ohio State University (Michael E. Moritz College of Law) 55 West 12th Avenue, John Deaver Drinko Hall Columbus, OH 43210-1391 614-292-8810 Fax: 614-292-1383 lawadmit@osu.edu	358				$17,000	$30,000	4				4		88	37	4	4	4	750	22	48	22	1	50 (41)	560,969	228,646
Oklahoma City University (School of Law) 2501 North Blackwelder Avenue Oklahoma City, OK 73106-1493 405-208-5354 Fax: 405-208-5814 lawadmit@okcu.edu	360	$50	Aug 1	March 1	$27,900 ($18,600)	$27,900 ($18,600)	4				4	4	90	60	4	4	4	533 (90)	27	41	16	12	40 (56)	322,061	147,684
Pace University (School of Law) 78 North Broadway White Plains, NY 10603 914-422-4210 Fax: 914-989-8714 calexander@law.pace.edu	362	$65	March 1	Feb 15	$39,546 ($29,660)	$39,546 ($29,660)	4		4		4	4	88	37	4	4	4	562 (185)	25	59	18	6	44 (98)	398,968	938,300
Pennsylvania State University (Dickinson School of Law) 100 Beam Building University Park, PA 16802-1910 814-867-1251 Fax: 717-241-3503 dsladmit@psu.edu	364	$60	March 1	March 1	$33,600 ($1,217/hr)	$33,600 ($1m217/hr)	4				4	4	88	35	4	4	4	573 (82)	25	44	19	3	53 (11)	530,783	1,497,012
Pepperdine University (School of Law) 24255 Pacific Coast Highway Malibu, CA 90263 310-506-4631 Fax: 310-506-7668	366			April 1	$29,000	$29,000	4				4	4	88	57	4		4	680	23	51	17	5	30	342,450	87,000
Phoenix School of Law 4041 N. Central Ave. Suite 100 Phoenix, AZ 85012-3330 (602) 682-6800	368	$50			$13,720 ($10,300)				4		4	4	87	67	4			102 (126)	32	51	19	4	15 (13)	124,613	508,704
Pontifical Catholic University of Puerto Rico (School of Law) 2250 Avenida las Americas suite 543 Ponce, PR 00717-9997 787-841-2000, ext. 1836 Fax 787-840-4620	370		n/av	Check			4				4	4	94	82		4	4	220 (220)	24	50		11	14 (18)	135,000	15,000
Quinnipiac University (School of Law) 275 Mt. Carmel Avenue Hamden, CT 06518-1908 203-582-3400 Fax: 203-582-3339 ladm@quinnipiac.edu	372	$40	March 1	April 15	$40,000 ($28,000)	$40,000 ($28,000)	4				4	4	86	45	4	4	4	291 (124)	25	51	13	3	35 (33)	193,400	248,090

#	School	App Fee	Date 1	Date 2	Tuition A	Tuition B									Enrollment							
374	**Regent University (School of Law)** — 1000 Regent University Drive, Virginia Beach, VA 23464-9800; 757-352-4584; Fax: 757-352-4139; lawschool@regent.edu	$50	June 1	July 1	$29,250 ($21,450)	$29,250 ($21,450)	4		4	90	73	4	4		396 (26)	25	49	15		28 (25)	136,136	265,148
376	**Roger Williams University (School of Law)** — Ten Metacom Avenue, Bristol, RI 02809-5171; 401-254-4555; Fax: 401-254-4516; admissions@rwu.edu	$60	March 15	Feb 15	$34,950	$34,950	4		4	90	48	4	4		550 (30)	25	51	11	2	33 (30)	301,907	1,083,880
378	**Rutgers University/Camden (School of Law)** — Fifth and Penn Streets, Camden, NJ 08102; 856-225-6102; Fax: 856-225-6537; admissions@camlaw.rutgers.edu	$65	April 1	July 1	$21,486 ($17,920)	$21,486 ($26,660)	4		4	84	32	4	4		620 (191)	25	40	21		51 (57)	512,000	150,000
380	**Rutgers University/Newark (School of Law)** — Center for Law and Justice, 123 Washington St., Newark, NJ 07102; 973-353-5557/5554; Fax: 973-353-3459; lawinfo@andromeda.rutgers.edu	$60	March 15	March 1	$19,225 ($12,730)	$28,230 ($18,814)	4		4	84	34 to 35	4	4		558 (260)	27	43	38	2	55 (31)	353,600	163,600
382	**Saint John's University (School of Law)** — 8000 Utopia Parkway, Queens, NY 11439; 718-990-6474; Fax: 718-990-2526; lawinfo@stjohns.edu	$60	April 1		$42,200 ($31,650)	$42,200 ($31,650)	4		4	86	58	4	4		737 (178)	23	47	25	3	64 (76)	376,546	189,558
384	**Saint Louis University (School of Law)** — 3700 Lindell Boulevard, St. Louis, MO 63108; 314-977-2800; Fax: 314-977-1464; admissions@law.slu.edu	$55	March 1	March 1	$34,180 ($24,940)	$34,180 ($24,940)	4	4	4	91	37-39	4	4		691 (266)	25	48	18	5	68 (45)	657,923	262,976
386	**Saint Mary's University (School of Law)** — One Camino Santa Maria, San Antonio, TX 78228-8601; 210-436-3523; Fax: 210-431-4202; wwilson@stmarytx.edu	$55	March 1	March 31	$26,520 ($15,912)	$26,520 ($15,912)	4		4	90	46	4	4		681 (181)	25	43	34	16	36 (53)	635,241	415,495
388	**Saint Thomas University (School of Law)** — 16401 NW 37th Avenue, Miami Gardens, FL 33054; 305-623-2310; fkhan@stu.edu	$60	May 1	May 1	$27,840	$27,840	4		4	90	60	4	4		625	25	53	47	21	27 (32)	330,143	1,251,432
390	**Samford University (Cumberland School of Law)** — 800 Lakeshore Drive, Birmingham, AL 35229; 205-726-2702; Fax: 205-726-2057; law.admissions@samford.edu	$50	Feb 28	March 1	$31,478	$31,478	4		4	90	47	4	4		493	24	45	8	3	34 (21)	205,466	120,539

INSTITUTION	Profile Page	APPLICATIONS Fee	APPLICATIONS Deadline	APPLICATIONS Financial Aid Deadline	TUITION In State Full Time (Part Time)	TUITION Out of State Full Time (Part Time)	CALENDAR Fall	CALENDAR Winter	CALENDAR Spring	CALENDAR Summer	PROGRAMS Day	PROGRAMS Evening	PROGRAMS Credits for JD	PROGRAMS Required Credits for Courses	PROGRAMS Transferable Summer Courses	PROGRAMS Joint Degree	PROGRAMS Graduate Law Degree	ENROLLED STUDENT BODY Full Time (Part Time)	ENROLLED STUDENT BODY Average Age First Year	ENROLLED STUDENT BODY % Women	ENROLLED STUDENT BODY % Minority	ENROLLED STUDENT BODY Attrition Rate %	FACULTY Full Time (Part Time)	LIBRARY Volumes	LIBRARY Microforms
Santa Clara University (School of Law) 500 El Camino Real, Santa Clara, CA 95053, 408-554-4800, Fax: 408-554-7897, lawadmissions@scu.edu	392	$75	Feb 1	Feb 1	$35,250 ($24,676)	$35,250 ($24,676)	4				4	4	86	42	4	4	4	728 (217)	26	49	42	12	45 (31)	369,154	1,110,627
Seattle University (School of Law) 901 12th Avenue, Sullivan Hall, P.O. Box 222000, Seattle, WA 98122-4340, 206-398-4200, Fax: 206-398-4058, lawadmis@seattleu.edu	394	$60	March 1	March 1	$35,340 ($29,450)	$35,340 ($29,450)	4			4	4	4	90	44	4	4		808 (228)	27	51	29	2	63 (43)	388,860	218,919
Seton Hall University (School of Law) One Newark Center, Newark, NJ 07102-5210, 973-642-8747, Fax: 973-642-8876, admitme@shu.edu	396	$65	April 1	April 1	$38,040 ($28,725)	$38,040 ($28,725)	4				4	4	85	44	4	4	4	770 (450)	25	41	18	2	67 (96)	443,681	498,403
South Texas College of Law 1303 San Jacinto Street, Houston, TX 77002-7000, 713-646-1810, Fax: 713-646-2906, admissions@stcl.edu	398	$50	Feb 15	May 1	$23,010 ($15,340)	$23,010 ($15,340)	4		4		4	4	90	46	4	4	4	936 (316)	24	45	24	6	60 (64)	246,568	276,704
Southern Illinois University (School of Law) Lesar Law Building, Mail Code 6804, Carbondale, IL 62901, 618-453-8858, Fax: 618-453-8921, lawadmit@siu.edu	400	$50	March 1	April 1	$11,022	$29,925	4				4		90	48	4	4	4	382 (1)	26	38	8	13	35 (10)	421,497	203,178
Southern Methodist University (Dedman School of Law) Office of Admissions, P.O. Box 750110, Dallas, TX 75275-0110, 214-768-2550, Fax: 214-768-2549, lawadmit@smu.edu	402	$75	Feb 15	June 1	$38,406 ($28,805)	$38,406 ($28,805)					4	4	87	37		4	4	572 (330)	25	47	23	3	47 (30)	637,217	140,625
Southern University and A & M College (Law Center) Post Office Box 9294, Baton Rouge, LA 70813-9294, 225-771-5340, Fax: 225-771-2121, vwilkerson@sulc.edu	404			April 15	$7,000 ($2,000)	$13,000 ($7,200)	4				4		96	75	4	4		413 (20)	27	48	69	10	28 (24)	453,396	206,603

School	No.	App Fee	Date 1	Date 2	Tuition 1	Tuition 2																		
Southwestern University (Law School) 3050 Wilshire Boulevard Los Angeles, CA 90010-1106 213-738-6717 Fax: 213-383-1688 admissions@swlaw.edu	406	$60	April 1	June 1	$33,410 ($20,126)	$33,410 ($20,126)	4		4		4	87	52	4	4	698 (274)	27	51	35	8	58 (33)	483,433	63,061
Stanford University (Stanford Law School) Crown Quadrangle, 559 Nathan Abbott Way Stanford, CA 94305-8610 650-723-4985 Fax: 650-723-0838 admissions@law.stanford.edu	408	$75	Feb 1	March 15	$42,420	$42,420	4		4		4	111	29	4		539	25	47	35		49	484,986	71,806
State University of New York (University at Buffalo Law School) 309 O'Brian Hall Buffalo, NY 14260 716-645-2907 Fax: 716-645-6676 lwiley@buffalo.edu	410	$75	March 15	March 1	$16,010	$16,010	4		4		4	90	34	4		718	25	46	11	2	60 (123)	296,539	285,936
Stetson University (Stetson University College of Law) 1401 61st Street South Gulfport, FL 33707 727-562-7802 Fax: 727-343-0136 zuppo@law.stetson.edu	412	$55	March 15	open	$31,420 ($21,700)	$31,420 ($21,700)	4		4	4	4	88	52	4	4	876 (208)	24	53	23	3	52 (36)	420,000	53,670
Suffolk University (Law School) 120 Tremont Street Boston, MA 02108-4977 617-573-8144 Fax: 617-523-1367	414	$60	March 1	March 1	$39,550 ($29,664)	$39,550 ($29,664)	4		4		4	84	43	4	4	1079 (603)	25	47	17	7	92 (133)	378,478	160,122
Syracuse University (College of Law) Office of Admissions and Financial Aid, Suite 340 Syracuse, NY 13244-1030 315-443-1962 Fax: 315-443-9568	416	$70	April 1	Feb 15	$41,000	$41,000	4		4		4	87	40	4	4	659 (7)	24	45	19		59 (54)	218,058	255,018
Temple University (James E. Beasley School of Law) 1719 N. Broad Street Philadelphia, PA 19122 215-204-5949 Fax: 215-204-1185 lawadmis@temple.edu	418			n/app	$16,000 ($12,000)	$26,000 ($20,000)	4		4		4	87	40	4	4	1060	26	48	24	3	59 (212)	573,568	179,200
Texas Southern University (Thurgood Marshall School of Law) 3100 Cleburne Avenue Houston, TX 77004 713-313-7114 Fax: 713-313-1049 cgardner@tmslaw.tsu.edu	420	$55	April 1	April 1	$12,000	$16,000	4		4		4	90	70	4	4	632	27	46	80	35	34 (19)	251,722	62,907
Texas Tech University (School of Law) 1802 Hartford Avenue Lubbock, TX 79409 806-742-3990, ext. 273 Fax: 806-742-4617 donna.williams@ttu.edu	422	$50	March 15	April 15	$12,975	$20,385	4		4		4	90	55	4	4	637	24	42	25	5	38 (24)	331,191	675,175

INSTITUTION	Profile Page	APPLICATIONS Fee	APPLICATIONS Deadline	APPLICATIONS Deadline Financial Aid	TUITION In State Full Time (Part Time)	TUITION Out of State Full Time (Part Time)	CALENDAR Fall	CALENDAR Winter	CALENDAR Spring	CALENDAR Summer	PROGRAMS Day	PROGRAMS Evening	PROGRAMS Credits for JD	PROGRAMS Required Credits for Courses	PROGRAMS Transferable Summer Courses	PROGRAMS Joint Degree	PROGRAMS Graduate Law Degree	ENROLLED STUDENT BODY Full Time (Part Time)	Average Age First Year	% Women	% Minority	Attrition Rate %	FACULTY Full Time (Part Time)	LIBRARY Volumes	LIBRARY Microforms
Texas Wesleyan University (School of Law) 1515 Commerce Street Fort Worth, TX 76102 817-212-4040 Fax: 817-212-4141 lawadmissions@law.txwes.edu	424	$55	March 31	May 15	$25,250 ($17,900)	$25,250 ($17,900)	✓	✓		✓	✓	✓	90	50	✓		✓	522 (271)	28	51	16	4	35 (19)	274,945	750,960
Thomas Jefferson School of Law 2121 San Diego Avenue San Diego, CA 92110 619-297-9700 Fax: 619-294-4713 info@tjsl.edu	426	$50	open	Feb 15	$37,700 ($25,400)	$37,700 ($25,400)	✓				✓	✓	88	55	✓	✓	✓	649 (241)	26	45	33		43 (27)	102,936	135,156
Thomas M. Cooley Law School 300 South Capitol Avenue Lansing, MI 48901 517-371-5140 Fax: 517-334-5718 admissions@cooley.edu	428		open	Rolling	$27,210 ($16,326)	$27,210 ($16,326)	✓	✓			✓	✓	90	63	✓	✓	✓	538 (3185)	29	48	21	21	91 (140)	577,975	132,377
Touro College (Jacob D. Fuchsberg Law Center) 225 Eastview Drive Central Islip, NY 11722 631-761-7010 Fax: 631-761-7019 gjustice@tourolaw.edu	430		rolling	April 15	$26,000	$26,000	✓				✓		87	51 to 52	✓	✓	✓	725	26	45	23	5	31 (41)	429,683	225,964
Tulane University (Law School) Weinmann Hall, 6329 Freret Street New Orleans, LA 70118 504-865-5930 Fax: 504-865-6710 admissions@law.tulane.edu	432	$60	March 15	Feb 15	$37,200	$37,200	✓				✓	✓	88	32	✓	✓	✓	815	24	42	20	5	39 (75)	401,949	261,651
University of Akron (School of Law) 302 Buchtel Common Akron, OH 44325-2901 330-972-7331 Fax: 330-258-2343 lthorpe@uakron.edu	434		March 1	May 1	$16,808 ($13,466)	$28,088 ($22,470)	✓				✓	✓	88	44	✓	✓	✓	280 (237)	26	45	14	23	30 (27)	288,287	416,266
University of Alabama (School of Law) Box 870382 Tuscaloosa, AL 35487-0382 205-348-5440 Fax: 205-348-3917 admissions@law.ua.edu	436	$40	March 31	March 31	$12,000	$23,000	✓				✓		90	36	✓	✓	✓	615	25	39	9	4	45 (55)	438,444	143,115
University of Arizona (James E. Rogers College of Law) 120 E. Speedway P.O. Box 210176 Tucson, AZ 85721-0176 520-621-3477 Fax: 520-621-9140 admissions@law.arizona.edu	438			March 1	$13,000	$22,000	✓				✓		85	39	✓	✓	✓	480	25	50	29	1	30 (55)	410,000	426,000

School	No.	Fee	Deadline	Deadline	Res. Tuition	Non-Res. Tuition						Credits				Enrollment							
University of Arkansas (School of Law) Robert A. Leflar Law Center, Waterman Hall Fayetteville, AR 72701 479-575-3937 Fax: 479-575-3102 jkmiller@uark.edu	440		April 1	April 1	$9,279	$19,946	4				4	90	43	4	4	398	25	41	17		26 (20)	327,581	166,629
University of Arkansas at Little Rock (UALR William H. Bowen School of Law) 1201 McMath Avenue Little Rock, AR 72202-5142 501-324-9903 Fax: 501-324-9909 lawadm@ualr.edu	442		April 15	March 1	$11,285	$22,851	4				4	90	45	4	4	311 (145)	27	48	23	1	38 (82)	317,304	578,702
University of Baltimore (School of Law) 1420 North Charles Street Baltimore, MD 21201-5779 410-837-4459 Fax: 410-837-4450 lwadmiss@ubmail.ubalt.edu; j zavrotny@ubalt.edu	444	$40		March 1	$9,489 ($1,218)	$15,568 ($786)	4				4	90	41	4	4	657 (425)	26	52	13	7	48 (92)	365,150	193,533
University of California (Hastings College of the Law) 200 McAllister Street San Francisco, CA 94102 415-565-4623 Fax: 415-581-8946 admiss@uchastings.edu	446	$75	March 1	March 1	$21,303	$32,528	4				4	86	34	4	4	1262	24	53	32	2	60 (117)	707,264	71,568
University of California at Berkeley (School of Law) 215 Boalt Hall Berkeley, CA 94720 510-642-2274 Fax: 510-643-6222 adissions@law.berkeley.edu	448	$75		March 2	$27,000	$40,000	4				4	85	32	4	4	864	25	55	32	1	93 (38)	682,682	188,598
University of California at Davis (School of Law) Martin Luther King, Jr. Hall - 400 Mrak Hall Drive Davis, CA 95616-5201 530-752-6477 admissions@lawucdavis.edu	450	$75	Feb 1	March 2	$34,528	$45,474	4				4	88	33	4	4	606	24	53	37	5	49 (14)	302,516	768,833
University of California at Los Angeles (UCLA School of Law) P.O. Box 951445 Los Angeles, CA 90095-1445 310-825-2080 Fax: 310-206-7227 admissions@law.ucla.edu	452	$75	Feb 1	March 2	$35,327	$45,967	4				4	87	35	4	4	1011	25	48	33	2	110 (46)	676,524	20,313
University of Chicago (Law School) 1111 East 60th Street Chicago, IL 60637 773-702-9484 Fax: 773-834-0942 admissions@law.uchicago.edu	454	$75	Feb 1	March 1	$43,998	$43,998	4				4	105	40	4	4	593	24	45	28	1	52 (31)	624,758	11,712
University of Cincinnati (College of Law) P.O. Box 210040 Cincinnati, OH 45221-0040 513-556-6805 Fax: 513-556-2391 admissions@law.uc.edu	456	$35	March 1	March 1	$19,942	$34,776	4				4	90	36	4	4	391	25	42	16	1	32	428,753	875,904

196 Guide to Law Schools

INSTITUTION	Profile Page	Fee	Deadline	Deadline Financial Aid	TUITION In State Full Time (Part Time)	TUITION Out of State Full Time (Part Time)	Fall	Winter	Spring	Summer	Day	Evening	Credits for JD	Required Credits for Courses	Transferable Summer Courses	Joint Degree	Graduate Law Degree	ENROLLED Full Time (Part Time)	Average Age First Year	% Women	% Minority	Attrition Rate %	FACULTY Full Time (Part Time)	Volumes	Microforms
University of Colorado (Law School) Campus Box 403, Wolf Law Building Boulder, CO 80309-0403 303-492-7203 Fax: 303-492-2542	458	$65	March 15	April 1	$23,562	$31,626	✓				✓		89	40	✓	✓	✓	547	24	50	20	1	41 (21)	741,484	1,634,139
University of Connecticut (School of Law) 55 Elizabeth Street Hartford, CT 06105 860-570-5159 Fax: 860-570-5153 admissions@law.uconn.edu	460	$60	March 1	March 1	$19,608 ($16,340)	$41,328 ($34,440)	✓				✓	✓	86	36	✓	✓	✓	483 (232)	26	47	21	1	44 (44)	545,754	222,856
University of Dayton (School of Law) 300 College Park Dayton, OH 45469-2760 937-229-3555 Fax: 937-229-4194 lawinfo@notes.udayton.edu	462	$50	May 1	March 1	$32,684	$32,684	✓				✓		90	79	✓	✓	✓	500	26	42	14	16	28 (52)	186,051	877,452
University of Denver (Sturm College of Law) 2255 E. Evans Avenue Denver, CO 80208 303-871-6135 Fax: 303-871-6992 admissions@law.du.edu	464	$60	March 1	open	$35,460 ($26,004)	$35,460 ($26,004)	✓				✓	✓	90	44	✓	✓	✓	786 (232)	28	47	18	5	65 (56)	234,419	177,768
University of Detroit Mercy (School of Law) 651 East Jefferson Avenue Detroit, MI 48226 313-596-0264 Fax: 313-596-0280 udmlawao@udmercy.edu	466	$50	April 15	April 1	$32,090 ($25,688)	$32,090 ($25,688)	✓				✓	✓	90	34	✓	✓	✓	586 (144)	25	46	18	15	52 (35)	226,804	168,320
University of Florida (Fredric G. Levin College of Law) 141 Bruton-Geer Hall, P.O. Box 117622 Gainesville, FL 32611-7622 352-273-0890 Fax: 352-392-4087 madorno@law.ufl.edu	468	$30	Jan 15	April 7	$14,228	$33,592	✓				✓		88	36	✓	✓	✓	1106	24	48	23	3	75 (47)	643,282	318,270
University of Georgia (School of Law) Hirsch Hall, 225 Herty Drive Athens, GA 30602-6012 706-542-7060 Fax: 706-542-5556 ugajd@uga.edu	470	$50	March 1	July 1	$14,448	$30,226	✓				✓		88	42	✓	✓	✓	710	23	49	20	2	49 (20)	390,000	504,653
University of Hawaii at Manoa (William S. Richardson School of Law) 2515 Dole Street Honolulu, HI 96822 808-956-7966 Fax: 808-956-3813 lawadm@hawaii.edu	472	$60	March 1	March 1	$15,192 ($12,666)	$28,176 ($23,480)	✓				✓		89	42	✓	✓	✓	285 (41)	26	48	60	3	42 (15)	248,838	875,305

No.	School	App Fee	Deadline 1	Deadline 2	Tuition (res)	Tuition (nonres)																			
474	University of Houston (Law Center) 100 Law Center Houston, TX 77204-6060 713-743-2280 Fax: 713-743-2194 lawadmissions@uh.edu	$70	Nov 1	April 1	$8,293 ($5,529)	$11,998 ($7,999)	4			4	4	90	34	4	4	4	762 (234)	24	45	32	2	51 (77)	542,164	1,624,790
476	University of Idaho (College of Law) P.O. Box 442321 Moscow, ID 83844-2321 208-885-2300 Fax: 208-885-5709 jfinney@uidaho.edu	$50	Feb 15	Feb 15	$11,776	$21,856	4			4	4	90	39	4	4	4	319	26	40	12	3	33 (14)	167,549	102,842
478	University of Illinois (College of Law) 504 East Pennsylvania Avenue Champaign, IL 61820 217-244-6415 Fax: 217-244-1478 admissions@law.uiuc.edu	$50	March 15	April 1	$23,000	$33,000	4			4	4	90	33	4	4	4	587	24	40	26	2	40 (46)	615,739	928,746
480	University of Iowa (College of Law) 320 Melrose Avenue Iowa City, IA 52242 319-335-9095 Fax: 319-335-9646 law-admissions@uiowa.edu	$60	March 1	open	$20,146	$37,852	4			4	4	84	33	4	4	4	590	25	44	15	2	48 (14)	833,170	474,296
482	University of Kansas (School of Law) 205 Green Hall, 1535 W. 15th Street Lawrence, KS 66045 785-864-4378 Fax: 785-864-5054 admitlaw@ku.edu	$55	March 15	March 1	$14,101	$25,375	4		4	4	4	90	37 to 38	4	4	4	499 (16)	23	39	16	2	39 (14)	360,139	101,732
484	University of Kentucky (College of Law) 209 Law Building Lexington, KY 40506-0048 606-257-7938 Fax: (859) 323-1061 lawadmissions@email.uky.edu	$50	March 1	April 1	$13,204	$24,010	4			4	4	90	34	4	4	4	426	23	43	9	5	26 (28)	477,877	221,124
486	University of La Verne (College of Law) 320 East D Street Ontario, CA 91764 909-460-2001 Fax: 909-460-2082 lawadm@ulv.edu	$60	July 1	May 15	$31,590 ($23,690)		4			4	4	88	60	4	4	4	205 (105)	26	42	31	22	19 (12)	97,233	208,841
488	University of Louisville (Louis D. Brandeis School of Law) University of Louisville Belknap Campus-Wilson W. Wyatt Hall Louisville, KY 40292 502-852-6364 Fax: 502-852-8971 brandon.hamilton@louisville.edu	$50	April 1	June 1	$14,440 ($12,610)	$28,980 ($25,956)	4			4	4	90	44	4	4	4	368 (67)	24	45	8	5	34 (9)	417,747	190,390
490	University of Maine (School of Law) 246 Deering Avenue Portland, ME 04102 207-780-4341 Fax: 207-780-4239 mainelaw@usm.maine.edu	$50	March 1	Feb 15	$18,025	$28,105	4			4	4	90	56	4	4	4	251 (7)	27	53	6	3	18 (7)	330,999	132,739

INSTITUTION	Profile Page	APPLICATIONS			TUITION		CALENDAR				PROGRAMS							ENROLLED STUDENT BODY					FACULTY	LIBRARY	
		Fee	Deadline	Deadline Financial Aid	In State Full Time (Part Time)	Out of State Full Time (Part Time)	Fall	Winter	Spring	Summer	Day	Evening	Credits for JD	Required Creits for Courses	Transferable Summer Courses	Joint Degree	Graduate Law Degree	Full Time (Part Time)	Average Age First Year	% Women	% Minority	Attrition Rate %	Full Time (Part Time)	Volumes	Microforms
University of Maryland (School of Law) 500 West Baltimore Street Baltimore, MD 21201 410-706-3492 Fax: 410-706-1793 admissions@law.umaryland.edu	492	$65	March 1	March 1	$19,744 ($14,790)	$31,023 ($23,369)	4				4		85	34 to 35	4	4		678 (153)	25	55	35	1	56 (99)	353,820	141,718
University of Memphis (Cecil C. Humphreys School of Law) 1 North Front Street Memphis, TN 38103-2189 901-678-5403 Fax: 901-678-0741 lawadmissions@memphis.edu	494	$25	March 1	April 1	$11,950 ($10,697)	$33,822 ($29,583)	4				4		90	57	4	4		392 (28)	26	42	14	3	23 (26)	274,325	105,352
University of Miami (School of Law) P.O. Box 248087, 1311 Miller Drive Coral Gables, FL 33124-8087 305-284-2523 Fax: 305-284-4400 admissions@law.miami.edu	496	$60	Feb 4	Feb 1	$37,418	$37,418	4				4		88	72	4	4	4	1351 (33)	24	45	30	2	80 (104)	431,381	218,280
University of Michigan (Law School) 625 South State Street Ann Arbor, MI 48109-1215 734-764-0537 Fax: 734-647-3218 law.jd.admissions@umich.edu	498	$60	Feb 15	rolling	$43,010	$46,010	4			4	4		82	32	4	4	4	1117	24	44	23	4	87 (33)	1,002,273	1,673,989
University of Minnesota (Law School) 229 19th Avenue S. Minneapolis, MN 55455 612-625-3487 Fax: 612-626-1874 jdadmissions@umn.edu	500	$75	April 1	April 1	$25,324	$34,726	4				4		88	33	4	4	4	850	25	45	18	4	66 (121)	1,083,918	366,973
University of Mississippi (L.Q.C. Lamar Hall) P.O. Box 1848 Lamar Law Center University, MS 38677 662-915-6910 Fax: 662-915-1289 bvinson@olemiss.edu	502	$40	March 1		$9,377	$18,997	4			4	4		90	36 to 37	4	4	4	517	23	44	14	2	26 (16)	336,487	172,860
University of Missouri-Columbia (School of Law) 103 Hulston Hall Columbia, MO 65211 573-882-6042 Fax: 573-882-9625 heckmn@missouri.edu	504	$55	March 1	March 1	$14,883	$29,385	4				4		89	45	4	4	4	445	25	38	13	3	22 (13)	401,578	124,907
University of Missouri-Kansas City (School of Law) 500 East 52nd Street Kansas City, MO 64110-2499 816-235-1644 Fax: 816-235-5276 brooks@umkc.edu	506	$50			$14,316 ($8,590)	$28,266 ($16,960)	4				4	4	91	54	4	4	4	489 (26)	25	40	13	13	33 (41)	224,325	124,033

No.	School / Contact																			
508	**University of Montana** (School of Law) Missoula, MT 59812 406-243-2698 Fax: 406-243-2576 heidi.fanslow@umontana.edu		March 1		$10,000	$20,000	4				4		90	56		4	4	245		27	51	7		22 (21)	123,661	134,480
510	**University of Nebraska-Lincoln** (College of Law) P.O. Box 830902 Lincoln, NE 68583-0902 402-472-2161 Fax: 402-472-5185 lawadm@unl.edu	$25	March 1	May 1	$9,158	$23,603	4	4	4	4	93	45	4	4	393 (5)	24	40	89	6	36 (23)	243,206	175,351
512	**University of Nevada, Las Vegas** (William S. Boyd School of Law) 4505 Maryland Parkway, Box 451003 Las Vegas, NV 89154-1003 702-895-2440 Fax: 702-895-2414 request@law.unlv.edu	$50	March 15	Feb 1	$18,000 ($643/hr)	$30,000 ($1,071/hr)	4	4	4	4	89	41	4	4	370 (118)	27	47	29		52 (23)	330,808	198,454
514	**University of New Mexico** (School of Law) MSC11-6070, 1 University of New Mexico Albuquerque, NM 87131-0001 505-277-0958 Fax: 505-277-9958 witherington@law.unm.edu	$50	Feb 15	March 1	$10,561	$24,467	4	4	4	4	86	41	4	4	347	28	51	45		37 (20)	433,064	39,325
516	**University of North Carolina at Chapel Hill** (School of Law) Campus Box 3380 Van Hecke-Wettach Hall Chapel Hill, NC 27599-3380 919-962-5109 Fax: 919-843-7939 law_admissions@unc.edu		Feb 1	Dec 31	$14,000	$26,000	4	4	4	4	86	33	4	4	699	23	52	24	3	44 (61)	527,954	32,207
518	**University of North Dakota** (School of Law) Box 9003 Grand Forks, ND 58202 701-777-2104 Fax: 701-777-2217 linda.kohoutek@thor.law.und.nodak.edu			Check	$7,000	$14,000	4	4	4	4	90	34	4	4	205	26	52	11	6	11 (16)	251,320	129,554
520	**University of Notre Dame** (Notre Dame Law School) P.O. Box 780 Notre Dame, IN 46556-0780 574-631-6626 Fax: 574-631-5474 lawadmit@nd.edu	$60	March 15	Feb 15	$39,320	$39,320	4	4	4	4	90	42	4	4	548 (1)	24	42	23	1	53 (43)	356,733	315,657
522	**University of Oklahoma** (College of Law) Andrew M. Coats Hall 300 Timberdell Road Norman, OK 73019 405-325-4728 Fax: 405-325-0502 rlucas@ou.edu	$50	March 15	March 1	$12,218	$21,045	4	4	4	4	90	41	4	4	550	24	43	21	2	39 (29)	364,449	81,119
524	**University of Oregon** (School of Law, William W. Knight Law Center) 1221 University of Oregon Eugene, OR 97403-1221 541-346-3846 Fax: 541-346-3984 admissions@law.uoregon.edu	$50	March 1	March 1	$22,328	$27,818	4	4	4	4	85	36	4	4	544 (9)	26	45	18	1	33 (51)	205,324	185,420

INSTITUTION	Profile Page	APPLICATIONS Fee	Deadline	Deadline Financial Aid	TUITION In State Full Time (Part Time)	TUITION Out of State Full Time (Part Time)	CALENDAR Fall	CALENDAR Winter	CALENDAR Spring	CALENDAR Summer	PROGRAMS Day	Evening	Credits for JD	Required Credits for Courses	Transferable Summer Courses	Joint Degree	Graduate Law Degree	ENROLLED STUDENT BODY Full Time (Part Time)	Average Age First Year	% Women	% Minority	Attrition Rate %	FACULTY Full Time (Part Time)	LIBRARY Volumes	Microforms
University of Pennsylvania (Law School) 3400 Chestnut Street Philadelphia, PA 19104-6204 215-898-7400 Fax: 215-898-9606 admissions@law.upenn.edu	526	$75	Feb 15	March 1	$43,680	$43,680	4				4	4	89	28		4	4	790	24	47	28	1	74 (82)	879,269	129,458
University of Pittsburgh (School of Law) 3900 Forbes Avenue Pittsburgh, PA 15260 412-648-1413 Fax: 412-648-1318 Mccall@law.pitt.edu	528	$55	March 1	April 1	$24,368	$32,364	4				4	4	88	34		4	4	709 (12)	24	47	16	1	54 (97)	470,958	204,232
University of Puerto Rico (School of Law) P.O. Box 23349, UPR Station Rio Piedras, PR 00931-3349 787-999-9551 Fax: 787-999-9564 arosario-lebron@law.upr.edu	530	$20	Feb 15	May 1	$3,200 ($1,544)	$3,200	4				4	4	92	46		4	4	535 (182)	24	52		5	30 (66)	283,745	172,059
University of Richmond (School of Law) 28 Westhampton Way Richmond, VA 23173 804-289-8189 Fax: 804-287-6516 lawadmissions@richmond.edu	532	$35	Feb 15	March 1	$32,450	$32,450	4			4	4	4	86	35	4	4	4	465 (1)	24	48	17	1	48 (74)	407,871	194,283
University of Saint Thomas (School of Law) 1000 LaSalle Ave. Minneapolis, MN 55403 651-962-4895 Fax: 651-962-4876 lawschool@stthomas.edu	534	$50	July 1	July 1	$34,472	$34,472	4				4	4	88	46	4	4	4	457 (2)	25	45	14	3	36 (61)	207,979	881,232
University of San Diego (School of Law) 5998 Alcala Park San Diego, CA 92110 619-260-4528 Fax: 619-260-2218 jdinfo@sandiego.edu	536	$50	Feb 1	March 2	$37,560 ($26,670)	$37,560 ($26,670)	4				4	4	85	35	4	4	4	824 (325)	24	44	29	2	56 (39)	529,802	226,282
University of San Francisco (School of Law) 2130 Fulton Street San Francisco, CA 94117-1080 415-422-6586 Fax: 415-422-5442 lawadmissions@usfca.edu	538	$60	Feb 1	Feb 15	$33,790 ($24,200)	$33,790 ($24,200)	4				4	4	86	48	4	4	4	556 (156)	26	52	37	9	29 (64)	136,407	216,954
University of South Carolina (School of Law) 701 South Main Streetquarter Columbia, SC 29208 803-777-6605 Fax: 803-777-7751 usclaw@law.sc.edu	540	$60	March 1	March 1	$19,034	$38,014	4				4		90	46	4	4	4	685 quarter	24	42	12	3	31 (21)	500,000	2,718

#	School / Contact	App fee	Deadline	Deadline	Tuition (res)	Tuition (nonres)														
542	**University of South Dakota (School of Law)** 414 East Clark Street, Vermillion, SD 57069-2390 · 605-677-5443 · Fax: 605-677-5417 · law.school@usd.edu	$35	March 1		$5,203 ($2,822)	$15,083 ($7,500)	4		4	90	46	4	4	202 (2)	26	50	7	3	15	213,077	46,922
544	**University of Southern California (Gould School of Law)** Los Angeles, CA 90089-0071 · 213-740-2523 · admissions@law.usc.edu	$70	Feb 1	March 1	$46,264	$46,264	4		4	88	33	4	4	598	23	47	38	1	50 (105)	429,267	106,285
546	**University of Tennessee (College of Law)** 1505 W. Cumberland Avenue, Knoxville, TN 37996-1810 · 865-974-4131 · Fax: 865-974-1572 · lawadmit@utk.edu	$15	Feb 15	March 1	$11,196	$29,640	4		4	89	38	4	4	471	23	47	21	2	28 (41)	590,896	46,903
548	**University of Texas at Austin (School of Law)** 727 East Dean Keeton Street, Austin, TX 78705 · 512-232-1200 · Fax: 512-471-2765 · admissions@law.utexas.edu	$70	Feb 1	March 31	$21,000	$36,000	4		4	86	38	4	4	1441	24	43	33	1	87 (93)	1,046,921	350,983
550	**University of the District of Columbia (David A. Clarke School of Law)** 4200 Connecticut Avenue, N.W., Washington, DC 20008 · 202-274-7341 · Fax: 202-274-5583 · vcarry@udc.edu; lawadmission@udc.edu	$35	March 15	March 31	$7,350 ($5,250)	$14,700 ($10,500)	4		4	90	75	4	4	266 (27)	28	60	28	5	20 (17)	257,000	114,989
552	**University of the Pacific (McGeorge School of Law)** 3200 Fifth Avenue, Sacramento, CA 95817 · 916-739-7105 · Fax: 916-739-7301 · mcgeorge@pacific.edu	$50	May 1	open	$38,556 ($25,632)	$38,556 ($25,632)	4		4	88	59	4	4	660 (377)	25	50	50	14	55 (57)	509,762	294,936
554	**University of Toledo (College of Law)** 2801 West Bancroft Street, Toledo, OH 43606-3390 · 419-530-4131 · Fax: 419-530-4345 · law.utoledo.edu	$40	July 1	open	$16,272 ($12,204)	$280,008 ($21,006)	4		4	89	42	4	4	346 (148)	26	40	10	8	31 (18)	360,833	137,340
556	**University of Tulsa (College of Law)** 3120 East Fourth Place, Tulsa, OK 74104-2499 · 918-631-2406 · Fax: 918-631-3630 · april-fox@utulsa.edu	$30	open	April 1	$28,876 ($18,572)	$28,876 ($18,572)	4		4	88	50 to 53	4	4	389 (40)	28	39	16	2	29 (28)	410,962	1,066,843
558	**University of Utah (S.J. Quinney College of Law)** 332 South 1400 East Room 101, Salt Lake City, UT 84112 · 801-581-7479 · Fax: 801-581-6897 · aguilarr@law.utah.edu	$60	Feb 15		$17,950	$34,046	4		4	88	40	4	4	401	28	41	13	2	42 (72)	340,000	103,000
560	**University of Virginia (School of Law)** 580 Massie Road, Charlottesville, VA 22903-1738 · 434-924-7351 · Fax: 434-982-2128 · lawadmit@virginia.edu	$75	March 1	March 1	$38,800	$43,800	4		4	86	29	4	4	1122	24	44	20	1	76 (94)	876,458	275,048

INSTITUTION	Profile Page	Fee	Deadline	Deadline Financial Aid	In State Full Time (Part Time)	Out of State Full Time (Part Time)	Fall	Winter	Spring	Summer	Day	Evening	Credits for JD	Required Credits for Courses	Transferable Summer Courses	Joint Degree	Graduate Law Degree	Full Time (Part Time)	Average Age First Year	% Women	% Minority	Attrition Rate %	Full Time (Part Time)	Volumes	Microforms
University of Washington (School of Law) Box 353020 Seattle, WA 98195-3020 206-543-4078 Fax: 206-543-5671 lawadm@u.washington.edu	562	$50	Jan 15	Feb 28	$22,267	$32,777	4				4		135 quarters	49	4	4	4	561	26	55	21	2	46 (46)	617,260	187,870
University of Wisconsin (Law School) 975 Bascom Mall Madison, WI 53706 608-262-5914 Fax: 608-263-3191 admissions@law.wisc.edu	564	$56	March 1	March 1	$16,426 ($686/hr)	$36,350 ($1,516/hr)	4				4		90	40 to 45	4	4	4	792 (33)	25	46	23		50 (59)	449,048	168,407
University of Wyoming (College of Law) Dept. 3035, 1000 East University Avenue Laramie, WY 82071 307-766-6416 Fax: 307-766-6417 dburke@uwyo.edu	566	$50	March 1	March 1	$8,952	$20,142	4				4		89	37	4	4	4	226	26	48	13	2	23 (10)	322,174	152,066
Valparaiso University (School of Law) Wesemann Hall, 656 S. Greenwich Street Valparaiso, IN 46383-6493 219-465-7821 Fax: 219-465-7808 law.admissions@valpo.edu	568	$60	June 1	March 1	$30,510 ($1,196/hr)	$30,510 ($1,196/hr)	4				4	4	90 units	57	4	4	4	486 (56)	25	46	18	15	37 (40)	332,337	936,822
Vanderbilt University (Law School) 131 21st Avenue South Nashville, TN 37203 615-322-6452 Fax: 615-322-1531 admissions@law.vanderbilt.edu	570	$50	March 15	Feb 15	$43,700	$43,700	4				4		88	38		4	4	594	23	48	18	8	48 (75)	480,079	740,667
Vermont Law School P.O. Box 96, Chelsea Street South Royalton, VT 05068-0096 802-831-1239 Fax: 802-831-1174 admiss@vermontlaw.edu	572	$60	March 1	March 1	$39,995	$39,995	4				4		87	52		4	4	567	26	50	9		59 (14)	254,127	122,219
Villanova University (School of Law) 299 N. Spring Mill Road Villanova, PA 19085 610-519-7010 Fax: 610-519-6291 admissions@law.villanova.edu	574	$75	March 1	March 1	$34,860	$34,860	4				4		88	44		4	4	754	23	44	17	1	45 (65)	345,482	1,150,098
Wake Forest University (School of Law) P.O. Box 7206, Reynolda Station Winston-Salem, NC 27109 336-758-5437 Fax: 336-758-4632 admissions@law.wfu.edu	576	$60	March 15	May 1	$35,450	$35,450	4				4		89	41	4	4	4	465 (10)	24	44	20	3	39 (18)	419,496	

School	No.	Fee	Deadline	Deadline	Tuition	Tuition					%	%				Enroll.						Vol.	Vol.
Washburn University (School of Law) 1700 College Topeka, KS 66621 785-670-1185 Fax: 785-670-1120 admissions@washburnlaw.edu	578	$40	Nov 1	June 1	$16,080	$25,080	4		4	4	90	44	4	4	4	441	25	40		4	33 (51)	395,673	179,562
Washington and Lee University (School of Law) Lewis Hall Lexington, VA 24450 540-458-8503 Fax: 540-458-8586 lawadm@wlu.edu	580	$50	March 1	Feb 15	$38,062	$38,062	4		4	4	85	37	4	4	4	390	24	43	19	1	39 (21)	444,532	187,924
Washington University in St. Louis (School of Law) Box 1120, One Brookings Drive St. Louis, MO 63130 314-935-4525 Fax: 314-935-8778 admiss@wulaw.wustl.edu	582			March 1	$36,000	$36,000	4		4	4	85	35	4	4	4	875	23	41	21		54 (107)	660,000	1,389,966
Wayne State University (Law School) 471 West Palmer Street Detroit, MI 48202 313-577-3937 Fax: 313-993-8129 emjackson@wayne.edu	584	$50	March 15	June 30	$22,331 ($11,909)	$24,537 ($13,086)	4		4	4	86	35	4	4	4	457 (112)	25	50	15	6	43 (24)	627,452	224,071
West Virginia University (College of Law) P.O. Box 6130 Morgantown, WV 26506 304-293-5304 Fax: 304-293-6891 wvulaw.Admissions@mail.wvu.edu	586			March 1	$10,644	$24,010	4		4	4	91	37	4	4	4	490	26	44	8		19 (21)	347,393	550,200
Western New England College (School of Law) 1215 Wilbraham Road Springfield, MA 01119 413-782-1406 Fax: 413-796-2067 admissions@law.wnec.edu	588	$50	March 15	rolling	$34,378 ($25,784)	$34,378 ($25,784)	4		4	4	88	46	4	4	4	389 (149)	25	53	11	1	38 (36)	362,091	227,772
Western State University (College of Law) 1111 North State College Blvd Fullerton, CA 92831 714-459-1101 Fax: 714-441-1748 adm@wsulaw.edu	590	$50	June 1	March 2	$32,600 ($21,800)	$32,600 ($21,800)	4	4		4	88	72	4		4	276 (141)	26	50	34		25 (23)	208,080	99,070
Whittier College (Whittier Law School) 3333 Harbor Blvd. Costa Mesa, CA 92626 714-444-4141, ext. 121 Fax: 714-444-0250 info@law.whittier.edu	592			May 1	$29,860 ($19,500)	$29,860 ($19,500)	4		4	4	87	40	4	4	4	503 (385)	28	52	42	31	28 (41)	421,678	133,552
Widener University (Widener University School of Law) 4601 Concord Pike, P.O. Box 7474 Wilmington, DE 19803-0474 302-477-2162 Fax: 302-477-2224 law.admissions@law.widener.edu	594	$60	May 15	open	$33,540 ($24,620)	$33,540 ($24,620)	4		4	4	88	57	4	4	4	612 (363)	24	44	8	28	61 (68)	258,433	332,319

INSTITUTION	Profile Page	APPLICATIONS Fee	APPLICATIONS Deadline	APPLICATIONS Deadline Financial Aid	TUITION In State Full Time (Part Time)	TUITION Out of State Full Time (Part Time)	CALENDAR Fall	CALENDAR Winter	CALENDAR Spring	CALENDAR Summer	PROGRAMS Day	PROGRAMS Evening	PROGRAMS Credits for JD	PROGRAMS Required Credits for Courses	PROGRAMS Transferable Summer Courses	PROGRAMS Joint Degree	PROGRAMS Graduate Law Degree	ENROLLED STUDENT BODY Full Time (Part Time)	ENROLLED STUDENT BODY Average Age First Year	ENROLLED STUDENT BODY % Women	ENROLLED STUDENT BODY % Minority	ENROLLED STUDENT BODY Attrition Rate %	FACULTY Full Time (Part Time)	LIBRARY Volumes	LIBRARY Microforms
Widener University (Widener University School of Law) 3800 Vartan Way, P.O. Box 69381 Harrisburg, PA 17106-9381 717-541-3903 Fax: 717-541-3999 law.admissions@law.widener.edu	596	$60	May 15	open	$33,540 ($24,920)	$33,540 ($24,620)	✓				✓	✓	88	66	✓	✓		358 (103)	23	48	10	13	30 (30)	258,433	332,319
Willamette University (College of Law) 245 Winter Street S.E. Salem, OR 97301 503-370-6282 Fax: 503-370-6087 law-admission@willamette.edu	598	$50	March 1	March 1	$29,600	$29,600	✓				✓		90	40	✓	✓	✓	424	26	42	15	4	37 (22)	299,123	156,790
William Mitchell College of Law 875 Summit Avenue St. Paul, MN 55105-3076 651-290-6343 Fax: 651-290-6414 admissions@wmitchell.edu	600	$50	May 1	March 15	$32,340 ($23,400)	$32,340 ($23,400)	✓				✓	✓	86	46	✓	✓	✓	603 (418)	27	51	11	11	36 (229)	356,269	154,517
Yale University (Yale Law School) P.O. Box 208329 New Haven, CT 06520-8329 203-432-4995 admissions.law@yale.edu	602	$75	Feb 15	March 15	$43,750	$43,750	✓		✓		✓		83	21		✓	✓	620	25	48	35		67 (42)	874,393	40,781
Yeshiva University (Benjamin N. Cardozo School of Law) 55 Fifth Avenue New York, NY 10003 212-790-0274 Fax: 212-790-0482 lawinfo@yu.edu	604	$70	April 1	April 15	$44,600	$44,600	✓				✓		84	55			✓	1020 (101)	24	50	22	3	57 (76)	560,325	1,338,310

Regional Maps Locating ABA-Approved Law Schools

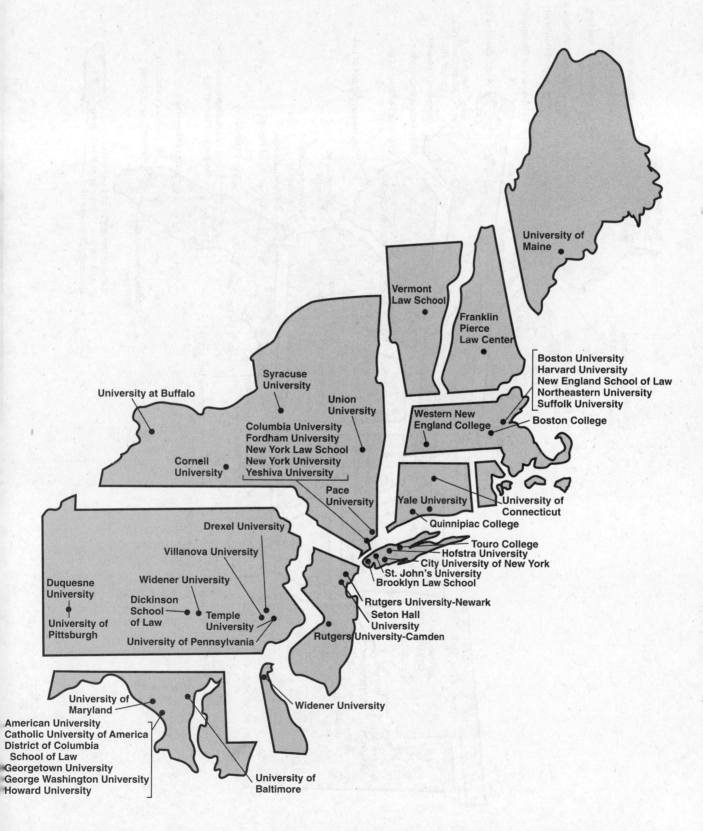

University of Maine

Vermont Law School

Franklin Pierce Law Center

Boston University
Harvard University
New England School of Law
Northeastern University
Suffolk University

Boston College

Syracuse University

University at Buffalo

Union University

Western New England College

Columbia University
Fordham University
New York Law School
New York University
Yeshiva University

Cornell University

Pace University

Yale University

University of Connecticut

Quinnipiac College

Drexel University

Villanova University

Touro College
Hofstra University
City University of New York
St. John's University
Brooklyn Law School

Duquesne University

Widener University

Dickinson School of Law

Temple University

Rutgers University-Newark
Seton Hall University

University of Pittsburgh

University of Pennsylvania

Rutgers University-Camden

University of Maryland

Widener University

American University
Catholic University of America
District of Columbia School of Law
Georgetown University
George Washington University
Howard University

University of Baltimore

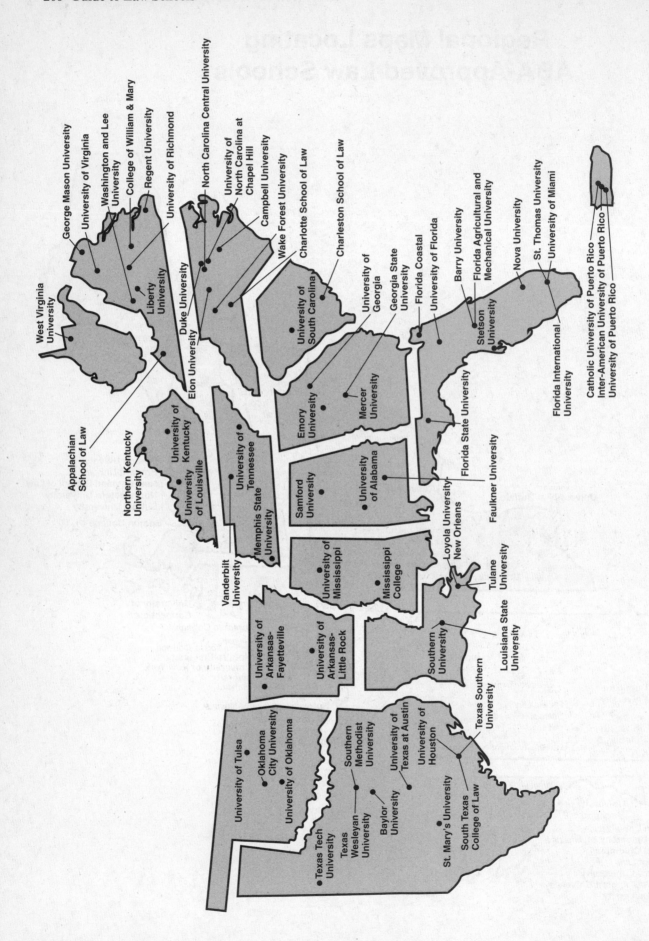

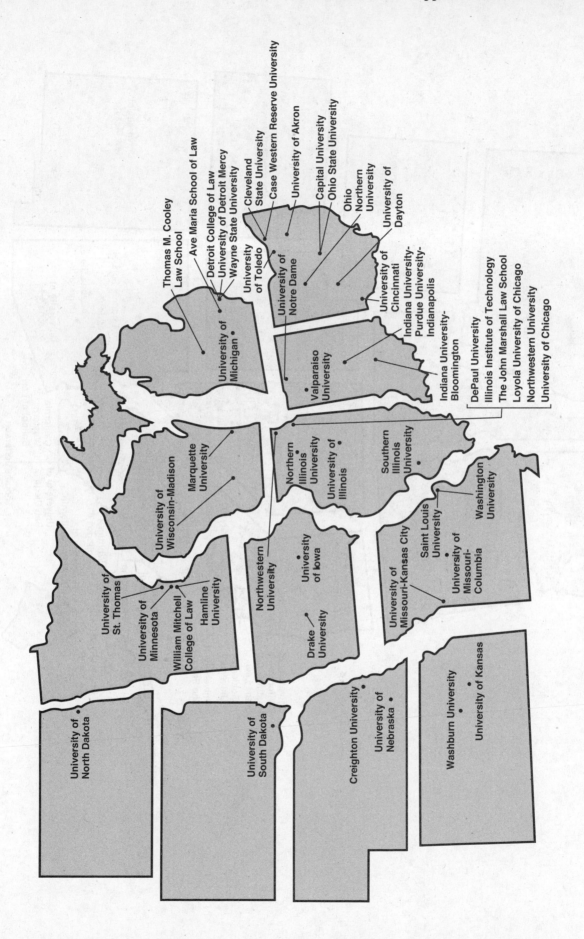

Thomas M. Cooley Law School
Ave Maria School of Law
Detroit College of Law
University of Detroit Mercy
Wayne State University
University of Michigan

University of Toledo

Cleveland State University
Case Western Reserve University
University of Akron
Capital University
Ohio State University
Ohio Northern University
University of Dayton

University of Notre Dame

University of Cincinnati

Indiana University-Purdue University-Indianapolis

Indiana University-Bloomington

Valparaiso University

DePaul University
Illinois Institute of Technology
The John Marshall Law School
Loyola University of Chicago
Northwestern University
University of Chicago

University of Wisconsin-Madison

Marquette University

Northern Illinois University

University of Illinois

Southern Illinois University

Washington University

University of Missouri-Kansas City

Saint Louis University

University of Missouri-Columbia

University of St. Thomas
University of Minnesota
William Mitchell College of Law
Hamline University

Northwestern University

University of Iowa

Drake University

University of North Dakota

University of South Dakota

Creighton University

University of Nebraska

Washburn University

University of Kansas

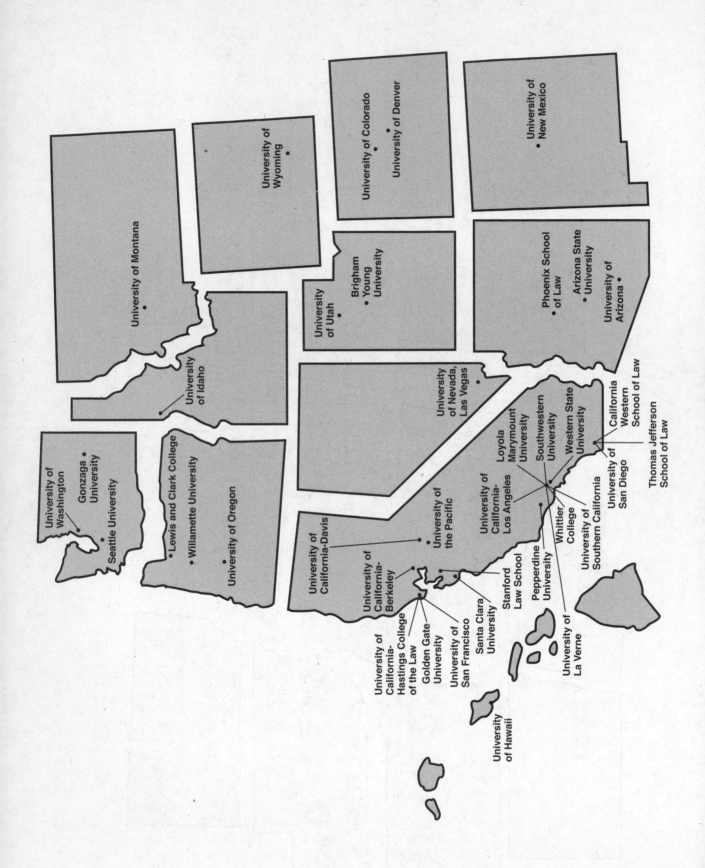

CHAPTER 15

Profiles of ABA-Approved Law Schools

The school profiles included in Barron's *Guide to Law Schools* comprise the listing of 198 law schools that are fully or provisionally approved by the American Bar Association and grant the J.D. degree. (One ABA-approved law school, the Judge Advocate General's School, located in Charlottesville, Virginia, and associated with the U.S. Army, is not included in our listings because it offers post-J.D. programs only.) The schools are arranged in alphabetical order by the name of the institution to which they are attached or, for independent law schools, by the name of the school. Also included for your convenience is a listing of the law schools by state.

So that you may use the profiles to best advantage, an explanation of the entries follows.

THE HEADING

The first-page heading of each profile presents the official name of the parent college or university (if any) and of the law school and the law school mailing address. The page two heading of each entry contains phone and fax numbers, followed by e-mail and web addresses; names and phone numbers of admissions and financial aid contacts; and a map showing the location within the respective state of each school.

THE CAPSULE

The capsule of each profile provides basic information about the law school. Wherever *n/av* is used in the capsule, it means the information was not available. Wherever *none* or *n/app* is used in the capsule, it means the category was not applicable to the law school.

Application filing dates and fees lead off the capsule.

Accrediting agencies, and **degrees granted** fill out this section of the capsule.

Accreditation Every school profiled is fully or provisionally approved by the American Bar Association. This means that the law school has met the educational standards set by the ABA regarding faculty, curricula, facilities, and other matters to qualify its graduates for admission to the Bar. In addition, membership in the Association of American Law Schools (AALS) is also indicated. Schools are not eligible for AALS membership until they have graduated three classes and have been in operation for five years. AALS membership is complementary to, but *not* competitive with, ABA approval.

Degrees Granted Law schools today offer the J.D. (Juris Doctor) degree, rather than the traditional LL.B. This recognizes the fact that virtually all law schools now require a B.A. for admission and that the curriculum of the law school represents graduate-level work. Law schools offering post-law school graduate work leading to such degrees as the LL.M. (Master of Laws), M.C.L. (Master of Comparative Law), and J.S.D. (Doctor of the Science of Law) degrees are noted.

These data are followed by **enrollment** figures for men, women, and minorities, and out-of-state students in the first-year class. Actual figures and percentages are both given.

This section also includes the number of applicants, accepted candidates, and enrolled first-year students.

The current **class profile** includes LSAT scoring and passing-the-bar information.

Finally, **tuition and fees** are graphically displayed for both in- and out-of-state applicants, showing comparisons with average nationwide figures. It is important to remember that tuition costs generally change at least yearly, and that changes can be substantial. Students are therefore urged to contact individual law schools for the most current tuition figures.

Also shown in this section is the percentage of current law students receiving **financial aid.**

Admissions The **admissions** section leads off the law school's descriptive passages, where some of the capsule information is reinforced.

The subsection *Requirements* includes whether a bachelor's degree is an absolute necessity and lists the factors considered in the admissions decision, such as LSAT percentile, GPA, and any nonacademic requirements. Virtually all of the law schools require the LSAT and a bachelor's degree, although some schools admit students without a bachelor's degree in exceptional cases. Very few schools require specific undergraduate courses or degrees or an admissions interview. Although not actual requirements, there are some qualities that schools seek in their applicants, such as preferred LSAT percentiles and GPAs. Where available, these preferred qualities also are given.

The subsection *Procedure* lists the application deadlines for various sessions, when the LSAT should be taken, the application fee, and when students are notified of the admissions decision. If a school makes admissions decisions on a rolling basis, it decides on each application as soon as possible after the file is complete and does not specify a notification deadline. As a general rule, it is best to submit applications as early as possible. Many schools require a tuition deposit to hold a place in the class. In some cases the deposit is refundable; in some, it is partially refundable; and in some, it is nonrefundable. Most schools participate in the Law School Data Assembly Service (LSDAS); if the school uses this application service, it is noted in this section.

The subsection *Special* describes admissions programs and includes information on special recruiting procedures and considerations for minority and disadvantaged students; whether the school's requirements for out-of-state students differ and whether transfer students are admitted. Although requirements for transfer with advanced standing differ from school to school, in general the applicant must have been in good standing at the school he or she is transferring from and must have completed a minimum of one year of law school study. Preadmissions courses offered by the school are also described.

Costs As noted in the explanation for the capsule, costs change from year to year; therefore, students are urged to contact the individual law schools for the most current figures. This section gives costs for tuition, additional fees, room and board, and books and supplies.

Financial Aid This section describes the availability of financial aid. It includes the percentage of students who receive aid; the types and sources of aid available, such as scholarships, grants, loans, part-time jobs, and assistantships; and the criteria for aid awards. The size of the average scholarship or grant is noted. Information on aid application deadlines and notification dates is also provided.

THE GENERAL DESCRIPTION

About the Law School This paragraph indicates, in general, whether the law school is part of a university or college, when it was founded, whether it is public or private, and its religious affiliation, if any. The school's educational philosophy, primary goals, and major characteristics are noted. Because law school programs often make use of law-related institutions, such as courts, jails, and public defenders' offices, the school's proximity to such institutions is noted. There is also information on the law school's facilities: the campus (its size, the type of area in which it is located, and its proximity to a large city); whether housing is available on campus; and whether the housing office helps students find off-campus accommodations. This section also describes the percentage of the campus accessible to physically disabled persons.

Calendar This section describes whether courses are offered for full-time and/or part-time students and whether they are offered during the day and/or evening. It also describes the minimum and maximum lengths of time allowed for completion of the program, when new students may enter the program, the availability of summer sessions, and the availability of transferable summer credits.

Programs Entries list the degrees granted, including graduate law degrees and joint degrees.

The subsection *Required* describes the number of credits needed for the J.D. and the minimum grade point average that must be maintained. The specific mandatory course requirements are listed, as well as any additional requirements for graduation. At some law schools required courses make up a major portion of the curriculum, whereas at others there are fewer required courses, allowing more room for electives. The majority of schools have a fairly even mix of mandatory and elective courses, although in most cases first-year courses are prescribed. Many law schools permit students to take a limited number of relevant graduate courses offered by other schools or departments of the institution.

Special programs are described in the subsection *Electives*. Clinical training programs offer a wide range of activities allied with, but separate from, traditional classroom studies. They cover such areas as working with legal aid societies and antipoverty groups; doing research for consumer-protection agencies; working with public defender programs or as interns in federal, district, or county attorneys' offices; and engaging in a multitude of legal or quasilegal activities. Some law schools offer a variety of programs and special activities, which allow all students to participate in some way. Other law schools have narrow or limited programs, or limit the number of students who may participate. Some schools have special or unusual seminars; some have programs involving study abroad; and some allow students to pursue independent study, usually under the supervision of a member of the law school faculty. Some schools also have tutorial or remedial programs. The most widely taken electives are listed here.

The subsection *Graduation Requirements* describes the minimum grade point average a student must maintain, whether or not there is an upper-division writing requirement, and what other requirements must be fulfilled.

Organizations Virtually all law schools have student-edited law reviews; some law schools publish more than one law review and some publish other types of legal journals and newspapers as well. Students selected to work on these publications gain valuable research, writing, and editing experience. Most schools also have moot court programs and engage in intramural and interschool competitions. Other campus activities and organizations, such as special interest or academic clubs and sororities and fraternities, are also listed in this section.

Library This section lists the resources of the law library, such as the total number of hardcopy volumes, the number of microform volume equivalents, the number of serial publications, and special collections or depositories. Computerized legal-research databases, such as LEXIS and WESTLAW, are noted, as well as the ratio of library volumes to faculty and to students, and the ratio of seats in the library to students. Recent improvements to the library are also described.

Faculty The number of full-time and part-time faculty members is given here. The percentage of full-time faculty members with a graduate law degree is noted. The ratio of full-time students to full-time faculty in an average class and in a clinic are noted here. In addition to regular classroom lectures, those law schools that have a regular program of inviting legal scholars, attorneys, and other notable speakers to campus to lecture on law-related topics are indicated. If the school has a chapter of the Order of the Coif, a national law school honor society, this is also noted here; the number of faculty who are members as well as the number of recent graduates who became members are sometimes given. Only students who are in the top 10 percent of their class are eligible for membership.

Students This paragraph gives an idea of the mix of backgrounds at a school. It includes, where available, data on the geographic distribution of the student body and on how many students enter directly from undergraduate school, have a graduate degree, or have full-time work experience. The average age of entering students is given, as is the age range. The attrition rate and reasons for discontinuing law study are noted.

The **Placement** sidebar is the final section offered for each school entry. Displayed here is information concerning the number of J.D.s awarded the previous academic year, followed by a listing of the placement services and special features available to students. Statistics relating to job interviews and job placement (and average starting salaries) follow. Finally, a breakdown of placement history is presented.

INDEX BY STATE OF ABA-APPROVED LAW SCHOOLS

ALABAMA
Faulkner University
Samford University
University of Alabama

ARIZONA
Arizona State University
Phoenix School of Law
University of Arizona

ARKANSAS
University of Arkansas
University of Arkansas at Little Rock

CALIFORNIA
California Western School of Law
Chapman University
Golden Gate University
Loyola Marymount University
Pepperdine University
Santa Clara University
Southwestern University
Stanford University
Thomas Jefferson School of Law
University of California
University of California at Berkeley
University of California at Davis
University of California at Los Angeles
University of La Verne
University of San Diego
University of San Francisco
University of Southern California
University of the Pacific
Western State University
Whittier College

COLORADO
University of Colorado
University of Denver

CONNECTICUT
Quinnipiac University
University of Connecticut
Yale University

DELAWARE
Widener University

DISTRICT OF COLUMBIA
American University
Catholic University of America
George Washington University
Georgetown University
Howard University
University of the District of Columbia

FLORIDA
Barry University
Florida Agricultural and Mechanical University
Florida Coastal
Florida International University
Florida State University
Nova Southeastern University
Saint Thomas University
Stetson University
University of Florida
University of Miami

GEORGIA
Atlanta's John Marshall Law School
Emory University
Georgia State University

Mercer University
University of Georgia

HAWAII
University of Hawaii at Manoa

IDAHO
University of Idaho

ILLINOIS
De Paul University
Illinois Institute of Technology
John Marshall Law School
Loyola University Chicago
Northern Illinois University
Northwestern University
Southern Illinois University
University of Chicago
University of Illinois

INDIANA
Indiana University
Indiana University-Purdue University at Indianapolis
University of Notre Dame
Valparaiso University

IOWA
Drake University
University of Iowa

KANSAS
University of Kansas
Washburn University

KENTUCKY
Northern Kentucky University
University of Kentucky
University of Louisville

LOUISIANA
Louisiana State University
Loyola University of New Orleans
Southern University and A & M College
Tulane University

MAINE
University of Maine

MARYLAND
University of Baltimore
University of Maryland

MASSACHUSETTS
Boston College
Boston University
Harvard University
New England School of Law
Northeastern University
Suffolk University
Western New England College

MICHIGAN
Ave Maria School of Law
Michigan State University
Thomas M. Cooley Law School
University of Detroit Mercy
University of Michigan
Wayne State University

MINNESOTA
Hamline University
University of Minnesota
University of Saint Thomas
William Mitchell College of Law

MISSISSIPPI
Mississippi College
University of Mississippi

MISSOURI
Saint Louis University
University of Missouri-Columbia
University of Missouri-Kansas City
Washington University in St. Louis

MONTANA
University of Montana

NEBRASKA
Creighton University
University of Nebraska-Lincoln

NEVADA
University of Nevada, Las Vegas

NEW HAMPSHIRE
Franklin Pierce Law Center

NEW JERSEY
Rutgers University/Camden
Rutgers University/Newark
Seton Hall University

NEW MEXICO
University of New Mexico

NEW YORK
Albany Law School
Brooklyn Law School
City University of New York
Columbia University
Cornell University
Fordham University
Hofstra University
New York Law School
New York University
Pace University
Saint John's University
State University of New York
Syracuse University
Touro College
Yeshiva University

NORTH CAROLINA
Campbell University
Charlotte School of Law
Duke University
Elon University
North Carolina Central University
University of North Carolina at Chapel Hill
Wake Forest University

NORTH DAKOTA
University of North Dakota

OHIO
Capital University
Case Western Reserve University
Cleveland State University
Ohio Northern University
Ohio State University
University of Akron
University of Cincinnati
University of Dayton
University of Toledo

OKLAHOMA
Oklahoma City University
University of Oklahoma
University of Tulsa

OREGON
Lewis and Clark College
University of Oregon
Willamette University

PENNSYLVANIA
Drexel University
Duquesne University
Pennsylvania State University
Temple University
University of Pennsylvania
University of Pittsburgh
Villanova University
Widener University

PUERTO RICO
Inter American University of Puerto Rico
Pontifical Catholic University of Puerto Rico
University of Puerto Rico

RHODE ISLAND
Roger Williams University

SOUTH CAROLINA
Charleston School of Law
University of South Carolina

SOUTH DAKOTA
University of South Dakota

TENNESSEE
University of Memphis
University of Tennessee
Vanderbilt University

TEXAS
Baylor University
Saint Mary's University
South Texas College of Law
Southern Methodist University
Texas Southern University
Texas Tech University
Texas Wesleyan University
University of Houston
University of Texas at Austin

UTAH
Brigham Young University
University of Utah

VERMONT
Vermont Law School

VIRGINIA
Appalachian School of Law
College of William & Mary
George Mason University
Liberty University
Regent University
University of Richmond
University of Virginia
Washington and Lee University

WASHINGTON
Gonzaga University
Seattle University
University of Washington

WEST VIRGINIA
West Virginia University

WISCONSIN
Marquette University
University of Wisconsin

WYOMING
University of Wyoming

80 New Scotland Avenue
Albany, NY 12208

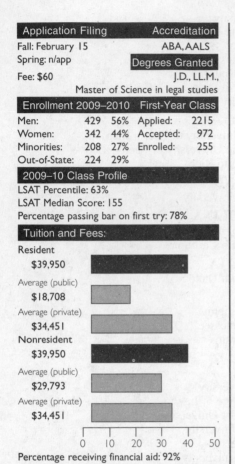

Application Filing	Accreditation
Fall: February 15	ABA, AALS
Spring: n/app	**Degrees Granted**
Fee: $60	J.D., LL.M.,
	Master of Science in legal studies

Enrollment 2009–2010		First-Year Class	
Men:	429 56%	Applied:	2215
Women:	342 44%	Accepted:	972
Minorities:	208 27%	Enrolled:	255
Out-of-State:	224 29%		

2009–10 Class Profile
LSAT Percentile: 63%
LSAT Median Score: 155
Percentage passing bar on first try: 78%

Tuition and Fees:

Resident
$39,950

Average (public)
$18,708

Average (private)
$34,451

Nonresident
$39,950

Average (public)
$29,793

Average (private)
$34,451

0 10 20 30 40 50

Percentage receiving financial aid: 92%

ADMISSIONS
In the fall 2009 first-year class, 2215 applied, 972 were accepted, and 255 enrolled. Four transfers enrolled. The median LSAT percentile of the most recent first-year class was 63; the median GPA was 3.3 on a scale of 4.0.

Requirements
Applicants must have a bachelor's degree and take the LSAT. The most important admission factors include academic achievement, LSAT results, and general background. No specific undergraduate courses are required. Candidates are not interviewed.

Procedure
The priority application deadline for fall entry is February 15. Applicants should submit an application form, LSAT results, transcripts, a personal statement, the TOEFL when applicable, a nonrefundable application fee of $60, and 2 letters of recommendation. Notification of the admissions decision is on a rolling basis. The latest acceptable LSAT test date for fall entry is February. The law school uses the LSDAS.

Special
The law school recruits minority and disadvantaged students through current minority students who assist the Admissions Office by recruiting at colleges and universities with large minority populations, by offering tuition scholarships and grants that are awarded to more than half of the accepted minority applicants, and by increased outreach by minority alumni. Requirements are not different for out-of-state students. Transfer students must have one year of credit and have attended an ABA-approved law school.

Costs
Tuition and fees for the 2009-2010 academic year are $39,950 for all full-time students. Tuition for part-time students is $29,325 per year. Books and supplies run $1100.

Financial Aid
About 92% of current law students receive some form of aid. The average annual amount of aid from all sources combined, including scholarships, loans, and work contracts, is $44,000; maximum, $54,500. Awards are based on need and merit, along with diversity. Required financial statement is the FAFSA. The aid application deadline for fall entry is rolling. Special funds for minority or disadvantaged students include diversity scholarships and full or partial tuition waivers. First-year students are notified about their financial aid application at time of acceptance.

About the Law School
Albany Law School was established in 1851 and is independent. The 6-acre campus is in an urban area 150 miles north of New York City. The primary mission of the law school is to provide students with a quality education in accordance with ethical principles and professional standards. The curriculum is traditional, yet innovative, and stresses legal knowledge, professional skills, thought habits, and contemporary techniques and technologies. Students have access to federal, state, county, city, and local agencies, courts, correctional facilities, law firms, and legal aid organizations in the Albany area. The school is located in Albany, the state capital. Facilities of special interest to law students are the New York State Legislature, State House, and all government agencies. Inexpensive off-campus housing is readily available as well as privately owned dorm-style housing adjacent to campus. About 98% of the law school facilities are accessible to the physically disabled.

Calendar
The law school operates on a traditional semester basis. Courses for full-time students are offered days only and must be completed within 3 years. For part-time students, courses are offered days only and must be completed within 4 years. New full- and part-time students are admitted in the fall. There is a 7-week summer session. Transferable summer courses are offered.

Programs
In addition to the J.D., the law school offers the LL.M. and Master of Science in legal studies. The following joint degrees may be earned: J.D./M.B.A. (Juris Doctor/Master of Business Administration), J.D./M.P.A. (Juris Doctor/Master of Public Administration), J.D./M.R.P. (Juris Doctor/Master of Regional Planning), J.D./M.S. (Juris Doctor/Master of Science in bioethics and in legal studies), and J.D./M.S.W. (Juris Doctor/Master of Social Work).

Required
To earn the J.D., candidates must complete 87 total credits, of which 42 are for required courses. They must maintain a minimum GPA of 1.7 in the required courses. The following first-year courses are required of all students: Constitutional Law I and II, Contracts I and II, Criminal Law, Evidence, Introduction to Civil Procedure, Introduction to Lawyering, Legal Methods, Property I and II, and Torts. Required upper-level courses consist of an upper-class writing requirement and The Legal Professional/Professional Responsibility seminar. The required orientation program for first-year students is a weeklong program that includes a "Legal Methods" class, social activities, and administrative activities.

Phone: 518-445-2326
Fax: 518-445-2369
E-mail: admissions@albanylaw.edu
Web: www.albanylaw.edu

Contact

Gail Bensen, Director of Admissions, 518-445-2326 for general inquiries; Andrea Wedler, Director of Financial Aid, 518-445-2357 for financial aid information.

NEW YORK

Electives

Students must take 24 credits in their area of concentration. The Albany Law School offers concentrations in corporate law, criminal law, environmental law, family law, intellectual property law, international law, labor law, litigation, securities law, tax law, commercial law, constitutional law, civil procedure, health law, estate law, government administration and regulation, court administration, and perspectives on law and legal systems. In addition, a clinical program enables upper-level students to obtain practical experience in a public law office. A classroom component is available; students may earn 12 credits, 2 to 6 each semester. Clinics include the Civil Rights and Disabilities Law Project, Health Law Project, Litigation Project, Domestic Violence Project, Securities Arbitration Project, and Low-Income Taxpayer's Project. Seminars, worth 2 or 3 credits each semester, and research assistantships are open to upper-level students. Internships in government agencies are offered through the Government Law Center, and externships in public law offices are arranged through the Placement Clinic. Annual special lecture series include the Justice Jackson and the Edward L. Sobota Memorial Lecture Series. Summer study abroad may be arranged through other ABA-accredited law schools for upper-level students. Albany Law School offers the Nairobi International Institute in partnership with Widener University School of Law, the International Human Rights Internship Program, and the University of Paris Exchange Program. Tutorial programs include the Lewis A. Swyer Academic Success Program, which provides small-group and individual instruction in legal reasoning, case analysis and synthesis, writing, and study skills. Entering students who have been out of the academic environment for several years, those whose academic backgrounds differ substantially, and those with language, physical, or emotional handicaps are eligible. In addition to an extensive Diversity Scholarship program, a number of programs are sponsored by faculty, alumni, and student organizations for those students with unusual backgrounds, including those minorities who historically have been underrepresented in the legal profession. Several societies offer lectures, symposia, and other events, including the International Law Society and Environmental Law Society. The most widely taken electives are Business Organizations, Evidence, and New York Practice.

Graduation Requirements

In order to graduate, candidates must have a GPA of 2.0 and have completed the upper-division writing requirement.

Organizations

Students edit the *Albany Law Review, Albany Law Journal of Science and Technology*, the *Albany Government Law Review*, the student newspaper *The Issue*, and the yearbook *The Verdict*. Intraschool moot court competitions include the Domenick L. Gabrielli Appellate Advocacy Competition, the Karen C. McGovern Senior Prize Trials, and the Donna Jo Morse Client Counseling Competition. Other interschool competitions include ABA Client Counseling, ABA Negotiations, ABA National Appellate Advocacy, First Amendment, Products Liability, Civil Rights, Constitutional, Criminal Procedure, Entertainment, Environmental Law, Evidence, Health Law, International, Labor, National Security, Privacy, and Securities Law. Law student organizations, local chapters of national associations, and campus clubs include the Environmental Law Society, International Law Society, Intellectual Property Law Society, Phi Alpha Delta, Student Lawyers Guild, Amnesty International, Black Law Students Association, Latino Law Students Association, and Asian Pacific American Law Students Association.

Library

The law library contains 292,198 hardcopy volumes and 2,020,246 microform volume equivalents, and subscribes to 1159 serial publications. Such on-line databases and networks as CALI, CIS Universe, DIALOG, Infotrac, Legal-Trac, LEXIS, LOIS, Matthew Bender, NEXIS, OCLC First Search, WESTLAW, New York Legislature Retrieval System, and Court of Appeals on-line information service are available to law students for research. Special library collections include a U.S. government documents depository, New York State documents research depository, and a New York Court of Appeals oral argument videotape repository. The ratio of library volumes to faculty is 5963 to 1 and to students is 379 to 1. The ratio of seats in the library to students is 1 to 6.

Placement

J.D.s awarded:	248

Services available through: a separate law school placement center

Services: on-campus interviews with law firms, government agencies, public interest organizations, and businesses; off-campus interview programs in selected cities; job fairs and employer information sessions; career education programs; workshops; and panel discussions

Special features: The law school graduate employment rate has exceeded the national average for more than a quarter of a century

Full-time job interviews:	150 employers
Summer job interviews:	150 employers
Placement by graduation:	n/av
Placement within 9 months:	97% of class
Average starting salary:	$40,000 to $175,000
Areas of placement:	
Private practice 2-10 attorneys	28%
Private practice 11-25 attorneys	8%
Private practice 26-50 attorneys	3%
Private practice 51-100 attorneys	9%
Business/industry	18%
Government	16%
Judicial clerkships	9%
Public interest	6%
Academic	2%
Military	1%

Faculty

The law school has 49 full-time and 48 part-time faculty members, of whom 35 are women. About 25% of full-time faculty have a graduate law degree in addition to the J.D. The ratio of full-time students to full-time faculty in an average class is 14 to 1; in a clinic, 8 to 1. The law school has a regular program of bringing visiting professors and other distinguished lecturers and visitors to campus.

Students

About 44% of the student body are women; 27%, minorities; 2%, African American; 5%, Asian American; 4%, Hispanic; 1%, Native American; and 2%, foreign national. The majority of students come from New York (71%). The average age of entering students is 23; age range is 20 to 47. About 49% of students enter directly from undergraduate school and 49% have worked full-time prior to entering law school. About 1% drop out after the first year for academic or personal reasons; 99% remain to receive a law degree.

Washington College of Law

4801 Massachusetts Avenue, N.W.
Washington, DC 20016-8186

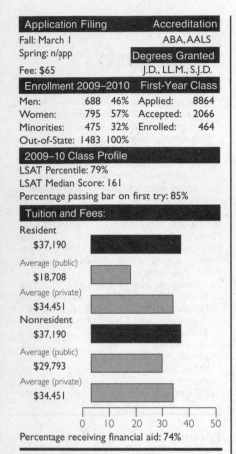

Application Filing	Accreditation
Fall: March 1	ABA, AALS
Spring: n/app	**Degrees Granted**
Fee: $65	J.D., LL.M., S.J.D.

Enrollment 2009–2010		First-Year Class	
Men:	688 46%	Applied:	8864
Women:	795 57%	Accepted:	2066
Minorities:	475 32%	Enrolled:	464
Out-of-State:	1483 100%		

2009–10 Class Profile
LSAT Percentile: 79%
LSAT Median Score: 161
Percentage passing bar on first try: 85%

Tuition and Fees:

Resident
$37,190

Average (public)
$18,708

Average (private)
$34,451

Nonresident
$37,190

Average (public)
$29,793

Average (private)
$34,451

0 10 20 30 40 50

Percentage receiving financial aid: 74%

ADMISSIONS

In a recent year, 8864 applied, 2066 were accepted, and 464 enrolled. Seventy-four transfers enrolled. The median LSAT percentile of the most recent first-year class was 79; the median GPA was 3.42 on a scale of 4.0. The lowest LSAT percentile accepted was 32; the highest was 99. Figures in the above capsule and in this profile are approximate.

Requirements
Applicants must have a bachelor's degree and take the LSAT. The most important admission factors include academic achievement, GPA, and LSAT results. No specific undergraduate courses are required. Candidates are not interviewed.

Procedure
Applicants should submit an application form, LSAT results, transcripts, a nonrefundable application fee of $65, 1 letters of recommendation, and a personal statement. Notification of the admissions decision is begins late December. The latest acceptable LSAT test date for fall entry is February. The law school uses the LSDAS. Check with school for current application deadlines.

Special
The law school recruits minority and disadvantaged students in collaboration with the Office of Admissions and Office of Diversity Services. Every effort is made to attend recruiting events that are targeted to enroll the most diverse class possible. Requirements are not different for out-of-state students. Transfer students must have one year of credit, have attended an ABA-approved law school, and academic achievement.

Costs

Tuition and fees for the 2009-2010 academic year are approximately $37,190 for all full-time students. Tuition for part-time students is approximately $23,222 per year. On-campus room and board costs about $13,635 annually; books and supplies run about $1015.

Financial Aid

In a recent year, about 74% of current law students received some form of aid. The average annual amount of aid from all sources combined, including scholarships, loans, and work contracts, was $38,268; maximum, $50,493. Awards are based on need and merit. Required financial statements are the FAFSA and Need Access Application. Special funds for minority or disadvantaged students include need-based grants and donor restricted scholarships. First-year students are notified about their financial aid application at within 2 weeks of acceptance if application is made by the filing deadline. Check with the school for current application deadline.

About the Law School

American University Washington College of Law was established in 1896 and is a private institution. The campus is in an urban area in Washington, D.C., 3 miles from downtown. The primary mission of the law school is to provide an individualized, high-quality legal education by engaging the community, the nation, and the world through a vision that integrates theory and practice, doctrine and experiential learning, and skills and values, all in a diverse and demanding environment.

Students have access to federal, state, county, city, and local agencies, courts, correctional facilities, law firms, and legal aid organizations in the Washington area. including the U.S. Congress, U.S. Supreme Court, Library of Congress, IMF, World Bank, and other NGO's. Facilities of special interest to law students more than 1000 approved extern sites at federal agencies, courts, trade associations, and public interest organizations. Housing for students is easily found in many apartment buildings and rental houses, which are located nearby. All law school facilities are accessible to the physically disabled.

Calendar

The law school operates on a traditional semester basis. Courses for full-time students are offered both day and evening and must be completed within 5 years. For part-time students, courses are offered both day and evening and must be completed within 6 years. New full- and part-time students are admitted in the fall. There is a 9-week summer session. Transferable summer courses are offered.

Programs

In addition to the J.D., the law school offers the LL.M. and S.J.D. Students may take relevant courses in other programs and apply credit toward the J.D.; a maximum of 6 credits may be applied. The following joint degrees may be earned: J.D./M.A. (Juris Doctor/Master of Arts in international affairs), J.D./M.B.A. (Juris Doctor/Master of Business Administration), and J.D./M.S. (Juris Doctor/Master of Science in law, justice, and society).

Required
To earn the J.D., candidates must complete 86 total credits, of which 32 are for required courses. They must maintain a minimum GPA of 2.0 in the required courses. The following first-year courses are required of all students: Civil Procedure, Constitutional Law, Contracts, Criminal Law, Legal Rhetoric I and II, Property, and Torts. Required upper-level courses consist of Criminal Procedure I and Legal Ethics. The required orientation program for first-year students is 3 days and includes registration, dean's and faculty welcome, academic orientation, technology and financial aid sessions, a reception, and Student Bar Association social activities.

Phone: 202-274-4101
Fax: 202-274-4107
E-mail: wcladmit@wcl.american.edu
Web: www.wcl.american.edu

Contact

Admissions Office, 202-274-4101 for general inquiries; Financial Aid Office, 202-274-4040 for financial aid information.

DISTRICT OF COLUMBIA

Electives

The Washington College of Law offers concentrations in corporate law, criminal law, environmental law, family law, intellectual property law, international law, juvenile law, labor law, litigation, securities law, tax law, torts and insurance, and human rights law, arbitration, international, environment, and administrative law. In addition, clinical experiences offered to students include the Civil Practice Clinic for 14 credits, International Human Rights Law Clinic for 14 credits, and Community and Economic Development Clinic for 14 credits. Internships, available with government agencies, international organizations, and nonprofit entities, are under faculty supervision. The Independent Study Program permits directed research under faculty supervision. The Field Component Program offers field work with the Securities and Exchange Commission, the Commodities Futures Trading Commission, the State Department, and the National Association of Securities Dealers. Special lecture series include an extensive series of conferences and speaker series that deal with topics of contemporary interest. In addition, student organizations sponsor lectures and panel discussions on a range of topics. Study abroad consists of summer programs in Chile (study involving legal structures in Latin America), Istanbul, London/Paris/Geneva (international business, human rights, and environmental law); a semester exchange: Paris-X Nanterre, France; Hong Kong Exchange; Canada, Mexico, Netherlands, Belgium, Finland, Germany, Australia, Spain; and dual degree programs in Spain and Canada. There is a Peer Counseling Program. An academic support program is available for all students, but remedial programs are not provided. The Office of Diversity Services offers minority programs and advisory services. The most widely taken electives are Evidence, Business Associations, and Administrative Law.

Graduation Requirements

In order to graduate, candidates must have a GPA of 2.0, have completed the upper-division writing requirement, and a lawyering skills requirement.

Organizations

Students edit the *American University Law Review*, *Administrative Law Review*, (ABA Section Publication), *American University International Law Review*, *American University Journal of Gender, Social Policy and the Law*, *American Jurist*, Business Law Brief, Criminal Law Brief, Human Rights Brief, Modern American, and sustainable Development Law and Policy. Three moot court competitions are Alvina Reckman Myers First-Year Moot Court Competition, the Inter-American Moot Court Competition, and the Burton D. Wechsler First Amendment Moot Court Competition. Students participate in approximately 12 competitions, including the Jean Pictet Competition, and the VIS Moot International Arbitration Team. Law student organizations, include Equal Justice Foundation, Law and Government Society, Women's Law Association, Local chapters of national associations include American Constitution Society, Black Law Students Association, Hispanic Law Students Association, Lambda Law Society, Federalist Society, and Phi Delta Phi.

Library

The law library contains 592,065 hardcopy volumes and 92,643 microform volume equivalents, and subscribes to 8247 serial publications. Such on-line databases and networks as CALI, CIS Universe, DIALOG, Dow-Jones, Infotrac, Legal-Trac, LEXIS, LOIS, Mathew Bender, NEXIS, OCLC First Search, RLIN, WESTLAW, Wilsonline Indexes, and HeinOnline, Access UN, UN Human Rights, UN Treaty, BNA, CCH, and MOML are available to law students for research. Special library collections include European Community and U.S. government depositories as well as the Baxter Collection in International Law, Administrative Conference of the U.S. Cicchino Collection, Goodman Collection of Rare Books, Iran-Contra Affair, Judicial Documents Collection, and the National Bank Rev. Collection. Recently, the library The library occupies 51,157 net square feet in a state-of-the-art facility. There are 644 wired or wireless seats. Laboratories are available for research and law related applications. The ratio of library volumes to faculty is 5862 to 1 and to students is 399 to 1. The ratio of seats in the library to students is 1 to 2.

Faculty

The law school has 101 full-time and 180 part-time faculty members, of whom 110 are women. According to AAUP standards

Placement

J.D.s awarded:	555

Services available through: a separate law school placement center

Services: mock interview programs, access to alumni mentors and regional recruitment programs in Atlanta, Boston, New York and the West Coast.

Special features: 6 full-time career counselors all with JDs. Several counselors have specific areas of focus including international, judicial, public interest, government, and alumni counseling.

Full-time job interviews:	45 employers
Summer job interviews:	131 employers
Placement by graduation:	85% of class
Placement within 9 months:	99% of class
Average starting salary:	$48,000 to $135,000

Areas of placement:

Private practice 2-10 attorneys	13%
Private practice 11-25 attorneys	4%
Private practice 26-50 attorneys	3%
Private practice 51-100 attorneys	2%
23% Private practice 101+ attorneys;	
1% solo pract	27%
Business/industry	18%
Government	13%
Judicial clerkships	11%
Public interest	7%
Academic	2%

for Category I institutions, faculty salaries are average. About 21% of full-time faculty have a graduate law degree in addition to the J.D.; about 22% of part-time faculty have one. The ratio of full-time students to full-time faculty in an average class is 14 to 1; in a clinic, 8 to 1. The law school has a regular program of bringing visiting professors and other distinguished lecturers and visitors to campus. There is a chapter of the Order of the Coif; 186 graduates are members.

Students

About 57% of the student body are women; 32%, minorities; 8%, African American; 11%, Asian American; 12%, Hispanic; and 1%, Native American. The majority of students come from the Northeast (54%). The average age of entering students is 24; age range is 20 to 47. About 5% drop out after the first year for academic or personal reasons; 95% remain to receive a law degree.

P.O. Box 2825
Grundy, VA 24614

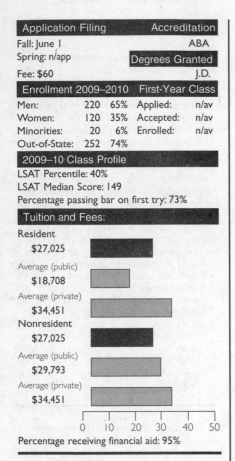

Application Filing		Accreditation
Fall: June 1		ABA
Spring: n/app		Degrees Granted
Fee: $60		J.D.

Enrollment 2009–2010 First-Year Class

Men:	220	65%	Applied:	n/av
Women:	120	35%	Accepted:	n/av
Minorities:	20	6%	Enrolled:	n/av
Out-of-State:	252	74%		

2009–10 Class Profile
LSAT Percentile: 40%
LSAT Median Score: 149
Percentage passing bar on first try: 73%

Tuition and Fees:

Resident
$27,025

Average (public)
$18,708

Average (private)
$34,451

Nonresident
$27,025

Average (public)
$29,793

Average (private)
$34,451

0   10   20   30   40   50
Percentage receiving financial aid: 95%

ADMISSIONS

Some figures in the above capsule and in this profile are approximate. Seven transfers enrolled in a recent year. The median LSAT percentile of the most recent first-year class was 40; the median GPA was 3.08 on a scale of 4.0. The lowest LSAT percentile accepted was 32; the highest was 55.

Requirements

Applicants must have a bachelor's degree and take the LSAT. Minimum acceptable GPA is 2.0 on a scale of 4.0. The most important admission factors include GPA, LSAT results, and academic achievement. No specific undergraduate courses are required. Candidates are not interviewed.

Procedure

The application deadline for fall entry is June 1. Applicants should submit an application form, LSAT results, transcripts, a personal statement, a nonrefundable application fee of $60, and 2 letters of recommendation. Notification of the admissions decision is after December 31. The latest acceptable LSAT test date for fall entry is February. The law school uses the LSDAS.

Special

The law school recruits minority and disadvantaged students by attending events at schools with minority student populations, distributing targeted literature, and through its mentoring program. Requirements are not different for out-of-state students. Transfer students must have a 2.0 GPA at an ABA-approved or state-approved law school. Preadmissions courses consist of a 4-week Pre-Admission Summer Opportunity program.

Costs

Tuition and fees for the 2009-2010 academic year are $27,025 for all full-time students. Books and supplies run $1500.

Financial Aid

About 95% of current law students receive some form of aid. The average annual amount of aid from all sources combined, including scholarships, loans, and work contracts, is $31,171; maximum, $41,090. Awards are based on need and merit. Required financial statement is the FAFSA. Students applying for need-based aid are required to complete a need assessment application to determine eligibility. The aid application deadline for fall entry is July 1. First-year students are notified about their financial aid application at time of acceptance.

About the Law School

Appalachian School of Law was established in 1997 and is a private institution. The 3.2-acre campus is in a small town in downtown Grundy, Virginia. The primary mission of the law school is to train lawyers to be community leaders. Students have access to federal, state, county, city, and local agencies, courts, correctional facilities, law firms, and legal aid organizations in the Grundy area. There is an adequate supply of rental properties off campus. All law school facilities are accessible to the physically disabled.

Calendar

The law school operates on a traditional semester basis. Courses for full-time students are offered days only and must be completed within 5 years. There is no part-time program. New students are admitted in the fall. There is no summer session. Transferable summer courses are not offered.

Programs

Required

To earn the J.D., candidates must complete 90 total credits, of which 69 are for required courses. They must maintain a minimum GPA of 2.0 in the required courses. The following first-year courses are required of all students: Civil Procedure I and II, Contracts I and II, Criminal Law, Introduction to Law, Legal Process I and II, Property I and II, and Torts. Required upper-level courses consist of 2 practicum courses, a seminar, Business Associations, Constitutional Law I and II, Criminal Procedure, Dispute Resolution, Estates and Trusts, Evidence, Externship, Family Law, Payment Systems, Professional Responsibility, and Secured Transactions. The required orientation program for first-year students is 1 week, covering skills needed to be a successful law student, core issues of professionalism, and an introduction to Central Appalachia. A substantive component of the Torts course is also included.

Electives

Students must take 13 credits in their area of concentration. The Appalachian School of Law offers concentrations in ADR/Lawyers as Problem Solver. All students take a 2-credit seminar in their third year. The seminars have included Cyberlaw, Environmental Law, and First Amendment. Students also participate in a 3-credit internship during the summer after their first year. Judicial Chambers, prosecutors' and public defenders' offices, and legal aid organizations are typical placements. An Academic Success Program is open to all first-year students. The most widely taken electives are Remedies, Advanced Torts, and Conflict of Laws.

Graduation Requirements

In order to graduate, candidates must have a GPA of 2.0 and have completed the upper-division writing requirement.

Phone: 276-935-4349
800-895-7411
Fax: 276-935-8496
E-mail: npruitt@asl.edu
Web: www.asl.edu

Contact
Nancy Pruitt, Director of Student Services, 800-895-7411 for general inquiries; Hannah Sawyers, Financial Aid Officer, 800-895-7411 for financial aid information.

VIRGINIA

Organizations
The primary law review is the *Appalachian Journal of Law*. Students also edit the *Appalachian Natural Resources Law Journal*. There is a National Appellate Advocacy Competition, Wechsler National Criminal Law Competition, Gabrielli National Family Law Competition, ATLA Student Trial Advocacy Competition, ABA Client Counseling Competition, and ABA Negotiation Competition. Law student organizations, local chapters of national organizations, and campus organizations include the Black Law Students Association, Federalist Society, Equal Justice Works, Phi Alpha Delta, ATLA, Phi Delta Phi, Democratic Society, Republican Law Students Association, and Appalachian Women in Law.

Library
The law library contains 128,552 hardcopy volumes and 104,163 microform volume equivalents, and subscribes to 917 serial publications. Such on-line databases and networks as CALI, CIS Universe, DIALOG, Dow-Jones, Infotrac, LegalTrac, LEXIS, LOIS, Matthew Bender, NEXIS, OCLC First Search, WESTLAW, CCH, BNA, and HeinOnline are available to law students for research. Special library collections include Appalachian Collection, government document depository, and 4th Circuit briefs. The ratio of library volumes to faculty is 6428 to 1 and to students is 378 to 1.

Faculty
The law school has 20 full-time and 4 part-time faculty members, of whom 10 are women. About 33% of full-time faculty have a graduate law degree in addition to the J.D. The ratio of full-time students to full-time faculty in an average class is 21 to 1. The law school has a regular program of bringing visiting professors and other distinguished lecturers and visitors to campus.

Students
About 35% of the student body are women; 6%, minorities; 1%, African American; 1%, Asian American; and 3%, Hispanic. The majority of students come from Virginia (26%). The average age of entering students is 26; age range is 21 to 55. About 46% of students enter directly from undergraduate school.

Placement

J.D.s awarded:	108
Services available through: a separate law school placement center	
Special features: on-line job board, subscriptions to job databases, bimonthly career services newsletter, and job search counseling	
Full-time job interviews:	6 employers
Summer job interviews:	5 employers
Placement by graduation:	41% of class
Placement within 9 months:	64% of class
Average starting salary:	$26,000 to $68,000
Areas of placement:	
Solo practice	5%
Private practice 2-10 attorneys	34%
Private practice 11-25 attorneys	3%
Government	19%
Business/industry	12%
Judicial clerkships	8%
Public interest	7%
Military	3%

ARIZONA STATE UNIVERSITY

Sandra Day O'Connor College of Law

1100 S. McAllister Ave. - Box 877906
Tempe, AZ 85287-7906

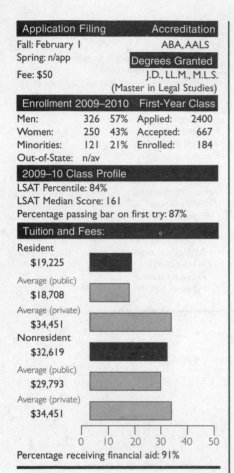

Application Filing	Accreditation
Fall: February 1	ABA, AALS
Spring: n/app	**Degrees Granted**
Fee: $50	J.D., LL.M., M.L.S.
	(Master in Legal Studies)

Enrollment 2009–2010			First-Year Class	
Men:	326	57%	Applied:	2400
Women:	250	43%	Accepted:	667
Minorities:	121	21%	Enrolled:	184
Out-of-State:	n/av			

2009–10 Class Profile

LSAT Percentile: 84%
LSAT Median Score: 161
Percentage passing bar on first try: 87%

Tuition and Fees:

Resident
$19,225

Average (public)
$18,708

Average (private)
$34,451

Nonresident
$32,619

Average (public)
$29,793

Average (private)
$34,451

0 10 20 30 40 50

Percentage receiving financial aid: 91%

ADMISSIONS

In the fall 2009 first-year class, 2400 applied, 667 were accepted, and 184 enrolled. Fifty-seven transfers enrolled. The median LSAT percentile of the most recent first-year class was 84; the median GPA was 3.6 on a scale of 4.3. The lowest LSAT percentile accepted was 26; the highest was 99.

Requirements

Applicants must have a bachelor's degree and take the LSAT. No specific undergraduate courses are required. Candidates are not interviewed.

Procedure

The application deadline for fall entry is February 1. Applicants should submit an application form, LSAT results, transcripts, a personal statement, TOEFL, a nonrefundable application fee of $50, a resumé no longer than 3 typed pages, and statements explaining affirmative answers to the conduct questions. Notification of

the admissions decision is November to May on a rolling basis. The latest acceptable LSAT test date for fall entry is February. The law school uses the LSDAS.

Special

The law school recruits minority and disadvantaged students by means of special mailings, personal contact, the involvement of current students and alumni, affordable tuition rates, and scholarship programs. Requirements are not different for out-of-state students. Transfer students must have one year of credit and have attended an ABA-approved law school.

Costs

Tuition and fees for the 2009-2010 academic year are $19,225 for full-time in-state students and $32,619 for out-of-state students. On-campus room and board costs about $10,660 annually; books and supplies run $1850.

Financial Aid

About 91% of current law students receive some form of aid. The average annual amount of aid from all sources combined, including scholarships, loans, and work contracts, is $31,326; maximum, $70,179. Awards are based on need and merit. Required financial statement is the FAFSA. The aid application deadline for fall entry is rolling. Special funds for minority or disadvantaged students include Diversity Legal Writing Program funds; Bureau of Reclamation funds for Native American students; and various privately funded scholarships. First-year students are notified about their financial aid application throughout spring and summer.

About the Law School

Arizona State University Sandra Day O'Connor College of Law was established in 1967 and is a public institution. The 700-acre campus is in an urban area in downtown Tempe, part of the Phoenix Metroplex. The primary mission of the law school is is pioneering a new model for twenty-first century legal education, one that reinvents the modern law school as not just an institution that trains lawyers, but as a multifaceted legal studies center that engages in developing solutions to the world's global challenges and that seeks to educated a broad cross-section of contem-

porary society. Students have access to federal, state, county, city, and local agencies, courts, correctional facilities, law firms, and legal aid organizations in the Tempe area. More than 150 externships are available. Facilities of special interest to law students opportunities abound in Phoenix, the fifth largest city in the U.S. and the largest state capital. It is home to the Chief Judge of the 9th Circuit Court of Appeals, a federal courthouse, the Arizona Supreme Court, Arizona Court of Appeals, and the Arizona legislature. Housing for students is available on campus and designated specifically for graduate students. Housing is found off campus. All law school facilities are accessible to the physically disabled.

Calendar

The law school operates on a traditional semester basis. Courses for full-time students are offered both day and evening and must be completed within 84 months. There is no part-time program. New students are admitted in the fall. There is a 2 five- week, and 1 eight-week summer session. Transferable summer courses are offered.

Programs

In addition to the J.D., the law school offers the LL.M. and M.L.S. (Master in Legal Studies). Students may take relevant courses in other programs and apply credit toward the J.D.; a maximum of 6 credits may be applied. The following joint degrees may be earned: J.D./M.B.A. (Juris Doctor/Master of Business Administration), J.D./M.D. (Juris Doctor/Doctor of Medicine with Mayo Medical School), J.D./M.H.S.M. (Juris Doctor/Master of Health Sector Management), J.D./Ph.D. (Juris Doctor/Ph.D. in justice and social inquiry), and J.D/Ph.D. (Juris Doctor/Ph.D. in Psychology).

Required

To earn the J.D., candidates must complete 88 total credits, of which 39 are for required courses. The following first-year courses are required of all students: Bridging The Gap - Pathways To Success In Law School and the Profession, Civil Procedure, Constitutional Law I, Contracts, Criminal Law, Law and the Regulatory State, Legal Advocacy, Legal Method and Writing, Property, and Torts. Required upper-level courses consist of Criminal Procedure or Consti-

Phone: 480-965-1474
Fax: 480-727-7930
E-mail: *chitra.damania@asu.edu*
Web: www.law.asu.edu

Contact

Chitra Damania, Director of Admissions, 480-965-1474 for general inquiries; Joseph Lindsay, Director of Financial Aid, 480-965-1474 for financial aid information.

ARIZONA

tutional Law II and Professional Responsibility. The required orientation program for first-year students is a program lasting several days that introduces students to legal professionalism and to the practicalities of legal study.

Electives

Students must take 16 credits in their area of concentration. The Sandra Day O'Connor College of Law offers concentrations in environmental law, intellectual property law, international law, tax law, certificates in Indian law, health law, and law science, and technology. In addition, current offerings include a Criminal Practice Clinic, a Civil Justice Clinic, and a Technology Ventures Clinic, each worth 6 credits. Third-year students are given preference for clinics and seminars; 25 to 30 seminars per semester are offered (worth 2 or 3 credit hours). Externships and field work allow upper-level students to gain up to 12 credits while working in one of the more than 150 organized externships. A number of research opportunities are also available for students. Professor Joe Feller's Natural Resources Field Seminar provides an opportunity to observe first-hand some of the places and resources discussed in the courses on Water Law and Natural Resources Law. The course is held in Northern Arizona, north of the Grand Canyon. Visiting old-growth forests, an ecological restoration project, the site of the Bridger fire, desert rangelands, and the Colorado River in Glen Canyon, participants meet with federal and state resource managers and scientists to discuss the application and implementation of environmental laws. The college sponsors numerous annual lecture series and several major symposia yearly. Study abroad is possible through a semester exchange program with Universidad Torcuato Di Tella, Buenos Aires, University of Victoria, British Columbia, National University, Singapore, and Université René Descartes, Paris, France, and Bocconi University School of Law, Milan, Italy. There is an Academic Success Program available. A number of Phoenix firms offer minority Legal Writing Programs. The most widely taken electives are Evidence, Business Associations, and Trusts and Estates.

Graduation Requirements

In order to graduate, candidates must have a GPA of 2.0, have completed the upper-division writing requirement, and complete 88 credit hours including the required courses, the graduation writing requirement, the seminar writing requirement, and the practical skills requirement.

Organizations

Students edit the *Arizona State Law Journal*. Students also assist faculty in editing *Jurimetrics: The Journal of Law, Science, and Technology*. Students also publish their own newspaper: *Res Ipsa Loquitur*. Students are urged to participate in the ABA Dispute Resolution Section's "Representation in Mediation" Competition, the Jessup International Moot Court Competition, and a Client Counseling Competition. Other competitions include the Judge Tang Essay Competition, the Oplinger Closing Argument Competition, the Jenckes Competition, and numerous other writing competitions. Student organizations include Government and Public Interest Law, Law and Science Student Association, and Corporate ad Business Law Student Association. Local chapters of national associations include the American Bar Association Law Student Division, John P. Morris Black Law Students Association, and Native American Law Student Association. Other organizations affiliated campuswide include Phi Alpha Delta, the ASU Graduate and Professional Association, and the Chicano/Latino Law Student Association.

Library

The law library contains 275,773 hardcopy volumes and 142,341 microform volume equivalents, and subscribes to 3740 serial publications. Such on-line databases and networks as CALI, CIS Universe, Infotrac, Legal-Trac, LEXIS, LOIS, NEXIS, OCLC First Search, WESTLAW, Wilsonline Indexes, and Academic Universe are available to law students for research. Special library collections include Anglo-American case reports and statutes and special collections of Indian law, Mexican law, law and technology, and English legal history. Recently, the library made improvements to include the establishment of an institutional repository of faculty publications, the creation of a Tribal Law portal for the website to assist students and faculty with Indian legal research, and the creation of new research guides on Foreclosure law, Bankruptcy and Immigration. The ratio of library volumes to faculty is 4838 to 1 and to students is 463 to 1. The ratio of seats in the library to students is 1 to 1.

Faculty

The law school has 57 full-time and 37 part-time faculty members, of whom 23 are women. According to AAUP standards for Category I institutions, faculty salaries are below average. About 7% of full-time faculty have a graduate law degree in addition to the J.D.; about 4% of part-time faculty have one. The ratio of full-time students to full-time faculty in an average class is 9 to 1; in a clinic, 7 to 1. The law school has a regular program of bringing visiting professors and other distinguished lecturers and visitors to campus. There is a chapter of the Order of the Coif; 20 faculty are members.

Students

About 43% of the student body are women; 21%, minorities; 2%, African American; 3%, Asian American; 10%, Hispanic; 6%, Native American; other 11%, Foreign national, 2%; unknown, 9%. The average age of entering students is 26; age range is 20 to 51. About 32% of students enter directly from undergraduate school, 8% have a graduate degree, and 66% have worked full-time prior to entering law school. About 4% drop out after the first year for academic or personal reasons; 98% remain to receive a law degree.

Placement

J.D.s awarded:	170
Services available through: a separate law school placement center	
Services: on campus and out-of-state job fairs.	
Special features: personal individualized service for students and graduates.	
Full-time job interviews:	17 employers
Summer job interviews:	55 employers
Placement by graduation:	91% of class
Placement within 9 months:	99% of class
Average starting salary:	$37,000 to $160,000
Areas of placement:	
Private practice 2-10 attorneys	25%
Private practice 11-25 attorneys	2%
Private practice 26-50 attorneys	6%
Private practice 51-100 attorneys	5%
Government	17%
Business/industry	10%
Public interest	9%
Judicial clerkships	7%
Academic	3%
Military	1%

ATLANTA'S JOHN MARSHALL LAW SCHOOL

1422 W. Peachtree St., NW
Atlanta, GA 30309

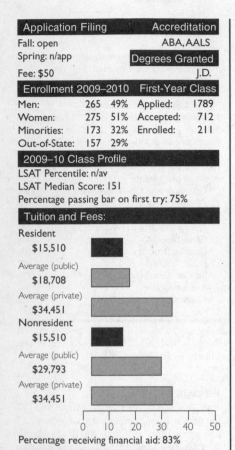

Application Filing	Accreditation
Fall: open	ABA, AALS
Spring: n/app	
	Degrees Granted
Fee: $50	J.D.

Enrollment 2009–2010		First-Year Class	
Men:	265 49%	Applied:	1789
Women:	275 51%	Accepted:	712
Minorities:	173 32%	Enrolled:	211
Out-of-State:	157 29%		

2009–10 Class Profile
LSAT Percentile: n/av
LSAT Median Score: 151
Percentage passing bar on first try: 75%

Tuition and Fees:

Resident
$15,510

Average (public)
$18,708

Average (private)
$34,451

Nonresident
$15,510

Average (public)
$29,793

Average (private)
$34,451

0 10 20 30 40 50

Percentage receiving financial aid: 83%

ADMISSIONS
In the fall 2009 first-year class, 1789 applied, 712 were accepted, and 211 enrolled. Fourteen transfers enrolled. The median GPA of the most recent first-year class was 2.97. The lowest LSAT percentile accepted was 25; the highest was 75.

Requirements
Applicants must have a bachelor's degree and take the LSAT. Minimum acceptable GPA is 2.0 on a scale of 4.0. The most important admission factors include LSAT results, GPA, and general background. No specific undergraduate courses are required. Candidates are not interviewed.

Procedure
The application deadline for fall entry is open. Applicants should submit an application form, LSAT results, transcripts, a personal statement, a nonrefundable application fee of $50, 2 letters of recommendation, TOEFL if required, and resumé an optional. Notification of the

admissions decision is on a rolling basis. The latest acceptable LSAT test date for fall entry is June. The law school uses the LSDAS.

Special
The law school recruits minority and disadvantaged students through college visits, advertisements, and referrals. Requirements are not different for out-of-state students. Transfer students must have one year of credit, have attended an ABA-approved law school, and must be in good academic standing at the school from which they are transferring.

Costs
Tuition and fees for the 2009-2010 academic year are $15,510 for all full-time students. Tuition for part-time students is $9366 per year. Books and supplies run $1200.

Financial Aid
About 83% of current law students receive some form of aid. The average annual amount of aid from all sources combined, including scholarships, loans, and work contracts, is $30,000; maximum, $51,720. Awards are based on need. Required financial statement is the FAFSA. The aid application deadline for fall entry is open. First-year students are notified about their financial aid application at time of enrollment.

About the Law School
Atlanta's John Marshall Law School was established in 1933 and is a private institution. The campus is in an urban area midtown Atlanta. The primary mission of the law school is to prepare competent and professional lawyers who possess a strong social conscience, continually demonstrate high ethical standards, and are committed to the improvement of the legal system and society. Students have access to federal, state, county, city, and local agencies, courts, correctional facilities, law firms, and legal aid organizations in the Atlanta area. Facilities of special interest to law students include more new classrooms, new trial and appellate courtrooms, and a café serving breakfast, lunch, and dinner. There is unlimited access to wireless Internet, online legal databases, and state of the art technology in multiple class-

rooms allowing for interactive learning experiences. Housing for students is available in the local Atlanta rental market. All law school facilities are accessible to the physically disabled.

Calendar
The law school operates on a traditional semester basis. Courses for full-time students are offered both day and evening and must be completed within 4 years. For part-time students, courses are offered both day and evening and must be completed within 5 years. New full- and part-time students are admitted in the fall. There is a 7-week summer session. Transferable summer courses are offered.

Programs
Students may take relevant courses in other programs and apply credit toward the J.D.; a maximum of 30 credits credits may be applied.

Required
To earn the J.D., candidates must complete 88 total credits, of which 63 are for required courses. They must maintain a minimum GPA of 2.0 in the required courses. The following first-year courses are required of all students: Civil Procedure I and II; Contracts I and II; Legal Research, Writing, and Analysis I and II; Real Property I and II; and Torts I and II. Required upper-level courses consist of Business Organizations; Constitutional Law I and II; Criminal Law, Criminal Procedure; Evidence; Legal Drafting; Legal Research, Writing, Analysis III; Professional Responsibility; Remedies; and Sales and Secured Transactions. Students are not required to take clinical courses but the law school does offer the opportunity to obtain clinical hours through its Pro-Bono and Externship Program. The required orientation program for first-year students is a comprehensive 4-day program.

Electives
The Atlanta's John Marshall Law School offers concentrations in corporate law, criminal law, entertainment law, environmental law, family law, intellectual property law, international law, juvenile law, labor law, litigation, securities law, sports law, tax law, torts and insurance, and pub-

Phone: 404-872-3593
Fax: 404-873-3802
E-mail: *admissions@johnmarshall.edu*
Web: *www.johnmarshall.edu*

Contact

Shannon Keef, Director, 404-872-3593 for general inquiries; James Smith, Director of Financial Aid, 404-872-3593 for financial aid information.

GEORGIA

Placement

J.D.s awarded:	106
Services available through: the university placement center	
Special features: On-campus interviews, resume forwarding, 1000 + job postings a year	
Full-time job interviews:	n/av
Summer job interviews:	n/av
Placement by graduation:	97% of class
Placement within 9 months:	94% of class
Average starting salary:	$60,069
Areas of placement:	
Private practice 2-10 attorneys	64%
Judicial Clerkships	5%
Government	10%
Business/Industry	15%
Public Interest	4%
Academic	2%

lic law. In addition, seminars are available for students with advanced standing in such areas as Privacy Law, Death Penalty, and Forensic Evidence, for 2 credits each. There are numerous internship opportunities offered in various areas of law. The Directed Research Program for 2 credits involves comprehensive individual research projects under the supervision of a faculty member, resulting in a scholarly paper. An Externship Program worth 2 to 4 credits is available. Students are placed in a public law office and work under the supervision of a licensed attorney, certified under the third-year practice act of the Georgia Supreme Court. The Fred Gray Social Justice Seminar and the Annual Bobby Lee Cook Practical Legal Symposium draw some of Georgia's top attorneys as featured presenters. Study abroad, including a Micronesian Externship Program, for 2 to 3 credits is available to all students in good standing. Academic support is available to all students. Minority programs include the Black Law Students Association, Georgia Association of Black Women Lawyers, Caribbean Law Students Association, and the Lambda Law Society. Special interest group programs include the Corporate Law Society, Federalist Society, Animal Legal Defense Fund Organization, Public Defenders Club, Prosecutor's Club, Labor and Employment Law Society, Health Law Society, and Immigration Law Club. The most widely taken electives are Georgia Practice and Procedure, Environmental Law, and Sports and Entertainment Law.

Graduation Requirements

In order to graduate, candidates must have a GPA of 2.0 and have completed the upper-division writing requirement.

Organizations

The primary law review is *Atlanta's JMLS Law Review*. Students edit the student newspaper *SBA Newsletter*. Other publications include *Dean's Weekly Announcements*. Moot court competitions include the Frederick Douglas Moot Court Competition, NACD Trial Competition Team, and ABA Appellate Advocacy Team. Other competitions include the American Trial Lawyers Association Competition Team, ABA Client Interviewing and Counseling Competition, and National Moot Court

Competition. Law student organizations, local chapters of national associations, and campus organizations include the Sports and Entertainment Law Society, Intellectual Property Club, Health Law Society, American Trial Lawyers Association, Sigma Delta Kappa-Alpha Chi Chapter, and Phi Alpha Delta-Hollowell Chapter, Georgia Association of Women Lawyers, Student Bar Associaton, and Black Law Students Association.

Library

The law library contains 96,000 hard-copy volumes and 711,151 microform volume equivalents, and subscribes to 402 serial publications. Such on-line databases and networks as CALI, Infotrac, Legal-Trac, LEXIS, Mathew Bender, NEXIS, OCLC First Search, WESTLAW, HeinOnline, BNA.LOM, Pacer, LLMC.COM, CCH New Business and Finance ProQuest, SSLN, JSTOR, and Lexis Congressional are available to law students for research. Recently, the library redesigned lobby and replaced chairs. The ratio of library volumes to faculty is 2743 to 1 and to students is 178 to 1. The ratio of seats in the library to students is 1 to 3.

Faculty

The law school has 35 full-time and 21 part-time faculty members, of whom 28 are women. About 1% of full-time faculty have a graduate law degree in addition to the J.D.; about 2% of part-time faculty have one. The ratio of full-time students to full-time faculty in an average class is 13 to 1. The law school has a regular program of bringing visiting professors and other distinguished lecturers and visitors to campus.

Students

About 51% of the student body are women; 32%, minorities; 19%, African American; 3%, Asian American; and 3%, Hispanic. The majority of students come from Georgia (71%). The average age of entering students is 24; age range is 21 to 55. About 60% of students enter directly from undergraduate school, 20% have a graduate degree, and 40% have worked full-time prior to entering law school. About 8% drop out after the first year for academic or personal reasons; 74% remain to receive a law degree.

AVE MARIA SCHOOL OF LAW

3475 Plymouth Road
Ann Arbor, MI 48105

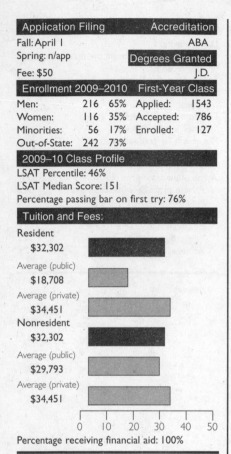

Application Filing	Accreditation
Fall: April 1	ABA
Spring: n/app	**Degrees Granted**
Fee: $50	J.D.

Enrollment 2009–2010		First-Year Class	
Men:	216 65%	Applied:	1543
Women:	116 35%	Accepted:	786
Minorities:	56 17%	Enrolled:	127
Out-of-State:	242 73%		

2009–10 Class Profile
LSAT Percentile: 46%
LSAT Median Score: 151
Percentage passing bar on first try: 76%

Tuition and Fees:

Resident
$32,302

Average (public)
$18,708

Average (private)
$34,451

Nonresident
$32,302

Average (public)
$29,793

Average (private)
$34,451

0 10 20 30 40 50

Percentage receiving financial aid: 100%

ADMISSIONS

In a recent year, 1543 applied, 786 were accepted, and 127 enrolled. The median LSAT percentile of the most recent first-year class was 46; the median GPA was 3.15 on a scale of 4.0. The lowest LSAT percentile accepted was 16; the highest was 98. Figures in the above capsule and in this profile are approximate.

Requirements
Applicants must have a bachelor's degree and take the LSAT. The most important admission factors include academic achievement, letter of recommendation, and character, personality. No specific undergraduate courses are required. Candidates are not interviewed.

Procedure
Applicants should submit an application form, LSAT results, transcripts, a personal statement, TOEFL score, if applicable, a nonrefundable application fee of $50, and 2 letters of recommendation. Notifica-

tion of the admissions decision is on a rolling basis. The latest acceptable LSAT test date for fall entry is June. The law school uses the LSDAS. Check with the school for the current application deadlines.

Special
The law school recruits minority and disadvantaged students through visits to historically Black colleges and universities, mailings to minority students, participation in events sponsored by minority organizations, attendance at minority student conferences, and hosting an annual program for high school students entitled "A Pathway to Law.". Requirements are not different for out-of-state students. Transfer students must have one year of credit, have a minimum GPA of 3, have attended an ABA-approved law school, and transcripts and letter of good standing from ABA-approved law school.

Costs
Tuition and fees for the 2009-2010 academic year are approximately $32,302 for all full-time students. Books and supplies run about $900.

Financial Aid
In a recent year, about 100% of current law students received some form of aid. The average annual amount of aid from all sources combined, including scholarships, loans, and work contracts, was approximately $44,775; maximum, $51,990. Awards are based on need and merit. Required financial statement is the FAFSA. Check with the school for the current application deadline. First-year students are notified about their financial aid application at time of acceptance.

About the Law School
Ave Maria School of Law was established in 1999 and is a private institution. The 11-acre campus is in a suburban area near the Detroit metropolitan area. The primary mission of the law school is to educate lawyers with the finest professional skills, characterized by the harmony of faith and reason, and the Catholic intellectual tradition. Students have access to federal, state, county, city, and local agencies, courts, correctional facilities, law firms, and legal aid organizations in the Ann Arbor area. Facilities of special interest

to law students include a renovated facility with a comprehensive library. Classrooms and library seating are equipped with power and internet connectivity and classrooms have state-of-the-art teaching technologies. Housing for students in Ann Arbor and neighboring communities; and a wide variety of housing options are offered. All law school facilities are accessible to the physically disabled.

Calendar
The law school operates on a traditional semester basis. Courses for full-time students are offered both day and evening and must be completed within 5 years. There is no part-time program. New students are admitted in the fall. There is no summer session. Transferable summer courses are not offered.

Programs
Students may take relevant courses in other programs and apply credit toward the J.D.; a maximum of 8 credits may be applied.

Required
To earn the J.D., candidates must complete 90 total credits, of which 60 are for required courses. They must maintain a minimum GPA of 1.0 in the required courses. The following first-year courses are required of all students: Civil Procedure I and II, Contracts I and II, Criminal Law, Moral Foundations of the Law I and II, Property I and II, Research, Writing, and Advocacy I and II, and Torts I and II. Required upper-level courses consist of Business Organizations, Constitutional Law, Criminal Procedure, Evidence, Federal Taxation, Jurisprudence, Law, Ethics and Public Policy, Professional Responsibility, and Research, Writing, and Advocacy III. The required orientation program for first-year students is a week long and includes programs to develop effective study strategies, meetings with faculty and administrators, and exposure to perspectives on legal study and practice.

Electives
In addition, Clinics include the Women's Immigrant Rights Clinic (4 credits), Asylum Clinic (4 credits), Patent Law Clinic (2 credits), and Advanced Clinic (1 to 2 credits). Completion of first-year courses is

Phone: 734-827-8063
Fax: 734-622-0123
E-mail: info@avemarialaw.edu
Web: www.avemarialaw.edu

Contact

Administrative Assistant, 734-827-8063 for general inquiries; Director of Financial Aid, 734-827-8051 for financial aid information.

MICHIGAN

required. Seminars include First Amendment, Bioethics, and National Security Law. Upper-level students are eligible to enroll in several 2-credit seminars which are generally limited to a maximum of 16 students. The Externship Program allows students to complement their classroom experience with work experience in a variety of legal settings, including working for a state or federal judge, assisting at a local prosecutor's office, or working for a government agency. Externships are offered for 1 or 2 credits per semester; students may enroll in a maximum of 2 credits per semester with an overall maximum of 4 credits. Externships are available to upper-level students with a minimum GPA of 2.667. Under the supervision of a faculty member, students may pursue directed research up to 2 credits per semester for an overall maximum of 4 credits. Students may participate in the Volunteer Tax Assistance Program. The distinguished Speaker Series brings a number of local and national speakers to reflect on their roles in the profession. The Ave Maria Lecture is an annual address from a nationally-recognized public figure. Students are permitted to enroll in summer study abroad programs with advance permission. The Academic Support Program offers activities and services throughout the year designed to help students perform to the best of their abilities. It is staffed by a full-time attorney. While the Academic Support Program offers services to all students, one-on-one programs are designed for at-risk students to provide targeted assistance. The law school has recently hosted annual meetings of the Society of Catholic School Scientists and University Faculty for life. The most widely taken electives are Trial Advocacy, Employment Law, and Trusts and Estates.

Graduation Requirements

In order to graduate, candidates must have a GPA of 2.0, have completed the upper-division writing requirement, and minimum of 6 full-time semesters, and the recommendation of faculty.

Organizations

The primary law review is the *Ave Maria Law Review*. Internal moot court competitions include the St. Thomas More Moot Court Competition (first-year students),

the Ave Maria Intramural Appellate Competition, and the Ave Maria Intramural Trial Competition. The law school participates in several competitions annually, including the State of Michigan Moot Court Competition, the ABA National Client Counseling Competition, and the Herbert Wechsler Criminal Law Moot Court Competition. Law student organizations, local chapters of national associations, and campus organizations include Business Law Society, Women Lawyers Association, Minority Law Students Association, Delta Theta Phi, Phi Alpha Delta, Federalist Society, Law Partners, Lex Vitae Society, and Intellectual Property Group.

Library

The law library contains 117,104 hardcopy volumes and 5319 microform volume equivalents, and subscribes to 1027 serial publications. Such on-line databases and networks as CALI, CIS Universe, Infotrac, Legal-Trac, LEXIS, Mathew Bender, NEXIS, OCLC First Search, WESTLAW, Wilsonline Indexes, and 40 total on-line databases, digital congressional, U.S. Supreme Court are available to law students for research. Special library collections include Canon Law, and Bioethics. Recently, the library SMART whiteboard installed in seminar rooms. The ratio of library volumes to faculty is 4182 to 1 and to students is 353 to 1. The ratio of seats in the library to students is 1 to 1.

Faculty

The law school has 28 full-time and 10 part-time faculty members, of whom 13 are women. About 29% of full-time faculty have a graduate law degree in addition to the J.D. The ratio of full-time students to full-time faculty in an average class is 28 to 1; in a clinic, 10 to 1. The law school has a regular program of bringing visiting professors and other distinguished lecturers and visitors to campus.

Students

About 35% of the student body are women; 17%, minorities; 2%, African American; 7%, Asian American; 7%, Hispanic; and 1%, Native American. The majority of students come from the Midwest (50%). The average age of entering students is 25; age range is 21 to 43. About 49% of students enter directly from undergraduate school,

Placement

J.D.s awarded:	123
Services available through: a separate law school placement center	
Services: educational programs on careers	
Special features: Mock Interview Program for first-year students and Lawyer-Mentor Program.	
Full-time job interviews:	8 employers
Summer job interviews:	10 employers
Placement by graduation:	35% of class
Placement within 9 months:	74% of class
Average starting salary:	$46,300 to $60,000
Areas of placement:	
Private practice 2-10 attorneys	19%
Private practice 11-25 attorneys	8%
Private practice 26-50 attorneys	2%
Private practice 51-100 attorneys	5%
Business/industry	24%
Judicial clerkships	17%
Government	14%
501+ Attorneys 3%,	
Solo practitioners 3%	6%
Public interest	3%
Academic	2%

5% have a graduate degree, and 50% have worked full-time prior to entering law school. About 4% drop out after the first year for academic or personal reasons; 84% remain to receive a law degree.

School of Law

6441 East Colonial Drive
Orlando, FL 32807

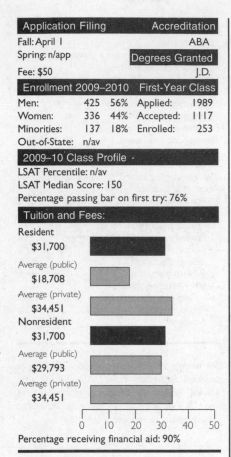

Application Filing		Accreditation
Fall: April 1		ABA
Spring: n/app		Degrees Granted
Fee: $50		J.D.

Enrollment 2009–2010		First-Year Class	
Men:	425 56%	Applied:	1989
Women:	336 44%	Accepted:	1117
Minorities:	137 18%	Enrolled:	253
Out-of-State:	n/av		

2009–10 Class Profile
LSAT Percentile: n/av
LSAT Median Score: 150
Percentage passing bar on first try: 76%

Tuition and Fees:

Resident
$31,700

Average (public)
$18,708

Average (private)
$34,451

Nonresident
$31,700

Average (public)
$29,793

Average (private)
$34,451

0 10 20 30 40 50

Percentage receiving financial aid: 90%

ADMISSIONS

In the fall 2009 first-year class, 1989 applied, 1117 were accepted, and 253 enrolled. Ten transfers enrolled. The median GPA of the most recent first-year class was 3.3.

Requirements

Applicants must have a bachelor's degree and take the LSAT. No specific undergraduate courses are required. Candidates are not interviewed.

Procedure

The application deadline for fall entry is April 1. Applicants should submit an application form, LSAT results, transcripts, a personal statement, a nonrefundable application fee of $50, and 2 (supplemental) letters of recommendation. Notification of the admissions decision is on a rolling basis. The latest acceptable LSAT test date for fall entry is February. The law school uses the LSDAS.

Special

The law school recruits minority and disadvantaged students through the Early Start Program, a 4-week summer program held prior to orientation. Requirements are not different for out-of-state students. Transfer students must have one year of credit, have a minimum GPA of 2.5, and have attended an ABA-approved law school.

Costs

Tuition and fees for the 2009-2010 academic year are $31,700 for all full-time students. Tuition for part-time students is $23,920 per year.

Financial Aid

About 90% of current law students receive some form of aid. The average annual amount of aid from all sources combined, including scholarships, loans, and work contracts, is $38,707. Required financial statement is the FAFSA. The aid application deadline for fall entry is June. First-year students are notified about their financial aid application after a seat deposit is received (commitment to enroll).

About the Law School

Barry University School of Law was established in 1999 and is a private institution. The 20-acre campus is in an urban area 15 minutes from downtown Orlando. The primary mission of the law school is to provide a learning environment that challenges students to accept intellectual, personal, ethical, spiritual, and social responsibilities. Students have access to federal, state, county, city, and local agencies, courts, correctional facilities, law firms, and legal aid organizations in the Orlando area. Facilities of special interest to law students include a 2-story 20,000-square-foot law center building, a 9,000-square-foot moot court building, a 9,000-square-foot administration building, and a 36,000-square-foot law library. Housing for students is plentiful off campus.

Calendar

The law school operates on a traditional semester basis. Courses for full-time students are offered both day and evening and must be completed within 6 semesters. For part-time students, courses are offered evenings only and must be completed within 8 semesters. New full- and part-time students are admitted in the fall. There is a summer session. Transferable summer courses are offered.

Programs

Required

To earn the J.D., candidates must complete 90 total credits, of which 53 to 55 are for required courses. They must maintain a minimum GPA of 1.8 in the required courses. The following first-year courses are required of all students: Civil Procedure, Constitutional Law, Contracts, Criminal Law, Legal Methods, Legal Research and Writing I and II, Property, and Torts. Required upper-level courses consist of Business Organizations, Commercial Course, Evidence, Federal Taxation, Perspectives Course, and Professional Responsibility. The required orientation program for first-year students is 5 days including instruction on legal briefing, a mock class, a practitioner's panel, and time/stress management.

Electives

The School of Law offers a concentration in family law. In addition, clinics include the Children and Families Clinic, Immigration Clinic, and Earth Justice Clinic. Various internships are available. Externships include Mediation, Public Defender's Office, Judicial, State Attorney's Office, and Business. Study abroad in Spain is available (joint program with St. Thomas Law). Tutorial programs include the Academic Success Program.

Graduation Requirements

In order to graduate, candidates must have a GPA of 2.0 and have completed the upper-division writing requirement.

Organizations

Students edit *Barry University Law Review*, the student newspaper *The Advocate*, and *Moot Points*. Law student organizations, local chapters of national associations, and campus organizations include Moot Court Board, St. Thomas More Society, Trial Advocacy Team, Phi Alpha Delta, Delta Theta Phi, Christian Legal Society, Hispanic American Associa-

Phone: 321-206-5600
866-JD-BARRY
Fax: 321-206-5662
E-mail: *acruz@mail.barry.edu*
Web: *http://barry.edu/law*

Contact
Helia Hull, Associate Dean, 321-206-5600 for general inquiries; Connie Allman, 321-206-5621 or 866-JD-BARRY for financial aid information.

tion, James C. Collier Black Law Students Association, Environmental Law Society, Real Estate Committee, and Asian American Law Student Association.

Library
The law library contains 200,000 hardcopy volumes and 92,839 microform volume equivalents, and subscribes to 1600 serial publications. Such on-line databases and networks as CALI, Legal-Trac, LEXIS, LOIS, NEXIS, OCLC First Search, and WESTLAW are available to law students for research. Recently, the library added wireless research capability. The ratio of library volumes to faculty is 7143 to 1 and to students is 280 to 1. The ratio of seats in the library to students is 1 to 2.

Faculty
The law school has 24 full-time and 54 part-time faculty members, of whom 30 are women. According to AAUP standards for Category IIA institutions, faculty salaries are below average. About 60% of full-time faculty have a graduate law degree in addition to the J.D. The ratio of full-time students to full-time faculty in an average class is 19 to 1.

Students
About 44% of the student body are women; 18%, minorities; 4%, African American; 4%, Asian American; 9%, Hispanic; and 1%, Native American. The average age of entering students is 25; age range is 20 to 59. About 3% drop out after the first year for academic or personal reasons; 97% remain to receive a law degree.

Placement	
J.D.s awarded:	173
Services available through: the university placement center	
Full-time job interviews:	n/av
Summer job interviews:	n/av
Placement by graduation:	n/av
Placement within 9 months:	n/av
Average starting salary:	n/av
Areas of placement:	
Private practice 2-100 attorneys	58%
Business/industry	16%
Government	15%
Public interest	7%
Academic	3%
Judicial clerkships	1%

School of Law

One Bear Place #97288
Waco, TX 76798-7288

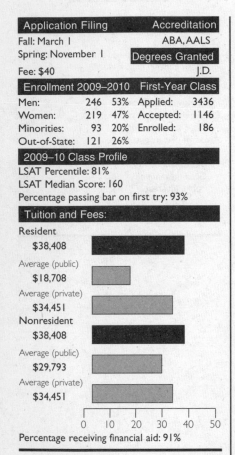

Application Filing	Accreditation
Fall: March 1	ABA, AALS
Spring: November 1	
Fee: $40	**Degrees Granted**
	J.D.

Enrollment 2009–2010			First-Year Class	
Men:	246	53%	Applied:	3436
Women:	219	47%	Accepted:	1146
Minorities:	93	20%	Enrolled:	186
Out-of-State:	121	26%		

2009–10 Class Profile
LSAT Percentile: 81%
LSAT Median Score: 160
Percentage passing bar on first try: 93%

Tuition and Fees:

Resident
$38,408

Average (public)
$18,708

Average (private)
$34,451

Nonresident
$38,408

Average (public)
$29,793

Average (private)
$34,451

0 10 20 30 40 50

Percentage receiving financial aid: 91%

ADMISSIONS

In the fall 2009 first-year class, 3436 applied, 1146 were accepted, and 186 enrolled. 1 transfer enrolled. The median LSAT percentile of the most recent first-year class was 81; the median GPA was 3.62 on a scale of 4.0. The lowest LSAT percentile accepted was 71; the highest was 87.

Requirements
Applicants must have a bachelor's degree and take the LSAT. The most important admission factors include LSAT results, GPA, and general background. No specific undergraduate courses are required. Candidates are not interviewed.

Procedure
The application deadline for fall entry is March 1. Applicants should submit an application form, LSAT results, transcripts, a personal statement, LSDAS, a nonrefundable application fee of $40, 2 letters of recommendation, and a personal statement. Notification of the admissions

decision is 4 to 6 weeks after the application deadline. The latest acceptable LSAT test date for fall entry is December. The law school uses the LSDAS.

Special
The law school recruits minority and disadvantaged students the same as non-minority students. A member of the Law School faculty serves as the Minority Law Student Adviser. Requirements are not different for out-of-state students. Transfer students must have 1 year of credit, have a minimum GPA of 3, have attended an ABA-approved law school, and to be competitive with the applicant pool, the applicants should be in the top 5 to 10% of their class at a comparable law school.

Costs

Tuition and fees for the 2009-2010 academic year are $38,408 for all full-time students. On-campus room and board costs about $9708 annually; books and supplies run $2007.

Financial Aid

About 91% of current law students receive some form of aid. The average annual amount of aid from all sources combined, including scholarships, loans, and work contracts, is $38,234; maximum, $56,884. Awards are based on need and merit. Required financial statement is the FAFSA. The aid application deadline for fall entry is February 15. Special funds for minority or disadvantaged students include a limited number of scholarships ranging from one-third to full tuition for students who have overcome educational and/or emotional disadvantages or other personal hardship experiences. First-year students are notified about their financial aid application before enrollment.

About the Law School

Baylor University School of Law was established in 1849 and is a private institution. The 432-acre campus is in an urban area 92 miles south of Dallas. The primary mission of the law school is to train students in all facets of the law including theoretical analysis, practical application, legal writing and advocacy, negotiation, and counseling skills to equip them to practice effectively in any area of the law. Students have access to federal, state, county, city, and local agencies, courts, correctional

facilities, law firms, and legal aid organizations in the Waco area. Facilities of special interest to law students include a $33 million, state-of-the-art 128,000 square foot facility. Housing for students consists of private and university rental housing, including numerous rooms and condominiums near the Baylor campus and other properties throughout the city of Waco. All law school facilities are accessible to the physically disabled.

Calendar

The law school operates on a quarter basis. Courses for full-time students are offered days only and must be completed within 5 years. There is no part-time program. New students are admitted in the fall, spring, and summer. There is a 11-week summer session. Transferable summer courses are offered.

Programs

Students may take relevant courses in other programs and apply credit toward the J.D.; a maximum of 12 credits may be applied. The following joint degrees may be earned: J.D./M.B.A. (Juris Doctor/Master of Business Administration), J.D./M. Tax (Juris Doctor/Master of Taxation), and J.D/M.P.P.A. (Juris Doctor/Master of Public Policy Administration).

Required
To earn the J.D., candidates must complete 126 total credits, of which 78 are for required courses. They must maintain a minimum GPA of 2.0 in the required courses. The following first-year courses are required of all students: Appellate Advocacy and Procedure, Civil Procedure, Contracts I and II, Criminal Law, Criminal Procedure, Introduction to Law and Lawyering, Legal Analysis, Research, and Communication I, II, and III, Legislative, Administrative Process and Procedure, Property I and II, and Torts I and II. Required upper-level courses consist of Basic Tax and Accounting for Lawyers, Business Organization I, Constitutional Law, Practice Court II, Practice Court III, Professional Responsibility, and Trusts and Estates Remedies. All students must take clinical courses. The required orientation program for first-year students is a 3-day program that covers introduction to the legal profession and life as a law student.

Phone: 254-710-1911
800-BAYLOR
Fax: 254-710-2316
E-mail: *becky_beck@baylor.edu*
Web: *law.baylor.edu*

Contact

Becky L. Beck, Assistant Dean of Admissions, 254-710-2529 for general inquiries; Office of Financial Aid, Baylor University, 254-710-2611 for financial aid information.

TEXAS ®

Placement

J.D.s awarded:	130

Services available through: a separate law school placement center, the university placement center, and reciprocity may be requested from other law schools.

Services: resource library; use of telephone/fax/typewriter for job search purposes

Special features: the Direct Contact Program, Resume Collection Program, job search skills programs, mock interviews, guest speaker panel discussions, and participation in various job fairs in Texas as well as out of state.

Full-time job interviews:	17 employers
Summer job interviews:	47 employers
Placement by graduation:	n/av
Placement within 9 months:	98% of class
Average starting salary:	$51,000 to $93,122

Areas of placement:

Private practice 2-10 attorneys	25%
Private practice 11-25 attorneys	11%
Private practice 26-50 attorneys	8%
Private practice 51-100 attorneys	3%
private practice 100+ attorneys, Solo, Private Pra	17%
Government	12%
Judicial clerkships	10%
Business/industry	10%
Academic	2%
Public interest	1%
Military	1%

Electives

The School of Law offers concentrations in criminal law, international law, litigation, business transactions, administrative law, estate planning, and business litigation. In addition, the 2-quarter Practice Court Program is required in the third year and includes rigorous hands-on training. Students are required to complete at least 4 mini trials and 1 large trial along with several other exercises. There are real-life client opportunities for pro bono divorce cases and other client opportunities for penalty cases. A Supreme Court seminar is available. Internships are available in the District Attorney's Office, U.S. Attorney's Office, U.S. District Court, U.S. Bankruptcy Court, Texas Attorney General's Office-Child Support Division, Legal Services Office, and others for 2 hours of credit, and the Texas Supreme Court and Court of Criminal Appeals for 5 hours of credit. Independent studies for 1 or 2 hours of credit are available for second- and third-year students under faculty supervision. Field work opportunities are available in a number of offices such as General Counsel for Texas Life Insurance Co. Special lecture series include the Frank Wilson Memorial, W.R. White Memorial, R. Matt Dawson Lecture Series, and the John William Minton and Florence Dean Minton Endowed Law School Lecture Series. Students may study in Guadalajara, Mexico and earn up to 5 credits during a 2-week program in August. A faculty-conducted tutorial program is available for students placed on academic probation as well as for other interested students. There is a designated faculty Minority Student Adviser and a Diversity in Law Students Association. There is an Environmental Law program once a year and various speakers throughout the year. The most widely taken electives are Client Counseling, Alternative Dispute Resolution, Advanced Criminal Procedure, Administration of Estates, Appellate Procedure, Trusts and Estates II, and Secured Transactions.

Graduation Requirements

In order to graduate, candidates must have a GPA of 2.0 and have completed the upper-division writing requirement.

Organizations

The primary law review is the Baylor Law Review. Moot court competitions include the Dawson and Sodd Fall Moot Court and the Strasburger, Price Spring Moot Court, and the Wortham Top Gun Competition. Intrascholastic competitions are the Naman, Howell, Smith and Lee Client Counseling Competition, and the Bob Wortham Mock Trial Tournament of Champions. Interscholastic competitions include the National Trial, National Moot Court, National Appellate Advocacy, Texas Young Lawyers Moot Court, National Negotiations, and National Client Counseling. Law student organizations, local chapters of national associations, and campus clubs and organizations include Women's Legal Society, American Constitution Society, Civil Rights Society, Baylor University Student Bar Association, Diversity in Law Association, Civil Rights Society, R.E.B Baylor Chapter of Phi Alpha, James P. Alexander Senate of Delta Theta Phi, and the Hemphill Inn Chapter of Phi Delta Phi.

Library

The law library contains 241,927 hardcopy volumes and 127,451 microform volume equivalents, and subscribes to 2212 serial publications. Such on-line databases and networks as CALI, DIALOG, LegalTrac, LEXIS, LOIS, NEXIS, OCLC First Search, RLIN, WESTLAW, and NEXIS are available to law students for research. Special library collections include the Frank M. Wilson Rare Book Room Collection, which contains first editions and rare printings of legal writings, novels, and research titles relating to law. Recently, the library moved into a spacious facility with a state-of-the-art computer laboratory and wireless connectivity throughout and a view of the Brazos River. The ratio of library volumes to faculty is 8960 to 1 and to students is 520 to 1. The ratio of seats in the library to students is 1 to 2.

Faculty

The law school has 27 full-time and 29 part-time faculty members, of whom 11 are women. According to AAUP standards for Category I institutions, faculty salaries are well below average. About 25% of full-time faculty have a graduate law degree in addition to the J.D.; about 3% of part-time faculty have one. The ratio of full-time students to full-time faculty in an average class is 25 to 1; in a clinic, 2 to 1. The law school has a regular program of bringing visiting professors and other distinguished lecturers and visitors to campus.

Students

About 47% of the student body are women; 20%, minorities; 2%, African American; 9%, Asian American; 9%, Hispanic; and 1%, Native American. The majority of students come from Texas (74%). The average age of entering students is 23; age range is 18 to 46. About 76% of students enter directly from undergraduate school, 3% have a graduate degree, and 21% have worked full-time prior to entering law school. About 4% drop out after the first year for academic or personal reasons; 96% remain to receive a law degree.

Law School

885 Centre Street
Newton, MA 02459

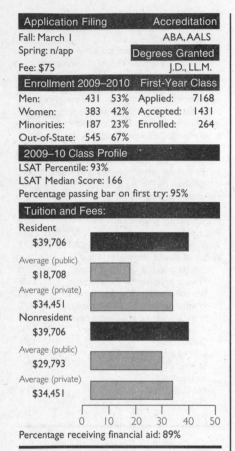

Application Filing	Accreditation
Fall: March 1	ABA, AALS
Spring: n/app	

Degrees Granted
Fee: $75	J.D., LL.M.

Enrollment 2009–2010		First-Year Class	
Men:	431 53%	Applied:	7168
Women:	383 42%	Accepted:	1431
Minorities:	187 23%	Enrolled:	264
Out-of-State:	545 67%		

2009–10 Class Profile
LSAT Percentile: 93%
LSAT Median Score: 166
Percentage passing bar on first try: 95%

Tuition and Fees:

Resident
$39,706

Average (public)
$18,708

Average (private)
$34,451

Nonresident
$39,706

Average (public)
$29,793

Average (private)
$34,451

0   10   20   30   40   50

Percentage receiving financial aid: 89%

ADMISSIONS

In the fall 2009 first-year class, 7168 applied, 1431 were accepted, and 264 enrolled. Fourteen transfers enrolled. The median LSAT percentile of the most recent first-year class was 93; the median GPA was 3.53 on a scale of 4.0.

Requirements

Applicants must have a bachelor's degree and take the LSAT. Minimum acceptable GPA is 2.0 on a scale of 4.0. The most important admission factors include academic achievement, character, personality, and undergraduate curriculum. No specific undergraduate courses are required. Candidates are not interviewed.

Procedure

The application deadline for fall entry is March 1. Applicants should submit an application form, LSAT results, a personal statement, a nonrefundable application fee of $75, 2 letters of recommendation, and the LSDAS report. Notification of the admissions decision is on a rolling basis.

The latest acceptable LSAT test date for fall entry is February. The law school uses the LSDAS.

Special

The law school recruits minority and disadvantaged students through a program of active outreach by the Admissions Committee and minority student organizations. Requirements are not different for out-of-state students. Transfer students must have one year of credit and have attended an ABA-approved law school; applicants are considered on a space-available basis.

Costs

Tuition and fees for the 2009-2010 academic year are $39,706 for all full-time students. Books and supplies run $1300.

Financial Aid

About 89% of current law students receive some form of aid. The average annual amount of aid from all sources combined, including scholarships, loans, and work contracts, is $38,962; maximum, $56,546. Awards are based on need and merit. Required financial statements are the FAFSA and the Need Access on-line application. The aid application deadline for fall entry is March 15. Special funds for minority or disadvantaged students include additional tuition remission. First-year students are notified about their financial aid application at the beginning of February on a rolling basis as files are completed.

About the Law School

Boston College Law School was established in 1929 and is a private institution. The 40-acre campus is in a suburban area 6 miles west of downtown Boston. The primary mission of the law school is to provide a quality legal education in the Jesuit, Catholic tradition to a highly qualified and diverse group of men and women to prepare them to serve their communities and serve as leaders in the profession. Students have access to federal, state, county, city, and local agencies, courts, correctional facilities, law firms, and legal aid organizations in the Newton area. Facilities of special interest to law students include a $16 million library, a $13 million classroom building with

state-of-the-art audiovisual and computing capabilities, and a Career Resources Center. Housing for students is extensive; there is ample rental housing in Newton and the surrounding communities. All law school facilities are accessible to the physically disabled.

Calendar

The law school operates on a traditional semester basis. Courses for full-time students are offered days only and must be completed within 4 years. There is no part-time program. New students are admitted in the fall. There is no summer session. Transferable summer courses are not offered.

Programs

In addition to the J.D., the law school offers the LL.M. Students may take relevant courses in other programs and apply credit toward the J.D.; a maximum of 12 credits may be applied. The following joint degrees may be earned: J.D./M.A. (Juris Doctor/Master of Arts in education), J.D./M.A.P. (Juris Doctor/Master of Arts in Philosophy), J.D./M.B.A. (Juris Doctor/Master of Business Administration), J.D./M.Ed. (Juris Doctor/Master of Education), and J.D./M.S.W. (Juris Doctor/Master of Social Work).

Required

To earn the J.D., candidates must complete 85 total credits, of which 36 and up are for required courses. They must maintain a minimum GPA of 2.0 in the required courses. The following first-year courses are required of all students: Civil Procedure, Constitutional Law, Contracts, Criminal Law, Legal Research and Writing, Property, and Torts. Required upper-level courses consist of class meeting lawyering skill, class meeting perspective on law and justice, Constitutional Law II, and Professional Responsibility. The required orientation program for first-year students is a day followed by 2 sessions on subsequent days. Orientation covers introduction to the law school, perspectives on differences, and legal ethics orientation.

Electives

The Law School offers concentrations in corporate law, criminal law, environmen-

Phone: 617-552-4351
Fax: 617-552-2917
E-mail: bclawadm@bc.edu
Web: www.bc.edu/lawschool

Contact
Rita C. Jones, Assistant Dean Admissions and Fin, 617-552-4351 for general inquiries; Rita C. Jones, Assistant Dean Admissions and Fin, 617-552-4351 for financial aid information.

MASSACHUSETTS

tal law, family law, intellectual property law, international law, juvenile law, litigation, securities law, tax law, torts and insurance, and clinical programs. In addition, clinics include the Civil Litigation Clinic, Women and the Law Clinic, the Criminal Justice Clinic, Housing Clinic, and Community Enterprise Clinic, each worth 7 credits. Internships include the Semester in Practice and the Attorney General's Program. Special lecture series include the Legal History Roundtable, Criminal Law Roundtable, and faculty workshops. A London program is offered to second-and third-year students for 13 credits. The International Criminal Tribunals (ICT) offers a unique opportunity to work onsite at the criminal tribunal established by the UN Security Council. Tutorial programs are available to students who require them. Programming for minority students is sponsored by student groups. Minority students are actively recruited. The most widely taken electives are Taxation, Corporations, and Evidence.

Graduation Requirements
In order to graduate, candidates must have a GPA of 2.0.

Organizations
Students edit the *Boston College Law Review, Boston College Environmental Affairs Law Review, Boston College International and Comparative Law Review, Boston College Third World Law Journal, Uniform Commercial Code Reporter Digest*, and the online newsletter, *The Counselor*. Moot court competitions include the Wendell F. Grimes Moot Court, Jessup International Moot Court, and National Moot Court competitions. Other competitions include the Mock Trial, Negotiations, Client Counseling, Administrative Law Moot Court, Braxton Craven Moot Court, Bankruptcy Moot Court, European Union Law Moot Court, Frederick Douglass Moot Court, Saul Lefkowitz, Trademark Moot Court, and Immigration Law Moot Court. Law student organizations include International Law Society, Public Interest Law Foundation, and Environmental Law Society. Local chapters of national associations include the ABA-Law Student Division, National Lawyers Guild, and Phi Alpha Delta. Campus clubs and other organizations include the Black Law Students Association, Lambda, Latino Law Students Association, Asian Pacific American Law Students Association, South Asian Law Student Association, and Jewish Law Student Association.

Library
The law library contains 481,235 hardcopy volumes and 231,805 microform volume equivalents, and subscribes to 2549 serial publications. Such on-line databases and networks as CALI, CIS Universe, DIALOG, Infotrac, Legal-Trac, LEXIS, LOIS, Mathew Bender, NEXIS, OCLC First Search, RLIN, WESTLAW, Wilsonline Indexes, Access UN, HeinOnline, CCH Internet, Research Network, Congressional Quarterly, Environment and Safety Library, and Bloomberg Law are available to law students for research. Special library collections include Daniel R. Coquillette Rare Book collection and the U.S. Government Documents Depository. The ratio of library volumes to faculty is 7291 to 1 and to students is 591 to 1. The ratio of seats in the library to students is 1 to 1.

Faculty
The law school has 66 full-time and 35 part-time faculty members, of whom 41 are women. According to AAUP standards for Category I institutions, faculty salaries are above average. About 17% of full-time faculty have a graduate law degree in addition to the J.D. The ratio of full-time students to full-time faculty in an average class is 13 to 1; in a clinic, 6 to 1. The law school has a regular program of bringing visiting professors and other distinguished lecturers and visitors to campus. There is a chapter of the Order of the Coif.

Students
About 42% of the student body are women; 23%, minorities; 4%, African American; 12%, Asian American; 7%, Hispanic; and 15%, Foreign National. The majority of students come from Massachusetts (33%). The average age of entering students is 24; age range is 20 to 43. About 40% of students enter directly from undergraduate school, 14% have a graduate degree, and 60% have worked full-time prior to entering law school. About 2% drop out after the first year for academic or personal reasons; 98% remain to receive a law degree.

Placement

J.D.s awarded:	245

Services available through: a separate law school placement center

Special features: Mandatory 1L meeting with assigned Career Service counselors, dedicated public service counselor, over 80 skills workshops and career panels and programs offered yearly, on-campus and off-campus recruitment programs in 8 national cities, and two government/public interest consortium programs.

Full-time job interviews:	400 employers
Summer job interviews:	400 employers
Placement by graduation:	86% of class
Placement within 9 months:	97% of class
Average starting salary:	$26,400 to $160,000

Areas of placement:

Private practice 2-10 attorneys	8%
Private practice 51-100 attorneys	6%
Judicial clerkships	53%
Government	7%
Business/industry	5%
Academic	4%
Public interest	3%

School of Law

765 Commonwealth Avenue
Boston, MA 02215

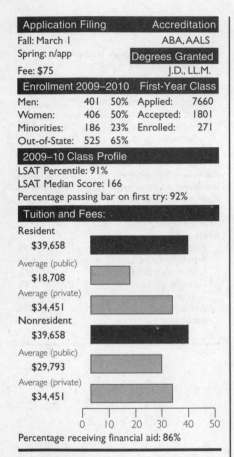

Application Filing	Accreditation
Fall: March 1	ABA, AALS
Spring: n/app	**Degrees Granted**
Fee: $75	J.D., LL.M.

Enrollment 2009–2010		First-Year Class	
Men:	401 50%	Applied:	7660
Women:	406 50%	Accepted:	1801
Minorities:	186 23%	Enrolled:	271
Out-of-State:	525 65%		

2009–10 Class Profile
LSAT Percentile: 91%
LSAT Median Score: 166
Percentage passing bar on first try: 92%

Tuition and Fees:

Resident
    $39,658

Average (public)
    $18,708

Average (private)
    $34,451

Nonresident
    $39,658

Average (public)
    $29,793

Average (private)
    $34,451

0 10 20 30 40 50
Percentage receiving financial aid: 86%

ADMISSIONS

In the fall 2009 first-year class, 7660 applied, 1801 were accepted, and 271 enrolled. Twenty-five transfers enrolled. The median LSAT percentile of the most recent first-year class was 91; the median GPA was 3.7 on a scale of 4.3. The lowest LSAT percentile accepted was 44; the highest was 99.

Requirements
Applicants must have a bachelor's degree and take the LSAT. The law school takes a holistic approach to the review of applications. No specific undergraduate courses are required. Candidates are not interviewed.

Procedure
The application deadline for fall entry is March 1. Applicants should submit an application form, LSAT results, transcripts, TOEFL for international students only, a nonrefundable application fee of $75, and 2 letters of recommendation. Notification of the admissions decision is on a rolling basis. The latest acceptable LSAT test date for fall entry is February. The law school uses the LSDAS.

Special
The law school recruits minority and disadvantaged students by means of the Candidate Referral Service, LSAC forums, active minority groups on campus, alumni contacts, and the recruiting efforts of the Associate Director of Academic and Multicultural Affairs. Requirements are not different for out-of-state students. Transfer students must have one year of credit, have attended an ABA-approved law school, and must submit a transfer application.

Costs

Tuition and fees for the 2009-2010 academic year are $39,658 for all full-time students. On-campus room and board costs about $11,808 annually; books and supplies run $1374.

Financial Aid

About 86% of current law students receive some form of aid. The average annual amount of aid from all sources combined, including scholarships, loans, and work contracts, is $46,924; maximum, $57,234. Awards are based on need and merit. Required financial statements are the FAFSA and Need Access Form. The aid application deadline for fall entry is March 1. Special funds for minority or disadvantaged students include Martin Luther King Jr., Whitney Young, Norbert Simmons, and Barbara Jordan fellowships and scholarships. First-year students are notified about their financial aid application at time of acceptance.

About the Law School

Boston University School of Law was established in 1872 and is a private institution. The 132-acre campus is in an urban area in Boston. The primary mission of the law school is to prepare a diverse student body for the ethical practice of law around the globe, with perspectives and analyses that enrich a comprehensive understanding and adapt to changing needs. Students have access to federal, state, county, city, and local agencies, courts, correctional facilities, law firms, and legal aid organizations in the Boston area. The school hosts the American Society for Law, Medicine, and Ethics, the Morin Center for Banking and Financial Law Studies, and the Pike Institute of Law and Disability. Facilities of special interest to law students are the university's new fitness and recreation center the Tsai Performance Center, rowing and sailing programs on the Charles River, and all the amenities of Boston, such as the Boston Symphony, opera, theater, and sports. Housing for students is available as rental apartment units within walking distance of the school or as suburban accommodations easily reached by mass transportation lines. There is a new graduate student apartment building. About 98% of the law school facilities are accessible to the physically disabled.

Calendar

The law school operates on a traditional semester basis. Courses for full-time students are offered days only and must be completed within 3 years. Graduate studies are offered part-time both day and evening. New full- and part-time students are admitted in the fall. There is no summer session. Transferable summer courses are not offered.

Programs

In addition to the J.D., the law school offers the LL.M. Students may take relevant courses in other programs and apply credit toward the J.D.; a maximum of 16 credits may be applied. The following joint degrees may be earned: J.D./LL.M. (Juris Doctor/Master of Laws in banking and financial law, taxation, and European law), J.D./M.A. (Juris Doctor/Master of Arts in law and international relations, philosophy, and perseriation studies), J.D./M.B.A. (Juris Doctor/Master of Business Administration in law and health sector management), J.D./M.P.H. (Juris Doctor/Master of Public Health), and J.D./M.S. (Juris Doctor/Master of Science in law and masscommunication).

Required
To earn the J.D., candidates must complete 84 total credits, of which 33 are for required courses. They must maintain a minimum GPA of 2.0 in the required courses. The following first-year courses are required of all students: Civil Procedure, Constitutional Law, Contracts, Criminal Law, Legal Writing and Research, Legislation, Property, and Torts. Required upper-level courses consist of Professional Responsibility. All students choose from voluntary clinical and externship program offerings that include: Civil Litigation, Criminal Law, Legislative Policy and Drafting, Africa i-Parliaments and Legislative Counsel Clinics. The required orientation program

Phone: 617-353-3100
Fax: 617-353-0578
E-mail: *bulawadm@bu.edu*
Web: *www.bu.edu/LAW*

Contact

Alissa Leonard, Director of Admissions and Financial Aid, 617-353-3100 for general inquiries; Alissa Leonard, Director of Admissions and Financial Aid, 617-353-3100 for financial aid information.

MASSACHUSETTS

for first-year students is a 1½ day program including building tours, panel discussions, faculty talks, and social events.

Electives

The School of Law offers concentrations in corporate law, intellectual property law, international law, litigation, and health law, and business organizations and finance law. In addition, clinics for upper-level students include 3 to 8 credits in Legislative Services, Criminal Trial Advocacy, and Civil Litigation Clinic. More than 70 seminars for varying credit are open to upper-level students. Semester-in-practice options include a human rights externship in Geneva, government lawyering in Washington, D.C., a death penalty externship at the Southern Center for Human Rights in Atlanta, and an independent proposal externship outside of Boston. A variety of other externships, geared toward individual student interest, are offered for various credit levels. Independent Study with a faculty member (supervised research and writing) is offered to upper-level students for 1 to 3 credits. Special lecture series include the Distinguished Speaker Series, Shapiro Lecture, Legal History Lectures, Intellectual Property Speaker Series, Law and Economics seminar, faculty workshops, and Faculty Brown Bag lunch talks. The school offers 13 academic-year study-abroad programs: in Lyon, Beijing, Geneva, Hamburg, Madrid, Singapore, Paris, Oxford, Tel Aviv, Leiden, Buenos Aires, Florence, and Hong Kong. The Student Affairs Office coordinates a Voluntary Academic Support Program for first-year students whose first-semester grades indicate that they need assistance. The program is offered in the second semester of the first year for no credit. The classes focus on outlining and exam-taking skills. Individualized academic support for second- and third-year students is available. In addition, the Student Affairs Office, together with minority student organizations, sponsors an orientation program for incoming minority students. Additional programming includes 2 weeks of diversity sessions and a minority alumni student networking event. A Student Organization Activities Fair, sponsored by the Student Bar Association, introduces students to school organizations and groups. The most widely taken electives are Corporations, Evidence, Federal Income Taxation.

Graduation Requirements

In order to graduate, candidates must have a GPA of 2.3, have completed the upper-division writing requirement, and have researched and written a major paper on a topic of their choice, which is supervised and evaluated by faculty.

Organizations

Students edit the *Boston University Law Review, American Journal of Law and Medicine, Annual Review of Banking and Financial Law, Boston University International Law Journal, Public Interest Law Journal*, and *Journal of Science and Technology Law*. All first-year students participate in the intramural J. Newton Esdaile Moot Court program during the spring semester. Second-year students may participate in the Edward C. Stone Appellate Moot Court Competition in the fall; the top advocates from the Stone Competition advance to the Homer Albers Prize Moot Court Competition during the spring semester of their second year. Teams of third-year students are sent to national intramural competitions such as National Moot Court, National Appellate Advocacy, and Craven Constitutional Law. Students may participate in the Association of Trial Lawyers of America National Student Trial Advocacy Competition and the ABA Negotiation and Client Counseling competitions. The law school supports more than 30 student organizations, including Student Bar Association, Women's Law Association, and Corporate Law Society. Other organizations include the Arts Law Association; Civil Liberties Association, and Communications, Entertainment, and Sports Law Association. There are local chapters of Federalist Society, Phi Alpha Delta, and Phi Delta Phi.

Library

The law library contains 659,182 hardcopy volumes and 321,809 microform volume equivalents, and subscribes to 3615 serial publications. Such on-line databases and networks as CALI, CIS Universe, DIALOG, Dow-Jones, Infotrac, Legal-Trac, LEXIS, LOIS, NEXIS, OCLC First Search, WESTLAW, and Wilsonline Indexes, and The law school has access to more than 100 electronic databases. Special library collections include intellectual property, banking and financial law, health law, human rights, tax law, and

Placement

J.D.s awarded:	272

Services available through: a separate law school placement center
Services: extensive off-campus interview programs in 8 cities and numerous specialty job fairs; job search strategy and interview workshops; numerous presentations on areas of practice and law-related careers featuring alumni

Full-time job interviews:	128 employers
Summer job interviews:	128 employers
Placement by graduation:	97% of class
Placement within 9 months:	100% of class
Average starting salary:	$48,000 to $160,000

Areas of placement:

Private practice 2-10 attorneys	3%
Private practice 11-25 attorneys	2%
Private practice 26-50 attorneys	2%
Private practice 51-100 attorneys	4%
Private practice 101-501+ attorneys 57% Private pr	58%
Academic	7%
Judicial clerkships	6%

international law collections. The ratio of library volumes to faculty is 11,771 to 1 and to students is 816 to 1. The ratio of seats in the library to students is 1 to 1.

Faculty

The law school has 56 full-time and 79 part-time faculty members, of whom 53 are women. According to AAUP standards for Category I institutions, faculty salaries are average. About 19% of full-time faculty have a graduate law degree in addition to the J.D.; about 13% of part-time faculty have one. The ratio of full-time students to full-time faculty in an average class is 37 to 1; in a clinic, 11 to 1. The law school has a regular program of bringing visiting professors and other distinguished lecturers and visitors to campus.

Students

About 50% of the student body are women; 23%, minorities; 5%, African American; 12%, Asian American; and 6%, Hispanic. The majority of students come from Massachusetts (35%). The average age of entering students is 24; age range is 21 to 44. About 15% of students have a graduate degree. About 4% drop out after the first year for academic or personal reasons; 95% remain to receive a law degree.

BRIGHAM YOUNG UNIVERSITY

J. Reuben Clark Law School

342 JRCB Brigham Young University
Provo, UT 84602

Application Filing			Accreditation
Fall: March 1			ABA, AALS
Spring: n/app			**Degrees Granted**
Fee: $50			J.D., LL.M.

Enrollment 2009–2010			First-Year Class	
Men:	302	66%	Applied:	733
Women:	156	34%	Accepted:	216
Minorities:	78	17%	Enrolled:	147
Out-of-State:	224	49%		

2009–10 Class Profile
LSAT Percentile: 89%
LSAT Median Score: 163
Percentage passing bar on first try: 93%

Tuition and Fees:

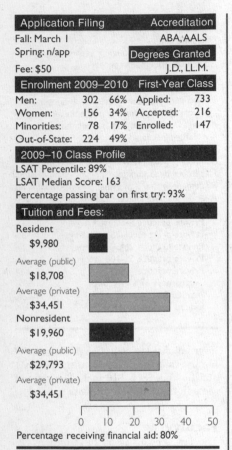

Resident
$9,980

Average (public)
$18,708

Average (private)
$34,451

Nonresident
$19,960

Average (public)
$29,793

Average (private)
$34,451

Percentage receiving financial aid: 80%

ADMISSIONS
In the fall 2009 first-year class, 733 applied, 216 were accepted, and 147 enrolled. Eight transfers enrolled. The median LSAT percentile of the most recent first-year class was 89; the median GPA was 3.74 on a scale of 4.0. The lowest LSAT percentile accepted was 26; the highest was 99.

Requirements
Applicants must have a bachelor's degree and take the LSAT. The most important admission factors include LSAT results, GPA, and a personal statement. No specific undergraduate courses are required. Candidates are not interviewed.

Procedure
The application deadline for fall entry is March 1. Applicants should submit an application form, LSAT results, transcripts, a personal statement, a nonrefundable application fee of $50, 2 letters of recommendation, and ecclesiastical endorsement, and Dean's certification. Notification of the admissions decision is no later than April 15. The latest acceptable LSAT test date for fall entry is December. The law school uses the LSDAS.

Special
The law school recruits minority and disadvantaged students by direct mail, law forums, visiting undergraduate institutions, and personal contact from students, alumni, and friends of the law school. The school works closely with the Minority Law Students Association in recruiting minority students. Requirements are not different for out-of-state students. Transfer students must have one year of credit, have attended an ABA-approved law school, and must be in the top third of the class in their prior school.

Costs
Tuition and Fees for the 2009-2010 academic year are$9,980 for full- time in-state students and $19,960 for out-of-state students. On-campus room and board costs about $6550 annually; books and supplies run $1850.

Financial Aid
About 80% of current law students receive some form of aid. The average annual amount of aid from all sources combined, including scholarships, loans, and work contracts, is $10,000; maximum, $17,000. Awards are based on need and merit. Required financial statements are the CSS Profile and the FAFSA. The aid application deadline for fall entry is June 1. Special funds for minority or disadvantaged students include funds available to any student based on merit. First-year students are notified about their financial aid application at time of acceptance.

About the Law School
Brigham Young University J. Reuben Clark Law School was established in 1973 and is a private institution. The 544-acre campus is in a suburban area 45 miles south of Salt Lake City. The primary mission of the law school is to affirm the strength brought to the law by a student's personal religious conviction. The school encourages public service and professional excellence and the promotion of fairness and virtue founded upon the rule of law. Students have access to federal, state, county, city, and local agencies, courts, correctional facilities, law firms, and legal aid organizations in the Provo area. The World Family Policy Center and the International Center for Law and Religion Studies afford opportunities for international involvement with issues of global importance. The school provides each student with a personal study carrel within the law library, which is wired to the Internet, Lexis and Westlaw, and a place where books and personal effects may be secured. Individual study rooms and family support rooms (wired to classrooms for audio and video) are located in the library. Housing for students is available within easy access of the school. All law school facilities are accessible to the physically disabled.

Calendar
The law school operates on a traditional semester basis. Courses for full-time students are offered days only and must be completed within 3 years. There is no part-time program. New students are admitted in the fall. There is no summer session. Transferable summer courses are not offered.

Programs
In addition to the J.D., the law school offers the LL.M. Students may take relevant courses in other programs and apply credit toward the J.D.; a maximum of 9 credits may be applied. The following joint degrees may be earned: J.D./M.Acc. (Juris Doctor/Master of Accountancy), J.D./M.B.A. (Juris Doctor/Master of Business Administration), J.D./M.Ed. (Juris Doctor/Master of Education), J.D./M.P.A. (Juris Doctor/Master of Public Administration), and J.D./M.P.P. (Juris Doctoe/Master of Public Policy).

Required
To earn the J.D., candidates must complete 90 total credits, of which 36 are for required courses. They must maintain a minimum GPA of 2.7 in the required courses. The following first-year courses are required of all students: Civil Procedure, Contracts, Criminal Law, Introduction to Advocacy I and II, Perspectives on Law, Property, Structures of the Constitution, and Torts. Required upper-level

Phone: 801-422-4277
Fax: 801-422-0389
E-mail: *kucharg@law.byu.edu*
Web: *www.law.byu.edu*

Contact
Gaelynn Kuchar, Admissions Director, 801-422-4277 for general inquiries.

UTAH

courses consist of a substantial paper, Advanced Legal Research, and Professional Responsibility. The required orientation program for first-year students is a 4-day program that includes an introduction to the study of law and legal research.

Electives
The law school has LawHelp seminars worth up to 15 credits in which second- and third- year students provide legal services to clients under the direction of an attorney. Each first-year student has 1 class taught in seminar/small section form; 41 seminars are available for second-and third-year students. Students are allowed up to 15 credit hours for judicial, prosecutorial, government, private law firm, and public interest internships; 2 credit hours for research programs; and 15 for field work. The Career Services Office offers a weekly lecture series course, which features guest speakers from practice area specialties. Student organizations sponsor speakers on topics ranging from practical lawyering skills to jurisprudential theory. Students interested in study-abroad programs sponsored by other law schools may transfer credit. Each first-year course has a weekly tutorial. Additionally, the Academic Success Program includes study skills workshops, and individual tutors. Minority recruiting includes the Minority Law School night, the Diversity Job Fair, and outreach to the multi-cultural offices at many undergraduate institutions. A joint student/faculty law school discovery committee is geared to expanding the school's diversity. The most widely taken electives are Constitutional Law, Secured Transactions, and Wills and Estates.

Graduation Requirements
In order to graduate, candidates must have a GPA of 2.7, have completed the upper-division writing requirement, and The grading scale is a 1.6 to 4.0 scale.

Organizations
Students edit the *Brigham Young University Law Review*, *BYU Journal of Public Law*, and *BYU Education and Law Journal*. The *Clark Memorandum* is a semi-annual Law Society and alumni magazine. *Amicus Briefs* is constantly updated online. The school sends teams to the Jessup International Moot Court Competition and 5 other competitions annu-

ally. Other competitions include the John Welch Award for Outstanding Writing, the A.H. Christensen Advocacy Award, the Woody Deem Trial Advocacy Competition, BYU Research and Writing Award, and Le Boeuf Bankruptcy Scholar Award. Law student organizations include Minority Law Students Association, Women's Law Forum, and Government and Politics Legal Society. Local chapters of national associations include Public Interest Law Foundation (NAPIL), Federalist Society, and Phi Delta Phi. Campus clubs and other organizations include the Student Intellectual Property Association (SIPLA), International and Comparative Law Society, and Sports and Entertainment Law Society (SPENT).

Library
The law library contains 523,234 hardcopy volumes and 157,007 microform volume equivalents, and subscribes to 4447 serial publications. Such on-line databases and networks as CALI, CIS Universe, DIALOG, Dow-Jones, Infotrac, Legal-Trac, LEXIS, LOIS, NEXIS, OCLC First Search, RLIN, WESTLAW, Wilsonline Indexes, and Hein Online, BNA, CCH, RIA, Making of Modern Law: Legal Treatises, Making of Modern Law: U.S. Supreme Court Records and Briefs, LLMC-Digital, LexisNexis Congressional Universe, Tax Notes, GLIN, Pratt's Banking Law Library, Index to Foreign Legal Periodicals, Constitutions of the Countries of the World, International Law in Domestic Courts, and Foreign Law Guide are available to law students for research. Special library collections include U.S. government documents and Utah State documents depositories, American Indian Law Collection, and Canadian and UK Collections. Recently, the library re-designed the library webpage and instituted a web-content management system, and remodeled portions of the Law School to create a 1,400-square-foot student study commons area. The ratio of library volumes to faculty is 13,417 to 1 and to students is 1163 to 1. The ratio of seats in the library to students is 1 to 1.

Faculty
The law school has 39 full-time and 38 part-time faculty members, of whom 21 are women. About 4% of full-time faculty have a graduate law degree in addition to the J.D. The ratio of full-time students to

Placement

J.D.s awarded:	150

Services available through: a separate law school placement center

Services: weekly lecture series course that features attorneys speaking on different areas of practice, resume review service, and workshops

Special features: networking groups, practice area, tutorials, a professional development skills training course, satellite interviewing programs, attorney mock interviewing programs, video interviews, a judicial clerkship handbook, a job hunt handbook, a legal career planning handbook, and alumni receptions.

Full-time job interviews:	32 employers
Summer job interviews:	78 employers
Placement by graduation:	78% of class
Placement within 9 months:	96% of class
Average starting salary:	$31,000 to $195,000

Areas of placement:

Private practice 2-10 attorneys	13%
Private practice 11-25 attorneys	7%
Private practice 26-50 attorneys	2%
Private practice 51-100 attorneys	5%
Private practice 101+ attorneys	26%
Solo practice	3%
Business/industry	13%
Government	8%
Military	5%
Public interest	1%
Academic	1%
Judicial clerkship	16%

full-time faculty in an average class is 17 to 1. The law school has a regular program of bringing visiting professors and other distinguished lecturers and visitors to campus. There is a chapter of the Order of the Coif; 27 faculty and 493 graduates are members.

Students
About 34% of the student body are women; 17%, minorities; 1%, African American; 7% Asian American; 7%, Hispanic; 2%, Native American; and 1%, foreign nationals. The majority of students come from Utah (51%). The average age of entering students is 25; age range is 19 to 53. About 5% of students have worked full-time prior to entering law school. About 1% drop out after the first year for academic or personal reasons; 99% remain to receive a law degree.

BROOKLYN LAW SCHOOL

250 Joralemon Street
Brooklyn, NY 11201

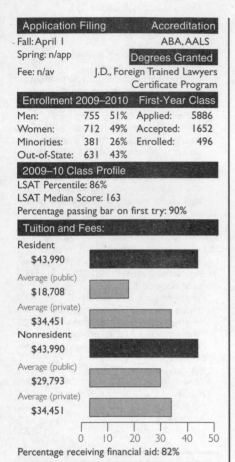

Application Filing	Accreditation
Fall: April 1	ABA, AALS
Spring: n/app	**Degrees Granted**
Fee: n/av	J.D., Foreign Trained Lawyers Certificate Program

Enrollment 2009–2010		First-Year Class	
Men:	755 51%	Applied:	5886
Women:	712 49%	Accepted:	1652
Minorities:	381 26%	Enrolled:	496
Out-of-State:	631 43%		

2009–10 Class Profile
LSAT Percentile: 86%
LSAT Median Score: 163
Percentage passing bar on first try: 90%

Tuition and Fees:

Resident
$43,990

Average (public)
$18,708

Average (private)
$34,451

Nonresident
$43,990

Average (public)
$29,793

Average (private)
$34,451

0 10 20 30 40 50

Percentage receiving financial aid: 82%

ADMISSIONS
In the fall 2009 first-year class, 5886 applied, 1652 were accepted, and 496 enrolled. Twenty-two transfers enrolled. The median LSAT percentile of the most recent first-year class was 86; the median GPA was 3.46 on a scale of 4.0. The highest LSAT percentile was 99.

Requirements
Applicants must have a bachelor's degree, be 18 years old, and take the LSAT. The most important admission factors include college attended, GPA, and LSAT results. No specific undergraduate courses are required. Candidates are not interviewed.

Procedure
The application deadline for fall entry is April 1. There is no application fee. Applicants should submit an application form, LSAT results, transcripts, a personal statement, 2 letters of recommendation from faculty, and transcripts (via LSDAS), and Dean's Certification Form. Notification of the admissions decision is on a rolling basis beginning January. The latest

acceptable LSAT test date for fall entry is June. The law school uses the LSDAS.

Special
The law school recruits minority and disadvantaged students by means of recruitment visits to historically black colleges and universities; various minority law career days and professional school forums sponsored by colleges and/or national minority student organizations; assistance from school chapters of Asian, Black, and Latin American Law Student Associations in recruitment efforts; the LSDAS Candidate Referral Service (CRS); and a series of orientation programs for prospective students, hosted at the law school. Requirements are not different for out-of-state students. Transfer students must have a minimum GPA of 3, have attended an ABA-approved law school, and have a letter of good standing from the dean of the current school. The law school must be a member of AALS; 35 credits are the maximum allowable.

Costs
Tuition and fees for the 2009-2010 academic year are $43,990 for all full-time students. Tuition for part-time students is $33,074 per year. On-campus room and board costs about $16,420 annually; books and supplies run $1100.

Financial Aid
About 82% of current law students receive some form of aid. The average annual amount of aid from all sources combined, including scholarships, loans, and work contracts, is $35,044; maximum, $66,335. Awards are based on need and merit. Aid takes the form of grants, loans, and work-study. Required financial statements are the FAFSA and Need Access Form, and the IRS Form 1040 for the applicant as well as their parents' Forms 1040. Also required are the school's financial assistance application forms. No application is required for merit-based awards. The aid application deadline for fall entry is open. Special funds for minority or disadvantaged students include the Geraldo Rivera Scholarship; MLK, Jr. Scholarship; Judith Bregman Scholarship; William Randolph Hearst Scholarship; Edgardo Lopez Scholarship; James McClendon Jr. Scholarship; Lark-Barranco Scholarship; and the Opportunity Grant. First-year students are notified about their financial aid application at time of acceptance

for merit scholarships. Need-based award notification is during the late spring or early summer prior to enrollment.

About the Law School
Brooklyn Law School was established in 1901 is independent. The 1-acre campus is in an urban area in New York City. The primary mission of the law school is to train practicing attorneys as well as help students develop the intellectual capacity required to succeed whether they choose to practice law or pursue an alternative career with a legal background. Students have access to federal, state, county, city, and local agencies, courts, correctional facilities, law firms, and legal aid organizations in the Brooklyn area. Nearby are the U.S. district court, appellate court, state supreme and family courts, city civil and criminal courts, U.S. attorney's office, and Legal Aid Society. Housing is guaranteed for first-year students. All law school facilities are accessible to the physically disabled.

Calendar
The law school operates on a traditional semester basis. Courses for full-time students are offered both day and evening. Electives may be taken in the evening division and must be completed within 4 years. For part-time students, courses are offered evenings only. Periodically, a part-time day division is created and must be completed within 5 years. New full- and part-time students are admitted in the fall. There is a 6- to 7-week summer session. Transferable summer courses are offered.

Programs
In addition to the J.D., the law school offers the Foreign Trained Lawyers Certificate Program. The following joint degrees may be earned: J.D./M.A. (Juris Doctor/Master of Arts in law and in political science), J.D./M.B.A. (Juris Doctor/Master of Business Administration), J.D./M.S. (Juris Doctor/Master of Science in library and information science, city and regional planning, and urban environmental systems management or historic preservation), and J.D./M.U.P. (Juris Doctor/Master of Urban Planning).

Required
To earn the J.D., candidates must complete 86 total credits, of which 31 are for required courses. They must maintain a minimum GPA of 2.0 in the required courses. The following first-year courses

Phone: 718-780-7906
Fax: 718-780-0395
E-mail: *admitq@brooklaw.edu*
Web: *brooklaw.edu*

Contact

Dean of Admissions and Financial Aid, 718-780-7906 for general inquiries; Nancy Zahzam, Financial Aid Director, 718-780-7915 (nancy.zahzam@brooklaw.edu) for financial aid information.

NEW YORK

are required of all students: Civil Procedure, Constitutional Law, Contracts, Criminal Law, Legal Process, Legal Writing, Property, and Torts. Required upper-level courses consist of an upper-class writing requirement and Legal Profession. The required orientation program for first-year students is held a week before classes begin where students receive faculty and student advisers, start the Introduction to the Study of Law course and the First-Year Legal Writing Program, and participate in workshops.

Electives

Students must take 55 credits in their area of concentration. The Brooklyn Law School offers concentrations in corporate law, criminal law, entertainment law, family law, intellectual property law, international law, juvenile law, labor law, litigation, media law, securities law, sports law, tax law, torts and insurance, and international business, public interest, and human rights. Any student who has completed the first year of study may take clinics in bankruptcy, community development, and criminal practice. Seminars range from 1 to 2 credits. All students who have completed their first year of study may enroll in internships with judges, criminal justice agencies, and a wide range of organizations in areas such as environmental law, children's rights, business regulation, and intellectual property. Up to 3 credits may be earned by any upper-level student who, under the supervision of a faculty member, researches and writes a paper of publishable quality. The Media and Society Lecture Series brings new members from around the country to address current issues involving the media. The Abraham L. Pomerantz lectures focus on corporate or securities law topics and related professional responsibility issues. Summer study sponsored by the Law School in Bologna, Italy and Beijing, China is available. There is an exchange program with Bucerius University in Hamburg, Germany, and University of Essex in England. Upper-level students may also pursue study abroad through other law schools if they demonstrate, in writing, special need and obtain the written approval of the Associate Dean for Academic Affairs. First-year students may take advantage of year-long support services offered through the Academic Success Program. A summer Legal Process course and various tutorial programs specifically target affirmative action stu-

dents. Special interest groups include the Edward V. Sparer Public Interest Fellowship Program; the Center for the Study of International Business Law Fellowship Program; the Center for Law, Language, and Cognition; Center for Health, Science, and Public Policy; and the International Human Rights Fellowship. The most widely taken electives are Corporations, Evidence, and Criminal Procedure.

Graduation Requirements

In order to graduate, candidates must have a GPA of 2.3, have completed the upper-division writing requirement, and pass the Legal Profession course.

Organizations

Students edit the *Brooklyn Law Review; Brooklyn Journal of International Law; Journal of Law and Public Policy; Brooklyn Journal of Corporate, Financial and Commercial Law*, and *The Docket*. Moot court teams annually compete in 15 to 18 tournaments including the ABA's National Moot Court Competition; Phillip C. Jessup International Law Moot Competition; and the National First Amendment Competition, co-sponsored by Vanderbilt University and the Freedom Forum. Other competitions include the Texas Young Lawyer's Association National Trial Competition, College of Trial Lawyers the Dominick L. Gabriella Family Law Competition, and the Ruby R. Vale Interschool Corporate Moot Court Competition. Law student organizations, include the Association of Trial Lawyers of America, National Lawyers Guild, and Legal Association of Women. Local chapters of national association include the Brooklyn Law Students for the Public Interest; BLS Students Against Domestic Violence, and Entertainment, Arts and Sports Law Society, other campus organizations include the Student Bar Association; and Asian, Black, and Latin American Law Student associations.

Library

The law library contains 580,994 hardcopy volumes and 1,600,012 microform volume equivalents, and subscribes to 1024 serial publications. Such on-line databases and networks as CALI, CIS Universe, DIALOG, Legal-Trac, LEXIS, LOIS, OCLC First Search, WESTLAW, Wilsonline Indexes, and CCH Tax Service, CCH Health and HR, CIS Statistical Universe, IndexMaster, HeinOnline, LawPro, UN Access, UN Treaty, JSTOR,

Placement

J.D.s awarded:	499

Services available through: a separate law school placement center

Services: on-line job listings; specialized public interest counseling through the law school's Office of Public Service Program

Special features: a network of 18,000 alumni; assigning every first-year student to career counselors during the first semester.

Full-time job interviews:	45 employers
Summer job interviews:	114 employers
Placement by graduation:	80% of class
Placement within 9 months:	92% of class
Average starting salary:	$35,000 to $170,000

Areas of placement:

Private practice 2-10 attorneys	19%
Private practice 11-25 attorneys	3%
Private practice 26-50 attorneys	4%
Private practice 51-100+ attorneys	28%
Government	15%
Business/industry	12%
Judicial clerkships	6%
Public interest	6%

BNA All, RIA Checkpoint, Isino Law, NatLaw and Justis, LEXIS NEXIS Serials, LEXIS NEXIS Congressional, Bloomberg, Making of Modern Law are available to law students for research. Special library collections include a selective U.S. government depository, selective New York depository, joint international library program, and a consortium collection. The ratio of library volumes to faculty is 7645 to 1 and to students is 413 to 1. The ratio of seats in the library to students is 1 to 2.

Faculty

The law school has 75 full-time and 121 part-time faculty members, of whom 73 are women. The law school has a regular program of bringing visiting professors and other distinguished lecturers and visitors to campus.

Students

About 49% of the student body are women; 26%, minorities; 5%, African American; 15%, Asian American; and 6%, Hispanic. The majority of students come from New York (57%). The average age of entering students is 25; age range is 20 to 46. About 25% of students enter directly from undergraduate school, 8% have a graduate degree, and 65% have worked full-time prior to entering law school. About 7% drop out after the first year for academic or personal reasons; 93% remain to receive a law degree.

CALIFORNIA WESTERN SCHOOL OF LAW

225 Cedar Street
San Diego, CA 92101-3046

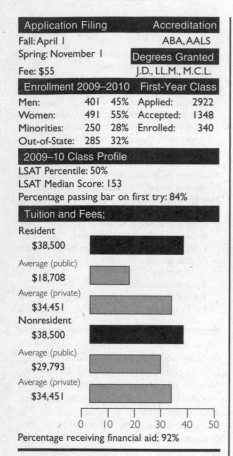

Application Filing	Accreditation
Fall: April 1	ABA, AALS
Spring: November 1	Degrees Granted
Fee: $55	J.D., LL.M., M.C.L.

Enrollment 2009–2010		First-Year Class	
Men:	401 45%	Applied:	2922
Women:	491 55%	Accepted:	1348
Minorities:	250 28%	Enrolled:	340
Out-of-State:	285 32%		

2009–10 Class Profile
LSAT Percentile: 50%
LSAT Median Score: 153
Percentage passing bar on first try: 84%

Tuition and Fees:

Resident
$38,500

Average (public)
$18,708

Average (private)
$34,451

Nonresident
$38,500

Average (public)
$29,793

Average (private)
$34,451

0   10   20   30   40   50

Percentage receiving financial aid: 92%

ADMISSIONS
In the fall 2009 first-year class, 2922 applied, 1348 were accepted, and 340 enrolled. Six transfers enrolled. The median LSAT percentile of the most recent first-year class was 50; the median GPA was 3.28 on a scale of 4.0. The lowest LSAT percentile accepted was 25; the highest was 75.

Requirements
Applicants must have a bachelor's degree and take the LSAT. The most important admission factors include LSAT results, GPA, writing ability, personal statements, optional diversity statements, and work experience. No specific undergraduate courses are required. Candidates are not interviewed.

Procedure
The application deadline for fall entry is April 1. Applicants should submit an application form, LSAT results, transcripts, a personal statement, a nonre-

fundable application fee of $55, 2 letters of recommendation, and resume. Notification of the admissions decision is on a rolling basis. The latest acceptable LSAT test date for fall entry is February. The law school uses the LSDAS.

Special
The law school recruits minority and disadvantaged students through a combined effort with the Office of Admissions and the Office of Diversity Services, which coordinates the diversity recruitment program and maintains working relationships with law firms, alumni, professional and community organizations, and college administrators who provide valuable resources for minority students. Requirements are not different for out-of-state students. Transfer students must have one year of credit, have a minimum average of 70, have attended an ABA-approved law school, and submit an official transcript and 2 letters of recommendation, preferably from a law school dean or professors. Preadmissions courses consist of the 6-week Summer Enrichment Program, a 3-credit course that is an introduction to law school and the American legal system, and an Introduction to Legal Skills (Legal Writing and Legal Analysis) course.

Costs
Tuition and fees for the 2009-2010 academic year are $38,500 for all full-time students. Tuition for part-time students is $27,100 per year. Books and supplies run $1867.

Financial Aid
About 92% of current law students receive some form of aid. The average annual amount of aid from all sources combined, including scholarships, loans, and work contracts, is $48,499; maximum, $60,498. Awards are based on need and merit. Required financial statements are the FAFSA and California Western School of Law financial aid application. The aid application deadline for fall entry is April 1. Special funds for minority or disadvantaged students include scholarships. First-year students are notified about their financial aid application at time of acceptance.

About the Law School
California Western School of Law was established in 1924 and is a private institution. The 200,000-square-foot campus is in an urban area in San Diego. The primary mission of the law school is to educate lawyers who will be creative problem solvers who will contribute to improving the lives of their clients and the quality of justice in society. Students have access to federal, state, county, city, and local agencies, courts, correctional facilities, law firms, and legal aid organizations in the San Diego area. The San Diego Law Library is within walking distance. Facilities of special interest to law students are within walking distance and include courts, law firms, city, state, and federal agencies, and county law library. Housing for students is off campus. The school has a housing coordinator to assist students with finding housing. Most students live within 5 to 10 minutes of school. About 95% of the law school facilities are accessible to the physically disabled.

Calendar
The law school operates on a trimester basis. Courses for full-time students are offered days only and must be completed within 5 years. For part-time students, courses are offered days only and must be completed within 6 years. New full- and part-time students are admitted in the fall and spring. There is a 15-week summer session. Transferable summer courses are offered.

Programs
In addition to the J.D., the law school offers the LL.M. and M.C.L. Students may take relevant courses in other programs and apply credit toward the J.D.; a maximum of 12 credits may be applied. The following joint degrees may be earned: J.D./M.B.A. (Juris Doctor/Master of Business Administration), J.D./M.S.W. (Juris Doctor/Master of Social Work), and J.D./Ph.D. (Juris Doctor/Ph.D. in political science or history).

Required
To earn the J.D., candidates must complete 89 total credits, of which 43 are for required courses. They must maintain a minimum GPA of 74.0 in the required courses. The following first-year courses are required of all students: Civil Proce-

Phone: 619-525-1401
800-255-4252
Fax: 619-615-1401
E-mail: admissions@cwsl.edu
Web: www.californiawestern.edu

Contact
Admissions Office, 619-525-1401 for general inquiries; William Kahler, Director of Financial Aid, 619-525-7060 for financial aid information.

CALIFORNIA

dure I and II, Contracts I and II, Criminal Law, Legal Skills I and II, Property I and II, and Torts I. Required upper-level courses consist of Constitutional Law I, Criminal Procedure, Evidence, Legal Skills III, Professional Responsibility, and Torts II. The required orientation program for first-year students is a 1-day general orientation.

Electives

The California Western School of Law offers concentrations in corporate law, criminal law, entertainment law, environmental law, family law, intellectual property law, international law, juvenile law, labor law, litigation, media law, sports law, telecommunication law, and biotechnology law. In addition, there is a wide variety of specialized seminar courses open to upper-level students. The school has an internship program open to upper-level students; students may take up to 10 credit hours and will receive 1 credit hour for a weekly seminar. Students may assist faculty as research assistants. Special lecture series include the Faculty Speakers Series, the Scholar in Residence Series, and S. Houston Lay International Law and Relations Series. Students may participate in a study-abroad program and transfer up to 8 credit hours of work from consortium schools. California Western sponsors study-abroad programs in New Zealand, Malta, England (London), and Ireland (Galway). Tutorial programs include Introduction to Legal Skills, the Enrichment Program, and the Bar Prep Program. The Office of Diversity Services coordinates a mentor program for students with local minority lawyers, and sponsors tutorials. The school sponsors more than 30 student organizations that cover a wide range of interests and topics. The most widely taken electives are Alternative Dispute Resolution, Constitutional Law II, and Business Organizations.

Graduation Requirements

In order to graduate, candidates must have a GPA of 74.0, have completed the upper-division writing requirement, and a practicum course.

Organizations
Students edit the *California Western Law Review*, the *California Western International Law Journal*, the *Environmental* *Law Newsletter* and the student newspaper the *Commentary*. Moot court competitions include the National Appellate Advocacy, Roger J. Traynor Moot Court, and Phillip C. Jessup International Law. Other competitions include the William C. Lynch Appellate Competition. Law student organizations include Public Interest Law Foundation, Phi Alpha Delta, and Student Bar Association. Local chapters of national associations include La Raza Law Students Association, Women's Law Caucus, and Black Law Students Association. Other campus organizations include Entertainment Sports Law Society, International Law Society, and Family Law Society.

Library
The law library contains 345,342 hardcopy volumes and 161,909 microform volume equivalents, and subscribes to 5006 serial publications. Such on-line databases and networks as CALI, CIS Universe, DIALOG, Legal-Trac, LEXIS, LOIS, Mathew Bender, NEXIS, OCLC First Search, WESTLAW, Wilsonline Indexes, Lexis Nexis Congressional, JSTOR, and Live Edgar are available to law students for research. Special library collections include collections on problem solving, constitutional and human rights law, military law, and international law. California Western is a partial California Depository Library. The ratio of library volumes to faculty is 6641 to 1 and to students is 358 to 1. The ratio of seats in the library to students is 1 to 2.

Faculty
The law school has 52 full-time and 87 part-time faculty members, of whom 62 are women. About 25% of full-time faculty have a graduate law degree in addition to the J.D.; about 10% of part-time faculty have one. The ratio of full-time students to full-time faculty in an average class is 18 to 1; in a clinic, 1 to 1. The law school has a regular program of bringing visiting professors and other distinguished lecturers and visitors to campus.

Students
About 55% of the student body are women; 28%, minorities; 3%, African American; 14%, Asian American; 10%, Hispanic; 1%, Native American; and 10%, unknown. The majority of students come from Cali-

Placement

J.D.s awarded:	247

Services available through: a separate law school placement center

Services: nonlegal career alternatives, judicial clerkships, and decision-making counseling

Special features: intensive individual planning and counseling, Alumni Career Advisor/ mentor program, minority career development program, government legal careers job fair, public interest job fair, 5 career counselors on staff, a Pro Bono Program, and practice area/career option panels.

Full-time job interviews:	10 employers
Summer job interviews:	40 employers
Placement by graduation:	47% of class
Placement within 9 months:	91% of class
Average starting salary:	$50,000 to $200,000

Areas of placement:

Private practice 2-10 attorneys	41%
Private practice 11-25 attorneys	3%
Private practice 26-50 attorneys	6%
Private practice 51-100 attorneys	3%
Private practice 100+ attorneys	7%
Business/industry	13%
Government	12%
Public interest	7%
Judicial clerkships	5%
Military	2%
Academic	1%

fornia (68%). The average age of entering students is 27; age range is 20 to 59. About 4% of students have a graduate degree. About 18% drop out after the first year for academic or personal reasons; 72% remain to receive a law degree.

CAMPBELL UNIVERSITY

Norman Adrian Wiggins School of Law

225 Hillsborough Street, Suite 401
Releigh, NC 24603

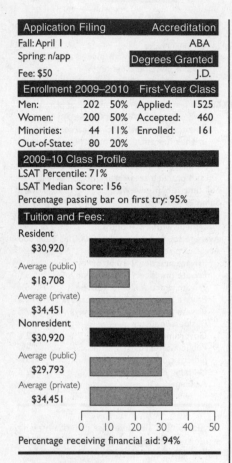

Application Filing			Accreditation
Fall: April 1			ABA
Spring: n/app			**Degrees Granted**
Fee: $50			J.D.

Enrollment 2009–2010			First-Year Class	
Men:	202	50%	Applied:	1525
Women:	200	50%	Accepted:	460
Minorities:	44	11%	Enrolled:	161
Out-of-State:	80	20%		

2009–10 Class Profile

LSAT Percentile: 71%
LSAT Median Score: 156
Percentage passing bar on first try: 95%

Tuition and Fees:

Resident
$30,920

Average (public)
$18,708

Average (private)
$34,451

Nonresident
$30,920

Average (public)
$29,793

Average (private)
$34,451

0 10 20 30 40 50

Percentage receiving financial aid: 94%

ADMISSIONS

In the fall 2009 first-year class, 1525 applied, 460 were accepted, and 161 enrolled. Four transfers enrolled. The median LSAT percentile of the most recent first-year class was 71; the median GPA was 3.37 on a scale of 4.0.

Requirements
Applicants must have a bachelor's degree and take the LSAT. The most important admission factors include LSAT results, GPA, and a personal interview. No specific undergraduate courses are required. Candidates are interviewed.

Procedure
The application deadline for fall entry is April 1. Applicants should submit an application form, LSAT results, transcripts, a personal statement, a nonrefundable application fee of $50, and 2 letters of recommendation. Notification of the admissions decision is on a rolling basis. The latest acceptable LSAT test

date for fall entry is February. The law school uses the LSDAS.

Special
The law school recruits minority and disadvantaged students by visiting minority organizations and hosting minority organizations and events. Requirements are not different for out-of-state students. Transfer students must have one year of credit and have attended an ABA-approved law school. The school conducts a summer Performance Based Admission Program. Students admitted to this program take 2 law courses over a 7-week period during the summer from May to July. Whether an applicant is offered admission to the fall class is based on an applicant's performance on the final examination administered in each course.

Costs

Tuition and fees for the 2009-2010 academic year are $30,920 for all full-time students. Books and supplies run $2000.

Financial Aid

About 94% of current law students receive some form of aid. The average annual amount of aid from all sources combined, including scholarships, loans, and work contracts, is $48,866; maximum, $55,980. Awards are based on need and merit. Required financial statement is the FAFSA. The aid application deadline for fall entry is open. First-year students are notified about their financial aid application at time of acceptance.

About the Law School

Campbell University Norman Adrian Wiggins School of Law was established in 1976 and is a private institution. The 110,000 sq.ft. campus is in an urban area located in downtown Raleigh. The primary mission of the law school is to build futures, shape careers, and combine theory and practice to provide a solid foundation for the practice of law, while instilling ethical and professional responsibility. Students have access to federal, state, county, city, and local agencies, courts, correctional facilities, law firms, and legal aid organizations in the Releigh area. Facilities of special interest to law students include a 4000 sq.ft. students commons with a coffee shop on the second floor of the law

school. All law school facilities are accessible to the physically disabled.

Calendar

The law school operates on a traditional semester basis. Courses for full-time students are offered days only and must be completed within 5 years. There is no part-time program. New students are admitted in the fall. There is a 7-week summer session. Transferable summer courses are not offered.

Programs

The following joint degrees may be earned: J.D./M.B.A. (Juris Doctor/Master of Business Administration), J.D./M.P.A. (Juris Doctor/Master of Public Administration in conjunction with North Carolina State University (Dual Degree), and J.D./M.T.W.M. (Juris Doctor/Master in Trust and Wealth Management).

Required
To earn the J.D., candidates must complete 90 total credits, of which 67 are for required courses. They must maintain a minimum average of 75in the required courses. The following first-year courses are required of all students: Advocacy, Civil Procedure I, Constitutional and Courts, Contracts I and II, Criminal Law, Legal Research and Writing, Practical Skills and Values, Professional Responsibility Lecture Series, Property I and II, and Torts I and II. Required upper-level courses consist of Business Organizations, Commercial Law I and II, Constitutional Law I, Criminal Procedure, Evidence, Income Taxation, Jurisprudence, Perspectives on Professionalism and Leadership or Perspectives, Professional Responsibility and Ethics, Trial Advocacy, and Wills and Trusts. The required orientation program for first-year students is typically 3 days focused on an introduction to the study of law.

Electives
The Norman Adrian Wiggins School of Law offers concentrations in litigation and business law. In addition, clinics include Trial Advocacy, a required "simulated" clinic offering 7 credit hours over 2 semesters, an Elder Law Clinic,worth 8 credit hours, and Juvenile Justice Mediation, worth 3 credit hours. Seminars include

Phone: 919-865-5988
334-4111, ext. 4650
Fax: 919-865-5886
Web: law.campbell.edu

Contact

Admissions, 910-865-5988 for general inquiries; Samatha Collinash, Assistant Director, 919-865-5990 for financial aid information.

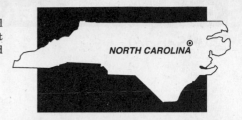

Environmental Law, Insurance Law, and Intellectual Property. Public-service internships are available to second- and third-year students for a maximum of 4 credit hours. Externships are available. The Professionalism Lecture Series is required of all first-year students. Special interest group programs include Campbell Law Innocence Project. The law school has an Academic Success Program to assist students. The most widely taken electives are Family Law, Remedies, and Workers' Compensation.

Graduation Requirements
In order to graduate, candidates must have a minimum of 75.

Organizations

Students edit the *Campbell Law Review* and the *Campbell Law Observer*. Moot Court competitions entered by students are the ABA National Appellate Advocacy, National Moot Court, John Marshall National Moot Court, and the International Arbitration Competition. Other competitions are the National Trial, American Trial Lawyers Association, National Student Trial Advocacy, ABA Client Counseling and Negotiation Competition, and the NITA Tournament of Champions Trial Competition. Law student organizations, local chapters of national associations, and campus organizations include the Student Bar Association, ABA-Law Student Division, Black Law Students Association, Delta Theta Phi-Bryan Senate and Phi Alpha Delta fraternities, the Christian Legal Society, Academy of Trial Lawyers, and Women in Law.

Library

The law library contains 106,265 hardcopy volumes and 87,368 microform volume equivalents, and subscribes to 2588 serial publications. Such on-line databases and networks as CALI, CIS Universe, Dow-Jones, Infotrac, Legal-Trac, LEXIS, LOIS, Mathew Bender, NEXIS, OCLC First Search, WESTLAW, Wilsonline Indexes, Current Index to Legal Periodicals, Full Text and Retrospective, Making of Modern Law, Legal Treatises, Making of Modern Law: Historic Trials, Making of Modern Law: Supreme Court, BNA Premier, English Collection Online Law Module, Audio Case Files, RIA Checkpoint, LMC Digital, Religion Case Law Reporter, Legal Forms, Index Maser, Historical Statistics of the United States Oxford International Encyclopedia of Legal History, and HeinOnline are available to law students for research. Special library collections include Trial Advocacy, Ethics and Jurisprudence, Public Interest Law, Church-State resources, and Federal Taxation. The ratio of library volumes to faculty is 4251 to 1 and to students is 264 to 1. The ratio of seats in the library to students is 1 to 2.

Faculty

The law school has 25 full-time and 40 part-time faculty members, of whom 14 are women. About 20% of full-time faculty have a graduate law degree in addition to the J.D.; about 2% of part-time faculty have one. The ratio of full-time students to full-time faculty in an average class is 17 to 1; in a clinic, 8 to 1.

Students

About 50% of the student body are women; 11%, minorities; 4%, African American; 2%, Asian American; 2%, Hispanic; and 1%, Native American. The majority of students come from North Carolina (80%). The average age of entering students is 26; age range is 22 to 58. About 9% drop out after the first year for academic or personal reasons; 91% remain to receive a law degree.

Placement

J.D.s awarded:	109
Services available through: a separate law school placement center	
Services: in- and out-of-state job fairs	
Special features: targeted mailings sent to regions of North Carolina, press releases issued on student activities, alumni assistance in specific areas of job search, a separate placement resource center and library, and a North Carolina job fair	
Full-time job interviews:	16 employers
Summer job interviews:	28 employers
Placement by graduation:	67% of class
Placement within 9 months:	94% of class
Average starting salary:	$54,500 to $63,500
Areas of placement:	
Private practice 2-10 attorneys	59%
Private practice 11-25 attorneys	9%
Private practice 26-50 attorneys	8%
Private practice 51-100 attorneys	14%
Government	12%
Business/industry	9%
Judicial clerkships	5%
Public interest	5%

CAPITAL UNIVERSITY

Law School

303 East Broad Street
Columbus, OH 43215-3200

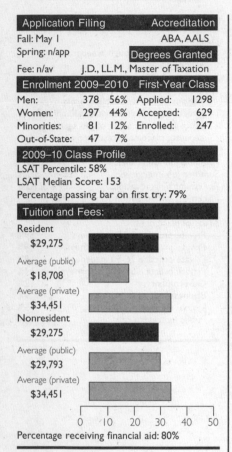

Application Filing	Accreditation
Fall: May 1	ABA, AALS
Spring: n/app	
	Degrees Granted
Fee: n/av	J.D., LL.M., Master of Taxation

Enrollment 2009–2010			First-Year Class	
Men:	378	56%	Applied:	1298
Women:	297	44%	Accepted:	629
Minorities:	81	12%	Enrolled:	247
Out-of-State:	47	7%		

2009–10 Class Profile
LSAT Percentile: 58%
LSAT Median Score: 153
Percentage passing bar on first try: 79%

Tuition and Fees:

Resident
$29,275

Average (public)
$18,708

Average (private)
$34,451

Nonresident
$29,275

Average (public)
$29,793

Average (private)
$34,451

0 10 20 30 40 50

Percentage receiving financial aid: 80%

ADMISSIONS

In the fall 2009 first-year class, 1298 applied, 629 were accepted, and 247 enrolled. Figures in the above capsule and in this profile are approximate. Ten transfers enrolled in a recent year. The median LSAT percentile of the most recent first-year class was 58; the median GPA was 3.2 on a scale of 4.0. The lowest LSAT percentile accepted was 18; the highest was 93.

Requirements
Applicants must have a bachelor's degree and take the LSAT. Minimum acceptable GPA is 2.0 on a scale of 4.0. The most important admission factors include academic achievement, LSAT results, and faculty recommendation. No specific undergraduate courses are required. Candidates are not interviewed.

Procedure
Applicants should submit an application form, LSAT results, transcripts, 2 letters of recommendation, also an essay or personal statement, and a $100 tuition deposit for accepted students; a second $100 seat deposit is also. Notification of the admissions decision is on a rolling basis. The latest acceptable LSAT test date for fall entry is February. Check with the school for current application deadlines. The law school uses the LSDAS.

Special
The law school recruits minority and disadvantaged students by means of targeted mailings, use of minority students, faculty, and alumni in the recruitment process, and financial assistance programs. Requirements are not different for out-of-state students. Transfer students must have one year of credit and have attended an ABA-approved law school. Preadmissions courses consist of an Academic Success Protocol.

Costs

Tuition and fees for the 2009-2010 academic year are $29,275 for all full-time students. Tuition for part-time students is $19,525 per year. Books and supplies run $1400.

Financial Aid

In a recent year, about 80% of current law students received some form of aid. The average annual amount of aid from all sources combined, including scholarships, loans, and work contracts, was $23,385; maximum, $42,750. Awards are based on need and merit. Required financial statement is the FAFSA. Check with the school for current application deadlines. Special funds for minority or disadvantaged students include teaching and research assistantships, grants and scholarships, work-study awards, low-interest student loans, and endowed scholarships. First-year students are notified about their financial aid application at time of acceptance.

About the Law School

Capital University Law School was established in 1903 and is a private institution. The campus is in an urban area in the Discovery District of downtown Columbus. The primary mission of the law school is to provide solid legal education to the next generation of leaders in the legal profession through student-centered teaching, cutting-edge academic programs, service to the legal profession, and commitment to diversity. Students have access to federal, state, county, city, and local agencies, courts, correctional facilities, law firms, and legal aid organizations in the Columbus area. There are extensive externship and mentoring programs. Facilities of special interest to law students include Capital's family advocacy clinic, general legal clinic, National Center for Adoption Law and Policy, and Tobacco Public Policy Center. Housing for students is available off campus; the university helps students find suitable housing. All law school facilities are accessible to the physically disabled.

Calendar

The law school operates on a traditional semester basis. Courses for full- and part-time students are offered both day and evening and must be completed within 7 years. New full- and part-time students are admitted in the fall. There is a 10- and 5-week summer session. Transferable summer courses are offered.

Programs

In addition to the J.D., the law school offers the LL.M. and Master of Taxation. Students may take relevant courses in other programs and apply credit toward the J.D.; a maximum of 9 credits may be applied. The following joint degrees may be earned: J.D./LL.M. (Juris Doctor/Master of Laws in taxation), J.D./M.B.A. (Juris Doctor/Master of Business Administration), J.D./M.S.A. (Juris Doctor/Master of Sports Administration), J.D./M.S.N. (Juris Doctor/Master of Science in Nursing), and J.D./M.T.S. (Juris Doctor/Master of Theological Studies).

Required
To earn the J.D., candidates must complete 89 total credits, of which 46 are for required courses. They must maintain a minimum GPA of 2.0 in the required courses. The following first-year courses are required of all students: Civil Procedure I, Constitutional Law I, Contracts I and II, Criminal Law, Legal Writing I and II, Property I and II, and Torts I and II. Required upper-level courses consist of a writing or research requirement, Civil Procedure II, Constitutional Law II, Evidence, Federal Personal Income Tax, Legal Drafting, a Perspective course, and

Phone: 614-236-6500
Fax: 614-236-6972
E-mail: admissions@law.capital.edu
Web: law.capital.edu

Contact

Assistant Dean of Admission and Financial Aid, 614-236-6310 for general inquiries; Christine Mc Donough, Assistant Director, 614-236-6350 for financial aid information.

Professional Responsibility. The required orientation program for first-year students is 2½ days and includes a mock classroom discussion, ethics panels, reading and briefing exercises, and meetings with faculty and peer advisors.

Electives

Students must take 11 to 15 credits in their area of concentration. The law school offers concentrations in environmental law, family law, labor law, governmental affairs, labor and employment, publicly held companies, small business entities, and alternative dispute resolution. In addition, clinics in general, civil, and criminal litigation are available to students who have qualified as legal interns. Several seminars are offered each year in a variety of subjects. Externships are available through the local, state, and federal courts and through several government agencies and nonprofit organizations. Students may serve as research assistants for law professors or enroll in independent studies. All students must satisfy an upper-class scholarship requirement. Field work may be done through the externship programs, as well as the clinics. Special lecture series include the Sullivan Lectures, Wells Conference, and faculty symposia. All students are welcome to participate in the 1L Academic Success Protocol conducted during the first year of instruction in which students are extensively trained in effective exam-taking and legal problem-solving skills. A second-year, 1-credit legal analysis course is available to 2L students. One-on-one academic coaching is available to all students at any time. The law school's office of multicultural affairs offers programs for minority students. Special interest group programs include the National Center for Adoption Law and Policy, Center for Dispute Resolution, graduate tax and business law programs, and Tobacco Public Policy Center. The most widely taken electives are Business Associations I and II, Payment Systems, and Secured Transactions.

Graduation Requirements

In order to graduate, candidates must have a GPA of 2.0, have completed the upper-division writing requirement, Professional Responsibility, Legal Drafting Practicum, and a Perspective Requirement.

Organizations

Students edit *The Capital University Law Review*, the newspaper *Res Ipsa Loquitur*, and the *Adoption Law News Summary*. Moot court competitions include National Moot Court, Sports Law, and Labor Law competitions. Other competitions include Negotiation, First Year Moot Court, Environmental Law, Frederick Douglass Competition, Jessup International Competition, Tax Law Competition, and Mock Trial. Student organizations include the ABA-Law Student Division, Black Law Students Association, and the Intellectual Property Law Society. There are local chapters of the Federalist Society, Christian Legal Society, and Phi Alpha Delta. Other law student organizations include Corporate and Business Law Society, Environmental Law Society, and Sports and Entertainment Law.

Library

The law library contains 258,223 hardcopy volumes and 55,144 microform volume equivalents, and subscribes to 2400 serial publications. Such on-line databases and networks as CALI, CIS Universe, LEXIS, NEXIS, OCLC First Search, WESTLAW, OhioLink, JSTOR, HeinOnline, CCH Tax, BNA All, CCH Business, and CCHHHR are available to law students for research. Special library collections include American Law of Taxation. Recently, the library instituted a virtual tour. The ratio of library volumes to faculty is 6979 to 1 and to students is 382 to 1. The ratio of seats in the library to students is 1 to 2.

Faculty

The law school has 37 full-time and 63 part-time faculty members, of whom 25 are women. According to AAUP standards for Category IIA institutions, faculty salaries are average. About 25% of full-time faculty have a graduate law degree in addition to the J.D. The ratio of full-time students to full-time faculty in an average class is 16 to 1; in a clinic, 8 to 1. The law school has a regular program of bringing visiting professors and other distinguished lecturers and visitors to campus.

Students

About 44% of the student body are women; 12%, minorities; 7%, African American; 2%, Asian American; and 2%, His-

panic. The majority of students come from Ohio (93%). The average age of entering students is 27; age range is 21 to 52. About 60% of students enter directly from undergraduate school and 11% have a graduate degree. About 11% drop out after the first year for academic or personal reasons; 89% remain to receive a law degree.

Placement

J.D.s awarded:	236
Services available through: a separate law school placement center	
Special features: a career library, recruiting conferences, on-campus interviews, and on-line access to law student and graduate postings from 6/9 Ohio law schools; access to graduate job postings from over 40 law schools..	
Full-time job interviews:	7 employers
Summer job interviews:	26 employers
Placement by graduation:	n/av
Placement within 9 months:	95% of class
Average starting salary:	$39,781 to $75,724
Areas of placement:	
Private practice 2-10 attorneys	26%
Private practice 11-25 attorneys	6%
Private practice 26-50 attorneys	2%
Private practice 51-100 attorneys	2%
Private practice 101+ attorneys and solo practice	10%
Government	20%
Business/industry	20%
Public interest	6%
Academic	4%
Judicial clerkships	3%
Military	1%

11075 East Boulevard
Cleveland, OH 44106

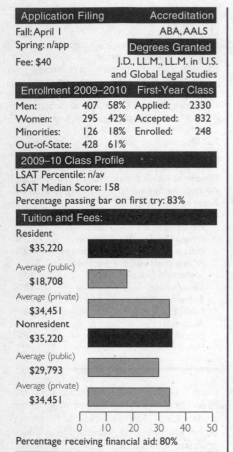

Application Filing	Accreditation
Fall: April 1	ABA, AALS
Spring: n/app	**Degrees Granted**
Fee: $40	J.D., LL.M., LL.M. in U.S. and Global Legal Studies

Enrollment 2009–2010		First-Year Class	
Men:	407 58%	Applied:	2330
Women:	295 42%	Accepted:	832
Minorities:	126 18%	Enrolled:	248
Out-of-State:	428 61%		

2009–10 Class Profile

LSAT Percentile: n/av
LSAT Median Score: 158
Percentage passing bar on first try: 83%

Tuition and Fees:

Resident
$35,220

Average (public)
$18,708

Average (private)
$34,451

Nonresident
$35,220

Average (public)
$29,793

Average (private)
$34,451

0   10   20   30   40   50

Percentage receiving financial aid: 80%

ADMISSIONS

In a recent year, 2330 applied, 832 were accepted, and 248 enrolled. Twenty-three transfers enrolled. The median GPA of the most recent first-year class was 3.39. Figures in the above capsule and in this profile are approximate.

Requirements

Applicants must have a bachelor's degree and take the LSAT. The most important admission factors include academic achievement, LSAT results, and GPA. No specific undergraduate courses are required. Candidates are not interviewed.

Procedure

Applicants should submit an application form, a nonrefundable application fee of $40, and a personal statement, resume, LSDAS Report. Notification of the admissions decision is between January 1 and May 1. The latest acceptable LSAT test date for fall entry is February. The law

school uses the LSDAS. Check with the school for the current application deadlines.

Special

The law school recruits minority and disadvantaged students by means of attendance at law school fairs likely to be attended by minority and disadvantaged students, financial assistance, the Pre-Law Conference for People of Color, and co-sponsoring of the Midwest Minority Recruitment Fair. Requirements are not different for out-of-state students. Transfer students must have one year of credit, have attended an ABA-approved law school, and have performed very well at the school from which they are transferring.

Costs

Tuition and fees for the 2009-2010 academic year was approximately $35,220 for all full-time students. Books and supplies run approximately $1240.

Financial Aid

In a recent year, about 80% of current law students received some form of aid. The average annual amount of aid from all sources combined, including scholarships, loans, and work contracts, was approximately $36,052; maximum, $51,855. Awards are based on need. Required financial statements are the FAFSA and either copies of the student's previous year's federal tax return or a student's statement of income (if the student was not required to file a tax return) if selected for verification by FAFA. Check with the school for current application deadline. Special funds for minority or disadvantaged students include leadership grants which may be offered to candidates with outstanding academic credentials, whose interesting backgrounds will enhance the quality of the student body. First-year students are notified about their financial aid application at approximately 4 weeks after the aid application is complete and the student has been admitted.

About the Law School

Case Western Reserve University School of Law was established in 1892 and is a private institution. The 128-acre campus is in an urban area 4 miles east of down-

town Cleveland. The primary mission of the law school is To prepare leaders in the practice of law, public and community service, and commerce; to provide enlightenment to the legal profession and the larger society; and to foster an accessible, fair, and reliable system of justice. Students have access to federal, state, county, city, and local agencies, courts, correctional facilities, law firms, and legal aid organizations in the Cleveland area. Cleveland is home to many of the nation's top law firms and Fortune 500 companies. Facilities of special interest to law students the state-of-the-art computer laboratory and moot court room, along with a legal clinic that operates as a law firm within the law school setting. Housing for students Affordable housing is available nearby. All law school facilities are accessible to the physically disabled.

Calendar

The law school operates on a traditional semester basis. Courses for full-time students are offered both day and evening and must be completed within 3 years. New full- and part-time students are admitted in the fall. There is a 6-week summer session. Transferable summer courses are offered.

Programs

In addition to the J.D., the law school offers the LL.M. and LL.M. in U.S. and Global Legal Studies. Students may take relevant courses in other programs and apply credit toward the J.D.; a maximum of 9 credits may be applied. The following joint degrees may be earned: J.D./M.A (Juris Doctor/Master of Bioethics), J.D./M.A. (Juris Doctor/Master of Arts in legal history), J.D./M.B.A. (Juris Doctor/Master of Business Administration), J.D./M.D. (Juris Doctor/Doctor of Medicine), J.D./M.N.O. (Juris Doctor/Master of Nonprofit Management), J.D./M.P.H. (Juris Doctor/Master of Public Health), J.D./M.P.S. (Juris Doctor/Master of Political Science), J.D./M.S. (Juris Doctor/Master of Science in Biochemistry), and J.D./M.S.S.A. (Juris Doctor/Master of Science in Social Work).

Required

To earn the J.D., candidates must complete 88 total credits, of which 39 are for required courses. They must maintain a minimum GPA of 2.33 in the required

Phone: 216-368-3600
800-756-0036
Fax: 216-368-1042
E-mail: lawadmissions@case.edu
Web: law.case.edu

Contact

Assistant Dean of Admissions, 216-368-3600 for general inquiries; Director of Financial Aid, 216-368-3602 for financial aid information.

OHIO

courses. The following first-year courses are required of all students: a Perspectives course, CASE ARC: CORE I and II, Civil Procedure, Constitutional Law, Contracts, Criminal Law, Property, and Torts. Required upper-level courses consist of a substantial research paper, CASE ARC: CORE lll and FPS, and Professional Responsibility. more than 50 clinical course positions are available to third-year students.The required orientation program for first-year students is an intensive week-long orientation that includes 17 hours of instruction in the innovative CASE ARC Integrated Lawyering Skills Program.

Electives

Students must take 15 credits in their area of concentration. The School of Law offers concentrations in corporate law, criminal law, international law, litigation, and health law, law technology, public law. In addition, Clinical courses provide students with the opportunity to sit first chair and represent clients in a variety of cases. A wide range of seminars is limited to 12 students and range from copyright in the Digital Millennium to Wrongful Convictions. Judicial externships with federal district and circuit court judges are available to selected students for 3 credits. Supervised research with faculty is worth 2 credit hours, and is offered to second- and third-year students. Field work is also available for credit through the Coast Guard Defense Lab and the Terrorism Prosecution Lab. Special lecture series include the Klatsky Seminar in Human Rights and the Distinguished Intellectual Property Lecture. A study-abroad program is available in Russia, Canada, Mexico, and Australia. An academic assistance program offers tutorial assistance to first- and second-year students, primarily on exam technique and general writing skills. The school is actively involved in the recruitment of students who will enhance the diversity of the student body and legal profession. In addition to an extensive recruitment travel, there is an annual Minority Scholars Day. The most widely taken electives are Evidence, Business Associations, Criminal Procedure, Wills and Trusts.

Graduation Requirements

In order to graduate, candidates must have a GPA of 2.33, have completed the upper-division writing requirement, and CASE ARC Integrated Lawyering Skills Program; Professional Responsibility.

Organizations

Students edit the *Case Western Reserve Law Review, Health Matrix:The Journal of Law-Medicine, Journal of International Law, Canada-United States Law Journal, the Internet Law Journal*, and the newspaper *The Docket*. Students compete in the local Dean Dunmore Moot Court competition; the National Moot Court, held regionally and in New York; Niagara, Canada-U.S. relations; and the local Jessup competition sponsored by the International Law Society. Other competitions include the Jonathan M. Ault Mock Trial in Houston. Law student organizations, local chapters of national associations, and campus organizations include Big Buddies, the Student Intellectual Property Law Association, the Student International Law Association, the Student Health Law Association, Phi Delta Phi, Women's Law Association, and J. Reuben Clark Law Society.

Library

The law library contains 307,071 hardcopy volumes and 104,733 microform volume equivalents, and subscribes to 968 serial publications. Such on-line databases and networks as CALI, CIS Universe, Infotrac, Legal-Trac, LEXIS, LOIS, Mathew Bender, NEXIS, OCLC First Search, WESTLAW, Wilsonline Indexes, and Academic Universe, HeinOnline, JSTOR, NetLibrary, BNA are available to law students for research. Special library collections include U.S. government documents depository, Canadian government documents depository. Recently, the library The library was recently completely remodeled and the physical facilities and the network connections upgraded, including multimedia technology and wireless access. The ratio of library volumes to faculty is 5483 to 1 and to students is 437 to 1.

Faculty

The law school has 56 full-time and 73 part-time faculty members, of whom 43 are women. According to AAUP standards for Category I institutions, faculty salaries are average. The ratio of full-time students to full-time faculty in an average

J.D.s awarded:	239

Services available through: a separate law school placement center
Services: videoconference interviews; mock interviews
Special features: National relationships that create extraordinary opportunities and connect Case law students with prospective employers. Recently, the fall and spring interview programs included on-campus interviews, and off-campus interview trips to Washington, D.C., Chicago, New York City, Southern California, and New England.

Full-time job interviews:	n/av
Summer job interviews:	n/av
Placement by graduation:	73% of class
Placement within 9 months:	98% of class
Average starting salary:	$32,000 to $150,000

Areas of placement:

Private practice 2-10 attorneys	24%
Private practice 11-25 attorneys	9%
Private practice 26-50 attorneys	10%
Private practice 51-100 attorneys	3%
Business/industry	20%
Government	9%
Public interest	8%
Judicial clerkships	6%
Military	3%
Academic	2%

class is 14 to 1; in a clinic, 8 to 1. The law school has a regular program of bringing visiting professors and other distinguished lecturers and visitors to campus. There is a chapter of the Order of the Coif; 100 faculty and 10 graduates are members.

Students

About 42% of the student body are women; 18%, minorities; 4%, African American; 9%, Asian American; and 1%, Hispanic. The majority of students come from Ohio (39%). The average age of entering students is 25; age range is 21 to 49. About 32% of students enter directly from undergraduate school and 16% have a graduate degree.

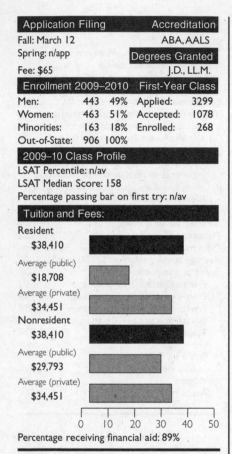

Application Filing	Accreditation
Fall: March 12	ABA, AALS
Spring: n/app	**Degrees Granted**
Fee: $65	J.D., LL.M.

Enrollment 2009–2010		First-Year Class	
Men:	443 49%	Applied:	3299
Women:	463 51%	Accepted:	1078
Minorities:	163 18%	Enrolled:	268
Out-of-State:	906 100%		

2009–10 Class Profile

LSAT Percentile: n/av
LSAT Median Score: 158
Percentage passing bar on first try: n/av

Tuition and Fees:

Resident
$38,410

Average (public)
$18,708

Average (private)
$34,451

Nonresident
$38,410

Average (public)
$29,793

Average (private)
$34,451

0   10   20   30   40   50

Percentage receiving financial aid: 89%

ADMISSIONS

In the fall 2009 first-year class, 3299 applied, 1078 were accepted, and 268 enrolled. Nine transfers enrolled. The median GPA of the most recent first-year class was 3.33.

Requirements

Applicants must have a bachelor's degree and take the LSAT. The most important admission factors include LSAT results, GPA, and letter of recommendation. No specific undergraduate courses are required. Candidates are not interviewed.

Procedure

The application deadline for fall entry is March 12. Applicants should submit an application form, LSAT results, transcripts, a nonrefundable application fee of $65, and 2 letters of recommendation. Notification of the admissions decision is on a rolling basis. The latest acceptable LSAT test date for fall entry is February. The law school uses the LSDAS.

Special

The law school recruits minority and disadvantaged students by visiting colleges and geographical areas with large minority populations. Minority applicants are encouraged to write brief background statements as part of the admissions process. Special consideration is given to applicants who plan to attend the Council on Legal Education Opportunity (CLEO) program and to Pre Law Summer Institute (PLSI) for Native American Students. Requirements are not different for out-of-state students. Transfer students must have one year of credit, have attended an ABA-approved law school, and be in good standing, and be competitive in class rank.

Costs

Tuition and fees for the 2009-2010 academic year are $38,410 for all full-time students. Books and supplies run $1500.

Financial Aid

About 89% of current law students receive some form of aid. The average annual amount of aid from all sources combined, including scholarships, loans, and work contracts, is $44,676; maximum, $64,170. Awards are based on need and merit, along with along with community service in conjunction with other considerations. Required financial statement is the FAFSA. The aid application deadline for fall entry is July 15. Special funds for minority or disadvantaged students include scholarships that are merit based. First-year students are notified about their financial aid application at time of acceptance.

About the Law School

Catholic University of America Columbus School of Law was established in 1898 and is a private institution. The 154-acre campus is in an urban area in a noncommercial area, accessible by public. The primary mission of the law school is to provide a small, diverse student body with a quality legal education and to prepare students for the ethical practice of law. Students have access to federal, state, county, city, and local agencies, courts, correctional facilities, law firms, and legal aid organizations in the Washington area. The Library of Congress and the U.S. Supreme Court are nearby. Facilities of special interest to law students consist of a new law school facility, completed in 1994,

that houses all components of the school. Law students also have access to the university's athletic complex, including a pool, Nautilus equipment, sauna, tennis courts, and a track. Housing for students are available in a variety of apartments and private rooms that are within easy traveling distance. All law school facilities are accessible to the physically disabled.

Calendar

The law school operates on a traditional semester basis. Courses for full-time students are offered days only and must be completed within 5 years. For part-time students, courses are offered evenings only and must be completed within 6 years. New full- and part-time students are admitted in the fall. There is a 7 to 8-week summer session. Transferable summer courses are offered.

Programs

In addition to the J.D., the law school offers the LL.M. Students may take relevant courses in other programs and apply credit toward the J.D.; a maximum of If the student is not a credits may be applied. The following joint degrees may be earned: J.D./J.C.L. (Juris Doctor/Licentiate of Canon Law), J.D./M.A. (Juris Doctor/Master of Arts in politics, philosophy, history,), J.D./M.L.S. (Juris Doctor/Master of Library Science), and J.D./M.S.W. (Juris Doctor/Master of Social Work).

Required

To earn the J.D., candidates must complete 84 total credits, of which 33 are for required courses. They must maintain a minimum GPA of 2.1 in the required courses. The following first-year courses are required of all students: Civil Procedure, Constitutional Law, Contracts, Criminal Law, Lawyering Skills, Property, Social Justice and the Law, and Torts. Required upper-level courses consist of Professional Responsibility. The required orientation program for first-year students occurs during the first week and consists of the beginning of the Lawyering Skills course, a general introduction to the law library and the law school, study skills, and social activities.

Phone: 202-319-5151
Fax: 202-319-6285
E-mail: *admissions@law.edu*
Web: *www.law.edu*

Contact
Office of Admissions, 202-319-5151 for general inquiries; David Schrock, Financial Aid Director, 202-319-5143 for financial aid information.

DISTRICT OF COLUMBIA

Electives
The Columbus School of Law offers concentrations in corporate law, criminal law, entertainment law, environmental law, family law, intellectual property law, international law, juvenile law, labor law, litigation, maritime law, media law, securities law, sports law, tax law, torts and insurance, and communications law, securities and corporate law, public policy, law and religion, and jurisprudence. In addition, The law school has 4 one-semester and 2 year-long clinics offering from 6 to 12 credits including General Practice, Families & the Law, and Advocacy for the Elderly. Seminars are also open only to upper-level students. Students from the law school participate in nearly 200 externship placements annually in all organizations, and law firms of all sizes and specialties. Students may serve as research assistants to law faculty members. Field work opportunities are available through the general externship program as well as the Immigration and Human Rights Clinic and seminars such as the Public Policy Practicum and the Education Law Practicum. Special lecture series are the Pope John XXIII Lectures, the Brendan F. Brown Distinguished Lectures and Scholars-in-Residence, and the Mirror of Justice Lectures. The International Business and Trade Summer Law Program is a 6-week summer program that takes place at the historic Jagiellonian University in Krakow, Poland is open to students who have completed their first year of law school and are in good standing. Student groups and individual faculty members conduct informal tutorial sessions. A Writing Consultant is available for individualized legal writing assistance. The most widely taken electives are Evidence, Corporations, and Family Law.

Graduation Requirements
In order to graduate, candidates must have a GPA of 2.15, have completed the upper-division writing requirement, and .

Organizations
Student-edited publications include *The Catholic University of America Law Review*. Other law reviews include *the Journal of Contemporary Health Law and Policy, and CommLaw Conspectus*. Moot Court teams compete in the Sutherland Cup Competition, National Telecommunications Law Competition and Jessup Cup

International Law Competition. Other competitions include the Securities Law Competition, and the Trials Competition. Student organizations include the Students for Public Interest Law, Advocates for Life, and Communications Law Students, Law student organizations include the student divisions of the ABA, the American Society of International Law, and Black Law Students Organization. Local chapters of national associations include Thurgood Marshall American Inn of Court and Pope John Paul II Guild of Catholic Lawyers.

Library
The law library contains 203,232 hardcopy volumes and 199,613 microform volume equivalents, and subscribes to 5276 serial publications. Such on-line databases and networks as CALI, CIS Universe, Infotrac, Legal-Trac, LEXIS, LOIS, NEXIS, OCLC First Search, WESTLAW, and Wilsonline Indexes are available to law students for research. Special library collections include a partial U.S. government depository that can be accessed through hard copy, CD-ROMs, and the Internet. The collection also includes large concentrations in Congressional documents, international law, law and religion, military law, telecommunications law, and UN documents. Recently, the library added compact shelving to increase shelving capacity by 24,000 volumes. Three video playback rooms, 6 study rooms, the wainscoted two-story Clark Reading Room, and multiple lounge areas offer ample room for students to study and relax. The ratio of library volumes to faculty is 3332 to 1 and to students is 214 to 1. The ratio of seats in the library to students is 1 to 2.

Faculty
The law school has 91 full-time and 87 part-time faculty members, of whom 54 are women. According to AAUP standards for Category 1 institutions, faculty salaries are below average. The ratio of full-time students to full-time faculty in an average class is 15 to 1. The law school has a regular program of bringing visiting professors and other distinguished lecturers and visitors to campus.

Students
About 51% of the student body are women; 18%, minorities; 5%, African American;

Placement
J.D.s awarded:	245

Services available through: a separate law school placement center

Special features: individual and group consultations, on-campus interviewing, consortium interviewing conferences, resume collection service, workshops on planning and executing a job search, writing resumes and cover letters, developing interviewing skills, building legal credentials, understanding specific legal markets, and a broad range of programming and networking opportunities.

Full-time job interviews:	75 employers
Summer job interviews:	n/av
Placement by graduation:	n/av
Placement within 9 months:	93% of class
Average starting salary:	$28,000 to $135,000

Areas of placement:
Private practice 2-10 attorneys	42%
Government	27%
Business/industry	13%
Judicial clerkships	12%
Public interest	2%
Academic	2%

10%, Asian American; and 3%, Hispanic. The average age of entering students is 26; age range is 21 to 46. About 10% drop out after the first year for academic or personal reasons.

CHAPMAN UNIVERSITY

School of Law

One University Drive
Orange, CA 92866

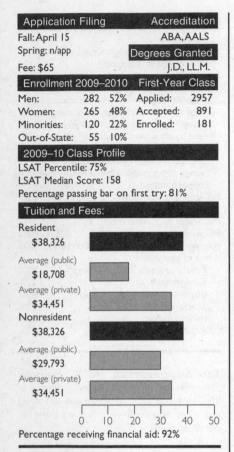

Application Filing		Accreditation	
Fall: April 15		ABA, AALS	
Spring: n/app		**Degrees Granted**	
Fee: $65		J.D., LL.M.	
Enrollment 2009–2010		**First-Year Class**	
Men:	282 52%	Applied:	2957
Women:	265 48%	Accepted:	891
Minorities:	120 22%	Enrolled:	181
Out-of-State:	55 10%		

2009–10 Class Profile
LSAT Percentile: 75%
LSAT Median Score: 158
Percentage passing bar on first try: 81%

Tuition and Fees:

Resident
$38,326

Average (public)
$18,708

Average (private)
$34,451

Nonresident
$38,326

Average (public)
$29,793

Average (private)
$34,451

Percentage receiving financial aid: 92%

ADMISSIONS

In the fall 2009 first-year class, 2957 applied, 891 were accepted, and 181 enrolled. Three transfers enrolled. The median LSAT percentile of the most recent first-year class was 75; the median GPA was 3.43 on a scale of 4.0. The lowest LSAT percentile accepted was 32; the highest was 96.

Requirements
Applicants must have a bachelor's degree and take the LSAT. Minimum acceptable GPA is 2.0 on a scale of 4.0. The most important admission factors include undergraduate curriculum, writing ability, and academic achievement. No specific undergraduate courses are required. Candidates are not interviewed.

Procedure
The application deadline for fall entry is April 15. Applicants should submit an application form, transcripts, a personal statement, TOEFL, where indicated, a nonrefundable application fee of $65, 2 letters od recommendation submitted to LSDAS (maximum of 3) and résumé, and LSDAS report (which includes LSAT, transcripts, and letters of recommendation). Notification of the admissions decision is usually within 6 to 8 weeks. The latest acceptable LSAT test date for fall entry is February. The law school uses the LSDAS.

Special
The law school recruits minority and disadvantaged students at colleges and universities that have a high percentage of minority and disadvantaged students, by advertising in and supporting publications reaching the various ethnic and disadvantaged communities, and by hosting and attending special events. Requirements are not different for out-of-state students. Transfer students must have one year of credit, 2 letters of recommendation (one from a law professor), an official law transcript, a letter of good standing, and an updated LSDAS Report.

Costs

Tuition and fees for the 2009-2010 academic year are $38,326 for all full-time students. Tuition for part-time students is $30,476 per year. On-campus room and board costs about $13,968 annually; books and supplies run $1560.

Financial Aid

About 92% of current law students receive some form of aid. The average annual amount of aid from all sources combined, including scholarships, loans, and work contracts, is $50,608; maximum, $63,223. Awards are based on need and merit, along with merit-based scholarships, and loans based on need. Required financial statement is the FAFSA. The aid application deadline for fall entry is March 2. Students receive an offer of aid after an offer of admissions is made, provided the application is complete.

About the Law School

Chapman University School of Law was established in 1995 and is a private institution. The 52-acre campus is in a suburban area in Orange, California. The primary mission of the law school is to provide personalized education in a challenging academic environment that stimulates intellectual inquiry, embraces diverse ideas and viewpoints, and fosters competent, ethical lawyering. Students have access to federal, state, county, city, and local agencies, courts, correctional facilities, law firms, and legal aid organizations in the Orange area. Facilities of special interest to law students include a state-of-the-art law building, with drop ports throughout, digital document cameras, touch screen computers at podiums, electronic courtrooms, assisted-listening devices, and an outstanding law library. Limited university-owned housing is available for law school students. Various apartment complexes are within proximity of the law school. All law school facilities are accessible to the physically disabled.

Calendar

The law school operates on a traditional semester basis. Courses for full-time students are offered both day and evening and beyond the first-year curriculum and must be completed within 5 years. For part-time students, courses are offered days only and must be completed within 6 years. New full- and part-time students are admitted in the fall. There is a 7-week summer session. Transferable summer courses are offered.

Programs

In addition to the J.D., the law school offers the LL.M., LL.M. in Taxation, and LL.M. in Prosecutional Science. Students may take relevant courses in other programs and apply credit toward the J.D.; a maximum of 8 credits may be applied. The following joint degrees may be earned: J.D./M.B.A. (Juris Doctor/Master of Business Administration) and J.D./M.F.A. (Juris Doctor/Master of Fine Arts in film and television).

Required
To earn the J.D., candidates must complete 88 total credits, of which 51 to 52 are for required courses. They must maintain a minimum GPA of 2.0 in the required courses. The following first-year courses are required of all students: Civil Procedure I and II, Contracts I and II, Criminal Law, Legal Research and Writing I and II, Property I and II, and Torts I and II. Required upper-level courses consist of a

Phone: 714-628-2500
877-Chaplaw
Fax: 714-628-2501
E-mail: *metten@chapman.edu*
Web: *chapman.edu/law*

Contact

Annette Metten, Admissions Coordinator, 714-628-2525 for general inquiries; Kathleen Clark, Director of Financial, 714-628-2510 (lawfinaid@chapman.edu) for financial aid information.

CALIFORNIA

writing requirement, Constitutional Law I and II, Corporations, Evidence, Federal Income Tax, Lawyering Skills, and Professional Responsibility. The required orientation program for first-year students lasts approximately 3 days and includes an introduction to the process of legal education and analysis, professionalism oath, legal education in practice, as well as informal social events and information sessions on navigating through the law school experience.

Electives

The School of Law offers concentrations in entertainment law, environmental law, international law, tax law, and land use/ real estate, and advocacy and dispute resolution. In addition, a U.S. Tax Court Clinic, Ninth Circuit Appellate Advocacy Clinic, Constitutional Jurisprudence Clinic, Family Violence Clinic, AmVets Clinic for military personel, Mediation Clinic, Entertainment Law Clinic, Tax Appeals Clinic, and Elder Law Clinic are available for students for varying academic credit. A variety of seminar-type courses for upperclassmen is offered, ranging from 2 to 4 credits. Various externship opportunities, including judicial externships, are available to students in good standing; credits vary with a maximum of 10 total. Special lecture series include the Distinguished Jurist in Residence Program, Chapman Dialogues, International Law Lecture Series, and Entertainment Law Lecture Series open to all students for no credit. There is a study-abroad program in England, and Australia. The Academic Achievement Program offers lectures and workshops, individualized tutoring for students, early bar preparation, and referrals to university or outside programs or support services designed to meet identified special student needs. Remedial programs include additional legal writing and research courses. Minority programs include Diversity Week. The most widely taken electives are Externships, Wills and Trusts, and Criminial Police Practice.

Graduation Requirements

In order to graduate, candidates must have a GPA of 2.0, have completed the upper-division writing requirement, and have satisfied ABA residency requirements.

Organizations

Students edit the *The Chapman Law Review, Nexus, A Journal of Opinion, Criminal Justice Journal*, and the student newspaper, *The Chapman Law Courier*. Moot court competitions include ABA National Appellate Advocacy Competition, Traynor Moot Court, and Thomas Tang Moot Court Competition. Other competitions include American Trial Lawyers Association Competition, Vis International Arbitration Competition, International Arbitration Competition, ABA Client Counseling Competition, National Environmental Law Moot Court Competition, National Moot Court Competition, and Luke Charles Moore Invitational Moot Court Competition. Law student organizations include the Land Resources Society, Tax Law Society, and Entertainment and Sports Law Society. There are local chapters of the Federalist Society, Phi Alpha Delta, and National Lawyers Guild. Other campus organizations include the Student Bar Association, International Law Society, and Minority Law Students Association.

Library

The law library contains 303,429 hardcopy volumes and 206,609 microform volume equivalents, and subscribes to 236 serial publications. Such on-line databases and networks as CALI, LEXIS, LOIS, OCLC First Search, WESTLAW, Wilsonline Indexes, and BNA Online are available to law students for research. The library maintains special collections to support the financial aid and placement areas of the law school. The monograph collection is growing to support multiuple disciplines. The ratio of library volumes to faculty is 5835 to 1 and to students is 563 to 1. The ratio of seats in the library to students is 1 to 549.

Faculty

The law school has 52 full-time and 40 part-time faculty members, of whom 26 are women. According to AAUP standards for Category IIA institutions, faculty salaries are well above average. About 11% of full-time faculty have a graduate law degree in addition to the J.D. The ratio of full-time students to full-time faculty in an average class is 10 to 1; in a clinic, 5 to

Placement

J.D.s awarded:	159

Services available through: a separate law school placement center
Services: information sessions, panels, law firm nights, mock interviews, a mentor and e-mentor program, off-site recruiting events, cover letter review counseling, and assistance for postgraduate judicial clerkships.
Special features: Provide specialized counseling for L.L.M. students.

Full-time job interviews:	19 employers
Summer job interviews:	19 employers
Placement by graduation:	86% of class
Placement within 9 months:	97% of class
Average starting salary:	$27,040 to $160,000

Areas of placement:

Solo practice; Private practice 100+ attorneys	19%
Private practice 2-10 attorneys	29%
Private practice 11-25 attorneys	3%
Private practice 26-50 attorneys	4%
Private practice 51-100 attorneys	2%
Academic	20%
Government	8%
Business/industry	8%
Judicial clerkships	3%
Military	2%
Public interest	1%

1. The law school has a regular program of bringing visiting professors and other distinguished lecturers and visitors to campus.

Students

About 48% of the student body are women; 22%, minorities; 1%, African American; 14%, Asian American; 7%, Hispanic; and 1%, Native American. The majority of students come from California (90%). The average age of entering students is 25; age range is 20 to 50. About 47% of students enter directly from undergraduate school and 6% have a graduate degree. About 10% drop out after the first year for academic or personal reasons; 82% remain to receive a law degree.

P.O. Box 535
Charleston, SC 29402

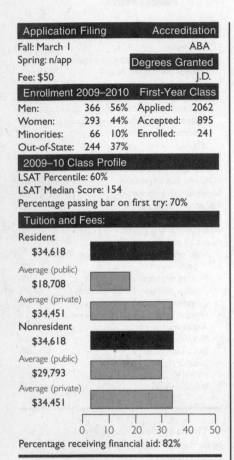

Application Filing	Accreditation
Fall: March 1	ABA
Spring: n/app	Degrees Granted
Fee: $50	J.D.

Enrollment 2009–2010		First-Year Class	
Men:	366 56%	Applied:	2062
Women:	293 44%	Accepted:	895
Minorities:	66 10%	Enrolled:	241
Out-of-State:	244 37%		

2009–10 Class Profile
LSAT Percentile: 60%
LSAT Median Score: 154
Percentage passing bar on first try: 70%

Tuition and Fees:

Resident
$34,618

Average (public)
$18,708

Average (private)
$34,451

Nonresident
$34,618

Average (public)
$29,793

Average (private)
$34,451

0 10 20 30 40 50

Percentage receiving financial aid: 82%

ADMISSIONS
In the fall 2009 first-year class, 2062 applied, 895 were accepted, and 241 enrolled. Three transfers enrolled. The median LSAT percentile of the most recent first-year class was 60; the median GPA was 3.2 on a scale of 4.0.

Requirements
Applicants must have a bachelor's degree and take the LSAT. The most important admission factors include general background, commitment to public service, and LSAT results. No specific undergraduate courses are required. Candidates are interviewed.

Procedure
The application deadline for fall entry is March 1. Applicants should submit an application form, LSAT results, transcripts, a personal statement, a nonrefundable application fee of $50, 2 letters of recommendation, and Dean's Certification. Notification of the admissions deci-

sion is December through August. The latest acceptable LSAT test date for fall entry is February. The law school uses the LSDAS.

Special
The law school recruits minority and disadvantaged students through visits to HBCUs, a minority recruitment day, and CRS/LSDAS. Requirements are not different for out-of-state students. Transfer students must have 1 year of credit and have attended an ABA-approved law school.

Costs
Tuition and fees for the 2009-2010 academic year are $34,618 for all full-time students. Tuition for part-time students is $27,824 per year. Books and supplies run $1250.

Financial Aid
About 82% of current law students receive some form of aid. The average annual amount of aid from all sources combined, including scholarships, loans, and work contracts, is $34,000; maximum, $53,868. Awards are based on need and merit. Required financial statements are the FAFSA and School Specific Scholarship Application. The aid application deadline for fall entry is April 1. Special funds for minority or disadvantaged students Student Success Initiative and school scholarship. First-year students are notified about their financial aid application after acceptance, and prior to enrollment.

About the Law School
Charleston School of Law was established in 2003 and is a private institution. The campus is in an urban area in historic Charleston, South Carolina. The primary mission of the law school is to prepare graduates for public service. Students have access to federal, state, county, city, and local agencies, courts, correctional facilities, law firms, and legal aid organizations in the Charleston area. Facilities of special interest to law students include a moot court room. The law library is located in restored historic warehouse. Housing for students is not available on campus; numerous options are available in the area. All law school facilities are accessible to the physically disabled.

Calendar
The law school operates on a traditional semester basis. Courses for full-time students are offered both day and evening and must be completed within 84 months. For part-time students, courses are offered evenings only and must be completed within 84 months. New full- and part-time students are admitted in the fall. There is an 8- and a 2-week summer session. Transferable summer courses are offered.

Programs

Required
To earn the J.D., candidates must complete 88 total credits, of which 63 are for required courses. They must maintain a minimum GPA of 2.0 in the required courses. The following first-year courses are required of all students: Civil Procedure I and II, Contracts I and II, Legal Writing and Research I and II, Property I and II, and Torts I and II. Required upper-level courses consist of a skills course, advanced writing requirement, Business Associations, Commercial Law, Constitutional Law I and II, Criminial Law, Criminial Procedure, Evidence, Professional Responsibility, Secured Transactions, and Wills, Trusts, and Estates. The required orientation program for first-year students lasts 2½ days.

Electives
After the first year, students may complete an externship with more than 100 options from public defender, to solicitor, to various judges. Damages, Mass Torts, Information Privacy Law, and Advanced Appellate Advocacy seminars are offered. Internships are available through the Public Defender, Solicitor, and Heirs Property Project. Field work consists of externship placement in more than 100 sites. Research positions with faculty members and tutorial programs include Academic Success Program. Special lecture series consist of a professionalism series (3 of 6 required per semester). Cooperative study abroad program with Stetson is available. Minority programs are offered through the Office of Student Diversity and Mentoring. The most widely taken electives are Damages, Trial Advocacy, and Equity.

Phone: 843-377-2143
Fax: 843-329-0491
E-mail: jbenfield@charlestonlaw.org
Web: charlestonlaw.edu

Contact
Associate Dean, 843 377-2143 for general inquiries; Mike Parrish, Director of Financial Aid, 843 377-4901 for financial aid information.

SOUTH CAROLINA

Graduation Requirements

In order to graduate, candidates must have a GPA of 2.0, have completed the upper-division writing requirement, and have completed 30 hours of documented pro bono work, a skills course, and a professionalism series.

Organizations
Students edit the *Charleston Law Review, Federal Courts Law Review*, and *MALABU (Maritime Law Bulletin)*. Law student organizations, local chapters of national associations, and campus organizations include SBA, BLSA, Women in Law, Environmental Law Society, Real Estate Law, and International Law Society.

Library
The law library contains 26,267 hard-copy volumes, and subscribes to 800 serial publications. Such on-line databases and networks as CALI, CIS Universe, Legal-Trac, LEXIS, LOIS, Mathew Bender, OCLC First Search, WESTLAW, Wilsonline Indexes, Hein Online, BNA, CCH, and RIA are available to law students for research. The ratio of library volumes to faculty is 820 to 1 and to students is 39 to 1. The ratio of seats in the library to students is 1 to 8

Faculty
The law school has 32 full-time and 33 part-time faculty members, of whom 25 are women. The ratio of full-time students to full-time faculty in an average class is 60 to 1; in a clinic, 18 to 1. The law school has a regular program of bringing visiting professors and other distinguished lecturers and visitors to campus.

Students
About 44% of the student body are women; 10%, minorities; 6%, African American; 1%, Asian American; 1%, Hispanic; and 1%, Native American. The majority of students come from South Carolina (63%). The average age of entering students is 23; age range is 20 to 52. About 70% of students enter directly from undergraduate school, 30% have a graduate degree, and 25% have worked full-time prior to entering law school. About 3% drop out after the first year for academic or personal reasons; 97% remain to receive a law degree.

Placement

J.D.s awarded:	184
Services available through: a separate law school placement center	
Special features: a Director of Public Service and Pro Bono who administers the Pro Bono Program through the placement office.	
Full-time job interviews:	3 employers
Summer job interviews:	15 employers
Placement by graduation:	n/av
Placement within 9 months:	67% of class
Average starting salary:	$39,000 to $74,000
Areas of placement:	
Private practice	43%
Judicial clerkships	31%
Government	14%
Business/industry	7%
Public interest	4%
Academic	1%

CHARLOTTE SCHOOL OF LAW

2145 Suttle Avenue
Charlotte, NC 28208

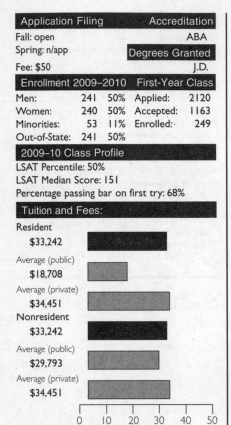

Application Filing	Accreditation
Fall: open	ABA
Spring: n/app	

	Degrees Granted
Fee: $50	J.D.

Enrollment 2009–2010		First-Year Class	
Men:	241 50%	Applied:	2120
Women:	240 50%	Accepted:	1163
Minorities:	53 11%	Enrolled:	249
Out-of-State:	241 50%		

2009–10 Class Profile

LSAT Percentile: 50%
LSAT Median Score: 151
Percentage passing bar on first try: 68%

Tuition and Fees:

Resident
$33,242

Average (public)
$18,708

Average (private)
$34,451

Nonresident
$33,242

Average (public)
$29,793

Average (private)
$34,451

0 10 20 30 40 50

Percentage receiving financial aid: 90%

ADMISSIONS

In the fall 2009 first-year class, 2120 applied, 1163 were accepted, and 249 enrolled. Five transfers enrolled. The median LSAT percentile of the most recent first-year class was 50; the median GPA was 3.11 on a scale of 4.6. The lowest LSAT percentile accepted was 140; the highest was 168.

Requirements

Applicants must have a bachelor's degree, and take the LSAT. No specific undergraduate courses are required. Candidates are not interviewed.

Procedure

The application deadline for fall entry is open. Applicants should submit an application form, LSAT results, transcripts, a personal statement, and an application fee of $50, that is waived if applying for the first time electronically. Notification of the admissions decision is rolling. The latest acceptable LSAT test date for fall

entry is June. The law school uses the LSDAS.

Special

Requirements are not different for out-of-state students. Transfer students must have attended an ABA-approved law school and be currently enrolled in law school. Preadmissions courses consist of AAMPLE, the on-line summer conditional admit program.

Costs

Tuition and fees for the 2009-2010 academic year are $33,242 for all full-time students. Tuition and fees for part-time students is $26,892. Books and supplies run $1925.

Financial Aid

About 90% of current law students receive some form of aid. The average annual amount of aid from all sources combined, including scholarships, loans, and work contracts, is $12,725; maximum, $56,485. Awards are based on merit. Required financial statement is the FAFSA. The aid application deadlines for fall entry is the end of the academic term. First-year students are notified about their financial aid application at time of acceptance.

About the Law School

Charlotte School of Law was established in 2006 and is independent. The 4-acre campus is in Charlotte, North Carolina. The primary mission of the law school is to ensure students are equipped with practical skills that will allow them to thrive in a profesional setting, to motivate and energize the student community in evey aspect of the law school experience, and to place a strong emphasis on serving the underserved through community service and pro bono work. Students have access to federal, state, county, city, and local agencies, courts, correctional facilities, law firms, and legal aid organizations in the Charlotte area. Facilities of special interest to law students include a 4-story modern state of the art building. All law school facilities are accessible to the physically disabled.

Calendar

The law school operates on a traditional semester basis. Courses for full-time stu-

dents are offered both day and evening and must be completed within 5 years. For part-time students, courses are offered both day and evening and must be completed within 7 years. New full- and part-time students are admitted in the fall and spring. There are 2-5-week summer sessions. Transferable summer courses are offered.

Programs

Required

To earn the J.D., candidates must complete 90 total credits, of which 60 are for required courses. They must maintain a minimum GPA of 2.0 in the required courses. The following first-year courses are required of all students: Civil Procedure I and II, Contracts I and II, Lawyering Process I and II, Passport to Effective Practice, Property I and II, and Torts I and II. Required upper-level courses consist of a skills course, an advanced writing course, Business Associations, Commercial Law, Constitutional Law I and II, Criminal Procedure, Evidence, Professional Responsibility, and Wills and Trusts. The required orientation program for first-year students is 3 to 4 days.

Electives

In addition, clinics include Business Law Clinic (3 credits), Parent Representation Clinic (3 credits), and Wrongful Conviction Clinic (2 credits). Seminars include Art Law Clinic (2 credits), Business Drafting Seminar (2 to 3 credits), and White Collar Crime Seminar (2 to 3 credits). Internships and externships are available. The law school offers externship fieldwork for 2 to 4 credits. This upper-level elective provides an opportunity for students to learn "in role". As part of the students services program, the law school provides students with academic support services through the Charlotte Law Program for Academic Success. Charlotte Law has several student organizations to support students of color such as the Latin American Law Society, Charlotte Law Diversity Alliance, and Black Law Students Association.

Graduation Requirements

In order to graduate, candidates must have a GPA of 2.0, have completed the

Phone: 704-971-8542
Fax: 704-971-8599
E-mail: admissions@charlottelaw.edu
Web: charlottelaw.edu

Contact

Carrie Mansfield, 704-971-8542 for general inquiries; Laren Mack, Financial Aid Director, 704-971-8546 for financial aid information.

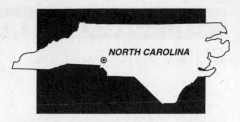

NORTH CAROLINA

upper-division writing requirement, and have completed 8 Pro-bono hours, and 10 hours community of service.

Organizations

Students edit the *Charlotte Law Review* and the student newspaper, *The Docket*. Moot Court competitions include the Jessup International Law Competition, Gibbons Criminal Law Competition, Saul Lefkowitch Intellectual Property Moot Court Competition, and the Frederick Douglass Moot Court Competition. Other competitions include American Association of Justice (AAJ) (formerly the Academy of Trial Lawyers), Student Trial Advocacy Competition, and National Trial Competition in Atlanta, Georgia. Law student organizations, local chapters of national associations, and campus clubs and organizations include Women in Law, International Law Society, Environmental Law Society, Federalist Society, Delta Theta Phi, Phi Alpha Delta, Phi Delta Phi, Public Interest Law Society, Charlotte Law Cares, and Real Estate Society.

Library

The law library contains 196,308 hardcopy volumes and 99,339 microform volume equivalents, and subscribes to 13,473 serial publications. Such on-line databases and networks as CALI, Legal-Trac, LEXIS, LOIS, Mathew Bender, NEXIS, OCLC First Search, WESTLAW, eLibrary,

HeinOnline, JSTOR Loislaw, LexisNexis Congressional, LLMC Digital, Making of Modern Law, Oxford Scholarship Online, ProQuest, Supreme Court Database, U.S. Supreme Court Records and Briefs, BNA, and CCH are available to law students for research. Recently, the library moved to the new school building. The ratio of library volumes to faculty is 8923 to 1 and to students is 408 to 1. The ratio of seats in the library to students is 1 to 2.

Faculty

The law school has 22 full-time and 27 part-time faculty members, of whom 25 are women. About 18% of part-time faculty have a graduate law degree in addition to the J.D. The ratio of full-time students to full-time faculty in an average class is 45 to 1; in a clinic, 6 to 1. The law school has a regular program of bringing visiting professors and other distinguished lecturers and visitors to campus.

Students

About 50% of the student body are women; 11%, minorities; 6%, African American; 1%, Asian American; 4%, Hispanic; and 1%, Native American. The majority of students come from North Carolina (50%). The average age of entering students is 28; age range is 20 to 55. About 10% drop out after the first year for academic or personal reasons; 90% remain to receive a law degree.

Placement

J.D.s awarded:	64
Services available through: a separate law school placement center	
Services: full-service	
Full-time job interviews:	n/aav
Summer job interviews:	n/av
Placement by graduation:	n/av
Placement within 9 months:	n/av
Average starting salary:	n/av
Areas of placement:	n/av

CITY UNIVERSITY OF NEW YORK

CUNY School of Law

65-21 Main Street
Flushing, NY 11367-1300

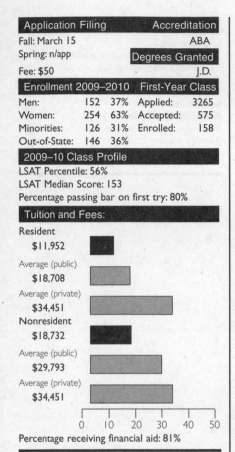

Application Filing	Accreditation
Fall: March 15	ABA
Spring: n/app	**Degrees Granted**
Fee: $50	J.D.

Enrollment 2009–2010		First-Year Class	
Men:	152 37%	Applied:	3265
Women:	254 63%	Accepted:	575
Minorities:	126 31%	Enrolled:	158
Out-of-State:	146 36%		

2009–10 Class Profile
LSAT Percentile: 56%
LSAT Median Score: 153
Percentage passing bar on first try: 80%

Tuition and Fees:

Resident
$11,952

Average (public)
$18,708

Average (private)
$34,451

Nonresident
$18,732

Average (public)
$29,793

Average (private)
$34,451

0 10 20 30 40 50

Percentage receiving financial aid: 81%

ADMISSIONS

In the fall 2009 first-year class, 3265 applied, 575 were accepted, and 158 enrolled. Three transfers enrolled. The median LSAT percentile of the most recent first-year class was 56; the median GPA was 3.31 on a scale of 4.0. The lowest LSAT percentile accepted was 36; the highest was 98.

Requirements
Applicants must have a bachelor's degree and take the LSAT. The most important admission factors include academic achievement, a letter of recommendation and a demonstrated commitment to public interest/public service. No specific undergraduate courses are required. Candidates are not interviewed.

Procedure
The application deadline for fall entry is March 15. Applicants should submit an application form, LSAT results, transcripts, a personal statement, a nonre-

fundable application fee of $50, 2 letters of recommendation, a personal statement, and the LSDAS. Notification of the admissions decision is begins in January. The latest acceptable LSAT test date for fall entry is February. The law school uses the LSDAS.

Special
The law school recruits minority and disadvantaged students through programs similar to those used by most other law schools. Requirements are not different for out-of-state students. Transfer students must have one year of credit, have attended an ABA-approved law school, and have demonstrated a commitment to public interest/public service.

Costs

Tuition and fees for the 2009-2010 academic year are $11,952 for full-time in-state students and $18,732 for out-of-state students. Books and supplies run $70.

Financial Aid

About 81% of current law students receive some form of aid. The average annual amount of aid from all sources combined, including scholarships, loans, and work contracts, is $34,409; maximum, $43,335. Awards are based on need and merit. Required financial statement is the FAFSA. The aid application deadline for fall entry is May 3. Special funds for minority or disadvantaged students include the Professional Opportunity Scholarship, CLEO, and various other scholarships. First-year students are notified about their financial aid application on a rolling basis.

About the Law School

City University of New York CUNY School of Law was established in 1983 and is a public institution. The campus is in an urban area in the New York City borough of Queens. The primary mission of the law school is to train lawyers to serve the underprivileged and disempowered and to make a difference in their communities. Students have access to federal, state, county, city, and local agencies, courts, correctional facilities, law firms, and legal aid organizations in the Flushing area. There are several notable in-house clinical programs. Facilities of special interest to law students include a 3-story build-

ing adjacent to the Queens College campus, which houses classrooms, the library, lounge, administrative offices, day-care center, and cafeteria. Housing for students is available off campus. About 99% of the law school facilities are accessible to the physically disabled.

Calendar

The law school operates on a traditional semester basis. Courses for full-time students are offered both day and evening. There is no part-time program. New students are admitted in the fall. There is an 8-week summer session. Transferable summer courses are offered.

Programs

Students may take relevant courses in other programs and apply credit toward the J.D.; a maximum of 6 credits may be applied.

Required
To earn the J.D., candidates must complete 91 total credits, of which 60 are for required courses. They must maintain a minimum GPA of 2.3 in the required courses. The following first-year courses are required of all students: Civil Procedure I, Law and a Market Economy I and II: Contracts, Law and Family Relations, Lawyering Seminar: Work of a Lawyer I and II, Legal Process, Legal Research I and II, Liberty, Equality, and Due Process, and Responsibility for Injurious Conduct I and II: Torts and Criminal Law. Required upper-level courses consist of a clinic or concentration, Constitutional Structures and the Law, Law and a Market Economy III: Property, Lawyering and the Public Interest I: Evidence, Lawyering Seminar III, and Public Institutions and Law. All students must take clinical courses. The required orientation program for first-year students is a 1-week academic, skills, and social program, including court visits.

Electives
Students must take 12 to 16 credits in their area of concentration. The CUNY School of Law offers concentrations in criminal law, environmental law, family law, international law, juvenile law, labor law, litigation, health, mediation, domestic violence, elder law, immigration, human rights, civil rights, and com-

Phone: 718-340-4210
Fax: 718-340-4435
E-mail: mail.law.cuny.edu
Web: www.law.cuny.edu

Contact

Yvonne Cherena-Pacheco, Assistant Dean for Enrollment, 718-340-4210 for general inquiries; Angela Joseph, Director of Financial Aid, 718-340-4292 for financial aid information.

NEW YORK

munity economic development. In addition, all students must enroll in a clinic (12 to 16 credits) or a concentration (12 credit internship). Current clinic offerings include Immigrant and Refugee Rights, Elder Law, Battered Women's Rights, Defender, International Women's Human Rights, Mediation, and Community Economic Development. All third-year students at CUNY law represent clients under the supervision of attorneys at one of the largest law firms in Queens- Main Street Legal Services, Inc.- situated on the law school campus. Each first-year student takes 2 4-credit Lawyering Seminars. Limited to 24 students, these seminars imbed lawyering skills such as legal analysis, legal research, legal writing, interviewing, counseling, and negotiating in doctrine taught in first-year courses. Second-year students choose a Lawyering Seminar in an area of interest. Recent Lawyering Seminar offerings include Trial Advocacy, Civil Pre-Trial Process, Mediation, Criminal Defense, Juvenile Rights, Nonprofit Representation, Economic Justice, Community Economic Development, and Writing from a Judicial Perspective. In addition, at least 4 upper-division classes are taught in a 20:1 ratio. Internships are available in connection with the concentration program in placements related to specially-designed courses. Current areas are civil rights/discrimination and health law. Students spend 2 full days in the field and 8 hours in class. Field work is connected to concentrations and to a 3-credit summary school course—Public Interest/Public Service. Special lecture series are sponsored by various student organizations. A professional skills center and a writing center are available to support students. Special offerings are also available to 2nd and 3rd semester students who are experiencing difficulty. The most widely taken electives are NY Practice, Criminal Procedure, and Business Associations.

Graduation Requirements

In order to graduate, candidates must have a GPA of 2.3, have completed the upper-division writing requirement, and clinic/concentration.

Organizations

Students edit the *New York City Law Review*, and participate in the annual Moot Court Competition, Phillip C. Jessup International Law Moot Court Competition, and the John J. Gibbons Criminal Procedure Competition. They also participate in the Immigration Law Moot Court Competition, the annual Domenick L. Gabrielli National Family Moot Court Competition, and the annual Nassau Academy of Law Moot Court Competition. Student organizations, local chapters of national associations, and campus organizations include the Labor Coalition for Workers' Rights and Economic Justice, Domestic Violence Coalition, Mississippi Project, National Lawyers Guild, American Civil Liberties Union, Black Law Students Association, Public Interest Law Organization, International Law Organization, and OUTLaws.

Library

The law library contains 284,829 hardcopy volumes and 1,063,674 microform volume equivalents, and subscribes to 3077 serial publications. Such on-line databases and networks as CALI, DIALOG, Dow-Jones, Infotrac, Legal-Trac, LEXIS, LOIS, Mathew Bender, NEXIS, OCLC First Search, WESTLAW, Wilsonline Indexes, CIAD, Earthscape, LLMC Digital, HeinOnline, Gale Virtual Reference Library, Global Jurist, Index to Foreign Legal Periodicals, IndexMaster, and BNA are available to law students for research. Special library collections include a U.S. Government Printing Office depository; the school is a member of the New York Joint International Law Program Consortium. Recently, the library maintains a large number of student access computer terminals, microform readers, microform reader-printers, and wireless network. The ratio of library volumes to faculty is 7698 to 1 and to students is 702 to 1. The ratio of seats in the library to students is 1 to 1.

Faculty

The law school has 37 full-time and 11 part-time faculty members, of whom 28 are women. According to AAUP standards for Category IIA institutions, faculty salaries are above average. About 37% of full-time faculty have a graduate law degree in addition to the J.D.; about 11% of part-time faculty have one. The ratio of full-time students to full-time faculty in an average class is 10 to 1; in a clinic, 8 to 1. The law school has a regular program of bringing visiting professors and other distinguished lecturers and visitors to campus.

Placement

J.D.s awarded:	121
Services available through: a separate law school placement center	
Services: counseling, seminars, workshops, and panels with local practitioners, faculty, and alumni	
Special features: The Career Planning Office is responsible for helping students find meaningful work. Special focus is placed on public interest careers.	
Full-time job interviews:	11 employers
Summer job interviews:	5 employers
Placement by graduation:	42% of class
Placement within 9 months:	92% of class
Average starting salary:	$41,000 to $55,000
Areas of placement:	
Private practice 2-10 attorneys	27%
Private practice 51-100 attorneys	1%
Public interest	27%
Government	19%
Judicial clerkships	11%
Business/industry	11%
Academic	4%

Students

About 63% of the student body are women; 31%, minorities; 8%, African American; 11%, Asian American; and 11%, Hispanic. The majority of students come from New York (64%). The average age of entering students is 26; age range is 21 to 55. About 12% of students have a graduate degree. Less than 1% drop out after the first year for academic or personal reasons; almost 100% remain to receive a law degree.

Cleveland-Marshall College of Law

2121 Euclid Avenue LB138
Cleveland, OH 44115-2214

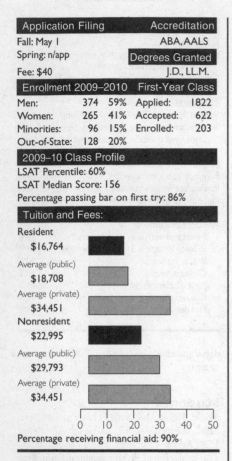

Application Filing	Accreditation
Fall: May 1	ABA, AALS
Spring: n/app	**Degrees Granted**
Fee: $40	J.D., LL.M.

Enrollment 2009–2010		First-Year Class	
Men:	374 59%	Applied:	1822
Women:	265 41%	Accepted:	622
Minorities:	96 15%	Enrolled:	203
Out-of-State:	128 20%		

2009–10 Class Profile
LSAT Percentile: 60%
LSAT Median Score: 156
Percentage passing bar on first try: 86%

Tuition and Fees:

Resident
$16,764

Average (public)
$18,708

Average (private)
$34,451

Nonresident
$22,995

Average (public)
$29,793

Average (private)
$34,451

0   10   20   30   40   50

Percentage receiving financial aid: 90%

ADMISSIONS

In the fall 2009 first-year class, 1822 applied, 622 were accepted, and 203 enrolled. Twenty transfers enrolled. The median LSAT percentile of the most recent first-year class was 60; the median GPA was 3.44 on a scale of 4.0. The lowest LSAT percentile accepted was 11; the highest was 98.

Requirements
Applicants must have a bachelor's degree and take the LSAT. Minimum acceptable GPA is 2.0 on a scale of 4.0. The most important admission factors include academic achievement, LSAT results, and general background. No specific undergraduate courses are required. Candidates are not interviewed.

Procedure
The application deadline for fall entry is May 1. Applicants should submit an application form, LSAT results, transcripts, a personal statement, TOEFL, if English is not the primary language, a nonrefund-able application fee of $40, 2 letters of recommendation, and a personal statement. Notification of the admissions decision is on a rolling basis beginning in December. The latest acceptable LSAT test date for fall entry is June. The law school uses the LSDAS.

Special
The law school recruits minority and disadvantaged students by means of the Legal Career Opportunities Program (LCOP), a special admissions program for applicants whose background and experience deserve special consideration. The Admissions Committee invites applicants whose test scores or undergraduate GPA are not strong but whose skills, accomplishments, and other qualifications merit consideration. The Admissions Committee seeks to admit candidates who have encountered adversity but have a record of accomplishment, either academic or professional. LCOP begins in the early part of June and continues through mid-July; students earn 2 or 3 semester credits, depending on the summer course that is offered, and credit is applied to the J.D. degree. Requirements are not different for out-of-state students. Transfer students must have a minimum GPA of 3.0 and have attended an ABA-approved law school.

Costs

Tuition and fees for the 2009-2010 academic year are $16,764 for full-time in-state students and $22,995 for out-of-state students. Tuition for part-time students is $12,895 in-state and $17,689 out-of-state. On-campus room and board costs about $13,000 annually; books and supplies run $5800.

Financial Aid

About 90% of current law students receive some form of aid. The average annual amount of aid from all sources combined, including scholarships, loans, and work contracts, is $18,076; maximum, $36,152. Awards are based on need and merit. Required financial statements are the FAFSA and Law Aid Application. The aid application deadline for fall entry is May 1. There are special funds for minority or disadvantaged students. Students who complete the admissions and financial aid materials are considered for these funds. First-year students are notified about their financial aid application at time of acceptance.

About the Law School

Cleveland State University Cleveland-Marshall College of Law was established in 1897 and is a public institution. The 120-acre campus is in an urban area in downtown Cleveland. The primary mission of the law school is to foster a more just society through legal education, service, and scholarship, and to enable a diverse population of students to become accomplished, ethical citizen-lawyers who will make significant contributions to the region, the nation, and the world. Students have access to federal, state, county, city, and local agencies, courts, correctional facilities, law firms, and legal aid organizations in the Cleveland area. Facilities of special interest to law students are the intramural competitions, student health services, library, university and law recreation center, Cleveland Public Library, physical education facilities, University Circle Cultural Arts Center, Playhouse Square, student counseling services, professional sports team, museums, and the Rock 'N Roll Hall of Fame and Museum. Housing for students is available on campus, in the city, and in nearby suburbs, many within a 15- to 20-minute commuting distance. All law school facilities are accessible to the physically disabled.

Calendar

The law school operates on a traditional semester basis. Courses for full-time students are offered during the day only in the first year; afterward, in the day and evening, and must be completed within 6 years. For part-time students, courses are offered both day and evening and must be completed within 6 years. New full- and part-time students are admitted in the fall. There is a 7½ -week summer session. Transferable summer courses are offered.

Programs

In addition to the J.D., the law school offers the LL.M. Students may take relevant courses in other programs and apply credit toward the J.D.; a maximum of 8 credits may be applied. The following joint degrees may be earned: J.D./M.A.E.S. (Juris Doctor/Master of Environmental Studies), J.D./M.B.A. (Juris Doctor/Master of Business Administration), J.D./M.P.A. (Juris Doctor/Master

Phone: 216-687-2304

866-687-2304

Fax: 216-687-6881

E-mail: *christophe.lcak@law.csuohio.edu*

Web: *www.law.csuohio.edu*

Contact

Christopher Lucak, Assistant Dean for Admissions, 216-687-2304 for general inquiries and financial aid information.

OHIO

of Public Administration), J.D./M.S.E.S. (Juris Doctor/Master of Environmental Science), and J.D/M.U.P.D.D. (Juris Doctor/Master of Urban Planning, Design and Development).

Required

To earn the J.D., candidates must complete 90 total credits, of which 41 are for required courses. They must maintain a minimum GPA of 2.0 in the required courses. The following first-year courses are required of all students: Civil Procedure, Contracts, Criminal Law, Legal Writing, Property, and Torts. Required upper-level courses consist of Constitutional Law, Evidence, and Legal Profession. Students must take a skills course, which includes clinical courses. The required orientation program for first-year students is 5 days and includes social activities, legal writing and demonstration classes, library tours, peer adviser meetings, and technology setup.

Electives

Students must take 18 to 26 credits in their area of concentration. The Cleveland-Marshall College of Law offers concentrations in corporate law, criminal law, international law, labor law, litigation, civil litigation, and dispute resolution. In addition, the Employment Law Clinic offers from 6 to 10 credits, the Urban Development Law Clinic offers from 2 to 10 credits, the Fair Housing Clinic offers from 2 to 8 credits, the Environmental Law Clinic offers 2 to 4 credits, and the Community Health Advocacy Law Clinic offers 3 credits. Upper-level students may take seminars and up to 3 hours of independent research; seminar papers fulfill the upper-level writing requirement. A judicial externship is worth 6 credits; students work 24 hours a week in a federal or state appellate court. A U.S. attorney externship is worth 4 credits; students are placed in a civil or criminal U.S. attorney's office. There are independent/public service externships worth 4 to 6 hours. Special lecture series include the Cleveland-Marshall Lecture Series, the Criminal Law Forums, and Labor and Employment Lecture Series. Students may participate in study-abroad programs run by ABA/AALS-approved law schools. Cleveland-Marshall also sponsors an ABA/AALS summer program in St. Petersburg, Russia. First-year students admitted to the Legal Career Opportunities Program are offered a course in Legal Process. An Academic Excellence program is offered.

Cleveland-Marshall has a Manager of Student Affairs who oversees minority programs. A variety of special interest group programs are available. The most widely taken electives are Advocacy, Business, and Employment Law.

Graduation Requirements

In order to graduate, candidates must have a GPA of 2.0, have completed the upper-division writing requirement, and have completed a course with an administrative component of law, evidence, and legal profession. A perspective course, a skills course, and a third semester of Legal Writing are also required.

Organizations

Students edit the *Cleveland State Law Review*, the *Journal of Law and Health*, and the newspaper *The Gavel*. The college sends teams to various competitions throughout the United States, including the National Appellate Advocacy, International Environmental Law, and National Criminal Procedure competitions. Other competitions include the Jessup International Law, Entertainment and Communication Law, National Animal Advocacy, Information Technology and Privacy Law, and Evidence competitions. Law student organizations, local chapters of national associations, and campus organizations include Entertainment and Sports Law Association, Federalist Society, Student Public Interest Law Organization, ABA-Law Student Division, Delta Theta Phi, Black Law Students Association, Criminal Law Society, and the Association for Environmental Law and Sustainability.

Library

The law library contains 538,989 hardcopy volumes and 234,094 microform volume equivalents, and subscribes to 1828 serial publications. Such on-line databases and networks as CALI, CIS Universe, LEXIS, NEXIS, WESTLAW, Wilsonline Indexes, SCHOLAR, OhioLINK, HeinOnline, LLMC Online, Gongwer, EPIC, and OCLC are available to law students for research. Special library collections include federal government documents. Recently, the library added a 4-story structure with 85,000 square feet, including a 52-seat computer laboratory, 207 student carrels, and 17 group-study rooms. The ratio of library volumes to faculty is 12,536 to 1 and to students is 843 to 1. The ratio of seats in the library to students is 5 to 6.

Placement

J.D.s awarded:	201

Services available through: a separate law school placement center

Services: practice interviews, matching students with local attorneys for interest interviews, and career-related workshops

Special features: There is individualized counseling, skills and cover letter development, references and resources, and job postings containing more than 1000 employment opportunities annually.

Full-time job interviews:	14 employers
Summer job interviews:	31 employers
Placement by graduation:	73% of class
Placement within 9 months:	90% of class
Average starting salary:	$36,000 to $120,000

Areas of placement:

Private practice 2-10 attorneys	23%
Private practice 11-25 attorneys	4%
Private practice 26-50 attorneys	5%
Private practice 51-100+ attorneys	35%
Business/industry	23%
Solo practice	4%
Government	10%
Judicial clerkships	5%
Public interest	3%
Academic	3%
Military	2%

Faculty

The law school has 43 full-time and 34 part-time faculty members, of whom 31 are women. According to AAUP standards for Category I institutions, faculty salaries are well below average. About 20% of full-time faculty have a graduate law degree in addition to the J.D. The ratio of full-time students to full-time faculty in an average class is 17 to 1; in a clinic, 4 to 1. The law school has a regular program of bringing visiting professors and other distinguished lecturers and visitors to campus.

Students

About 41% of the student body are women; 15%, minorities; 9%, African American; 3%, Asian American; and 3%, Hispanic. The majority of students come from the Midwest (83%). The average age of entering students is 26; age range is 21 to 54. About 41% of students enter directly from undergraduate school and 10% have a graduate degree. About 17% drop out after the first year for academic or personal reasons; 83% remain to receive a law degree.

Cleveland State University   **257**

William & Mary Law School

P.O. Box 8795
Williamsburg, VA 23187-8795

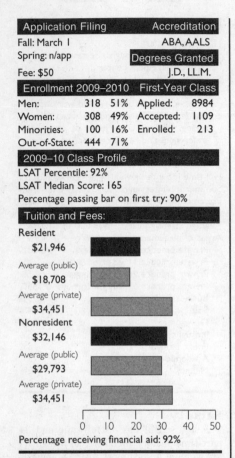

Application Filing	Accreditation
Fall: March 1	ABA, AALS
Spring: n/app	**Degrees Granted**
Fee: $50	J.D., LL.M.

Enrollment 2009–2010		First-Year Class	
Men:	318 51%	Applied:	8984
Women:	308 49%	Accepted:	1109
Minorities:	100 16%	Enrolled:	213
Out-of-State:	444 71%		

2009–10 Class Profile
LSAT Percentile: 92%
LSAT Median Score: 165
Percentage passing bar on first try: 90%

Tuition and Fees:

Resident
$21,946

Average (public)
$18,708

Average (private)
$34,451

Nonresident
$32,146

Average (public)
$29,793

Average (private)
$34,451

0 10 20 30 40 50

Percentage receiving financial aid: 92%

ADMISSIONS

In the fall 2009 first-year class, 8984 applied, 1109 were accepted, and 213 enrolled. Three transfers enrolled. The median LSAT percentile of the most recent first-year class was 92; the median GPA was 3.66 on a scale of 4.0. The lowest LSAT percentile accepted was 20; the highest was 99.

Requirements
Applicants must have a bachelor's degree and take the LSAT. Minimum acceptable GPA is 2.0 on a scale of 4.0. All factors in a candidate's background are considered important in the application process. No specific undergraduate courses are required. Candidates are interviewed.

Procedure
The application deadline for fall entry is March 1. Applicants should submit an application form, LSAT results, transcripts, a personal statement, a nonrefundable application fee of $50, and 2 letters of recommendation. Notification of

the admissions decision is from November through April. The latest acceptable LSAT test date for fall entry is February. The law school uses the LSDAS.

Special
The law school recruits minority and disadvantaged students by means of on- and off-campus recruitment, brochures, grant proposals, LSDAS Candidate Referral Services, BLSA Programs, DiscoverLaw.org, and financial aid. Requirements are not different for out-of-state students. Transfer students must have attended an ABA-approved law school and have approximately 26 credit hours.

Costs

Tuition and fees for the 2009-2010 academic year are $21,946 for full-time in-state students and $32,146 for out-of-state students. On-campus room and board costs about $13,650 annually; books and supplies run $1300.

Financial Aid

About 92% of current law students receive some form of aid. The average annual amount of aid from all sources combined, including scholarships, loans, and work contracts, is $33,142; maximum, $61,737. Awards are based on need and merit. Required financial statement is the FAFSA. The aid application deadline for fall entry is February 15. Diversity is a factor in awarding scholarships. First-year students are notified about their financial aid application from November through April.

About the Law School

College of William & Mary, William & Mary Law School, was established in 1779 and is a public institution. The 1200-acre campus is in a small town 45 miles west of Norfolk, 45 miles east of Richmond. The primary mission of the law school is to provide students with a superior legal education in a close-knit collegial environment and to offer the opportunity to confront the demands of constructive citizenship and leadership. Students have access to federal, state, county, city, and local agencies, courts, correctional facilities, law firms, and legal aid organizations in the Williamsburg area. The National Center for State Courts and Colonial Williamsburg are nearby. Facilities of special interest to law students include the Center

for Legal and Court Technology, the world center for courtroom technology research, housed within the McGlothlin Courtroom, the world's most technologically advanced courtroom. The project has an extensive student staff, trains all second-year students in hands-on courtroom technology use, and supports the law school activities and courses, such as the legal technology seminar and technology augmented trial advocacy. The law school is a wireless facility allowing access to on-line Internet services throughout the building and adjacent patios and lawns. Housing for students is available on-campus in graduate apartments located next to the law school building. Commercial apartments, townhouses, and other area housing are available as well. Williamsburg is "family friendly" with many neighborhoods and services for those students with children. All law school facilities are accessible to the physically disabled.

Calendar

The law school operates on a traditional semester basis. Courses for full-time students are offered days only and must be completed within 3 years. There is no part-time program. New students are admitted in the fall. There is a 4-week summer session. Transferable summer courses are offered.

Programs

In addition to the J.D., the law school offers the LL.M. Students may take relevant courses in other programs and apply credit toward the J.D.; a maximum of 6 credits may be applied. The following joint degrees may be earned: J.D./M.A. (Juris Doctor/Master of Arts in American studies), J.D./M.B.A. (Juris Doctor/Master of Business Administration), and J.D./M.P.P. (Juris Doctor/Master of Public Policy).

Required
To earn the J.D., candidates must complete 86 total credits, of which 34 are for required courses. They must maintain a minimum GPA of 1.8 in the required courses. The following first-year courses are required of all students: Civil Procedure, Constitutional Law, Criminal Law, Legal Skills, Property, and Torts. Required upper-level courses consist of Ethics and Legal Skills. The required orientation program for first-year stu-

Phone: 757-221-3785
Fax: 757-221-3261
E-mail: lawadm@wm.edu
Web: www.law.wm.edu

Contact

Faye F. Shealy, Associate Dean, 757-221-3785 for general inquiries; Ed Irish, Director of Student Financial Aid, 757-221-2420 for financial aid information.

VIRGINIA

dents is a 1-week program designed to introduce legal analysis, legal vocabulary, legal teaching methods, legal writing, and the law firm structure of the Legal Skills Program.

Electives

In addition, clinics, worth 3 credits, combine a classroom component with supervised work in an office setting and include domestic violence, children's advocacy, veteran's benefits, and federal tax practice. Seminars, worth 2 to 3 credits, are open to both second- and third-year students (size limited to 15 to 25 students) and include civil rights, corporate drafting, and legal technology. Internships, worth 1 to 3 credits, include Attorney General Practice, Virginia Court of Appeals, Criminal Litigation, Non-Profit Organizations, and Private Practice/ In-House Counsel. Research programs, worth 1 to 2 credits, include independent research, advanced research, and directed reading. They are open to second- and third-year students and must be completed with a supervising professor. Field work is offered through an externship program open to second- and third-year students for 1 to 3 credits. Externships require a minimum of 40 hours of work, a synopsis of work done, a journal, and an evaluation by the supervising attorney or judge. Placements may be made with a judge, nonprofit organization, private practice, or government agency. Special lectures include the Institute of Bill of Rights Law, Cutler Lectures, and George Wythe Lectures. Study abroad is available in the summer in Madrid, Spain, with most classes worth 2 credits and open to any second- or third-year student who applies from an ABA accredited law school. In addition, semester abroad exchange programs are available to second- and third-year students in China, Japan, New Zealand, Spain, Austria, and Luxemborg. Tutorial programs are available to any first-year student. Minority programs are arranged by minority student organizations. Special interest group programs are arranged by individual student organizations. The most widely taken electives are criminal procedure, evidence, and business associations.

Graduation Requirements

In order to graduate, candidates must have a GPA of 2.0 and have completed the upper-division writing requirement.

Organizations

Students edit the *William and Mary Law Review, William & Mary Bill of Rights Journal, William and Mary Journal of Women in the Law, William and Mary Environmental Law and Policy Review, William and Mary Law Review*, and *William and Mary Business Law Review*. Ten teams compete each year at competitions such as the National Tournament, ABA Tournament, and Vanderbilt University First Amendment Invitational Tournament. Each year the school sponsors the National Trial Team competitions and the Bushrod T. Washington Moot Court Tournament, which is open to first-year students.The William B. Spong, Jr. Invitational Moot Court Tournament attracts 24 teams from throughout the nation annually. The Alternative Dispute Resolution team hosts an ABA competition every 3 to 5 years. Law student organizations, local chapters of national associations, and campus organizations include the Sports and Entertainment Law Society, International Law Society, Military Law Society, Lesbian and Gay Student Association, Black Law Students Association, Phi Alpha Delta, Christian Legal Society, Public Service Fund, and George Wythe Society.

Library

The law library contains 406,000 hardcopy volumes and 929,860 microform volume equivalents, and subscribes to 4234 serial publications. Such on-line databases and networks as CALI, Legal-Trac, LEXIS, LOIS, Matthew Bender, NEXIS, OCLC First Search, WESTLAW, First Search, VIVA, and LexisNexis Academic Factiva are available to law students for research. Special library collections include Thomas Jefferson, and George Wythe law collections, environmental law, Roman law, constitutional law, jurisprudence, and intellectual property. Recently, the library was expanded and completely renovated. The ratio of library volumes to faculty is 11,600 to 1 and to students is 649 to 1. The ratio of seats in the library to students is 1 to 1.

Faculty

The law school has 35 full-time and 70 part-time faculty members, of whom 31 are women. According to AAUP standards for Category 1 institutions, faculty salaries are below average. About 11% of full-

Placement

J.D.s awarded:	192

Services available through: a separate law school placement center and students have access to the University's other career services offices

Services: video conference interviews, summer public service fellowships, post-graduate public service fellowships, 34 off-campus interview programs, loan repayment assistance, judicial clerkships, and externships for academic credit

Special features: The career services staff includes professionals who have significant experience in career counseling, practicing law, and lawyer recruiting and hiring. The emphasis is on individualized career planning for students with extensive programs and resources designed to enable them to make informed career choices.

Full-time job interviews:	51 employers
Summer job interviews:	174 employers
Placement by graduation:	88% of class
Placement within 9 months:	97% of class
Average starting salary:	$33,700 to $225,000

Areas of placement:

Private practice 2-10 attorneys	12%
Private practice 11-25 attorneys	2%
Private practice 26-50 attorneys	2%
Private practice 51-100 attorneys	6%
Judicial clerkships	14%
Government	8%
Business/industry	7%
Military	7%
Public interest	4%

time faculty have a graduate law degree in addition to the J.D.; about 6% of part-time faculty have one. The ratio of full-time students to full-time faculty in an average class is 34 to 1; in a clinic, 6 to 1. The law school has a regular program of bringing visiting professors and other distinguished lecturers and visitors to campus. There is a chapter of the Order of the Coif; 12 faculty and 574 graduates are members.

Students

About 49% of the student body are women; 16%, minorities; 12%, African American; 3%, Asian American; 1%, Hispanic; and 19%, unknown. The majority of students come from Virginia (29%). The average age of entering students is 24; age range is 18 to 50. About 52% of students enter directly from undergraduate school, 8% have a graduate degree, and 48% have worked full-time prior to entering law school. About 1% drop out after the first year for academic or personal reasons; 99% remain to receive a law degree.

School of Law

435 West 116th Street
New York, NY 10027

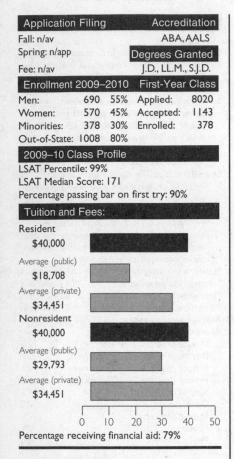

Application Filing		Accreditation	
Fall: n/av		ABA, AALS	
Spring: n/app		**Degrees Granted**	
Fee: n/av		J.D., LL.M., S.J.D.	

Enrollment 2009–2010		First-Year Class	
Men:	690 55%	Applied:	8020
Women:	570 45%	Accepted:	1143
Minorities:	378 30%	Enrolled:	378
Out-of-State:	1008 80%		

2009–10 Class Profile
LSAT Percentile: 99%
LSAT Median Score: 171
Percentage passing bar on first try: 90%

Tuition and Fees:

Resident
$40,000

Average (public)
$18,708

Average (private)
$34,451

Nonresident
$40,000

Average (public)
$29,793

Average (private)
$34,451

0   10   20   30   40   50

Percentage receiving financial aid: 79%

ADMISSIONS

In a recent year, 8020 applied, 1143 were accepted, and 378 enrolled. Forty-eight transfers enrolled. The median LSAT percentile of the most recent first-year class was 99; the median GPA was 3.67 on a scale of 4.0. The lowest LSAT percentile accepted was 50; the highest was 99. Figures in the above capsule and in this profile are approximate.

Requirements
Applicants must have a bachelor's degree and take the LSAT. No specific undergraduate courses are required. Candidates are not interviewed.

Procedure
Applicants should submit an application form, LSAT results, transcripts, and 2 letters of recommendation. Notification of the admissions decision is December through April. The latest acceptable LSAT test date for fall entry is December. The law school uses the LSDAS.

Special
The law school recruits minority and disadvantaged students through outreach efforts, counseling initiatives, and national database searches with invitations to apply. Requirements are not different for out-of-state students. Transfer students must have one year of credit, have attended an ABA-approved law school, and have completed the first year with distinction at an ABA-approved law school or at an accredited Canadian law school.

Costs

Tuition and fees for the 2009-2010 academic year are approximately $40,000 for all full-time students. On-campus room and board costs about is approximately $16,950 annually; books and supplies run $950.

Financial Aid

In a recent year, about 79% of current law students received some form of aid. The average annual amount of aid from all sources combined, including scholarships, loans, and work contracts, was approximately $47,000; maximum, $65,000. Awards are based on need along with financial aid grants are awarded on the basis of need; a small number of merit-based awards are also offered. Required financial statements are the FAFSA and Need Access application. First-year students are notified about their financial aid application at time of acceptance. Check with the school for current application deadlines.

About the Law School

Columbia University School of Law was established in 1858 and is a private institution. The 36-acre campus is in an urban area the Morningside Heights section of northwest Manha. The primary mission of the law school is to serve as one of the world's leading centers of research and scholarship regarding law and its role in society. Students have access to federal, state, county, city, and local agencies, courts, correctional facilities, law firms, and legal aid organizations in the New York area. The city of New York offers students a broad range of opportunities. Facilities of special interest to law students The law school recently completed a $133 million expansion and renewal project. Across the street from Greene Hall, the law school's main building, is William C. Warren hall, home to the *Columbia Law review*, Morn-

ingside Heights Legal Services, and then Center for Public Interest Law. Housing for students includes on-campus apartments, available to both single students and couples; the Off-Campus Housing Office (OCHA) helps students find off-campus housing. All admitted first-year students who apply for housing by May 1 are guaranteed some type of university housing for all 3 years of the J.D. program. About 98% of the law school facilities are accessible to the physically disabled.

Calendar

The law school operates on a traditional semester basis. Courses for full-time students are offered days only. There is no part-time program. New students are admitted in the fall. There is no summer session. Transferable summer courses are not offered.

Programs

In addition to the J.D., the law school offers the LL.M. and S.J.D. Students may take relevant courses in other programs and apply credit toward the J.D.; a maximum of 10 credits may be applied. The following joint degrees may be earned: J.D./ M.B.A. (Juris Doctor/Master of Business Administration), J.D./M.A., M.Phil., or P (Juris Doctor/Master of Arts or Doctor of Philosophy), J.D./M.F.A. (Juris Doctor/Master of Arts in theater arts), J.D./M.I.A. (Juris Doctor/Master of International Affairs), J.D./M.P.A. (Juris Doctor/Master of Public Administration), J.D./M.P.H. (Juris Doctor/Master of Public Health), J.D./M.S. (Juris Doctor/Master of Science in journalism or urban planning), and J.D./M.S.W. (Juris Doctor/Master of Social Work).

Required
To earn the J.D., candidates must complete 83 total credits, of which 35 are for required courses. The following first-year courses are required of all students: Civil Procedure, Constitutional Law, Contracts, Criminal Law, Critical Legal Thought, Foundation of the Regulatory State, Foundation Year Moot Court, Law and Contemporary Society, Law and Economics, Law and Social Science, Lawyering Across Multiple Legal Orders, Legal Methods and Legal Writing and Research, Legislation, Property, The Rule of Law:perspectives on Legal Thought, and Torts. Required upper-level courses consist of a minimum of 2 writing credits earned, a pro bono ser-

Phone: 212-854-2670
Fax: 212-854-1109
E-mail: admissions@law.columbia.edu
Web: www.law.columbia.edu

Contact

Admissions Office, 212-854-2674 for general inquiries; Assistant Dean of Registration and, 212-854-6522 for financial aid information.

NEW YORK

vice requirement (40 hours in second and third, and Profession of Law (focusing on professional ethics). Clinics are electives. The required orientation program for first-year students lasts 2 days and starts before the Legal Methods course begins.

Electives

The School of Law offers concentrations in corporate law, criminal law, entertainment law, environmental law, family law, international law, labor law, litigation, media law, securities law, sports law, tax law, torts and insurance, and constitutional law, human rights law, labor law, history and philosophy of law, health care and the law, and education law. In addition, Clinics such as child advocacy, law and the arts, environmental law, human rights, lawyering in the digital age, mediation, nonprofit organizations/small business, and prisoners and families offer client-based experiences to upper-class students for 5 to 7 points. 130 seminars are offered annually in such areas as Constitutional Law, Corporate Law, and Human Rights for 2 points (generally). Admission to a seminar is by lottery. Additional training through internships is available through arrangements with city agencies and consumer advocacy groups; clerkships with criminal, appellate, and federal court judges; and the pro bono service requirement. Research may be done as part of the legal writing requirement. Credit may be earned in journal work, independent, or supervised research. Law school lectures regularly bring leading figures from business, politics, entertainment, and areas of the law and judiciary to Columbia. There is a 4-year double degree program with the University of Paris, giving students a J.D. and Maitrise en Droit; a 3-year J.D./D.E.S.S. with the Institut d'Etudes Politique Sciences, a 4-year program with the University of London, giving students a J.D. and LL.B., a 3-year program with the University of London where students receive a Columbia J.D. and University of London LL.M., and a 3-year program with the Institute for Law and Finance (Johann Wolfgang Goethe Universuty, Frankfurt) where students receive a Columbia J.D. and Institute for Law and France LL.M. Students may also elect to initiate a study abroad program in additional countries.

Graduation Requirements

In order to graduate, candidates must have completed the upper-division writing requirement and satisfied degree require-

ments (including pro bono service) and a course in professional responsibility and ethics in the third year.

Organizations

Students edit the *Columbia Law Review, Columbia Journal of Environmental Law, Columbia Human Rights Law Review, Columbia Journal of Law and Social Problems, Columbia Journal of Transactional Law, Columbia Journal of Asian Law, American Review of International Arbitration, Columbia-VLA Journal of Law and the Arts, Columbia Business Law Review, Columbia Journal of Gender and the Law, Parker School Journal of East European Law, Columbia Journal of European Law, Columbia Science and Technology Law Review*, and *National Black Law Journal*. Students also edit the newspaper *Columbia Law School News* and the yearbook *Pegasus*. The Moot Court Committee sponsors the Harlan Fiske Stone Honor Competition and the Jerome Michael Jury Trials. Students also participate, with distinction, in the Jessup International Moot Court Competition. Other competitions include the Frederick Douglass National Competition and Native American Law Students Moot Court Competition.

Library

The law library contains 1,092,534 hardcopy volumes and 235,424 microform volume equivalents, and subscribes to 6472 serial publications. Such on-line databases and networks as CALI, CIS Universe, DIALOG, Infotrac, Legal-Trac, LEXIS, LOIS, Mathew Bender, NEXIS, OCLC First Search, RLIN, WESTLAW, Wilson-line Indexes, and Jutastat, CCH, PLC Global, UN ODS, TIARA TREATIES, BNA, China Law and Practice, Constitutions of the World (Oceana), Foreign Law Guide, Hein Online, Indexmaster, Inter-Am Database, Arbitration Online, LLMC digital, Making of Modern Law, PACER, BNA International/Intellectual Property, and others. are available to law students for research. Special library collections include a notable collection on foreign law, Roman law, and a large rare book collection of more than 30,000 volumes, Perlin/Rosenberg Papers, as well as papers from the Nuremberg Trials and the South African Treason Trials. The reference staff (all with J.D.s and M.L.S.s taught the Legal Research program for second-year students. The ratio of library volumes to faculty is 11,148 to 1 and to students is

880 to 1. The ratio of seats in the library to students is 1 to 4.

Faculty

The law school has 98 full-time and 69 part-time faculty members, of whom 51 are women. According to AAUP standards for Category I institutions, faculty salaries are well above average. About 15% of full-time faculty have a graduate law degree in addition to the J.D.; about 10% of part-time faculty have one. The ratio of full-time students to full-time faculty in an average class is 13 to 1; in a clinic, 8 to 1. The law school has a regular program of bringing visiting professors and other distinguished lecturers and visitors to campus.

Students

About 45% of the student body are women; 30%, minorities; 10%, African American; 18%, Asian American; 7%, Hispanic; and 7%, international students. The majority of students come from New York (20%). The average age of entering students is 24. About 33% of students enter directly from undergraduate school and 11% have a graduate degree.

CORNELL UNIVERSITY

Law School

Myron Taylor Hall
Ithaca, NY 14853-4901

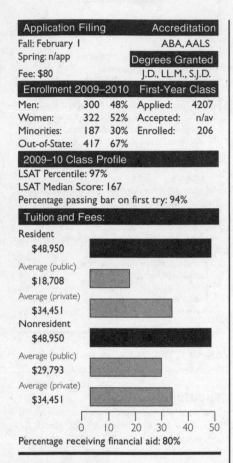

Application Filing		Accreditation	
Fall: February 1		ABA, AALS	
Spring: n/app		**Degrees Granted**	
Fee: $80		J.D., LL.M., S.J.D.	

Enrollment 2009–2010		First-Year Class	
Men:	300 48%	Applied:	4207
Women:	322 52%	Accepted:	n/av
Minorities:	187 30%	Enrolled:	206
Out-of-State:	417 67%		

2009–10 Class Profile
LSAT Percentile: 97%
LSAT Median Score: 167
Percentage passing bar on first try: 94%

Tuition and Fees:

Resident
$48,950

Average (public)
$18,708

Average (private)
$34,451

Nonresident
$48,950

Average (public)
$29,793

Average (private)
$34,451

0 10 20 30 40 50

Percentage receiving financial aid: 80%

ADMISSIONS
In the fall 2009 first-year class, 4207 applied and 206 enrolled. Ten transfers enrolled. The median LSAT percentile of the most recent first-year class was 97; the median GPA was 3.63 on a scale of 4.0.

Requirements
Applicants must have a bachelor's degree and take the LSAT. No specific undergraduate courses are required. Candidates are not interviewed.

Procedure
The application deadline for fall entry is February 1. Applicants should submit an application form, LSAT results, a non-refundable application fee of $80, 2 letters of recommendation, and a personal statement. Transcripts must be sent via the LSDAS. Notification of the admissions decision is mid to late December (early action). The latest acceptable LSAT test date for fall entry is October (early action) December (regular decision). The law school uses the LSDAS.

Special
The law school recruits minority and disadvantaged students by aggressively encouraging them to apply. In addition, a student's minority or disadvantaged status is considered to be a positive part of the application; offers of financial aid are also made. Requirements are not different for out-of-state students. Transfer students must have 1 year of credit, have attended an ABA-approved law school, and must be in the top 10% of the class.

Costs
Tuition and fees for the 2009-2010 academic year are $48,950 for all full-time students. On-campus room and board costs about $11,000 annually; books and supplies run $850.

Financial Aid
About 80% of current law students receive some form of aid. The average annual amount of aid from all sources combined, including scholarships, loans, and work contracts, is $40,000; maximum, $67,250. Awards are based on need and merit. Required financial statements are the FAFSA and Need Access. The aid application deadline for fall entry is March 15. Special funds for minority or disadvantaged students include need-based enhanced grants. First-year students are notified about their financial aid application shortly after acceptance.

About the Law School
Cornell University Law School was established in 1888 and is a private institution. The 745-acre campus is in a small town 250 miles northwest of New York City. The primary mission of the law school is to teach law within the context of humanity. Students have access to federal, state, county, city, and local agencies, courts, correctional facilities, law firms, and legal aid organizations in the Ithaca area. A full range of opportunities consistent with a small city is available to students. Facilities of special interest to law students are the Legal Aid Clinic, Berger International Legal Studies Program, and the Legal Information Institute. Housing for students is ample both on and off campus. About 90% of the law school facilities are accessible to the physically disabled.

Calendar
The law school operates on a traditional semester basis. Courses for full-time students are offered days only and must be completed within 3 years. There is no part-time program. New students are admitted in the fall. There is a 4-week summer session. Transferable summer courses are offered.

Programs
In addition to the J.D., the law school offers the LL.M. and S.J.D. Students may take relevant courses in other programs and apply credit toward the J.D.; a maximum of 12 credits may be applied. The following joint degrees may be earned: J.D./D.M.A. (Juris Doctor/Doctor of Musical Arts), J.D./D.V.M. (Juris Doctor/Doctor of Veterinary Medicine), J.D./M.A. (Juris Doctor/Master of Arts), J.D./M.A.T. (Juris Doctor/Master of Teaching), J.D./M. Arch. (Juris Doctor/Master of Architecture), J.D./M.B.A. (Juris Doctor/Master of Business Administration), J.D./M.D. (Juris Doctor/Doctor of Medicine), J.D./M. Eng. (Juris Doctor/Master of Engineering), J.D./M.F.A. (Juris Doctor/Master of Fine Arts), J.D./M.F.S. (Juris Doctor/Master of Food Science), J.D./M.H.A. (Juris Doctor/Master of Health Administration), J.D./M.I.L.R. (Juris Doctor/Master of Industrial and Labor Relations), J.D./M.L.A. (Juris Doctor/Master of Landscape Architecture), J.D./M.M.H. (Juris Doctor/Master of Hospitality Management), J.D./M.P.A. (Juris Doctor/Master of Public Administration), J.D./M.P.S. (Juris Doctor/Master of Professional Studies), J.D./M.R.P. (Juris Doctor/Master of Regional Planning), J.D./M.S. (Juris Doctor/Master of Science), and J.D./Ph.D. (Juris Doctor/Doctor of Philosophy).

Required
To earn the J.D., candidates must complete 84 total credits, of which 36 are for required courses. They must maintain a minimum GPA of 2.3 in the required courses. The following first-year courses are required of all students: Civil Procedure, Constitutional Law, Contracts, Criminal Law, Lawyering, Property, and Torts. Required upper-level courses consist of a writing requirement (2 writing courses) and Professional Responsibility course. The required orientation program for first-year students is a 2-day introduction to the school.

NEW YORK

Phone: 607-255-5141
Fax: 607-255-7193
E-mail: *lawadmit@postoffice.law.cornell.edu*
Web: *lawschool.cornell.edu*

Contact

Admissions Office, 607-255-5141 for general inquiries; Financial Aid Office, 607-255-6292 for financial aid information.

Electives

Students must take 14 credits in their area of concentration. The Law School offers concentrations in advocacy, business law and regulation, general practice, and public law. In addition, clinics, worth 4 to 6 credits, include the Legal Aid Clinic, Women and Law Clinic, and Youth Law Clinic. Multiple seminars in the upper-division are open to a maximum of 16 students per semester. Internships include the judicial externship, Neighborhood Legal Services, Criminal Justice, and legislative. Full-term externships are worth 12 credits at approved sites. Special lecture series are the Berger International Lecture Series, the Robert S. Stevens Lecture Series, the Berger Program in International Law, Clarke Lectures (part of Clarke program in East Asian Law and Culture), and Cyrus Mehri lecture series in public interest with 14 partner schools. A minority orientation program and a diversity weekend for admitted applicants are held. The most widely taken electives are Corporations, Evidence, and Federal Income Taxation.

Graduation Requirements

In order to graduate, candidates must have a GPA of 2.3, have completed the upper-division writing requirement, first-year Lawyering Program, and Professional Responsibility course.

Organizations

Students edit the *Cornell Law Review, Cornell Journal of Law and Public Policy, Cornell International Law Journal, LII Bulletin-NY, LII Bulletin-Patent*, the student newspaper *Tower*, and the *Cornell Law Forum*. A variety of moot court competitions, such as the Cuccia Cup, Jessup, and Niagara CISG, are held, mostly at the school. Law student organizations include the Herbert W. Briggs Society of International Law, Cornell Law Students Association, and Environment Law Association. There are local chapters of National Lawyers Guild, Phi Delta Phi, and Order of the Coif.

Library

The law library contains 670,000 hardcopy volumes and 5500 microform volume equivalents, and subscribes to 6387 serial publications. Such on-line databases and networks as CALI, CIS Universe, DIALOG, Dow-Jones, Infotrac, Legal-Trac, LEXIS, LOIS, Mathew Bender, NEXIS, OCLC First Search, RLIN, WESTLAW, and Wilsonline Indexes are available to law students for research. Special library collections include international and foreign law, a U.S. government documents depository, the Bennett Collection of Statutory Materials, Donovan Nuremberg Trials Collection, and rare books. Recently, the library updated its web site. The ratio of library volumes to faculty is 12,641 to 1 and to students is 1077 to 1. The ratio of seats in the library to students is 1 to 1.

Faculty

The law school has 53 full-time and 60 part-time faculty members, of whom 30 are women. According to AAUP standards for Category 1 institutions, faculty salaries are above average. About 30% of full-time faculty have a graduate law degree in addition to the J.D.; about 1% of part-time faculty have one. The ratio of full-time students to full-time faculty in an average class is 10 to 1; in a clinic, 8 to 1. The law school has a regular program of bringing visiting professors and other distinguished lecturers and visitors to campus. There is a chapter of the Order of the Coif; 30 faculty and 18 graduates are members.

Students

About 52% of the student body are women; 30%, minorities; 45%, African American; 10%, Asian American; 5%, Hispanic; and 1%, Native American. The majority of students come from the Northeast (56%). The average age of entering students is 23; age range is 20 to 45. About 30% of students enter directly from undergraduate school, 10% have a graduate degree, and 70% have worked full-time prior to entering law school.

Placement

J.D.s awarded:	188

Services available through: a separate law school placement center
Services: off-campus job fairs in major U.S. cities
Special features: The Public Interest Low Income Protection Plan for loan forgiveness and moderate payback plans program is for students who intend to work in the public or nonprofit sector. Public Interest Foundation and work-study grants are available for summer public interest work..

Full-time job interviews:	125 employers
Summer job interviews:	302 employers
Placement by graduation:	95% of class
Placement within 9 months:	99% of class
Average starting salary:	$46,000 to $145,000

Areas of placement:

Private practice 11-25 attorneys	2%
Private practice 26-50 attorneys	2%
Private practice 51-100 attorneys	5%
Private practice 100+ attorneys, Unknown 5%	73%
Judicial clerkships	14%
Public interest	3%
Government	1%

CREIGHTON UNIVERSITY

School of Law

2500 California Plaza
Omaha, NE 68178

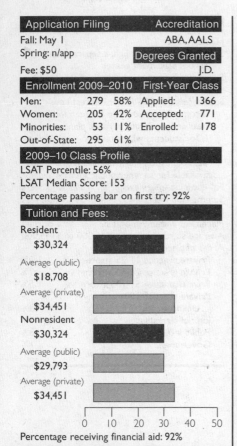

Application Filing		Accreditation
Fall: May 1		ABA, AALS
Spring: n/app		**Degrees Granted**
Fee: $50		J.D.

Enrollment 2009–2010		First-Year Class	
Men:	279 58%	Applied:	1366
Women:	205 42%	Accepted:	771
Minorities:	53 11%	Enrolled:	178
Out-of-State:	295 61%		

2009–10 Class Profile
LSAT Percentile: 56%
LSAT Median Score: 153
Percentage passing bar on first try: 92%

Tuition and Fees:

Resident
$30,324

Average (public)
$18,708

Average (private)
$34,451

Nonresident
$30,324

Average (public)
$29,793

Average (private)
$34,451

0   10   20   30   40   50

Percentage receiving financial aid: 92%

ADMISSIONS

In the fall 2009 first-year class, 1366 applied, 771 were accepted, and 178 enrolled. Seven transfers enrolled. The median LSAT percentile of the most recent first-year class was 56; the median GPA was 3.43 on a scale of 4.33. The lowest LSAT percentile accepted was 30; the highest was 94.

Requirements

Applicants must have a bachelor's degree and take the LSAT. The most important admission factors include LSAT results, GPA, and general background. No specific undergraduate courses are required. Candidates are not interviewed.

Procedure

The application deadline for fall entry is May 1. Applicants should submit an application form, LSAT results, transcripts, a personal statement, a nonrefundable application fee of $50, and 2 letters of recommendation. Notification of the admissions decision is on a rolling basis. The

latest acceptable LSAT test date for fall entry is June. The law school uses the LSDAS.

Special

The law school recruits minority and disadvantaged students by means of a substantial Diversity Scholarship Program, attending law and graduate fairs, participating in LSAC's DiscoverLaw.org program, and providing application fee waivers. Requirements are not different for out-of-state students. Transfer students must have one year of credit and have attended an ABA-approved law school.

Costs

Tuition and fees for the 2009-2010 academic year are $30,324 for all full-time students. On-campus room and board costs about $13,500 annually; books and supplies run $3085.

Financial Aid

About 92% of current law students receive some form of aid. The average annual amount of aid from all sources combined, including scholarships, loans, and work contracts, is $41,654; maximum, $68,617. Awards are based on need and merit. Loans are need-based, whereas scholarships are merit-based. Required financial statement is the FAFSA. The aid application deadline for fall entry is March 1. Special funds for minority or disadvantaged students include a substantial scholarship program for Native American, African American, Asian American, and Hispanic American applicants. First-year students are notified about their financial aid application at time of acceptance.

About the Law School

Creighton University School of Law was established in 1904 and is a private institution. The 129-acre campus is in an urban area near downtown Omaha. The primary mission of the law school is to train lawyers to practice in every jurisdiction in the United States and to prepare men and women to render morally responsible services in all phases of the administration of justice. Students have access to federal, state, county, city, and local agencies, courts, correctional facilities, law firms, and legal aid organizations in the Omaha area. The state's capital and legislature

are 45 minutes away by car. Facilities of special interest to law students include the Ahmanson Law Center, which houses all functions of the law school under one roof. The law school has full range and wireless coverage throughout the building. The law school is adjacent to the Harper Student Center. Housing for students is available in a university-owned high-rise apartment complex located 2 blocks from the law school, exclusively for use by professional students and families. Additional privately owned apartment complexes are located within walking distance. About 99% of the law school facilities are accessible to the physically disabled.

Calendar

The law school operates on a traditional semester basis. Courses for full-time students are offered both day and evening and must be completed within 3 years. For part-time students, courses are offered both day and evening and must be completed within 6 years. New full- and part-time students are admitted in the fall. There is a 5- to 6-week summer session. Transferable summer courses are offered.

Programs

Students may take relevant courses in other programs and apply credit toward the J.D.; a maximum of 6 credits may be applied. The following joint degrees may be earned: J.D./M.A. (Juris Doctor/Master of Arts in international relations), J.D./M.B.A. (Juris Doctor/Master of Business Administration), and J.D./M.S. (Juris Doctor/Master of Science in information technology management and negotiation and dispute resolution).

Required

To earn the J.D., candidates must complete 94 total credits, of which 57 are for required courses. They must maintain a minimum GPA of 2.0 in the required courses. The following first-year courses are required of all students: Civil Procedure I and II, Constitutional Law I and II, Contracts I and II, Legal Research, Legal Writing and Lawyering Skills I, Property I and II, and Torts I and II. Required upper-level courses consist of Business Associations, Criminal Procedure, Evidence, Legal Writing and Lawyering Skills II, Professional Responsibility, Secured Transactions in Personal Property, and

Phone: 402-280-2586
800-282-5835
Fax: 402-280-3161
E-mail: *lawadmit@creighton.edu*
Web: *www.creighton.edu/law*

Contact
Andrea D. Bashara, Assistant Dean, 402-280-2586 for general inquiries; Paula Kohles, Associate Director, 402-280-2731 for financial aid information.

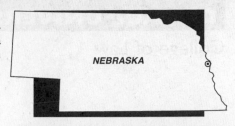

NEBRASKA

Trusts and Estates I. The required orientation program for first-year students is a 1 ½ = day program that includes an introduction to the Socratic method and preparing for the first day of class, financial aid presentation, a technology orientation, and mentor groups.

Electives
Students must take 18 credits in their area of concentration. The School of Law offers concentrations in corporate law, criminal law, international law, and litigation. In addition, clinics include the Milton R. Abrahams Legal Clinic, and the Community Economic Development Clinic, which are worth 2 to 4 credits and are open to third-year students who have completed all required courses. Seminars, worth 2 and 3 credits, include the Comparative Criminal Procedure, International Human Rights Law and Mediation Seminar. Internships are offered to eligible upper-level students in many different city, county, and federal offices and legal aid offices. Participants serve as law clerks to the various attorneys and judges, for 3 nonclassroom hours. Students may select research topics and write papers for credit under the guidance of a faculty member. Special lecture series include the annual TePoel Lecture Series, Lane Foundation Lectures, and the Koley Lectures. The law school has an exchange program with Universidad Pontificia Comillas in Madrid, Spain. Students may earn up to 12 hours of law school credit through the exchange program. The Black Law Students Association and Latino Law Students Association offer tutorial programs to members. The law school has a Director of Academic Excellence to assist students in developing their skills for academic success. Tutors are available for first-year courses. A Legal Writing Center is available to assist students in developing their writing skills. The most widely taken electives are Conflict of Laws, Federal Income Taxation, and Criminal Law.

Graduation Requirements
In order to graduate, candidates must have a GPA of 2.0, and have completed the upper-division writing requirement.

Organizations
Students edit the *Creighton Law Review*. Moot court opportunities include the second-year intramural ABA regional, national, and international tournaments as well as invitational tournaments. Other competitions include the Negotiation Competition, Client Counseling, ABA National Criminal Justice Trial Advocacy Competition, Jessup International Moot Court Competition, and essay competitions. Student organizations include J. Reuben Clark, Fellowship of Christian Law Students, and American Constitution Society for Law and Policy. There are local chapters of Phi Alpha Delta, Phi Delta Phi, and the American Bar Association-Law Student Division. Other student organizations include the Public Interest Law Forum, Women's Law Student Association, and International Law Society.

Library
The law library contains 384,395 hardcopy volumes and 175,086 microform volume equivalents, and subscribes to 1606 serial publications. Such on-line databases and networks as CALI, CIS Universe, Infotrac, Legal-Trac, LEXIS, LOIS, Matthew Bender, NEXIS, OCLC First Search, WESTLAW, Wilsonline Indexes, HeinOnline, CCH, United Nations Treaty Collection, Academic Universe, Making of Modern Law, RIA Checkpoint, ILP and ILP Retro, Intelliconnect, and LLMC Digital are available to law students for research. The law library is a selective U.S. government depository consisting of a complete Congressional Information Service Legislative History service from 1970 to the present, Nebraska Appellate and Supreme Court briefs, and a rare book collection containing approximately 750 British and American legal texts from the 15th through the 19th centuries. Recently, the library expanded access to wireless network and enhanced the wireless security. The ratio of library volumes to faculty is 12,400 to 1 and to students is 794 to 1. The ratio of seats in the library to students is 1 to 2.

Faculty
The law school has 31 full-time and 39 part-time faculty members, of whom 20 are women. According to AAUP standards for Category IIA institutions, faculty salaries are average. About 29% of full-time faculty have a graduate law degree in addition to the J.D. The ratio of full-time students to full-time faculty in an average class is 18 to 1; in a clinic, 6 to 1. The law

Placement

J.D.s awarded:	146
Services available through: a separate law school placement center	
Special features: web page (job postings are password protected)	
Full-time job interviews:	21 employers
Summer job interviews:	21 employers
Placement by graduation:	57% of class
Placement within 9 months:	93% of class
Average starting salary:	$25,000 to $190,000
Areas of placement:	
Private practice 2-10 attorneys	22%
Private practice 11-25 attorneys	2%
Private practice 26-50 attorneys	9%
Private practice 51-100+ attorneys	7%
Private practice, unreported size	9%
Government	21%
Business/industry	21%
Judicial clerkships	5%
Public interest	2%
Military	2%

school has a regular program of bringing visiting professors and other distinguished lecturers and visitors to campus.

Students
About 42% of the student body are women; 11%, minorities; 2%, African American; 4%, Asian American; and 4%, Hispanic. The majority of students come from Nebraska (39%). The average age of entering students is 23; age range is 21 to 50. About 55% of students enter directly from undergraduate school and 4% have a graduate degree. About 6% drop out after the first year for academic or personal reasons; 89% remain to receive a law degree.

DE PAUL UNIVERSITY

College of Law

25 East Jackson Boulevard
Chicago, IL 60604

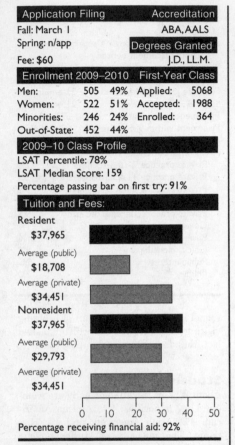

Application Filing		Accreditation
Fall: March 1		ABA, AALS
Spring: n/app		Degrees Granted
Fee: $60		J.D., LL.M.

Enrollment 2009–2010			First-Year Class	
Men:	505	49%	Applied:	5068
Women:	522	51%	Accepted:	1988
Minorities:	246	24%	Enrolled:	364
Out-of-State:	452	44%		

2009–10 Class Profile

LSAT Percentile: 78%
LSAT Median Score: 159
Percentage passing bar on first try: 91%

Tuition and Fees:

Resident
$37,965

Average (public)
$18,708

Average (private)
$34,451

Nonresident
$37,965

Average (public)
$29,793

Average (private)
$34,451

Percentage receiving financial aid: 92%

ADMISSIONS

In the fall 2009 first-year class, 5068 applied, 1988 were accepted, and 364 enrolled. Twenty-six transfers enrolled. The median LSAT percentile of the most recent first-year class was 78; the median GPA was 3.4 on a scale of 4.0. The lowest LSAT percentile accepted was 33; the highest was 99.

Requirements
Applicants must have a bachelor's degree and take the LSAT. No specific undergraduate courses are required. Candidates are not interviewed.

Procedure
The application deadline for fall entry is March 1. Applicants should submit an application form, LSAT results, transcripts, a personal statement, a nonrefundable application fee of $60, and 1 letter of recommendation. Accepted students must pay 2 deposits, which total $400. Notification of the admissions decision is on a rolling basis. The latest acceptable LSAT test date for fall entry is February. The law school uses the LSDAS.

Special
The law school recruits minority and disadvantaged students by attending recruitment programs at historically black colleges and other universities with a substantial number of minority students. The College of Law also recruits minority students through direct mail and a number of on-campus programs. In addition, scholarships are awarded. Requirements are not different for out-of-state students. Transfer students must have one year of credit, have a minimum GPA of 2, have attended an ABA-approved law school, and submit their LSDAS reports, law school transcripts, letter of recommendation, and letters of good standing.

Costs

Tuition and fees for the 2009-2010 academic year are $37,965 for all full-time students. Tuition for part-time students is $24,820 per year. On-campus room and board costs about $29,907 annually; books and supplies run $1500.

Financial Aid

About 92% of current law students receive some form of aid. The average annual amount of aid from all sources combined, including scholarships, loans, and work contracts, is $43,860; maximum, $80,885. Awards are based on need and merit. Required financial statement is the FAFSA. The aid application deadline for fall entry is March 1. Scholarship awards are available to students who contribute to diversity and have financial need. All students are eligible for consideration. First-year students are notified about their financial aid application after March 1.

About the Law School

De Paul University College of Law was established in 1898 and is a private institution. The campus is in an urban area in downtown Chicago. The primary mission of the law school is to train and educate men and women who will ethically and competently represent the legal profession in urban and international settings and in private practice, business, or government. Students have access to federal, state, county, city, and local agencies, courts, correctional facilities, law firms, and legal aid organizations in the Chicago area. Extensive clinical and externship opportunities are available. Facilities of special interest to law students include amphitheater-style video-equipped classrooms, a state-of-the-art moot court room, a legal clinic, new student housing, and the law library. Housing for students is available in an 18-story downtown Chicago residence. The Office of Admission also assists students in locating off-campus apartments and studios. About half of the student body is from out of state. All law school facilities are accessible to the physically disabled.

Calendar

The law school operates on a traditional semester basis. Courses for full-time students are offered both day and evening and must be completed within 5 years. Part-time students may take some upper-level day and must be completed within 5 years. New full- and part-time students are admitted in the fall. There is a 7-week summer session. Transferable summer courses are offered.

Programs

In addition to the J.D., the law school offers the LL.M. and International Law. Students may take relevant courses in other programs and apply credit toward the J.D.; a maximum of 10 hours credits may be applied. The following joint degrees may be earned: J.D./M.A. (Juris Doctor/Master in International Studies), J.D./M.B.A. (Juris Doctor/Master of Business Administration), J.D./M.S. (Juris Doctor/Master in Public Service Management), and J.D./M.S. or J.D./M.A. (Juris Doctor/Master in Computer Science).

Required
To earn the J.D., candidates must complete 86 total credits, of which 40 are for required courses. They must maintain a minimum GPA of 2.0 in the required courses. The following first-year courses are required of all students: Civil Procedure, Constitutional Process I, Contracts, Criminal Law, Legal Analysis, Research and Communication I and II, Property, and Torts. Required upper-level courses consist of Legal Analysis, Research and Communication III, Legal Profession, a professional skills couse, and a writing course. The required orientation program for first-year students is a 2-day program for full-time students and a 3-evening program for part-time students.

Phone: 312-362-6831
800-428-7453
Fax: 312-362-5280
E-mail: *lawinfo@depaul.edu*
Web: *law.depaul.edu*

Contact

Priscilla Miller, Associate Director, 312-362-6831 for general inquiries; Office of Financial Aid, 312-362-8091 for financial aid information.

ILLINOIS

Electives

The College of Law offers concentrations in corporate law, criminal law, entertainment law, family law, intellectual property law, international law, juvenile law, labor law, litigation, media law, securities law, sports law, tax law, torts and insurance, health law, information technology, arts and museum law, international human rights law, and public interest law. In addition, upper-level students may enroll in legal clinics such as Technology and Intellectual Property Clinic, Criminal Appeals, Death Penalty, Immigration and Asylum Law, and Family and Child Law. Each clinic is worth 3 hours of credit. Seminars are 3-credit hour courses taken during the last year of legal studies. The College of Law also offers numerous internships. Students work with a government agency (such as the State Attorney's Office, the Public Defender's Office, or the judiciary) or other nonprofit and for-profit organizations. Students may undertake an independent study project in which they develop an in-depth, publishable research paper under the guidance of a professor. Courses with a field work component are offered in Commercial Law, Criminal Justice, Environmental Law, Family Law, Judicial, Intellectual Property, Labor Law, Tax Law, Health Law, International Human Rights, and Mediation, as well as a legal clinic. An annual Visiting Scholar program is offered. Students may study abroad in an exchange program in conjunction with University College in Dublin, Ireland, as well as summer programs offered in Beijing, China; Chiapas, Mexico; San Jose, Costa Rica; Sydney, Australia; Bvenos, Aires; and Prague, Czech Republic. An extensive Academic Support Program under the supervision of 2 full-time education specialists is offered. A wide-range of services and activities for students-of-color are provided by DePaul's Black, Latino, and Asian student associations. An Assistant Dean of Multicultural Affairs is on the staff of the law school. Special interest programs include the Women's Law Caucus, Public Interest Law Association, Human Rights Bar Association, Environmental Law Society, Labor Law Society, International Law Society, and Gay and Lesbian Society. The College also sponsors the following institutes: Health Law Institute; Center for Intellectual Property and Information Technology; Schiller, DuCanto & Fleck Family Law Center; International Human Rights Law Institute; Center for Justice in

Capital Cases; International Aviation Law Institute; and the Center for Law and Science. The most widely taken electives are Litigation Strategies, Alternate Dispute Resolution, and Corporate Law.

Graduation Requirements

In order to graduate, candidates must have a GPA of 2.0, have completed the upper-division writing requirement, and a required seminar.

Organizations

Students edit the *De Paul Law Review, Health Care Law Journal, Business & Commercial Law Journal, Intellectual Property Law Digest, Journal of Art, Technology and Intellectual Property Law, Journal of Sports Law and Contemporary Problems*, and the *Journal of Social Justice*. Students participate in an annual international moot court competition. The Moot Court Society enters national and international competitions. Negotiations, Client Counseling, and Jessup International Moot Court competitions are held annually. Law student organizations, local chapters of national associations, and campus clubs and organizations include the Women's Law Caucus, Student Bar Association, Phi Alpha Delta, Phi Delta Phi, Decalogue Society, Federalist Society for Law & Public Policy Studies, International Law Society, and Justinian Society of Lawyers.

Library

The law library contains 402,000 hard-copy volumes and 190,418 microform volume equivalents, and subscribes to 6000 serial publications. Such on-line databases and networks as CALI, CIS Universe, Infotrac, Legal-Trac, LEXIS, LOIS, NEXIS, OCLC First Search, WESTLAW, Wilsonline Indexes, BNA-ALL, Making of Modern Law, and CCH Tax are available to law students for research. Special library collections include an official U.S. government depository and tax law, health law, and human rights law collections. The ratio of library volumes to faculty is 6700 to 1 and to students is 391 to 1. The ratio of seats in the library to students is 1 to 2.

Faculty

The law school has 60 full-time and 66 part-time faculty members, of whom 45 are women. According to AAUP standards for Category I institutions, faculty salaries are below average. About 30%

Placement

J.D.s awarded:	362

Services available through: a separate law school placement center and the university placement center

Services: career and advisory programs are available as well as an Alumni Job Newsletter, in-office fax, copier, scanner and Network, Internet, LEXIS, and WESTLAW capabilities.

Special features: The De Paul College of Law Alumni Board is very active in career planning and placement programs, and supports a proactive approach to students and alumni career development. Eastlaw and Yahoo groups are also used to inform students of job opportunities. The office offers an on-line, document, and digital libraries as well as an on-line event calendar.

Full-time job interviews:	18 employers
Summer job interviews:	46 employers
Placement by graduation:	81% of class
Placement within 9 months:	94% of class
Average starting salary:	$26,000 to $256,000

Areas of placement:

Private practice 2-10 attorneys	46%
Private practice 11-25 attorneys	16%
Private practice 26-50 attorneys	8%
Private practice 51-100 attorneys	6%
Private practice 101+ attorneys/Solo practice; un	24%
Business/industry	21%
Government	11%
Public interest	4%
Judicial clerkships	3%
Academic	2%
Military	1%

of full-time faculty have a graduate law degree in addition to the J.D.; about 10% of part-time faculty have one. The ratio of full-time students to full-time faculty in an average class is 13 to 1; in a clinic, 8 to 1. The law school has a regular program of bringing visiting professors and other distinguished lecturers and visitors to campus. There is a chapter of the Order of the Coif; 50 faculty are members.

Students

About 51% of the student body are women; 24%, minorities; 7%, African American; 6%, Asian American; and 11%, Hispanic. The majority of students come from Illinois (56%). The average age of entering students is 24; age range is 20 to 52. About 35% of students enter directly from undergraduate school and 9% have a graduate degree. About 3% drop out after the first year for academic or personal reasons; 97% remain to receive a law degree.

DRAKE UNIVERSITY

Law School

2507 University Avenue
Des Moines, IA 50311

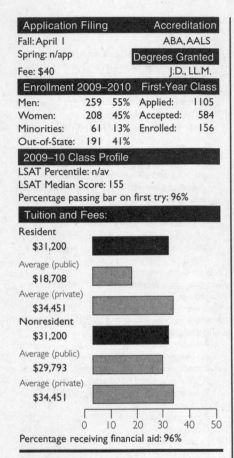

Application Filing			Accreditation
Fall: April 1			ABA, AALS
Spring: n/app			**Degrees Granted**
Fee: $40			J.D., LL.M.

Enrollment 2009–2010			First-Year Class	
Men:	259	55%	Applied:	1105
Women:	208	45%	Accepted:	584
Minorities:	61	13%	Enrolled:	156
Out-of-State:	191	41%		

2009–10 Class Profile
LSAT Percentile: n/av
LSAT Median Score: 155
Percentage passing bar on first try: 96%

Tuition and Fees:

Resident
$31,200

Average (public)
$18,708

Average (private)
$34,451

Nonresident
$31,200

Average (public)
$29,793

Average (private)
$34,451

0   10   20   30   40   50

Percentage receiving financial aid: 96%

ADMISSIONS

In the fall 2009 first-year class, 1105 applied, 584 were accepted, and 156 enrolled. Three transfers enrolled. The median GPA of the most recent first-year class was 3.42.

Requirements

Applicants must have a bachelor's degree and take the LSAT. The most important admission factors include LSAT results, GPA, and undergraduate curriculum. No specific undergraduate courses are required. Candidates are not interviewed.

Procedure

The application deadline for fall entry is April 1. Applicants should submit an application form, LSAT results, transcripts, TOEFL (for international students), a nonrefundable application fee of $40, 2 letters of recommendation, and a personal statement. Notification of the admissions decision is within 4 to 6 weeks after the file is complete. Notification begins in late January. The latest acceptable LSAT test date for fall entry is June. The law school uses the LSDAS.

Special

The law school recruits minority and disadvantaged students by means of targeted efforts at nationally identified feeder schools for students of color, the use of the Candidate Referral Service (CRS), and an on-campus recruitment event. Requirements are not different for out-of-state students. Transfer students must have 1 year of credit, have attended an ABA-approved law school, and generally, rank in the upper half of their current law school class and have certification of good academic standing and eligibility to re-enroll at that school.

Costs

Tuition and fees for the 2009-2010 academic year are $31,200 for all full-time students. On-campus room and board costs about $15,600 annually; books and supplies run $1300.

Financial Aid

About 96% of current law students receive some form of aid. The maximum annual amount of aid from all sources combined, including scholarships, loans, and work contracts, is $48,760. Awards are based on need and merit. Loans are offered on the basis of need. The school offers numerous scholarships, some based on merit, some on merit and need. Required financial statement is the FAFSA. The aid application deadline for fall entry is March 1. Special funds for minority or disadvantaged students include Law Opportunity scholarships, which are awards for entering students from educationally or economically disadvantaged backgrounds or who contribute to the diversity of the class and demonstrate financial need. First-year students are notified about their financial aid application some time after admission and before a seat deposit is required.

About the Law School

Drake University Law School was established in 1865 and is a private institution. The 120-acre campus is in an urban area 5 miles northwest of downtown Des Moines. Students have access to federal, state, county, city, and local agencies, courts, correctional facilities, law firms, and legal aid organizations in the Des Moines area. There are legal clinics, insurance companies, corporate offices, and internships. Facilities of special interest to law stu-

dents are the Constitutional Law Center, Agricultural Law Center;, Neal and Bea Smith Legal Clinic, Legislative Practice Center, Health Law and Policy Center, Joan and Lyle Middleton Center for Children's Rights, and the Intellectual Property Law Center. Housing for students consists of university-owned and privately owned apartments located within walking distance of the campus; housing is also available in city suburbs just 15 minutes from campus. About 99% of the law school facilities are accessible to the physically disabled.

Calendar

The law school operates on a traditional semester basis. Courses for full-time students are offered days only and must be completed within 6 years. For part-time students, courses are offered days only and must be completed within 6 years. New full- and part-time students are admitted in the fall and summer. There is a 7-week summer session. Transferable summer courses are offered.

Programs

In addition to the J.D., the law school offers the LL.M. Students may take relevant courses in other programs and apply credit toward the J.D.; a maximum of 6 credits may be applied. The following joint degrees may be earned: J.D./M.A. (Juris Doctor/Master of Arts in political science), J.D./M.B.A. (Juris Doctor/ Master of Business Administration), J.D./M.H.A. (Juris Doctor/Master of Health Administration), J.D./M.P.A. (Juris Doctor/ Master of Public Administration), J.D./M.P.H. (Juris Doctor/Master of Public Health), J.D./M.S. (Juris Doctor/ Master of Science in agricultural economics), J.D./M.S.W. (Juris Doctor/ Master of Social Work), and J.D./Pharm.D. (Juris Doctor/Doctor of Pharmacy).

Required

To earn the J.D., candidates must complete 90 total credits, of which 41 are for required courses. They must maintain a minimum GPA of 2.0 in the required courses. The following first-year courses are required of all students: Civil Procedure I and II, Constitutional Law I, Contracts I and II, Criminal Law, Legal Research, Writing, and Appellate Practice, Property, and Torts. Required upper-level courses consist

Phone: 515-271-2782
800-44-DRAKE, ext. 2782
Fax: 515-271-1990
E-mail: *lawadmit@drake.edu*
Web: *www.law.drake.edu*

Contact
Andrew Englis, Associate Director of Admission and Financial Aid, 515-271-2782; 800-44-DRAKE, ext. 2782 for general inquiries; Kara Blanchard, Director of Admission and Financial Aid, 515-271-2782; 800-44-DRAKE, ext. 2782 for financial aid information.

IOWA

of Advanced Writing Seminar, Constitutional Law II, Evidence, and Legal Ethics and Professional Responsibility. All students who have completed 45 hours of class may take the clinical courses as electives. The required orientation program for first-year students is 3 days and includes a formal welcome, registration instructions, law school tour, fee payment session, small group meetings, computer training, sessions on professionalism, and the noncredit Introduction to Law course.

Electives
The Law School offers concentrations in corporate law, criminal law, environmental law, family law, intellectual property law, international law, juvenile law, labor law, litigation, securities law, tax law, torts and insurance, agricultural law, constitutional law, and public interest law. In addition, the law school's clinical programs include the General Civil Practice Clinic, Criminal Defense Clinic, Elder Law Clinic, and the Middleton Children's Rights Clinic. Generally, students must have completed 45 hours of classroom credit prior to enrolling; however, prerequisites vary. To enroll in seminars, students must have completed 30 hours with a 2.0 GPA. Generally, 1 to 3 hours of credit may be granted for a seminar course. Internships are available in administrative law, the legislature, the judiciary, insurance, environmental law, securities, probate, health law, and others. Credit varies from 1 to 4 credit hours and prerequisites vary. Independent research may be undertaken for 1 to 3 credit hours and is graded on a credit/no credit basis. Special lecture series include the Constitutional Law Resource Center Speaker Series, the Dwight D. Opperman Lecture in Constitutional Law and the Intellectual Property Law Center Symposia. Drake offers a 4-week summer abroad program in Nantes, France worth up to 6 credits; credit may also be accepted from programs offered by other law schools. The most widely taken electives are Trial Advocacy, Client Representation and Litigation, and Advanced Client Representation and Litigation.

Graduation Requirements
In order to graduate, candidates must have a GPA of 2.0, have completed the upper-division writing requirement, have completed 6 semesters for residence credit and 90 hours for academic credit, and have satisfied the advanced writing requirement through either independent study or course work.

Organizations
Students edit the *Drake Law Review* and the *Drake Journal of Agricultural Law*. Moot court teams are sent to the C. Edwin Moore Appellate Advocacy, National Moot Court, and National Appellate Advocacy competitions. Other competitions include the National Mock Trial Competition, Client Counseling Competition, Negotiations Competition, and Environmental Moot Court. Law student organizations, local chapters of national associations, and campus organizations include the Student Bar Association, Drake Law Women, International Law Society, Student Bar Association, Delta Theta Phi Law Fraternity, American Bar Association-Student Division, Order of Barristers, and American Association for Justice.

Library
The law library contains 330,000 hardcopy volumes and 117,967 microform volume equivalents, and subscribes to 3333 serial publications. Such on-line databases and networks as CALI, CIS Universe, DIALOG, Infotrac, Legal-Trac, LEXIS, LOIS, NEXIS, OCLC First Search, WESTLAW, Wilsonline Indexes, and RIA Checkpoint are available to law students for research. Special library collections include a government depository; agricultural, tax, computer, and constitutional law collections; Neal Smith Congressional Archives; and National Bar Association Archives. Recently, the school completed a $8.5 million, 70,000-square-foot library. In addition to the on-line catalog and automated circulation system, the library provides computer access with several computer laboratories and Ethernet connections throughout the library, at carrels, tables, and study rooms, including Internet access from any student workstation in the library. A wireless network is accessible throughout the library and law school. The ratio of library volumes to faculty is 8684 to 1 and to students is 707 to 1. The ratio of seats in the library to students is 1 to 1.

Faculty
The law school has 38 full-time and 33 part-time faculty members, of whom 26 are women. About 24% of full-time faculty have a graduate law degree in addition to

Placement

J.D.s awarded:	136
Services available through: a separate law school placement center	
Services: workshops, panel speakers, mentors, networking opportunities, mock interviews, job fairs	
Special features: a nationwide network of alumni in specific geographic and practice areas that has been developed to assist students with employment opportunities. ILS must participate in required workshops and mandatory counseling appointments.	
Full-time job interviews:	32 employers
Summer job interviews:	24 employers
Placement by graduation:	n/av
Placement within 9 months:	97% of class
Average starting salary:	$37,500 to $110,000
Areas of placement:	
Private practice 2-10 attorneys	25%
Private practice 11-25 attorneys	5%
Private practice 26-50 attorneys	3%
Private practice 51-100 attorneys	6%
Private practice 100 + attorneys/unknown	11%
Business/industry	20%
Government	10%
Judicial clerkships	9%
Public interest	6%
Military	2%
Academic	2%

the J.D. The ratio of full-time students to full-time faculty in an average class is 14 to 1; in a clinic, 7 to 1. The law school has a regular program of bringing visiting professors and other distinguished lecturers and visitors to campus. There is a chapter of the Order of the Coif; 11 faculty and 631 graduates are members.

Students
About 45% of the student body are women; 13%, minorities; 7%, African American; 2%, Asian American; 3%, Hispanic; and 1%, Native American. The majority of students come from the Midwest (82%). The average age of entering students is 25; age range is 21 to 51. About 40% of students enter directly from undergraduate school and 6% have a graduate degree. About 4% drop out after the first year for academic or personal reasons; 96% remain to receive a law degree.

DREXEL UNIVERSITY

Earle Mack School of Law

3320 Market Street
Philadelphia, PA 15282

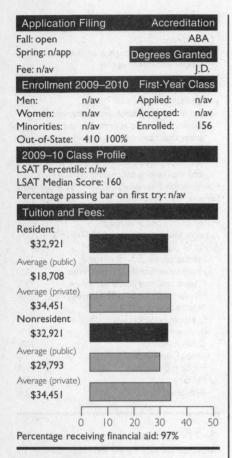

Application Filing	Accreditation
Fall: open	ABA
Spring: n/app	Degrees Granted
Fee: n/av	J.D.

Enrollment 2009–2010		First-Year Class	
Men:	n/av	Applied:	n/av
Women:	n/av	Accepted:	n/av
Minorities:	n/av	Enrolled:	156
Out-of-State:	410 100%		

2009–10 Class Profile
LSAT Percentile: n/av
LSAT Median Score: 160
Percentage passing bar on first try: n/av

Tuition and Fees:

Resident
$32,921

Average (public)
$18,708

Average (private)
$34,451

Nonresident
$32,921

Average (public)
$29,793

Average (private)
$34,451

Percentage receiving financial aid: **97%**

ADMISSIONS

In a recent year, 156 enrolled. The median GPA of the most recent first-year class was 3.42. The lowest LSAT percentile accepted was 25; the highest was 75. Figures in the above capsule and in this profile are approximate.

Requirements
Applicants must take the LSAT.

Procedure
Applicants should submit an application form, LSAT results, at least 2 letters of recommendation, and LSDAS registration. Notification of the admissions decision is rolling basis. The law school uses the LSDAS. Check with the school for the current application deadlines.

Special
The law school recruits minority and disadvantaged students Through affiliation agreements with minority ethnic, and religious bar associations. Student also are encourage to attend bar association events and events encouraging diversity in the profession. The Philadelphia Trial Lawyers Association has initiated a mentoring program that pairs trial lawyers with students of color. Requirements are not different for out-of-state students. Transfer students must have attended an ABA-approved law school and Transfer applications will be considered only between the applicant's first and second seats of law school.

Costs

Tuition and fees for the 2009-2010 academic year are approximately $32,921 for all full-time students.

Financial Aid

In a reent year, about 97% of current law students received some form of aid. Awards are based on need and merit. Required financial statement is the FAFSA. Special funds for minority or disadvantaged students are available. First-year students are notified about their financial aid application at December 1. Check with the school for the current application deadline.

About the Law School

Drexel University Earle Mack School of Law was established in 2006 and is a private institution in Philadelphia. The primary mission of the law school is to provide knowledge of the law, training in practical skills, and commitment to professionalism.

Calendar

The law school operates on a trimester basis. For part-time students, courses are offered both day and evening. There is no part-time program. New students are admitted in the fall and summer. There is a summer session.

Programs

The following joint degrees may be earned: J.D./Ph.D. (Program in Law Psychology).

Required
The following first-year courses are required of all students: Interviewing counseling and negotiation, Introduction to Law, Legal Methods, and Research. Required upper-level courses consist of Drafting Appealate Advocacy, Drafting Litigation, Drafting Perspective, and Employment Discrimination. The optional orientation program for first-year students 4 days.

Electives
The Earle Mack School of Law offers concentrations in health law, business and entrepreneurship law. In addition, clinics include the Civil Litigation Field Clinic, Criminal Litigation Field Clinic, and Public Health and Environmental Law Field Clinic. There is an Academic Skills Program that is available to all students.

Organizations

Library

The law library contains 48,148 hard-copy volumes.

Phone: 215-895 1LAW
Fax: 215-571-4769

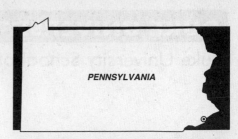

PENNSYLVANIA

Faculty

The law school has 24 full-time and 25 part-time faculty members. The ratio of full-time students to full-time faculty in an average class is 16 to 1.

Students

The average age of entering students is 25; age range is 21 to 48.

Placement	
J.D.s awarded:	n/av
Services available through:	
Full-time job interviews:	n/av
Summer job interviews:	n/av
Placement by graduation:	n/av
Placement within 9 months:	n/av
Average starting salary:	n/av
Areas of placement:	
Private practice 51-100 attorneys	25%
Judicial clerkships	40%
Business/industry	15%
Government	10%
Public interest	10%

DUKE UNIVERSITY

Duke University School of Law

Science Drive and Towerview Road,
Box 90362
Durham, NC 27708-0362

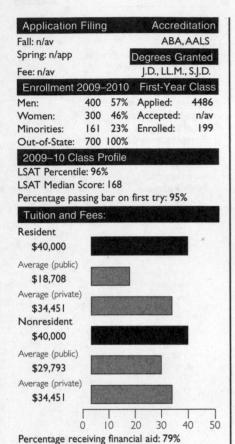

Application Filing		Accreditation	
Fall: n/av		ABA, AALS	
Spring: n/app		**Degrees Granted**	
Fee: n/av		J.D., LL.M., S.J.D.	
Enrollment 2009–2010		**First-Year Class**	
Men:	400 57%	Applied:	4486
Women:	300 46%	Accepted:	n/av
Minorities:	161 23%	Enrolled:	199
Out-of-State:	700 100%		

2009–10 Class Profile
LSAT Percentile: 96%
LSAT Median Score: 168
Percentage passing bar on first try: 95%

Tuition and Fees:

Resident
$40,000

Average (public)
$18,708

Average (private)
$34,451

Nonresident
$40,000

Average (public)
$29,793

Average (private)
$34,451

0   10   20   30   40   50

Percentage receiving financial aid: 79%

ADMISSIONS

In a recent year, 4486 applied and 199 enrolled. Twenty transfers enrolled. The median LSAT percentile of the most recent first-year class was 96; the median GPA was 3.72 on a scale of 4.0. Figures in the above capsule and in this profile are approximate.

Requirements

Applicants must have a bachelor's degree and take the LSAT. No specific undergraduate courses are required. Candidates are not interviewed.

Procedure

Applicants should submit an application form, LSAT results, transcripts, 2 academic letters letters of recommendation, and 1 certification from an academic dean. Notification of the admissions decision is on a rolling basis. The latest acceptable LSAT test date for fall entry is December. The law school uses the LSDAS. Check with the school for the current application deadlines.

Special

The law school recruits minority and disadvantaged students Through minority student organizations, faculty, and alumni and by encouraging participation in the Admited Students Weekend and/or other visits to the Law School. Requirements are not different for out-of-state students. Transfer students must have one year of credit, have attended an ABA-approved law school, and must be eligible to re-enroll and otherwise be in good standing at the current law school.

Costs

Tuition and fees for the 2009-2010 academic year are approximately $40,000 for all full-time students.

Financial Aid

In a recent year, about 79% of current law students received some form of aid. The average annual amount of aid from all sources combined, including scholarships, loans, and work contracts, was $38,680; maximum, $50,042. Awards are based on need and merit. Required financial statement is the FAFSA. Check with the school for the current application deadline. Special funds for minority or disadvantaged students consist of a need-based scholarships. First-year students are notified about their financial aid application at shortly after acceptance.

About the Law School

Duke University Duke University School of Law was established in 1930 and is a private institution. The campus is in an urban area in Durham. The primary mission of the law school is is to prepare students for responsible and productive lives in the legal profession by providing a rigorous education, a collaborative, supportive, and diverse enviroment, and to provide leadership in improving the law and legal institutions through research, and public service. Students have access to federal, state, county, city, and local agencies, courts, correctional facilities, law firms, and legal aid organizations in the Durham area. Facilities of special interest to law students Duke Law School is located in a single building engineered for both wired and wireless communications. All classrooms and the moot court room have been built, or renovated, within the past five years and are state-of-the-art. Housing for students is limited on campus, but

there are ample rental units in the surrounding area. All law school facilities are accessible to the physically disabled.

Calendar

The law school operates on a traditional semester basis. Courses for full-time students are offered days only and must be completed within 3 years. There is no part-time program. New students are admitted in the fall and summer. There is a 9-week summer session. Transferable summer courses are not offered.

Programs

In addition to the J.D., the law school offers the LL.M. and S.J.D. Students may take relevant courses in other programs and apply credit toward the J.D.; a maximum of 3 credits may be applied. The following joint degrees may be earned: J.D./LL.M. (Juris Doctor/Master of Laws in comparative and international law), J.D./M.A. (Juris Doctor/Master of Arts in cultural anthropology and English,), J.D./M.B.A. (Juris Doctor/Master of Business Administration), J.D./M.D. (Juris Doctor/Doctor of Medicine), J.D./M.E.M. (Juris Doctor/Master of Environmental Management), J.D./M.P.P. (Juris Doctor/Master of Public Policy), J.D./M.S. (Juris Doctor/Master of Science in mechanical engineering), J.D./M.T.S. (Juris Doctor/Master of Theological Studies), and J.D./Ph.D. (Juris Doctor/Doctor of Philosophy in political science).

Required

To earn the J.D., candidates must complete 84 total credits, of which 32 are for required courses. They must maintain a minimum GPA of 2.1 in the required courses. The following first-year courses are required of all students: Civil Procedure, Constitutional Law, Contracts, Criminal Law, Legal Research and Writing, Property, and Torts. Required upper-level courses consist of Ethics/Professional Responsibility. All clinical courses are electivesThe required orientation program for first-year students occurs the week before the start of classes.

Electives

The Duke University School of Law offers concentrations in include intellectual property, international law, national security law, enviromental studies, and business. For students interested in structuring study in a particular field, the law

Phone: 919-613-7020
Fax: 919-613-7257
E-mail: *nash@law.duke.edu*
Web: *http://admissions.law.duke.edu*

Contact

Associate Dean for Admissions, 919-613-7020 for general inquiries; Assistant Director of Financial Aid, 919-613-7004 for financial aid information.

NORTH CAROLINA

school offers individual academic advising on coursework and progression study. In addition, There are six in-house legal clinics. The Guantanamo Defense Clinic assists the Chief Defense Counsel for Guantanamo detainees with trial preparation. In the AIDS Legal Assistance Project, students help clients with HIV/AIDS prepare wills, apply for government benefits, and handle other issues. The Children's Education Law Clinic represents of low-income children in special education, school discipline, and disability benefits cases. The Community Enterprise Law Clinic help students develop transactional skills in a community development law setting. The Low-Income Tax Payer Cllinic helps clients in disputes with the IRS. In Wrongful Convictions, students investigate prisoners' claims of actual innocence, and in Animal Law, students investigate issues of animal cruelty and pursue animal-protection law reform advocacy. In each clinic, students provide between 75 and 100 hours of client work. Clinics are open to all upper-class students. Seminars are offered in Bioethics, Corporate Reorganization, Entertainment Law, National Security Law, and many others. Has ab international externship program in wich students earn credit for law placements at agencies such as the U.S. Trade Representative Office and the State Department. 3L students can develop a "capstone" project that integrates advanced knowledge in a particular subject with a hands-on practice component. Some capstone projects are extensions of successful clinic experiences; others include writing an appellate brief or preparing congressional testimony with a faculty member, or working with a law reform commission. A student may take up to 3 semester hours of independent research toward their J.D. degree. Rules vary for J.D./LL.M. and LL.M. students. All independent research taken for credit is completed in cooperation with faculty. The Pro Bono Project connects volunteer law students with attorneys in nonprofit and governmental organizations as well as with attorneys engaged in private pro bono practice. Study abroad is possible through the Summer Institutes in Transnational Law in Geneva or Hong Kong. This program is required of incoming J.D./LL.M. students, and is also open to J.D. students. Students may accrue up to 6 hours of academic credit. Remediation is provided when needed. Charting Courses is an annual event designed to foster inter-

active dialogue among Duke Law School's African-American students, alumni, faculty, and administrators. All minorities are welcome to attend. Duke Law School has over 50 student organizations, with the majority having special interest programming. The most widely taken electives are Business Associations, Evidence, and Intellectual Property.

Graduation Requirements
In order to graduate, candidates must have a GPA of 2.1, have completed the upper-division writing requirement, and Ethics/Professional Responsibility.

Organizations

Students edit the *Duke Law Journal*, *Law and Contemporary Problems*, *Alaska Law Review*, *Duke Journal of Comparative and International Law*, *Duke Environmental Law and Policy Forum*, *Duke Journal of Gender Law and Policy*, and *Duke Law and Technology Review* (eJournal featuring student-written essays called issue briefs or iBriefs), *Duke Journal of Constitutional Law and Public Policy* the *The Devil's Advocate*, the *Alibi*, a literary magazine; *The Herald* (an on-line magazine for students, faculty, and staff); *Duke Law Magazine*; and *Duke Business Journal*, the *The Duke Law Daily*. Moot court competitions include the Jessup International Law Moot Court, National Moot Court, and ABA National Appellate Practice Advocacy Competition. The Moot Court Board Organizes and conducts the annual Hardt Cup competition for first-year students and the Dean's Cup for second - and third-year students. There are more than 50 student organizations.

Library

The law library contains 622,400 hardcopy volumes and 78,067 microform volume equivalents, and subscribes to 7016 serial publications. Such on-line databases and networks as CALI, CIS Universe, DIALOG, Infotrac, Legal-Trac, LEXIS, LOIS, Mathew Bender, NEXIS, OCLC First Search, RLIN, WESTLAW, Wilson-line Indexes, and CCH Business and Tax, LLMC Digital, U.N. treaty collection, RIA Checkpoint, HeinOnline, Index to Foreign Legal Periodicals, Pacer, Foreign Law Guide, Current Index to Legal Periodicals, and others. are available to law students for research. Special library collections include The library has more than 500 seats for individual and collaborative

Placement

J.D.s awarded:	n/av
Services available through: a separate law school placement center	
Services: alumni network, on-campus interviewing by employers, judges, and government,	
Full-time job interviews:	250 employers
Summer job interviews:	350 employers
Placement by graduation:	95% of class
Placement within 9 months:	100% of class
Average starting salary:	$42,000 to $135,000
Areas of placement:	
Judicial clerkships	16%
Academic	4%
Business/industry	1%

study in a wireless enviroment. The ratio of library volumes to faculty is 11,316 to 1 and to students is 960 to 1. The ratio of seats in the library to students is 1 to 1.

Faculty

The law school has 55 full-time and 67 part-time faculty members, of whom 41 are women. According to AAUP standards for Category 1 institutions, faculty salaries are well above average. About 18% of full-time faculty have a graduate law degree in addition to the J.D.; about 1% of part-time faculty have one. The ratio of full-time students to full-time faculty in an average class is 2 to 1; in a clinic, 11 to 1. The law school has a regular program of bringing visiting professors and other distinguished lecturers and visitors to campus. There is a chapter of the Order of the Coif.

Students

About 46% of the student body are women; 23%, minorities; 12%, African American; 7%, Asian American; 4%, Hispanic; and 14%, race/ethnicity unknown; foreign national-5%. The majority of students come from the South (34%). The average age of entering students is 25; age range is 20 to 38. About 35% of students enter directly from undergraduate school and 10% have a graduate degree. About 1% drop out after the first year for academic or personal reasons; 99% remain to receive a law degree.

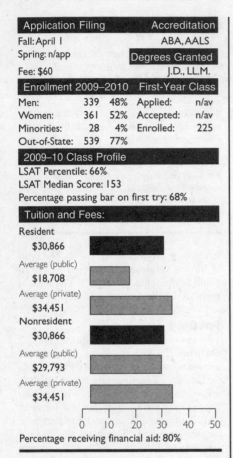

Application Filing		Accreditation
Fall: April 1		ABA, AALS
Spring: n/app		**Degrees Granted**
Fee: $60		J.D., LL.M.

Enrollment 2009–2010		First-Year Class	
Men:	339 48%	Applied:	n/av
Women:	361 52%	Accepted:	n/av
Minorities:	28 4%	Enrolled:	225
Out-of-State:	539 77%		

2009–10 Class Profile
LSAT Percentile: 66%
LSAT Median Score: 153
Percentage passing bar on first try: 68%

Tuition and Fees:

Resident
$30,866

Average (public)
$18,708

Average (private)
$34,451

Nonresident
$30,866

Average (public)
$29,793

Average (private)
$34,451

0   10   20   30   40   50

Percentage receiving financial aid: 80%

ADMISSIONS

In the fall 2009 first-year class, 225 enrolled. The median LSAT percentile of the most recent first-year class was 66; the median GPA was 3.5 on a scale of 4.0.

Requirements

Applicants must have a bachelor's degree and take the LSAT. The most important admission factors include academic achievement, LSAT results, life experience, and occupational and professional work experience. No specific undergraduate courses are required. Candidates are not interviewed.

Procedure

The application deadline for fall entry is April 1 for day students and May 1 for evening students. Applicants should submit an application form, LSAT results, transcripts, TOEFL for foreign students, a nonrefundable application fee of $60, and 2 letters of recommendation. Notification of the admissions decision is on a rolling basis. The latest acceptable LSAT test date for fall entry is December for day students. The law school uses the LSDAS.

Special

The law school recruits minority and disadvantaged students by means of Candidate Referral Service minority search, law fairs, contact with minority coordinators, and assistance with scholarships and grants. Requirements are not different for out-of-state students. Transfer students must have one year of credit, and have attended an ABA-approved law school; admission depends on space availability.

Costs

Tuition and fees for the 2009-2010 academic year are $30,866 for all full-time students. Tuition for part-time students is $23,874 per year. On-campus room and board costs about $9900 annually; books and supplies run $1100.

Financial Aid

About 80% of current law students receive some form of aid. Awards are based on need and merit, along with minority status. Required financial statements are the FFS, the CSS Profile, and the FAFSA. The aid application deadline for fall entry is May 31. Special funds for minority or disadvantaged students consist of scholarships and grants. First-year students are notified about their financial aid application at time of acceptance.

About the Law School

Duquesne University School of Law was established in 1911 and is a private institution. The 47-acre campus is in an urban area in Pittsburgh. The primary mission of the law school is to educate students in the fundamental principles of law, to assist students in forming sound judgment, and to develop facility in legal research and writing. Students have access to federal, state, county, city, and local agencies, courts, correctional facilities, law firms, and legal aid organizations in the Pittsburgh area. Varied clinical programs supervised by the school allow students to gain practical experience. Facilities of special interest to law students are the District Attorney's Office Clinical Program, the Department of Environmental Resources Clinical Program, in-house Economic and Community Development Clinic, Neighborhood Legal Services Clinic, and Civil and Family Justice. Housing for students is available off campus. All law school facilities are accessible to the physically disabled.

Calendar

The law school operates on a traditional semester basis. Courses for full-time students are offered days only and must be completed within 4 years. For part-time students, courses are offered both day and evening and must be completed within 5 years. New full- and part-time students are admitted in the fall. There is a 5-week summer session. Transferable summer courses are offered.

Programs

In addition to the J.D., the law school offers the LL.M. The following joint degrees may be earned: J.D./M.A.H.E. (Juris Doctor/Master of Arts in Healthcare Ethics), J.D./M.B.A. (Juris Doctor/Master of Business Administration), J.D./M.Div. (Juris Doctor/Master of Divinity in conjunction with Pittsburgh), and J.D./M.S.E.S.M. (Juris Doctor/Master of Science in Environmental Science and Management).

Required

To earn the J.D., candidates must complete 86 total credits, of which 56 are for required courses. They must maintain a minimum GPA of 3.0 in the required courses. The following first-year courses are required of all students: Civil Procedure I, Contracts, Criminal Law and Procedure (second year for evening students), Legal Process and Procedure, Legal Research and Writing, Property (second year for evening students), and Torts. Required upper-level courses consist of Basic Federal Income Taxation, Commercial Transactions I and II, Constitutional Law, Corporations, Evidence, and Professional Responsibility. The required orientation program for first-year students consists of 1 week of sessions on requirements in the first year and handling stress. Students meet with their faculty adviser and student mentors.

Electives

The School of Law offers concentrations in corporate law, criminal law, environmental law, family law, international

Phone: 412-396-6296
Fax: 412-396-1073
E-mail: *campion@duq.edu*
Web: *law.duq.edu*

Contact

Jospeh P. Campion Jr., Director of Admissions, 412-396-6296 for general inquiries; Richard Esposito, Financial Aid Director, 412-396-6607 for financial aid information.

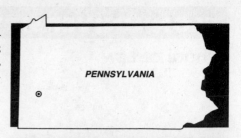

PENNSYLVANIA

law, labor law, litigation, securities law, tax law, torts and insurance, intellectual property, and health care. In addition, clinics, which are considered all upper-division classes worth 3 credits, include the U.S. Attorney's Program, District Attorney's Program, and Pennsylvania Department of Environmental Resources Program. Also open to upper-division students are internships and seminars, both worth 2 to 3 credits. Seminar topics include labor arbitration, collective bargaining, and trial tactics. Upper-division students are eligible to serve as faculty research assistants. Special lectures are given by the guest speakers who visit the school throughout the year. Law students may request permission to participate in study-abroad programs offered by other ABA-approved law schools. There are summer study-abroad programs in China, Ireland, and Vatican City. The Black Law Students Association sponsors a tutoring program. Special interest programs are offered by the Public Interest Law Association, Health Care Law Association, Law Review, *Juris* magazine, Black Law Students Association, Corporate Law Society, and Women's Law Association.

Graduation Requirements

In order to graduate, candidates must have a GPA of 3.0 and have completed the upper-division writing requirement.

Organizations

Students edit the *Duquesne Law Review*; *Juris*, a newsmagazine; and the *Duquesne Business Law Journal*. Moot courts include a trial moot court, an appellate moot court, a corporate moot court, and a tax moot court. Law student organizations, local chapters of national associations, and campus organizations include the Environmental Law Association, the Intellectual Property & Technological Law Society, Health Care Law Association, Phi Alpha Delta, Association of Trial Lawyers of America, ABA-Law Student Division, and Criminal Law Association.

Library

The law library contains 230,261 hardcopy volumes and 74,366 microform volume equivalents, and subscribes to 2999 serial publications. Such on-line databases and networks as CALI, CIS Universe, Infotrac, Legal-Trac, LEXIS, LOIS, NEXIS, OCLC First Search, WESTLAW, and Innovative Millennium are available to law students for research. The Law library entered into a unique public/private agreement to manage the Allegment County Law Library. Students have full access to this library, U.S. government documents depository, and extensive Pennsylvania legal reseach collection. Recently, the library updated group study rooms and library furnishings, installed a wireless network, and hired 2 additional reference librarians to assist students. The ratio of library volumes to faculty is 8856 to 1 and to students is 329 to 1. The ratio of seats in the library to students is 1 to 2.

Faculty

The law school has 26 full-time and 34 part-time faculty members, of whom 20 are women. According to AAUP standards for Category I institutions, faculty salaries are well below average. About 32% of full-time faculty have a graduate law degree in addition to the J.D.; about 10% of part-time faculty have one. The ratio of full-time students to full-time faculty in an average class is 19 to 1. The law school has a regular program of bringing visiting professors and other distinguished lecturers and visitors to campus.

Students

About 52% of the student body are women; 5%, minorities; 3%, African American; 2%, Asian American; and 1%, Hispanic. The majority of students come from Pennsylvania (23%). The average age of entering students is 22; age range is 20 to 48. About 25% of students have worked full-time prior to entering law school. About 2% drop out after the first year for academic or personal reasons; 95% remain to receive a law degree.

Placement

J.D.s awarded:	n/av
Services available through: a separate law school placement center and and a full-time Career Services Office for law students	
Special features: individual counseling for students, videotaped mock interviews, and focus groups for nontraditional students	
Full-time job interviews:	8 employers
Summer job interviews:	38 employers
Placement by graduation:	60% of class
Placement within 9 months:	89% of class
Average starting salary:	$30,000 to $125,000
Areas of placement:	
Private practice 2-500 attorneys, unknown	50%
Business/industry	17%
Judicial clerkships	12%
Government	11%
Public interest	8%
Academic	2%

School of Law

201 North Greene Street
Greensboro, NC 27401

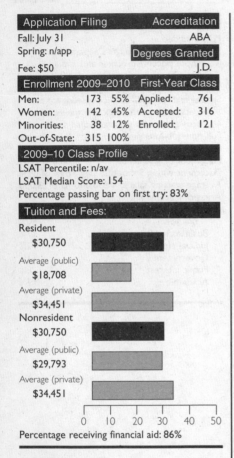

Application Filing		Accreditation
Fall: July 31		ABA
Spring: n/app		**Degrees Granted**
Fee: $50		J.D.

Enrollment 2009–2010		First-Year Class	
Men:	173 55%	Applied:	761
Women:	142 45%	Accepted:	316
Minorities:	38 12%	Enrolled:	121
Out-of-State:	315 100%		

2009–10 Class Profile
LSAT Percentile: n/av
LSAT Median Score: 154
Percentage passing bar on first try: 83%

Tuition and Fees:

Resident
$30,750

Average (public)
$18,708

Average (private)
$34,451

Nonresident
$30,750

Average (public)
$29,793

Average (private)
$34,451

0   10   20   30   40   50

Percentage receiving financial aid: 86%

ADMISSIONS
In the fall 2009 first-year class, 761 applied, 316 were accepted, and 121 enrolled. Three transfers enrolled. The median GPA of the most recent first-year class was 3.29.

Requirements
Applicants must have a bachelor's degree. The most important admission factors include general background, leadership experience, GPA, and LSAT results. Candidates are not interviewed.

Procedure
The application deadline for fall entry is July 31. Applicants should submit an application form, LSAT results, transcripts, a personal statement, a nonrefundable application fee of $50, 2 letters of recommendation, and a resume (optional). Notification of the admissions decision is by December 31, for early decision; other decisions on a rolling basis. The latest acceptable LSAT test date for fall entry is June. The law school uses the LSDAS.

Special
The law school recruits minority and disadvantaged students through Diversity Day at the law school, attendance at recruitment events hosted by and for minority applicants, and scholarships to aid diverse students. Requirements are not different for out-of-state students. Transfer students must have one year of credit and have attended an ABA-approved law school.

Costs
Tuition and fees for the 2009-2010 academic year are $30,750 for full-time in-state students. Books and supplies run $1600.

Financial Aid
About 86% of current law students receive some form of aid. The average annual amount of aid from all sources combined, including scholarships, loans, and work contracts, is $36,221. Awards are based on need and merit. Required financial statement is the FAFSA. Special funds for minority or disadvantaged students include Elon Law scholarships and the ABA Legal Opportunity Scholarship. First-year students are notified about their financial aid application at time of acceptance for scholarships.

About the Law School
Elon University School of Law was established in 2005 and is a private institution. The campus is in an urban area in Greensboro, North Carolina. The primary mission of the law school is to emphasize strong classroom instruction, practical experiences, and leadership development to equip graduates to take on the challenges of the 21st century. Students have access to federal, state, county, city, and local agencies, courts, correctional facilities, law firms, and legal aid organizations in the Greensboro area. Other resources include the Center for Engaged Learning & the Law. Facilities of special interest to law students include the North Carolina Business Court, housed in the law school. Housing for students is available off campus. All law school facilities are accessible to the physically disabled.

Calendar
The law school operates on a modified semester (4-1-4) basis. Courses for full-time students are offered both day and evening and must be completed within 84 months. There is no part-time program. New students are admitted in the fall. There are 2-5 week-week summer sessions.

Programs
Required
To earn the J.D., candidates must complete 90 total credits, of which 49 are for required courses. They must maintain a minimum GPA of 2.80 in the required courses. The following first-year courses are required of all students: Civil Procedure I and II, Community Communication I and II, Contracts I and II, Criminial Law, Lawyering, Leadership, and Professionalism, Legal Method, Property I and II, and Torts I and II. Required upper-level courses consist of Business Associations, Constitutional Law I and II, Criminial Procedure, Evidence, Leadership and Public Law, and Professional Responsibility. The required orientation program for first-year students is a 1-week program which involves an introduction to the law school program and services, as well as a "boot camp" introducing students to the subjects and methods of instruction and evaluation during the first year.

Electives
Students must take 10 credits in their area of concentration. The School of Law offers concentrations in corporate law, litigation, public interest, and gerneral practice. In addition, second- and third-year students may take clinics such as the Juvenile Clinic, Housing and Domestic Relations Clinic, and Wills Clinic for 3 credit hours each. Available seminars include Negotiation and Mediation, Interviewing and Counseling, and Separation of Powers, also for 3 credit hours each. Research program include Advanced Legal Research. Field work includes Legal Aid. There is the Joseph M. Bryan Distinguished Leadership Lecture Series and the tutorial prpogram, L.E.T.S. Study. The most widely taken electives are First Amendent, Wills and Trusts, and Remedies.

Phone: 336-279-9200
1-888 ELON LAW
Fax: 336-279-8199
E-mail: *law@elon.edu*
Web: *law.elon.edu*

Contact

Admissions Office, Elon University School of Law, 1-888-ELON LAW for general inquiries.

NORTH CAROLINA

Graduation Requirements

In order to graduate, candidates must have a GPA of 2.8 and have completed the upper-division writing requirement.

Organizations

Students edit the *Elon Law Review* and the newspaper, *Res Ipsa*. Moot court competitions include William C. Vis International Commercial Arbitration Moot, ABA National Appellate Advocacy Competition, J. Braxton Craven Moot Court Competition, and John Marshall Moot Court Competition. Law students organizations, local chapters of national associations, and campus organizations include Family Law Sociaty, Black Law Students Association, Outlaw, Delta Theta Phi, Phi Alpha Delta, Federalist Society, Intervarsidy Christian Fellowship, Public Interest Law Society, and Innocence Project.

Library

The law library contains 169,180 hardcopy volumes and 91,000 microform volume equivalents, and subscribes to 161 serial publications. Such on-line databases and networks as CALI, CIS Universe, Infotrac, Legal-Trac, LEXIS, LOIS, NEXIS, OCLC First Search, WESTLAW, DARTS, FLG, CCH, HEIN Online, and Leadership Library on the Internet are available to law students for research. Recently, the library established Online Chat Reference and Jump Start, a program of legal research and preparedness for summer practice. The ratio of library volumes to faculty is 8056 to 1 and to students is 537 to 1. The ratio of seats in the library to students is 1 to 2.

Faculty

The law school has 21 full-time and 33 part-time faculty members, of whom 20 are women. According to AAUP standards for Category IIA institutions, faculty salaries are average. About 29% of full-time faculty have a graduate law degree in addition to the J.D. The ratio of full-time students to full-time faculty in an average class is 17 to 1; in a clinic, 10 to 1. The law school has a regular program of bringing visiting professors and other distinguished lecturers and visitors to campus.

Students

About 45% of the student body are women; 12%, minorities; 6%, African American; 3%, Asian American; and 2%, Hispanic. The average age of entering students is 23. About 6% drop out after the first year for academic or personal reasons; 94% remain to receive a law degree.

Placement	
J.D.s awarded:	107
Services available through: a separate law school placement center	
Full-time job interviews:	n/av
Summer job interviews:	n/av
Placement by graduation:	n/av
Placement within 9 months:	n/av
Average starting salary:	n/av
Areas of placement:	n/av

EMORY UNIVERSITY

School of Law

Gambrell Hall, 1301 Clifton Road, N.E.
Atlanta, GA 30322

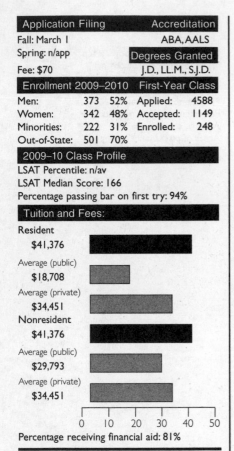

Application Filing		Accreditation
Fall: March 1		ABA, AALS
Spring: n/app		Degrees Granted
Fee: $70		J.D., LL.M., S.J.D.

Enrollment 2009–2010		First-Year Class	
Men:	373 52%	Applied:	4588
Women:	342 48%	Accepted:	1149
Minorities:	222 31%	Enrolled:	248
Out-of-State:	501 70%		

2009–10 Class Profile

LSAT Percentile: n/av
LSAT Median Score: 166
Percentage passing bar on first try: 94%

Tuition and Fees:

Resident
$41,376

Average (public)
$18,708

Average (private)
$34,451

Nonresident
$41,376

Average (public)
$29,793

Average (private)
$34,451

Percentage receiving financial aid: 81%

ADMISSIONS

In the fall 2009 first-year class, 4588 applied, 1149 were accepted, and 248 enrolled. Twenty-two transfers enrolled. The median GPA of the most recent first-year class was 3.57.

Requirements

Applicants must have a bachelor's degree and take the LSAT. The most important admission factors include LSAT results, GPA, and academic achievement. No specific undergraduate courses are required. Candidates are not interviewed.

Procedure

The application deadline for fall entry is March 1. Applicants should submit an application form, LSAT results, transcripts, a personal statement, TOEFL for foreign applicants, a nonrefundable application fee of $70, 2 letters of recommendation, and resumé or list of extracurricular activities. Notification of the admissions decision is from January to May. The latest acceptable LSAT test date for fall

entry is February. The law school uses the LSDAS.

Special

The law school recruits minority and disadvantaged students by visiting historically black colleges, attending college law fairs in the fall, sending mailings to minority students, and hosting several special on-site visits throughout the year. Requirements are not different for out-of-state students. Transfer students must have 1 year of credit, have attended an ABA-approved law school, and have a ranking of at least the top 50% of the class, although the top 20% to 25% is preferred. Preadmissions courses consist of the occasional CLEO summer institutes and a small program sponsored by the Georgia Legislature for minority students and students from disadvantaged backgrounds. Four students are chosen by Emory to participate in summer law classes held at the University of Georgia. Passing grades in the courses allow them to enroll at Emory Law School in the fall.

Costs

Tuition and fees for the 2009-2010 academic year are $41,376 for all full-time students. On-campus room and board costs about $16,516 annually; books and supplies run $2000.

Financial Aid

About 81% of current law students receive some form of aid. The average annual amount of aid from all sources combined, including scholarships, loans, and work contracts, is $41,748. Awards are based on need and merit, along with both merit and need; loans are either need or non-need, depending on the loan. Required financial statement is the FAFSA. The aid application deadline for fall entry is April 1. Special funds for minority or disadvantaged students include scholarships based on merit and need. First-year students are notified about their financial aid application some time shortly after students are accepted but before a tuition deposit is required.

About the Law School

Emory University School of Law was established in 1916 and is a private institution. The 600-acre campus is in an

urban area 7 miles northeast of Atlanta. The law school is dedicated to integrative, international, and interdisciplinary legal study and is committed to promoting scholarly excellence in a diverse community. The school educates leaders in society based on a common quest for knowledge, pursuit of public service, and advocacy for justice. Students have access to federal, state, county, city, and local agencies, courts, correctional facilities, law firms, and legal aid organizations in the Atlanta area. Students have access to national and regional businesses. Facilities of special interest to law students are the more than 45 clinics with federal agencies, judges, public interest offices, and businesses. Housing for students is readily available from the University and private parties in the immediate area, which offers many different options, such as apartments, condos, and rental homes. All law school facilities are accessible to the physically disabled.

Calendar

The law school operates on a traditional semester basis. Courses for full-time students are offered both day and evening and must be completed within 6 years. There is no part-time program. New students are admitted in the fall. There is no summer session. Transferable summer courses are not offered.

Programs

In addition to the J.D., the law school offers the LL.M. and S.J.D. Students may take relevant courses in other programs and apply credit toward the J.D.; a maximum of 6 credits may be applied. The following joint degrees may be earned: J.D./M.A. (Juris Doctor/Master of Arts in judaic studies), J.D./M.B.A. (Juris Doctor/Master of Business Administration), J.D./M.Div. (Juris Doctor/Master of Divinity), J.D./M.P.H. (Juris Doctor/Master of Public Health), J.D./M.T.S. (Juris Doctor/Master of Theological Studies), J.D./Ph.D. (Juris Doctor/Doctor of Philosophy in religion), and J.D./REES (Juris Doctor/Russian East European Studies Certificate).

Required

To earn the J.D., candidates must complete 90 total credits, of which 47 are for required courses. They must maintain a minimum GPA of 2.25 in the

Phone: 404-727-6801
Fax: 404-727-2477
E-mail: erosenz@law.emory.edu
Web: www.law.emory.edu

Contact

Ethan Rosenzweig, Assistant Dean of Admission, 404-727-6857 for general inquiries; Brenda Hill, Associate Director of Financial Aid, 404-727-6039 for financial aid information.

GEORGIA

required courses. The following first-year courses are required of all students: Civil Procedure I and II, Constitutional Law, Contracts, Criminal Law, Legal Methods, Legal Writing, Research, and Appellate Advocacy, Property, and Torts. Required upper-level courses consist of a writing requirement, Business Associations, Evidence, Legal Profession, and Trial Techniques. The required orientation program for first-year students is a 2-day period prior to registration and 1 day of optional activities that introduce students to the university and the law school communities. Students also attend a small section class during orientation.

Electives

The School of Law offers concentrations in corporate law, environmental law, intellectual property law, international law, litigation, tax law, law and religion, child advocacy, feminist jurisprudence, and legal theory. In addition, clinics are available to second- and third-year students for 3 credits, generally. Seminars are also open to second- and third-year students for 3 hours of academic credit. During the summer, most students have paid internships with firms, businesses, government offices, or public interest agencies. A small number of students may be offered research assistantships. Field placements are open to second- and third-year students for academic credit with more than 50 local businesses and federal and state courts and agencies. Students may take advantage of ABA accredited law school study abroad programs. Tutorials are offered to all students by professors on an individual basis. Academic assistance is made available to any student by request. Special consideration is given to minority students in the admissions process; and the diversity office offers programs and initiatives to build community and prepare students for success in diverse legal communities. The most widely taken electives are Criminal Procedure, Individual Tax, and Family Law.

Graduation Requirements

In order to graduate, candidates must have a GPA of 2.25 and have completed the upper-division writing requirement.

Organizations

Student-edited publications are the *Emory Law Journal, Emory International Law Review,* and *Emory Bankruptcy Journal.* Annually, moot court teams participate in internal competitions, the Georgia Intra-State Moot Court, the National First Amendment Moot Court, and the Jessup International Law Moot Court competitions, among others. Other competitions include the Frederick Douglass Moot Court Competition, the Negotiation Competition, and the National Hispanic Bar Association Moot Court Competition. Law student organizations include the Alternative Dispute Resolutions Society, the Emory Public Interest Committee, and the Health Law Society. Local chapters of national associations include the Association of Trial Lawyers of America, the Federalist Society for Law and Public Policy, and Phi Alpha Delta. Campus clubs and other organizations include Legal Association of Women Students, Black Law Students Association, and Emory Gay and Lesbian Advocates.

Library

The law library contains 308,364 hardcopy volumes and 107,514 microform volume equivalents, and subscribes to 3867 serial publications. Such on-line databases and networks as CALI, CIS Universe, DIALOG, Dow-Jones, Infotrac, Legal-Trac, LEXIS, LOIS, Mathew Bender, NEXIS, OCLC First Search, RLIN, WESTLAW, and Wilsonline Indexes are available to law students for research. Special library collections include a European Union depository and a federal depository. Recently, the library expanded electronic resources and wireless Internet access throughout the library and law school. The ratio of library volumes to faculty is 4818 to 1 and to students is 431 to 1. The ratio of seats in the library to students is 1 to 1.

Faculty

The law school has 64 full-time and 42 part-time faculty members, of whom 39 are women. According to AAUP standards for Category I institutions, faculty salaries are above average. The ratio of full-time students to full-time faculty in an average class is 11 to 1; in a clinic, 2 to 1. The law school has a regular program of bringing visiting professors and other distinguished lecturers and visitors to campus. There is a chapter of the Order of the Coif.

Placement

J.D.s awarded:	221

Services available through: a separate law school placement center

Special features: personal advising and programming designed to assist students, specific advising in public interest law by the Associate Director of Career Services, and off-campus job fairs in New York, Washington, D.C., Chicago, Dallas, and Los Angeles, among others.

Full-time job interviews:	n/av
Summer job interviews:	n/av
Placement by graduation:	97% of class
Placement within 9 months:	95% of class
Average starting salary:	$52,000 to $145,000

Areas of placement:

Private practice 2-10 attorneys	9%
Private practice 11-25 attorneys	4%
Private practice 26-50 attorneys	6%
Private practice 51-100 attorneys	2%
Private practice 101+ attorneys	50%
Business/industry	11%
Judicial clerkships	9%
Government	9%
Public interest	2%

Students

About 48% of the student body are women; 31%, minorities; 10%, African American; 13%, Asian American; 12%, Hispanic; 5%, foreign. The majority of students come from the South (31%). The average age of entering students is 23; age range is 20 to 50. About 45% of students enter directly from undergraduate school. About 2% drop out after the first year for academic or personal reasons; 98% remain to receive a law degree.

Thomas Goode Jones School of Law

5345 Atlanta Highway
Montgomery, AL 36109

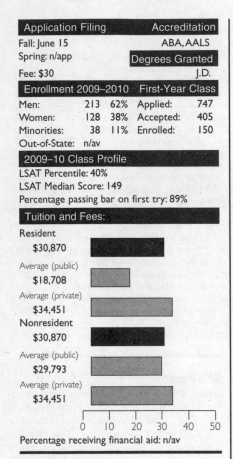

Application Filing		Accreditation
Fall: June 15		ABA, AALS
Spring: n/app		Degrees Granted
Fee: $30		J.D.

Enrollment 2009–2010		First-Year Class	
Men:	213 62%	Applied:	747
Women:	128 38%	Accepted:	405
Minorities:	38 11%	Enrolled:	150
Out-of-State:	n/av		

2009–10 Class Profile

LSAT Percentile: 40%
LSAT Median Score: 149
Percentage passing bar on first try: 89%

Tuition and Fees:

Resident
$30,870

Average (public)
$18,708

Average (private)
$34,451

Nonresident
$30,870

Average (public)
$29,793

Average (private)
$34,451

0 10 20 30 40 50

Percentage receiving financial aid: n/av

ADMISSIONS

In the fall 2009 first-year class, 747 applied, 405 were accepted, and 150 enrolled. One transfer enrolled. The median LSAT percentile of the most recent first-year class was 40; the median GPA was 3.08 on a scale of 4.0.

Requirements
Applicants must have a bachelor's degree and take the LSAT. No specific undergraduate courses are required. Candidates are not interviewed.

Procedure
The application deadline for fall entry is June 15. Applicants should submit an application form, LSAT results, transcripts, a personal statement, and a nonrefundable application fee of $30; letters of recommendation are welcome but not required. The latest acceptable LSAT test date for fall entry is June. The law school uses the LSDAS.

Special
Requirements are not different for out-of-state students. Transfer students must have attended an ABA-approved law school and must be in good standing and can transfer a maximum of 30 credit hours.

Costs

Tuition and fees for the 2009-2010 academic year are $30,870 for all full-time students. Books and supplies run $3000.

Financial Aid

Required financial statement is the FAFSA.

About the Law School

Faulkner University Thomas Goode Jones School of Law was established in 1928 and is a private institution. The campus is in an urban area. Students have access to federal, state, county, city, and local agencies, courts, correctional facilities, law firms, and legal aid organizations in the Montgomery area. Housing for students is not available on campus. All law school facilities are accessible to the physically disabled.

Calendar

The law school operates on a traditional semester basis. Courses for full-time students are offered days only. There is no part-time program. New students are admitted in the fall. There is an 8-week summer session. Transferable summer courses are offered.

Programs

Required
To earn the J.D., candidates must complete 90 total credits, of which 51 are for required courses. The following first-year courses are required of all students: Civil Procedure, Contracts, Criminal Law, Legal Research and Writing, Property, and Torts. Required upper-level courses consist of Business Associations, Constitutional Law, Evidence, Practice Skills, Professional Responsibility, and Remedies. The required orientation program for first-year students is a 4-day introduction

to analytical reasoning, legal research and writing, the court system, and professionalism.

Electives
The Thomas Goode Jones School of Law offers concentrations in corporate law, criminal law, entertainment law, environmental law, family law, intellectual property law, international law, juvenile law, labor law, litigation, securities law, sports law, tax law, torts and insurance, and alternative dispute resolution. Students may participate in the Elder Law Clinic, Family Violence Clinic, and the Mediation Clinic.

Graduation Requirements
In order to graduate, candidates must have a GPA of 2.0, and have completed the upper-division writing requirement, and practical skills or oral advocacy course.

Organizations

Students edit the *Faulkner Law Review*. Students participate in the National Moot Court Competition, ABA National Appellate Competition, National Health Law Moot Court Competition, and Buffalo/Niagara National Mock Trial Competition. Other competitions include National Trial Competition, Thurgood Marshall Mock Trial Competition, ABA Employment Law National Mock Trial Competition, William Daniel National Criminal Law Mock Trial Competition, AAJ National Trial Competition, and ABA Representation in Mediation Competition. Law student organizations, local chapters of national associations, and campus clubs and organizations include the Christian Legal Society, Women Students Association, Federalist Society, American Constitution Society, American Association for Justice, Black Law Students Association, Phi Alpha Delta, Animal Law Society, Board of Advocates, and Jones Law Republicans.

Phone: 334-386-7210
800-879-9816
Fax: 334-386-7223
E-mail: *law@faulkner.edu*
Web: *www.faulkner.edu/law*

Contact

Andrew R. Matthews, Assistant Dean for Student Services, 334-386-7210 for general inquiries; William G. Jackson, Director of Financial Aid, 334-386-7195 for financial aid information.

ALABAMA

Faculty

The law school has 29 full-time faculty members, of whom 10 are women. About 15% of full-time faculty have a graduate law degree in addition to the J.D. The ratio of full-time students to full-time faculty in an average class is 40 to 1; in a clinic, 12 to 1. The law school has a regular program of bringing visiting professors and other distinguished lecturers and visitors to campus. There is a chapter of the Order of the Coif with a current membership of 1.

Students

About 38% of the student body are women; 13%, minorities; 7%, African American; 2%, Asian American; 2%, Hispanic; and 2%, Native American.

Placement	
J.D.s awarded:	65
Services available through: a separate law school placement center	
Full-time job interviews:	n/av
Summer job interviews:	n/av
Placement by graduation:	n/av
Placement within 9 months:	n/av
Average starting salary:	n/av
Areas of placement:	n/av

FLORIDA AGRICULTURAL AND MECHANICAL UNIVERSITY

Florida A & M University College of Law

201 N. Beggs Avenue
Orlando, FL 32801

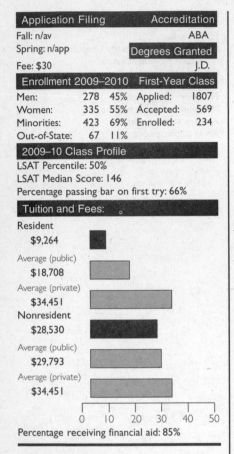

Application Filing		Accreditation
Fall: n/av		ABA
Spring: n/app		
Fee: $30		**Degrees Granted**
		J.D.

Enrollment 2009–2010		First-Year Class	
Men:	278 45%	Applied:	1807
Women:	335 55%	Accepted:	569
Minorities:	423 69%	Enrolled:	234
Out-of-State:	67 11%		

2009–10 Class Profile
LSAT Percentile: 50%
LSAT Median Score: 146
Percentage passing bar on first try: 66%

Tuition and Fees:

Resident
$9,264

Average (public)
$18,708

Average (private)
$34,451

Nonresident
$28,530

Average (public)
$29,793

Average (private)
$34,451

0   10   20   30   40   50

Percentage receiving financial aid: 85%

ADMISSIONS

In the fall 2009 first-year class, 1807 applied, 569 were accepted, and 234 enrolled. One transfer enrolled. The median LSAT percentile of the most recent first-year class was 50; the median GPA was 3.07 on a scale of 4.0.

Requirements
Applicants must have a bachelor's degree and take the LSAT. The most important admission factors include academic achievement, LSAT results, public service, and writing ability. Candidates are not interviewed.

Procedure
The priority application deadline for fall entry is April 1. Applicants should submit an application form, LSAT results, transcripts, TOEFL, an application fee of $30, 2 letters of recommendation, and a personal statement. Notification of the admissions decision is on a rolling basis. The latest acceptable LSAT test date for

fall entry is February. The law school uses the LSDAS.

Special
Requirements are not different for out-of-state students. Transfer students are accepted on a case-by-case basis. Transfer students must have attended an ABA-approved law school. A Maximum of 30 credit hours may be given for work at another ABA approved law school.

Costs

Tuition and fees for the 2009-2010 academic year are $9264 for full-time in-state students and $28,530 for out-of-state students. Tuition for part-time students is $6855 in-state and $20,983 out-of-state. Books and supplies run $1000.

Financial Aid

About 85% of current law students receive some form of aid. The average annual amount of aid from all sources combined, including scholarships, loans, and work contracts, is $29,206; maximum, $55,000. Federal aid is based on need. Scholarships are based on merit. Required financial statement is the FAFSA. The aid application deadline for fall entry is March 1. There is a grant available for black students in the day program based on merit that has the possibility of renewal each year. First-year students are notified about their financial aid application at time of acceptance.

About the Law School

Florida Agricultural and Mechanical University Florida A & M University College of Law was established in 2000 and is a public institution. The campus is in an urban area of Orlando. The primary mission of the law school is to cultivate, through its faculty professionalism, respect, and responsibility toward others. Students have access to federal, state, county, city, and local agencies, courts, correctional facilities, law firms, and legal aid organizations in the Orlando area. Facilities of special interest to law students include the state of the art moot court room. All law school facilities are accessible to the physically disabled.

Calendar

The law school operates on a traditional semester basis. Courses for full-time students are offered both day and evening and must be completed within 5 years. For part-time students, courses are offered both day and evening and must be completed within 6 years. New full- and part-time students are admitted in the fall. There is a 10-week summer session.

Programs

Required
To earn the J.D., candidates must complete 90 total credits, of which 61 are for required courses. They must maintain a minimum GPA of 2.0 in the required courses. The following first-year courses are required of all students: Civil Procedure I and II, Constitutional Law I, Contracts I and II, Legal Methods I and II, Property I and II, and Torts I and II. Required upper-level courses consist of Business Organizations, Clinical Program/Pro Bono, Constitutional Law II, Criminal Law, Criminal Procedure, Estates and Trusts, Evidence, Family Law, Florida Constitutional Law, Florida Practice, and Professional Responsibility. All students must take clinical courses. The required orientation program for first-year students is a 1 week program designed to facilitate a student's entry into law schools. Case briefing, study skills, debt and time management, and professionalism are covered.

Electives
The Florida A & M University College of Law offers concentrations in international law. In addition, all upper-division students are eligible to participate in clinics. Some clinics have prerequisites. Clinics offer 6 to 12 credits and include Community Economic Development, Homelessness and Legal Advocacy, Guardian or Trial Practice, and Evidence. All upper-division students are also eligible to participate in seminars worth 2 credits. All upper-division students are eligible to participate in internship programs. Internships usually are awarded 1 or 2 credits depending on the student effort required. The Academic Success and Bar Preparation Program provides tutorial assistance to students.

Phone: 407-254-3268

E-mail: famulaw.admissions@famu.edu

Web: law.famu.edu

Contact

Office of Admissions, 407-254-3286 for general inquiries; Kareman Campbell, 407-254-4016 for financial aid information.

Graduation Requirements

In order to graduate, candidates must have a GPA of 2.0 and have completed the upper-division writing requirement.

Organizations

Students edit the *Florida A&M University College- Law Review* and the newspaper, *The FAMU Lawyer*. Other publications include *The Record*. Moot court competitions include the American Bar Association (ABA) Moot Court Competition, Frederick Douglas Moot Court Competition, and Saul Lefkowitz Moot Court Competition. Other competitions include the BMI Cardozo Entertainment Communications Law Moot Court Competition, and Thurgood Marshall Mock Trial Competition. Law student organizations include the Student Bar Association, Black Law Students Association, and Women's Law Caucus. Local chapters of national associations include the Phi Alpha Delta Law Fraternity, International Hispanic American Law Students Association, and Federalist Law Society. Campus clubs and other organizations include the Criminal Law Association, Christian Legal Society, and Enterntainment, Arts and Sports Law Society.

Library

The law library contains 368,923 hardcopy volumes and 128,224 microform volume equivalents, and subscribes to 2072 serial publications. Such on-line databases and networks as CALI, CIS Universe, Infotrac, Legal-Trac, LEXIS, LOIS, NEXIS, OCLC First Search, WESTLAW,

Wilsonline Indexes, CCH Business and Tax, RIA, HeinOnline, and BNA are available to law students for research. Special library collections include Virgil Hawkins Collection and International Law Collection. Recently, the library added the International Law Special Collection. The ratio of library volumes to faculty is 8020 to 1 and to students is 602 to 1. The ratio of seats in the library to students is 1 to 1.

Faculty

The law school has 46 full-time and 11 part-time faculty members, of whom 25 are women. According to AAUP standards for Category IIA institutions, faculty salaries are average. About 17% of full-time faculty have a graduate law degree in addition to the J.D. The ratio of full-time students to full-time faculty in an average class is 18 to 1. The law school has a regular program of bringing visiting professors and other distinguished lecturers and visitors to campus.

Students

About 55% of the student body are women; 69%, minorities; 49%, African American; 3%, Asian American; 16%, Hispanic; and 1%, Native American. The majority of students come from Florida (89%). The average age of entering students is 31; age range is 21 to 66. About 14% of students enter directly from undergraduate school, 18% have a graduate degree, and 86% have worked full-time prior to entering law school. About 3% drop out after the first year for academic or personal reasons; 97% remain to receive a law degree.

Placement

J.D.s awarded:	164
Services available through: a separate law school placement center	
Services: Individual one-to-one mentoring pairing a law student with a practitioner in his/her area of interest	
Special features: Speaker's Series (special guest speakers)	
Full-time job interviews:	n/av
Summer job interviews:	n/av
Placement by graduation:	65% of class
Placement within 9 months:	90% of class
Average starting salary:	$35,000 to $110,000
Areas of placement:	
Private practice 2-10 attorneys	30%
Private practice 11-25 attorneys	5%
Government	22%
Unknown	23%
Business/industry	8%
Public interest	8%
Judicial clerkships	2%
Military	2%

School of Law

8787 Baypine Rd.
Jacksonville, FL 32256

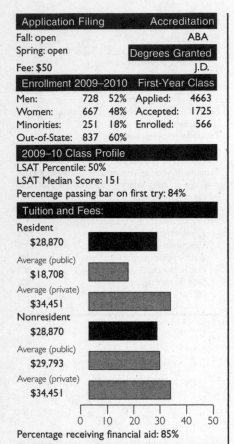

Application Filing		Accreditation
Fall: open		ABA
Spring: open		Degrees Granted
Fee: $50		J.D.

Enrollment 2009–2010		First-Year Class	
Men:	728 52%	Applied:	4663
Women:	667 48%	Accepted:	1725
Minorities:	251 18%	Enrolled:	566
Out-of-State:	837 60%		

2009–10 Class Profile
LSAT Percentile: 50%
LSAT Median Score: 151
Percentage passing bar on first try: 84%

Tuition and Fees:

Resident
$28,870

Average (public)
$18,708

Average (private)
$34,451

Nonresident
$28,870

Average (public)
$29,793

Average (private)
$34,451

0 10 20 30 40 50

Percentage receiving financial aid: 85%

ADMISSIONS

In a recent year, 4663 applied, 1725 were accepted, and 566 enrolled. Thirty-five transfers enrolled. The median LSAT percentile of the most recent first-year class was 50; the median GPA was 3.17 on a scale of 4.0. The lowest LSAT percentile accepted was 25; the highest was 95. Figures in the above capsule and in this profile are approximate.

Requirements
Applicants must have a bachelor's degree and take the LSAT. Minimum acceptable GPA is 2.0 on a scale of 4.0. The most important admission factors include LSAT results, GPA, and life experience. No specific undergraduate courses are required. Candidates are not interviewed.

Procedure
Applicants should submit an application form, LSAT results, a nonrefundable application fee of $50, and 2 letters of recommendation. Notification of the admissions decision is on a rolling basis. The latest acceptable LSAT test date for fall entry is June. The law school uses the LSDAS. Check with the school for the current application deadlines.

Special
The law school recruits minority and disadvantaged students through law forums, career fairs, and scholarships. Requirements are not different for out-of-state students. Transfer students must have a minimum GPA of 2 and have attended an ABA-approved law school.

Costs

Tuition and fees for the 2009-2010 academic year are approximately $28,870 for all full-time students. Tuition for part-time students is approximately $23,360 per year. Books and supplies run about $1200.

Financial Aid

In a recent year, about 85% of current law students received some form of aid. The average annual amount of aid from all sources combined, including scholarships, loans, and work contracts, was approximately $18,500; maximum, $27,750. Awards are based on need and merit. Required financial statements are the FAFSA and Institutional application. First-year students are notified about their financial aid application at time of acceptance. Check with the school for the current application deadline.

About the Law School

Florida Coastal School of Law was established in 1996 is independent. The 5-acre campus is in a suburban area near downtown Jacksonville and the beach. The primary mission of the law school is to distinguish itself as a forward-looking, globally interactive, and culturally diverse institution dedicated to having a positive impact on its students, the community, the legal profession, and the justice system. Students have access to federal, state, county, city, and local agencies, courts, correctional facilities, law firms, and legal aid organizations in the Jacksonville area. Facilities of special interest to law students include the Information Resources and Technology Division; the Center for Strategic Governance and

Information Initiatives, and an on-campus teen court. Housing for students includes a large variety of close and affordable off-campus apartments and homes. All law school facilities are accessible to the physically disabled.

Calendar

The law school operates on a traditional semester basis. Courses for full-time students are offered both day and evening and must be completed within 5 years. For part-time students, courses are offered both day and evening and must be completed within 6 years. New full- and part-time students are admitted in the fall and spring. There is an 8-week summer session. Transferable summer courses are offered.

Programs

Students may take relevant courses in other programs and apply credit toward the J.D.; a maximum of 6 credits may be applied.

Required
To earn the J.D., candidates must complete 87 total credits, of which 56 are for required courses. They must maintain a minimum GPA of 2.0 in the required courses. The following first-year courses are required of all students: Civil Procedure I and II, Contracts I and II, Criminal Law, Lawyering Process I and II, Property I and II, and Torts I and II. Required upper-level courses consist of an advanced writing requirement, Business Associations, Constitutional Law I and II, Criminal Procedure, Evidence, Family Law, Professional Responsibility, and Sales. All students must take clinical courses. The required orientation program for first-year students is 2 1/2 days and includes interactions with faculty, staff, and students; the role of the lawyer and professionalism; the responsibilities of the future lawyer and student ethics; Academic Success programs; and a reception.

Electives
The School of Law offers concentrations in corporate law, criminal law, entertainment law, environmental law, family law, international law, juvenile law, labor law, litigation, maritime law, media law, secu-

Phone: 904-680-7710
877-210-2591
Fax: 904-680-7776
E-mail: *admissions@fcsl.edu*
Web: *www.fcsl.edu*

Contact
Office of Admissions, 904-680-7710 for general inquiries; Office of Admissions, 904-680-7710 for financial aid information.

rities law, sports law, tax law, and intellectual property, and public interest law. In addition, third-year clinics include Criminal, Civil, Municipal, Domestic Violence, and Caribbean Law Clinic. Students may earn up to 6 credits in each clinic. Seminars are available to upper-division students only. These include Environmental Law, Sports Law, Appellate Advocacy, and Maritime Law, each worth 3 credit hours each. Other seminars may be offered periodically depending upon the interest of students and faculty. Internships with federal and state court judges can be taken for 3 or 4 credit hours. Students must have completed Professional Responsibility, Evidence, and Constitutional Law. Advanced Legal Research, worth 2 credit hours, is open to upper-division students. Independent study with a full-time faculty member is also available for up to 2 credit hours. The School of Law invites practitioners, judges, and other public figures to speak on a variety of topics, including legal practice, legal education, and jurisprudence. An Academic Success program is aimed at serving two groups of students: (1) incoming students considered at risk because of low LSAT scores or low GPA; (2) or students who are re-entering school after a long absence; and (3) current students who are at risk or on academic probation. The program consists of workshops on a variety of topics, including case briefing, study aids, and exam-taking. In addition, the School of Law has tutors for all first-year classes. Students may also meet with the program director to deal with individual problem issues. The most widely taken electives are Remedies, Trusts and Estates, and Florida Practice and Procedure.

Graduation Requirements
In order to graduate, candidates must have a GPA of 2.0 and have completed the upper-division writing requirement.

Organizations
Students edit the *Florida Coastal School of Law Review* and the newspaper, *Coastal Tidings*. Moot court competitions include the Robert Orseck Memorial Moot Court and the E. Earl Zehemer Memorial Moot Court. Law student organizations include the Student Bar Association, Black Law Students Association, and CAPIL. There is a local chapter of ABA-Law Students Division, Phi Alpha Delta, and Law and Technology Society. Other organizations include the Environmental and Land Use Club, Hispanic American Law Students Association, and Sports Law Association.

Library
The law library contains 223,820 hardcopy volumes and 469,002 microform volume equivalents, and subscribes to 3125 serial publications. Such on-line databases and networks as CALI, CIS Universe, Infotrac, Legal-Trac, LEXIS, LOIS, Matthew Bender, NEXIS, OCLC First Search, WESTLAW, and CCH Internet Tax, HR and Business Networks, UN Treaty Collection, and Hein On-line are available to law students for research. Recently, the library added staff to provide services to patrons. The ratio of library volumes to faculty is 3610 to 1 and to students is 210 to 1. The ratio of seats in the library to students is 1 to 8.

Faculty
The law school has 62 full-time and 45 part-time faculty members, of whom 50 are women. About 13% of full-time faculty have a graduate law degree in addition to the J.D.; about 7% of part-time faculty have one. The ratio of full-time students to full-time faculty in an average class is 18 to 1; in a clinic, 12 to 1. The law school has a regular program of bringing visiting professors and other distinguished lecturers and visitors to campus.

Students
About 48% of the student body are women; 18%, minorities; 11%, African American; 3%, Asian American; 3%, Hispanic; and 1%, Native American. The majority of students come from Florida (40%). The average age of entering students is 27; age range is 21 to 68. About 50% of students enter directly from undergraduate school, 20% have a graduate degree, and 50% have worked full-time prior to entering law school. About 8% drop out after the first year for academic or personal reasons; 92% remain to receive a law degree.

Placement
J.D.s awarded:	82
Services available through: a separate law school placement center	
Services: job opportunity list service, job fairs	
Special features: extensive programming on a variety of career development topics including practice areas, work environments, alternative careers, and transition from school to the work force.	
Full-time job interviews:	6 employers
Summer job interviews:	5 employers
Placement by graduation:	40% of class
Placement within 9 months:	90% of class
Average starting salary:	$35,000 to $80,000
Areas of placement:	
Private practice 2-10 attorneys	63%
Government	18%
Business/industry	18%

FLORIDA INTERNATIONAL UNIVERSITY

College of Law

FIU College of Law, RDB 1055
Miami, FL 33199

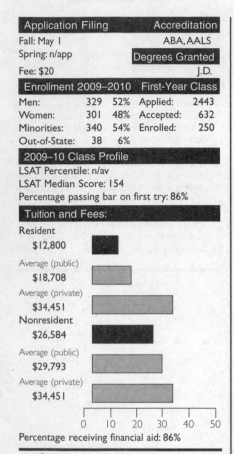

Application Filing	Accreditation
Fall: May 1	ABA, AALS
Spring: n/app	**Degrees Granted**
Fee: $20	J.D.

Enrollment 2009–2010		First-Year Class	
Men:	329 52%	Applied:	2443
Women:	301 48%	Accepted:	632
Minorities:	340 54%	Enrolled:	250
Out-of-State:	38 6%		

2009–10 Class Profile
LSAT Percentile: n/av
LSAT Median Score: 154
Percentage passing bar on first try: 86%

Tuition and Fees:

Resident
$12,800

Average (public)
$18,708

Average (private)
$34,451

Nonresident
$26,584

Average (public)
$29,793

Average (private)
$34,451

0 10 20 30 40 50

Percentage receiving financial aid: 86%

ADMISSIONS

In the fall 2009 first-year class, 2443 applied, 632 were accepted, and 250 enrolled. Seven transfers enrolled. The median GPA of the most recent first-year class was 3.4. The lowest LSAT percentile accepted was 151; the highest was 156.

Requirements
Applicants must have a bachelor's degree and take the LSAT. Minimum acceptable GPA is 2.0 on a scale of 4.0. The most important admission factors include GPA, LSAT results, and writing ability. No specific undergraduate courses are required. Candidates are not interviewed.

Procedure
The application deadline for fall entry is May 1. Applicants should submit an application form, LSAT results, transcripts, a personal statement, a nonrefundable application fee of $20, and 3 letters of recommendation. Notification of the admissions decision is on a rolling basis. The latest acceptable LSAT test date for fall

entry is February. The law school uses the LSDAS.

Special
The law school recruits minority and disadvantaged students by participation and sponsorship of pipeline initiatives, minority targeted events, application fee waiver programs, and direct mailing campaigns. Requirements are not different for out-of-state students. Transfer students must have 1 year of credit and have attended an ABA-approved law school.

Costs

Tuition and fees for the 2009-2010 academic year are $12,800 for full-time in-state students and $26,584 for out-of-state students. Tuition for part-time students is $9682 in-state and $20,021 out-of-state. On-campus room and board costs about $10,680 annually; books and supplies run $2652.

Financial Aid

About 86% of current law students receive some form of aid. The average annual amount of aid from all sources combined, including scholarships, loans, and work contracts, is $34,239; maximum, $50,496. Awards are based on need and merit. Required financial statement is the FAFSA. The aid application deadline for fall entry is February 1. First-year students are notified about their financial aid application at time of acceptance.

About the Law School

Florida International University College of Law was established in 2000 and is a public institution. The 584-acre campus is in an urban area Miami Dade County, Florida. The primary mission of the law school is to serve the citizens of the state of Florida, particularly south Florida, by providing access to the legal profession through a high quality educational program. Students have access to federal, state, county, city, and local agencies, courts, correctional facilities, law firms, and legal aid organizations in the Miami area. Housing for students is in a wing of a residence hall. All law school facilities are accessible to the physically disabled.

Calendar

The law school operates on a traditional semester basis. Courses for full-time students are offered both day and evening and must be completed within 7 years. For part-time students, courses are offered both day and evening and must be completed within 7 years. New full- and part-time students are admitted in the fall. There is a 12-week summer session. Transferable summer courses are offered.

Programs

Students may take relevant courses in other programs and apply credit toward the J.D.; a maximum of 6 credits credits may be applied. The following joint degrees may be earned: J.D./M.A.L.A.C.S. (Juris Doctor/Master of Latin American and Caribbean Studies), J.D./M.B.A. (Juris Doctor/Master of Business Administration), J.D./M.I.B. (Juris Doctor/Master of International Business), J.D./M.P.A. (Juris Doctor/Master of Public Administration), J.D./M.S. Psych (Juris Doctor/Master of Psychology), J.D./M.S.C.J. (Juris Doctor/Master of Criminal Justice), J.D./M.S.E. (Juris Doctor/Master of Environmental Studies), and J.D./M.S.W. (Juris Doctor/Master of Social Work).

Required
To earn the J.D., candidates must complete 90 total credits, of which 31 are for required courses. They must maintain a minimum GPA of 2.0 in the required courses. The following first-year courses are required of all students: Civil Procedure, Constitutional Law, Contracts, Criminal Law, Introduction to International and Comparative Law, Legal Skills and Values I and II, Property, and Torts. Required upper-level courses consist of 2 Litigation and Alternative Dispute Resolution courses, International and Comparative Law, Legal Skills and Values III, and Professional Responsibility. The required orientation program for first-year students is 3 days including coaching by legal writing instructors on writing briefs and preparing for class in a series of mock classes.

Electives
Clinics, open to second- and third-year students, include Community Development Clinic, Criminal Law Clinic, Immigration and Human Rights Clinic, and

Phone: (305) 348-8006
Fax: (305) 348-2965
E-mail: miroa@fiu.edu
Web: http://law.fiu.edu

Contact

Alma O. Miro', Director of Admissions and Financ, 305-348-8006 for general inquiries; Alma O. Miro', Director of Admissions and Financ, 305-348-8006 for financial aid information.

Juvenile Justice Judicial Clinic. All second-, third-, and fourth-year students are eligible to enroll in a seminar. Seminars include Critical Race Theory, Constitutional Theory, and Islamic Law, 2 credits each. Internships may be done under the supervision of a professor, most are done in international or foreign settings. Research programs include the Legal Skills and Values program. All students are required to complete 30 hours of community service with a pro bono organization. Special lecture series include the Faculty Colloquia Series. Study abroad is available in Sevilla, Spain. The College of Law has a comprehensive tutorial and academic support program, which is headed by the Assistant Dean of the Academic Support Program. The most widely taken electives are Evidence, Business Organizations, and Sales.

Graduation Requirements

In order to graduate, candidates must have a GPA of 2.0, and have completed the upper-division writing requirement, which must be completed as part of a seminar.

Organizations

The primary law review is the *Florida International University College of Law, Law Review*. Moot court competitions include the Wechler First Amendment Moot Court Competition, Orseck Memorial Moot Court Competition, and the National Moot Court Competition. Other competitions include the ABA Negotiations Competition, Bedell Trial Advocacy Competition, and ATLA Trial Competition. Law student organizations include the Black Law Students Association, Student Bar Association, and Hispanic Law Students Association. Local chapters of national associations include Phi Alpha Delta, Federalist Society, American Inns of Court, and Student Government Association.

Library

The law library contains 213,410 hardcopy volumes and 123,491 microform volume equivalents, and subscribes to 1500 serial publications. Such on-line databases and networks as CALI, CIS Universe, Infotrac, Legal-Trac, LEXIS, Mathew Bender, NEXIS, OCLC First Search, RLIN, WESTLAW, Wilsonline Indexes, and many others are available to law students for research. Special library collections include Cuba, Latin America, and Caribbean legal materials, as well as those on international and comparative law, national security and human rights. Recently, the library added a new Cuban collection, and has longer hours. The ratio of library volumes to faculty is 6669 to 1 and to students is 339 to 1. The ratio of seats in the library to students is 1 to 2.

Faculty

The law school has 32 full-time and 21 part-time faculty members, of whom 26 are women. According to AAUP standards for Category I institutions, faculty salaries are well below average. About 45% of full-time faculty have a graduate law degree in addition to the J.D. The ratio of full-time students to full-time faculty in an average class is 40 to 1; in a clinic, 8 to 1. The law school has a regular program of bringing visiting professors and other distinguished lecturers and visitors to campus.

Students

About 48% of the student body are women; 54%, minorities; 9%, African American; 2%, Asian American; 43%, Hispanic; 1%, Native American; and 1%, foreign nationals, 41%, whites, 3% unknown. The majority of students come from Florida (94%). The average age of entering students is 26; age range is 19 to 58. About 5% drop out after the first year for academic or personal reasons; 83% remain to receive a law degree.

Placement

J.D.s awarded:	118
Services available through: a separate law school placement center	
Special features: Public Service Fellows Program, mock interviews, workshop series, and one on one counseling	
Full-time job interviews:	12 employers
Summer job interviews:	19 employers
Placement by graduation:	21% of class
Placement within 9 months:	86% of class
Average starting salary:	$42,000 to $110,000
Areas of placement:	
Private practice 2-10 attorneys	52%
Private practice 11-25 attorneys	3%
Private practice 26-50 attorneys	6%
Private practice 51-100 attorneys	9%
Public interest	4%
Business/industry	14%
Judicial clerkships	1%
Government	8%

FLORIDA STATE UNIVERSITY

College of Law

425 W. Jefferson St.
Tallahassee, FL 32306-1601

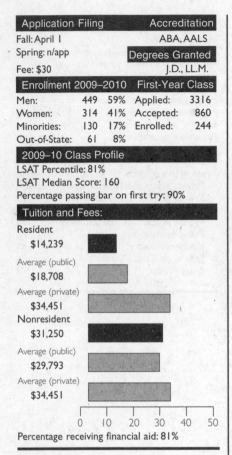

Application Filing	Accreditation
Fall: April 1	ABA, AALS
Spring: n/app	Degrees Granted
Fee: $30	J.D., LL.M.

Enrollment 2009–2010		First-Year Class	
Men:	449 59%	Applied:	3316
Women:	314 41%	Accepted:	860
Minorities:	130 17%	Enrolled:	244
Out-of-State:	61 8%		

2009–10 Class Profile
LSAT Percentile: 81%
LSAT Median Score: 160
Percentage passing bar on first try: 90%

Tuition and Fees:

Resident
$14,239

Average (public)
$18,708

Average (private)
$34,451

Nonresident
$31,250

Average (public)
$29,793

Average (private)
$34,451

0 10 20 30 40 50

Percentage receiving financial aid: 81%

ADMISSIONS

In the fall 2009 first-year class, 3316 applied, 860 were accepted, and 244 enrolled. Twenty-seven transfers enrolled. The median LSAT percentile of the most recent first-year class was 81; the median GPA was 3.53 on a scale of 4.0. The highest LSAT percentile was 98.

Requirements
Applicants must have a bachelor's degree and take the LSAT. The most important admission factors include, LSAT results, GPA, and academic achievement. No specific undergraduate courses are required. Candidates are not interviewed.

Procedure
The application deadline for fall entry is April 1. Applicants should submit an application form, LSAT results, transcripts, a personal statement, a nonrefundable application fee of $30, 2 letters of recommendation, and a resume. Notification of the admissions decision is on a rolling basis. The latest acceptable LSAT

test date for fall entry is February. The law school uses the LSDAS.

Special
The law school recruits minority and disadvantaged students through the LSDAS-CRS, by sponsoring special programs throughout the year, by recruiting at colleges and universities, and through electronic outreach. Requirements are not different for out-of-state students. Transfer students must have one year of credit and be in the top third of their class.

Costs

Tuition and fees for the 2009-2010 academic year are $14,239 for full-time in-state students and $31,250 for out-of-state students. On-campus room and board costs about $9000 annually; books and supplies run $1000.

Financial Aid

About 81% of current law students receive some form of aid. The average annual amount of aid from all sources combined, including scholarships, loans, and work contracts, is $22,750; maximum, $48,250. Awards are based on need and merit. Approximately 35% of the entering class received a scholarship for the first year. Awards range from $1000 to $15,000. Required financial statement is the FAFSA. The aid application deadline for fall entry is April 1. Special funds for minority or disadvantaged students include diversity enhancement scholarships. First-year students are notified about their financial aid application at time of acceptance on a rolling basis.

About the Law School

Florida State University College of Law was established in 1966 and is a public institution. The 1620-acre campus (including the Panama City and Ringling campus) is in a suburban area in Tallahassee, the state capital. The primary mission of the law school is to ensure, through a multi-disciplinary teaching approach, that students are prepared for a rapidly changing legal profession and can successfully compete anywhere. Students have access to federal, state, county, city, and local agencies, courts, correctional facilities, law firms, and legal aid organizations in the Tallahassee area. The State Legisla-

tive and the State and Supreme Court law libraries, located nearby, are available for students. Housing for students is available in dorms for single students and apartments for both single and married students are available. A housing office helps students find off-campus accommodations. All law school facilities are accessible to the physically disabled.

Calendar

The law school operates on a traditional semester basis. Courses for full-time students are offered both day and evening and must be completed within 3 years. There is no part-time program. New students are admitted in the fall. There is a 7-week summer session. Transferable summer courses are offered.

Programs

In addition to the J.D., the law school offers the LL.M. Students may take relevant courses in other programs and apply credit toward the J.D.; a maximum of 6 credits may be applied. The following joint degrees may be earned: J.D./M.B.A. (Juris Doctor/Master of Business Administration), J.D./M.P.A. (Juris Doctor/Master of Public Administration), J.D./M.S. (Juris Doctor/Master of Science in economics or international affairs), J.D./M.S. L.I.S. (Juris Doctor/Master of Science in library information studies), J.D./M.S.P. (Juris Doctor/Master of Science in Urban and Regional Planning), and J.D./M.S.W. (Juris Doctor/Master of Social Work).

Required
To earn the J.D., candidates must complete 88 total credits, of which 36 are for required courses. They must maintain a minimum average grade of 69 in the required courses. The following first-year courses are required of all students: Civil Procedure, Constitutional Law I, Contracts I and II, Criminal Law, Legal Writing and Research I and II, Property I and II, and Torts. Required upper-level courses consist of a skills training course, a writing requirement course, Constitutional Law II, and Professional Responsibility. All students must complete 20 hours of civil pro bono work. The required orientation program for first-year students is a 2-day program that includes an introduction to legal education, research and writing, and ethics/professionalism.

Phone: 850-644-3787
Fax: 850-644-7284
E-mail: *admissions@law.fsu.edu*
Web: *www.law.fsu.edu*

Contact
Jennifer Kessinger, Director of Admissions and Records, 850-644-3787 for general inquiries; Gail Rogers, 850-644-5716 for financial aid information.

Electives

The College of Law offers concentrations in corporate law, criminal law, environmental law, international law, litigation, tax law, and law, business, and economics. In addition, the college offers more than 60 externship placements, either full- or part- time, including judicial clerkships, administrative agency placements, and many civil and criminal lawyering programs. A variety of specialized seminars are offered, such as business reorganization, cyberlaw, and energy law. The college offers an in-house legal clinic, the Public Interest Law Center, which represents children, persons with disabilities, and victims of domestic violence. A total of 20 hours of pro bono service in the field is required for graduation. Special lecture series include the Mason Ladd Memorial Lectures, Distinguished Lectures in Environmental Law, and numerous Faculty Enrichment Speakers. Study abroad is available during the summer terms at Oxford University in England through exchange programs with Griffith University in Brisbane Australia, and with Erasmus University in Rotterdam, the Netherlands. There is a summer program for minority undergraduate students. The most widely taken electives are Evidence, Business Associations, and Gratuitious Transfers.

Graduation Requirements

In order to graduate, candidates must have a minimum grade average of 69., have completed the upper-division writing requirement, and 20 hours of pro bono work, 6 semester residency requirement, and the skills training requirement.

Organizations
The primary law review is the *Florida State University Law Review*. Other law journals include the *Journal of Land Use and Environmental Law*, begun in 1983 and the state's first and only student publication in environmental and land law use. Students also edit the *Journal of Transnational Law and Policy*. The *Florida State University Business Review* is a joint effort between law and business students. The college's moot court team participates in many regional and national competitions each year, including the Florida Bar Robert Orseck Moot Court Competition, Juvenile Law National Moot Court Competition, and the John Gib-

bons National Constitutional Criminal Law Moot Court Competition. The mock trial team takes part in 2 state-wide competitions as well as regional and national competitions each year. Law school organizations include the Student Bar Association, Black Students Association and the LAWtinos. Local chapters of national associations include the Women's Law Symposium Dispute Resolution Society and OUTLaw. Law school organizations include Phi Alpha Delta; Christian Legal Society; and Entertainment, Art, and Sports Law Society.

Library
The law library contains 525,173 hardcopy volumes and 1,065,200 microform volume equivalents, and subscribes to 3580 serial publications. Such on-line databases and networks as CALI, CIS Universe, Dow-Jones, Infotrac, Legal-Trac, LEXIS, Mathew Bender, NEXIS, OCLC First Search, WESTLAW, Wilsonline Indexes, and more than 500 databases are available to law students for research. Special library collections include rare English, American, and Floridian legal materials, including a first edition of Blackstone's Commentaries, and videotapes of oral arguments before the Florida Supreme Court of cases since 1985. Recently, the library added new student seating. The ratio of library volumes to faculty is 8901 to 1 and to students is 688 to 1. The ratio of seats in the library to students is 1 to 2.

Faculty
The law school has 59 full-time and 29 part-time faculty members, of whom 40 are women. According to AAUP standards for Category I institutions, faculty salaries are well below average. About 7% of full-time faculty have a graduate law degree in addition to the J.D. The ratio of full-time students to full-time faculty in an average class is 14 to 1; in a clinic, 12 to 1. The law school has a regular program of bringing visiting professors and other distinguished lecturers and visitors to campus. There is a chapter of the Order of the Coif; 39 faculty and 554 graduates are members.

Students
About 41% of the student body are women; 17%, minorities; 8%, African American; 2%, Asian American; 6%, Hispanic; Fewer than 1% Native Americans, and fewer

Placement

J.D.s awarded:	233

Services available through: a separate law school placement center and the university placement center

Services: various workshops/lectures on specific placement topics such as Internet job hunting, judicial clerkships, and job searches beyond OCI and practice area panels.

Special features: job postings available online for students and alumni along with a "Mach Speed Mock Interview" event.

Full-time job interviews:	24 employers
Summer job interviews:	50 employers
Placement by graduation:	76% of class
Placement within 9 months:	98% of class
Average starting salary:	$31,800 to $160,000

Areas of placement:

Private practice 2-10 attorneys	26%
Private practice 11-25 attorneys	5%
Private practice 26-50 attorneys	5%
Private practice 51-100 attorneys	4%
Private practice 101-500 attorneys	9%
Government	23%
Business/industry	10%
Public interest	9%
Military	3%
Judicial clerkships	2%
Academic	1%

than 1%, Puerto Rican. The majority of students come from the South (94%). The average age of entering students is 23; age range is 20 to 45. About 43% of students enter directly from undergraduate school. About 3% drop out after the first year for academic or personal reasons; 97% remain to receive a law degree.

School of Law

140 West 62nd Street
New York, NY 10023

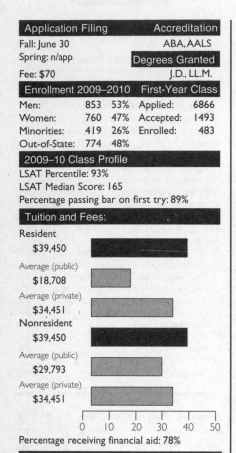

Application Filing		Accreditation	
Fall: June 30		ABA, AALS	
Spring: n/app		**Degrees Granted**	
Fee: $70		J.D., LL.M.	
Enrollment 2009–2010		**First-Year Class**	
Men:	853 53%	Applied:	6866
Women:	760 47%	Accepted:	1493
Minorities:	419 26%	Enrolled:	483
Out-of-State:	774 48%		
2009–10 Class Profile			
LSAT Percentile: 93%			
LSAT Median Score: 165			
Percentage passing bar on first try: 89%			

Tuition and Fees:

Resident
  $39,450

Average (public)
  $18,708

Average (private)
  $34,451

Nonresident
  $39,450

Average (public)
  $29,793

Average (private)
  $34,451

0   10   20   30   40   50

Percentage receiving financial aid: 78%

ADMISSIONS

In a recent year, 6866 applied, 1493 were accepted, and 483 enrolled. Twenty-six transfers enrolled. The median LSAT percentile of the most recent first-year class was 93; the median GPA was 3.56 on a scale of 4.0. The lowest LSAT percentile accepted was 62; the highest was 99. Figures in the above capsule and in this profile are approximate.

Requirements

Applicants must have a bachelor's degree and take the LSAT. The most important admission factors include LSAT results, GPA, and general background. No specific undergraduate courses are required. Candidates are not interviewed.

Procedure

Applicants should submit an application form, LSAT results, transcripts, TOEFL, if the student is from a non-English-speaking country, a nonrefundable application fee of $70, and a personal statement. LSAT results and transcripts should be submitted through LSDAS. Notification of the admissions decision is 6 to 8 weeks

after application is complete. The latest acceptable LSAT test date for fall entry is February. The law school uses the LSDAS. Check with the school for current application deadlines.

Special

The law school recruits minority and disadvantaged students by means of attendance at forums and law fairs, LSDAS Candidate Referral Service, alumni assistance, and current minority students contacting accepted minority applicants. Requirements are not different for out-of-state students. Transfer students must have a minimum GPA of 3, have attended an ABA-approved law school, and fulfill a 2-year residency requirement at Fordham.

Costs

Tuition and fees for the 2009-2010 academic year are approximately $39,450 for all full-time students. Books and supplies run about $1400.

Financial Aid

In a recent year, about 78% of current law students received some form of aid. The average annual amount of aid from all sources combined, including scholarships, loans, and work contracts, was approximately $31,340; maximum, $56,120. Awards are based on need along with with approximately 10% based on merit. Required financial statement is the FAFSA. Special funds for minority or disadvantaged students include funds contributed by benefactors of the school. Also, some funds are specifically allocated to assist these groups. First-year students are notified about their financial aid application at after acceptance, when their file is complete. Check with the school for the current application deadline.

About the Law School

Fordham University School of Law was established in 1905 and is a private institution. The 8-acre campus is in an urban area in the Lincoln Center area of New York City. The primary mission of the law school is to offer a complete legal education providing students with an understanding of legal doctrine and a solid foundation of analytical reasoning, lawyering skills, and professional values that they use in law practice or law-related profes-

sions; to contribute to the development of the law; and to serve the wider community. Students have access to federal, state, county, city, and local agencies, courts, correctional facilities, law firms, and legal aid organizations in the New York area. Lincoln Center, with its many cultural attractions, is nearby. Housing for students is available in a 250-bed, 20-story university residence hall connected to the law school, or within the immediate neighborhood or greater metropolitan area. All law school facilities are accessible to the physically disabled.

Calendar

The law school operates on a traditional semester basis. Courses for full-time students are offered both day and evening and must be completed within 3 years. For part-time students, courses are offered both day and evening and must be completed within 4 years. New full- and part-time students are admitted in the fall. There is an 8-week summer session. Transferable summer courses are offered.

Programs

In addition to the J.D., the law school offers the LL.M. Students may take relevant courses in other programs and apply credit toward the J.D.; a maximum of 13 credits may be applied. The following joint degrees may be earned: J.D./M.A. (Juris Doctor/Master of Arts international political economy), J.D./M.B.A. (Juris Doctor/Master of Business Administration), and J.D./M.S.W. (Juris Doctor/Master of Social Work).

Required

To earn the J.D., candidates must complete 83 total credits, of which 39 are for required courses. They must maintain a minimum GPA of 1.9 in the required courses. The following first-year courses are required of all students: Civil Procedure, Constitutional Law, Contracts, Criminal Justice, Legal Process, Legal Writing and Research, Property, and Torts. Required upper-level courses consist of Corporations and Partnerships and Professional Responsibility. The required orientation program for first-year students is a 2-day general orientation program and a 1-week legal process course.

Phone: 212-636-6810
Fax: 212-636-7984
E-mail: lawadmissions@law.fordham.edu
Web: http://law.fordham.edu

Contact

Assistant Dean, Admissions, 212-636-6810 for general inquiries; Financial Aid Director, 212-636-6815 for financial aid information.

NEW YORK

Electives

The School of Law offers concentrations in corporate law, criminal law, entertainment law, environmental law, family law, international law, juvenile law, labor law, litigation, maritime law, media law, securities law, sports law, tax law, torts and insurance, and European Community law, trial advocacy, public interest law, and professional responsibility. In addition, Clinics, which are open to upper-class students who have satisfied prerequisites, include Criminal Defense, Immigration Law, and Community Economic Development. Seminars, usually worth 2 or 3 credits, are also open to upper-class students; a selection of recent offerings includes Advanced Copyright Law, Civil Rights, and Environmental Law. After the first year, students may participate in a broad range of actual practice settings in federal and state courts, administrative agencies, prosecutors' and defenders' offices, and nonprofit agencies for 2 credits. Research is done through the Stein Institute of Law and Ethics Research fellowships and the Crowley International Human Rights Program. Field work may be undertaken in the Crowley International Human Rights Program and in the noncredit Pro Bono program, where students assist in preparing cases under the direction of attorneys from the Legal Aid Society and various public agencies and nonprofit organizations through Fordham's Public Interest Center. Special lecture series include John F. Sonnett Lectures by distinguished judges and litigators; Stein Lectures in ethics and professional responsibility; Noreen E. McNamara Lectures by outstanding women in the profession; and Robert L. Levine Lectures by distinguished legal scholars. Students may study abroad for up to 1 year for up to 24 credits in approved subjects. The law school operates a summer program in Dublin and Belfast and SKKU in South Korea. The noncredit Academic Enrichment Program provides training in briefing cases, study strategies, and exam-taking techniques. The school contributes to the CLEO program. The Student Bar Association funds several student-run minority organizations. Public service programs include a nonlegal community service project; advocacy projects for battered women, low-income tenants, and unemployed individuals; and student-funded fellowships for summer work at public interest organizations. The most widely taken electives are Income Taxation, New York Practice, and Evidence.

Graduation Requirements

In order to graduate, candidates must have a GPA of 1.9 and have completed the upper-division writing requirement.

Organizations

Students edit the *Fordham Law Review*, *Fordham Urban Law Journal*, *Fordham International Law Journal*, *Fordham Environmental Law Journal*, *Fordham Entertainment, Mass Media, Intellectual Property Journal*, and *Fordham Journal of Corporate and Financial Law*. Moot court competitions include the intramural William Hughes Mulligan and the I. Maurice Wormser and the interschool Irving R. Kaufman Securities Law Competition. Teams also compete at the National Moot Court, Jessup International Law, Craven Constitutional Law, Cardozo Entertainment Law, National Trial Advocacy, National Tax, and National Products Liability competitions. There are approximately 40 student-run organizations at the law school, including the Student Bar Association, Fordham Law Women, and Stein Scholars. There are local chapters of the Federalist Society, National Lawyers Guild, BLSA, LALSA, APALSA and Phi Alpha Delta. Campus clubs include Habitat for Humanity, Equal Justice Works and the Sports Law Association.

Library

The law library contains 384,966 hardcopy volumes and 241,265 microform volume equivalents, and subscribes to 4880 serial publications. Such on-line databases and networks as CALI, CIS Universe, DIALOG, Dow-Jones, Infotrac, Legal-Trac, LEXIS, LOIS, NEXIS, OCLC First Search, RLIN, WESTLAW, and Wilson-line Indexes are available to law students for research. Special library collections include an EEC collection and a federal documents depository. Recently, the library acquired the INNOPACQ on-line catalog system and retroconverted the card catalog to a machine readable form. Also, an Automated Circulation System was installed, and a LAN for student computers and the computer classroom and laboratory. A wireless network was installed throughout the library. There was also new office construction and new circulation and reference areas. The ratio of library volumes to faculty is 5274 to 1 and to students is 239 to 1. The ratio of seats in the library to students is 1 to 3.

Placement

J.D.s awarded:	481

Services available through: a separate law school placement center

Services: self-assessment seminars, mock interviews, networking/job prospecting workshops

Special features: The school designs its own programs to ensure that students have opportunities to interact with alumni and employers..

Full-time job interviews:	250 employers
Summer job interviews:	315 employers
Placement by graduation:	86% of class
Placement within 9 months:	99% of class
Average starting salary:	$60,000 to $140,000

Areas of placement:

Private practice 2-10 attorneys	7%
Private practice 11-25 attorneys	8%
Private practice 26-50 attorneys	4%
Private practice 51-100 attorneys	3%
Private practice 100+ attorneys	52%
Government	11%
Business/industry	6%
Judicial clerkships	4%
Public interest	3%
Academic	2%

Faculty

The law school has 73 full-time and 117 part-time faculty members, of whom 67 are women. According to AAUP standards for Category I institutions, faculty salaries are average. About 45% of full-time faculty have a graduate law degree in addition to the J.D.; about 8% of part-time faculty have one. The ratio of full-time students to full-time faculty in an average class is 49 to 1; in a clinic, 8 to 1. The law school has a regular program of bringing visiting professors and other distinguished lecturers and visitors to campus. There is a chapter of the Order of the Coif.

Students

About 47% of the student body are women; 26%, minorities; 6%, African American; 11%, Asian American; 8%, Hispanic; and 1%, Native American. The majority of students come from the Northeast (73%). The average age of entering students is 24; age range is 20 to 52. About 31% of students enter directly from undergraduate school, 19% have a graduate degree, and 50% have worked full-time prior to entering law school. About 2% drop out after the first year for academic or personal reasons; 98% remain to receive a law degree.

Fordham University   **291**

FRANKLIN PIERCE LAW CENTER

2 White Street
Concord, NH 03301

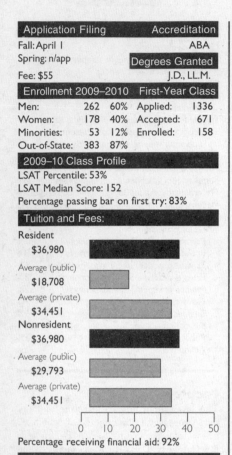

Application Filing	Accreditation
Fall: April 1	ABA
Spring: n/app	Degrees Granted
Fee: $55	J.D., LL.M.

Enrollment 2009–2010		First-Year Class	
Men:	262 60%	Applied:	1336
Women:	178 40%	Accepted:	671
Minorities:	53 12%	Enrolled:	158
Out-of-State:	383 87%		

2009–10 Class Profile
LSAT Percentile: 53%
LSAT Median Score: 152
Percentage passing bar on first try: 83%

Tuition and Fees:

Resident
$36,980

Average (public)
$18,708

Average (private)
$34,451

Nonresident
$36,980

Average (public)
$29,793

Average (private)
$34,451

0   10   20   30   40   50

Percentage receiving financial aid: 92%

ADMISSIONS

In the fall 2009 first-year class, 1336 applied, 671 were accepted, and 158 enrolled. Three transfers enrolled. The median LSAT percentile of the most recent first-year class was 53; the median GPA was 3.35 on a scale of 4.3. The lowest LSAT percentile accepted was 17; the highest was 94.

Requirements
Applicants must have a bachelor's degree and take the LSAT. The most important admission factors include maturity, academic achievement, and motivation. No specific undergraduate courses are required. Candidates are interviewed.

Procedure
The application deadline for fall entry is April 1. Applicants should submit an application form, LSAT results, transcripts, a personal statement, TOEFL for non-English speaking (native), a non-refundable application fee of $55, and 2 letters of recommendation. Notification

of the admissions decision is on a rolling basis. The latest acceptable LSAT test date for fall entry is February. The law school uses the LSDAS.

Special
The law school recruits minority and disadvantaged students by participating in minority programs such as the Council on Legal Education Opportunity (CLEO) and the Puerto Rican Legal Defense Fund, actively recruiting self-identified minorities through the Law School Admission Council, and offering diversity scholarships. Students are also invited to submit a supplemental statement addressing their challenges and achievements. Requirements are not different for out-of-state students. Transfer students must have one year of credit, have a minimum GPA of 3.0, and have attended an ABA-approved law school.

Costs

Tuition and fees for the 2009-2010 academic year are $36,980 for all full-time students. Books and supplies run $1400.

Financial Aid

About 92% of current law students receive some form of aid. The average annual amount of aid from all sources combined, including scholarships, loans, and work contracts, is $46,375; maximum, $56,644. Awards are based on need and merit. Required financial statements are the FAFSA and Pierce Law application, and tax return. The aid application deadline for fall entry is open. Special funds for minority or disadvantaged students include diversity scholarships that are available to members of groups currently underrepresented in the law center community. They are awarded based on academic and community involvement factors. First-year students are notified about their financial aid application on a rolling basis after application and acceptance.

About the Law School

Franklin Pierce Law Center was established in 1973 and is independent. The 1-acre campus is in a small town 70 miles north of Boston, Massachusetts. Students have access to federal, state, county, city, and local agencies, courts, correctional

facilities, law firms, and legal aid organizations in the Concord area. Facilities of special interest to law students consist of the attorney general offices and city, state, and federal court clerkships. Housing for students is available around the school's residential setting. About 95% of the law school facilities are accessible to the physically disabled.

Calendar

The law school operates on a traditional semester basis. Courses for full-time students are offered both day and evening and must be completed within 3 years. There is no part-time program. New students are admitted in the fall. There is a 7-week summer session. Transferable summer courses are offered.

Programs

In addition to the J.D., the law school offers the LL.M. and Technology and Law, and Master of International Criminial Law and Justice. Students may take relevant courses in other programs and apply credit toward the J.D.; a maximum of 8 credits may be applied. The following joint degrees may be earned: J.D./M.C.T. (Juris Doctor/Master of Commerce and Technology Law), J.D./M.I.C.L.J. (Juris Doctor/Master of International Criminal Law and Justice), and J.D./M.I.P. (Juris Doctor/Master of Intellectual Property).

Required
To earn the J.D., candidates must complete 85 total credits, of which 39 are for required courses. They must maintain a minimum GPA of 2.0 in the required courses. The following first-year courses are required of all students: 1 legal perspective course, Civil Procedure, Constitutional Law, Contracts, Legal Skills I and II, Property, and Torts. Required upper-level courses consist of Administrative Law, Criminal Procedure I, and Professional Responsibility. The required orientation program for first-year students is a 3-day orientation program.

Electives
The Franklin Pierce Law Center offers concentrations in corporate law, criminal law, entertainment law, family law, intellectual property law, international law, juvenile law, litigation, tax law, legal

Phone: 603-228-9217
Fax: 603-228-1074
E-mail: *admissions@piercelaw.edu*
Web: *piercelaw.edu*

Contact

Katie McDonald, Assistant Dean for Admissions, 603-228-9217 for general inquiries; Susan Ahern, Financial Aid Officer, 603-513-5123 for financial aid information.

NEW HAMPSHIRE

services, and regulatory and administrative law. In addition, Pierce Law operates 6 clinics in offices designed to emulate a state-of-the-art law office; second- and third-year students represent actual clients in a range of matters. Students receive either 4 or 5 credits. Clinics include the Intellectual Property & Business Transaction Clinic, Administrative Advocacy Clinic, Consumer & Commercial Law Clinic, Criminal Practice Clinic, Appellate Defender Program, and IP Amicus Clinic. Research seminars are offered in medical decision making, supreme court issues, and advanced legal research. Externships are available to students after the third semester. Externships are part time for 4 credits or full time for 12 credits. The school has a large number of regular placements and students may design their own externship as long as it is appropriate for the number of credits and with an experienced practitioner who has committed to educating the student. Second- and third-year students may also take independent study with a specific faculty member for a maximum of 4 credits. Periodically, speakers are invited to the school to lecture on a variety of subjects, including civil rights, health law, patent law, and corporate law. Study abroad is possible through programs provided by ABA-approved schools. In addition, Pierce Law sponsors the Intellectual Property Seminar Institute in Beijing, China (with Tsinghua University) and the eLaw Summer Institute in Cork, Ireland (with University College Cork). Computer tutorial programs are offered to all students. The Academic Success Program works with students individually and in small groups. Teaching assistants are available for individual consultation; all first-year courses have teaching assistants for discussion and explanation. The most widely taken electives are Evidence, and Copyright and Trademarks.

Graduation Requirements

In order to graduate, candidates must have a GPA of 2.0, have completed the upper-division writing requirement, and have completed 85 credits, have 6 full-time semesters of residency, offset all credits below C- with an equal number of credits of B- or above, have satisfied any terms of academic probation or financial obligation, and not be the subject of an alleged Honor Code violation.

Organizations

Student-edited publications are *IDEA: The Journal Of Law and Technology* and *Pierce Law Review. The Annual Survey of New Hampshire Law*, which publishes articles focusing on recent opinions of the New Hampshire Supreme Court, is a 4-credit, 2-semester course in which second-year students write articles and a third-year student serves as editor. Moot court competitions include the required appellate argument for second semester first-year students. Students annually enter the Giles Sutherland Rich Intellectual Property Moot Court, Saul Lefkowitz Moot Court Competition, National Health Law Competition, Association of Trial Lawyers of America, and Student Trial Advocacy Competition. Students enter legal essay writing contests on a volunteer basis. Law student organizations, local chapters of national associations and campus organizations, include Student Intellectual Property Association, Women Law Students Association, Licensing Executive Society, Minority Law Students Association, Phi Alpha Delta, International Law Students Association, Student Bar Association, and Black Law Students Association.

Library

The law library contains 307,364 hardcopy volumes and 663,822 microform volume equivalents, and subscribes to 1256 serial publications. Such on-line databases and networks as CALI, Legal-Trac, LEXIS, LOIS, NEXIS, WESTLAW, Jstor, BNA IP Library, CCH IP Library, U.S.L.W., Oceana Tiara, CCH Tay Research Network, Making of Modern Law, Oxford Reports on International Law Tax, U.S. Government Periodicals, Inoex, World Trademark & Law Report, and ABA/BNA Lawyers Manual on Professional Conduct are available to law students for research. Special library collections include an intellectual property special collection, a repository for the World Intellectual Property Organization (WIPO), and a federal GPO selective depository. The ratio of library volumes to faculty is 12,295 to 1 and to students is 699 to 1. The ratio of seats in the library to students is 1 to 2.

Faculty

The law school has 25 full-time and 30 part-time faculty members, of whom 19

Placement

J.D.s awarded:	143

Services available through: a separate law school placement center

Services: video interviews and playbacks; workshops on information interviewing; career planning for students interested in intellectual property, business, public interest, and general practice; externships for academic credit

Special features: individual and personal service to its students, with emphasis on helping students network; and nationwide academic externship opportunities

Full-time job interviews:	33 employers
Summer job interviews:	33 employers
Placement by graduation:	65% of class
Placement within 9 months:	96% of class
Average starting salary:	$37,200 to $135,000

Areas of placement:

Private practice 2-10 attorneys	19%
Private practice 11-25 attorneys	8%
Private practice 26-50 attorneys	6%
Private practice 51-100 attorneys	8%
Private practice 101+ attorneys	12%
Solo practice	3%
Government	12%
Judicial clerkships	10%
Public interest	4%
Military	1%
Academic	1%
Business/industry	14%

are women. About 17% of full-time faculty have a graduate law degree in addition to the J.D. The ratio of full-time students to full-time faculty in an average class is 14 to 1; in a clinic, 4 to 1. The law school has a regular program of bringing visiting professors and other distinguished lecturers and visitors to campus.

Students

About 40% of the student body are women; 12%, minorities; 1%, African American; 6%, Asian American; 3%, Hispanic; and 2%, International. The majority of students come from the Northeast (42%). The average age of entering students is 27; age range is 21 to 51. About 33% of students enter directly from undergraduate school, 17% have a graduate degree, and 67% have worked full-time prior to entering law school. About 8% drop out after the first year for academic or personal reasons; 90% remain to receive a law degree.

School of Law

3301 Fairfax Drive
Arlington, VA 22201

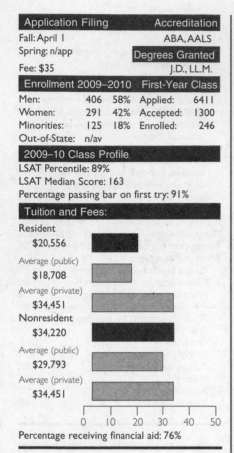

Application Filing		Accreditation
Fall: April 1		ABA, AALS
Spring: n/app		
		Degrees Granted
Fee: $35		J.D., LL.M.

Enrollment 2009–2010			First-Year Class	
Men:	406	58%	Applied:	6411
Women:	291	42%	Accepted:	1300
Minorities:	125	18%	Enrolled:	246
Out-of-State:	n/av			

2009–10 Class Profile
LSAT Percentile: 89%
LSAT Median Score: 163
Percentage passing bar on first try: 91%

Tuition and Fees:

Resident
$20,556

Average (public)
$18,708

Average (private)
$34,451

Nonresident
$34,220

Average (public)
$29,793

Average (private)
$34,451

0 10 20 30 40 50

Percentage receiving financial aid: 76%

ADMISSIONS

In the fall 2009 first-year class, 6411 applied, 1300 were accepted, and 246 enrolled. Twenty-eight transfers enrolled. The median LSAT percentile of the most recent first-year class was 89; the median GPA was 3.72 on a scale of 4.0. The lowest LSAT percentile accepted was 44; the highest was 99.

Requirements
Applicants must have a bachelor's degree and take the LSAT. The most important admission factors include LSAT results, class rank, and GPA. No specific undergraduate courses are required. Candidates are not interviewed.

Procedure
The application deadline for fall entry is April 1. Applicants should submit an application form, LSAT results, transcripts, a personal statement, LSDAS Report (transcript must be submitted directly to LSAC) a nonrefundable application fee of $35, 2 letters of recommendation, and a 500-word personal statement. Notification of the admissions decision is December through April. The latest acceptable LSAT test date for fall entry is February. The law school uses the LSDAS.

Special
The law school recruits minority and disadvantaged students through the Law Services' Candidate Referral Service, Law School Forums, regional law fairs, and CLEO. Requirements are not different for out-of-state students. Transfer students must have one year of credit, have a minimum GPA of 3.0, and have attended an ABA-approved law school.

Costs

Tuition and fees for the 2009-2010 academic year are $20,556 for full-time in-state students and $34,220 for out-of-state students. Tuition for part-time students is $16,721 in-state and $27,945 out-of-state.

Financial Aid

About 76% of current law students receive some form of aid. The average annual amount of aid from all sources combined, including scholarships, loans, and work contracts, is $24,076. Awards are based on merit. Required financial statement is the FAFSA. The aid application deadline for fall entry is March 1. First-year students are notified about their financial aid application between the time of acceptance and the first day of school.

About the Law School

George Mason University School of Law was established in 1979 and is a public institution. The 1-acre campus is in a suburban area 2 miles south of Washington, D.C. The primary mission of the law school is to provide superior legal education programs leading to the first professional degree in law, the Juris Doctor. The school stresses the case method. Students have access to federal, state, county, city, and local agencies, courts, correctional facilities, law firms, and legal aid organizations in the Arlington area. Housing for students is not available on the metro campus. All law school facilities are accessible to the physically disabled.

Calendar

The law school operates on a traditional semester basis. Courses for full-time students are offered days only and must be completed within 3 years. For part-time students, courses are offered evenings only and must be completed within 4 years. New full- and part-time students are admitted in the fall. There is an 8-week summer session. Transferable summer courses are offered.

Programs

In addition to the J.D., the law school offers the LL.M. The following joint degrees may be earned: J.D./M.A. (Juris Doctor/Master of Arts in economics), J.D./M.P.P. (Juris Doctor/Master of Public Policy), and J.D./Ph.D. (Juris Doctor/Doctor of Philosophy in economics).

Required
To earn the J.D., candidates must complete 89 total credits, of which 40 are for required courses. They must maintain a minimum GPA of 2.15 in the required courses. The following first-year courses are required of all students: Civil Procedure, Contracts I and II, Criminal Law, Economic Foundations of Legal Studies, Legal Research, Writing, and Analysis I and II, Property, The Founders' Constitution, and Torts. Required upper-level courses consist of a minimum of 2 upper-level courses in which substantial papers are required, Appellate Writing and Legal Drafting, Constitutional Law I, and Professional Responsibility. The required orientation program for first-year students is presented during the first week of school. The program lasts 2 days and consists of presentations by the administration, legal writing classes, and small group meetings with faculty alumni, and student advisers.

Electives
The School of Law offers concentrations in corporate law, criminal law, intellectual property law, international law, litigation, securities law, tax law, patent law, regulatory law, technology law, legal and economic theory, personal law, international business law, and homeland and national security law. Clinics are limited to upper-level students and are worth 3 credits. Seminars, taken in the second, third, or fourth year, consist of a minimum of 2 upper-level courses in which substantial papers are required or there is a satisfaction of track thesis requirement. Internships are limited to upper-level stu-

Phone: 703-993-8010
Fax: 703-993-8088
E-mail: aprice1@gmu.edu
Web: www.law.gmu.edu

Contact

Alison H. Price, Associate Dean and Director of Admissions, 703-993-8264 for general inquiries; Jevita Rogers, Office of Financial Aid, 703-993-2353 for financial aid information.

VIRGINIA

dents and are worth 2 to 3 credits, up to a maximum of 4 credits. The Law and Economics Center administers a series of interdisciplinary symposia, lectures, and conferences devoted to current topics in law and economics. The National Center for Technology and Law also hosts conferences and programs. There is a University of Hamburg (Germany) exchange program in Law and Economics. Tutorial programs consist of Fundamental Skills Saturday sessions and daylong spring session for students in academic jeopardy. Minority programs include the L. Douglas Wilder Seminar Series. Special interest groups include GLBT forums and panels and J. Reuben Clark Law Society Conference sponsorship. The most widely taken electives are Evidence, Administrative Law, and Business Associations.

Graduation Requirements
In order to graduate, candidates must have a GPA of 2.15 and have completed the upper-division writing requirement.

Organizations

Students edit the *George Mason University Law Review*, *Civil Rights Law Journal*, *Journal of International Commercial Law*, *Journal of Law, Economics and Policy*, and the newspaper *The Docket*. The school sponsors several in-house competitions each year, and sends teams to numerous national and regional competitions. Other competitions include the Law and Economics Competition, Trial Advocacy Association Competition, and the Mediation Advocacy Competition. Law student organizations include the Business Law Society, National Security Law Society, and the Intellectual Property Law Society. Local chapters of national associations include the Student Bar Association, Association for Public Interest Law, and the Black Law Students Association. Campus clubs and other organizations include local chapters of the ABA-Law Student Division, Phi Delta Phi (Lewis Powell Inn), and Phi Alpha Delta (George Mason Chapter).

Library

The law library contains 488,944 hardcopy volumes and 233,330 microform volume equivalents. Such on-line databases and networks as CALI, CIS Universe, DIALOG, Dow-Jones, LEXIS, LOIS, NEXIS, OCLC First Search, WESTLAW, Wilsonline Indexes, ALADIN, VIVA, TWEN, BNA, Index to Legal Periodicals, Law Library Microform Consortium Digital, HeinOnline, RIA Checkpoint, LEXIS NEXIS Congressional Research Digital Collection, Making of Modern Law, and Westlaw Business are available to law students for research. Special library collections include business, economic theory and history, ethics and philosophy, banking, patent law, and law and economics. The school is also a participant in the Federal Government Documents Depository. The ratio of library volumes to faculty is 10,187 to 1 and to students is 702 to 1.

Faculty

The law school has 48 full-time and 139 part-time faculty members, of whom 49 are women. According to AAUP standards for Category I institutions, faculty salaries are below average. About 42% of full-time faculty have a graduate law degree in addition to the J.D.; about 9% of part-time faculty have one. The law school has a regular program of bringing visiting professors and other distinguished lecturers and visitors to campus.

Students

About 42% of the student body are women; 18%, minorities; 3%, African American; 10%, Asian American; 4%, Hispanic; and 1%, Native American. The average age of entering students is 25. About 15% of students have a graduate degree. About 1% drop out after the first year for academic or personal reasons; 97% remain to receive a law degree.

Placement

J.D.s awarded:	230

Services available through: a separate law school placement center
Services: mock interview program, Myers-Briggs assessment, career advisory network, job fairs
Special features: required first-year counseling sessions; open door office hours; combined career counseling, academic advising, and alumni services office

Full-time job interviews:	35 employers
Summer job interviews:	86 employers
Placement by graduation:	96% of class
Placement within 9 months:	99% of class
Average starting salary:	$32,500 to $240,000

Areas of placement:

Private practice 2-10 attorneys	17%
Private practice 11-25 attorneys	4%
Private practice 26-50 attorneys	1%
Private practice 51-100 attorneys	1%
Private practice 100+ attorneys	23%
Government	15%
Judicial clerkships	13%
Business/industry	10%
Public interest	8%
Academic	5%
Military	2%

2000 H Street, N.W.
Washington, DC 20052

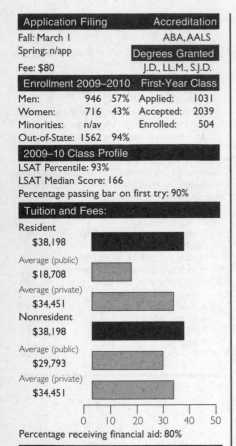

Application Filing	Accreditation
Fall: March 1	ABA, AALS
Spring: n/app	**Degrees Granted**
Fee: $80	J.D., LL.M., S.J.D.

Enrollment 2009–2010		First-Year Class	
Men:	946 57%	Applied:	1031
Women:	716 43%	Accepted:	2039
Minorities:	n/av	Enrolled:	504
Out-of-State:	1562 94%		

2009–10 Class Profile
LSAT Percentile: 93%
LSAT Median Score: 166
Percentage passing bar on first try: 90%

Tuition and Fees:

Resident
$38,198

Average (public)
$18,708

Average (private)
$34,451

Nonresident
$38,198

Average (public)
$29,793

Average (private)
$34,451

0   10   20   30   40   50

Percentage receiving financial aid: 80%

ADMISSIONS

In a recent year, 10311 applied, 2039 were accepted, and 504 enrolled. The median LSAT percentile of the most recent first-year class was 93; the median GPA was 3.71 on a scale of 4.0. The lowest LSAT percentile accepted was 41; the highest was 100. Figures in the above capsule and in this profile are approximate.

Requirements
Applicants must have a bachelor's degree and take the LSAT. The most important admission factors include academic achievement, LSAT results, and writing ability. No specific undergraduate courses are required. Candidates are not interviewed.

Procedure
Applicants should submit an application form, LSAT results, transcripts, a non-refundable application fee of $80, and two letters of recommendation are recommended, but not required. Notification

of the admissions decision is as soon as a decision is made. The latest acceptable LSAT test date for fall entry is February, but only in certain cases. The law school uses the LSDAS. Check with the school for the application deadlines.

Special
The law school recruits minority and disadvantaged students by participating in law forums throughout the country and visiting schools with large minority populations. In addition, each admitted applicant is contacted by a currently enrolled student. Requirements are not different for out-of-state students. Transfer students must have one year of credit, have attended an ABA-approved law school, and ; admissions decisions are based on the applicant's law school record and the amount of space available.

Costs

Tuition and fees for the 2009-2010 academic year are approximately $38,198 for all full-time students. Tuition for part-time students is approximately $25,540 per year. On-campus room and board costs about $12,150 annually; books and supplies run about $1100.

Financial Aid

In a recent year, about 80% of current law students received some form of aid. The average annual amount of aid from all sources combined, including scholarships, loans, and work contracts, was approximately $34,822; maximum, $53,540. Awards are based on need and merit. Required financial statements are the CSS Profile and the FAFSA. First-year students are notified about their financial aid application at some time after admission, providing all files are complete. Check with the school for the current application deadline.

About the Law School

George Washington University Law School was established in 1865 and is a private institution. The campus is in an urban area in downtown Washington, D.C. The primary mission of the law school is to offer students the opportunity to study and observe lawmaking at its source, by combining a wide variety of courses in public law with the traditional fields of

law. Students have access to federal, state, county, city, and local agencies, courts, correctional facilities, law firms, and legal aid organizations in the Washington area. Extensive clinical opportunities exist in the nation's capital. Housing for students consists of a limited number of spaces available on campus in efficiency, 1- and 2-bedroom apartments.

Calendar

The law school operates on a traditional semester basis. Courses for full-time students are offered both day and evening and must be completed within 3 years. For part-time students, courses are offered both day and evening and must be completed within 4 years. New full- and part-time students are admitted in the fall. There is a 7-week summer session. Transferable summer courses are offered.

Programs

In addition to the J.D., the law school offers the LL.M. and S.J.D. Students may take relevant courses in other programs and apply credit toward the J.D.; a maximum of 6 credits may be applied. The following joint degrees may be earned: J.D./M.A. (Juris Doctor/Master of Arts in international affairs, history,), J.D./M.B.A. (Juris Doctor/Master of Business Administration), J.D./M.P.A. (Juris Doctor/Master of Public Administration), J.D./M.P.H. (Juris Doctor/Master of Public Health), J.D./M.P.P. (Juris Doctor/Master of Public Policy), LL.M./M.A. (Master of Laws/Master of Arts), and LL.M./M.P.H (Master of Laws/Master of Public Health).

Required
To earn the J.D., candidates must complete 84 total credits, of which 34 are for required courses. They must maintain a minimum GPA of 1.67 in the required courses. The following first-year courses are required of all students: Civil Procedure I and II, Constitutional Law I, Contracts I and II, Criminal Law, Introduction to Advocacy, Legal Researching and Writing, Property, and Torts. Required upper-level courses consist of Professional Responsibility and Ethics. The required orientation program for first-year students is a 3-day program that includes registration.

Phone: 202-994-7230
Fax: 202-994-3597
E-mail: *jd@law.gwu.edu*
Web: *www.law.gwu.edu*

Contact
Office of Law Admissions, 202-994-7230 for general inquiries; Law Financial Aid Office, 202-994-6592 for financial aid information.

DISTRICT OF COLUMBIA

Electives
The Law School offers concentrations in corporate law, criminal law, environmental law, family law, intellectual property law, international law, labor law, litigation, securities law, tax law, torts and insurance, and government contracts, intellectual property, and constitutional law. In addition, Clinics, worth 2 to 4 credits, include the Consumer Mediation Clinic, Domestic Violence Clinic, and Immigration Clinic, all open to upper-level students. The Federal Sentencing Seminar (2 credits), Sexuality and the Law Seminar (2 or 3 credits), and Law in Cyberspace (2 or 3 credits) are all open to second- or third-year students. Internships are available to second- and third-year students for 1 to 4 credits a semester, for a maximum of 8 credits. Students arrange independent projects with state or federal public interest organizations. Through the Enrichment Program, speakers are brought to the law school for lectures and informal seminars that are open to all students. The law school offers 2 summer study abroad programs: An international human rights program is offered with Oxford University and an intellectual property program is offered with the Munich I.P. Law Center. Third-year students serving as Resource Fellows assist other students who are in academic difficulty. The Writing Center serves as a resource for all students. Minority programs are sponsored by groups such as the Black Law Students Association, Hispanic Law Students Association, and Asian/Pacific American Law Students Association and East Asian Law Society. Special interest groups include the Law Association for Women, Christian Law Society, Law Students for the Arts, International Law Society, Student Animal Defense Fund, Lambda Law and politically-oriented groups. The most widely taken electives are Federal Income Taxation, Evidence, and Corporations.

Graduation Requirements
In order to graduate, candidates must have a GPA of 1.67, have completed the upper-division writing requirement, and completion of the required curriculum.

Organizations
Students edit the *George Washington Law Review, George Washington International Law Journal, International Law in Domestic Courts*, and the newspaper *Nota Bene*. The *American Intellectual Property Law Association Quarterly Journal*, a publication of the AIPLA, is housed at the law school. The Moot Court Board sponsors the Van Vleck Appellate Moot Court competition, the Jessup Cup Competition in international law, and the Giles S. Rich in patent law. Teams participate in other moot court competitions around the country. In-house alternative dispute resolution competitions are held in negotiations and client counseling. Law student organizations, local chapters of national associations, and campus clubs and organizations include the Equal Justice Foundation, Evening Law Student Association, International Law Society, the Student Bar Association, Legal Support Group, Black Law Students Association, Environmental Law Society, Phi Alpha Delta, Phi Delta Phi, and the Federalist Society.

Library
The law library contains 611,190 hardcopy volumes and 130,195 microform volume equivalents, and subscribes to 4304 serial publications. Such on-line databases and networks as CALI, CIS Universe, DIALOG, Legal-Trac, LEXIS, LOIS, Mathew Bender, NEXIS, OCLC First Search, RLIN, WESTLAW, and Wilsonline Indexes are available to law students for research. Special library collections include collections of unique materials in the areas of environmental law, intellectual property law, international law, government procurement law, and legal history. Recently, the library constructed additional student conference rooms, added additional shelving, installed wireless network, constructed a special room with temperature and humidity controls for rare book collection. The ratio of library volumes to faculty is 6112 to 1 and to students is 368 to 1. The ratio of seats in the library to students is 1 to 7.

Faculty
The law school has 100 full-time and 288 part-time faculty members, of whom 128 are women. According to AAUP standards for Category I institutions, faculty salaries are above average. The ratio of full-time students to full-time faculty in an average class is 16 to 1; in a clinic, 8 to 1. The law school has a regular program of bringing visiting professors and other distinguished lecturers and visitors to campus. There is a chapter of the Order of the Coif.

Placement
J.D.s awarded:	506
Services available through: a separate law school placement center	
Special features: on-line job listings, and an evening student counselor.	
Full-time job interviews:	600 employers
Summer job interviews:	n/av
Placement by graduation:	93% of class
Placement within 9 months:	95% of class
Average starting salary:	$90,000 to $135,000
Areas of placement:	
Private practice; 12% unknown	62%
Government	11%
Judicial clerkships	10%
Business/industry	9%
Public interest	4%
Academic	1%

Students
About 43% of the student body are women; 8%, African American; 10%, Asian American; 7%, Hispanic; 1%, Native American; and 11%, Students who did not report ethnicity on application. The majority of students come from the Northeast (34%). The average age of entering students is 24; age range is 20 to 55. About 32% of students enter directly from undergraduate school, 34% have a graduate degree, and 67% have worked full-time prior to entering law school. About 1% drop out after the first year for academic or personal reasons; 99% remain to receive a law degree.

Law Center

600 New Jersey Avenue, N.W.
Washington, DC 20001

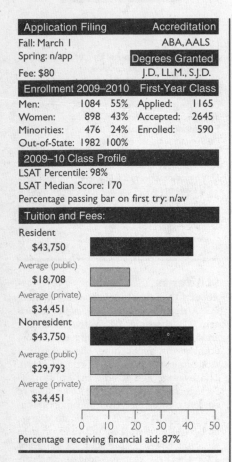

Application Filing		Accreditation	
Fall: March 1		ABA, AALS	
Spring: n/app		**Degrees Granted**	
Fee: $80		J.D., LL.M., S.J.D.	
Enrollment 2009–2010		**First-Year Class**	
Men:	1084 55%	Applied:	1165
Women:	898 43%	Accepted:	2645
Minorities:	476 24%	Enrolled:	590
Out-of-State:	1982 100%		

2009–10 Class Profile
LSAT Percentile: 98%
LSAT Median Score: 170
Percentage passing bar on first try: n/av

Tuition and Fees:

Resident
$43,750

Average (public)
$18,708

Average (private)
$34,451

Nonresident
$43,750

Average (public)
$29,793

Average (private)
$34,451

0 10 20 30 40 50

Percentage receiving financial aid: 87%

ADMISSIONS

In the fall 2009 first-year class, 11653 applied, 2645 were accepted, and 590 enrolled. Eighty transfers enrolled. The median LSAT percentile of the most recent first-year class was 98; the median GPA was 3.68 on a scale of 4.0. The lowest LSAT percentile accepted was 56; the highest was 99.

Requirements
Applicants must have a bachelor's degree and take the LSAT. The most important admission factors include academic achievement, LSAT results, and life experience. No specific undergraduate courses are required. Candidates are interviewed.

Procedure
The application deadline for fall entry is March 1. Applicants should submit an application form, LSAT results, transcripts, a personal statement, a nonrefundable application fee of $80, 1 letter of recommendation, and transcripts must be received through the LSDAS; a resume is also required. Notification of the admissions decision is approximately 6 to 12 weeks. The latest acceptable LSAT test date for fall entry is February. The law school uses the LSDAS.

Special
The law school recruits minority and disadvantaged students by means of an outreach program that encourages qualified minority and disadvantaged students to apply. Requirements are not different for out-of-state students. Transfer students must have one year of credit and have attended an ABA-approved law school.

Costs

Tuition and fees for the 2009-2010 academic year are $43,750 for all full-time students. Tuition for part-time students is $31,900 per year. On-campus room and board costs about $21,225 annually; books and supplies run $1025.

Financial Aid

About 87% of current law students receive some form of aid. The average annual amount of aid from all sources combined, including scholarships, loans, and work contracts, is $52,145; maximum, $66,000. Awards are based on need and merit. Required financial statements are the CSS Profile, the FAFSA, and Need Access Application. The aid application deadline for fall entry is March 1. First-year students are notified about their financial aid application after acceptance and completion of financial aid requirements. Awards are given on a rolling basis.

About the Law School

Georgetown University Law Center was established in 1870 and is a private institution. The 6.7-acre campus is in an urban area in Washington, D.C. Drawing on its Jesuit heritage, Georgetown Law has a strong tradition of public service and is dedicated to the principle that law is but a means, justice is the end. Students have access to federal, state, county, city, and local agencies, courts, correctional facilities, law firms, and legal aid organizations in the Washington area. Other resources include the U.S. Supreme Court, federal courts, the U.S. Congress, and major federal departments and agencies, many of which are within walking distance. The Law Center campus includes 5 buildings. The Hotung International Law Center contains its own international and comparative law library, a state-of-the-art moot court room, and extensive classroom and meeting space; the sport and fitness complex has a cyber café and lounge, lap pool, basketball and racquetball courts, spinning and aerobic rooms, and weight-lifting facilities. Additionally, McDonough Hall has classrooms, a cafeteria, administrative and student organization offices, and student lounges; Williams Library, a state-of-the-art facility with group study lounges, a computer laboratory, and student journal offices; and the Gewirz Student Center, the Law Center's on-campus residential facility, which also includes the Law Center's child care and student health facilities. On-campus housing is available in the Gewirz Student Center, which offers furnished apartment units. Law students are supported through a variety of other housing programs. All law school facilities are accessible to the physically disabled.

Calendar

The law school operates on a traditional semester basis. Courses for full-time students are offered both day and evening and must be completed within 5 years. For part-time students, required courses and electives are offered in the evening (students have the option of taking other coursework during the day and evening, and must be completed within 6 years. New full- and part-time students are admitted in the fall. There is a 7-week summer session. Transferable summer courses are offered.

Programs

In addition to the J.D., the law school offers the LL.M. and S.J.D. LL.M. concentrations are available in international legal studies. Students may take relevant courses in other programs and apply credit toward the J.D.; a maximum of 6 credits may be applied. The following joint degrees may be earned: J.D./Govt. (Juris Doctor/Doctor in Government), J.D./LL.M. (Juris Doctor/Master of Laws in taxation), J.D./M.A.A.S. (Juris Doctor/Master of Arts in Arab studies), J.D./M.A.G.E.S. (Juris Doctor/Master of Arts in German and European studies), J.D./M.A.L.A.S (Juris Doctor/Master of Arts Latin American studies), J.D./M.A.R.E.E.S. (Juris Doctor/Master of Arts in Russian and East European studies), J.D./M.A.S.S.P. (Juris Doctor/Master of Arts in Security Studies), J.D./M.B.A. (Juris Doctor/Master of Business Administration), J.D./M.P.H. (Juris Doctor/Master of Public Policy), J.D./M.S.F.S. (Juris Doctor/Master of Foreign Science), and J.D./Phil. (Juris Doctor/Master of Arts or Doctor of Philosophy).

Phone: 202-662-9010
Fax: 202-662-9439
E-mail: *admis@law.georgetown.edu*
Web: *www.law.georgetown.edu*

Contact
Andrew Cornblatt, Dean of Admissions, Associate Vice Presidet for Graduate Enrollment, 202-662-9010 for general inquiries; Charles Pruett, Director of Financial Aid, 202-662-9210 for financial aid information.

Required

To earn the J.D., candidates must complete 85 total credits, of which 33 are for required courses. They must maintain a minimum GPA of 1.67 in the required courses. The following first-year courses are required of all students: Bargain, Exchange and Liability, Civil Procedure, Constitutional Law I, Contracts, Criminal Justice, Democracy and Coercion, Elective (1), Government Processes, Law in a Global Context, Legal Justice Seminar, Legal Practice: Writing and Analysis, Legal Process and Society, Legal Research and Writing, Property, Property in Time, and Torts. Required upper-level courses consist of Legal Writing seminar or a supervised research and writing project and Professional Responsibility. The required orientation program for first-year students is a 4-day program encompassing social, cultural, and legal events throughout the week on and off campus.

Electives

The Law Center offers concentrations in corporate law, criminal law, entertainment law, environmental law, family law, intellectual property law, international law, juvenile law, labor law, litigation, maritime law, securities law, tax law, torts and insurance, commercial law, constitutional law and government, and administrative law and government. In addition, The Law Center offers 13 in-house clinical courses with credits from 6 to 14 per semester. Clinics include appellate advocacy, criminal defense, and civil rights. More than 200 seminars are offered on such topics as environmental law, intellectual property law, and international law. Many students pursue externships with government agencies, judges, and other organizations. The Law Center also offers a unique international internship program through which students can intern abroad with law firms, nongovernmental organizations, and corporate in-house legal departments. Supervised research projects may be undertaken for 2 credits under the guidance of a faculty member. Some courses involve field work. Several special lecture series held each academic year bring prominent legal scholars, judges, lawyers, and business executives to the Law Center. The Law Center offers a summer law program in London with distinguished professors from Europe and the U.S., as well as the opportunity to study abroad for a semester at prestigious institutions in Europe, Asia, and India. Students have the unique opportunity to study for a semester in London at Georgetown's own Center for Transnational Legal Studies, a partnership of 20 leading schools

from 5 continents. The tutorial program is open to all students; however, it is primarily designed for first-year students. Each of the first-year sections is assigned an upperclass tutor who meets with students on a weekly basis. A writing center is open to all students. These programs are not remedial. They do, however, provide academic support. A diversity clerkship program is offered by the Center Services Office, and other educational programs are sponsored by the Career Services Office and minority students groups. The Law Center's Loan Repayment Assistance Program (LRAP), one of the strongest in the country, assists graduates in public interest and government jobs with their law school loans. In addition, the Public Interest Law Scholars Program (PILS) provides scholarships and other assistance to 8 members of each entering class, and the student-run Equal Justice Foundation provides stipends to students accepting unpaid summer internships with nonprofit or government organizations.

Graduation Requirements

In order to graduate, candidates must have a GPA of 2.0, have completed the upper-division writing requirement, and have completed the Professional Responsibility course.

Organizations
Student-edited publications include the *Georgetown Law Journal, American Criminal Law Review, Georgetown Journal of Gender and the Law, Georgetown Immigration Law Journal, Georgetown International Environmental Law Review, Georgetown Journal of Legal Ethics, The Tax Lawyer, Georgetown Journal of Law and Public Policy, Georgetown Journal on Poverty Law and Policy, Georgetown Journal of International Law, Georgetown Journal of Law, Modern Critical Race Perspective,* and the newspaper, *Georgetown Law Weekly.* Georgetown competes in more than a dozen moot court competitions, including the Philip C. Jessup International Law Moot Court Competition, the ABA National Appellate Advocacy Competition, and the European Tax College Moot Court Competition. Georgetown also fields teams in more than a dozen mock trial and alternative dispute resolution competitions, including the American Association for Justice's Student Trial Advocacy Competition, the Texas Young Lawyer's Association National Trial Competition, and the Vis International Commercial Arbitration Moot. There are 75 student organizations, including Alternative Dispute Resolution Society, Equal

Placement	
J.D.s awarded:	650
Full-time job interviews:	280 employers
Summer job interviews:	700 employers
Placement by graduation:	93% of class
Placement within 9 months:	97% of class
Average starting salary:	$50,000 to $160,000
Areas of placement:	
Private practice 2-10 attorneys	2%
Private practice 11-25 attorneys	1%
Private practice 26-50 attorneys	1%
Private practice 51-100 attorneys	3%
Judicial clerkships	8%
Government	6%
Business/industry	5%
Public interest	5%
Military	2%

Justice Foundation, the Federalist Society, and American Constitution Society. There are local chapters of the Student Bar Association, Christian Legal Society, and International Law Society.

Library
The law library contains 593,978 hardcopy volumes and 591,932 microform volume equivalents, and subscribes to 5460 physicial periodicals and over 50,000 electronic serials. Such on-line databases and networks as CALI, CIS Universe, DIALOG, Legal-Trac, LEXIS, Mathew Bender, NEXIS, OCLC First Search, WESTLAW, Wilsonline Indexes, and OCLC, and FirstSearch are available to law students for research. The library provides free digital scanners to students. The ratio of library volumes to faculty is 3908 to 1 and to students is 300 to 1. The ratio of seats in the library to students is 1 to 2.

Faculty
The law school has 152 full-time and 231 part-time faculty members, of whom 106 are women. According to AAUP standards for Category I institutions, faculty salaries are above average. The ratio of full-time students to full-time faculty in an average clinic is 7 to 1. There is a chapter of the Order of the Coif.

Students
About 43% of the student body are women; 24%, minorities; 9%, African American; 9%, Asian American; 5%, Hispanic; and 3%, foreign nationals. The average age of entering students is 24; age range is 20 to 52. About 33% of students enter directly from undergraduate school, 8% have a graduate degree, and 67% have worked full-time prior to entering law school.

College of Law

P.O. Box 4037
Atlanta, GA 30302-4037

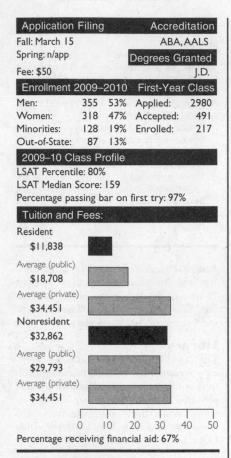

Application Filing			Accreditation
Fall: March 15			ABA, AALS
Spring: n/app			

Degrees Granted	
Fee: $50	J.D.

Enrollment 2009–2010			First-Year Class	
Men:	355	53%	Applied:	2980
Women:	318	47%	Accepted:	491
Minorities:	128	19%	Enrolled:	217
Out-of-State:	87	13%		

2009–10 Class Profile
LSAT Percentile: 80%
LSAT Median Score: 159
Percentage passing bar on first try: 97%

Tuition and Fees:

Resident
$11,838

Average (public)
$18,708

Average (private)
$34,451

Nonresident
$32,862

Average (public)
$29,793

Average (private)
$34,451

0   10   20   30   40   50

Percentage receiving financial aid: 67%

ADMISSIONS

In the fall 2009 first-year class, 2980 applied, 491 were accepted, and 217 enrolled. Twelve transfers enrolled. The median LSAT percentile of the most recent first-year class was 80; the median GPA was 3.45 on a scale of 4.0. The lowest LSAT percentile accepted was 43; the highest was 97.

Requirements
Applicants must have a bachelor's degree and take the LSAT. The most important admission factors include academic achievement, LSAT results, and GPA. No specific undergraduate courses are required. Candidates are not interviewed.

Procedure
The application deadline for fall entry is March 15. Applicants should submit an application form, LSAT results, transcripts, a personal statement, LSDAS report, TOEFL for applicants whose native language is not English, a non-refundable application fee of $50, and 2

letters of recommendation. Notification of the admissions decision begins in January. The latest acceptable LSAT test date for fall entry is February. The law school uses the LSDAS.

Special
The law school recruits minority and disadvantaged students by means of visiting other colleges and universities during graduate and professional program days, speaking to prelaw clubs and classes, and recruiting at schools with large minority student populations. The law school also conducts high school visits and cosponsors a law camp for high school students in the summer. Requirements are not different for out-of-state students. Transfer students must have one year of credit, have attended an ABA-approved law school, and have a letter from the dean of the student's previous law school stating that the student is in good standing and is eligible to return to the school, and stating the student's class ranking.

Costs

Tuition and fees for the 2009-2010 academic year are $11,838 for full-time in-state students and $32,862 for out-of-state students. On-campus room and board costs about $10,986 annually; books and supplies run $750.

Financial Aid

About 67% of current law students receive some form of aid. The average annual amount of aid from all sources combined, including scholarships, loans, and work contracts, is $17,415; maximum, $30,000. Awards are based on need and merit. There are also loans that are need- and non-need-based. Required financial statement is the FAFSA. The aid application deadline for fall entry is April 1. Special funds for minority or disadvantaged students include scholarships. First-year students are notified about their financial aid application at time of acceptance.

About the Law School

Georgia State University College of Law was established in 1982 and is a public institution. The 34-acre campus is in an urban area in the city of Atlanta. The primary mission of the law school is to provide both part- and full-time programs that are designed for students wishing to

gain a knowledge of the law, of legal institutions, and of legal processes. The college is equally committed to part- and full-time legal studies. Students have access to federal, state, county, city, and local agencies, courts, correctional facilities, law firms, and legal aid organizations in the Atlanta area. A variety of institutions and law-related agencies are located in the metropolitan Atlanta area. Facilities of special interest to law students include the Richard B. Russell Federal Building; Federal Reserve Bank; state capitol building; state legislature; federal, state, and local court systems; and offices of the U.S. attorney, state attorney general, and county and city district attorneys. Housing for students is on a first-come, first-served basis in the University Lofts, which accommodates 2000 students in modern apartments. All law school facilities are accessible to the physically disabled.

Calendar

The law school operates on a traditional semester basis. Courses for both full- and part- time students are offered both day and evening and must be completed within 6 years. New full- and part-time students are admitted in the fall. There is a 7-week summer session. Transferable summer courses are offered.

Programs

Students may take relevant courses in other programs and apply credit toward the J.D.; a maximum of 14 semester hour credits may be applied. The following joint degrees may be earned: J.D./M.A. (Juris Doctor/Master of Arts in philosophy), J.D./M.B.A. (Juris Doctor/Master of Business Administration), J.D./M.C.R.P. (Juris Doctor/Master of City and Regional Planning), J.D./M.P.A. (Juris Doctor/Master of Public Administration), and J.D./M.S.H.A. (Juris Doctor/Master of Health Administration).

Required
To earn the J.D., candidates must complete 90 total credits, of which 43 are for required courses. They must maintain a minimum GPA of 2.2 in the required courses. The following first-year courses are required of all students: Civil Procedure I and II, Contracts I and II, Criminal Law, Legal Bibliography, Property I and II, Research Writing and Advocacy I and II, and Torts I and II. Required upper-

Phone: 404-413-9200
Fax: 404-413-9203
E-mail: cjgeorge@gsu.edu
Web: www.law.gsu.edu

Contact

Cheryl Jester-George, Director of Admissions, 404-413-9004 for general inquiries; Louis Scott, Director of Financial Aid, 404-413-2137 for financial aid information.

level courses consist of Constitutional Law, Evidence, Litigation, and Professional Responsibility. The required orientation program for first-year students occurs in the first week of the fall semester and is designed to introduce some of the first-year required courses, college personnel, and facilities and to familiarize students with procedures.

Electives

Students must take 47 hours in their area of concentration. The College of Law offers concentrations in corporate law, criminal law, environmental law, family law, international law, labor law, litigation, sports law, tax law, torts and insurance, and health law. In addition, second- and third-year students may earn 3 to 6 semester hours by enrolling in the Tax Clinic and the Center for Law, Health and Society's Health Law Partnership (HeLP) Clinic. Students in the Tax Clinic assist individual clients in preparing their cases for presentation before the Small Claims Division of the U.S. Tax Court and the Administrative Appeals Office of the Internal Revenue Service. Students in the HeLP Clinic have opportunities to work on cases related to children's health and welfare. Seminars are offered to students who have completed the prerequisites and are normally worth 2 semester hours. Internships include working for local district attorneys, solicitors, and defenders; clerking for county, state, and federal judges; and placement in a variety of other governmental or public interest organizations. Independent research for 1 to 2 semester hours of credit may be selected by third-year students upon approval by a faculty adviser and the administration. Field work includes pro bono work. Special lecture series include the Henry J. Miller Distinguished Lecture Series. The College of Law offers 2 study-abroad programs. Law students can participate in the Summer Academy for International Commercial Arbitration conducted in Europe, which includes visits to arbitral institutions in Vienna, Budapest, Prague, and Venice. Law and graduate students may also participate in "The Urban Environment: Law, Policy and Culture--The Rio Experience." The administration offers an academic enrichment program for students who need or desire additional help in required courses. Minority and special interest programs are usually sponsored by student organizations and/or faculty members. The most widely taken electives

are Basic Tax; Wills, Trusts, and Estates; and Criminal Procedure.

Graduation Requirements

In order to graduate, candidates must have a GPA of 2.2 and have completed the upper-division writing requirement.

Organizations

The primary law review is the *Georgia State University Law Review*. Students edit *The Docket*, *The Black Letter Law*, and *The Federalist*. The Moot Court Society competes 7 or 8 times a year. Other competitions include the National Moot Court Competition, sponsored by the Association of the Bar of New York City; National Appellate Advocacy Competition, sponsored by the ABA; William W. Daniel Mock Trial Invitational; and Lone Star Classic Mock Trial Competition. Student organizations include the Student Trial Lawyers Association, Intellectual Property Law Society, and Hispanic Students Bar Association. Local chapters of national associations include the Association of Women Law Students, Black Law Students Association, Environmental Law Society, and Student Health Lawyers Association. Other groups include Delta Theta Phi, Phi Alpha Delta, and Phi Delta Phi law fraternities.

Library

The law library contains 160,054 hardcopy volumes and 191,256 microform volume equivalents, and subscribes to 2161 serial publications. Such on-line databases and networks as CALI, CIS Universe, Legal-Trac, LEXIS, LOIS, NEXIS, OCLC First Search, WESTLAW, Wilsonline Indexes, HeinOnline, Galileo, BNA, Making of Modern Law, Juris, and Oxford are available to law students for research. Special library collections include a U.S. depository and collections in health law and environmental law. Recently, the library converted shelf space to additional study room. Additionally, all study rooms were upgraded with overhead protectors and an on-line reservation system. The ratio of library volumes to faculty is 2910 to 1 and to students is 238 to 1. The ratio of seats in the library to students is 1 to 2.

Faculty

The law school has 55 full-time and 50 part-time faculty members, of whom 40

Placement

J.D.s awarded:	185

Services available through: a separate law school placement center

Services: programming and counseling on career options for lawyers, and participating in national and regional job fairs

Special features: state-of-the-art Internet-based job listings service for students and alumni, personalized, one-on-one job search planning sessions for first-year, second-year, and third-year students in addition to alumni transitioning into other practice areas and legal-related or alternative careers

Full-time job interviews:	17 employers
Summer job interviews:	60 employers
Placement by graduation:	n/av
Placement within 9 months:	98% of class
Average starting salary:	$38,000 to $160,000

Areas of placement:

Private practice 2-10 attorneys	23%
Private practice 11-25 attorneys	8%
Private practice 26-50 attorneys	3%
Private practice 51-100 attorneys	2%
Private practice 100+ attorneys	17%
Business/industry	18%
Government	8%
Public interest	6%
Judicial clerkships	4%
Academic	4%
Military	2%

are women. According to AAUP standards for Category I institutions, faculty salaries are well below average. About 17% of full-time faculty have a graduate law degree in addition to the J.D.; about 10% of part-time faculty have one. The ratio of full-time students to full-time faculty in an average class is 11 to 1; in a clinic, 4 to 1. The law school has a regular program of bringing visiting professors and other distinguished lecturers and visitors to campus.

Students

About 47% of the student body are women; 19%, minorities; 5%, African American; 4%, Asian American; 1%, Hispanic; and 14%, (students may select multiracial as an ethnic classification). The majority of students come from Georgia (87%). The average age of entering students is 26; age range is 21 to 55. About 55% of students enter directly from undergraduate school, 10% have a graduate degree, and 30% have worked full-time prior to entering law school. About 11% drop out after the first year for academic or personal reasons; 89% remain to receive a law degree.

School of Law

536 Mission Street
San Francisco, CA 94105-2968

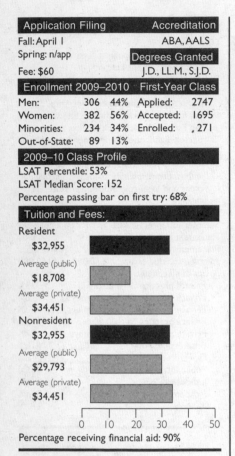

Application Filing		Accreditation
Fall: April 1		ABA, AALS
Spring: n/app		**Degrees Granted**
Fee: $60		J.D., LL.M., S.J.D.

Enrollment 2009–2010			First-Year Class	
Men:	306	44%	Applied:	2747
Women:	382	56%	Accepted:	1695
Minorities:	234	34%	Enrolled:	271
Out-of-State:	89	13%		

2009–10 Class Profile
LSAT Percentile: 53%
LSAT Median Score: 152
Percentage passing bar on first try: 68%

Tuition and Fees:

Resident
$32,955

Average (public)
$18,708

Average (private)
$34,451

Nonresident
$32,955

Average (public)
$29,793

Average (private)
$34,451

0   10   20   30   40   50

Percentage receiving financial aid: 90%

ADMISSIONS

In a recent year, 2747 applied, 1695 were accepted, and 271 enrolled. Six transfers enrolled. The median LSAT percentile of the most recent first-year class was 53; the median GPA was 3.08 on a scale of 4.0. The lowest LSAT percentile accepted was 11; the highest was 96. Figures in the above capsule and in this profile are approximate.

Requirements
Applicants must have a bachelor's degree and take the LSAT. The most important admission factors include academic achievement, LSAT results, and life experience. No specific undergraduate courses are required. Candidates are not interviewed.

Procedure
Applicants should submit an application form, LSAT results, transcripts, a personal statement, a nonrefundable application fee of $60, 2 letters of recommendation, and a resume. Notification of the admis-

sions decision is 4 to 6 weeks after the application. The latest acceptable LSAT test date for fall entry is February. The law school uses the LSDAS. Check with the school for application deadlines.

Special
The law school recruits minority and disadvantaged students by targeting recruiting to underrepresented communities, supporting the CLEO program, the law school's diversity scholarship program, and participation in the LSAC-sponsored minority programs. Requirements are not different for out-of-state students. Transfer students must have one year of credit, have attended an ABA-approved law school, and are subject to the availability of seats, the personal statement, and a competitive review of the students' academic record from the first year of law school.

Costs

Tuition and fees for the 2009-2010 academic year are approximately $32,955 for all full-time students. Tuition for part-time students is approximately $23,145 per year. Books and supplies run about $1200.

Financial Aid

In a recent year, about 90% of current law students received some form of aid. The average annual amount of aid from all sources combined, including scholarships, loans, and work contracts, was approximately $43,000; maximum, $54,270. Awards are based on need and merit. Required financial statements are the FAFSA and institutional form. Special funds for minority or disadvantaged students include a scholarship fund reserved for minority students or those from disadvantaged backgrounds. First-year students are notified about their financial aid application at time of acceptance. Check with the school for current application deadline.

About the Law School

Golden Gate University School of Law was established in 1901 and is a private institution. The campus is in an urban area in the legal and financial district in downtown. The primary mission of the law school is to educate lawyers in

a humanistic yet rigorous environment through a balance of traditional legal theory courses and clinical experiences. Students have access to federal, state, county, city, and local agencies, courts, correctional facilities, law firms, and legal aid organizations in the San Francisco area. Many internships, externships, and other clinical programs take advantage of government offices, courts, and law firms in the city. Facilities of special interest to law students The law school, which occupies an architecturally acclaimed building that includes classrooms, a moot court room, student computer laboratories, faculty and staff offices, and a law library. A new student services center just opened. Housing for students is not available on campus, but the housing office helps students find accommodations off campus. All law school facilities are accessible to the physically disabled.

Calendar

The law school operates on a traditional semester basis. Courses for full-time students are offered both day and evening and must be completed within 3 years (84 months maximum). For part-time students, courses are offered evenings only and must be completed within 4 years (84 months maximum). New full- and part-time students are admitted in the fall. There is a 7-week summer session. Transferable summer courses are offered.

Programs

In addition to the J.D., the law school offers the LL.M. and S.J.D. The following joint degrees may be earned: J.D./M.B.A. (Juris Doctor/Master of Business Administration) and J.D./Ph.D. (Juris Doctor/Doctor of Philosophy in clinical psychology).

Required
To earn the J.D., candidates must complete 88 total credits, of which 57 are for required courses. They must maintain a minimum GPA of 2.15 in the required courses. The following first-year courses are required of all students: Civil Procedure I and II, Contracts I and II, Criminal Law, Property I and II, Torts I and II, and Writing and Research I and II. Required upper-level courses consist of Appellate Advocacy, Business Associations, Constitutional Law I and II, Criminal Procedure I, Evidence, Professional Responsibility,

Phone: 415-442-6630
800-GGU-4YOU
E-mail: *lawadmit@ggu.edu*
Web: *www.ggu.edu/law*

Contact

Admissions Office, 415-442-6630 for general inquiries; Director of Financial Aid, 415-442-6635 for financial aid information.

CALIFORNIA

Solving Legal Problems, and Wills and Trusts. Students are encouraged to enroll in any of the many clinics.The required orientation program for first-year students is a 4-day program held before classes begin.

Electives

The School of Law offers concentrations in corporate law, criminal law, environmental law, intellectual property law, international law, labor law, litigation, tax law, and real estate law, and public interest law. In addition, The school offers 2 on-site clinics, and 10 field placement clinics. Clinics include Environmental Law and Justice, Women's Employment Rights, Civil Practice, and Public Interest/Government. Seminars are worth 2 credits, and prerequisites vary. Topics include Asian Pacific Trade, Social Justice, Domestic Violence Seminar, and Settlement of Litigation Disputes. Full- and part-time internships with law firms, government agencies, and judges are offered. There is also an Honors Lawyering Program through which students spend 2 semesters working as legal apprentices. Students may pursue independent research under the direction of faculty members. Courses are offered in Advanced Legal Research, Solving Legal Problems, and Tax Research. Special lecture series are offered annually. Summer study abroad is possible in Paris, France. An Academic Success Program develops skills and legal analysis and exam writing. Elective and required courses are offered in legal analysis, legal methods, and legal reasoning; special problems courses are offered in substantive areas of law. There is a diversity scholarship program, specialized course offerings, and certificates of specialization. The most widely taken electives are Tax, Remedies, and Intellectual Property.

Graduation Requirements

In order to graduate, candidates must have a GPA of 2.15, have completed the upper-division writing requirement, and Students take writing courses in each of their 3 years in law school.

Organizations

Students edit the *Golden Gate University Law Review, Annual Survey of International and Comparative Law*, and *Environmental Law Journal*. Teams attend

various national and international contests, including the Jessup International Moot Court Competition, Environmental Law Moot Court, and Intellectual Property Moot Court. Other competitions attended are the National Mock Trial Competition, Association of Trial Lawyers of America Competition, and the ABA's Criminal Justice Trial Competition, among others. Law student organizations, local chapters of national associations, and campus clubs and organizations include Student Bar Association, Queer Law Student Association, Asian Pacific American Law Student Association, Latino/a American Law Student Association, Black Law Students Association, National Lawyers Guild, Phi Delta Phi, Federalist Society, Public Interest Law Foundation, Environmental Law Society, and International Law Society.

Library

The law library contains 377,000 hardcopy volumes and 238,000 microform volume equivalents, and subscribes to 3600 serial publications. Such on-line databases and networks as CALI, DIALOG, Dow-Jones, Infotrac, Legal-Trac, LEXIS, LOIS, Matthew Bender, NEXIS, and WESTLAW are available to law students for research. Special library collections include a depository for both California and federal documents and the archives of the National Educational Foundation. Its collections emphasize taxation, real estate, land use, and individual rights. Recently, the library began an expansion that will add a 100-seat reading room. The ratio of library volumes to faculty is 9195 to 1 and to students is 548 to 1. The ratio of seats in the library to students is 1 to 2.

Faculty

The law school has 41 full-time and 67 part-time faculty members, of whom 46 are women. About 11% of full-time faculty have a graduate law degree in addition to the J.D.; about 8% of part-time faculty have one. The ratio of full-time students to full-time faculty in an average class is 19 to 1; in a clinic, 6 to 1. The law school has a regular program of bringing visiting professors and other distinguished lecturers and visitors to campus.

Students

About 56% of the student body are women; 34%, minorities; 3%, African Ameri-

Placement

J.D.s awarded:	249
Services available through: a separate law school placement center	
Services: encourages private firms and public agencies to list job opportunities, solicits on-campus interviews	
Special features: computer-assisted job search through LCS on-line.	
Full-time job interviews:	28 employers
Summer job interviews:	28 employers
Placement by graduation:	n/av
Placement within 9 months:	82% of class
Average starting salary:	$30,000 to $200,000
Areas of placement:	
Solo practice	3%
Private practice 2-10 attorneys	26%
Private practice 11-25 attorneys	6%
Private practice 26-50 attorneys	1%
Private practice 51-100 attorneys	8%
Business/industry	28%
Government	17%
Academic	6%
Public interest	4%
Judicial clerkships	1%

can; 18%, Asian American; 6%, Hispanic; 1%, Native American; and 12%, other, or unknown, foreign, 1%. The majority of students come from California (87%). The average age of entering students is 26; age range is 20 to 57. About 20% of students enter directly from undergraduate school, 6% have a graduate degree, and 43% have worked full-time prior to entering law school. About 27% drop out after the first year for academic or personal reasons; 73% remain to receive a law degree.

GONZAGA UNIVERSITY

School of Law

Box 3528 Spokane,
WA 99220-3528

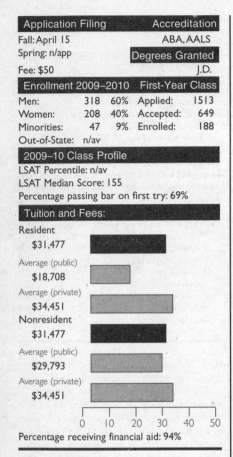

Application Filing			Accreditation
Fall: April 15			ABA, AALS
Spring: n/app			**Degrees Granted**
Fee: $50			J.D.

Enrollment 2009–2010			First-Year Class	
Men:	318	60%	Applied:	1513
Women:	208	40%	Accepted:	649
Minorities:	47	9%	Enrolled:	188
Out-of-State:	n/av			

2009–10 Class Profile
LSAT Percentile: n/av
LSAT Median Score: 155
Percentage passing bar on first try: 69%

Tuition and Fees:

Resident
$31,477

Average (public)
$18,708

Average (private)
$34,451

Nonresident
$31,477

Average (public)
$29,793

Average (private)
$34,451

0 10 20 30 40 50

Percentage receiving financial aid: 94%

ADMISSIONS

In the fall 2009 first-year class, 1513 applied, 649 were accepted, and 188 enrolled. Four transfers enrolled. The median GPA of the most recent first-year class was 3.3.

Requirements
Applicants must have a bachelor's degree and take the LSAT. The most important admission factors include academic achievement, LSAT results, and general background. No specific undergraduate courses are required. Candidates are not interviewed.

Procedure
The application deadline for fall entry is April 15. Applicants should submit an application form, LSAT results, transcripts, TOEFL for international applicants, a nonrefundable application fee of $50, 2 letters of recommendation, a resume, LSDAS report, and a personal statement. Notification of the admissions decision is after January 1. The latest acceptable LSAT test date for fall entry is February. The law school uses the LSDAS.

Special
The law school recruits minority and disadvantaged students by means of targeted mailings, on-line chat rooms, law school forums and fairs, alumni referrals, prelaw advisors, open houses, and campus visits. A recent law school graduate is hired full-time to focus on minority recruiting. Requirements are not different for out-of-state students. Transfer students must have 1 year of credit, must have attended an ABA-approved law school, are accepted on a space available basis, and must be in good standing and eligible to return to their previous law school.

Costs

Tuition and fees for the 2009-2010 academic year are $31,477 for full-time in-state students. Books and supplies run $1000.

Financial Aid

About 94% of current law students receive some form of aid. The average annual amount of aid from all sources combined, including scholarships, loans, and work contracts, is $31,320; maximum, $46,032. Awards are based on need and merit. Required financial statement is the FAFSA. The aid application deadline for fall entry is February 1. Special funds for minority or disadvantaged students include scholarships. First-year students are notified about their financial aid application within 1 month of acceptance if the FAFSA is complete.

About the Law School

Gonzaga University School of Law was established in 1912 and is a private institution. The 94-acre campus is in an urban area 1½ miles from downtown Spokane. The primary mission of the law school is to preserve and develop a humanistic, Catholic, and Jesuit legal education. Students have access to federal, state, county, city, and local agencies, courts, correctional facilities, law firms, and legal aid organizations in the Spokane area. Facilities of special interest to law students include the Chastek Law Library, the Foley Library Center, computer labs, the Rudolf fitness center, and the McCarthy Arena. Housing for students consists of university housing, and private apartments, often within a 10-block radius of the law school. About 90% of the law school facilities are accessible to the physically disabled.

Calendar

The law school operates on a traditional semester basis. Courses for full-time students are offered days only and must be completed within 5 years. There is no part-time program. New students are admitted in the fall. There are 2 five week summer sessions. Transferable summer courses are offered.

Programs

The following joint degrees may be earned: J.D./M.Acc. (Juris Doctor/Master of Accounting), J.D./M.B.A. (Juris Doctor/Master of Business Administration), and J.D./M.S.W. (Juris Doctor/ Master of Social Work).

Required
To earn the J.D., candidates must complete 90 total credits, of which 49 are for required courses. They must maintain a minimum GPA of 2.2 in the required courses. The following first-year courses are required of all students: Civil Procedure, Contracts, Criminal Law, Legal Research Writing I and II, Litigation Skills and Professionalism Lab, Perspectives on the Law, Property, Torts, and Transactional Skills and Professionalism Lab. Required upper-level courses consist of a public service requirement, clinic or externship, Constitutional Law (Civil Liberties), Constitutional Law (Government Structure), Evidence, Legal Writing and Research III and IV, and Professional Responsibility. All students must take clinical courses. The required orientation program for first-year students consists of 3 days of introduction to the legal system, introduction to the law, and information regarding Gonzaga.

Electives
The School of Law offers concentrations in environmental law and public interest law, and business law. In addition, upper-level students who have completed or are enrolled in 60 credits must participate in either in-house or outplacement clin-

Phone: 509-313-5532
800-793-1710
Fax: 509-313-3697
E-mail: *admissions@lawschool.gonzaga.edu*
Web: *http://www.law.gonzaga.edu*

Contact

Susan Lee, Director of Admissions, 509-313-5532 or 800 793-1710 for general inquiries; Joan Henning, Coordinator of Financial Services, 509-313-3859 for financial aid information.

WASHINGTON

ics for a minimum of 3 credits up to 15 credits. Various 2-credit upper-level seminars are offered, including those on the First Amendment, International Human Rights, Ethical Problems in the Representation of Children, Death Penalty, and Employment Discrimination. Internships are available when 60 credits have been completed. Directed research programs, worth 1 or 2 credits, must be supervised by a faculty member. Special lecture series include the William O. Douglass Lecture, Paul and Lita Luvera Lecture, International Law Symposium, public issues, and various law forums. There is a summer law program in Florence, Italy. Tutorial programs are available at a student's request. The Academic Resource Program provides tutorial assistance to participating first-year students. The Student Bar Association sponsors group tutorials for all first-year courses. Minority programs are sponsored by the Multicultural Law Caucus, Black Law Students Association, Hispanic Law Caucus, Sexual Orientation Diversity Alliance, Indian Law Caucus, and Asian Pacific Islander Law Caucus. Special interest group programs include the Public Interest Law Project, Street Law, Property Law Interest Group, and Criminal Defense Law Caucus. The most widely taken electives are Environmental Law, Tax Law, and International Law.

Graduation Requirements
In order to graduate, candidates must have a GPA of 2.2 and 90 credit hours and 30 hours of public service.

Organizations

Students edit the *Gonzaga Law Review*, *Gonzaga Journal of International Law*, a journal specializing in international law, business, political, and socioeconomic issues (website www.law.gonzaga.edu/), and the student newspaper, *The Advocate*. Moot court competitions include the National Appellate Advocacy, Jessup Cup, and National Moot Court. Teams also take part in the Negotiation, National Trial, Client Counseling, Tax, Saul Lefkowitz, and Giles Rich Patent competitions. Law student organizations, local chapters of national associations, and campus organizations include the Women's Law Caucus, International Law Society, Multicultural

Law Caucus, Student Bar Association, Gonzaga Public Interest Law Project, Environmental Law Caucus, Phi Alpha Delta, ACLU, and National Native American Law Students Association.

Library

The law library contains 167,286 hardcopy volumes and 141,329 microform volume equivalents, and subscribes to 2461 serial publications. Such on-line databases and networks as CALI, CIS Universe, DIALOG, Infotrac, Legal-Trac, LEXIS, LOIS, NEXIS, OCLC First Search, WESTLAW, Wilsonline Indexes, OCLC, Foreign Law Guide, constitutions of the countries of the world, United Nations treaty collection, Washington Lawyers Practice Manual Clearing House Review, LexisNexis Congressional, Checkpoint, Hein Online, and LLMC-Digital are available to law students for research. Special library collections include ABA Archives, American Indian Selected Publications, Canon Law Materials, Federal Legislative Histories, Hein's American Law Institution Publications, Hein's Legal Thesis and Dissertations, Karol Llewellyn Papers, Scrapbooks of the Honorable Richard Guy; selected nineteenth century treatises, Washington Supreme Court and Court of Appeal briefs, and Federal Depository Library. Recently, the library purchased 315 new study chairs. The ratio of library volumes to faculty is 4920 to 1 and to students is 318 to 1. The ratio of seats in the library to students is 1 to 1.

Faculty

The law school has 34 full-time and 42 part-time faculty members, of whom 17 are women. The ratio of full-time students to full-time faculty in an average class is 15 to 1; in a clinic, 6 to 1.

Students

About 40% of the student body are women; 9%, minorities; 4%, Asian American; 3%, Hispanic; and 1%, Native American. The average age of entering students is 25; age range is 20 to 41. About 14% drop out after the first year for academic or personal reasons; 86% remain to receive a law degree.

Placement

J.D.s awarded:	175

Services available through: a separate law school placement center
Services: on-campus interviews, workshops, Resource Library, Spring Career Fest, consortium, and Public Interest Career Fest
Special features: counseling on employment and mock interviews, cover letter and resume review, presentations and workshops on areas of practice, and graduate/alumni networking events in other cities.

Full-time job interviews:	9 employers
Summer job interviews:	32 employers
Placement by graduation:	n/av
Placement within 9 months:	94% of class
Average starting salary:	$62,000 to $70,000
Areas of placement:	
Private practice 2-10 attorneys	21%
Private practice 11-25 attorneys	5%
Private practice 26-50 attorneys	7%
Private practice 51-100 attorneys	1%
Private practice - size unknown	20%
Government	15%
Business/industry	13%
Judicial clerkships	8%
Public interest	6%
Military	2%
Academic	2%

School of Law

1536 Hewitt Avenue
St. Paul, MN 55104-1284

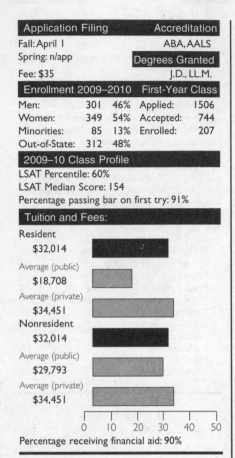

Application Filing		Accreditation
Fall: April 1		ABA, AALS
Spring: n/app		Degrees Granted
Fee: $35		J.D., LL.M.

Enrollment 2009–2010		First-Year Class	
Men:	301 46%	Applied:	1506
Women:	349 54%	Accepted:	744
Minorities:	85 13%	Enrolled:	207
Out-of-State:	312 48%		

2009–10 Class Profile
LSAT Percentile: 60%
LSAT Median Score: 154
Percentage passing bar on first try: 91%

Tuition and Fees:

Resident
$32,014

Average (public)
$18,708

Average (private)
$34,451

Nonresident
$32,014

Average (public)
$29,793

Average (private)
$34,451

0 10 20 30 40 50

Percentage receiving financial aid: 90%

ADMISSIONS

In the fall 2009 first-year class, 1506 applied, 744 were accepted, and 207 enrolled. One transfer enrolled. The median LSAT percentile of the most recent first-year class was 60; the median GPA was 3.42 on a scale of 4.0. The lowest LSAT percentile accepted was 15; the highest was 93.

Requirements
Applicants must have a bachelor's degree and take the LSAT. The most important asmission factors include writing ability, GPA, and LSAT results. No specific undergraduate courses are required. Candidates are not interviewed.

Procedure
The application deadline for fall entry is April 1. Applicants should submit an application form, LSAT results, transcripts, a personal statement, a nonrefundable application fee of $35, and 2 letters of recommendation. Notification

of the admissions decision is 2 to 6 weeks after the file is completed. The latest acceptable LSAT test date for fall entry is February. The law school uses the LSDAS.

Special
The law school recruits minority and disadvantaged students through strategic recruitment, diversity scholarships, and an admissions recruitment program geared specifically for minority students. The school also participates in CLEO. Requirements are not different for out-of-state students. Transfer students must have one year of credit, have attended an ABA-approved law school, and submit a letter of good standing and a transcript from the previous institution. Preadmissions courses consist of a 20-hour Legal Method/Practice class offered as part of orientation.

Costs

Tuition and fees for the 2009-2010 academic year are $32,014 for all full-time students. Tuition for part-time students is $23,078 per year. On-campus room and board costs about $12,226 annually; books and supplies run $2000.

Financial Aid

About 90% of current law students receive some form of aid. The average annual amount of aid from all sources combined, including scholarships, loans, and work contracts, is $30,000; maximum, $49,685. Awards are based on need and merit. Required financial statement is the FAFSA. The aid application deadline for fall entry is open. Special funds for minority or disadvantaged students include the equivalent of 8 1/2 full-tuition scholarships. First-year students are notified about their financial aid application at time of acceptance.

About the Law School

Hamline University School of Law was established in 1972 and is a private institution. The 50-acre campus is in an urban area located between St. Paul and Minneapolis. The primary mission of the law school is to educate students to apply legal knowledge with disciplined imagination, a global perspective, and creative conflict resolution skills. Students have access to federal, state, county, city, and

local agencies, courts, correctional facilities, law firms, and legal aid organizations in the St. Paul area. The state capital is minutes away from the campus in St. Paul. Facilities of special interest to law students include an expanded Law Center designed for interaction with a moot court room with state-of-the-art technology. The library addition provides increased study space and the entire building has wireless Internet access. The law building is in the middle of campus with easy access to dining, athletic, and extra curricular activity spaces. Housing for students is readily available, both on and off campus. On campus, there is apartment-style housing, as well as dorm space. All law school facilities are accessible to the physically disabled.

Calendar

The law school operates on a traditional semester basis. Courses for full-time students are offered both day and evening and must be completed within 7 years. For part-time students, courses are offered on weekends, and must be completed within 7 years. New full- and part-time students are admitted in the fall. There is an 8-week summer session. Transferable summer courses are offered.

Programs

In addition to the J.D., the law school offers the LL.M. Students may take relevant courses in other programs and apply credit toward the J.D.; a maximum of 12 credits may be applied. The following joint degrees may be earned: J.D./M.A.N.M. (Juris Doctor/Master of Arts in Nonprofit Management), J.D./M.A.O.L. (Juris Doctor/Master of Arts in Organizational Leadership), J.D./M.A.P.A. (Juris Doctor/Master of Arts in Public Administration), J.D./M.B.A. (Juris Doctor/Master of Business Administration), and J.D./M.F.A. (Juris Doctor/Master of Fine Arts in Creative Writing).

Required
To earn the J.D., candidates must complete 88 total credits, of which 35 are for required courses. They must maintain a minimum GPA of 2.0 in the required courses. The following first-year courses are required of all students: Civil Procedure I and II, Constitutional Law I, Contracts I and II, Criminal Law, Legal

Phone: 651-523-2461
800-388-3688
Fax: 651-523-3064
E-mail: lawadm@gw.hamline.edu
Web: web.hamline.edu/law

Contact

Office of Admissions, 651-523-2461 or 800-388-3688 for general inquiries; Lynette Wahl, Associate Director of Financial Aid, 651-523-2280 for financial aid information.

MINNESOTA

Research and Writing I and II, Property, and Torts I. Required upper-level courses consist of a legal perspectives course, a seminar course, a skills course, and Professional Responsibility. Students must take a skills course, and clinics are one way to meet that requirement. The required orientation program for first-year students is 2 days, and consists of an introduction to the school, campus, and legal studies and professional responsibility.

Electives

The School of Law offers concentrations in corporate law, criminal law, international law, juvenile law, labor law, alternative dispute resolution, commercial law, government and regulatory affairs, health law, intellectual property, and social justice. In addition, 3- or 4-credit clinics provide upper-level students with practical experience in such areas as child advocacy, immigration law, public interest law, unemployment compensation law, alternative dispute resolution, trial practice, and education law. In seminars, 15 upper-level students per semester engage in an in-depth study of a selected topic for 3 credits. Internships for 3 to 12 credits offer upper-level students the opportunity to work with expert practitioners in various types of legal practice. Upper-level students may be research assistants for professors. Credit is given only if research assistance is structured as an independent study. Special lectures are open to the school community and to the public. Credit is not given. Opportunities for study abroad consist of summer programs at the University of Bergen (Norway), Queen Mary University of London (England), Central European University (Budapest, Hungary), and January term programs at Hebrew University (Jerusalem) and Puerto Rico. The Academic Success Program, which includes help with legal writing and substantive review of courses, is offered to students who need remedial assistance. Offerings include special scholarships programs and student organizations for minority students coordinated by the Assistant Dean for Student and Multicultural Affairs. A variety of student organizations exists to fit every interest. The most widely taken electives are Corporations, Evidence, and Criminal Procedure.

Graduation Requirements

In order to graduate, candidates must have a GPA of 2.0 and have completed the upper-division writing requirement. Students must take Professional Responsibility, a seminar, a skills course, and a Legal Perspectives course.

Organizations

Students edit the *Hamline Law Review*, the *Hamline Journal of Public Law and Policy*, and the *Journal of Law and Religion*. There are many moot court competitions, including National Moot Court, Frederick Douglass, and Rich Intellectual Property Competition. Other competitions include Client Counseling and Negotiation. Law student organizations, local chapters of national organizations, and campus organizations include the Student Bar Association, Women's Legal Caucus, Multicultural Law Students Association, Delta Theta Phi, Phi Alpha Delta, ABA-Law School Division, Minnesota Justice Foundation, International Society, and Center for International Students.

Library

The law library contains 154,942 hardcopy volumes and 130,432 microform volume equivalents, and subscribes to 911 serial publications. Such on-line databases and networks as CALI, CIS Universe, DIALOG, Infotrac, Legal-Trac, LEXIS, LOIS, NEXIS, OCLC First Search, WESTLAW, Wilsonline Indexes, and CD-ROM are available to law students for research. Special library collections include a U.S. government selective depository collection. Recently, the library installed new seating and carpeting and signage. The ratio of library volumes to faculty is 3443 to 1 and to students is 238 to 1. The ratio of seats in the library to students is 1 to 2.

Faculty

The law school has 45 full-time and 84 part-time faculty members, of whom 54 are women. About 26% of full-time faculty have a graduate law degree in addition to the J.D. The ratio of full-time students to full-time faculty in an average class is 26 to 1; in a clinic, 8 to 1. The law school has a regular program of bringing visiting professors and other distinguished lecturers and visitors to campus.

Placement

J.D.s awarded:	190
Services available through: a separate law school placement center	
Special features: extensive career programming.	
Full-time job interviews:	31 employers
Summer job interviews:	43 employers
Placement by graduation:	n/av
Placement within 9 months:	93% of class
Average starting salary:	$36,500 to $240,000
Areas of placement:	
Private practice 2-10 attorneys	28%
Private practice 11-25 attorneys	2%
Private practice 26-50 attorneys	1%
Private practice 51-100 attorneys	5%
Private practice solo; unknown practice size	5%
Business/industry	27%
Judicial clerkships	15%
Government	8%
Public interest	7%
Military	1%
Academic	1%

Students

About 54% of the student body are women; 13%, minorities; 3%, African American; 5%, Asian American; 4%, Hispanic; and 1%, Native American. The majority of students come from the Midwest (85%). The average age of entering students is 26; age range is 19 to 63. About 35% of students enter directly from undergraduate school, 10% have a graduate degree, and 65% have worked full-time prior to entering law school. About 4% drop out after the first year for academic or personal reasons; 96% remain to receive a law degree.

Harvard Law School

Cambridge, MA 02138

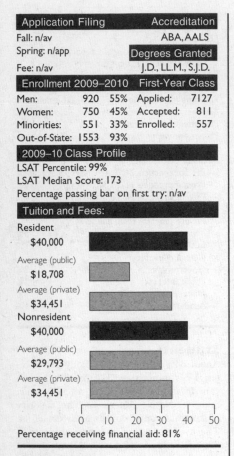

Application Filing		Accreditation	
Fall: n/av		ABA, AALS	
Spring: n/app		**Degrees Granted**	
Fee: n/av		J.D., LL.M., S.J.D.	

Enrollment 2009–2010			First-Year Class	
Men:	920	55%	Applied:	7127
Women:	750	45%	Accepted:	811
Minorities:	551	33%	Enrolled:	557
Out-of-State:	1553	93%		

2009–10 Class Profile
LSAT Percentile: 99%
LSAT Median Score: 173
Percentage passing bar on first try: n/av

Tuition and Fees:

Resident
$40,000

Average (public)
$18,708

Average (private)
$34,451

Nonresident
$40,000

Average (public)
$29,793

Average (private)
$34,451

0 10 20 30 40 50

Percentage receiving financial aid: 81%

ADMISSIONS

In a recent year, 7127 applied, 811 were accepted, and 557 enrolled. Twenty-six transfers enrolled. The median LSAT percentile of the most recent first-year class was 99; the median GPA was 3.81 on a scale of 4.0. Figures in the above capsule and in this profile are approximate.

Requirements
Applicants must have a bachelor's degree and take the LSAT. No specific undergraduate courses are required. Candidates are not interviewed.

Procedure
Applicants should submit an application form, LSAT results, transcripts, 2 letters of recommendation, and students are urged to visit the school. A personal statement and a college certification form are required. Accepted students must make a deposit of $500. Notification of the admissions decision is on a rolling basis. The latest acceptable LSAT test date for fall entry is December. The law school uses

the LSDAS. Check with the school for the current application deadlines.

Special
The law school recruits minority and disadvantaged students by encouraging all who would like to study law at Harvard to apply. Requirements are not different for out-of-state students. Transfer students must have one year of credit, have attended an ABA-approved law school, and have outstanding records in college and in the first year of law school.

Costs

Tuition and fees for the 2009-2010 academic year are approximately $40,000 for all full-time students. On-campus room and board costs about $16,179 annually; books and supplies run about $1050.

Financial Aid

In a recent year, about 81% of current law students received some form of aid. The average annual amount of aid from all sources combined, including scholarships, loans, and work contracts, is $42,823; maximum, $54,000. Awards are based on need along with . Required financial statements are the CSS Profile, the FAFSA, and Need Access. First-year students are notified about their financial aid application at some time after admission. Assuming a timely aid application, students are not required to submit a deposit to reserve a place in the class until a financial aid decision has been made. Check with the school for the current application deadline.

About the Law School

Harvard University Harvard Law School was established in 1817 and is a private institution. The campus is in an urban area Cambridge, Massachusetts. The primary mission of the law school is to stress an understanding of the principles of law and a mastery of such skills as oral advocacy, research, and legal writing, and to educate lawyers to be capable of addressing legal problems in a changing society. Students have access to federal, state, county, city, and local agencies, courts, correctional facilities, law firms, and legal aid organizations in the Cambridge area. externship clinical practice sites. Housing for students consists of law school dormitories, Harvard-affiliated housing,

and off-campus housing. There is housing for single and married students. All law school facilities are accessible to the physically disabled.

Calendar

The law school operates on a traditional semester basis. Courses for full-time students are offered days only and must be completed within 3 years. There is no part-time program. New students are admitted in the fall. There is no summer session. Transferable summer courses are not offered.

Programs

In addition to the J.D., the law school offers the LL.M. and S.J.D. Students may take relevant courses in other programs and apply credit toward the J.D.; a maximum of 10 credits through cross credits may be applied. The following joint degrees may be earned: J.D./LL.M. (Juris Doctor/Master of Laws (University of Cambridge, England)), J.D./M.A. (Juris Doctor/Master of Arts), J.D./M.A.L.D. (Juris Doctor/Master of Arts in Law and Diplomacy with Tufts), J.D./M.B.A. (Juris Doctor/Master of Business Administration), J.D./M.P.A. (Juris Doctor/Master of Public Administration), J.D./M.P.H (Juris Doctor/Master of Public Health), J.D./M.P.P. (Juris Doctor/Master of Public Policy), and J.D./Ph.D. (Juris Doctor/Doctor of Philosophy).

Required
To earn the J.D., candidates must complete 82 total credits, of which 30 are for required courses. They must maintain a minimum GPA of n/av.0 in the required courses. The following first-year courses are required of all students: an elective, Civil Procedure, Contracts, Criminal Law, Lawyering, Property, and Torts. Required upper-level courses consist of a professional responsibility requirement and a written work requirement. The required orientation program for first-year students lasts 2 days and is described as comprehensive.

Electives
The Law School has no formal program of offering concentrations in particular specialties. However, because the curriculum is so extensive, it allows for many different paths of study. Students are encouraged to discuss their plans with

Phone: 617-495-3179
E-mail: jdadmiss@law.harvard.edu
Web: law.harvard.edu

Contact
Admissions Office, 617-495-3109, fax 617-436-7290 for general inquiries.

MASSACHUSETTS

faculty members involved in relevant areas of study and are encouraged to take courses in a number of different fields, as well as in other parts of the University. The school offers a broad array of clinical opportunities to students. Through Harvard's Hale and Dorr Legal Services Center, students can focus on a number of practice areas, including the Community Enterprise Project, Medical and Legal Services Unit, Family and Children's Law Practice, Immigration Law, Housing Law and Litigation, and the General Practice Unit. The Criminal Justice institute is Harvard Law School's curriculum-based clinical program in criminal law. The Harvard Defenders is a student-operated organization dedicated to providing quality legal representation to people with low income in criminal show-cause hearings and welfare fraud. The Harvard Legal Aid Bureau is a student-run legal services office dedicated to providing legal assistance to low-income people and to creating a clinical education environment in which its members learn from legal practice. The Harvard Mediation Program (HMP) works to resolve disputes both in and out of the courts in the Boston area. Students can participate also in a wide variety of externships for credit, including the Harvard Immigration and Refugee Clinic, Office of Attorney General, U.S. and District Attorneys offices as well as numerous government agencies and nonprofit organizations. More than 30 courses offer clinical field work experience and more than 2 others include simulated exercises. There are 75 seminars, including those on affirmative action, the federal budgetary process, and corporate theory. Internships are available for credit. Research programs may be conducted with the Center for Criminal Justice; the Berman Center for Internet & Society; Petrie-Flom Center for Health Law Policy, Biotechnology and Bioethics; Child Advocacy Program; Human Rights Program; East Asian Legal Studies; International Tax Program; Program on International Financial Systems; European Law Research Center; Program in Law and Economics; Program on the Legal Profession; Program on Negotiation; International and Comparative Legal Studies; International Tax Program; and Islamic Legal Studies. Field work is available in business, civil and criminal, mediation, and environmental law. A number of courses provide students with field work in local courts and government agencies,

and others provide instruction in aspects of legal practice through simulated casework and a problem-oriented approach. Special lecture series include the BSA Speaker Series, the DSAC Brown-Bag Lunch Discussion Series, East Asian Legal Studies Speaker Program, HLS Forum, Human Rights Program Speaker Series, and Introduction to the World of Law. Law students may propose a 1 semester course of study at a foreign institution. The most widely taken electives are Constitutional Law, Taxation, and Corporations.

Graduation Requirements
In order to graduate, candidates must have completed the upper-division writing requirement.

Organizations
Students edit the *Harvard Law Review, Blackletter Law Journal, Civil Rights-Civil Liberties Law Review, Human Rights Journal, Journal of Law and Public Policy, Journal of Law and Technology, Journal on Legislation, Journal of Law & Gender, International Law Journal, Environmental Law Review, Latino Law Review, Negotiation Law Review,* the student newspaper, the *Harvard Law Record,* and a yearbook. Moot court opportunities include the Ames Competition, which offers moot court competitions for first-year and upper-class students. The school also participates in interschool contests, including the Willston Legislative Drafting Competition and the Jessup International Law Moot Court Competition. Students may choose to participate in more than 80 student organizations and 14 publications.

Library
The law library contains 1,723,645 hardcopy volumes and 1,973,552 microform volume equivalents, and subscribes to 15,303 serial publications. Such on-line databases and networks as CALI, DIALOG, LEXIS, LOIS, NEXIS, WESTLAW, and Harvard On-Line Library Information System (HOLLIS), HeinOnline, CCH Research Network, Compustat, Index master, LawMemo.com, LawTRIO, Lawyers Weekly USA, LLMC Digital, Mass. Social Law Library, Pike & Fischer, Quicklaw, TRACfed are available to law students for research. Special library collections include a comprehensive collection of Anglo American reports and treatises, and a

Placement
Services available through: a separate law school placement center and separate Office of Public Interest Advising
Services: on-campus interviews for first, second- and third-year students.

Full-time job interviews:	800 employers
Summer job interviews:	n/av
Placement by graduation:	96% of class
Placement within 9 months:	99% of class
Areas of placement:	
Private practice	60%
Judicial clerkships	29%
Public interest	4%
Government	3%
Business/industry	3%
Academic	1%

special collection on international law as well as rare books and a 30,000-item art collection. The ratio of library volumes to faculty is 13,058 to 1 and to students is 1035 to 1. The ratio of seats in the library to students is 1 to 2.

Faculty
The law school has 132 full-time and 71 part-time faculty members, of whom 64 are women. According to AAUP standards for Category I institutions, faculty salaries are well above average. About 27% of full-time faculty have a graduate law degree in addition to the J.D. The law school has a regular program of bringing visiting professors and other distinguished lecturers and visitors to campus.

Students
About 45% of the student body are women; 33%, minorities; 11%, African American; 12%, Asian American; 6%, Hispanic; and 1%, Native American. The majority of students come from the Northeast (27%). The average age of entering students is 24; age range is 20 to 37. About 41% of students enter directly from undergraduate school and 12% have a graduate degree. About 1% drop out after the first year for academic or personal reasons; 99% remain to receive a law degree.

School of Law

121 Hofstra University
Hempstead, NY 11549

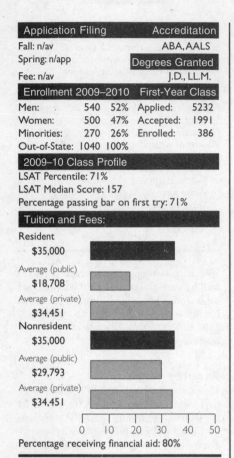

Application Filing	Accreditation
Fall: n/av	ABA, AALS
Spring: n/app	Degrees Granted
Fee: n/av	J.D., LL.M.

Enrollment 2009–2010		First-Year Class	
Men:	540 52%	Applied:	5232
Women:	500 47%	Accepted:	1991
Minorities:	270 26%	Enrolled:	386
Out-of-State:	1040 100%		

2009–10 Class Profile
LSAT Percentile: 71%
LSAT Median Score: 157
Percentage passing bar on first try: 71%

Tuition and Fees:

Resident
$35,000

Average (public)
$18,708

Average (private)
$34,451

Nonresident
$35,000

Average (public)
$29,793

Average (private)
$34,451

Percentage receiving financial aid: 80%

ADMISSIONS

In a recent year, 5232 applied, 1991 were accepted, and 386 enrolled. Twenty-four transfers enrolled. The median LSAT percentile of the most recent first-year class was 71; the median GPA was 3.3 on a scale of 4.0. The lowest LSAT percentile accepted was 8; the highest was 99. Figures in the above capsule and in this profile are approximate.

Requirements
Applicants must have a bachelor's degree and take the LSAT. The most important admission factors include academic achievement, LSAT results, and general background. No specific undergraduate courses are required. Candidates are not interviewed.

Procedure
Applicants should submit an application form, LSAT results, transcripts, and 1 letters of recommendation. Notification of the admissions decision is on a rolling basis. The latest acceptable LSAT test

date for fall entry is February, generally. The law school uses the LSDAS. Check with the school for current application deadlines.

Special
The law school recruits minority and disadvantaged students by means of student, faculty, graduate, and administrator visits to a diverse range of institutions to increase the number of law students from traditionally excluded groups. Scholarships are also available. Requirements are not different for out-of-state students. Transfer students must have one year of credit and have attended an ABA-approved law school.

Costs

Tuition and fees for the 2009-2010 academic year are approximately $35,000 for all full-time students. Tuition for part-time students is approximately $25,000 per year. On-campus room and board costs about $10,815 annually; books and supplies run $1100.

Financial Aid

In a recent year, about 80% of current law students received some form of aid. The average annual amount of aid from all sources combined, including scholarships, loans, and work contracts, was $35,000. Awards are based on need and merit. Required financial statements are the FAFSA and Need Access application. First-year students are notified about their financial aid application at time of acceptance. Check with the school for current application deadlines.

About the Law School

Hofstra University School of Law was established in 1970 and is a private institution. The 240-acre campus is in a suburban area 25 miles east of New York City. The primary mission of the law school is to prepare students for success in the practice of law by combining rigorous intellectual discussion with hands-on training in the skills required to excel in today's competitive legal environment. Students have access to federal, state, county, city, and local agencies, courts, correctional facilities, law firms, and legal aid organizations in the Hempstead area. Facilities of special interest to law stu-

dents are all university facilities, including the university library center, athletic facilities, cultural programs, and social events. Housing for students on and near campus in suite and apartment style residence halls. All law school facilities are accessible to the physically disabled.

Calendar

The law school operates on a traditional semester basis. Courses for full-time students are offered days only and must be completed within 3 years. For part-time students, courses are offered days only and must be completed within 4 years. New full- and part-time students are admitted in the fall. There is a 7-week summer session. Transferable summer courses are offered.

Programs

In addition to the J.D., the law school offers the LL.M. The following joint degrees may be earned: J.D./M.B.A. (Juris Doctor/Master of Business Administration) and J.D./M.S. (Juris Doctor/Master of Science in Taxation).

Required
To earn the J.D., candidates must complete 87 total credits, of which 39 are for required courses. They must maintain a minimum GPA of 2.0 in the required courses. The following first-year courses are required of all students: Appellate Advocacy, Civil Procedure I and II, Contracts I and II, Criminal Law, Introduction to International & Comparative Law, Legal Writing and Research, Property, and Torts I and II. Required upper-level courses consist of Constitutional Law I and II, Lawyer's Ethics or Ethics and Economics of Law Practice, and Upperclass writing requirements I and II. The required orientation program for first-year students is a 3-day program that includes legal method classes taught by faculty members, general lectures, panels concerning student services, and social activities.

Electives
The School of Law offers concentrations in corporate law, criminal law, environmental law, family law, international law, juvenile law, labor law, litigation, securities law, tax law, torts and insurance, and

NEW YORK

Phone: 516-463-5916
Fax: 516-463-6264
E-mail: *lawadmissions@hofstra.edu*
Web: *hofstra.edu/law*

Contact
Assistant Dean for Enrollment Management, 516-463-5916 for general inquiries; Director of Financial Aid, 516-463-5929 for financial aid information.

constitutional law, and health law. In addition, students may enroll in the Housing Rights, Criminal Justice, Child Advocacy, Mediation, Not-For-Profit Organizations, Securities Arbitration, or Political Asylum clinics. Each are worth 6 credits. Upperclass students may choose from a large number of 2- to 3-credit seminars. First-year students take 1 required substantive course in a small section of 25 to 30 students. Students may enroll in the Externship Program for 3 credits; they may work for judges or in nonprofit or government agencies, dealing with civil and criminal matters. Faculty-supervised independent study is worth from 2 to 6 credits. The law school offers special problems seminars, in which 3 to 5 students work closely with a professor in a tutuorial setting on a topic of current interest. In addition, the law school offers an extensive Pro Bono Student Volunteer Program. A Visiting Scholar Program brings to the law school a distinguised scholar for a visit of 3 to 4 days; the visiting scholar teaches classes, gives a lecture, and meets informally with students and faculty. Annually scheduled lectures involve experts in bankruptcy law, family law, legal ethics, and health law, as well as features by distinguished jurists, scholars, and practicners. The law school offers summer programs in Nice, France, in Sydney, Australia, and in Sorrento, Italy. A winter study abroad in Curacao is also available. Hofstra law students may also participate in a seminar abroad with any other E.A.C.L.E. institution. An exchange program with Soochow University (China) will be available shortly. Students must meet with the Assistant Dean for Student Affairs with any request for student tutorial support services. The Director of Multicultural Student Affairs is responsible for minority student affairs, minority recruitment and admissions, the coordination of the law school's Enhancement Program and the coordination of the Dwight L. Greene Scholarship Program. Specific initiatives to support the students of color include: an Open House for minority applicants, Law Day for admitted students of color, a Minority Student Orientation Program for incoming students, a first-year reception, mentoring programs, and other programs throughout the year. Chapters of BALSA, LALSA, and APALSA are very active at the law school. The most widely taken electives are Business Organizations; Criminal Procedure; and Wills, Trusts and Estates.

Graduation Requirements
In order to graduate, candidates must have a GPA of 2.0, have completed the upper-division writing requirement, and completed 2 upper-level writing requirements.

Organizations
Students edit the *Hofstra Law Review, Hofstra Labor and Employment Law Journal, Family Court Review, Journal or International Business and Law*, and the law school student newspaper, *Conscience*. Teams compete annually in the following national competition; the National Moot Court Competition, the Robert F. Wagner, Jr. Labor & Employment Law Competition, the Conrad L. Duberstein Competition and the Phillip Jessup International Law Competition. Students also participate in the Nassau County Bar Association's Long Island Moot Court Competition sponsored by the Nassau Academy of Law and also intramural competitions sponsored by the Hofstra Law School Moot Court Association. Law student organizations include the Corporate Law Society, Hofstra Law Women, and The International Law Society. There are local chapters of Asian-Pacific American Law Students Association, Black American Law Students Association, Latino American Law Students Association, and Phi Alpha Delta. Hofstra University supports more than 100 student cultural, media, sports, creative, service, and politically and socially active clubs.

Library
The law library contains 550,765 hardcopy volumes and 1,823,120 microform volume equivalents, and subscribes to 1200 serial publications. Such on-line databases and networks as CALI, CIS Universe, DIALOG, Infotrac, Legal-Trac, LEXIS, LOIS, NEXIS, WESTLAW, and Child Law Practice, AccessUN, ADRworld, Berkeley, CIAO, CILP, Legal Trac, LLMC, NLRB, RIA, and Smart CLIP are available to law students for research. Special library collections include records and briefs of U.S. Supreme Court cases (1832 to the present) and of the New York Court of Appeals and Appellate Division; federal depository materials; and all U.N. documents (1976 to the present) on microfiche. Additional microfiche holdings are the ABA archival collection (1878 to the present) and the

Placement	
J.D.s awarded:	n/av
Services available through: a separate law school placement center	
Full-time job interviews:	21 employers
Summer job interviews:	34 employers
Placement by graduation:	n/av
Placement within 9 months:	98% of class
Average starting salary:	$35,000 to $125,000
Areas of placement:	
Private practice 2-10 attorneys	29%
Private practice 11-25 attorneys	9%
Private practice 26-50 attorneys	7%
Private practice 51-100 attorneys	4%
Private practice 101-500 attorneys, 4% unknown	12%
Government	13%
Business/industry	12%
Judicial clerkships	6%
Public interest	2%
Academic	2%

archival collection of the American Law Institute. The ratio of library volumes to faculty is 13,769 to 1 and to students is 537 to 1. The ratio of seats in the library to students is 1 to 3.

Faculty
The law school has 40 full-time and 59 part-time faculty members, of whom 24 are women. According to AAUP standards for Category I institutions, faculty salaries are average. About 25% of full-time faculty have a graduate law degree in addition to the J.D.; about 7% of part-time faculty have one. The ratio of full-time students to full-time faculty in an average class is 21 to 1; in a clinic, 10 to 1.

Students
About 47% of the student body are women; 26%, minorities; 7%, African American; 7%, Asian American; and 6%, Hispanic. The average age of entering students is 24; age range is 19 to 70. About 53% of students enter directly from undergraduate school, 10% have a graduate degree, and 46% have worked full-time prior to entering law school. About 11% drop out after the first year for academic or personal reasons; 89% remain to receive a law degree.

Hofstra University **311**

2900 Van Ness Street, N.W.
Washington, DC 20008

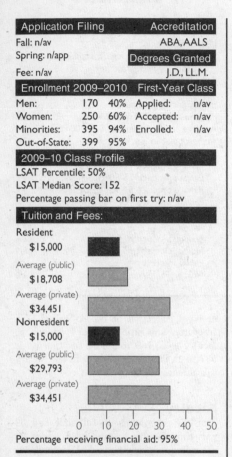

Application Filing		Accreditation	
Fall: n/av		ABA, AALS	
Spring: n/app		**Degrees Granted**	
Fee: n/av		J.D., LL.M.	

Enrollment 2009–2010		First-Year Class	
Men:	170 40%	Applied:	n/av
Women:	250 60%	Accepted:	n/av
Minorities:	395 94%	Enrolled:	n/av
Out-of-State:	399 95%		

2009–10 Class Profile
LSAT Percentile: 50%
LSAT Median Score: 152
Percentage passing bar on first try: n/av

Tuition and Fees:

Resident
$15,000

Average (public)
$18,708

Average (private)
$34,451

Nonresident
$15,000

Average (public)
$29,793

Average (private)
$34,451

Percentage receiving financial aid: 95%

ADMISSIONS
In a recent year, ten transfers enrolled. The median LSAT percentile of the most recent first-year class was 50; the median GPA was 3.2 on a scale of 4.0. Figures in the above capsule and in this profile are approximate.

Requirements
Applicants must have a bachelor's degree and take the LSAT. Minimum acceptable LSAT percentile is 35 and minimum acceptable GPA is 3.0 on a scale of 4.0. The most important admission factors include general background, GPA, and LSAT results. No specific undergraduate courses are required. Candidates are not interviewed.

Procedure
Applicants should submit an application form, LSAT results, transcripts, 2 letters of recommendation, and a personal statement, and the Dean's survey. Notification of the admissions decision is on a rolling basis. The latest acceptable LSAT test

date for fall entry is February. The law school uses the LSDAS. Check with the school for current application deadlines.

Special
Requirements are not different for out-of-state students. Transfer students must have one year of credit, have a minimum GPA of 3, have attended an ABA-approved law school, and be ranked in the upper one-quarter to one-third of their class.

Costs
Tuition and fees for the 2009-2010 academic year are approximately $15,000 for all full-time students. On-campus room and board costs about $12,891 annually; books and supplies run about $1351.

Financial Aid
In a recent year, about 95% of current law students received some form of aid. The average annual amount of aid from all sources combined, including scholarships, loans, and work contracts, was approximately $18,000; maximum, $36,000. Awards are based on merit. Required financial statement is the FAFSA. First-year students are notified about their financial aid application at time of acceptance. Check with the school for current application deadline.

About the Law School
Howard University was established in 1869 and is a private institution. The 22-acre campus is in an urban area in northwest Washington DC. The primary mission of the law school is The mission of Howard University School of Law includes the provision of quality education for any student, with emphasis on the educational opportunities for those students from traditionaly underserved communities. Students have access to federal, state, county, city, and local agencies, courts, correctional facilities, law firms, and legal aid organizations in the Washington area. Students have access to the Washington Consortium of Law Libraries, which offers use of all law libraries in the D.C. metropolitan area. Facilities of special interest to law students include the superior moot court room. Housing for students is limited on campus; most students live off campus. All law school facilities are accessible to the physically disabled.

Calendar
The law school operates on a traditional semester basis. Courses for full-time students are offered both day and evening and must be completed within 5 Years. For part-time students, courses are offered both day and evening. New students are admitted in the fall and spring. There is no summer session. Transferable summer courses are offered.

Programs
In addition to the J.D., the law school offers the LL.M. (master's specialization in international law and comparitive law). Students may take relevant courses in other programs and apply credit toward the J.D.; a maximum of 30 credits may be applied. The following joint degrees may be earned: J.D./M.B.A. (Juris Doctor/Master of Business Administration).

Required
To earn the J.D., candidates must complete 88 total credits, of which n/av are for required courses. They must maintain a minimum GPA of 72.0 in the required courses. The following first-year courses are required of all students: Civil Procedure, Constitutional Law I, Contracts, Criminal Law, Legal Method, Legal Research and Writing, Property, and Torts I & II. Required upper-level courses consist of Constitutional Law II, Evidence, Legal Writing II, Legal Writing III, Professional Responsibility, and Skills. The required orientation program for first-year students is two weeks long, and includes an introduction to legal methods.

Electives
In addition, clinics in a wide range of areas are available to third-year students; 4 to 12 credits are offered for each clinic. Second and third-year students may take seminars for 3 credits. Internships are available to third-year students for 3 credits. Third-year students may also participate in research for 2 credits. All students may attend tutorials, and special lectures for no credit. After the first year of study, students may undertake a study-abroad program. ABA-approved courses worth 2 credits each are offered at HUSL/University of Western Capetown, South Africa. The most widely taken electives are Federal Tax; Wills, Trusts, and Estates; and Administrative Law.

Phone: 202-806-8008
Fax: 202-806-8162
E-mail: admissions@law.howard.edu
Web: www.law.howard.edu

Contact

Dean of Admissions, 202-806-8008 for general inquiries; Financial Aid Officer, 202-806-8005 for financial aid information.

DISTRICT OF COLUMBIA

Graduation Requirements

In order to graduate, candidates must have completed the upper-division writing requirement.

Organizations

Students edit the *Howard Law Journal, Social the Justice Law Review* and the newspaper, *the Barrister*. Moot court competitions include ABA National Appellate Advocacy-Northeast Regional, Frederick Douglass National, and Huver I. Brown. Law student organizations, local chapters of national association, and campus clubs and organizations include ABA, Phi Alpha Delta, NBLSA, Student Bar Association, Entertaiment Law Association, International Law Society, Black Law Students Association, and Public Interest Law Society.

Library

The law library contains 428,494 hardcopy volumes and 54,000 microform volume equivalents, and subscribes to 1643 serial publications. Such on-line databases and networks as CALI, DIALOG, Legal-Trac, LEXIS, Matthew Bender, WEST-LAW, and Internet are available to law students for research. Special library collections include Fats Waller Litigation Files and a civil rights collection. Recently, the library implemented a Web-based library catalog, developed library home-page research tools, and distributed CD-ROM materials for the library LAN.

The ratio of library volumes to faculty is 12,985 to 1 and to students is 1033 to 1. The ratio of seats in the library to students is 1 to 3.

Faculty

The law school has 33 full-time and 23 part-time faculty members, of whom 19 are women. According to AAUP standards for Category 1 institutions, faculty salaries are well below average. About 10% of full-time faculty have a graduate law degree in addition to the J.D.; about 4% of part-time faculty have one. The ratio of full-time students to full-time faculty in an average class is 17 to 1; in a clinic, 8 to 1. The law school has a regular program of bringing visiting professors and other distinguished lecturers and visitors to campus.

Students

About 60% of the student body are women; 94%, minorities; 87%, African American; 4%, Asian American; 4%, Hispanic; and 5%, Caucasian. The majority of students come from the Northeast (39%). The average age of entering students is 25; age range is 21 to 48. About 80% of students enter directly from undergraduate school, 7% have a graduate degree, and 20% have worked full-time prior to entering law school. About 5% drop out after the first year for academic or personal reasons; 94% remain to receive a law degree.

Placement

J.D.s awarded:	n/av
Services available through: a separate law school placement center	
Special features: Summer Clerkship Program (for the summer following a student's first-year) and workshops and seminars featuring Howard Law alumni and other practitioners regarding legal career settings, practice specialities, and employment trends; first-year summer clerkship program (through partnerships with major law firms and corporations; summer associate training program; workshops and seminars on job search skills, legal careers settings and practice specialties and employment trends.	
Full-time job interviews:	109 employers
Summer job interviews:	169 employers
Placement by graduation:	80% of class
Placement within 9 months:	94% of class
Average starting salary:	$30,000 to $150,000
Areas of placement:	
Private practice 2-10 attorneys	5%
Private practice 11-25 attorneys	1%
Private practice 26-50 attorneys	3%
Private practice 51-100 attorneys	3%
Government	30%
Business/industry	19%
unknown	19%
Judicial clerkships	16%
Public interest	3%
Academic	1%

ILLINOIS INSTITUTE OF TECHNOLOGY

Chicago-Kent College of Law

565 West Adams Street
Chicago, IL 60661

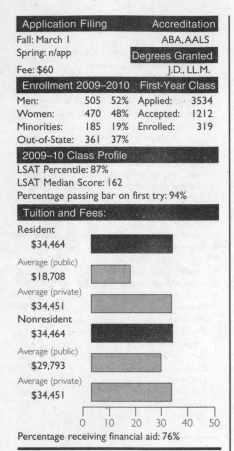

Application Filing	Accreditation
Fall: March 1	ABA, AALS
Spring: n/app	**Degrees Granted**
Fee: $60	J.D., LL.M.

Enrollment 2009–2010		First-Year Class	
Men:	505 52%	Applied:	3534
Women:	470 48%	Accepted:	1212
Minorities:	185 19%	Enrolled:	319
Out-of-State:	361 37%		

2009–10 Class Profile
LSAT Percentile: 87%
LSAT Median Score: 162
Percentage passing bar on first try: 94%

Tuition and Fees:

Resident
$34,464

Average (public)
$18,708

Average (private)
$34,451

Nonresident
$34,464

Average (public)
$29,793

Average (private)
$34,451

0 10 20 30 40 50

Percentage receiving financial aid: 76%

ADMISSIONS

In a recent year, 3534 applied, 1212 were accepted, and 319 enrolled. Forty-four transfers enrolled. The median LSAT percentile of the most recent first-year class was 87; the median GPA was 3.6 on a scale of 4.0. The highest LSAT percentile was 99. Figures in the above capsule and in this profile are approximate.

Requirements
Applicants must have a bachelor's degree and take the LSAT. No specific undergraduate courses are required. Candidates are not interviewed.

Procedure
Applicants should submit an application form, LSAT results, transcripts, a personal statement, a nonrefundable application fee of $60, 1 academic preferred letters of recommendation, and admitted applicants must submit a nonrefundable seat deposit, payable in 2 installments in April and June. Notification of the admissions decision is on a rolling basis. The latest acceptable LSAT test date for fall entry is February. The law school uses the LSDAS.

Check with the school for the current application deadlines.

Special
The law school recruits minority and disadvantaged students through minority student law days, direct mail, and events sponsored by minority law student groups. Chicago-Kent also hosts the PreLaw Undergraduate Scholars program ("PLUS"), a rigorous four-week summer program that is designed to provide undergraduate students with a "taste" of the law school experience .The program is primarily directed at undergraduate students from disadvantaged groups that are underrepresented in the legal profession. Requirements are not different for out-of-state students. Transfer students must have one year of credit, have attended an ABA-approved law school, and a letter of good standing from the dean of their law school and 1 letter of recommendation.

Costs

Tuition and fees for the 2009-2010 academic year are approximately $34,464 for all full-time students. Tuition for part-time students is approximately $25,350 per year. On-campus room and board costs about $15,331 annually; books and supplies run about $1000.

Financial Aid

In a recent year, about 76% of current law students received some form of aid. The average annual amount of aid from all sources combined, including scholarships, loans, and work contracts, was approximately $38,452; maximum, $74,116. Awards are based on need and merit. Required financial statement is the FAFSA. Special funds for minority or disadvantaged students are available. First-year students are notified about their financial aid application at time of acceptance. Check with the school for the current application deadlines.

About the Law School

Illinois Institute of Technology Chicago-Kent College of Law was established in 1888 and is a private institution. The campus is in an urban area in downtown Chicago. The primary mission of the law school is to provide students with a solid grounding in legal theory and ethics, along with innovative approaches to teaching

and skills training. Students have access to federal, state, county, city, and local agencies, courts, correctional facilities, law firms, and legal aid organizations in the Chicago area. Facilities of special interest to law students include a state-of-the-art building that houses the law school and the university's Stuart School of Business. Housing for students is available in nearby urban and suburban neighborhoods and on-campus housing is available on the university's main campus. All law school facilities are accessible to the physically disabled.

Calendar

The law school operates on a traditional semester basis. Courses for full-time students are offered both day and evening and must be completed within 5 years. For part-time students, courses are offered both day and evening and must be completed within 6 years. New full- and part-time students are admitted in the fall. There is an 8-week summer session. Transferable summer courses are offered.

Programs

In addition to the J.D., the law school offers the LL.M. Students may take relevant courses in other programs and apply credit toward the J.D.; a maximum of 12 credits may be applied. The following joint degrees may be earned: J.D./LL.M. (Juris Doctor/Master of Laws in taxation or financial services), J.D./M.B.A. (Juris Doctor/Master of Business Administration), J.D./M.E.M. (Juris Doctor/Master of Science in Environmental Management), J.D./M.P.A. (Juris Doctor/Master of Public Administration), J.D./M.P.H. (Juris Doctor/Master of Public Health), and J.D./M.S. (Juris Doctor/Master of Science in financial markets & trading).

Required
To earn the J.D., candidates must complete 87 total credits, of which 42 are for required courses. They must maintain a minimum GPA of 2.3 in the required courses. The following first-year courses are required of all students: Civil Procedure, Contracts, Criminal Law, Legal Writing I and II, Legislative Process, Property, and Torts. Required upper-level courses consist of Constitutional Law, Legal Writing III and IV, Professional Responsibility, and Seminar. The required orientation program for first-year students is a 3-day program combining introductory programs, library

Phone: 312-906-5020
Fax: 312-906-5274
E-mail: admit@kentlaw.edu
Web: www.kentlaw.edu

Contact

Assistant Dean for Admissions, 312-906-5020 for general inquiries; Ada Chin, Director of Financial Aid, 312-906-5180 for financial aid information.

ILLINOIS

tours, computer training, legal research and writing, and small sessions with current students and faculty.

Electives

Students must take 20 credits in their area of concentration. The Chicago-Kent College of Law offers concentrations in criminal law, environmental law, intellectual property law, international law, labor law, litigation, and The law school offers certificate programs in seven areas: Environmental and Energy Law, Intellectual Property Law, International and Comparative Law, Labor and Employment Law, Litigation and Alternative Dispute Resolution, Public Interest Law, and Criminal Litigation. In addition, Students may take clinical work in areas including criminal, civil, employment discrimination, and others through the Chicago-Kent-Law Offices for 3-4 credits. One seminar of 2 hours credit is required of all students. Recently offered seminars include Bioethics and the Law, Race-Conscious Remedies, and Current Energy Issues. An Advanced Externship Program places students with public agencies and teaching attorneys in areas such as environmental, bankruptcy, and international. A Judicial Externship program places students in clerkships with federal judges. Students can take Individual Research for 1 credit per semester, working under the supervision of a professor. Special lecture series include the Morris Lecture in International and Comparative Law, the Piper Lecture in Labor Law, and the Green Lecture in Law and Technology. Study abroad is possible through programs in England, Germany, Denmark, France, Norway, China, Mexico, New Zealand Switzerland. The college accepts credits from most ABA-accredited law school study abroad programs. The Academic Support Program is offered to students based on factors including LSAT score, undergraduate and graduate GPA, undergraduate course of study, years out of school native language, and disabilities. The Office of Student Professional Development assists in the recruitment of minority students and students from historically disadvantaged backgrounds through visits to high schools and colleges, collaboration with college counselors, and pre-law advisers, and community outreach. A certificate program for J.D. students in environmental and energy law includes a series of electives in land use, energy and environmental law as well as

interdisciplinary classes in the economic analysis of environmental problems. There are similar certificate programs in other areas. The most widely taken electives are Evidence, Commercial Law Survey, and Business Organizations.

Graduation Requirements

In order to graduate, candidates must have a GPA of 2.3, have completed the upper-division writing requirement, and required courses, 87 credits.

Organizations

Students edit the *Chicago-Kent Law Review*, which is published 3 times a year. The *Journal of Intellectual Property, Employee Rights* and *Employment Policy Journal*, and the *Journal of International and Comparative Law* and the *Seventh Circuit Review*. The student newspaper is *The Commentator*. The Moot Court Honor Society, which enters its members in more than 10 intercollegiate competitions annually, sponsors the Ilana Diamond Rovner Appellate Advocacy Competition. First-year students compete in the Charles Evans Hughes Moot Court Competition. The College of Law's more than 30 law student organizations plus local chapters of national associations, and campus organizations include the Environmental Law Society, International Law Society, the Intellectual Property Law Society, the Society of Women in Law, Asian-Pacific American, Black and Hispanic-Latino Law Students Associations, Association of Trial Lawyers of America, Phi-Alpha Delta, and National Lawyers Guild.

Library

The law library contains 550,789 hardcopy volumes and 145,312 microform volume equivalents, and subscribes to 2500 serial publications. Such on-line databases and networks as CALI, CIS Universe, DIALOG, Dow-Jones, Infotrac, Legal-Trac, LEXIS, LOIS, NEXIS, OCLC First Search, RLIN, WESTLAW, Wilsonline Indexes, and Internet, EPIC, ProQuest, Illinet, and Lexis Congressional are available to law students for research. Special library collections include a depository of federal documents, a special collection on law and the aging, as well as international organization documents (UN, EU, GATT, among others). The ratio of library volumes to faculty is 7545 to 1 and to students is 565 to 1. The ratio of seats in the library to students is 1 to 2.

Placement	
J.D.s awarded:	363
Services available through: a separate law school placement center	
Full-time job interviews:	22 employers
Summer job interviews:	51 employers
Placement by graduation:	71% of class
Placement within 9 months:	97% of class
Average starting salary:	$30,000 to $145,000
Areas of placement:	
Private practice 2-10 attorneys	22%
Private practice 11-25 attorneys	9%
Private practice 26-50 attorneys	3%
Private practice 51-100 attorneys	3%
Business/industry	19%
Government	15%
Judicial clerkships	5%
Public interest	3%
Academic	1%

Faculty

The law school has 73 full-time and 153 part-time faculty members, of whom 63 are women. According to AAUP standards for Category 1 institutions, faculty salaries are average. About 12% of full-time faculty have a graduate law degree in addition to the J.D.; about 8% of part-time faculty have one. The ratio of full-time students to full-time faculty in an average class is 38 to 1; in a clinic, 9 to 1. The law school has a regular program of bringing visiting professors and other distinguished lecturers and visitors to campus. There is a chapter of the Order of the Coif; 45 faculty and 619 graduates are members.

Students

About 48% of the student body are women; 19%, minorities; 6%, African American; 8%, Asian American; 5%, Hispanic; and 1%, Native American. The majority of students come from the Midwest (80%). The average age of entering students is 24; age range is 19 to 69. About 41% of students enter directly from undergraduate school, 12% have a graduate degree, and 59% have worked full-time prior to entering law school. About 10% drop out after the first year for academic or personal reasons; 90% remain to receive a law degree.

INDIANA UNIVERSITY

Maurer School of Law

211 S. Indiana Avenue
Bloomington, IN 47405-7001

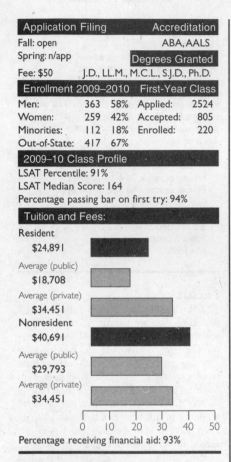

Application Filing	Accreditation
Fall: open	ABA, AALS
Spring: n/app	**Degrees Granted**
Fee: $50	J.D., LL.M., M.C.L., S.J.D., Ph.D.

Enrollment 2009–2010		First-Year Class	
Men:	363 58%	Applied:	2524
Women:	259 42%	Accepted:	805
Minorities:	112 18%	Enrolled:	220
Out-of-State:	417 67%		

2009–10 Class Profile
LSAT Percentile: 91%
LSAT Median Score: 164
Percentage passing bar on first try: 94%

Tuition and Fees:

Resident
$24,891

Average (public)
$18,708

Average (private)
$34,451

Nonresident
$40,691

Average (public)
$29,793

Average (private)
$34,451

0 10 20 30 40 50

Percentage receiving financial aid: 93%

ADMISSIONS

In the fall 2009 first-year class, 2524 applied, 805 were accepted, and 220 enrolled. Six transfers enrolled. The median LSAT percentile of the most recent first-year class was 91; the median GPA was 3.7 on a scale of 4.0. The lowest LSAT percentile accepted was 17; the highest was 99.

Requirements
Applicants must have a bachelor's degree and take the LSAT. The most important admission factors include LSAT results, GPA, faculty letters of recommendation, and academic achievement. No specific undergraduate courses are required. Candidates are not interviewed.

Procedure
The application deadline for fall entry is open. Applicants should submit an application form, LSAT results, transcripts, a personal statement, a nonrefundable application fee of $50, 2 letters of recommendation, a residence form included in the application packet (required of all applicants regardless of residence), and

a resume (recommended). Notification of the admissions decision is early December until the class is filled. The latest acceptable LSAT test date for fall entry is December or earlier is preferred but will accept in February or June. The law school uses the LSDAS.

Special
The law school recruits minority and disadvantaged students by participating in law fairs and private visits at historic minority colleges and universities as well as in major urban areas. Also by participating in activities of minority-focused organizations such as the National Society of Black Engineers. Requirements are not different for out-of-state students. Transfer students must have one year of credit, have attended an ABA-approved law school, have a superior law school record, have credentials comparable to the class in which they wish to transfer (in terms of LSAT score and GPA), and provide reasons for transfer. Space availability is also a factor in the acceptance decision.

Costs

Tuition and fees for the 2009-2010 academic year are $24,891 for full-time in-state students and $40,691 for out-of-state students. On-campus room and board costs about $14,116 annually; books and supplies run $1800.

Financial Aid

About 93% of current law students receive some form of aid. The average annual amount of aid from all sources combined, including scholarships, loans, and work contracts, is $44,403; maximum, $82,279. Awards are based on need and merit. The basis of award varies by type of award. Required financial statement is the FAFSA. The aid application deadline for fall entry is March 1. Special funds for minority or disadvantaged students include Education Opportunity Fellowships, which reduce nonresident tuition to the resident level, and outside private donor scholarships for disadvantaged students. The law school participates in the Indiana Conference for Legal Education Opportunity, which provides scholarships and other programs for minority or disadvantaged students. First-year students are notified about their financial aid application at time of admission for scholarships and mid-June for loan packages.

About the Law School

Indiana University Maurer School of Law was established in 1842 and is a public institution. The 1931-acre campus is in an urban area 50 miles southwest of Indianapolis. The primary mission of the law school is to provide its graduates with a rich combination of legal reasoning and practical lawyering skills in a collegial and supportive culture characterized by constant open interaction among students and between students and faculty. Students have access to federal, state, county, city, and local agencies, courts, correctional facilities, law firms, and legal aid organizations in the Bloomington area. Facilities of special interest to law students clinics are housed in a separate off-campus building, allowing students to meet and serve their clients in a typical law firm environment. The School of Law is 100% wireless, allowing students to access the Internet and conduct legal research everywhere. Housing for students includes excellent on-campus housing as well as a variety of affordable private housing units in the neighborhood adjacent to the law school. All law school facilities are accessible to the physically disabled.

Calendar

The law school operates on a traditional semester basis. Courses for full-time students are offered and a few advanced courses are taught in the evening and must be completed within 3 years. There is no part-time program. New students are admitted in the fall and summer. There is a 5-week summer session. Transferable summer courses are offered.

Programs

In addition to the J.D., the law school offers the LL.M., M.C.L., S.J.D., and Ph.D. Students may take relevant courses in other programs and apply credit toward the J.D.; a maximum of 6 credits may be applied. The following joint degrees may be earned: J.D./M.A. (Juris Doctor/Master of Arts in Journalism), J.D./M.A. or M.S. (Juris Doctor/Master of Arts or Master of Science in telecommunications), J.D./M.B.A. (Juris Doctor/Master of Business Administration), J.D./M.B.A.A. (Juris Doctor/Master of Business Administration in accounting), J.D./M.P.A. (Juris Doctor/Master of Professional Accountancy), J.D./M.S. (Juris Doctor/Master of Science in library and information sciences), and

Phone: 812-855-4765
Fax: 812-855-0555
E-mail: Lawadmis@indiana.edu
Web: www.law.indiana.edu

Contact

Frank Motley, Assistant Dean for Admissions, 812-855-4765 for general inquiries; Paul Leopold, Director of Financial Aid, 812-855-7746 for financial aid information.

INDIANA

J.D./M.S.E.S. (Juris Doctor/Master of Science in environmental science).

Required

To earn the J.D., candidates must complete 88 total credits, of which 31 are for required courses. They must maintain a minimum GPA of 2.3 in the required courses. The following first-year courses are required of all students: Civil Procedure, Constitutional Law, Contracts, Criminal Law, Legal Research and Writing I and II, Property, The Legal Profession, and Torts. required upper-level courses consist of at least 1 course in which writing is used as a means of instruction. All students must take clinical courses. The required orientation program for first-year students is a 2-day program.

Electives

The Maurer School of Law offers concentrations in corporate law, criminal law, entertainment law, environmental law, family law, intellectual property law, international law, juvenile law, labor law, litigation, maritime law, media law, securities law, sports law, tax law, torts and insurance, communications law, Internet law, and cybersecurity. In addition, second and third-year students may enroll (with varying credits given) in any of the 11 clinics offered including the Elmore Entrepreneurship Law Clinic, the Conservation Law Clinic, and the Community Legal Services Clinic. Ten to 14 seminars are offered each semester for second and third-year students. Recent seminar offerings include Counterinsurgency and the Law, Voting Rights, and Biotechnological Innovation and the Law. Internships are available during all 3 years of law study with a variety of public agencies, nonprofit organizations, faculty members, and public interest groups. The School of Law sponsors guest lecturers on a near-weekly basis throughout the year, including a program of Jurists-in-Residence in which distinguished legal practitioners present one or more lectures and participate in classes. Students may study abroad in Poland, Germany, France, Spain, China, Hong Kong, New Zealand, and England. Summer law study programs are offered in London, Oxford, Paris, Dublin, Florence, Barcelona, and Moscow. There is a voluntary Academic Enhancement Program with group instruction and one-on-one instruction available. The Law School participates in the Indiana Conference for Legal Education Opportunity. Minority

students find support and enrichment of the law school experience from the Black Law Students Association, the Latino Law Students Association, and the Asian Pacific Islander Law Students Association. The most widely taken electives are Business Law, Intellectual Property, and Trial Practice/Litigation.

Graduation Requirements

In order to graduate, candidates must have a GPA of 2.3, have completed the upper-division writing requirement, and must be in residence in an approved law school for 6 semesters of full-time study.

Organizations

Students edit the *Indiana Law Journal, Federal Communications Law Journal, Indiana Journal of Global Legal Studies*, and the student newspaper, *Indiana Daily Student*. Students participate in the Sherman Minton Moot Court Competition, Jessup International Moot Court Competition, and Telecommunications Moot Court Competition. Other competitions include the Trial Practice Competition and Negotiations Competition. Student organizations include the Intellectual Property Association, International Law Society, and the Public Interest Law Foundation. Local chapters of national associations include the American Constitution Society, Federalist Society for Law and Public Studies, and American Bar Association - Law Student Division.

Library

The law library contains 463,190 hardcopy volumes and 1,677,604 microform volume equivalents, and subscribes to 10,242 serial publications. Such on-line databases and networks as CALI, CIS Universe, DIALOG, Dow-Jones, Infotrac, Legal-Trac, LEXIS, LOIS, Mathew Bender, NEXIS, OCLC First Search, WEST-LAW, Wilsonline Indexes, GPO Access, HeinOnline, BNA Library, CCH Library, Making of Modern Law, and U.S. Supreme Court Recorder (1832-1978) are available to law students for research. Special library collections include being a depository for records and briefs of the U.S. Supreme Court, Indiana Court of Appeals, and Indiana Supreme Court. Additionally, the library is a selective depository for U.S. government publications and houses a rare books and archives collection. The ratio of library volumes to faculty is 9774

Placement

J.D.s awarded:	212

Services available through: a separate law school placement center
Services: job fairs and career planning seminars, videotaped mock interview program, judicial clerkship series, workshops covering all aspects of job searches and speed interview workshops

Full-time job interviews:	32 employers
Summer job interviews:	82 employers
Placement by graduation:	89% of class
Placement within 9 months:	96% of class
Average starting salary:	$38,000 to $165,000

Areas of placement:

Private practice 2-10 attorneys	8%
Private practice 11-25 attorneys	6%
Private practice 26-50 attorneys	5%
Private practice 51-100 attorneys	3%
Private practice 101-500+ attorneys	23%
Government	17%
Business/industry	17%
Judicial clerkships	11%
Public interest	6%
Academic	4%

to 1 and to students is 725 to 1. The ratio of seats in the library to students is 1 to 1.

Faculty

The law school has 55 full-time and 34 part-time faculty members, of whom 26 are women. According to AAUP standards for Category I institutions, faculty salaries are below average. About 31% of full-time faculty have a graduate law degree in addition to the J.D. The ratio of full-time students to full-time faculty in an average class is 10 to 1; in a clinic, 5 to 1. The law school has a regular program of bringing visiting professors and other distinguished lecturers and visitors to campus. There is a chapter of the Order of the Coif; 32 faculty are members.

Students

About 42% of the student body are women; 18%, minorities; 7%, African American; 6%, Asian American; and 5%, Hispanic. The majority of students come from the Midwest (61%). The average age of entering students is 24; age range is 20 to 39. About 45% of students enter directly from undergraduate school, 7% have a graduate degree, and 46% have worked full-time prior to entering law school. About 1% drop out after the first year for academic or personal reasons; 99% remain to receive a law degree.

INDIANA UNIVERSITY-PURDUE UNIVERSITY AT INDIANAPOLIS

Indiana University School of Law-Indianapolis

530 West New York Street
Indianapolis, IN 46202-3225

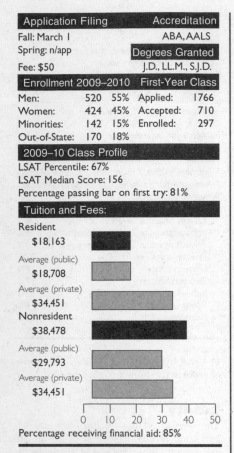

Application Filing		Accreditation	
Fall: March 1		ABA, AALS	
Spring: n/app		**Degrees Granted**	
Fee: $50		J.D., LL.M., S.J.D.	
Enrollment 2009–2010		**First-Year Class**	
Men:	520 55%	Applied:	1766
Women:	424 45%	Accepted:	710
Minorities:	142 15%	Enrolled:	297
Out-of-State:	170 18%		

2009–10 Class Profile
LSAT Percentile: 67%
LSAT Median Score: 156
Percentage passing bar on first try: 81%

Tuition and Fees:

Resident
$18,163

Average (public)
$18,708

Average (private)
$34,451

Nonresident
$38,478

Average (public)
$29,793

Average (private)
$34,451

Percentage receiving financial aid: 85%

ADMISSIONS

In the fall 2009 first-year class, 1766 applied, 710 were accepted, and 297 enrolled. Eighteen transfers enrolled. The median LSAT percentile of the most recent first-year class was 67; the median GPA was 3.5 on a scale of 4.0. The lowest LSAT percentile accepted was 15; the highest was 98.

Requirements

Applicants must have a bachelor's degree and take the LSAT. The most important admission factors include undergraduate curriculum, LSAT results, and academic achievement. The student's academic program is weighed into the GPA assessment. No specific undergraduate courses are required. Candidates are not interviewed.

Procedure

The application deadline for fall entry is March 1. Applicants should submit an application form, LSAT results, transcripts, a personal statement, a nonrefundable application fee of $50, and 2 letters of recommendation. Notification of the admissions decision is on a rolling basis. The latest acceptable LSAT test date for fall entry is February. The law school uses the LSDAS.

Special

The law school recruits minority and disadvantaged students by means of Minority Law Day, visits to historically black colleges and universities, visits to areas and universities with high Latino populations, CLEO, ICLEO, and LSDAS candidate referral search. Requirements are not different for out-of-state students. Transfer students must have one year of credit and have attended an ABA-approved law school; acceptance depends on space availability.

Costs

Tuition and fees for the 2009-2010 academic year are $18,163 for full-time in-state students and $38,478 for out-of-state students. Tuition for part-time students is $14,065 in-state and $29,640 out-of-state. On-campus room and board costs about $14,460 annually; books and supplies run $1100.

Financial Aid

About 85% of current law students receive some form of aid. The average annual amount of aid from all sources combined, including scholarships, loans, and work contracts, is $27,785; maximum, $76,435. Awards are based on need and merit. If awards are from a private donor, requirements differ. Required financial statement is the FAFSA. The aid application deadline for fall entry is March 1. Special funds for minority or disadvantaged students consist of awards from private donors as well as Indiana CLEO for underrepresented groups in the legal field. First-year students are notified about their financial aid application at time of acceptance.

About the Law School

Indiana University School of Law-Indianapolis was established in 1895 and is a public institution. The campus is in an urban area in Indianapolis. The primary mission of the law school is to provide a legal education that will equip graduates with highly refined analytical and problem-solving skills, compassion, and ethics. Students have access to federal, state, county, city, and local agencies, courts, correctional facilities, law firms, and legal aid organizations in the Indianapolis area. Facilities of special interest to law students include the Indiana Supreme Court and the NCAA. Housing is available for single students in university-owned housing. Most students live in off-campus apartments. All law school facilities are accessible to the physically disabled.

Calendar

The law school operates on a traditional semester basis. Courses for full-time students are offered days only and must be completed within 5 years. For part-time students, courses are offered evenings only and must be completed within 5 years. New full- and part-time students are admitted in the fall. There is an 8-week summer session. Transferable summer courses are offered.

Programs

In addition to the J.D., the law school offers the LL.M. and S.J.D. The following joint degrees may be earned: J.D./M.B.A. (Juris Doctor/Master of Business Administration), J.D./M.H.A. (Juris Doctor/Master of Health Administration), J.D./M.L.S (Juris Doctor/Master of Library Science), J.D./M.P.A. (Juris Doctor/Master of Public Affairs), J.D./M.P.H. (Juris Doctor/Master of Public Health), J.D./M.Phil (Juris Doctor/Master of Arts in Philosophy with concentration in health and biothics), and J.D./M.S.W. (Juris Doctor/Master of Social Work).

Required

To earn the J.D., candidates must complete 90 total credits, of which 35 are for required courses. They must maintain a minimum GPA of 2.3 in the required courses. The following first-year courses are required of all students: Civil Procedure I and II, Contracts I and II, Criminal Law, Legal Writing I and II, Property, and Torts. Required upper-level courses consist of Legal Writing III and Professional Responsibility. The required orientation program for first-year students is 2 days in the fall and covers case briefing, outlining, library use, and basic computer use.

Electives

The Indiana University School of Law-Indianapolis offers concentrations in

Phone: 317-274-2459
Fax: 317-278-4780
E-mail: khmiller@iupui.edu
Web: indylaw.indiana.edu

Contact

Karen Miller, Assistant Director for Admissions, 317-274-2459 for general inquiries; Jennifer Vines, Financial Aid Representative, 317-278-2862 for financial aid information.

INDIANA
⊙

corporate law, criminal law, intellectual property law, international law, labor law, litigation, tax law, health law, international human rights, and state and local government law. In addition, halfway through their studies, students may take clinics in Civil Practice, Disability, Criminal Defense, Appellate Practice, Wrongful Conviction, and Immigration Law. Clients are represented by students under the supervision of faculty. Seminars are available for 2 credits in areas such as evidence, international law, health law, and American legal history. Externships for students are offered in banking; commercial; environmental; immigration; corporate; criminal defense; international, federal, state, and local government law; with federal and state courts and agencies; public defender; and prosecution. Credit varies from none to 2 hours. Research opportunities are available through the Center for Law and Health and the law journals. A special lecture series is active at the law school with various speakers and topics of interest. Summer study abroad is available in China and the Croatia program. Tutorial programs are offered through the Dean's Tutorial Society, led by students and led by a faculty member. A Minority Law Day is held for prospective students. Indiana CLEO is available for underrepresented groups in the legal profession. The most widely taken electives are International Law, Health Law, and Advocacy Skills.

Graduation Requirements
In order to graduate, candidates must have a GPA of 2.3 and have completed the upper-division writing requirement.

Organizations

Students edit the *Indiana Law Review, Indiana International and Comparative Law Review,* and the *Indiana Health Law Review.* Moot court teams are sent annually to the ABA-National Appellate Advocacy Competition, the Privacy Competition in Chicago, and the Philip C. Jessup International Law Competition. Teams also compete in the Client Counseling and Law and European Law competitions. Law student organizations, local chapters of national associations, and campus organizations include the Equal Justice Works, LAMBDA Law Society, Sports and

Entertainment Law Society, International Law Society, Black Law Students Association, and Phi Alpha Delta.

Library

The law library contains 609,151 hardcopy volumes and 66,847 microform volume equivalents, and subscribes to 3416 serial publications. Such on-line databases and networks as CALI, CIS Universe, DIALOG, Dow-Jones, Infotrac, Legal-Trac, LEXIS, Matthew Bender, NEXIS, OCLC First Search, WESTLAW, Wilsonline Indexes, HeinOnline, CCH Intelliconnect, BNA, LLMC, RIA Checkpoint, Making of Modern Law, and Oxford Scholarship Online are available to law students for research. Special library collections include United States government and United Nations publications. Recently, the library increased access to electronic resources. The ratio of library volumes to faculty is 9825 to 1 and to students is 645 to 1. The ratio of seats in the library to students is 1 to 1.

Faculty

The law school has 62 full-time and 73 part-time faculty members, of whom 49 are women. According to AAUP standards for Category IIA institutions, faculty salaries are average. About 48% of full-time faculty have a graduate law degree in addition to the J.D.; about 29% of part-time faculty have one. The ratio of full-time students to full-time faculty in an average class is 10 to 1; in a clinic, 8 to 1. The law school has a regular program of bringing visiting professors and other distinguished lecturers and visitors to campus.

Students

About 45% of the student body are women; 15%, minorities; 8%, African American; 4%, Asian American; 2%, Hispanic; and 1%, Native American. The majority of students come from Indiana (82%). The average age of entering students is 26; age range is 21 to 59. About 34% of students enter directly from undergraduate school, 14% have a graduate degree, and 66% have worked full-time prior to entering law school. About 1% drop out after the first year for academic or personal reasons; 99% remain to receive a law degree.

INTER AMERICAN UNIVERSITY OF PUERTO RICO

School of Law

P.O. Box 70351
San Juan, PR 00936-8351

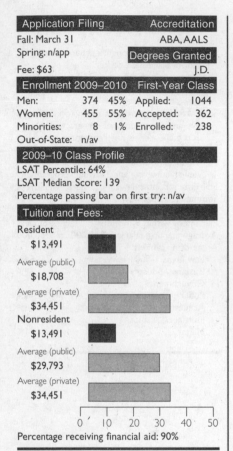

Application Filing		Accreditation	
Fall: March 31		ABA, AALS	
Spring: n/app		**Degrees Granted**	
Fee: $63			J.D.

Enrollment 2009–2010		First-Year Class	
Men:	374 45%	Applied:	1044
Women:	455 55%	Accepted:	362
Minorities:	8 1%	Enrolled:	238
Out-of-State:	n/av		

2009–10 Class Profile
LSAT Percentile: 64%
LSAT Median Score: 139
Percentage passing bar on first try: n/av

Tuition and Fees:

Resident
$13,491

Average (public)
$18,708

Average (private)
$34,451

Nonresident
$13,491

Average (public)
$29,793

Average (private)
$34,451

0 10 20 30 40 50

Percentage receiving financial aid: 90%

ADMISSIONS

In the fall 2009 first-year class, 1044 applied, 362 were accepted, and 238 enrolled. Seventeen transfers enrolled. The median LSAT percentile of the most recent first-year class was 64; the median GPA was 3.37 on a scale of 4.0. The lowest LSAT percentile accepted was 2; the highest was 86.

Requirements
Applicants must have a bachelor's degree and take the LSAT. Minimum acceptable LSAT percentile is 2 and minimum acceptable GPA is 2.5 on a scale of 4.0. The most important admission factors include GPA, and LSAT, and EXADEP results. No specific undergraduate courses are required. Candidates are not interviewed.

Procedure
The application deadline for fall entry is March 31. Applicants should submit an application form, LSAT results, transcripts, EXADEP scores, a nonrefundable application fee of $63, and have full profi-

ciency in Spanish, and accepted students must pay a $125 seat deposit. Notification of the admissions decision is by May 20. The latest acceptable LSAT test date for fall entry is February. The law school uses the LSDAS.

Special
Requirements are different for out-of-state students in that they are required to submit evidence of their authorization to study in Puerto Rico, as well as the documents required by the Immigration and Naturalization Office of the U.S. Department of Justice. Transfer students must have a minimum GPA of 3, have attended an ABA-approved law school, and they are admitted for fall, spring, or summer session. The school offers a compulsory 3-week summer preparation course for students admitted to the J.D. program.

Costs

Tuition and fees for the 2009-2010 academic year are $13,491 for all full-time students. Tuition for all part-time students is $10,484.

Financial Aid

About 90% of current law students receive some form of aid. The average annual amount of aid from all sources combined, including scholarships, loans, and work contracts, is $9443; maximum, $32,727. Awards are based on need and merit. Although law students do not qualify for Pell Grant awards, the free application for federal student aid is required. Required financial statement is the FAFSA. The aid application deadline for fall entry is August 13, and for spring entry it is January 15. First-year students are notified about their financial aid application at time of acceptance.

About the Law School

Inter American University of Puerto Rico School of Law was established in 1961 and is a private institution. The campus is in an urban area in metropolitan San Juan. The primary mission of the law school is to train professionals competent for public and private practice through a broad background in history and development of the law, particularly how it affects contemporary Puerto Rican legal issues and institutions, and also

to promote legal research and continued legal education of its alumni and others in the legal profession. Students have access to federal, state, county, city, and local agencies, courts, correctional facilities, law firms, and legal aid organizations in the San Juan area. The school's location grants students access to additional resources such as the University of Puerto Rico Law School and the Puerto Rico Bar Association. Facilities of special interest to law students include the moot courtroom and law library. Housing for students is available in the neighborhood for those students who reside outside the metropolitan area. The school does not provide housing facilities. All law school facilities are accessible to the physically disabled.

Calendar

The law school operates on a traditional semester basis. Courses for full-time students are offered both day and evening and must be completed within 3 to 6 years. For part-time students, courses are offered both day and evening and must be completed within 4 to 8 years. New full- and part-time students are admitted in the fall. There is a 4- to 5-week summer session. Transferable summer courses are not offered.

Programs

The following joint degrees may be earned: J.D./M.B.A. (Juris Doctor/Master of Business Administration).

Required
To earn the J.D., candidates must complete 92 total credits, of which 62 are for required courses. They must maintain a minimum GPA of 2.0 in the required courses. The following first-year courses are required of all students: Civil Procedure-Successions, Constitutional Law I, Criminal Law, Criminal Procedure, Family Law, Introduction to Law, Property Law, Research Analysis and Writing, and Torts. Required upper-level courses consist of Administrative Law, Constitutional Law II, Criminal Procedure, Ethics of the Legal Professional, Evidence, General Theory Obligations and Contracts, History of Puerto Rican Law, Litigation: Theory, Doctrine, and Practice, and Mortgage Law. All students must take clinical courses. The required orientation program for first-year students is a summer

Contact

Dean of Students, 787-751-1912, ext. 2011 for general inquiries; Ricardo Crespo, Director of Financial Aid, (787) 751-1912, ext. 2014 for financial aid information.

PUERTO RICO

introductory course and a program during the week preceding the fall semester.

Electives

The Legal Aid Clinic involves students in offering legal advice, handling cases before courts and administrative agencies, and drafting legal documents for 4 credits. Seminars provide in-depth study in various areas of law and are worth 3 credits each. Tutorial programs for 2 credits are available in courts and government agencies. The most widely taken electives are Labor Law, Employment Law, and Commercial Law.

Graduation Requirements

In order to graduate, candidates must have a GPA of 2.0 and have completed the upper-division writing requirement.

Organizations

The primary law review is the *Revista Juridica de la Universidad Interamerica de Puerto Rico*, which is edited by students, professors, and scholars. Other law reviews include *CLAVE*, The student newspaper is the *Student Council Bulletin*. Other publications include *AD REM*. Moot court competitions include the Animal Law Moot Court and closing animal competitions. Student council members serve on law school committees. There are local chapters of the ABA-Law Student Division, National Law Students Association, Phi Alpha Delta-Luis Munoz Morales chapter, and the National Hispanic Bar Association - Law Student Division. Other organizations include the Students' Cooperative Bookstore.

Library

The law library contains 202,325 hardcopy volumes and 353,804 microform volume equivalents, and subscribes to 2646 serial publications. Such on-line databases and networks as CALI, Infotrac, Legal-Trac, LEXIS, OCLC First Search, RLIN, WESTLAW, Internet, LIBIS (the university's library), MICROJURIS (Puerto Rican Law Data Base), JTS (Jurisprudence of Supreme Court), HEIN Online and Lex Juris are available to law students for research. Special library collections include Domingo Toledo Alamo, Jose Ramon Velez Torres, Hipolito Marcano Antonio Fernos-Isern. Also, 3 private collections of civil law books include rare books. Recently, the library began a 5-year reclasification project. The ratio of library volumes to faculty is 8796 to 1 and to students is 244 to 1. The ratio of seats in the library to students is 1 to 2.

Faculty

The law school has 23 full-time and 31 part-time faculty members, of whom 23 are women. About 84% of full-time faculty have a graduate law degree in addition to the J.D.; about 34% of part-time faculty have one. The ratio of full-time students to full-time faculty in an average class is 13 to 1; in a clinic, 4 to 1. The law school has a regular program of bringing visiting professors and other distinguished lecturers and visitors to campus.

Students

About 55% of the student body are women and 1% are minorities. All students come from Puerto Rico. The average age of entering students is 24; age range is 21 to 50. About 90% of students enter directly from undergraduate school and 10% have a graduate degree. About 8% drop out after the first year for academic or personal reasons; 92% remain to receive a law degree.

Placement

J.D.s awarded:	132
Services available through: the university placement center and Office of the Dean of Students-Career Placement Office	
Special features: International Law Internships.	
Full-time job interviews:	35 employers
Summer job interviews:	14 employers
Placement by graduation:	20% of class
Placement within 9 months:	91% of class
Average starting salary:	$28,000 to $68,000
Areas of placement:	
Private practice 2-10 attorneys	10%
Private practice 11-25 attorneys	10%
Private practice 26-50 attorneys	10%
Private practice 51-100 attorneys	7%
Government	23%
Business/industry	21%
Judicial clerkships	9%
Academic	3%
Public interest	1%

JOHN MARSHALL LAW SCHOOL

315 South Plymouth Court
Chicago, IL 60604

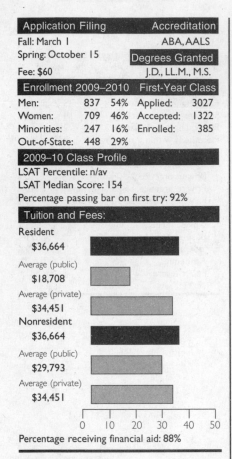

Application Filing		Accreditation
Fall: March 1		ABA, AALS
Spring: October 15		**Degrees Granted**
Fee: $60		J.D., LL.M., M.S.

Enrollment 2009–2010			First-Year Class	
Men:	837	54%	Applied:	3027
Women:	709	46%	Accepted:	1322
Minorities:	247	16%	Enrolled:	385
Out-of-State:	448	29%		

2009–10 Class Profile
LSAT Percentile: n/av
LSAT Median Score: 154
Percentage passing bar on first try: 92%

Tuition and Fees:

Resident
$36,664

Average (public)
$18,708

Average (private)
$34,451

Nonresident
$36,664

Average (public)
$29,793

Average (private)
$34,451

0 10 20 30 40 50

Percentage receiving financial aid: 88%

ADMISSIONS
In the fall 2009 first-year class, 3027 applied, 1322 were accepted, and 385 enrolled. Twenty-six transfers enrolled. The median GPA of the most recent first-year class was 3.3.

Requirements
Applicants must have a bachelor's degree and take the LSAT. The most important admission factors include life experience, LSAT results, and academic achievement. No specific undergraduate courses are required. Candidates are not interviewed.

Procedure
The application deadline for fall entry is March 1. Applicants should submit an application form, LSAT results, transcripts, TOEFL or TWE if applicable, a nonrefundable application fee of $60, and LSDAS report. Notification of the admissions decision is 2 to 5 weeks after their file is complete. The latest acceptable LSAT test date for fall entry is June. The law school uses the LSDAS.

Special
The law school recruits minority and disadvantaged students through special mailings and outreach to minority institutions and diversity mock trial competitions. Requirements are not different for out-of-state students. Transfer students must have a minimum GPA of 2.75 and have attended an ABA-approved law school. Preadmissions courses consist of Summer College to Assess Legal Education Skills (SCALES), a noncredit introductory program designed to provide an opportunity for law school applicants to demonstrate their readiness and suitability for law school. Students who succcessfully complete the requirements of SCALES are offered regular admission into Law School in August.

Costs
Tuition and fees for the 2009-2010 academic year are $36,664 for all full-time students. Tuition for part-time students is $25,324 in-state. Books and supplies run $2226.

Financial Aid
About 88% of current law students receive some form of aid. The maximum annual amount of aid from all sources combined, including scholarships, loans, and work contracts, is $60,120. Awards are based on need and merit. Required financial statement is the FAFSA. The aid application deadline for fall entry is June 1. First-year students are notified about their financial aid application at time of acceptance.

About the Law School
John Marshall Law School was established in 1899 and is independent. The campus is in an urban area in Chicago. The primary mission of the law school is to provide students with an intellectually challenging foundation in legal principles and a rigorous background in lawyering skills. Students have access to federal, state, county, city, and local agencies, courts, correctional facilities, law firms, and legal aid organizations in the Chicago area. Housing for students is readily available and assistance is provided through the admissions office. All law school facilities are accessible to the physically disabled.

Calendar
The law school operates on a traditional semester basis. Courses for full-time students are offered both day and evening and must be completed within 5 years. For part-time students, courses are offered both day and evening and Saturdays. and must be completed within 6 years. New full- and part-time students are admitted in the fall and spring. There is an 8-week summer session. Transferable summer courses are offered.

Programs
In addition to the J.D., the law school offers the LL.M. and M.S. in intellectual property, taxation, real estate, employee benefits, information technology, and privacy law. Students may take relevant courses in other programs and apply credit toward the J.D.; a maximum of 6 credits may be applied. The following joint degrees may be earned: J.D./M.B.A. (Juris Doctor/Master of Business Administration) and J.D./M.P.A. (Juris Doctor/ Master of Public Administration).

Required
To earn the J.D., candidates must complete 90 total credits, of which 48 are for required courses. They must maintain a minimum GPA of 2.25 in the required courses. The following first-year courses are required of all students: Civil Procedure I, Constitutional Law I, Contracts I and II, Criminal Law, Lawyering Skills I and II, Property, and Torts. Required upper-level courses consist of Civil Procedure II, Constitutional Law II, Evidence, Lawyering Skills Drafting, Moot Court-Herzog, Professional Responsibility, and Trial Advocacy. All students must take clinical courses. The required orientation program for first-year students is 3 days for day students and 4 evenings for evening students entering with the August class, and 4 evenings for day and evening students entering with the January class. The program consists of both academic and administrative presentations.

Electives
The John Marshall Law School offers concentrations in corporate law, international law, litigation, tax law, advocacy and dispute resolution, business, estate planning, general practice, informatics, intellectual property, real estate, information technology law, and public interest law,. In addition, clinics are open to students with at least 53 hours and prior approval.

Phone: 312-987-1406
800-537-4280
Fax: 312-427-5136
E-mail: *admission@jmls.edu*
Web: *www.jmls.edu*

Contact

Admission and Student Affairs, 312-987-1406 for general inquiries; Yara Santana, Director, 312-427-2737, ext. 510 for financial aid information.

ILLINOIS

Clinics offer from 2 to 4 credits per semester and are with the Chicago Corporation Counsel, Fair Housing, Legal Aid Bureau, Illinois Attorney General, intellectual property law, judicial and legislative clerkships, Legal Aid Bureau, Public Defender, State's Attorney of Cook County, Travelers and Immigrants Aid, the U.S. Attorney, Northern District of Illinois, and John Marshall's Deteraus Legal Support Center and Clinic. Seminars are worth 2 to 3 credits, and are in the areas of banking, business planning, computers, constitutional law, counseling and negotiating, estate planning, information law, rights of prisoners, scientific evidence, intellectual property, international criminal law, taxation, and trial advocacy. Research programs, worth 1 to 2 credits, are open to students who have at least 59 hours. A scholarly paper must be produced from research supervised by a faculty member. There is an ABA-approved Intellectual Property Law Summer Prigram in Beijing. Special interest groups are the Center for Information Technology and Privacy Law, Center for Intellectual Property Law, Fair Housing Legal Support Center, Center for Advocacy, and Dispute Resolution, Center for Real Estate Law, Center for Tax Law and Employee Benefits, and Center for International Law. The most widely taken electives are Corporations, Estates and Trusts, and Commercial Law.

Graduation Requirements

In order to graduate, candidates must have a GPA of 2.25 and have completed 4 semesters of Lawyering Skills.

Organizations

Student-edited publications are *The John Marshall Law Review*, the *Journal of Computer and Information Law*, the *Review of Intellectual Property Law*, and the student newspaper *Decisive Utterance*. Teams are sent annually to more than 20 interscholastic moot court and trial competitions. The John Marshall Law School hosts the annual International Moot Court Competition in Information Technology and Privacy Law and the annual National Criminal Justice Trial Advocacy Competition with the American Bar Association. Law student organizations, local chapters of national associations, and campus organizations include Phi Alpha Delta, Phi Delta Phi, Delta Theta Phi, Student Bar Association, Illinois State Bar Association-Law Student Division, ABA-Law Student Division, Asian and Pacific Island Law Students Association, Black Law Students Association, and Latino Law Students Association.

Library

The law library contains 409,154 hardcopy volumes and 158,195 microform volume equivalents, and subscribes to 5011 serial publications. Such on-line databases and networks as CALI, LEXIS, NEXIS, OCLC First Search, WESTLAW, Wilsonline Indexes, Hein-Online BNA-All, JSTOR, ILCLE, Smartbook, and Kluwer International are available to law students for research. Special library collections include a U.S. government documents depository, Chinese language intellectual property law collection, and animal rights law collection (National Anti-Vivisection Society). Library space went through major renovations in 2008 including new furnishings and flooring, more study rooms, improved lighting, upgraded wireless, and multiple electronic databases. The ratio of library volumes to faculty is 5604 to 1 and to students is 265 to 1. The ratio of seats in the library to students is 1 to 2.

Faculty

The law school has 73 full-time and 110 part-time faculty members, of whom 59 are women. About 25% of full-time faculty have a graduate law degree in addition to the J.D. 25% of full-time faculty have a graduate law degree in addition to the J.D. The ratio of full-time students to full-time faculty in an average class is 14.4 to 1.

Students

About 46% of the student body are women; 16%, minorities; 8%, African American; 6%, Asian American; 8%, Hispanic; and 1%, Native American. The majority of students come from Illinois (71%). The average age of entering students is 23; age range is 21 to 52. About 33% of students enter directly from undergraduate school, 14% have a graduate degree, and 40% have worked full-time prior to entering law school. About 9% drop out after the first year for academic or personal reasons; 80% remain to receive a law degree.

Placement

J.D.s awarded:	403
Services available through: a separate law school placement center and career services office	
Special features: Mentor Program, Mandatory Career services training for first-year students in November followed by required one-on-one counseling sessions with an assigned counselor..	
Full-time job interviews:	30 employers
Summer job interviews:	30 employers
Placement by graduation:	n/av
Placement within 9 months:	89% of class
Average starting salary:	$78,500
Areas of placement:	
Private practice 2-10 attorneys	33%
Private practice 11-25 attorneys	6%
Private practice 26-50 attorneys	4%
Private practice 51-100 attorneys	5%
Business/industry	23%
Government	13%
Private practice 100+ attorneys	7%
Academic	3%
Judicial clerkships	2%
Public interest	2%
Military	2%

LEWIS AND CLARK COLLEGE

Lewis and Clark Law School

10015 Southwest Terwilliger Boulevard Portland, OR 97219

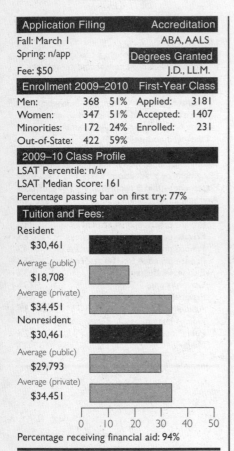

Application Filing		Accreditation
Fall: March 1		ABA, AALS
Spring: n/app		

Degrees Granted		
Fee: $50		J.D., LL.M.

Enrollment 2009–2010		First-Year Class	
Men:	368 51%	Applied:	3181
Women:	347 51%	Accepted:	1407
Minorities:	172 24%	Enrolled:	231
Out-of-State:	422 59%		

2009–10 Class Profile
LSAT Percentile: n/av
LSAT Median Score: 161
Percentage passing bar on first try: 77%

Tuition and Fees:

Resident
$30,461

Average (public)
$18,708

Average (private)
$34,451

Nonresident
$30,461

Average (public)
$29,793

Average (private)
$34,451

0   10   20   30   40   50

Percentage receiving financial aid: 94%

ADMISSIONS
In the fall 2009 first-year class, 3181 applied, 1407 were accepted, and 231 enrolled. Forty-five transfers enrolled. The median GPA of the most recent first-year class was 3.52. The lowest LSAT percentile accepted was 17; the highest was 99.

Requirements
Applicants must have a bachelor's degree and take the LSAT. The most important admission factors include LSAT results, GPA, and writing ability. No specific undergraduate courses are required. Candidates are not interviewed.

Procedure
The application deadline for fall entry is March 1. Applicants should submit an application form, LSAT results, transcripts, a personal statement, a nonrefundable application fee of $50, 2 letters of recommendation, an essay, resumé, LSDAS report of undergraduate work, and optional statements on extracurricular activities or special circumstances.

Notification of the admissions decision is on a rolling basis. The latest acceptable LSAT test date for fall entry is February. The law school uses the LSDAS.

Special
The law school recruits minority and disadvantaged students by having law school representatives visit undergraduate institutions with significant ethnic enrollment; by inviting prelaw advisers from undergraduate schools with large ethnic minority populations to visit the campus; by partnering with the Oregon State Bar to attract and retain ethnic minority students in Oregon; and by contacting ethnic minority candidates who take the LSAT. Requirements are not different for out-of-state students. Transfer students must have one year of credit, have attended an ABA-approved law school, and achieved strong academic standing at the school from which the student is transferring, and present a compelling reason for wishing to transfer to Lewis and Clark.

Costs
Tuition and fees for the 2009-2010 academic year are $30,461 for all full-time students. Tuition for part-time students is $22,851 per year. Books and supplies run $1050.

Financial Aid
About 94% of current law students receive some form of aid. The average annual amount of aid from all sources combined, including scholarships, loans, and work contracts, is $38,184; maximum, $47,578. Awards are based on need and merit. Required financial statement is the FAFSA. The aid application deadline for fall entry is March 1. Special funds for minority or disadvantaged students consist of scholarship funds from the college, Oregon State Bar funds, and a special Native American Scholarship. First-year students are notified about their financial aid application at time of acceptance. Loans are determined after applicants are admitted; scholarships are granted with the offer of admission.

About the Law School
Lewis and Clark College Lewis and Clark Law School was established in 1884 and is a private institution. The 31-acre campus

is in a suburban area within Portland. The primary mission of the law school is to train and educate students about the law and about being ethical, well-rounded professionals. The school also strives to advance the knowledge, skills, and professionalism of legal practitioners. Students have access to federal, state, county, city, and local agencies, courts, correctional facilities, law firms, and legal aid organizations in the Portland area. The American Inns of Court; clinical internship seminars; externships, and the Oregon student appearance rule, which allows students to appear in court, are available to students. Facilities of special interest to law students include a 640-acre wilderness park bordering the campus and the undergraduate school, which has indoor and outdoor pools, a gymnasium, and tennis and racquetball courts. Housing for students consists of a wide variety of off-campus apartments and houses that students share at reasonable rents. Campus-owned houses are available for law students to rent. All law school facilities are accessible to the physically disabled.

Calendar
The law school operates on a traditional semester basis. Courses for full-time students are offered both day and evening and must be completed within 5 years. For part-time students, courses are offered both day and evening and must be completed within 6 years. New full- and part-time students are admitted in the fall. There are 2- 5-week summer sessions. Transferable summer courses are not offered.

Programs
In addition to the J.D., the law school offers the LL.M. The following joint degrees may be earned: J.D./L.L.M. (Juris Doctor/Master of Laws in environmental and natural resources law).

Required
To earn the J.D., candidates must complete 88 total credits, of which 28-35 are for required courses. They must maintain a minimum GPA of 1.7 in the required courses. The following first-year courses are required of all students: Civil Procedure I and II, Constitutional Law I, Contracts, Criminal Procedure I (full-time students), Legal Analysis and Writ-

Phone: 503-768-6613
800-303-4860
Fax: 503-768-6793
E-mail: *lawadmss@lclark.edu*
Web: *http://Law.Lclark.edu*

Contact

Admissions Office, 503-768-6613 or 800-303-4860 for general inquiries; Diana Meyer, Assistant Director of Financial Services, 503-768-7090 for financial aid information.

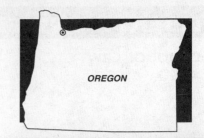

OREGON

ing I and II, Legal Elements, Property (full-time students), and Torts. Required upper-level courses consist of Constitutional Law II, Criminal Law (part-time students), Professionalism, Property (part-time students), and Seminar. The required orientation program for first-year students a 2-day program consisting of student registration and introduction to legal analysis.

Electives

The Lewis and Clark Law School offers concentrations in corporate law, criminal law, environmental law, family law, international law, labor law, litigation, securities law, tax law, torts and insurance, employment law, and animal law. In addition, the law school operates a clinic in downtown Portland. The clinic serves indigent clients and performs civil work in the areas of consumer, landlord-tenant, employment law, and tax law. It is available to all upper-division students for 4 credits. Students interested in environmental law may participate in the Pacific Environmental Advocacy Center, the International Environmental Law Project, and clinical internship seminars. Seminars available for 2 to 3 credits in a variety of subjects are limited to 20 students and usually require a paper. Each upper-division student must take 1 seminar to graduate. A 3-hour seminar is offered in conjunction with a 10-hour per week placement in areas including criminal law, natural resources and, intellectual property. The school also offers full semester or summer externships, which require a substantial paper in addition to working full time in an approved placement with significant faculty supervision. Students may work as research assistants to faculty members, write for law reviews, and perform independent research projects for credit with faculty. Special lecture series include the Higgins Visit and the distinguished visitors series. There are also faculty colloquia and speakers invited by various student groups. The school has partnerships with the summer abroad program at the University of San Diego and with the China program at the University of Missouri-Kansas City. Students participate in study-abroad programs with any ABA law schools and apply these credits at Lewis and Clark. An academic support program that focuses on study skills and group support is available to students. The school actively recruits ethnic minor-

ity candidates any actively participates and hosts diversity pipline programs. Students may participate in a wide variety of student organizations including, but not limited to, the Business Law Society, Environmental Law Caucus, Minority Law Student Association, Student Animal Legal Defense Fund, and the Public Interest Law Project. The most widely taken electives are Business/Corporate Law, Environmental, and Intellectual Property.

Graduation Requirements

In order to graduate, candidates must have a GPA of 2.0 and have completed the upper-division writing requirement.

Organizations

The primary law review is the *Environmental Law Review*. Other student-edited publications include *Lewis and Clark Law Review* and the *Animal Law Review*. Moot court competitions consist of a negotiation competition, environmental law, moot court and tax moot court. A writing competition for the best paper in the area of international law is sponsored by the law firm of Ragen, Davis, and Wright. Law student organizations include Intellectual Property Society Public Interest Project, and Minority Law Student Association. Other campus organizations include OutLaw, Students Advocating Business and Enviormental Responsibility, and Phi Delta Phi. Local chapters of national associations include Student Bar Association, Student Animal Legal Defense Fund, and National Lawyers Guild.

Library

The law library contains 220,765 hardcopy volumes and 311,765 microform volume equivalents, and subscribes to 1575 serial publications. Such on-line databases and networks as CALI, CIS Universe, Legal-Trac, LEXIS, LOIS, NEXIS, OCLC First Search, WESTLAW, and UN Treaty Collections, HeinOnline, JSTOR, OED Online, BNA Online, and Making of Modern Law are available to law students for research. Special library collections include the Milton Pearl Environmental Law Collection, Tax/Estate Planning Collection, the Federal Patent and Trademark Depository Library, and Samuel Johnson Public Land Law papers. Recently, the library was completely remodeled to add 17,200 square feet of space, increased the

Placement

J.D.s awarded:	238

Services available through: a separate law school placement center

Services: extensive resource library, 2 mentor programs, a video mock interview program, monthly jobs newsletter, a comprehensive web site with links, on-campus interview program, and public interest/pro bono honors program.

Full-time job interviews:	11 employers
Summer job interviews:	32 employers
Placement by graduation:	n/av
Placement within 9 months:	96% of class
Average starting salary:	$67,834
Areas of placement:	
Private practice 2-10 attorneys	34%
Private practice 11-25 attorneys	6%
Private practice 26-50 attorneys	2%
Private practice 51-100 attorneys	2%
Business/industry	20%
Government	17%
Public interest	11%
Judicial clerkships	6%
Academic	2%

number of group study rooms, networked all library seats (375), and added wireless capability. The ratio of library volumes to faculty is 4014 to 1 and to students is 423 to 1. The ratio of seats in the library to students is 1 to 2.

Faculty

The law school has 55 full-time and 71 part-time faculty members, of whom 47 are women. About 15% of full-time faculty have a graduate law degree in addition to the J.D. The ratio of full-time students to full-time faculty in an average class is 38 to 1; in a clinic, 3 to 1. The law school has a regular program of bringing visiting professors and other distinguished lecturers and visitors to campus.

Students

About 51% of the student body are women; 24%, minorities; 3%, African American; 9%, Asian American; 5%, Hispanic; 4%, Native American; 2% international students and 9% race/ethnicity unknown. The majority of students come from Oregon (41%). The average age of entering students is 26; age range is 21 to 58. About 4% drop out after the first year for academic or personal reasons; 89% remain to receive a law degree.

School of Law

1971 University Blvd.
Lynchburg, VA 24502

Application Filing	Accreditation
Fall: n/av	ABA, AALS
Spring: n/app	**Degrees Granted**
Fee: n/av	J.D.

Enrollment 2009–2010		First-Year Class	
Men:	110 65%	Applied:	n/av
Women:	60 35%	Accepted:	n/av
Minorities:	26 15%	Enrolled:	n/av
Out-of-State:	170 100%		

2009–10 Class Profile

LSAT Percentile: n/av
LSAT Median Score: 150
Percentage passing bar on first try: 89%

Tuition and Fees:

Resident
$25,260

Average (public)
$18,708

Average (private)
$34,451

Nonresident
$25,260

Average (public)
$29,793

Average (private)
$34,451

0 10 20 30 40 50

Percentage receiving financial aid: 100%

ADMISSIONS

In a recent year, three transfers enrolled. The median GPA of the most recent first-year class was 3.16. Figures in the above capsule and in this profile are approximate.

Requirements

Applicants must have a bachelor's degree and take the LSAT. The most important admission factors include motivations, general background, and LSAT results. No specific undergraduate courses are required. Candidates are interviewed.

Procedure

Applicants should submit an application form, LSAT results, transcripts, a personal statement, and 2 letters of recommendation. Notification of the admissions decision is within 30 days of completed file. The latest acceptable LSAT test date for fall entry is February. Check with the school for current application deadlines. The law school uses the LSDAS.

Special

The law school recruits minority and disadvantaged students through campus visits, advertising, special events, and CLEO membership. Requirements are not different for out-of-state students. Transfer students must have one year of credit, have a minimum GPA of 2, and a letter from previous law school.

Costs

Tuition and fees for the 2009-2010 academic year are approximately $25,260 for all full-time students. Books and supplies run approximately $2900.

Financial Aid

In a recent year, about 100% of current law students receive some form of aid. The maximum annual amount of aid from all sources combined, including scholarships, loans, and work contracts, was approximately $42,800. Awards are based on merit. Required financial statement is the FAFSA. Special funds for minority or disadvantaged students include one minority scholarship category. Check with the school for current application deadline. First-year students are notified about their financial aid application at during application process.

About the Law School

Liberty University School of Law was established in 2004 and is a private institution. The 5000-acre campus is in an urban area Central Virginia in the Blue Ridge Mountains. The primary mission of the law school is to equip future leaders in law with a superior legal education in Fidelity to the Christian faith expressed through the Holy Scriptures. Students have access to federal, state, county, city, and local agencies, courts, correctional facilities, law firms, and legal aid organizations in the Lynchburg area. The law school has a partnership with Liberty Counsel, a public interest law firm with an office in Lynchburg. Facilities of special interest to law students include a 330-seat ceremonial courtroom with a 9-seat bench, which is an exact replica of the U.S. Supreme Court bench; wireless access throughout law school; proximity of law library to classrooms; and a massive fitness center. Housing for students consists of affordable off-campus apartments and

homes. All law school facilities are accessible to the physically disabled.

Calendar

The law school operates on a traditional semester basis. Courses for full-time students are offered and are primarily day only; particular courses are and must be completed within 7 years. There is no part-time program. New students are admitted in the fall. There is no summer session. Transferable summer courses are not offered.

Programs

Required

To earn the J.D., candidates must complete 90 total credits, of which 69 are for required courses. They must maintain a minimum GPA of 2.0 in the required courses. The following first-year courses are required of all students: Civil Procedure I and II, Contracts I and II, Foundations of Law I and II, Lawyering Skills I and II, Property I and II, and Torts I and II. Required upper-level courses consist of Business Associations, Constitutional Law I and II, Criminal Law, Criminal Procedure, Evidence, Jurisprudence or Legal History, Lawyering Skills III and IV, Lawyering Skills V and VI, Professional Responsibility, Taxation of Individuals, and Wills, Trusts, and Estates. The required orientation program for first-year students is 3½ days of case briefing, other academic preparation, and student activities.

Electives

In addition, The law school offers clinical experience in the Constitutional Law Clinic. The school offers seminars in First Amendment Law, Juvenile Law, and School Law. Non-paid, non-credit internships in government and nonprofit organizations are available to students. Fieldwork includes a Criminal Law Externship and a Judicial Clerk Externship. The law school hosts a Speakers Forum bringing in members of the bench and bar as well as hosting a broad range of special lectures. Tutorial and remedial programs include the Academic Support Program. Special interest groups include the Alternative Dispute Resolution (ADR) Board and the Moot Court Board. The most widely

Phone: 434-592-5300
Fax: 434-592-0202
E-mail: law@liberty.edu
Web: law.liberty.edu

Contact

Office of Admissions and Financial Aid, (434) 592-5300 for general inquiries; Coordinator of Financial Aid, (434) 592-5431 for financial aid information.

VIRGINIA

taken electives are Real Estate Transactions, Family Law, and State and Local Government.

Graduation Requirements

In order to graduate, candidates must have a GPA of 2.0 and have completed the upper-division writing requirement.

Organizations

Students edit the *Liberty University Law Review*. Students participate in the Thurgood A. Marshall Memorial Moot Court Competition, Regent National Constitutional Law Moot Court Competition, and the ABA Appellate Advocacy Competition. Other competitions include the Robert R. Merhige National Environmental Negotiation Competition, ABA Client Counseling Competition, and the ABA Negotiation Competition. Law student organizations include the Moot Court Board, and the ADR Board. Local chapters of national associations include the Student Bar Association, Federalist Society, and the Christian Legal Society. Other campus organizations include the International Law Society.

Library

The law library contains 94,815 hard-copy volumes and 155,383 microform volume equivalents, and subscribes to 770 serial publications. Such on-line databases and networks as CALI, CIS Universe, Infotrac, Legal-Trac, LEXIS, NEXIS, OCLC First Search, WESTLAW, Wilsonline Indexes, and BNA, CCH, CILP, LSN, LLMC, RIA, HeinOnline, Fastcase, plus others are available to law students for research. The ratio of library volumes to faculty is 4990 to 1 and to students is 578 to 1. The ratio of seats in the library to students is 1 to 1.

Faculty

The law school has 19 full-time and 6 part-time faculty members, of whom 8 are women. According to AAUP standards for Category II A institutions, faculty salaries are well below average. About 26% of full-time faculty have a graduate law degree in addition to the J.D. The law school has a regular program of bringing visiting professors and other distinguished lecturers and visitors to campus.

Students

About 35% of the student body are women; 15%, minorities; 8%, African American; 2%, Asian American; 2%, Hispanic; 2%, Native American; and 86%, Caucasian, Foreign National, or Unknown. The majority of students come from Canada (1%). The average age of entering students is 26; age range is 20 to 54. About 10% of students have a graduate degree. About 10% drop out after the first year for academic or personal reasons; 90% remain to receive a law degree.

Placement	
J.D.s awarded:	n/av
Services available through: a separate law school placement center	
Full-time job interviews:	n/av
Summer job interviews:	n/av
Placement by graduation:	n/av
Placement within 9 months:	n/av
Average starting salary:	n/av
Areas of placement:	n/av

Paul M. Hebert Law Center

202 Law Center, 1 East Campus Drive
Baton Rouge, LA 70803

Application Filing	Accreditation
Fall: March 1	ABA, AALS
Spring: n/app	**Degrees Granted**
Fee: $50	J.D., LL.M., M.C.L., Diploma in Civil (Comparative) Law (D.C.L.)

Enrollment 2009–2010		First-Year Class	
Men:	329 55%	Applied:	1407
Women:	269 45%	Accepted:	422
Minorities:	60 10%	Enrolled:	235
Out-of-State:	167 28%		

2009–10 Class Profile
LSAT Percentile: 72%
LSAT Median Score: 157
Percentage passing bar on first try: 90%

Tuition and Fees:

Resident
$14,470

Average (public)
$18,708

Average (private)
$34,451

Nonresident
$25,570

Average (public)
$29,793

Average (private)
$34,451

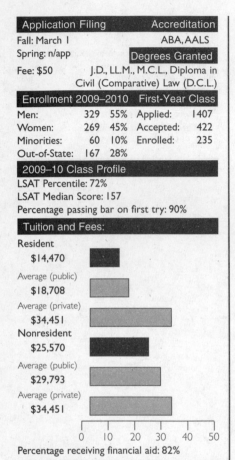

0 10 20 30 40 50

Percentage receiving financial aid: 82%

ADMISSIONS

In the fall 2009 first-year class, 1407 applied, 422 were accepted, and 235 enrolled. Three transfers enrolled. The median LSAT percentile of the most recent first-year class was 72; the median GPA was 3.44 on a scale of 4.0. The lowest LSAT percentile accepted was 25; the highest was 98.

Requirements
Applicants must have a bachelor's degree and take the LSAT. The most important admission factors include academic achievement, LSAT results, and letter of recommendation. No specific undergraduate courses are required. Candidates are not interviewed.

Procedure
The application deadline for fall entry is March 1. Applicants should submit an application form, LSAT results, transcripts, a personal statement, a nonre-fundable application fee of $50, 2 letters of recommendation, and a $500 seat deposit credited toward tuition. Notification of the admissions decision is on a rolling basis. The latest acceptable LSAT test date for fall entry is February. The law school uses the LSDAS.

Special
The law school recruits minority and disadvantaged students by means of an active recruiting program that identifies students through test scores and information received through the Law Services Candidate Referral Program. Requirements are not different for out-of-state students. Transfer students must have one year of credit, have attended an ABA-approved law school, have reasons for seeking a transfer, and provide information on their overall first-year academic performance.

Costs

Tuition and fees for the 2009-2010 academic year are $14,470 for full-time in-state students and $25,570 for out-of-state students. On-campus room and board costs about $11,081 annually; books and supplies run $1700.

Financial Aid

About 82% of current law students receive some form of aid. Awards are based on need and merit. Required financial statements are the FFS and the FAFSA. The aid application deadline for fall entry is April 1. First-year students are notified about their financial aid application shortly after applying.

About the Law School

Louisiana State University Paul M. Hebert Law Center was established in 1906 and is a public institution. The campus is in an urban area in Baton Rouge. The primary mission of the law school is to produce highly competent and ethical lawyers capable of serving the cause of justice in private practice, in public service, and in commerce and industry, both in Louisiana and elsewhere; to support and assist the continuing professional endeavors of our alumni; and to be of service to all members of the legal profession of this state. Students have access to federal, state, county, city, and local agen-cies, courts, correctional facilities, law firms, and legal aid organizations in the Baton Rouge area. Legislative and executive branches of state government are also accessible to students. Housing for students is available in residence halls, as well as rooms and apartments in privately owned facilities and university facilities. All law school facilities are accessible to the physically disabled.

Calendar

The law school operates on a traditional semester basis. Courses for full-time students are offered days only and must be completed within 4 years. There is no part-time program. New students are admitted in the fall. There is a 7-week summer session. Transferable summer courses are offered.

Programs

In addition to the J.D., the law school offers the LL.M., M.C.L., and Diploma in Civil (Comparative) Law (D.C.L.). Students may take relevant courses in other programs and apply credit toward the J.D.; a maximum of 12 hours may be applied. The following joint degrees may be earned: J.D./D.C.L. (Juris Doctor/Diploma in Civil Law), J.D./M.B.A. (Juris Doctor/Master of Business Administration), J.D./M.M.C. (Juris Doctor/Master of Mass Communications), and J.D./M.P.A. (Juris Doctor/Master of Public Administration).

Required
To earn the J.D., candidates must complete 94 total credits, of which 70 are for required courses. They must maintain a minimum GPA of 2.0 in the required courses. The following first-year courses are required of all students: Administration of Criminal Justice I, Basic Civil Procedure I and II, Civil Law Property, Constitutional Law I, Contracts, Criminal Law, Legal Research and Writing I and II, Legal Traditions and Systems, Obligations, and Torts. Required upper-level courses consist of Evidence, Legal Profession, and Trial Advocacy. The required orientation program for first-year students is a day and a half and includes tours and a student activities expo. It also provides some 2 hours with students, about 1 hour with faculty, and a 2-hour Professionalism Program sponsored by the Louisiana State Bar Association.

Phone: 225-578-8646
Fax: 225-578-8647
E-mail: lynell.cadray@law.lsu.edu
Web: /www.law.lsu.edu

Contact

Lynell Cadray, Assistant Vice Chancellor for Enrollment and Director of Admissions, 225-578-8646 for general inquiries; Mary Parker, Executive Director, 225-578-3103 for financial aid information.

LOUISIANA

Electives

The Paul M. Hebert Law Center offers concentrations in corporate law, criminal law, environmental law, family law, international law, juvenile law, labor law, litigation, maritime law, media law, securities law, tax law, and torts and insurance. In addition, third-year students may take clinical courses in preparing for trials and oral arguments, generally worth 2 credits. Seminars are offered for 2 hours of credit. With faculty approval, students may conduct supervised independent research. Special lecture series are the Edward Douglass White Lectures, the James J. Bailey Lectures, and the John H. Tucker, Jr. Lectures. Students may study for 6 weeks during the summer in France. Freshman tutorial programs are available. There are externships whereby 5 students may be selected to work under the supervision of any agency and the instructor in certain courses.

Graduation Requirements

In order to graduate, candidates must have a GPA of 2.0, and have completed the upper-division writing requirement by taking a seminar in which they must submit a paper.

Organizations

Students edit the *Louisiana Law Review* and the newspaper *Civilian*. Moot court competitions include the Tullis Moot Court at the Law Center and at the regional and national Jessup Moot Court and National Moot Court competitions. Teams also participate in the F. Lee Bailey, Frederick Douglass, and Entertainment Law moot courts, and the American Trial Lawyers and Louisiana State Bar Association, Young Lawyers Division, Mock Trial competitions. Law student organizations, local chapters of national associations, and campus organizations include the Student Bar Association the Moot Court Board, the Public Interest Law Society, the LSU Law ACLU, Phi Alpha Delta, Phi Delta Phi, the Tax Club, the Black Law Students Association, and the Legal Association of Women.

Library

The law library contains 848,000 hardcopy volumes and 2,153,035 microform volume equivalents, and subscribes to 8221 serial publications. Such on-line databases and networks as CALI, CIS Universe, DIALOG, Dow-Jones, LEXIS, LOIS, NEXIS, OCLC First Search, WESTLAW, Wilsonline Indexes, ONLINE public access catalog, HeinOnline, LLMC Digital, JSTOR, and BNA ALL are available to law students for research. Special library collections include a digital library, a U.S. government document depository, a depository for Louisiana Supreme Court and Court of Appeals briefs and records, and international, comparative, and foreign law collections, include Roman Law, and Judge Paul M. Hebert Nuremberg War Crimes Trial Archive. Recently, the library renovated to add office space, an electronic classroom, a microform room, and a reserve room. The ratio of library volumes to faculty is 22,316 to 1 and to students is 1418 to 1. The ratio of seats in the library to students is 1 to 1.

Faculty

The law school has 38 full-time and 50 part-time faculty members, of whom 21 are women. According to AAUP standards for Category I institutions, faculty salaries are below average. About 27% of full-time faculty have a graduate law degree in addition to the J.D.; about 8% of part-time faculty have one. The ratio of full-time students to full-time faculty in an average class is 16 to 1; in a clinic, 10 to 1. The law school has a regular program of bringing visiting professors and other distinguished lecturers and visitors to campus. There is a chapter of the Order of the Coif.

Students

About 45% of the student body are women; 10%, minorities; 8%, African American; 1%, Asian American; and 1%, Hispanic. The majority of students come from Louisiana (72%). The average age of entering students is 24; age range is 21 to 52. About 80% of students enter directly from undergraduate school, 10% have a graduate degree, and 20% have worked full-time prior to entering law school. About 2% drop out after the first year for academic or personal reasons; 98% remain to receive a law degree.

Placement

J.D.s awarded:	n/av
Services available through: a separate law school placement center and Law Center Career Services	
Services: participation in 20 U.S.-wide job fairs and a judicial clerkship preparation course	
Special features: resume quick check, mock interviews for students, individual counseling, guest speakers, special programs, a career services library, and a judicial clerkship preparation course.	
Full-time job interviews:	38 employers
Summer job interviews:	78 employers
Placement by graduation:	n/av
Placement within 9 months:	92% of class
Average starting salary:	$27,500 to $160,000
Areas of placement:	
Private practice 2-10 attorneys	26%
Private practice 11-25 attorneys	16%
Private practice 26-50 attorneys	11%
Private practice 51-250 attorneys, self employed	7%
Judicial clerkships	21%
Government	9%
Business/industry	3%
Public interest	1%

Loyola Law School

919 Albany Street
Los Angeles, CA 90015

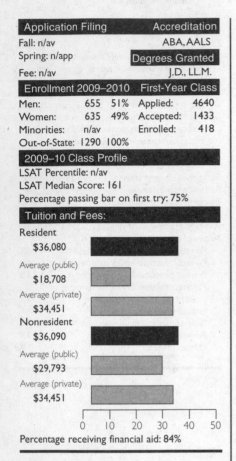

Application Filing	Accreditation
Fall: n/av	ABA, AALS
Spring: n/app	
Fee: n/av	**Degrees Granted**
	J.D., LL.M.

Enrollment 2009–2010   First-Year Class

Men:	655	51%	Applied:	4640
Women:	635	49%	Accepted:	1433
Minorities:	n/av		Enrolled:	418
Out-of-State:	1290	100%		

2009–10 Class Profile

LSAT Percentile: n/av
LSAT Median Score: 161
Percentage passing bar on first try: 75%

Tuition and Fees:

Resident
$36,080

Average (public)
$18,708

Average (private)
$34,451

Nonresident
$36,090

Average (public)
$29,793

Average (private)
$34,451

0   10   20   30   40   50

Percentage receiving financial aid: 84%

ADMISSIONS
In the fall 2009 first-year class, 4640 applied, 1433 were accepted, and 418 enrolled. The median GPA of the most recent first-year class was 3.44.

Requirements
Applicants must have a bachelor's degree and take the LSAT. The most important admission factors include academic achievement, LSAT results, and general background. No specific undergraduate courses are required. Candidates are not interviewed.

Procedure
Applicants should submit an application form, LSAT results, transcripts, a personal statement, TOEFL (where applicable), and 1 letters of recommendation. Notification of the admissions decision is December through June. The latest acceptable LSAT test date for fall entry is February. The law school uses the LSDAS.

Special
The law school recruits minority and disadvantaged students with programs such as the Open House, campus visits by faculty, and financial support for outstanding minority applicants. Additionally, there is a Summer Institute program for students who need additional preparation prior to law school. Requirements are not different for out-of-state students. Transfer students must have one year of credit, have attended an ABA-approved law school, and have above average performance at the prior law school.

Costs
Tuition and fees for the 2009-2010 academic year are $36,080 for full-time in-state students and $36,090 for out-of-state students. Tuition for part-time students is $24,260 per year. Books and supplies run $1000.

Financial Aid
About 84% of current law students receive some form of aid. The average annual amount of aid from all sources combined, including scholarships, loans, and work contracts, is $39,200; maximum, $56,300. Awards are based on need and merit. Required financial statement is the FAFSA. First-year students are notified about their financial aid application at time of acceptance.

About the Law School
Loyola Marymount University Loyola Law School was established in 1920 and is a private institution. The 2.5-acre campus is in an urban area ½ mile west of downtown Los Angeles. The primary mission of the law school is to educate men and women who will be leaders of both the legal profession and society, demonstrating in their practice of law and public service the highest standards of personal integrity, professional ethics, and a deep concern for social justice in the Jesuit Marymount tradition. Students have access to federal, state, county, city, and local agencies, courts, correctional facilities, law firms, and legal aid organizations in the Los Angeles area. Housing for students is not available on campus, but there is a housing referral service. All law school facilities are accessible to the physically disabled.

Calendar
The law school operates on a traditional semester basis. Courses for full-time students are offered both day and evening and must be completed within 5 years. For part-time students, courses are offered both day and evening and must be completed within 5 years. New full- and part-time students are admitted in the fall. There is a 7½ -week summer session. Transferable summer courses are offered.

Programs
In addition to the J.D., the law school offers the LL.M. Students may take relevant courses in other programs and apply credit toward the J.D.; a maximum of 6 credits may be applied. The following joint degrees may be earned: J.D./M.B.A. (Juris Doctor/Master of Business Administration).

Required
To earn the J.D., candidates must complete 87 total credits, of which 41 are for required courses. They must maintain a minimum GPA of 2.1 in the required courses. The following first-year courses are required of all students: Civil Procedure, Constitutional Law I, Contracts, Criminal Law, Legal Research and Writing, Property, and Torts. Required upper-level courses consist of a writing course, Constitutional Law II, Ethical Lawyering, and Evidence. The required orientation program for first-year students is 2 to 3 days.

Electives
The Loyola Law School offers concentrations in corporate law, criminal law, entertainment law, environmental law, family law, intellectual property law, international law, juvenile law, labor law, litigation, media law, securities law, sports law, tax law, torts and insurance, and . In addition, clinics are open to advanced students in good academic standing for a maximum of 14 clinical credits. Seminars and research programs are open to advanced students; these students are also eligible for internships, field work, and study-abroad programs. Seminars are generally worth 2 units each. The law school offers 4 study abroad programs: Costa Rica, Bologna, Italy, Beijing China, and

Phone: 213-736-1074
Fax: 213-736-6523
E-mail: admissions@lls.edu
Web: www.lls.edu

Contact
Assistant Dean of Admissions, 213-736-8128 for general inquiries; Dean for Enrollment Management, 213-736-1140 for financial aid information.

London, England. Tutorials are available to students with academic need. The most widely taken electives are Trust & Wills, Remedies, and Business Associations.

Graduation Requirements
In order to graduate, candidates must have a GPA of 2.0, have completed the upper-division writing requirement, and 58 resident credits in addition to 40 hours of community service work.

Organizations
The primary student-edited law reviews are *Loyola of Los Angeles Law Review*, *Loyola of Los Angeles International and Comparative Law Review*, *Loyola of Los Angeles Entertainment Law Review*, and the campus electronic newsletter "In Brief". Annual moot court competitions include the Jessup International Moot Court, National Civil Trial Competition, and ABA competition. Other competitions include the Byrne Trial Advocacy Competition, which includes on- and off-campus competitions in the fall and spring, the Black Law Students Association (BLSA) Moot Court Competitions, the Hispanic National Ba Association (HWBA) Moot Court Competition, and VIS Arbitration Moot Court. Law student organizations, include the Women's Law Association, Asian Pacific American Law Student's Association (APALSA), and Business Law Association. Local chapters of national associations include Phi Alpha Delta, National Lawyers Guild, and Public Interest Law Assocation. Other campus organizations include the Entertainment and Sports Law Society, Criminal Law Society, and St. Thomas More Honor Society.

Library
The law library contains 592,499 hard-copy volumes and 117,616 microform volume equivalents, and subscribes to 7019 serial publications. Such on-line databases and networks as CALI, CIS Universe, Infotrac, Legal-Trac, LEXIS, LOIS, Mathew Bender, NEXIS, OCLC First Search, RLIN, WESTLAW, Wilsonline Indexes, and Congressional Masterfile I and II, Congressional Universe, State Net, and ORION are available to law students for research. Special library collections include federal and state depositories and foreign collections of selected European, Latin American, and Pacific Rim countries. A complete U.S. legislative history from 1970 to the present includes all available records and briefs of the U.S. Supreme Court, law and popular culture, and a CBS News O.J. Simpson archive. Recently, the library The renovated library features generous study carrels with electrical outlets, comfortable lounge seating, 24 group study rooms, and 6 multi-media rooms. The library's Computer Resource Center offers 199 workstations and 700 Network connections throughout the library for laptop computer connections. The ratio of library volumes to faculty is 7900 to 1 and to students is 458 to 1.

Faculty
The law school has 75 full-time and 59 part-time faculty members, of whom 46 are women. The ratio of full-time students to full-time faculty in an average class is 16 to 1. The law school has a regular program of bringing visiting professors and other distinguished lecturers and visitors to campus. There is a chapter of the Order of the Coif.

Students
About 49% of the student body are women. The average age of entering students is 23.

Placement

J.D.s awarded:	n/av
Services available through: a separate law school placement center	
Services: information on practice areas, computer-assisted job search, and on-campus interview programs	
Special features: numerous workshops and panel discussions, an extensive resource library, special programs for students interested in pursuing government or public interest careers, and programs promoting issues of diversity and minority recruitment and hiring..	
Full-time job interviews:	n/av
Summer job interviews:	n/av
Placement by graduation:	n/av
Placement within 9 months:	97% of class
Average starting salary:	$60,000 to $125,000
Areas of placement:	
Private practice 2-100 attorneys	59%
Business/industry	21%
Public interest	9%
Government	8%
Judicial clerkships	3%
Academic	2%

LOYOLA UNIVERSITY CHICAGO

School of Law

25 East Pearson Street
Chicago, IL 60611

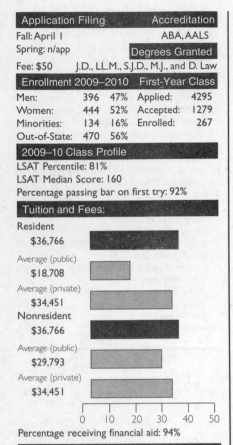

Application Filing	Accreditation
Fall: April 1	ABA, AALS
Spring: n/app	Degrees Granted
Fee: $50	J.D., LL.M., S.J.D., M.J., and D. Law

Enrollment 2009–2010		First-Year Class	
Men:	396 47%	Applied:	4295
Women:	444 52%	Accepted:	1279
Minorities:	134 16%	Enrolled:	267
Out-of-State:	470 56%		

2009–10 Class Profile

LSAT Percentile: 81%
LSAT Median Score: 160
Percentage passing bar on first try: 92%

Tuition and Fees:

Resident
$36,766

Average (public)
$18,708

Average (private)
$34,451

Nonresident
$36,766

Average (public)
$29,793

Average (private)
$34,451

0 10 20 30 40 50

Percentage receiving financial aid: 94%

ADMISSIONS

In the fall 2009 first-year class, 4295 applied, 1279 were accepted, and 267 enrolled. Twelve transfers enrolled. The median LSAT percentile of the most recent first-year class was 81; the median GPA was 3.47 on a scale of 4.0. The lowest LSAT percentile accepted was 26; the highest was 99.

Requirements

Applicants must have a bachelor's degree and take the LSAT. The most important admission factors include academic achievement, GPA, and LSAT results. No specific undergraduate courses are required. Candidates are not interviewed.

Procedure

The application deadline for fall entry is April 1. Applicants should submit an application form, LSAT results, transcripts, a personal statement, a nonrefundable application fee of $50, and 2 academic letters of recommendation. Notification of the admissions decision is within 4 weeks

of receipt of a completed application. The latest acceptable LSAT test date for fall entry is February. The law school uses the LSDAS.

Special

The law school recruits minority and disadvantaged students through national law forums and university-sponsored law days. Requirements are not different for out-of-state students. Transfer students must have one year of credit, have a minimum GPA of 3, have attended an ABA-approved law school; typically, students in the top 25% of their class are considered.

Costs

Tuition and fees for the 2009-2010 academic year are $36,766 for all full-time students. Tuition for part-time students is $27,716 per year. On-campus room and board costs about $13,200 annually; books and supplies run $1298.

Financial Aid

About 94% of current law students receive some form of aid. The average annual amount of aid from all sources combined, including scholarships, loans, and work contracts, is $34,500; maximum, $56,764. Awards are based on need and merit. Required financial statement is the FAFSA. The aid application deadline for fall entry is March 1. Special funds for minority or disadvantaged students include a variety of merit-based scholarships. First-year students are notified about their financial aid application 2 to 3 weeks after the law school receives results of the FAFSA.

About the Law School

Loyola University Chicago School of Law was established in 1908 and is a private institution. The campus is in an urban area in Chicago. The primary mission of the law school is to encourage the development of a sense of professional responsibility and respect for the judicial process, and an understanding of the social, moral, and ethical values inherent in the practice of law. Students have access to federal, state, county, city, and local agencies, courts, correctional facilities, law firms, and legal aid organizations in the Chicago area. Facilities of special interest to law students consist of the Water Tower campus, housing a cafeteria, coffee shop, and

bookstore. Loyola also has a campus in Rome, Italy. The law school is in the heart of Chicago's North Michigan Avenue shopping/tourist district, within blocks of Lake Michigan and cultural attractions including the Museum of Contemporary Art. Housing for students is available in a residence hall across from the law school, in apartments within walking distance of the law school, and in various Chicago neighborhoods. All law school facilities are accessible to the physically disabled.

Calendar

The law school operates on a traditional semester basis. Courses for full-time and part-time students are offered both day and evening and must be completed within 7 years. New full- and part-time students are admitted in the fall. There is a 10-week summer session. Transferable summer courses are offered.

Programs

In addition to the J.D., the law school offers the LL.M., S.J.D., M.J., and D. Law. Students may take relevant courses in other programs and apply credit toward the J.D.; a maximum of 9 credits may be applied. The following joint degrees may be earned: J.D./M.A. (Juris Doctor/ Master of Arts in political science), J.D./M.B.A. (Juris Doctor/ Master of Business Administration), and J.D./M.S.W. (Juris Doctor/ Master of Social Work).

Required

To earn the J.D., candidates must complete 86 total credits, of which 34 are for required courses. They must maintain a minimum GPA of 2.0 in the required courses. The following first-year courses are required of all students: Civil Procedure I, Constitutional Law I, Contracts, Criminal Law, Legal Research, Legal Writing I and II, Perspective Elective, Property I, and Torts. Required upper-level courses consist of Advocacy and Professional Responsibility. The required orientation program for first-year students is 3 half-days.

Electives

The School of Law offers concentrations in corporate law, criminal law, family law, international law, juvenile law, labor law, litigation, tax law, health law, and public interest law. With the exceptions of health

Phone: 312-915-7170
800-545-5744
Fax: 312-915-7906
E-mail: law-admissions@luc.edu
Web: www.luc.edu/law

Contact

Pamela A. Bloomquist, Assistant Dean, Law Admission and Financial Assistance, 312-915-7170 for general inquiries; Joseph Donahue, Financial Aid Counselor, 312-915-7170 for financial aid information.

ILLINOIS

law, tax law, advocacy, and child law, none of the concentrations are formalized. In addition, clinical legal experience is gained through the Loyola University Community Law Center, the Federal Tax Clinic, the Child Law Clinic, and the Business Law Clinic. Seminars, of which there are a variety, are offered for 2 to 3 credit hours to all students after the first year. Second- and third-year law students receive 3 hours credit for teaching a course called Street Law in Chicago-area high schools. Externships are available every semester; supervised experience is offered in judicial, criminal, corporate, health law, child law, and government for 2 or 3 credit hours. Individualized research projects, under the supervision of a faculty member, are available every semester for 1 to 2 hours credit. Special lecture series include the Philip H. Corboy Lecture, the Wing-Tat Lee Lecture on international and comparative law, the Christopher T. Hurley Lecture, and the Law and Literature Lecture. Study-abroad programs include the Rome Program and the Beijing Program, each 4-5-week summer programs offering 4 or 5 elective courses for 2 credits each. There is a 2-week London Advocacy Program and a Chile immersion program. Tutors are assigned to each first-year course section. Loyola's Academic Enhancement Program is conducted during the spring semester. The voluntary program provides extensive tutoring and faculty mentors to students who fall within the lower 20% of the first-year class. Minority programs include the Dean's Diversity Committe and the minority mentorship program. The Child Advocacy Program utilizes interdisciplinary instruction and field experience to train students to become child advocates. The Public Interest Law Program provides law students with opportunities to explore public interest law through the legal clinic. The most widely taken electives are Evidence, Business Organization, Federal Income Taxation.

Graduation Requirements
In order to graduate, candidates must have a GPA of 2.0 and 86 hours that fulfill all required courses.

Organizations

Student-edited publications include the *Loyola Law Journal, Loyola Consumer Law Review, Annals of Health Law, Public Interest Law Reporter, Children's Legal Rights Journal*, and the *International Law Review*. A monthly newsletter is published by the law school administration with student assistance. Moot court competitions include the National Moot Court, Jessup Competition, and Wagner (labor law). Other competitions include the National Mock Trial Competition and the Client Counseling Competition and Negotiations Competition, sponsored by the ABA. Loyola also participates annually in the Intra-school Moot Court Competition, Chicago Bar, Illinois Bar, Niagara, Sutherland Rich (intellectual property), National Juvenile Law, National Health Law, ABA, Hispanic Bar, Frederick Douglass, Willem Vis, and Thomas Tang competitions. Law student organizations, include the Health Law Society, Child Law Society, and National Lawyers Guild. There are more than 30 active student organizations that provide the law community with a broad range of legal topics and interests. Local chapters of national associations include Phi Alpha Delta and Decalogue Society. Other campus organizations include Black Law Students Association, American Society of International Law, Latin American Law Students Association.

Library

The law library contains 398,495 hardcopy volumes and 220,923 microform volume equivalents, and subscribes to 4516 serial publications. Such on-line databases and networks as CALI, CIS Universe, Infotrac, Legal-Trac, LEXIS, LOIS, NEXIS, OCLC First Search, WESTLAW, Wilsonline Indexes, and CCH, BNA, HeinOnline, Pegasus, WorldCat, LLMC-Digital, CIAO, Constitutions of the U.S. (National and State), and SmartBooks. are available to law students for research. Special library collections include a G.P.O. depository, an Illinois depository, and a collection on medical jurisprudence, papers of justice Mary Ann McMorrow, and Law and Popular Culture. Wireless access is available throughout the library. The ratio of library volumes to faculty is 8302 to 1 and to students is 474 to 1. The ratio of seats in the library to students is 1 to 2.

Faculty

The law school has 48 full-time and 113 part-time faculty members, of whom 69 are women. According to AAUP standards for Category I institutions, faculty salaries are below average. About 10% of full-time

Placement

J.D.s awarded:	304

Services available through: a separate law school placement center

Services: job listings websites available to students and alumni founding member PSLawNet (public service law database)

Special features: mock interviews, minority job fairs, the Patent Law Interview Program, the Midwest Public Interest Law Career Conference, 3 computer terminals and printer for resume and cover letter production and career research, the Public Service Law Network Worldwide Internet database, host of many networking and mentoring events.,

Full-time job interviews:	15 employers
Summer job interviews:	40 employers
Placement by graduation:	62% of class
Placement within 9 months:	88% of class
Average starting salary:	$47,167 to $115,077

Areas of placement:

Private practice 2-10 attorneys	39%
Private practice 11-25 attorneys	11%
Private practice 26-50 attorneys	4%
Private practice 51-100 attorneys	7%
Business/industry	17%
Government	12%
Public interest	4%
Judicial clerkships	3%
Academic	1%

faculty have a graduate law degree in addition to the J.D. The ratio of full-time students to full-time faculty in an average class is 15 to 1; in a clinic, 8 to 1. The law school has a regular program of bringing visiting professors and other distinguished lecturers and visitors to campus.

Students

About 52% of the student body are women; 16%, minorities; 5%, African American; 4%, Asian American; 5%, Hispanic; 1%, Native American; and 8%, 10% unknown; foreign national. The majority of students come from Illinois (44%). The average age of entering students is 24; age range is 21 to 59. About 33% of students enter directly from undergraduate school, 10% have a graduate degree, and 66% have worked full-time prior to entering law school. About 1% drop out after the first year for academic or personal reasons; 95% remain to receive a law degree.

School of Law

7214 St. Charles Avenue
New Orleans, LA 70118

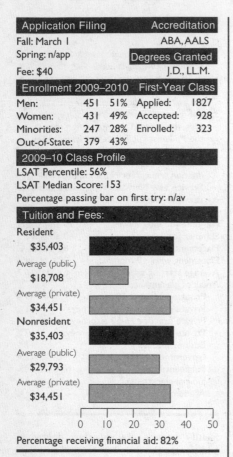

Application Filing	Accreditation
Fall: March 1	ABA, AALS
Spring: n/app	**Degrees Granted**
Fee: $40	J.D., LL.M.

Enrollment 2009–2010		First-Year Class	
Men:	451 51%	Applied:	1827
Women:	431 49%	Accepted:	928
Minorities:	247 28%	Enrolled:	323
Out-of-State:	379 43%		

2009–10 Class Profile
LSAT Percentile: 56%
LSAT Median Score: 153
Percentage passing bar on first try: n/av

Tuition and Fees:

Resident
$35,403

Average (public)
$18,708

Average (private)
$34,451

Nonresident
$35,403

Average (public)
$29,793

Average (private)
$34,451

0 10 20 30 40 50

Percentage receiving financial aid: 82%

ADMISSIONS

In the fall 2009 first-year class, 1827 applied, 928 were accepted, and 323 enrolled. Eight transfers enrolled. The median LSAT percentile of the most recent first-year class was 56; the median GPA was 3.27 on a scale of 4.0. The lowest LSAT percentile accepted was 23; the highest was 96.

Requirements
Eary admits may be admitted with 3/4's of their degree requirements. Applicants must take the LSAT. Minimum acceptable GPA is 2.0 on a scale of 4.0. The most important admission factors include LSAT results, GPA, and academic achievement. No specific undergraduate courses are required. Candidates are not interviewed.

Procedure
The priority application deadline for fall entry is March 1. Applicants should submit an application form, LSAT results, transcripts, a personal statement, a nonrefundable application fee of $40, and 3

recommended letters of recommendation. Notification of the admissions decision is 4 to 6 weeks after the file is complete. The latest acceptable LSAT test date for fall entry is generally December for full-time students. The law school uses the LSDAS.

Special
The law school recruits minority and disadvantaged students through alumni involvement, recruitment at institutions with traditionally minority-dominated enrollment, the use of CLEO, and the purchase of names and addresses of minority prospects from LSAC. Requirements are not different for out-of-state students. Transfer students must have one year of credit, have attended an ABA-approved law school, and have entering LSAT and undergraduate GPA eligible for acceptance at Loyola and above average law school GPA.

Costs

Tuition and fees for the 2009-2010 academic year are $35,403 for all full-time students. Tuition for part-time students is $24,333 per year. On-campus room and board costs about $10,600 annually; books and supplies run $1500.

Financial Aid

About 82% of current law students receive some form of aid. The average annual amount of aid from all sources combined, including scholarships, loans, and work contracts, is $35,000; maximum, $55,703. Awards are based on need and merit. Required financial statement is the FAFSA. The aid application deadline for fall entry is June 1. Special funds for minority or disadvantaged students consist of grants based on merit alone. First-year students are notified about their financial aid application at time of acceptance. Scholarships/grant notification is sent with the acceptance letter. Loan notification begins in March and is sent as acceptance is made and complete FAFSA is received.

About the Law School

Loyola University of New Orleans School of Law was established in 1914 and is a private institution. The 4.2-acre campus is in an urban area of New Orleans. The primary mission of the law school is to educate future members of the bar to be skilled advocates and sensitive counselors-

at-law committed to ethical standards in pursuit of human dignity for all. Students have access to federal, state, county, city, and local agencies, courts, correctional facilities, law firms, and legal aid organizations in the New Orleans area. Facilities of special interest to law students include the U.S. Court of Appeals for the Fifth Circuit, the Supreme Court of the State of Louisiana, the U.S. Court for the Eastern District of Louisiana, and the Louisiana Legislature. Housing for students is available in a residence hall located directly across the street from the law school building; there is no married student housing on campus. All law school facilities are accessible to the physically disabled.

Calendar

The law school operates on a traditional semester basis. For full-time students required courses are offered day only; electives, day and evening, and must be completed within 5 years. For part-time students, required courses are offered, evening only; electives, day and evening and must be completed within 5 years. New full- and part-time students are admitted in the fall. There is an 8-week summer session. Transferable summer courses are offered.

Programs

In addition to the J.D., the law school offers the LL.M. The following joint degrees may be earned: J.D./M.B.A. (Juris Doctor/Master of Business Administration), J.D./M.P.A. (Juris Doctor/Master of Public Administration), and J.D./M.U.R.P. (Juris Doctor/Master of Urban and Regional Planning).

Required
To earn the J.D., candidates must complete 90 total credits, of which 53 are for required courses. They must maintain a minimum GPA of 2.0 in the required courses. The following first-year courses are required of all students: Civil Law Property I or Common Law Property I, Civil Law Property II or Common Law Property II, Civil Procedure I and II, Common Law Contracts for Civil Law Students or Contracts I, Conventional Obligations or Contracts II, Criminal Law, Legal Profession, Legal Research and Writing, Moot Court, and Torts I and II. Required upper-level courses consist of Administration of Criminal Justice I, Business Organiza-

Phone: 504-861-5575
Fax: 504-861-5772
E-mail: *ladmit@loyno.edu*
Web: *law.loyno.edu*

Contact

K. Michele Allison-Davis, Assistant Dean of Admissions, 504-861-5575 for general inquiries; Nadine Lauret, Assistant Director of Financial Aid, 504-861-5551 for financial aid information.

LOUISIANA

tions I, Constitutional Law I, Donations or Civil Law of Persons or Security Rights or Community Property (choose 2), Evidence, Law and Poverty, Sales and Leases (Civil Law Division only), and Successions or Trusts and Estates. All students must complete 8 skills points in order to graduate. Loyola has a mandatory skills curriculum; courses that students must take for 8 skills points are drawn from the following categories: office practice, trial practice, appellate practice, and pro bono practice.The required orientation program for first-year students is held for 8 days prior to the beginning of classes. Students attend a 13-hour Legal Methods course designed to provide the fundamentals of briefing cases, classroom interaction, outlining for exams and other essentials needed to begin law school confidently. Students also complete requirements for registration, receive welcoming remarks from university officials, meet professors, and meet with upper-level students.

Electives

The School of Law offers concentrations in corporate law, criminal law, entertainment law, environmental law, family law, international law, litigation, maritime law, tax law, civil law, and public interest law. In addition, there are several clinics for third-year students who may earn a total of 9 credit hours for 3 semesters (including the summer semester). At the Public Law Center, students participate in legislative and administrative advocacy, and at the Loyola Law Clinic, students participate in a clinical setting, working on both civil and criminal cases, as well as mediation. Seminars are offered as part of the regular curriculum. Credit is usually 2 hours. Second- and third-year law students in the upper third of their class may participate in externship programs. Students devote at least 12 hours a week to various assignments for a total of 4 credits earned over 2 semesters. Independent research projects may be undertaken under the supervision of a professor for 1 or 2 credit hours, depending on the project. A Street Law course is available. Loyola offers several lecture series that promote the legal profession. No credit is given and attendance is voluntary. There are study-abroad programs in Cuernavaca, Mexico; Brazil or Costa Rica; Moscow and St. Petersburg, Russia; Budapest, Hungary; and Vienna, Austria. All programs are open to second- and

third-year students who may earn a total of 6 to 8 credits. Second- and third-year students may serve as Teacher Assistants (T.A.) in the Legal Research and Writing and Moot Court programs. The Academic Success Program is maintained for students who need assistance with organizing and preparing for classes and exams. Diversity grants based on merit are available for entering first-year students. The most widely taken electives are Mediation, Family Law, and Negotiable Instruments.

Graduation Requirements

In order to graduate, candidates must have a GPA of 2.0, have completed the upper-division writing requirement, and have fulfilled the Perspective requirement, 1 of 3 possible courses that give a philosophical and historical perspective on law.

Organizations

Students edit the *Loyola Law Review*, *Loyola Journal of Public Interest Law*, *Maritime Law Journal*, *Loyola Intellectual Property and High Technology Law Annual*, and the newspaper, *The Code*. Moot court competitions include the National Moot Court Competition, Stetson International Environment Moot Court Competition, and National Mardi Gras Invitational Competition. Other competitions include the William C. Vis International Commercial Arbitration Competition, Frederick Douglass Moot Court Competition (participation by the Black Law Students Association), the Thomas Tang Competition (participation by the Asian Pacific American Law Student Association), Pepperdine Entertainment Law Competition, Jerome Prince Memorial Evidence Competition, First Amendment Competition, and St. John's Duberstein Bankruptcy Competition. Law student organizations, local chapters of national associations, and campus organizations include the Student Bar Association, Black Law Students Association, Hispanic-American Law Students Association, Delta Theta Phi, Phi Delta Phi, National Lawyers Guild, Communications Law Society, JD/MBA Society, and Loyola Environmental Law Society.

Library

The law library contains 404,868 hardcopy volumes and 178,132 microform volume equivalents, and subscribes to 3549 serial publications. Such on-line databases and networks as CALI, CIS Universe, DIALOG, Infotrac, Legal-Trac, LEXIS, NEXIS, OCLC First Search, WESTLAW,

Placement

J.D.s awarded:	288
Services available through: a separate law school placement center and the university placement center	
Services: coordination of speakers for various employment opportunities, a student news and job information monthly newsletter, and a resume bank	
Full-time job interviews:	70 employers
Summer job interviews:	n/av
Placement by graduation:	55% of class
Placement within 9 months:	87% of class
Average starting salary:	n/av
Areas of placement:	
Private practice all size firms	62%
Government	12%
Business/industry	11%
Judicial clerkships	10%
Public interest	4%
Academic	1%

and Wilsonline Indexes are available to law students for research. Special library collections include French, Quebec, and Scottish law; U.S. government documents and Louisiana state documents; and GATT depository. Recently, the library added 2 new computer laboratories with more than 59 computers and on-line catalog, and wireless Internet access. All new furniture has also been purchased. The ratio of library volumes to faculty is 8097 to 1 and to students is 459 to 1. The ratio of seats in the library to students is 1 to 2.

Faculty

The law school has 50 full-time and 57 part-time faculty members, of whom 32 are women. According to AAUP standards for Category IIA institutions, faculty salaries are average. About 24% of full-time faculty have a graduate law degree in addition to the J.D. The ratio of full-time students to full-time faculty in an average class is 17 to 1; in a clinic, 10 to 1. The law school has a regular program of bringing visiting professors and other distinguished lecturers and visitors to campus.

Students

About 49% of the student body are women; 28%, minorities; 15%, African American; 5%, Asian American; 8%, Hispanic; and 1%, Native American. The majority of students come from Louisiana (57%). The average age of entering students is 25; age range is 21 to 56. About 3% drop out after the first year for academic or personal reasons; 99% remain to receive a law degree.

Office of Admissions,
P.O. Box 1881 Milwaukee,
WI 53201-1881

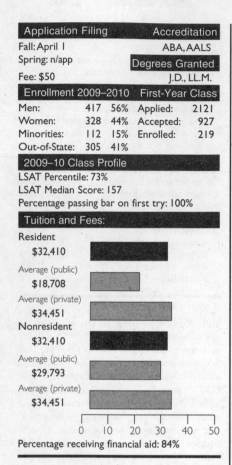

Application Filing	Accreditation
Fall: April 1	ABA, AALS
Spring: n/app	
Fee: $50	Degrees Granted
	J.D., LL.M.

Enrollment 2009–2010			First-Year Class	
Men:	417	56%	Applied:	2121
Women:	328	44%	Accepted:	927
Minorities:	112	15%	Enrolled:	219
Out-of-State:	305	41%		

2009–10 Class Profile
LSAT Percentile: 73%
LSAT Median Score: 157
Percentage passing bar on first try: 100%

Tuition and Fees:

Resident
$32,410

Average (public)
$18,708

Average (private)
$34,451

Nonresident
$32,410

Average (public)
$29,793

Average (private)
$34,451

0 10 20 30 40 50

Percentage receiving financial aid: 84%

ADMISSIONS
In the fall 2009 first-year class, 2121 applied, 927 were accepted, and 219 enrolled. Fifteen transfers enrolled. The median LSAT percentile of the most recent first-year class was 73; the median GPA was 3.39 on a scale of 4.0.

Requirements
Applicants must have a bachelor's degree and take the LSAT. No specific undergraduate courses are required. Candidates are not interviewed.

Procedure
The application deadline for fall entry is April 1. Applicants should submit an application form, LSAT results, transcripts, a personal statement, the TOEFL for students from non-English-speaking countries, a nonrefundable application fee of $50, 1 letters of recommendation, and accepted students must pay a nonrefundable $350 first tuition deposit and a $350 second tuition deposit; both are applied

to the first-semester tuition. Notification of the admissions decision is on a rolling basis. The latest acceptable LSAT test date for fall entry is February. The law school uses the LSDAS.

Special
The law school recruits minority and disadvantaged students through CRS, contacts with current students and alumni of color, targeted recruitment, and visits to Law Forums and college campuses with significant minority representation. Requirements are not different for out-of-state students. Transfer students must have one year of credit, have attended an ABA-approved law school, and must complete 54 credits at Marquette.

Costs
Tuition and fees for the 2009-2010 academic year are $32,410 for all full-time students. Tuition for part-time students is $10,360 per year. Books and supplies run $1200.

Financial Aid
About 84% of current law students receive some form of aid. Awards are based on need and merit. Required financial statement is the FAFSA. The aid application deadline for fall entry is March 1. Special funds for minority or disadvantaged students include targeted scholarships. First-year students are notified about their financial aid application at after acceptance but prior to enrollment if financial aid forms were filed in a timely fashion.

About the Law School
Marquette University Law School was established in 1892 and is a private institution. The 80-acre campus is in an urban area adjacent to downtown Milwaukee. The primary mission of the law school is to offer a balanced curriculum noted for its comprehensive teaching of both the theory and practice of law and to instill in students a sense of professional responsibility. Marquette graduates are admitted to the Wisconsin bar without taking the bar exam. Students have access to federal, state, county, city, and local agencies, courts, correctional facilities, law firms, and legal aid organizations in the Milwaukee area. The municipal courthouse is located 2 blocks away. The federal

courthouse is approximately one-half mile away. Facilities of special interest to law students include the Legal Research Center, Sensenbrenner Hall, and fitness and recreation centers. Housing for students consists of campus area apartments. The Office of Residence Life assists students with off-campus accommodations. About 99% of the law school facilities are accessible to the physically disabled.

Calendar
The law school operates on a traditional semester basis. Courses for full-time students are offered both day and evening and must be completed within 4 years. For part-time students, courses are offered both day and evening and must be completed within 6 years. New full- and part-time students are admitted in the fall. There is a 2 summer-week summer session. Transferable summer courses are offered.

Programs
In addition to the J.D., the law school offers the LL.M. Students may take relevant courses in other programs and apply credit toward the J.D.; a maximum of 9 credits may be applied. The following joint degrees may be earned: J.D. (certificate in dispute resolution), J.D./M.A. (Juris Doctor/Master of Arts in bioethics, international affair), and J.D./M.B.A. (Juris Doctor/Master of Business Administration, Master of Bus).

Required
To earn the J.D., candidates must complete 90 total credits, of which 38 are for required courses. They must maintain a minimum GPA of 2.0 in the required courses. The following first-year courses are required of all students: Civil Procedure, Constitutional Law, Contracts, Criminal Law, Law and Ethics of Lawyering, Legal Writing and Research, Property, and Torts. Required upper-level courses consist of a Perspectives course, a process elective, a public law elective, a seminar, a workshop course, Advanced Legal Research, Evidence, The Law Governing Lawyers, and Trusts and Estates. The required orientation program for first-year students takes place in the days prior to the start of the semester and includes all aspects of law school. Students meet

Phone: 414-288-6767
Fax: 414-288-0676
E-mail: law.admission@marquette.edu
Web: http://law.marquette.edu

Contact

Law School Office of Admissions, 414-288-6767 for general inquiries; Office of Student Financial Aid, 414-288-4000 for financial aid information.

WISCONSIN

with professors and upper-class students in small groups.

Electives

The Law School offers concentrations in corporate law, criminal law, environmental law, family law, international law, juvenile law, labor law, litigation, sports law, tax law, torts and insurance, and constitutional law, and intellectual property. In addition, clinical training is available through the Prosecutor Clinic, Defender Clinic, Unemployment Compensation Clinic, and Small Claims Mediation Clinic. Seminars provide students with an opportunity to work intensely under faculty supervision. Internships are available in both appellate and trial courts, including the Wisconsin Supreme Court the U.S. Court of Appeals for the Seventh Circuit, and the Milwaukee County Circuit Courts. Research programs provide students with an appreciation of the relationship of law to other disciplines and an understanding of the process through which legal doctrine is formed as well as comparisons of the American legal system with other legal systems. Supervised field-work programs provide students with the opportunity to intern with a variety of governmental and public service agencies. There is an Academic Support Program for first-year students. The school actively recruits minority students. The most widely taken electives are skills courses, upper-level electives in specific doctrinal areas, and clinical courses.

Graduation Requirements

In order to graduate, candidates must have a GPA of 2.0 and have completed the upper-division writing requirement.

Organizations

Students edit the *Marquette Law Review, Marquette Sports Law Review, Marquette Intellectual Property Law Review, Marquette Elder's Advisor*, and the *Federation of Insurance and Corporate Counsel Quarterly*. Moot court competitions include the Jenkins Moot Court, sports law, and alternative dispute resolution competitions. National competitions include the National Moot Court, Philip C. Jessup International, Giles Rich Intellectual Property, and Sports Law Moot Court. Law student organizations, local chapters of national associations, and campus organizations include the Student Bar Association, Health Law Society, Environmental Law Society, Public Interest Law Society, Sports Law Society, Black Law Students Association, Delta Theta Phi, Phi Alpha Delta, and Phi Delta Phi.

Library

The law library contains 362,586 hardcopy volumes and 163,520 microform volume equivalents, and subscribes to 3200 serial publications. Such on-line databases and networks as CALI, CIS Universe, Infotrac, Legal-Trac, LEXIS, LOIS, NEXIS, OCLC First Search, WESTLAW, Wilsonline Indexes, and BNA, HeinOnline, and CIS Congressional are available to law students for research. Special library collections include a federal depository. Recently, the library added new chairs and tables plus a soft seating area. The ratio of library volumes to faculty is 7554 to 1 and to students is 487 to 1. The ratio of seats in the library to students is 1 to 2.

Faculty

The law school has 48 full-time and 71 part-time faculty members, of whom 47 are women. According to AAUP standards for Category I institutions, faculty salaries are below average. About 8% of full-time faculty have a graduate law degree in addition to the J.D. The ratio of full-time students to full-time faculty in an average class is 19 to 1; in a clinic, 8 to 1. The law school has a regular program of bringing visiting professors and other distinguished lecturers and visitors to campus.

Students

About 44% of the student body are women; 15%, minorities; 5%, African American; 4%, Asian American; 5%, Hispanic; and 1%, Native American. The majority of students come from the Midwest (83%). The average age of entering students is 25; age range is 19 to 45. About 49% of students enter directly from undergraduate school and 11% have a graduate degree. About 9% drop out after the first year for academic or personal reasons; 91% remain to receive a law degree.

Placement

J.D.s awarded:	216
Services available through: a separate law school placement center	
Services: mock interviews	
Special features: personal counseling with students, access to a computer and a laser printer in the office to prepare resumes and cover letters, and access to an on-line WESTLAW database of lawyers and judicial clerkships.	
Full-time job interviews:	18 employers
Summer job interviews:	38 employers
Placement by graduation:	66% of class
Placement within 9 months:	93% of class
Average starting salary:	$32,000 to $170,000
Areas of placement:	
Private practice 2-10 attorneys	32%
Private practice 11-25 attorneys	11%
Private practice 26-50 attorneys	3%
Private practice 51-100 attorneys	2%
Private practice 101+ attorneys	3%
Solo practice	14%
Business/industry	14%
Government	9%
Public interest	5%
Judicial clerkships	4%
Academic	3%
Military	1%

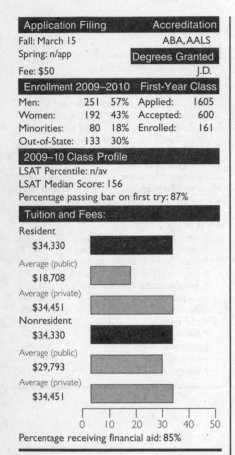

Application Filing			Accreditation
Fall: March 15			ABA, AALS
Spring: n/app			Degrees Granted
Fee: $50			J.D.

Enrollment 2009–2010		First-Year Class	
Men:	251 57%	Applied:	1605
Women:	192 43%	Accepted:	600
Minorities:	80 18%	Enrolled:	161
Out-of-State:	133 30%		

2009–10 Class Profile
LSAT Percentile: n/av
LSAT Median Score: 156
Percentage passing bar on first try: 87%

Tuition and Fees:

Resident
$34,330

Average (public)
$18,708

Average (private)
$34,451

Nonresident
$34,330

Average (public)
$29,793

Average (private)
$34,451

0   10   20   30   40   50

Percentage receiving financial aid: 85%

ADMISSIONS

In the fall 2009 first-year class, 1605 applied, 600 were accepted, and 161 enrolled. Six transfers enrolled. The median GPA of the most recent first-year class was 3.43.

Requirements
Applicants must have a bachelor's degree and take the LSAT. The most important admission factors include LSAT results, GPA, and writing ability. All factors in the application process are important and evaluated. No specific undergraduate courses are required. Candidates are not interviewed.

Procedure
The application deadline for fall entry is March 15. Applicants should submit an application form, LSAT results, transcripts, a personal statement, a nonrefundable application fee of $50, 2 letters of recommendation, and a personal statement to be used as a writing sample. Notification of the admissions decision is on a rolling basis. The latest acceptable LSAT test date for fall entry is February. The law school uses the LSDAS.

Special
The law school recruits minority and disadvantaged students by visiting colleges that are traditionally minority schools and by using the Candidate Referral Service of Law Services to identify qualified minority students. The law school also hosts events on campus. Requirements are not different for out-of-state students. Transfer students must have 1 year of credit, have attended an ABA-approved law school, and be in top 50% of their class, submit a letter of good standing from their dean, have 2 letters of recommendation from their professors, subscribe to LSDAS, and submit a current transcript of all law schools attended to Mercer.

Costs

Tuition and fees for the 2009-2010 academic year are $34,330 for all full-time students. On-campus room and board costs about $14,620 annually; books and supplies run $1380.

Financial Aid

About 85% of current law students receive some form of aid. The average annual amount of aid from all sources combined, including scholarships, loans, and work contracts, is $43,361; maximum, $50,900. Awards are based on need and merit. Students are awarded merit scholarships and need- and non-need based loans. Required financial statements are the FAFSA and institutional application. The aid application deadline for fall entry is April 1. Special funds for minority or disadvantaged students include the National CLEO Program and Georgia Fellowship Program. First-year students are notified about their financial aid application at at the time of application to law school.

About the Law School

Mercer University Walter F. George School of Law was established in 1873 and is a private institution. The 130-acre campus is in an urban area 80 miles south of Atlanta. The primary mission of the law school is to produce genuinely good lawyers, in an ethical and pragmatic sense, who are well-equipped to begin their careers in the practice of law. Students have access to federal, state, county, city, and local agencies, courts, correctional facilities, law firms, and legal aid organizations in the Macon area. Facilities of special interest to law students include a 4-story reproduction of Independence Hall that sits atop Coleman Hill about a mile from the Main Mercer University campus. Students have 24-hour access to the building and law library. In addition, each first year law student receives a laptop computer. Housing for students consists of privately owned and university owned apartments available within walking distance of the school, and multiple apartment complexes throughout the city. All law school facilities are accessible to the physically disabled.

Calendar

The law school operates on a traditional semester basis. Courses for full-time students are offered and summer school offers evening classes and must be completed within 3 years. For part-time students, courses are offered and summer school offers evening classes and must be completed within 7 years. New full- and part-time students are admitted in the fall. There is a 7 -week summer session. Transferable summer courses are offered.

Programs

Students may take relevant courses in other programs and apply credit toward the J.D.; a maximum of 12 hours for JD/MBA degree and 6 hours for Business certificate program credits may be applied. The following joint degrees may be earned: J.D./M.B.A. (Juris Doctor/Master of Business Administration).

Required
To earn the J.D., candidates must complete 91 total credits, of which 59 are for required courses. They must maintain a minimum GPA of an overall average of 76 in the required courses. The following first-year courses are required of all students: American Constitutional System, Contracts, Criminal Law, Introduction to Law Study, Introduction to Legal Research, Jurisdiction and Judgments, Legal Analysis, Legal Profession, Legal Writing I, Property, Sales, and Torts. Required upper-level courses consist of Civil Lawsuits, Evidence, Introduction to

Phone: 478-301-2605
800-637-2378
Fax: 478-301-2989
E-mail: Sutton_me@law.mercer.edu
Web: www.Law.Mercer.edu

Contact

Marilyn E. Sutton, Assistant Dean of Admissions and Financial Aid, 478-301-2605 for general inquiries; Stephanie Powell, Director of Financial Aid, 478-301-2064 for financial aid information.

GEORGIA

Alternative Dispute Resolution, Introduction to Counseling, Law of Lawyering, Legal Writing II, and Statutory Law and Analysis. All students must take Introduction to Counseling and Introduction to Dispute Resolution courses. Each student also must elect at least 1 course from a list of advanced skills courses that use simulations of law practice situations.The required orientation program for first-year students is a 1-week, Introduction to Law Study course, taught before the start of regular first-year courses. It carries 1 hour of credit, has an exam, and is graded. Additional information is offered in a 3-day session before the start of classes.

Electives

The Walter F. George School of Law offers concentrations in corporate law, criminal law, environmental law, family law, intellectual property law, international law, labor law, litigation, media law, securities law, tax law, torts and insurance, legal writing, research and drafting certificate program, and law and public service program. In addition, clinics include the Public Defender Criminal Defense Clinic, worth 3 credits; the Habeaus Project for second- and third-year students, worth 4 credits. Each student must elect at least 1 seminar in the third year or 2 credit hours. Approximately 15 seminars are offered each year on a range of subjects from legal ethics to mass media. Supervised internships of 2 to 4 credit hours may be arranged under the Public Interest Practicum Program. Judicial Field Placement, a 3 to 4 credit course for second-year students, places students with federal and state court judges to serve as clerks. There is a weekly classroom component as well. Mercer offers numerous lecture series including the John James lecture, Law Review Symposium, and Ethics and Professionalism symposium. Study abroad programs are available in conjunction with Stetson University Law School. An academic tutorial program offers one-on-one mentoring to any student in academic difficulty. Minority programs include Mercer's BLSA organization, which conducts minority orientation prior to the first year. Various minority groups on campus visit HBC schools during the year and work with BLSA and minority student organizations. Mercer Pro Bono Clinic and Public Interest Foundation provide volunteer services for local legal aid organizations. The most widely taken electives are

Business Associations, Criminal Procedure, and Domestic Relations.

Graduation Requirements

In order to graduate, candidates must have completed the upper-division writing requirement.

Organizations

Students edit the *Mercer Law Review*, and the *Journal of Southern Legal History*. National moot court competitions held annually are the National Moot Court, Gabrielli National Family Law, and Gibbons National Criminal Procedure. Other competitions include the Georgia Intrastate, Vale National Corporate Law, National Negotiation, National Client Counseling, National Civil Rights, and Frederick Douglass competitions. Law student organizations include the Association of Women Law Students, Student Bar Association, and Project Equality. There are local chapters of Phi Alpha Delta, Phi Delta Phi, and Black Law Student Association. Other campus organizations include Environmental Law Society, International Law Society, and Legal Aid Volunteer Association.

Library

The law library contains 195,673 hardcopy volumes and 147,045 microform volume equivalents, and subscribes to 3155 serial publications. Such on-line databases and networks as CALI, CIS Universe, LEXIS, NEXIS, OCLC First Search, WESTLAW, Wilsonline Indexes, Galileo, CQ Researcher, LLMC digital, HeinOnline, JSTOR, CCH, CIA, and BNA are available to law students for research. Special library collections include Georgia legal research materials, federal depository library, and Southern legal history. Recently, the library installed soft seating and space for collaborative work. The ratio of library volumes to faculty is 10,957 to 1 and to students is 791 to 1. The ratio of seats in the library to students is 1 to 1.

Faculty

The law school has 32 full-time and 39 part-time faculty members, of whom 20 are women. According to AAUP standards for Category IIA institutions, faculty salaries are average. About 18% of full-time faculty have a graduate law degree

Placement	
J.D.s awarded:	159

Services available through: a separate law school placement center
Special features: videotaped practice interviews and critiques, job fairs and consortia, and seminars and educational panels on types of practice and interviewing..

Full-time job interviews:	10 employers
Summer job interviews:	35 employers
Placement by graduation:	55% of class
Placement within 9 months:	88% of class
Average starting salary:	$33,000 to $145,000

Areas of placement:

Private practice 2-10 attorneys	23%
Private practice 11-25 attorneys	13%
Private practice 26-50 attorneys	6%
Private practice 51-100 attorneys	4%
2% solo, 2% unknown,	16%
Government	14%
Judicial clerkships	8%
Business/industry	5%
Military	4%
Academic	4%
Public interest	3%

in addition to the J.D.; about 18% of part-time faculty have one. The ratio of full-time students to full-time faculty in an average class is 12 to 1. The law school has a regular program of bringing visiting professors and other distinguished lecturers and visitors to campus.

Students

About 43% of the student body are women; 18%, minorities; 9%, African American; 6%, Asian American; 1%, Hispanic; 1%, Native American; and 1%, Chicano/Mexican, Puerto Rican. The majority of students come from the South (90%). The average age of entering students is 23; age range is 19 to 37. About 4% drop out after the first year for academic or personal reasons; 96% remain to receive a law degree.

College of Law

230 Law College Bldg.
East Lansing, MI 48824-1300

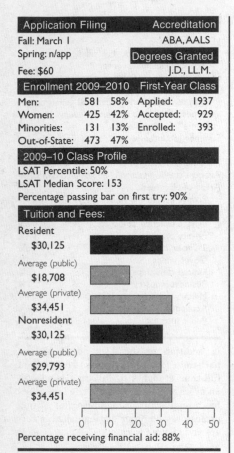

Application Filing	Accreditation
Fall: March 1	ABA, AALS
Spring: n/app	Degrees Granted
Fee: $60	J.D., LL.M.

Enrollment 2009–2010		First-Year Class	
Men:	581 58%	Applied:	1937
Women:	425 42%	Accepted:	929
Minorities:	131 13%	Enrolled:	393
Out-of-State:	473 47%		

2009–10 Class Profile
LSAT Percentile: 50%
LSAT Median Score: 153
Percentage passing bar on first try: 90%

Tuition and Fees:

Resident
$30,125

Average (public)
$18,708

Average (private)
$34,451

Nonresident
$30,125

Average (public)
$29,793

Average (private)
$34,451

0 10 20 30 40 50

Percentage receiving financial aid: 88%

ADMISSIONS

In a recent year, 1937 applied, 929 were accepted, and 393 enrolled. Forty-four transfers enrolled. The median LSAT percentile of the most recent first-year class was 50; the median GPA was 3.32 on a scale of 4.0. The lowest LSAT percentile accepted was 10; the highest was 97.

Requirements
Applicants must have a bachelor's degree and take the LSAT. The most important admission factors include GPA, LSAT results, and academic achievement. No specific undergraduate courses are required. Candidates are not interviewed.

Procedure
Applicants should submit an application form, LSAT results, transcripts, ACT, SAT I, GRE, and GMAT, a nonrefundable application fee of $60, 2 letters required letters of recommendation, and Accepted students must submit a nonrefundable tuition deposit of $700, which is credited toward tuition. Notification of the admis-

sions decision is on a rolling basis. The latest acceptable LSAT test date for fall entry is February. The law school uses the LSDAS. Check with the school for current application deadlines.

Special
The law school recruits minority and disadvantaged students by means of conducting special interviews for acceptance purposes, awarding half- and full-tuition scholarships, and sponsoring an annual Minority Recruitment Conference. Requirements are not different for out-of-state students. Transfer students must have one year of credit, have a minimum GPA of 3, have attended an ABA-approved law school, and be in good academic standing, and be eligible to return to the law school they currently attend.

Costs

Tuition and fees for the 2009-2010 academic year are approximately $30,125 for all full-time students. Tuition for part-time students is approximately $24,970 per year. On-campus room and board costs about $9962 annually; books and supplies run $1292.

Financial Aid

In a recent year, about 88% of current law students received some form of aid. The average annual amount of aid from all sources combined, including scholarships, loans, and work contracts, was approximately $32,235; maximum, $45,418. Awards are based on need and merit. Required financial statement is the FAFSA. Special funds for minority or disadvantaged students are available. First-year students are notified about their financial aid application at time of acceptance. Check with the school for the current application deadline.

About the Law School

Michigan State University College of Law was established in 1891 and is a private institution. The 5000+-acre campus is in a suburban area just outside the state capital. The primary mission of the law school is to provide a rigorous educational program which prepares a diverse community of students to be national and international leaders. Students have

access to federal, state, county, city, and local agencies, courts, correctional facilities, law firms, and legal aid organizations in the East Lansing area. Through the externship programs, a number of local courts are used officially as training forums for students. Facilities of special interest to law students include the law library, classrooms, offices for faculty, administrators and student organizations, study and lounge facilities, the Moot Court, the expanded computer laboratory, and the Career Services Office. The building supports wireless technology. Housing for students is available both on and off campus. On-campus housing includes both residence halls and apartments. All law school facilities are accessible to the physically disabled.

Calendar

The law school operates on a traditional semester basis. Courses for full-time students are offered both day and evening and must be completed within 3 years. For part-time students, courses are offered both day and evening and must be completed within 5 years. New full- and part-time students are admitted in the fall. There is an 8-week summer session. Transferable summer courses are offered.

Programs

In addition to the J.D., the law school offers the LL.M. Students may take relevant courses in other programs and apply credit toward the J.D.; a maximum of 6 credits may be applied. The following joint degrees may be earned: J.D./M.A. (Juris Doctor/Master of Arts), J.D./M.B.A. (Juris Doctor/Master of Business Administration), J.D./M.L.R.H.R. (Juris Doctor/Master of Labor Relations and Human Resources), J.D./M.P.A. (Juris Doctor/Master of Public Administration), and J.D./M.S. (Juris Doctor/Master of Science).

Required
To earn the J.D., candidates must complete 88 total credits, of which 44 are for required courses. They must maintain a minimum GPA of 2.0 in the required courses. The following first-year courses are required of all students: Civil Procedure I and II, Constitutional Law I, Contracts I and II, Property, Research, Writing, and Advocacy I and II, Torts, and

Phone: 517-432-0222
844-9352
Fax: 517-432-0098
Web: www.law.msu.edu

Contact

Assistant Dean, 517-432-0222 for general inquiries; 517-432-6810, for financial aid information.

MICHIGAN

Writing Skills Workshop. Required upper-level courses consist of Business Enterprises, Constitutional Law II, Criminal Law, Evidence, and Professional Responsibility. The required orientation program for first-year students consists of 3 days of intensive study in research and writing. Students are taught research skills, use of library techniques, how to brief a case, and how to write an exam.

Electives

Students must take 14 credits in their area of concentration. The College of Law offers concentrations in corporate law, criminal law, environmental law, family law, international law, litigation, media law, tax law, and health law certificate in law and social work, indigenous law, intellectual property & communications law, and public law and regulation. In addition, Clinics include the Rental House Clinic, Tax Clinic, Small Business and Nonprofit Clinic, and the Chance at Childhood Clinic. Many seminars in specialized areas are offered each year, allowing students to explore areas of interest in depth with expert faculty members. The MSU Law Career Services assists students in identifying, preparing for and applying for internships, including judicial clerkships. In addition to the MSU Law Review, there are 6 additional student-run publications. Students may also enroll in directed studies and apply for positions as research assistants. Various externship programs are available, including a federal externship in Washington, D.C. and a Summer International Externship Program in Canada. There are student-faculty, and alumni-sponsored lecture series featuring experts on current matters of law. The Law College offers a cooperative study program with the University of Ottawa and a joint J.D./LL.B. program. Through the Canadian summer program, students participate in the Houses of Parliament in Ottawa and Montreal. The Law College also sponsors a summer abroad program in Guadalajara, Mexico and law students participate in other ABA-approved programs. The Law College houses the Office of Diversity Services. There are also a variety of student organizations that focus on issues and services for minority students. The most widely taken electives are Environmental Law, Intellectual Property, and Sports Law.

Graduation Requirements

In order to graduate, candidates must have a GPA of 2.0 and have completed the upper-division writing requirement.

Organizations

Students edit the *Michigan State Law Review*, *Michigan State Journal of International Law*, *Michigan State Journal of Medicine and Law*, *Michigan State Entertainment and Sports Law Journal*, *Michigan State Journal of Gender and Law*, *Michigan State Journal of Business and Securities Law*, and the student newspaper, *Res Ipsa Loquitor*. A Moot Court offers intramural competitions. The Law College participates in regional, national, and international moot court competitions, including the Cathy Bennett National Trial Competition, Jessup International Moot Court Competition, and Pepperdine Entertainment Law Competition. The Law College hosts the National Trial Advocacy Competition, which attracts 18 competing school teams each fall. Law student organizations include Women's Law Caucus, Jewish Legal Society, and Christian Legal Society. Local chapters of national associations include ABA-Student Division, Amnesty International, and Phi Alpha Delta. Campus clubs and other organizations include the Association of Trial Lawyers, Military Law Society, and Public Interest Society.

Library

The law library contains 133,882 hard-copy volumes and 152,890 microform volume equivalents, and subscribes to 4088 serial publications. Such on-line databases and networks as CALI, CIS Universe, Infotrac, Legal-Trac, LEXIS, LOIS, NEXIS, OCLC First Search, WESTLAW, Wilsonline Indexes, and BNA-ALL are available to law students for research. Special library collections include international, labor, and taxation; a Government Printing Office depository; and law practice materials. Recently, the library constructed 3 additional group study rooms and upgraded the 40-station computer laboratory. The ratio of library volumes to faculty is 3523 to 1 and to students is 133 to 1. The ratio of seats in the library to students is 1 to 3.

Faculty

The law school has 38 full-time and 41 part-time faculty members, of whom 27

Placement

J.D.s awarded:	284
Services available through: a separate law school placement center	
Special features: Symplicity, On-line job listing service.	
Full-time job interviews:	19 employers
Summer job interviews:	35 employers
Placement by graduation:	n/av
Placement within 9 months:	92% of class
Average starting salary:	$35,000 to $145,000
Areas of placement:	
Private practice 2-10 attorneys	29%
Private practice 11-25 attorneys	9%
Private practice 26-50 attorneys	5%
Private practice 51-100 attorneys	6%
Business/industry	18%
Government	12%
Unknown	9%
Judicial clerkships	5%
Public interest	5%
Military	2%
Academic	2%

are women. According to AAUP standards for Category I institutions, faculty salaries are average. About 30% of full-time faculty have a graduate law degree in addition to the J.D.; about 20% of part-time faculty have one. The ratio of full-time students to full-time faculty in an average class is 18 to 1; in a clinic, 6 to 1. The law school has a regular program of bringing visiting professors and other distinguished lecturers and visitors to campus.

Students

About 42% of the student body are women; 13%, minorities; 4%, African American; 4%, Asian American; 3%, Hispanic; and 1%, Native American. The majority of students come from the Midwest (70%). The average age of entering students is 23; age range is 20 to 51. About 44% of students enter directly from undergraduate school and 3% have a graduate degree. About 5% drop out after the first year for academic or personal reasons; 92% remain to receive a law degree.

School of Law

151 E. Griffith Street
Jackson, MS 39201

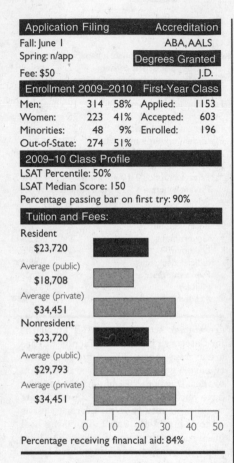

Application Filing		Accreditation
Fall: June 1		ABA, AALS
Spring: n/app		

		Degrees Granted
Fee: $50		J.D.

Enrollment 2009–2010   First-Year Class

Men:	314	58%	Applied:	1153
Women:	223	41%	Accepted:	603
Minorities:	48	9%	Enrolled:	196
Out-of-State:	274	51%		

2009–10 Class Profile

LSAT Percentile: 50%
LSAT Median Score: 150
Percentage passing bar on first try: 90%

Tuition and Fees:

Resident
$23,720

Average (public)
$18,708

Average (private)
$34,451

Nonresident
$23,720

Average (public)
$29,793

Average (private)
$34,451

0   10   20   30   40   50

Percentage receiving financial aid: 84%

ADMISSIONS

In a recent year, 1153 applied, 603 were accepted, and 196 enrolled. Two transfers enrolled. The median LSAT percentile of the most recent first-year class was 50; the median GPA was 3.21 on a scale of 4.0. The highest LSAT percentile was 93. figures in the above capsule and in this profile are approximate.

Requirements
Applicants must have a bachelor's degree and take the LSAT. The most important admission factors include LSAT results, GPA, and academic achievement. No specific undergraduate courses are required. Candidates are not interviewed.

Procedure
Applicants should submit an application form, LSAT results, transcripts, a personal statement, and a nonrefundable application fee of $50. Notification of the admissions decision is on a rolling basis. The latest acceptable LSAT

test date for fall entry is February. The law school uses the LSDAS. Check with the school for current application deadline.

Special
The law school recruits minority and disadvantaged students by means of recruiting at historically black institutions. Scholarship and stipends are designated for tuition for minority students. Requirements are not different for out-of-state students. Transfer students must have one year of credit, have a minimum GPA of 2, have attended an ABA-approved law school, and submit an LSDAS report and 2 letters of recommendation from their current law faculty, as well as a letter of good standing from their current law school dean.

Costs

Tuition and fees for the 2009-2010 academic year are $23,720 for all full-time students. Books and supplies run $900.

Financial Aid

About 84% of current law students receive some form of aid. The average annual amount of aid from all sources combined, including scholarships, loans, and work contracts, is $22,000; maximum, $42,170. Awards are based on need and merit, along with . Required financial statement is the FAFSA. First-year students are notified about their financial aid application at time of acceptance.

About the Law School

Mississippi College School of Law was established in 1975 and is a private institution. The campus is in an urban area in Jackson. The primary mission of the law school is to impart to its students quality education within the context of a Christian institution and to instill in them the highest degree of professional proficiency and integrity. Students have access to federal, state, county, city, and local agencies, courts, correctional facilities, law firms, and legal aid organizations in the Jackson area. Housing for students is available off campus. Some on-campus housing at the Clinton campus may be available. All law school facilities are accessible to the physically disabled.

Calendar

The law school operates on a traditional semester basis. Courses for full-time students are offered days only and must be completed within 3 years. For part-time students, courses are offered There is no part-time program. New students are admitted in the fall. There is a 9-week summer session. Transferable summer courses are offered.

Programs

The following joint degrees may be earned: J.D./M.B.A. (Juris Doctor/Master of Business Administration).

Required
To earn the J.D., candidates must complete 90 total credits, of which 36 are for required courses. They must maintain a minimum GPA of 2.0 in the required courses. The following first-year courses are required of all students: Civil Procedure I and II, Contracts I and II, Criminal Law, Legal Analysis, Legal Research and Legal Writing, Property I, and Torts I and II. Required upper-level courses consist of a writing requirement, Appellate Advocacy, Constitutional Law, and Professional Responsibility and Ethics. The required orientation program for first-year students is a 3-day program that includes how to brief a case, an introduction to basic legal methods, and the development of the Anglo-American legal system.

Electives
The School of Law offers concentrations in corporate law, family law, litigation, and general and government related areas. In addition, seminars are open to all upperclass students and are usually worth 2 credit hours. The externship program is a small, select program that provides closely supervised externships with legal/judicial offices and governmental agencies; 2 credit hours are generally given. Legal research and writing programs provide an opportunity to work directly with a faculty member on a topic of the student's choice for 2 credit hours. Field work is possible through the extern program, which is open to upper-class students. Placement is with government and nonprofit entities for 1 to 3 hours during a semester to provide hands-on training. A remedial writing workshop is offered to first-year

MISSISSIPPI

Phone: 601-925-7152
800-738-1236
E-mail: *pevans@mc.edu*
Web: *http:// law.mc.edu*

Contact

Patricia H. Evans, Assistant Dean of Admissions, 601-925-7150 for general inquiries; Jackie Banes, 601-925-7110 for financial aid information.

students exhibiting need based upon a written submission; no credit is offered. A 3 credit-hour special interest program, Comparative Legal Systems: Civil Law and Common Law, is offered to students interested in Louisiana law. The most widely taken electives are Trial Practice, Pretrial Practice, and Counseling and Negotiations.

Graduation Requirements

In order to graduate, candidates must have a GPA of 2.0 and have completed the upper-division writing requirement.

Organizations

Students edit the *Mississippi College Law Review* and the student paper, *Legal Eye*. The moot court board conducts the appellate competitions. Law student organizations include the Law Student Association, Women's Student Bar Association, and Environmental Club. There are local chapters of Phi Alpha Delta and Phi Delta Phi.

Library

The law library contains 346,941 hardcopy volumes and 217,570 microform volume equivalents, and subscribes to 3100 serial publications. Such on-line databases and networks as CALI, CIS Universe, DIALOG, LEXIS, LOIS, Mathew Bender, NEXIS, WESTLAW, and Wilsonline Indexes are available to law students for research. Special library collections include a partial government printing office depository for U.S. government documents. Recently, the library renovated 2nd and 3rd floors. The ratio of library volumes to faculty is 15,770 to 1 and to students is 647 to 1. The ratio of seats in the library to students is 1 to 1.

Faculty

The law school has 22 full-time and 42 part-time faculty members, of whom 25 are women. According to AAUP standards for Category IIA institutions, faculty salaries are well below average. About 35% of full-time faculty have a graduate law degree in addition to the J.D. The ratio of full-time students to full-time faculty in an average class is 18 to 1; in a clinic, 18 to 1.

Students

About 41% of the student body are women; 9%, minorities; 7%, African American; 1%, Asian American; and 1%, Hispanic. The majority of students come from Mississippi (49%). The average age of entering students is 26; age range is 21 to 53. About 70% of students enter directly from undergraduate school, 10% have a graduate degree, and 20% have worked full-time prior to entering law school. About 7% drop out after the first year for academic or personal reasons; 93% remain to receive a law degree.

Placement

J.D.s awarded:	162
Services available through: a separate law school placement center	
Services: work study program	
Special features: .	
Full-time job interviews:	32 employers
Summer job interviews:	32 employers
Placement by graduation:	50% of class
Placement within 9 months:	87% of class
Average starting salary:	$45,770 to $95,333
Areas of placement:	
Private practice 2-10 attorneys	30%
Private practice 11-25 attorneys	4%
Private practice 26-50 attorneys	4%
Private practice 51-100 attorneys	11%
Business/industry	13%
Government	11%
Judicial clerkships	8%
Public interest	5%
Academic	1%

Mississippi College   **343**

154 Stuart Street
Boston, MA 02116

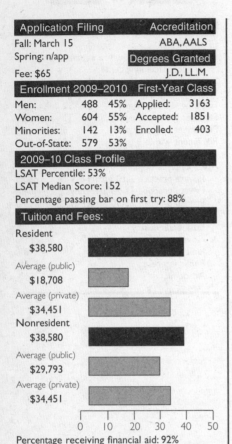

Application Filing	Accreditation
Fall: March 15	ABA, AALS
Spring: n/app	Degrees Granted
Fee: $65	J.D., LL.M.

Enrollment 2009–2010		First-Year Class	
Men:	488 45%	Applied:	3163
Women:	604 55%	Accepted:	1851
Minorities:	142 13%	Enrolled:	403
Out-of-State:	579 53%		

2009–10 Class Profile
LSAT Percentile: 53%
LSAT Median Score: 152
Percentage passing bar on first try: 88%

Tuition and Fees:

Resident
$38,580

Average (public)
$18,708

Average (private)
$34,451

Nonresident
$38,580

Average (public)
$29,793

Average (private)
$34,451

0   10   20   30   40   50

Percentage receiving financial aid: 92%

ADMISSIONS

In the fall 2009 first-year class, 3163 applied, 1851 were accepted, and 403 enrolled. Four transfers enrolled. The median LSAT percentile of the most recent first-year class was 53; the median GPA was 3.22 on a scale of 4.0. The lowest LSAT percentile accepted was 36; the highest was 95.

Requirements

Applicants must have a bachelor's degree and take the LSAT. Minimum acceptable GPA is 2.0 on a scale of 4.0. The most important admission factors include motivations, GPA, and LSAT results. No specific undergraduate courses are required. Candidates are not interviewed.

Procedure

The application deadline for fall entry is March 15. Applicants should submit an application form, LSAT results, transcripts, a personal statement, a nonrefundable application fee of $65, 2 letters of recommendation, a personal statement, and the LSDAS Report. Notification of the admissions decision is on a rolling basis. The latest acceptable LSAT test date for fall entry is February. The law school uses the LSDAS.

Special

The law school recruits minority and disadvantaged students by means of attendance at minority recruitment fairs as well as recruitment at institutions and cities with large minority populations; participation in CLEO and CRS searches through LSAC; connecting minority applicants with minority alumni and current students; and scholarships. Requirements are not different for out-of-state students. Transfer students must have 1 year of credit, a minimum average of C+, and a dean's letter of good standing.

Costs

Tuition and fees for the 2009-2010 academic year are $38,580 for all full-time students. Tuition for part-time students is $28,960 per year. Books and supplies run $1250.

Financial Aid

About 92% of current law students receive some form of aid. The average annual amount of aid from all sources combined, including scholarships, loans, and work contracts, is $38,604; maximum, $60,622. Awards are based on need and merit. Required financial statements are the FAFSA, the institutional application, and federal tax returns. The aid application deadline for fall entry is April 8. Special funds for minority or disadvantaged students include the MacLean Grant for disadvantaged students and the Jacqueline Lloyd Grant for minority students. First-year students are notified about their financial aid application at time of acceptance.

About the Law School

New England Law/Boston was established in 1908 and is independent. The campus is in an urban area in Boston. The primary mission of the law school is to provide the opportunity for quality legal education and ethical training to men and women, especially those who might otherwise not have that opportunity. Students have access to federal, state, county, city, and local agencies, courts, correctional facilities, law firms, and legal aid organizations in the Boston area. Boston is the state capital, and as such offers many opportunities to law students. Facilities of special interest to law students are the Clinical Law Office, a school-sponsored neighborhood law office that provides clinical training and assists low-income litigants, and other clinical programs with the attorney general, Massachusetts Revenue Department, and other agencies. Housing for students is not available on campus; however, assistance is provided for finding housing and roommates. About 98% of the law school facilities are accessible to the physically disabled.

Calendar

The law school operates on a traditional semester basis. Courses for full-time students are offered both day and evening and must be completed within 5 years. For part-time students, courses are offered both day and evening and must be completed within 6 years. New full- and part-time students are admitted in the fall. There is an 8-week summer session. Transferable summer courses are offered.

Programs

In addition to the J.D., the law school offers the LL.M. Students may take relevant courses in other programs and apply credit toward the J.D.; a maximum of 6 credits may be applied.

Required

To earn the J.D., candidates must complete 86 total credits, of which 43 are for required courses. They must maintain a minimum GPA of 2.0 in the required courses. The following first-year courses are required of all students: Civil Procedure, Constitutional Law, Contracts, Legal Methods, Property, and Torts. Required upper-level courses consist of Criminal Law, Criminal Procedure I, Evidence, and Law and Ethics of Lawyering. The required orientation program for first-year students is a 2-day full-time, 3-day part-time program with panel discussions on legal issues and lectures on the legal process, how to brief a case, and the procedures of a civil case.

Phone: 617-422-7210
Fax: 617-422-7201
E-mail: admit@admin.nesl.edu
Web: www.nesl.edu

Contact
Michelle L'etoile, Director of Admissions, 617-422-7210 for general inquiries; Eric Krupski, Director of Financial Aid, 617-422-7298 for financial aid information.

MASSACHUSETTS

Electives

New England Law/Boston offers concentrations in corporate law, criminal law, environmental law, family law, international law, litigation, and tax law. In addition, clinics are available to second- and third-year day division students and third- and fourth-year evening division students for 2 to 6 credits. All upperclass students may take electives for 2 to 3 credits. Final-year students may undertake research programs for a 2 credit maximum per year. New England Law, in cooperation with 3 other law schools, sponsors 6 summer abroad programs and 3 semester abroad programs. Students may spend a summer studying in Prague, Chile, Ireland, London, or Malta. Students may also spend a semester studying in the Netherlands, or at the University of Paris X in Nanterre. The school will accept credit for courses taken in any summer-abroad program approved by the American Bar Association. A tutorial program, the Academic Excellence program, is offered. A noncredit remedial research and writing program is open to first-year students. Noncredit minority programs are open to all students. The most widely taken electives are Wills, Estates and Trusts, Business Organization and UCC: Sales.

Graduation Requirements

In order to graduate, candidates must have a GPA of 2.0, have completed the upper-division writing requirement, and have 86 credits.

Organizations
Students edit *New England Law Review*, *New England Journal on Criminal and Civil Confinement*, and the student newspaper, *Due Process*. Other publications include the *New England Journal of International and Comparative Law*. Students participate in an annual in-house Honors Moot Court Competition and Trial Competition. Other competitions include the National Appellate Moot Court Competition, National Trial Competition, National Tax Moot Court, Jessup International Moot Court, Environmental Moot Court, Frederick Douglass Moot Court, and occasionally the ABA Appellate Advocacy Competition. Student organizations include the Student Bar Association, Public Interest Law Association, and Minority Students Association. There are local

chapters of the ABA-Law Student Division, Phi Alpha Delta, and Phi Delta Phi.

Library
The law library contains 320,682 hardcopy volumes and 857,787 microform volume equivalents, and subscribes to 893 serial publications. Such on-line databases and networks as CALI, CIS Universe, DIALOG, Dow-Jones, Infotrac, Legal-Trac, LEXIS, LOIS, Mathew Bender, NEXIS, OCLC First Search, RLIN, WESTLAW, Wilsonline Indexes, and CD-ROMs, the Internet, JSTOR, and BNA are available to law students for research. Special library collections include women and the law, Portia Law School archives, a Massachusetts continuing legal education depository, all standard legal research materials such as court reports, statutes, treatises, restatements, and legal periodicals. Recently, the library added improved lighting and new furniture in the basement levels, 25 additional study spaces and 2 additional group study rooms. The ratio of library volumes to faculty is 9162 to 1 and to students is 293 to 1. The ratio of seats in the library to students is 1 to 2.

Faculty
The law school has 35 full-time and 68 part-time faculty members, of whom 39 are women. About 22% of full-time faculty have a graduate law degree in addition to the J.D.; about 23% of part-time faculty have one. The ratio of full-time students to full-time faculty in an average class is 23 to 1; in a clinic, 8 to 1. The law school has a regular program of bringing visiting professors and other distinguished lecturers and visitors to campus.

Students
About 55% of the student body are women; 13%, minorities; 2%, African American; 5%, Asian American; and 2%, Hispanic. The majority of students come from the Northeast (70%). The average age of entering students is 26; age range is 21 to 66. About 17% drop out after the first year for academic or personal reasons; 83% remain to receive a law degree.

Placement

J.D.s awarded:	313
Services available through: a separate law school placement center	
Services: computerized job search resources and assistance with judicial clerkships	
Special features: individual and group counseling services as well as strong alumni contacts.	
Full-time job interviews:	11 employers
Summer job interviews:	11 employers
Placement by graduation:	50% of class
Placement within 9 months:	90% of class
Average starting salary:	$30,000 to $160,000
Areas of placement:	
Private practice 2-10 attorneys	27%
Private practice 11-25 attorneys	4%
Private practice 26-50 attorneys	2%
Private practice 51-100 attorneys	1%
Private Practice 101+ Attorney	10%
Business/industry	27%
Government	14%
Judicial clerkships	11%
Public interest	4%
Academic	2%
Military	1%

NEW YORK LAW SCHOOL

185 West Broadway
New York, NY 10013-2960

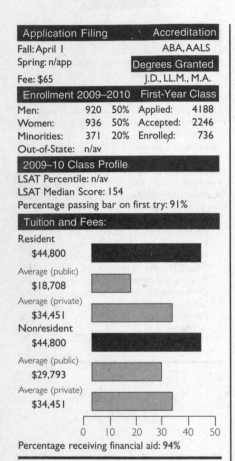

Application Filing	Accreditation
Fall: April 1	ABA, AALS
Spring: n/app	**Degrees Granted**
Fee: $65	J.D., LL.M., M.A.

Enrollment 2009–2010			First-Year Class	
Men:	920	50%	Applied:	4188
Women:	936	50%	Accepted:	2246
Minorities:	371	20%	Enrolled:	736
Out-of-State:	n/av			

2009–10 Class Profile

LSAT Percentile: n/av
LSAT Median Score: 154
Percentage passing bar on first try: 91%

Tuition and Fees:

Resident
$44,800

Average (public)
$18,708

Average (private)
$34,451

Nonresident
$44,800

Average (public)
$29,793

Average (private)
$34,451

0 10 20 30 40 50

Percentage receiving financial aid: 94%

ADMISSIONS

In the fall 2009 first-year class, 4188 applied, 2246 were accepted, and 736 enrolled. Twenty-two transfers enrolled. The median GPA of the most recent first-year class was 3.3.

Requirements

Applicants must have a bachelor's degree and take the LSAT. No specific undergraduate courses are required. Candidates are not interviewed.

Procedure

The application deadline for fall entry is April 1. Applicants should submit an application form, LSAT results, a personal statement, a nonrefundable application fee of $65, and 1 to 3 letters of recommendation. Notification of the admissions decision is on a rolling basis. The latest acceptable LSAT test date for fall entry is February. The law school uses the LSDAS.

Special

The law school recruits minority and disadvantaged students through diversity recruitment efforts initiated by the minority recruitment coordinator in the Admissions Office. Requirements are not different for out-of-state students. Transfer students must have 1 year of credit, have attended an ABA-approved law school, and have a bachelor's degree from a regionally accredited college or university.

Costs

Tuition and fees for the 2009-2010 academic year are $44,800 for all full-time students. Tuition for part-time students is $34,500 per year. On-campus room and board costs about $16,840 annually; books and supplies run $1300.

Financial Aid

About 94% of current law students receive some form of aid. The average annual amount of aid from all sources combined, including scholarships, loans, and work contracts, is $47,272; maximum, $67,615. Awards are based on need. Scholarships are awarded on the basis of merit. NYLS need-based grants are awarded on the basis of financial need. Required financial statement is the FAFSA. The aid application deadline for fall entry is April 15. Special funds for minority or disadvantaged students Are part of the regular scholarship and grant process. First-year students are notified about their financial aid application contingent upon its completion.

About the Law School

New York Law School was established in 1891 is independent. The campus is in an urban area in the historic TriBeCa district of New York City. The primary mission of the law school is to deliver a sense of public service in law students, melding the theoretical and the practical to provide a strong foundation of legal knowledge as well as diverse perspectives. Students have access to federal, state, county, city, and local agencies, courts, correctional facilities, law firms, and legal aid organizations in the New York area. Facilities of special interest to law students the Communications Media Center, which promotes learning about mass communications law; the Center for New York City Law, which focuses on urban

governmental and legal processes; and the Center for International Law, which supports teaching and research in that field. Housing for students consists of an apartment building in the East Village with rooms for 99 students in shared two-and- three-bedroom apartments located 20 minutes from the school by subway. All law school facilities are accessible to the physically disabled.

Calendar

The law school operates on a traditional semester basis. Courses for full-time students are offered both day and evening and must be completed within 3 years. For part-time students, courses are offered both day and evening and must be completed within 4 years. New full- and part-time students are admitted in the fall. There is an 8-week summer session. Transferable summer courses are offered.

Programs

In addition to the J.D., the law school offers the LL.M. and M.A. Students may take relevant courses in other programs and apply credit toward the J.D.; a maximum of 10 credits may be applied. The following joint degrees may be earned: J.D./M.B.A. (Juris Doctor/Master of Business Administration).

Required

To earn the J.D., candidates must complete 86 total credits, of which 38 are for required courses. They must maintain a minimum GPA of 2.0 in the required courses. The following first-year courses are required of all students: Civil Procedure, Contracts, Criminal Law, Lawyering, Legal Reasoning, Writing and Research, Legislation and Regulation, Property, Torts, and Written and Oral Advocacy. Required upper-level courses consist of advanced writing requirement, Constitutional Law I and II, Evidence, and Professional Responsibility. Clinical programs are included in the Lawyering Skills program, where faculty-supervised students represent clients with current legal matters pending before various federal and state courts and administrative agencies. The required orientation program for first-year students is a week long, is intergrated into the first week of classes, and designed to ease the anxieties of incoming students by having them

Phone: 212-431-2888
877-YES-NYLS
Fax: 212-966-1522
E-mail: *admissions@nyls.edu*
Web: *www.nyls.edu*

Contact

William D. Perez, Assistant Dean, 212-431-2888 or 877-YES-NYLS for general inquiries; Office of Admissions and Financial Aid, 212-431-2828 for financial aid information.

NEW YORK

meet informally with professors and fellow students at planned social events as well as introducing them to the rigors of law studies.

Electives

The New York Law School offers concentrations in corporate law, criminal law, entertainment law, environmental law, family law, intellectual property law, international law, labor law, litigation, media law, securities law, tax law, torts and insurance, business and commercial law, constitutional law, procedure and evidence, property and real estate, public interest law, administrative law and practice, and immigration law. In addition, Clinics are available in Criminal Law, Mediation, Elder Law, Securities Arbitration, and Urban Law. Students gain additional legal practice experience through workshop courses. These courses link a seminar in a specialized body of law to field placements in offices and agencies practicing in that area of the law. Externships and judicial internships provide opportunities to do actual legal work, in private or public law offices or in judges' chambers, while being supervised by a practitioner at the placement site and meeting with a faculty member at the school. Special lecture series include the Steifel Symposium, Fall Executive Speakers Series, New York City Law Breakfasts, Solomon Lecture, Professional Development Seminar, Faculty Lecture Series, Dean's Roundtable, Spotlight on Women, CV Starr Lecture, Otto Walter Lecture Series, and Faculty Presentation Day. Independent study programs are available. Students may participate in study abroad programs offered by other law schools. The Academic Support Program consists of a condensed introductory course in legal methods in the summer followed by weekly tutorial meetings with second- and third-year teaching fellows through the first academic year. The admission/financial aid officers have responsibility for minority recruitment and enrollment initiatives in conjunction with the Office of Student Life, Asian American Law Students Association, Black Law Students Association, Latino Law Students Association, South Asian Law Students Association, and Stonewall Law Students Association. Special interest group programs include Media Law Project, Domestic Violence Project, New York Law School Civil Liberties Union, Public Interest Coalition,

and Trial Lawyers Association. The most widely taken electives are Commercial Transactions; Corporations; and Wills, Trusts, and Future Interests.

Graduation Requirements

In order to graduate, candidates must have a GPA of 2.0 and have completed the upper-division writing requirement.

Organizations

Students edit the *New York Law School Law Review*, and the student newspaper *De Novo* Students may participate in the Froessel Moot Court intramural competition. Students become members of the Moot Court Association by invitation and may represent the school in intramural competitions held at law schools nationwide. The Robert F. Wagner Labor Law Moot Court competition is hosted by the school each spring. Law student organizations include Business Law Society, International Law Society, Stonewall Law Students Association, Evening Students Association, Legal Association for Women, and Civil Liberties Union. There are local chapters of Phi Alpha Delta, Phi Delta Phi, and Amnesty International.

Library

The law library contains 534,789 hardcopy volumes and 175,305 microform volume equivalents, and subscribes to 4250 serial publications. Such on-line databases and networks as CALI, CIS Universe, DIALOG, Legal-Trac, LEXIS, NEXIS, OCLC First Search, WESTLAW, Wilsonline Indexes, Law Schools On-line, Index to UN documents, and 25 other CD-ROM databases are available to law students for research. Special library collections include the U.S. government documents depository and special collections in communications rights law, alternative dispute resolution, and labor law. Recently, the library added, a new, glass-enclosed 235,000-square-foot academic building, which extends 5 stories aboveground and 4 below - doubling the size of the campus. The new building, featuring the Mendik Law Library, lounge areas with WiFi, and an open-air terrace with a view of Manhattan on the fifth floor, is almost exclusively student-centered--wuth classrooms, lounges, study rooms, dining facilities, and the library. The ratio of library volumes to faculty is 7130 to 1 and to students is 288

Placement

J.D.s awarded:	437

Services available through: a separate law school placement center
Services: more than 200 law firms participate in recruitment programs
Special features: a resource library, which contains a collection of job search and career planning materials, information on law firms, corporations, government agencies, the judiciary, public interest organizations, a computerized database; and an alumni network.

Full-time job interviews:	53 employers
Summer job interviews:	n/av
Placement by graduation:	n/av
Placement within 9 months:	91% of class
Average starting salary:	$25,000 to $160,000

Areas of placement:

Private practice 26-50 attorneys	43%
Business/industry	23%
Government	14%
Public interest	6%
Unknown	6%
Judicial clerkships	4%
Academic	4%

to 1. The ratio of seats in the library to students is 1 to 3.

Faculty

The law school has 75 full-time and 123 part-time faculty members, of whom 74 are women. About 35% of full-time faculty have a graduate law degree in addition to the J.D.; about 22% of part-time faculty have one. The ratio of full-time students to full-time faculty in an average class is 23 to 1; in a clinic, 19 to 1. The law school has a regular program of bringing visiting professors and other distinguished lecturers and visitors to campus.

Students

About 50% of the student body are women; 20%, minorities; 5%, African American; 9%, Asian American; and 8%, Hispanic. The average age of entering students is 25; age range is 20 to 57. About 40% of students enter directly from undergraduate school, 9% have a graduate degree, and 62% have worked full-time prior to entering law school. About 11% drop out after the first year for academic or personal reasons; 89% remain to receive a law degree.

New York Law School **347**

NEW YORK UNIVERSITY

School of Law

161 Avenue of the Americas,
5th Floor
New York, NY 10013

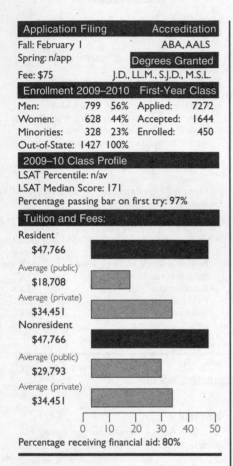

Application Filing	Accreditation
Fall: February 1	ABA, AALS
Spring: n/app	**Degrees Granted**
Fee: $75	J.D., LL.M., S.J.D., M.S.L.

Enrollment 2009–2010		First-Year Class	
Men:	799 56%	Applied:	7272
Women:	628 44%	Accepted:	1644
Minorities:	328 23%	Enrolled:	450
Out-of-State:	1427 100%		

2009–10 Class Profile
LSAT Percentile: n/av
LSAT Median Score: 171
Percentage passing bar on first try: 97%

Tuition and Fees:

Resident
$47,766

Average (public)
$18,708

Average (private)
$34,451

Nonresident
$47,766

Average (public)
$29,793

Average (private)
$34,451

0   10   20   30   40   50

Percentage receiving financial aid: 80%

ADMISSIONS

In the fall 2009 first-year class, 7272 applied, 1644 were accepted, and 450 enrolled. Thirty-seven transfers enrolled. The median GPA of the most recent first-year class was 3.72.

Requirements
Applicants must have a bachelor's degree and take the LSAT. Applicants must be at least 18 years old. No specific undergraduate courses are required. Candidates are not interviewed.

Procedure
The application deadline for fall entry is February 1. Applicants should submit an application form, LSAT results, transcripts, a personal statement, a nonrefundable application fee of $75, and 1 letter of recommendation. Notification of the admissions decision is by late April. The latest acceptable LSAT test date for fall entry is December. The law school uses the LSDAS.

Special
NYU seeks to enroll a student body from a broad spectrum of society, including members of groups under represented in the profession as well as persons who have experienced socio-economic and/or educational disavantage. Requirements are not different for out-of-state students. Transfer students must have one year of credit, and have attended an ABA-approved law school. They must submit all college and law school transcripts, LSAT scores, a letter of recommendation from a law school professor, and a statement of good standing from a dean. The school attended must be a member of the AALS or be approved by the Section on Legal Education of the ABA.

Costs

Tuition and fees for the 2009-2010 academic year are $47,766 for all full-time students. On-campus room and board costs about $20,914 annually; books and supplies run $1370.

Financial Aid

About 80% of current law students receive some form of aid. Awards are based on need and merit. Required financial statements are the FAFSA and Institutional Application. The aid application deadline for fall entry is April 15. First-year students are notified about their financial aid application at time of acceptance.

About the Law School

New York University School of Law was established in 1835 and is a private institution. The campus is in an urban area in New York City. The primary mission of the law school is to produce men and women who are leaders of the bar, public and private, in a world that operates across national boundaries. Students have access to federal, state, county, city, and local agencies, courts, correctional facilities, law firms, and legal aid organizations in the New York area. Facilities of special interest to law students include Vanderbilt Hall and Furman Hall, which contains classrooms, faculty and administrative offices, and the library; D'Agostino and Mercer student residences, with meeting rooms, student journal offices, and a conference center. Housing for students is available for virtually all first-year students who request it, including couples

and families; 2 law school-owned apartment buildings are within 4 blocks of the campus. About 95% of the law school facilities are accessible to the physically disabled.

Calendar

The law school operates on a traditional semester basis. Courses for full-time students are offered both day and evening but classes are primarily during the day and must be completed within 6 semesters. There is no part-time program. New students are admitted in the fall. There is no summer session. Transferable summer courses are not offered.

Programs

In addition to the J.D., the law school offers the LL.M., S.J.D., and M.S.L. in Law and Jewish Civilization. Students may take relevant courses in other programs and apply credit toward the J.D.; a maximum of 10 credits may be applied (12 for joint degree students). The following joint degrees may be earned: J.D./J.D. (Juris Doctor/Juris Doctor with Osgoode Hall Law School), J.D./LL.M. (Juris Doctor/Master of Laws in taxation), J.D./M.A. (Juris Doctor/ Master of Arts in economics, philosophy, etc.), J.D./M.B.A. (Juris Doctor/Master of Business Administration), J.D./M.P.A. (Juris Doctor/Master of Public Administration with Princeton University and Harvard University), J.D./ M.P.P. (Juris Doctor/Master of Public Policy with Harvard University), J.D./ M.S.W. (Juris Doctor/Master of Social Work), J.D./M.U.P. (Juris Doctor/Master of Urban Planning), and J.D.M.A., Ph.D. (Juris Doctor/Master of Arts) and J.D./J.D. (Juris Doctor/Juris Doctor with Melbourne Law School).

Required
To earn the J.D., candidates must complete 83 total credits, of which 38 to 42 are for required courses. The following first-year courses are required of all students: Contracts, Criminal Law, Elective, Lawyering, Procedure, Property, The Administrative and Regulatory State, and Torts. Required upper-level courses consist of 1 upper-level writing requirement, Constitutional Law, and Professional Responsibility. Clinics and advocacy courses are electives. The required orientation program for first-year students is a 7-day

Phone: 212-998-6060
Fax: 212-995-4527
E-mail: *law.moreinfo@nyu.edu*
Web: *www.law.nyu.edu*

Contact

Office of Admissions, 212-998-6060 for general inquiries; Kendra Simes, Director of Student Financial Service, 212-998-6050 for financial aid information.

NEW YORK

academic and social orientation period before the start of classes, followed by a series of optional weekly programs during the first term.

Electives

The School of Law offers concentrations in corporate law, criminal law, entertainment law, environmental law, family law, intellectual property law, international law, juvenile law, labor law, litigation, maritime law, media law, securities law, sports law, tax law, torts and insurance, global law, public interest law, real estate law, constitutional law, interdisciplinary law, and innovation. In addition, clinics provide simulated and actual trial experience; they include the Equal Justice and Capital Defender Clinic, Civil Rights Clinic, and International Human Rights Clinic. There are 29 clinics offered. Seminars are offered in areas such as constitutional law; corporate and commercial law; legal political and social philosophy, and international law. The law school provides guaranteed summer funding to all first-and second-year students who want to work in and public interest and government positions. These summer internships are with public interest organizations worldwide. Additionally, Root-Tilden-Kern Scholars participate in a 10-week internship in public interest law. Students may arrange with faculty to conduct research and/or act as research assistants. Students may also register for Directed Research which requires a substantial paper that may fulfill part of the upper-level writing requirement. Research is also part of the law school's specialized programs and fellowships. For example the Hays Civil Liberties Program, open to selected third-year students; the Criminal Justice Fellowships; and fellowships or other programs in areas such as International Law, Philosophy and the Law, and Law and Economics. Among others, special lecture series include the Leadership in Public Interest Series, the National Center on Philanthropy and the Law Speaker Series, the Jean Monnet Center Speaker Series, the Environmental Law Society Speaker Series, and the Leadership Program in Law and Business Speaker Series. Study abroad is possible through a 1-semester exchange program with the Universities of Paris, Amsterdam, Copenhagen, and Cape Town, as well as universities in Belgium, Italy, Brazil, Canada, England, Germany, Japan, Australia, Argentina, and Singapore. Tutorial

assistance is available through the Office of Student Affairs. The law school's 25 centers and institutes, as well as its over 60 student organizations, present programs throughout the year. The most widely taken electives are Colloquia (faculty-student discussions); all clinical program and advocacy courses; and seminars.

Graduation Requirements

In order to graduate, candidates must have completed the upper-division writing requirement and attend 6 semesters of classes on a full time basis.

Organizations

Students edit the *New York University Law Review*, *Annual Survey of American Law*, *Journal of International Law and Politics*, *Environmental Law Journal*, *Review of Law and Social Change*, *Journal of Legislation and Public Policy*, *Journal of Law & Business*, *Journal of Law & Liberty* the newspaper, *The Commentator*, and the *Moot Court Board casebook*. Members of the Moot Court Board enter intra-school and nationwide competitions, as well as develop moot court cases for use in nationwide competitions. The law school administers the Orison S. Marden Competition, and the Immigration Law Competition. There are more than 60 funded law student organizations on campus, including the Student Bar Association. For a full listing of student organizations, go to the school's web site at *www.law.nyu.edu/studentorgs/sba/organizations*.

Library

The law library contains 1,098,972 hardcopy volumes and 146,070 microform volume equivalents, and subscribes to 32,669 serial publications. Such on-line databases and networks as CALI, CIS Universe, DIALOG, Dow-Jones, Legal-Trac, LEXIS, NEXIS, OCLC First Search, RLIN, WESTLAW, Wilsonline Indexes, CCH, and many foreign and international Internet databases are available to law students for research. Special library collections include the Anglo-American collection, which includes recognized strengths in tax, legal history, intellectual property, constitutional law, the law of democratic institutions, public international law, and a depository for U.S. government documents and European Union documents. The law school building provides library

Placement

J.D.s awarded:	471

Services available through: a separate law school placement center

Special features: Early Interview Week each August, including employers nationwide; Public Interest/Government and International Job Fairs, mentoring programs and co-sponsorship of events, panels and programs with student groups. Annual Career Fair in January along with networking, interviewing and resume development workshops throughout the year along with individualized counseling..

Full-time job interviews:	n/av
Summer job interviews:	n/av
Placement by graduation:	98% of class
Placement within 9 months:	98% of class
Average starting salary:	$57,354 to $160,000

Areas of placement:

Private practice 51-100 attorneys	75%
Judicial clerkships	11%
Public interest	9%
Government	2%
Business/industry	2%
Academic	1%

space as well as an underground tunnel connecting the library and the new building. Additionally, there is ILLIAD for book ordering and an Interlibrary loan, as well as an online Electronic Resource Management System for more precise and faster research. The ratio of library volumes to faculty is 8792 to 1 and to students is 770 to 1.

Faculty

The law school has 125 full-time and 70 part-time faculty members, of whom 59 are women. According to AAUP standards for Category I institutions, faculty salaries are above average. The ratio of full-time students to full-time faculty in an average class is 9 to 1; in a clinic, 8 to 1. The law school has a regular program of bringing visiting professors and other distinguished lecturers and visitors to campus. There is a chapter of the Order of the Coif.

Students

About 44% of the student body are women; 23%, minorities; 6%, African American; 11%, Asian American; and 6%, Hispanic. The average age of entering students is 24; age range is 19 to 44. About 28% of students enter directly from undergraduate school and 11% have a graduate degree. All students remain to receive a law degree.

School of Law

640 Nelson Street
Durham, NC 27707

Application Filing		Accreditation
Fall: March 31		ABA
Spring: n/app		**Degrees Granted**
Fee: $40		J.D.

Enrollment 2009–2010		First-Year Class	
Men:	237 39%	Applied:	3089
Women:	364 61%	Accepted:	531
Minorities:	331 55%	Enrolled:	204
Out-of-State:	120 20%		

2009–10 Class Profile
LSAT Percentile: n/av
LSAT Median Score: 145
Percentage passing bar on first try: 79%

Tuition and Fees:

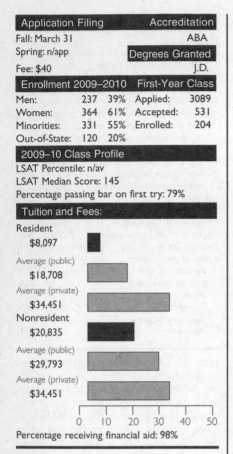

Resident
$8,097

Average (public)
$18,708

Average (private)
$34,451

Nonresident
$20,835

Average (public)
$29,793

Average (private)
$34,451

0 10 20 30 40 50

Percentage receiving financial aid: 98%

ADMISSIONS

In the fall 2009 first-year class, 3089 applied, 531 were accepted, and 204 enrolled. The median GPA of the most recent first-year class was 3.24. The lowest LSAT percentile accepted was 143; the highest was 150.

Requirements
Applicants must have a bachelor's degree and take the LSAT. The most important admission factors include academic achievement, motivation, and general background. No specific undergraduate courses are required. Candidates are not interviewed.

Procedure
The application deadline for fall entry is March 31. Applicants should submit an application form, LSAT results, transcripts, a nonrefundable application fee of $40, and 2 letters of recommendation. Accepted students who intend to enroll must submit a non-refundable $100 seat

deposit. Notification of the admissions decision is on a rolling basis. The latest acceptable LSAT test date for fall entry is February. The law school uses the LSDAS.

Special
The law school recruits minority and disadvantaged students by attending recruitment events, posting diversity links on the school's website, and by hosting a Performance-Based Admissions Program, which is designed to identify applicants who have the potential to succeed in law school but whose undergraduate transcripts and LSAT scores do not meet traditional standards. Requirements are not different for out-of-state students. Transfer students must have a minimum GPA of 2.0, have attended an ABA-approved law school, have 1 year of residence at the law school, and be in good standing with the previous law school.

Costs

Tuition and fees for the 2009-2010 academic year are $8097 for full-time in-state students and $20,835 for out-of-state students. Tuition for part-time students is $8097 in-state and $20,835 out-of state for a 4- year program. On-campus room and board costs about $9457 annually; books and supplies run $2100.

Financial Aid

About 98% of current law students receive some form of aid. The average annual amount of aid from all sources combined, including scholarships, loans, and work contracts, is $22,500; maximum, $42,231. Awards are based on need and merit. Required financial statement is the FAFSA. The aid application deadline for fall entry is June 30. Special funds for minority or disadvantaged students include Title III grants and scholarships. First-year students are notified about their financial aid application at time of acceptance.

About the Law School

North Carolina Central University School of Law was established in 1939 and is a public institution. The 135-acre campus is in an urban area 20 miles from Raleigh, 5 miles from Research Triangle Park. The primary mission of the law school is to provide a challenging and broad-based educational program designed to stimu-

late intellectual inquiry, and foster in each student a sense of community service, professional responsibility, and personal integrity. The law school student body is diverse in terms of gender, ethnicity, economic, and experiential backgrounds. Students have access to federal, state, county, city, and local agencies, courts, correctional facilities, law firms, and legal aid organizations in the Durham area adjacent to corporate and legal employers in Research Triangle Park, N.C. Facilities of special interest to law students include a modern law library, computer laboratory, academic support programs, individual offices for student organizations, Wi-Fi access throughout the building, and Smart-Board technology in each classroom. Some on-campus housing is available for single students, but married students must live off campus. About 95% of the law school facilities are accessible to the physically disabled.

Calendar

The law school operates on a traditional semester basis. Courses for full-time students are offered days only (special elective classes may meet in the evening) and must be completed within 3 years. For part-time students, courses are offered evenings only and must be completed within 4 years. New full- and part-time students are admitted in the fall. There is a 5½-week summer session. Transferable summer courses are offered.

Programs

Students may take relevant courses in other programs and apply credit toward the J.D.; a maximum of 6 hours credits may be applied. The following joint degrees may be earned: J.D./M.B.A. (Juris Doctor/Master of Business Administration) and J.D./M.L.S. (Juris Doctor/Master of Library and Information Services).

Required
To earn the J.D., candidates must complete 88 total credits, of which 59 are for required courses. They must maintain a minimum GPA of 2.0 in the required courses. The following first-year courses are required of all students: Civil Procedure I and II, Contracts I and II, Criminal Law, Legal Reasoning and Analysis, Legal Research and Persuasion, Property I and II, and Torts I and II. Required upper-

Phone: 919-530-6333
Fax: 919-530-6339
E-mail: sbrownb@nccu.edu
Web: web.nccu.edu/law

Contact

Sandra Brown Bechtold (Admissions Coordinator), 919-530-5243 for general inquiries; Steve Douglas (Assistant Dean, Financial Aid), 919-530-6365 for financial aid information.

NORTH CAROLINA

level courses consist of Advanced Legal Writing I and II (Senior Writing Evening Program, Business Associations (Corporations Evening Program), Constitutional Law I, Decedents' Estates, Evidence, Legal Letters (Day), N.C. Distinctions, Professional Responsibility, Sales and Secured Transactions, Senior Writing (Evening), and Taxation. Although not required, students are encouraged to enroll in the clinical program. There is a model law office that houses clinical facilities.The required orientation program for first-year students lasts 2 days and includes preenrollment seminars.

Electives

Students must take 12 credits in their area of concentration. The School of Law offers certificates in Dispute Resolution and Biotechnology and Pharmaceutical Law concentrations. In addition, the Clinical Experience Program consists of preliminary courses in the pre-trial process, local rules, mock client interview, and practice with mock trials and oral arguments in Civil Litigation or Criminal Litigation. For field placements, students work with in-house attorneys in various specialty areas or extern with government officials, legal services agencies, and attorneys in North Carolina. Clinics may be taken by third-year students who receive 2 to 4 credit hours for their work. The Pro Bono Clinic offers many opportunities for second- and third-year students to volunteer in local special interest agencies and organizations. The law school offers approximately 15 seminar classes where the attendance is capped at 20 students. The seminars require 3 writing assignments in such classes as employment discrimination, critical race theory, and sexuality and the law. A number of internships with companies, judges, and practitioners are available. The law school is a member of an inter-institutional enrollment program that includes Duke University School of Law and University of North Carolina School of Law. The law school offers a General Externship Program for students to extern in specialty areas of the law. Placements must be approved by the Clinic Director and are available to second- and third-year students. There are also field components to the Domestic Violence, Criminal, and Civil clinics. The law school offers summer study in Costa Rica. An academic support program is available to students for assistance

with specific academic needs, problems, and adjustment expectations. Tutorials in each first-year substantive course and selected upper-level courses are open to all interested students. In addition, the law school offers a noncredit writing laboratory for 1 hour every week in the fall and spring semesters. There are active student organizations for the Innocence Project, Sports and Entertainment Law, Public Interest Law, Intellectual Property, and many other areas. The most widely taken electives are Clinical Program, Criminal Procedure, and Trial Practice.

Graduation Requirements

In order to graduate, candidates must have a GPA of 2.0, have completed the upper-division writing requirement, and satisfy oral and practical skills components.

Organizations

Students edit *The North Carolina Central Law Review* and the *Review of Biotechnology and Pharmaceutical Law*. Moot court competitions include the J. Braxton Craven, Jr. Memorial Moot Court Competition; Saul Lefkowitz Moot Court Competition; and the Ernest B. Fullwood Moot Court Competition. Other competitions include the Trial Advocacy Competition, National Trial Competition, and the Association of Trial Lawyers of America (ATLA) Trial Competition. Law student organizations include the Student Bar Association, Black Law Students Association, and the Public Interest Law Association. There are local chapters of Phi Alpha Delta and Phi Delta Phi. Other organizations include Women's Caucus, Sports and Entertainment Law Association, and Outlaw Alliance.

Library

The law library contains 388,660 hardcopy volumes and 1,074,887 microform volume equivalents, and subscribes to 818 serial publications. Such on-line databases and networks as CALI, CIS Universe, Infotrac, LEXIS, LOIS, OCLC First Search, and WESTLAW are available to law students for research. Special library collections include depository for state and federal documents. The ratio of library volumes to faculty is 13,402 to 1 and to students is 647 to 1. The ratio of seats in the library to students is 1 to 2.

Placement

J.D.s awarded:	189
Services available through: a separate law school placement center	
Services: workshop sessions on various practice areas; mock interviews; and participation in job fairs	
Special features: placement programs that bring in recruiters from government, private firms, legal services, and corporations.	
Full-time job interviews:	7 employers
Summer job interviews:	32 employers
Placement by graduation:	n/av
Placement within 9 months:	83% of class
Average starting salary:	n/av
Areas of placement:	
Private practice 2-100	53%
Government	22%
Public interest	7%
Judicial clerkships	6%
Business/industry	6%
Academic	1%
Unknown	5%

Faculty

The law school has 29 full-time and 20 part-time faculty members, of whom 27 are women. According to AAUP standards for Category IIA institutions, faculty salaries are average. About 35% of full-time faculty have a graduate law degree in addition to the J.D. The ratio of full-time students to full-time faculty in an average class is 17 to 1. The law school has a regular program of bringing visiting professors and other distinguished lecturers and visitors to campus.

Students

About 61% of the student body are women; 55%, minorities; 49%, African American; 3%, Asian American; 3%, Hispanic; 1%, Native American; and 4%, Foreign National and unreported. The majority of students come from North Carolina (80%). The average age of entering students is 23; age range is 21 to 60. About 14% of students enter directly from undergraduate school and 13% have a graduate degree. About 13% drop out after the first year for academic or personal reasons; 96% remain to receive a law degree.

NORTHEASTERN UNIVERSITY

School of Law

400 Huntington Avenue
Boston, MA 02115

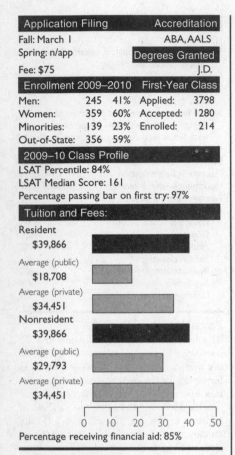

Application Filing		Accreditation
Fall: March 1		ABA, AALS
Spring: n/app		
		Degrees Granted
Fee: $75		J.D.

Enrollment 2009–2010		First-Year Class	
Men:	245 41%	Applied:	3798
Women:	359 60%	Accepted:	1280
Minorities:	139 23%	Enrolled:	214
Out-of-State:	356 59%		

2009–10 Class Profile
LSAT Percentile: 84%
LSAT Median Score: 161
Percentage passing bar on first try: 97%

Tuition and Fees:

Resident
$39,866

Average (public)
$18,708

Average (private)
$34,451

Nonresident
$39,866

Average (public)
$29,793

Average (private)
$34,451

0   10   20   30   40   50

Percentage receiving financial aid: 85%

ADMISSIONS
In the fall 2009 first-year class, 3798 applied, 1280 were accepted, and 214 enrolled. Twenty-three transfers enrolled. The median LSAT percentile of the most recent first-year class was 84; the median GPA was 3.4 on a scale of 4.0. The lowest LSAT percentile accepted was 23; the highest was 99.

Requirements
Applicants must have a bachelor's degree and take the LSAT. The most important admission factors include general background, LSAT results, and GPA. No specific undergraduate courses are required. Candidates are not interviewed.

Procedure
The application deadline for fall entry is March 1. Applicants should submit an application form, LSAT results, transcripts, a personal statement, TOEFL, if indicated, a nonrefundable application fee of $75, 2 letters of recommendation, and resume. Notification of the admissions

decision is on a modified rolling basis. The latest acceptable LSAT test date for fall entry is February. The law school uses the LSDAS.

Special
The law school recruits minority and disadvantaged students by targeting historically black colleges and universities, providing scholarships, and being a member of CLEO. Requirements are not different for out-of-state students. Transfer students must have one year of credit, have attended an ABA-approved law school, and must submit 1 recommendation from the dean of their current law school attesting to their good standing and eligibility, and at least 1 letter from a first-year law professor.

Costs
Tuition and fees for the 2009-2010 academic year are $39,866 for all full-time students. On-campus room and board costs about $17,700 annually; books and supplies run $1500.

Financial Aid
About 85% of current law students receive some form of aid. The average annual amount of aid from all sources combined, including scholarships, loans, and work contracts, is $48,322; maximum, $65,691. Awards are based on need and merit. Required financial statements are the FAFSA, institutional application, and federal tax returns. The aid application deadline for fall entry is February 15. First-year students are notified about their financial aid application at time of acceptance and upon completion of financial aid application information .

About the Law School
Northeastern University School of Law was established in 1898 and is a private institution. The 67-acre campus is in an urban area in Boston. The primary mission of the law school is to fuse theory and practice with ethical and social justice ideals so students understand what lawyers do, how they do it, and the difference they can make in the lives of others. Students have access to federal, state, county, city, and local agencies, courts, correctional facilities, law firms, and legal aid organizations in the Boston area. Housing for

students is available on campus. All law school facilities are accessible to the physically disabled.

Calendar
The law school operates on a semester basis the first year and on a quarter basis the second and third years. Courses for full-time students are offered days only and must be completed within 5 years. There is no part-time program. New students are admitted in the fall. There is a 12-week summer session. Transferable summer courses are offered.

Programs
Students may take relevant courses in other programs and apply credit toward the J.D.; a maximum of 12 credits may be applied. The following joint degrees may be earned: J.D./M.A. (Juris Doctor/Master of Arts in sustainable international development), J.D./M.B.A. (Juris Doctor/Master of Business Administration), J.D./M.E.L.P. (Juris Doctor/Master in Environmental Law and Policy), J.D./M.P.H. (Juris Doctor/Master of Public Health), J.D./M.S. (Juris Doctor/Master of Science in accounting), and J.S./M.S./Ph.D. (Juris Doctor/Master of Science/Doctor of Philosophy).

Required
To earn the J.D., candidates must complete 87 total credits, of which 37 are for required courses. The following first-year courses are required of all students: Civil Procedure, Constitutional Issues, Contracts, Criminal Justice, Legal Skills in social context, Property, and Torts. Required upper-level courses consist of Professional Responsibility. Students are required to complete 4 supervised legal internships under the school's program of cooperative legal education. In the second and third year of school, students alternate every 3 months between full-time class work and full-time co-op work. The school also offers traditional clinical courses as electives for upper-level students. The required orientation program for first-year students is 2 to 3 days and introduces students to the first-year curriculum, faculty, law school, and university services.

Phone: 617-373-2395
Fax: 617-373-8865
E-mail: c.taubman@neu.edu
Web: www.slaw.neu.edu

Contact
Carrie Taubman, Assistant Dean and Director, 617-373-2395 for general inquiries; Linda Schoendorf, Director of Financial Aid, 617-373-4620 for financial aid information.

MASSACHUSETTS

Electives
The School of Law offers concentrations in corporate law, criminal law, environmental law, family law, intellectual property law, international law, labor law, litigation, tax law, public interest, advocacy, and human rights. In addition, clinical courses for upper-level students include Certiorari Clinic/Criminal Appeals for 3 credits, Criminal Advocacy for 7 credits, Poverty Law and Practice for 6 credits. Public Health Legal Clinic for 6 credits, Domestic Violence for 6 credits, and Prisoner's Rights for 6 credits. Seminars include Global Aids Policy Seminar, International Human Rights Legal Research Seminar, Balancing Liberty and Security Seminar, Professional Responsibility Seminar, Teaching the Constitution Seminar, and Transactional Drafting Seminar. Research assistantships are available with individual professors. Students are required to complete 4 distinct cooperative legal education externship quarters during the second and third year of school, alternating every 3 months between full-time classes and full-time work. Special lecture series include the Northeastern Law Forum, Gordon Lecture Doynard Fellows Program, and Givelber Distinguished Lecture Program. Study abroad is possible as well as international co-op placements. There are many academic support programs, including the Legal Writing Workshop, Legal Analysis Workshop, and Analytical Skills Workshop. Upper-level courses include Advanced Legal Research, Legal Research and Writing, and Academic Success Legal Analysis, a-1 credit bar preparation course. Minority students may take advantage of the Analytical Skills Workshop. Special interest group programs include the Tobacco Products Liability Project, Prisoner's Assistance Project, Domestic Violence Institute, Human Rights and the Global Economy, and Public Health Advocacy Institute. The most widely taken electives are Evidence, Corporations, Federal Courts and the Federal System, and Trusts and Estates.

Graduation Requirements
In order to graduate, candidates must have completed the upper-division writing requirement, cooperative education, and a public interest requirement.

Organizations
Students edit the *Northeastern University Law Journal* primarily Moot court competitions include the Frederick Douglass Moot Court Competition, ABA National Appellate Advocacy, and National Trial Moot Court. Law student organizations include Jewish Law Students, Legal Environmental Advocacy Forum (LEAP), and International Law Society. Local chapters of national associations include National Lawyers Guild, Queer Caucus, and Jewish Law Students Association. Other organizations include the Black Law Students Association, Asian Pacific Law Students Association, and Latino/Latina Law Students Association.

Library
The law library contains 335,453 hardcopy volumes and 201,355 microform volume equivalents, and subscribes to 13,687 serial publications. Such on-line databases and networks as CALI, CIS Universe, DIALOG, Infotrac, Legal-Trac, LEXIS, LOIS, Mathew Bender, NEXIS, OCLC First Search, WESTLAW, Wilsonline Indexes, Social Law Library's on-line database, BNA core with Tax Management; Hein Online; CIAO; Constitutions of the Countries of the World; Environment Law Reporter; Government Search; and Treaties and International Agreements Online are available to law students for research. Students have access to more than 300 additional databases and research netwroks through the university library. Special library collections include the Sara Ehrmann Collection on the death penalty and the Pappas Public Interest Law Collection. Recently, the library Underwent extensive renovations and gained about 4000 square feet of space for collections and researchers. Added amenities include a large computer classroom, a sun-filled reading room, and a convenient street-level entrance. The ratio of library volumes to faculty is 9318 to 1 and to students is 557 to 1. The ratio of seats in the library to students is 1 to 1.

Faculty
The law school has 36 full-time and 45 part-time faculty members, of whom 37 are women. According to AAUP standards for Category I institutions, faculty salaries are average. About 9% of full-time faculty have a graduate law degree in addition to the J.D.; about 12% of part-time faculty

Placement

J.D.s awarded:	221

Services available through: a separate law school placement center

Services: a Career Resource Library, materials prepared by the Office of Career Services on career-related topics, on-campus interview programs, and participation in numerous job fairs and informational programs.

Special features: The director of the office is an attorney and the associate director has a master's degree in management. The Career Services Office works in collaboration with the Office of Cooperative Legal Education to provide career counseling as well as to guarantee one year of practical legal experience (4, 3-month, full-time legal internships) prior to graduation. Approximately 40% of graduates obtain their first job from one of their internships.

Full-time job interviews:	16 employers
Summer job interviews:	39 employers
Placement by graduation:	n/av
Placement within 9 months:	94% of class
Average starting salary:	$36,000 to $160,000

Areas of placement:

Private practice 2-10 attorneys	9%
Private practice 11-25 attorneys	6%
Private practice 26-50 attorneys	4%
Private practice 51-100 attorneys	2%
private practice-100+ attorneys	13%
Business/industry	26%
Public interest	16%
Judicial clerkships	13%
Government	8%
Academic	3%

have one. The ratio of full-time students to full-time faculty in an average class is 17 to 1; in a clinic, 6 to 1. The law school has a regular program of bringing visiting professors and other distinguished lecturers and visitors to campus.

Students
About 60% of the student body are women; 23%, minorities; 8%, African American; 6%, Asian American; 8%, Hispanic; and 1%, Native American. The majority of students come from Massachusetts (41%). The average age of entering students is 25; age range is 20 to 51. About 26% of students enter directly from undergraduate school, 9% have a graduate degree, and 74% have worked full-time prior to entering law school. About 1% drop out after the first year for academic or personal reasons; 99% remain to receive a law degree.

College of Law

Swen Parson Hall, Room 151
De Kalb, IL 60115-2890

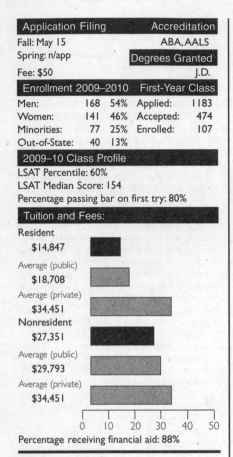

Application Filing		Accreditation
Fall: May 15		ABA, AALS
Spring: n/app		**Degrees Granted**
Fee: $50		J.D.

Enrollment 2009–2010		First-Year Class	
Men:	168 54%	Applied:	1183
Women:	141 46%	Accepted:	474
Minorities:	77 25%	Enrolled:	107
Out-of-State:	40 13%		

2009–10 Class Profile

LSAT Percentile: 60%
LSAT Median Score: 154
Percentage passing bar on first try: 80%

Tuition and Fees:

Resident
$14,847

Average (public)
$18,708

Average (private)
$34,451

Nonresident
$27,351

Average (public)
$29,793

Average (private)
$34,451

Percentage receiving financial aid: 88%

ADMISSIONS

In the fall 2009 first-year class, 1183 applied, 474 were accepted, and 107 enrolled. One transfer enrolled. The median LSAT percentile of the most recent first-year class was 60; the median GPA was 3.23 on a scale of 4.0. The lowest LSAT percentile accepted was 17; the highest was 89.

Requirements
Applicants must have a bachelor's degree and take the LSAT. The most important admission factors include academic achievement, LSAT results, and letter of recommendation. No specific undergraduate courses are required. Candidates are not interviewed.

Procedure
The application deadline for fall entry is May 15. Applicants should submit an application form, LSAT results, transcripts, a personal statement, a nonrefundable application fee of $50, 2 letters of recommendation, LSDAS report, and resume. Notification of the admissions decision is on a rolling basis. The latest acceptable LSAT test date for fall entry is June. The law school uses the LSDAS.

Special
The law school recruits minority and disadvantaged students through the BLSA, LLSA, ALSN, and the Women's Law Caucus who work closely with the Admissions Office to increase the student body's diversity. Graduate Assistants in the Office of Admission participate in various recruiting events throughout the year, including the Annual Illinois Latino Law Forum. Requirements are not different for out-of-state students. Transfer students must have one year of credit and have attended an ABA-approved law school.

Costs

Tuition and fees for the 2009-2010 academic year are $14,847 for full-time in-state students and $27,351 for out-of-state students. On-campus room and board costs about $10,032 annually; books and supplies run $1500.

Financial Aid

About 88% of current law students receive some form of aid. The average annual amount of aid from all sources combined, including scholarships, loans, and work contracts, is $20,378; maximum, $42,764. Awards are based on need and merit. Required financial statements are the FAFSA and in-house financial aid verification form. The aid application deadline for fall entry is March 1. Special funds for minority or disadvantaged students include scholarships for partial- or full-tuition waivers (some with stipends) available to culturally and/or financially disadvantaged individuals. First-year students are notified about their financial aid application after acceptance.

About the Law School

Northern Illinois University College of Law was established in 1979 and is a public institution. The 755-acre campus is in a small town 65 miles west of Chicago. The primary mission of the law school is to prepare students to become effective, creative, and ethical lawyers, ready to serve the legal needs of their communities. Students have access to federal, state, county, city, and local agencies, courts, correctional facilities, law firms, and legal aid organizations in the DeKalb area. Facilities of special interest to law students include a full service law library, adjacent to the main university library; a computer laboratory for law students; 2 courtrooms; and 7 smart classrooms equipped with updated technology. Housing for students includes Neptune Hall, one block away from the law school, whose first floor is designated and equipped for law students. There are also affordable apartment options surrounding the campus. All law school facilities are accessible to the physically disabled.

Calendar

The law school operates on a traditional semester basis. Courses for full-time students are offered. Primarily during the day (there are some upper-division wvwning courses) and must be completed within 3 years. For part-time students, courses are offered days only and must be completed within 5 years. New full- and part-time students are admitted in the fall. There is a 6-week summer session. Transferable summer courses are offered.

Programs

Students may take relevant courses in other programs and apply credit toward the J.D.; a maximum of 6 credits may be applied. The following joint degrees may be earned: J.D./M.B.A. (Juris Doctor/Master of Business Administration) and J.D./M.P.A. (Juris Doctor/Master of Public Administration).

Required
To earn the J.D., candidates must complete 90 total credits, of which 43 are for required courses. They must maintain a minimum GPA of 2.0 in the required courses. The following first-year courses are required of all students: Basic Legal Research I and II, Civil Procedure, Constitutional Law I, Contract I and II, Criminal Law, Legal Writing, Advocacy I and II, Property, and Torts I and II. Required upper-level courses consist of a writing seminar, Constitutional Law II, Lawyering Skills, and Professional Responsibility. Students are not required to take clinical courses but must take a skills course. The required orientation program for first-year students is a week-long orientation

Phone: 815-753-8595
892-3050
Fax: 815-753-5680
E-mail: lawadm@niu.edu
Web: hiu.edu/law

Contact

Admissions Staff, 815-753-8595 for general inquiries; Sandra Polanco, Assistant Director of Admissions and Financial Aid, 815-753-9485 for financial aid information.

ILLINOIS

introducing briefing cases, case synthesis, outlining, exam preparation, and ethics and professionalism.

Electives

The Zeke Giorgi Legal Clinic offers clinics in criminal defense, domestic abuse, elder law, and mediation. Clinics are 4 credit hours. All students must complete a 3-hour seminar in their fourth or fifth semester. The College of Law offers a 6-credit hour study abroad program in Agen, France every summer. Comparative Labor and Employment Law; Disability Law; and Women, Law and the Global Economy. Seminars include Externships are offered in the Judicial Externship Program, which places students with state and federal judges; civil and criminal externships are also available with state criminal prosecutors and public defenders, and appellate defender externships are available at the Illinois Appellate Defender Office. There is the annual Riley Lecture Series on Professionalism, the annual Law Review Symposium, and the Marla Dickerson Lecture Series. Seminars include Comparative Labor and Employment Law; Disability Law; and Women, Law and the Global Economy. The Academic Support Program is available for students who may need additional support during the first and second year of law school. Each minority group has a student organization. Speakers on a variety of topics are sponsored by the Women's Law Caucus, International Law Society, BLSA, and LLSA. The most widely taken electives are Agency, Corporations, and Real Estate Transactions.

Graduation Requirements

In order to graduate, candidates must have a GPA of 2.0 and have completed the upper-division writing requirement.

Organizations

The *Northern Illinois University Law Review* is a student-edited publication. Teams compete at the National Moot Court, Chicago Bar Association, and International Information Technology and Privacy Law competitions. Other competitions include the ABA Client Counseling, the ABA National Appellate Advocacy, and National Trial Advocacy, Negotiation, and Alternative Dispute Resolution. Student organizations include the International Law Society, Women's Law Caucus, and the Public Interest Law Society. There are local chapters of Phi Alpha Delta and Delta Theta Phi. Other organizations include the BLSA, LLSA, and Moot Court Society.

Library

The law library contains 262,244 hardcopy volumes and 98,075 microform volume equivalents, and subscribes to 1650 serial publications. Such on-line databases and networks as CALI, CIS Universe, Legal-Trac, LEXIS, LOIS, NEXIS, OCLC First Search, WESTLAW, BNA, HeinOnline, Versus Law, CCH Intelliconnect, RIA, GovSearch, IICLE, Making of Modern Law-Sub-collections: Trials; Eighteenth Century Collections Online; and Legal Documents are available to law students for research. Special library collections include a selective federal document depository. The ratio of library volumes to faculty is 10,927 to 1 and to students is 849 to 1. The ratio of seats in the library to students is 1 to 2.

Faculty

The law school has 24 full-time and 14 part-time faculty members, of whom 16 are women. According to AAUP standards for Category I institutions, faculty salaries are well below average. About 13% of full-time faculty have a graduate law degree in addition to the J.D. The ratio of full-time students to full-time faculty in an average class is 20 to 1; in a clinic, 7 to 1. The law school has a regular program of bringing visiting professors and other distinguished lecturers and visitors to campus.

Students

About 46% of the student body are women; 25%, minorities; 7%, African American; 7%, Asian American; 10%, Hispanic; and 1%, Native American. The majority of students come from Illinois (87%). The average age of entering students is 25; age range is 21 to 54. About 40% of students enter directly from undergraduate school, 6% have a graduate degree, and 60% have worked full-time prior to entering law school. About 10% drop out after the first year for academic or personal reasons; 90% remain to receive a law degree.

Placement

J.D.s awarded:	92

Services available through: a separate law school placement center and the university placement center

Services: participating in regional and national job fairs

Special features: individual career counseling for students and alumni about traditional and nontraditional jobs for law graduates.

Full-time job interviews:	12 employers
Summer job interviews:	10 employers
Placement by graduation:	40% of class
Placement within 9 months:	90% of class
Average starting salary:	$42,000 to $52,000

Areas of placement:

Private practice 2-10 attorneys	42%
Private practice 11-50 attorneys	10%
Private practice 101 + attorneys, solo practice	6%
Government	15%
Business/industry	13%
Public interest	5%
Military	4%
Judicial clerkships	2%
Academic	2%

Salmon P. Chase College of Law

Louie B. Nunn Hall
Highland Heights, KY 41099

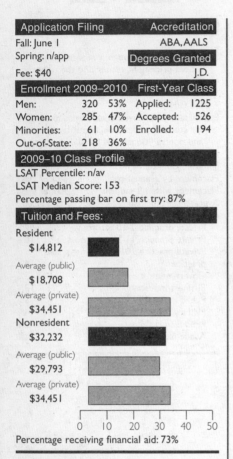

Application Filing		Accreditation
Fall: June 1		ABA, AALS
Spring: n/app		Degrees Granted
Fee: $40		J.D.

Enrollment 2009–2010		First-Year Class	
Men:	320 53%	Applied:	1225
Women:	285 47%	Accepted:	526
Minorities:	61 10%	Enrolled:	194
Out-of-State:	218 36%		

2009–10 Class Profile
LSAT Percentile: n/av
LSAT Median Score: 153
Percentage passing bar on first try: 87%

Tuition and Fees:

Resident
$14,812

Average (public)
$18,708

Average (private)
$34,451

Nonresident
$32,232

Average (public)
$29,793

Average (private)
$34,451

0 10 20 30 40 50

Percentage receiving financial aid: 73%

ADMISSIONS

In the fall 2009 first-year class, 1225 applied, 526 were accepted, and 194 enrolled. Ten transfers enrolled. The median GPA of the most recent first-year class was 3.35.

Requirements

Applicants must have a bachelor's degree and take the LSAT. The most important admission factors include LSAT results, GPA, and writing ability. No specific undergraduate courses are required. Candidates are not interviewed.

Procedure

The application deadline for fall entry is June 1. Applicants should submit an application form, LSAT results, transcripts, a personal statement, a nonrefundable application fee of $40, answers to all applicable essay questions, and 2 letters of recommendation must be submitted to LSDAS. A $150 acceptance deposit must be submitted after an offer has been made and a $300 registration deposit is required preceding enrollment. Notification of the admissions

decision is on a rolling basis. The latest acceptable LSAT test date for fall entry is February, but will consider June scores. The law school uses the LSDAS.

Special

The law school recruits minority and disadvantaged students by participating in prelaw and career fairs geared toward diverse attendees; collaborating with the Black Law Students Association and the Latino Law Group; offering diversity scholarships; participating in programs sponsored by the Law School Admissins Council; and hosting Diversity Days on campus. Requirements are not different for out-of-state students. Transfer students must have a minimum GPA of 3.0, have attended an ABA-approved law school, must be in good standing and eligible to continue study, and must provide an official transcript documenting acceptably high-quality performance.

Costs

Tuition and fees for the 2009-2010 academic year are $14,812 for full-time in-state students and $32,232 for out-of-state students. Tuition for part-time students is $11,410 in-state and $24,810 out-of-state. On-campus room and board costs about $9956 annually; books and supplies run $1000.

Financial Aid

About 73% of current law students receive some form of aid. The average annual amount of aid from all sources combined, including scholarships, loans, and work contracts, is $24,763; maximum, $45,757. Awards are based on need and merit, with a number of scholarships based on merit, need, or a combination of both. Required financial statement is the FAFSA. The aid application deadline for fall entry is March 1. Special funds for minority or disadvantaged students include designated scholarship funds. First-year students are notified about their financial aid application at time of acceptance, after processing the aid application.

About the Law School

Northern Kentucky University Salmon P. Chase College of Law was established in 1893 and is a public institution. The 300-acre campus is in a suburban area 7 miles southeast of Cincinnati. The primary mission of the law school is to provide an

intellectually rigorous education in legal theory and professional skills and to instill the ideals of ethics, leadership, and public engagement. Students have access to federal, state, county, city, and local agencies, courts, correctional facilities, law firms, and legal aid organizations in the Highland Heights area. The school is located in a major metropolitan area that provides a wide variety of opportunities for law students. Facilities of special interest to law students include the Center for Excellence in Advocacy and the Transactional Law Practice Center, which provide opportunities for students to be practice ready upon graduation. Housing for students is available on campus through NKU's Office of University Housing, including suites or apartments. There are also several private, off-campus apartment communities nearby. All law school facilities are accessible to the physically disabled.

Calendar

The law school operates on a traditional semester basis. Courses for full-time students are offered days only, with some electives being offered on Saturdays, and must be completed within 3½ years. For part-time students, courses are offered both day and evening and Saturdays and must be completed within 5 years. New full- and part-time students are admitted in the fall. There is a 2-8-week summer session. Transferable summer courses are offered.

Programs

The following joint degrees may be earned: J.D./M.B.A. (Juris Doctor/Master of Business Administration).

Required

To earn the J.D., candidates must complete 90 total credits, of which 48 are for required courses. They must maintain a minimum GPA of 2.0 in the required courses. The following first-year courses are required of all students: Basic Legal Skills I and II, Civil Procedure I and II, Contracts I and II, Legal Analysis and Problem Solving, Property I and II, and Torts I and II. Required upper-level courses consist of Constitutional Law I and II, Criminal Law, Criminal Procedure, Evidence, and Professional Responsibility. Students are allowed to use a maximum of 18 non-classroom hours of credit toward graduation. The required orienta-

Phone: 859-572-5490
888-465-7316
Fax: 859-572-6081
E-mail: brayg@nku.edu
Web: http://chaselaw.nku.edu

Contact
Gina Bray, Admissions Specialist, 859-572-5490 for general inquiries; Leah Stewart, Director, Student Financial Assist, 859-572-6437 for financial aid information.

KENTUCKY

tion program for first-year students consists of Legal Analysis and Problem Solving (LAPS), which is a 2-week 1-credit required course that takes place before the fall semester begins. LAPS focuses on the skills needed in the first semester of law school such as case briefing and participation in the Socratic method. Information about law school requirements and student services such as Student Success Initiatives, and professionalism matters are provided as well. LAPS continues through the fall semester with both required and optional meetings on matters such as outlining and exam answering. It also provides small group study opportunities led by upper-level law students.

Electives
Students must take 15 credits in their area of concentration. The Salmon P. Chase College of Law offers concentrations in labor law, tax law, and certificate programs in Advocacy and in Transactional Law. In addition, students may earn academic credit while working under the supervision of licensed practicing attorneys in specialized externship clinics such as the Kentucky Innocence Project, the Constitutional Litigation Clinic, and the Local Government Law Center. Externships are also available in the areas of intellectual property, criminal prosecution, criminal defense, labor law, children's law, and government agencies and offices. The Chase Local Government Law Center clinical internship allows students to research and draft answers to questions from local governments, to participate in the drafting of model ordinances for cities and counties, and to be involved in the development and production of local government practice guides on matters ranging from criminal law to land use and zoning. Seminars include Business, Technology, and Regulation; Constitutional Law Seminar, and Criminal Law/Justice Seminar. An active supervised independent research program is offered. Public policy research opportunities are available through the in-house Local Government Law Center. The Law Review sponsors a national symposium twice each year. Chase's Student Success Initiatives program provides a wide range of workshops, one-on-one help with writing or question and answer sessions provided by Chase faculty. The Student Success Initiative program also addresses remedial issues. Individual assistance is available from

Chase's Office of Student Success Initiatives. Professional and social activities, as well as special tutorial assistance are available in conjunction with the Black Lawyers Association of Cincinnati (BLAC) and the Cincinnati Bar Association/BLAC Lawyers' Association Roundtable. A variety of programs throughout the year are sponsored by the Chase Public Interest Group, Student Bar Association, International Law Society, and National Women's Law Caucus. The most widely taken electives are Alternative Dispute Resolution, Modern Real Estate Transactions, and Employment Discrimination.

Graduation Requirements
In order to graduate, candidates must have a GPA of 2.0 and have completed the upper-division writing requirement.

Organizations
The primary law review is the Northern Kentucky Law Review. Students participate in a variety of moot court competitions at numerous locations, including the Evan A. Evans Constitutional Law Moot Court Competition, August A. Rendigs Jr. National Moot Court Competition, and the Robert F. Wagner National Labor and Employment Law Moot Court Competition. Other competitions include the National Trial Advocacy Competition, AAJ Student Trial Advocacy Competition, and the Jerome Prince Memorial Evidence Moot Court Competition. Law student organizations include the Chase Public Interest Group, Black Law Students Association, and the Chase IP Society. The International Law Students Association, Intellectual Property Society, and the Chase Latino Law Association are represented on campus.

Library
The law library contains 335,312 hardcopy volumes and 173,343 microform volume equivalents, and subscribes to 2301 serial publications. Such on-line databases and networks as CALI, CIS Universe, Infotrac, Legal-Trac, LEXIS, Mathew Bender, NEXIS, OCLC First Search, WESTLAW, Wilsonline Indexes, and Kentucky Virtual Library, BNA-Online, CCH Online, and HeinOnline. are available to law students for research. Special library collections include Kentucky Appellate Court Briefs. Recently, the library added more student seating. The ratio of library volumes to faculty is 12,775 to 1 and to

Placement

J.D.s awarded:	132

Services available through: a separate law school placement center

Services: information and advising legal career path

Special features: Workshops and job fairs, including participation in the Tri-State Diversity Recruitment Program, Alumni Speaker Series, BLAC-CBA Roundtable Minority Clerkship Program, Equal Justice Works Career Fair, Loyola Patent Law Program, Indianapolis Bar Association Diversity Job Fair, and Southeastern Intellectual Property Job Fair.

Full-time job interviews:	15 employers
Summer job interviews:	32 employers
Placement by graduation:	53% of class
Placement within 9 months:	93% of class
Average starting salary:	$28,000 to $140,000

Areas of placement:

Private practice 2-10 attorneys	31%
Private practice 11-25 attorneys	2%
Private practice 26-50 attorneys	2%
Private practice 51-100 attorneys	3%
Private practice 101+ attorneys	6
Solo practice	7%
Business/industry	21%
Government	10%
Judicial clerkships	8%
Public Interest	7%
Military	1%
Academic	1%

students is 612 to 1. The ratio of seats in the library to students is 1 to 3.

Faculty
The law school has 29 full-time and 14 part-time faculty members, of whom 12 are women. About 31% of full-time faculty have a graduate law degree in addition to the J.D.; about 4% of part-time faculty have one. The ratio of full-time students to full-time faculty in an average class is 42 to 1; in a clinic, 4 to 1. The law school has a regular program of bringing visiting professors and other distinguished lecturers and visitors to campus.

Students
About 47% of the student body are women; 10%, minorities; 5%, African American; 2%, Asian American; and 1%, Hispanic. The majority of students come from Kentucky (64%). The average age of entering students is 27; age range is 21 to 53. About 26% of students enter directly from undergraduate school and 13% have a graduate degree. About 6% drop out after the first year for academic or personal reasons; 94% remain to receive a law degree.

School of Law

357 East Chicago Avenue
Chicago, IL 60611

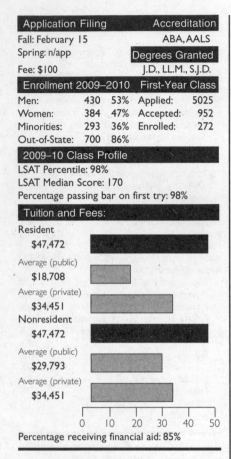

Application Filing	Accreditation
Fall: February 15	ABA, AALS
Spring: n/app	**Degrees Granted**
Fee: $100	J.D., LL.M., S.J.D.

Enrollment 2009–2010		First-Year Class	
Men:	430 53%	Applied:	5025
Women:	384 47%	Accepted:	952
Minorities:	293 36%	Enrolled:	272
Out-of-State:	700 86%		

2009–10 Class Profile
LSAT Percentile: 98%
LSAT Median Score: 170
Percentage passing bar on first try: 98%

Tuition and Fees:

Resident
$47,472

Average (public)
$18,708

Average (private)
$34,451

Nonresident
$47,472

Average (public)
$29,793

Average (private)
$34,451

0 10 20 30 40 50

Percentage receiving financial aid: 85%

ADMISSIONS

In the fall 2009 first-year class, 5025 applied, 952 were accepted, and 272 enrolled. Seventy-six transfers enrolled. The median LSAT percentile of the most recent first-year class was 98; the median GPA was 3.72 on a scale of 4.0. The lowest LSAT percentile accepted was 20; the highest was 100.

Requirements
Applicants must have a bachelor's degree and take the LSAT for the accelerated J.D. program, applicants may take either the LSAT ot the GMAT. The most important admission factors include academic achievement, life experience, and personal interview. No specific undergraduate courses are required. Candidates are interviewed.

Procedure
The application deadline for fall entry is February 15. Applicants should submit an application form, LSAT results, transcripts, a personal statement, a nonrefundable appli-

cation fee of $100, 1 letter of recommendation, and a resume. Registration with LSDAS is required. Interviews are strongly encouraged. Notification of the admissions decision is by April 30. The latest acceptable LSAT test date for fall entry is February. The law school uses the LSDAS.

Special
The law school recruits minority and disadvantaged students through the efforts of the Director of Diversity Education and Outreach. Requirements are not different for out-of-state students. Transfer students must have one year of credit, have attended an ABA-approved law school, and have earned a minimum of 30 credit hours.

Costs

Tuition and fees for the 2009-2010 academic year are $47,472 for all full-time students. On-campus room and board costs about $12,376 annually; books and supplies run $1418.

Financial Aid

About 85% of current law students receive some form of aid. Awards are based on need and merit. Required financial statements are the FAFSA and Need Access Financial Aid Application Form. The aid application deadline for fall entry is February 1. First-year students are notified about their financial aid application before April 30 if all required documents are received by the Office of Admission and Financial Aid before the February 1 deadline.

About the Law School

Northwestern University School of Law was established in 1859 and is a private institution. The 20-acre campus is in an urban area in Chicago. The primary mission of the law school is to advance the understanding of law and legal institutions and to produce graduates who are prepared to lead and succeed in a rapidly changing world. Students have access to federal, state, county, city, and local agencies, courts, correctional facilities, law firms, and legal aid organizations in the Chicago area. The Arthur Rubloff Building, an addition to the school, houses the American Bar Foundation. Facilities of special interest to law students consist of 1 fully equipped, modern courtroom. The Bluhm Legal Clinic is housed in a modern and spacious facility and mirrors the set-

ting of major urban law firms. About 90% of the law school facilities are accessible to the physically disabled.

Calendar

The law school operates on a traditional semester basis. Courses for full-time students are offered both day and evening and must be completed within 3 years (there is also an accelerated 2-year J.D. program).There is no part-time program. New students are admitted in the fall and summer (students in the accelerated J.D. program). There is a 10-week summer session for the J.D./M.B.A. and accelerated J.D. programs only.. Transferable summer courses are not offered.

Programs

In addition to the J.D., the law school offers the S.J.D. and LL.M. with a certificate in mangement, LL.M. in Taxation; LL.M. in International Human Rights; 2-year J.D. for students with a Foreign law degree. Students may take relevant courses in other programs and apply credit toward the J.D.; a maximum of 10 credits may be applied. The following joint degrees may be earned: J.D./D.E.S.S. (Juris Doctor with Science Po in Paris, France), J.D./LL.M. (Juris Doctor/ Master of Laws in Taxation and International), J.D./M.B.A. (Juris Doctor/Master of Business Administration), and J.D./Ph.D. (Juris Doctor/Doctor of Philosophy).

Required
To earn the J.D., candidates must complete 83 total credits, of which 29 are for required courses. They must maintain a minimum GPA of 2.25 in the required courses. The following first-year courses are required of all students: Civil Procedure, Communication and Legal Reasoning, Constitutional Law, Contracts, Criminal Law, Property, and Torts. Required upper-level courses consist of a senior research project and Legal Ethics. The required orientation program for first-year students is 1 week before classes begin. First-year students register and receive class assignments, meet with their faculty advisers, tour the school, and attend team-building and diversity workshops as well as social functions.

Electives
The School of Law offers concentrations in corporate law, international law, litigation, dispute resolution, law and

Phone: 312-503-8465
Fax: 312-503-0178
E-mail: admissions@law.northwestern.edu
Web: www.law.northwestern.edu

Contact

Johann Lee, Assistant Dean, 312-503-8465 for general inquiries and for financial aid information.

ILLINOIS

social policy, and academic career track. In addition, clinics are open to second- and third-year students. A sequence of simulation-based courses offered in the second year includes Clinical Trial Advocacy and Pre-Trial Litigation, as well as case-based instruction. Students also take clinically based Evidence, which presents the principles of evidence in the context of simulated cases. Course credits vary between 3 and 4 hours. Students can represent clients through the Children and Family Justice Center, Small Business Opportunity Center, Center for International Human Rights, Center on Wrongful Conviction, Investor Protection Center, MacArthur Justice Center, and the Appellate Advocacy Program. Seminars are offered in legal history, civil rights litigation, race relations, and other areas. Through the Owen L. Coon/James L. Rahl Senior Research Program, a third-year student may earn up to 14 credits for advanced research under the personal supervision of 1 or more faculty members. Completion of this project fulfills the graduation writing requirement. Directed reading and research, supervised by faculty members, is available to second-year students. Practicums consist of a 10- to 12- hour-per-week field work component and a weekly 2-hour seminar. Practicums are available in the areas of corporate counsel, judicial, mediation, public interest, and criminal law. Annually, the Rosenthal Lecture Series brings preeminent figures in law and related fields to the school. The Pope and John Lecture on Professionalism deals with ethics and professional responsibility. The Howard J. Trienens Visiting Judicial Scholar Program brings leading jurists to the school to lecture on legal issues and to meet informally with students. The Brodsky Family Northwestern JD-MBA Lecture Series brings prominent figures in law and business. Study-abroad opportunities include Catholic University of Leuven, Belgium; Free University of Amsterdam, The Netherlands; Tel Aviv University, Israel; Universidad Torcuato Di Tella in Argentina; Bond University, Australia; University of the Andes in Chile; Bucerius Law School in Germany; National University of Singapore; University of Lucerne in Switzerland; and Instituto de Empresa in Spain. Tutorial programs are offered through the Dean of Students on an individual basis. The Director of Diversity Education and Outreach provides academic admission, placement counseling, and other supportive services. The most widely taken electives are Evidence, Business Association, and Estates and Trusts.

Graduation Requirements

In order to graduate, candidates must have a GPA of 2.25 and have completed the upper-division writing requirement, and Professional Skills and Perspective electives.

Organizations

Student-edited publications include the *Northwestern University Law Review, Journal of Criminal Law and Criminology, Northwestern Journal of International Law and Business, Northwestern Journal of Technology and Intellectual Property, Journal of International Human Rights, Journal of Social Policy*, and the newspaper, *The Pleader*. Annual moot court competitions are the Arlyn Miner First-Year Moot Court Program, Julius H. Miner Moot Court, Philip C. Jessup International Law Moot Court, and William C. Vis International Commercial Arbitration Moot Court. Other competitions are the John Paul Stevens Prize for academic excellence, Lowden-Wigmore Prizes for best student paper in international law, Arlyn Miner Book Award for the best brief by a first-year student, Harold D. Shapiro Prize for best student in an international economics relations class, the West Publishing Company Awards for scholastic achievement, and the Nathan Burkhan Memorial Competition for best paper on copyright law. Law student organizations, local chapters of national associations, and campus organizations include Order of the Coif; Amnesty International; Feminists for Social Change; National Lawyers Guild; The Federalist Society; ABA-Law Student Division; Diversity Coalition; SERV (Student Effort to Rejuvenate Volunteering); and Wigmore Follies, an annual student-run variety show.

Library

The law library contains 779,880 hard-copy volumes and 88,914 microform volume equivalents, and subscribes to 8334 serial publications. Such on-line databases and networks as CALI, CIS Universe, DIALOG, Dow-Jones, Infotrac, Legal-Trac, LEXIS, LOIS, NEXIS, OCLC First Search, RLIN, WESTLAW, Wilsonline Indexes, CCH Access, and RIA Checkpoint are available to law students for research. Special library collections include domestic and international law and rare and special collections, including Supreme Court papers of Justice Arthur J. Goldberg. Recently, the library installed a wireless network and digital microform reader/printer. The ratio of library volumes to faculty is 8862 to 1 and to students is 958 to 1. The ratio of seats in the library to students is 1 to 1.

Placement

J.D.s awarded:	273

Services available through: a separate law school placement center

Services: arrangement of job fairs for off-campus interviews, on-line searchable resume database service

Full-time job interviews:	820 employers
Summer job interviews:	820 employers
Placement by graduation:	98% of class
Placement within 9 months:	99% of class
Average starting salary:	$45,000 to $160,000

Areas of placement:

Private practice 51-100 attorneys	74%
Judicial clerkships	12%
Business/industry	5%
Public interest	5%
Government	2%
Academic	2%

Faculty

The law school has 88 full-time and 64 part-time faculty members, of whom 54 are women. According to AAUP standards for Category I institutions, faculty salaries are well above average. About 5% of full-time faculty have a graduate law degree in addition to the J.D. The ratio of full-time students to full-time faculty in an average class is 10 to 1; in a clinic, 7 to 1. The law school has a regular program of bringing visiting professors and other distinguished lecturers and visitors to campus. There is a chapter of the Order of the Coif; 40 faculty and 20 graduates are members.

Students

About 47% of the student body are women; 36%, minorities; 8%, African American; 15%, Asian American; 8%, Hispanic; and 1%, Native American. The majority of students come from the Midwest (29%). The average age of entering students is 26; age range is 21 to 40. About 3% of students enter directly from undergraduate school, 13% have a graduate degree, and 97% have worked full-time prior to entering law school. About 1% drop out after the first year for academic or personal reasons; 99% remain to receive a law degree.

Shepard Broad Law Center

3305 College Avenue
Fort Lauderdale, FL 33314-7721

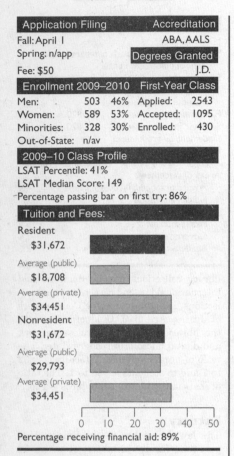

Application Filing	Accreditation
Fall: April 1	ABA, AALS
Spring: n/app	Degrees Granted
Fee: $50	J.D.

Enrollment 2009–2010		First-Year Class	
Men:	503 46%	Applied:	2543
Women:	589 53%	Accepted:	1095
Minorities:	328 30%	Enrolled:	430
Out-of-State:	n/av		

2009–10 Class Profile
LSAT Percentile: 41%
LSAT Median Score: 149
Percentage passing bar on first try: 86%

Tuition and Fees:

Resident
$31,672

Average (public)
$18,708

Average (private)
$34,451

Nonresident
$31,672

Average (public)
$29,793

Average (private)
$34,451

0   10   20   30   40   50

Percentage receiving financial aid: 89%

ADMISSIONS

In the fall 2009 first-year class, 2543 applied, 1095 were accepted, and 430 enrolled. Eighteen transfers enrolled. The median LSAT percentile of the most recent first-year class was 41; the median GPA was 3.2 on a scale of 4.0. The lowest LSAT percentile accepted was 5; the highest was 90.

Requirements
Applicants must have a bachelor's degree and take the LSAT. The most important admission factors include undergraduate curriculum, life experience, and academic achievement. No specific undergraduate courses are required. Candidates are not interviewed.

Procedure
The application deadline for fall entry is April 1. Applicants should submit an application form, LSAT results, transcripts, a nonrefundable application fee of $50, and 2 letters of recommendation are suggested. Notification of the admissions

decision is on a rolling basis. The latest acceptable LSAT test date for fall entry is February. The law school uses the LSDAS.

Special
The law school recruits minority and disadvantaged students by means of on-campus minority programs, attendance at historically black college fairs, and participation in and maintenance of a good relationship with the CLEO program. Requirements are not different for out-of-state students. Transfer students must have one year of credit, have attended an ABA-approved law school, have no grade below C in required courses, and provide a letter of good standing from the current dean. Foreign attorneys are also admitted. Preadmissions courses consist of (AAM-PLE) alternative admissions programs where students must earn at least a C+ average for 2 courses.

Costs

Tuition and fees for the 2009-2010 academic year are $31,672 for all full-time students. Tuition for part-time students is $23,878 per year. On-campus room and board costs about $13,624 annually; books and supplies run $2626.

Financial Aid

About 89% of current law students receive some form of aid. The average annual amount of aid from all sources combined, including scholarships, loans, and work contracts, is $29,353. Awards are based on need and merit. Loans are need-based. Most scholarships are merit-based; some are need-based. Required financial statements is the FAFSA. No statements are required for merit-based aid. The aid application deadline for fall entry is March 1. Special funds for minority or disadvantaged students include scholarship funds. First-year students are notified about their financial aid application when the application for aid is complete.

About the Law School

Nova Southeastern University Shepard Broad Law Center was established in 1974 and is a private institution. The 232-acre campus is in a suburban area 3 miles west of Fort Lauderdale, Florida. The primary mission of the law school is to ensure that students develop the knowledge, skills,

and values that are at the heart of becoming trusted, highly adept professional lawyers who are respected for serving their clients, their communities, and justice. Students have access to federal, state, county, city, and local agencies, courts, correctional facilities, law firms, and legal aid organizations in the Fort Lauderdale area. Facilities of special interest to law students include the law center's building, the Leo C. Goodwin Sr. Hall. All students can access computing facilities from anywhere in the building using wireless technology. Housing for students is in 4 university-owned apartment buildings; there are also numerous apartments available near the campus. All law school facilities are accessible to the physically disabled.

Calendar

The law school operates on a traditional semester basis. Courses for full-time students are offered both day and evening and must be completed within 5 years. For part-time students, courses are offered evenings only (some day classes are available) and must be completed within 6 years. New full- and part-time students are admitted in the fall. There is an 8-week summer session. Transferable summer courses are offered.

Programs

Students may take relevant courses in other programs and apply credit toward the J.D.; a maximum of 4 (8 in joint-degree) credits may be applied. The following joint degrees may be earned: J.D./M.B.A. (Juris Doctor/Master of Business Administration), J.D./M.S. (Juris Doctor/Master of Science in computer science, dispute), and J.D./M.U.R.P. (Juris Doctor/Masters of Urban and Regional Planning).

Required
To earn the J.D., candidates must complete 90 total credits, of which 57 are for required courses. The following first-year courses are required of all students: Civil Procedure, Constitutional Law I, Contracts, Criminal Law, Lawyering Skills and Values I and II, Legal Study Skills I and II, Property, and Torts. Required upper-level courses consist of Advanced Lawyering Skills and Values (2 semesters), Advanced Legal Analysis, an upper-class

Phone: 954-262-6117
800-986-6529
Fax: 954-262-3844
E-mail: *admission@nsu.law.nova.edu*
Web: *www.nsulaw.nova.edu*

Contact

Beth Hall, Assistant Dean of Admissions, 954-262-6117 for general inquiries; Marsheila Bryant, Counselor, Financial Aid, 800-522-3243 for financial aid information.

writing requirement, Business Entities, Constitutional Law II, Criminal Procedure, Evidence, Family Law, Professional Responsibility, and Wills and Trusts. The required orientation program for first-year students includes an introduction to the law school experience before classes begin; other sessions are held during the semester.

Electives

The Shepard Broad Law Center offers concentrations in corporate law, criminal law, environmental law, international law, litigation, tax law, torts and insurance, children and family, and health law. In addition, the clinics offer 12 credits to students who work with families and children, an environmental group, an international agency, a prosecutor or public defender, a corporation or business firm, a personal injury firm, or a mediation program. Some of these clinical opportunities are available for 6 to 8 credits, and a mediation program is offered for 8 credits. Upper-level students may take seminars for 2 to 3 credits. As interns, students earn 2 credits researching for a judge or serving as a Guardian ad Litem. The Career Development Office sponsors lecture series on various types of law practices. The Law Center offers a dual-degree program with the University of Barcelona and similar opportunities in other countries. Tutorial programs consist of the Academic the Critical Skills Program. Special interest group programs are the Individuals with Disabilities Project and Guardian ad Litem. Both offer credit for working to protect the rights of the disabled and children. The most widely taken electives are Sales, Remedies, and Florida Constitutional Law.

Graduation Requirements

In order to graduate, candidates must have a GPA of 2.0, have completed the upper-division writing requirement, and passed all required courses.

Organizations

Students edit the *Nova Law Review*, the *Journal of International and Comparative Law*, and the student newspaper *Broadly Speaking*. Intramural moot court competitions are held in the fall for upper-class students and in the winter for first-year students; the Law Center frequently hosts

a Round Robin Moot Court Competition. A team competes in the American Trial Lawyers Association trial competition as well as other moot court and trial competitions. Law student organizations include the Business Law Students Association, Christian Legal Society, and Jewish Law Students Association. Local chapters of national association include Hispanic Law Students Association, Black Law Students Association, and Asian/Pacific Islands Law Students Association. Campus organizations include the International Law Society, Entertainment and Sports Law Society, and the Student Bar Association.

Library

The law library contains 330,000 hardcopy volumes and 145,222 microform volume equivalents, and subscribes to 913 serial publications. Such on-line databases and networks as CALI, CIS Universe, DIALOG, Dow-Jones, Infotrac, Legal-Trac, LEXIS, LOIS, Mathew Bender, NEXIS, OCLC First Search, WESTLAW, Wilsonline Indexes, and approximately 29,000 on-line databases are available to law students for research. Special library collections include state, federal, and United Nations depositories and collections in tax, criminal law, international law, children/family, jurisprudence, admiralty, trial practice, and law and popular culture. Recently, the library expanded the computer laboratory and permanent learning center facilities, including interactive video, CD-ROM, and computer-assisted instruction stations. The ratio of library volumes to faculty is 5842 to 1 and to students is 305 to 1. The ratio of seats in the library to students is 1 to 2.

Faculty

The law school has 58 full-time and 50 part-time faculty members, of whom 41 are women. According to AAUP standards for Category 1 institutions, faculty salaries are well below average. About 30% of full-time faculty have a graduate law degree in addition to the J.D.; about 13% of part-time faculty have one. The ratio of full-time students to full-time faculty in an average class is 63 to 1; in a clinic, 15 to 1. The law school has a regular program of bringing visiting professors and other distinguished lecturers and visitors to campus.

Placement

J.D.s awarded:	258

Services available through: a separate law school placement center

Services: Southeastern Minority Job Fair, Southeastern Intellectual Property Job Fair, Public Interest Law Day, and Loyola (Chicago) Patent Law Interview Program.

Special features: on-line job posting system and a monthly alumni job bulletin.

Full-time job interviews:	25 employers
Summer job interviews:	25 employers
Placement by graduation:	n/av
Placement within 9 months:	82% of class
Average starting salary:	$39,000 to $123,000

Areas of placement:

Private practice 2-10 attorneys	32%
Private practice 11-25 attorneys	9%
Private practice 26-50 attorneys	7%
Private practice 51-100 attorneys	3%
large firm, sole practitioner, unknown employer	11%
Government	10%
Business/industry	9%
Public interest	7%
Judicial clerkships	3%
Academic	1%

Students

About 53% of the student body are women; 30%, minorities; 5%, African American; 5%, Asian American; and 19%, Hispanic. The average age of entering students is 26; age range is 20 to 52. About 14% drop out after the first year for academic or personal reasons; 86% remain to receive a law degree.

OHIO NORTHERN UNIVERSITY

Claude W. Pettit College of Law

525 South Main Street
Ada, OH 45810

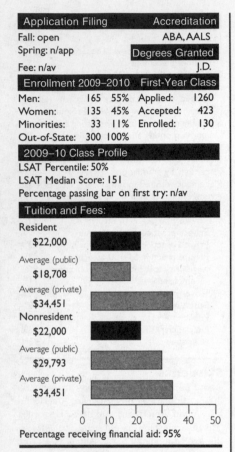

ADMISSIONS
In a recent year, 1260 applied, 423 were accepted, and 130 enrolled. The median LSAT percentile of the most recent first-year class was 50; the median GPA was 3.32 on a scale of 4.0. The lowest LSAT percentile accepted was 14; the highest was 93.

Requirements
Applicants must have a bachelor's degree and take the LSAT. Minimum acceptable GPA is 2.0 on a scale of 4.0. No specific undergraduate courses are required. Candidates are not interviewed.

Procedure
Applicants should submit an application form, LSAT results, transcripts, maximum of 3 letters of recommendation, and a resume, and a personal statement. Notification of the admissions decision is on a rolling basis. The latest acceptable LSAT test date for fall entry is June. The law school uses the LSDAS. Check with

the school for the current application deadlines.

Special
The law school recruits minority and disadvantaged students by means of on-site college recruitment, CRS mailings, and campus visit days. Requirements are not different for out-of-state students. Transfer students must have attended an ABA-approved law school and provide a letter of good standing, a transcript of law school work, undergraduate transcripts, and the LSDAS report.

Costs
Tuition and fees for the 2009-2010 academic year are approximately $22,000 for all full-time students. On-campus room and board costs about $6570 annually; books and supplies run about $900.

Financial Aid
In a recent year, about 95% of current law students received some form of aid. The average annual amount of aid from all sources combined, including scholarships, loans, and work contracts, was approximately $29,300. Awards are based on need and merit. Required financial statements are the FAFSA and the school's financial aid application. First-year students are notified about their financial aid application at time of acceptance. Check with school for current application deadline.

About the Law School
Ohio Northern University Claude W. Pettit College of Law was established in 1885 and is a private institution. The 280-acre campus is in a small town 80 miles northeast of Columbus. The primary mission of the law school is to educate and train students from diverse backgrounds to become responsible and successful practitioners capable of exemplary legal service in roles throughout society. Students have access to federal, state, county, city, and local agencies, courts, correctional facilities, law firms, and legal aid organizations in the Ada area. Facilities of special interest to law students include the Lima Legal Aid Office, ONU Legal Aid Clinic, and Legal Services of Northern Ohio. Housing for students is available on campus and reasonable off-campus housing is also available. About 90% of the law school

facilities are accessible to the physically disabled.

Calendar
The law school operates on a traditional semester basis. Courses for full-time students are offered days only and must be completed within 5 years. There is no part-time program. New students are admitted in the fall and summer. There is an 8-week summer session. Transferable summer courses are offered.

Programs
Required
To earn the J.D., candidates must complete 87 total credits, of which 45 are for required courses. They must maintain a minimum GPA of 2.0 in the required courses. The following first-year courses are required of all students: Civil Procedure I and II, Contracts I and II, Criminal Law, Legal Research and Writing I and II, Property I and II, and Torts I and II. Required upper-level courses consist of Business Organizations I, Constitutional Law I, Evidence, Federal Income Tax, and Legal Profession. Students must complete 10 hours of skills courses chosen from a wide range of options. The required orientation program for first-year students comprises a 2-day introduction to university and law school procedures and the instructional approach followed by 4 special continuing orientation programs.

Electives
In addition, clinics include Legal Aid, Bankruptcy, and Transactional Clinics. Seminars are open to second- and third-year students and include Kids Who Kill, Women and the Law, and Land Use Planning Seminar. There are Civil and Criminal Internship Programs. Students are required to do a major research project, worth 2 credits, as part of the seminar requirement. Field work includes judicial externships with state and federal courts, criminal externships, and governmental-legislative externships. The Annual Kormendy Lecture Series sponsors prominent national legal figures. Recent lecturers have included Justice Clarence Thomas and Professor Deborah Rhode, Stanford School of Law. The college will give credit for ABA-approved law schools' study-abroad programs with prior approval. There is an Icelandic Study Exchange

Phone: 419-772-2211
877-452-9668
Fax: 419-772-3042
Web: www.law.onu.edu

Contact

Director of Law Admissions, 419-772-2211 for general inquiries; Financial Aid Director, 419-772-2272 for financial aid information.

OHIO

Program. The Academic Support Program includes student tutors for all required courses. Minority students benefit from the Black Law Students Association-sponsored study groups and the EXCEL-Academic Success Program. The Asian-Pacific-American Law Student Association also sponsors special programs. Special interest groups include International Law Society, Legal Association of Women, and Environmental Law Society. The most widely taken electives are Criminal Procedure, Decedents' Estates and Trusts, and Commercial Transactions.

Graduation Requirements
In order to graduate, candidates must have a GPA of 2.0 and have completed the upper-division writing requirement.

Organizations

Students edit the *Ohio Northern University Law Review*. Teams compete in the Jessup International Law Competition, Tax Competitions, and ABA Nationals. Law student organizations include Sports Law Society, Street Law, and International Law. Local chapters of national associations include Environmental Law Society, Federalist Society, and Constitutional Law Society. Campus clubs include the Student Bar Association, Legal Association of Women, Black Law Students Association.

Library

The law library contains 222,422 hardcopy volumes and 115,944 microform volume equivalents, and subscribes to 2245 serial publications. Such on-line databases and networks as CALI, CIS Universe, DIALOG, Infotrac, Legal-Trac, LEXIS, LOIS, Matthew Bender, NEXIS, OCLC First Search, WESTLAW, and Wilsonline Indexes are available to law students for research. Special library collections include a federal government depository and developing Celebrezze archives. Recently, the library upgraded the computer laboratory and a wireless network. The ratio of library volumes to faculty is 12,357 to 1 and to students is 762 to 1. The ratio of seats in the library to students is 1 to 1.

Faculty

The law school has 18 full-time and 7 part-time faculty members, of whom 7 are women. According to AAUP standards for Category IIB institutions, faculty salaries are above average. About 28% of full-time faculty have a graduate law degree in addition to the J.D. The ratio of full-time students to full-time faculty in an average class is 15 to 1; in a clinic, 6 to 1. The law school has a regular program of bringing visiting professors and other distinguished lecturers and visitors to campus.

Students

About 45% of the student body are women; 11%, minorities; 7%, African American; 1%, Asian American; 2%, Hispanic; 1%, Native American; and 1%, Indian. The majority of students come from the Northeast (25%). The average age of entering students is 25; age range is 20 to 57. About 71% of students enter directly from undergraduate school. About 3% drop out after the first year for academic or personal reasons; 85% remain to receive a law degree.

Placement

J.D.s awarded:	n/av
Services available through: a separate law school placement center	
Services: Spring Recruiting Conference and Spring Public Interest Career Fair	
Special features: An active membership in NALP and the Ohio Law Placement Consortium (OLPC), through which the college participates in a variety of joint recruiting projects throughout the year.	
Full-time job interviews:	13 employers
Summer job interviews:	23 employers
Placement by graduation:	n/av
Placement within 9 months:	94% of class
Average starting salary:	$30,000 to $110,000
Areas of placement:	
Private practice 2-10 attorneys	58%
Private practice 11-25 attorneys	6%
Private practice 51-100 attorneys	8%
Government	15%
Business/industry	14%
101-501+ attorneys	8%
Judicial clerkships	6%
Public interest	3%
Military	3%

Michael E. Moritz College of Law

55 West 12th Avenue,
John Deaver Drinko Hall
Columbus, OH 43210-1391

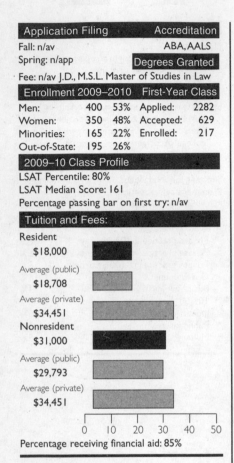

Application Filing		Accreditation
Fall: n/av		ABA, AALS
Spring: n/app		Degrees Granted
Fee: n/av		J.D., M.S.L. Master of Studies in Law

Enrollment 2009–2010		First-Year Class	
Men:	400 53%	Applied:	2282
Women:	350 48%	Accepted:	629
Minorities:	165 22%	Enrolled:	217
Out-of-State:	195 26%		

2009–10 Class Profile
LSAT Percentile: 80%
LSAT Median Score: 161
Percentage passing bar on first try: n/av

Tuition and Fees:

Resident
$18,000

Average (public)
$18,708

Average (private)
$34,451

Nonresident
$31,000

Average (public)
$29,793

Average (private)
$34,451

0 10 20 30 40 50

Percentage receiving financial aid: 85%

ADMISSIONS

In the fall 2009 first-year class, 2282 applied, 629 were accepted, and 217 enrolled. Figures in the above capsule and in this profile are approximate. Ten transfers enrolled. The median LSAT percentile of the most recent first-year class was 80; the median GPA was 3.5 on a scale of 4.0. The highest LSAT percentile was 99.

Requirements
Applicants must have a bachelor's degree and take the LSAT. The most important admission factors include academic achievement, undergraduate curriculum, and life experience. No specific undergraduate courses are required. Candidates are not interviewed.

Procedure
Applicants should submit an application form, LSAT results, transcripts, 2 letters of recommendation, and the Academic Records Office Evaluation from their undergraduate school. Notification of the admissions decision is on a rolling basis.

The latest acceptable LSAT test date for fall entry is February. Check with the school for current application deadlines. The law school uses the LSDAS.

Special
The law school recruits minority and disadvantaged students through participation in CLEO and as a part of the overall recruitment program. Requirements are not different for out-of-state students. Transfer students must have one year of credit and have attended an ABA-approved law school.

Costs
Tuition and fees for the 2009-2010 academic year are $18,000 for full-time in-state students and $31,000 for out-of-state students. On-campus room and board costs about $7000 annually; books and supplies run $3000.

Financial Aid
In a recent year, about 85% of current law students received some form of aid. The average annual amount of aid from all sources combined, including scholarships, loans, and work contracts, was $16,929; maximum, $26,259. Awards are based on need and merit. Required financial statement is the FAFSA. There are special funds for minority or disadvantaged students, including CLEO participation. First-year students are notified about their financial aid application shortly after acceptance.

About the Law School
Ohio State University Michael E. Moritz College of Law was established in 1891 and is a public institution. The 3200-acre campus is in an urban area 2 miles north of downtown Columbus. The primary mission of the law school is to produce lawyers from a base of scholarship, education, and service; the approach is broad-based and academically oriented. Students have access to federal, state, county, city, and local agencies, courts, correctional facilities, law firms, and legal aid organizations in the Columbus area. Facilities of special interest to law students include the state legislature and state supreme court. Housing for students is available in 3 campus dormitories reserved for graduate and professional students; there are plenty of

off-campus housing facilities sufficient for all students. There is also an apartment complex adjacent to the law school. All law school facilities are accessible to the physically disabled.

Calendar
The law school operates on a traditional semester basis. Courses for full-time students are offered days only and must be completed within 5 years. There is no part-time program. New students are admitted in the fall. There is an 8-week summer session. Transferable summer courses are offered.

Programs
In addition to the J.D., the law school offers the M.S.L. Master of Studies in Law. Students may take relevant courses in other programs and apply credit toward the J.D.; a maximum of 5 credits may be applied. The following joint degrees may be earned: J.D./M.B.A. (Juris Doctor/Master of Business Administration), J.D./M.H.A. (Juris Doctor/Master of Health and Hospital Administration), and J.D./M.P.A. (Juris Doctor/Master of Public Administration).

Required
To earn the J.D., candidates must complete 88 total credits, of which 37 are for required courses. They must maintain a minimum GPA of 2.0 in the required courses. The following first-year courses are required of all students: Civil Procedure, Constitutional Law, Contracts, Criminal Law, Legal Research, Legislation, Property, Torts, and Writing and Analysis. Required upper-level courses consist of 2 courses with a writing component, Appellate Practice, and Professional Responsibility. The required orientation program for first-year students is 2 days and covers case briefing, professional responsibility, and college policies and offices. There are also 2 days of student-sponsored social activities.

Electives
The Michael E. Moritz College of Law offers concentrations in corporate law, criminal law, family law, international law, juvenile law, labor law, litigation, media law, securities law, tax law, torts and insurance, alternative dispute resolu-

Phone: 614-292-8810
Fax: 614-292-1383
E-mail: lawadmit@osu.edu
Web: www.osu.edu/units/law

Contact

Kathy S. Northern, Associate Dean, 614-292-8810 for general inquiries; Robert L. Solomon, Assistant Dean, 614-292-8807 for financial aid information.

tion, international law and civil rights. In addition, second- and third-year students may take clinics. Second-year students take simulation clinics such as pretrial litigation, negotiation, and client counseling. They may also participate in the legislation, special education, and mediation clinics. Third-year students may act as legal interns representing clients under faculty supervision in the Civil Law, Juvenile Law, and Prosecutorial and Defense Practica. At least 1 seminar must be taken by second- or third-year students; seminars range from creative and constitutional aspects of law to those devoted to a student's research of a specific legal area. Internships are available with certain federal and state judges and through the D.C. Summer Program. Research programs include opportunities for independent study. There are field work opportunities to work for the public and private sector; opportunities to do volunteer work, such as the Volunteer Income Tax Assistance (VITA) program. Special lectures are supported by the Ohio State Law Forum, which invites distinguished academicians, jurists, and practitioners; speakers are also invited by faculty and student groups. Study abroad is possible through the Oxford Summer Program and is open to students from the college and all other accredited law schools. Students can earn 3 or 6 hours of credit during the summer. Study abroad at Oxford is also possible through the Spring Semester Program. A legal methods program, designed to help certain first-year students who may need more time and attention adapting to law school, is available. The Black Law Students Association, Caribbean Law Students Associations, Hispanic Law Students Association, Asian Law Students Association, and Middle Eastern Law Students Association sponsor various events and programs. There are approximately 50 special interest student organizations that include the sports and entertainment law society, pro bono research group, public interest law forum, women's law caucus, health law society, and J. Rueben Clark Society. The most widely taken electives are those that are directly bar-related (Evidence, Corporations), international law offerings, and alternative dispute resolution offerings.

Graduation Requirements
In order to graduate, candidates must have a GPA of 2.0, have completed the upper-division writing requirement, and an ethics course.

Organizations

Students edit the *Ohio State Law Journal, Journal on Dispute Resolution, Ohio State Journal of Criminal Law, I/S: A Journal of Law and Policy for the Information Society, Entrepenurial Business Law Journal*, and the student newspaper *Hearsay*. Other student organizations have newsletters, which they publish periodically. Appellate Practice is the first moot court experience required of all students. The college has 12 separate moot court teams. There are also several National Trial Competition teams and 2 negotiation teams. There are also intraschool Moot Court, Negotiation, and Trial Competitions. Law student organizations and campus organizations include Law School Democrats, Law School Republicans, Military Law Association, Student Bar Association, Pro Bono Research Group, and International Law Society. There are local chapters of legal fraternities as well as a student section of the American Bar Association.

Library

The law library contains 560,969 hardcopy volumes and 228,646 microform volume equivalents, and subscribes to 7876 serial publications. Such on-line databases and networks as DIALOG, LEXIS, WESTLAW, LCS, and OCLC are available to law students for research. Special library collections include a government depository, a large foreign law collection, and materials on dispute resolution. Recently, the library added 64,000 square feet to the existing library space, including 12 study rooms, and added 300 carrels and 40 word processors. The ratio of library volumes to faculty is 11,219 to 1 and to students is 772 to 1. The ratio of seats in the library to students is 1 to 1.

Faculty

The law school has 50 full-time and 41 part-time faculty members, of whom 27 are women. According to AAUP standards for Category I institutions, faculty salaries are average. The ratio of full-time students to full-time faculty in an average class is 20 to 1; in a clinic, 15 to 1. There is a chapter of the Order of the Coif.

Placement

J.D.s awarded:	n/av
Services available through: a separate law school placement center	
Services: practice interviews with local attorneys and job search workshops	
Special features: encouragement to do judicial clerkships.	
Full-time job interviews:	52 employers
Summer job interviews:	89 employers
Placement by graduation:	74% of class
Placement within 9 months:	n/av
Average starting salary:	$42,500 to $90,000
Areas of placement:	
Private practice 2-10 attorneys	52%
Government	15%
Business/industry	14%
Judicial clerkships	12%
Academic	4%
Public interest	3%

Students

About 48% of the student body are women; 22%, minorities; 8%, African American; 10%, Asian American; and 4%, Hispanic. The majority of students come from Ohio (74%). The average age of entering students is 22; age range is 21 to 47. About 12% of students have a graduate degree. About 1% drop out after the first year for academic or personal reasons; 99% remain to receive a law degree.

School of Law

2501 North Blackwelder Avenue
Oklahoma City, OK 73106-1493

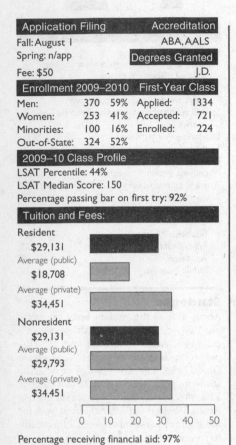

Application Filing		Accreditation	
Fall: August 1		ABA, AALS	
Spring: n/app		Degrees Granted	
Fee: $50			J.D.

Enrollment 2009–2010		First-Year Class	
Men:	370 59%	Applied:	1334
Women:	253 41%	Accepted:	721
Minorities:	100 16%	Enrolled:	224
Out-of-State:	324 52%		

2009–10 Class Profile

LSAT Percentile: 44%
LSAT Median Score: 150
Percentage passing bar on first try: 92%

Tuition and Fees:

Resident
$29,131

Average (public)
$18,708

Average (private)
$34,451

Nonresident
$29,131

Average (public)
$29,793

Average (private)
$34,451

0   10   20   30   40   50

Percentage receiving financial aid: 97%

ADMISSIONS

In the fall 2009 first-year class, 1334 applied, 721 were accepted, and 224 enrolled. Three transfers enrolled. The median LSAT percentile of the most recent first-year class was 44; the median GPA was 3.2 on a scale of 4.0. The lowest LSAT percentile accepted was 15; the highest was 97.

Requirements
Applicants must have a bachelor's degree and take the LSAT. Minimum acceptable GPA is 2.0 on a scale of 4.0. The most important admission factors include academic achievements, GPA, and LSAT results. No specific undergraduate courses are required. Candidates are not interviewed.

Procedure
The application deadline for fall entry is August 1. Applicants should submit an application form, LSAT results, transcripts, a personal statement, a nonrefundable application fee of $50, 2 letters of recommendation, and a personal statement, and a resume. Notification of the admissions decision is as soon as a decision has been made. The latest acceptable LSAT test date for fall entry is June. The law school uses the LSDAS.

Special
The law school recruits minority and disadvantaged students through directed mailings and visits to campuses with high minority concentrations, which are complemented by events at the law school co-hosted by minority student organizations throughout the academic year. Upon acceptance, minority and diversity candidates are contacted by students, and alumni who answer questions and ease concerns about cost, prospects for success, and the job market. Requirements are not different for out-of-state students. Transfer students must have attended an ABA-approved law school and complete their last 45 hours at the school, be in good standing at their former law school, and submit a letter from the dean along with official transcripts. The law school offers a limited number of students whose academic credentials may not qualify them for regular admission the opportunity to participate in the Alternate Summer Admissions Program. This 7-week program includes Legal Method and Legal Writing. Students must pass both courses to be admitted in the regular fall program.

Costs

Tuition and fees for the 2009-2010 academic year are $29,131 for all full-time students. Tuition for part-time students is $19,766 per year. On-campus room and board costs about $8400 annually; books and supplies run $1800.

Financial Aid

About 97% of current law students receive some form of aid. The average annual amount of aid from all sources combined, including scholarships, loans, and work contracts, is $24,780; maximum, $45,609. Awards are based on need and merit. Some scholarships are awarded solely on merit; some on merit and need. Financial aid is awarded on the basis of need. Scholarships lower the loan eligibility for all students. Required financial statements are the FAFSA. The aid application deadline for fall entry is March 1. First-year students are notified about their financial aid application at approximately 1 to 2 weeks after their financial file is completed.

About the Law School

Oklahoma City University School of Law was established in 1907 and is a private institution. The 104-acre campus is in an urban area about 2 miles from state capitol building. The primary mission of the law school is to help students become

responsible professionals through a rigorous program of instruction that focuses on students' intellectual and professional development and enables them to become leaders in law, business, government, and civic life; and to improve law and legal institutions through research and scholarship. Students have access to federal, state, county, city, and local agencies, courts, correctional facilities, law firms, and legal aid organizations in the Oklahoma City area. Oklahoma City, as the state capital, is a major center for law, business, health care, and government. Facilities of special interest to law students include the nearby state capitol complex, which contains the Supreme Court, the Court of Criminal Appeals, the Court of Civil Appeals, the state legislature, and various state administrative and regulatory agencies. The law school is also near the U.S. District Court and numerous other federal and state entities, law firms, the Oklahoma Medical Center, and business institutions. Housing for students is in on-campus residence halls and an on-campus apartment complex. Many inexpensive private apartments are also available in the metro area. All law school facilities are accessible to the physically disabled.

Calendar

The law school operates on a traditional semester basis. Courses for full-time students are offered both day and evening and must be completed within 4 years. For part-time students, courses are offered both day and evening and must be completed within 5 years. New full- and part-time students are admitted in the fall. There is a 7½-week summer session. Transferable summer courses are offered.

Programs

The following joint degrees may be earned: J.D./M.B.A. (Juris Doctor/Master of Business Administration).

Required
To earn the J.D., candidates must complete 90 total credits, of which 60 are for required courses. They must maintain a minimum GPA of 2.0 in the required courses. The following first-year courses are required of all students: Civil Procedure I and II, Contracts I and II, Criminal Law, Legal Analysis, Legal Research and Writing I, and II, Property, and Torts. Required upper-level courses consist of Administrative Law, Agency and Unincorporated Business Associations, Commercial Paper, Constitutional

Phone: 405-208-5354
866-529-6281
Fax: 405-208-5814
E-mail: *lawadmit@okcu.edu*
Web: *www.okcu.edu/law*

Contact
Bernard Jones, Assistant Dean for Admissions, 405-208-5354 or 800-633-7242 for general inquiries; Jennifer Killman, Senior Counselor, 405-208-5419 for financial aid information.

OKLAHOMA

Placement

J.D.s awarded:	145

Services available through: a separate law school placement center and the university placement center

Special features: The Professional and Career Development Center is staffed by 4 full-time career services personnel who help students develop career goals and plans, locate resources including alumni mentors, and find employment.

Full-time job interviews:	4 employers
Summer job interviews:	12 employers
Placement by graduation:	n/av
Placement within 9 months:	83% of class
Average starting salary:	$22,000 to $120,000

Areas of placement:

Private practice 2-10 attorneys	55%
Private practice 11-25 attorneys	22%
Private practice 26-50 attorneys	2%
Private practice 51-100 attorneys	2%
Private practice 101+ attorneys	2%
Business/industry	14%
Government	13%
Public interest	6%
Academic	3%
Military	2%

Law I and II, Consumer Bankruptcy, Corporations, Criminal Procedure I, Evidence, Income Tax Law, Legal Profession, Sales and Leases, Secured Transactions, and Willis, Trussts, and Estates. The required orientation program for first-year students is a 6-day program that includes a course on Legal Analysis for academic credit.

Electives
The School of Law offers certificates in business law, health law, public law, and client representation in alternative dispute resolution. In addition, the law school offers an extensive externship program through which students earn academic credit while working under the guidance of attorneys and judges in numerous settings, including the federal and state courts, corporate ;ega; departments, government agencies, and the criminal justice system. Approximately 6 seminars are offered each semester on advanced topics. Recent seminars include Bioethics, Current Developments in Corporate Law, and Tribal Law. Students who obtain a Legal Intern's license (authorized by the state of Oklahoma) and have a sponsoring attorney may appear alone in court on certain matters. With a supervising attorney present, they may handle any court proceeding. Students may conduct research through seminars, advanced research courses, supervised papers, or directed research projects. They may also assist faculty members as research assistants. An externship program is offered with live-client placements in many courts and governmental business offices in or near Oklahoma City. The Native American Legal Resource Center also offers clinical opportunities. The annual Quinlan Lecture Series presents a nationally preeminent legal scholar or jurist. The annual Brennan Lecture presents a national prominent scholar or jurist in the field of state constitutional law. The Center on State Constitutional Law and Government presents several prominent state and local public officials each year. OCU co-sponsors 4 summer international programs (4 credit hours each) in Tianjn, China; Granada, Spain; Freiburg, Germany/The Hague, The Netherlands; and Buenos Aires, Argentina. The academic achievement program includes individual tutoring by faculty and upper-class students, programming by the Director of Academic Achievement, and a bar exam preparation program. Students with writing difficulties may seek help from the University Writing Center. The law school's Native American Legal Resource Center works closely with Indian tribes in the state of Oklahoma and administers numerous federal grants to assist tribes. There are numerous opportunities to engage in pro bono services. The most widely taken electives are Consumer Bankruptcy, Agency and Unincorporated Business Associations, and Administrative Law.

Graduation Requirements
In order to graduate, candidates must have a GPA of 2.0 and have completed the upper-division writing requirement.

Organizations
The Oklahoma City University Law Review publishes 3 issues annually. The Student Bar Association publishes *The Verdict*, a bimonthly newsletter. Moot court competitions include the ABA National Appellate Moot Court Competition, Jessup International Law Moot Court Competition, and AAJ Trial Competition. Other competitions include the ACTL National Trial Competition, Frederick Douglass National Moot Court Competition, Native American Law Moot Court Competitions, ACS National Appellate Moot Court Competititon, and ABA National Mediation Moot Court Competition. Law student organizations include Black Law Students Association, Hispanic Law Students Association, and ABA-Law Student Division. There are local chapters of Hand Inn (Phi Delta Phi) and The Vaughn Chapter (Phi Alpha Delta) national associations. Campus organizations include Sports and Entertainment Law Assocaition, American Constitution Society, and Federalist Society.

Library
The law library contains 322,061 hard-copy volumes and 147,684 microform volume equivalents, and subscribes to 1118 serial publications. Such on-line databases and networks as CALI, CIS Universe, Infotrac, Legal-Trac, LEXIS, LOIS, NEXIS, OCLC First Search, WESTLAW, Wilsonline Indexes, and Index Master, Legal-Trac, LLMC Digital, HeinOnline, JSTOR, Index to Legal Periodicals, Audio Case Files, Befress Legal Journal, CCH Internet Tax Research, Constitutions of the Countries of the World, eBrary, EBSCO, Foreign Law Guide, NewsBank, Oxford English Dictionary, RIA Checkpoint Academic Advantage, U.S. Congressional Serial Set (LexisNexis), WorldCat, A to Z List of Journals, and BNA databases are available to law students for research. Special library collections include the Native American collection with a concentration on the Indian tribes of Oklahoma. Recently, the library upgraded wired and wireless connections, made databases available off campus through a proxy server, and added an on-line reposity for faculty scholarship and phone interface for searching the library catalog. The ratio of library volumes to faculty is 10,735 to 1 and to students is 517 to 1. The ratio of seats in the library to students is 1 to 2.

Faculty
The law school has 40 full-time and 56 part-time faculty members, of whom 41 are women. About 30% of full-time faculty have a graduate law degree in addition to the J.D. The ratio of full-time students to full-time faculty in an average class is 18 to 1; in a clinic, 8 to 1. The law school has a regular program of bringing visiting professors and other distinguished lecturers and visitors to campus.

Students
About 41% of the student body are women; 16%, minorities; 3%, African American; 3%, Asian American; 4%, Hispanic; 5%, Native American; and 8%, Mexican American, Puerto Rican, Foreign nationals, and unknown. The majority of students come from Oklahoma (48%). The average age of entering students is 27; age range is 21 to 53. About 64% of students enter directly from undergraduate school and 8% have a graduate degree. About 12% drop out after the first year for academic or personal reasons; 88% remain to receive a law degree.

School of Law

78 North Broadway
White Plains, NY 10603

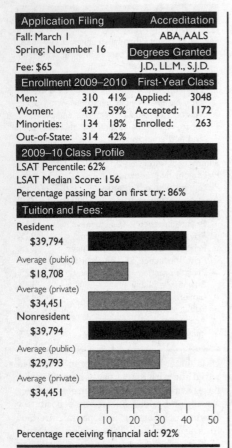

Application Filing		Accreditation
Fall: March 1		ABA, AALS
Spring: November 16		**Degrees Granted**
Fee: $65		J.D., LL.M., S.J.D.

Enrollment 2009–2010		First-Year Class	
Men:	310 41%	Applied:	3048
Women:	437 59%	Accepted:	1172
Minorities:	134 18%	Enrolled:	263
Out-of-State:	314 42%		

2009–10 Class Profile
LSAT Percentile: 62%
LSAT Median Score: 156
Percentage passing bar on first try: 86%

Tuition and Fees:

Resident
$39,794

Average (public)
$18,708

Average (private)
$34,451

Nonresident
$39,794

Average (public)
$29,793

Average (private)
$34,451

0   10   20   30   40   50

Percentage receiving financial aid: 92%

ADMISSIONS

In the fall 2009 first-year class, 3048 applied, 1172 were accepted, and 263 enrolled. Thirty-one transfers enrolled. The median LSAT percentile of the most recent first-year class was 62; the median GPA was 3.41 on a scale of 4.0. The lowest LSAT percentile accepted was 30; the highest was 98.

Requirements
Applicants must have a bachelor's degree and take the LSAT. Minimum acceptable GPA is 2.0 on a scale of 4.0. The most important admission factors include LSAT results, GPA, personal interview, work experience, academic achievement, and diversity. No specific undergraduate courses are required. Candidates are interviewed.

Procedure
The application deadline for fall entry is March 1. Applicants should submit an application form, LSAT results, transcripts, a personal statement, a nonrefundable application fee of $65, 2 letters of recommendation, and TOEFL or TWE test scores if applicable. Notification of the admissions decision is on a rolling basis. The latest

acceptable LSAT test date for fall entry is February. The law school uses the LSDAS.

Special
The law school recruits minority and disadvantaged students by hosting a Law Day for minority students each year and visiting historically black colleges. Since 1999, Pace Law has cohosted the Puerto Rican Legal Defense and Education Fund Program. There are diversity pages on the Prospective Student pages to aid applicants in the admission/financial aid process and to provide contact with the school's minority network. Requirements are not different for out-of-state students. Transfer students must have one year of credit, have attended an ABA-approved law school, and have a maximum of 30 transfer credits from state-approved law schools.

Costs

Tuition and fees for the 2009-2010 academic year are $39,794 for all full-time students. Tuition for part-time students is $29,856 per year. On-campus room and board costs about $15,720 annually; books and supplies run $1800.

Financial Aid

About 92% of current law students receive some form of aid. The average annual amount of aid from all sources combined, including scholarships, loans, and work contracts, is $37,000; maximum, $59,464. Awards are based on need and merit. Required financial statement is the FAFSA. The aid application deadline for fall entry is February 15. Special funds for minority or disadvantaged students include diversity scholarship/grant funds for first-year students in an effort to provide financial assistance for those who are underrepresented in the legal community. First-year students are notified about their financial aid application at time of acceptance from March 15 through August 30.

About the Law School

Pace University School of Law was established in 1976 and is a private institution. The 12-acre campus is in a suburban area in White Plains, New York. The primary mission of the law school is to permit students the flexibility to build their own program of legal study on the foundation of basic legal principles and skills. Students have access to federal, state, county, city, and local agencies, courts, correctional facilities, law firms, and legal aid organizations in the White Plains area. Major state courts for

the New York State Ninth Judicial District, county and federal courts, county government, and the district attorney's office are within walking distance. Facilities of special interest to law students include the Judicial Institute of the State of New York, an innovative center for judicial education, which is housed in a state-of-the-art facility at Pace; Women's Justice Center; Land Use Law Center; Real Estate Law Institute; and Institute for International Commercial Law. Housing for students includes an on-campus residence hall, providing single rooms. The university also assists students in locating off-campus accommodations close to campus. All law school facilities are accessible to the physically disabled.

Calendar

The law school operates on a traditional semester basis. Courses for full-time students are offered days only during the first year and must be completed within minimum 3 years. For part-time students, courses are offered both day and evening and must be completed within minimum 4 years. New full-time students are admitted in the fall and spring; part-time, fall. There is a 7-week summer session. Transferable summer courses are offered.

Programs

In addition to the J.D., the law school offers the LL.M. and S.J.D. Students may take relevant courses in other programs and apply credit toward the J.D.; a maximum of 10 credits may be applied. The following joint degrees may be earned: J.D./M.A. (Juris Doctor/Master of Arts in women's studies with Sarah Lawrence College), J.D./M.B.A. (Juris Doctor/Master of Business Administration with Pace University), J.D./M.E.M. (Juris Doctor/Master of Environmental Management with Yale School), J.D./M.P.A. (Juris Doctor/Master of Public Administration with Pace University), and J.D./M.S. (Juris Doctor/Master of Science in environmental policy with Bard College).

Required
To earn the J.D., candidates must complete 88 total credits, of which 37 are for required courses. They must maintain a minimum GPA of 2.3 in the required courses. The following first-year courses are required of all students: Civil Procedure I and II, Constitutional Law, Contracts, Criminal Law, Legal Research and Writing I and II, Property I, and Torts. Required upper-level courses consist of electives from more than

Phone: 914-422-4210
Fax: 914-989-8714
E-mail: *calexander@law.pace.edu*
Web: *www.law.pace.edu*

Contact

Cathy M. Alexander, Assistant Dean of Admissions, 914-422-4210 for general inquiries; Adriana Pace, Associate Director, Financial Aid, 914-422-4050 for financial aid information.

NEW YORK

100 courses, Federal Income Tax I, Professional Responsibility, an upper-level skills requirement, and an upper-level writing requirement. A skills course is required, but it can be a clinical, externship, or simulation course. The required orientation program for first-year students consists of a 3-day program prior to the beginning of fall semester classes, with a substantive law component that emphasizes briefing techniques and lectures.

Electives

The School of Law offers concentrations in corporate law, criminal law, environmental law, family law, intellectual property law, international law, juvenile law, labor law, litigation, maritime law, securities law, tax law, torts and insurance, health, land use, and real estate. In addition, Pace offers 6 clinics, including criminal defense, post-conviction exoneration, environmental protection, and representation of immigrants, medical patients, and stockholders with complaints against stockbrokers. Clinics are generally 6 credits per semester. They are available to upper-level students who have taken prerequisite courses. Pace offers more than 30 seminars, including The Supreme Court and the Constitution, Feminist Legal Theory, and Comparative Environmental Law: Brazil--U.S. (taught in Brazil). Externships include serving as clerks for federal, state, and family court judges; assisting in criminial prosecutions; working in federal and state environmental agencies in New York and Washington, D.C.; clerking in law firms with international law practices in New York and abroad; working in public interest organizations; and helping missions of small island states in the United Nations on matters involving global warming. Students serve as research assistants for professors and in the Environmental Law Center, the Land Use Center, the Women's Justice Center, the Energy and Climate Center, and the International Commercial Law Institute. All students take Legal Research and Writing in their first year, may take upper-level Advanced Legal Research, and must complete an upper-level research and writing project. The school hosts 5 academic lectures each year: Dyson Lecture, Garrison and Kerlin Lecture in Environmental Law, Blank Lecture on Ethics, Hopkins Lecture, and Sloan Lecture on International Law. A semester at the University College of London Faculty of Laws is avail-

able each spring for second- and third-year students as well as visting students from other ABA-accredited institutions. Tutorial programs include the Academic Support Program and the Dean's Scholar program. Minority programs include Legal Education Opportunity (LEO). Pace has active student organizations in various areas of law, including property entertainment and sports, family, land use and real estate, and criminal law. The most widely taken electives are Family Law, Environmental Law, and International Law.

Graduation Requirements

In order to graduate, candidates must have a GPA of 2.3 and have completed the upper-division writing requirement.

Organizations

Students edit the *Pace Law Review*, the *Pace Environmental Law Review*, the *Pace International Law Review*, the student newspaper *Hearsay*, and the *Journal of Court Innovation*. The Moot Court Committee sponsors the required competition for first-year students and an advanced competition for second- and third-year students and sends teams to national and international competitions. These include the National Environmental Moot Court, International Criminal Moot Court, and Willem C. Vis International Commercial Arbitration moot competitions. Other competitions include Client Counseling, sponsored by the American Bar Association, Environmental Law, National Moot Court, Unified Moot Court, Frederick Douglass Moot Court, International Environmental Moot Court, and Pace/Gray's Inn Moot Court competitions. Student organizations include the Student Bar Association, Women's Association of Law Students, and the Environmental Law Society. Phi Alpha Delta has a local chapter. Other organizations include International Law Society, Health Law Society, and Latino/Black Law Students Organization.

Library

The law library contains 398,968 hardcopy volumes and 938,300 microform volume equivalents, and subscribes to 1549 serial publications. Such on-line databases and networks as CALI, CIS Universe, Infotrac, Legal-Trac, LEXIS, LOIS, Matthew Bender, NEXIS, WESTLAW, and BNA are available to law students for research. Special library collections include a selective U.S. government depository and David Sive and Law School Archives. Recently, the entire library was

Placement

J.D.s awarded:	253

Services available through: a separate law school placement center and the university placement center

Services: seminars and workshops, on-line job listings for students and alumni, databases and guides for judicial clerkships, and private and public sector employment and fellowship opportunities

Special features: videotaped mock interviews, alumni adviser, mentor programs, a career newsletter, and bulletin of career information

Full-time job interviews:	13 employers
Summer job interviews:	13 employers
Placement by graduation:	n/av
Placement within 9 months:	92% of class
Average starting salary:	$46,000 to $160,000
Areas of placement:	
Private practice 2-10 attorneys	20%
Private practice 11-25 attorneys	6%
Private practice 26-50 attorneys	3%
Private practice 51-100 attorneys	2%
Private practice 501+ attorneys	7%
Government	17%
Business/industry	17%
Public interest	7%
Academic	7%
Judicial clerkships	5%

completely renovated. The wireless network was upgraded. The ratio of library volumes to faculty is 9067 to 1 and to students is 534 to 1. The ratio of seats in the library to students is 1 to 1.

Faculty

The law school has 44 full-time and 98 part-time faculty members, of whom 52 are women. According to AAUP standards for Category I institutions, faculty salaries are average. About 5% of full-time faculty have a graduate law degree in addition to the J.D.; about 2% of part-time faculty have one. The ratio of full-time students to full-time faculty in an average class is 16 to 1; in a clinic, 8 to 1. The law school has a regular program of bringing visiting professors and other distinguished lecturers and visitors to campus.

Students

About 59% of the student body are women; 18%, minorities; 4%, African American; 7%, Asian American; 6%, Hispanic; and 12%, did not disclose. The majority of students come from the Northeast (83%). The average age of entering students is 25; age range is 18 to 60. About 6% drop out after the first year for academic or personal reasons; 84% remain to receive a law degree.

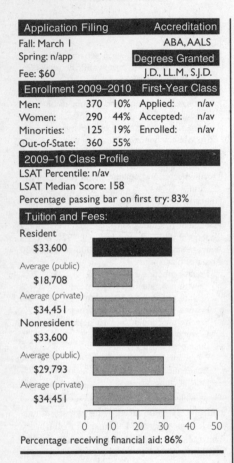

Application Filing	Accreditation
Fall: March 1	ABA, AALS
Spring: n/app	Degrees Granted
Fee: $60	J.D., LL.M., S.J.D.

Enrollment 2009–2010		First-Year Class	
Men:	370 10%	Applied:	n/av
Women:	290 44%	Accepted:	n/av
Minorities:	125 19%	Enrolled:	n/av
Out-of-State:	360 55%		

2009–10 Class Profile

LSAT Percentile: n/av
LSAT Median Score: 158
Percentage passing bar on first try: 83%

Tuition and Fees:

Resident
$33,600

Average (public)
$18,708

Average (private)
$34,451

Nonresident
$33,600

Average (public)
$29,793

Average (private)
$34,451

0   10   20   30   40   50

Percentage receiving financial aid: 86%

ADMISSIONS

In a recent year, twenty-seven transfers enrolled. The median GPA of the most recent first-year class was 3.43. Some figures in the above capsule and in this profile are approximate.

Requirements

Applicants must have a bachelor's degree and take the LSAT. The most important admission factors include LSAT results, GPA, and academic achievement. No specific undergraduate courses are required. Candidates are not interviewed.

Procedure

Applicants should submit an application form, LSAT results, transcripts, a personal statement, a nonrefundable application fee of $60, 2 (preferably academic) letters of recommendation, a record of work experience, and 2 statements: a 1-page personal statement and 1-page of interest in Pennsylvania State University, Dickinson School of Law. Notification of the admissions decision is on a rolling basis. The latest acceptable LSAT test date for fall entry is February. The law school uses the LSDAS. Check with the school for the current application deadlines.

Special

The law school recruits minority and disadvantaged students by means of minority forums such as the LSAT Candidate Referral Service, recruitment outreach to historically black colleges, and outreach by current minority students and minority alumni. Requirements are not different for out-of-state students. Transfer students must have one year of credit, have attended an ABA-approved law school, and be in the top 25% of the previous law school in order to be competitive for available space.

Costs

Tuition and fees for the 2009-2010 academic year are approximately $33,600 for all full-time students. On-campus room and board costs about $10,674 annually; books and supplies run $1360.

Financial Aid

About 86% of a recent year, law students received some form of aid. The average annual amount of aid from all sources combined, including scholarships, loans, and work contracts, was approximately $32,805; maximum, $47,884. Awards are based on need and merit. Required financial statements are the FAFSA and Penn State Dickinson Financial Aid Application. Check with the school for the current application deadline. First-year students are notified about their financial aid application at time of acceptance.

About the Law School

Pennsylvania State University Dickinson School of Law was established in 1834 and is a public institution. The 20-acre campus is in a small town 24 miles southwest of Harrisburg. The primary mission of the law school is to offer students a rich and diverse academic program with a myriad of elective courses, joint degree programs, and clinical offerings designed to meet the needs and aspirations of today's law students. Students have access to federal, state, county, city, and local agencies, courts, correctional facilities, law firms, and legal aid organizations in the University Park area. The Penn State School of International Affairs is housed administratively within the Dickinson School of Law. The Dale F. Shugart Community Law Center in Carlisle, only a few blocks from the law school, houses several in-house legal clinics. Students enjoy affordable housing within a short walk or drive of either campus. Penn State offers limited on-campus housing for graduate students in University Park. About 98% of the law school facilities are accessible to the physically disabled.

Calendar

The law school operates on a traditional semester basis. Courses for full-time students are offered days only and must be completed within 4.5 years. For part-time students, courses are offered days only and must be completed within 7 years. New full- and part-time students are admitted in the fall. There is a 9-week summer session. Transferable summer courses are offered.

Programs

In addition to the J.D., the law school offers the LL.M. and S.J.D. Students may take relevant courses in other programs and apply credit toward the J.D.; a maximum of 6 credits may be applied. The following joint degrees may be earned: J.D./M.A. (Juris Doctor/Master of Arts in educational theory and policy), J.D./M.Agr. (Juris Doctor/Master in Agriculture), J.D./M.B.A. (Juris Doctor/Master of Business Administration), J.D./M.E.P.C. (Juris Doctor/ Master of Environmental Pollution Control), J.D./M.Ed. (Juris Doctor/Master of Education in college student affairs, higher education, and educational leadership), J.D./M.P.A. (Juris Doctor/Master of Public Administration), J.D./M.S. (Juris Doctor/ Master of Science in forest resources,, educational leadership, and human resources and employment relations), J.D./M.S.I.S. (Juris Doctor/Master of Science in Information Systems), and J.D./Ph.D. (Juris Doctor/Doctor of Philosophy in educational leadership, higher education, and Forest resources or wildlife and fisheries science).

Required

To earn the J.D., candidates must complete 88 total credits, of which 35 are for required courses. They must maintain a minimum GPA of 2.0 in the required courses. The following first-year courses are required of all students: Civil Procedure, Constitutional Law, Contracts, Criminal Law, Legal Analysis, Research and Writing I and II, Property, and Torts. Required upper-level courses consist of Professional Responsibility and a sales or secured transactions seminar. The required orientation program for first-

Phone: 814-867-1251
800-840-1122
Fax: 717-241-3503
E-mail: *dsladmit@psu.edu*
Web: *www.dsl.psu.edu*

Contact

Director of Admissions, 717-240-5207 for general inquiries; Financial Aid Director, 717-240-5256 for financial aid information.

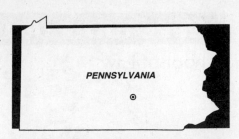

PENNSYLVANIA

year students lasts 2 1/2 days and is designed to introduce new students to the academic life of law school. Students receive instruction on how to read and brief cases and attend sessions on professionalism. There are several opportunities for students to meet and mingle with classmates, professors, and staff members.

Electives

The Dickinson School of Law offers concentrations in corporate law, criminal law, entertainment law, environmental law, family law, intellectual property law, international law, juvenile law, labor law, litigation, maritime law, media law, securities law, sports law, tax law, torts and insurance, and dispute resolution. In addition, in-house clinics include the Arts, Sports and Entertainment Law Clinic, Children's Advocacy Clinic, and Disability Law Clinic. Students earn credit for no more than 3 semesters of clinic work and a maximum of 11 credits. A student cannot enroll in more than 1 clinic during a semester. Seminars, worth 2 to 3 credits, include the United Nations and International Law Seminar, Advanced Corporate Tax Seminar, and Advanced Evidence Seminar. Students can earn academic credit working without compensation in a government, nonprofit, or public setting, similar to the field, placement clinic settings. Internships are typically taken in the summer for 3 credits. The law school offers a Washington, D.C. Semester Program through which students may spend the final semester of law school working for a government agency or nonprofit organization in Washington, D.C. Research programs (Independent Study) may be arranged with full-time faculty. A maximum of 4 credits may be earned during the student's J.D. degree enrollment. A field placement clinic is a 3-credit course, normally taken for 2 semesters for a total of 6 credits, in which students have the opportunity to work and learn outside of the law school in a variety of field placements in public service, government law offices, and judges' chambers. Special lecture series include the Penn State Institute for Sports Law, Policy and Research lecture series; the Polisher Tax lecture Series; the Senior Speakers Dinner; the Speakers Trust Fund; and the Faculty Development Series. Study-abroad programs include the Florence, Rome and Siena Study Abroad Program (5 to 6 credits); the Capitals of Europe Program (6 credits); and the Montreal Summer Study Program in Arbitra-

tion in Montreal, Quebec (5 to 6 credits). A peer-to-peer tutoring program for first-year students is part of the law school's effort to promote academic success. Tutors are second- and third-year law students who have demonstrated a high level of competence in the first-year curriculum. In addition, faculty-conducted academic success workshops are offered throughout the year. Students may also receive one-on-one assistance from a writing specialist. The most widely taken electives are Corporations, Sales, and Trusts and Estates.

Graduation Requirements

In order to graduate, candidates must have a GPA of 2.0, have completed the upper-division writing requirement, and each student must successfully complete a seminar, and the Professional Responsibility course.

Organizations

The primary law review is the *Penn State Law Review*. Other law reviews include the *Penn State International Review* the *Penn State Environmental Law Review*, and the *World Arbitration and Mediation Review*. *Res Ipsa Loquitur* is the student yearbook. The school generally fields as many as 10 teams in various interscholastic moot court competitions. The competitions include Jessup International, National Appellate, and National Trial. Other competitions include a securities law competition, an international commercial arbitration competition, and a labor law competition. Law student organizations, local chapters of national associations, and campus organizations include PILF, International Law Society, the Federalist Society, ABA-Law Student Division, Amnesty International, Toastmasters International, Women's Law Caucus, Minority Law Students Association, and Phi Alpha Delta.

Library

The law library contains 530,783 hardcopy volumes and 1,497,012 microform volume equivalents, and subscribes to 1200 serial publications. Such on-line databases and networks as CALI, CIS Universe, DIALOG, Dow-Jones, Infotrac, Legal-Trac, LEXIS, LOIS, NEXIS, OCLC First Search, RLIN, WESTLAW, Wilson-line Indexes, HeinOnline, BNA, CCH, LLMC, Digital, MOML, IFLP, LexisNexis Congressional, Proquest, U.S. Supreme Court Records and Briefs, UNTS, and AccessUN, CQ Electronic Library are

Placement

J.D.s awarded:	165
Services available through: a separate law school placement center	
Services: digitally recorded practice interviews	
Special features: high-end videoconferencing equipment for students to interview remotely	
Full-time job interviews:	40 employers
Summer job interviews:	50 employers
Placement by graduation:	59% of class
Placement within 9 months:	92% of class
Average starting salary:	$36,369 to $118,750
Areas of placement:	
Private practice 2-10 attorneys	18%
Private practice 11-25 attorneys	5%
Private practice 26-50 attorneys	4%
Private practice 51-100 attorneys	6%
Private practice 101+ attorneys and size unknown	21%
Judicial clerkships	14%
Business/industry	14%
Government	12%
Public interest	3%
Academic	2%

available to law students for research. Special library collections include a U.S. government depository, European Community and United Nations documents, and Pennsylvania briefs and records.The ratio of library volumes to faculty is 10,015 to 1 and to students is 810 to 1. The ratio of seats in the library to students is 1 to 3.

Faculty

The law school has 53 full-time and 11 part-time faculty members, of whom 30 are women. About 43% of full-time faculty have a graduate law degree in addition to the J.D.; about 14% of part-time faculty have one. The ratio of full-time students to full-time faculty in an average class is 9 to 1; in a clinic, 9 to 1. The law school has a regular program of bringing visiting professors and other distinguished lecturers and visitors to campus.

Students

About 44% of the student body are women; 19%, minorities; 7%, African American; 6%, Asian American; and 5%, Hispanic. The majority of students come from Pennsylvania (45%). The average age of entering students is 25; age range is 21 to 62. About 36% of students enter directly from undergraduate school and 9% have a graduate degree. About 3% drop out after the first year for academic or personal reasons; 97% remain to receive a law degree.

School of Law

24255 Pacific Coast Highway
Malibu, CA 90263

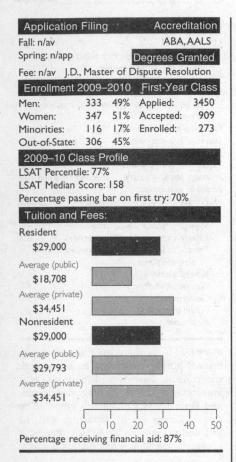

Application Filing		Accreditation
Fall: n/av		ABA, AALS
Spring: n/app		**Degrees Granted**
Fee: n/av	J.D., Master of Dispute Resolution	

Enrollment 2009–2010		First-Year Class	
Men:	333 49%	Applied:	3450
Women:	347 51%	Accepted:	909
Minorities:	116 17%	Enrolled:	273
Out-of-State:	306 45%		

2009–10 Class Profile
LSAT Percentile: 77%
LSAT Median Score: 158
Percentage passing bar on first try: 70%

Tuition and Fees:

Resident
$29,000

Average (public)
$18,708

Average (private)
$34,451

Nonresident
$29,000

Average (public)
$29,793

Average (private)
$34,451

0   10   20   30   40   50

Percentage receiving financial aid: 87%

ADMISSIONS
In a recent year, 3450 applied, 909 were accepted, and 273 enrolled. Thirty transfers enrolled. The median LSAT percentile of the most recent first-year class was 77; the median GPA was 3.3 on a scale of 4.0. Figures in the above capsule and in this profile are approximate.

Requirements
Applicants must have a bachelor's degree and take the LSAT. No specific undergraduate courses are required. Candidates are not interviewed.

Procedure
Applicants should submit an application form, 2 letters of recommendation, and resume, personal statement, response to School of Law's mission, and a seat deposit. Notification of the admissions decision is on a rolling basis. The latest acceptable LSAT test date for fall entry is February. The law school uses the LSDAS.

Special
The law school recruits minority and disadvantaged students by actively encouraging applications from ethnic minorities. Requirements are not different for out-of-state students. Transfer students must have one year of credit, have attended an ABA-approved law school, and submit an official law school transcript, a letter from the dean indicating the student's eligibility to continue his or her studies and indicating the student's class rank, and supply a photocopy of the current school's LSDAS report. The student must rank in the top 30% of the first-year law class.

Costs
Tuition and fees for the 2009-2010 academic year are approximately $29,000 for all full-time students. On-campus room and board costs about $12,970 annually; books and supplies run about $700.

Financial Aid
In a recent year, about 87% of current law students received some form of aid. The maximum annual amount of aid from all sources combined, including scholarships, loans, and work contracts, was approximately $37,084. Awards are based on need and merit, along with need-based financial aid awards are generally a combination of grants, loans, and work-study employment. Required financial statement is the FAFSA. Special funds for minority or disadvantaged students consist of the Diversity Scholarship, based on academic and personal achievement. First-year students are notified about their financial aid application at 2 weeks after acceptance notification, if completed. Check with the school for the current application deadline.

About the Law School
Pepperdine University School of Law was established in 1969 and is a private institution. The 830-acre campus is in a small town 30 miles north of Los Angeles, California. The primary mission of the law school is to provide highly qualified students with a distinctive and solid legal education. The school maintains a Christian emphasis. Students have access to federal, state, county, city, and local agencies, courts, correctional facilities, law firms, and legal aid organizations in the Malibu area. Facilities of special interest to law students include the Odell McConnell Law Center, which overlooks the Pacific Ocean; the facility contains an auditorium-classroom, law library, classrooms, an atrium, an appellate courtroom, a trial courtroom, cafeteria, lounges, and student services offices. Housing for students is limited on campus; on-campus apartments house 4 students in each of the 36 apartments. All law school facilities are accessible to the physically disabled.

Calendar
The law school operates on a traditional semester basis. Courses for full-time students are offered days only. There is no part-time program. New students are admitted in the fall. There is a 7 1/2-week summer session. Transferable summer courses are offered.

Programs
In addition to the J.D., the law school offers the Master of Dispute Resolution. The following joint degrees may be earned: J.D./M.B.A. (Juris Doctor/Master of Business Administration), J.D./M.D.R. (Juris Doctor/Master of Dispute Resolution), and J.D./M.P.P. (Juris Doctor/Master of Public Policy).

Required
To earn the J.D., candidates must complete 88 total credits, of which 57 are for required courses. They must maintain a minimum GPA of 72.0 in the required courses. The following first-year courses are required of all students: Civil Pleadings and Procedure I and II, Contracts I and II, Criminal Law, Criminal Procedure, Legal Research and Writing I and II, Real Property I and II, and Torts I and II. Required upper-level courses consist of Constitutional Law I and II, Corporations, Evidence, Federal Income Taxation, Legal Ethics, Remedies, and Wills and Trusts. The required orientation program for first-year students is a 4-day program that includes introduction to legal ethics, the socratic method, case briefing, note taking, outlining, and legal research and writing.

Electives
The School of Law offers concentrations in corporate law, criminal law, entertainment law, environmental law, family law, international law, labor law, tax law, and

Phone: 310-506-4631
Fax: 310-506-7668
Web: http://law.pepperdine.edu

Contact
Director of Admissions, 310-506-4631 for general inquiries; Director of Financial Aid, 310-506-4633 for financial aid information.

tort law, property law, intellectual property law, advocacy and dispute resolution, public interest, technology and entrepreneurship, and constitutional law. In addition, clinical opportunities are available with the District Attorney's Office of Los Angeles and Ventura counties, and with state and federal court judges in Los Angeles and Ventura counties. Also, smaller programs offer training in corporate and securities law, tax law, juvenile law, domestic arbitration, labor law, consumer protection, trade regulation, and with various media industries. Second- and third-year students may study in the London Law Program during the fall and summer semesters. Courses are taught by British and American faculty. The most widely taken electives are the London Law Program, entertainment and sports law courses, and technology and entrepreneurship.

Graduation Requirements
In order to graduate, candidates must have a GPA of 72.0.

Organizations
Students edit the *Pepperdine Law Review*, *National Association of Administrative Law Journal*, and *Dispute Resolution Journal*. First-year students participate in an appellate advocacy experience. Upper-level students compete for places on teams that attend the National Moot Court and other competitions. Each spring there is the Dalsimer Moot Court intra-school competition. Law student organizations are the Student Bar Association, Asian Pacific American Law Students Association, and Black Law Students Association. There are local chapters of Delta Theta Phi, Phi Alpha Delta, and Phi Delta Phi.

Library
The law library contains 342,450 hardcopy volumes and 87,000 microform volume equivalents, and subscribes to 1300 serial publications. Such on-line databases and networks as DIALOG, LEXIS, and WESTLAW are available to law students for research. Recently, the library installed 49 computer workstations and 70 open network connections. The ratio of library volumes to faculty is 11,415 to 1 and to students is 504 to 1.

Faculty
The law school has 30 full-time faculty members, of whom 8 are women. According to AAUP standards for Category IIA institutions, faculty salaries are well above average. The law school has a regular program of bringing visiting professors and other distinguished lecturers and visitors to campus.

Students
About 51% of the student body are women; 17%, minorities; 5%, African American; 6%, Asian American; 5%, Hispanic; and 1%, Native American. The majority of students come from California (55%). The average age of entering students is 23; age range is 20 to 55. About 6% of students have a graduate degree. About 5% drop out after the first year for academic or personal reasons.

Placement	
J.D.s awarded:	n/av
Services available through: The School of Law Career Development Office	
Services: co-sponsor workshops on practice specialties	
Special features: seminars to assist students in preparing resumes and improving job search and interviewing skills, counseling expertise in practice areas and alternative careers.	
Full-time job interviews:	220 employers
Summer job interviews:	n/av
Placement by graduation:	59% of class
Placement within 9 months:	95% of class
Average starting salary:	n/av
Areas of placement:	n/av

4041 N. Central Ave. Suite 100
Phoenix, AZ 85012-3330

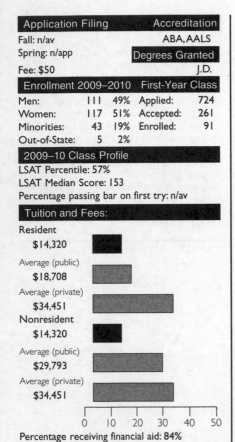

Application Filing			Accreditation	
Fall: n/av			ABA, AALS	
Spring: n/app			**Degrees Granted**	
Fee: $50				J.D.

Enrollment 2009–2010		First-Year Class	
Men:	111 49%	Applied:	724
Women:	117 51%	Accepted:	261
Minorities:	43 19%	Enrolled:	91
Out-of-State:	5 2%		

2009–10 Class Profile
LSAT Percentile: 57%
LSAT Median Score: 153
Percentage passing bar on first try: n/av

Tuition and Fees:

Resident
$14,320

Average (public)
$18,708

Average (private)
$34,451

Nonresident
$14,320

Average (public)
$29,793

Average (private)
$34,451

0 10 20 30 40 50

Percentage receiving financial aid: 84%

ADMISSIONS
In a recent year, 724 applied, 261 were accepted, and 91 enrolled. Five transfers enrolled. The median LSAT percentile of the most recent first-year class was 57; the median GPA was 3.27 on a scale of 4.0. The lowest LSAT percentile accepted was 15; the highest was 94. Figures in the above capsule and in this profile are approximate.

Requirements
Applicants must have a bachelor's degree and take the LSAT. Minimum acceptable LSAT percentile is 13 and minimum acceptable GPA is 2.0 on a scale of 4.0. The most important admission factors include academic achievement, writing ability, and life experience. No specific undergraduate courses are required. Candidates are not interviewed.

Procedure
Applicants should submit an application form, LSAT results, transcripts, a personal statement, a nonrefundable application fee of $50, 2 letters of recommendation, and copy of resume, and LSDAS report. Notification of the admissions decision is immediately after decision is made. The latest acceptable LSAT test date for fall entry is December. The law school uses the LSDAS.

Special
The law school recruits minority and disadvantaged students recruitment through minority bar associations, and at institutions with a large minority population. Requirements are not different for out-of-state students. Transfer students must have attended an ABA-approved law school.

Costs
Tuition and fees for the 2009-2010 academic year are approximately $14,320 for full-time in-state students. Tuition for part-time students is approximately $10,900 in-state. On-campus room and board costs about $5040 annually; books and supplies run about $1120.

Financial Aid
In a recent year, about 84% of current law students received some form of aid. The average annual amount of aid from all sources combined, including scholarships, loans, and work contracts, was approximately $25,934; maximum, $48,982. First-year students are notified about their financial aid application at time of acceptance. Check with the school for current application deadline.

About the Law School
Phoenix School of Law was established in 2005 is independent. The campus is in an urban area in Phoenix. The primary mission of the law school is student centered, practice ready, and serving the underserved. Students have access to federal, state, county, city, and local agencies, courts, correctional facilities, law firms, and legal aid organizations in the Phoenix area.

Calendar
The law school operates on a traditional semester basis. Courses for full-time students are offered days only and must be completed within 5 years. For part-time students, courses are offered both day and evening and must be completed within 6 years. New full- and part-time students are admitted in the fall and spring. There is a 7-weeks-week summer session. Transferable summer courses are offered.

Programs
Students may take relevant courses in other programs and apply credit toward the J.D.; a maximum of 6 credits may be applied.

Required
To earn the J.D., candidates must complete 87 total credits, of which 67 are for required courses. The following first-year courses are required of all students: Civil Procedure I and II, Contracts I and II, Criminal Law, Lawyering Process I and II, Property I and II, and Torts I and II. Required upper-level courses consist of Business Associations, Commercial Law, Constitutional Law I and II, Criminal Procedure, Evidence, Family Law/Community Property, General Practice Skills, Professional Responsibility, and Trusts and Estates. The required orientation program for first-year students lasts 3 days (4 hour session each day).

Electives
In addition, Students may take clinics (worth 3 credit hours) and externships (worth 2 or 3 credit hours) as long as they have a 2.0 GPA. The most widely taken electives are Environmental Law, Pre-Trial Practice, and Administrative Law.

Graduation Requirements
In order to graduate, candidates must have a GPA of 2.0, have completed the upper-division writing requirement, and 30 Pro Bono hours.

Organizations
Students edit the *Phoenix Law Review* and the student newspaper, *The Sidebar*. Moot court competitions for students include the ABA Moot Court Competition, National Moot Court Competition, and the John J. Gibbons Criminal Procedure Moot Court Competition. Other competitions include Judge Thomas Tang Competition and National Association of Women's Lawyers - Selma Moidel Smith Law Student Writing Competition. Law student

Contact
Communications Manager, (602) 682-6830 for general inquiries; Financial Aid Coordinator, (602) 682-6842 for financial aid information.

ARIZONA

organizations, local chapters of national associations, and campus organizations include Federalist Society, International Law Society, Intellectual Property Law Society, Phoenix Law Women Association, Black Law Students Association, Public Interest Law Project, Alternative Dispute Resolution, Juggling Club, and Hispanic Law Students Association.

Library
The law library contains 124,613 hard-copy volumes and 508,704 microform volume equivalents, and subscribes to 1202 serial publications. Such on-line databases and networks as CALI, CIS Universe, Legal-Trac, LEXIS, NEXIS, WESTLAW, and Hein Online, CCH, BNA, and Pro Quest are available to law students for research. Special library collections include Academic Success and the Center for Professional Development. Recently, the library Moved into a new library. The ratio of library volumes to faculty is 8308 to 1 and to students is 547 to 1.

Faculty
The law school has 15 full-time and 13 part-time faculty members, of whom 11 are women. The ratio of full-time students to full-time faculty in an average class is 28 to 1; in a clinic, 5 to 1. The law school has a regular program of bringing visiting professors and other distinguished lecturers and visitors to campus.

Students
About 51% of the student body are women; 19%, minorities; 2%, African American; 2%, Asian American; 13%, Hispanic; and 2%, Native American. The majority of students come from Arizona (98%). The average age of entering students is 32; age range is 23 to 55. About 19% of students have a graduate degree. About 4% drop out after the first year for academic or personal reasons.

Placement	
Services available through: a separate law school placement center	
Full-time job interviews:	n/av
Summer job interviews:	n/av
Placement by graduation:	n/av
Placement within 9 months:	n/av
Average starting salary:	n/av
Areas of placement:	n/av

PONTIFICAL CATHOLIC UNIVERSITY OF PUERTO RICO

School of Law

2250 Avenida las Americas suite 543
Ponce, PR 00717-9997

Application Filing

Fall: n/av
Spring: n/app

Fee: n/av

Accreditation

ABA

Degrees Granted

J.D., LL.M.

Enrollment 2009–2010

			First-Year Class	
Men:	220	5%	Applied:	n/av
Women:	220	50%	Accepted:	n/av
Minorities:	n/av		Enrolled:	n/av
Out-of-State:	440	100%		

2009–10 Class Profile

LSAT Percentile: 13%
LSAT Median Score: n/av
Percentage passing bar on first try: n/av

Tuition and Fees:

Resident
  n/av

Average (public)
  $18,708

Average (private)
  $34,451

Nonresident
  n/av

Average (public)
  $29,793

Average (private)
  $34,451

```
0    10   20   30   40   50
```

Percentage receiving financial aid: 52%

ADMISSIONS

In a recent year, the median LSAT percentile of the most recent first-year class was 13; the median GPA was 2.9 on a scale of 4.0.

Requirements

Applicants must have a bachelor's degree and take the LSAT. Minimum acceptable GPA is 2.5 on a scale of 4.0. The most important admission factors include GPA, LSAT results, and general background. No specific undergraduate courses are required. Candidates are not interviewed.

Procedure

Applicants should submit an application form, transcripts, and PAEG. The latest acceptable LSAT test date for fall entry is June. The law school uses the LSDAS. Check with the school for the current application deadlines.

Special

Requirements are not different for out-of-state students. Transfer students must have a minimum GPA of 2. Preadmissions courses consist of allowing students with an undergraduate GPA of lower than 2.5 or who don't achieve adequate scores on the admissions exam to enroll in special remedial courses and then be admitted conditionally.

Financial Aid

In a recent year, about 52% of current law students received some form of aid. The average annual amount of aid from all sources combined, including scholarships, loans, and work contracts, was approximately $2000. Awards are based on need and merit. Check with the school for current application deadlines.

About the Law School

Pontifical Catholic University of Puerto Rico School of Law was established in 1961 and is a private institution. The 92-acre campus is in an urban area 60 miles from San Juan. The primary mission of the law school is to develop lawyers with a thorough training in the law and a practical mastery of legal techniques within the context of Catholic teachings. Students have access to federal, state, county, city, and local agencies, courts, correctional facilities, law firms, and legal aid organizations in the Ponce area. Housing for students is available.

Calendar

The law school operates on a traditional semester basis. Courses for full- time students are offered both day and evening. For part- time students, courses are offered both day and evening. New full- and part-time students are admitted in the fall. There is a summer session. Transferable summer courses are not offered.

Programs

In addition to the J.D., the law school offers the LL.M. Students may take relevant courses in other programs and apply credit toward the J.D. The following joint degrees may be earned: J.D./M.B.A. (Juris Doctor/Master of Business Administration).

Required

To earn the J.D., candidates must complete 94 total credits, of which 82 are for required courses. The following first-year courses are required of all students: Constitutional Law, Criminal Procedure, Family Law, Inroduction to Law, Legal Bibliography and Writing, Logic and Redaction, Moral and Dogmatic Theory, Obligations, and Property Law. Required upper-level courses consist of Administrative Law, Advanced Logical Analysis, Appellate Practice, Civil Procedure I and II, Corporations, Evidence, Federal Jurisdiction, Legal Clinics, Legal Ethics, Mercantile law, Mortgages, Negotiable Instruments, Notarial Law, Special Contracts, Special Logical Procedures, Successions and Donations, and Torts.

Electives

In addition, Clinical training is provided through the school's downtown Ponce Legal Aid Clinic for indigent clients and through judicial clerkships in superior and federal district courts and placements with district attorney's offices. The Center for Legal and Social Investigations allows for research under the supervision of a faculty director.

Phone: 787-841-2000, ext. 1836
Fax: 787-840-4620
Web: www.pucpr.edu

Contact

Associate Dean, (787) 841-2000, ext. 341 for general inquiries; Director, (787) 841-2000 for financial aid information.

PUERTO RICO

Organizations

The primary law review is the *Revista de Derecho Puertorriqueno*, which is edited by a student board. Law student organizations include the Law Student Division of the American Bar Association, National Law Students of Puerto Rico, and the Women's Rights Organization. Local chapters of national associations are Delta Theta Phi and Phi Alpha Delta.

Library

The law library contains 135,000 hard-copy volumes and 15,000 microform volume equivalents. Special library collections include include deposits of U.S. government and United Nations documents.

Faculty

The law school has 14 full-time and 18 part-time faculty members. About 50% of full-time faculty have a graduate law degree in addition to the J.D. The ratio of full-time students to full-time faculty in an average class is 12 to 1.

Students

About 50% of the student body are women. The average age of entering students is 24; age range is 21 to 51. About 50% of students enter directly from undergraduate school. About 11% drop out after the first year for academic or personal reasons.

Placement	
J.D.s awarded:	n/av
Services available through: a separate law school placement center	
Full-time job interviews:	n/av
Summer job interviews:	n/av
Placement by graduation:	n/av
Placement within 9 months:	n/av
Average starting salary:	$14,000 to $24,000
Areas of placement:	
Academic	50%
unknown	50%

QUINNIPIAC UNIVERSITY

School of Law

275 Mt. Carmel Avenue
Hamden, CT 06518-1908

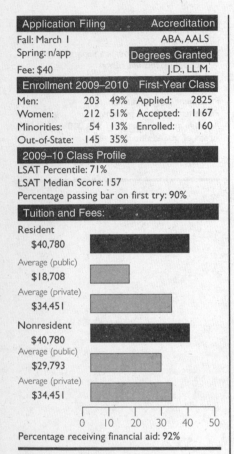

Application Filing		Accreditation
Fall: March 1		ABA, AALS
Spring: n/app		

Degrees Granted	
Fee: $40	J.D., LL.M.

Enrollment 2009–2010   First-Year Class

Men:	203	49%	Applied:	2825
Women:	212	51%	Accepted:	1167
Minorities:	54	13%	Enrolled:	160
Out-of-State:	145	35%		

2009–10 Class Profile

LSAT Percentile: 71%
LSAT Median Score: 157
Percentage passing bar on first try: 90%

Tuition and Fees:

Resident
$40,780

Average (public)
$18,708

Average (private)
$34,451

Nonresident
$40,780

Average (public)
$29,793

Average (private)
$34,451

Percentage receiving financial aid: 92%

ADMISSIONS

In the fall 2009 first-year class, 2825 applied, 1167 were accepted, and 160 enrolled. Four transfers enrolled. The median LSAT percentile of the most recent first-year class was 71; the median GPA was 3.31 on a scale of 4.0. The lowest LSAT percentile accepted was 36; the highest was 99.

Requirements
Applicants must have a bachelor's degree and take the LSAT. The most important admission factors include undergraduate curriculum, LSAT results, and life/work experience, ethic background, and writing skills. No specific undergraduate courses are required. Candidates are not interviewed.

Procedure
The application deadline for fall entry is March 1. Applicants should submit an application form, LSAT results, transcripts, a personal statement, a nonre-

fundable application fee of $40, 2 letters of recommendation, and résumé. Notification of the admissions decision is on a rolling basis. The latest acceptable LSAT test date for fall entry is February. The law school uses the LSDAS.

Special
The law school recruits minority and disadvantaged students by means of student search, community outreach programs, the CLEO program, minority days on campus, and attendance at various minority programs. Requirements are not different for out-of-state students. Transfer students must have 1 year of credit, have attended an ABA-approved law school, have a letter of good standing from the dean of the law school from which the student is transferring, and submit law school class rank.

Costs

Tuition and fees for the 2009-2010 academic year are $40,780 for all full-time students. Tuition for part-time students is $28,780 per year. Books and supplies run $1200.

Financial Aid

About 92% of current law students receive some form of aid. The average annual amount of aid from all sources combined, including scholarships, loans, and work contracts, is $42,168; maximum, $66,880. Awards are based on need and merit. Required financial statement is the FAFSA. The aid application deadline for fall entry is April 15. Special funds for minority or disadvantaged students are available. First-year students are notified about their financial aid application at time of acceptance.

About the Law School

Quinnipiac University School of Law was established in 1978 and is a private institution. The 500-acre campus is in a suburban area 90 miles north of New York City; 2 hours from Boston. The primary mission of the law school is to educate students, through theory in classrooms and practice in clinics and externships, to be prepared to practice law in any environment in the 21st century. Students have access to federal, state, county, city, and local agencies, courts, correctional facilities, law

firms, and legal aid organizations in the Hamden area. Facilities of special interest to law students include the School of Law Library, Fitness Center, and Grand Courtroom. Housing for students is available off-campus in the area; the Office of Admissions assists students with housing opportunities. All law school facilities are accessible to the physically disabled.

Calendar

The law school operates on a traditional semester basis. Courses for full-time students are offered both day and evening and must be completed within 84 months. For part-time students, courses are offered both day and evening and must be completed within 84 months. New full- and part-time students are admitted in the fall. There is a 7-week summer session. Transferable summer courses are offered.

Programs

In addition to the J.D., the law school offers the LL.M. Students may take relevant courses in other programs and apply credit toward the J.D.; a maximum of 9 credits may be applied. The following joint degrees may be earned: J.D./M.B.A. (Juris Doctor/Master of Business Administration).

Required
To earn the J.D., candidates must complete 86 total credits, of which 45 are for required courses. They must maintain a minimum GPA of 2.0 in the required courses. The following first-year courses are required of all students: Civil Procedure I and II, Constitutional Law, Contracts I and II, Criminal Law, Legal Skills I and II, Property, and Torts. Required upper-level courses consist of Administrative Law, Business Organizations, Commercial Law, Evidence, Federal Income Taxation, Lawyer's Professional Responsibility, and Trusts and Estates. The required orientation program for first-year students is a 2-day general introductory program to the school, the faculty, the administration, and the students.

Electives
Students must take 15 to 21 credits in their area of concentration. The School of Law offers concentrations in criminal law, family law, intellectual property law,

Phone: 203-582-3400
800-462-1944
Fax: 203-582-3339
E-mail: ladm@quinnipiac.edu
Web: www.law.quinnipiac.edu

Contact

Ed Wilkes, Executive Dean, Enrollment Services, 203-582-3400 for general inquiries; Odette Franceskino, Director of Financial Aid, 203-582-3405 for financial aid information.

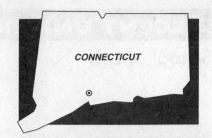
CONNECTICUT

juvenile law, litigation, tax law, health law, and dispute resolution. In addition, students may participate in a Civil Clinic during the day, for 4 to 8 credits, or during the evening for 3 to 4 credits. There is also a Tax Law Clinic. Seminars are varied. Quinnipiac offers 9 externship programs in areas such as public interest, corporate counsel, judicial, legislative, criminal justice, family and juvenile law, legal services, mediation, and field placement II. There are various research programs. Special lecture series include the Quinnipiac-Yale Dispute Resolution Lecture Series. There is an ABA-accredited summer program in Ireland with Trinity College (Dublin). An academic support program and writing program are available to students at the law school. A supplemental bar review class, offered free of charge to Quinnipiac graduates, is offered. There is a special minority recruitment and information day at the law school. The Thurgood Marshall Awards reception in the evening recognizes individual achievement and service to the school and community. The most widely taken electives are Criminal Procedure, Tax, and Trusts and Estates.

Graduation Requirements

In order to graduate, candidates must have a GPA of 2.0 and have completed the upper-division writing requirement.

Organizations

Students edit the *Quinnipiac Law Review*, *Quinnipiac Probate Law Journal*, *Quinnipiac Health Law Journal*, and the student newspaper, *The Quinnipiac Legal Times*. Moot court competitions are the National Appellate Advocacy Competition, Albert Mugel Tax Moot Court Competition, and Domick Gabrielli National Family Law Moot Court competition. The Mock Trial Society competes in the American Association for Justice Student Trial Advocacy National Competition, Texas Young Lawyers Association Competition, and the American Bar Association Criminal Justice Division Mock Trial Competition. There are more than 30 student organizations on campus. These, including local chapters of national associations and campus organizations, are Tax Law Society, APALSA, Public Interest Law Project, Student Bar Association, Women's Law Society, the Black Students Association, Phi Alpha Delta, and Phi Delta Phi.

Library

The law library contains 193,400 hardcopy volumes and 248,090 microform volume equivalents, and subscribes to 2573 serial publications. Such on-line databases and networks as CALI, CIS Universe, DIALOG, Infotrac, Legal-Trac, LEXIS, LOIS, Mathew Bender, NEXIS, OCLC First Search, WESTLAW, Wilsonline Indexes, CILP, Constitution of Countries of the World, Criminal Justice periodicals, IFLP, LLMC-Digital, Qcat Online Catalog, RIA Checkpoint, Statistical Universe, Congressional Universe, Hein Online, and BNA are available to law students for research. Special library collections include a federal government depository library collection, a tax collection, a Connecticut collection, and a health law collection. In addition to numerous hardwired electrical and network connections through out the library, there is a wireless network, and the library also has Facebook and Twitter pages. The ratio of library volumes to faculty is 5525 to 1 and to students is 466 to 1. The ratio of seats in the library to students is 1 to 1.

Faculty

The law school has 35 full-time and 33 part-time faculty members, of whom 21 are women. According to AAUP standards for Category IIA institutions, faculty salaries are well above average. About 31% of full-time faculty have a graduate law degree in addition to the J.D. The ratio of full-time students to full-time faculty in an average class is 12 to 1; in a clinic, 6 to 1. The law school has a regular program of bringing visiting professors and other distinguished lecturers and visitors to campus.

Students

About 51% of the student body are women; 13%, minorities; 3%, African American; 5%, Asian American; 4%, Hispanic; and 1%, Native American. The majority of students come from Connecticut (65%). The average age of entering students is 25; age range is 21 to 57. About 54% of students enter directly from undergraduate school, 12% have a graduate degree, and 40% have worked full-time prior to entering law school. About 3% drop out after the first year for academic or personal reasons; 97% remain to receive a law degree.

Placement

J.D.s awarded:	113
Services available through: a separate law school placement center	
Services: counseling on cover letter preparation, mock interviews, educational and informational programs, and participation in national career fairs	
Special features: staff members with J.D. degrees counsel students and develop employment opportunities for students and graduates. There is also on Alumni Career Networking Event.	
Full-time job interviews:	20 employers
Summer job interviews:	20 employers
Placement by graduation:	n/av
Placement within 9 months:	95% of class
Average starting salary:	$20,000 to $253,000
Areas of placement:	
Private practice 2-10 attorneys	15%
Private practice 11-25 attorneys	5%
Private practice 26-50 attorneys	1%
Private practice 51-100 attorneys	3%
Private practice 101-250 attorneys; solo practice	11%
Business/industry	28%
Government	23%
Judicial clerkships	11%
Public interest	2%
Academic	1%

School of Law

1000 Regent University Drive Virginia Beach, VA 23464-9800

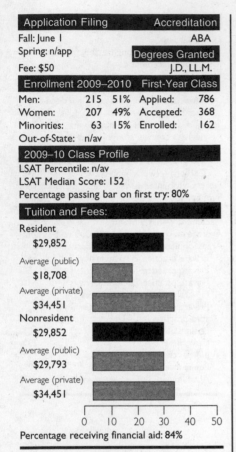

Application Filing		Accreditation
Fall: June 1		ABA
Spring: n/app		Degrees Granted
Fee: $50		J.D., LL.M.

Enrollment 2009–2010		First-Year Class	
Men:	215 51%	Applied:	786
Women:	207 49%	Accepted:	368
Minorities:	63 15%	Enrolled:	162
Out-of-State:	n/av		

2009–10 Class Profile

LSAT Percentile: n/av
LSAT Median Score: 152
Percentage passing bar on first try: 80%

Tuition and Fees:

Resident
$29,852

Average (public)
$18,708

Average (private)
$34,451

Nonresident
$29,852

Average (public)
$29,793

Average (private)
$34,451

Percentage receiving financial aid: 84%

ADMISSIONS

In the fall 2009 first-year class, 786 applied, 368 were accepted, and 162 enrolled. The median GPA of the most recent first-year class was 3.37.

Requirements

Applicants must have a bachelor's degree and take the LSAT. Minimum acceptable GPA is 2.0 on a scale of 4.0. The most important admission factors include academic achievement, LSAT results, and GPA. No specific undergraduate courses are required. Candidates are not interviewed.

Procedure

The application deadline for fall entry is June 1. Applicants should submit an application form, LSAT results, transcripts, a personal statement, a nonrefundable application fee of $50, and 3 letters of recommendation. Notification of the admissions decision is on a rolling basis. The latest acceptable LSAT test date for fall entry is June. The law school uses the LSDAS.

Special

The law school recruits minority and disadvantaged students through recruitment travel, referrals, CRS mailings, and special scholarships. Requirements are not different for out-of-state students. Transfer students must have one year of credit, have a minimum GPA of 2.3, and have attended an ABA-approved law school.

Costs

Tuition and fees for the 2009-2010 academic year are $29,852 for all full-time students. Tuition for part-time students is $22,052 per year. On-campus room and board costs about $9450 annually; books and supplies run $1620.

Financial Aid

About 84% of current law students receive some form of aid. The average annual amount of aid from all sources combined, including scholarships, loans, and work contracts, is $37,150; maximum, $49,972. Awards are based on need and merit, along with leadership and public interest awards. Required financial statement is the FAFSA. The aid application deadline for fall entry is July 1. Special funds for minority or disadvantaged students consist of law school grants and scholarships available to qualified students. First-year students are notified about their financial aid application as prospective students.

About the Law School

Regent University School of Law was established in 1986 and is a private institution. The 80-acre campus is in a suburban area 7 miles southeast of Norfolk, Virginia. The primary mission of the law school is to train lawyers to participate effectively and professionally in the private and public sectors of this nation while affirming their understanding of the relationship between Christian principles and the practice of law. Students have access to federal, state, county, city, and local agencies, courts, correctional facilities, law firms, and legal aid organizations in the Virginia Beach area. Facilities of special interest to law students include a 134,000 square-foot law center equipped with the latest technology in audiovisual equipment, such as cameras for simultaneous broadcasting. There is also a 350-seat moot court/city council chamber. Housing for students consists of university-owned and operated apartments. All law school facilities are accessible to the physically disabled.

Calendar

The law school operates on a traditional semester basis. Courses for full-time students are offered days only and must be completed within 5 years. For part-time students, courses are offered days only and must be completed within 6 years. New full- and part-time students are admitted in the fall. There is a 7-week summer session. Transferable summer courses are not offered.

Programs

In addition to the J.D., the law school offers the LL.M. The following joint degrees may be earned: J.D./M.A. (Juris Doctor/Master of Arts in communication, counseling, government, journalism, and organizational (leadership), J.D./M.B.A. (Juris Doctor/Master of Business Administration), and J.D./M.Div. (Juris Doctor/Master of Divinity).

Required

To earn the J.D., candidates must complete 90 total credits, of which 73 are for required courses. They must maintain a minimum GPA of 2.0 in the required courses. The following first-year courses are required of all students: Christian Foundations of Law, Civil Procedure I and II, Contracts I and II, Legal Analysis Research and Writing I and II, Property I and II, and Torts I and II. Required upper-level courses consist of Business Associations, Constitutional Criminal Procedure, Constitutional Law I and II, Criminal Law, Evidence, Professional Responsibility, Professional Skills Practicum, and UCC I. Clinical courses are offered but not required. The required orientation program for first-year students is a 4-day program including a legal study skills workshop covering preparation for class, case briefing, outlining, and exam preparation and taking, and a student affairs orientation covering law school policies and procedure. The optional fifth day consists of a community service project.

Electives

The School of Law offers concentrations in corporate law, criminal law, family law,

Phone: 757-352-4584
877-267-5072
Fax: 757-352-4139
E-mail: *lawschool@regent.edu*
Web: *www.regent.edu/law/admissions*

Contact

Bonnie G. Creef, Director of Admissions and Financial Aid, 757-352-4584 for general inquiries; Tom Foley, Assistant Director of Admissions and Financial Aid, 757-226-4584 for financial aid information.

intellectual property law, international law, litigation, and tax law. The school lists courses in areas of concentration as a curricular guide; students need not declare concentration to graduate. In addition, third-year students may participate in the Litigation Clinic for 3 credits. Second- or third-year students may take any seminar offered, including Race and the Law for 3 credits, Gender and the Law for 3 credits, and Elder Law for 3 credits. Internships are available as research assistants or law clerks for public interest law firms, local legal aid offices, prosecutors' and public defenders' offices, and the court system. Research programs include Advanced Legal Research and Writing, Academic Legal Scholarship, and Independent Studies. Independent Study may be taken for 1 to 2 hours of credit each. Practical experience may also be gained through externships, for a maximum of 5 hours of credit, in an approved study program with a public interest or nonprofit, firm a judicial officer, or an attorney working in the feseral or state government. A variety of distinguished guests come to campus each year to address the law school community. These have included Justices Scalia and Thomas of the U.S. Supreme Court, Chief Justice Leroy Hassell of the Virginia Supreme Court, Dr. Robert P. George of Princeton University, and Judge Andrew Napolitiano, author and legal analyst. Study abroad includes a summer session in Strasbourg, France which emphasizes international human rights and jurisprudence, for a total of 6 credits, and a summer session in Haifa, Israel, which emphasizes biblical law, Qur'anic law, and the modern Israeli legal system, for a total of 3 credits. The school also has student exchange relationships with educational instutions in Spain, China and South Korea. Selected students are required to participate in the school's Academic Success Program, which consists of a 2-week pre-orientation summer program. Study skills workshops during the academic year, and one-on-one academic advising.The School of Law has an active Black Law Students Association (BLSA) and has hosted several BLSA events. The most widely taken electives are Family Law, UCC II, and wills, Trusts & Estates.

Graduation Requirements

In order to graduate, candidates must have a GPA of 2.0, have completed the upper-division writing requirement, an upper-division oral skills requirement, and a bar prepartation course (for non-honors students).

Organizations

Students edit the *Regent University Law Review, Regent University Journal of International Law*, and *Reget Journal of Law & Public Policy*. Moot court competitions for students include the ABA National Appellate Advocacy Competition, the National Constitutional Law Moot Court Competition, and the William B. Spong, Jr. Memorial Moot Court Competition at William and Mary. Other competitions include ABA Negotiations Competition, sponsored by the ABA-Law Student Division; the Robert Mehrige, Jr. National Environmental Negotiations Competition, sponsored by the University of Richmond; and the National Pretrial Competition, sponsored by Stetson University. Law student organizations include the Student Bar Association, Moot Court Board, and the Alternative Dispute Resolution, and Client Counseling Board. Local chapters of national associations include the Christian Legal Society, Federalist Society, and The American Inns of Court. Other campus organizations include Regent Students for Life, International Law Society, and Public Interest Legal Advocates of Regent.

Library

The law library contains 136,136 hardcopy volumes and 265,148 microform volume equivalents, and subscribes to 577 serial publications. Such on-line databases and networks as CALI, CIS Universe, DIALOG, Dow-Jones, Infotrac, Legal-Trac, LEXIS, LOIS, NEXIS, OCLC First Search, WESTLAW, and AccessUN, Arbitration Law OnLine, Halsbury's Laws Direct, HeinOnline, IndexMaster, Lawyers Weekly USA Online, Legal Scholarship Network (LSN), LexisNexis US Serials Set Digital Collection, LLMC-Digital, Making of Modern Law, Legal Treatises 1800-1926, RIA Checkpoint, Treaties and International Agreements Online, Virginia Lawyers Weekly Online, and Virginia Supreme Court Records and Briefs. are available to law students for research. Special library collections include the Founders Collection, John Brabner-Smith Library and Papers, Ralph Johnson Bunche Library, Mary Elizabeth Menefee Collection of Law & Film, First Amendment & Civil Rights

Placement

J.D.s awarded:	140

Services available through: a separate law school placement center

Special features: extensive career planning and professional development seminars, participation in career planning programs, panel discussions, and mock interviews, as well as one-to-one counseling of law students. Examples of fall programs include topics such as Interview Skills Workshop, Résumé Preparation, Focusing on a Litigation Career, and Solo Practice.

Full-time job interviews:	4 employers
Summer job interviews:	10 employers
Placement by graduation:	71% of class
Placement within 9 months:	91% of class
Average starting salary:	$49,439 to $115,000

Areas of placement:

Private practice 2-10 attorneys	34%
Private practice 11-25 attorneys	2%
Private practice 26-50 attorneys	4%
Private practice 51-100 attorneys	1%
Government	14%
Judicial clerkships	11%
Business/industry	11%
Public interest	9%
Military	6%
Academic	5%
Law Firm Private practice, firm size unknown	5%

Collection, and Early American Political Sermons. Recently, the library completely redesigned the layout of the public space. The ratio of library volumes to faculty is 4737 to 1 and to students is 299 to 1. The ratio of seats in the library to students is 1 to 1.

Faculty

The law school has 28 full-time and 25 part-time faculty members, of whom 12 are women. About 11% of full-time faculty have a graduate law degree in addition to the J.D.; about 8% of part-time faculty have one. The ratio of full-time students to full-time faculty in an average class is 22 to 1; in a clinic, 7 to 1. The law school has a regular program of bringing visiting professors and other distinguished lecturers and visitors to campus.

Students

About 49% of the student body are women; 15%, minorities; 7%, African American; 5%, Asian American; 2%, Hispanic; and 1%, Native American. The average age of entering students is 25; age range is 19 to 58.

Regent University   **381**

ROGER WILLIAMS UNIVERSITY

School of Law

Ten Metacom Avenue Bristol,
RI 02809-5171

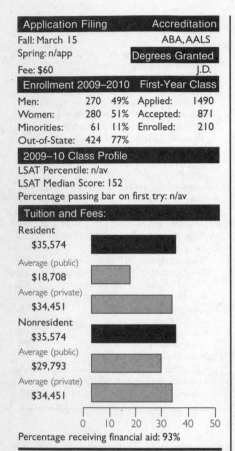

Application Filing		Accreditation	
Fall: March 15		ABA, AALS	
Spring: n/app		Degrees Granted	
Fee: $60		J.D.	
Enrollment 2009–2010		First-Year Class	
Men:	270 49%	Applied:	1490
Women:	280 51%	Accepted:	871
Minorities:	61 11%	Enrolled:	210
Out-of-State:	424 77%		

2009–10 Class Profile
LSAT Percentile: n/av
LSAT Median Score: 152
Percentage passing bar on first try: n/av

Tuition and Fees:

Resident
$35,574

Average (public)
$18,708

Average (private)
$34,451

Nonresident
$35,574

Average (public)
$29,793

Average (private)
$34,451

0   10   20   30   40   50

Percentage receiving financial aid: 93%

ADMISSIONS

In the fall 2009 first-year class, 1490 applied, 871 were accepted, and 210 enrolled. The median GPA of the most recent first-year class was 3.3.

Requirements
Applicants must have a bachelor's degree and take the LSAT. Minimum acceptable GPA is 2.0 on a scale of 4.0. The most important admission factors include LSAT results, GPA, and academic achievement. No specific undergraduate courses are required. Candidates are not interviewed.

Procedure
The application deadline for fall entry is March 15. Applicants should submit an application form, LSAT results, transcripts, a personal statement, the TOEFL, a nonrefundable application fee of $60, and 1 letter of recommendation. Notification of the admissions decision is on a rolling basis. The latest acceptable LSAT test

date for fall entry is June. The law school uses the LSDAS.

Special
The law school recruits minority and disadvantaged students by actively recruiting diverse students from local area colleges and universities, and by actively supporting diverse students once admitted through student organizations, academic support, and other programs. The Office of Admissions works closely with the Office of Diversity and Outreach to increase diversity by actively recruiting at historically black colleges and universities and major law school admissions fairs. Requirements are not different for out-of-state students. Transfer students must have a minimum GPA of 2.0, have attended an ABA-approved law school, and have a letter of good standing from their prior law school.

Costs

Tuition and fees for the 2009-2010 academic year are $35,574 for all full-time students. On-campus room and board costs about $9942 annually; books and supplies run $1748.

Financial Aid

About 93% of current law students receive some form of aid. The average annual amount of aid from all sources combined, including scholarships, loans, and work contracts, is $44,754; maximum, $57,022. Awards are based on merit along with leadership activities and public interest background. Required financial statement is the FAFSA. The aid application deadline for fall entry is February 15. First-year students are notified about their financial aid application once they are accepted and the necessary financial aid paperwork has been completed.

About the Law School

Roger Williams University School of Law was established in 1992 and is a private institution. The 140-acre campus is in a small town in the small, historic seacoast town of Bristol. The primary mission of the law school is to prepare students for the competent and ethical practice of law. Students have access to federal, state, county, city, and local agencies, courts, correctional facilities, law firms, and legal

aid organizations in the Bristol area. There are also state library archives and libraries at Brown University, University of Rhode Island, Providence College, and Rhode Island Historical Society. Facilities of special interest to law students include the Criminal Defense and Immigration clinics located in Providence, as well as the Mediation Clinic in Bristol. Housing for students is available in 1-bedroom apartments and townhouses 2 miles from campus. Nearby Bristol and Warren have numerous apartments available in private homes and apartment complexes. All law school facilities are accessible to the physically disabled.

Calendar

The law school operates on a traditional semester basis. Courses for full-time students are offered both day and evening and must be completed within 84 months. There is no part-time program. New students are admitted in the fall. There is a 7-week summer session. Transferable summer courses are offered.

Programs

Students may take relevant courses in other programs and apply credit toward the J.D.; a maximum of 9 to 15 credits may be applied. The following joint degrees may be earned: J.D./M.M.A. (Juris Doctor/Master of Marine Affairs), J.D./M.S. (Juris Doctor/Master of Science in Labor Relations and Human Resources), and J.D./M.S.C.J. (Juris Doctor/Master of Science in Criminal Justice).

Required
To earn the J.D., candidates must complete 90 total credits, of which 48 are for required courses. They must maintain a minimum GPA of 2.0 in the required courses. The following first-year courses are required of all students: Civil Procedure I and II, Contracts I and II, Criminal Law, Legal Methods I and II, Property, and Torts I and II. Required upper-level courses consist of Constitutional Law I and II, Criminal Procedure, Evidence, Professional Responsibility, and Upper Level Legal Methods. The required orientation program for first-year students is held 3 days prior to the first day of classes and includes an introduction to the judicial system and the study of law, case

Phone: 401-254-4555
800-633-2727
Fax: 401-254-4516
E-mail: admissions@rwu.edu
Web: http://law.rwu.edu

Contact
Michael W. Boylen, Assistant Dean of Admissions, 401-254-4555 for general inquiries; Denise Rousseau, Assistant Director, Financial Aid, 401-254-4510 for financial aid information.

RHODE ISLAND

briefing, exam-taking techniques, professionalism, student services introductions, and social events.

Electives
Third-year students may participate in the Criminal Defense Clinic, the Mediation Clinic, or the Immigration Clinic, for 6 credits. Seminars, available to second- and third-year students, span the breath of the curriculum. They are worth 2 credits each. Special legal perspectives courses are worth 1 credit. Internships for third-year students consist of judicial and public interest clerkships worth 5 credits. There is faculty-supervised directed research for 1 or 2 credits. Students are required to perform 20 hours of public service prior to graduation. A special lecture series includes topics on Marine Affairs and Public Interest Law. Study abroad is available through the London Summer Program. There are workshops on studying, case briefing, course outlining, and exam taking. The school has a rigorous Academic Support Program. The school's Office of Diversity and Outreach sponsors a variety of programs designed to address the needs of a diverse student body. The school has a wide range of special interest student groups. The most widely taken electives are Wills and Trusts, Business Organizations, and Sales.

Graduation Requirements
In order to graduate, candidates must have a GPA of 2.0 and have completed the upper-division writing requirement.

Organizations
Students edit the *Roger Williams University Law Review*. The primary internal competition is the Esther Clark Moot Court Competition. Students also participate in the National Moot Court Competition and the John R. Brown Admiralty Moot Court Competition. Other competitions include Mock Trial, and Mediation, Negotiation, and Client Counseling Law student organizations include the Maritime Law Society, Multicultural Law Students Association, and Sports and Entertainment Law Society. Local chapters of national associations include the American Trial Lawyers Association, ABA, and National Association of Public Interest Lawyers. Other campus organizations

include Women's Law Caucus, LGBT Alliance, and the Federalist Society.

Library
The law library contains 301,907 hardcopy volumes and 1,083,880 microform volume equivalents, and subscribes to 3363 serial publications. Such on-line databases and networks as CALI, CIS Universe, Legal-Trac, LEXIS, LOIS, NEXIS, OCLC First Search, RLIN, WESTLAW, Wilsonline Indexes, BNA, HeinOnline, CCH Intelliconnect, CILP, Social Law Lib. Mass. Admin. Law, RIA Checkpoint, Constitutions Suite Online, Foreign Law Guide, United Nations Treaty Collection, Justis, Making of Modern Law, Oxford Reports on International Law, and Index to Foreign Legal Periodicals are available to law students for research. Special library collections include Rhode Island Law, the State Justice Institute depository, Maritime Law, and Portuguese-American Comparative Law. Recently, the library provided electrical connections for laptops on study tables. The ratio of library volumes to faculty is 9421 to 1 and to students is 565 to 1. The ratio of seats in the library to students is 1 to 1.

Faculty
The law school has 33 full-time and 30 part-time faculty members, of whom 23 are women. About 20% of full-time faculty have a graduate law degree in addition to the J.D.; about 9% of part-time faculty have one. The ratio of full-time students to full-time faculty in an average class is 40 to 1; in a clinic, 10 to 1. The law school has a regular program of bringing visiting professors and other distinguished lecturers and visitors to campus.

Students
About 51% of the student body are women; 11%, minorities; 2%, African American; 3%, Asian American; 5%, Hispanic; 1%, Native American; and 11%, unknown/other. The majority of students come from the Northeast (56%). The average age of entering students is 25; age range is 21 to 50. About 48% of students enter directly from undergraduate school and 4% have a graduate degree.

Placement

J.D.s awarded:	184

Services available through: a separate law school placement center

Special features: Legal Career Options Day, Government/Small Firm Day, Rhode Island State Government Internship Program, extensive one-on-one counseling sessions, Mock Interview Program, coordinated programs with the Rhode Island Bar Association, and an alumni job newsletter.

Full-time job interviews:	11 employers
Summer job interviews:	15 employers
Placement by graduation:	n/av
Placement within 9 months:	86% of class
Average starting salary:	$28,000 to $250,000

Areas of placement:

Private practice 2-10 attorneys	23%
Private practice 11-25 attorneys	3%
Private practice 26-50 attorneys	2%
Private practice 51-100 attorneys	1%
Business/industry	21%
Unknown	15%
Judicial clerkships	13%
Public interest	8%
Military	7%
Government	6%
Academic	1%

RUTGERS UNIVERSITY/CAMDEN

School of Law

Fifth and Penn Streets Camden, NJ 08102

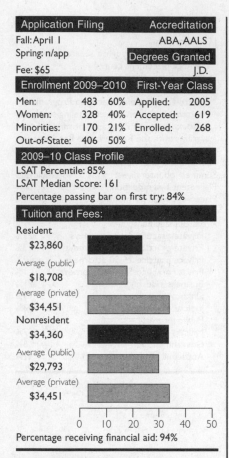

Application Filing		Accreditation
Fall: April 1		ABA, AALS
Spring: n/app		
		Degrees Granted
Fee: $65		J.D.

Enrollment 2009–2010		First-Year Class	
Men:	483 60%	Applied:	2005
Women:	328 40%	Accepted:	619
Minorities:	170 21%	Enrolled:	268
Out-of-State:	406 50%		

2009–10 Class Profile
LSAT Percentile: 85%
LSAT Median Score: 161
Percentage passing bar on first try: 84%

Tuition and Fees:

Resident
$23,860

Average (public)
$18,708

Average (private)
$34,451

Nonresident
$34,360

Average (public)
$29,793

Average (private)
$34,451

0 10 20 30 40 50

Percentage receiving financial aid: 94%

ADMISSIONS
In the fall 2009 first-year class, 2005 applied, 619 were accepted, and 268 enrolled. Fifty-six transfers enrolled. The median LSAT percentile of the most recent first-year class was 85; the median GPA was 3.46 on a scale of 4.0. The lowest LSAT percentile accepted was 45; the highest was 98.

Requirements
Applicants must have a bachelor's degree and take the LSAT. Minimum acceptable LSAT percentile is 45 and minimum acceptable GPA is 2.5 on a scale of 4.0. The most important admission factors include general background, GPA, and LSAT results. No specific undergraduate courses are required.

Procedure
The application deadline for fall entry is April 1. Applicants should submit an application form, LSAT results, transcripts, a personal statement, a nonrefundable application fee of $65, and 2 letters of recommendation. Notification of the admissions decision is on a rolling basis. The latest

acceptable LSAT test date for fall entry is June. The law school uses the LSDAS.

Special
The law school recruits minority and disadvantaged students by means of mail, student organizations, interviews, campus visits, and law forums. Requirements are not different for out-of-state students. Transfer students must have one year of credit and have attended an ABA-approved law school.

Costs
Tuition and fees for the 2009-2010 academic year are $23,860 for full-time in-state students and $34,360 for out-of-state students. Tuition for part-time students is $19,198 in-state and $27,938 out-of-state. On-campus room and board costs about $11,465 annually; books and supplies run $1313.

Financial Aid
About 94% of current law students receive some form of aid. The average annual amount of aid from all sources combined, including scholarships, loans, and work contracts, is $28,767; maximum, $58,000. Awards are based on need and merit. Required financial statement is the FAF-SA. The aid application deadline for fall entry is July 1. Special funds for minority or disadvantaged students include funds that are available from state, university, and school programs. First-year students are notified about their financial aid application at time of acceptance.

About the Law School
Rutgers University/Camden School of Law was established in 1926 and is a public institution. The 25-acre campus is in an urban area adjacent to the Center City district of Philadelphia and 1 mile from the Library Bell. The primary mission of the law school is to provide a dynamic program of professional training, distinguished legal scholarship, and service to the bar and community. Students have access to federal, state, county, city, and local agencies, courts, correctional facilities, law firms, and legal aid organizations in the Camden area. Facilities of special interest to law students include computer laboratories, e-mail accounts, Internet connections, and on-line legal research. Housing for students is available in a 6-story apartment complex that houses 248 students in 62 graduate apartments. Off-campus housing on the Delaware River is also available.

About 90% of the law school facilities are accessible to the physically disabled.

Calendar
The law school operates on a traditional semester basis. Courses for full- and part-time students are offered both day and evening and must be completed within 5 years. New full-time students are admitted in the fall; part-time, fall and summer. There is a 7-week summer session. Transferable summer courses are offered.

Programs
Students may take relevant courses in other programs and apply credit toward the J.D.; a maximum of 6 credits may be applied. The following joint degrees may be earned: J.D./D.O. (Juris Doctor/Doctor of Osteopathic Medicine), J.D./M.B.A. (Juris Doctor/Master of Business Administration), J.D./M.C.R.P. (Juris Doctor/Master of City and Regional Planning), J.D./M.D. (Juris Doctor/Doctor of Medicine), J.D./M.P.A. (Juris Doctor/Master of Public Administration), J.D./M.P.A.P. (Juris Doctor/Master of Public Affairs and Politics), and J.D./M.S.W. (Juris Doctor/Master of Social Work).

Required
To earn the J.D., candidates must complete 84 total credits, of which 32 are for required courses. They must maintain a minimum GPA of 2.0 in the required courses. The following first-year courses are required of all students: Civil Procedure, Constitutional Law, Contracts, Criminal Law, Legal Research and Writing, Moot Court I, Property, and Torts. Required upper-level courses consist of elective courses with writing components and Professional Responsibility. The required orientation program for first-year students is 2 days prior to the start of classes; there is a briefing on reading and analyzing cases, library usage, legal writing, professional responsibility, and general study techniques, as well as an introduction to computer usage and student organizations and social events.

Electives
The School of Law offers concentrations in corporate law, criminal law, environmental law, family law, international law, labor law, litigation, tax law, health law, and public interest law. In addition, clinics, which are worth 4 to 6 course credits, include a Small Business Counseling Clinic, Child and Family Advocacy Clinic, Children's Justice Clinic, Domestic Vio-

Phone: 856-225-6102
800-466-7561
Fax: 856-225-6537
E-mail: admissions@camlaw.rutgers.edu
Web: www.camlaw.rutgers.edu

Contact

Maureen B. O'Boyle, Associate Director of Admissions, 856-225-6102 for general inquiries; Linda Taylor-Burch, 856-225-6039 for financial aid information.

lence Clinic, and a Civil Practice Clinic. The Pro Bono/Public Interest program enables students to represent clients, under the supervision of attorneys, in domestic violence, children's SSI disability benefits, death penalty, immigration, and bankruptcy cases. As part of its Lawyering Program, the law school has many seminars covering a wide variety of areas of practice, including Business Ethics and Law, Citizenship, Civil Disobedience, Law Politics and Democracy, Patent Prosecution, Sex Discrimination, and Marshall Brennan Fellows. Each seminar is limited to 14 students, and credit available ranges from 2 to 3 course credits. The law school offers extensive opportunities for students to earn academic credit while working for various public and private nonprofit agencies and for state and federal judges. In addition to the work, students attend seminars relating to the work done in their placement. Rutgers has placed students in externships in virtually every federal and state agency in the New Jersey, Philadelphia, and Delaware area. Credit for externships can range from 3 to 6 credits. Third-year law students may take independent study for 1 to 2 credits under the supervision of a faculty member. Select students can also participate in several programs, including the Eagleton Fellowship Program, that give them an opportunity to work closely with the New Jersey state executive branch. These programs and fellowships often have a significant research component. The annual state Constitution Law Lecture and Corman Distinguished Lecture bring nationally known scholars and jurists to the law school. Students can study abroad through any other ABA-approved program. Students have studied in Paris, Rome, London, Japan, and a variety of other countries. There are individual and group tutorials in the school's Academic Success Program, as well as workshops on study techniques, test taking, and individual subject review for all students. The law school has several noncredit minority programs designed to provide a support system for minority students and increase the presence of minority students on campus. The most widely taken electives are Evidence, Commercial Law, and Business Organizations.

Graduation Requirements

In order to graduate, candidates must have a GPA of 2.0 and have completed the upper-division writing requirement.

Organizations

Students edit the *Rutgers Law Journal*, the *Rutgers Journal of Law and Public Policy*, and the *Rutgers Journal of Law and Religion*. A highlight of the upper-level curriculum is the Judge James A. Hunter III Advanced Moot Court Program. Other moot court competitions include the National Moot Court Competition and Jessup International Moot Court Competition. Other competitions include the Gibbons National Criminal Procedure Moot Court Competition, Admiralty Moot Court Competition, National Black Law Students Association Frederick Douglass Competition, National Latino Law Students Association Moot Court Competition, and the Environmental Moot Court Competition. Law student organizations include the Student Bar Association, Association for Public Interest Law, and the Francis Deak International Law Society. There are local chapters and clubs of all major national law student organizations, including Phi Alpha Delta law fraternity, Women's Law Caucus, Black Law Students Association, Hispanic Students Association, Student Bar Association, Latino Law Students Association, and Asian/Pacific American Students Association.

Library

The law library contains 512,000 hardcopy volumes and 150,000 microform volume equivalents, and subscribes to 1953 serial publications. Such on-line databases and networks as CALI, Dow-Jones, Legal-Trac, LEXIS, LOIS, Matthew Bender, NEXIS, OCLC First Search, WESTLAW, and Wilsonline Indexes are available to law students for research. Special library collections include a historical collection of Soviet and Eastern European legal matters and a U.S. government depository library. Recently, the library renovated some of its space with, 2 seminar rooms, a Wi-Fi network, and a lounge area. The ratio of library volumes to faculty is 10,039 to 1 and to students is 631 to 1. The ratio of seats in the library to students is 1 to 2.

Faculty

The law school has 51 full-time and 57 part-time faculty members, of whom 40 are women. According to AAUP standards for Category IIA institutions, faculty salaries are well above average. About 40% of full-time faculty have a graduate law degree in addition to the J.D.; about 20% of part-time

Placement

J.D.s awarded:	240

Services available through: a separate law school placement center and University Career Services Center for joint degree candidates

Services: assistance with LEXIS, WESTLAW, and the Internet career searches; fall and spring on-campus interview programs

Special features: interview workshops, on-campus interview programs, career forums, resource library, and participation in a consortium with the law schools of the University of Pennsylvania, Temple, and Villanova; full-service Career Services Office with 3 full-time professional career services staff members in addition to 1 full-time pro bono coordinator and public interest adviser; videotaped mock interviews, individualized and small group career workshops, career panels, and several alumni and attorney mentoring programs

Full-time job interviews:	150 employers
Summer job interviews:	150 employers
Placement by graduation:	75% of class
Placement within 9 months:	92% of class
Average starting salary:	$45,000 to $110,000

Areas of placement:

Private practice 2-10 attorneys	5%
Private practice 11-25 attorneys	9%
Private practice 26-50 attorneys	12%
Private practice 51-100 attorneys	15%
Unknown firm size	1%
Judicial clerkships	40%
Business/industry	9%
Government	6%
Public interest	2%
Military	1%

faculty have one. The ratio of full-time students to full-time faculty in an average class is 13 to 1; in a clinic, 8 to 1. The law school has a regular program of bringing visiting professors and other distinguished lecturers and visitors to campus.

Students

About 40% of the student body are women; 21%, minorities; 6%, African American; 9%, Asian American; 5%, Hispanic; 1%, Native American; and 1%, foreign. The majority of students come from New Jersey (50%). The average age of entering students is 25; age range is 21 to 45. About 38% of students enter directly from undergraduate school, 7% have a graduate degree, and 48% have worked full-time prior to entering law school. About 2% drop out after the first year for academic or personal reasons; 96% remain to receive a law degree.

School of Law

Center for Law and Justice,
123 Washington St.
Newark, NJ 07102

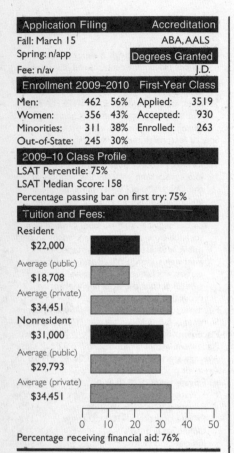

Application Filing	Accreditation
Fall: March 15	ABA, AALS
Spring: n/app	Degrees Granted
Fee: n/av	J.D.

Enrollment 2009–2010		First-Year Class	
Men:	462 56%	Applied:	3519
Women:	356 43%	Accepted:	930
Minorities:	311 38%	Enrolled:	263
Out-of-State:	245 30%		

2009–10 Class Profile
LSAT Percentile: 75%
LSAT Median Score: 158
Percentage passing bar on first try: 75%

Tuition and Fees:

Resident
$22,000

Average (public)
$18,708

Average (private)
$34,451

Nonresident
$31,000

Average (public)
$29,793

Average (private)
$34,451

0 10 20 30 40 50

Percentage receiving financial aid: 76%

ADMISSIONS

In the fall 2009 first-year class, 3519 applied, 930 were accepted, and 263 enrolled. Figures in the above capsule and in this profile are approximate. Twenty-five transfers enrolled. The median LSAT percentile of the most recent first-year class was 75; the median GPA was 3.33 on a scale of 4.0. The highest LSAT percentile was 99.

Requirements
Applicants must have a bachelor's degree and take the LSAT. The most important admission factors include academic achievement, LSAT results, and GPA. No specific undergraduate courses are required. Candidates are not interviewed.

Procedure
Applicants should submit an application form, LSAT results, transcripts, a personal statement, a nonrefundable application fee, 1 letter of recommendation, sent to law services, and LSAT results and transcripts sent through the LSDAS, and a personal statement. Notification of the admissions decision is on a rolling basiic. The latest acceptable LSAT test date for fall entry is February. Check with the school for current application deadlines. The law school uses the LSDAS.

Special
The law school recruits minority and disadvantaged students through participation in LSAC forums, participation in Puerto Rican Legal Defense Fund Law Day, visits to historically black colleges, black, Latino, and Asian law days, and contact with high school and college students. The Minority Student Program is open to disadvantaged students of all races. Requirements are not different for out-of-state students. Transfer students must have one year of credit, have a minimum GPA of 3.0, have attended an ABA-approved law school, and have a letter of good standing.

Costs

Tuition and fees for the 2009-2010 academic year are $22,000 for full-time in-state students and $31,000 for out-of-state students. Tuition for part-time students is $14,000 in-state and $20,000 out-of-state. On-campus room and board costs about $13,000 annually; books and supplies run $1300.

Financial Aid

In a recent year, about 76% of current law students received some form of aid. Awards are based on need and merit, although most financial aid and scholarships are awarded on the basis of need. Limited merit scholarships and a number of need and merit scholarships are also available. Required financial statement is the FAFSA. The aid application deadline for fall entry is March 1. Special funds for minority or disadvantaged students consist of the Ralph Bunche Fellowships, which yield tuition remission and a stipend; the C. Clyde Ferguson Scholarships, which yield full in-state tuition and housing for New Jersey residents; Marie Slocum Scholarship; Judge Herbert Tate, Sr. Scholarship; Judge John Dios Scholarship; and other scholarships. First-year students are notified about their financial aid application several weeks after an offer of admission.

About the Law School

Rutgers University/Newark School of Law was established in 1908 and is a public institution. The 11-acre campus is in an urban area in the city of Newark, 8 miles southwest of New York. The primary mis-
sion of the law school is to prepare students for professional practice by offering high-quality education in all fields of law, as well as to preserve and expand knowledge as part of a national community of legal scholars, and to serve the public by working to achieve social justice through law. Students have access to federal, state, county, city, and local agencies, courts, correctional facilities, law firms, and legal aid organizations in the Newark area. Also nearby are the American Civil Liberties Union and public interest organizations. Facilities of special interest to law students are the federal courts and county and state court complexes, which are located in downtown Newark, the Newark Museum and Public Library, and the New Jersey Performing Arts Center, which is located just a few blocks away. The Center For Law and Justice is a technologically advanced building, and its courtroom is periodically used for hearing oral arguments by the state appellate court. Housing for students is available on campus--a third of students live on campus. Most students live in nearby communities. All law school facilities are accessible to the physically disabled.

Calendar

The law school operates on a traditional semester basis. Courses for full-time students are offered both day and evening and must be completed within 5 years. For part-time students, courses are offered both day and evening and must be completed within 6 years. New full- and part-time students are admitted in the fall. There is a 7-week summer session. Transferable summer courses are offered.

Programs

Students may take relevant courses in other programs and apply credit toward the J.D.; a maximum of 12 credits may be applied. The following joint degrees may be earned: J.D./M.A. (Juris Doctor/Master of Arts in criminal justice, political science), J.D./M.B.A. (Juris Doctor/Master of Business Administration), J.D./M.C.R.P. (Juris Doctor/Master in City and Regional Planning), J.D./M.D. (Juris Doctor/Doctor of Medicine), J.D./M.S.W. (Juris Doctor/Master of Social Work), and J.D./Ph.D (Juris Doctor/Doctor of Philosophy).

Required
To earn the J.D., candidates must complete 84 total credits, of which 34 to 35 are

Phone: 973-353-5557/5554
Fax: 973-353-3459
E-mail: *lawinfo@andromeda.rutgers.edu*
Web: *http://law.newark.rutgers.edu*

Contact

Anita Walton, Assistant Dean for Admissions, 973-353-5557/5554 for general inquiries; Nicky Fornarotto, Coordinator for Financial Aid, 973-353-1702 for financial aid information.

for required courses. They must maintain a minimum GPA of 1.67 in the required courses. The following first-year courses are required of all students: a required freshman elective, Civil Procedure, Constitutional Law, Contracts, Criminal Law, Legal Research and Writing I and II, Property, and Torts. Required upper-level courses consist of an upper-level writing requirement and Professional Responsibility. All students may elect to choose among extensive in-house clinical programming. The required orientation program for first-year students is 3 days and covers Professional Responsibility registration, student services, health and safety issues, an Introduction to Legal Research course, and provides opportunities to meet upper-class students and all student organization representatives.

Electives

The School of Law offers concentrations in corporate law, criminal law, entertainment law, environmental law, family law, international law, juvenile law, labor law, litigation, media law, securities law, sports law, tax law, torts and insurance, constitutional law, health law, and intellectual property. In addition, students can earn up to 8 credits per semester for clinics. Clinics are open only to upper-level students, and some require students to be in their final year. Clinics include Constitutional Rights, Women's Rights, Environmental Law, Urban Legal, Federal Tax, Special Education, Women and Aids, Domestic Violence, Child Advocacy Project, and Transactional Law/Community Development. Some 20 seminars are offered each semester for 2 credits each. They are open to all upper-level students and offer the opportunity to write a substantial legal paper that meets the writing requirement. Upper-level students with grades of B- or better may engage in internships with state or federal magistrates, justices, or judges for 3 credits; they are supported by a weekly in house seminar. Externships are available with the Attorney General's office, the Security and Exchange Commission, and the National Labor Relations Board. An Intellectual Property Externship is also offered. Students may assist full-time faculty members in their research for 2 or 3 credits. Independent research may be undertaken by upper-level students for 2 or 3 credits with faculty permission. Special lecture series include

Miller, Stoffer, and Weintraub lectureships, which are given annually. Students may enroll for up to 12 credits in an ABA/AALS sponsored semester-abroad program. Approximately 25 students engage in this study, from China to Greece and at the University of Leiden-Holland. First-year students are tutored by upper-level students with good grades; tutors may earn 2 credits. The Minority Student Program is dependent on socio-economic status, regardless of race. The school also has programs on behalf of women, minority groups, and gay and lesbian groups. The most widely taken electives are Evidence, Business Associations, and Copyright.

Graduation Requirements

In order to graduate, candidates must have a GPA of 2.0 and have completed the upper-division writing requirement.

Organizations

Students edit the *Rutgers Law Review, Computer and Technology Law Journal, Women's Rights Law Reporter, Race and the Law Review*, Bankruptcy Law Journal, Alternative Dispute Resolution Journal, and *Rutgers Law Record*. Students compete in the Nathan Baker Mock Trial, David Cohn Moot Court, and the ABA Negotiations competitions. Students participate in approximately 25 to 30 writing competitions, among them the Nathan Burkan Copyright Competition. Law student organizations, local chapters of national associations, and campus organizations include Student Bar Association, Public Interest Law Foundation, Federalist Society, Student Lawyers Guild, Association of Black Law Students, Intellectual Property Law Society, Medicine and Health Law Society, Women's Law Forum, and International Law Students Society.

Library

The law library contains 353,600 hardcopy volumes and 163,600 microform volume equivalents, and subscribes to 3120 serial publications. Such on-line databases and networks as DIALOG, LEXIS, NEXIS, RLIN, and WESTLAW are available to law students for research. Special library collections include depositories for U.S. and New Jersey documents. Recently, the library installed INNOPAC, an automated serials and acquisition system and on-line public access catalog. The ratio of library

Placement

J.D.s awarded:	198

Services available through: a separate law school placement center

Services: extensive on-campus interviewing program as well as co-sponsorship of off-campus job fairs; career panels on specific practice areas, judicial clerkships, networking and job search skills

Special features: individual counseling, the alumni/ae job hotline, updated daily, and videotaped mock interviews.

Full-time job interviews:	59 employers
Summer job interviews:	68 employers
Placement by graduation:	n/av
Placement within 9 months:	98% of class
Average starting salary:	$35,000 to $192,000

Areas of placement:

Private practice 2-10 attorneys	11%
Private practice 11-25 attorneys	11%
Private practice 26-50 attorneys	11%
Private practice 51-100 attorneys	11%
Judicial clerkships	28%
Business/industry	13%
Government	5%
Public interest	3%
Military	2%
Academic	2%

volumes to faculty is 6429 to 1 and to students is 432 to 1. The ratio of seats in the library to students is 1 to 2.

Faculty

The law school has 55 full-time and 31 part-time faculty members, of whom 32 are women. According to AAUP standards for Category I institutions, faculty salaries are above average. About 6% of full-time faculty have a graduate law degree in addition to the J.D. The ratio of full-time students to full-time faculty in an average class is 17 to 1; in a clinic, 8 to 1. There is a chapter of the Order of the Coif; 37 faculty and 186 graduates are members.

Students

About 43% of the student body are women; 38%, minorities; 13%, African American; 12%, Asian American; 10%, Hispanic; and 1%, Native American. The majority of students come from the Northeast (90%). The average age of entering students is 27; age range is 21 to 55. About 40% of students enter directly from undergraduate school, 23% have a graduate degree, and 34% have worked full-time prior to entering law school. About 2% drop out after the first year for academic or personal reasons; 97% remain to receive a law degree.

School of Law

8000 Utopia Parkway
Queens, NY 11439

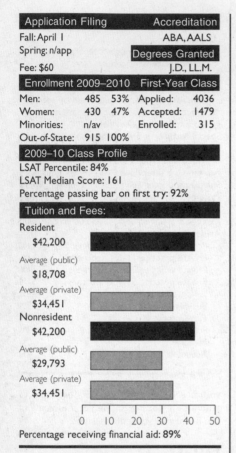

Application Filing		Accreditation	
Fall: April 1		ABA, AALS	
Spring: n/app		Degrees Granted	
Fee: $60		J.D., LL.M.	

Enrollment 2009–2010		First-Year Class	
Men:	485 53%	Applied:	4036
Women:	430 47%	Accepted:	1479
Minorities:	n/av	Enrolled:	315
Out-of-State:	915 100%		

2009–10 Class Profile
LSAT Percentile: 84%
LSAT Median Score: 161
Percentage passing bar on first try: 92%

Tuition and Fees:

Resident
$42,200

Average (public)
$18,708

Average (private)
$34,451

Nonresident
$42,200

Average (public)
$29,793

Average (private)
$34,451

Percentage receiving financial aid: 89%

ADMISSIONS

In the fall 2009 first-year class, 4036 applied, 1479 were accepted, and 315 enrolled. Eight transfers enrolled. The median LSAT percentile of the most recent first-year class was 84; the median GPA was 3.48 on a scale of 4.0.

Requirements
Applicants must have a bachelor's degree and take the LSAT. No specific undergraduate courses are required. Candidates are not interviewed.

Procedure
The application deadline for fall entry is April 1. Applicants should submit an application form, LSAT results, transcripts, a personal statement, a nonrefundable application fee of $60, and up to 3 letters of recommendation. Notification of the admissions decision is on a rolling basis. The latest acceptable LSAT test date for fall entry is February. The law school uses the LSDAS.

Special
The law school recruits minority and disadvantaged students through special visits to historically black colleges and universities, open houses, need-based and academic scholarships to improve diversity, and the Summer Institute Program. Requirements are not different for out-of-state students. Transfer students must have one year of credit and have attended an ABA-approved law school. Preadmissions courses consist of the Summer Institute, a conditional admissions program for individuals who have suffered the effects of discrimination, chronic financial hardship, and/or other social, educational, or physical disadvantages to such an extent that their undergraduate performance or LSAT score cannot otherwise warrant unconditional acceptance into the entering class.

Costs

Tuition and fees for the 2009-2010 academic year are $42,200 for all full-time students. Tuition for part-time students is $31,650 per year. On-campus room and board costs about $13,670 annually; books and supplies run $1400.

Financial Aid

About 89% of current law students receive some form of aid. Awards are based on need and merit. Required financial statement is the FAFSA. Check with the school for current deadlines. First-year students are notified about their financial aid application at time of acceptance.

About the Law School

Saint John's University School of Law was established in 1925 and is a private institution. The 100-acre campus is in a suburban area in New York City (Queens county). The primary mission of the law school is to prepare students to enter the legal profession with excellent lawyering skills and a commitment to high principles of professionalism and community service. Students have access to federal, state, county, city, and local agencies, courts, correctional facilities, law firms, and legal aid organizations in the Queens area. There are a variety of year-long programs at the law school, including clinics, externships, colloquia, and trial and appellate experiences. Facilities of special interest

to law students include a renovated moot court room and adjoining classrooms, providing faculty and students with state-of-the-art learning spaces. There is state-of-the-art technology in all classrooms, including wireless capability throughout the law school. Housing for students is available at the university, and assistance is provided in locating area housing. A roommate list is also available. All law school facilities are accessible to the physically disabled.

Calendar

The law school operates on a traditional semester basis. Courses for full-time students are offered both day and evening and must be completed within 3 years. For part-time students, courses are offered both day and evening and must be completed within 4 years. New full- and part-time students are admitted in the fall. There is an 8-week summer session. Transferable summer courses are offered.

Programs

In addition to the J.D., the law school offers the LL.M. Students may take relevant courses in other programs and apply credit toward the J.D.; a maximum of 3 credits may be applied. The following joint degrees may be earned: J.D./B.A.-B.S. (Juris Doctor/Bachelor of Arts and/or Bachelor of Science), J.D./LL.M. (Juris Doctor/Master of Laws in bankruptcy and in U.S. legal studies), J.D./M.A. (Juris Doctor/Master of Arts in government and politics), and J.D./M.B.A. (Juris Doctor/Master of Business Administration).

Required
To earn the J.D., candidates must complete 86 total credits, of which 58 are for required courses. They must maintain a minimum GPA of 2.0 in the required courses. The following first-year courses are required of all students: Civil Procedure, Constitutional Law, Contracts I and II, Criminal Law, Introduction to Law, Legal Analysis and Writing, Property, and Torts. Required upper-level courses consist of Professional Responsibility. The required orientation program for first-year students is held throughout a 2-week long program in which students participate in sessions and take Introduction to Law.

Phone: 718-990-6474
Fax: 718-990-2526
E-mail: lawinfo@stjohns.edu
Web: www.law.stjohns.edu

Contact

Admissions Office, 718-990-6474 for general inquiries; Jorge Rodriguez, Assistant Vice President/Executive Director, 718-990-6403 for financial aid information.

NEW YORK

Electives

The School of Law offers concentrations in corporate law, criminal law, entertainment law, environmental law, family law, intellectual property law, international law, juvenile law, labor law, litigation, maritime law, securities law, sports law, tax law, torts and insurance, estate administration, and real estate (property). Clinics include the Elder Law Clinic, the Domestic Violence Clinic, and the Prosecution Clinic. Seminars include Civil Practice, Constitutional Rights, and Race and the Law. They also have the opportunity to be placed with administrative, city, state, and federal judges in the Judicial Externship. Research programs include the St. Thomas More Institute for Legal Research. Each year the school hosts guest speakers, Judge-in-Residence and Scholar-in-Residence programs, and various other symposia. Students may study at the law school's Rome, Italy campus and earn a minimum of 4 credits during the month long program. Tutorial programs include academic support and the Writing Center. The law school's remedial program hosts a Conditional Admit Program called the Summer Institute. The most widely taken electives are New York Practice, Criminal Procedure I, and Family Law.

Graduation Requirements

In order to graduate, candidates must have a GPA of 2.0, have completed the upper-division writing requirement, and the Advanced Writing requirement, which is intended to ensure that all students have the opportunity after the first year to compose at least 1 scholarly writing for which they must analyze, synthesize, organize, and present substantive material.

Organizations

The primary law review is the *St. John's Law Review*. Other law reviews include the *Journal of Civil Rights and Economic Development, Journal of Catholic Legal Studies, New York International Law Review, American Bankruptcy Institute Law Review* and *N.Y. Litigator*. The student newspaper is *The Forum* and the yearbook is *Res Gestae*. Moot court competitions include John J. Gibbons National Criminal Procedure Moot Court, Sutherland Cup Moot Court, and Domenick L. Gabrielli National Moot Court competitions. The law school hosts the Conrad B. Duberstein Moot Court Competition. Oth-

er competitions include the Intra-School, First Year Trial, Client Counseling, Criminal Law Institute, and Civil Trial Institute competitions. Law student organizations, local chapters of national associations, and campus organizations include Student Bar Association, Labor Relations and Employment Law Society, and Environmental Law Society. There are local chapters of Delta Theta Phi, Phi Alpha Delta, and Phi Delta Phi. Campus clubs and other organizations include the Corporate and Securities Law Society, Admiralty Law Society, and Family Law Society.

Library

The law library contains 376,546 hardcopy volumes and 189,558 microform volume equivalents, and subscribes to 4000 serial publications. Such on-line databases and networks as CALI, CIS Universe, DIALOG, Infotrac, Legal-Trac, LEXIS, Mathew Bender, NEXIS, OCLC First Search, WESTLAW, Wilsonline Indexes, SUNY/OCLC, HeinOnline, and LLMC Digital are available to law students for research. Special library collections include United Nations Depository, New York State Depository, Civil Rights, Bankruptcy, and U.S. Depository. The ratio of library volumes to faculty is 5884 to 1 and to students is 412 to 1. The ratio of seats in the library to students is 1 to 2.

Faculty

The law school has 64 full-time and 76 part-time faculty members, of whom 51 are women. According to AAUP standards for Category I institutions, faculty salaries are average. About 34% of full-time faculty have a graduate law degree in addition to the J.D.; about 14% of part-time faculty have one. The ratio of full-time students to full-time faculty in an average class is 14 to 1; in a clinic, 8 to 1. The law school has a regular program of bringing visiting professors and other distinguished lecturers and visitors to campus.

Students

About 47% of the student body are women; 6%, African American; 9%, Asian American; 8%, Hispanic; and 1%, Foreign National. The average age of entering students is 23; age range is 19 to 53. About 40% of students enter directly from undergraduate school and 4% have a graduate degree. About 3% drop out after the first year for academic or personal reasons.

Placement

J.D.s awarded:	285

Services available through: a separate law school placement center

Services: Career Services posts all job listings and administers its fall and spring recruitment programs using an on-line web-based system.

Special features: Technology is utilized extensively by Career Services to communicate with students. An internal web site contains internship and fellowship postings, and provides access to Career Services information such as handbooks and directories, announcements, a calendar of events, links to job searches, and links to other web sites.

Full-time job interviews:	40 employers
Summer job interviews:	44 employers
Placement by graduation:	78% of class
Placement within 9 months:	96% of class
Average starting salary:	$42,000 to $16,000

Areas of placement:

Private practice 2-10 attorneys	17%
Private practice 11-25 attorneys	5%
Private practice 26-50 attorneys	6%
Private practice 51-100 attorneys	5%
25% Private practice 101+	25%
Government	17%
Business/industry	15%
Judicial clerkships	4%
Public interest	3%
Academic	3%

Saint John's University

389

SAINT LOUIS UNIVERSITY

School of Law

3700 Lindell Boulevard
St. Louis, MO 63108

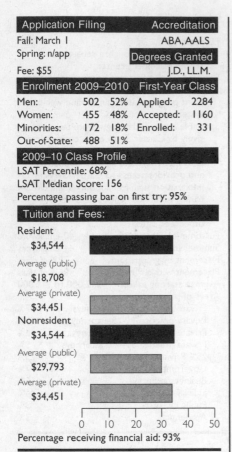

Application Filing			Accreditation
Fall: March 1			ABA, AALS
Spring: n/app			**Degrees Granted**
Fee: $55			J.D., LL.M.

Enrollment 2009–2010			First-Year Class	
Men:	502	52%	Applied:	2284
Women:	455	48%	Accepted:	1160
Minorities:	172	18%	Enrolled:	331
Out-of-State:	488	51%		

2009–10 Class Profile

LSAT Percentile: 68%
LSAT Median Score: 156
Percentage passing bar on first try: 95%

Tuition and Fees:

Resident
$34,544

Average (public)
$18,708

Average (private)
$34,451

Nonresident
$34,544

Average (public)
$29,793

Average (private)
$34,451

Percentage receiving financial aid: 93%

ADMISSIONS

In the fall 2009 first-year class, 2284 applied, 1160 were accepted, and 331 enrolled. Seven transfers enrolled. The median LSAT percentile of the most recent first-year class was 68; the median GPA was 3.41 on a scale of 4.0. The lowest LSAT percentile accepted was 17; the highest was 99.

Requirements

Applicants must have a bachelor's degree and take the LSAT. The most important admission factors include LSAT results and GPA. No specific undergraduate courses are required. Candidates are not interviewed.

Procedure

The application deadline for fall entry is March 1. Applicants should submit an application form, LSAT results, transcripts, a personal statement, TOEFL where applicable, a nonrefundable application fee of $55, and 2 letters of recom-

mendation. Accepted students must pay a $150 deposit to reserve a place and a $300 final deposit to confirm attendance. Notification of the admissions decision is on a rolling basis. The latest acceptable LSAT test date for fall entry is February. The law school uses the LSDAS.

Special

The law school recruits minority and disadvantaged students actively through the Summer Institute, scholarships for diversity, active minority student associations and the Minority Clerkship Program, and by recruiting at colleges and universities throughout the United States. Requirements are not different for out-of-state students. Transfer students must have one year of credit, have attended an ABA-approved law school, and rank in the top third of the law class.

Costs

Tuition and fees for the 2009-2010 academic year are $34,544 for all full-time students. Tuition for part-time students is $25,122 per year. Books and supplies run $660.

Financial Aid

About 93% of current law students receive some form of aid. The average annual amount of aid from all sources combined, including scholarships, loans, and work contracts, is $34,180; maximum, $50,790. Awards are based on need and merit. Required financial statements are the FAFSA and Financial Aid Award Letter. The aid application deadline for fall entry is March 1. Special funds for minority or disadvantaged students include scholarships up to full tuition. First-year students are notified about their financial aid application at time of acceptance.

About the Law School

Saint Louis University School of Law was established in 1843 and is a private institution. The 300-acre campus is in an urban area in mid-town St. Louis. The primary mission of the law school is to advance the understanding and the development of law, and prepare students to achieve professional success and personal satisfaction through leadership and service to others. The School of Law is guided by the Jesuit tradition of academic

excellence, freedom of inquiry, and respect for individual differences. Students have access to federal, state, county, city, and local agencies, courts, correctional facilities, law firms, and legal aid organizations in the St. Louis area. Housing for students consists of off-campus housing, which is readily available and affordable. All law school facilities are accessible to the physically disabled.

Calendar

The law school operates on a traditional semester basis. Courses for full-time students are offered both day and evening and must be completed within 3 years. For part-time students, courses are offered both day and evening and must be completed within 5 years (4-year plan includes summer). New full- and part-time students are admitted in the fall. There is an 8-week summer session. Transferable summer courses are offered.

Programs

In addition to the J.D., the law school offers the LL.M. Students may take relevant courses in other programs and apply credit toward the J.D.; a maximum of 6 credits may be applied. The following joint degrees may be earned: (Others are available through the graduate school.), J.D./Ph.D (Juris Doctor/Ph.D. in Health Core Ethics), J.D./M.A. (Juris Doctor/Master of Arts in public administration), J.D./M.A. (Juris Doctor/Master of Arts in urban affairs), J.D./M.B.A. (Juris Doctor/Master of Business Administration), J.D./M.H.A. (Juris Doctor/Master of Health Care Administration), J.D./M.P.H. (Juris Doctor/Master of Public Health in Health Policy), and J.D./M.S.W. (Juris Doctor/Master of Social Work).

Required

To earn the J.D., candidates must complete 91 total credits, of which 37 to 39 are for required courses. They must maintain a minimum GPA of 2.0 in the required courses. The following first-year courses are required of all students: Civil Procedure I and II, Constitutional Law I, Contracts I and II, Criminal Law, Legal Research and Writing I and II, Property, and Torts. Required upper-level courses consist of a humanities based course, a seminar, Legal Profession (Professional Ethics), and Professional Skills. Student

Phone: 314-977-2800
800-SLU-FOR-U
Fax: 314-977-1464
E-mail: admissions@law.slu.edu
Web: www.law.slu.edu

Contact

Assistant Dean and Director of Admissions, 314-977-2800 for general inquiries; Jackie Koerner, Financial Aid Coordinator, 314-977-3369 for financial aid information.

MISSOURI

must take a professional skills course but it does not need to be a clinic. The required orientation program for first-year students is 3 days including a day of service.

Electives

The School of Law offers concentrations in corporate law, criminal law, environmental law, international law, labor law, litigation, tax law, health law, and urban development. In addition, clinical training includes the Civil Clinic, Judicial Process Clinic, and the Externship Program, all for 3 to 6 credits. An average of 18 seminars for 2 credits are offered each semester. Internships are available through clinical externship and judicial clerkship clinical programs. Law school students have opportunities for directed research with individual faculty members for 1 to 6 hours. Fieldwork consists of a Corporate Counsel Practitioner Program for 3 credits. Special lecture series include the Richard Childress Memorial Lecture Series, Adler-Rosecan Lecture, Center for Health Law Distinguished Speaker Series, First 100 years of Women Speaker Series, and the James Millstone Lecture. Summer study-abroad is available in Berlin, German; Cork, Ireland; Bern, Switzerland; Paris or Orleans, France; and Madrid, Spain. All students have open access to academic advising and support. Intensive programs for students struggling after 1 semester are offered. Minority programs consist of the Summer Institute and a Minority Clerkship Program. Special interest group programs include the William C. Wefel Center for Employment Law, Center for Health Law Studies, and Center for International Comparative Law. The most widely taken electives are Health Law, Employment Law/Business, and International Law.

Graduation Requirements

In order to graduate, candidates must have a GPA of 2.0.

Organizations

Students edit the *Saint Louis University Law Journal*, *Public Law Review*, and *Saint Louis University Journal of Health Law and Policy*. Students may participate in the Jessup International Moot Court Program, National Health Law Moot Court Competition, and Intellectual Property Moot Court Competitions. Other

competitions include the Client Counseling Competition, ABA Negotiations Competition, and various regional and national Trial Advocacy Competitions. Law student organizations, local chapters of national associations, and campus organizations include Public Interest Law Group, Black Law Students Association, Latin American Law Students Association, Hispanic Law Students Association, Phi Alpha Delta, Delta Theta Phi, Phi Delta Phi, ABA-Student Division, and Public Interest Law Group.

Library

The law library contains 657,923 hardcopy volumes and 262,976 microform volume equivalents, and subscribes to 2701 serial publications. Such on-line databases and networks as CALI, CIS Universe, DIALOG, Infotrac, LEXIS, LOIS, NEXIS, OCLC First Search, WESTLAW, Wilsonline Indexes, BNA, CCH, HeinOnline, CIAO, and JSTOR are available to law students for research. Special library collections include the Leonor K. Sullivan Congressional Papers, the Leo C. Brown Arbitration Papers, the Irish Law Collection, the Jewish Law Collection, the Polish Law Collection, and all areas of health law. Recently, the library installed additional group and individual study rooms, and opened an off-site storage facility. The ratio of library volumes to faculty is 9675 to 1 and to students is 687 to 1. The ratio of seats in the library to students is 1 to 2.

Faculty

The law school has 68 full-time and 45 part-time faculty members, of whom 44 are women. About 26% of full-time faculty have a graduate law degree in addition to the J.D. The ratio of full-time students to full-time faculty in an average class is 35 to 1; in a clinic, 3 to 1. The law school has a regular program of bringing visiting professors and other distinguished lecturers and visitors to campus.

Students

About 48% of the student body are women; 18%, minorities; 7%, African American; 5%, Asian American; 3%, Hispanic; and 1%, Native American. The majority of students come from the Midwest (69%). The average age of entering students is 25; age range is 20 to 55. About 50% of students enter directly from undergradu-

Placement

J.D.s awarded:	303
Services available through: a separate law school placement center	
Services: special programs on various areas of practice, such as health law, international, corporate, government, public interest, and judicial clerkships	
Special features: an extensive career library with a computer search service.	
Full-time job interviews:	75 employers
Summer job interviews:	60 employers
Placement by graduation:	66% of class
Placement within 9 months:	89% of class
Average starting salary:	n/av
Areas of placement:	
Private practice 2-10 attorneys	28%
Private practice 11-25 attorneys	14%
Private practice 26-50 attorneys	5%
Private practice 51-100 attorneys	5%
Private practice 100+ attorneys	10%
Business/industry	17%
Public interest	11%
Government	7%
Judicial clerkships	3%

ate school and 50% have worked full-time prior to entering law school. About 5% drop out after the first year for academic or personal reasons; 87% remain to receive a law degree.

SAINT MARY'S UNIVERSITY

School of Law

One Camino Santa Maria
San Antonio, TX 78228-8601

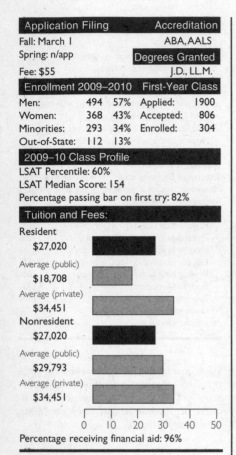

Application Filing		Accreditation
Fall: March 1		ABA, AALS
Spring: n/app		
		Degrees Granted
Fee: $55		J.D., LL.M.

Enrollment 2009–2010			First-Year Class	
Men:	494	57%	Applied:	1900
Women:	368	43%	Accepted:	806
Minorities:	293	34%	Enrolled:	304
Out-of-State:	112	13%		

2009–10 Class Profile
LSAT Percentile: 60%
LSAT Median Score: 154
Percentage passing bar on first try: 82%

Tuition and Fees:

Resident
$27,020

Average (public)
$18,708

Average (private)
$34,451

Nonresident
$27,020

Average (public)
$29,793

Average (private)
$34,451

0 10 20 30 40 50

Percentage receiving financial aid: 96%

ADMISSIONS

In the fall 2009 first-year class, 1900 applied, 806 were accepted, and 304 enrolled. Five transfers enrolled. The median LSAT percentile of the most recent first-year class was 60; the median GPA was 3.21 on a scale of 4.0. The lowest LSAT percentile accepted was 18; the highest was 94.

Requirements

Applicants must have a bachelor's degree and take the LSAT. Minimum acceptable GPA is 2.0 on a scale of 4.0. The most important admission factors include LSAT results, academic achievement, and general background. No specific undergraduate courses are required. Candidates are not interviewed. All factors are considered by the admissions staff.

Procedure

The application deadline for fall entry is March 1. Applicants should submit an application form, a personal statement, a nonrefundable application fee of $55, and as many as 5 letters of recommendation may be accepted. Notification of the admissions decision is beginning in November and ending in May. The latest acceptable LSAT test date for fall entry is February. The law school uses the LSDAS.

Special

The law school recruits minority and disadvantaged students trough both the regular admissions selection process and the Summer Skills Enhancement Program. Requirements are not different for out-of-state students. Transfer students must have 1 year of credit, have a minimum GPA of 2.5, and have attended an ABA-approved law school.

Costs

Tuition and fees for the 2009-2010 academic year are $27,020 for all full-time students. Tuition for part-time students is $16,412 per year. On-campus room and board costs about $8072 annually; books and supplies run $1300.

Financial Aid

About 96% of current law students receive some form of aid. The average annual amount of aid from all sources combined, including scholarships, loans, and work contracts, is $29,183; maximum, $38,000. Awards are based on need. Required financial statement is the FAFSA. The aid application deadline for fall entry is March 31. Special funds for minority or disadvantaged students include funds based on need. First-year students are notified about their financial aid application at time of acceptance.

About the Law School

Saint Mary's University School of Law was established in 1948 and is a private institution. The 135-acre campus is in a suburban area in San Antonio, Texas. The primary mission of the law school is to offer a solid curriculum of traditional legal studies and to teach students the practical skills and habits necessary to practice effective public service advocacy. Students have access to federal, state, county, city, and local agencies, courts, correctional facilities, law firms, and legal aid organizations in the San Antonio area. Housing for students is available in on-campus resident dormitory facilities for single students only. Information and application forms may be obtained from the Director of Housing. All law school facilities are accessible to the physically disabled.

Calendar

The law school operates on a traditional semester basis. Courses for full-time students are offered both day and evening and must be completed within 5 years. For part-time students, courses are offered evenings only and must be completed within 7 years. New full- and part-time students are admitted in the fall. There is a 5 1/2-week summer session. Transferable summer courses are offered.

Programs

In addition to the J.D., the law school offers the LL.M. The following joint degrees may be earned: J.D./M.A. (Juris Doctor/Master of Arts in accounting, communication arts,), J.D./M.B.A. (Juris Doctor/Master of Business Administration), J.D./M.P.A (Juris Doctor/Master of Public Administration in justice administration), and J.D./M.S. (Juris Doctor/Master of Science in computer science and engineering.

Required

To earn the J.D., candidates must complete 90 total credits, of which 46 are for required courses. They must maintain a minimum GPA of 2.0 in the required courses. The following first-year courses are required of all students: Civil Procedure, Constitutional Law, Contracts I and II, Criminal Law, Legal Research and Writing II, Legal Writing I, Property I and II, and Torts I and II. Required upper-level courses consist of Business and Commercial Transactions, Civil and Criminal Litigation, Evidence, Persons and Property, Philosophy of Law and Lawyers, Practice Skills, Professional Responsibility, Public and International Law, and Texas Civil Procedure I. Although not required, law students are urged to participate in clinics for credit in the third year or as volunteers in the first and second years. The required orientation program for first-year students consists of a 1-day orientation session during which first-year law students receive an introduction to successful legal studies at St. Mary's.

Phone: 210-436-3523
866-639-5831
Fax: 210-431-4202
E-mail: *wwilson@stmarytx.edu*
Web: *www.stmarytx.edu*

Contact

William Wilson, Ph.D., 210-436-3523 for general inquiries; Director of Financial Assistance, 210-431-6743 for financial aid information.

TEXAS

Electives

The School of Law offers concentrations in corporate law, criminal law, environmental law, family law, international law, juvenile law, labor law, litigation, maritime law, securities law, tax law, and torts and insurance. In addition, Civil Justice Clinic, Criminal Justice Clinic, and Immigration and Human Rights Clinic are open to second- and third-year students. Limited to an enrollment of 12 students, seminars are opportunities for research and discussion on advanced or special issues. Past seminars have included Natural Resource Protection Law; Doing Business with Mexico; International Law; Mediation; Health Care Crisis; First Amendment/Reporter Privilege; and International Arbitration. Two judicial internships, in Austin, Texas are offered for 4 credit hours. Students are required to do field work in the clinical programs. St. Mary's sponsors conferences and symposia on such diverse topics as United Nations Law and Legal Research, and Human Rights in the Americas. St. Mary's Center for Terrorism Law's Distinguished Speaker Series brings nationally recognized experts to present on various topics in the field of terrorism. St. Mary's Institute on World Legal Problems is conducted 5 weeks each summer, during July and August, at the University of Innsbruck, Austria. Beginning in the second semester of the first year, students who scored poorly in their first-semester examinations are required to attend small-group tutorials. Each year, 20 students are accepted into the Law Skills Enhancement Program. The Minority Law Students Association, the Black Allied Law Students Association, and the Asian-Pacific American Law Students Association offer tutorials to first-year students who are members. Special-interest groups include the Society of Legal Entrepreneurs, Education Law Association, and Environmental Law Society. Several student groups, including the Women's Bar Association, and the Minority Law Students Association, have developed mentor relationships with local bar associations. The most widely taken electives are Wills and Estates, Trusts, and Business Associations.

Graduation Requirements

In order to graduate, candidates must have a GPA of 2.0 and have completed the upper-division writing requirement.

Organizations

Students edit the *St. Mary's University School of Law Journal* and *The Scholar: St. Mary's Law Review on Minority Issues*. Moot court competitions include the Norvell Moot Court Competition, the Walker Moot Court, and the National ABA Regional Moot Court competition. Other competitions include the Shannon Thurmond Giltner Novice Mock Trial, National Mock Trial, and the ABA Client-Counseling. Law student organizations are the Student Bar Association, Family Law Association, and William Sessions American Inn of Court. Local chapters of national associations are Delta Theta Phi, Delta Alpha Delta, and Harlan Society. Campus clubs and other organizations include the Student Aggie Bar Association, the Longhorn Bar Association, and Hispanic Law Association.

Library

The law library contains 635,241 hardcopy volumes and 415,495 microform volume equivalents, and subscribes to 3583 serial publications. Such on-line databases and networks as CALI, CIS Universe, Infotrac, Legal-Trac, LEXIS, LOIS, Mathew Bender, NEXIS, OCLC First Search, WESTLAW, IndexMaster, Access UN, CCH Legal Research Network, Checkpoint, CCH Tax Research Network, Foreign Law Guide, HeinOnline, Inter AM Legal Periodicals Index, Lexis Congressional Universe, LLMC Digital, LoisLaw, United Nations Treaty, World Catalog are available to law students for research. Special library collections include Mexican legal materials, microtext of records and briefs of the United States Supreme Court, and legal documents from the United Nations and from American, British, Canadian, and international law. The library is a depository for U.S. government documents. Recently, the library wireless Internet access was added, and a closed circuit security system was installed in 2006. The ratio of library volumes to faculty is 17,646 to 1 and to students is 737 to 1. The ratio of seats in the library to students is 1 to 3.

Faculty

The law school has 36 full-time and 53 part-time faculty members, of whom 29 are women. According to AAUP standards for Category IIA institutions, faculty salaries are average. About 44% of full-time faculty have a graduate law degree in addition to the J.D. The ratio of full-time students to full-time faculty in an average class is 21 to 1; in a clinic, 4 to 1. The law school has a regular program of bringing visiting professors and other distinguished lecturers and visitors to campus.

Students

About 43% of the student body are women; 34%, minorities; 3%, African American; 5%, Asian American; 25%, Hispanic; and 1%, Native American. The majority of students come from Texas (87%). The age range of entering students is 20 to 60. About 16% drop out after the first year for academic or personal reasons; 84% remain to receive a law degree.

School of Law

16401 NW 37th Avenue
Miami Gardens, FL 33054

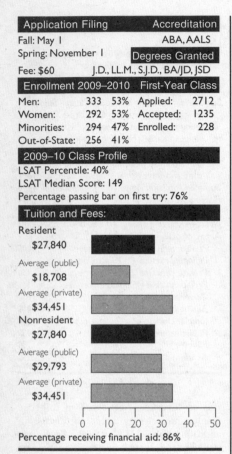

Application Filing	Accreditation
Fall: May 1	ABA, AALS
Spring: November 1	Degrees Granted
Fee: $60	J.D., LL.M., S.J.D., BA/JD, JSD

| Enrollment 2009–2010 | First-Year Class |

Men:	333	53%	Applied:	2712
Women:	292	53%	Accepted:	1235
Minorities:	294	47%	Enrolled:	228
Out-of-State:	256	41%		

2009–10 Class Profile

LSAT Percentile: 40%
LSAT Median Score: 149
Percentage passing bar on first try: 76%

Tuition and Fees:

Resident
$27,840

Average (public)
$18,708

Average (private)
$34,451

Nonresident
$27,840

Average (public)
$29,793

Average (private)
$34,451

0 10 20 30 40 50

Percentage receiving financial aid: 86%

ADMISSIONS

In a recent year, 2712 applied, 1235 were accepted, and 228 enrolled. Four transfers enrolled. The median LSAT percentile of the most recent first-year class was 40; the median GPA was 3.08 on a scale of 4.0. The lowest LSAT percentile accepted was 11; the highest was 92. Figures in the above capsule and in this profile are approximate.

Requirements

Applicants must have a bachelor's degree and take the LSAT. Minimum acceptable LSAT percentile is 15 and minimum acceptable GPA is 2.0 on a scale of 4.0. The most important admission factors include LSAT results, academic achievement, and general background. No specific undergraduate courses are required. Candidates are not interviewed.

Procedure

Applicants should submit an application form, LSAT results, transcripts, a personal statement, a nonrefundable application fee of $60, and 1 letters of recommendation. Notification of the admissions decision is on a rolling basis. The latest acceptable LSAT test date for fall entry is June. The law school uses the LSDAS. Check with the school for current application deadlines.

Special

The law school recruits minority and disadvantaged students through recruiting at various historically black colleges and universities, and direct mail to target population using Candidate Referral Service (CRS). Requirements are not different for out-of-state students. Transfer students must have one year of credit, have a minimum GPA of 2.65, have attended an ABA-approved law school, and have a letter of good standing.

Costs

Tuition and fees for the 2009-2010 academic year is approximately $27,840 for all full-time students. On-campus room and board costs about $8800 annually; books and supplies run about $1000.

Financial Aid

In a recent year, about 86% of current law students received some form of aid. The average annual amount of aid from all sources combined, including scholarships, loans, and work contracts, was approximately $34,347; maximum, $47,762. Awards are based on need and merit. Required financial statement is the FAFSA. Check with the school for current application deadlines. First-year students are notified about their financial aid application at time of acceptance.

About the Law School

Saint Thomas University School of Law was established in 1984 and is a private institution. The campus is in a suburban area 15 miles northwest of downtown Miami. The primary mission of the law school is to provide a personalized, value-oriented legal education to a diverse student body, including those from groups traditionally underrepresented by and within the legal profession. Students have access to federal, state, county, city, and local agencies, courts, correctional facilities, law firms, and legal aid organizations in the Miami Gardens area. Housing for students include on-campus dormitories and a variety of off-campus housing, located within a few miles of the campus. All law school facilities are accessible to the physically disabled.

Calendar

The law school operates on a traditional semester basis. Courses for full-time students are offered both day and evening and must be completed within 5 years. For part-time students, courses are offered and There is no part-time program. and must be completed within n/app. New students are admitted in the fall and spring. There is a 7 weeks-week summer session. Transferable summer courses are offered.

Programs

In addition to the J.D., the law school offers the LL.M., S.J.D., and BA/JD, Environmental Justice, JSD Intercultural Human Rights. The following joint degrees may be earned: J.D./M.B.A (Juris Doctor/Master of Business Administration in Internation), J.D./M.B.A. (Juris Doctor/Master of Business Administration in Sports), J.D./M.S (Juris Doctor/Master of Science in Marriage and Family), J.D./M.S. (Juris Doctor/Master of Science in Sports Administration), and J.D/M.B.A (Juris Doctor/Master of Business Administration in Accounting).

Required

To earn the J.D., candidates must complete 90 total credits, of which 60 are for required courses. They must maintain a minimum GPA of 2.5 in the required courses. The following first-year courses are required of all students: Advanced Legal Research and Writing, Civil Procedure I and II, Contracts I and II, Criminal Law, Legal Analysis, Writing, and Research, and Torts I and II. Required upper-level courses consist of Agency and Partnership, Appellate Advocacy, Constitutional Law I and II, Corporations, Criminal Law, Criminal Procedure I, Evidence, Professional Responsibility, Property I and II, Senior Writing Requirement, and Wills and Trusts. All students must take clinical courses. The required orientation program for first-year students is a 2-day program during which students register, are introduced to legal research

FLORIDA

Phone: 305-623-2310
800-245-4569
E-mail: fkhan@stu.edu
Web: www.stu.edu

Contact
Director of Admissions, 305-623-2384 for general inquiries; Office of Financial Aid, 305-628-6900 for financial aid information.

and writing, learn how to brief a case, meet faculty, administration, and staff, and learn about student organizations.

Electives
In addition, The law school sponsors two in-house full year clinics: Immigration Clinic (6 credits each semester) and Tax Clinic (4 credits each semester). The law school offers a wide range of 2 credit seminars available to upper-class students, including Church-State Relation, Comparative Law, Cyberlaw, Exploring Principles of Earth Jurisprudence, Environmental Law, Genetics and the Law, Health Law Policy, Land Use Planning, Rule of Law, Sixth Amendment in Modern Jurisprudence, and Women and the Law. The law school's Clinical Program includes internships in the Appellate Litigation (full year, 4 credits each semester), Bankruptcy Clinic (4 credits per semester), Civil Practice (4 or 12 credits per semester), Criminal Practice (12 credits per semester), Elder Law (4 credits per semester), Family Court (full year - 4 credits each semester), Florida Supreme Court (12 credits per semester), Judicial (4 credits per semester), and the Pax Romana United Nations Clinic (12 credits per semester). A lecture series every fall features presentations geared primarily to first-year students on effective note taking, time management and student strategies, stress management, the importance of writing well, and effective exam preparation. St. Thomas sponsors a month-long summer-abroad program in Spain. In addition, upper-class students may take up to 7 credits in an ABA-accredited summer-abroad program sponsored by law schools other than St. Thomas. Legal fraternities and other student organizations offer lecture series, mentoring programs, and other projects. The most widely taken electives are Family Law, White Collar Crime, and Law and Literature.

Graduation Requirements
In order to graduate, candidates must have a GPA of 2.5, have completed the upper-division writing requirement, and study law in residence for 96 weeks, pursue the entire study of law as a full-time student for 6 semesters or the equivalent, the last 2 of which must be at St. Thomas, complete 40 hours of pro bono work, pass a competency exam, satisfy the Senior Writing Requirement, and complete six credits of Professional Skills Courses.

Organizations
Students edit the *St. Thomas Law Review*, *Intercultural Human Rights Law Review* and the newspaper *Plead the Fifth*. Moot court competitions include the Phillip Jessup International Law Moot Court, National Entertainment Law Moot Court, and the National Labor Law Moot Court. Other competitions include the American Bar Association National Trial Tournament, the American Trail Lawyers Association National Trial Tournament, the National Trial Advocacy Competition, and the Frederick Douglass Trial Advocacy Competition. Student organizations include the Caribbean Association of Law Students, St. Thomas More Catholic Law Society, and Tax Law Society. Local chapters of national associations include the American Bar Association/Law Student Division (ABA/LSD), Asian Pacific American Law Student Association (APALSA), and Black Law Student Association (BLSA). Campus clubs and organizations include the Entertainment and Sports Law Society, Florida Association for Women Lawyers (FAWL), and Cuban American Bar Association (CABA), Law Student Division.

Library
The law library contains 330,143 hardcopy volumes and 1,251,432 microform volume equivalents, and subscribes to 2976 serial publications. Such on-line databases and networks as CALI, CIS Universe, DIALOG, Legal-Trac, LEXIS, LOIS, Matthew Bender, NEXIS, OCLC First Search, WESTLAW, and Wilsonline Indexes are available to law students for research. Recently, the library made available a wireless network with capacity for 1054 connections. The ratio of library volumes to faculty is 12,228 to 1 and to students is 528 to 1. The ratio of seats in the library to students is 1 to 1.

Faculty
The law school has 27 full-time and 32 part-time faculty members, of whom 26 are women. About 36% of full-time faculty have a graduate law degree in addition to the J.D.; about 3% of part-time faculty have one. The ratio of full-time students to full-time faculty in an average class is 18 to 1; in a clinic, 8 to 1. The law school has a regular program of bringing visiting professors and other distinguished lecturers and visitors to campus.

Placement

J.D.s awarded:	211

Services available through: a separate law school placement center

Services: providing monthly newsletter for students, monthly job listings for alumni, and written guides on aspects of job search and career planning, conducting workshops and seminars, participating in southeastern job fairs, sponsoring guest speakers on areas of legal practice, judicial clerkships, and alternative careers, participating in minority opportunity programs and mentoring programs with alumni and the Florida Bar Association and the Broward and Dade County Bar Associations.

Special features: individualized attention for all students. The Office conducts mandatory individual meetings with first-year students, sets aside 4 hours daily for appointments with advanced and graduating students, and schedules exit interviews.

Full-time job interviews:	13 employers
Summer job interviews:	19 employers
Placement by graduation:	n/av
Placement within 9 months:	74% of class
Average starting salary:	$38,000 to $40,000

Areas of placement:

Solo practice-3%; 100+ attorneys-4%; unknown-2%	10%
Private practice 2-10 attorneys	33%
Private practice 11-25 attorneys	9%
Private practice 26-50 attorneys	2%
Private practice 51-100 attorneys	3%
Business/industry	22%
Government	13%
Public interest	8%
Judicial clerkships	2%
Academic	1%

Students
About 53% of the student body are women; 47%, minorities; 9%, African American; 4%, Asian American; 31%, Hispanic; and 6%, international students and those with unknown ethnic group. The majority of students come from Florida (59%). The average age of entering students is 25; age range is 20 to 54. About 66% of students enter directly from undergraduate school, 5% have a graduate degree, and 34% have worked full-time prior to entering law school. About 21% drop out after the first year for academic or personal reasons; 79% remain to receive a law degree.

Saint Thomas University   **395**

SAMFORD UNIVERSITY

Cumberland School of Law

800 Lakeshore Drive
Birmingham, AL 35229

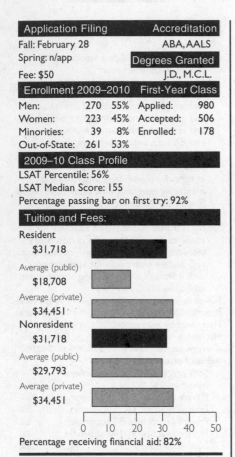

Application Filing	Accreditation
Fall: February 28	ABA, AALS
Spring: n/app	**Degrees Granted**
Fee: $50	J.D., M.C.L.

Enrollment 2009–2010			First-Year Class	
Men:	270	55%	Applied:	980
Women:	223	45%	Accepted:	506
Minorities:	39	8%	Enrolled:	178
Out-of-State:	261	53%		

2009–10 Class Profile
LSAT Percentile: 56%
LSAT Median Score: 155
Percentage passing bar on first try: 92%

Tuition and Fees:

Resident
$31,718

Average (public)
$18,708

Average (private)
$34,451

Nonresident
$31,718

Average (public)
$29,793

Average (private)
$34,451

Percentage receiving financial aid: 82%

ADMISSIONS

In the fall 2009 first-year class, 980 applied, 506 were accepted, and 178 enrolled. Twelve transfers enrolled. The median LSAT percentile of the most recent first-year class was 56; the median GPA was 3.31 on a scale of 4.0.

Requirements
Applicants must have a bachelor's degree and take the LSAT. The most important admission factors include LSAT results, GPA, and academic achievement. No specific undergraduate courses are required. Candidates are not interviewed.

Procedure
The application deadline for fall entry is February 28. Applicants should submit an application form, a personal statement, a nonrefundable application fee of $50, 2 letters of recommendation, LSAT results, transcripts, and letters of recommendation must come from LSDAS. Notification of the admissions decision is on a rolling

basis. The latest acceptable LSAT test date for fall entry is February. The law school uses the LSDAS.

Special
The law school recruits minority and disadvantaged students by means of recruiting at historically black colleges and universities. The Black Law Students Association is active in on-campus recruiting. Also, alumni actively assist with student recruitment. Requirements are not different for out-of-state students. Transfer students must have 1 year of credit, have a minimum GPA of 3, have attended an ABA-approved law school, and have attended an AALS- and ABA-approved school, and have a letter of good standing from the dean of the former law school.

Costs

Tuition and fees for the 2009-2010 academic year are $31,718 for all full-time students. Books and supplies run $2000.

Financial Aid

About 82% of current law students receive some form of aid. The average annual amount of aid from all sources combined, including scholarships, loans, and work contracts, is $242,000; maximum, $53,990. Awards are based on need and merit. Required financial statement is the FAFSA. The aid application deadline for fall entry is March 1. Special funds for minority or disadvantaged students include full or partial tuition scholarships. First-year students are notified about their financial aid application at time of acceptance.

About the Law School

Samford University Cumberland School of Law was established in 1847 and is a private institution. The 300-acre campus is in a suburban area 6 miles from downtown Birmingham. The primary mission of the law school is to educate students to be responsible lawyers, trained to exercise their professional skills competently with sensitivity to the needs and concerns of their clients, and to act in strict accord with the highest ethical standards. Students have access to federal, state, county, city, and local agencies, courts, correctional facilities, law firms, and legal aid organizations in the Birming-

ham area. Facilities of special interest to law students include an $8.4 million, 61,000-square-foot freestanding library connected to the Law School building by a covered breezeway on the second floor, easily accessible to physically disabled students. Housing for students is available off campus in any number of nearby neighborhoods. Assistance in obtaining apartment rental information is provided by an apartment locator service. About 95% of the law school facilities are accessible to the physically disabled.

Calendar

The law school operates on a traditional semester basis. Courses for full-time students are offered days only and must be completed within 4 years. There is no partitime program. New part-time students are admitted in the fall. There is a 9-week summer session. Transferable summer courses are offered.

Programs

In addition to the J.D., the law school offers the M.C.L. Students may take relevant courses in other programs and apply credit toward the J.D.; a maximum of 12 credits may be applied. The following joint degrees may be earned: J.D./M.Acc. (Juris Doctor/Master of Accounting), J.D./M.B.A. (Juris Doctor/Master of Business Administration), J.D./M.Div. (Juris Doctor/Master of Divinity), J.D./M.P.A. (Juris Doctor/Master of Public Administration), J.D./M.P.H. (Juris Doctor/Master of Public Health), J.D./M.S. (Juris Doctor/Master of Science in environmental management), and J.D./M.T.S. (Juris Doctor/Master of Theological Studies).

Required
To earn the J.D., candidates must complete 90 total credits, of which 47 are for required courses. They must maintain a minimum GPA of 2.0 in the required courses. The following first-year courses are required of all students: Civil Procedure I and II, Contracts I and II, Criminal Law, Evidence, Lawyering and Legal Reasoning I and II, Real Property, and Torts. Required upper-level courses consist of Business Organizations, Constitutional Law I and II, Payment Systems or Secured Transactions, Professional Responsibility, and Wills, Trusts and Estates. The required orientation program for first-

Phone: 205-726-2702
800-888-7213
Fax: 205-726-2057
E-mail: *law.admissions@samford.edu*
Web: *cumberland.samford.edu*

Contact

Jennifer Y Simms, Assistant Dean, 800-888-7213 for general inquiries; Laine Smith, Director of Financial Aid, 800-888-7245 for financial aid information.

ALABAMA

year students is designed to introduce new students to the school, the faculty, and the curriculum. Entering students begin the required Lawyering and Legal Reasoning course and receive instruction on the briefing of cases and demonstration of law school teaching methods. This 6-credit hour, 2-semester course provides students with intensive hands-on experience in practical lawyering skills.

Electives
The Cumberland School of Law offers concentrations in corporate law, criminal law, environmental law, family law, intellectual property law, international law, juvenile law, labor law, litigation, securities law, tax law, torts and insurance, and Trial Advocacy. In addition the Center for Advocacy and Clinical Education offers upper-level students externships for 3 credit hours. Seminars are offered for 2 credit hours. Research programs are directed by individual professors and are aimed at upper-level students. Field work placement is available with government agencies, federal judges, litigation placements, and corporations. Special lecture series include the Cordell Hull Speakers Forum, the Ray Rushton Distinguished Lecturer Series, the Thurgood Marshall Speakers' Forum, the Faculty Colloquium, and the Work in Progress Program. Study-abroad programs include international and comparative law at Sidney Sussex College, Cambridge, England, and the Federal University of Ceasa, Fortaleza, Brazil. A writing laboratory is available for students who need additional coaching in this critical skill. The Black Law Students Association sponsors a tutorial program, a mentor program, a speakers forum, and special recognition events. Special interest group programs include Women in Law, Community Service Organization, Trial Advocacy Board, and Henry Upson Sims Moot Court Board. The most widely taken electives are Mediation, Basic Skills in Trial Advocacy, and Law Office Practice and Management.

Graduation Requirements
In order to graduate, candidates must have a GPA of 2.0 and have completed the upper-division writing requirement.

Organizations

Students edit the *Cumberland Law Review*, the *American Journal of Trial Advocacy*, and the newspaper *Pro Confesso*. Moot court competitions include the Justice Janie Shores Moot Court, Gordon T. Saad, and the Robert Donworth Freshman. Other competitions include Mock Trial, Herbert W. Peterson Senior, Judge James O. Haley Federal Court, Parham H. Williams Freshman Mock Trial, Albert P. Brewer Client Counseling, Negotiation, and Representation in Mediation Competition. Student organizations include the Association of Trial Lawyers of America, ABA-Student Division, and Federalist Society. Local chapters of national organizations include Phi Alpha Delta and Phi Delta Phi. Other organizations include the State Student Bar Associations of Alabama, Florida, Georgia, and other southern states.

Library

The law library contains 205,466 hardcopy volumes and 120,539 microform volume equivalents, and subscribes to 750 serial publications. Such on-line databases and networks as CALI, Legal-Trac, LEXIS, LOIS, NEXIS, WESTLAW, and HeinOnline are available to law students for research. Special library collections include Constitutional Law, Ethics, Legal History, and Trial Practice. Recent library omprovements include additional electronic databases. The ratio of library volumes to faculty is 6043 to 1 and to students is 416 to 1. The ratio of seats in the library to students is 1 to 1.

Faculty

The law school has 34 full-time and 21 part-time faculty members, of whom 20 are women. According to AAUP standards for Category IIA institutions, faculty salaries are average. About 22% of full-time faculty have a graduate law degree in addition to the J.D. The ratio of full-time students to full-time faculty in an average class is 18 to 1; in a clinic, 10 to 1. The law school has a regular program of bringing visiting professors and other distinguished lecturers and visitors to campus.

Students

About 45% of the student body are women; 8%, minorities; 5%, African American; 1%, Asian American; 1%, Hispanic; 1%, Native American; and 1%, foreign national. The majority of students come from Alabama (47%). The average age of enter-

Placement

J.D.s awarded:	163

Services available through: a separate law school placement center
Services: national and regional law fairs
Special features: numerous workshops and programs focused on interviewing, job search skills, and legal career specialties, in addition to a resource lilbrary for students. The office manages on-campus interviews and job postings through Symplicity to assist employers in meeting their hiring needs. The office staff also meet regularly with employers across the South to gather information on hiring trends and to market students and graduates.

Full-time job interviews:	9 employers
Summer job interviews:	42 employers
Placement by graduation:	58% of class
Placement within 9 months:	94% of class
Average starting salary:	$30,000 to $175,000

Areas of placement:

Private practice 2-10 attorneys	26%
Private practice 11-25 attorneys	12%
Private practice 26-50 attorneys	6%
Private practicc 51-100 attorneys	8%
Private practice 100 + attorneys	15%
Business/industry	11%
Government	10%
Judicial clerkships	3%
Academic	2%
Military	1%
Solo practice	3%
Unknown firm size	2%

ing students is 24; age range is 21 to 60. About 90% of students enter directly from undergraduate school and 10% have a graduate degree. About 3% drop out after the first year for academic or personal reasons; 91% remain to receive a law degree.

500 El Camino Real
Santa Clara, CA 95053

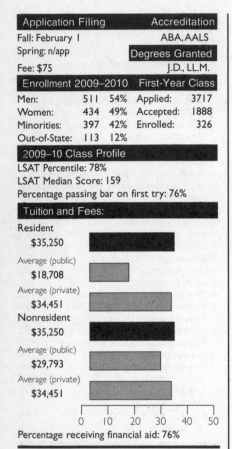

Application Filing		Accreditation	
Fall: February 1		ABA, AALS	
Spring: n/app		Degrees Granted	
Fee: $75		J.D., LL.M.	

Enrollment 2009–2010		First-Year Class	
Men:	511 54%	Applied:	3717
Women:	434 49%	Accepted:	1888
Minorities:	397 42%	Enrolled:	326
Out-of-State:	113 12%		

2009–10 Class Profile
LSAT Percentile: 78%
LSAT Median Score: 159
Percentage passing bar on first try: 76%

Tuition and Fees:

Resident
$35,250

Average (public)
$18,708

Average (private)
$34,451

Nonresident
$35,250

Average (public)
$29,793

Average (private)
$34,451

0   10   20   30   40   50

Percentage receiving financial aid: 76%

ADMISSIONS

In a recent year, 3717 applied, 1888 were accepted, and 326 enrolled. Twenty-seven transfers enrolled. The median LSAT percentile of the most recent first-year class was 78; the median GPA was 3.36 on a scale of 4.0. The lowest LSAT percentile accepted was 40; the highest was 99. Figures in the above capsule and in this profile are approximate.

Requirements
Applicants must have a bachelor's degree and take the LSAT. The most important admission factors include LSAT results, undergraduate curriculum, and GPA. No specific undergraduate courses are required. Candidates are not interviewed.

Procedure
Applicants should submit an application form, LSAT results, transcripts, a nonrefundable application fee of $75, and are optional letters of recommendation. Notification of the admissions decision is January through May. The latest acceptable LSAT test date for fall entry is February.

The law school uses the LSDAS. Check with the school for current application deadlines.

Special
The law school recruits minority and disadvantaged students by means of ethnic student organizations that advise the faculty admissions committee and by providing substantial financial assistance. Requirements are not different for out-of-state students. Transfer students must have one year of credit, have attended an ABA-approved law school, and have a letter of good standing from their prior school.

Costs

Tuition and fees for the 2009-2010 academic year are approximately $35,250 for all full-time students. Tuition for part-time students is approximately $24,676 per year. On-campus room and board costs about $12,528 annually; books and supplies run about $674.

Financial Aid

In a recent year, about 76% of current law students received some form of aid. The average annual amount of aid from all sources combined, including scholarships, loans, and work contracts, was approximately $38,474; maximum, $54,828. Awards are based on need and merit. Required financial statement is the FAFSA. Special funds for minority or disadvantaged students consist of the Law Faculty Scholarship and Diversity Scholarship. First-year students are notified about their financial aid application at the time of acceptance for scholarships; other aid decisions are made known upon completion of financial aid applications. Check with the school for the current application deadlines.

About the Law School

Santa Clara University School of Law was established in 1912 and is a private institution. The 104-acre campus is in a suburban area less than 1 mile west of San Jose and 45 miles sou. The primary mission of the law school is wholly consistent with the Jesuit purpose in professional education: to train men and women of competence, conscience, and compassion. Students have access to federal, state, county, city, and local agencies, courts, correctional facilities, law firms, and legal aid organizations in the Santa Clara area. The area is

widely known as Silicon Valley. Local law firms have specialties that serve the needs of the high-tech industry and advise the school. Facilities of special interest to law students are Heafey Law Library; Bergin Hall faculty office building; Bannan Hall, which houses classrooms and the law student lounge; Katherine and George Alexander Community Law Center; Loyal Hall, which houses the Law Career Center, Legal Research and Writing Faculty, Law Review, Northern California Innocence Project, Center for Public Interest and Social Justice, Center for Global Law and Policy, and High Tech Law Institute. Housing for students is limited on campus to 20 2- or 3-person apartments and 20 studio apartments; housing of all types is readily available off campus. About 97% of the law school facilities are accessible to the physically disabled.

Calendar

The law school operates on a traditional semester basis. Courses for full-time students are offered both day and evening and must be completed within 5 years. For part-time students, courses are offered both day and evening and must be completed within 5 years. New full- and part-time students are admitted in the fall. There is a 7 1/2- 8-week summer session. Transferable summer courses are offered.

Programs

In addition to the J.D., the law school offers the LL.M. and international and comparative law. Students may take relevant courses in other programs and apply credit toward the J.D.; a maximum of 12 credits may be applied. The following joint degrees may be earned: J.D./M.B.A. (Juris Doctor/Master of Business Administration).

Required
To earn the J.D., candidates must complete 86 total credits, of which 42 are for required courses. They must maintain a minimum GPA of 2.33 in the required courses. The following first-year courses are required of all students: Constitutional Law I, Contracts, Criminal Law, Legal Research and Writing, Pleading and Civil Procedure, Property, and Torts. Required upper-level courses consist of Advocacy, Constitutional Law II, Evidence, and The Legal Profession. The required orientation program for first-year students is a 3-day introduction to the study of law.

Phone: 408-554-4800
Fax: 408-554-7897
E-mail: *lawadmissions@scu.edu*
Web: *scu.edu/law*

Contact

Assistant Dean for Admission, 408-554-4800 for general inquiries; Financial Aid Counselor, 408-554-4447 for financial aid information.

Electives

The School of Law offers concentrations in corporate law, criminal law, environmental law, intellectual property law, international law, litigation, tax law, and high tech law, and public interest law. In addition, through the on-campus Law Clinic Office, upper-division students practice law under the supervision of faculty. Students participate in all phases of a case, from the initial client interview through trial and may receive 3 to 6 units. The focus of the Criminal Law Clinic is the Northern California Innocence Project. Fifteen to 20 seminars are offered each year in areas such as social justice and public interest law, sports law, drug abuse law, high technology and intellectual property, and international law. Internships are in high-tech, civil practice and the criminal justice system. Judicial externships are offered with the California Supreme Court and other state and federal courts. Faculty members engage students as research assistants for a variety of projects. During the academic year, students have access to the courts and legal community of the San Francisco Bay Area. The voluntary Pro Bono Project matches students and alumni for work on pro bono cases. The school hosts lectures on topics ranging from intellectual property issues to current events in international law. The Institute of International and Comparative Law sponsors Summer Law study-abroad programs in Strasbourg, France; Geneva, Switzerland; Oxford, England; Hong Kong; Singapore; Seoul, Korea; Tokyo, Japan; Munich, Germany; Istanbul, Turkey; Sydney, Australia; The Hague, Netherlands; San Jose, Costa Rica; Vienna, Bratislava, and Budapest. In addition, students have an opportunity to spend a semester abroad at 1 of 14 universities in countries. The Academic Success Program offers personal and tutorial support to students identified through the admission process as needing academic support, and students recommended by their first-year instructors. Tutorial support emphasizes legal analysis and uses the writing of briefs, outlines, and exams to develop this skill. The Assistant Dean for Admissions and Financial Aid acts as a mentor to students of color. The minority alumni network actively supports current students. Students may earn a certificate in public interest law by taking 14 units, plus a unit of Public Interest Seminar, and completing a practicum. Certificates are also offered in international law and high-technology law with varying requirements. The most widely taken electives are Wills and Trusts, Patents, and International Law.

Graduation Requirements

In order to graduate, candidates must have a GPA of 2.33, have completed the upper-division writing requirement, and have completed 86 semester units and the required course of study.

Organizations

Students edit the *Santa Clara Law Review, Computer and High Technology Law Journal,* and the *Santa Clara Journal of International Law.* The student newspaper is *The Advocate.* Moot court competitions include the Jessup International Moot Court, Traynor Moot Court, and the Giles Rich Moot Court. Other competitions include ABA Client Counseling Competition, ABA National Trial Competition, and the Negotiation Competition. Student organizations, local chapters of national associations, and campus organizations include Intellectual Property Association, Public Interest Coalition, International Law Society, Phi Alpha Delta, Phi Delta Phi, Amnesty International, ACLU, Student Bar Association, BALSA, and Women in Law.

Library

The law library contains 369,154 hardcopy volumes and 1,110,627 microform volume equivalents, and subscribes to 4406 serial publications. Such on-line databases and networks as CALI, CIS Universe, DIALOG, Dow-Jones, Infotrac, Legal-Trac, LEXIS, LOIS, NEXIS, OCLC First Search, RLIN, WESTLAW, Wilsonline Indexes, and Link+, Indexmaster, Hein Online, CIAO, CCH Internet Research JSTOR, and UN Readex Bureau of National Affairs, BE Press, BNA's Core Package, Daily Journal Online, ILP, Oxford University Press, Vault, Westpack and other databases available through the university's main library. are available to law students for research. Special library collections include the proceedings of the House Judiciary Committee on the Watergate Hearings. Recently, the library remodeled reference desk and offices, and upgraded laboratory computers. The ratio of library volumes to faculty is 8203 to 1 and to students is 391 to 1. The ratio of seats in the library to students is 1 to 2.

Placement

J.D.s awarded:	281

Services available through: a separate law school placement center and Law Career Services

Special features: fall and spring on-campus interview programs, career-oriented workshops and events, web site with current listings and job search tips, extensive resource library, and reciprocity with other Bay area and ABA-accredited law schools.

Full-time job interviews:	32 employers
Summer job interviews:	78 employers
Placement by graduation:	71% of class
Placement within 9 months:	90% of class
Average starting salary:	$38,000 to $145,000

Areas of placement:

Private practice 2-10 attorneys	15%
Private practice 11-25 attorneys	4%
Private practice 26-50 attorneys	4%
Private practice 51-100 attorneys	4%
Private practice 101+ attorneys; 7%	
unknown	32%
Business/industry	27%
Government	9%
Public interest	3%
Judicial clerkships	1%
Academic	1%

Faculty

The law school has 45 full-time and 31 part-time faculty members, of whom 35 are women. According to AAUP standards for Category IIA institutions, faculty salaries are well above average. About 3% of full-time faculty have a graduate law degree in addition to the J.D. The ratio of full-time students to full-time faculty in an average class is 16 to 1; in a clinic, 20 to 1. The law school has a regular program of bringing visiting professors and other distinguished lecturers and visitors to campus. There is a chapter of the Order of the Coif; 8 faculty and 129 graduates are members.

Students

About 49% of the student body are women; 42%, minorities; 4%, African American; 27%, Asian American; and 9%, Hispanic. The majority of students come from California (88%). The average age of entering students is 26; age range is 17 to 60. About 12% drop out after the first year for academic or personal reasons; 95% remain to receive a law degree.

SEATTLE UNIVERSITY

School of Law

901 12th Avenue, Sullivan Hall,
P.O. Box 222000
Seattle, WA 98122-4340

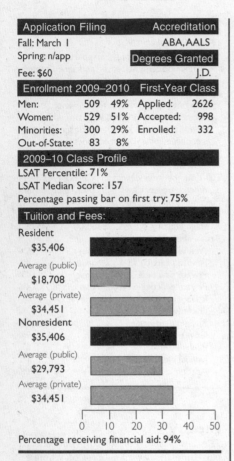

Application Filing		Accreditation
Fall: March 1		ABA, AALS
Spring: n/app		Degrees Granted
Fee: $60		J.D.

Enrollment 2009–2010			First-Year Class	
Men:	509	49%	Applied:	2626
Women:	529	51%	Accepted:	998
Minorities:	300	29%	Enrolled:	332
Out-of-State:	83	8%		

2009–10 Class Profile

LSAT Percentile: 71%
LSAT Median Score: 157
Percentage passing bar on first try: 75%

Tuition and Fees:

Resident
$35,406

Average (public)
$18,708

Average (private)
$34,451

Nonresident
$35,406

Average (public)
$29,793

Average (private)
$34,451

Percentage receiving financial aid: 94%

ADMISSIONS

In the fall 2009 first-year class, 2626 applied, 998 were accepted, and 332 enrolled. Twenty-three transfers enrolled. The median LSAT percentile of the most recent first-year class was 71; the median GPA was 3.35 on a scale of 4.0. The lowest LSAT percentile accepted was 17; the highest was 99.

Requirements

Applicants must have a bachelor's degree and take the LSAT. The most important admission factors include GPA, LSAT results, and character, personality. No specific undergraduate courses are required. Candidates are not interviewed.

Procedure

The application deadline for fall entry is March 1. Applicants should submit an application form, LSAT results, transcripts, a personal statement, the TOEFL for international students educated abroad, a nonrefundable application fee of $60, 2 letters of recommendation, and

resume. Notification of the admissions decision is January 1 to May 1. The latest acceptable LSAT test date for fall entry is February. The law school uses the LSDAS.

Special

The law school recruits minority and disadvantaged students through admission officer visits, minority community service organizations, minority prelaw and bar associations, candidate referral services, prelaw adviser mailings, and a fee waiver program. Requirements are not different for out-of-state students. Transfer students must have 1 year of credit, have attended an ABA-approved law school, and be in good academic standing and in the top third of their class.

Costs

Tuition and fees for the 2009-2010 academic year are $35,406 for all full-time students. Tuition for part-time students is $29,494 per year. On-campus room and board costs about $11,448 annually; books and supplies run $903.

Financial Aid

About 94% of current law students receive some form of aid. The average annual amount of aid from all sources combined, including scholarships, loans, and work contracts, is $41,241; maximum, $56,658. Awards are based on need and merit. Required financial statement is the FAFSA. The aid application deadline for fall entry is March 1. Special funds for minority or disadvantaged students range from $3000 to 3 full-tuition awards and may be renewable, with conditions, for the full term of legal studies. First-year students are notified about their financial aid application within 3 weeks of the offer of admission.

About the Law School

Seattle University School of Law was established in 1972 and is a private institution. The 48-acre campus is in an urban area on Seattle's First Hill. The primary mission of the law school is to educate outstanding lawyers who are leaders for a just and humane world. Students have access to federal, state, county, city, and local agencies, courts, correctional facilities, law firms, and legal aid organizations in the Seattle area. They have access to Appellate Court, U.S. District Court, and Superior Court as well as the King County Youth Detention Center. Facilities of special interest to law students include

Sullivan Hall, which contains classrooms and seminar spaces equipped with data ports for each seat and desk space large enough to accommodate a laptop computer for every student. The entire building is wired for the use of on-line legal research services such as Westlaw and other Internet uses. There is an on-line electronic teaching laboratory. The law school is also wireless. All law school facilities are accessible to the physically disabled.

Calendar

The law school operates on a traditional semester basis. Courses for full-time students are offered both day and evening and must be completed within 7 years. New full- and part-time students are admitted in the fall and summer. There is a 6- to 8-week summer session. Transferable summer courses are offered.

Programs

Students may take relevant courses in other programs and apply credit toward the J.D.; a maximum of 4 credits may be applied. The following joint degrees may be earned: J.D./M.A.C. (Juris Doctor/Master of Professional Accounting), J.D./M.A.C.J. (Juris Doctor/Master of Arts in Criminal Justice), J.D./M.B.A. (Juris Doctor/Master of Business Administration), J.D./M.I.B (Juris Doctor/Master of International Business), J.D./M.P.A. (Juris Doctor/Master of Public Administration), J.D./M.S. (Juris Doctor/Master of Science in finance), J.D./M.S.A.L (Juris Doctor/Master of Sports Administration and Leadership), and J.J./M.A.T.L. (Juris Doctor/Master of Arts in Transformational Leadership).

Required

To earn the J.D., candidates must complete 90 total credits, of which 44 are for required courses. They must maintain a minimum GPA of 2.0 in the required courses. The following first-year courses are required of all students: Civil Procedure, Contracts, Criminal Law, Legal Writing, Property, and Torts. Required upper-level courses consist of a professional skills course (choose from several options), Constitutional Law, Evidence, Legal Writing II, and Professional Responsibility. The required orientation program for first-year students consists of a 2-day series of workshops and, throughout the year, seminars on both academic and nonacademic issues.

Phone: 206-398-4200
800-471-1767
Fax: 206-398-4058
E-mail: lawadmis@seattleu.edu
Web: www.law.seattleu.edu

Contact

Carol Cochran, Assistant Dean for Admission, 206-398-4200 for general inquiries; Kathleen Koch, Assistant Dean for Student Financial Services, 206-398-4250 for financial aid information.

WASHINGTON

Electives

Students must take 15 to 25 credits in their area of concentration. The School of Law offers concentrations in corporate law, criminal law, environmental law, family law, intellectual property law, international law, labor law, litigation, tax law, health, commercial law, estate planning, inequality/poverty law, and real estate law. In addition, clinics include the Youth Advocacy Clinic, a 6-credit course in which third-year students, supervised by faculty members, represent clients as youth or status offenders. Seminars are available in numerous limited-enrollment advanced classes, worth 2 to 3 credits, with subjects ranging from First Amendment to Tax Policy to Human Rights. Part-time externships, worth 3 to 4 credits, are available for students in the judiciary and with several preapproved agencies and governmental organizations. Full-time judicial externships, worth 15 credits, are also available. Research programs include work with faculty members conducting research in subjects such as involuntary commitment of the mentally ill and freedom of the press and the First Amendment; independent study on topics of student interest is also encouraged. More than 80% of students are employed in law-related field work positions each year with corporate firms, partnerships, federal, state, and local public agencies, and nonprofit associations. The Alumni/ae Lecture Series brings distinguished scholars, jurists, and practitioners to campus to comment on compelling legal issues. Students may participate in study-abroad programs sponsored by other ABA law schools and receive up to 6 credits. The school has study-abroad programs in Brazil, Ireland, and South Africa. The Academic Resource Center, staffed by a tenured professor and full-time J.D. alumna, offers tutorial services as well as group workshops and seminars. The Access Admission Program, designed for historically disadvantaged, physically challenged, and older applicants (limited to 30 students a year), is an intensive program integrating first-year classes with group instruction. Minority programs are conducted through the Black Law Students Association, Latino Law Student Society, and Asian/Pacific Islander Law Students Association. Special interest group programs include activities by the Environmental Law Society, International Law Society, and Entertainment/Sports

Law Society. The most widely taken electives are Administrative Law, Business Entities, and Intellectual Property.

Graduation Requirements

In order to graduate, candidates must have a GPA of 2.0 and have completed the upper-division writing requirement.

Organizations

Students edit the *Seattle University Law Review, the Seattle Journal of Social Justice*, and the newspaper *The Prolific Reporter*. Moot court competitions include Jessup International Law, Pace Environmental Law, and Frederick Douglass. Other competitions include National Appellate Moot Court Competition, Association of Trial Lawyers of America, Client Counseling, and Negotiation. Law student organizations include the Student Bar Association, Public Interest Law Foundation, and Federalist Society. Other organizations include Amnesty International, Black Law Students Association, and Human Rights Network. There are local chapters of American Trial Lawyers Association, Phi Alpha Delta, and American Civil Liberties Union.

Library

The law library contains 388,860 hardcopy volumes and 218,919 microform volume equivalents, and subscribes to 2455 serial publications. Such on-line databases and networks as CALI, CIS Universe, DIALOG, Legal-Trac, LEXIS, LOIS, NEXIS, OCLC First Search, WESTLAW, and 40 e-resources, including database encyclopedias, e-books, and e-journals, are available to law students for research. Special library collections include a U.S. government documents depository, Mc Naughton's Recreational Reading Collection, Walker Collection, Faculty Read Book Collection, and Jerome McCristal Culp Jr. Collection of Race Gender and Seprals. Every library carrel, table, and study area provides Internet access. Extensive compact shelving ensures onsite access to all library materials. A Document Delivery Center offers students printing and photocopying services. The library website features research guides, a blog, and an audio tour. The ratio of library volumes to faculty is 6172 to 1 and to students is 375 to 1. The ratio of seats in the library to students is 1 to 2.

Placement

J.D.s awarded:	357

Services available through: a separate law school placement center

Services: comprehensive lists of judges, courts, and application requirements for judicial clerkships

Special features: résumé and cover letter writing workshops; mock interviews; career panels highlighting various areas of law practice; brown bag sessions to review job hunting, application, and interviewing process; career counseling by all-attorney staff; daily job postings on-line; sessions offered both day and evenings to accommodate all students.

Full-time job interviews:	8 employers
Summer job interviews:	62 employers
Placement by graduation:	54% of class
Placement within 9 months:	94% of class
Average starting salary:	$44,500 to $130,000

Areas of placement:

Private practice 2-10 attorneys	26%
Private practice 11-25 attorneys	3%
Private practice 26-50 attorneys	3%
Private practice 51-100 attorneys	2%
Private practice 101-500 attorneys 6%, Solo 3%	9%
Business/industry	31%
Government	12%
Judicial clerkships	6%
Public interest	5%
Academic	1%

Faculty

The law school has 63 full-time and 43 part-time faculty members, of whom 42 are women. According to AAUP standards for Category IIA institutions, faculty salaries are average. About 15% of full-time faculty have a graduate law degree in addition to the J.D. The ratio of full-time students to full-time faculty in an average class is 12 to 1; in a clinic, 8 to 1. The law school has a regular program of bringing visiting professors and other distinguished lecturers and visitors to campus.

Students

About 51% of the student body are women; 29%, minorities; 3%, African American; 13%, Asian American; 5%, Hispanic; 1%, Native American; and 5%, multicultural. The majority of students come from Washington (92%). The average age of entering students is 27; age range is 20 to 52. About 20% of students enter directly from undergraduate school, 12% have a graduate degree, and 78% have worked full-time prior to entering law school. About 2% drop out after the first year for academic or personal reasons; 90% remain to receive a law degree.

SETON HALL UNIVERSITY

School of Law

One Newark Center Newark, NJ
07102-5210

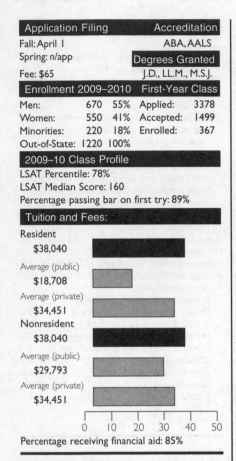

Application Filing	Accreditation
Fall: April 1	ABA, AALS
Spring: n/app	**Degrees Granted**
Fee: $65	J.D., LL.M., M.S.J.

Enrollment 2009–2010		First-Year Class	
Men:	670 55%	Applied:	3378
Women:	550 41%	Accepted:	1499
Minorities:	220 18%	Enrolled:	367
Out-of-State:	1220 100%		

2009–10 Class Profile
LSAT Percentile: 78%
LSAT Median Score: 160
Percentage passing bar on first try: 89%

Tuition and Fees:

Resident
$38,040

Average (public)
$18,708

Average (private)
$34,451

Nonresident
$38,040

Average (public)
$29,793

Average (private)
$34,451

0 10 20 30 40 50

Percentage receiving financial aid: 85%

ADMISSIONS

In a recent year, 3378 applied, 1499 were accepted, and 367 enrolled. Eighteen transfers enrolled. The median LSAT percentile of the most recent first-year class was 78; the median GPA was 3.45 on a scale of 4.0. The lowest LSAT percentile accepted was 44; the highest was 99. Figures in the above capsule and in this profile are approximate.

Requirements
Applicants must have a bachelor's degree and take the LSAT. The most important admission factors include academic achievement, LSAT results, and GPA. No specific undergraduate courses are required. Candidates are not interviewed.

Procedure
Applicants should submit an application form, LSAT results, transcripts, a personal statement, the TOEFL for non-English speaking applicants, a nonrefundable application fee of $65, and 2 letters of recommendation. Notification of the admissions decision is on a rolling basis

typically between. The latest acceptable LSAT test date for fall entry is February. The law school uses the LSDAS. Cfheck with the school for the current application deadlines.

Special
The law school recruits minority and disadvantaged students by reaching out to historically black colleges and minority bar associations to encourage applications from highly qualified students of color. The Partners in Excellence (PIE) Program, the Legal Education Opportunities (LEO) Institute, and the Dorothy Day Scholarship are intended to help in the recruitment of a diverse pool of students. Requirements are not different for out-of-state students. Transfer students must have one year of credit, have attended an ABA-approved law school, and be in the top 20% of the law class. Preadmissions courses consist of the Pre-Legal Institute, and Legal Education Opportunities Program for admission to law school for the educationally disadvantaged.

Costs

Tuition and fees for the 2009-2010 academic year are approximately $38,040 for all full-time students. Tuition for part-time students is approximately $28,725 per year. Books and supplies run about $1000.

Financial Aid

In a recent year, about 85% of current law students received some form of aid. The average annual amount of aid from all sources combined, including scholarships, loans, and work contracts, was approximately $33,500; maximum, $51,180. Awards are based on need and merit. Required financial statement is the FAFSA. Special funds for minority or disadvantaged students are need-based from the law school and external sources. First-year students are notified about their financial aid application at time of acceptance. Check with the school for the current application deadline.

About the Law School

Seton Hall University School of Law was established in 1951 and is a private institution. The 2-acre campus is in an urban area in Newark. The primary mission of the law school is to provide an excellent legal education to students who are highly qualified for the study of law, to disseminate knowledge, and to provide an environment for

research and writing. Students have access to federal, state, county, city, and local agencies, courts, correctional facilities, law firms, and legal aid organizations in the Newark area. The law school's location is home to many firms, offering students opportunities as interns, clerks, and summer associates. Nearby are government offices and federal and county courthouses. Housing for students Ample and affordable rental housing is available in the vicinity. All law school facilities are accessible to the physically disabled.

Calendar

The law school operates on a traditional semester basis. Courses for full-time students are offered both day and evening and must be completed within 6 years. For part-time students, courses are offered both day and evening and must be completed within 6 years. New full- and part-time students are admitted in the fall. There is an 8-week summer session. Transferable summer courses are offered.

Programs

In addition to the J.D., the law school offers the LL.M. and M.S.J. Students may take relevant courses in other programs and apply credit toward the J.D.; a maximum of 12 credits may be applied. The following joint degrees may be earned: B.S./J.D. (Bachelor of Science/Juris Doctor), J.D./M.A.D.I.R. (Juris Doctor/Master of Arts in Diplomacy and International Rel), J.D./M.B.A. (Juris Doctor/Master of Business Administration), J.D./M.D. (Juris Doctor/Doctor of Medicine), and M.D./M.S.J. (Doctor of Medicine/Master of Science in Jurisprudence).

Required
To earn the J.D., candidates must complete 85 total credits, of which 44 are for required courses. They must maintain a minimum GPA of 2.0 in the required courses. The following first-year courses are required of all students: Civil Procedure, Constitutional Law, Contracts, Criminal Law, Legal Research and Legal Writing, Property, and Torts. Required upper-level courses consist of Appellate Advocacy, Business Associations, Evidence, Federal Income Taxation, Persuasion and Advocacy, and Professional Responsibility. Students may apply to the particular clinic they seek to join. The required orientation program for first-year students is a 2-day program commencing immediately before the start of

Phone: 973-642-8747
888-415-7271
Fax: 973-642-8876
E-mail: *admitme@shu.edu*
Web: *http://law.shu.edu*

Contact

Dean of Admissions and Financial Resource, 973-642-8747 or 888-415-7271 for general inquiries; Director of Financial Resource Management, 973-642-8744 for financial aid information.

NEW JERSEY

classes with activities continuing into the first week of classes.

Electives

Students must take 13 credits in their area of concentration. The School of Law offers concentrations in intellectual property law and health law. In addition, the Center for Social Justice's for-credit clinical programs and pro bono program allow students to engage in a legal apprenticeship with an average of 15 hours per week performing legal duties, such as interviewing and counseling clients, conferring with adversaries, taking depositions, conducting research, and participating in trials. Students acquire the practical skills, knowledge, and experience that both train them and make them more attractive to prospective employers. Students may apply to the particular clinic they seek to join. The clinical programs include the Civil Litigation Clinic, Family Law Clinic, Immigration and Human Rights Clinic, Impact Litigation Clinic, and the Pro Bono Program. There is a minimum cumulative GPA of 2.6 with certain course prerequisites. Students are encouraged to enroll in at least 1 or 2 seminars or small group courses in subjects that interest them. The Advanced Writing Requirement is a required seminar course to meet graduation standards and is 2 to 3 credits per course. Elective seminars include Drafting, Simulation, and Skills courses, offered for 2 to 4 credits each. Internships include judicial, not-for-profit organizations, and federal and state government. Research program opportunities, offered to second- and third-year students, include independent research, seminars, and the opportunity to serve as a faculty research assistant. The Center for Social Justice sponsors a pro bono program that places students in a variety of legal settings during all 3 years of the law school. The law school sponsors innumerable programs. Recent speakers have included Janet Reno, Scott Turow, Akhil Amar, Cornell West, Arthur Miller, Randy Barnett, Erwin Chemerinsky, and Maya Angelou. There are summer study-abroad programs in Italy, Egypt, and Ireland. Academic support services are available to students in academic difficulty. Minority programs include the Partners in Excellence (PIE) Program, which seeks to attract a diverse pool of highly talented students who will enrich the academic life of the law school, and the Legal Educa-

tion Opportunities (LEO) Institute, which is intended to provide educationally disadvantaged students the opportunity to demonstrate their ability to succeed in the study of law. The most widely taken electives are Criminal Procedure, Estates and Trusts, and Commercial Law Survey.

Graduation Requirements

In order to graduate, candidates must have a GPA of 2.0, have completed the upper-division writing requirement, and have completed 85 credits of academic work. Not more than 10 of these credits may be completed with a grade of F, D, or D+. No student may attempt more than 95 credits of academic work.

Organizations

Students edit the *Seton Hall Law Review, Journal of Sports and Entertainment Law, Seton Hall Legislative Journal, Seton Hall Circuit Review*, and the newspaper *Res Ipsa Loquitur*. Moot court competitions include National Moot Court Competition, National Appellate Advocacy, and Craven's Constitutional Law Moot Court Competition. Other competitions include Alternative Dispute Resolution and various writing competitions. Law student organizations, local chapters of national associations, and campus organizations include Jewish Law Society, Public Interest Network, Entertainment and Sports Law Society, St. Thomas More Society, Health Law Forum, Women's Law Forum, Black Law Students Association, Federalist Society, and American Constitution Society.

Library

The law library contains 443,681 hardcopy volumes and 498,403 microform volume equivalents, and subscribes to 7485 serial publications. Such on-line databases and networks as LEXIS, NEXIS, WEST-LAW, and BNA, CCH, European Union Law Library, Journal of Legal Scholarship, Legal Scholarship Network, LOIS-LAW, Tax Analysts, LLMC, RIA Checkpoint, Environmental Law Reporter, Global Jurist, Indexmaster, HeinOnline, and New York Legal Publishing Corporation are available to law students for research. Special library collections include the Rodino Papers and depositories for federal and New Jersey State documents. Recently, the library provided full wireless coverage on all library levels. The ratio of library volumes to faculty is 6622 to 1 and

Placement

J.D.s awarded:	410

Services available through: a separate law school placement center
Services: mentor programs, mock interviews, summer public interest fellowships, loan forgiveness program, externship program
Special features: an evening placement counselor, public interest director, newsletters, on-line services, clerkship counselor.

Full-time job interviews:	100 employers
Summer job interviews:	100 employers
Placement by graduation:	90% of class
Placement within 9 months:	97% of class
Average starting salary:	$55,000 to $75,000

Areas of placement:

Private practice 2-10 attorneys	18%
Private practice 11-25 attorneys	10%
Private practice 26-50 attorneys	5%
Private practice 51-100 attorneys	8%
Judicial clerkships	35%
Business/industry	15%
Government	5%
Public interest	3%
Academic	1%

to students is 364 to 1. The ratio of seats in the library to students is 1 to 2.

Faculty

The law school has 67 full-time and 96 part-time faculty members, of whom 53 are women. According to AAUP standards for Category I institutions, faculty salaries are below average. About 25% of full-time faculty have a graduate law degree in addition to the J.D.; about 10% of part-time faculty have one. The ratio of full-time students to full-time faculty in an average class is 15 to 1; in a clinic, 6 to 1. The law school has a regular program of bringing visiting professors and other distinguished lecturers and visitors to campus. There is a chapter of the Order of the Coif; 10 faculty are members.

Students

About 41% of the student body are women; 18%, minorities; 4%, African American; 8%, Asian American; 5%, Hispanic; and 2%, foreign national. The average age of entering students is 25; age range is 21 to 47. About 33% of students enter directly from undergraduate school, 11% have a graduate degree, and 66% have worked full-time prior to entering law school. About 2% drop out after the first year for academic or personal reasons; 97% remain to receive a law degree.

1303 San Jacinto Street
Houston, TX 77002-7000

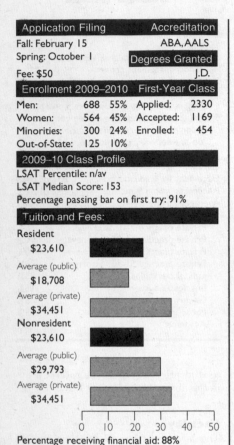

Application Filing		Accreditation	
Fall: February 15		ABA, AALS	
Spring: October 1		**Degrees Granted**	
Fee: $50			J.D.

Enrollment 2009–2010		First-Year Class	
Men:	688 55%	Applied:	2330
Women:	564 45%	Accepted:	1169
Minorities:	300 24%	Enrolled:	454
Out-of-State:	125 10%		

2009–10 Class Profile
LSAT Percentile: n/av
LSAT Median Score: 153
Percentage passing bar on first try: 91%

Tuition and Fees:

Resident
$23,610

Average (public)
$18,708

Average (private)
$34,451

Nonresident
$23,610

Average (public)
$29,793

Average (private)
$34,451

0 10 20 30 40 50

Percentage receiving financial aid: 88%

ADMISSIONS

In a recent year, 2330 applied, 1169 were accepted, and 454 enrolled. Three transfers enrolled. The median GPA of the most recent first-year class was 3.21. Figures in the above capsule and in this profile are approximate.

Requirements
Applicants must have a bachelor's degree and take the LSAT. The most important admission factors include LSAT results, GPA, and life experience. No specific undergraduate courses are required. Candidates are not interviewed.

Procedure
Applicants should submit an application form, a nonrefundable application fee of $50, 2 letters of recommendation, and personal statement, and a resume. Notification of the admissions decision is on a rolling basis. The latest acceptable LSAT test date for fall entry is February. The law school uses the LSDAS. Check with

the school for the current application deadlines.

Special
The law school recruits minority and disadvantaged students by offering application fee waivers for those with documented need. South Texas considers ethnicity and disadvantaged backgrounds in the admissions process and offers scholarships to those who qualify. Requirements are not different for out-of-state students. Transfer students must have one year of credit, have attended an ABA-approved law school, and be ranked in the upper 10% of the current law school class, and be able to provide a letter of good standing.

Costs

Tuition and fees for the 2009-2010 academic year are approximately $23,610 for all full-time students. Tuition for part-time students is approximately $15,940 per year. Books and supplies run about $1700.

Financial Aid

In a recent year, about 88% of current law students received some form of aid. The average annual amount of aid from all sources combined, including scholarships, loans, and work contracts, was approximately $30,315; maximum, $49,393. Awards are based on need and merit. Required financial statement is the FAFSA. Special funds for minority or disadvantaged students include Enhancement Scholarships for continuing students. First-year students are notified about their financial aid application at at the time of application. Check with the school for the current application deadlines.

About the Law School

South Texas College of Law was established in 1923 is independent. The campus is in an urban area in downtown Houston. The primary mission of the law school is to provide an accessible legal education, distinguished by its excellence, to a diverse body of students committed to serving their communities and the profession. Students have access to federal, state, county, city, and local agencies, courts, correctional facilities, law firms, and legal aid organizations in the Houston area. South Texas is only one of two American

law schools housing two appellate courts on a permanent basis. Facilities of special interest to law students include its 4 Centers of Excellence and its skills and clinical programs: Advocacy Program, the Frank Evans Center for Conflict Resolution, the Corporate Compliance Center, and the Transactional Practice Center. Housing for students is not available on campus. However, high-rise apartments are within walking distance of the campus. Apartment locators are available, usually at no cost. All law school facilities are accessible to the physically disabled.

Calendar

The law school operates on a traditional semester basis. Courses for full- and part-time students are offered both day and evening and must be completed within 7 years.. New full-time students are admitted in the fall and spring; part-time, fall. There is an 8-week summer session. Transferable summer courses are offered.

Programs

The following joint degrees may be earned: J.D./M.B.A. (Juris Doctor/Master of Business Administration).

Required
To earn the J.D., candidates must complete 90 total credits, of which 46 are for required courses. They must maintain a minimum GPA of 2.0 in the required courses. The following first-year courses are required of all students: Civil Procedure, Constitutional Law, Contracts I and II, Criminal Law, Legal Research and Writing I and II, Property I, and Torts I and II. Required upper-level courses consist of 2 hours of Professional Skills, Evidence, Federal Income Tax, Professional Responsibility, Property II, and Substantial research paper. Students can satisfy this requirement through participation in academic internships, on-site clinics, and upper division skills training courses. The required orientation program for first-year students is 3- or 4-days and is generally scheduled the week prior to the beginning of classes, formatted to accommodate both full- and part-time students.

Phone: 713-646-1810
Fax: 713-646-2906
E-mail: admissions@stcl.edu
Web: www.stcl.edu

Contact

Director of Admissions, 713-646-1810 for general inquiries; Director of Financial Aid, 713-646-1820 for financial aid information.

TEXAS

Electives

The South Texas College of Law offers concentrations in environmental law, international law, and Advocacy, Alternative Dispute Resolution, and Transactional law. In addition, Upper-level students can earn a maximum of 6 semester hours of credit in clinics including the Criminal Process Clinic, Judicial Process Clinic and the Public Interest Clinic. Seminars are offered for 2 hours of credit. Internships are normally offered during the fall, spring, and summer and are limited to a maximum of 6 credit hours. Each year, the College hosts the Fred Parks Distinguished Lecture Series and the Turner Lecture Series in Professionalism. South Texas co-sponsors a number of ABA-approved summer abroad programs, in addition to 2 cooperative semester abroad programs. South Texas also administers an academic assistance program that includes individual counseling and study skills seminars on the outlining process, as well as preparing for and taking exams. The most widely taken electives are Corporations, Criminal Procedure, and Wills, Trusts, and Estates.

Graduation Requirements

In order to graduate, candidates must have a GPA of 2.0 and have completed the upper-division writing requirement.

Organizations

Students edit the *South Texas Law Review, Corporate Counsel Review, Currents: International Trade Law Journal, Corporate Counsel Review*, and the newspaper, *Annotations*. Students enrolled in the Moot Court Competition course are selected to participate in numerous national moot court and mock trial competitions held annually. South Texas has more than 25 registered organizations in which students can participate. Students at South Texas have the opportunity to become members of numerous active student organizations representing a wide range of interests. There are local chapters of Phi Delta Phi, Phi Alpha Delta, and Delta Theta Phi.

Library

The law library contains 246,568 hardcopy volumes and 276,704 microform volume equivalents, and subscribes to 4345 serial publications. Such on-line databases and networks as CALI, CIS Universe, Infotrac, Legal-Trac, LEXIS, LOIS, Matthew Bender, NEXIS, OCLC First Search, WESTLAW, and Wilsonline Indexes are available to law students for research. Special library collections include A U.S. government selective depository and a rare books collection, college archives, and various manuscript collections. Recently, the library completed construction on The Fred Parks Law Library. Floors 1 to 5 of the building are comprised of classrooms, seminar and conference rooms with additional carrel space, 2-person study rooms, faculty study rooms, and soft seating. The 6th floor is a flexible combination of classroom and ceremonial space with an adjoining outdoor terrace. In addition, each seat within the library is wired for a laptop computer connection and the entire library also installed with wireless connectivity. The ratio of library volumes to faculty is 4109 to 1 and to students is 197 to 1. The ratio of seats in the library to students is 1 to 2.

Faculty

The law school has 60 full-time and 64 part-time faculty members, of whom 40 are women. About 28% of full-time faculty have a graduate law degree in addition to the J.D. The ratio of full-time students to full-time faculty in an average class is 20 to 1; in a clinic, 19 to 1. The law school has a regular program of bringing visiting professors and other distinguished lecturers and visitors to campus.

Students

About 45% of the student body are women; 24%, minorities; 4%, African American; 11%, Asian American; 9%, Hispanic; 1%, Native American; and 75%, White. The majority of students come from Texas (90%). The average age of entering students is 24; age range is 19 to 60. About 33% of students enter directly from undergraduate school. About 6% drop out after the first year for academic or personal reasons.

Placement

J.D.s awarded:	357

Services available through: a separate law school placement center and Career Resources Center publicizes various job fairs and maintains a library of placement opportunities.

Special features: seminars and speaker programs, skills training workshops, alumni mentor program, tours and visits to local and out-of-city courts, area corporations and law firms, networking breakfasts, 6 to 8 job fairs each year, and coordination of campus interviews.

Full-time job interviews:	18 employers
Summer job interviews:	60 employers
Placement by graduation:	n/av
Placement within 9 months:	80% of class
Average starting salary:	$70,000 to $135,000

Areas of placement:

Private practice 2-10 attorneys	38%
Private practice 11-25 attorneys	7%
Private practice 26-50 attorneys	2%
Private practice 51-100 attorneys	2%
Business/industry	17%
9% Self-employed; 4% 101+ attorneys; 3% size unkno	16%
Government	11%
Judicial clerkships	3%
Public interest	2%
Military	1%
Academic	1%

School of Law

Lesar Law Building, Mail Code 6804
Carbondale, IL 62901

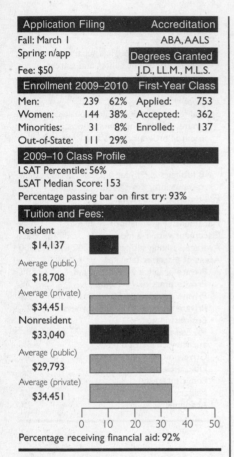

Application Filing	Accreditation
Fall: March 1	ABA, AALS
Spring: n/app	Degrees Granted
Fee: $50	J.D., LL.M., M.L.S.

Enrollment 2009–2010		First-Year Class	
Men:	239 62%	Applied:	753
Women:	144 38%	Accepted:	362
Minorities:	31 8%	Enrolled:	137
Out-of-State:	111 29%		

2009–10 Class Profile

LSAT Percentile: 56%
LSAT Median Score: 153
Percentage passing bar on first try: 93%

Tuition and Fees:

Resident
$14,137

Average (public)
$18,708

Average (private)
$34,451

Nonresident
$33,040

Average (public)
$29,793

Average (private)
$34,451

0 10 20 30 40 50

Percentage receiving financial aid: 92%

ADMISSIONS

In the fall 2009 first-year class, 753 applied, 362 were accepted, and 137 enrolled. Eight transfers enrolled. The median LSAT percentile of the most recent first-year class was 56; the median GPA was 3.25 on a scale of 13.0. The lowest LSAT percentile accepted was 13; the highest was 96.

Requirements
Applicants must have a bachelor's degree and take the LSAT. The most important admission factors include LSAT results, GPA, academic achievement, and answers on the Admission Committee Memorandum. No specific undergraduate courses are required. Candidates are not interviewed.

Procedure
The application deadline for fall entry is March 1. Applicants should submit an application form, LSAT results, transcripts, a personal statement, a nonrefundable application fee of $50, 2 recommended letters of recommendation, and the Admissions Committee Memorandum. Notification of the admissions decision is as early as possible. The latest acceptable LSAT test date for fall entry is February. The law school uses the LSDAS.

Special
The law school recruits minority and disadvantaged students by means of the Candidate Referral Service; special programs at the School of Law, including an Open House for admitted applicants; networking, and contacting institutions that serve underrepresented students. Requirements are not different for out-of-state students. Transfer students must have one year of credit, have attended an ABA-approved law school, and may be admitted if it appears likely that they will successfully complete the School of Law curriculum. Factors considered include the applicant's law school record, class rank, law school attended, LSAT, and GPA.

Costs

Tuition and fees for the 2009-2010 academic year are $14,137 for full-time in-state students and $33,040 for out-of-state students. On-campus room and board costs about $10,458 annually; books and supplies run $1150.

Financial Aid

About 92% of current law students receive some form of aid. Awards are based on need and merit. Required financial statement is the FAFSA. The aid application deadline for fall entry is April 1. First-year students are notified about their financial aid application at time of acceptance.

About the Law School

Southern Illinois University School of Law was established in 1973 and is a public institution. The 3290-acre campus is in a rural area 100 miles southeast of St. Louis, Missouri. The primary mission of the law school is to train lawyers who will be competent to practice law now and in the future, exhibit leadership, and adhere to the ethical standards of the legal profession. Students have access to federal, state, county, city, and local agencies, courts, correctional facilities, law firms, and legal aid organizations in the Carbondale area. Facilities of special interest to law students include 24-hour keypad access to the law building and library, a wireless network, and distance-learning capabilities allowing live correspondence with national law schools. The courtroom and classrooms are stocked with the latest technology. The law library houses a vast collection of legal authorities to meet the demanding research needds of the prospective lawyer. Housing for students is available in dorms across the street from the law school. There is also plenty of off-campus housing available within 10 minutes of the law school. All law school facilities are accessible to the physically disabled.

Calendar

The law school operates on a traditional semester basis. Courses for full-time students are offered days only and must be completed within 5 years. There is no part-time program. New students are admitted in the fall. There is an 8-week summer session. Transferable summer courses are offered.

Programs

In addition to the J.D., the law school offers the LL.M. and M.L.S. Students may take relevant courses in other programs and apply credit toward the J.D.; a maximum of 6 credits may be applied. The following joint degrees may be earned: J.D./M. Acct. (Juris Doctor/Master of Accounting), J.D./M.B.A. (Juris Doctor/Master of Business Administration), J.D./M.D. (Juris Doctor/Doctor of Medicine), J.D./M.P.A. (Juris Doctor/Master of Public Administration), J.D./M.S.ECE (Juris Doctor/Master of Science in Electrical and Computer Engineering), J.D./M.S.Ed. (Juris Doctor/Master of Educational Administration), J.D./M.S.W. (Juris Doctor/Master of Social Work), and J.D./Ph.D. (Juris Doctor/Doctor of Philosophy in political science).

Required
To earn the J.D., candidates must complete 90 total credits, of which 48 are for required courses. They must maintain a minimum GPA of 2.3 in the required courses. The following first-year courses are required of all students: Civil Procedure I, Contracts I and II, Criminal Law, Lawyering Skills I and II, Legislative and Administrative Process, Property I and II, and Torts. Required upper-level

Phone: 618-453-8858
800-739-9187
Fax: 618-453-8921
E-mail: *lawadmit@siu.edu*
Web: *www.lawsiu.edu*

Contact

Akami Marik, Field Representative, 618-453-8858 or 800-739-9187 for general inquiries; Linda Clemons Director of Financial Aid, 618-453-3102 for financial aid information.

ILLINOIS

courses consist of a writing requirement, Civil Procedure II, Constitutional Law, Evidence, and Legal Profession. All students must choose from a menu of skills courses. The required orientation program for first-year students involves 3 half-day programs of presentations aimed at providing vital information to entering students.

Electives

The School of Law offers concentrations in corporate law, criminal law, environmental law, family law, intellectual property law, international law, labor law, litigation, sports law, tax law, and torts and insurance. In addition, 2 in-house clinics are offered to upper-level law students for up to 6 hours of credit; the elder law clinic and the domestic violence clinic. Senior seminares are available to students who have completed 31 semester hours. Students must fulfill the senior writing requirements upon graduation by taking the Senior Writing Seminar, Designated Elective Course, Law Journal Credit, Journal of Legal Medicine Credit, or Advanced Appelate Moot Court. Senior law students may enroll for up to 6 hours in externships; credit is earned by working in a public interest or legal services agency or for local prosecutors and public defenders, for local judges, or for local and state agencies. Independent research and a writing credit is allowed under certain conditions. Each year the law school hosts the Lesar Lecture Series and the Dr. Arthur Grayson Distinguished Lecture (Law and Medicine). The law school sponsors a summer study-abroad program in Ireland. All first-year students participate in the Academic Success Program, which includes structured study groups led by upper-class students. The school makes individual accommodations to the needs of its disabled students. The most widely taken electives are Criminal Procedure, Introduction to Commercial Law, and Corporations.

Graduation Requirements

In order to graduate, candidates must have a GPA of 2.3, have completed the upper-division writing requirement, and must maintain a 2.3 GPA for courses taken during the third year of law school.

Organizations

Students edit the *Southern Illinois University Law Journal* and the *Journal of Legal Medicine*. The Moot Court Board sends teams to numerous competitions, including the ABA National Appellate Advocacy Competition, Criminal Procedure Moot Court Competition, Gibbons National Criminal Procedure Moot Court Competition, and Weschler First Amendment Moot Court Competition. The student division of the ABA holds an annual intraschool Client Interviewing and Counseling Competition as well as a Negotiation Competition. Students also participate in the National Trial Competition. Law student organizations, include the Black Law Students Association, Lesbian and Gay Law Students Association, and Women's Law Forum. Local chapters of national association include the Amnesty International, Federalist Society, and ABA/Law School Division.Campus organizations include the Environmental Law Society, International Law Society, and Student Bar Association.

Library

The law library contains 421,497 hardcopy volumes and 203,178 microform volume equivalents, and subscribes to 1051 serial publications. Such on-line databases and networks as CALI, CIS Universe, DIALOG, Infotrac, Legal-Trac, LEXIS, LOIS, Mathew Bender, NEXIS, OCLC First Search, WESTLAW, Wilsonline Indexes, and Access UN, CCH Tax, CILP, Global Newsbank, HeinOnline, News Illinois, PDR, Shepard's Citation Service, Britannica, BNA Databases, CALI, Current Index to Legal Periodicals, Illinois Administrative Code Annotations, Illinois Institute for Continuing Legal Education (IICLE) Smart Books, and others. are available to law students for research. Special library collections include a federal government selective depository library and Illinois State comprehensive document depository. Recently, the library upgraded carpeting, painted, and added public computer stations. The ratio of library volumes to faculty is 12,042 to 1 and to students is 1104 to 1. The ratio of seats in the library to students is 1 to 1.

Faculty

The law school has 35 full-time and 10 part-time faculty members, of whom 18

Placement

J.D.s awarded:	104
Services available through: a separate law school placement center	
Full-time job interviews:	5 employers
Summer job interviews:	9 employers
Placement by graduation:	n/av
Placement within 9 months:	80% of class
Average starting salary:	$35,000 to $60,000
Areas of placement:	
Private practice 2-10 attorneys	29%
Private practice 11-25 attorneys	7%
Private practice 51-100 attorneys	2%
Private practice other firm size	8%
Government	24%
Business/industry	14%
Public interest	7%
Academic	3%
Judicial clerkships	2%
Military	2%

are women. According to AAUP standards for Category I institutions, faculty salaries are well below average. About 18% of full-time faculty have a graduate law degree in addition to the J.D. The ratio of full-time students to full-time faculty in an average class is 27 to 1. The law school has a regular program of bringing visiting professors and other distinguished lecturers and visitors to campus.

Students

About 38% of the student body are women; 8%, minorities; 3%, African American; 2%, Asian American; 2%, Hispanic; and 1%, Native American. The majority of students come from Illinois (71%). The average age of entering students is 26; age range is 21 to 48. About 38% of students enter directly from undergraduate school and 6% have a graduate degree. About 13% drop out after the first year for academic or personal reasons; 87% remain to receive a law degree.

SOUTHERN METHODIST UNIVERSITY

Dedman School of Law

Office of Admissions, P.O. Box 750110
Dallas, TX 75275-0110

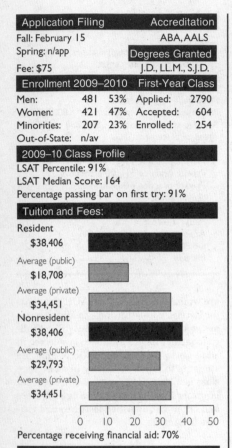

Application Filing	Accreditation
Fall: February 15	ABA, AALS
Spring: n/app	**Degrees Granted**
Fee: $75	J.D., LL.M., S.J.D.

Enrollment 2009–2010		First-Year Class	
Men:	481 53%	Applied:	2790
Women:	421 47%	Accepted:	604
Minorities:	207 23%	Enrolled:	254
Out-of-State:	n/av		

2009–10 Class Profile
LSAT Percentile: 91%
LSAT Median Score: 164
Percentage passing bar on first try: 91%

Tuition and Fees:

Resident
$38,406

Average (public)
$18,708

Average (private)
$34,451

Nonresident
$38,406

Average (public)
$29,793

Average (private)
$34,451

0 10 20 30 40 50

Percentage receiving financial aid: 70%

ADMISSIONS

In the fall 2009 first-year class, 2790 applied, 604 were accepted, and 254 enrolled. Forty-one transfers enrolled. The median LSAT percentile of the most recent first-year class was 91; the median GPA was 3.76 on a scale of 4.0. The highest LSAT percentile was 99.

Requirements
Applicants must have a bachelor's degree and take the LSAT. Minimum acceptable GPA is 2.0 on a scale of 4.0. No specific undergraduate courses are required. Candidates are not interviewed.

Procedure
The application deadline for fall entry is February 15. Applicants should submit an application form, LSAT results, transcripts, a personal statements, a nonrefundable application fee of $75, 2 letters of recommendation, a resume, and optional statements. Notification of the admissions decision is on a rolling basis beginning

December. The latest acceptable LSAT test date for fall entry is February. The law school uses the LSDAS.

Special
The law school recruits minority and disadvantaged students by means of school visitations, special mailings, and a Minority Pre-Law Symposium held every year in the spring. Requirements are not different for out-of-state students. Transfer students must have one year of credit, and have attended an ABA-approved law school. Admission for transfers is highly competitive. The student must be in good standing at previous law school.

Costs

Tuition and fees for the 2009-2010 academic year are $38,406 for all full-time students. Tuition for part-time students is $28,805 per year. Books and supplies run $1800.

Financial Aid

About 70% of current law students receive some form of aid. Awards are based on need and merit. Required financial statements are the FAFSA and others, depending on the type of scholarship being sought. The aid application deadline for fall entry is June 1. Special funds for minority or disadvantaged students include scholarships, which are available on a need and merit basis and are designed to promote the diversity of the student body and the legal profession and to assist those who have had fewer academic opportunities. First-year students are notified about their financial aid application at time of acceptance, beginning May 1 and on a rolling basis until the first day of classes.

About the Law School

Southern Methodist University Dedman School of Law was established in 1925 and is a private institution. The 6-acre campus is in a suburban area 5 miles north of downtown Dallas. The primary mission of the law school is to prepare students for the competent and ethical practice of law through a curriculum that combines training in the science and method of law, knowledge of the substance and procedure of law, understanding of the role of law in an international society, and practical experience in handling professional

problems. Students have access to federal, state, county, city, and local agencies, courts, correctional facilities, law firms, and legal aid organizations in the Dallas area. Facilities of special interest to law students include the fully computerized Underwood Law Library, built in 1972, and Carr Collins Hall, remodeled in 2005, which houses admissions, an expanded Office of Career Services, financial aid, a public service department, and a dining hall. All classrooms are equipped with multimedia presentation facilities and wireless access. Housing for students consists of both single- and married-student housing, available on campus on a first-come, first-served basis. All law school facilities are accessible to the physically disabled.

Calendar

The law school operates on a traditional semester basis. Courses for full-time students and part- time students are offered both day and evening and must be completed within 5 years. New full- and part-time students are admitted in the fall. There is a 7-week summer session. Transferable summer courses are not offered.

Programs

In addition to the J.D., the law school offers the LL.M. and S.J.D. Students may take relevant courses in other programs and apply credit toward the J.D.; a maximum of 6 credits may be applied. The following joint degrees may be earned: J.D./M.A. (Juris Doctor/Master of Arts in applied economics) and J.D./M.B.A. (Juris Doctor/Master of Business Administration).

Required
To earn the J.D., candidates must complete 87 total credits, of which 37 are for required courses. They must maintain a minimum GPA of 2.0 in the required courses. The following first-year courses are required of all students: Civil Procedure, Constitutional Law I, Contracts, Criminal Law, Legal Research, Writing, and Advocacy, Property, and Torts. Required upper-level courses consist of a general writing requirement, an edited writing seminar, Constitutional Law II, Professional Responsibility, and Professional Skills course. Clinical courses are available for students who have completed

Phone: 214-768-2550
888-768-5291
Fax: 214-768-2549
E-mail: *lawadmit@smu.edu*
Web: *law.smu.edu*

Contact

Office of Admissions, 214-768-2550 for general inquiries; Stan Eddy, Financial Aid Counselor, 214-768-3348 for financial aid information.

TEXAS

44 hours and have met certain pre-requisites. The required orientation program for first-year students consists of a 2-day introduction to the study of law.

Electives

The Dedman School of Law offers concentrations in corporate law, criminal law, environmental law, family law, intellectual property law, international law, litigation, securities law, and tax law. In addition, child advocacy, civil, consumer advocacy, criminal defense, criminal prosecution, small business, and federal taxpayers clinics are offered. Clinics may be taken by students who have completed 44 hours and in good academic standing (2.0) and have met certain course prerequisites. Seminars include such topics as Advanced Commercial Law, Antitrust, and Civil Rights. Directed Research is worth a maximum of 3 hours. Field work may be done through Directed Studies, and is worth 1 to 2 hours. A mandatory 30 hours of pro bono legal work is required for graduation. The special lecture series includes the Murrah Lecture and the Tate Lecture. A 6-week summer program at University College in Oxford, England is provided for students who wish to study abroad. In addition students can participate in other approved study-abroad programs. The Academic Skills Assessment program (ASAP) is available by invitation only to first-year law students. The non-credit Student Mentoring program is available for all first-year law students. Minority programs include Minority Law Day, the ABA Diversity Clerkship Program, Southeastern Minority Job Fair, Sunbelt Minority Job Fair, the Black/Hispanic/Asian Pacific American Law Students Associations, and Multicultural Orientation. Special interest group programs include the Board of Advocates, Student Bar Association, Association of Public Interest Law, and Association of Law and Politics.

Graduation Requirements

In order to graduate, candidates must have a GPA of 2.0, have completed the upper-division writing requirement, and a 30-hour pro bono work requirement.

Organizations

Students edit the *SMU Law Review, Journal of Air Law and Commerce, The International Lawyer, SMU Science* and *Technology Law Review,* and *Law and Business Review of the Americas.* Moot court competitions include the Jackson and Walker, Phillip C. Jessup International Moot Court, and Howie and Sweeney competitions. Other competitions include the ABA Client Counseling, ABA Negotiations, Hispanic National Bar Association Moot Court, Thomas Tang Moot Court, John Marshall IT Moot Court, and others. Local chapters of national associations, include BLSA, APALSA, HLSA, Criminal Law Association, and Corporate Law Association, Law student organizations include Student Bar Association, Board of Advocates, and Barristers. Other law student orgainzations include Federalist Law Society, OWLS, and Phi Alpha Delta.

Library

The law library contains 637,217 hardcopy volumes and 140,625 microform volume equivalents, and subscribes to 4987 serial publications. Such on-line databases and networks as CALI, CIS Universe, Infotrac, Legal-Trac, LEXIS, LOIS, Mathew Bender, NEXIS, OCLC First Search, WESTLAW, Wilsonline Indexes, and HeinOnline, Lexis/Nexis Congressional, Oceana Online, Access UN, BNA, CCH, Foreign Law Guide, Inter Am, Law Into China, Lawtel Eu, Making of Modern Law, Oxford Scholarship online, and others. are available to law students for research. Special library collections include a rare book room with 9000 volumes; papers and professional library of Sir Joseph Gold; Dallas (Texas) Independent School District Desegregation Litigation Papers; and Steinberg collection of Jewish law. Recently, the library was refurbished with updated chairs, tables, carpet, and paint, and a wireless network was installed throughout. The ratio of library volumes to faculty is 13,558 to 1 and to students is 706 to 1. The ratio of seats in the library to students is 1 to 1.

Faculty

The law school has 47 full-time and 30 part-time faculty members, of whom 23 are women. According to AAUP standards for Category I institutions, faculty salaries are average. About 40% of full-time faculty have a graduate law degree in addition to the J.D. The ratio of full-time students to full-time faculty in an average class is 15 to 1; in a clinic, 8 to 1. The law

Placement	
J.D.s awarded:	283
Services available through: a separate law school placement center, and the university placement center	
Special features: 7 professionals on staff, including 5 SMU law graduates.	
Full-time job interviews:	25 employers
Summer job interviews:	100 employers
Placement by graduation:	72% of class
Placement within 9 months:	99% of class
Average starting salary:	$62,400 to $160,000
Areas of placement:	
Private practice attorneys	65%
Business/industry	23%
Government	5%
Judicial clerkships	2%
Academic	3%
Public interest	2%

school has a regular program of bringing visiting professors and other distinguished lecturers and visitors to campus. There is a chapter of the Order of the Coif; 90 graduates are members.

Students

About 47% of the student body are women; 23%, minorities; 5%, African American; 7%, Asian American; 9%, Hispanic; 1%, and Native American. The average age of entering students is 25; age range is 21 to 53. About 11% of students have a graduate degree. About 3% drop out after the first year for academic or personal reasons; 97% remain to receive a law degree.

SOUTHERN UNIVERSITY AND A & M COLLEGE

Law Center

Post Office Box 9294
Baton Rouge, LA 70813-9294

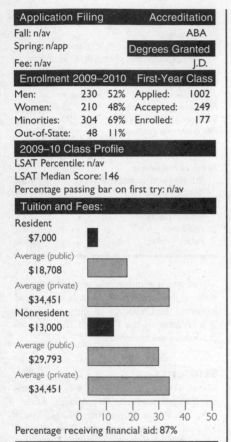

Application Filing		Accreditation	
Fall: n/av			ABA
Spring: n/app		Degrees Granted	
Fee: n/av			J.D.

Enrollment 2009–2010			First-Year Class	
Men:	230	52%	Applied:	1002
Women:	210	48%	Accepted:	249
Minorities:	304	69%	Enrolled:	177
Out-of-State:	48	11%		

2009–10 Class Profile
LSAT Percentile: n/av
LSAT Median Score: 146
Percentage passing bar on first try: n/av

Tuition and Fees:

Resident
$7,000

Average (public)
$18,708

Average (private)
$34,451

Nonresident
$13,000

Average (public)
$29,793

Average (private)
$34,451

0   10   20   30   40   50

Percentage receiving financial aid: 87%

ADMISSIONS

In the fall 2009 first-year class, 1002 applied, 249 were accepted, and 177 enrolled. Figures in the above capsule and in this profile are approximate. One transfer enrolled. The median GPA of the most recent first-year class was 2.8.

Requirements

Applicants must have a bachelor's degree and take the LSAT. Minimum acceptable GPA is 2.0 on a scale of 4.0. The most important admission factors include LSAT results, GPA, and academic achievement. No specific undergraduate courses are required. Candidates are not interviewed.

Procedure

Applicants should submit an application form, LSAT results, transcripts, 2 letters of recommendation, and a personal statement. Notification of the admissions decision is begins in February. The latest acceptable LSAT test date for fall entry is

February. Check with the school for current application deadlines. The law school uses the LSDAS.

Special

The law school recruits minority and disadvantaged students by participating in various programs at minority feeder schools. Requirements are not different for out-of-state students. Transfer students must have one year of credit, have a minimum GPA of 2.5, have attended an ABA-approved law school, and matriculate at least 1 year at the law center if transferring from a Louisiana law school, and 2 if transferring from others.

Costs

Tuition and fees for the 2009-2010 academic year are $7000 for full-time in-state students and $13,000 for out-of-state students. Tuition for part-time students is $3000 in-state and $8000 out-of-state. On-campus room and board costs about $8000 annually; books and supplies run $1900.

Financial Aid

In a recent year, about 87% of current law students received some form of aid. The average annual amount of aid from all sources combined, including scholarships, loans, and work contracts, was $17,022; maximum, $21,622. Awards are based on need and merit. Required financial statement is the FAFSA. Check with the school for current application deadlines. First-year students are notified about their financial aid application at time of acceptance.

About the Law School

Southern University and A & M College Law Center was established in 1947 and is a public institution. The campus is in an urban area in Baton Rouge. The primary mission of the law school is to prepare students for the practice of law with specific emphasis upon minorities and the disadvantaged; the program of study is designed to give students a comprehensive knowledge of both the civil law and common law and knowledge of a lawyer's ethics and responsibility to society. Students have access to federal, state, county, city, and local agencies, courts, correctional facilities, law firms, and legal aid organi-

zations in the Baton Rouge area. Facilities of special interest to law students are the WESTLAW and LEXIS Laboratory, the Law Review, and the computer laboratory. Housing for students is convenient and ample. About 90% of the law school facilities are accessible to the physically disabled.

Calendar

The law school operates on a traditional semester basis. Courses for full-time students are offered days only and must be completed within 5 years. There is no part-time program. New full- and part-time students are admitted in the fall. There is a 6-week summer session. Transferable summer courses are offered.

Programs

The following joint degree may be earned: J.D./M.P.A. (Juris Doctor/Master of Public Administration).

Required

To earn the J.D., candidates must complete 96 total credits, of which 75 are for required courses. They must maintain a minimum GPA of 2.0 in the required courses. The following first-year courses are required of all students: Basic Civil Procedure, Civil Law Property, Constitutional Law I, Contracts, Criminal Law, Family Law, Legal Research, Legal Writing I and II, Obligations, and Torts I and II. Required upper-level courses consist of Advanced Legal Writing I and II, Agency and Partnership, Civil Procedure I and II, Commercial Papers, Conflict of Laws, Constitutional Law II, Corporations, Criminal Procedure, Evidence, Federal Jurisdiction and Procedure, Professional Responsibility, Sales and Leases, Security Devices, Successions and Donations, and Trial Advocacy. The required orientation program for first-year students is a 1- or 2-day program, with emphasis on analysis, reading comprehension, case briefing, and communication skills.

Electives

Administrative, Juvenile, Criminal, Elderly, Tax, and Domestic Law clinics are limited to third-year students who may earn 6 credit hours. Seminars are available in various subject areas for second- and

Phone: 225-771-5340
800-537-1135
Fax: 225-771-2121
E-mail: vwilkerson@sulc.edu
Web: www.sulc.edu

Contact

Velma Wilkerson, Admissions Coordinator, 225-771-5340 for general inquiries; Jerome Harris, Director of Financial Aid, 225-771-2141 for financial aid information.

LOUISIANA

third-year students. Individual student research projects are available for 1 credit hour under the supervision of a professor. Nationally recognized legal scholars are invited each semester to lecture on current issues. At least 3 lectures are scheduled during the school year. First-year students are required to participate in 1 monthly session and tutorial programs 2 times a week. The most widely taken electives are Civil Rights, Law Office Practice, and Workers' Compensation.

Graduation Requirements

In order to graduate, candidates must have a GPA of 2.0 and a residency requirement (6 semesters).

Organizations

Students edit the *Southern University Law Review* and the student newspaper, *The Public Defender*. Moot court competitions include the annual National Moot Court competition, the In-House Round Robin, and Thurgood Marshall competitions. Student organizations, local chapters of national associations, and campus organizations include Student Bar Association, Black Law Students Association, Student Trial Lawyers Association, Phi Alpha Delta, Delta Theta Phi, ABA-Law Student Division, Environmental Law Society, Women in Law, and Sports and Entertainment Legal Association.

Library

The law library contains 453,396 hardcopy volumes and 206,603 microform volume equivalents, and subscribes to 731 serial publications. Such on-line databases and networks as CALI, DIALOG, LegalTrac, LEXIS, LOIS, NEXIS, OCLC First Search, and WESTLAW are available to law students for research. Special library collections include civil rights and civil law collections, state and federal depositories, and South African Law Collection. The ratio of library volumes to faculty is 16,193 to 1 and to students is 1098 to 1. The ratio of seats in the library to students is 1 to 65.

Faculty

The law school has 28 full-time and 24 part-time faculty members, of whom 19 are women. According to AAUP standards for Category IIA institutions, faculty salaries are well below average. About 20% of full-time faculty have a graduate law degree in addition to the J.D.; about 15% of part-time faculty have one. The ratio of full-time students to full-time faculty in an average class is 15 to 1; in a clinic, 12 to 1. The law school has a regular program of bringing visiting professors and other distinguished lecturers and visitors to campus.

Students

About 48% of the student body are women; 69%, minorities; 68%, African American; 1%, Asian American; and 31%, Caucasian. The majority of students come from the South (96%). The average age of entering students is 27; age range is 22 to 54. About 60% of students enter directly from undergraduate school, 20% have a graduate degree, and 40% have worked full-time prior to entering law school. About 10% drop out after the first year for academic or personal reasons; 90% remain to receive a law degree.

Placement	
J.D.s awarded:	n/av
Services available through: a separate law school placement center	
Special features: web site information on job opportunities and newsletters from other campuses.	
Full-time job interviews:	7 employers
Summer job interviews:	17 employers
Placement by graduation:	74% of class
Placement within 9 months:	26% of class
Average starting salary:	n/av
Areas of placement:	
Private practice 2-10 attorneys	24%
Private practice 11-25 attorneys	2%
Private practice 26-50 attorneys	3%
Private practice 51-100 attorneys	5%
Judicial clerkships	21%
Unknown	14%
Government	10%
Business/industry	6%
Academic	5%
Public interest	2%
Solo practice	8%

Law School

3050 Wilshire Boulevard
Los Angeles, CA 90010-1106

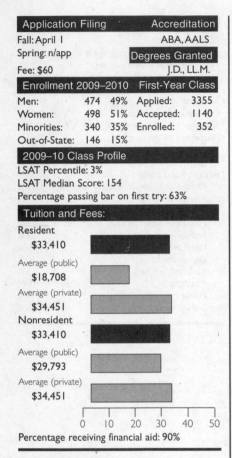

Application Filing	Accreditation
Fall: April 1	ABA, AALS
Spring: n/app	**Degrees Granted**
Fee: $60	J.D., LL.M.

Enrollment 2009–2010		First-Year Class	
Men:	474 49%	Applied:	3355
Women:	498 51%	Accepted:	1140
Minorities:	340 35%	Enrolled:	352
Out-of-State:	146 15%		

2009–10 Class Profile
LSAT Percentile: 3%
LSAT Median Score: 154
Percentage passing bar on first try: 63%

Tuition and Fees:

Resident
$33,410

Average (public)
$18,708

Average (private)
$34,451

Nonresident
$33,410

Average (public)
$29,793

Average (private)
$34,451

0 10 20 30 40 50

Percentage receiving financial aid: 90%

ADMISSIONS

In a recent year, 3355 applied, 1140 were accepted, and 352 enrolled. Thirty-two transfers enrolled. The median LSAT percentile of the most recent first-year class was 3; the median GPA was 3.29 on a scale of 4.0. Figures in the above capsule and in this profile are approximate.

Requirements
Applicants must have a bachelor's degree and take the LSAT. The most important admission factors include motivations, LSAT results, and GPA. No specific undergraduate courses are required. Candidates are not interviewed.

Procedure
Applicants should submit an application form, LSAT results, transcripts, a personal statement, a nonrefundable application fee of $60, and up to 3 letters of recommendation are strongly recommended. Notification of the admissions decision is on a rolling basis. The latest acceptable LSAT test date for fall entry is February, although June may be accepted. The law school uses the LSDAS. Check with the school for current application deadlines.

Special
The law school recruits minority and disadvantaged students by means of participation by admissions staff in minority recruitment programs at undergraduate campuses around the country, a Law Day program held at the law school for minority junior college and university students, admissions receptions on campus, public service announcements in print and broadcast media, scholarship programs, and programs for prospective students sponsored by minority student organizations at the law school. Requirements are not different for out-of-state students. Transfer students must have one year of credit, have a minimum GPA of 2, have attended an ABA-approved law school, and have a maximum of 43 transferable semester units; they must also submit a letter of good standing from that school's dean. Preadmissions courses consist of Introduction to Legal Writing: a Seminar for Pre-Law Students, a 4-week, noncredit course that provides a foundation in specialized legal writing skills.

Costs

Tuition and fees for the 2009-2010 academic year are approximately $33,410 for all full-time students. Tuition for part-time students is approximately $20,126 per year.

Financial Aid

In a recent year, about 90% of current law students received some form of aid. The average annual amount of aid from all sources combined, including scholarships, loans, and work contracts, was approximately $25,000; maximum, $45,000. Awards are based on need and merit. Required financial statements are the FAFSA and the school's financial aid application. Check with the school for the current application deadlines. Special funds for minority or disadvantaged students consist of approximately a dozen different scholarship funds, the most significant of which is the John J. Schumacher Minority Leadership Scholarship Program for outstanding academic and leadership potential. First-year students are notified about their financial aid application at within 2 weeks of acceptance.

About the Law School

Southwestern University Law School was established in 1911 and is a private institution. The 2-acre campus is in an urban area in Los Angeles. The primary mission of the law school is to produce, through full-time, part-time, traditional and non-traditional Juris Doctorate and Master of Laws programs, highly skilled graduates who are capable of integrating theory and practice to meet the challenges of the twenty-first century. Students have access to federal, state, county, city, and local agencies, courts, correctional facilities, law firms, and legal aid organizations in the Los Angeles area. plus all the resources of a major metropolitan center. Housing for students is not available on campus; however, apartments and homes are located nearby. About 99% of the law school facilities are accessible to the physically disabled.

Calendar

The law school operates on a traditional semester basis. Courses for full-time students are offered days only and with some evening electives available and must be completed within 5 years. For part-time students, courses are offered both day and evening and must be completed within 5 years. New full- and part-time students are admitted in the fall. There is an 8-week summer session. Transferable summer courses are offered.

Programs

In addition to the J.D., the law school offers the LL.M. in Entertainment and Media Law, and in General Studies.

Required
To earn the J.D., candidates must complete 87 total credits, of which 52 are for required courses. They must maintain a minimum GPA of 2.0 in the required courses. The following first-year courses are required of all students: an elective option, Civil Procedure I and II, Contracts I and II, Criminal Law, Legal Analysis, Writing and Skills I and II, Property, and Torts. Required upper-level courses consist of a seminar that satisfies a writing requirement, Business Associations, Constitutional Law I and II, Evidence, and Legal Profession. Simulation training is part of required courses such as Legal Analysis, Writing and Skills and electives such as Civil Pre-Trial Practice; Interviewing, Counseling and Negotiating; and Trial AdvocacyThe required orientation program for first-year students is a week-long program.

Electives
The Law School offers concentrations in corporate law, criminal law, entertain-

Phone: 213-738-6717
Fax: 213-383-1688
E-mail: *admissions@swlaw.edu*
Web: *www.swlaw.edu*

Contact

Admissions Director, 213-738-6717 for general inquiries; Financial Aid Director, 213-738-6719 for financial aid information.

ment law, environmental law, family law, intellectual property law, international law, juvenile law, labor law, litigation, media law, sports law, tax law, torts and insurance, and technology, innovation and commercialization. In addition, A Children's Rights Clinic, Immigration Rights Clinic, externships, and a simulated clinical experience are available through courses such as Legal Analysis, Writing and Skills; Interviewing, Counseling and Negotiation; and Trial Advocacy. Credit varies per experience (2 to 10 units). Seminars offered for 2 units require in-depth research, analysis, and writing. Titles encompass many areas of the law, including intellectual property, international law, and private and public sector administrative issues. Practical experience may be gained through more than 100 part- and full-time externships available in the judiciary; public interest law firms; federal, state, and local government offices; and entertainment industry settings. Two to ten units per externship placement may be earned on a credit/no credit basis. A limited number of judicial externships in Mexican and Argentine courts is also available through the summer program in Guatajuato, Mexico and Buenos Aires, Argentina, as well as legal organizations through the summer program in Vancouver, British Columbia, Canada. Paid faculty research assistant positions are available. Special lecture series include the Law Review Distinguished Lecture Series, Faculty Speakers Committee Lecture Series, Career Development Panels, Public Interest Law Speakers, Treusch Public Service Lecture, "Conversations with" Entertainment Law Series, and a variety of speakers presented by student organizations. The Entertainment Law Institute, Law Review, and Law Journal also sponsor scholarly symposia. Study-abroad programs featuring international and comparative law courses taught by school faculty and other international legal experts are offered in Vancouver, British Columbia, Canada; Buenos Aires, Argentina; London; and in Guatajuato, Mexico. The Academic Support Program is available for a selected number of entering students the summer prior to matriculation, and for interested students throughout the academic year. Southwestern has a Diversity Affairs Director to provide counseling and programming to students from admissions to graduation and beyond. Other programs offered for minority students include a Minority

Career Development seminar, other panel presentations by minority attorneys and judges, and job search skills reviews sponsored by the Placement Office in conjunction with minority bar and law student associations. A number of ethnic/minority law student organizations each have their own programming as well. A Diversity Day for prospective students provides information on admissions and financial aid processes, and the law school also hosts regional job fairs and alumni roundtables for BLSA, APALSA, LLSA and LGBT organizations, among others. The most widely taken electives are Copyright, Trial Advocacy, and Wills and Trusts.

Graduation Requirements

In order to graduate, candidates must have a GPA of 2.0 and have completed the upper-division writing requirement.

Organizations

Students edit the *Southwestern University Law Review*, the *Southwestern Journal of Law and Trade in the Americas*, a law journal devoted to the legal and economic issues of North, Central, and South America; the *Journal of International Media and Entertainment Law*, a joint publication with the ABA Forum on Communications Law; and the student newspaper, *The Commentator*. Moot court competitions include the National Telecommunications Moot Court Competition, Stetson International Environmental Law Moot Court Competition, and the Burton D. Wechsler First Amendment Moot Court Competition. A formal Trial Advocacy Honors Program fields several teams at competitions around the country. Teams also compete in the National Black Law Students Association's Frederick Douglass Moot Court, Interscholastic Client Counseling, and the Interscholastic Negotiation Competitions. Law student organizations, local chapters of national associations, and campus organizations include the Women's Law Association, Entertainment and Sports Law Society, International Law Society, Phi Alpha Delta Law Fraternity, American Association for Justice, National Lawyers Guild, OUTlaw, Media Law Forum, and Environmental Law Forum.

Library

The law library contains 483,433 hardcopy volumes and 63,061 microform volume equivalents, and subscribes to 4663 serial publications. Such on-line databases

Placement

J.D.s awarded:	258

Services available through: the school's placement center

Services: videotaped mock interviews conducted by alumni practitioners

Placement by graduation:	85% of class
Placement within 9 months:	97% of class
Average starting salary:	$52,000 to $140,000

Areas of placement:

Private practice 2-10 attorneys	26%
Private practice 11-25 attorneys	8%
Private practice 26-50 attorneys	7%
Private practice 51-100 attorneys	10%
Business/industry	15%
Government	14%
Unknown	10%
Judicial clerkships	5%
Public interest	4%
Academic	1%

and networks as CALI, LEXIS, LOIS, NEXIS, WESTLAW, Wilsonline Indexes, and HeinOnline, Index to Foreign Legal Periodicals, Index to Legal Periodicals, IndexMaster, Legal Scholarship Network, LLMC Digital, Marcive, Shepard's Online, Smart CILP, United Nations Treatises, and World Trade Law.net are available to law students for research. The ratio of library volumes to faculty is 8335 to 1 and to students is 497 to 1. The ratio of seats in the library to students is 1 to 2.

Faculty

The law school has 58 full-time and 33 part-time faculty members, of whom 32 are women. About 20% of full-time faculty have a graduate law degree in addition to the J.D. The ratio of full-time students to full-time faculty in an average class is 16 to 1. The law school has a regular program of bringing visiting professors and other distinguished lecturers and visitors to campus.

Students

About 51% of the student body are women; 35%, minorities; 5%, African American; 16%, Asian American; 12%, Hispanic; and 1%, Native American. The majority of students come from California (85%). The average age of entering students is 27; age range is 20 to 55. About 30% of students enter directly from undergraduate school, 12% have a graduate degree, and 35% have worked full-time prior to entering law school. About 8% drop out after the first year for academic or personal reasons; 80% remain to receive a law degree.

Stanford Law School

Crown Quadrangle,
559 Nathan Abbott Way
Stanford, CA 94305-8610

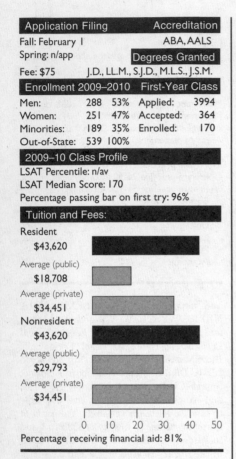

Application Filing		Accreditation	
Fall: February 1		ABA, AALS	
Spring: n/app		Degrees Granted	
Fee: $75		J.D., LL.M., S.J.D., M.L.S., J.S.M.	

Enrollment 2009–2010		First-Year Class	
Men:	288 53%	Applied:	3994
Women:	251 47%	Accepted:	364
Minorities:	189 35%	Enrolled:	170
Out-of-State:	539 100%		

2009–10 Class Profile
LSAT Percentile: n/av
LSAT Median Score: 170
Percentage passing bar on first try: 96%

Tuition and Fees:

Resident
$43,620

Average (public)
$18,708

Average (private)
$34,451

Nonresident
$43,620

Average (public)
$29,793

Average (private)
$34,451

Percentage receiving financial aid: 81%

ADMISSIONS

In the fall 2009 first-year class, 3994 applied, 364 were accepted, and 170 enrolled. Twelve transfers enrolled. The median GPA of the most recent first-year class was 3.87.

Requirements
Applicants must have a bachelor's degree and take the LSAT. No specific undergraduate courses are required. Candidates are not interviewed.

Procedure
The application deadline for fall entry is February 1. Applicants should submit an application form, LSAT results, transcripts, a personal statement, a nonrefundable application fee of $75, 2 letters of recommendation, and a statement of good standing from the undergraduate dean. Notification of the admissions decision is on a rolling basis. The latest acceptable LSAT test date for fall entry is December. The law school uses the LSDAS.

Special
The law school recruits minority and disadvantaged students by attending law forums and Law Days, and making individual school visits. Requirements are not different for out-of-state students. Transfer students must have one year of credit and have attended an ABA-approved law school.

Costs

Tuition and fees for the 2009-2010 academic year are $43,620 for all full-time students. On-campus room and board costs about $17,532 annually; books and supplies run $1815.

Financial Aid

About 81% of current law students receive some form of aid. The maximum annual amount of aid from all sources combined, including scholarships, loans, and work contracts, is $66,288. Awards are based on need. Required financial statements are the FAFSA and Need Access Form. The aid application deadline for fall entry is March 15. First-year students are notified about their financial aid application upon receipt of the Need Access and FAFSA analyses.

About the Law School

Stanford Law School was established in 1893 and is a private institution. The 6109-acre campus is in a suburban area 35 miles south of San Francisco. The primary mission of the law school is to be a national and world leader in the education of lawyers and in the expansion of legal knowledge through research with the ultimate aim of improving the legal orders of the domestic and global communities. Students have access to federal, state, county, city, and local agencies, courts, correctional facilities, law firms, and legal aid organizations in the Stanford area. Housing for students is guaranteed to all new students who apply for housing by a specified date and are willing to live anywhere on campus. Law students are given priority for Munger Residence Hall. All law school facilities are accessible to the physically disabled.

Calendar

The law school operates on a traditional semester basis. Courses for full-time students are offered days only and must be completed within 10 trimesters. There is no part-time program. New students are admitted in the fall. There is no summer session. Transferable summer courses are not offered.

Programs

In addition to the J.D., the law school offers the LL.M., S.J.D., M.L.S., and J.S.M. Students may take relevant courses in other programs and apply credit toward the J.D.; a maximum of 15 credits may be applied. The following joint degrees may be earned: J.D./M.A. (Juris Doctor/Master of Arts with Johns Hopkins University), J.D./M.B.A. (Juris Doctor/Master of Business Administration), J.D./M.P.A. (Juris Doctor/Master of Public Administration with Princeton University), J.D./M.S. (Juris Doctor/Master of Science), and J.D./Ph.D. (Juris Doctor/Master of Philosphy). The law school will consider requests for joint programs on an individually designed basis.

Required
To earn the J.D., candidates must complete 111 total credits, of which 29 are for required courses. The following first-year courses are required of all students: Civil Procedure, Constitutional Law, Contracts, Criminal Law, Federal Litigation, Legal Research and Writing, Property, and Torts. The required orientation program for first-year students is a 2-day program that includes introductions to policies, programs, and resources.

Electives
The Stanford Law School offers concentrations in corporate law, criminal law, entertainment law, environmental law, family law, intellectual property law, international law, juvenile law, labor law, litigation, maritime law, media law, securities law, sports law, tax law, and torts and insurance. In addition, the law school offers courses with clinical components from 2 to 12 units of credit in a variety of areas. A variety of seminars, worth 2 to 3 units, is offered to upper-level students each year. Externships, from 4 to 12 units of credit, are offered to upper-level students each year, typically in the Bay area. The law school offers 3 types of directed research comprising from 1 to 13

Phone: 650-723-4985
Fax: 650-723-0838
E-mail: admissions@law.stanford.edu
Web: law.stanford.edu

Contact
Office of Admissions, 650-723-4985 for general inquiries; Dewayne Barnes, Associate Director of Financial Aid, 650-723-9247 for financial aid information.

units of credit. This is an opportunity for students beyond the first-year program in law to research problems in any field of law. A wide variety of lecture series are sponsored by both the law school and its student organizations. The law school also offers foreign study options with a number of schools. The most widely taken electives are Evidence, Corporations, and Tax.

Graduation Requirements
In order to graduate, candidates must have completed the upper-division writing requirement and at least 1 advanced course that contains 1 or more units of ethics instruction, and a course comprising substantial instruction in professional skills.

Organizations
The primary law review is the *Stanford Law Review*. Students also edit the *Environmental Law Journal, Stanford Journal of Law, Business and Finance, Stanford Journal of Civil Rights and Civil Liberties,* and *Stanford Technology Law Review*. The Kirkwood Moot Court Competition is held in February each year. Law student organizations include Stanford Law Students Association. Local chapters of national associations include American Constitution Society and Federalist Society.

Library
The law library contains 484,986 hardcopy volumes and 71,806 microform volume equivalents. Such on-line databases and networks as CALI, CIS Universe, DIALOG, Infotrac, Legal-Trac, LEXIS, LOIS, NEXIS, OCLC First Search, RLIN, WESTLAW, Wilsonline Indexes, and NEXIS, plus extensive other sources via local and national networks are available to law students for research. Special library collections include U.S. government documents and California state documents. Recently, the library reclassified the Library of Congress titles and renovated the Reading Room. The ratio of library volumes to faculty is 9898 to 1 and to students is 900 to 1. The ratio of seats in the library to students is 1 to 1.

Faculty
The law school has 49 full-time faculty members, of whom 15 are women. According to AAUP standards for Category I institutions, faculty salaries are well above average. The ratio of full-time students to full-time faculty in an average class is 9 to 1. The law school has a regular program of bringing visiting professors and other distinguished lecturers and visitors to campus. There is a chapter of the Order of the Coif.

Students
About 47% of the student body are women; 35%, minorities; 9%, African American; 14%, Asian American; 10%, Hispanic; and 2%, Native American. The average age of entering students is 25; age range is 21 to 40. About 30% of students enter directly from undergraduate school and 25% have a graduate degree.

Placement

J.D.s awarded:	176
Services available through: a separate law school placement center	
Services: Externships are coordinated through the Director of Public Interest Programs	
Special features: counseling and advising students regarding job search, career decisions, and public service	
Full-time job interviews:	n/av
Summer job interviews:	n/av
Placement by graduation:	n/av
Placement within 9 months:	99% of class
Average starting salary:	n/av
Areas of placement:	
Private practice	61%
Judicial clerkships	23%
Public interest	6%
Business/industry	5%
Government	4%
Academic	1%

University at Buffalo Law School

309 O'Brian Hall
Buffalo, NY 14260

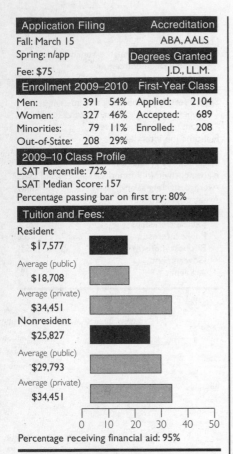

Application Filing	Accreditation
Fall: March 15	ABA, AALS
Spring: n/app	**Degrees Granted**
Fee: $75	J.D., LL.M.

Enrollment 2009–2010		First-Year Class	
Men:	391 54%	Applied:	2104
Women:	327 46%	Accepted:	689
Minorities:	79 11%	Enrolled:	208
Out-of-State:	208 29%		

2009–10 Class Profile
LSAT Percentile: 72%
LSAT Median Score: 157
Percentage passing bar on first try: 80%

Tuition and Fees:

Resident
$17,577

Average (public)
$18,708

Average (private)
$34,451

Nonresident
$25,827

Average (public)
$29,793

Average (private)
$34,451

0 10 20 30 40 50

Percentage receiving financial aid: 95%

ADMISSIONS

In the fall 2009 first-year class, 2104 applied, 689 were accepted, and 208 enrolled. Forty-one transfers enrolled. The median LSAT percentile of the most recent first-year class was 72; the median GPA was 3.52 on a scale of 4.0. The lowest LSAT percentile accepted was 26; the highest was 98.

Requirements
Applicants must have a bachelor's degree and take the LSAT. Minimum acceptable LSAT percentile is 44 and minimum acceptable GPA is 2.0 on a scale of 4.0. The most important admission factors include writing ability, LSAT results, and academic achievement. No specific undergraduate courses are required. Candidates are not interviewed.

Procedure
The application deadline for fall entry is March 15. Applicants should submit an application form, LSAT results, transcripts, a personal statement, TOEFL for international applicants, a nonrefundable application fee of $75, 2 letters of recommendation, and a resume. Notification of the admissions decision is as early as December. The latest acceptable LSAT test date for fall entry is February. The law school uses the LSDAS.

Special
The law school recruits minority and disadvantaged students through targeted recruitment efforts at colleges with significant minority student populations and participation in a tuition waiver program for EOP, HEOP, and SEEK students. Requirements are not different for out-of-state students. Transfer students must have one year of credit, have attended an ABA-approved law school, and have submitted 1 letter of reference from law professors, a letter of good standing from the initial law school, the first page of the LSDAS report, an official law school transcript, the law school application, and the $75 application fee.

Costs

Tuition and fees for the 2009-2010 academic year are $17,577 for full-time in-state students and $25,827 for out-of-state students. On-campus room and board costs about $12,113 annually; books and supplies run $1127.

Financial Aid

About 95% of current law students receive some form of aid. The average annual amount of aid from all sources combined, including scholarships, loans, and work contracts, is $20,932; maximum, $16,010. Awards are based on need and merit. Required financial statement is the FAFSA. The aid application deadline for fall entry is March 1. Special funds for minority or disadvantaged students include graduate tuition waivers based on participation in an EOP, HEOP, or SEEK program while an undergraduate. There is also a fellowship opportunity available to admitted applicants that have maintained an undergraduate grade point average of 3.0 or better and is either a member of an underrepresented minority or has overcome significant obstacles in the pursuit of their education. First-year students are notified about their financial aid application at time of acceptance.

About the Law School

State University of New York University at Buffalo Law School was established in 1887 and is a public institution. The 154-acre campus is in a suburban area 3 miles north of Buffalo in Amherst, New York. The primary mission of the law school is to provide an outstanding legal education through interdisciplinary teaching that emphasizes the role lawyers and the law play within the broader context of American Society while providing practice-ready attorneys. Students have access to federal, state, county, city, and local agencies, courts, correctional facilities, law firms, and legal aid organizations in the Buffalo area. Other resources include the University at Buffalo undergraduate and graduate schools and libraries. Facilities of special interest to law students include the nation's only fully functioning state court housed on a university campus. Housing for students is available in apartment-style on-campus housing, as well as ample graduate student housing. All law school facilities are accessible to the physically disabled.

Calendar

The law school operates on a 4-1-4 modified semester, other 3-1-3 basis. Courses for full-time students are offered both day and evening, with occasional evening classes, and must be completed within 5 years. There is no part-time program. New students are admitted in the fall. There is a 7-week summer session. Transferable summer courses are offered.

Programs

In addition to the J.D., the law school offers the LL.M. Students may take relevant courses in other programs and apply credit toward the J.D.; a maximum of 9 credits may be applied. The following joint degrees may be earned: J.D./M.A. (Juris Doctor/Master of Applied Economics), J.D./M.B.A. (Juris Doctor/Master of Business Administration), J.D./M.L.S (Juris Doctor/Master of Library Science), J.D./M.P.H. (Juris Doctor/Master of Public Health), J.D./M.S.W. (Juris Doctor/Master of Social Work), J.D./M.U.P. (Juris Doctor/Master of Urban Planning), J.D./Ph.D. (Juris Doctor/Doctor of Philosophy in selected disciplines), and J.D./Pharm.D. (Juris Doctor/Doctor of Pharmacy).

Required
To earn the J.D., candidates must complete 90 total credits, of which 34 are for required courses. The following first-year courses are required of all students: Civil Procedure, Constitutional Law, Contracts, Criminal law, Legal Profession and Eth-

Phone: 716-645-2907
Fax: 716-645-6676
E-mail: lwiley@buffalo.edu
Web: www.law.buffalo.edu

Contact
Lillie Wiley-Upshaw, Vice Dean, 716-645-2907 for general inquiries; Brezetta Stevenson, Financial Aid Coordinator, 716-645-7324 for financial aid information.

NEW YORK

ics, Property, Research and Writing (2 semesters), and Torts. Required upper-level courses consist of a seminar. The required orientation program for first-year students lasts 1 week and includes an introduction to faculty, administrators, and student organizations as well as an introductory course on legal methods, reasoning, argument, legal institutions, ethics and the profession.

Electives
The University at Buffalo Law School offers concentrations in corporate law, criminal law, environmental law, family law, intellectual property law, international law, litigation, tax law, health law, technology and intellectual property, affordable housing, and community. In addition, upper-division students may take clinical courses for 3 to 4 credit hours each semester for up to 4 semesters after the first year of law school. Topics include affordable housing; elder law; community economic development; securities law; mediation; environment and policy law; environment and development; and women, children and social justice. Upper-division students must take at least one 3-credit hour seminar. Numerous seminars are offered and students may enroll in multiple seminars. Externships are available in public interest, governmental, and international settings. Upper-division students may take individual research for 3 to 6 credit hours and may participate in any of several law school research centers. Field placements are associated with various courses including child welfare, criminal law, legislative externships, and judicial clerkships. Special lecture series include the Mitchell Lecture and Baldy Center Lecture Series. There are summer internships abroad with leading human rights organizations through the Buffalo Human Rights Center. There is also a semester long program entitled the University of Buffalo Law School's New York City Program in Finance and Law, which requires a student to live in New York City for one semester. Academic support is available for students in need with a full-time faculty member. Special interest group programs include the Buffalo Public Interest Law Program, Domestic Violence Task Force, and Prison Task Force. The most widely taken electives are Corporations, Evidence, and Federal Income Tax I.

Graduation Requirements
In order to graduate, candidates must have completed the upper-division writing requirement and 90 credit hours. Grades of A, A–, B+, B, B, or C must be earned in at least 80 hours. A 3 credit hour seminar is also required.

Organizations
Students edit the *Buffalo Law Review, Buffalo Human Rights Law Review, Buffalo Women's Law Journal, Buffalo Intellectual Property Law Journal, Buffalo Interest Law Journal*, and the newspaper, *The Opinion*. Other publications include the *New Criminal Law Review, Buffalo Human Rights Law Review*, and the *ABA Journal of Affordable Housing and Community Development Law*. Moot court competitions include the Desmond Intramural held in November, the Mugel National Tax Moot Court held in the spring, and the Herbert Wechsler National Criminal Moot Court. Other competitions include Jessup International Moot Court Competition, First Year Moot Court Competition, Buffalo-Niagara Invitational Mock Trial Tournament, and Frederick Douglas Moot Court. Law student organizations, local chapters of national associations, and campus organizations include the Asian American Law Students Association, Black Law Students Association, Latin American Law Students Association, Sports and Entertainment Law Society, Alternative Dispute Resolution Group, Buffalo Criminal Law Society, Association of Trial Lawyers of America, Phi Alpha Delta, and American Civil Liberties Union.

Library
The law library contains 296,539 hardcopy volumes and 285,936 microform volume equivalents, and subscribes to 6627 serial publications. Such on-line databases and networks as CALI, Dow-Jones, Infotrac, LEXIS, LOIS, Mathew Bender, NEXIS, OCLC First Search, WESTLAW, Wilsonline Indexes, LRS (New York Legislation), and 100 web-based databases accessible on the library network are available to law students for research. Special library collections include a U.S. government document depository, the Morris L. Cohen Rare Book collection, the papers of John Lord O'Brian, Berman Human Rights Collections, and a substantial United Nations documents collection. Recently, the library added a reading room for law students only outfitted with new furniture. The ratio of library volumes to faculty is 4942 to 1 and to students is 413 to 1. The ratio of seats in the library to students is 1 to 1.

Placement

J.D.s awarded:	247

Services available through: a separate law school placement center and the university placement center

Services: alumni mentoring program, alumni career panels, training and skills-building programs that provide networking opportunities

Special features: an employment bulletin that is sent free to graduates, a unique IL mentorship program, required individual career counseling for ILS, and 3LS, robust programming and podcast seriles

Full-time job interviews:	25 employers
Summer job interviews:	37 employers
Placement by graduation:	77% of class
Placement within 9 months:	96% of class
Average starting salary:	$22,000 to $165,000

Areas of placement:

Private practice 2-10 attorneys	24%
Private practice 11-25 attorneys	5%
Private practice 26-50 attorneys	9%
Private practice 51-100 attorneys	6%
Business/industry	11%
Government	8%
Public interest	7%
Judicial clerkships	5%
Solo practice; firm size unknown,	5%
Academic	4%
Military	3%

Faculty
The law school has 60 full-time and 123 part-time faculty members, of whom 71 are women. According to AAUP standards for Category I institutions, faculty salaries are average. About 26% of full-time faculty have a graduate law degree in addition to the J.D.; about 4% of part-time faculty have one. The ratio of full-time students to full-time faculty in an average class is 12 to 1; in a clinic, 10 to 1. The law school has a regular program of bringing visiting professors and other distinguished lecturers and visitors to campus.

Students
About 46% of the student body are women; 11%, minorities; 5%, African American; 6%, Asian American; 4%, Hispanic; 1%, Native American; and 13%, race/ethnicity unknown. The majority of students come from New York (71%). The average age of entering students is 25; age range is 20 to 58. About 35% of students enter directly from undergraduate school, 31% have a graduate degree, and 39% have worked full-time prior to entering law school. About 2% drop out after the first year for academic or personal reasons; 96% remain to receive a law degree.

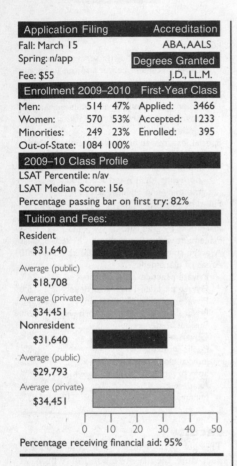

Application Filing		Accreditation
Fall: March 15		ABA, AALS
Spring: n/app		Degrees Granted
Fee: $55		J.D., LL.M.

Enrollment 2009–2010		First-Year Class	
Men:	514 47%	Applied:	3466
Women:	570 53%	Accepted:	1233
Minorities:	249 23%	Enrolled:	395
Out-of-State:	1084 100%		

2009–10 Class Profile

LSAT Percentile: n/av
LSAT Median Score: 156
Percentage passing bar on first try: 82%

Tuition and Fees:

Resident
$31,640

Average (public)
$18,708

Average (private)
$34,451

Nonresident
$31,640

Average (public)
$29,793

Average (private)
$34,451

0   10   20   30   40   50

Percentage receiving financial aid: 95%

ADMISSIONS

In the fall 2009 first-year class, 3466 applied, 1233 were accepted, and 395 enrolled. Twelve transfers enrolled. The median GPA of the most recent first-year class was 3.46.

Requirements

Applicants must have a bachelor's degree and take the LSAT. No specific undergraduate courses are required. Candidates are not interviewed.

Procedure

The application deadline for fall entry is March 15. Applicants should submit an application form, LSAT results, transcripts, a personal statement, (TOEFL if necessary), a nonrefundable application fee of $55, 1 is required; 3 recommended letters of recommendation, and a personal statement and resume (optional). Notification of the admissions decision is on a rolling basis. The latest acceptable LSAT test date for fall entry is February. The law school uses the LSDAS.

Special

The law school recruits minority and disadvantaged students by means of CRS mailings, CLEO, law school forums, college campus visits, to HBCU, Doorways Scholars Reception, and Minority Youth Prelaw Conference. Requirements are not different for out-of-state students. Transfer students must have one year of credit, have attended an ABA-approved law school, and submit a complete official transcript, register for the LSDAS, and provide official documentation from the dean of the applicants law school confirming current standing and law school rank.

Costs

Tuition and fees for the 2009-2010 academic year are $31,640 for all full-time students. Tuition for part-time students is $21,920 per year.

Financial Aid

About 95% of current law students receive some form of aid. The average annual amount of aid from all sources combined, including scholarships, loans, and work contracts, is $18,959; maximum, $53,346. Awards are based on need and merit. Required financial statement is the FAFSA. The aid application deadline for fall entry is open. Special funds for minority or disadvantaged students include Stetson diversity scholarships and matching CLEO scholarships. First-year students are notified about their financial aid application after the confirmation deposit is paid.

About the Law School

Stetson University Stetson University College of Law was established in 1900 and is a private institution. The 21-acre campus is in a suburban area. The main campus is 20 miles SW of Tampa the satellite campus is in Tampa. The primary mission of the law school is to prepare students to competently, professionally, ethically, and compassionately engage in the practice of law, serve in related professions, and pursue public service. Students have access to federal, state, county, city, and local agencies, courts, correctional facilities, law firms, and legal aid organizations in the Gulfport area. Facilities of special interest to law students include 7 courtrooms. Housing for students is available in residence halls, 2-bedroom apartments, and school-owned houses; also, housing options are available in the community.

All law school facilities are accessible to the physically disabled.

Calendar

The law school operates on a traditional semester basis. Courses for full-time students are offered both day and evening and must be completed within 2<1/2>to 3 years. For part-time students, courses are offered evenings only; however, part-time students may take electives during the day and evening and must be completed within 4 years. New full-time students are admitted in the fall and spring; part-time, fall. There is a summer session. Transferable summer courses are offered.

Programs

In addition to the J.D., the law school offers the LL.M. Students may take relevant courses in other programs and apply credit toward the J.D.; a maximum of 12 credits may be applied. The following joint degrees may be earned: J.D./M.B.A. (Juris Doctor/Master of Business Administration), J.D./M.D. (Juris Doctor/Doctor of Medicine), and J.D./M.P.H. (Juris Doctor/Master of Public Health).

Required

To earn the J.D., candidates must complete 88 total credits, of which 52 are for required courses. They must maintain a minimum GPA of 2.25 in the required courses. The following first-year courses are required of all students: Agency and Unincorporated Organizations, Civil Procedure, Contracts I and II, Criminal Law, Real Property I and II, Research and Writing I and II, and Torts. Required upper-level courses consist of a scholary writing requirement, administrative law requirement, Code area requirement, Constitutional Law, Evidence, Professional Responsibility, and Skills area requirement. The required orientation program for first-year students is a 3-day program that introduces the students to the three C's of professionalism-character, competence, and commitment. The competence (or academic portion) is led by full-time faculty members. The orientation includes pro bono activities and character development activities.

Electives

Students must take 18 credits in their area of concentration. The Stetson University

Phone: 727-562-7802
877-LAW STET
Fax: 727-343-0136
E-mail: *zuppo@law.stetson.edu*
Web: *www.law.stetson.edu*

Contact
Laura Zuppo, Executive Director of Admissions, 727-562-7802 for general inquiries and for financial aid information.

J.D.s awarded: 352

FLORIDA

College of Law offers concentrations in international law, litigation, and advocacy; elder law; and higher education law and policy. In addition, clinic programs, available to third-year students, include the Civil Poverty Clinic, Elder Consumer Protection Clinic, Labor Law Clinic, Local Government Clinic, Prosecution Clinic, and Public Defender Clinic. Most clinics are for 5 credit hours. Many seminars for second- and third-year students are offered each year. Internships with federal and state court judges (trial, appellate, and supreme court) are available for upper-level students for 4 credit hours or 12 hours for the supreme court. Practicum programs are available with state and federal agencies. There is a summer internship program in Washington, D.C. Individual research projects may be arranged for 1 or 2 credit hours. Inns of Court program, featuring a prominent speaker, is offered. Other programs are sponsored by faculty, student organizations, and the Office of Career Development. Second- and third-year students may participate in study-abroad programs offered through Stetson and other law schools. Stetson sponsors summer-abroad programs in Granada, Spain; Tianjin, China; Buenos, Argentina; and the Hague, The Netherlands. There is also a winter intercession program in the Cayman Islands and a spring break travel abroad program. Individual tutors are available for students. Stetson has a comprehensive Academic Success Program. Minority programs include the Southern Regional Black Law Students Association, Host for annual Academic Retreat, Doorways Scholars Reception, and Minority Youth Prelaw conference. Stetson is also a CLEO sponsor. Special interest group programs include an honors program for top students, Black Law Students Association, Student Bar Association, Ambassador program, HBA, AALSA, SALSA, and LAMBDA. The most widely taken electives are Trial Advocacy, Alternative Dispute Resolution, and Criminal Procedure.

Graduation Requirements
In order to graduate, candidates must have a GPA of 2.25, have completed the upper-division writing requirement, and have completed 20 hours of public service.

Organizations
Students edit the *Stetson Law Review*, the peer-edited journals *Journal of Inter-* *national Aging Law and Policy*, *Journal of Wildlife and Policy*, and the student newspaper *The Brief*. Annually, students compete in 16 to 18 competitions, including the National Moot Court, Willem C. Vis International Commercial Arbitration Moot, and the Jessup International Moot Court competitions. Other competitions include state, regional and national mock trial competitions; regional and national client counseling competitions; regional and national mediation competitions; and regional and national negotiation competitions. Law student organizations, local chapters of national associations, and campus organizations include the Elder Law Society, Environment Law Society, International Law Society, Phi Alpha Delta, Phi Delta Phi, Business Law Society, Student Bar Association, ABA-Law Student Division, and Black Law Students Association.

Library
The law library contains 420,000 hardcopy volumes and 53,670 microform volume equivalents, and subscribes to 2607 serial publications. Such on-line databases and networks as CALI, CIS Universe, DIALOG, Infotrac, Legal-Trac, LEXIS, LOIS, Mathew Bender, NEXIS, OCLC First Search, WESTLAW, BNA Antitrust and Trade Regulation Report, BNA Criminal Law Reporter, BNA Family Law Report, BNA Labor and Employment Law Libray, Sage the Annals of the American Academy of Political and Social Science, Value Line Research and Historial Reports, and Sage Journal of Sport and Social Issues are available to law students for research. Special library collections include a depository for selected U.S. government publications and Nuremburg Trials historial archival collection. Recently, the library added a new courtroom seminar room in the Tampa library, 24/7 student swipe card access, and vending machines for drinks and snacks. The ratio of library volumes to faculty is 8077 to 1 and to students is 387 to 1. The ratio of seats in the library to students is 1 to 2.

Faculty
The law school has 52 full-time and 36 part-time faculty members, of whom 32 are women. According to AAUP standards for Category IIA institutions, faculty salaries are above average. About 35% of full-time faculty have a graduate law degree in

Placement
Services available through: a separate law school placement center
Services: on-campus interviewing programs in the fall and spring semesters
Special features: resourse room for student use, including computers for job searches on LexisNexis and WESTLAW, a fax machine, and a laser printer for resume and cover letter production; open 24/7

Full-time job interviews:	68 employers
Summer job interviews:	68 employers
Placement by graduation:	n/av
Placement within 9 months:	96% of class
Average starting salary:	$42,000 to $110,000

Areas of placement:

Private practice 2-10 attorneys	18%
Private practice 11-25 attorneys	12%
Private practice 26-50 attorneys	7%
Private practice 51-100 attorneys	4%
private practice 101+ attorneys and solo practice	11%
Government	21%
Business/industry	13%
Public interest	7%
Judicial clerkships	5%
Military	2%
Academic	1%

addition to the J.D.; about 5% of part-time faculty have one. The ratio of full-time students to full-time faculty in an average class is 18 to 1; in a clinic, 10 to 1. The law school has a regular program of bringing visiting professors and other distinguished lecturers and visitors to campus.

Students
About 53% of the student body are women; 23%, minorities; 7%, African American; 3%, Asian American; 9%, Hispanic; and 1%, Native American. The average age of entering students is 24; age range is 19 to 55. About 3% drop out after the first year for academic or personal reasons; 97% remain to receive a law degree.

SUFFOLK UNIVERSITY

Law School

120 Tremont Street
Boston, MA 02108-4977

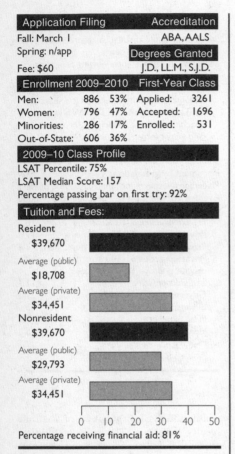

Application Filing		Accreditation
Fall: March 1		ABA, AALS
Spring: n/app		**Degrees Granted**
Fee: $60		J.D., LL.M., S.J.D.

Enrollment 2009–2010		First-Year Class	
Men:	886 53%	Applied:	3261
Women:	796 47%	Accepted:	1696
Minorities:	286 17%	Enrolled:	531
Out-of-State:	606 36%		

2009–10 Class Profile
LSAT Percentile: 75%
LSAT Median Score: 157
Percentage passing bar on first try: 92%

Tuition and Fees:

Resident
$39,670

Average (public)
$18,708

Average (private)
$34,451

Nonresident
$39,670

Average (public)
$29,793

Average (private)
$34,451

Percentage receiving financial aid: 81%

ADMISSIONS
In the fall 2009 first-year class, 3261 applied, 1696 were accepted, and 531 enrolled. Fourteen transfers enrolled. The median LSAT percentile of the most recent first-year class was 75; the median GPA was 3.3 on a scale of 4.0.

Requirements
Applicants must have a bachelor's degree and take the LSAT. The most important admission factors include academic achievement, GPA, and LSAT results. No specific undergraduate courses are required. Candidates are interviewed.

Procedure
The application deadline for fall entry is March 1. Applicants should submit an application form, LSAT results, transcripts, a personal statement, TOEFL, a nonrefundable application fee of $60, and 1 letter of recommendation. Accepted students must pay $200 tuition deposit by April 15; a second deposit of $300 is

due June 1. Notification of the admissions decision is on a rolling basis. The latest acceptable LSAT test date for fall entry is February. The law school uses the LSDAS.

Special
The law school recruits minority and disadvantaged students by means of an admissions committee, which gives consideration to students who have overcome economic and social disadvantages or have been subjected to discrimination of any form. Requirements are not different for out-of-state students. Transfer students must have one year of credit, have a minimum GPA of 3, have attended an ABA-approved law school, and be in good academic standing. The application must be completed by early June. The dean of each previous law school must provide a letter of good standing and a final transcript.

Costs
Tution and fees for the 2009/10 acedemic year are $36,670 for all full-time students. Tution for all part-time students is $29,754. Books and supplies run $900.

Financial Aid
About 81% of current law students receive some form of aid. The average annual amount of aid from all sources combined, including scholarships, loans, and work contracts, is $39,606; maximum, $61,452. Awards are based on need and merit. Required financial statements are the FAFSA, Need Access form, and a federal income tax return. The aid application deadline for fall entry is March 1. Special funds for minority or disadvantaged students are available through a number of financial assistance programs. First-year students are notified about their financial aid application on a rolling basis, beginning March 1st, for accepted students.

About the Law School
Suffolk University Law School was established in 1906 and is a private institution. The campus is in an urban area in downtown Boston on the Freedom Trail. The primary mission of the law school is to give capable men and women the opportunity to study law regardless of background or circumstances. Now one of the largest law schools in the country, Suffolk University Law School has remained

true to its mission to provide excellent education and training for a diverse student body. Students have access to federal, state, county, city, and local agencies, courts, correctional facilities, law firms, and legal aid organizations in the Boston area. Facilities of special interest to law students Include the Center for International Legal Studies, Juvenile Justice Center, and Rappaport Center for Law and Public Services. Housing for students is not available on campus, but assistance for obtaining housing in the area is available. All law school facilities are accessible to the physically disabled.

Calendar
The law school operates on a traditional semester basis. Courses for full-time students are offered both day and evening and must be completed within 3 years. For part-time students, courses are offered both day and evening and must be completed within 4 years. New full- and part-time students are admitted in the fall. There is a 10-week summer session. Transferable summer courses are offered.

Programs
In addition to the J.D., the law school offers the LL.M. and S.J.D. The following joint degrees may be earned: J.D./M.B.A. (Juris Doctor/Master of Business Administration), J.D./M.P.A. (Juris Doctor/Master of Public Administration), J.D./M.S.C.J. (Juris Doctor/Master of Criminal Justice), J.D./M.S.F. (Juris Doctor/Master of Science in Finance), and J.D./M.S.I.E. (Juris Doctor/Master of Science in International Economics).

Required
To earn the J.D., candidates must complete 84 total credits, of which 43 are for required courses. They must maintain a minimum GPA of 2.0 in the required courses. The following first-year courses are required of all students: Civil Procedure, Constitutional Law, Contracts, Criminal Law, Legal Practice Skills, Property, and Torts. Required upper-level courses consist of Base Menu courses, Professional Responsibility, and Skills Menu courses. Clinical courses are not required, but are strongly recommended. The required orientation program for first-year students includes an introduction to classmates, professors, and law school administra-

Phone: 617-573-8144
Fax: 617-523-1367
Web: www.law.suffolk.edu

Contact
Gail Ellis, Dean of Admissions, 617-573-8144 for general inquiries; Kristi Jovell, Director of Financial Aid, 617-573-8147 for financial aid information.

MASSACHUSETTS

tors in various receptions and programs. New students also meet with upper-class students and are trained on the school's computer systems. They participate in a program aimed at preparing them on what to expect during their first year of law school and are introduced to case briefing, outlining, and time management.

Electives
Students must take 18 to 25 credits in their area of concentration. The Law School offers concentrations in intellectual property law, international law, labor law, litigation, health and biomedical law, business law, and financial services. In addition, clinic programs include the Suffolk Defenders, Suffolk Prosecutors, and Battered Women's Clinic. Seminars are available in such areas as advanced evidence, family law practice, and jurisprudence. The Civil and Judicial Internship Program allows students to gain 2 to 5 credits per semester for supervised legal work performed for government or non-profit agencies, private law firms and companies, and state and federal courts. Many students act as research assistants for individual faculty members. Work-study programs are available. The Donahue Lecture Series presents 3 to 4 national scholars who lecture on various topics in legal education. Students may participate in study-abroad programs. A summer study-abroad program is available at the University of Lund in Lund, Sweden. Tutorial programs are available through the Academic Support Program and the Peer Mentoring Program. There are multicultural groups such as the Asian Pacific American Law Students Association, Black Law Students Association, Hispanic Law Students Association, Native American Law Students Association, and South Asian Law Students Association. There are 46 student groups. The most widely taken electives are Evidence, Family Law, and Corporations.

Graduation Requirements
In order to graduate, candidates must have a GPA of 2.0 and have completed the upper-division writing requirement.

Organizations
The primary law review is the *Suffolk University Law Review*. Other law reviews include the *Suffolk Transnational Law*

Review; the *Journal of High Technology*, an on-line publication; the *Journal of Health and Biomedical Law*; and the *Journal of Trial and Appellate Advocacy*. The Student newspaper is the *Dicta*. Moot court competitions include the Justice Tom C. Clark Appellate Advocacy Competition, the Walter H. McLaughlin Appellate Advocacy Competition, 2nd Year Day/3rd Year Mock Trial Competition, 3rd Year Day/4th Year Evening Mock Trial Competition, Burton D. Wechsler First Amendment Moot Court Competition, and National Civil Trial Competition. Law students organizations include the International Law Society, Student Bar Association, Phi Alpha Delta, Phi Delta Phi, the National Lawyers Guild, National Women's Law Student Association, Shelter Legal Services, ISAIL, and SPILG.

Library
The law library contains 378,478 hard-copy volumes and 160,122 microform volume equivalents, and subscribes to 219,186 serial publications. Such on-line databases and networks as CALI, CIS Universe, DIALOG, Infotrac, Legal-Trac, LEXIS, LOIS, NEXIS, OCLC First Search, WESTLAW, Wilsonline Indexes, and membership in the New England Law Library Consortium and BNA are available to law students for research. Special library collections include a collection of biographical material on lawyers and judges, famous trials, law and literature, environmental law, criminal law, intellectual property law, biomedical law, and trial practice materials. Recently, the library added upgrades to students computer labs and created on-line tutorials for students. The ratio of library volumes to faculty is 4113 to 1 and to students is 225 to 1. The ratio of seats in the library to students is 1 to 1.

Faculty
The law school has 92 full-time and 133 part-time faculty members, of whom 68 are women. According to AAUP standards for Category IIA institutions, faculty salaries are well above average. About 38% of full-time faculty have a graduate law degree in addition to the J.D.; about 20% of part-time faculty have one. The ratio of full-time students to full-time faculty in an average class is 17 to 1; in a clinic, 10 to 1. The law school has a regular program of bringing visiting professors and other distinguished lecturers and visitors to campus.

Placement

J.D.s awarded:	476

Services available through: a separate law school placement center
Services: professional directories, notices of employment, judicial clerkship information, library facilities for employment information, and panel discussions
Special features: the fall on-campus Recruitment Program, to which the Career Services Office invites law firms, corporations, legal services offices, and state and federal agencies to interview students for employment. The school is also a member of the Massachusetts Law School Consortium and the Northeast Law School Consortium, which sponsors other recruitment and career-related programs..

Full-time job interviews:	22 employers
Summer job interviews:	47 employers
Placement by graduation:	53% of class
Placement within 9 months:	86% of class
Average starting salary:	$44,000 to $95,000

Areas of placement:
Private practice 2-10 attorneys	20%
Private practice 11-25 attorneys	5%
Private practice 26-50 attorneys	3%
Private practice 51-100 attorneys	11%
Business/industry	28%
Government	13%
Judicial clerkships	11%
Academic	3%
Public interest	2%
Military	1%
Unknown	1%

Students
About 47% of the student body are women; 17%, minorities; 3%, African American; 9%, Asian American; 4%, Hispanic; and 8%, mixed race or unknown. The majority of students come from the Northeast (80%). The average age of entering students is 25; age range is 21 to 61. About 26% of students enter directly from undergraduate school and 10% have a graduate degree. About 7% drop out after the first year for academic or personal reasons; 93% remain to receive a law degree.

College of Law

Office of Admissions and Financial Aid,
Suite 340
Syracuse, NY 13244-1030

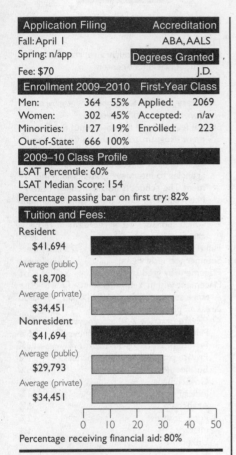

Application Filing		Accreditation
Fall: April 1		ABA, AALS
Spring: n/app		
Fee: $70		**Degrees Granted**
		J.D.

Enrollment 2009–2010		First-Year Class	
Men:	364 55%	Applied:	2069
Women:	302 45%	Accepted:	n/av
Minorities:	127 19%	Enrolled:	223
Out-of-State:	666 100%		

2009–10 Class Profile

LSAT Percentile: 60%
LSAT Median Score: 154
Percentage passing bar on first try: 82%

Tuition and Fees:

Resident
$41,694

Average (public)
$18,708

Average (private)
$34,451

Nonresident
$41,694

Average (public)
$29,793

Average (private)
$34,451

0 10 20 30 40 50

Percentage receiving financial aid: 80%

ADMISSIONS

In a recent year, 2069 applied and 223 enrolled. The median LSAT percentile of the most recent first-year class was 60; the median GPA was 3.29 on a scale of 4.0. Figures in the above capsule and in this profile are approximate.

Requirements

Applicants must have a bachelor's degree and take the LSAT. The most important admission factors include GPA, LSAT results, and academic achievement. No specific undergraduate courses are required. Candidates are not interviewed.

Procedure

Applicants should submit an application form, LSAT results, transcripts, a personal statement, a nonrefundable application fee of $70, 2 letters of recommendation, and a resumé. Notification of the admissions decision is on a rolling basis from January to March. The latest acceptable LSAT test date for fall entry is February.

The law school uses the LSDAS. Check with the school for current application deadlines.

Special

The law school recruits minority and disadvantaged students by means of an in-house Legal Education Opportunity Program, students of color law forums, the CLEO program, and by application review. Requirements are not different for out-of-state students. Transfer students must have one year of credit, have a minimum GPA of 3, and have attended an ABA-approved law school.

Costs

Tuition and fees for the 2009-2010 academic year are approximately $41,694 for all full-time students. On-campus room and board costs about $11,270 annually; books and supplies run about $1250.

Financial Aid

In a recent year, about 80% of current law students received some form of aid. Awards are based on need and merit. Required financial statements are the FAFSA and the College of Law application form, tax returns, and W2s. Special funds for minority or disadvantaged students include need-based tuition grants. First-year students are notified about their financial aid application at time of acceptance. Check with the school for current application deadlines.

About the Law School

Syracuse University College of Law was established in 1895 and is a private institution. The 200-acre campus is in an urban area 3 miles east of Syracuse. The primary mission of the law school is guided by the philosophy that the best way to educate lawyers to practice in today's world is to engage them in a process of interdisciplinary learning while teaching them to apply what they learn in the classroom to real legal issues, problems, and clients. Students have access to federal, state, county, city, and local agencies, courts, correctional facilities, law firms, and legal aid organizations in the Syracuse area. Facilities of special interest to law students . Housing for students is available both on and off campus. On-campus hous-

ing options include apartment complexes for law and graduate students. About 87% of the law school facilities are accessible to the physically disabled.

Calendar

The law school operates on a traditional semester basis. Courses for full-time students are offered days only and must be completed within 4<½>years. For part-time students, courses are offered days only and must be completed within 4<½>years. New full- and part-time students are admitted in the fall. There is a 7-week summer session. Transferable summer courses are offered.

Programs

Students may take relevant courses in other programs and apply credit toward the J.D.; a maximum of 6 credits may be applied. The following joint degrees may be earned: J.D./M.A. (Juris Doctor/ Master of Arts in international relations), J.D./M.B.A. (Juris Doctor/Master of Business Administration), J.D./M.P.A. (Juris Doctor/Master of Public Administration), J.D./M.S. (Juris Doctor/Master of Science in communications, environmenta), and J.D./M.S. or Ph.D. (Juris Doctor/Master of Science or Doctor of Philosophy in envi).

Required

To earn the J.D., candidates must complete 87 total credits, of which 40 are for required courses. They must maintain a minimum GPA of 2.2 in the required courses. The following first-year courses are required of all students: Civil Procedure, Constitutional Law I, Contracts, Criminal Law, Legal Communication and Research, Legislation and Policy, Property, and Torts. Required upper-level courses consist of a writing requirement, Constitutional Law II, Professional Responsibility, and Third-semester research and writing course. The required orientation program for first-year students is a 5-day program that includes academic sessions, book discussions, alumni and students panels, professionalism programs, and social activities.

Electives

Students must take 15 to 20 credits in their area of concentration. The College of Law offers concentrations in corporate

Contact

Admissions Office, 315-443-1962 for general inquiries; Director of Financial Aid, 315-443-1963 for financial aid information.

NEW YORK

law, environmental law, family law, intellectual property law, international law, labor law, litigation, tax law, and technology commercialization law, law and economics, national security and counterterrorism, Indigenous law, and disability law. In addition, second- and third-year students may take clinics for 12 credits in Community Development Law, Disabilities Rights, Children's Rights and Family Law, and 6 credits in the Low Income Taxpayer Clinic, the Securities Arbitration/Consumer Law Clinic, and the Elder Law Clinic. Second- and third-year students may also earn 1 to 2 credits per semester for seminars. A study-abroad summer program is available in London. Tutorial programs are offered to first-year students. Minority programs include the Legal Education Opportunity Program.

Graduation Requirements
In order to graduate, candidates must have a GPA of 2.2 and have completed the upper-division writing requirement.

Organizations

Law students edit the *Syracuse Law Review, Journal of International Law and Commerce, The Labor Lawyer, The Law & Technology Journal*, and *The Digest*. Annually, students compete in the Mackenzie Lewis Competition, Lionel O. Grossman Trial Competition, and Jessup Moot Court competition. Law student organizations include Black Law Students Association, Phi Alpha Delta, Asian-Pacific American Law Students Association, Law Student Senate, Syracuse Public Interest Network, and Latin American Law Students Association.

Library

The law library contains 218,058 hardcopy volumes and 255,018 microform volume equivalents, and subscribes to 3300 serial publications. Such on-line databases and networks as CALI, CIS Universe, DIALOG, Infotrac, Legal-Trac, LEXIS, LOIS, NEXIS, OCLC First Search, WESTLAW, Wilsonline Indexes, and BNA, HeinOnline, Heins Foreign and International Law Resources, Heins U.S. Congressional Documents, LexisNexis Congressional, LLMC Digital, U.S. Serial Set Digital Collection, and Index to Foreign Legal Periodicals are available to law students for research. Special library collections include legal history, legal education, New York state law, tax law and policy, Law of Indigenous Peoples, trial practice skills, and law technology and management. The law library is depository for U.S. Government documents. Recently, the library was refurbished with updated lighting, chairs and carpet. Facilities include 8 group study rooms, 2 computer clusters, an information commons, and numerous spaces for group and individual study. The law library is wireless, and service points are expanded through the law library website, which offers remote access to electronic research databases, library information, and service request forms, 24 hours a day. The ratio of library volumes to faculty is 3696 to 1 and to students is 327 to 1. The ratio of seats in the library to students is 1 to 2.

Faculty

The law school has 59 full-time and 54 part-time faculty members, of whom 34 are women. According to AAUP standards for Category I institutions, faculty salaries are below average. About 25% of full-time faculty have a graduate law degree in addition to the J.D. The ratio of full-time students to full-time faculty in an average class is 21 to 1; in a clinic, 10 to 1. The law school has a regular program of bringing visiting professors and other distinguished lecturers and visitors to campus. There is a chapter of the Order of the Coif.

Students

About 45% of the student body are women; 19%, minorities; 4%, African American; 10%, Asian American; 3%, Hispanic; 1%, Native American; and 4%, Foreign nationals. The average age of entering students is 24; age range is 21 to 47. About 7% of students have a graduate degree.

Placement

J.D.s awarded:	206
Services available through: a separate law school placement center	
Services: workshop on networking, career speaker series, identifying clerkship opportunities	
Special features: individual counseling for law students.	
Full-time job interviews:	n/av
Summer job interviews:	n/av
Placement by graduation:	n/av
Placement within 9 months:	90% of class
Average starting salary:	$36,700 to $113,000
Areas of placement:	
Private practice 2-10 attorneys	20%
Private practice 11-25 attorneys	6%
Private practice 26-50 attorneys	5%
Private practice 51-100 attorneys	6%
Private practice firm 100+	10%
Business/industry	16%
Judicial clerkships	15%
Government	13%
Public interest	4%
Academic	3%
Military	2%

James E. Beasley School of Law

1719 N. Broad Street
Philadelphia, PA 19122

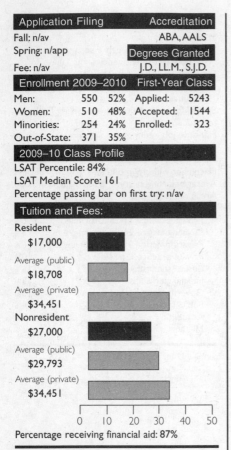

Application Filing		Accreditation	
Fall: n/av		ABA, AALS	
Spring: n/app		Degrees Granted	
Fee: n/av		J.D., LL.M., S.J.D.	

Enrollment 2009–2010		First-Year Class	
Men:	550 52%	Applied:	5243
Women:	510 48%	Accepted:	1544
Minorities:	254 24%	Enrolled:	323
Out-of-State:	371 35%		

2009–10 Class Profile
LSAT Percentile: 84%
LSAT Median Score: 161
Percentage passing bar on first try: n/av

Tuition and Fees:

Resident
$17,000

Average (public)
$18,708

Average (private)
$34,451

Nonresident
$27,000

Average (public)
$29,793

Average (private)
$34,451

0 10 20 30 40 50

Percentage receiving financial aid: 87%

ADMISSIONS

In the fall 2009 first-year class, 5243 applied, 1544 were accepted, and 323 enrolled. Figures in the above capsule and in this profile are approximate. Eight transfers enrolled. The median LSAT percentile of the most recent first-year class was 84; the median GPA was 3.35 on a scale of 4.0. The lowest LSAT percentile accepted was 20; the highest was 99.

Requirements
Applicants must have a bachelor's degree and take the LSAT. Minimum acceptable GPA is 2.35 on a scale of 4.0. No specific undergraduate courses are required. Candidates are not interviewed.

Procedure
Applicants should submit an application form, LSAT results, transcripts, TOEFL (when English is not a student's primary language), 3 recommended letters of recommendation, and a personal statement. Notification of the admissions decision is on a rolling basis. The latest acceptable LSAT test date for fall entry is February.

Check with the school for current application deadlines. The law school uses the LSDAS.

Special
The law school recruits minority and disadvantaged students through visits to colleges and cities with large minority populations; faculty and student contact with minority applicants; special programs sponsored by minority student organizations in conjunction with the Law School Annual Open House; and the LSAC Candidate Referral Service. The Sp.A.C.E. program, the law school's discretionary admissions process, seeks to identify applicants whose GPA and LSAT scores may not fully represent their abilities and potential, including minority applicants and economically disadvantaged applicants. Requirements are not different for out-of-state students. Transfer students must have one year of credit, have attended an ABA-approved law school, and have attended an ABA/AALS member law school and rank in the top 20% of their class after completion of 1 year. Availability of seats is also a factor in admission.

Costs

Tuition and fees for the 2009-2010 academic year are $17,000 for full-time in-state students and $27,000 for out-of-state students. Tuition for part-time students is $13,000 in-state and $21,000 out-of-state. On-campus room and board costs about $11,000 annually; books and supplies run $1600.

Financial Aid

In a recent year, about 87% of current law students received some form of aid. The average annual amount of aid from all sources combined, including scholarships, loans, and work contracts, was $21,958; maximum, $43,382. Awards may be based on merit only, need only, or a combination of need and merit. Required financial statement is the FAFSA. Check with the school for current application deadlines. Special funds for minority or disadvantaged students include a limited number of partial tuition scholarships that are awarded to students admitted through the Sp.A.C.E. program (the discretionary admissions process) who have outstanding performance records and demonstrated financial need. First-year students are notified about their financial aid application after admission, and when their financial aid forms are received and processed.

About the Law School

Temple University James E. Beasley School of Law was established in 1895 and is a public institution. The 87-acre campus is in an urban area 2 miles north of downtown Philadelphia. The law school is committed to excellence in teaching, scholarship, and service and believes that legal education must provide practical and theoretical knowledge. The school seeks to maintain and strengthen its tradition of accessibility and diversity to pursue the goals of excellence in higher education and equal justice under the law. Students have access to federal, state, county, city, and local agencies, courts, correctional facilities, law firms, and legal aid organizations in the Philadelphia area. The Temple Legal Aid Office is housed in the law school's main building. Facilities of special interest to law students include Barrack Hall, with student services offices, classrooms, and student organization offices; the law school complex consists of Klein Hall with a large moot court room, 2 trial courtrooms; an 11-level open-stack law library with 2 multilevel reading rooms; wired and wireless network access throughout the library and law school buildings; 750 study carrels, table seats; and Shusterman Hall, a legal conference center. Housing for students on campus is apartment-style; many students choose off-campus housing. All law school facilities are accessible to the physically disabled.

Calendar

The law school operates on a traditional semester basis. Courses for full-time students are offered days only and must be completed within 3 years. For part-time students, courses are offered both day and evening and must be completed within 4 years. New full- and part-time students are admitted in the fall. There is a 6 to 8-week summer session. Transferable summer courses are offered.

Programs

In addition to the J.D., the law school offers the LL.M. and S.J.D. Students may take relevant courses in other programs and apply credit toward the J.D.; a maximum of 12 credits may be applied. The following joint degrees may be earned: J.D./LL.M. (Juris Doctor/Master of Laws in taxation), J.D./LL.M. (Juris Doctor/Master of Laws in transnational law), and J.D./M.B.A. (Juris Doctor/ Master of Business Administration).

Phone: 215-204-5949
800-560-1428
Fax: 215-204-1185
E-mail: lawadmis@temple.edu
Web: www.temple.edu/lawschool

Contact

Admissions Staff, 215-204-8925 or 800-560-1428 for general inquiries; Financial Aid Office, 215-204-8943 or 800-560-1428 for financial aid information.

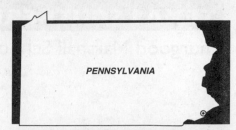

PENNSYLVANIA

Required

To earn the J.D., candidates must complete 87 total credits, of which 40 are for required courses. They must maintain a minimum GPA of 2.0 in the required courses. The following first-year courses are required of all students: Civil Procedure I, Constitutional Law, Contracts I and II, Criminal Law I, Legal Decision Making, Legal Writing and Research, Property, and Torts. Required upper-level courses consist of 2 writing requirements and Professional Responsibility. The school offers, but does not require, participation in an extensive selection of clinical opportunities.The required orientation program for first-year students consists of a 5-day program that provides an overview of academic requirements, faculty regulations, university and law school services, financial aid, general placement information, and social activities.

Electives

The James E. Beasley School of Law offers concentrations in corporate law, criminal law, environmental law, family law, international law, juvenile law, litigation, securities law, tax law, torts and insurance, trial advocacy, public interest law, technology law, intellectual property law, and constitutional and civil rights law. In addition, extensive clinics worth 3 or 4 credits per semester, are offered to third and fourth year students in the areas of civil litigation, criminal litigation, transactional work, and mediation. There is an extensive number of writing seminar courses, each of which is worth 3 credits per semester. All students are required to take 2 upper-level writing courses. Three writing seminars include Race & Ethnicity, Constitutional Law and Foreign Policy, and the Law of Electronic Commerce. Special lecture series include Dean's Invitational Forums, Honorable Clifford Scott Green Lecture, Herbert H. Kolsby Lecture, Friel-Scanlan Lecture, and Institute for International and Comparative Law lecture series. Summer sessions, worth from 2 to 6 credits, are available in Rome, Italy; Athens, Greece; and Tel Aviv, Israel. A full semester abroad is offered in Tokyo, Japan; Beijing, China; and Cork, Ireland. Students also have the option of designing an individualized study abroad program at law school throughout the world. There is a faculty mentoring program. Special interest group programs include the Pub-

lic Interest Scholars Program. The most widely taken electives are Evidence, Business Associations, and Taxation.

Graduation Requirements

In order to graduate, candidates must have a GPA of 2.0, have completed the upper-division writing requirement, and Professional Responsibility.

Organizations

Students edit the *Temple Law Review, Temple International and Comparative Law Journal, Temple Environmental Law and Technology Journal, Temple Journal of Science, Technology, and Environmental Law,* and the newspaper *Class Action.* Moot court competitions include the I. Herman Stern and Samuel J. Polsky Moot Court competitions, held annually at the school; students also attend other competitions throughout the country. Outside competitions include the Jessup International, ABA National Negotiation, National Invitational Tournament of Champions, National Trial Competition, National Association of Criminal Defense Lawyers, and American Trial Lawyers Association Competition. More than 30 different student organizations flourish at the law school. There are local chapters of the Black Law Students Association, Moot Court, and National Lawyers Guild.

Library

The law library contains 573,568 hardcopy volumes and 179,200 microform volume equivalents, and subscribes to 3048 serial publications. Such on-line databases and networks as CALI, CIS Universe, DIALOG, Dow-Jones, Infotrac, Legal-Trac, LEXIS, LOIS, Mathew Bender, NEXIS, OCLC First Search, RLIN, WESTLAW, Wilsonline Indexes, and HeinOnline, PA Code Online, CCH Tax Online, EAHorney, Gale Yellowbooks, Berkeley Online Journals, BNA Online, and WestPac are available to law students for research. Special library collections include the Anglophonic collection, African collection, Rawle history collection, Ellsberg Watergate collection, Temple Trial collection, U.S. government depository and depository for briefs and records for Pennsylvania. Recently, the library installed a reference desk, innovative circulation acquisition and cataloging system, renovated administrative offices, and made structural changes

Placement

J.D.s awarded:	n/av
Services available through: a separate law school placement center	
Full-time job interviews:	61 employers
Summer job interviews:	85 employers
Placement by graduation:	70% of class
Placement within 9 months:	93% of class
Average starting salary:	$30,000 to $160,000
Areas of placement:	
Private practice 2-10 attorneys	13%
Private practice 11-25 attorneys	8%
Private practice 26-50 attorneys	4%
Private practice 51-100 attorneys	4%
Private practice 101+ attorneys	17%
Government	14%
Judicial clerkships	9%
Public interest	7%
Unknown	4%
Academic	2%
Business/industry	17%

to improve acoustics and lighting. The ratio of library volumes to faculty is 9721 to 1 and to students is 549 to 1.

Faculty

The law school has 59 full-time and 212 part-time faculty members, of whom 81 are women. According to AAUP standards for Category I institutions, faculty salaries are average. About 29% of full-time faculty have a graduate law degree in addition to the J.D. The ratio of full-time students to full-time faculty in an average class is 17 to 1. The law school has a regular program of bringing visiting professors and other distinguished lecturers and visitors to campus.

Students

About 48% of the student body are women; 24%, minorities; 8%, African American; 11%, Asian American; 4%, Hispanic; and 4%, Native American. The majority of students come from Pennsylvania (65%). The average age of entering students is 26; age range is 19 to 52. About 26% of students enter directly from undergraduate school, 16% have a graduate degree, and 74% have worked full-time prior to entering law school. About 3% drop out after the first year for academic or personal reasons; 97% remain to receive a law degree.

Thurgood Marshall School of Law

3100 Cleburne Avenue
Houston, TX 77004

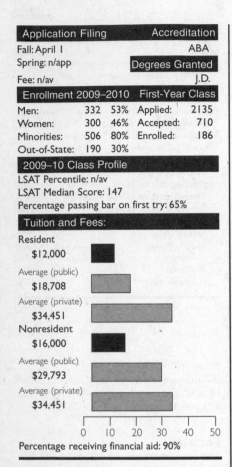

Application Filing	Accreditation
Fall: April 1	ABA
Spring: n/app	

	Degrees Granted
Fee: n/av	J.D.

Enrollment 2009–2010		First-Year Class	
Men:	332 53%	Applied:	2135
Women:	300 46%	Accepted:	710
Minorities:	506 80%	Enrolled:	186
Out-of-State:	190 30%		

2009–10 Class Profile
LSAT Percentile: n/av
LSAT Median Score: 147
Percentage passing bar on first try: 65%

Tuition and Fees:

Resident
$12,000

Average (public)
$18,708

Average (private)
$34,451

Nonresident
$16,000

Average (public)
$29,793

Average (private)
$34,451

0   10   20   30   40   50

Percentage receiving financial aid: 90%

ADMISSIONS

In the fall 2009 first-year class, 2135 applied, 710 were accepted, and 186 enrolled. Figures in the above capsule and in this profile are approximate. One transfer enrolled. The median GPA of the most recent first-year class was 2.91.

Requirements

Applicants must have a bachelor's degree and take the LSAT. The most important admission factors include LSAT results, GPA, and motivations. No specific undergraduate courses are required. Candidates are not interviewed.

Procedure

Applicants should submit an application form, LSAT results, a personal statement, a nonrefundable application fee, and 2 letters of recommendation. Notification of the admissions decision is between February and May (majority). The latest acceptable LSAT test date for fall entry is February. Check with the school for current application deadlines. The law school uses the LSDAS.

Special

The law school recruits minority and disadvantaged students through the Office of Admissions' Candidate Referral Service program and college campus visits. The majority of students are members of minority groups. Requirements are not different for out-of-state students. Transfer students must have attended an ABA-approved law school and have been academically successful at the first school of attendance.

Costs

Tuition and fees for the 2009-2010 academic year are $12,000 for full-time in-state students and $16,000 for out-of-state students. On-campus room and board costs about $7000 annually; books and supplies run $1900.

Financial Aid

In a recent year, about 90% of current law students received some form of aid. The average annual amount of aid from all sources combined, including scholarships, loans, and work contracts, was $20,500; maximum, $23,725. Awards are based on need and merit. Required financial statement is the FAFSA. Check with the school for current application deadlines. First-year students are notified about their financial aid application after the financial aid forms are processed and before enrollment if the application was submitted before the deadline.

About the Law School

Texas Southern University Thurgood Marshall School of Law was established in 1947 and is a public institution. The 6-acre campus is in an urban area 7 miles south of downtown Houston. The primary mission of the law school is in keeping with its designation by the Texas Legislature as a special purpose institution for urban programming, to meet not only the needs of students in general, but of minority and disadvantaged students as well. Students have access to federal, state, county, city, and local agencies, courts, correctional facilities, law firms, and legal aid organizations in the Houston area. There are also adjunct faculty in certain areas of specialty and 2 writing-skills specialists. There is a strong clinical program and a very competitive moot court program. Facilities of special interest to law students include several computer rooms offering terminals for on-line legal research as well as for off-line student use. Housing for students consists of a privately managed campus apartment community, for which law students receive priority consideration. All law school facilities are accessible to the physically disabled.

Calendar

The law school operates on a traditional semester basis. Courses for full-time students are offered days only and must be completed within 4 years. There is no part-time program. New students are admitted in the fall. There is a 9-week summer session. Transferable summer courses are offered.

Programs

Students may take relevant courses in other programs and apply credit toward the J.D.; a maximum of 6 credits may be applied. The following joint degrees may be earned: J.D./M.B.A. (Juris Doctor/Master of Business Administration) and J.D./M.P.A. (Juris Doctor/Master of Public Administration).

Required

To earn the J.D., candidates must complete 90 total credits, of which 70 are for required courses. They must maintain a minimum GPA of 2.0 in the required courses. The following first-year courses are required of all students: Civil Procedure, Contracts I and II, Criminal Law, Lawyering Process/Legal Writing I and II, Property I and II, and Torts I and II. Required upper-level courses consist of a writing seminar, Appellate Litigation, Basic Federal Income Taxation, Business Associations, Commercial Law, Constitution Law, Consumer Rights, Criminal Procedure, Evidence, Federal Jurisdiction and Procedure, Professional Responsibility, Texas Practice, Trial Simulation, and Wills and Trusts. The required orientation program for first-year students consists of a 1-week introduction and lectures on skills.

Phone: 713-313-7114
Fax: 713-313-1049
E-mail: cgardner@tmslaw.tsu.edu
Web: www.tsulaw.edu

Contact

Carolyn Gardner, Admissions Officer, 713-313-7114 for general inquiries; Karen Percival, Financial Aid Counselor, 713-313-7243 for financial aid information.

TEXAS

Electives

The Thurgood Marshall School of Law offers concentrations in litigation and tax law. In addition, clinics include criminal law, administrative law, and civil law. Seminars include criminal trial practice, writing, and First Amendment. Internships are available through the clinics offered, including a judicial internship with federal and state judges. Research programs allow for independent research and thesis research. A special lecture series, the Quodlibet, is a faculty- and student-sponsored program on current legal issues that are debated by faculty. Students may participate in study-abroad programs sponsored by other ABA-approved law schools. Each first-year section is assigned a student tutor who reviews substantive materials, discusses hypotheticals, and provides study help for each professor's class. The Legal Education Advancement Program (LEAP) is a 6-week summer program to develop oral and written legal analysis skills. Minority students are offered the third-year Mentor Program in which students are assigned alumni mentors in the third year through the bar examination. Academic counseling on course selection and personal goals is available. The most widely taken electives are The most widely taken electives are Estate Planning, Legal Clinics, and Oil and Gas Law.

Graduation Requirements

In order to graduate, candidates must have a GPA of 2.0 and have completed the upper-division writing requirement.

Organizations

The primary law review is the *Thurgood Marshall Law Review*. The student magazine is *The Solicitor*. The James M. Douglas Board of Advocates sponsors numerous moot court and mock trial programs. Law student organizations include the Student Bar Association, Black Law Students Association, and Chicano Law Students Association. There are local chapters of Asian Pacific American Law Students Association, Phi Alpha Delta, and Phi Delta Phi.

Library

The law library contains 251,722 hardcopy volumes and 62,907 microform volume equivalents, and subscribes to 465 serial publications. Such on-line databases and networks as CALI, CIS Universe, Infotrac, Legal-Trac, LEXIS, LOIS, Mathew Bender, OCLC First Search, WESTLAW, Legal-Trac, and 19th Century are available to law students for research. Special library collections include the Dominion Reports, federal government depositories, and civil rights. The ratio of library volumes to faculty is 7403 to 1 and to students is 398 to 1. The ratio of seats in the library to students is 1 to 3.

Faculty

The law school has 34 full-time and 19 part-time faculty members, of whom 14 are women. About 39% of full-time faculty have a graduate law degree in addition to the J.D. The ratio of full-time students to full-time faculty in an average class is 60 to 1; in a clinic, 10 to 1.

Students

About 46% of the student body are women; 80%, minorities; 49%, African American; 7%, Asian American; 26%, Hispanic; and 17%, Caucasian, 18%; other 1%. The majority of students come from Texas (70%). The average age of entering students is 27; age range is 20 to 35. About 60% of students enter directly from undergraduate school, 10% have a graduate degree, and 40% have worked full-time prior to entering law school. About 35% drop out after the first year for academic or personal reasons; 65% remain to receive a law degree.

Placement

J.D.s awarded:	140
Services available through: a separate law school placement center	
Services: participation in numerous job fairs in and out of state.	
Special features: Attorneys address students about legal career opportunities and participate in interview role-playing. Resumes are also individually critiqued. In addition, mock interview seminars are conducted, as well as workshops in preparation for summer legal internships.	
Full-time job interviews:	n/av
Summer job interviews:	28 employers
Placement by graduation:	72% of class
Placement within 9 months:	72% of class
Average starting salary:	$47,000
Areas of placement:	
Private practice 2-10 attorneys	88%
Government	7%
Business/industry	4%
Public interest	2%

TEXAS TECH UNIVERSITY

School of Law

1802 Hartford Avenue
Lubbock, TX 79409

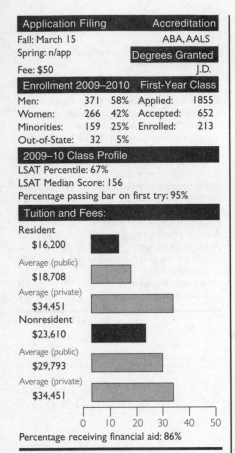

Application Filing		Accreditation
Fall: March 15		ABA, AALS
Spring: n/app		**Degrees Granted**
Fee: $50		J.D.

Enrollment 2009–2010		First-Year Class	
Men:	371 58%	Applied:	1855
Women:	266 42%	Accepted:	652
Minorities:	159 25%	Enrolled:	213
Out-of-State:	32 5%		

2009–10 Class Profile
LSAT Percentile: 67%
LSAT Median Score: 156
Percentage passing bar on first try: 95%

Tuition and Fees:

Resident
$16,200

Average (public)
$18,708

Average (private)
$34,451

Nonresident
$23,610

Average (public)
$29,793

Average (private)
$34,451

(scale: 0 10 20 30 40 50)

Percentage receiving financial aid: 86%

ADMISSIONS

In the fall 2009 first-year class, 1855 applied, 652 were accepted, and 213 enrolled. Ten transfers enrolled. The median LSAT percentile of the most recent first-year class was 67; the median GPA was 3.43 on a scale of 4.0. The lowest LSAT percentile accepted was 15; the highest was 95.

Requirements

Applicants must have a bachelor's degree and take the LSAT. The most important admission factors include LSAT results, GPA, and life experience. No specific undergraduate courses are required. Candidates are interviewed.

Procedure

The application deadline for fall entry is March 15. Applicants should submit an application form, LSAT results, transcripts, a personal statement, TOEFL, if necessary, a nonrefundable application fee of $50, 2 letters of recommendation,

and a resumé. Notification of the admissions decision is begins in November. The latest acceptable LSAT test date for fall entry is December. The law school uses the LSDAS.

Special

The law school recruits minority and disadvantaged students by encouraging campus visitation by minority faculty and students and recruiting at many universities. Requirements are not different for out-of-state students. Transfer students must have one year of credit, have attended an ABA-approved law school, have ranked in the upper 25% of the first-year class, and be in good standing.

Costs

Tuition and fees for the 2009-2010 academic year are $16,200 for full-time in-state students and $23,610 for out-of-state students. On-campus room and board costs about $8110 annually; books and supplies run $1000.

Financial Aid

About 86% of current law students receive some form of aid. The average annual amount of aid from all sources combined, including scholarships, loans, and work contracts, is $24,398; maximum, $37,121. Awards are based on need and merit. Required financial statement is the FAFSA. The aid application deadline for fall entry is April 15 (priority date); spring entry, October 1 (priority date); and summer entry, March 1 (priority date). Special funds for minority or disadvantaged students includes private scholarships. First-year students are notified about their financial aid application in March.

About the Law School

Texas Tech University School of Law was established in 1967 and is a public institution. The 1839-acre campus is in an urban area in Lubbock. The primary mission of the law school is to educate and train individuals for the ethical practice of law in the 21st century; to engage in productive, effective scholarship both within our academic community and within the larger academic community throughout our state and nation; and to render public service. Students have access to federal, state, county, city, and local agencies,

courts, correctional facilities, law firms, and legal aid organizations in the Lubbock area. A medical school/teaching hospital is nearby. Housing for students is available on-campus, as well as numerous rental properties close to the law school and throughout the city. All law school facilities are accessible to the physically disabled.

Calendar

The law school operates on a traditional semester basis. Courses for full-time students are offered days only and must be completed within 3 years. There is no part-time program. New students are admitted in the fall. There is a 2-5 week-week summer session. Transferable summer courses are offered.

Programs

Students may take relevant courses in other programs and apply credit toward the J.D.; a maximum of 12 hours credits may be applied. The following joint degrees may be earned: J.D./M.B.A. (Juris Doctor/Master of Business Administration), J.D./M.D. (Juris Doctor/Doctor of Medicine), J.D./M.P.A. (Juris Doctor/Master of Public Administration), J.D./M.S. (Juris Doctor/Master of Science in agricultural and applied economics), J.D./M.S.A.C. (Juris Doctor/Master of Accounting), J.D./M.S.B.T. (Juris Doctor/Master of Science in Biotechnology), J.D./M.S.E. (Juris Doctor/Master of Science in Engineering and in Entomology), J.D./M.S.E.T. (Juris Doctor/Master of Science in Environmental Toxicology), J.D./M.S.H.T.S. (Juris Doctor/Master of Science in Horticulture and Turfgrass Science), J.D./M.S.P.F.P. (Juris Doctor/Master of Science in Personal Financial Planning), and J.D./M.S.S.S. (Juris Doctor/Master of Science in Soil) and J.D./M.S.C.S.(Juris Doctor/Master of Science in Crop Science).

Required

To earn the J.D., candidates must complete 90 total credits, of which 55 are for required courses. They must maintain a minimum GPA of 2.0 in the required courses. The following first-year courses are required of all students: Civil Procedure, Constitutional Law, Contracts, Criminal Law, Legal Practice I and II, Property, and Torts. Required upper-level courses consist of Business Entities,

TEXAS

Phone: 806-742-3990, ext. 273
Fax: 806-742-4617
E-mail: donna.williams@ttu.edu
Web: www.law.ttu.edu

Contact
Admissions Assistant, 806-742-3990, ext. 273 for general inquiries; Donna Williams, Admissions Counselor, 806-742-3985 for financial aid information.

Commercial Law, Criminal Procedure, Evidence, Income Taxation, Professional Responsibility, and Wills and Trusts. The required orientation program for first-year students is 3 1/2 days. The program introduces students to professionalism and to basic legal skills, ethics, and analysis.

Electives
The School of Law offers concentrations in corporate law, criminal law, environmental law, intellectual property law, international law, litigation, securities law, and tax law. The School of Law also has certificate programs in Business Law, Health Law, and Law and Science. Third-year students may take clinics including Low Income Tax (2 credits), Civil Litigation (4 credits), and Criminal Justice (4 credits). Second- and third-year students, who have completed prerequisites, may take seminar courses. A number of externships are available to second- and third-year students for credit. Independent research programs are available for advanced students and in conjunction with the 3 Centers of Excellence. There are various special lecture series including the Sandra Day O'Connor Lecture Series. There is a Summer Law Institute in Guanajuato, Mexico and an exchange program in Lyon, France and Melbourne, Australia. There is an Academic Success Program available for students needing tutorial help. Student organizations regularly sponsor programs for their members and the larger community. There are more than 50 special interest student groups that sponsor programs. The most widely taken electives are Texas Pretrial Procedure, Texas Trial and Appellate, and Family Law.

Graduation Requirements
In order to graduate, candidates must have a GPA of 2.0 and have completed the upper-division writing requirement.

Organizations
Students edit the *Texas Tech Law Review, Texas Tech Journal of Texas Administrative Law Journal, The Texas Bank Lawyer, Estate Planning and Community Property Journal* and *Texas Tech Lawyer Alumni Magazine*. Moot court competitions include the ABA National Appellate Advocacy Competition, National Moot Court Competition, and Philip C. Jessup International Law Moot Court Compe-

tition. Other competitions include the TYLA National Trial Competition, AAJ National Student Trial Advocacy Competition, and ABA Negotiation Competition. Law student organizations, local chapters of national associations, and campus organizations include Texas Tech Student Bar Association, Board of Barristers, Student Public Interest Initiative, Women's Caucus, Black Law Students Association, Volunteer Law Students Association, Delta Theta Phi, Phi Alpha Delta, and Phi Delta Phi.

Library
The law library contains 331,191 hardcopy volumes and 675,175 microform volume equivalents, and subscribes to 3194 serial publications. Such on-line databases and networks as CALI, CIS Universe, LEXIS, LOIS, Mathew Bender, NEXIS, OCLC First Search, WESTLAW, Wilsonline Indexes, RIA Checkpoint, Hein Online, BNA, Serial Set, UN Treaty Collection, LLMC, LSN, CCH Business, and CCH Legal Pro are available to law students for research. Special library collections include a federal government documents depository. Recently, the library installed Worldcat Local Catalog Interface and a fire suppression system in the server room, and upgraded the security system and the server and storage network. The ratio of library volumes to faculty is 5401 to 1 and to students is 297 to 1. The ratio of seats in the library to students is 1 to 3.

Faculty
The law school has 38 full-time and 24 part-time faculty members, of whom 19 are women. According to AAUP standards for Category I institutions, faculty salaries are well below average. About 49% of full-time faculty have a graduate law degree in addition to the J.D.; about 11% of part-time faculty have one. The ratio of full-time students to full-time faculty in an average class is 15 to 1; in a clinic, 11 to 1. The law school has a regular program of bringing visiting professors and other distinguished lecturers and visitors to campus. There is a chapter of the Order of the Coif; 17 faculty and 591 graduates are members.

Students
About 42% of the student body are women; 25%, minorities; 4%, African

Placement
J.D.s awarded:	206

Services available through: a separate law school placement center
Special features: participation in 4 off-campus recruitment programs in conjunction with various law schools.

Full-time job interviews:	5 employers
Summer job interviews:	56 employers
Placement by graduation:	40% of class
Placement within 9 months:	92% of class
Average starting salary:	$25,000 to $160,000

Areas of placement:
Private practice 2-10 attorneys	49%
Private practice 11-25 attorneys	15%
Private practice 26-50 attorneys	12%
Private practice 51-100 attorneys	2%
Government	17%
Business/industry	17%
Judicial clerkships	5%
Military	4%
Public interest	3%
Academic	1%

American; 4%, Asian American; 15%, Hispanic; and 1%, Native American. The majority of students come from Texas (95%). The average age of entering students is 24; age range is 21 to 49. About 5% drop out after the first year for academic or personal reasons; 89% remain to receive a law degree.

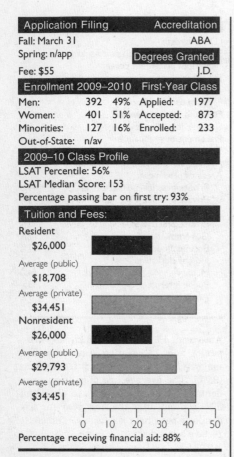

Application Filing		Accreditation
Fall: March 31		ABA
Spring: n/app		**Degrees Granted**
Fee: $55		J.D.

Enrollment 2009–2010		First-Year Class	
Men:	392 49%	Applied:	1977
Women:	401 51%	Accepted:	873
Minorities:	127 16%	Enrolled:	233
Out-of-State:	n/av		

2009–10 Class Profile
LSAT Percentile: 56%
LSAT Median Score: 153
Percentage passing bar on first try: 93%

Tuition and Fees:

Resident
$26,000
Average (public)
$18,708
Average (private)
$34,451
Nonresident
$26,000
Average (public)
$29,793
Average (private)
$34,451

Percentage receiving financial aid: 88%

ADMISSIONS

In the fall 2009 first-year class, 1977 applied, 873 were accepted, and 233 enrolled. Thirteen transfers enrolled. The median LSAT percentile of the most recent first-year class was 56; the median GPA was 3.17 on a scale of 4.33. The lowest LSAT percentile accepted was 33; the highest was 86.

Requirements
Applicants must have a bachelor's degree and take the LSAT. The most important admission factors include GPA, academic achievement, writing ability, and general background. No specific undergraduate courses are required. Candidates are not interviewed.

Procedure
The application deadline for fall entry is March 31. Applicants should submit an application form, LSAT results, transcripts, a personal statement, a nonrefundable application fee of $55, 2 letters of recommendation, and a resume. Notification of the admissions decision is on a rolling basis. The latest acceptable LSAT test date for fall entry is February. The law school uses the LSDAS.

Special
The law school recruits minority and disadvantaged students through personal meetings, on-campus events, LSAC forums, and phone and e-mail contact. Requirements are not different for out-of-state students. Transfer students must have one year of credit, have a minimum GPA of 3.0, have attended an ABA-approved law school, and provide a letter of good standing from the home law school, the application fee, a professor's recommendation, and a letter of request to transfer; a maximum of 30 hours can be transferred (pass/fail credits transfer).

Costs

Tuition and fees for the 2009-2010 academic year are $26,000 for all full-time students. Tuition for part-time students is $18,650 per year. Books and supplies run $1740.

Financial Aid

About 88% of current law students receive some form of aid. The maximum annual amount of aid from all sources combined, including scholarships, loans, and work contracts, is $41,675. Awards are based on need and merit. Required financial statement is the FAFSA. The aid application deadline for fall entry is May 15. Special funds for minority or disadvantaged students include diversity scholarship awards. First-year students are notified about their financial aid application at the time of acceptance or time of file completion, whichever is later.

About the Law School

Texas Wesleyan University School of Law was established in 1989 and is a private institution. The campus is in an urban area in downtown Fort Worth. The primary mission of the law school is to provide legal education to a diverse student body, recognizing the need for both knowledge and skills, as well as professionalism. Students have access to federal, state, county, city, and local agencies, courts, correctional facilities, law firms, and legal aid organizations in the Fort Worth area. There are numerous corporate headquarters throught out Dallas Fort Worth. Housing for students is at the main campus (a 10-minute drive); there are a variety of apartment and home options for rent and purchase. All law school facilities are accessible to the physically disabled.

Calendar

The law school operates on a traditional semester basis. Courses for full-time students are offered days only and must be completed within 6 years. For part-time students, courses are offered both day and evening and must be completed within 6 years. New full- and part-time students are admitted in the fall. There is a 7-week summer session. Transferable summer courses are offered.

Programs

Required
To earn the J.D., candidates must complete 90 total credits, of which 50 are for required courses. They must maintain a minimum GPA of 2.33 in the required courses. The following first-year courses are required of all students: Civil Procedure, Constitutional Law, Contracts, Criminal Law, Introduction to Law, Legal Analysis, Research, and Writing, Property, and Torts. Required upper-level courses consist of Business Associations, Criminal Procedure, Estates and Trusts, Evidence, and Professional Responsibility. All students must take clinical courses. The required orientation program for first-year students is a 3-day orientation that includes Introduction to Law class in Case Analysis, Legal History, Jurisprudence, Professionalism, Procedure, and Statutory Interpretation.

Electives
The School of Law offers concentrations in corporate law, criminal law, environmental law, family law, international law, litigation, tax law, and real estate law. In addition, there is a Law Clinic, Family Mediation Clinic, and Mediation Clinic. Seminars, open to upper-level students, include Law and Elderly, Computers and Law, and Race and Racism. After completing 45 hours and maintaining a minimum

Phone: 817-212-4040
800-733-9529
Fax: 817-212-4141
E-mail: lawadmissions@law.txwes.edu
Web: www.law.txwes.edu

Contact

Emily Finlow, Records Manager, 817-212-4040 for general inquiries; Doug Akins, Financial Aid Officer, 817-212-4090 for financial aid information.

TEXAS

GPA of 2.33, a student can earn up to 6 hours working with a private attorney under the supervision of a faculty member. Directed Research programs and Directed Readings are available. Special lecture series include the Eldon Mahon Lecture Series. An Academic Support Program provides assistance to students, including facilitated study groups and exam-taking workshops. Remedial programs include the Summer Enrichment Program. The most widely taken electives are Tax, Family Law, and Texas Procedure.

Graduation Requirements

In order to graduate, candidates must have a GPA of 2.33, and have completed the upper-division writing requirement, and 30 hours of pro bono legal services.

Organizations

Students edit the *Texas Wesleyan Law Review* and *The Rambler*. There are fall and spring intraschool moot court competitions, as well as the ABA/LSD National Moot Court, Texas Young Lawyers Moot Court, and Jessup International Moot Court competitions. Other competitions include the ABA/LSD National Negotiations competition. Law student organizations, local chapters of national associations, and campus organizations include Texas Aggie Wesleyan Legal Society, Intellectual Property Association, Wesleyan Innocence Project, Delta Theta Phi, Phi Delta Phi, Phi Alpha Delta, HLSA, BLSA, ABA/LSD, and Christian Legal Society.

Library

The law library contains 274,945 hardcopy volumes and 750,960 microform volume equivalents, and subscribes to 5173 serial publications. Such on-line databases and networks as CALI, CIS Universe, Legal-Trac, LEXIS, Matthew Bender, NEXIS, OCLC First Search, WESTLAW, Wilsonline Indexes, BNA ALL, HeinOnline, Audio CaseFiles, CCH Intelliconnect Network, Gammel's Laws of Texas--19th Century Texas Law Online, GPO Monthly Catalog, IndexMaster, LLMC Digital, Making of Modern Law, RIA Checkpoint, and Tax Analysts are available to law students for research. Special library collections include the Chief Justice Joe Greenhill, Sr. Collection. Recently, the library moved to a different facility, added carrel

seating, and increased its overall seating capacity. The ratio of library volumes to faculty is 7856 to 1 and to students is 347 to 1. The ratio of seats in the library to students is 1 to 2.

Faculty

The law school has 35 full-time and 19 part-time faculty members, of whom 20 are women. About 31% of full-time faculty have a graduate law degree in addition to the J.D. The ratio of full-time students to full-time faculty in an average class is 24 to 1; in a clinic, 8 to 1. The law school has a regular program of bringing visiting professors and other distinguished lecturers and visitors to campus.

Students

About 51% of the student body are women; 16%, minorities; 2%, African American; 2%, Asian American; 3%, Hispanic; 1%, Native American; and 1%, unknown. The average age of entering students is 28; age range is 21 to 52. About 12% of students have a graduate degree. About 4% drop out after the first year for academic or personal reasons; 96% remain to receive a law degree.

Placement

J.D.s awarded:	160
Services available through: a separate law school placement center and counseling on joining local and state bar associations, networking, and professional development	
Special features: job fairs, career services library, job search workshop, career services handbook and packet given to students at orientation, alumni outreach, on-line job bank, on-campus interviews	
Full-time job interviews:	25 employers
Summer job interviews:	25 employers
Placement by graduation:	39% of class
Placement within 9 months:	85% of class
Average starting salary:	$28,800 to $200,000
Areas of placement:	
Private practice 2-10 attorneys	34%
Private practice 11-25 attorneys	11%
Private practice 26-50 attorneys	6%
Private practice 51-100 attorneys	2%
Private practice 101-500 attorneys, or unknown	4%
Business/industry	29%
Government	11%
Judicial clerkships	2%
Public interest	1%

THOMAS JEFFERSON SCHOOL OF LAW

2121 San Diego Avenue
San Diego, CA 92110

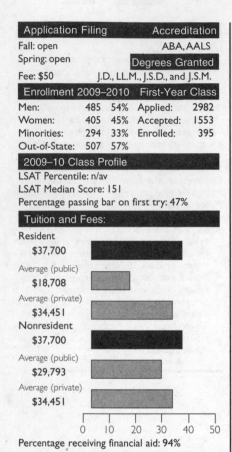

ADMISSIONS

In the fall 2009 first-year class, 2982 applied, 1553 were accepted, and 395 enrolled. Two transfers enrolled. The median GPA of the most recent first-year class was 2.96. The lowest LSAT percentile accepted was 20; the highest was 95.

Requirements

Applicants must take the LSAT. Minimum acceptable GPA is 2.0 on a scale of 4.0. The most important admission factors include LSAT results, academic achievement, and life experience. No specific undergraduate courses are required. Candidates are not interviewed.

Procedure

The application deadline for fall entry is open. Applicants should submit an application form, LSAT results, transcripts, a personal statement, a nonrefundable application fee of $50, 2 letters of recommendation, and a personal statement. The latest acceptable LSAT test date for fall entry is June. The law school uses the LSDAS.

Special

Requirements are not different for out-of-state students.

Costs

Tuition and fees for the 2009-2010 academic year are $37,700 for all full-time students. Tuition for part-time students is $25,400 per year. Books and supplies run $1700.

Financial Aid

About 94% of current law students receive some form of aid. The average annual amount of aid from all sources combined, including scholarships, loans, and work contracts, is $28,367; maximum, $64,060. Awards are based on need and merit. Required financial statements are the FAFSA and an institutional application. The aid application deadline for fall entry is February 15. First-year students are notified about their financial aid application at the time an application for admission is received.

About the Law School

Thomas Jefferson School of Law was established in 1969 and is a private institution. The campus is in an urban area the Old Town area of San Diego. The primary mission of the law school is to provide an outstanding legal education for a nationally-based student body in a collegiate and supportive environment with attention to newly emerging areas of law, particularly those related to technological development, globalization and the quest for social justice. Students have access to federal, state, county, city, and local agencies, courts, correctional facilities, law firms, and legal aid organizations in the San Diego area. There are also county law libraries available. Housing for students is not available on-site. The Student Services Department can assist with various housing alternatives. All law school facilities are accessible to the physically disabled.

Calendar

The law school operates on a traditional semester basis. Courses for full-time students are offered both day and evening and must be completed within 5 years. For part-time students, courses are offered both day and evening and must be completed within 6 years. New full- and part-time students are admitted in the fall and spring. There is an 8-week summer session. Transferable summer courses are offered.

Programs

In addition to the J.D., the law school offers the LL.M. and J.S.D., and J.S.M. Students may take relevant courses in other programs and apply credit toward the J.D.; a maximum of 8 credits may be applied. The following joint degrees may be earned: J.D./M.B.A. (Juris Doctor/Master of Business Administration).

Required

To earn the J.D., candidates must complete 88 total credits, of which 55 are for required courses. They must maintain a minimum GPA of 2.0 in the required courses. The following first-year courses are required of all students: Civil Procedure I and II, Contracts I and II, Criminal Law, Criminal Procedure, Legal Writing I, Property I, and Torts I and II. Required upper-level courses consist of Constitutional Law I and II, Corporations, Evidence, Legal Writing II, Professional Responsibility, Property II, and Remedies. The required orientation program for first-year students is 2 days.

Electives

The Thomas Jefferson School of Law offers concentrations in corporate law, criminal law, entertainment law, environmental law, family law, intellectual property law, international law, litigation, media law, sports law, tax law, and litigation, which includes dispute resolution, constitutional and civil rights, family law, government and administrative law, intellectual property, and health law. In addition, students can earn a maximum of 5 units by working in various government agencies, state and federal courts, or legal aid clinics. Small seminars are offered in specialty areas and are open to all students. Topics vary. A judicial internship program places qualified students in state and federal courts. Research assistantships are available through individual

Phone: 619-297-9700
800-936-7529
Fax: 619-294-4713
E-mail: info@tjsl.edu
Web: www.tjsl.edu

Contact

Michelle Allison, Associate Director of Admissions, 619-297-9700, ext. 1694 for general inquiries; Marc Berman, Director of Financial Assistance, 619-297-9700, ext. 1353 for financial aid information.

CALIFORNIA

instructors. Students can earn a maximum of 10 units while working in nonpaid positions at select governmnet agencies, corporations, law firms, and public-interest organizations. An Alumni Perspectives series annually features successful alumni who share their practice experience and expertise with students. Native American Law Students Association, Iranian Jurisprudence Society, Christian Legal Society, Jewish Student Union, Women's Law Association, La Raza, Pan Asian Lawyers Student Association, and Black Law Students Association offer mentoring and networking programs for minority students.

Graduation Requirements

In order to graduate, candidates must have a GPA of 2.0 and have completed the upper-division writing requirement.

Organizations

Students edit the *Thomas Jefferson Law Review*. Other publications include *The Thomas Jefferson School of Law News* and *The SBA Informer*. Moot court competitions include the National Appellate Advocacy Competition, William Jessup Moot Court Competition, and Pepperdine Entertainment Law Moot Court Competition. Other competitions include A.T.L.A. Mock Trial, Young Texas Lawyers Association Mock Trial, San Diego Defense Lawyers, Intra-School National Mock Trial, and William Daniel Mock Trial Competition. Law student organizations, include ABA/Law Student Division, Phi Alpha Delta, and Student Bar Association. Local chapters of national association include International Law Society, Public Interest Law Foundation, and Environmental Law Society. Other campus organizations include Black Law Students Association, Pan Asian Law Students Association, and La Razza Law Students Association.

Library

The law library contains 102,936 hardcopy volumes and 135,156 microform volume equivalents, and subscribes to 2603 serial publications. Such on-line databases and networks as CALI, CIS Universe, DIALOG, Infotrac, Legal-Trac, LEXIS, LOIS, Mathew Bender, NEXIS, OCLC First Search, WESTLAW, and United Nations Treaty Service; Legal Scholarship and Social Science Scholarship Net-

work, Hein Online. LLMC Digital; CCH Labor Relations Employment Practices, Wages/Hours are available to law students for research. Special library collections include Thomas Jefferson's writings and books, videos, and other material about Thomas Jefferson. Recently, the library expanded all areas of its treatise collection especially in the areas of international law, law and technology, and law and social justice. The ratio of library volumes to faculty is 6118 to 1 and to students is 158 to 1. The ratio of seats in the library to students is 1 to 3.

Faculty

The law school has 43 full-time and 27 part-time faculty members, of whom 28 are women. About 18% of full-time faculty have a graduate law degree in addition to the J.D. The ratio of full-time students to full-time faculty in an average class is 32 to 1. The law school has a regular program of bringing visiting professors and other distinguished lecturers and visitors to campus.

Students

About 45% of the student body are women; 33%, minorities; 7%, African American; 11%, Asian American; 14%, Hispanic; and 1%, Native American. The majority of students come from California (43%). The average age of entering students is 26; age range is 21 to 53.

Placement

J.D.s awarded:	n/av

Services available through: a separate law school placement center

Services: lecture series and panel presentations; access to on-campus and regional job fairs; access to on-line job posting system, and numerous on-line job posting sites.

Special features: All counselors are attorneys, and have practical legal experience including law firms, judicial clerk skills, public interest, and government.

Full-time job interviews:	8 employers
Summer job interviews:	16 employers
Placement by graduation:	22% of class
Placement within 9 months:	86% of class
Average starting salary:	$44,500 to $95,000

Areas of placement:

Private practice 2-10 attorneys	24%
Private practice 11-25 attorneys	5%
Private practice 26-50 attorneys	2%
Private practice 51-100 attorneys	1%
Private practice 100+ attorneys solo practice	27%
Government	8%
Judicial clerkships	6%
Public interest	3%
Academic	3%
Business/industry	2%

THOMAS M. COOLEY LAW SCHOOL

300 South Capitol Avenue
Lansing, MI 48901

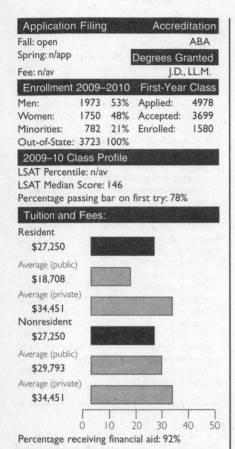

Application Filing	Accreditation
Fall: open	ABA
Spring: n/app	**Degrees Granted**
Fee: n/av	J.D., LL.M.

Enrollment 2009–2010		First-Year Class	
Men:	1973 53%	Applied:	4978
Women:	1750 48%	Accepted:	3699
Minorities:	782 21%	Enrolled:	1580
Out-of-State:	3723 100%		

2009–10 Class Profile
LSAT Percentile: n/av
LSAT Median Score: 146
Percentage passing bar on first try: 78%

Tuition and Fees:

Resident
$27,250

Average (public)
$18,708

Average (private)
$34,451

Nonresident
$27,250

Average (public)
$29,793

Average (private)
$34,451

0   10   20   30   40   50

Percentage receiving financial aid: 92%

ADMISSIONS

In a recent year, 4978 applied, 3699 were accepted, and 1580 enrolled. Fifteen transfers enrolled. The median GPA of the most recent first-year class was 3.03. The lowest LSAT percentile accepted was 79; the highest was 96. Figures in the above capsule and in this profile are approximate. Figures in the above capsule and in this profile are approximate.

Requirements
Applicants must take the LSAT. Minimum acceptable GPA is 2.0 on a scale of 4.0. The most important admission factors include GPA and LSAT results. No specific undergraduate courses are required. Candidates are not interviewed.

Procedure
Applicants should submit an application form, LSAT results, transcripts, and new students pay a $25 nonrefundable enrollment fee upon acceptance. Notification of the admissions decision is on a rolling

basis. The latest acceptable LSAT test date for fall entry is June. The law school uses the LSDAS. Check with the school for current application deadlines.

Special
The law school recruits minority and disadvantaged students through recruitment travel and by attending law forums and job fairs. Requirements are not different for out-of-state students. Transfer students must have one year of credit, have a minimum GPA of 2, have attended an ABA-approved law school, and students can transfer up to 30 credits for classes in which they have received a grade of C or better. They must be in good standing at their last school. Preadmissions courses consist of Qualifying school is available to promising candidates who do not meet standard admissions criteria.

Costs

Tuition and fees for the 2009-2010 academic year is approximately $27,250 for all full-time students. Tuition for part-time students is approximately $16,366 per year. Books and supplies run about $800.

Financial Aid

In a recent year, about 92% of current law students received some form of aid. The average annual amount of aid from all sources combined, including scholarships, loans, and work contracts, is about $18,500. Awards are based on need and merit. Required financial statement is the FAFSA. Special funds for minority or disadvantaged students include Rosa Park and Martin Luther King, Jr. scholarships. Both are awarded based on need and merit. First-year students are notified about their financial aid application at time of acceptance. Check with the school for the current application deadlines.

About the Law School

Thomas M. Cooley Law School was established in 1972 and is a private institution. The campus is in a suburban area at 3 campuses: in Lansing, Grand Rapids, and. The primary mission of the law school is to integrate the study of law with practical experience in government, business, and the courts. Students have access to federal, state, county, city, and local agencies,

courts, correctional facilities, law firms, and legal aid organizations in the Lansing area. An extensive externship program provides access to national lawyers' networks. Facilities of special interest to law students include a legal research library, at each campus and an Academic Resource Center. Housing for students includes university apartments, condos, and private houses. All law school facilities are accessible to the physically disabled.

Calendar

The law school operates on a traditional semester basis. Courses for full-time students are offered day, evening, and weekends and must be completed within 5 years. For part-time students, courses are offered day, evening, and weekends and must be completed within 6 years. New full- and part-time students are admitted in the fall, winter, and summer. There is a 15-week summer session. Transferable summer courses are offered.

Programs

In addition to the J.D., the law school offers the LL.M. Students may take relevant courses in other programs and apply credit toward the J.D.; a maximum of 9 (MPA) 9 (MBA) credits may be applied. The following joint degrees may be earned: J.D./M.B.A. (Juris Doctor/Master of Business Administration) and J.D./M.P.A. (Juris Doctor/Master of Public Administration through partner).

Required
To earn the J.D., candidates must complete 90 total credits, of which 63 are for required courses. They must maintain a minimum GPA of 2.0 in the required courses. The following first-year courses are required of all students: Civil Procedure I and II, Contracts I and II, Criminal Law, Criminal Procedure, Introduction to Law I, Professional Responsibility, Property I and II, Research and Writing, and Torts I and II. Required upper-level courses consist of Advanced Writing, Business Organizations, Constitutional Law I and II, Evidence, Remedies, Secured Transactions, Taxation, and Wills, Estates, and Trusts. All students must take clinical courses. The required orientation program for first-year students is a 2-day orientation program prior to start of the first semester.

Phone: 517-371-5140
800-874-3511
Fax: 517-334-5718
E-mail: admissions@cooley.edu
Web: www.cooley.edu

Contact
Asst. Dean for Admissions, 517-371-5140 ext. 2250 for general inquiries; Financial Aid Director, 517-371-5140 ext. 2216 for financial aid information.

MICHIGAN

Electives
The Thomas M. Cooley Law School offers concentrations in corporate law, environmental law, international law, litigation, and general practice, solo and small firm, administrative law, constitutional law, and civil rights. In addition, In-house clinics include the Sixty Plus Elder Law Clinic, Estate Planning Clinic, Public Defender Clinic, Innocence Project, and Domestic Violence Clinic for 3 to 6 credits. Practice seminars are conducted in alternate dispute resolution, appellate practice, and civil procedure worth 2 to 3 credits. Research and Writing, Advanced Research and Writing, and Law Practice courses provide training in brief writing and oral argument conducted before sitting Circuit Court judges. Directed Studies allow independent research and writing projects. Cooley has an extensive third-year externship program, which places senior students in work settings for 1 or 2 terms throughout the U.S. Special lecture series include the Krinock Lecture and professionalism lectures. The winter term offers study abroad in Australia and New Zealand; the summer term offers Canadian courses in Toronto. Through the Student Tutorial Services, upper-class students help new students form study groups. Faculty members may offer special seminars on study techniques. In addition, the Academic Resource Center coordinates tutorials on exam skills and study techniques and offers individual counseling. The Academic Resource Center provides free assistance for any student requesting it, including Testing Seminars, practice exams, individual counseling, and study skills seminars. Minority programs include BALSA, APALSA, Hispanic Law Society, African Legal Scholars Association, Gay Rights Alliance and Native American Law Students Association. Bar preparation programs are available for all students, and Professional Portfolio Program. The most widely taken electives are Law Practice, Trial Workshop, and Family Law.

Graduation Requirements
In order to graduate, candidates must have a GPA of 2.0 and have completed the upper-division writing requirement.

Organizations
Students edit the *Cooley Law Review*, the *Thomas M. Cooley Journal of Practical* *and Clinical Law*, the newspaper *Pillar*, and the *Benchmark*, a magazine published each trimester. The Law School competes in the Frederick Douglass Moot Court, Chicago Bar Association, Moot Court, and State of Michigan Moot Court. Other competitions include Environmental Law Moot Court, Evans Competition, National Trial Competition, NACDL, Criminal Justice Trial Advocacy Competition, and Client Counseling Competition. Law student organizations, local chapters of national associations, and campus organizations include the Black Law Students Association, the Criminal Law Society, the ABA-Law Student Division, Phi Delta Phi, International Law Society, ATLA, and Sports Law Club.

Library
The law library contains 577,975 hardcopy volumes and 132,377 microform volume equivalents, and subscribes to 5004 serial publications. Such on-line databases and networks as CALI, LEXIS, Matthew Bender, NEXIS, OCLC First Search, and WESTLAW are available to law students for research. Special library collections include a depository for U.S. government documents, a full set of Michigan Supreme Court records and briefs, and a Congressional Information Service Microfiche library. Recently, the library new library facilities at the Grand Rapids and Auburn Hills campuses housing special collections in tax and intellectual property. The ratio of library volumes to faculty is 6351 to 1 and to students is 160 to 1. The ratio of seats in the library to students is 1 to 4.

Faculty
The law school has 91 full-time and 140 part-time faculty members, of whom 79 are women. According to AAUP standards for Category IIA institutions, faculty salaries are well above average. About 10% of full-time faculty have a graduate law degree in addition to the J.D. The ratio of full-time students to full-time faculty in an average class is 65 to 1; in a clinic, 6 to 1. The law school has a regular program of bringing visiting professors and other distinguished lecturers and visitors to campus.

Students
About 48% of the student body are women; 21%, minorities; 10%, African American;

Placement
J.D.s awarded:	805
Services available through: a separate law school placement center	
Special features: a complete career library including audio and visual resources, weekly workshops and programs, job bulletins from more than 114 law schools nationwide, a newsletter, mock interview program, and on-campus interview program.	
Full-time job interviews:	11 employers
Summer job interviews:	9 employers
Placement by graduation:	47% of class
Placement within 9 months:	82% of class
Average starting salary:	$14,560 to $135,000
Areas of placement:	
Private practice 2-10 attorneys	20%
Private practice 11-25 attorneys	3%
Private practice 26-50 attorneys	1%
Private practice 51-100 attorneys	1%
Business/industry	20%
Government	17%
Judicial clerkships	8%
Public interest	6%
Academic	2%

5%, Asian American; 5%, Hispanic; and 10%, 4% Foreign nationals. The average age of entering students is 29; age range is 20 to 62. About 21% drop out after the first year for academic or personal reasons; 79% remain to receive a law degree.

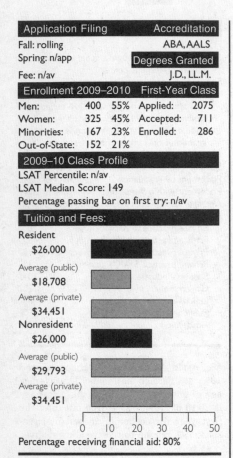

Application Filing		Accreditation
Fall: rolling		ABA, AALS
Spring: n/app		Degrees Granted
Fee: n/av		J.D., LL.M.

Enrollment 2009–2010		First-Year Class	
Men:	400 55%	Applied:	2075
Women:	325 45%	Accepted:	711
Minorities:	167 23%	Enrolled:	286
Out-of-State:	152 21%		

2009–10 Class Profile
LSAT Percentile: n/av
LSAT Median Score: 149
Percentage passing bar on first try: n/av

Tuition and Fees:

Resident
$26,000

Average (public)
$18,708

Average (private)
$34,451

Nonresident
$26,000

Average (public)
$29,793

Average (private)
$34,451

0 10 20 30 40 50

Percentage receiving financial aid: 80%

ADMISSIONS

In a recent year, 2075 applied, 711 were accepted, and 286 enrolled. Thirteen transfers enrolled. The median GPA of the most recent first-year class was 3.04. The lowest LSAT percentile accepted was 15; the highest was 88. Figures in the above capsule and in this profile are approximate.

Requirements
Applicants must have a bachelor's degree and take the LSAT. The most important admission factors include academic achievement, LSAT results, and general background. No specific undergraduate courses are required. Candidates are not interviewed.

Procedure
Applicants should submit an application form, LSAT results, transcripts, a personal statement, optional letters of recommendation, and a personal statement. Notification of the admissions decision is on a rolling basis. The latest acceptable

LSAT test date for fall entry is June. The law school uses the LSDAS. Check with the school for current application deadlines.

Special
The law school recruits minority and disadvantaged students by means of visits to historically black colleges, as well as colleges and universities with significant minority populations; the use of Law Services' Candidate Referral Service; Council on Legal Education Opportunity (CLEO); the Legal Education Access Program; and other projects. Requirements are not different for out-of-state students. Transfer students must have one year of credit and be in good academic standing, and submit a copy of the LSDAS Report, an official transcript, and a letter of good standing from the law school currently attended.

Costs

Tuition and fees for the 2009-2010 academic year are approximately $26,000 for all full-time students.

Financial Aid

In a recent year, about 80% of current law students received some form of aid. The average annual amount of aid from all sources combined, including scholarships, loans, and work contracts, was approximately $18,500; maximum, $45,111. Awards are based on need and merit. Required financial statement is the FAFSA. Special funds for minority or disadvantaged students consist of the Touro Grant, awarded based on financial need; Perkins Loan and College Work Study, awarded based on need; and incentive awards, based on need and merit. First-year students are notified about their financial aid application at after acceptance but before enrollment. Check with the school for current application deadlines.

About the Law School

Touro College Jacob D. Fuchsberg Law Center was established in 1980 and is a private institution. The 11.1-acre campus is in a suburban area approximately 40 miles east of New York City. The primary mission of the law school is to produce graduates ready for real-world practice. The student experience is characterized by extensive faculty-student interaction, innovative student support systems, and a

commitment to a lawyer's moral and ethical obligations. Students have access to federal, state, county, city, and local agencies, courts, correctional facilities, law firms, and legal aid organizations in the Central Islip area. The school is planning to relocate to become part of the Central Islip court complex, with a state-of-the-art interactive facility. Facilities of special interest to law students include law firms, local and New York City attorneys' offices, and public interest agencies and firms. Housing for students is available on-campus and off-campus. The school's Housing Information Network and mailings identify available accommodations and students who wish to share housing. About 98% of the law school facilities are accessible to the physically disabled.

Calendar

The law school operates on a traditional semester basis. Courses for full-time students are offered days only and must be completed within 6 years. For part-time students, courses are offered both day and evening and must be completed within 6 years. New full- and part-time students are admitted in the fall. There is a 4- and 7-week summer session. Transferable summer courses are offered.

Programs

In addition to the J.D., the law school offers the LL.M. in U.S. legal studies for foreign law graduates and in General. The following joint degrees may be earned: J.D./M.B.A. (Juris Doctor/Master of Business Administration (with Long Island University, C.W. Post), J.D./M.P.A. (Juris Doctor/Master of Public Administration in health care), and J.D./M.S.W. (Juris Doctor/Master of Social Work (with State University of New York at Srony Brook)).

Required
To earn the J.D., candidates must complete 87 total credits, of which 51 to 52 are for required courses. They must maintain a minimum GPA of 2.0 in the required courses. The following first-year courses are required of all students: Civil Procedure I and II, Contracts I and II, Criminal Law I, Legal Methods I and II, Property I, and Torts I and II. Required upper-level courses consist of Advanced Writing Requirement, Business Organizations I, Constitutional Law I and II, Evidence, Perspective Requirement, Professional

Phone: 631-761-7010
Fax: 631-761-7019
E-mail: gjustice@tourolaw.edu
Web: http://www.tourolaw.edu

Contact

Assistant Dean of Administration, 631-421-2244, ext. 302 for general inquiries; Associate Director of Financial, 631-421-2244, ext. 322 for financial aid information.

Responsibility, Property II, Public Interest Requirement, and Trusts and Estates. mThe required orientation program for first-year students is a 5-day program that deals mostly with legal methods and provides an introduction to law; case assignments are given in advance for students to read, brief, and discuss.

Electives

The Jacob D. Fuchsberg Law Center offers concentrations in corporate law, criminal law, family law, international law, litigation, torts and insurance, and public interest and civil rights, intellectual property, real estate, health law, and immigration law. In addition, clinical offerings include Family Law (6 credits), Criminal Law, (5 credits); and International Human Rights/ Immigration Litigation (4 credits). Seminars are open to all students who have satisfied the prerequisites: Law and Medicine: Selected Topics in Law, Medicine, and Ethics; Patent Practice Seminar; and Selected Topics in Corporate Law. Internships are arranged through the Career Planning Office for positions during the semester and in the summer. Externships are also available in-house, at the Law Center's Domestic Violence Project and at the Housing Rights Project. Second- and third-year students may apply to be paid research assistants for a faculty member. Also, students may take Independent Research for 1 to 3 credits. Field work may be done through Career Planning externships, through the pro bono requirement, and through clinical offerings. Annually, the Law Center hosts the 3 lecture series: Distinguished Jurist in Residence; Distinguished Public Interest Lawyer in Residence; and the Bruce K. Gould Book Award. Any student in good academic standing may take up to 6 credits at an ABA-approved summer program. Such programs are evaluated on a case-by-case basis. The Office of Student Affairs arranges summer placements abroad in London, Paris, Lisbon, Brussels, Cork, Tel Aviv, Jerusalem, and Moscow. The Writing Resources Clinic provides writing specialists to assist students. The Professional Development Program, designed to help first-year students adapt to the rigors of law school, provides teaching assistants in most required courses, as well as TA mentors and TA tutors for writing skills. Minority students may take advantage of the Legal Education Access Program (LEAP), which offers an orientation pro-

gram, a lecture series, discussion groups, mentor program, and individual counseling. Special interest groups include the Institute for Jewish Law and the Institute for Business Law and Technology. The most widely taken electives are New York Practice, Family Law, and Criminal Procedure.

Graduation Requirements

In order to graduate, candidates must have a GPA of 2.0, have completed the upper-division writing requirement, and have successfully completed 87 credits, including all the required courses and additional requirements (Perspective Requirement, Public Interest Requirement, and Advanced Writing Requirement).

Organizations

Students edit the *Touro Law Review,* the newspaper *The Restatement,* and the yearbook *Res Ipsa.* Students compete in the Albany Law School Family Law Moot Court Competition, Benjamin N. Cardozo National Moot Court in Entertainment Law, and Brooklyn Law School's Jerome Prince Invitational Evidence Competition. Other competitions include the New York State Bar Association Legal Ethics Writing Competition, the Nathan Burkan Copyright Law, Association of Trial Lawyers of America, and ABA Negotiation and Counseling competitions. Law student organizations include the Student Bar Association, Delta Theta Phi International Law Fraternity, and Women's Bar Association. There are local chapters of ABA-Law Student Division, National Jewish Students Network, and American Civil Liberties Union. Other organizations include BLSA, Jewish Law Students Association, and PILOT (public interest student organization).

Library

The law library contains 429,683 hardcopy volumes and 225,964 microform volume equivalents, and subscribes to 1400 serial publications. Such on-line databases and networks as CALI, Legal-Trac, LEXIS, NEXIS, OCLC First Search, WESTLAW, and full Internet access are available to law students for research. Special library collections include official depository for selected U.S. government publications, a selective New York State depository, an extensive Judaica collec-

Placement

J.D.s awarded:	n/av
Services available through: a separate law school placement center	
Services: employer panels, resource library, judicial clerkship screening committee, job prospectus, and alumni newsletter on-line daily.	
Full-time job interviews:	14 employers
Summer job interviews:	9 employers
Placement by graduation:	57% of class
Placement within 9 months:	78% of class
Average starting salary:	$40,000 to $63,000
Areas of placement:	
Private practice 2-10 attorneys	31%
Private practice 11-25 attorneys	6%
Private practice 26-50 attorneys	5%
Private practice 51-100 attorneys	2%
Private practice 100-250 attorneys	2%
Business/industry	23%
Government	21%
Public interest	5%
Academic	3%
Judicial clerkships	2%

tion, and rare English, American, and foreign legal works. Recently, the library added titles and volumes. The ratio of library volumes to faculty is 13,860 to 1 and to students is 598 to 1. The ratio of seats in the library to students is 1 to 2.

Faculty

The law school has 31 full-time and 41 part-time faculty members, of whom 18 are women. About 33% of full-time faculty have a graduate law degree in addition to the J.D. The ratio of full-time students to full-time faculty in an average class is 35 to 1; in a clinic, 8 to 1. The law school has a regular program of bringing visiting professors and other distinguished lecturers and visitors to campus.

Students

About 45% of the student body are women; 23%, minorities; 11%, African American; 6%, Asian American; and 7%, Hispanic. The majority of students come from New York (79%). The average age of entering students is 26; age range is 20 to 63. About 60% of students enter directly from undergraduate school, 25% have a graduate degree, and 64% have worked full-time prior to entering law school. About 5% drop out after the first year for academic or personal reasons; 90% remain to receive a law degree.

Law School

Weinmann Hall, 6329 Freret Street
New Orleans, LA 70118

Application Filing	Accreditation
Fall: March 15	ABA, AALS
Spring: n/app	**Degrees Granted**
Fee: $60	J.D., LL.M., S.J.D.

Enrollment 2009–2010		First-Year Class	
Men:	473 58%	Applied:	2990
Women:	342 42%	Accepted:	890
Minorities:	163 20%	Enrolled:	282
Out-of-State:	701 86%		

2009–10 Class Profile
LSAT Percentile: 87%
LSAT Median Score: 162
Percentage passing bar on first try: n/av

Tuition and Fees:

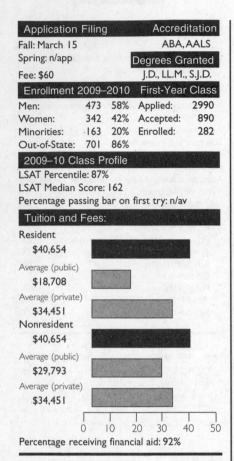

Resident
$40,654

Average (public)
$18,708

Average (private)
$34,451

Nonresident
$40,654

Average (public)
$29,793

Average (private)
$34,451

0 10 20 30 40 50

Percentage receiving financial aid: 92%

ADMISSIONS
In the fall 2009 first-year class, 2990 applied, 890 were accepted, and 282 enrolled. Fifteen transfers enrolled. The median LSAT percentile of the most recent first-year class was 87; the median GPA was 3.6 on a scale of 4.0. The lowest LSAT percentile accepted was 25; the highest was 99.

Requirements
Applicants must take the LSAT. The most important admission factors include academic achievement, LSAT results, and GPA. No specific undergraduate courses are required. Candidates are interviewed.

Procedure
The application deadline for fall entry is March 15. Applicants should submit an application form, LSAT results, transcripts, a personal statement, a nonrefundable application fee of $60, and up to 3 letters of recommendation. Notification of the admissions decision is from January 15 through the summer. The latest

acceptable LSAT test date for fall entry is February. The law school uses the LSDAS.

Special
The law school recruits minority and disadvantaged students by actively visiting undergraduate schools, using the CRS, and following up. Requirements are not different for out-of-state students. Transfer students must have one year of credit and have a good law school record.

Costs
Tuition and fees for the 2009-2010 academic year are $40,654 for all full-time students. Books and supplies run $1500.

Financial Aid
About 92% of current law students receive some form of aid. The average annual amount of aid from all sources combined, including scholarships, loans, and work contracts, is $50,000; maximum, $60,000. Awards are based on need and merit. Loans are based on need, while scholarships are based on merit and on need and merit combined. Required financial statement is the FAFSA. The aid application deadline for fall entry is February 15. Special funds for minority or disadvantaged students are available. First-year students are notified about their financial aid application in the spring.

About the Law School
Tulane University Law School was established in 1847 and is a private institution. The 110-acre campus is in an urban area in uptown New Orleans. The primary mission of the law school is to provide the best possible professional training so that graduates will become effective and ethical lawyers with skills that qualify them to practice law anywhere in the United States or the world. Students have access to federal, state, county, city, and local agencies, courts, correctional facilities, law firms, and legal aid organizations in the New Orleans area. There are five levels of courts in New Orleans: state trial, appellate, and supreme, and federal trial and appellate. Facilities of special interest to law students are the Reily Recreation Center, Freeman School of Business, and numerous cultural opportunities throughout the city. Housing for students is available in neighborhoods surrounding the

campus. About 95% of the law school facilities are accessible to the physically disabled.

Calendar
The law school operates on a traditional semester basis. Courses for full-time students are offered days, with a small number of elective courses offered during the evening, and must be completed within 6 semesters, although limited leaves of absence are granted. There is no part-time program. New students are admitted in the fall. Summer sesion consist of 6 weeks in New Orleans and 2 to 4 weeks abroad. Transferable summer courses are offered.

Programs
In addition to the J.D., the law school offers the S.J.D. and in admiralty, energy and environment, international and comparative law, American law, and American business law. The following joint degrees may be earned: J.D./M.A. (Juris Doctor/Master of Arts in Latin American studies), J.D./M.Acc (Juris Doctor/Master of Accounting), J.D./M.B.A. (Juris Doctor/Master of Business Administration), J.D./M.H.A. (Juris Doctor/ Master of Health Administration), J.D./M.P.H. (Juris Doctor/ Master of Public Health in environmental health), J.D./M.S. (Juris Doctor/ Master of Science in international development), and J.D./M/S.W. (Juris Doctor/ Master of Social Work).

Required
To earn the J.D., candidates must complete 88 total credits, of which 32 are for required courses. They must maintain a minimum GPA of 2.0 in the required courses. The following first-year courses are required of all students: Civil Procedure, Constitutional Law, Contracts I, Contracts II or Obligations I, Criminal Law, Legal Research and Writing, Property (Civil or Common), and Torts. Required upper-level courses consist of 30 hours of community service and Legal Profession. The required orientation program for first-year students is 1½ days of logistical information plus sessions on case briefing.

Electives
Students must take 15 to 16 credits in their area of concentration. The Law School offers concentrations in environ-

Phone: 504-865-5930
Fax: 504-865-6710
E-mail: admissions@law.tulane.edu
Web: www.law.tulane.edu

Contact
Susan Krinsky, Associate Dean for Admission, 504-865-5930 for general inquiries; Georgia Whiddon, 504-865-5931 for financial aid information.

LOUISIANA

Placement	
J.D.s awarded:	270
Services available through: a separate law school placement center	
Services: videotaped mock interviews, law firm tours and orientations, job fairs and placement consortia, and introduction to new cities	
Full-time job interviews:	100 employers
Summer job interviews:	100 employers
Placement by graduation:	60% of class
Placement within 9 months:	95% of class
Average starting salary:	$35,000 to $140,000
Areas of placement:	
Private practice 2-501 attorneys	59%
Judicial clerkships	10%
Government	9%
Public interest	6%
Business/industry	5%
Academic	1%
Unknown	12%

mental law, international law, maritime law, sports law, European legal studies, and civil law. In addition, 6 different clinics, including representation of actual clients, are available for third-year students for 8 credits. Second- and third-year students may earn 2 to 3 credits for seminars that are offered in various advanced legal areas and typically require an extensive research paper. Judicial and other externships, 1-year (2-semester) externship programs worth 4 credits, are offered to third-year students. Upper-level students may undertake directed research with individual faculty members for a maximum of 3 credits. Field work in some courses, particularly advanced environmental law, is offered. Many special lecture series are also offered each year. Students may earn 3 to 6 credits for the summer study-abroad program, offered in 6 countries and held for 2 to 4 weeks. In addition, some semester-long exchange programs are available with universities abroad. Selected first-year students may take the tutorial course, Legal Analysis, for 1 credit. Support and placement programs for minority students are sponsored by the school, including an assistant dean. Special interest group programs are provided by 40 student organizations. The most widely taken electives are Business Enterprises, Evidence, and Trusts and Estates.

Graduation Requirements
In order to graduate, candidates must have a GPA of 2.0, have completed the upper-division writing requirement, and have performed 30 hours of pro bono work.

Organizations
Students edit the *Tulane Law Review, Tulane Maritime Law Journal, Tulane Environmental Law Journal, Journal of Law and Sexuality, Tulane Journal of International and Comparative Law, Civil Law Forum, Sports Law Journal, Journal of Technology and Intellectual Property*, and the student newspaper *Dicta*. There are separate intraschool trial and appellate competitions for second- and third-year students, plus a variety of inter-school competitions, including the Jessup International, Negotiations, and Trial competitions. Law student organizations, local chapters of national associations, and campus organizations include the

Environmental Law Society, Public Interest Law Foundation, International Law Society, American Civil Liberties Union, Child Advocates, Tulane Law Women, Public Interest Law Foundation, BLSA, Federal Society, and American Constitution Society.

Library
The law library contains 401,949 hardcopy volumes and 261,651 microform volume equivalents, and subscribes to 1115 serial publications. Such on-line databases and networks as CALI, CIS Universe, DIALOG, Dow-Jones, Infotrac, Legal-Trac, LEXIS, LOIS, Matthew Bender, NEXIS, OCLC First Search, RLIN, WESTLAW, Wilsonline Indexes, BNA, HeinOnline, Making of Modern Law, LLMC Digital, RIA Checkpoint, and Kluwer Arbitration are available to law students for research. Special library collections include canon law, European law, civil law, maritime law, Roman law, and the Judge John Minor Wisdom Papers Collection. Recently, the library addded electronic database records to the online public access catalog and upgraded photocopier functions. The ratio of library volumes to faculty is 10,306 to 1 and to students is 493 to 1. The ratio of seats in the library to students is 1 to 1.

Faculty
The law school has 39 full-time and 75 part-time faculty members, of whom 24 are women. According to AAUP standards for Category I institutions, faculty salaries are below average. About 35% of full-time faculty have a graduate law degree in addition to the J.D.; about 24% of part-time faculty have one. The ratio of full-time students to full-time faculty in an average nonseminar class is 50 to 1; in a clinic, 14 to 1. The law school has a regular program of bringing visiting professors and other distinguished lecturers and visitors to campus. There is a chapter of the Order of the Coif; 80 faculty are members, and 10% of graduates are members.

Students
About 42% of the student body are women; 20%, minorities; 8%, African American; 3%, Asian American; 6%, Hispanic; 1%, Native American; and 3%, 2 or more ethnicities. The majority of students come from the South (36%). The average age of

entering students is 24; age range is 19 to 49. About 38% of students enter directly from undergraduate school, 8% have a graduate degree, and 81% have worked full-time prior to entering law school. About 5% drop out after the first year for academic or personal reasons; 92% remain to receive a law degree.

School of Law

302 Buchtel Common
Akron, OH 44325-2901

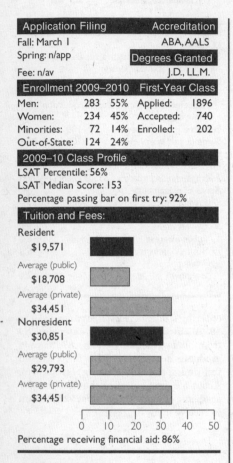

Application Filing	Accreditation
Fall: March 1	ABA, AALS
Spring: n/app	
	Degrees Granted
Fee: n/av	J.D., LL.M.

Enrollment 2009–2010			First-Year Class	
Men:	283	55%	Applied:	1896
Women:	234	45%	Accepted:	740
Minorities:	72	14%	Enrolled:	202
Out-of-State:	124	24%		

2009–10 Class Profile
LSAT Percentile: 56%
LSAT Median Score: 153
Percentage passing bar on first try: 92%

Tuition and Fees:

Resident
$19,571

Average (public)
$18,708

Average (private)
$34,451

Nonresident
$30,851

Average (public)
$29,793

Average (private)
$34,451

0 10 20 30 40 50

Percentage receiving financial aid: 86%

ADMISSIONS

In the fall 2009 first-year class, 1896 applied, 740 were accepted, and 202 enrolled. Three transfers enrolled. The median LSAT percentile of the most recent first-year class was 56; the median GPA was 3.39 on a scale of 4.0. The lowest LSAT percentile accepted was 15; the highest was 97.

Requirements

Applicants must have a bachelor's degree and take the LSAT. Minimum acceptable GPA is 2.0 on a scale of 4.0. The most important admission factors include LSAT results, GPA, and general background. No specific undergraduate courses are required. Candidates are not interviewed.

Procedure

The application deadline for fall entry is March 1. Applicants should submit an application form, LSAT results, transcripts, a personal statement, TOEFL for applicants whose first language is not English, and 2 to 3 letters of recommendation (strongly suggested, but not required). Notification of the admissions decision is 4 to 6 weeks after the application. The latest acceptable LSAT test date for fall entry is June. The law school uses the LSDAS.

Special

The law school recruits minority and disadvantaged students by means of publications, visiting colleges with a large percentage of minority students, sending mailings, holding recruitment days, participating in minority law fairs, granting scholarships, and advertising. In addition, minority law students and alumni contact minority admittees to welcome them. Requirements are not different for out-of-state students. Transfer students must have one year of credit, have attended an ABA-approved law school, and show strong academic performance. Preadmissions courses consist of optional legal skills workshops, traditionally offered in the summer.

Costs

Tuition and fees for the 2009-2010 academic year are $19,571 for full-time in-state students and $30,851 for out-of-state students. Tuition for part-time students is $15,898 in-state and $24,922 out-of-state. On-campus room and board costs about $9072 annually; books and supplies run $900.

Financial Aid

About 86% of current law students receive some form of aid. Awards are based on need and merit. Required financial statements are the FAFSA and the Institutional Aid Application. The aid application deadline for fall entry is May 1. First-year students are notified about their financial aid application as early as February for scholarships; soon thereafter for loans.

About the Law School

University of Akron School of Law was established in 1921 and is a public institution. The 170-acre campus is in an urban area 40 miles south of Cleveland, Ohio. The primary mission of the law school is to prepare students to become outstanding members of the bench and bar. Students have access to federal, state, county, city, and local agencies, courts, correctional facilities, law firms, and legal aid organizations in the Akron area. There is the Akron Municipal Court, Summit County Court, Ninth District Court of Appeals, and Federal Court. Facilities of special interest to law students include the Intellectual Property Center and the Legal Clinic. Housing for students is available on campus in graduate housing; many off-campus affordable housing options are available within walking distance or a short drive. All law school facilities are accessible to the physically disabled.

Calendar

The law school operates on a traditional semester basis. Courses for full-and part-time students are offered both day and evening and must be completed within 6 years. New full- and part-time students are admitted in the fall. There is a 5- and 10-week summer session. Transferable summer courses are offered.

Programs

In addition to the J.D., the law school offers the LL.M. Students may take relevant courses in other programs and apply credit toward the J.D.; a maximum of 6 graduate level credits may be applied. The following joint degrees may be earned: J.D./M.A.P. (Juris Doctor/Master of Applied Politics), J.D./M.B.A. (Juris Doctor/Master of Business Administration), J.D./M.P.A. (Juris Doctor/Master of Public Administration), J.D./M.S.M.H.R. (Juris Doctor/Master of Science in Management of Human Resources), and J.D./M.Tax. (Juris Doctor/Master of Taxation).

Required

To earn the J.D., candidates must complete 88 total credits, of which 44 are for required courses. They must maintain a minimum GPA of 2.0 in the required courses. The following first-year courses are required of all students: Civil Procedure I and II, Contracts I and II, Criminal Law, Introduction: Law and Legal Systems, Legal Analysis, Research, and Writing I and II, Legal Research, Property I and II, and Torts I and II. Required upper-level courses consist of a general writing requirement, Advanced Legal Research, Constitutional Law I and II, Evidence, Legal Drafting, and Professional Responsibility. Introduction to Law and Legal Systems is a 1-week course held during the first week of classes.

Electives

The School of Law offers concentrations in corporate law, criminal law, intellectual property law, international law, labor law,

Phone: 330-972-7331
800-4-AKRON-U
Fax: 330-258-2343
E-mail: lthorpe@uakron.edu
Web: www.uakron.edu/law

Contact
Lauri S. Thorpe, Assistant Dean, 330-972-7331, 800-4-AKRON-U, 330-972-6367 for general inquiries; University Financial Aid Office, 330-972-7032 for financial aid information.

OHIO

litigation, tax law, and public interest. In addition, the Trial Litigation and the Civil Litigation Clinics allow third-year students to be certified legal interns to represent clients in court; in the Clinical Seminar, students with strong academic records may clerk for judges. There is also a clinic in Appellate Review. Clinic students may be placed in-house or externally for credit after their first year. Students with an intern certificate may represent clients in civil and misdemeanor cases in court. The New Business Legal Clinic (NBLC) allows students to provide legal support to emerging businesses in the greater Akron area. Seminars include Feminist and Race Theory, International Investment, and Business Planning. Internships for academic credit (clinical seminars) are coordinated and monitored by the clinic staff. Public interest fellowships are coordinated by the Law Center Planning Office. Traditional employment opportunities are also coordinated through the Career Planning Office. All students must write a significant research paper in order to graduate. Individual studies and research may be taken under the guidance of a faculty member. Upper-division students may apply to become a research assistant for a law faculty member. Research may be in conjunction with a course. Field work is offered through the School of Law Legal Clinic for credit or the Career Planning and Placement Office or on a voluntary basis. Special lecture series are held during the fall and spring semesters in a wide variety of areas, with emphasis on intellectual property and constitutional law. Study abroad is only available through another ABA-accredited law school's study-abroad program. With permission of the associate dean, students may assume visiting status at another ABA-accredited law school and transfer credits back to Akron. The Academic Success Program provides individual and group workshop programming, including tutoring. Student mentors also assist individuals or groups in specific courses and in buildings skills for success in law school and practice. No formal remedial programs are required. The Black Law Students Association (BLSA) sponsors outlining and exam-taking seminars, adopt-a-school, scholarships, an annual dinner/dance, regional job fairs, Frederick Douglass Moot Court Competition, and travel to regional and national BLSA events. The Asian Latino Law Students Association (ALLSA) coordinates various service projects for the community involving law student volunteers. The Gay Straight Law Students Alliance coordinates co-curricular programming and community service projects. The school participates in a minority clerkship program with the bar association, leading law firms, and judges. The most widely taken electives are Administration of Criminal Justice; Wills, Trusts and Estates; and Corporations.

Graduation Requirements
In order to graduate, candidates must have a GPA of 2.0, have completed the upper-division writing requirement, and complete 8 credits: Legal Drafting, Advances Legal Research, and a skills component.

Organizations
Students edit the *Akron Law Review*, *Akron Tax Journal*, *Akron Intellectual Property Journal*, and *Strict Scrutiny*, the on-line *Constitutional Law Journal*. The moot court team attends the ABA/LSD-National Appellate Advocacy competition, National Moot Court competition, New York Bar National Moot Court Competition, and Jessup International Law Competition. A trial team attends competitions sponsored by Association of Trial Lawyers of America, National Institute for Trial Advocacy, the Academy of Trial Lawyers of Allegheny County, PA, and other associations. Law student organizations, local chapters of national associations, and campus organizations include the Intellectual Property and Technology Law Association, National Association of Criminal Defense Lawyers, Sports and Entertainment Law Society, International Law Society, Student Bar Association, Law Association for Women's Rights, Phi Alpha Delta, Phi Delta Phi, and Black Law Students Association.

Library
The law library contains 288,287 hardcopy volumes and 416,266 microform volume equivalents, and subscribes to 3260 serial publications. Such on-line databases and networks as CALI, CIS Universe, Infotrac, Legal-Trac, LEXIS, Mathew Bender, NEXIS, OCLC First Search, WESTLAW, Wilsonline Indexes, and 100 databases on Ohiolink, BNA Core Plus, and LLMC Digital are available to law students for research. Special library collections include a government documents depository (intellectual property).

Placement
J.D.s awarded:	151

Services available through: a separate law school placement center, the university placement center, and the College of Business Placement Center

Special features: i

Full-time job interviews:	11 employers
Summer job interviews:	21 employers
Placement by graduation:	60% of class
Placement within 9 months:	82% of class
Average starting salary:	$30,000 to $156,000

Areas of placement:
Private practice 2-10 attorneys	29%
Private practice 11-25 attorneys	4%
Private practice 26-50 attorneys	5%
Private practice 51-100 attorneys	4%
Private Practice 100+ attorneys; self-employed	14%
Business/industry	23%
Government	19%
Judicial clerkships	5%
Public interest	5%
Academic	1%

Recently, the library installed a wireless network to allow students to use wireless laptops to access the Internet. The ratio of library volumes to faculty is 9610 to 1 and to students is 558 to 1. The ratio of seats in the library to students is 1 to 2.

Faculty
The law school has 30 full-time and 27 part-time faculty members, of whom 24 are women. According to AAUP standards for Category I institutions, faculty salaries are well below average. About 24% of full-time faculty have a graduate law degree in addition to the J.D. The ratio of full-time students to full-time faculty in an average class is 13 to 1; in a clinic, 7 to 1. The law school has a regular program of bringing visiting professors and other distinguished lecturers and visitors to campus.

Students
About 45% of the student body are women; 14%, minorities; 7%, African American; 4%, Asian American; 3%, Hispanic; and 1%, Native American. The majority of students come from Ohio (76%). The average age of entering students is 26; age range is 21 to 49. About 59% of students enter directly from undergraduate school and 7% have a graduate degree. About 23% drop out after the first year for academic or personal reasons; 77% remain to receive a law degree.

School of Law

Box 870382
Tuscaloosa, AL 35487-0382

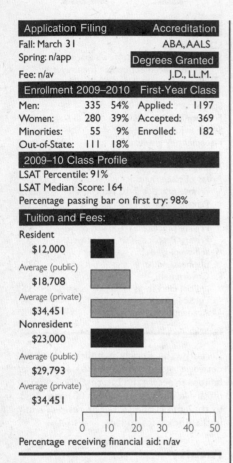

Application Filing	Accreditation
Fall: March 31	ABA, AALS
Spring: n/app	
	Degrees Granted
Fee: n/av	J.D., LL.M.

Enrollment 2009–2010			First-Year Class	
Men:	335	54%	Applied:	1197
Women:	280	39%	Accepted:	369
Minorities:	55	9%	Enrolled:	182
Out-of-State:	111	18%		

2009–10 Class Profile
LSAT Percentile: 91%
LSAT Median Score: 164
Percentage passing bar on first try: 98%

Tuition and Fees:

Resident
$12,000

Average (public)
$18,708

Average (private)
$34,451

Nonresident
$23,000

Average (public)
$29,793

Average (private)
$34,451

0   10   20   30   40   50

Percentage receiving financial aid: n/av

ADMISSIONS

In the fall 2009 first-year class, 1197 applied, 369 were accepted, and 182 enrolled. Figures in the above capsule and in this profile are approximate. The median LSAT percentile of the most recent first-year class was 91; the median GPA was 3.63 on a scale of 4.0.

Requirements
Applicants must have a bachelor's degree and take the LSAT. The most important admission factors include LSAT results, GPA, and academic achievement. No specific undergraduate courses are required. Candidates are not interviewed.

Procedure
Applicants should submit an application form, LSAT results, transcripts, the TOEFL for the LL.M. International Program and International J.D., and 2 personal statements, and supplemental information as required by the application questions. Notification of the admissions

decision is on a rolling basis. The latest acceptable LSAT test date for fall entry is February. Check with the school for current application deadlines. The law school uses the LSDAS.

Special
The law school recruits minority and disadvantaged students by means of recruiters visiting undergraduate institutions and mailings; participating annually in the Law Forums; and involving students, alumni, and faculty in recruitment efforts. Requirements are not different for out-of-state students. Transfer students must have one year of credit, have attended an ABA-approved law school, and have a collegiate academic record and an LSAT score that would have qualified the student for entry-level admission to the school. They must be in good standing at the current law school, as evidenced by a letter from the dean of that school, must not be on any kind of probationary status, and must rank academically high at that school.

Costs

Tuition and fees for the 2009-2010 academic year are $12,000 for full-time in-state students and $23,000 for out-of-state students. On-campus room and board costs about $1400 annually; books and supplies run $1600.

Financial Aid

In a recent year, the maximum annual amount of aid from all sources combined, including scholarships, loans, and work contracts, was $20,500. Awards are based on need and merit. The School of Law provides significant scholarship support to students. Applicants are considered automatically for scholarships. Required financial statement is the FAFSA. Check with the school for current application deadlines. Typically, financial aid is offered to first-year students at time of admission unless later in the admission process.

About the Law School

University of Alabama School of Law was established in 1872 and is a public institution. The campus is in a small town 60 miles southwest of Birmingham. The primary mission of the law school is to prepare future lawyers for their critical role in society, as well as to become a dynamic

part of the community. Students have access to federal, state, county, city, and local agencies, courts, correctional facilities, law firms, and legal aid organizations in the Tuscaloosa area. Facilities of special interest to law students include the moot court and trial advocacy rooms, student lounge, and student study areas. Housing for students is available in residence halls and university-owned and operated apartments and efficiency units. The majority of the law students live off campus. All law school facilities are accessible to the physically disabled.

Calendar

The law school operates on a traditional semester basis. Courses for full-time students are offered days only and must be completed within 3 years. There is no part-time program. New students are admitted in the fall. There is a 7-week summer session. Transferable summer courses are not offered.

Programs

In addition to the J.D., the law school offers the LL.M. Students may take relevant courses in other programs and apply credit toward the J.D.; a maximum of 6 credits may be applied. The following joint degrees may be earned: J.D./M.B.A. (Juris Doctor/Master of Business Administration) and J.D./Ph.D. (Juris Doctor/Doctor of Philosophy in Economics Dual Program).

Required
To earn the J.D., candidates must complete 90 total credits, of which 36 are for required courses. They must maintain a minimum GPA of 2.0 in the required courses. The following first-year courses are required of all students: Civil Procedure, Constitutional Law, Contracts, Criminal Law, Evidence, Legal Research, Legal Writing, Moot Court, Property, and Torts. Required upper-level courses consist of a seminar and The Legal Profession. The required orientation program for first-year students is a 2 1/2-day program geared toward making the transition into law school as smooth as possible.

Electives
The School of Law offers concentrations in corporate law, criminal law, environ-

Phone: 205-348-5440
Fax: 205-348-3917
E-mail: *admissions@law.ua.edu*
Web: *www.law.ua.edu*

Contact

Tom Ksobiech, Assistant Director of Admissions, 205-348-5440 for general inquiries; Noah Funderburg, Assistant Dean, 205-348-4508 for financial aid information.

ALABAMA

mental law, international law, litigation, and tax law. In addition, clinics are offered for 3 to 4 credit hours. Students may take 2-credit hour internships in which a student clerks for a judge. Seminars are small groups of second- and third-year students. Instruction is on a more informal and advanced basis than in basic courses. A written paper is required. First-year students are required to carry out a closely supervised program in legal research and writing. They must also participate in a moot court program in appellate advocacy involving substantial library research. A course in advanced legal research is offered as a 2-hour elective for upper-level students. Four credit externships are available during the summer and academic year in a great variety of placements. Special lecture series include the Hugo L. Black Lecture, established in 1996 to honor the U.S. Supreme Court Justice Hugo L. Black, who was a 1906 graduate of the law school, and the Daniel J. Meador Lecture, established in 1994 to honor Professor Meador, a 1951 graduate. Study abroad is available through a 4½-week program at the University of Fribourg and the Australian National University in Canberra, Australia. Students at Fribourg take 2 classes for 5 hours of credit. Several programs support a diversified student body. Special interest group programs include the Future Trial Lawyers Association, Dorbin Association (support group for women), Black Law Students Association, and the Alabama Public Interest Law Association to name a few. The most widely taken electives are Family Law, Criminal Procedure, Trial Advocacy, and First Amendment.

Graduation Requirements

In order to graduate, candidates must have a GPA of 2.0 and have completed the upper-division writing requirement.

Organizations

Students edit the *Alabama Law Review, Law and Psychology Review, Journal of the Legal Profession*, and *American Journal of Tax Policy*. The student newspaper is *Alabama Column*. The school participates annually in the National Moot Court, Phillip C. Jessup International Law Moot Court, and Frederick Douglass Moot Court competitions, and in competitions involving environmental law, labor law, bankruptcy law, intellectual property

law, and tax law. The law school also participates in 4 to 5 trial advocacy competitions each year and in 3 to 5 additional moot court competitions. Law school organizations, local chapters of national associations, and campus organizations include Phi Alpha Delta, Phi Delta Phi, Delta Theta Phi, Bench and Bar Society, Environmental Law Society, Law Spouses Club, and American Civil Liberties Union.

Library

The law library contains 438,444 hardcopy volumes and 143,115 microform volume equivalents, and subscribes to 3368 serial publications. Such on-line databases and networks as CALI, DIALOG, Infotrac, Legal-Trac, LEXIS, NEXIS, OCLC First Search, WESTLAW, OCLC, HeinOnline, Making of Modern Law, LLMC Digital, and BNA Online are available to law students for research. Special library collections include include several thousand photographs, the papers of former U.S. Senator Howell Heflin, former Congressman Kenneth A. Roberts, former director of the Federal Deposit Insurance Corporation George LeMaistre, and former professors John C. Payne and Jay Murphy. In addition, the Bounds Law Library maintains a replica of U.S. Supreme Court Justice Hugo L. Black's Alexandria, VA library. It also includes all decisions of appellate-level state and federal courts, all state and federal codes, Alabama and federal rules and regulations, and the decisions of selected agencies and of principal courts of the Commonwealth nations. There are also extensive treatise holdings. Recently, the library enhanced wireless capability and the on-line reserve system. The ratio of library volumes to faculty is 9743 to 1 and to students is 800 to 1. The ratio of seats in the library to students is 1 to 1.

Faculty

The law school has 45 full-time and 55 part-time faculty members, of whom 15 are women. According to AAUP standards for Category I institutions, faculty salaries are below average. About 30% of full-time faculty have a graduate law degree in addition to the J.D.; about 26% of part-time faculty have one. The ratio of full-time students to full-time faculty in an average class is 12 to 1; in a clinic, 5 to 1. The law school has a regular program of bringing visiting professors and other

Placement

J.D.s awarded:	190

Services available through: a separate law school placement center

Special features: fall and spring on-campus interviewing and resume forwarding programs and participation in job fairs, seminars, various publications, telephone and message/mail delivery service, LEXIS and WESTLAW computers; programs on nontraditional legal careers and other job possibilities..

Full-time job interviews:	12 employers
Summer job interviews:	61 employers
Placement by graduation:	85% of class
Placement within 9 months:	99% of class
Average starting salary:	$23,000 to $105,000

Areas of placement:

Private practice 2-10 attorneys	16%
Private practice 11-25 attorneys	9%
Private practice 26-50 attorneys	11%
Private practice 51-100 attorneys	7%
Judicial clerkships	17%
Government	9%
Business/industry	9%
Military	8%
Public interest	5%
Academic	4%

distinguished lecturers and visitors to campus. There is a chapter of the Order of the Coif; 28 faculty and 574 graduates are members.

Students

About 39% of the student body are women; 9%, minorities; 6%, African American; 1%, Asian American; 1%, Hispanic; and 1%, Native American. The majority of students come from Alabama (82%). The average age of entering students is 25. About 41% of students enter directly from undergraduate school, 14% have a graduate degree, and 51% have worked full-time prior to entering law school. About 4% drop out after the first year for academic or personal reasons; 96% remain to receive a law degree.

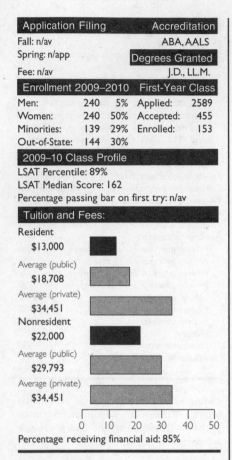

Application Filing			Accreditation	
Fall: n/av			ABA, AALS	
Spring: n/app			**Degrees Granted**	
Fee: n/av			J.D., LL.M.	

Enrollment 2009–2010			First-Year Class	
Men:	240	5%	Applied:	2589
Women:	240	50%	Accepted:	455
Minorities:	139	29%	Enrolled:	153
Out-of-State:	144	30%		

2009–10 Class Profile
LSAT Percentile: 89%
LSAT Median Score: 162
Percentage passing bar on first try: n/av

Tuition and Fees:

Resident
$13,000

Average (public)
$18,708

Average (private)
$34,451

Nonresident
$22,000

Average (public)
$29,793

Average (private)
$34,451

0 10 20 30 40 50

Percentage receiving financial aid: 85%

ADMISSIONS
In the fall 2009 first-year class, 2589 applied, 455 were accepted, and 153 enrolled. Figures in the above capsule and in this profile are approximate. Eight transfers enrolled. The median LSAT percentile of the most recent first-year class was 89; the median GPA was 3.5 on a scale of 4.0. The highest LSAT percentile was 99.

Requirements
Applicants must have a bachelor's degree and take the LSAT. The most important admission factors include academic achievement LSAT results and a personal statement. No specific undergraduate courses are required. Candidates are not interviewed.

Procedure
Applicants should submit an application form, LSAT results, transcripts, TOEFL for foreign applicants, 2 letters of recommendation, use of the LSDAS Report, a personal statement, and a resume.

Notification of the admissions decision is December through May. The latest acceptable LSAT test date for fall entry is February. Check with the school for current application deadlines. The law school uses the LSDAS.

Special
The law school recruits minority and disadvantaged students through a strong recruitment and retention program. Ethnicity is one of many qualitative factors considered by the Admissions Committee. Requirements are different for out-of-state students in that admission is slightly more competitive for nonresident students. Generally, 70% of enrollees are residents and 30% are nonresidents; however, more than 50% of admission offers go to nonresidents. Transfer students must have one year of credit, have attended an ABA-approved law school, and should be ranked in the top tenth to the top quarter of their class. Space in the class and nature of law school attended are always factors, as are undergraduate record, LSAT score, admissibility as a first-year applicant, personal statement, and letters of recommendation from law faculty with whom the applicant has studied.

Costs
Tuition and fees for the 2009-2010 academic year are $13,000 for full-time in-state students and $22,000 for out-of-state students. On-campus room and board costs about $9000 annually; books and supplies run $800.

Financial Aid
In a recent year, about 85% of current law students received some form of aid. The average annual amount of aid from all sources combined, including scholarships, loans, and work contracts, was $10,000; maximum, $30,000. Awards are based on need and merit. Required financial statement is the FAFSA. Check with the school for current application deadlines. There are special scholarships for Native Americans. First-year students are notified about their financial aid application between acceptance and enrollment; generally, between February and June.

About the Law School
University of Arizona James E. Rogers College of Law was established in 1925 and is a public institution. The 325-acre campus is in an urban area near downtown Tucson. The primary mission of the law school is to integrate the study of interdisciplinary issues with the traditional legal course of study in a small law school of approximately 480 students, with a rigorous yet collegial atmosphere. Students have access to federal, state, county, city, and local agencies, courts, correctional facilities, law firms, and legal aid organizations in the Tucson area. In addition, Arizona is home to many Native American tribes, all with their own tribal governments and trial court systems. All facilities are accessible and modern, including classrooms, a moot court room, seminar rooms, a student lounge, a library, a computer laboratory for students, and a fully equipped computerized courtroom. Housing for students includes plenty of affordable off-campus rental housing and a new graduate student apartment-type residence hall on campus. All law school facilities are accessible to the physically disabled.

Calendar
The law school operates on a traditional semester basis. Most courses for full-time students are offered days only; there are some late afternoon, early evening election courses for second- and third- year students. Course work must be completed within 3 years. There is no part-time program. New students are admitted in the fall. There is a 5-week summer session. Transferable summer courses are offered.

Programs
In addition to the J.D., the law school offers the LL.M in international trade law and LL.M. in indigenous peoples law and policy. Students may take relevant courses in other programs and apply credit toward the J.D.; a maximum of 6 credits may be applied. The following joint degrees may be earned: J.D./M.A. (Juris Doctor/Master of Arts in economics, American Indian studies, or women's studies), J.D./M.B.A. (Juris Doctor/Master of Business Administration), J.D./M.P.A. (Juris Doctor/Master of Public Administration), and J.D./Ph.D. (Juris Doctor/Doctor of Philosophy in psychology, philosophy, or economics).

Required
To earn the J.D., candidates must complete 85 total credits, of which 39 are for required courses. They must maintain

Phone: 520-621-3477
Fax: 520-621-9140
E-mail: *admissions@law.arizona.edu*
Web: *www.law.arizona.edu*

Contact

Dan Nunez, Admissions Office, 520-621-3477 for general inquiries; Henrietta Stover, Assistant Dean, Financial Services, 520-626-8101, Kim Marlow for financial aid information.

ARIZONA

a minimum GPA of 2.0 in the required courses. The following first-year courses are required of all students: Civil Procedure, Constitutional Law, Contracts, Criminal Procedure, Legal Analysis, Writing and Research, Property, and Torts. Required upper-level courses consist of an advanced writing seminar, Evidence, and Professional Responsibility. Many clinical and trial advocacy opportunities are available, but none are required. The required orientation program for first-year students 3 days and encompasses academic and cultural aspects of the law school experience; is 3 follow-up sessions during the first semester of school are held on ethics, stress, exam taking, and various other matters.

Electives

The James E. Rogers College of Law offers concentrations in corporate law, criminal law, environmental law, family law, international law, litigation, securities law, tax law, torts and insurance, Indian law, and human rights. In addition, clinics include a Domestic Violence Clinic, Child Advocacy Clinic, Indigenous Peoples Law Clinic, Immigration Law Clinics (3 to 5 units per credit) and Prosecution and Defense Clinics. These clinics are open to second- and third-year students who have completed Evidence and Ethics (Professional Responsibility). The college has a diverse set of offerings for its advanced research and writing seminars, ranging from the Warren Court to a death penalty seminar. Also offered is a rich variety of small seminars and colloquia. Internships may be taken with the state legislature, with the offices of U.S. senators and the White House Drug Policy Office, and with the Navajo, Tohono O'odham, and Pascua Yacqui tribal governments. Students may take up to 6 units of independent study with faculty supervision. Students may hear special lectures through the Isaac Marks Memorial Lectures, Rosentiel Scholar-in-Residence Program, McCormick Society lectures, and the Jeanne Kiewit Taylor Visiting Faculty Program. Chief Justice William Rehnquist teaches the history of the U.S. Supreme Court each January. Study abroad is possible in Puerto Rico at the University of Puerto Rico Law School. The College accepts credit for participation in ABA- approved international programs sponsored by other schools. All first-year students may participate in tutorial programs. Special scholarship efforts, mentoring, tutorial assistance, and a weeklong "Bridge Program" are offered to all students. The most widely taken electives are Federal Income Tax, Corporations, and Employment Law.

Graduation Requirements

In order to graduate, candidates must have a GPA of 2.0, have completed the upper-division writing requirement, and write a paper of "publishable quality" to fulfill the upper-division writing requirement.

Organizations

The primary law review is the *Arizona Law Review*. Students also edit *The Arizona Journal for International Law* and *The Journal of Psychology, Public Policy and Law*. Other publications include *Environmental Law Newsletter* and *The Bulletin*. Students may participate in a wide range of regional, national, and international moot court competitions. Other competitions include Richard Grand Damages, Grand Writing, and Jenkes competitions. Law student organizations, local chapters of national associations, and campus organizations include the Student Bar Association, Law Women's Association, Phi Alpha Delta, Phi Delta Phi, American Civil Liberties Union, ABA-Law Student Division, Black Law Students Association, LaRaza/Hispanic National Bar Association, Native American Law Student Association, and Asian American Law Student Association.

Library

The law library contains 410,000 hardcopy volumes and 426,000 microform volume equivalents, and subscribes to 3650 serial publications. Such on-line databases and networks as CALI, DIALOG, Dow-Jones, LEXIS, LOIS, NEXIS, OCLC First Search, and WESTLAW are available to law students for research. Special library collections include an extensive collection of materials on Latin American law, water law, and Indian law. Recently, the library refurbished and recarpeted the computer laboratory and library. There are also extensive electronic databases. The ratio of library volumes to faculty is 13,667 to 1 and to students is 863 to 1. The ratio of seats in the library to students is 1 to 1.

Faculty

The law school has 30 full-time and 55 part-time faculty members, of whom 36

Placement

J.D.s awarded:	n/av

Services available through: a separate law school placement center

Services: extensive career counseling and direction, creative programming, and participation of faculty and alumni

Special features: the college has a very active Career Services Office with 2 full-time attorneys on staff. The office takes a proactive approach to career services, educating, and assisting students.

Full-time job interviews:	70 employers
Summer job interviews:	110 employers
Placement by graduation:	65% of class
Placement within 9 months:	94% of class
Average starting salary:	$43,326 to $79,622

Areas of placement:

Private practice 2-10 attorneys	3%
Private practice 11-25 attorneys	8%
Private practice 26-50 attorneys	12%
Private practice 51-100 attorneys	15%
Judicial clerkships	22%
Government	17%
Business/industry	10%
Public interest	5%
LL.M. or Ph.D.	5%
Military	2%
Academic	1%

are women. According to AAUP standards for Category I institutions, faculty salaries are average. About 47% of full-time faculty have a graduate law degree in addition to the J.D.; about 2% of part-time faculty have one. The ratio of full-time students to full-time faculty in an average class is 15 to 1; in a clinic, 7 to 1. The law school has a regular program of bringing visiting professors and other distinguished lecturers and visitors to campus. There is a chapter of the Order of the Coif; 15 faculty and 370 graduates are members.

Students

About 50% of the student body are women; 29%, minorities; 5%, African American; 8%, Asian American; 12%, Hispanic; 4%, Native American; and 5%, foreign nationals. The majority of students come from Arizona (70%). The average age of entering students is 25; age range is 20 to 45. About 40% of students enter directly from undergraduate school, 22% have a graduate degree, and 60% have worked full-time prior to entering law school. About 1% drop out after the first year for academic or personal reasons; 98% remain to receive a law degree.

School of Law

Robert A. Leflar Law Center,
Waterman Hall
Fayetteville, AR 72701

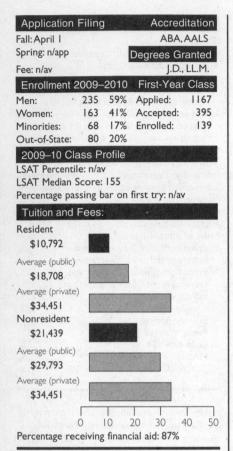

Application Filing	Accreditation
Fall: April 1	ABA, AALS
Spring: n/app	**Degrees Granted**
Fee: n/av	J.D., LL.M.

Enrollment 2009–2010		First-Year Class	
Men:	235 59%	Applied:	1167
Women:	163 41%	Accepted:	395
Minorities:	68 17%	Enrolled:	139
Out-of-State:	80 20%		

2009–10 Class Profile
LSAT Percentile: n/av
LSAT Median Score: 155
Percentage passing bar on first try: n/av

Tuition and Fees:

Resident
$10,792

Average (public)
$18,708

Average (private)
$34,451

Nonresident
$21,439

Average (public)
$29,793

Average (private)
$34,451

0 10 20 30 40 50

Percentage receiving financial aid: 87%

ADMISSIONS

In the fall 2009 first-year class, 1167 applied, 395 were accepted, and 139 enrolled. Seven transfers enrolled. The median GPA of the most recent first-year class was 3.49.

Requirements

Applicants must have a bachelor's degree and take the LSAT. The most important admission factors include LSAT results and GPA. No specific undergraduate courses are required. Candidates are not interviewed.

Procedure

The application deadline for fall entry is April 1. Applicants should submit an application form, LSAT results, and transcripts. And accepted students must submit a nonrefundable $75 preregistration fee, which is applied to the regular registration fee for the semester. Notification of the admissions decision is on a rolling basis. The latest acceptable LSAT test

date for fall entry is February. The law school uses the LSDAS.

Special

Requirements are different for out-of-state students in that index admission is granted to those nonresident applicants who have prediction indexes of 205 or above. If space permits, index admission is offered to other applicants. A small number of nonresidents who do not qualify for index admission may be admitted by the Admissions Committee. Transfer students must have one year of credit, have attended an ABA-approved law school, and contact the Associate Dean for Students at the school of law, indicating previous attendance at another school. Transfer students must complete the last 4 semesters at the University of Arkansas School of Law.

Costs

Tuition and fees for the 2009-2010 academic year are $10,792 for full-time in-state students and $21,439 for out-of-state students. On-campus room and board costs about $7732 annually; books and supplies run $1082.

Financial Aid

About 87% of current law students receive some form of aid. Awards are based on need and merit, along with the probability of success in law school. Required financial statement is the FAFSA. The aid application deadline for fall entry is April 1. Special funds for minority or disadvantaged students include selected scholarships.

About the Law School

University of Arkansas School of Law was established in 1924 and is a public institution. The campus is in a small town. The primary mission of the law school is to prepare students as lawyers who will provide professional service to their clients, who are interested in and capable of advancing legal process and reform, and who are prepared to fill the vital role of the lawyer as a community leader. Students have access to federal, state, county, city, and local agencies, courts, correctional facilities, law firms, and legal aid organizations in the Fayetteville area. Housing for students consists of on-campus residence

halls and sorority and fraternity houses. A housing service helps students find off-campus housing. All law school facilities are accessible to the physically disabled.

Calendar

The law school operates on a traditional semester basis. Courses for full-time students are offered days only and must be completed within 3 years. There is no part-time program. New students are admitted in the fall. There is a summer session. Transferable summer courses are offered.

Programs

In addition to the J.D., the law school offers the LL.M. Students may take relevant courses in other programs and apply credit toward the J.D.; a maximum of 6 credits may be applied. The following joint degrees may be earned: J.D./M.A. (Juris Doctor/Master of Arts in international law and politics), J.D./M.B.A. (Juris Doctor/Master of Business Administration), and J.D./M.P.A. (Juris Doctor/Master of Public Administration).

Required

To earn the J.D., candidates must complete 90 total credits, of which 43 are for required courses. They must maintain a minimum GPA of 2.0 in the required courses. The following first-year courses are required of all students: Civil Procedure A and B, Contracts A and B, Criminal Law, Legal Research and Writing I and II, Property A and B, and Torts. Required upper-level courses consist of Constitutional Law, Legal Research and Writing III, and Professional Responsibility. The required orientation program for first-year students is a 3-day introduction to the study of law that includes an introduction to the library, law school and campus tours, and university resources and student life planning suggestions.

Electives

The School of Law offers concentrations in agricultural law. In addition, Students with 48 or more hours and who have completed Civil Procedure A and B, Criminal Procedure, Basic Evidence, and Professional Responsibility may take the civil or criminal clinic. Upper-level students who have taken Professional Responsibility

Phone: 479-575-3102
Fax: 479-575-3937
E-mail: jkmiller@uark.edu
Web: Law.uark.edu/

ARKANSAS

may take the federal practice clinic. Seminars for 2 or 3 hours of credit are available to upper-level students. Seminars offered include Bankruptcy, Bioethics, and Comparative Law. Faculty may hire research assistants. Several scholarships are available for minority students.

Graduation Requirements

In order to graduate, candidates must have a GPA of 2.0 and have completed the upper-division writing requirement.

Organizations

Students edit the *University of Arkansas Law Review* the *Journal of Food Law and Policy* and the *Journal of Islamic Law and Culture.* The school participates in a variety of national and regional moot court competitions. Law student organizations, local chapters of national associations, and campus organizations include the Student Honor Council, Board of Advocates, Student Bar Association, Phi Alpha Delta, Phi Delta Phi, Black Law Students Association, Women's Law Student Association, Arkansas Coalition for Public Interest Law, and Christian Legal Society.

Library

The law library contains 327,581 hardcopy volumes and 166,629 microform volume equivalents, and subscribes to 3591 serial publications. Such on-line databases and networks as CALI, CIS Universe, Infotrac, Legal-Trac, LEXIS, LOIS, Mathew Bender, NEXIS, OCLC First Search, WESTLAW, Wilsonline Indexes, Making of Modern Law, and Records and Briefs of the United States Supreme Court are available to law students for research. Special library collections include a growing collection of agricultural law materials developed through the National Center for Agricultural Law Research and Information. The Young Law Library is a depository for federal documents, UN documents, and Arkansas State documents. Recently, the library expanded the Leflar Law Center, which created additional library space. A Rare Book, and Archive Room has been added. The ratio of library volumes to faculty is 12,600 to 1 and to students is 823 to 1. The ratio of seats in the library to students is 1 to 1.

Contact

James Miller, Associate Dean for Students, 479-575-3102 for general inquiries; Kattie Wing, Director, 479-575-3806 for financial aid information.

Faculty

The law school has 26 full-time and 20 part-time faculty members, of whom 13 are women. According to AAUP standards for Category I institutions, faculty salaries are well below average. About 33% of full-time faculty have a graduate law degree in addition to the J.D.

Students

About 41% of the student body are women; 17%, minorities; 9%, African American; 3%, Asian American; 3%, Hispanic; and 3%, Native American. The majority of students come from Arkansas (80%). The average age of entering students is 25.

Placement

J.D.s awarded:	122
Services available through: a separate law school placement center and the university placement center	
Special features: monthly placement newsletters, including internships and fellowships, and alumni and monthly job list postings by mail or e-mail, including those exchanged at other schools.	
Full-time job interviews:	18 employers
Summer job interviews:	37 employers
Placement by graduation:	49% of class
Placement within 9 months:	95% of class
Average starting salary:	n/av
Areas of placement:	
Solo Practice	2%
Private practice 2-10 attorneys	36%
Private practice 11-25 attorneys	7%
Private practice 26-50 attorneys	5%
Private practice 51-100 attorneys	1%
Private practice 100+ attorneys	12%
Government	11%
Public interest	5%
Judicial clerkships	3%
Academic	1%
Business/industry	17%

UALR William H. Bowen School of Law

1201 McMath Avenue
Little Rock, AR 72202-5142

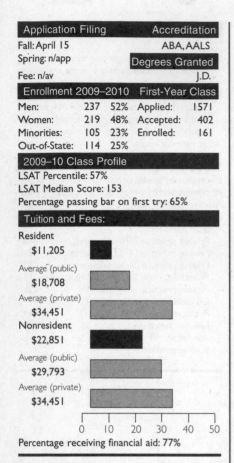

Application Filing	Accreditation
Fall: April 15	ABA, AALS
Spring: n/app	**Degrees Granted**
Fee: n/av	J.D.

Enrollment 2009–2010		First-Year Class	
Men:	237 52%	Applied:	1571
Women:	219 48%	Accepted:	402
Minorities:	105 23%	Enrolled:	161
Out-of-State:	114 25%		

2009–10 Class Profile
LSAT Percentile: 57%
LSAT Median Score: 153
Percentage passing bar on first try: 65%

Tuition and Fees:

Resident
$11,205

Average (public)
$18,708

Average (private)
$34,451

Nonresident
$22,851

Average (public)
$29,793

Average (private)
$34,451

0 10 20 30 40 50

Percentage receiving financial aid: 77%

ADMISSIONS

In the fall 2009 first-year class, 1571 applied, 402 were accepted, and 161 enrolled. Five transfers enrolled. The median LSAT percentile of the most recent first-year class was 57; the median GPA was 3.37 on a scale of 4.0. The lowest LSAT percentile accepted was 25; the highest was 99.

Requirements
Applicants must have a bachelor's degree and take the LSAT. The most important admission factors include LSAT results, GPA, and life experience. No specific undergraduate courses are required. Candidates are not interviewed.

Procedure
The application deadline for fall entry is April 15. Applicants should submit an application form, LSAT results, transcripts, and a prescribed-format personal statement. Notification of the admissions decision is on a rolling basis. The latest acceptable LSAT test date for fall entry is June. The law school uses the LSDAS.

Special
The law school recruits minority and disadvantaged students through scholarships that take diversity of life experiences into account, direct contact with undergraduate schools with high minority enrollment, and a Pre-Law Undergraduate Scholars Program targeting minority and disadvantaged students. Requirements are not different for out-of-state students. Transfer students must have attended an ABA-approved law school and have an official law school transcript showing completion of 20 semester hours, a letter of good standing stating class rank, LSAT score, official undergraduate transcript, a letter explaining the need to transfer, and an application.

Costs

Tuition and fees for the 2009-2010 academic year are $11,205 for full-time in-state students and $22,851 for out-of-state students. Books and supplies run $1400.

Financial Aid

About 77% of current law students receive some form of aid. The average annual amount of aid from all sources combined, including scholarships, loans, and work contracts, is $16,896; maximum, $20,058. Awards are based on need and merit. Required financial statement is the FAFSA. The aid application deadline for fall entry is March 1. Special funds for minority or disadvantaged students include scholarships based on diversity, including the Bowen Scholarship. First-year students are notified about their financial aid application at the time of admission application request.

About the Law School

University of Arkansas at Little Rock UALR William H. Bowen School of Law was established in 1975 and is a public institution. The 5-acre campus is in an urban area downtown, 6 miles from the main campus. The primary mission of the law school is to provide a high-quality legal education that equips students with the knowledge, skills, and ethical concepts to function as competent attorneys, public officials, business people, and other pro-

fessionals, and to think critically about the efficacy of the law and legal institutions and to work for their improvement. Students have access to federal, state, county, city, and local agencies, courts, correctional facilities, law firms, and legal aid organizations in the Little Rock area. Facilities of special interest to law students include all branches of state government as well as legal services and law firms. Housing for students consists of plentiful rental opportunities thoughout Little Rock along with privately owned law student housing adjacent to the law school. All law school facilities are accessible to the physically disabled.

Calendar

The law school operates on a traditional semester basis. Courses for full-time students are offered principally day, with some upper-level electives and must be completed within 6 years. For part-time students, courses are offered and principally evenings, with some upper-level electives during the day, and must be completed within 6 years. New full- and part-time students are admitted in the fall. There is an 8-week summer session. Transferable summer courses are offered.

Programs

Students may take relevant courses in other programs and apply credit toward the J.D.; a maximum of 6 credits for the joint degree may be applied. The following joint degrees may be earned: J.D./M.B.A. (Juris Doctor/Master of Business Administration), J.D./M.D. (Juris Doctor/Medical Doctor), J.D./M.P.A. (Juris Doctor/Master of Public Administration), J.D./M.P.H. (Juris Doctor/Master of Public Health), and J.D./M.P.S. (Juris Doctor/Master of Public Service.)

Required
To earn the J.D., candidates must complete 90 total credits, of which 45 are for required courses. They must maintain a minimum GPA of 2.0 in the required courses. The following first-year courses are required of all students: Civil Procedure I and II, Contracts I and II, Criminal Law, Legal Research I and II, Property I and II, Reasoning, Writing, and Advocacy I and II, and Torts. Required upper-level courses consist of Constitutional Law, Evidence, Lawyering Skills I and II, and Legal

Phone: 501-324-9903
Fax: 501-324-9909
E-mail: lawadm@ualr.edu
Web: law.ualr.edu

Contact

Jean M. Probasco, Registrar, 501-324-9903 for general inquiries; Director of Student Services, 501 569-3130 for financial aid information.

ARKANSAS

Profession. The required orientation program for first-year students is 4 days long and covers the academic and personal skills needed to succeed in law school.

Electives

The UALR William H. Bowen School of Law offers concentrations in corporate law, criminal law, family law, international law, juvenile law, labor law, litigation, securities law, tax law, and torts and insurance. Of special curricular note are the 3 clinics; litigation (worth 6 hours), mediation (worth 4 hours), and tax clinic (worth 4 hours). Upper-level students can choose from a number of seminar topics (worth 2 credits) as well as write their own independent paper (1 to 2 credits) under the supervision of a faculty member. Outside speakers participate in an annual symposium, and nationally notable speakers offer several lectures a year. The law school has a public interest externship program in which students earn academic credit working with government agencies, the state legislature, and judges. The law school accepts any ABA-accredited study-abroad program. A number of scholarships are available to students. Many factors are considered in the awarding of scholarships, including race, ethnicity, and background. An ongoing tutorial program directed by the associate dean and staffed by upper-level students who teach study skills is available to first-year students. An academic mentoring program is available to all first-year students. The most widely taken electives are Family Law, Debtor-Creditor, and Business Associations.

Graduation Requirements

In order to graduate, candidates must have a GPA of 2.0 and have completed the upper-division writing requirement and the upper-level jurisprudential requirement, which can be fulfilled by a number of courses.

Organizations

Students edit the *University of Arkansas at Little Rock Law Review*. Other law reviews include the faculty-edited *Journal of Appellate Practice and Process*. The student newspaper is *The Student Bar Association Forum*. There is also the alumni publication *Hearsay*. Moot court competitions include First Amendment National

Moot Court and ABA Young Lawyers National Moot Court Competition. Other competitions include the Henry Woods Trial Competition; National Trial Competition, an intraschool Moot Court Competition; and an Advocacy Slam. Law student organizations, local chapters of national associations, and campus organizations include Phi Alpha Delta, Phi Delta Phi, Delta Theta Phi, Black Law Students Association, The Federalist Society, American Bar Association, Community Outreach Opportunity League, Student Bar Association, and Pulaski County Bar-Law Student Division.

Library

The law library contains 317,304 hardcopy volumes and 578,702 microform volume equivalents. Such on-line databases and networks as CALI, CIS Universe, DIALOG, Infotrac, Legal-Trac, LEXIS, LOIS, NEXIS, OCLC First Search, WESTLAW, Wilsonline Indexes, HeinOnline, LLMC Digital, Versus Law, BNA, Intelliconnect, and Lexis Congressional EBSCOhost are available to law students for research. Special library collections include a federal documents depository, a state documents depository going back to 1993, and Arkansas Supreme Court records and briefs for 1836-1926. Recently, the library added a wireless network and on-line interlibrary loans and expanded access to electronic resources. The ratio of library volumes to faculty is 8350 to 1 and to students is 696 to 1. The ratio of seats in the library to students is 1 to 1.

Faculty

The law school has 38 full-time and 82 part-time faculty members, of whom 55 are women. The ratio of full-time students to full-time faculty in an average class is 15 to 1; in a clinic, 8 to 1. The law school has a regular program of bringing visiting professors and other distinguished lecturers and visitors to campus.

Students

About 48% of the student body are women; 23%, minorities; 13%, African American; 3%, Asian American; 5%, Hispanic; 1%, Native American; and 2%, international. The majority of students come from Arkansas (75%). The average age of entering students is 27; age range is 21 to 67. About 69% of students enter

Placement

J.D.s awarded:	127

Services available through: a separate law school placement center

Services: computer access to WESTLAW, NALPLine, brown-bag lunches on various aspects of career planning and the job search

Special features: the Symplicity on-line management system and membership the Intercollegiate Job Bank.

Full-time job interviews:	3 employers
Summer job interviews:	17 employers
Placement by graduation:	51% of class
Placement within 9 months:	95% of class
Average starting salary:	$40,000 to $65,000

Areas of placement:

Private practice 2-10 attorneys	26%
Private practice 11-25 attorneys	11%
Private practice 26-50 attorneys	2%
Private practice 51-100 attorneys	2%
Private practice 100+ attorneys, Solo, unknown	11%
Business/industry	14%
Judicial clerkships	13%
Government	13%
Academic	5%
Public interest	4%

directly from undergraduate school. About 1% drop out after the first year for academic or personal reasons; 99% remain to receive a law degree.

School of Law

1420 North Charles Street
Baltimore, MD 21201-5779

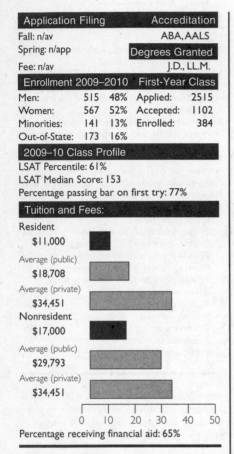

Application Filing	Accreditation
Fall: n/av	ABA, AALS
Spring: n/app	**Degrees Granted**
Fee: n/av	J.D., LL.M.

Enrollment 2009–2010		First-Year Class	
Men:	515 48%	Applied:	2515
Women:	567 52%	Accepted:	1102
Minorities:	141 13%	Enrolled:	384
Out-of-State:	173 16%		

2009–10 Class Profile

LSAT Percentile: 61%
LSAT Median Score: 153
Percentage passing bar on first try: 77%

Tuition and Fees:

Resident
$11,000

Average (public)
$18,708

Average (private)
$34,451

Nonresident
$17,000

Average (public)
$29,793

Average (private)
$34,451

0 10 20 30 40 50

Percentage receiving financial aid: 65%

ADMISSIONS

In the fall 2009 first-year class, 2515 applied, 1102 were accepted, and 384 enrolled. Figures in the above capsule and in this profile are approximate. Fifteen transfers enrolled. The median LSAT percentile of the most recent first-year class was 61; the median GPA was 3.23 on a scale of 4.0. The lowest LSAT percentile accepted was 23; the highest was 93.

Requirements

Applicants must have a bachelor's degree and take the LSAT. The most important admission factors include work experience, GPA, and LSAT results. No specific undergraduate courses are required. Candidates are not interviewed.

Procedure

Applicants should submit an application form, a personal statement, 2 letters of recommendation, personal statement, and a resume. LSAT scores, transcripts, and letters of recommendation must come through LSDAS. Notification of the admissions decision is on a rolling basis. The latest acceptable LSAT test date for fall entry is February. Check with the school for current application deadlines. The law school uses the LSDAS.

Special

The law school recruits minority and disadvantaged students by means of an on-campus minority law forum, recruiting at historically black colleges, recruiting minorities during visits to undergraduate institutions, and through the Baltimore Scholar Program. Requirements are not different for out-of-state students. Transfer students must have one year of credit, have attended an ABA-approved law school, and have files individually reviewed by committee, which does so subject to availability of space.

Costs

Tuition and fees for the 2009-2010 academic year are $11,000 for full-time in-state students and $17,000 for out-of-state students. Tuition for part-time students is $1400 in-state and $1000 out-of-state. Books and supplies run $700.

Financial Aid

In a recent year, about 65% of current law students received some form of aid. The average annual amount of aid from all sources combined, including scholarships, loans, and work contracts, was $18,000; maximum, $30,000. Awards are based on need and merit, along with need only for federal programs; scholarships are based on need and/or merit. Required financial statement is the FAFSA. Check with the school for current application deadlines. First-year students are notified about their financial aid application in May.

About the Law School

University of Baltimore School of Law was established in 1925 and is a public institution. The campus is in an urban area in Baltimore. The primary mission of the law school is to draw together students and faculty from a variety of backgrounds in a common search for knowledge and understanding. Students have access to federal, state, county, city, and local agencies, courts, correctional facilities, law firms, and legal aid organizations in the Baltimore area. Area corporations and nonprofit organizations are also accessible. Facilities of special interest to law students consist of 2 small personal computer laboratories for student use, on-line databases and networks, and a wireless campus. Housing for students is available off campus; there is a roommate referral service offered. Nearby, many apartments range from inexpensive studios to luxury apartment buildings. All law school facilities are accessible to the physically disabled.

Calendar

The law school operates on a traditional semester basis. Courses for full-time students are offered both day and evening and must be completed within 5 years. For part-time students, courses are offered both day and evening and must be completed within 6 years. New full- and part-time students are admitted in the fall. There is an 8-week summer session. Transferable summer courses are offered.

Programs

In addition to the J.D., the law school offers the LL.M. Students may take relevant courses in other programs and apply credit toward the J.D.; a maximum of 6 credits may be applied. The following joint degrees may be earned: J.D./M.B.A. (Juris Doctor/ Master of Business Administration), J.D./M.P.A. (Juris Doctor/ Master of Public Administration), J.D./M.S. (Juris Doctor/Master of Science in criminal justice and negotiations and conflict management), and J.D./Ph.D. (Juris Doctor/ Doctor of Philosophy in policy sciences).

Required

To earn the J.D., candidates must complete 90 total credits, of which 41 are for required courses. They must maintain a minimum GPA of 2.0 in the required courses. The following first-year courses are required of all students: Civil Procedure I and II, Constitutional Law, Contracts I and II, Criminal Law, Legal Analysis, Research, and Writing I and II, Property, and Torts or Introduction to Lawyering/Torts. Required upper-level courses consist of 2 upper-level research and writing projects, an advocacy requirement, Constitutional Law II, Evidence, Legal Analysis, Research, Writing III (Moot Court), and Professional Respon-

Phone: 410-837-4459
Fax: 410-837-4450
E-mail: *lwadmiss@ubmail.ubalt.edu; jzavrotny@ubalt.edu*
Web: *law.ubalt.edu*

Contact

Jeffrey Zavrotny, Director, 410-837-4454 for general inquiries; Marlene Telak, Program Administration, 410-837-4763 for financial aid information.

sibility. Clinical courses are offered as part of upper-level elective courses.The required orientation program for first-year students is 3 days; students meet with faculty and peer advisers, attend case analysis and other seminars, and attend an Information Fair on school services and student activities.

Electives

Students must take 36 credits in their area of concentration. The School of Law offers concentrations in corporate law, criminal law, family law, intellectual property law, international law, litigation, tax law, civil rights, estate planning, public and government law, and real estate practice. In addition, clinics offer the opportunity to work under the direct supervision of attorneys. Upper-level students undertake the representation of real clients in actual cases and perform all tasks necessary for proper representation. Students earn 6 credits in the Criminal Practice Clinic, Family Law Clinic, Appellate Advocacy Clinic, Civil Advocacy Clinic, Tax Clinic, Community Development Clinic, Immigrant Rights Clinic, and Family Mediation Clinic. Seminars are 3-credit advanced discussion classes that require independent research, writing, and discussion leadership by students. The Internship Program allows upper-level students to learn about the lawyering and judicial process by working closely with supervising attorneys and judges. Internships, worth 3 to 4 credits, include the Attorney Practice Internship and Judicial Internship and are open to any upper-level student in good standing. Special lecture series include the Liss Memorial Lectures, A.M. Law Series, Hoffberger Center for Professional Ethics, and the Center for International and Comparative Law. Study abroad is open to any student after the first year of study. The school offers a program in international comparative law in conjunction with the University of Aberdeen, Scotland; Curacao (Winter Intersession); and summer abroad in Haifa, Israel. First-year students may receive tutorial assistance through the Law Achievement Workshop, which consists of weekly tutorial sessions for almost every first-year class. Other tutorial programs are handled on an individual basis. Programs for minority students include the Law Achievement Workshop, Attorney Mentors, Exam Writing Workshop, Afro-American Lectures in

Law, and Black Law Student Orientation. The most widely taken electives are Business Organizations; Criminal Procedure I, and Family Law.

Graduation Requirements

In order to graduate, candidates must have a GPA of 2.0, have completed the upper-division writing requirement, and fulfill the upper-level advocacy requirement and perspective course requirement.

Organizations

Students edit *The University of Baltimore Law Review*, the *University of Baltimore Law Forum*, the *University of Baltimore Journal of Environmental Law*, the *University of Baltimore Intellectual Property Journal*, and the newspaper *Official Reporter*. Annually, teams compete at the American Trial Lawyers Association and Trial Advocacy and Client Counseling competitions, as well as the Client Negotiation Moot Court, Pace National Environmental Law Moot Court, Tax Moot Court, and Trial Advocacy competitions. Law student organizations include the Intellectual Property Legal Society, Christian Legal Society, and Criminal Law Association. There are local chapters of Phi Alpha Delta, Phi Delta Kappa, and Phi Delta Phi. Campus clubs and other organizations include BLSA, APALSA, and WBA.

Library

The law library contains 365,150 hardcopy volumes and 193,533 microform volume equivalents, and subscribes to 765 serial publications. Such on-line databases and networks as CALI, CIS Universe, Legal-Trac, LEXIS, LOIS, NEXIS, OCLC First Search, WESTLAW, and Wilsonline Indexes are available to law students for research. Special library collections include a U.S. government selective depository. Recently, the library added a 28-seat PC laboratory with offline LEXIS and WESTLAW printers. The ratio of library volumes to faculty is 7607 to 1 and to students is 337 to 1. The ratio of seats in the library to students is 1 to 3.

Faculty

The law school has 48 full-time and 92 part-time faculty members, of whom 48 are women. According to AAUP standards for Category IIA institutions, faculty sala-

Placement

J.D.s awarded:	292

Services available through: a separate law school placement center

Services: some 20 different panels and workshops on job search techniques, specialty areas, and career opportunities

Special features: University of Baltimore/University of Maryland Public Interest Career Fair; Greater Washington Baltimore Public Service Career Fair, and EXPLOR, a summer legal experience program for first year students

Full-time job interviews:	20 employers
Summer job interviews:	30 employers
Placement by graduation:	93% of class
Placement within 9 months:	94% of class
Average starting salary:	$27,500 to $145,000

Areas of placement:

Private practice 2-25 attorneys	21%
Private practice 26-100 attorneys	5%
Private practice 101+ attorneys	5%
Solo practice	10%
Judicial clerkships	23%
Business/industry	18%
Government	13%
5% private practice 100+ attorneys;	
solo practice;	10%
Public interest	5%
Academic	3%
Military	1%

ries are well above average. About 30% of full-time faculty have a graduate law degree in addition to the J.D. The ratio of full-time students to full-time faculty in an average class is 19 to 1; in a clinic, 6 to 1. The law school has a regular program of bringing visiting professors and other distinguished lecturers and visitors to campus.

Students

About 52% of the student body are women; 13%, minorities; 8%, African American; 5%, Asian American; 2%, Hispanic; and 1%, Native American. The majority of students come from Maryland (84%). The average age of entering students is 26; age range is 22 to 58. About 7% drop out after the first year for academic or personal reasons; 93% remain to receive a law degree.

Hastings College of the Law

200 McAllister Street
San Francisco, CA 94102

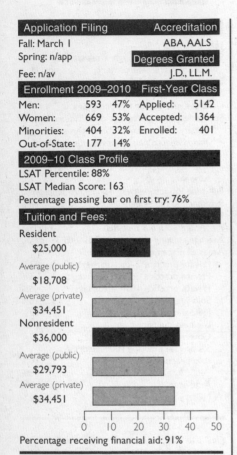

Application Filing			Accreditation	
Fall: March 1			ABA, AALS	
Spring: n/app			**Degrees Granted**	
Fee: n/av			J.D., LL.M.	
Enrollment 2009–2010			**First-Year Class**	
Men:	593	47%	Applied:	5142
Women:	669	53%	Accepted:	1364
Minorities:	404	32%	Enrolled:	401
Out-of-State:	177	14%		

2009–10 Class Profile
LSAT Percentile: 88%
LSAT Median Score: 163
Percentage passing bar on first try: 76%

Tuition and Fees:

Resident
$25,000

Average (public)
$18,708

Average (private)
$34,451

Nonresident
$36,000

Average (public)
$29,793

Average (private)
$34,451

0   10   20   30   40   50

Percentage receiving financial aid: 91%

ADMISSIONS

In the fall 2009 first-year class, 5142 applied, 1364 were accepted, and 401 enrolled. Figures in the above capsule and in this profile are approximate. Figures in the above capsule and in this profile are approximate. Forty-one transfers enrolled. The median LSAT percentile of the most recent first-year class was 88; the median GPA was 3.57 on a scale of 4.0. The lowest LSAT percentile accepted was 33; the highest was 100.

Requirements
Applicants must have a bachelor's degree and take the LSAT. The most important admission factors include academic achievement, LSAT results, and GPA. No specific undergraduate courses are required. Candidates are not interviewed.

Procedure
Applicants should submit an application form, LSAT results, transcripts, a personal statement, a nonrefundable applica-

tion fee, and 2 letters of recommendation. Notification of the admissions decision is January through May. The latest acceptable LSAT test date for fall entry is February. The law school uses the LSDAS.

Special
The law school recruits minority and disadvantaged students by enrolling 20% of the class through the LEOP program, an alternative means of evaluating disadvantaged students, through specific outreach initiatives and Candidate Referral Service, and through a holistic evaluation process. Requirements are not different for out-of-state students. Transfer students must have one year of credit, have a minimum GPA of 3.0, have attended an ABA-approved law school, and the school must be AALS-approved.

Costs

Tuition and fees for the 2009-2010 academic year are $25,000 for full-time in-state students and $36,000 for out-of-state students. On-campus room and board costs about $15,000 annually; books and supplies run $1200.

Financial Aid

In a recent year, about 91% of current law students received some form of aid. The average annual amount of aid from all sources combined, including scholarships, loans, and work contracts, was $36,064; maximum, $54,638. Awards are based on need and merit. Required financial statements are the FAFSA and the entering student financial aid supplement form. Check with the school for current application deadlines. First-year students are notified about their financial aid application as soon after acceptance as possible.

About the Law School

University of California Hastings College of the Law was established in 1878 and is a public institution. The campus is in an urban area in San Francisco. The primary mission of the law school is to prepare new members of the legal profession who are capable of and willing to serve all segments of the public as lawyers, judges, legislators, legal scholars, and in other roles in society. Students have access to federal, state, county, city, and local agencies, courts, correctional facilities,

law firms, and legal aid organizations in the San Francisco area. Facilities of special interest to law students include the Public Interest Clearinghouse, the Public Law Research Institute, and the Land Conservation Institute. Housing for students is offered at McAllister Tower, which accommodates approximately 450 students. There are studios, 1-bedroom, and 2-bedroom units available. About 90% of the law school facilities are accessible to the physically disabled.

Calendar

The law school operates on a traditional semester basis. Courses for full-time students are offered days only and must be completed within 3 years. For part-time students, courses are offered and There is no part-time program. New students are admitted in the fall. There is no summer session. Transferable summer courses are not offered.

Programs

In addition to the J.D., the law school offers the LL.M. Students may take relevant courses in other programs and apply credit toward the J.D.; a maximum of 6 units may be applied. The following joint degrees may be earned: J.D./M.A. (Juris Doctor/Master of Arts), J.D./M.B.A. (Juris Doctor/Master of Business Administration), J.D./M.P.H. (Juris Doctor/Master of Public Health), and J.D./M.P.P. (Juris Doctor/Master of Public Policy).

Required
To earn the J.D., candidates must complete 86 total credits, of which 34 are for required courses. They must maintain a minimum GPA of 2.0 in the required courses. The following first-year courses are required of all students: a statutory course, Civil Procedure, Contracts, Criminal Law, Legal Writing and Research, Moot Court, Property, and Torts. Required upper-level courses consist of a professional skills course, Professional Responsibility, and seminar or independent study with a substantial writing component. The required orientation program for first-year students is a 2 1/2-day program that includes mock classes taught by first-year faculty, assignments, discussions of study habits, test-taking, diversity issues, and career opportunities.

Contact
Greg Canada, Director of Admissions, 415-565-4885 for general inquiries; Linda Bisesi, Director of Financial Aid, 415-565-4624 for financial aid information.

CALIFORNIA

Electives
Students must take 20 to 24 credits in their area of concentration. The Hastings College of the Law offers concentrations in criminal law, international law, litigation, tax law, and public interest law. In addition, upper-level students may act as judicial externs for one of the state or federal courts. Students also may participate in a clinical seminar and gain practice experience under the supervision of an attorney. Clinics include Civil Justice, Civil Practice, Criminal Practice, Environmental Law, Workers' Rights, Immigration, and Local Government Law. Enrollment in seminars is limited to 24 second- and third-year students. Upper-level students whose academic work is of superior quality may conduct research under the supervision of a full-time faculty member. There are exchange programs with Leiden University, Austral University, Bocconi University, Bucerius Law School, Copenhagen University, University of New South Wales, and Wuhan University. The Legal Education Opportunity Program (LEOP) offers academic support to selected students with backgrounds that include some serious disadvantage that has been encountered and overcome. Incoming students have a special 1-week orientation introducing them to case briefing, legal writing, and analysis. Other programs for LEOP students include the First-Year Study Program for the California bar examination, which is taught by and for LEOP students. An exchange program in Environmental Law is offered with the Vermont Law School. The most widely taken electives are Constitutional Law, Evidence, and Criminal Procedure.

Graduation Requirements
In order to graduate, candidates must have a GPA of 2.0 and have completed the upper-division writing requirement.

Organizations
Students edit the *Hastings Law Journal, The Constitutional Law Quarterly, International and Comparative Law Review, Communications* and *Entertainment Law Journal, Women's Law Journal, Race and Poverty, Business Law Review,* and *North/Northwest Journal of Environmental Law and Policy.* The student newspaper is the *Hastings Law News.* Moot court competitions include the Giles Sutherland Rich Moot Court, National Appellate Advocacy,

and the Frederick Douglass Moot Court. Two credit hours are awarded for participation. Among the 40 student organizations are the Associated Students of Hastings, La Raza Law Students Association, and the Black Law Students Association. There are local chapters of the National Lawyers Guild, Phi Delta Phi, and Amnesty International.

Library
The law library contains 707,264 hardcopy volumes and 71,568 microform volume equivalents, and subscribes to 7858 serial publications. Such on-line databases and networks as CALI, CIS Universe, Legal-Trac, LEXIS, LOIS, OCLC First Search, WESTLAW, Wilsonline Indexes, ABI/Inform, BNA Core, CCH Internet Tax Library, CCH Internet Business and Finance Library, HeinOnline, PsycINFO, and U.S. Supreme Court Records and Briefs are available to law students for research. Special library collections include a state and federal depository, a state and federal records and briefs collection, and documents of the U.S. Supreme Court, U.S. Court of Appeals for the Ninth Circuit, and California appellate courts. Recently, the library renovated and upgraded the library facility with a wireless network, plug-in connections to the school's network, and an expanded computer laboratory. The ratio of library volumes to faculty is 11,788 to 1 and to students is 560 to 1. The ratio of seats in the library to students is 1 to 2.

Faculty
The law school has 60 full-time and 117 part-time faculty members, of whom 72 are women. According to AAUP standards for Category I institutions, faculty salaries are well below average. About 28% of full-time faculty have a graduate law degree in addition to the J.D. The ratio of full-time students to full-time faculty in an average class is 21 to 1; in a clinic, 18 to 1. The law school has a regular program of bringing visiting professors and other distinguished lecturers and visitors to campus. There is a chapter of the Order of the Coif; 48 faculty and 1630 graduates are members.

Students
About 53% of the student body are women; 32%, minorities; 3%, African American; 24%, Asian American; 7%, Hispanic;

Placement
J.D.s awarded:	421

Services available through: a separate law school placement center
Special features: The center is a co-sponsor of an annual public interest and public service conference; it also conducts on-campus interviewing twice a year.

Full-time job interviews:	200 employers
Summer job interviews:	225 employers
Placement by graduation:	61% of class
Placement within 9 months:	94% of class
Average starting salary:	$26,000 to $150,000

Areas of placement:
Private practice 2-10 attorneys	14%
Private practice 11-25 attorneys	6%
Private practice 26-50 attorneys	4%
Private practice 51-100 attorneys	4%
Private practice 101-500 attorneys	45%
Business/industry	9%
Government	8%
Judicial clerkships	4%
Public interest	4%
Academic	2%

and 1%, Native American. The majority of students come from California (86%). The average age of entering students is 24; age range is 20 to 47. About 6% of students' have a graduate degree. About 2% drop out after the first year for academic or personal reasons; 98% remain to receive a law degree.

School of Law

215 Boalt Hall
Berkeley, CA 94720

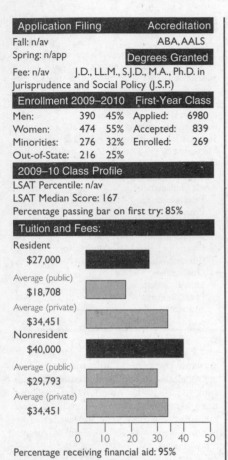

Enrollment 2009–2010   First-Year Class

Men:	390	45%	Applied:	6980
Women:	474	55%	Accepted:	839
Minorities:	276	32%	Enrolled:	269
Out-of-State:	216	25%		

2009–10 Class Profile

LSAT Percentile: n/av
LSAT Median Score: 167
Percentage passing bar on first try: 85%

Tuition and Fees:

Resident
$27,000

Average (public)
$18,708

Average (private)
$34,451

Nonresident
$40,000

Average (public)
$29,793

Average (private)
$34,451

0 10 20 30 40 50

Percentage receiving financial aid: 95%

ADMISSIONS

In the fall 2009 first-year class, 6980 applied, 839 were accepted, and 269 enrolled. Figures in the above capsule and in this profile are approximate. Sixty transfers enrolled. The median GPA of the most recent first-year class was 3.79. The lowest LSAT percentile accepted was 35; the highest was 100.

Requirements
Applicants must have a bachelor's degree and take the LSAT. The most important admission factors include academic achievement, LSAT results, and life experience. No specific undergraduate courses are required. Candidates are not interviewed.

Procedure
Applicants should submit an application form, LSAT results, transcripts, a nonrefundable application fee, and a personal statement. Although letters of recommendation are not mandatory, they are highly recommended. Notification of the admissions decision is from January to May. The latest acceptable LSAT test date for fall entry is December. Check with the school for current application deadlines. The law school uses the LSDAS.

Special
The law school recruits minority and disadvantaged students by participating in outreach activities at a wide variety of institutions, including HBCU's and HACU's. The law school also actively recruits all admitted students, including those from underrepresented minority groups. Requirements are not different for out-of-state students. Transfer students must have one year of credit, have attended an ABA-approved law school, and be in the top 5% at their home law school.

Costs

Tuition and fees for the 2009-2010 academic year are $27,000 for full-time in-state students and $40,000 for out-of-state students. Books and supplies run $1500.

Financial Aid

In a recent year, about 95% of current law students received some form of aid. The maximum annual amount of aid from all sources combined, including scholarships, loans, and work contracts, was $60,648. Awards are based on need and merit. Required financial statements are the FAFSA and Need Access. Chedk with the school for current application deadlines. The aid application deadline for fall entry is March 2. First-year students are notified about their financial aid application at in late spring.

About the Law School

University of California at Berkeley School of Law was established in 1903 and is a public institution. The campus is in an urban area 12 miles east of San Francisco. The primary mission of the law school is to educate men and women not only for the practice of law, but for all the varied roles lawyers perform in a modern society. Students have access to federal, state, county, city, and local agencies, courts, correctional facilities, law firms, and legal aid organizations in the Berkeley area. All other facilities of the Berkeley campus are available to law students. Housing for students is available at the law studio apartment complex, International House, and off campus. All law school facilities are accessible to the physically disabled.

Calendar

The law school operates on a traditional semester basis. Courses for full-time students are offered days only and must be completed within 3 years. There is no part-time program. New students are admitted in the fall. There is no summer session. Transferable summer courses are not offered.

Programs

In addition to the J.D., the law school offers the LL.M., S.J.D., M.A., and Ph.D. in Jurisprudence and Social Policy (J.S.P.). Students may take relevant courses in other programs and apply credit toward the J.D.; a maximum of varies credits may be applied. The following joint degrees may be earned: J.D./M.A. (Juris Doctor/ Master of Arts in Asian studies, jurisprudence), J.D./M.A.L.D. (Juris Doctor/ Master of Arts in law and diplomacy), J.D./M.B.A. (Juris Doctor/Master of Business Administration), J.D./M.C.P. (Juris Doctor/Master of City and Regional Planning), J.D./M.J. (Juris Doctor/Master of Journalism), J.D./M.P.P. (Juris Doctor/ Master of Public Policy), J.D./M.S.W. (Juris Doctor/Master of Social Work), and J.D./Ph.D. (Juris Doctor/Doctor of Philosophy in legal history, jurisprudence, economics, and history).

Required
To earn the J.D., candidates must complete 85 total credits, of which 32 are for required courses. The following first-year courses are required of all students: Civil Procedure, Contracts, Criminal Law, Legal Writing, Research, Advocacy, Property, and Torts. Required upper-level courses consist of Constitutional Law and Professional Responsibility. The required orientation program for first-year students consists of 2 days of basic material for new students including the curriculum and services in August, and 1 day in October for information regarding final exams, grading, and so on.

Phone: 510-642-2274
Fax: 510-643-6222
E-mail: *adissions@law.berkeley.edu*
Web: *www.law.berkeley.edu*

Contact

Edward Tom, Director, 510-642-2274 for general inquiries; Dennis Tominaga, Director, 510-642-1568 for financial aid information.

Electives

The School of Law offers concentrations in corporate law, environmental law, international law, law and technology, social justice/public interest, intellectual property, comparative legal studies, and law and economics. In addition, clinics, mostly open to second-and third-year students, include Death Penalty, International Human Rights Law, and Technology and Public Policy. Field work may be done at the East Bay Community Law Center and in the other clinics. Special lecture series are offered through various centers. Study abroad is available on a case-by-case basis. Special interest group programs include the Center for Social Justice and the Center for Law and Technology. The most widely taken electives are Evidence, Civil Procedures II, and Corporations.

Graduation Requirements

In order to graduate, candidates must have completed the upper-division writing requirement.

Organizations

Students edit *The California Law Review, Berkeley Business Law Journal, Ecology Law Quarterly, Berkeley Technology Law Journal, Berkeley Journal of Employment and Labor Law, Berkeley Journal of International Law, Berkeley Women's Law Journal, African American Law and Policy Report, La Raza Law Journal, California Criminal Law Review*, and *Asian Law Journal.* The *Cross-Examiner* is the student newspaper. Annual moot court competitions are held at the school and include the McBaine and Jessup competitions. Law student organizations, local chapters of national associations, and campus organizations include the Asian Pacific American Law Students, Law Students of African Descent, La Raza, Federalist Society, National Lawyers Guild, Phi Alpha Delta, and the ABA/Law Student Division.

Library

The law library contains 682,682 hardcopy volumes and 188,598 microform volume equivalents, and subscribes to 8200 serial publications. Such on-line databases and networks as CIS Universe, DIALOG, Legal-Trac, LEXIS, NEXIS, RLIN, and WESTLAW are available to law students for research. Special library collections include the Robbins Collection of ecclesiastical, foreign, comparative, and international law. Recently, the library began a major renovation of its main reading room. The ratio of library volumes to faculty is 7341 to 1 and to students is 790 to 1. The ratio of seats in the library to students is 1 to 2.

Faculty

The law school has 93 full-time and 38 part-time faculty members, of whom 55 are women. According to AAUP standards for Category I institutions, faculty salaries are above average. About 3% of full-time faculty have a graduate law degree in addition to the J.D. The ratio of full-time students to full-time faculty in an average class is 33 to 1; in a clinic, 13 to 1. The law school has a regular program of bringing visiting professors and other distinguished lecturers and visitors to campus. There is a chapter of the Order of the Coif; 8 faculty are members.

Students

About 55% of the student body are women; 32%, minorities; 6%, African American; 16%, Asian American; 13%, Hispanic; and 3%, Native American. The majority of students come from California (75%). The average age of entering students is 25; age range is 20 to 47. About 40% of students enter directly from undergraduate school, 11% have a graduate degree, and 60% have worked full-time prior to entering law school. About 1% drop out after the first year for academic or personal reasons; 98% remain to receive a law degree.

Placement

J.D.s awarded:	275

Services available through: a separate law school placement center and the university placement center

Services: A searchable job database is available on the school's web site.

Special features: fall and spring on-campus interview programs, a career symposium for first year students, a mentor program, mock interviews, a speaker series on law specialties, as well as individual counseling sessions with counselors who have all practiced law themselves. A full-time counselor focuses on public interest/public sector careers, fellowships, and judicial clerkship advising.

Full-time job interviews:	150 employers
Summer job interviews:	335 employers
Placement by graduation:	99% of class
Placement within 9 months:	99% of class
Average starting salary:	$30,000 to $180,000

Areas of placement:

Private practice unknown size	70%
Judicial clerkships	12%
Public interest	10%
Government	6%
Business/industry	2%

UNIVERSITY OF CALIFORNIA AT DAVIS

School of Law

Martin Luther King, Jr. Hall
400 Mrak Hall Drive
Davis, CA 95616-5201

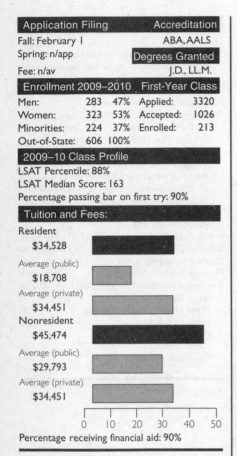

Application Filing	Accreditation
Fall: February 1	ABA, AALS
Spring: n/app	**Degrees Granted**
Fee: n/av	J.D., LL.M.

Enrollment 2009–2010		First-Year Class	
Men:	283 47%	Applied:	3320
Women:	323 53%	Accepted:	1026
Minorities:	224 37%	Enrolled:	213
Out-of-State:	606 100%		

2009–10 Class Profile
LSAT Percentile: 88%
LSAT Median Score: 163
Percentage passing bar on first try: 90%

Tuition and Fees:

Resident
$34,528

Average (public)
$18,708

Average (private)
$34,451

Nonresident
$45,474

Average (public)
$29,793

Average (private)
$34,451

Percentage receiving financial aid: 90%

ADMISSIONS

In the fall 2009 first-year class, 3320 applied, 1026 were accepted, and 213 enrolled. Eleven transfers enrolled. The median LSAT percentile of the most recent first-year class was 88; the median GPA was 3.52 on a scale of 4.0. The lowest LSAT percentile accepted was 52; the highest was 100.

Requirements
Applicants must have a bachelor's degree and take the LSAT. The most important admission factors include LSAT results, GPA, and personal statements. No specific undergraduate courses are required. Candidates are not interviewed.

Procedure
The application deadline for fall entry is February 1. Applicants should submit an application form, LSAT results, transcripts, a personal statement, and 2 letters of recommendation. Notification of the admissions decision is from January to April (wait list June to August). The latest

acceptable LSAT test date for fall entry is December prior to August enrollment. The law school uses the LSDAS.

Special
The law school recruits minority and disadvantaged students by means of visits to undergraduate campuses, the Candidate Referral Service, graduate/professional information days, and the LSAC forums and various outreach programs and events. Requirements are different for out-of-state students in that they pay tuition not required of California residents. All admission requirements are the same; however, international applicants must provide a TOEFL score. Transfer students must have one year of credit, have attended an ABA-approved law school, and admitted students must be in the top 5% to 10% of their first-year class.

Costs

Tuition and fees for the 2009-2010 academic year are $34,528 for full-time in-state students and $45,474 for out-of-state students. Books and supplies run $1014.

Financial Aid

About 90% of current law students receive some form of aid. The average annual amount of aid from all sources combined, including scholarships, loans, and work contracts, is $34,491; maximum, $51,439. Awards are based on need. Required financial statements are the FAFSA and Need Access. The aid application deadline for fall entry is March 2. First-year students are notified about their financial aid application once they have been admitted.

About the Law School

University of California at Davis School of Law was established in 1965 and is a public institution. The 5200-acre campus is in a small town 15 miles west of Sacramento. The primary mission of the law school is to be a nationally and internationally recognized leader in the development and dissemination of legal knowledge, as well as the training of students to become socially responsible lawyers committed to professional excellence and high ethical standards, and to promote public service through law reform and professional activities. Students have access to federal, state, county, city, and local agencies, courts, correctional facilities, law firms, and legal aid organizations in the

Davis area. Other resources include the state capital 15 miles away. Facilities of special interest to law students include the instructional computer laboratory; the library, which allows 24-hour access; a day care co-op where care is provided by parents for children 12 months and younger; and wireless Internet access through-out the law school building and in the courtyard. Housing for students is available on- and off campus through the ASUCD Community Housing Listing Service and a variety of community resource listings (e.g., newspapers); rental rates are reasonable and consistently lower than those in San Francisco and Los Angeles. All law school facilities are accessible to the physically disabled.

Calendar

The law school operates on a traditional semester basis. Courses for full-time students are offered days only and must be completed within 3 years. There is no part-time program. New students are admitted in the fall. There is no summer session. Transferable summer courses are not offered.

Programs

In addition to the J.D., the law school offers the LL.M. and Masters in International Commercial Law (MICL) (summer program). Students may take relevant courses in other programs and apply credit toward the J.D.; a maximum of 10 semester units credits may be applied. The following joint degrees may be earned: J.D./M.A. (Juris Doctor/Master of Arts in most programs offered by UC) and J.D./M.B.A. (Juris Doctor/Masters in Business Administration).

Required
To earn the J.D., candidates must complete 88 total credits, of which 33 are for required courses. They must maintain a minimum GPA of 2.0 in the required courses. The following first-year courses are required of all students: Civil Procedure, Constitutional Law, Contracts, Criminal Law, Introduction to Law, Legal Research and Legal Writing, Property, and Torts. Required upper-level courses consist of a skills requirement, an advanced legal writing project, and Professional Responsibility. The required orientation program for first-year students is an introductory week that includes meeting the Academic Assistance Program tutors, a

Phone: 530-752-6477
E-mail: *admissions@lawucdavis.edu*
Web: *www.law.ucdavis.edu*

Contact

Sharon L. Pinkney, Assistant Dean for Admission, 530-752-6477 for general inquiries; Lawrence Gallardo, Financial Aid Director, 530-752-6573 for financial aid information.

tour of the law library, a photo session, class registration, a financial aid information session, dean's orientation, and social activities. The primary focus is a 1-unit course, Introduction to Law.

Electives

Students must take 15 credits in their area of concentration. The School of Law offers concentrations in environmental law, international law, and a certificate program in public interest law; the law school provides for a number of specialized studies including intellectual property and business law. In addition, clinics are open to upper-level students. Placements are available with selected public agencies, judges, and some private attorneys through such formal clinical programs as Administration of Criminal Justice (2 to 6 or 12 units), Civil Rights (2 to 6 units), and Employment Relations (2 to 6 units). Seminars for 2 or 3 credits, open to upper-level students, include areas of constitutional law, criminal law, and estate planning. An extensive array of seminars for 2 to 3 credits are open to upper-level students. Internships are available through clinics; additional opportunities are available in tax and public interest. In the second or third year, all students must complete a writing project (an individually authored work of rigorous intellectual effort). Special lecture series include Bodenheimer Lecture on the Family and Barrett Lecture on Constitutional Law. Exchange programs with China University of Political Science and Law, University College Dublin, and University of Copenhagen are available. The UCDC Law Program is a uniquely collaborative semester-long externship program in Washington, D.C., combining a weekly seminar with a full-time field placement to offer law students an unparralleled opportunity to learn how federal statutes, regulations and policies are made, changed and understood in the nation's capital. From Introduction Week to the week of the bar exam, the Academic Success Program offers tutorial assistance, study aids, sample practice exams, study and exam skills workshops, individual academic counseling, and study plan and learning styles assessments. All programs are designed to help students improve their academic performance in law school and the profession. The Academic Success Program is staffed by a Director and 14 to 16 second- and third-year law student tutors. Proposition 209

in the state of California precludes establishing programs designed solely for any particular group based on race, ethnicity, or sex. Special interest group programs include the King Hall Pro Bono Program, the Public Interest Law Program, and the Environmental and Natural Resource Law Program. The most widely taken electives are Evidence, Business Association, and Trust Wills.

Graduation Requirements

In order to graduate, candidates must have a GPA of 2.0, have completed the upper-division writing requirement, and the required course Professional Responsibility.

Organizations

Students edit the *UC Davis Law Review* and the newspaper, *Advocate*. Moot court competitions held annually include the Moot Court Trial Competition, Client Counseling, and National Moot Court. Other competitions include the Frances Newall Carr Competition-Intra School Mock Trial, and National Negotiation Competition. Student organizations, local chapters of national associations, and campus organizations include the ABA-Law Student Division, Phi Alpha Delta, Phi Delta Phi, Tax Law Society, Advocates for the Rights of Children, Criminal Law Association, King Hall Legal Foundation, American Constitution Society, and the Federalist Society.

Library

The law library contains 302,516 hardcopy volumes and 768,833 microform volume equivalents, and subscribes to 4249 serial publications. Such on-line databases and networks as CALI, CIS Universe, DIALOG, Legal-Trac, LEXIS, Mathew Bender, NEXIS, OCLC First Search, WESTLAW, California Digital Libraries, RIA Checkpoint, SSRN, Hein OnLine, TRAC, MELVYL, CA Continuing Education of the Bar Online Publication, BNA & CCH Topical Online databases, and knowledge MOSAIC are available to law students for research. Special library collections include federal and California documents depositories. Special emphasis is in intellectual property environmental law, international law, immigration, and civil rights. Recently, the library instituted an Advanced Legal Research course, a faculty liaison program, and virtual

Placement

J.D.s awarded:	191

Services available through: a separate law school placement center

Special features: There is a career services library as well as career-related panels and presentations. UC Davis has its own internal Public Interest Program.

Full-time job interviews:	47 employers
Summer job interviews:	123 employers
Placement by graduation:	95% of class
Placement within 9 months:	98% of class
Average starting salary:	$30,000 to $125,000

Areas of placement:

Private practice 2-10 attorneys	17%
Private practice 11-25 attorneys	7%
Private practice 26-50 attorneys	6%
Private practice 51-100+ attorneys	19%
Private practice solo	3%
Public interest	13%
Judicial clerkships	11%
Business/industry	8%
Government	7%
Academic	1%
Military	1%

reference. The ratio of library volumes to faculty is 6174 to 1 and to students is 499 to 1. The ratio of seats in the library to students is 1 to 1.

Faculty

The law school has 49 full-time and 14 part-time faculty members, of whom 28 are women. According to AAUP standards for Category I institutions, faculty salaries are above average. About 8% of full-time faculty have a graduate law degree in addition to the J.D. The ratio of full-time students to full-time faculty in an average class is 35 to 1; in a clinic, 10 to 1. The law school has a regular program of bringing visiting professors and other distinguished lecturers and visitors to campus. There is a chapter of the Order of the Coif; 26 faculty and 502 graduates are members.

Students

About 53% of the student body are women; 37%, minorities; 2%, African American; 24%, Asian American; 7%, Hispanic; and 1%, Native American. The average age of entering students is 24; age range is 20 to 52. About 29% of students enter directly from undergraduate school and 7% have a graduate degree. About 5% drop out after the first year for academic or personal reasons; 90% remain to receive a law degree.

UNIVERSITY OF CALIFORNIA AT LOS ANGELES

UCLA School of Law

P.O. Box 951445
Los Angeles, CA 90095-1445

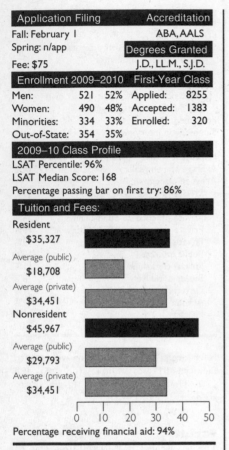

Application Filing	Accreditation
Fall: February 1	ABA, AALS
Spring: n/app	**Degrees Granted**
Fee: $75	J.D., LL.M., S.J.D.

Enrollment 2009–2010		First-Year Class	
Men:	521 52%	Applied:	8255
Women:	490 48%	Accepted:	1383
Minorities:	334 33%	Enrolled:	320
Out-of-State:	354 35%		

2009–10 Class Profile
LSAT Percentile: 96%
LSAT Median Score: 168
Percentage passing bar on first try: 86%

Tuition and Fees:

Resident
$35,327

Average (public)
$18,708

Average (private)
$34,451

Nonresident
$45,967

Average (public)
$29,793

Average (private)
$34,451

Percentage receiving financial aid: 94%

ADMISSIONS

In the fall 2009 first-year class, 8255 applied, 1383 were accepted, and 320 enrolled. Forty-six transfers enrolled. The median LSAT percentile of the most recent first-year class was 96; the median GPA was 3.75 on a scale of 4.0. The lowest LSAT percentile accepted was 47; the highest was 99.

Requirements
Applicants must have a bachelor's degree and take the LSAT. No specific undergraduate courses are required. Candidates are not interviewed.

Procedure
The application deadline for fall entry is February 1. Applicants should submit an application form, LSAT results, transcripts, a personal statement, a nonrefundable application fee of $75, at least 2 but no more than 3 letters of recommendation, and a résumé. Notification of the admissions decision is on a rolling basis. The latest acceptable LSAT test date for

fall entry is February. The law school uses the LSDAS.

Special
The law school recruits minority and disadvantaged students by means of visits to undergraduate schools, participation in LSAC forums, and programs arranged by law school administration and law student organizations. Requirements are not different for out-of-state students. Transfer students must have one year of credit and have attended an ABA-approved law school. Preadmissions courses consist of an intensive 8-day summer program for 40 incoming students held in early August to familiarize students with the study of law.

Costs

Tuition and fees for the 2009-2010 academic year are $35,327 for full-time in-state students and $45,967 for out-of-state students. On-campus room and board costs about $13,407 annually; books and supplies run $6885.

Financial Aid

About 94% of current law students receive some form of aid. The average annual amount of aid from all sources combined, including scholarships, loans, and work contracts, is $42,373; maximum, $67,036. Awards are based on need and merit. Required financial statements are the FAFSA. Those who wish to receive need-based grants must submit the Need Access application at www.needaccess.org. The aid application deadline for fall entry is March 2. Special funds for minority or disadvantaged students are available. First-year students are notified about their financial aid application once they are admitted and after their FAFSA and/or Need Access applications have been submitted.

About the Law School

University of California at Los Angeles UCLA School of Law was established in 1948 and is a public institution. The 419-acre campus is in an urban area. The primary mission of the law school is to educate students who go on to be leaders in our society. UCLA Law's central purpose is to train attorneys who will attain high levels of professional excellence and integrity who will experience civic responsibility. Students have access to federal, state, county, city, and local agencies, courts, correctional facilities, law firms, and legal aid organizations in the Los

Angeles area. Housing for students is available in both university-owned and privately owned apartments. University Apartments South offers housing for married students and single parents as well as single graduate and professional school students. UCLA recently opened Weyburn Terrace, an 840-apartment complex for single graduate students that is within walking distance of the campus. About 99% of the law school facilities are accessible to the physically disabled.

Calendar

The law school operates on a traditional semester basis. Courses for full-time students are offered days only and must be completed within 5 years. There is no part-time program. New students are admitted in the fall. There is no summer session. Transferable summer courses are not offered.

Programs

In addition to the J.D., the law school offers the LL.M. and S.J.D. Students may take relevant courses in other programs and apply credit toward the J.D.; a maximum of 6 semester units may be applied. The following joint degrees may be earned: J.D./M.A. (Juris Doctor/Master of Arts in Afro-American studies, American Indian studies), J.D./M.B.A. (Juris Doctor/Master of Business Administration), J.D./M.P.H. (Juris Doctor/Master of Public Health), J.D./M.P.P. (Juris Doctor/Master of Public Policy), J.D./M.S.W. (Juris Doctor/Master of Social Welfare), and J.D./Ph.D. (Juris Doctor/Doctorate of Philosophy).

Required
To earn the J.D., candidates must complete 87 total units, of which 35 are for required courses. They must maintain a minimum GPA of 2.0 in the required courses. The following first-year courses are required of all students: Civil Procedure, Constitutional Law I, Contracts, Criminal Law, Lawyering Skills, Property, and Torts. Required upper-level courses consist of Professional Responsibility and upper-division writing. The required orientation program for first-year students is a 2 1/2-day program designed to acquaint first-year students with classmates, professors, and deans and with the study of law and how to handle a variety of administrative tasks. It incorporates workshops, panels, and group discussions and sessions with law faculty.

Phone: 310-825-2080
Fax: 310-206-7227
E-mail: admissions@law.ucla.edu
Web: www.law.ucla.edu

Contact

Karman Hsu, Director of Admissions, 310-825-2080 for general inquiries; Biljana Vuletic, 310-825-2459 for financial aid information.

Electives

The UCLA School of Law offers concentrations in corporate law, criminal law, entertainment law, environmental law, family law, intellectual property law, international law, labor law, litigation, media law, securities law, sports law, and tax law. Academic specializations include critical race studies, public interest law and policy, business law and policy, entertainment and media law, and law and philosophy. In addition, there are more than 30 clinical offerings, with 300 clinical spots for students, including the Criminial Defense Clinic, International Justice Clinic, and Sports and the Law. Credit ranges from 2 to 10 units. Seminars are offered to advanced students, and credit ranges from 2 to 4 units; seminars include, among others, Music and Industry Law, International Human Rights, and National Security in the Information Economy. Full-time semester-long national and international externships are offered to students and are worth 13 units---11 units for placement and 2 units for a related seminar or tutorial taught by a faculty member. Students can work as extern law clerks to a federal judge or in a government agency, public interest law firm, or nonprofit organization. Students can also propose new agency externships tailored to their academic goals. Directed research, for which students must produce original scholarship of publishable quality, is worth 1 to 5 units. Special lecture series include International Law Speaker Series, Critical Race Speaker Series, Environmental Law Speaker Series, and Sexual Orientation Law Speaker Series. Students may spend one semester abroad through student exchange agreements with universities in several countries. The academic support program includes study groups led by academically successful second- and third-year students, exam and outlining workshops for all first-year students, individual academic counseling, and a summer program for 40 incoming first-year students. There are special sections in Constitutional Law, Evidence, Wills and Trusts, and Written Legal Analysis. Minority programs include Asian/Pacific Islander Law Students Association (APILSA), Black Law Students Association (BLSA), La Raza Law Students Association (La Raza), Native American Law Students Association (NALSA), and South Asian Law Students Association (SALSA). The most widely taken electives are Evidence, Constitutional Criminal Procedure, and Business Associations.

Graduation Requirements

In order to graduate, candidates must have a GPA of 2.0, have completed the upper-division writing requirement, and Complete the first-year curriculum, 6 semesters of residence credit in regular session, and a course of study in professional responsibility.

Organizations

Students edit the *UCLA Law Review*. Other student-edited publications include the *Asian Pacific American Law Journal*, *Chicano/Latino Law Review*, *National Black Law Journal*, *Pacific Basin Law Journal*, *Entertainment Law Review*, *Journal of Environmental Law and Policy*, *Journal of Islamic and Near Eastern Law*, *Journal of Law and Technology*, *Dukeminier Awards: Best Sexual Orientation Law Review Articles*, *Women's Law Journal*, and the *Journal of International Law and Foreign Affairs*. Moot Court Competitions include the UCLA Moot Court Honors Program, Sexual Orientation Law Moot Court Competition, and Jessup International Law Moot Court Competition. Law student organizations include the Environmental Law Society, International Law Society, and Mock Trial Association. Local chapters of national associations include the American Constitution Society, the Federalist Society, and many minority student organizations. Other campus clubs and organizations include Advocates for Children and Teens, Immigration Law Society and Sports Law Federation,.

Library

The law library contains 676,524 hardcopy volumes and 20,313 microform volume equivalents, and subscribes to 8283 serial publications. Such on-line databases and networks as CALI, CIS Universe, DIALOG, Infotrac, Legal-Trac, LEXIS, LOIS, Mathew Bender, NEXIS, OCLC First Search, RLIN, WESTLAW, Wilsonline Indexes, LLMC, Interam, HeinOnline, BNA Core, CCH IntelliConnect, Bloomberg, California Continuing Education of the Bar, and Making of Modern Law. are available to law students for research. Special library collections include a U.S. government depository, a California depository, an East Asian law collection, Aviation Law, Sexual Orientation Law, Women and the Law, Law and Popular Culture, and Law and Philosophy. The ratio of library volumes to faculty is 5244

Placement

J.D.s awarded:	363
Services available through: a separate law school placement center	
Services: a twice-yearly on-campus interview program; the office hosts public interest, government, and small firm events as well	
Special features: individual counseling and workshops on career planning and interviewing skills; on-line job listings can be accessed by students and alumni	
Full-time job interviews:	72 employers
Summer job interviews:	297 employers
Placement by graduation:	97% of class
Placement within 9 months:	99% of class
Average starting salary:	$32,000 to $168,000
Areas of placement:	
Private practice 2-10 attorneys	5%
Private practice 11-25 attorneys	4%
Private practice 26-50 attorneys	2%
Private practice 51-100 attorneys	3%
Judicial clerkships	9%
Public interest	9%
Government	7%
Business/industry	7%
Academic	2%
Military	1%

to 1 and to students is 515 to 1. The ratio of seats in the library to students is 1 to 1.

Faculty

The law school has 110 full-time and 46 part-time faculty members, of whom 50 are women. According to AAUP standards for Category I institutions, faculty salaries are above average. About 8% of full-time faculty have a graduate law degree in addition to the J.D.; about 13% of part-time faculty have one. The ratio of full-time students to full-time faculty in an average class is 11 to 1; in a clinic, 6 to 1. The law school has a regular program of bringing visiting professors and other distinguished lecturers and visitors to campus. There is a chapter of the Order of the Coif; 33 faculty and 10% of graduates are members.

Students

About 48% of the student body are women; 33%, minorities; 5%, African American; 18%, Asian American; 9%, Hispanic; and 1%, Native American. The majority of students come from California (65%). The average age of entering students is 25; age range is 19 to 40. About 35% of students enter directly from undergraduate school and 5% have a graduate degree. About 2% drop out after the first year for academic or personal reasons; 98% remain to receive a law degree.

Law School

1111 East 60th Street
Chicago, IL 60637

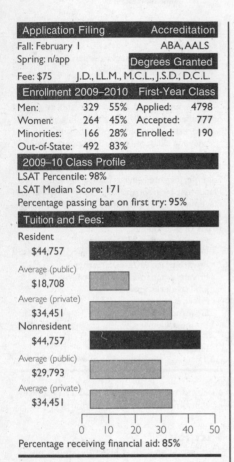

Application Filing		Accreditation
Fall: February 1		ABA, AALS
Spring: n/app		Degrees Granted
Fee: $75		J.D., LL.M., M.C.L., J.S.D., D.C.L.

Enrollment 2009–2010		First-Year Class	
Men:	329 55%	Applied:	4798
Women:	264 45%	Accepted:	777
Minorities:	166 28%	Enrolled:	190
Out-of-State:	492 83%		

2009–10 Class Profile

LSAT Percentile: 98%
LSAT Median Score: 171
Percentage passing bar on first try: 95%

Tuition and Fees:

Resident
$44,757

Average (public)
$18,708

Average (private)
$34,451

Nonresident
$44,757

Average (public)
$29,793

Average (private)
$34,451

0 10 20 30 40 50

Percentage receiving financial aid: 85%

ADMISSIONS

In the fall 2009 first-year class, 4798 applied, 777 were accepted, and 190 enrolled. Twenty-four transfers enrolled. The median LSAT percentile of the most recent first-year class was 98; the median GPA was 3.76 on a scale of 4.0.

Requirements

Applicants must have a bachelor's degree and take the LSAT. No specific undergraduate courses are required. Candidates are interviewed.

Procedure

The application deadline for fall entry is February 1. Applicants should submit an application form, LSAT results, transcripts, a nonrefundable application fee of $75, 2 letters of recommendation, a personal statement, and a resumé. Notification of the admissions decision is rolling starting in December. The latest acceptable LSAT test date for fall entry is December for most cases. The law school uses the LSDAS.

Special

The law school recruits minority and disadvantaged students by using the Law School Data Assembly Service's Candidate Referral Service and outreach at law school forums, colleges, and minority fairs. Requirements are not different for out-of-state students. Transfer students must have one year of credit, have attended an ABA-approved law school, and must be planning to spend at least 2 years at the law school.

Costs

Tuition and fees for the 2009-2010 academic year are $44,757 for all full-time students. On-campus room and board costs about $13,455 annually; books and supplies run $6105.

Financial Aid

About 85% of current law students receive some form of aid. Awards are based on need and merit. Required financial statement is the FAFSA. The aid application deadline for fall entry is March 1. First-year students are notified about their financial aid application at time of acceptance.

About the Law School

University of Chicago Law School was established in 1902 and is a private institution. The 203-acre campus is in an urban area 7 miles from downtown Chicago. The primary mission of the law school is to train well-rounded, critical, and socially conscious thinkers and doers. Three cornerstones provide the foundation for Chicago's educational mission: the life of the mind, participatory learning, and interdisciplinary inquiry. Students have access to federal, state, county, city, and local agencies, courts, correctional facilities, law firms, and legal aid organizations in the Chicago area. The clinics involve more than 120 students each year and permit them to represent clients with real-world legal problems under the guidance of clinical faculty. Facilities of special interest to law students include the law quadrangle, made up of buildings surrounding a reflecting pool and housing the law library, classrooms, offices, the legal aid clinics, an auditorium, and a moot court room. Housing for students consists of dormitories and a variety of apartments and single-family homes located in nearby

Hyde Park. About 90% of the law school facilities are accessible to the physically disabled.

Calendar

The law school operates on a quarter basis. Courses for full-time students are offered days only and must be completed within 3 years. There is no part-time program. New students are admitted in the fall. There is no summer session. Transferable summer courses are not offered.

Programs

In addition to the J.D., the law school offers the LL.M., M.C.L., J.S.D., D.C.L. Students may take relevant courses in other programs and apply credit toward the J.D.; a maximum of 12 credits may be applied.

Required

To earn th J.D., candidates must complete 105 total credits, of which 40 are for required courses. They must maintain a minimum GPA of 1.60 in the required courses. The following first-year courses are required of all students: 1 elective, Civil Procedure, Contracts, Criminal Law, Elements of the Law, Legal Research and Writing, Property, and Torts. Required upper-level courses consist of Professional Responsibillity. The optional orientation program for first-year students consists of 3 days of presentations, tours, and social events, including a dinner, a Lake Michigan boat cruise, and a picnic.

Electives

The Law School offers concentrations in corporate law, criminal law, entertainment law, environmental law, family law, intellectual property law, international law, juvenile law, labor law, litigation, maritime law, media law, securities law, sports law, tax law, torts and insurance, law and economics, and law and philosophy. In addition, clinics, available to second- and third-year students, include the Mandel Legal Aid Clinic, the Institute for Justice Clinic on Entrepreneurship, and the Exoneration Project. Seventy-two seminars are open to second- and third-year law students. The Career Services Center helps students locate summer internships. Nearly all of first-year students and 97% of second-year students

Phone: 773-702-9484
Fax: 773-834-0942
E-mail: admissions@law.uchicago.edu
Web: law.uchicago.edu

Contact
Admissions Office, 773-702-9484 for general inquiries; Kara Vargas, Director of Financial Aid, 773-702-9484 for financial aid information.

ILLINOIS

are employed during the summer. The Chicago Law Foundation, a student-run charitable organization, awards grants to students working in public-interest jobs during the summer. Also, the law school has funding available for public-interest work. Faculty-supervised research may be done in the individual research program for credit. Lectures, open to the law school community, occur several times a year in workshops such as Constitutional Law, International Law, and Law and Economics. Academic counselors, the Dean of Students, and the Associate Director of Student Affairs provide academic programming and counseling for students. The most widely taken electives are Evidence, Constitutional Law, and Corporations Law.

Graduation Requirements
In order to graduate, candidates must have a GPA of 1.68, have completed the upper-division writing requirement, and have a completed Professional Responsibility course.

Organizations
Students edit *The University of Chicago Law Review*, *The University of Chicago Legal Forum*, and *The Chicago Journal of International Law*. There are 4 faculty-edited journals: the *Supreme Court Review*, *Journal of Law and Economics*, *Journal of Legal Studies*, and *Law and Economics: Working Papers*. The student newspaper is *The Phoenix*. While first-year students have moot court practice in their Legal Research and Writing class, upper-level students participate in the Hinton Moot Court Program and selected outside moot court competitions. Other competitions include the annual trivia contest. The school has about 60 student organizations that include the Intellectual Property and Entertainment Law Society, and the International Law Society. Local chapters of national associations include the Black Law Students Association, the Federalist Society, and the American Constitution Society. Other organizations include Spring Break of Service, the Hemingway Society, and the Scales of Justice.

Library
The law library contains 624,758 hardcopy volumes and 11,712 microform vol-

ume equivalents, and subscribes to 6212 serial publications. Such on-line databases and networks as CALI, CIS Universe, DIALOG, Dow-Jones, Infotrac, Legal-Trac, LEXIS, NEXIS, OCLC First Search, RLIN, WESTLAW, HeinOnline, LLMC Digital, Bloomberg Law, CCH International, BNA-ALL, Access UN, Arbititration Law Online, and TRACFED are available to law students for research. Special library collections include a federal document depository, and Supreme Court briefs and records. Recently, the library was completely renovated. The ratio of library volumes to faculty is 12,905 to 1 and to students, 950 to 1. The ratio of seats in the library to students is 1 to 2.

Faculty
The law school has 52 full-time and 31 part-time faculty members, of whom 24 are women. According to AAUP standards for Category I institutions, faculty salaries are well above average. The ratio of full-time students to full-time faculty in an average class is 9 to 1; in a clinic, 10 to 1. The law school has a regular program of bringing visiting professors and other distinguished lecturers and visitors to campus. There is a chapter of the Order of the Coif.

Students
About 45% of the student body are women; 28%, minorities; 6%, African American; 11%, Asian American; 10%, Hispanic; and 1%, Native American. The majority of students come from the Midwest (29%). The average age of entering students is 24; age range is 21 to 42. About 32% of students enter directly from undergraduate school, 18% have a graduate degree, and 68% have worked full-time prior to entering law school. About 1% drop out after the first year for academic or personal reasons; 99% remain to receive a law degree.

Placement

J.D.s awarded:	196
Services available through: a separate law school placement center	
Services: Seminars and publications	
Special features: clerkship counseling	
Full-time job interviews:	275 employers
Summer job interviews:	592 employers
Placement by graduation:	99% of class
Placement within 9 months:	100% of class
Average starting salary:	$50,000 to $165,000
Areas of placement:	
Private practice	81%
Judicial clerkships	13%
Business/industry	3%
Government	2%
Public interest	1%

College of Law

P.O. Box 210040
Cincinnati, OH 45221-0040

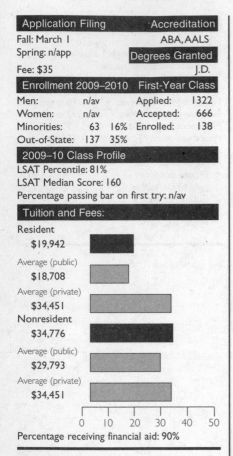

Application Filing	Accreditation
Fall: March 1	ABA, AALS
Spring: n/app	Degrees Granted
Fee: $35	J.D.

Enrollment 2009–2010		First-Year Class	
Men:	n/av	Applied:	1322
Women:	n/av	Accepted:	666
Minorities:	63 16%	Enrolled:	138
Out-of-State:	137 35%		

2009–10 Class Profile
LSAT Percentile: 81%
LSAT Median Score: 160
Percentage passing bar on first try: n/av

Tuition and Fees:

Resident
$19,942

Average (public)
$18,708

Average (private)
$34,451

Nonresident
$34,776

Average (public)
$29,793

Average (private)
$34,451

0   10   20   30   40   50

Percentage receiving financial aid: 90%

ADMISSIONS
In the fall 2009 first-year class, 1322 applied, 666 were accepted, and 138 enrolled. Twenty transfers enrolled. The median LSAT percentile of the most recent first-year class was 81; the median GPA was 3.6 on a scale of 4.0. The lowest LSAT percentile accepted was 26; the highest was 98.

Requirements
Applicants must have a bachelor's degree and take the LSAT. The most important admission factors include GPA, LSAT results, and academic achievement. No specific undergraduate courses are required. Candidates are not interviewed. A 6 member committee reads all fliles in their entirety under a fall review process.

Procedure
The application deadline for fall entry is March 1. Applicants should submit an application form, LSAT results, transcripts, a personal statement, TOEFL for international applicants, a nonrefundable application fee of $35, 2 letters of recommendation (through LSAC). Applicants may provide up to 4 letters of recommendation. Notification of the admissions decision is on a rolling basis. The latest acceptable LSAT test date for fall entry is February. The law school uses the LSDAS.

Special
The law school recruits minority and disadvantaged students by offering a diverse student body, faculty, and curriculum. Students from across a wide spectrum of ideas and ethnicities are attracted to this diverse program. Particular attention is given to providing competitive financial aid packages. Requirements are not different for out-of-state students. Transfer students must have 1 year of credit, have attended an ABA-approved law school, and supply their class rank, give the reason(s) for the transfer, and generally be in the top 20% of the class.

Costs
Tuition and fees for the 2009-2010 academic year are $19,942 for full-time in-state students and $34,776 for out-of-state students. On-campus room and board costs about $10,596 annually; books and supplies run $5850.

Financial Aid
About 90% of current law students receive some form of aid. The average annual amount of aid from all sources combined, including scholarships, loans, and work contracts, is $27,000; maximum, $49,700. Scholarships are awarded in an effort to attract an academically talented and diverse student body. Required financial statements are the FAFSA and a scholarship application is suggusted but not required. The aid application deadline for fall entry is March 1. First-year students are notified about their financial aid application within 4 weeks of acceptance.

About the Law School
University of Cincinnati College of Law was established in 1833 and is a public institution. The 473-acre campus is in an urban area in the Clifton area of Cincinnati. The primary mission of the law school is to provide students with an opportunity to equip themselves for effective and creative participation in the roles lawyers play in society. Students have access to federal, state, county, city, and local agencies, courts, correctional facilities, law firms, and legal aid organizations in the Cincinnati area. Students also have access to a variety of legal externships in Cincinnati and several clinical opportunities. Facilities of special interest to law students are the U.S. Court of Appeals for the Sixth Circuit and the District Court for the Southern District of Ohio; the 3000-plus members of the Cincinnati Bar Association; the more than 600 law firms; and the Legal Aid Society of Cincinnati. Housing for students is plentiful, and most law students live off campus in housing within walking distance of campus. The average rent is about $550 a month for a single apartment. All law school facilities are accessible to the physically disabled.

Calendar
The law school operates on a traditional semester basis. Courses for full-time students are offered days only. There is no part-time program. New students are admitted in the fall. There is no summer session. Transferable summer courses are offered.

Programs
Students may take relevant courses in other programs and apply credit toward the J.D.; a maximum of 8 credits may be applied. The following joint degrees may be earned: J.D./M.A. (Juris Doctor/Master of Arts in women's studies), J.D./M.A.P.S. (Juris Doctor/Master of Arts in Political Science), J.D./M.B.A. (Juris Doctor/Master of Business Administration), J.D./M.C.P. (Juris Doctor/Master of Community Planning), and J.D./M.S.W. (Juris Doctor/Master of Social Work).

Required
To earn the J.D., candidates must complete 90 total credits, of which 36 are for required courses. They must maintain a minimum GPA of 2.0 in the required courses. The following first-year courses are required of all students: Advocacy, Civil Procedure I and II, Constitutional Law I and II, Contracts, Criminal Law, Introduction to Law, Legal Research and Writing, Property, and Torts. Required upper-level courses consist of a seminar

Phone: 513-556-6805
Fax: 513-556-2391
E-mail: admissions@law.uc.edu
Web: www.law.uc.edu

Contact

Al Watson, Assistant Dean and Director of Admiss, 513-556-6805 for general inquiries; Al Watson, Assistant Dean and Director of Admiss, 513-556-6805 for financial aid information.

OHIO

requirement, Lawyering course, Legal Ethics, and writing requirements. Clinical courses are not required however, externships or a clinical experience are strongly encouraged. The required orientation program for first-year students is 1 week and includes the Introduction to Law course, registration, assignment of faculty and student advisers, a meeting with student advisers, a social event with upper-level students, information about the law library, and bar association membership opportunities.

Electives

The College of Law offers concentrations in corporate law, criminal law, environmental law, intellectual property law, international law, litigation, tax law, and international human rights. In addition, clinics include Sixth Circuit, Domestic Violence, and Ohio Innocence Project. Seminar topics include corporate law, constitutional law, and jurisprudence topics. An externship program is offered to 50 or 60 students and is worth 3 credit hours. Both judicial and legal externships are available. Individual research projects are also available. Speakers can be heard at the Human Rights Institute, which invites international human rights scholars, the Center for Corporate Law, Institute for Law and Psychiatry, and the Corporate Law symposium. The college has a student exchange program with the University of Canterbury, Christchurch, New Zealand. An academic success program is also available. The most widely taken electives are Corporations, Wills, and Secured Transactions.

Graduation Requirements

In order to graduate, candidates must have a GPA of 2.0, have completed the upper-division writing requirement, and have completed the Lawyering course.

Organizations

Students edit the *University of Cincinnati Law Review*, *Immigration and Nationality Law Review*, *Human Rights Quarterly*, and *Freedom Center Journal*. Students compete at the Jessup International Law Moot Court, the J. Braxton Craven, Jr. Memorial Moot Court, and the Giles Sutherland Rich Moot Court in patent law. Also, the College of Law hosts the National Product Liability Competition and participates in all other national competitions. Law student organizations and campus clubs include the ABA-Law Student Division, International Law Society, Intellectual Property Society. Student Bar Association, Moot Court, and Black Law Students Association. There are local chapters of Order of the Barristers and Order of the Coif.

Library

The law library contains 428,753 hard-copy volumes and 875,904 microform volume equivalents, and subscribes to 2643 serial publications. Such on-line databases and networks as CALI, CIS Universe, LEXIS, NEXIS, OCLC First Search, WESTLAW, HeinOnline, WORLDCAT, OHIOLINK, BNA Direct, JSTOR, ARTSTOR, FACTIVA, ABI/INFORM, Academic Search Complete and many more are available to law students for research. Special library collections include the Urban Morgan Human Rights Collection; the Segoe Collection on Land Use and Urban Planning; the Goldstein Collection on the Law of Church and State; manuscript collections: papers of William J. Butler, papers of Nathaniel R. Jones, records of Ohio 1987 Merit Plan constitutional amendment campaign regarding judicial selection, and a selective depository for U.S. federal government documents. The Law Library has 2,643 subscriptions in print, plus shared access to over 6,000 electronic titles. Recently, the library updated network and web file servers, replaced all 35 computer lab workstations, expanded wireless network access, and purchased a digital scanner/printer for microfiche and microfilm. The ratio of library volumes to faculty is 13,398 to 1 and to students is 1096 to 1. The ratio of seats in the library to students is 1 to 1.

Faculty

The law school has 32 full-time faculty members. According to AAUP standards for Category I institutions, faculty salaries are well below average. About 17% of full-time faculty have a graduate law degree in addition to the J.D. The ratio of full-time students to full-time faculty in an average class is 10 to 1. The law school has a regular program of bringing visiting professors and other distinguished lecturers and visitors to campus. There is a chapter of the Order of the Coif.

Placement

J.D.s awarded:	108
Services available through: a separate law school placement center	
Special features: individual counseling and planning, annual meetings to update students' professional plan, Legal Externship Program for credit, and Volunteer Opportunity Program for transcript recognition.	
Full-time job interviews:	15 employers
Summer job interviews:	49 employers
Placement by graduation:	72% of class
Placement within 9 months:	95% of class
Average starting salary:	$22,800 to $160,000
Areas of placement:	
Law Firm	50%
Business/industry	13%
Public interest	13%
Government	9%
Judicial clerkships	6%
Academic	5%
Military	3%

Students

About 42% of the student body are women; 16%, minorities; 6%, African American; 8%, Asian American; and 1%, Hispanic. The majority of students come from Ohio (65%). The average age of entering students is 25; age range is 20 to 36. About 60% of students enter directly from undergraduate school, 8% have a graduate degree, and 40% have worked full-time prior to entering law school. About 1% drop out after the first year for academic or personal reasons; 98% remain to receive a law degree.

UNIVERSITY OF COLORADO

Law School

Campus Box 403, Wolf Law Building
Boulder, CO 80309-0403

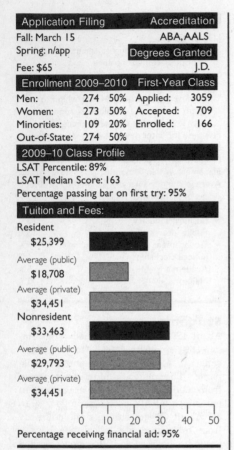

Application Filing	Accreditation
Fall: March 15	ABA, AALS
Spring: n/app	**Degrees Granted**
Fee: $65	J.D.

Enrollment 2009–2010		First-Year Class	
Men:	274 50%	Applied:	3059
Women:	273 50%	Accepted:	709
Minorities:	109 20%	Enrolled:	166
Out-of-State:	274 50%		

2009–10 Class Profile
LSAT Percentile: 89%
LSAT Median Score: 163
Percentage passing bar on first try: 95%

Tuition and Fees:

Resident
$25,399

Average (public)
$18,708

Average (private)
$34,451

Nonresident
$33,463

Average (public)
$29,793

Average (private)
$34,451

(bar chart axis: 0 10 20 30 40 50)

Percentage receiving financial aid: 95%

ADMISSIONS

In the fall 2009 first-year class, 3059 applied, 709 were accepted, and 166 enrolled. Sixteen transfers enrolled. The median LSAT percentile of the most recent first-year class was 89; the median GPA was 3.68 on a scale of 4.0. The lowest LSAT percentile accepted was 40; the highest was 99.

Requirements
Applicants must have a bachelor's degree and take the LSAT. All factors are considered important in the admission process. No specific undergraduate courses are required. Candidates are not interviewed.

Procedure
The application deadline for fall entry is March 15. Applicants should submit an application form, LSAT results, transcripts, a personal statement, a nonrefundable application fee of $65, 2 letters of recommendation, and a résumé. Notification of the admissions decision is December through May. The latest acceptable

LSAT test date for fall entry is February. The law school uses the LSDAS.

Special
The law school recruits minority and disadvantaged students by means of law school forums, candidate referral services through LSDAS, partnerships with organizations on campus, and special outreach by faculty, staff, and students. Requirements are not different for out-of-state students. Transfer students must have one year of credit, have attended an ABA-approved law school, and it is recommended that students be in the top 10% to 20% of their current law school class.

Costs

Tuition and fees for the 2009-2010 academic year are $25,399 for full-time in-state students and $33,463 for out-of-state students. On-campus room and board costs about $17,047 annually; books and supplies run $1749.

Financial Aid

About 95% of current law students receive some form of aid. The average annual amount of aid from all sources combined, including scholarships, loans, and work contracts, is $30,000; maximum, $45,000. Awards are based on need and merit; loans are based on need. Scholarships are usually based on a combination of need and merit. Required financial statements are the FAFSA and tax returns. The aid application deadline for fall entry is April 1. Special funds for minority or disadvantaged students include need-based, merit, and scholarships that advance the diversity of the student body. First-year students are notified about their financial aid application at at the time of the initial inquiry; information on financial aid is availlable on the web site and included in the catalog. Admitted students are encouraged to apply for financial aid as early as possible.

About the Law School

University of Colorado Law School was established in 1892 and is a public institution. The 873-acre campus is in a small town 30 miles northwest of Denver. The primary mission of the law school is to develop the skills, ethics, and habits to be an excellent lawyer with a strong sense of

the legal profession's greatest traditions and to develop an equal dedication to public service. Students have access to federal, state, county, city, and local agencies, courts, correctional facilities, law firms, and legal aid organizations in the Boulder area. Facilities of special interest to law students include the "green" Wolf Law Building, which contains all aspects of academic, administrative, clinical, research, career services, social, and audiovisual offerings for law students under one roof. Housing for students is primarily in apartments within 10 minutes of the law school. Less expensive accommodations are available in nearby towns. About 95% of the law school facilities are accessible to the physically disabled.

Calendar

The law school operates on a traditional semester basis. Courses for full-time students are offered days only and must be completed within 7 years. There is no part-time program. New students are admitted in the fall. There is a 3- and 5-week summer session. Transferable summer courses are offered.

Programs

Students may take relevant courses in other programs and apply credit toward the J.D.; the maximum number of credits that may be applied varries. The following joint degrees may be earned: J.D./ M.B.A. (Juris Doctor/Master of Business Administration), J.D./M.D. (Juris Doctor/ Doctor of Medicine), J.D./M.P.A. (Juris Doctor/Master of Public Administration), J.D./M.S. (Juris Doctor/Master of Science in Environmental Science), J.D./M.S.T. (Juris Doctor/Master of Science, Telecommunications), J.D./M.U.R.P. (Juris Doctor/Master of Urban and Regional Planning), and J.D./Ph.D (Juris Doctor/Doctor of Philosophy in Environmental Science).

Required
To earn the J.D., candidates must complete 89 total credits, of which 40 are for required courses. The following first-year courses are required of all students: Appellate Court Advocacy, Civil Procedure, Constitutional Law, Contracts, Criminal Law, Legal Writing, Property, and Torts. Required upper-level courses consist of a seminar and a practice requirement, Evidence, judy duty requirement, and

Contact

Admissions Office, 303-492-7203 for general inquiries; Kristine M Jackson, Assistant Dean for Admission and Financial Aid, 303-492-7203.

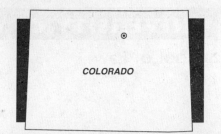

COLORADO

Professional Responsibility. The required orientation program for first-year students is 4 days and includes legal writing class, social activities, and an introduction to faculty, law school, and university facilities.

Electives

The Law School offers concentrations in corporate law, criminal law, environmental law, family law, intellectual property law, international law, juvenile law, labor law, litigation, media law, securities law, tax law, torts and insurance, and natural resources, civil rights law, constitutional law, health/medicine law, Indian law, legal ethics, public interest law, and trial law. In addition, clinics are available for either a year or 1 semester and a maximum of 14 credits may be awarded. Clinics include American Indian Law, Appellate Advocacy, Entrepreneurial Law, Juvenile Law, Wrongful Conviction, Civil Practice, Criminal Defense, Natural Resources Litigation, and Technology Law and Policy. A minimum of 1 seminar must be chosen from a variety of subjects. Externships allow students to earn up to 4 hours of academic credit for work in a governmental agency, private nonprofit institution or a private law office. Independent study is permitted for 1 credit. Field work is offered through some seminars, externships, and clinics. Special no-credit lectures are offered to all students on a variety of topics. Students may study abroad in Oxford, England; St. Petersburg and Moscow, Russia; Dubliln, Ireland; Paris, France; Barcelona, Spain; and Florence, Italy. A tutorial program is open to all first-year students who wish to participate. Students on academic probation are furnished with tutors. The most widely taken electives are Natural Resources and Environmental Law, Business Law, and Government and Public Law.

Graduation Requirements

In order to graduate, candidates must have a minimum average of 72, have completed the upper-division writing requirement, and submit a paper of publishable quality for the required seminar.

Organizations

Students edit the *University of Colorado Law Review, Colorado Journal of International Environmental Law and Policy*, and the *Journal on Telecommunications and High Technology Law*. The most successful teams in the Rothgerber Moot Court Competition participate in the National Moot Court Competition. The school also competes in the Jessup International Moot Court, held each year regionally, nationally, and internationally, and the Carrigan Cup Competition, an internal competition in which participants are selected for regional competitions leading to the national mock trial competition sponsored by the ABA. Other competitions deal with environmental law, American Indian law, and trademark law. Local chapters of national associations include Federalist Society for Law abd Public Policy Studies, National Lawyers Guild, and Student Trial Lawyers Association. There are local chapters of Phi Alpha Delta—Julius Caesar Chapter, American Bar Association Law Student Division, and ACLU. Law student organizations include Women's Law Caucus, Latino Law Students Association, and Environmental Law Society.

Library

The law library contains 741,484 hardcopy volumes and 1,634,139 microform volume equivalents, and subscribes to 4641 serial publications. Such on-line databases and networks as CALI, CIS Universe, DIALOG, Infotrac, Legal-Trac, LEXIS, LOIS, Mathew Bender, NEXIS, OCLC First Search, WESTLAW, Wilsonline Indexes, and HeinOnline, BNA All, LLMC Digital, and Digital Dissertation Factiva are available to law students for research. Special library collections include a federal publications depository and strengths in environmental and Native American Law and Constitutional Law. Recently, the library opened a state-of-the-art 59,000 square foot law library with 45% more space than the previous law library and all new furnishings. The ratio of library volumes to faculty is 18,085 to 1 and to students is 1356 to 1. The ratio of seats in the library to students is 1 to 1.

Faculty

The law school has 41 full-time and 21 part-time faculty members, of whom 21 are women. According to AAUP standards for Category I institutions, faculty salaries are below average. About 5% of full-time faculty have a graduate law degree in

Placement

J.D.s awarded:	166

Services available through: a separate law school placement center

Services: group information in addition to individual advising; access to computer career search resources; written documents providing job search information.

Special features: on-campus interview program, lunch-time informational sessions on job-seeking skills and various types of employment (traditional and nontraditional), Internet access to job postings, career workshops for law school graduates, a mock interview program, government/public interest career fair symposium series covering judicial, government, corporate, and private practice sectors, diversity hiring programs.

Full-time job interviews:	65 employers
Summer job interviews:	n/av
Placement by graduation:	64% of class
Placement within 9 months:	88% of class
Average starting salary:	$44,440 to $93,460

Areas of placement:

Private practice 2-10 attorneys	15%
Private practice 11-25 attorneys	4%
Private practice 26-50 attorneys	4%
Private practice 51-100 attorneys	5%
Private practice 100+ attorneys or employer firm	14%
Judicial clerkships	26%
Government	11%
Public interest	7%
Business/industry	6%
Military	4%
Academic	4%

addition to the J.D. The ratio of full-time students to full-time faculty in an average class is 12 to 1; in a clinic, 9 to 1. The law school has a regular program of bringing visiting professors and other distinguished lecturers and visitors to campus. There is a chapter of the Order of the Coif; 15 faculty and 656 graduates are members.

Students

About 50% of the student body are women; 20%, minorities; 3%, African American; 7%, Asian American; 7%, Hispanic; and 3%, Native American. The majority of students come from Colorado (50%). The average age of entering students is 24; age range is 21 to 48. About 45% of students enter directly from undergraduate school, 15% have a graduate degree, and 80% have worked full-time prior to entering law school. About 1% drop out after the first year for academic or personal reasons; 98% remain to receive a law degree.

School of Law

55 Elizabeth Street
Hartford, CT 06105

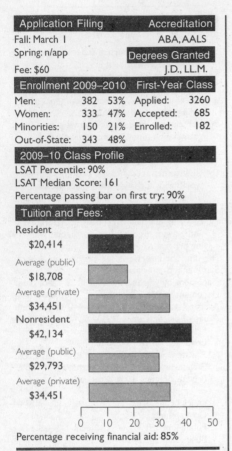

Application Filing	Accreditation
Fall: March 1	ABA, AALS
Spring: n/app	**Degrees Granted**
Fee: $60	J.D., LL.M.

Enrollment 2009–2010			First-Year Class	
Men:	382	53%	Applied:	3260
Women:	333	47%	Accepted:	685
Minorities:	150	21%	Enrolled:	182
Out-of-State:	343	48%		

2009–10 Class Profile
LSAT Percentile: 90%
LSAT Median Score: 161
Percentage passing bar on first try: 90%

Tuition and Fees:

Resident
$20,414

Average (public)
$18,708

Average (private)
$34,451

Nonresident
$42,134

Average (public)
$29,793

Average (private)
$34,451

0   10   20   30   40   50

Percentage receiving financial aid: 85%

ADMISSIONS

In the fall 2009 first-year class, 3260 applied, 685 were accepted, and 182 enrolled. Eighteen transfers enrolled. The median LSAT percentile of the most recent first-year class was 90; the median GPA was 3.38 on a scale of 4.0. The highest LSAT percentile was 99.

Requirements

Applicants must have a bachelor's degree and take the LSAT. The most important admission factors include LSAT results, GPA, and writing ability. No specific undergraduate courses are required. Candidates are not interviewed.

Procedure

The application deadline for fall entry is March 1. Applicants should submit an application form, LSAT results, transcripts, a personal statement, a nonrefundable application fee of $60, 2 letters of recommendation, and a résumé. Notification of the admissions decision is January through May. The latest acceptable LSAT

test date for fall entry is February. The law school uses the LSDAS.

Special

The law school recruits minority and disadvantaged students by attending recruiting fairs hosted by LSAC and HBCV as well as other minority majority institutions; hosting or co-hosting events such as balancing the scales and minority Law Day, and participating in LIAC's discoverlaw.org events. Minority Bar associations and student organizations also host events aimed at recruiting and informing future minority law students. Requirements are not different for out-of-state students. Transfer students must have one year of credit, have attended an ABA-approved law school, and should be within the top 10% of their class, and must show compelling reasons for transfer.

Costs

Tuition and fees for the 2009-2010 academic year are $20,414 for full-time in-state students and $42,134 for out-of-state students. Tuition for part-time students is $16,946 in-state and $35,046 out-of-state. Books and supplies run $1200.

Financial Aid

About 85% of current law students receive some form of aid. The average annual amount of aid from all sources combined, including scholarships, loans, and work contracts, is $23,159; maximum, $60,874. Awards are based on need; some loans are non-need-based. Required financial statements are the FAFSA and institutional financial aid application. The aid application deadline for fall entry is March 1. Special funds for minority or disadvantaged students include several grants that are awarded each year to entering students from economically and educationally disadvantaged backgrounds who demonstrate promise. First-year students are notified about their financial aid application at time of acceptance.

About the Law School

University of Connecticut School of Law was established in 1921 and is a public institution. The 21-acre campus is in an urban area in Hartford Connecticut, 2 hours from New York and 90 minutes from Boston. The primary mission of the

law school is to provide a legal education of high quality, serve the state and the bar, and prepare students to practice law in any jurisdiction. Students have access to federal, state, county, city, and local agencies, courts, correctional facilities, law firms, and legal aid organizations in the Hartford area. Housing for students is ample and affordable in the surrounding areas; there are no on-campus housing facilities.

Calendar

The law school operates on a traditional semester basis. Courses for full-time students are offered both day and evening after the first year and must be completed within 5 years. For part-time students, courses are offered both day and evening and must be completed within 6 years. New full- and part-time students are admitted in the fall. There is a 4½-week summer session. Transferable summer courses are offered.

Programs

In addition to the J.D., the law school offers the LL.M. Students may take relevant courses in other programs and apply credit toward the J.D.; a maximum of 6 credits may be applied. The following joint degrees may be earned: J.D./L.L.M. (Juris Doctor/Master of Laws, Insurance Law), J.D./M.B.A. (Juris Doctor/Master of Business Administration), J.D./M.L.S. (Juris Doctor/Master of Library Science), J.D./M.P.A. (Juris Doctor/Master of Public Affairs Administration), J.D./M.P.H. (Juris Doctor/Master of Public Health), and J.D./M.S.W. (Juris Doctor/Master of Social Work).

Required

To earn the J.D., candidates must complete 86 total credits, of which 36 are for required courses. They must maintain a minimum GPA of 2.3 in the required courses. The following first-year courses are required of all students: Civil Procedure, Constitutional Law, Contracts, Criminal Law, Lawyering Process, Moot Court, Property, Statutory/Regulatory Class, and Torts. Required upper-level courses consist of Legal Profession and the upper-class writing requirement. The required orientation program for first-year students is a 2-day event including presentations by the dean, faculty mem-

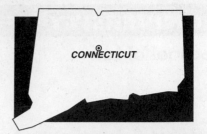

Contact

Karen DeMeola, Assistant Dean for Admissions, Student Finance, and Student Services, 860-570-5100 for general inquiries; Roberta Frick, Director of Financial Aid, 860-570-5147 for financial aid information.

bers, financial aid, and career services offices. In addition, the law school introduces students to practical lawyering and public service.

Electives

The School of Law offers concentrations in corporate law, criminal law, environmental law, family law, intellectual property law, international law, juvenile law, labor law, litigation, tax law, torts and insurance, legal theory, information technology law, property and land, child advocacy, and policy. In addition, clinics provide hands-on, practical training to upper-level students who earn up to 10 credits for their work; strong and widely recognized asylum and human rights, criminal law, appellate, child advocacy, immigration, intellectual property, and tax clinics are available. Seminars in a multitude of different substantive areas are available to upper-level students for typically 3 credits. Internships, research programs, and field work are available to upper-level students. Research positions are open to upper-level students under the direction of a faculty adviser. Special lecture series include Intellectual Property Teas; Law Review Symposia; and various human rights, international, diversity, and insurance law series. Study abroad is open to upper-level students for 1 semester in various countries, including England, the Netherlands, Ireland, France, Germany, Israel, Italy, or Puerto Rico. Exchange programs in environmental law with the University of Vermont Law School and University of London are also available. Students having academic difficulty meet weekly with a faculty or student tutor to review case briefing, writing, legal analysis, and exam techniques. No credit is granted. An academic support program is offered for students that includes 1 mini-course designed to introduce case briefing, writing, and legal analysis. Special interest group programs include the Tax Law Certificate Program, the Intellectual Property Certificate Program, the Certificate in Law and Public Policy, and the Certificate in Human Rights. The most widely taken electives are Evidence, Intellectual Property, and International Law.

Graduation Requirements

In order to graduate, candidates must have a GPA of 2.3 and have completed the upper-division writing requirement.

Organizations

Students edit the *Connecticut Law Review, Connecticut Journal of International Law, Connecticut Insurance Law Journal, Connecticut Intellectual Property Notes, Public Interest Law Journal,* and the student newspaper, *Pro Se.* Moot court competitions include the Alva P. Loiselle, William H. Hastie, and Willem Vis International Moot Court. Other competitions include the National Appellate Advocacy Competition, Family Law Competition, Craven Competition, and National Moot Court Competition. A wide range of intellectual, political, social, and special interest organizations and activities are available to students, including the Student Bar Association, Black, Latino, South Asian, Asian, and Women's Law Students Associations, and Public Interest Law Group. Among many others, there are local chapters of the Federalist Society, the American Constitution Society, the National Lawyers Guild, the Tax Law Society, the Connecticut Alliance of International Lawyers, and the Intellectual Property and Technology Law Society.

Library

The law library contains 545,754 hardcopy volumes and 222,856 microform volume equivalents, and subscribes to 5704 serial publications. Such on-line databases and networks as CALI, CIS Universe, Infotrac, Legal-Trac, LEXIS, LOIS, Mathew Bender, OCLC First Search, WESTLAW, Wilsonline Indexes, and more than 200 others are available to law students for research. Special library collections include a federal depository, Connecticut materials, an international collection, and an insurance law collection. Recently, the library instituted the law library blog; posted print library announcements in high student traffic location; implemented EZ Proxy; added a second semester of the Advanced Legal Research course; doubled annual student enrollment opportunity; and developed a process for notifying faculty of new book acquisitions. The ratio of library volumes to faculty is 12,404 to 1 and to students is 763 to 1. The ratio of seats in the library to students is 1 to 1.

Faculty

The law school has 44 full-time and 44 part-time faculty members, of whom 23 are women. According to AAUP standards for Category I institutions, faculty salaries

Placement

J.D.s awarded:	208
Services available through: a separate law school placement center	
Services: alumni mentor program, job bulletins, newsletter	
Special features: summer and permanent job résumé bank, presentations, workshops, seminars on career-related and job search projects	
Full-time job interviews:	n/av
Summer job interviews:	n/av
Placement by graduation:	n/av
Placement within 9 months:	92% of class
Average starting salary:	$31,200 to $180,000
Areas of placement:	
Private practice 2-10 attorneys	13%
Private practice 11-25 attorneys	6%
Private practice 26-50 attorneys	3%
Private practice 51-100 attorneys	8%
Private practice 100-250 attorneys	7%
Business/industry	14%
Judicial clerkships	13%
Government	10%
Public interest	2%
Academic	2%
Military	1%

are average. About 33% of full-time faculty have a graduate law degree in addition to the J.D. The ratio of full-time students to full-time faculty in an average class is 11 to 1; in a clinic, 8 to 1. The law school has a regular program of bringing visiting professors and other distinguished lecturers and visitors to campus.

Students

About 47% of the student body are women; 21%, minorities; 6%, African American; 8%, Asian American; 6%, Hispanic; and 1%, Native American. The majority of students come from Connecticut (52%). The average age of entering students is 26; age range is 20 to 74. About 40% of students enter directly from undergraduate school, 18% have a graduate degree, and 60% have worked full-time prior to entering law school. About 1% drop out after the first year for academic or personal reasons; 95% remain to receive a law degree.

UNIVERSITY OF DAYTON

School of Law

300 College Park
Dayton, OH 45469-2760

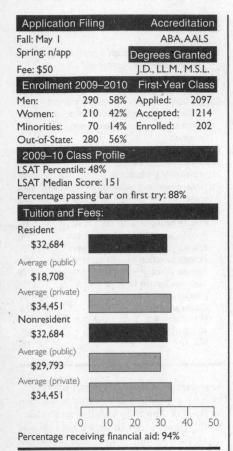

Application Filing	Accreditation
Fall: May 1	ABA, AALS
Spring: n/app	**Degrees Granted**
Fee: $50	J.D., LL.M., M.S.L.

Enrollment 2009–2010		First-Year Class	
Men:	290 58%	Applied:	2097
Women:	210 42%	Accepted:	1214
Minorities:	70 14%	Enrolled:	202
Out-of-State:	280 56%		

2009–10 Class Profile
LSAT Percentile: 48%
LSAT Median Score: 151
Percentage passing bar on first try: 88%

Tuition and Fees:

Resident
$32,684

Average (public)
$18,708

Average (private)
$34,451

Nonresident
$32,684

Average (public)
$29,793

Average (private)
$34,451

0   10   20   30   40   50
Percentage receiving financial aid: 94%

ADMISSIONS

In the fall 2009 first-year class, 2097 applied, 1214 were accepted, and 202 enrolled. Seven transfers enrolled. The median LSAT percentile of the most recent first-year class was 48; the median GPA was 3.16 on a scale of 4.0. The lowest LSAT percentile accepted was 13; the highest was 86.

Requirements
Applicants must have a bachelor's degree and take the LSAT. The most important admission factors include LSAT results, GPA, and writing ability. No specific undergraduate courses are required. Candidates are not interviewed.

Procedure
The application deadline for fall entry is May 1. Applicants should submit an application form, LSAT results, transcripts, a personal statement, a nonrefundable application fee of $50, 2 letters of recommendation, and an optional diversity statement. Notification of the admissions

decision is within 4 to 6 weeks of application completion. The latest acceptable LSAT test date for fall entry is February. The law school uses the LSDAS.

Special
The law school recruits minority and disadvantaged students by means of targeted mailings, recruiting at undergraduate schools, meeting with targeted student organizations, and some scholarship aid. Requirements are not different for out-of-state students. Transfer students must have one year of credit and have attended an ABA-approved law school. Applications are reviewed on a case-by-case basis, with class rank and the school attended being primary considerations.

Costs

Tuition and fees for the 2009-2010 academic year are $32,684 for all full-time students. Books and supplies run $1500.

Financial Aid

About 94% of current law students receive some form of aid. The average annual amount of aid from all sources combined, including scholarships, loans, and work contracts, is $37,053; maximum, $50,124. Awards are based on need and merit. Required financial statement is the FAFSA. The aid application deadline for fall entry is March 1. Special funds for minority or disadvantaged students are the Legal Opportunity Scholarships, awarded to entering students based on their diverse backgrounds and interests. First-year students are notified about their financial aid application at time of acceptance. Loan packages are awarded from winter to summer, scholarships at time of acceptance.

About the Law School

University of Dayton School of Law was established in 1974 and is a private institution. The 110-acre campus is in an urban area 1 mile south of downtown Dayton. The primary mission of the law school is to enroll a diverse group of women and men who are intellectually curious, who possess self-discipline, and who are well motivated, and to rigorously educate them in the substantive and procedural principles of public and private law. Students have access to federal, state,

county, city, and local agencies, courts, correctional facilities, law firms, and legal aid organizations in the Dayton area. Area corporations regularly employ students in their legal departments; some students are interns with the Ohio Supreme Court. Facilities of special interest to law students include the School of Law and University cafeterias, recreation areas, computer laboratories, child care, health services, and approximately 80 university-owned apartments within 2 blocks of the School of Law. Housing for students is convenient and readily available both on campus and off campus. University and private housing is within 5 to 15 minutes from the School of Law. All law school facilities are accessible to the physically disabled.

Calendar

The law school operates on a traditional semester basis. Courses for full-time students are offered both day and evening and must be completed within 2 to 3 years. There is no part-time program. New students are admitted in the fall. There is a 6-week summer session. Transferable summer courses are offered.

Programs

In addition to the J.D., the law school offers the LL.M. and M.S.L. Students may take relevant courses in other programs and apply credit toward the J.D.; a maximum of 6 credits may be applied. The following joint degrees may be earned: J.D./M.B.A. (Juris Doctor/Master of Business Administration).

Required
To earn the J.D., candidates must complete 90 total credits, of which 79 are for required courses. They must maintain a minimum GPA of 2.2 in the required courses. Prior to beginning classes, students must take Introduction to Legal Studies and Professionalism. The following first-year courses are required of all students: Civil Practice and Procedure, Contracts, Criminal Law, Criminial Procedure, Skills, Values and Ethics, Legal Profession I and II, Legislation, Real Property, and Torts I and II. Required upper-level courses consist of Business Organizations, Capstone Course/Clinical Experience, Commercial Transactions, Constitutional Law, Contracts II, Evi-

Phone: 937-229-3555
Fax: 937-229-4194
E-mail: *lawinfo@notes.udayton.edu*
Web: *http://law.udayton.edu*

Contact
Office of Admissions & Financial Aid, 937-229-3555 for general inquiries; Janet L. Hein, Assistant Dean, Director of Admissions and Financial Aid, 937-229-3555 for financial aid information.

OHIO

dence for the Litigator or Fundamentals of Evidence, Externship, Skills Proficiency, Professional Responsibility, Real Property II, and Wills and Trusts. The required orientation program for first-year students is a 3-day, one-credit initiation to the study of law, providing an overview of the legal system and an introduction to legal analysis and the use of the case method. Special emphasis is placed upon the role of the lawyer as counselor and professional responsibilities. Social gatherings take place.

Electives
The School of Law offers concentrations in criminal law, litigation, tax law, intellectual property, patent law, and computer/cyberspace law. In addition, A 4-credit clinic studies lawyer decision-making by placing students in the role of lawyer in real cases and by analyzing decisions made in that role. In field work and class sessins, students assume the responsibility of representing clients in a variety of legal matters under the supervision of professors while focusing on the role and skills of a lawyer, using simulation, review, and discussion and "case rounds" methodologies. A rigorous writing experience is a key component. More than 30 elective seminars are offered in topics as varied as Cybercrimes, Employment, Discrimination, Entertainment Law, Law and Education, and Health Care Law. All students are required to participate in a 4-credit, semester-long externship with a court government office or agency, public-interest organization, or business, during which the student performs the tasks of a lawyer under the mentorship and direction of an on-site lawyer supervisor. Special lecture series include the Scholarly Symposia Series, Law and Technology Seminars, and Bankruptcy Seminars. Study abroad includes Comparative Law offered during summer session in Italy and England. The Academic Success Program (ASP), a comparative academic support program, provides academic assistance to all students, with workshops throughout the year on class preparation, case synthesis out liningflow charting, and exam writing. A pre-orientation week-long intensisve preparation workshop is part of this program. The Road to Bar Passage Program provides guidence and support in the bar exam preparation process, including group informational meetings and individual bar exam counseling. The

Minority Summer Judicial Clerkship Program, Minority Summer Extenship Program, and regional minority career fairs are available. The most widely taken electives are Evidence, Tax, and Corporations.

Graduation Requirements
In order to graduate, candidates must have a GPA of 2.2 and have completed the upper-division writing requirement.

Organizations
Students edit the *University of Dayton Law Review*. Students typically participate in moot court competitions including bankruptcy law, patent law, and international law. There is a mock trial competition. Students also compete in the intercollegiate National Trial Competition. Law student organizations include Volunteer Student Law Project and the Intellectual Property Law Society. Local chapters of national associations include Phi Alpi Delta, ACLU, and St. Thomas More Society. Campus organizations include Habital for Humanity, Big Brothers/Big Sisters, and intramural sports teams.

Library
The law library contains 186,051 hardcopy volumes and 877,452 microform volume equivalents, and subscribes to 2394 serial publications. Such on-line databases and networks as CALI, LEXIS, OCLC First Search, WESTLAW, and Ohio LINK are available to law students for research. Recently, the library created a reception area, established a Bar Passage Collection, and became present facebook and twitter. The ratio of library volumes to faculty is 6645 to 1 and to students is 372 to 1. The ratio of seats in the library to students is 1 to 1.

Faculty
The law school has 28 full-time and 52 part-time faculty members, of whom 31 are women. According to AAUP standards for Category IIA institutions, faculty salaries are average. About 15% of full-time faculty have a graduate law degree in addition to the J.D. The ratio of full-time students to full-time faculty in an average class is 16 to 1; in a clinic, 5 to 1. The law school has a regular program of bringing visiting professors and other distinguished lecturers and visitors to campus.

Placement
J.D.s awarded:	150
Services available through: a separate law school placement center	
Full-time job interviews:	14 employers
Summer job interviews:	22 employers
Placement by graduation:	n/av
Placement within 9 months:	97% of class
Average starting salary:	$22,500 to $125,000
Areas of placement:	
Private practice 2-10 attorneys	37%
Private practice 11-25 attorneys	4%
Private practice 26-50 attorneys	8%
Private practice 51-100 attorneys	4%
Government	11%
Business/industry	11%
Judicial clerkships	9%
Self-employed private practice/ employed in firms	6%
Public interest	4%
Academic	3%
Military	2%
Legal publishing	2%

Students
About 42% of the student body are women; 14%, minorities; 7%, African American; 3%, Asian American; and 3%, Hispanic. The majority of students come from the Midwest (63%). The average age of entering students is 26; age range is 20 to 54. About 43% of students enter directly from undergraduate school, 12% have a graduate degree, and 57% have worked full-time prior to entering law school. About 16% drop out after the first year for academic or personal reasons; 80% remain to receive a law degree.

UNIVERSITY OF DENVER

Sturm College of Law

2255 E. Evans Avenue
Denver, CO 80208

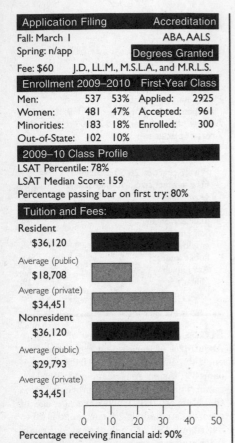

Application Filing

Fall: March 1
Spring: n/app
Fee: $60

Accreditation

ABA, AALS

Degrees Granted

J.D., LL.M., M.S.L.A., and M.R.L.S.

Enrollment 2009–2010   First-Year Class

Men:	537	53%	Applied:	2925
Women:	481	47%	Accepted:	961
Minorities:	183	18%	Enrolled:	300
Out-of-State:	102	10%		

2009–10 Class Profile

LSAT Percentile: 78%
LSAT Median Score: 159
Percentage passing bar on first try: 80%

Tuition and Fees:

Resident
$36,120

Average (public)
$18,708

Average (private)
$34,451

Nonresident
$36,120

Average (public)
$29,793

Average (private)
$34,451

Percentage receiving financial aid: 90%

ADMISSIONS

In the fall 2009 first-year class, 2925 applied, 961 were accepted, and 300 enrolled. Thirty-seven transfers enrolled. The median LSAT percentile of the most recent first-year class was 78; the median GPA was 3.51 on a scale of 4.0. The lowest LSAT percentile accepted was 33; the highest was 98.

Requirements

Applicants must have a bachelor's degree and take the LSAT. The most important admission factors include a personal statement, LSAT results, and GPA. No specific undergraduate courses are required. Candidates are not interviewed.

Procedure

The application deadline for fall entry is March 1. Applicants should submit an application form, LSAT results, transcripts, a personal statement, a nonrefundable application fee of $60, 2 letters of recommendation, and a résumé. Noti-

fication of the admissions decision is on a rolling basis. The latest acceptable LSAT test date for fall entry is February. The law school uses the LSDAS.

Special

The law school recruits minority and disadvantaged students by offering scholarships and working with student groups on recruitment and retention through the Office of Admissions. Requirements are not different for out-of-state students. Transfer students must have one year of credit and have attended an ABA-approved law school.

Costs

Tuition and fees for the 2009-2010 academic year are $36,120 for all full-time students. Tuition for part-time students is $26,632 per year. On-campus room and board costs about $9963 annually; books and supplies run $1749.

Financial Aid

About 90% of current law students receive some form of aid. The average annual amount of aid from all sources combined, including scholarships, loans, and work contracts, is $36,244; maximum, $52,657. Awards are based on need and merit. Award letters offer aid (scholarships, loans, work-study) up to the cost of attendance. Required financial statement is the FAFSA. The aid application deadline for fall entry is open. Special funds for minority or disadvantaged students include a variety of scholarships to support members of these groups. First-year students are notified about their financial aid application at time of acceptance.

About the Law School

University of Denver Sturm College of Law was established in 1892 and is a private institution. The 33-acre campus is in an urban area 10 minutes from downtown Denver. The primary mission of the law school is to provide an innovative, and technologically sophisticated legal education to a diverse student body of high academic quality. Students have access to federal, state, county, city, and local agencies, courts, correctional facilities, law firms, and legal aid organizations in the Denver area. Facilities of special interest to law students include the Frank H. Ricketson

Law Building, a green law building built in 2004. Housing for students consists of on-campus graduate student housing, as well as available near-campus neighborhood housing. All law school facilities are accessible to the physically disabled.

Calendar

The law school operates on a traditional semester basis. Courses for full-time and part-time students are offered both day and evening and must be completed within 7 years. New full- and part-time students are admitted in the fall. There is an 11-week summer session. Transferable summer courses are offered.

Programs

In addition to the J.D., the law school offers the LL.M. and M.S.L.A., M.R.L.S. Students may take relevant courses in other programs and apply credit toward the J.D.; a maximum of 10 credits may be applied. The following joint degrees may be earned: J.D./G.S.I.S. (Juris Doctor/ Graduate School International Studies), J.D./M.B.A. (Juris Doctor/Master of Business Administration), J.D./M.I.M. (Juris Doctor/Master of International Management), J.D./M.S.L.A. (Juris Doctor/Master of Science in Legal Administration), J.D./M.S.W. (Juris Doctor/Master of Social Work), and J.D./M.T. (Juris Doctor/Master in Taxation).

Required

To earn the J.D., candidates must complete 90 total credits, of which 44 are for required courses. They must maintain a minimum GPA of 2.3 in the required courses. The following first-year courses are required of all students: Civil Procedure, Contracts, Criminal Law, Lawyering Process, Property, and Torts. Required upper-level courses consist of Administrative Law, Constitutional Law, Evidence, and Legal Profession and Legal Writing. The required orientation program for first-year students consists of 3 days focused on programs, facilities, student support organizations, and procedures.

Electives

The Sturm College of Law offers concentrations in corporate law, environmental law, international law, and labor law. In addition, upper-level students receive 5 to

Phone: 303-871-6135
Fax: 303-871-6992
E-mail: admissions@law.du.edu
Web: www.law.du.edu

Contact
Susan Erlenborn, Assistant Director of admissions, 303-871-6135 for general inquiries; Iain Davis, Assistant Dean of Admissions and Financial Management, 303-871-6536 for financial aid information.

COLORADO

6 credit hours for a clinic. Clinics include Community Law, Civil Rights, Criminal Representation, Environmental Law, and Mediation/Arbitration. Seminars, offered to upper-level students, are worth 2 to 3 credit hours. Internships, open to upper-level students for 2 to 6 credits, are available in the offices of prosecutors; public defenders; the attorney general; and judicial, legislative, corporate, immigration, and natural resources agencies. Directed research may be undertaken under a professor's supervision. Research positions are open only to upper-level students for 2 to 3 credits.Students may elect to apply for study-abroad programs at other universities. The no-credit Academic Achievement Program is a tutorial program offered to first-year students. The most widely taken electives are Basic Tax, Corporations, and Trusts and Estates.

Graduation Requirements
In order to graduate, candidates must have a GPA of 2.3 and have completed the upper-division writing requirement.

Organizations
Students edit the *Denver University Law Review, Water Law Review, Sports and Entertainment Law Journal, Transportation Law Journal, Denver Journal of International Law and Policy,* and the student newspaper, *The Writ.* Moot court competitions running through the school year include the Negotiations Competition, Jessup International Law Competition, and Hoffman Cup Trial Competition. Other competitions include the National Civil Trial Competition, American Trial Lawyers, and Tournament of Champions. Among the student organizations are the Christian Legal Society, Colorado Council of Mediators Organization, Entertainment Law Society, and Health and Society Law. chapters of national associations include Delta Theta Phi, Phi Alpha Delta, and Phi Delta Phi. There are more than 40 student organizations.

Library
The law library contains 234,419 hardcopy volumes and 177,768 microform volume equivalents, and subscribes to 6920 serial publications. Such on-line databases and networks as CALI, CIS Universe, Infotrac, Legal-Trac, LEXIS, LOIS, Mathew Bender, NEXIS, OCLC

First Search, WESTLAW, and Wilsonline Indexes are available to law students for research. Special library collections include a government document selective depository and the Hughes Memorial Library Collection. The ratio of library volumes to faculty is 3606 to 1 and to students is 285 to 1. The ratio of seats in the library to students is 1 to 3.

Faculty
The law school has 65 full-time and 56 part-time faculty members, of whom 41 are women. According to AAUP standards for Category I institutions, faculty salaries are below average. About 20% of full-time faculty have a graduate law degree in addition to the J.D.; about 10% of part-time faculty have one. The ratio of full-time students to full-time faculty in an average class is 20 to 1; in a clinic, 10 to 1. The law school has a regular program of bringing visiting professors and other distinguished lecturers and visitors to campus.

Students
About 47% of the student body are women; 18%, minorities; 3%, African American; 6%, Asian American; 7%, Hispanic; 2%, Native American; and 5%, unknown. The majority of students come from Colorado (90%). The average age of entering students is 28; age range is 21 to 57. About 5% drop out after the first year for academic or personal reasons; 95% remain to receive a law degree.

Placement

J.D.s awarded:	352

Services available through: a separate law school placement center
Services: self-assessment and alternative careers
Special features: out-of-town alumni networks, DU alumni links, mentors, and individualized networking strategies.

Full-time job interviews:	15 employers
Summer job interviews:	57 employers
Placement by graduation:	61% of class
Placement within 9 months:	88% of class
Average starting salary:	$31,080 to $150,000

Areas of placement:

Private practice, 2-100 attorneys	52%
Business/industry	17%
Government	14%
Judicial clerkships	10%
Public interest	4%
Unknown	3%
Academic	1%

University of Denver   **471**

651 East Jefferson Avenue
Detroit, MI 48226

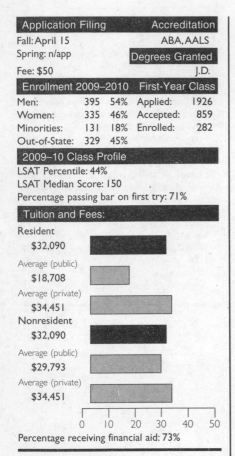

Application Filing	Accreditation
Fall: April 15	ABA, AALS
Spring: n/app	

	Degrees Granted
Fee: $50	J.D.

Enrollment 2009–2010   First-Year Class

Men:	395	54%	Applied:	1926
Women:	335	46%	Accepted:	859
Minorities:	131	18%	Enrolled:	282
Out-of-State:	329	45%		

2009–10 Class Profile

LSAT Percentile: 44%
LSAT Median Score: 150
Percentage passing bar on first try: 71%

Tuition and Fees:

Resident
$32,090

Average (public)
$18,708

Average (private)
$34,451

Nonresident
$32,090

Average (public)
$29,793

Average (private)
$34,451

```
0    10   20   30   40   50
```

Percentage receiving financial aid: 73%

ADMISSIONS

In the fall 2009 first-year class, 1926 applied, 859 were accepted, and 282 enrolled. One transfer enrolled. The median LSAT percentile of the most recent first-year class was 44; the median GPA was 3.16 on a scale of 4.0. The lowest LSAT percentile accepted was 15; the highest was 89.

Requirements

Applicants must have a bachelor's degree and take the LSAT. Minimum acceptable LSAT percentile is 15. The most important admission factors include academic achievement, LSAT results, and GPA. No specific undergraduate courses are required. Candidates are not interviewed.

Procedure

The application deadline for fall entry is April 15. Applicants should submit an application form, LSAT results, transcripts, a personal statement, TOEFL may be required in some instances., a

nonrefundable application fee of $50, 2 letters of recommendation, and a resume. Notification of the admissions decision is on a rolling basis. The latest acceptable LSAT test date for fall entry is February. The law school uses the LSDAS.

Special

The law school recruits minority and disadvantaged students by hosting an annual informational fair for prospective students of color, by attending law fairs at colleges and universities targeted to reach students of color and by using the LSAC Candidate Referral Service. Requirements are not different for out-of-state students. Transfer students must have one year of credit, have a minimum GPA of 3, have attended an ABA-approved law school, and be in good standing at his or her current law school. Preadmissions courses consist of an 8-week conditional admission program offered during the summer for minority and disadvantaged students who do not meet current admission standards, but who demonstrate potential for success in law school. Satisfactory demonstration of ability in the program permits admission as a regular student in the fall semester to the J.D. program.

Costs

Tuition and fees for the 2009-2010 academic year are $32,090 for all full-time students. Tuition for part-time students is $25,688 per year. Books and supplies run $1920.

Financial Aid

About 73% of current law students receive some form of aid. Scholarships are based on merit, while all other aid, except unsubsidized loans, is based on need. Required financial statement is the FAFSA. The aid application deadline for fall entry is April 1. First-year students are notified about their financial aid application at time of acceptance. Students are asked to apply for financial aid when they apply for admission. Awards are made after the student has been accepted and the file is complete.

About the Law School

University of Detroit Mercy School of Law was established in 1912 and is a private institution. The 4-acre campus is in an

urban area in downtown Detroit. The primary mission of the law school is to provide a rigorous legal education that integrates theory, doctrine, and practice and emphasizes legal writing, ethics, and public service. Students have access to federal, state, county, city, and local agencies, courts, correctional facilities, law firms, and legal aid organizations in the Detroit area. The career services office provides a wide array of resources to enable students to obtain short- and long-term positions in these areas. A full range of extracurricular activities and organizations like the St. Thomas More Society, the Student Bar Association, the Black Law Students Association, and Phi Alpha Delta offer the chance to exercise leadership skills and perform community service. Housing for students includes apartments and houses within walking distance or a short driving commute to the law school. The law school assists students with housing needs. All law school facilities are accessible to the physically disabled.

Calendar

The law school operates on a traditional semester basis. Courses for full-time students are offered both day and evening and must be completed within 3 years. For part-time students, courses are offered both day and evening and must be completed within 5 years. New full- and part-time students are admitted in the fall. There is a 7-week summer session. Transferable summer courses are offered.

Programs

The following joint degrees may be earned: J.D./L.E.D. (Juris Doctor/Bachelor of Laws (Mexico)), J.D./LL.B. (Juris Doctor/Bachelor of Laws (Canada)), and J.D./M.B.A. (Juris Doctor/Master of Business Administration).

Required

To earn the J.D., candidates must complete 90 total credits, of which 57 are for required courses. They must maintain a minimum GPA of 2.0 in the required courses. The following first-year courses are required of all students: Applied Legal Theory and Analysis, Civil Procedure, Contracts, Core Concepts, Property, and Torts. Required upper-level courses consist of 2 Law Firm Modules, Basic Federal Tax, Constitutional Law, Criminal Law,

Phone: 313-596-0264
866-428-1610 ext. 529
Fax: 313-596-0280
E-mail: udmlawao@udmercy.edu
Web: www.law.udmercy.edu

Contact

Associate Dean, Admissions and Student Affairs, 313-596-0264 for general inquiries; Denise Daniel, Financial Aid Coordinator, 313-596-0214 for financial aid information.

Evidence, Global Distribution Course, Professional Responsibility, and Upper-level Writing Requirement. All students must take a minimum of one clinical course. The required orientation program for first-year students is a 3-day session that includes presentations by faculty and administrators, alumni panel discussions, and an overview of the first-year curriculum. After this week, the Dean holds a continuing orientation session about once a month.

Electives

The School of Law offers concentrations in corporate law, criminal law, entertainment law, environmental law, family law, intellectual property law, international law, labor law, litigation, tax law, health law, and constitutional law. In addition, several 4-credit clinical opportunities are available for students including Immigration Law Clinic, Mobile Law Office, Mediation Clinic, and others. The school of law offers 2-credit seminars in selected law topics. A variety of 2-credit clinical externships is available to upper-class students. Students with a GPA of 2.5 may work under the supervision of faculty attorneys in preparing cases for local civil and criminal courts, federal district courts, non-profit legal agencies, and state and federal administrative courts. The clinic places students with such agencies as the Wayne County Prosecutor's Office, the U.S. Attorney's Office, the Attorney Grievance Commission, the American Civil Liberties Union, the City of Detroit Law Department, and local health care systems. Students may enroll to complete a research project of 1 to 2 credits. The law school holds an annual McElroy Lecture in Religion and Law and an Interfaith panel as well as frequent Dean's debates. UDM offers its International Opportunities Program in which students receive a $1000 loan. The loan is forgiven after the student successfully completes one of 20 approved programs and returns to UDM the following semester. There is an academic support program. Minority and disadvantaged students who do not meet the standards of those currently being admitted, but who have strong qualifications that indicate possible success in law school may be admitted to the Special Summer Program (SSP). Students who successfully complete the SSP may matriculate with the fall class. Through a consortium with

2 other law schools, students may choose from a wide array of intellectual property law electives. The most widely taken electives are Trial Practice, Estates and Trusts, and Criminal Procedure.

Graduation Requirements

In order to graduate, candidates must have a GPA of 2.0 and have completed the upper-division writing requirement.

Organizations

The primary law review is *The University of Detroit Mercy Law Review*. The student newspaper is *In Brief*. Moot court competitions include the Gallagher Competition, the G. Mennen Williams Annual Moot Court Competition, and Professional Responsibility Competition. Law student organizations include Sports and Entertainment Law Society, Student Animal Defense Fund, and Moot Court Board of Advocates. Local chapters of national associations include Phi Alpha Delta, Delta Theta Phi, and Black Law Students Association. Other campus organizations include the UDM Hockey Club, Women's Law Caucus, and St. Thomas More Society.

Library

The law library contains 226,804 hardcopy volumes and 168,320 microform volume equivalents, and subscribes to 3112 serial publications. Such on-line databases and networks as CALI, DIALOG, Legal-Trac, LEXIS, NEXIS, OCLC First Search, WESTLAW, Wilsonline Indexes, and LANs are available to law students for research. Special library collections include English and Canadian Law, government documents, records, legal periodical indexes on CD-ROM, and several hundred databases in related fields. Recently, the library installed 38 state-of-the-art computers for student use. The ratio of library volumes to faculty is 4130 to 1 and to students is 387 to 1. The ratio of seats in the library to students is 1 to 2.

Faculty

The law school has 52 full-time and 35 part-time faculty members, of whom 35 are women. About 14% of full-time faculty have a graduate law degree in addition to the J.D. The ratio of full-time students to full-time faculty in an average class is 14

Placement

J.D.s awarded:	215

Services available through: a separate law school placement center

Special features: The Career Services Office operates on-campus interview programs in the fall and spring, provides seminars and individual advice on such topics as interviewing and résumé preparation, and sponsors the weekly "Lunch with a Lawyer" series and the Alumni Mentor Program. The Career Services Office also provides employment letters for alumni and students, and an alumni job telephone hotline.

Full-time job interviews:	n/av
Summer job interviews:	n/av
Placement by graduation:	n/av
Placement within 9 months:	n/av
Average starting salary:	$64,448
Areas of placement:	
Private practice (size unknown)	57%
Business/industry	22%
Government	5%
Public interest	5%
Academic	5%
Judicial clerkships	4%

to 1; in a clinic, 14 to 1. The law school has a regular program of bringing visiting professors and other distinguished lecturers and visitors to campus.

Students

About 46% of the student body are women; 18%, minorities; 11%, African American; 4%, Asian American; 3%, Hispanic; 1%, Native American; and 20%, Foreign National. The majority of students come from Michigan (55%). The average age of entering students is 25; age range is 19 to 59. About 15% drop out after the first year for academic or personal reasons; 85% remain to receive a law degree.

Fredric G. Levin College of Law

141 Bruton-Geer Hall,
P.O. Box 117622
Gainesville, FL 32611-7622

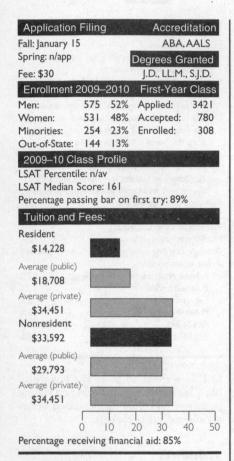

Application Filing	Accreditation
Fall: January 15	ABA, AALS
Spring: n/app	**Degrees Granted**
Fee: $30	J.D., LL.M., S.J.D.

Enrollment 2009–2010		First-Year Class	
Men:	575 52%	Applied:	3421
Women:	531 48%	Accepted:	780
Minorities:	254 23%	Enrolled:	308
Out-of-State:	144 13%		

2009–10 Class Profile
LSAT Percentile: n/av
LSAT Median Score: 161
Percentage passing bar on first try: 89%

Tuition and Fees:

Resident
$14,228

Average (public)
$18,708

Average (private)
$34,451

Nonresident
$33,592

Average (public)
$29,793

Average (private)
$34,451

0   10   20   30   40   50

Percentage receiving financial aid: 85%

ADMISSIONS
In the fall 2009 first-year class, 3421 applied, 780 were accepted, and 308 enrolled. Twenty-five transfers enrolled. The median GPA of the most recent first-year class was 3.67.

Requirements
Applicants must have a bachelor's degree and take the LSAT. No specific undergraduate courses are required. Candidates are not interviewed.

Procedure
The application deadline for fall entry is January 15. Applicants should submit an application form, LSAT results, transcripts, a personal statement, and a nonrefundable application fee of $30. Letters of recommendation are required, but 4 are recommended, and Candidates are strongly encouraged to use the LSDAS letter of recommendation option. Notification of the admissions decision is between December and late March. The latest

acceptable LSAT test date for fall entry is December. The law school uses the LSDAS.

Special
The College of Law is represented at a large number of Law Day programs in Florida and other southern states. This activity is supplemented by individual campus visits and other visits to historically black colleges in Florida and the south. The law school actively seeks a diverse student body. Requirements are not different for out-of-state students. Transfer students must have one year of credit, have attended an ABA-approved law school, must rank in at least the top 1/3 of their class to be considered, and must have finished the required first-year curriculum.

Costs
Tuition and fees for the 2009-2010 academic year are $14,228 for full-time in-state students and $33,592 for out-of-state students. On-campus room and board costs about $8030 annually; books and supplies run $990.

Financial Aid
About 85% of current law students receive some form of aid. The average annual amount of aid from all sources combined, including scholarships, loans, and work contracts, is $22,091; maximum, $47,289. Awards are based on need and merit. Required financial statements are the FAFSA and an additional application for merit/need-based scholarships and grants. The aid application deadline for fall entry is April 7. Special funds for minority or disadvantaged students include need-based grants. First-year students are notified about their financial aid application some time after acceptance but prior to enrollment.

About the Law School
University of Florida Fredric G. Levin College of Law was established in 1909 and is a public institution. The 2000-acre campus is in a suburban area in Gainsville, Florida. The primary mission of the law school is to offer excellence in educating professionals, advancing legal scholarship, serving the public, and fostering justice. Students have access to federal, state,

county, city, and local agencies, courts, correctional facilities, law firms, and legal aid organizations in the Gainesville area. Facilities of special interest to law students include a fully functional trial and appellate courtroom, audience gallery, and judges bench; an enlarged law library; and 2 new academic buildings with modern, comfortable classrooms equipped to offer the latest in teaching technology. Housing for students is available in university dormitories, family housing, and numerous nearby apartments. All law school facilities are accessible to the physically disabled.

Calendar
The law school operates on a traditional semester basis. Courses for full-time students are offered both day and evening and must be completed within 84 months. There is no part-time program. New students are admitted in the fall. There is an 8-week summer session. Transferable summer courses are offered.

Programs
In addition to the J.D., the law school offers the LL.M. and S.J.D. Students may take relevant courses in other programs and apply credit toward the J.D.; a maximum of 6 credits may be applied. The following joint degrees may be earned: J.D./M.A. (Juris Doctor/Master of Arts), J.D./M.B.A. (Juris Doctor/Master of Business Administration), J.D./M.D. (Juris Doctor/Doctor of Medicine), J.D./M.S. (Juris Doctor/Master of Science), and J.D./Ph.D. (Juris Doctor/Doctor of Philosophy).

Required
To earn the J.D., candidates must complete 88 total credits, of which 34 are for required courses. They must maintain a minimum GPA of 2.0 in the required courses. The following first-year courses are required of all students: Appellate Advocacy, Civil Procedure, Constitutional Law, Contracts, Criminal Law, Legal Research and Writing, Professional Responsibility, Property, and Torts. Required upper-level courses consist of an Advanced writing requirement and Legal Drafting. The required orientation program for first-year students is a 3-day comprehensive orientation to the profession and College of Law.

Phone: 352-273-0890
877-429-1297
Fax: 352-392-4087
E-mail: *madorno@law.ufl.edu*
Web: *http://www.law.ufl.edu*

Contact

Michell Adorno, Assistant Dean of Admissions, 352-273-0890 for general inquiries; Carol Huber, Director of Financial Aid, 352-273-0620 for financial aid information.

FLORIDA

Electives

The number of credits students must take in their area of concentration varies. The Fredric G. Levin College of Law offers concentrations in environmental law, family law, intellectual property law, international law, and estates and trust practice. In addition, clinics include Child Welfare Clinic for 9 credits, Mediation Clinic for 6 credits, Criminal Clinic for 6 credits, and Conservation Clinic for 3 credits. The clinics are open to students who have completed at least 48 hours and Professional Responsibility. Two-credit seminars covering a variety of legal topics are offered. They are open to students who have completed the first-year curriculum. A large number of for-credit externships are available with judges, prosecutor and defender's offices, and other governmental and nonprofit organizations as well as some "in-house counsel" positions. They are open to students who have completed the first-year curriculum. Special lecture series include Environmental and Land Use Law and Graduate Tax. Students may study abroad at Bar-Ilan University (Israel), John Wolfgang Goethe University (Germany), Leiden University (the Netherlands), Monash University (Australia), PUC-Rio (Brazil), Tel Aviv University (Israel), University of Montpellier (France), University of Cape Town (South Africa), University of Costa Rica, and University of Warsaw (Poland). First-semester students participate in the Academic Success Program. Academic Support workshops for students at risk of being placed on academic probation are available. The program is open to all students. The College's Office of Student Affairs offers programs, support, and services to minorities and diverse student groups. The most widely taken electives are Corporations, Evidence, and Estates and Trusts.

Graduation Requirements

In order to graduate, candidates must have a GPA of 2.0 and have completed the upper-division writing requirement.

Organizations

Students edit the *Florida Review*, *Florida International Law Journal*, *Journal of Law and Public Policy*, *Florida Tax Review*, *Journal of Technology Law and Policy*, and the student newspaper, *The Docket*. Moot court competitions include ABA National Appellate Advocacy Competition, National Security Law Competition, and Duberstein Bankruptcy Competition. Other competitions include the Thomas Tang Moot Court Competition, St. Johns National Civic Rights Mock Trial Competition, the Robert Orseck Florida Bar Competition, and the Sutherland Cup. Law student organizations, local chapters of national associations, and campus organizations include the Association for Public Interest Law, John Marshall Bar Association, BLSA, Gators for Alternative Dispute Association, International Law Society, American Bar Association-Law Student Division, Law College Council, Phi Alpha Delta, and Phi Delta Phi.

Library

The law library contains 643,282 hardcopy volumes and 318,270 microform volume equivalents, and subscribes to 7526 serial publications. Such on-line databases and networks as CALI, CIS Universe, Dow-Jones, Infotrac, Legal-Trac, LEXIS, Mathew Bender, NEXIS, OCLC First Search, RLIN, WESTLAW, Wilsonline Indexes, BNA, CCH, HeinOnline, and RIA are available to law students for research. Special library collections include Tax, U.S. government documents, and video and multimedia collections. Recently, the library installed an extensive wireless system. The ratio of library volumes to faculty is 8577 to 1 and to students is 582 to 1. The ratio of seats in the library to students is 1 to 1.

Faculty

The law school has 75 full-time and 47 part-time faculty members, of whom 49 are women. According to AAUP standards for Category I institutions, faculty salaries are below average. About 28% of full-time faculty have a graduate law degree in addition to the J.D. The ratio of full-time students to full-time faculty in an average class is 24 to 1; in a clinic, 8 to 1. The law school has a regular program of bringing visiting professors and other distinguished lecturers and visitors to campus. There is a chapter of the Order of the Coif; 19 faculty and 38 graduates are members.

Students

About 48% of the student body are women; 23%, minorities; 6%, African American; 7%, Asian American; 10%, Hispanic; and 1%, Native American. The majority of students come from Florida (87%). The average age of entering students is 24. About 49% of students enter directly from undergraduate school and 11% have a graduate degree. About 3% drop out after the first year for academic or personal reasons; 97% remain to receive a law degree.

Placement

J.D.s awarded:	430

Services available through: a separate law school placement center

Services: mock interviews, off-campus recruiting, on-line interview sign-up/job listings available 24/7, pro bono-public interest law, career programs, career library, Shadow Program, judicial clerkship program

Special features: More than 200 employers typically interview on campus in the fall and spring; 4 full-time professionals advise students and conduct programming and mock interviews.

Full-time job interviews:	27 employers
Summer job interviews:	102 employers
Placement by graduation:	76% of class
Placement within 9 months:	87% of class
Average starting salary:	$55,000 to $92,500

Areas of placement:

Private practice 2-10 attorneys	21%
Private practice 11-25 attorneys	9%
Private practice 26-50 attorneys	8%
Private practice 51-100 attorneys	5%
Private practice 101-500 attorneys	24%
Government	13%
Business/industry	8%
Judicial clerkships	5%
Public interest	5%
Academic	3%

UNIVERSITY OF GEORGIA

School of Law

Hirsch Hall, 225 Herty Drive
Athens, GA 30602-6012

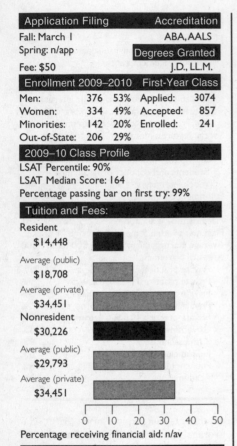

Application Filing		Accreditation	
Fall: March 1		ABA, AALS	
Spring: n/app		**Degrees Granted**	
Fee: $50		J.D., LL.M.	

Enrollment 2009–2010		First-Year Class	
Men:	376 53%	Applied:	3074
Women:	334 49%	Accepted:	857
Minorities:	142 20%	Enrolled:	241
Out-of-State:	206 29%		

2009–10 Class Profile
LSAT Percentile: 90%
LSAT Median Score: 164
Percentage passing bar on first try: 99%

Tuition and Fees:

Resident
$14,448

Average (public)
$18,708

Average (private)
$34,451

Nonresident
$30,226

Average (public)
$29,793

Average (private)
$34,451

0   10   20   30   40   50
Percentage receiving financial aid: n/av

ADMISSIONS
In the fall 2009 first-year class, 3074 applied, 857 were accepted, and 241 enrolled. Eighteen transfers enrolled. The median LSAT percentile of the most recent first-year class was 90; the median GPA was 3.7 on a scale of 4.3. The lowest LSAT percentile accepted was 40; the highest was 99.

Requirements
Applicants must take the LSAT. Minimum acceptable GPA is 2.0 on a scale of 4.0. No specific undergraduate courses are required. Candidates are not interviewed.

Procedure
The application deadline for fall entry is March 1. Applicants should submit an application form, LSAT results, transcripts, a personal statement, a nonrefundable application fee of $50, and 2 letters of recommendation. Notification of the admissions decision is from October through August. The latest acceptable

LSAT test date for fall entry is February. The law school uses the LSDAS.

Special
The law school recruits minority and disadvantaged students by means of the Candidate Referral Service of Law Services, LSAC Law Forums, and campus visitations. Requirements are not different for out-of-state students. Transfer students must have one year of credit, have attended an ABA-approved law school, and transfer from an AALS member school. A copy of the LSDAS Law School Report, law school transcript, dean's certification letter, and 2 letters of recommendation must be submitted.

Costs
Tuition and fees for the 2009-2010 academic year are $14,448 for full-time in-state students and $30,226 for out-of-state students. On-campus room and board costs about $13,920 annually; books and supplies run $1400.

Financial Aid
The average annual amount of aid from all sources combined, including scholarships, loans, and work contracts, is $21,682; maximum, $45,546. Awards are based on need and merit. Required financial statement is the FAFSA. The aid application deadline for fall entry is July 1. First-year students are notified about their financial aid application on or about February 1 for priority merit scholarships; on or about June 1 for need-based aid.

About the Law School
University of Georgia School of Law was established in 1859 and is a public institution. The 1289-acre campus is in a small town 65 miles northeast of Atlanta. Students have access to federal, state, county, city, and local agencies, courts, correctional facilities, law firms, and legal aid organizations in the Athens area. Students have access to the facilities of the University of Georgia. Facilities of special interest to law students are the Dean Rusk Center for International and Comparative Law, the Institute for Continuing Legal Education, and the Institution for Continuing Judicial Education. Housing for students is available on campus for single students in residence halls; stu-

dents with a spouse and/or children may live in University Village, an on-campus apartment complex. About 99% of the law school facilities are accessible to the physically disabled.

Calendar
The law school operates on a traditional semester basis. Courses for full-time students are offered days only and must be completed within 5 years. There is no part-time program. New students are admitted in the fall. There is a 7-week summer session. Transferable summer courses are offered.

Programs
In addition to the J.D., the law school offers the LL.M. Students may take relevant courses in other programs and apply credit toward the J.D.; a maximum of 6 credits may be applied. The following joint degrees may be earned: J.D./M.B.A. (Juris Doctor/Master of Business Administration), J.D./M.Ed. (Juris Doctor/Master of Education in sports studies), J.D./M.H.P. (Juris Doctor/Master of Historic Preservation), J.D./M.P.A. (Juris Doctor/Master of Public Administration), and J.D./M.S.W. (Juris Doctor/Master of Social Work).

Required
To earn the J.D., candidates must complete 88 total credits, of which 36 are for required courses. They must maintain a minimum GPA of 2.0 in the required courses. The following first-year courses are required of all students: Civil Procedure, Contracts and Sales, Criminal Law, Legal Research and Writing, Property, and Torts. Legal Profession is a required upper-level courses. Students must complete at least 1 practical skills course. Courses satisfying this requirement include the 11 service learning clinics. The required orientation program for first-year students is a 2-day program that provides an introduction to the school's activities, programs, and requirements, and to the case method and Socratic Method of teaching.

Electives
The School of Law offers concentrations in corporate law, criminal law, entertainment law, environmental law, family law, intellectual property law, international

Phone: 706-542-7060
Fax: 706-542-5556
E-mail: ugajd@uga.edu
Web: www.law.uga.edu

Contact
Paul Rollins, Director of Law Admissions, 706-542-7060 for general inquiries; Bonnie Joerschke, Director, Office of Student Fiancial Aid, 706-542-6147 for financial aid information.

GEORGIA

law, juvenile law, labor law, litigation, sports law, tax law, and torts and insurance. In addition, the clinics offered to students include the Criminal Defense Clinic, the Prosecutorial Clinic, and the Land Use Clinic, all of which have varying credit amounts. Seminars, worth 2 credits, and supervised research and independent projects, worth a maximum of 4 credits, are also open to upper-level students. Students may intern with the Civil Externship Clinic, the Public Interest Practicum, and the Global Internship Program. The Dean Rusk Center for International and Comparative Law provides research programs. Field work opportunities for students include Equal Justice Foundation Fellowships. Study abroad programs may be undertaken with permission and include the Georgia Law at Oxford, Brussels Seminar on Law and Institutions of the European Union and Community, and Georgia Law Summer Program in China. Several tutorial and mentoring programs are offered for no credit. The most widely taken electives are Constitutional Law I and II, Evidence, and Federal Income Tax.

Graduation Requirements
In order to graduate, candidates must have a GPA of 2.0 and have completed the upper-division writing requirement.

Organizations
Students edit the *Georgia Law Review*, *Georgia Journal of International and Comparative Law*, and *Journal of Intellectual Property Law*. Annually, moot court teams participate in 8 moot court competitions, including the National and the Phillip C. Jessup Moot Courts and the ABA National Moot Court competitions. Other competitions are the American Trial Lawyers Association and National Mock Trial competitions. Law student organizations include the Environmental Law Association, Student Animal Legal Defense Fund, and Business Law Society.There are local chapters of Black Law Students Association, Phi Alpha Delta, and ABA-Law Student Division. Campus clubs and other organizations include Equal Justice Foundation, Women Law Students Association, and Student Bar Association.

Library
The law library contains 390,000 hardcopy volumes and 504,653 microform volume equivalents, and subscribes to 7223 serial publications. Such on-line databases and networks as CALI, CIS Universe, Legal-Trac, LEXIS, LOIS, NEXIS, OCLC First Search, WESTLAW, and Wilsonline Indexes are available to law students for research. Special library collections include complete English and Canadian law collections and a European Community depository library. Recently, the library updated furnishings, task lighting, computer power outlets at every seat, and wireless Internet. The ratio of library volumes to faculty is 7959 to 1 and to students is 549 to 1. The ratio of seats in the library to students is 1 to 1.

Faculty
The law school has 49 full-time and 20 part-time faculty members, of whom 22 are women. According to AAUP standards for Category I institutions, faculty salaries are below average. About 18% of full-time faculty have a graduate law degree in addition to the J.D.; about 75% of part-time faculty have one. The ratio of full-time students to full-time faculty in an average class is 12 to 1. The law school has a regular program of bringing visiting professors and other distinguished lecturers and visitors to campus. There is a chapter of the Order of the Coif.

Students
About 49% of the student body are women; 20%, minorities; 12%, African American; 4%, Asian American; 1%, Hispanic; and 15%, multiracial and unknown, and foreign national. The majority of students come from Georgia (71%). The average age of entering students is 23; age range is 20 to 33. About 2% drop out after the first year for academic or personal reasons; 97% remain to receive a law degree.

Placement
J.D.s awarded:	230

Services available through: a separate law school placement center

Services: more than 20 separate informational programs, including forums on legal practice and settings, resume and cover letter writing, interviewing and other career-related topics; several initiatives matching more than 100 students with alumni for in-depth career advice, contacts information and experience; more than 6 days of mock interviews; more than 20 off-campus interview initiatives; fall and spring on-campus interview programs; on-line interview scheduling system, including a personal resume database; and video conference interviewing

Special features: visiting career consultants, a career lecture series and videotaping of mock interviews, shadow programs, mentor programs, and 12 or more interviewing consortia

Full-time job interviews:	87 employers
Summer job interviews:	87 employers
Placement by graduation:	87% of class
Placement within 9 months:	99% of class
Average starting salary:	$33,000 to $125,000
Areas of placement:	
Private practice 51-100 attorneys	58%
Judicial clerkships	17%
Government	11%
Business/industry	7%
Public interest	6%
Academic	1%

University of Georgia **477**

William S. Richardson School of Law

2515 Dole Street
Honolulu, HI 96822

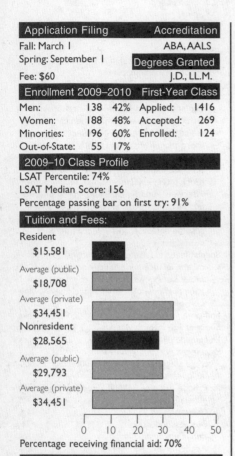

Application Filing		Accreditation	
Fall: March 1		ABA, AALS	
Spring: September 1		Degrees Granted	
Fee: $60		J.D., LL.M.	

Enrollment 2009–2010			First-Year Class	
Men:	138	42%	Applied:	1416
Women:	188	48%	Accepted:	269
Minorities:	196	60%	Enrolled:	124
Out-of-State:	55	17%		

2009–10 Class Profile
LSAT Percentile: 74%
LSAT Median Score: 156
Percentage passing bar on first try: 91%

Tuition and Fees:

Resident
$15,581

Average (public)
$18,708

Average (private)
$34,451

Nonresident
$28,565

Average (public)
$29,793

Average (private)
$34,451

Percentage receiving financial aid: 70%

ADMISSIONS

In the fall 2009 first-year class, 1416 applied, 269 were accepted, and 124 enrolled. Ten transfers enrolled. The median LSAT percentile of the most recent first-year class was 74; the median GPA was 3.45 on a scale of 4.0. The lowest LSAT percentile accepted was 23; the highest was 99.

Requirements
Applicants must have a bachelor's degree and take the LSAT. The most important admission factors include academic achievement, state or country of residence and LSAT results. No specific undergraduate courses are required. Candidates are not interviewed.

Procedure
The application deadline for fall entry is March 1. Applicants should submit an application form, LSAT results, transcripts, TOEFL, if applicable, a nonrefundable application fee of $60, 2 letters of recommendation, and residency declaration. Notification of the admissions decision is by mid April. The latest acceptable LSAT test date for fall entry is February. The law school uses the LSDAS.

Special
Requirements are not different for out-of-state students. Transfer students must have one year of credit, have attended an ABA-approved law school, have a law school rank at least in the top half of their class, 2 letters of recommendation including one from a law professor, and a complete application.

Costs

Tuition and fees for the 2009-2010 academic year are $15,581 for full-time in-state students and $28,565 for out-of-state students. Tuition for part-time students is $13,055 in-state and $23,869 out-of-state. On-campus room and board costs about $8600 annually; books and supplies run $7600.

Financial Aid

About 70% of current law students receive some form of aid. The average annual amount of aid from all sources combined, including scholarships, loans, and work contracts, is $31,000; maximum, $44,765. Awards are based on need and merit. Some merit grants are available. Required financial statement is the FAFSA. The aid application deadline for fall entry is March 1. Special funds for minority or disadvantaged students consist of grants from the Bishop Estate for Native Hawaiians and, through the University, special tuition waivers for state residents; Native Hawaiians qualify for resident tuition rates regardless of residency. First-year students are notified about their financial aid application some time after acceptance, which occurs in March or April, but before enrollment in August. Most students are notified about financial aid in June.

About the Law School

University of Hawaii at Manoa William S. Richardson School of Law was established in 1973 and is a public institution. The 300-acre campus is in a suburban area 2 miles east of Honolulu. The primary mission of the law school is to provide a professional legal education to highly qualified and diverse students in a collaborative, multidisciplinary educational community that is committed to teaching, scholarship, publlic service, ethical responsibility, and the pursuit of social and economic justice. Students have access to federal, state, county, city, and local agencies, courts, correctional facilities, law firms, and legal aid organizations in the Honolulu area. Students have access to virtually every aspect of the legal community as the law school is Hawaii's only law school; the legal community is active at the school via adjunct teaching, live client clinics, mentoring, and speaking. Facilities of special interest to law students consist of expertise, degree programs, and/or research units in ocean studies, resource management, land use, water resources, natural energy, and marine biology; additionally, there are Centers for Chinese, Hawaiian, Japanese, Korean, Pacific Island, Philippine, South Asian, and South East Asian Studies. Housing for students is very limited on campus; nearly all law students live off campus in nearby apartments. All law school facilities are accessible to the physically disabled.

Calendar

The law school operates on a traditional semester basis. Courses for full-time students are offered both day and evening and must be completed within 5 years. For part-time students, courses are offered evenings only. New full- and part-time students are admitted in the fall. There is a summer session. Transferable summer courses are offered.

Programs

In addition to the J.D., the law school offers the LL.M. Students may take relevant courses in other programs and apply credit toward the J.D.; a maximum of 10 credits may be applied. The following joint degrees may be earned: J.D./M.A. (Juris Doctor/Master of Arts in Asian studies), J.D./M.B.A. (Juris Doctor/Master of Business Adminstration), J.D./M.P.H. (Juris Doctor/Master of Public Health), J.D./M.S.W. (Juris Doctor/Master of Social Work), J.D./M.U.R.P. (Juris Doctor/Master of Urban and Regional Planning), and J.D./Ph.D. (Juris Doctor/Doctor of Philosophy in psychology).

Phone: 808-956-7966
Fax: 808-956-3813
E-mail: *lawadm@hawaii.edu*
Web: *law.hawaii.edu*

Contact

Director of Admissions, 808-956-7966 for general inquiries; Melissa K Skillings, Director of Financial Aid, 808-956-7966 for financial aid information.

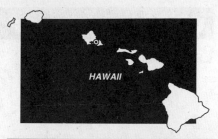

Required

To earn the J.D., candidates must complete 89 total credits, of which 42 are for required courses. They must maintain a minimum GPA of 2.0 in the required courses. The following first-year courses are required of all students: Appellate Advocacy, Civil Procedure I and II, Contracts I and II, Criminal Justice, Legal Bibliography, Legal Method Seminar, Real Property Law I, and Torts Process I and II. Required upper-level courses consist of 1 clinical course, Constitutional Law I, Pro Bono legal service (60 hours), Professional Responsibility, and Second Year Seminar. All students must take clinical courses. The required orientation program for first-year students is 1 week consisting of introductions to faculty, students, career issues, registration, and academic regulations; discussion of stress and personal issues; and a group introduction to the Legal Method Seminar.

Electives

The credits students must take in their area of concentration varies. The William S. Richardson School of Law offers concentrations in corporate law, criminal law, environmental law, family law, international law, labor law, litigation, maritime law, tax law, torts and insurance, Pacific Asian Legal Studies, and Native Hawaiian Law. In addition, clinics for 3 or 4 credits each are assigned by lottery to upper-level students who meet the prerequisites. Clinics include Prosecution, Elder Law, and Native Hawaiian Rights. Upper-level students are offered a variety of seminars in advanced legal studies and Pacific-Asian Legal Studies for 1 to 3 credits per seminar. The required Second Year Seminar is offered for 4 credits. One externship per semester may be taken by upper-level students; a maximum of 2 externships may be taken for 2 credits each. Alternatively, a 14-credit externship in an approved Pacific Island jurisdiction may be taken. Under the directed studies program, any upper-level student may elect to conduct special research for 1 to 3 credits. Research can be repeated. Field work is linked to those clinics that include live client representation as well as actual court appearances under a special state Supreme Court rule. Special lecture series are offered for no credit; any student may attend. Annually, there is a Distinguished Fujiyama Visiting Professor, a George

Johnson Visiting Scholar, and Jurist-in-Residence Program. There is also a Pacific-Asian Legal Studies lecture series for visiting Asian legal scholars. Study abroad can be accomplished by special arrangement for varying credits or by a full-semester externship in certain Pacific Island jurisdictions for 14 credits. Tutorial programs are available and administered through the Student Bar Association for no credit. Special interst group programs, offered for no credit, include the Filipino Law Students Association, 'Ahahui 'O Hawai'i (a Native Hawaiian organization), Advocates for Public Interest Law, and the Pacific-Asian Legal Studies Organization. The most widely taken electives are Evidence, Wills and Trusts, and Corporations.

Graduation Requirements

In order to graduate, candidates must have a GPA of 2.0 and have completed the upper-division writing requirement.

Organizations

Students edit the *University of Hawaii Law Review* and the *Asian-Pacific Law Policy Journal*. Students participate in the annual Susan McKay Moot Court Competition, the Environmental Law Moot Court, and the Jessup International Moot Court competition. Other competitions include Client Counseling. Law student organizations include the Student Bar Association, Environmental Law Society, and Hawaii Association of Women Law Students. Local chapters of national associations include the American Inns of Court, Phi Delta Phi, and Federalist Society.

Library

The law library contains 248,838 hardcopy volumes and 875,305 microform volume equivalents, and subscribes to 2736 serial publications. Such on-line databases and networks as DIALOG, Legal-Trac, LEXIS, NEXIS, WESTLAW, ERIC, and ABI/INFORM are available to law students for research. Special library collections include a partial federal government depository. Recently, the library upgraded its computer laboratory. The ratio of library volumes to faculty is 5925 to 1 and to students is 763 to 1. The ratio of seats in the library to students is 1 to 1.

Placement

J.D.s awarded:	88

Services available through: a separate law school placement center
Services: career information series
Special features: Nearly all placement activity is focused on the Hawaii market, as are on-campus interviews, since 95% of graduates remain in the state.

Full-time job interviews:	15 employers
Summer job interviews:	30 employers
Placement by graduation:	60% of class
Placement within 9 months:	100% of class
Average starting salary:	$32,000 to $160,000

Areas of placement:
Private practice 2-10 attorneys	13%
Private practice 11-25 attorneys	8%
Private practice 26-50 attorneys	7%
Private practice 51-100 attorneys	8%
Judicial clerkships	36%
Government	15%
Business/industry	12%

Faculty

The law school has 42 full-time and 15 part-time faculty members, of whom 29 are women. According to AAUP standards for Category I institutions, faculty salaries are average. About 37% of full-time faculty have a graduate law degree in addition to the J.D.; about 25% of part-time faculty have one. The ratio of full-time students to full-time faculty in an average class is 13 to 1; in a clinic, 12 to 1. The law school has a regular program of bringing visiting professors and other distinguished lecturers and visitors to campus.

Students

About 48% of the student body are women; 60%, minorities; 1%, African American; 54%, Asian American; 2%, Hispanic; and 1%, Native American. The majority of students come from Hawaii (83%). The average age of entering students is 26; age range is 22 to 59. About 20% of students enter directly from undergraduate school, 10% have a graduate degree, and 63% have worked full-time prior to entering law school. About 3% drop out after the first year for academic or personal reasons; 97% remain to receive a law degree.

Law Center

100 Law Center
Houston, TX 77204-6060

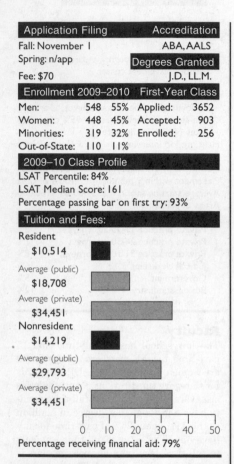

Application Filing	Accreditation
Fall: November 1	ABA, AALS
Spring: n/app	**Degrees Granted**
Fee: $70	J.D., LL.M.

Enrollment 2009–2010		First-Year Class	
Men:	548 55%	Applied:	3652
Women:	448 45%	Accepted:	903
Minorities:	319 32%	Enrolled:	256
Out-of-State:	110 11%		

2009–10 Class Profile
LSAT Percentile: 84%
LSAT Median Score: 161
Percentage passing bar on first try: 93%

Tuition and Fees:

Resident
$10,514

Average (public)
$18,708

Average (private)
$34,451

Nonresident
$14,219

Average (public)
$29,793

Average (private)
$34,451

0 10 20 30 40 50

Percentage receiving financial aid: 79%

ADMISSIONS

In the fall 2009 first-year class, 3652 applied, 903 were accepted, and 256 enrolled. Eight transfers enrolled. The median LSAT percentile of the most recent first-year class was 84; the median GPA was 3.34 on a scale of 4.0. The lowest LSAT percentile accepted was 15; the highest was 99.

Requirements
Applicants must have a bachelor's degree and take the LSAT. The most important admission factors include LSAT results, GPA, and general background. No specific undergraduate courses are required. Candidates are not interviewed.

Procedure
The application deadline for fall entry is November 1, May 15 for summer entry. Applicants should submit an application form, LSAT results, transcripts, a personal statement, a nonrefundable application fee of $70, 2 letters of recommendation,

(no more than 3 accepted) a résumé, and the LSDAS report. Notification of the admissions decision is December through July. The latest acceptable LSAT test date for fall entry is February (full-time) June (part-time). The law school uses the LSDAS.

Special
The law school recruits minority and disadvantaged students through a strong support system on campus, well-funded BLSA, HLSA, and ALSA organizations, and by visiting various colleges and hosting programs. Requirements are different for out-of-state students in that there is a 35% cap for nonresident students. Transfer students must have one year of credit, have attended an ABA-approved law school, and rank typically within the top of the first-year class.

Costs

Tuition and fees for the 2009-2010 academic year are $10,514 for full-time in-state students and $14,219 for out-of-state students. Tuition for part-time students is $7562 in-state and $10,032 out-of-state. On-campus room and board costs about $3769 annually; books and supplies run $550.

Financial Aid

About 79% of current law students receive some form of aid. The average annual amount of aid from all sources combined, including scholarships, loans, and work contracts, is $26,618; maximum, $35,368. Awards are based on need and merit; need-based financial aid is handled by the University's Director of Financial Aid. Scholarships are handled by the Scholarship Committee. Required financial statement is the FAFSA. The aid application deadline for fall entry is April 1. First-year students are notified about their financial aid application on a rolling basis as their financial aid file is complete, but no earlier than mid-April.

About the Law School

University of Houston Law Center was established in 1947 and is a public institution. The 540-acre campus is in an urban area 3 miles south of downtown Houston. The primary mission of the law school is to attract a student body characterized

by social and ethnic diversity that will be exposed to a diverse educational and social experience and that will enter the legal profession in positions of responsibility. Students have access to federal, state, county, city, and local agencies, courts, correctional facilities, law firms, and legal aid organizations in the Houston area. Special attention is given to accommodating students with disabilities. Housing for students is available, including housing for married students. The majority of students live 15 to 20 minutes from campus. About 95% of the law school facilities are accessible to the physically disabled.

Calendar

The law school operates on a traditional semester basis. Courses for full-time students are offered both day and evening (first-year courses are offered days only) and must be completed within 4 years. For part-time students, courses are offered both day and evening and (first-year courses are offered evenings only) and must be completed within 6 years. New full- and part-time students are admitted in the fall. There is a 5-week summer session. Transferable summer courses are offered.

Programs

In addition to the J.D., the law school offers the LL.M. Students may take relevant courses in other programs and apply credit toward the J.D.; a maximum of 12 to 15 hours depending on the program may be applied. The following joint degrees may be earned: J.D./M.A. (Juris Doctor/Master of Arts in history), J.D./M.B.A. (Juris Doctor/Master of Business Administration), J.D./M.D. (Juris Doctor/Doctor of Medicine), J.D./M.P.H. (Juris Doctor/Master of Public Health), J.D./M.S.W. (Juris Doctor/Master of Social Work), and J.D./Ph.D. (Juris Doctor/Doctor of Philosophy in medical humanities and in criminal justice).

Required
To earn the J.D., candidates must complete 90 total credits, of which 34 are for required courses. They must maintain a minimum GPA of 2.5 in the required courses. The following first-year courses are required of all students: a statutory elective, Constitutional Law, Contracts, Criminal Law, Legal Research, Legal

Phone: 713-743-2280
Fax: 713-743-2194
E-mail: lawadmissions@uh.edu
Web: www.law.uh.edu

Contact

Jamie Ann West, J.D., Assistant Dean, 713-743-2280 for general inquiries; Laura Neal, Financial Aid Counselor, 713-743-2269 for financial aid information.

TEXAS

Writing, Procedure, Property, and Torts. Required upper-level courses consist of Professional Responsibility and the senior writing requirement. The required orientation program for first-year students is 3 days of general information.

Electives

The Law Center offers concentrations in corporate law, criminal law, environmental law, family law, intellectual property law, international law, labor law, litigation, tax law, and health law. In addition, students may choose among 7 clinics, including Civil Practice, Consumer Law, Immigration Practice, Mediation, Transactional, Criminal Practice, and Health Law externships. Seminar courses are available in all areas. There are judicial internships at federal, state, district, and county municipal levels. Research programs include the Health Law and Policy Institute; Institute for Intellectual Property and Information Law; Center for Environment, Energy and Natural Resources Law; Center for Children, Law and Policy; Blakely Advocacy Institute; Institute for Higher Education Law and Governance; Texas Innocence Network; and the Criminal Justice Institute. Lecture series include the Baker Botts Lecture and Katz-Kiley Lecture. Study Abroad may be done through the North American Consortium on Legal Education (NACLE). The Academic Enrichment Program provides tutorial assistance. The One-L Mentoring Program helps new students acclimate to legal and life law school. The most widely taken electives are Commercial Transactions, Business Organizations, and Evidence.

Graduation Requirements

In order to graduate, candidates must have a GPA of 2.5 and have completed the upper-division writing requirement.

Organizations

Students edit the *Houston Law Review*, *Houston Journal of International law*, *Houston Journal of Health Law and Policy*, *Houston Business and Tax Law Journal*, *Journal of Consumer and Commercial Law*, and the *Environmental and Energy Law and Policy Journal*. Additional publications include *Health Law News* and the student newspaper, *Legalese*. Intrascholarship competitions include the Blakely-Butler Moot Court Competition, Hippard Mock Trial Competition, Newhouse Mediation Competition, and the Hofheinz Tournament of Champions. Law student organizations include Advocates, Corporate and Taxation Law Society, and the Energy and Environmental Law Society. The Law Center hosts local chapters of the ABA-Law Student Division, Phi Delta Phi, and Order of the Coif. Other organizations include the Student Bar Association, Black Law Students Association, Hispanic Law Students Association, Asian Law Students Association, Public Interest Law Organization, Outlaw (GLBT), and American Constitution Society for Law and Policy.

Library

The law library contains 542,164 hardcopy volumes and 1,624,790 microform volume equivalents, and subscribes to 775 serial publications. Such on-line databases and networks as CALI, CIS Universe, Legal-Trac, Lexis, Nexis, Lexis Nexis Academic, OCLC First Search, and WESTLAW are available to law students for research. Special library collections include a U.S. government depository, Mexican Law Collection, Admiralty and Maritime Law Collection, John R. Brown Archives, and Texas Supreme Court briefs. The ratio of library volumes to faculty is 10,642 to 1 and to students is 544 to 1. The ratio of seats in the library to students is 1 to 2.

Faculty

The law school has 51 full-time and 77 part-time faculty members, of whom 39 are women. According to AAUP standards for Category I institutions, faculty salaries are below average. About 28% of full-time faculty have a graduate law degree in addition to the J.D.; about 13% of part-time faculty have one. The ratio of full-time students to full-time faculty in an average class is 12 to 1; in a clinic, 8 to 1. The law school has a regular program of bringing visiting professors and other distinguished lecturers and visitors to campus. There is a chapter of the Order of the Coif; 28 faculty and over 700 graduates are members.

Students

About 45% of the student body are women; 32%, minorities; 8%, African Ameri-

Placement

J.D.s awarded:	286

Services available through: a separate law school placement center

Services: Public Interest/Public Sector Fellowship Program

Special features: A comprehensive career education series is held every year and includes networking events, speaker panels, and mock interviews for first-year students. UHLC participates in 10 off-campus recruitment programs during the year.

Full-time job interviews:	24 employers
Summer job interviews:	121 employers
Placement by graduation:	75% of class
Placement within 9 months:	96% of class
Average starting salary:	$20,000 to $350,000

Areas of placement:

Private practice 2-10 attorneys	18%
Private practice 11-25 attorneys	10%
Private practice 26-50 attorneys	2%
Private practice 51-100 attorneys	1%
Private practice 100+ attorneys	23%
Business/industry	21%
Government	10%
Judicial clerkships	4%
Public interest	4%
Academic	2%

can; 10%, Asian American; 9%, Hispanic; 1%, Native American; and 3%, Foreign Nationals. The majority of students come from Texas (89%). The average age of entering students is 24; age range is 20 to 63. About 31% of students enter directly from undergraduate school and 13% have a graduate degree. About 2% drop out after the first year for academic or personal reasons.

University of Houston **481**

College of Law

P.O. Box 442321
Moscow, ID 83844-2321

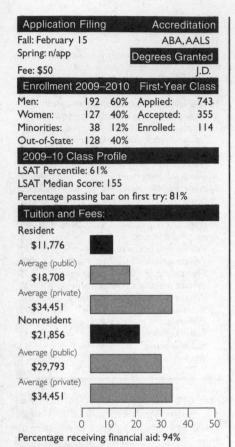

Application Filing		Accreditation	
Fall: February 15		ABA, AALS	
Spring: n/app		Degrees Granted	
Fee: $50			J.D.

Enrollment 2009–2010		First-Year Class	
Men:	192 60%	Applied:	743
Women:	127 40%	Accepted:	355
Minorities:	38 12%	Enrolled:	114
Out-of-State:	128 40%		

2009–10 Class Profile
LSAT Percentile: 61%
LSAT Median Score: 155
Percentage passing bar on first try: 81%

Tuition and Fees:

Resident
$11,776

Average (public)
$18,708

Average (private)
$34,451

Nonresident
$21,856

Average (public)
$29,793

Average (private)
$34,451

0   10   20   30   40   50

Percentage receiving financial aid: 94%

ADMISSIONS

In the fall 2009 first-year class, 743 applied, 355 were accepted, and 114 enrolled. Five transfers enrolled. The median LSAT percentile of the most recent first-year class was 61; the median GPA was 3.29 on a scale of 4.0. The lowest LSAT percentile accepted was 15; the highest was 93.

Requirements
Applicants must have a bachelor's degree and take the LSAT. The most important admission factors include state or country of residence, GPA, and LSAT results. No specific undergraduate courses are required. Candidates are not interviewed.

Procedure
The application deadline for fall entry is February 15. Applicants should submit an application form, LSAT results, transcripts, a personal statement, a nonrefundable application fee of $50. Letters o recommendation are not required, but up to 3 are recommended, and LSDAS

registration is required. Notification of the admissions decision is early April. The latest acceptable LSAT test date for fall entry is December (generally), February (in rare cases). The law school uses the LSDAS.

Special
The law school recruits minority and disadvantaged students through scholarships, application workshops for undergraduate minority groups, and recruiting at colleges and universities with distinctive programs to serve minority populations. Requirements are not different for out-of-state students. Transfer students must have one year of credit, have attended an ABA-approved law school, submit a letter of good standing, rank in the top half of class, and have competitive LSAT results and UGPA.

Costs

Tuition and fees for the 2009-2010 academic year are $11,776 for full-time in-state students and $21,856 for out-of-state students. On-campus room and board costs about $9292 annually; books and supplies run $1474.

Financial Aid

About 94% of current law students receive some form of aid. The average annual amount of aid from all sources combined, including scholarships, loans, and work contracts, is $24,000. Awards are based on need and merit. Required financial statements are the FAFSA and University of Idaho special forms. The aid application deadline for fall entry is February 15. Special funds for minority or disadvantaged students consist of scholarships. First-year students are notified about their financial aid application at time of acceptance.

About the Law School

University of Idaho College of Law was established in 1909 and is a public institution. The 160-acre campus is in a small town 85 miles southeast of Spokane, Washington. The primary mission of the law school is to prepare students for careers in law, business, and public service. Students have access to federal, state, county, city, and local agencies,

courts, correctional facilities, law firms, and legal aid organizations in the Moscow area. Facilities of special interest to law students include the law building, which recently underwent more than $1.5 million in renovations, including a new courtroom and new study carrels. Housing for students is available and includes many on- and off-campus options. All law school facilities are accessible to the physically disabled.

Calendar

The law school operates on a traditional semester basis. Courses for full-time students are offered days only and must be completed within 84 months. There is no part-time program. New students are admitted in the fall. There is an 8-week summer session. Transferable summer courses are not offered.

Programs

Students may take relevant courses in other programs and apply credit toward the J.D.; a maximum of 6 credits may be applied. The following joint degrees may be earned: J.D./M.Acct. (Juris Doctor/Master of Accountancy), J.D./M.B.A. (Juris Doctor/ Master of Business Administration in cooperation with Washington State University), J.D./M.S. (Juris Doctor/ Master of Science in environmental science), and J.D./M.S./Ph.D. (Juris Doctor/ Master of Science/Doctor of Philosophy in water resources management).

Required
To earn the J.D., candidates must complete 90 total credits, of which 39 are for required courses. They must maintain a minimum GPA of 2.0 in the required courses. The following first-year courses are required of all students: Civil Procedure I and II, Contracts I and II, Criminal Law, Legal Research and Writing, Property I and II, and Torts I and II. Required upper-level courses consist of an upper-division writing requirement, Constitutional Law I and II, and Professional Responsibility. The required orientation program for first-year students is a 4-day program covering study skills and case briefings and culminating with students participating as witnesses and jurors in the upper-level Trial Advocacy mock trials. The program also includes a half-day

Phone: 208-885-2300
Fax: 208-885-5709
E-mail: jfinney@uidaho.edu
Web: www.uidaho.edu/law

Contact

Jennifer Finney, Director of Admissions, 208-885-2300 for general inquiries; Rodd Dunn, Associate Director, 208-885-6312 for financial aid information.

IDAHO

Professionalism Workshop where current lawyers and judges discuss ethical issues with new students in small groups.

Electives

The College of Law offers concentrations in corporate law, criminal law, environmental law, litigation, and lawyering skills. In addition, third-year students may participate in one of 7 live clinics, including 9th Circuit Appellate, Tribal and Immigration, Small Business, Domestic Violence, Victims' Rights, Tax, and General Practice, for a maximum of 8 credits. Upper-level students may choose from seminars in several subject areas, including corporate law, dispute resolution, and environmental law, for 1 to 3 credits. The College of Law offers an extensive externship program, awarding class credit for summer placements in various government agencies, nonprofit organizations, and judicial offices for 1 to 8 credits. Any student may perform directed research upon a professor's approval for 1 to 2 credits. Third-year students may participate in the Semester-in-Practice program in Boise for up to 12 credits. The Sherman Bellwood Lectures bring learned individuals to the state of Idaho and the University of Idaho campus to allow students the opportunity to discuss, examine, and debate subjects related to the justice system. The speakers are prominent and highly regarded local, regional, and national leaders who cover a wide range of topics and have included several former United States Supreme Court Justices. Students may transfer in study-abroad credits earned through any ABA-approved study-abroad program. The College of Law has an Office of Academic Support run by a licensed attorney to assist students with their academic needs. Student organizations dedicated to promoting and supporting legal education among underrepresented groups include the Multicultural Law Caucus, Outlaw Alliance, Women's Law Caucus, Student Advocates for Hispanic/Latino Support and Awareness, and the Black Law Students Association. The most widely taken electives are in the areas of natural resources and water law and trial practice skills/clinics.

Graduation Requirements

In order to graduate, candidates must have a GPA of 2.0 and have completed the upper-division writing requirement.

Organizations

The *Idaho Law Review* is the primary law review. There is also the *University of Idaho Journal of Critical Studies ("The Crit")* and *inter alia* (student satire). Teams compete in the McNichols Moot Court competition, Duberstein Bankruptcy, and Environmental Law. Other competitions include the American Association for Justice Mock Trial competition. The Student Bar Association is the umbrella student government organization and coordinates the College of Law's 23 student organizations, including the Board of Student Advocates, Public Interest Law Group, and Environmental Law Society. Law student organizations, local chapters of national associations, and campus organizations include, among others, Phi Alpha Delta, American Civil Liberties Union, the Federalist Society, the Hunting and Fishing Club, Nontraditional Students Group, and Law School Support Association for spouses and partners of law students.

Library

The law library contains 167,549 hardcopy volumes and 102,842 microform volume equivalents, and subscribes to 5000 serial publications. Such on-line databases and networks as CALI, DIALOG, Legal-Trac, LEXIS, LOIS, NEXIS, OCLC First Search, WESTLAW, Wilsonline Indexes, Proquest Newspapers, BNA Tax Management Library, EBSCO databases, GPO Access, CIAO, CILP, LLMC Digital , HeinOnline, IndexMaster, and many others are available to law students for research. Special library collections include archives of Idaho materials, Idaho Supreme Court records and briefs, and Clagett historical materials. Recently, the library added new study carrels, new carpet, and new computers in computer laboratories. The ratio of library volumes to faculty is 5077 to 1 and to students is 525 to 1. The ratio of seats in the library to students is 1 to 1.

Faculty

The law school has 33 full-time and 14 part-time faculty members, of whom 22 are women. About 13% of full-time faculty have a graduate law degree in addition to the J.D. The ratio of full-time students to full-time faculty in an average class is 17 to 1. The law school has a regular program of bringing visiting professors and other distinguished lecturers and visitors to campus.

Placement

J.D.s awarded:	93

Services available through: a separate law school placement center and an in-house career services director.

Special features: a career services director who is a licensed attorney

Full-time job interviews:	29 employers
Summer job interviews:	n/av
Placement by graduation:	n/av
Placement within 9 months:	89% of class
Average starting salary:	$33,000 to $160,000

Areas of placement:

Private practice 2-10 attorneys	18%
Private practice 11-25 attorneys	12%
Private practice 26-50 attorneys	2%
Private practice 51-100 attorneys	1%
Judicial clerkships	24%
Government	19%
Public interest	8%
Business/industry	6%
Military	2%
Academic	2%

Students

About 40% of the student body are women and 12% are minorities. The majority of students come from Idaho (60%). The average age of entering students is 26; age range is 22 to 53. About 3% drop out after the first year for academic or personal reasons; 97% remain to receive a law degree.

UNIVERSITY OF ILLINOIS

College of Law

504 East Pennsylvania Avenue
Champaign, IL 61820

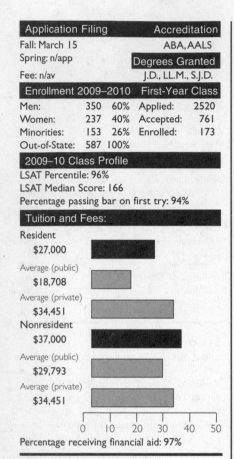

Application Filing		Accreditation
Fall: March 15		ABA, AALS
Spring: n/app		
		Degrees Granted
Fee: n/av		J.D., LL.M., S.J.D.

Enrollment 2009–2010			First-Year Class	
Men:	350	60%	Applied:	2520
Women:	237	40%	Accepted:	761
Minorities:	153	26%	Enrolled:	173
Out-of-State:	587	100%		

2009–10 Class Profile
LSAT Percentile: 96%
LSAT Median Score: 166
Percentage passing bar on first try: 94%

Tuition and Fees:

Resident
$27,000

Average (public)
$18,708

Average (private)
$34,451

Nonresident
$37,000

Average (public)
$29,793

Average (private)
$34,451

0   10   20   30   40   50

Percentage receiving financial aid: 97%

ADMISSIONS

In the fall 2009 first-year class, 2520 applied, 761 were accepted, and 173 enrolled. Figures in the above capsule and in this profile are approximate. Sixty transfers enrolled. The median LSAT percentile of the most recent first-year class was 96; the median GPA was 3.6 on a scale of 4.0. The lowest LSAT percentile accepted was 25; the highest was 99.

Requirements
Applicants must have a bachelor's degree and take the LSAT. The most important admission factors include character, personality, LSAT results, and GPA. No specific undergraduate courses are required. Candidates are not interviewed.

Procedure
Applicants should submit an application form, LSAT results, transcripts, a personal statement, a nonrefundable application fee, 2 letters of recommendation, and a resumé. Notification of the admissions decision is on a rolling basis beginning in December. The latest acceptable LSAT test date for fall entry is February. Check with the school for current application deadlines. The law school uses the LSDAS.

Special
The law school recruits minority and disadvantaged students by participating in recruiting fairs and visiting schools where there are a large number of minority students. Requirements are not different for out-of-state students. Transfer students must have one year of credit and have attended an ABA-approved law school.

Costs

Tuition and fees for the 2009-2010 academic year are $27,000 for full-time in-state students and $37,000 for out-of-state students. On-campus room and board costs about $11,000 annually; books and supplies run $1800.

Financial Aid

In a recent year, about 97% of current law students received some form of aid. The average annual amount of aid from all sources combined, including scholarships, loans, and work contracts, was $35,000; maximum, $48,218. Loans are need based and scholarships are merit based. Required financial statement is the FAFSA. Check with the school for current application deadlines. Special funds for minority or disadvantaged students are available. First-year students are notified about their financial aid application at the time application is made, and again in a letter of acceptance.

About the Law School

University of Illinois College of Law was established in 1897 and is a public institution. The 710-acre campus is in an urban area 130 miles south of Chicago. The primary mission of the law school is to serve the state, nation, and the world as a leading center of legal education, legal scholarship, and public service. Students have access to federal, state, county, city, and local agencies, courts, correctional facilities, law firms, and legal aid organizations in the Champaign area. Housing for students is available throughout the Champaign-Urbana area. In addition, there are several graduate student dorms available to law students. All law school facilities are accessible to the physically disabled.

Calendar

The law school operates on a traditional semester basis. Courses for full-time students are offered days only and must be completed within 3 years. There is no part-time program. New students are admitted in the fall. There is a summer session. The length of the session varies. Transferable summer courses are not offered.

Programs

In addition to the J.D., the law school offers the LL.M. and S.J.D. Students may take relevant courses in other programs and apply credit toward the J.D.; a maximum of 12 credits may be applied. The following joint degrees may be earned: J.D./ D.V.M. (Juris Doctor/ Doctor of Veterinary Medicine), J.D./M.B.A. (Juris Doctor/ Master of Business Administration), J.D./ M.C.S. (Juris Doctor/Master of Computer Science), J.D./M.D. (Juris Doctor/ Doctor of Medicine), J.D./M.Ed. (Juris Doctor/ Master of Education), J.D./M.H.R.I.R. (Juris Doctor/Master of Human Resources and Industrial Relations), J.D./M.S.Chem (Juris Doctor/Master of Science in Chemistry), J.D./M.S.Journ (Juris Doctor/Master Science in Journalism), J.D./M.S.N.R.E.S. (Juris Doctor/Master of Science in Natural Resources and Environmental Sciences), J.D./M.U.P. (Juris Doctor/Master of Urban Planning), and J.D./Ph.D.Ed. (Juris Doctor/Doctor of Philosophy in Education).

Required
To earn the J.D., candidates must complete 90 total credits, of which 33 are for required courses. They must maintain a minimum GPA of 2.0 in the required courses. The following first-year courses are required of all students: Civil Procedure, Constitutional Law I, Contracts, Criminal Law, Introduction to Advocacy, Legal Research, Legal Writing and Analysis, Property, and Torts. Required upper-level courses consist of Professional Responsibility and Upper-level Writing. The required orientation program for first-year students is a 2-day orientation filled with information and experiences

Phone: 217-244-6415
Fax: 217-244-1478
E-mail: admissions@law.uiuc.edu
Web: www.law.uiuc.edu

Contact

Paul Pless, Assistant Dean for Admissions and Financial Aid, 217-244-6415 for general inquiries and financial aid information.

designed to acclimate new students to the law school experience and expectations.

Electives

The College of Law offers concentrations in corporate law, criminal law, environmental law, family law, intellectual property law, international law, labor law, litigation, securities law, sports law, tax law, torts and insurance, and public interest law. In addition, clinics are open to second- and third-year students. Numerous seminars are generally limited-enrollment classes to ensure more individualized experiences and are offered each semester to all second- and third-year students. The topics vary widely to ensure timely coverage of relevant issues. Externships offer students the opportunity to receive law credit for uncompensated work with a nonprofit organization, government agency, or a judge. Students may work as research assistants for faculty members. They may also participate in individual research projects under the supervision of a faculty member, which result in a substantial research paper and corresponding academic credit for scholarly work. Courses that involve interaction with live clients include externships, clinics, legislative projects, and appellate defender work. Additional field work is available through the Prisoner's Rights Research Project. The David C. Baum Memorial Lectures are presented twice each year by distinguished scholars in the areas of civil liberties and civil rights. The Paul M. Van Arsdell, Jr. Memorial Lecture is presented annually on litigation and the legal profession. The Carl Vacketta/Piper Rudnick Lecture is presented annually on government and public affairs. Students may receive credit for ABA-approved study-abroad programs. The Academic Assistance Program offers group programs and individual counseling and tutoring. There are 7 minority student organizations. There are also minority career fairs, numerous speakers and lectures, and a student-chaired diversity committee. The most widely taken electives are Trial Advocacy, Business Associations, and Evidence.

Graduation Requirements

In order to graduate, candidates must have a GPA of 2.0, have completed the upper-division writing requirement, and have 90 semester hours of passing grades, 56 hours earned from the College of Law,

at least 4 full-time semesters at the College of Law, and passing grades in all required courses.

Organizations

Students edit *The University of Illinois Law Review, Elder Law Journal*, and the *Journal of Law, Technology, and Policy*. Law students write the highly regarded Illinois Law Update section of the *Illinois Bar Journal* and the *Illinois Business Law Journal*. Three moot court competitions are Frederick Green, Frederick Douglass, and Intellectual Property Moot Court competitions. Other competitions include ABA Negotiations, ABA Client Counseling competitions, and Trial Team. Law student organizations, local chapters of national associations, and campus clubs and organizations include Latino/Latina Law Students Association, Black Law Students Association, Street Law, American Association for Justice, Asian American Law Students Association, the Myra Bradwell Association for Women Law Students, the Student Bar Association, Public Interest Law Foundation, and Impact.

Library

The law library contains 615,739 hardcopy volumes and 928,746 microform volume equivalents. Such on-line databases and networks as CALI, CIS Universe, DIALOG, Dow-Jones, Infotrac, Legal-Trac, LEXIS, LOIS, NEXIS, OCLC First Search, WESTLAW, Wilsonline Indexes, and Making of Modern Law, are available to law students for research. Special library collections include a federal government depository, a European union depository, and an extensive collection of rare Anglo-American items. Recently, the library upgraded lighting and electrical outlets in the main reading room and added a teaching laboratory and 4 new study rooms. The ratio of library volumes to faculty is 15,393 to 1 and to students is 1049 to 1. The ratio of seats in the library to students is 1 to 6.

Faculty

The law school has 40 full-time and 46 part-time faculty members, of whom 33 are women. About 10% of full-time faculty have a graduate law degree in addition to the J.D. The ratio of full-time students to full-time faculty in an average class is 12

Placement

J.D.s awarded:	222
Services available through: a separate law school placement center, the university placement center, and other college placement offices	
Special features: Alumni-Student Job Search Conference, where more than 50 alumni provide counseling and programs for students about the job search process; professional staff of 3 attorneys	
Full-time job interviews:	27 employers
Summer job interviews:	90 employers
Placement by graduation:	83% of class
Placement within 9 months:	98% of class
Average starting salary:	n/av
Areas of placement:	
Private practice 2-10 attorneys	10%
Private practice 11-25 attorneys	7%
Private practice 26-50 attorneys	1%
Private practice 51-100 attorneys	3%
Private practice 100+ attorneys	35%
Business/industry	12%
Government	9%
Judicial clerkships	6%
Academic	3%
Military	2%
Public interest	1%

to 1; in a clinic, 8 to 1. The law school has a regular program of bringing visiting professors and other distinguished lecturers and visitors to campus. There is a chapter of the Order of the Coif.

Students

About 40% of the student body are women; 26%, minorities; 8%, African American; 12%, Asian American; 6%, Hispanic; and 1%, Native American. The average age of entering students is 24; age range is 20 to 43. About 55% of students enter directly from undergraduate school, 25% have a graduate degree, and 35% have worked full-time prior to entering law school. About 2% drop out after the first year for academic or personal reasons; 98% remain to receive a law degree.

College of Law

320 Melrose Avenue
Iowa City, IA 52242

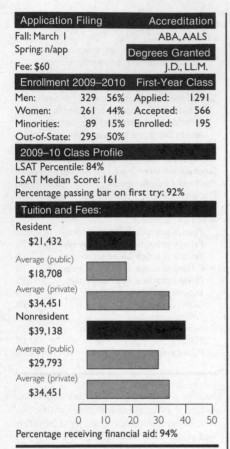

Application Filing	Accreditation
Fall: March 1	ABA, AALS
Spring: n/app	Degrees Granted
Fee: $60	J.D., LL.M.

Enrollment 2009–2010		First-Year Class	
Men:	329 56%	Applied:	1291
Women:	261 44%	Accepted:	566
Minorities:	89 15%	Enrolled:	195
Out-of-State:	295 50%		

2009–10 Class Profile
LSAT Percentile: 84%
LSAT Median Score: 161
Percentage passing bar on first try: 92%

Tuition and Fees:

Resident
$21,432

Average (public)
$18,708

Average (private)
$34,451

Nonresident
$39,138

Average (public)
$29,793

Average (private)
$34,451

0 10 20 30 40 50

Percentage receiving financial aid: 94%

ADMISSIONS

In the fall 2009 first-year class, 1291 applied, 566 were accepted, and 195 enrolled. Three transfers enrolled. The median LSAT percentile of the most recent first-year class was 84; the median GPA was 3.61 on a scale of 4.0.

Requirements
Applicants must have a bachelor's degree and take the LSAT. The most important admission factors include academic achievement, LSAT results, and motivations. No specific undergraduate courses are required. Candidates are not interviewed.

Procedure
The application deadline for fall entry is March 1. Applicants should submit an application form, LSAT results, transcripts, a personal statement, a nonrefundable application fee of $60 (domestic) and $100 (foreign), and 2 letters of recommendation. Prior standarized test scores may be submitted as well as TOEFL. Notification of the admissions decision is begins in December and is usually no later than April. The latest acceptable LSAT test date for fall entry is February, although a February score will put an applicant at a slight disadvantage. The law school uses the LSDAS.

Special
The law school recruits minority and disadvantaged students through extensive travel. Also the College of Law sponsors "Bridging the Gap," a minority pre-law seminar that is brought to potential applicants and prospects. The law school also supports Council on Legal Education Opportunity and the American Indian Pre-Law Summer Institute. Requirements are different for out-of-state students in that for applicants that are "on the fence," Iowa residents will have a slight advantage. Transfer students must have 1 year of credit, have attended an ABA-approved law school, and have credentials that would have made the students admissible as first-year students, have attended an ABA-accredited law school, and have ranked in the top 10% (non-residents) or 25% (residents) during the first year in law school.

Costs

On-campus room and board costs about $8004 annually; books and supplies run $2300.

Financial Aid

About 94% of current law students receive some form of aid. The average annual amount of aid from all sources combined, including scholarships, loans, and work contracts, is $38,383; maximum, $56,089. Awards are based on need and merit. Required financial statements are the FAFSA, the student's federal tax returns, and the institutional form. The aid application deadline for fall entry is open. Special funds for minority or disadvantaged students include the Law Opportunity Fellowship program, which funds a limited number of 3-year tuition and research assistant positions to persons from groups and backgrounds historically underrepresented in the legal profession. First-year students are notified about their financial aid application after admission and once all required financial aid documents are submitted to the university.

About the Law School

University of Iowa College of Law was established in 1865 and is a public institution. The 1900-acre campus is in a small town 115 miles east of Des Moines, 30 miles south of. Cedar Rapids, and 60 miles west of Moline, Illinois. The primary mission of the law school is to challenge students to set high standards for themselves and to strive for the best professional education they can obtain, resulting in graduates that make a positive and significant impact on society. Students have access to federal, state, county, city, and local agencies, courts, correctional facilities, law firms, and legal aid organizations in the Iowa City area. Facilities of special interest to law students include a $25 million law building that features state-of-the-art computer equipment, audiovisual technology, and 3 full-scale courtrooms. Housing for students Is available as graduate family housing for married or single parent students. Otherwise, students live in apartments, duplexes, and other rental options off campus. All law school facilities are accessible to the physically disabled.

Calendar

The law school operates on a traditional semester basis. Courses for full-time students are offered days only and must be completed within 84 months. There is no part-time program. New students are admitted in the fall. There is a 11-week summer session. Transferable summer courses are offered.

Programs

In addition to the J.D., the law school offers the LL.M. Students may take relevant courses in other programs and apply credit toward the J.D.; a maximum of 6 credits may be applied. The following joint degrees may be earned: J.D./M.A. (Juris Doctor/Master of Arts in urban and regional planning and), J.D./M.B.A. (Juris Doctor/Master of Business Administration), J.D./M.D. (Juris Doctor/Medical Doctor), J.D./M.H.A. (Juris Doctor/Master of Health Administration), J.D./M.P.H. (Juris Doctor/Master of Public Health), and J.D./Ph.D. (Juris Doctor/Doctorate of Higher Education).

Required
To earn the J.D., candidates must complete 84 total credits, of which 33 are for required courses. The following first-year courses are required of all students: Civil Procedure, Constitutional Law I, Contracts, Criminal Law, Introduction to Legal Reasoning, Legal Analysis Writing and Research I and II, Property, and Torts. Required upper-level courses consist of Constitutional Law II and Profession-

Phone: 319-335-9095
1-800-553-4692, ext. 9095
Fax: 319-335-9646
E-mail: *law-admissions@uiowa.edu*
Web: *www.law.uiowa.edu*

Contact

College of Law Admissions Staff, 319-335-9095 or 800-553-4692, ext. 9095 for general inquiries; Susan Palmer, Director of Financial Aid, 319-335-9142 for financial aid information.

IOWA

al Responsibility. Though not required, approximately 33% of law students participate in a clinic. The required orientation program for first-year students is 1 week; the 1-unit course component covers an overview of the American legal system, legal education, the legal profession, and perspectives on law. The program component covers academic and other support services, bar requirements, dealing with stress, professional conduct standards, community service, and social events.

Electives

The College of Law offers concentrations in corporate law, criminal law, intellectual property law, international law, litigation, securities law, and tax law. In addition, the highly practical clinical law programs give students the opportunity to gain experience in many different areas of substantive law, including, but not limited to, civil rights, employment law, and criminal defense. Clinics are open to students in their second and third years for up to 15 credit hours and usually fulfill the need for field work. Semester seminars are offered in a variety of subject areas. The seminars normally run for 2 semesters; 4 credits and upper-level writing units are awarded. If there is over-enrollment in the seminars, priority is given to third-year students and those seeking maximum credit. There are externship placements with a variety of outside agencies. They may be arranged in the summer or during the academic year. Credit for each externship varies and a maximum of 15 credits may be awarded under certain circumstances. Students may arrange an independent research project with faculty members in areas of mutual interest. Special guest lectures (by judges, professors, practitioners, politicians, and others) are open to students every semester. The college offers 4 study-abroad programs: the London Law Consortium (spring semester); the Summer Law Program in Comparative and International Law in Arcachon, France; a semester program at Catolica University in Lisbon, Portugal; and an Exchange Program with Bucerius Law School in Hamburg, Germany. In addition, students may receive credit for study-abroad programs sponsored by other ABA-approved law schools. The Academic Achievement Program (AAP) presents a variety of workshops during the year, with an emphasis on the needs of first-year students. Also, faculty members provide mentoring for students who need special assistance. The writing resource center works with stu-

dents individually to help strengthen writing skills vital to the study and practice of law. Minority students are involved in all law school opportunities, as well as in the minority student organizations. Special interest programs include the Women in Law Conference, Journal of Gender, Race and Justice symposium, and Transnational and Contemporary Problems Sympostion. The most widely taken electives are Clinics, Corporations, and Evidence.

Graduation Requirements

In order to graduate, candidates must have a GPA of 2.1, have completed the upper-division writing requirement, and fulfill a practical skills requirement.

Organizations

Students edit the *Iowa Law Review*, the *Journal of Corporation Law*, *Transnational Law and Contemporary Problems*, and the *Journal of Gender, Race, and Justice*. Newsletters are produced by the Organization of Women Law Students, the Iowa Society of International Law and Affairs, and the Iowa Student Bar Association. Moot court competitions include the Baskerville Competition, whose winners comprise the Chicago Moot Court team, the Van Oosterhout, to select the National Moot Court team, and the Jessup International Law Competition. Additionally, the Stephenson Competition offers an intramural competition for students interested in trial advocacy. Winners become the school's representatives to regional and national competitions. Law student organizations, local chapters of national associations, and campus organizations include AALSA (Asian American Law Students Association), BLSA (Black Law Students Association), Equal Justice Foundation, National Lawyers Guild, OWLSS (Organization for Women Law Students and Staff), American Constitutional Society, Phi Alpha Delta, the Federalist Society, and others.

Library

The law library contains 833,170 hardcopy volumes and 474,296 microform volume equivalents, and subscribes to 10,592 serial publications. Such on-line databases and networks as CIS Universe, DIALOG, Dow-Jones, Infotrac, Legal-Trac, LEXIS, LOIS, Mathew Bender, NEXIS, OCLC First Search, RLIN, WESTLAW, and Wilsonline Indexes are available to law students for research. Special library collections include a U.S. Government Printing

Placement

J.D.s awarded:	206

Services available through: a separate law school placement center
Services: a full-time professional provides individual advising, mock interview training, and videoconferencing for interviews
Special features: a judicial clerkship adviser

Full-time job interviews:	52 employers
Summer job interviews:	150 employers
Placement by graduation:	87% of class
Placement within 9 months:	99% of class
Average starting salary:	$30,000 to $165,000

Areas of placement:

Private practice 2-10 attorneys	10%
Private practice 11-25 attorneys	4%
Private practice 26-50 attorneys	5%
Private practice 51-100 attorneys	6%
Private practice 100+ attorneys and solo practice	26%
Government	17%
Business/industry	14%
Judicial clerkships	12%
Public interest	3%
Academic	3%

Office and Iowa depositories as well as a United Nations collection, civil rights, and a human rights collection. The ratio of library volumes to faculty is 17,358 to 1 and to students is 1412 to 1. The ratio of seats in the library to students is 1 to 1.

Faculty

The law school has 48 full-time and 14 part-time faculty members, of whom 23 are women. According to AAUP standards for Category I institutions, faculty salaries are average. About 8% of full-time faculty have a graduate law degree in addition to the J.D.; about 38% of part-time faculty have one. The ratio of full-time students to full-time faculty in an average class is 15 to 1; in a clinic, 7 to 1. The law school has a regular program of bringing visiting professors and other distinguished lecturers and visitors to campus. There is a chapter of the Order of the Coif; 48 faculty and 919 graduates are members.

Students

About 44% of the student body are women; 15%, minorities; 4%, African American; 6%, Asian American; 5%, Hispanic; and 1%, Native American. The majority of students come from the Midwest (78%). The average age of entering students is 25; age range is 20 to 53. About 8% of students have a graduate degree. About 2% drop out after the first year for academic or personal reasons; 94% remain to receive a law degree.

UNIVERSITY OF KANSAS

School of Law

205 Green Hall, 1535 W. 15th Street
Lawrence, KS 66045

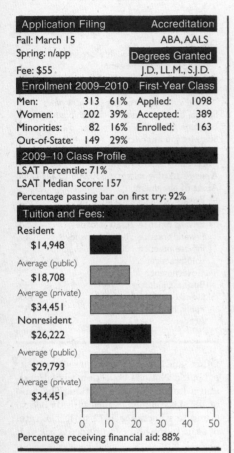

Application Filing	Accreditation
Fall: March 15	ABA, AALS
Spring: n/app	
Fee: $55	Degrees Granted
	J.D., LL.M., S.J.D.

Enrollment 2009–2010			First-Year Class	
Men:	313	61%	Applied:	1098
Women:	202	39%	Accepted:	389
Minorities:	82	16%	Enrolled:	163
Out-of-State:	149	29%		

2009–10 Class Profile
LSAT Percentile: 71%
LSAT Median Score: 157
Percentage passing bar on first try: 92%

Tuition and Fees:

Resident
$14,948

Average (public)
$18,708

Average (private)
$34,451

Nonresident
$26,222

Average (public)
$29,793

Average (private)
$34,451

0   10   20   30   40   50

Percentage receiving financial aid: 88%

ADMISSIONS

In the fall 2009 first-year class, 1098 applied, 389 were accepted, and 163 enrolled. Twenty-nine transfers enrolled. The median LSAT percentile of the most recent first-year class was 71; the median GPA was 3.5 on a scale of 4.0. The lowest LSAT percentile accepted was 15; the highest was 97.

Requirements
Applicants must have a bachelor's degree and take the LSAT. The most important admission factors include academic achievement, general background, and letter of recommendation. No specific undergraduate courses are required. Candidates are not interviewed.

Procedure
The application deadline for fall entry is March 15. Applicants should submit an application form, LSAT results, transcripts, a personal statement, a nonrefundable application fee of $55, and 2 letters of recommendation. International

students must submit the TOEFL. Notification of the admissions decision is on a rolling basis. The latest acceptable LSAT test date for fall entry is February; however, December is preferred. The law school uses the LSDAS.

Special
The law school recruits minority and disadvantaged students by means of recruiting in various geographic locations, at CLEO, and at PLSI. In addition, the law school hosts a diversity breakfast and uses the Law Services Candidate Referral System. Requirements are not different for out-of-state students. Transfer students must have one year of credit, and have attended an ABA-approved law school. No more than 30 hours from the student's previous law school can be transferred.

Costs

Tuition and fees for the 2009-2010 academic year are $14,948 for full-time in-state students and $26,222 for out-of-state students. On-campus room and board costs about $10,002 annually; books and supplies run $900.

Financial Aid

About 88% of current law students receive some form of aid. The average annual amount of aid from all sources combined, including scholarships, loans, and work contracts, is $24,344; maximum, $49,813. Awards are based on need and merit. Required financial statement is the FAFSA. The aid application deadline for fall entry is March 1. Special funds for minority or disadvantaged students consist of scholarships and financial aid. First-year students are notified about their financial aid application at any point in time from acceptance through the time of enrollment.

About the Law School

University of Kansas School of Law was established in 1878 and is a public institution. The 1000-acre campus is in a suburban area 40 miles west of Kansas City. The primary mission of the law school is to prepare students to be outstanding members of the legal profession, well educated in the law, with a commitment to professional achievement and public service. Students have access to federal,

state, county, city, and local agencies, courts, correctional facilities, law firms, and legal aid organizations in the Lawrence area. Facilities of special interest to law students include the Paul E. Wilson Defender Project, which allows students to counsel and perform legal service for indigent inmates of the U.S. Penitentiary at Leavenworth, the Kansas State Penitentiary, and Kansas Correctional Institution. Housing for students is available in a university residence hall or apartment complex and also in apartments or houses off campus. Family student housing is also available. All law school facilities are accessible to the physically disabled.

Calendar

The law school operates on a traditional semester basis. Courses for full-time students are offered days only and must be completed within 5 years. There is no part-time program. New students are admitted in the fall and summer. There are 2- five week summer sessions. Transferable summer courses are offered.

Programs

In addition to the J.D., the law school offers the LL.M. and S.J.D. Students may take relevant courses in other programs and apply credit toward the J.D.; a maximum of 6 hours of credit may be applied. The following joint degrees may be earned: J.D./M.A. (Juris Doctor/Master of Arts in East Asian languages and cultures, economics, global and indigenous nations, journalism, philosophy, and political science), J.D./M.B.A. (Juris Doctor/Master of Business Administration), J.D./M.P.A. (Juris Doctor/Master of Public Administration), J.D./M.S. (Juris Doctor/Master of Science in health services administration), J.D./M.S.W. (Juris Doctor/Master of Social Work), and J.D./M.U.P. (Juris Doctor/Master of Urban Planning).

Required
To earn the J.D., candidates must complete 90 total credits, of which 37 to 38 are for required courses. They must maintain a minimum GPA of 2.0 in the required courses. The following first-year courses are required of all students: Civil Procedure, Contracts, Criminal Law, Introduction to Constitutional Law, Lawyering Skills I and II, Property, and Torts I. Required upper-level courses consist of a

Phone: 785-864-4378
866-220-3654
Fax: 785-864-5054
E-mail: *admitlaw@ku.edu*
Web: *www.law.ku.edu*

Contact

Jacqlene Nance, Director of Admissions, 785-864-9212 for general inquiries; Brenda Maigaard, Director of Financial Aid, 785-864-5491 for financial aid information.

KANSAS

writing requirement, Commercial Law I, Evidence, Professional Responsibility, and a Professional Skills requirement. The required orientation program for first-year students is a 5-day program that includes sessions on lawyering skills, ethics in the legal profession, a mock class, small group sessions, tours of the building, and practical issues.

Electives

The School of Law offers concentrations in corporate law, criminal law, environmental law, family law, international law, juvenile law, labor law, litigation, media law, securities law, tax law, torts and insurance, agricultural law, civil rights law, constitutional law, energy law, industrial relations law, tribal law, and patent law. In addition, clinics are offered to second- and third-year students for 1 to 4 hours of credit. Clinics include Criminal Prosecution, the Paul E. Wilson Defender Project, and the Douglas County Legal Aid Clinic. Periodically, research workshops are offered for all students. Second- and third-year students may take advantage of available internship opportunities; usually no academic credit is awarded. Independent research seminars are available. Field work includes a judicial clerkship, an elder law externship, and a legislative clinic. Guest lecture programs are offered for no credit. Students may study at University College in London through the London Law Consortium, of which the University of Kansas is a member. Students may also study at the Summer Institute in Cambridge, England; Istanbul, Turkey; and Limerick, Ireland. They may also participate in other ABA-approved study-abroad programs. Tutorial programs are voluntary. The most widely taken electives are Business Associations I and II, Income Tax, and Family Law.

Graduation Requirements

In order to graduate, candidates must have a GPA of 2.0, have completed the upper-division writing requirement, and fulfill a Professional Skills requirement.

Organizations

Students edit the *Kansas Law Review, Kansas Journal of Law and Public Policy,* and the student newspaper, *The Brief Brief.* Other publications include the *KU Law Magazine.* Students compete in the National Moot Court, Jessup International Moot Court, and Criminal Procedure Moot Court Competitions. Other competitions include the First Amendment Moot Court and the Stetson International Environmental Moot Court Competitions. Law student organizations, local chapters of national associations, and campus organizations include the International Law Society, Women in Law, Public Interest Law Society, Traffic Court, Student Bar Association, the Federalist Society, Black Law Students Association, Phi Alpha Delta, and Native American Law Students Association.

Library

The law library contains 360,139 hardcopy volumes and 101,732 microform volume equivalents, and subscribes to 3702 serial publications. Such on-line databases and networks as CALI, LEXIS, NEXIS, WESTLAW, Wilsonline Indexes, RIA Checkpoint (Tax), BEP Journals, Environmental Law Reporter, Foreign Law Guide, CCH Intelliconnect, Elder Law Library Database, BNA ALL, Making of Modern Law, and HeinOnline are available to law students for research. Special library collections include selective government depositories for both state and federal documents, American judicial biographies, the International & Comparative Law Display, the Casad Collection, the Heller Collection, and the Hoeflich Rare Book Room. Recently, the library implemented a suggestion notebook; improved Blackboard and SSRN repository usage; and loaded more documents, papers, and articles into ScholarWorks. The ratio of library volumes to faculty is 9234 to 1 and to students is 699 to 1. The ratio of seats in the library to students is 1 to 1.

Faculty

The law school has 39 full-time and 14 part-time faculty members, of whom 23 are women. According to AAUP standards for Category I institutions, faculty salaries are average. About 8% of full-time faculty have a graduate law degree in addition to the J.D. The ratio of full-time students to full-time faculty in an average class is 12 to 1; in a clinic, 8 to 1. The law school has a regular program of bringing visiting professors and other distinguished lecturers and visitors to campus. There is a chapter of the Order of the Coif; 16 faculty and 800 graduates are members.

Placement

J.D.s awarded:	160
Services available through: a separate law school placement center	
Special features: a mentoring program that matches current law students with practicing alumni, Legal Career Options Day	
Full-time job interviews:	15 employers
Summer job interviews:	67 employers
Placement by graduation:	69% of class
Placement within 9 months:	94% of class
Average starting salary:	$24,000 to $160,000
Areas of placement:	
Private practice 2-10 attorneys	22%
Private practice 11-25 attorneys	9%
Private practice 26-50 attorneys	4%
Private practice 51-100 attorneys	4%
Private practice 101+ attorneys, solo practice	16%
Government	18%
Business/industry	15%
Judicial clerkships	7%
Public interest	4%
Academic	1%

Students

About 39% of the student body are women; 16%, minorities; 3%, African American; 5%, Asian American; 4%, Hispanic; and 4%, Native American. The majority of students come from Kansas (71%). The average age of entering students is 23; age range is 21 to 53. About 10% of students have a graduate degree. About 2% drop out after the first year for academic or personal reasons; 98% remain to receive a law degree.

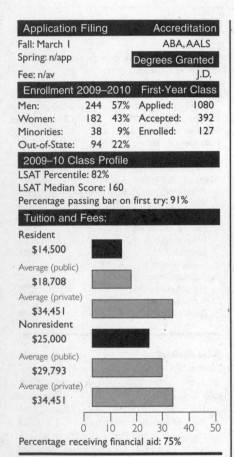

Application Filing		Accreditation
Fall: March 1		ABA, AALS
Spring: n/app		**Degrees Granted**
Fee: n/av		J.D.

Enrollment 2009–2010			First-Year Class	
Men:	244	57%	Applied:	1080
Women:	182	43%	Accepted:	392
Minorities:	38	9%	Enrolled:	127
Out-of-State:	94	22%		

2009–10 Class Profile
LSAT Percentile: 82%
LSAT Median Score: 160
Percentage passing bar on first try: 91%

Tuition and Fees:

Resident
$14,500

Average (public)
$18,708

Average (private)
$34,451

Nonresident
$25,000

Average (public)
$29,793

Average (private)
$34,451

0   10   20   30   40   50

Percentage receiving financial aid: 75%

ADMISSIONS

In the fall 2009 first-year class, 1080 applied, 392 were accepted, and 127 enrolled. Figures in the above capsule and in this profile are approximate. Seven transfers enrolled. The median LSAT percentile of the most recent first-year class was 82; the median GPA was 3.63 on a scale of 4.0. The lowest LSAT percentile accepted was 30; the highest was 97.

Requirements
Applicants must have a bachelor's degree and take the LSAT. The most important admission factors include writing ability, LSAT results, and GPA. No specific undergraduate courses are required. Candidates are not interviewed.

Procedure
Applicants should submit an application form, LSAT results, transcripts, a personal statement, TOEFL if a foreign student, a nonrefundable application fee, and 2 letters of recommendations are recommend but not required. Notification

of the admissions decision is weekly on a rolling basis. The latest acceptable LSAT test date for fall entry is February. Check with the school for current applicaion deadlines. The law school uses the LSDAS.

Special
The law school recruits minority and disadvantaged students by means of the Fall Diverse Student Visitation Conference, scholarships and stipends, visits to campuses, participation in KLEO, and general academic support offerings. Requirements are not different for out-of-state students. Transfer students must have one year of credit, have a minimum GPA of 2.7, and must provide reasons for wanting to transfer. As transfers are not encouraged, applications are reviewed on a case-by-case basis.

Costs

Tuition and fees for the 2009-2010 academic year are $14,500 for full-time in-state students and $25,000 for out-of-state students. On-campus room and board costs about $11,000 annually; books and supplies run $1000.

Financial Aid

In a recent year, about 75% of current law students received some form of aid. The average annual amount of aid from all sources combined, including scholarships, loans, and work contracts, was $20,500; maximum, $39,306. Awards are based on need and merit. Special funds are available that have specific criteria that must be met by the applicants. Required financial statement is the FAFSA. Check with the school for current application deadlines. Special funds for minority or disadvantaged students include tuition and monthly stipends available through the combined efforts of the college's and university's administration, plus Kentucky's KLEO program. First-year students are notified about their financial aid application 1 month after acceptance for scholarships, and in May for loans.

About the Law School

University of Kentucky College of Law was established in 1908 and is a public institution. The 673-acre campus is in an urban area 80 miles east of Louisville and 75 miles south of Cincinnati, Ohio. The

primary mission of the law school is to provide a legal education to individuals so that they might render a high quality of professional service to Kentucky and the nation. Students have access to federal, state, county, city, and local agencies, courts, correctional facilities, law firms, and legal aid organizations in the Lexington area. Additional opportunities are available in state agencies and the state judicial system. Facilities of special interest to law students include a civil law clinic; students have their own clients and caseloads under the supervision of a former trial attorney. Housing for students is plentiful both on and off campus. Most law students choose off-campus housing, some of which is located across the street from the law school. All law school facilities are accessible to the physically disabled.

Calendar

The law school operates on a traditional semester basis. Courses for full-time students are offered days only and are usually completed within 3 to 4 years. For part-time students, courses are offered and There is no part-time program. New students are admitted in the fall. There is an 8-week summer session. Transferable summer courses are offered.

Programs

Students may take relevant courses in other programs and apply credit toward the J.D.; a maximum of 6 credits may be applied. The following joint degrees may be earned: J.D./M.A. (Juris Doctor/Master of Arts in Diplomacy and International Commerce), J.D./M.B.A. (Juris Doctor/Master of Business Administration), and J.D./M.P.A. (Juris Doctor/Master of Public Administration).

Required
To earn the J.D., candidates must complete 90 total credits, of which 34 are for required courses. They must maintain a minimum GPA of 2.0 in the required courses. The following first-year courses are required of all students: Civil Procedure I and II, Constitutional Law I, Contracts and Sales I and II, Criminal Law, Legal Research and Writing, Property, and Torts. Required upper-level courses consist of a seminar with a writing requirement and Professional Responsibility. The required orientation program for first-

Phone: 606-257-7938
Fax: (859) 323-1061
E-mail: lawadmissions@email.uky.edu
Web: http://www.uky.edu/law

Contact

Jeanie Powell, Admissions Associate, 859-257-1678 for general inquiries; Student Financial Aid Office, 859-257-3172 for financial aid information.

KENTUCKY

year students is 2 days and includes an introduction to the community, to the case method, to the faculty, and to the current students.

Electives

The College of Law offers concentrations in corporate law, criminal law, environmental law, family law, intellectual property law, international law, juvenile law, labor law, litigation, securities law, sports law, tax law, torts and insurance. In addition, clinics include Prison Counsel for upper-level students for 3 credit hours and Civil-Law Clinic for upper-level students for 3 credit hours. Numerous seminars are offered, including Gender Discrimination, Housing Law, and Intellectual Property. Third-year students may participate in internships with prosecutors and with state and federal judges for 3 credit hours. An Innocence Project with the state public defender's office for 3 credit hours is also offered. Independent research may be done on topics of special interest for 1 to 3 credit hours. Third-year students receive 1 to 3 credit hours for clerking with judges in state district, circuit, and appellate division courts, or in either of 2 federal district courts. Third-year students also receive 1 to 3 credit hours working with local prosecutors and in the prison internship program. Study abroad is available via transient work at a number of ABA-approved law schools. Academic support is offered for all first-year students in the first semester and in later semesters for those in academic difficulty. An academic success program and tutorials are offered to minority students. The most widely taken electives are Evidence, Business Associations, and Tax.

Graduation Requirements

In order to graduate, candidates must have a GPA of 2.0 and have completed the upper-division writing requirement.

Organizations

Students edit the *Kentucky Law Journal, Journal of Natural Resources and Environmental Law*, and the newspaper *Week in Brief*. Students compete in the National Moot Court Competition, Jessup Competition, and First Amendment Moot Court Competition. Other competitions include the Trial Advocacy Competition, the Wilhelm Vis International Commercial Law Moot Court, and competitions in sports law, space law, and telecommunications law. Student organizations include the Student Bar Association, Black Law Students Association, and Women's Law Caucus. Other organizations include Intellectual Property Law Society, Health Law Society, and International Law Society. Henry Clay Inns of Court and several legal fraternities have local chapters.

Library

The law library contains 477,877 hardcopy volumes and 221,124 microform volume equivalents, and subscribes to 3810 serial publications. Such on-line databases and networks as CALI, CIS Universe, DIALOG, Dow-Jones, Legal-Trac, LEXIS, LOIS, Mathew Bender, NEXIS, OCLC First Search, and WESTLAW, are available to law students for research. Special library collections include human rights and mineral law and policy, as well as a selective government document depository. Recently, the library remodeled library study areas (now wireless). The ratio of library volumes to faculty is 18,380 to 1 and to students is 1122 to 1. The ratio of seats in the library to students is 1 to 1.

Faculty

The law school has 26 full-time and 28 part-time faculty members, of whom 16 are women. According to AAUP standards for Category I institutions, faculty salaries are below average. About 25% of full-time faculty have a graduate law degree in addition to the J.D.; about 10% of part-time faculty have one. The ratio of full-time students to full-time faculty in an average class is 15 to 1; in a clinic, 8 to 1. The law school has a regular program of bringing visiting professors and other distinguished lecturers and visitors to campus. There is a chapter of the Order of the Coif; 23 faculty and 450 graduates are members.

Students

About 43% of the student body are women; 9%, minorities; 6%, African American; 2%, Asian American; and 2%, Hispanic. The majority of students come from Kentucky (78%). The average age of entering students is 23; age range is 21 to 50. About 5% drop out after the first year for academic or personal reasons; 93% remain to receive a law degree.

Placement

J.D.s awarded:	124

Services available through: a separate law school placement center and the university placement center

Services: a computer database on Kentucky law firms and numerous recruitment conferences and job fairs

Special features: individual attention from an associate dean with 8 years of practice experience in a law firm setting

Full-time job interviews:	100 employers
Summer job interviews:	175 employers
Placement by graduation:	75% of class
Placement within 9 months:	99% of class
Average starting salary:	$24,000 to $120,000

Areas of placement:

Private practice 2-10 attorneys	27%
Private practice 11-25 attorneys	9%
Private practice 26-50 attorneys	3%
Private practice 51-100 attorneys	12%
Judicial clerkships	18%
Business/industry	11%
Government	10%
Public interest	9%
Academic	1%

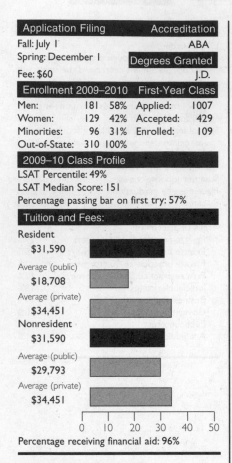

ADMISSIONS

In a recent year, 1007 applied, 429 were accepted, and 109 enrolled. Seven transfers enrolled. The median LSAT percentile of the most recent first-year class was 49; the median GPA was 3.3 on a scale of 4.33. The lowest LSAT percentile accepted was 33; the highest was 90. Figures in the above capsule and in this profile are approximate.

Requirements

Applicants must have a bachelor's degree and take the LSAT. Minimum acceptable LSAT percentile is 33 and minimum acceptable GPA is 2.0 on a scale of 4.33. The most important admission factors include LSAT results, GPA, and general background. No specific undergraduate courses are required. Candidates are not interviewed.

Procedure

Applicants should submit an application form, LSAT results, transcripts, and a nonrefundable application fee of $60. Notification of the admissions decision is 4 to 6 weeks after application is. The latest acceptable LSAT test date for fall entry is February. The law school uses the LSDAS. Check with the school for current application deadlines.

Special

The law school recruits minority and disadvantaged students Minority Outreach Programs and CLEO. Requirements are not different for out-of-state students. Transfer students must have one year of credit and competitive LSAT score, and undergraduate GPA, and letter of standing. Preadmissions courses consist of Legal Analysis and Writing.

Costs

Tuition and fees for the 2009-2010 academic year are approximately $31,590 for full-time in-state students. Tuition for part-time students is approximately $23,690 in-state. On-campus room and board costs about $16,833 annually; books and supplies run about $1386.

Financial Aid

In a recent year, about 96% of current law students received some form of aid. The average annual amount of aid from all sources combined, including scholarships, loans, and work contracts, is approximately $35,556; maximum, $53,797. Awards are based on need and merit. Required financial statement is the FAFSA. First-year students are notified about their financial aid application at time of acceptance. Check with the school for current application deadlines.

About the Law School

University of La Verne College of Law was established in 1970 and is a private institution. The 7-acre campus is in a suburban area Inland Southern California. The primary mission of the law school is to teach students to be effective legal professionals who use their skills an talents for the benefit of their communities, to imbue these students with pride in the legal profession, and to promote diversity within the law school community, accomplished by providing full- and part-time law programs with high academics standards. Students have access to federal, state, county, city, and local agencies, courts, correctional facilities, law firms, and legal aid organizations in the Ontario area. Facilities of special interest to law students n/av. Housing for students is not available for students on campus, but there is a student housing network which enables students to connect with others who are also seeking housing. Additional, listings of available housing options in the area are available.

Calendar

The law school operates on a traditional semester and traditional semester basis. Courses for full-time students are offered day only and must be completed within 3 years. For part-time students, courses are offered both day and evening and must be completed within 4 years. New full-time students are admitted in the fall; part-time, fall and spring. There is an 8-week summer session. Transferable summer courses are offered.

Programs

Students may take relevant courses in other programs and apply credit toward the J.D.; a maximum of varies credits may be applied. The following joint degrees may be earned: J.D./M.B.A. (Juris Doctor/Master of Business Administration) and J.D./M.P.A. (Juris Doctor/Master of Public Administration).

Required

To earn the J.D., candidates must complete 88 total credits, of which 60 are for required courses. They must maintain a minimum GPA of 2.00 in the required courses. The following first-year courses are required of all students: Civil Procedure, Contracts, Criminal Law, Legal Analysis and Writing, Legal Research I, Property, and Torts. Required upper-level courses consist of Appellate Advocacy, Business Organizations, Constitutional Law, Criminal Procedure, Evidence, Lawyering Skills Practicum, Professional Responsibility, and Wills and Trusts. The required orientation program for first-year students 2 day program, 7 hours total.

Electives

The College of Law offers concentrations in corporate law, criminal law, entertain-

Contact

Office of Admissions, 909-460-2001 for general inquiries; Financial Aid Coordinator, 909-460-2006 for financial aid information.

ment law, environmental law, family law, intellectual property law, international law, juvenile law, labor law, litigation, media law, securities law, sports law, tax law, and torts and insurance. In addition, clinics include the Disability Rights Legal Center (worth 3 to 6 units) and the Justice and Immigration Center (worth 6 units). There are also clinical externships. Seminars are open to upper division law students. Current seminar offerings are Law, Science and Medicine; Philosophy and Law; Environmental Law and Policy; and Global Issues in Constitutional Law. Internships are available. Credit is given for study abroad programs. Tutorial programs include the Peer Assistance Support System (PASS), Graduate Mentor Program, and workshops. There is also an Academic Support Program. The most widely taken electives are Entertainment Law, Real Estate Law, and Sales.

Graduation Requirements
In order to graduate, candidates must have a GPA of 2.0.

Organizations

The primary law review is the *Journal of Juvenile Law*. Moot court competitions include Roger J. Traynor California Moot Court Competition, National Criminal Procedure Moot Competition, and Frederick Douglass National Moot Court Competition. Law student organizations include Student Bar Association, Delta Theta Phi Law Fraternity, and Hispanic National Bar Association. Campus clubs and other organizations include Law Review, Asian Pacific American Law Student Association, Black Law Students Association, Entertainment Law Society, J. Reuben Clark Society, and Moot Court.

Library

The law library contains 97,233 hard-copy volumes and 208,841 microform volume equivalents, and subscribes to 2320 serial publications. Such on-line databases and networks as CALI, CIS Universe, Legal-Trac, LEXIS, LOIS, NEXIS, WEST-LAW, Wilsonline Indexes, and VersusLaw, LLMC Digital, HeinOnline, Legal Scholarship Network, Berkeley Electronic Press, and Philosopher's Index, CCH Legal Professional Library, RIA Checkpoint, BNA Core Plus Library, UN Treaty Database, and WorldTradeLaw.net are available to law students for research. Special library collections include a selective federal and California depository library. In a recent year, the library double the bandwidth of the wireless network. The ratio of library volumes to faculty is 5118 to 1 and to students is 674 to 1. The ratio of seats in the library to students is 1 to 1.

Faculty

The law school has 19 full-time and 12 part-time faculty members, of whom 13 are women. According to AAUP standards for Category I institutions, faculty salaries are well below average. About 47% of full-time faculty have a graduate law degree in addition to the J.D. The ratio of full-time students to full-time faculty in an average class is 11 to 1. The law school has a regular program of bringing visiting professors and other distinguished lecturers and visitors to campus.

Students

About 42% of the student body are women; 31%, minorities; 3%, African American; 14%, Asian American; and 13%, Hispanic. The average age of entering students is 26; age range is 21 to 55. About 22% drop out after the first year for academic or personal reasons; 69% remain to receive a law degree.

Placement

J.D.s awarded:	66
Services available through: a separate law school placement center	
Full-time job interviews:	n/av
Summer job interviews:	n/av
Placement by graduation:	97% of class
Placement within 9 months:	n/av
Average starting salary:	n/av
Areas of placement:	
Private practice 2-10 attorneys	48%
Private practice 11-25 attorneys	5%
Private practice 26-50 attorneys	14%
Private practice 51-100 attorneys	14%
Business/industry	14%
Government	11%

UNIVERSITY OF LOUISVILLE

Louis D. Brandeis School of Law

University of Louisville Belknap
Campus-Wilson W. Wyatt Hall
Louisville, KY 40292

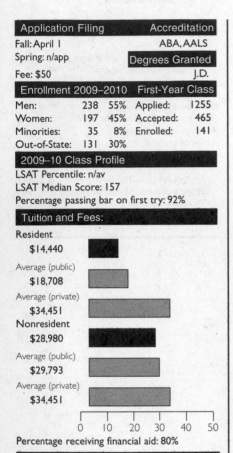

Application Filing	Accreditation
Fall: April 1	ABA, AALS
Spring: n/app	**Degrees Granted**
Fee: $50	J.D.

Enrollment 2009–2010		First-Year Class	
Men:	238 55%	Applied:	1255
Women:	197 45%	Accepted:	465
Minorities:	35 8%	Enrolled:	141
Out-of-State:	131 30%		

2009–10 Class Profile
LSAT Percentile: n/av
LSAT Median Score: 157
Percentage passing bar on first try: 92%

Tuition and Fees:

Resident
$14,440

Average (public)
$18,708

Average (private)
$34,451

Nonresident
$28,980

Average (public)
$29,793

Average (private)
$34,451

0 10 20 30 40 50

Percentage receiving financial aid: 80%

ADMISSIONS

In the fall 2009 first-year class, 1255 applied, 465 were accepted, and 141 enrolled. Seven transfers enrolled. The median GPA of the most recent first-year class was 3.5. The lowest LSAT percentile accepted was 16; the highest was 99.

Requirements
Applicants must have a bachelor's degree and take the LSAT. Minimum acceptable GPA is 2.0 on a scale of 4.0. The most important admission factors include general background, GPA, and LSAT results. No specific undergraduate courses are required. Candidates are not interviewed.

Procedure
The application deadline for fall entry is April 1. Applicants should submit an application form, LSAT results, transcripts, a personal statement, a nonrefundable application fee of $50, and 2 letters of recommendation. Notification of the admissions decision is on a rolling

basis. The latest acceptable LSAT test date for fall entry is February. The law school uses the LSDAS.

Special
The law school recruits minority and disadvantaged students by sponsoring a minority prelaw day and attending minority fairs and programs at other schools. Requirements are not different for out-of-state students. Transfer students must have one year of credit, have attended an ABA-approved law school, be in good standing, have met entrance requirements for the school had they applied for initial admission, and be in the upper quarter of their law school class. Preadmissions courses of vary from year to year.

Costs

Tuition and fees for the 2009-2010 academic year are $14,440 for full-time in-state students and $28,980 for out-of-state students. Tuition for part-time students is $602 per hour for residents and $1208 for non-residents and will not exceed the full-time rate at 10 hours or more of $7220 for residents. Books and supplies run $1000.

Financial Aid

About 80% of current law students receive some form of aid. Awards are based on need and merit. Required financial statement is the FAFSA. The aid application deadline for fall entry is June 1. Special funds for minority or disadvantaged students are available. First-year students are notified about their financial aid application prior to enrollment, usually by May 15.

About the Law School

University of Louisville Louis D. Brandeis School of Law was established in 1846 and is a public institution. The campus is in an urban area 4 miles south of downtown Louisville. The primary mission of the law school is to provide students with a quality legal education and prepare them for professional life through a curriculum that emphasizes fundamental lawyering skills and the development of professional values, while also affording students the opportunity to take advanced courses in a wide variety of specialty areas. Students have access to federal, state, county, city, and local agencies, courts, correctional

facilities, law firms, and legal aid organizations in the Louisville area. Facilities of special interest to law students include the school's physical facility that provides students with a large, comfortable environment in which to attend class and study. Many student gathering places and study group rooms are available. Housing for students is available in a university dormitory and in affordable rental housing close to campus. All law school facilities are accessible to the physically disabled.

Calendar

The law school operates on a traditional semester basis. Courses for full-time students are offered days only but full-time students may enroll in evening clases and must be completed within 5 years. For part-time students, courses are offered days and evenings and must be completed within 6 years. New full- and part-time students are admitted in the fall. There is an 8-week summer session. Transferable summer courses are offered.

Programs

Students may take relevant courses in other programs and apply credit toward the J.D.; a maximum of 6 credits may be applied. The following joint degrees may be earned: J.D./M.A.H. (Juris Doctor/Master of Arts in Humanities), J.D./M.A.P.S. (Juris Doctor/Master of Arts in Political Science), J.D./M.B.A. (Juris Doctor/Master of Business Administration), J.D./M. Div. (Juris Doctor/Master of Divinity), J.D./M.S. (Juris Doctor/Master of Science in Boethies), and J.D./M.S.S.W. (Juris Doctor/Master of Science in Social Work).

Required
To earn the J.D., candidates must complete 90 total credits, of which 44 are for required courses. They must maintain a minimum GPA of 2.0 in the required courses. The following first-year courses are required of all students: Basic Legal Skills, Civil Procedure, Contracts, Criminal Law, Legal Research, Property, and Torts. Required upper-level courses consist of 24 hours of core courses, a perspective course, a writing requirement, Constitutional Law I and II, and Professional Responsibility. The required orientation program for first-year students is 2½ days devoted to skills development and orienta-

Phone: 502-852-6364
800-334-8634
Fax: 502-852-8971
E-mail: *brandon.hamilton@louisville.edu*
Web: *www.law.louisville*

Contact
Admission Office, 502-852-6364 for general inquiries; Brando Hamilton, Assistant Dean for Admissions, 502-852-6364 for financial aid information.

KENTUCKY

tion to legal education and the profession. There is also time for social events.

Electives
The Louis D. Brandeis School of Law offers concentrations in corporate law, criminal law, entertainment law, environmental law, family law, intellectual property law, international law, juvenile law, labor law, litigation, securities law, sports law, tax law, torts and insurance, and disability law. In addition, there is a Law Clinic that focuses on the representation of low income clients in public housing and domestic violence cases. Law school students also participate in clinics hosted by the Louisville and Kentucky Bar Association. Clinical Externship, for upper-level students, provide the opportunity to perform law related work and gain practical experience with judges, clients through legal aid, Center for Women and Families, Public Defender's office, and the Internal Revenue Service, just to name a few. A wide variety of seminars is offered to second-, third, and fourth-year students in specialized fields of law; 2 to 3 credit hours are awarded. Several internships, worth 2 to 4 hours, are available, including a judicial, civil, criminal, and technology internship. All students are required to complete Legal Research, a 3-hour basic legal skills course, and a seminar that requires a substantial research paper. Special lecture series include the Brandeis and Harlan Lecture Series. Students may earn credit for participation in foreign study in an ABA-accredited program. Students with adequate language abilities may be foreign exchange students with several law schools throughout the world. The Academic Success Program provides structured study groups for all first year students. A library of academic resources is also available. Academic counseling is also required by those students who are on academic probation.The school has several minority recruting activities each year and a number of scholarships for minority students. A diversity committee presents programs to the student body on topics such as gay/lesbian issues and women in politics. The most widely taken electives are Secured Transactions and Negotiable Instruments, and Business Organizations.

Graduation Requirements
In order to graduate, candidates must have a GPA of 2.0, have completed the upper-division writing requirement, and have completed 30 hours of law-related public service at a placement approved by the school.

Organizations
Students edit *The University of Louisville Law Review, Journal of Law and Education*, and *Journal of Animal and Enviornmental Law*. Annually, students participate in the National Moot Court, the American Association of Trial Lawyers Mock Trial, and the ABA Negotiation Competition. Other competitions include a Trial Advocacy Moot Court exercise in a student's first year and the Pirtle-Washer Moot Court in a student's second year. Law student organizations, local chapters of national associations, and campus organizations include the Student Bar Association, Environmental Law Society, International Law Society, Delta Theta Phi, Phi Alpha Delta, the Federalist Society, Lambda Law Caucus, Black Law Students Association, and Women's Law Caucus.

Library
The law library contains 417,747 hardcopy volumes and 190,390 microform volume equivalents, and subscribes to 5200 serial publications. Such on-line databases and networks as CALI, CIS Universe, DIALOG, LEXIS, NEXIS, OCLC First Search, WESTLAW, Wilsonline Indexes, and an extensive collection of databases are available to law students for research. Special library collections include the Justice Brandeis papers, Justice Harlan papers, and a Supreme Court brief depository. Recently, the library upgraded the wireless, computer network and added furniture and a new lower level floor. The ratio of library volumes to faculty is 12,287 to 1 and to students is 960 to 1. The ratio of seats in the library to students is 1 to 1.

Faculty
The law school has 34 full-time and 9 part-time faculty members, of whom 18 are women. According to AAUP standards for Category I institutions, faculty salaries are well below average. About 30% of full-time faculty have a graduate law degree in addition to the J.D. The ratio of full-time students to full-time faculty in an average class is 14 to 1; in a clinic, 9 to 1. The law school has a regular program of bringing

Placement
J.D.s awarded:	124

Services available through: a separate law school placement center
Special features: participation in recruiting consortia in the southeast and Kentucky.

Full-time job interviews:	20 employers
Summer job interviews:	35 employers
Placement by graduation:	68% of class
Placement within 9 months:	97% of class
Average starting salary:	$37,000 to $103,000

Areas of placement:
Solo practice	3%
Private practice 2-10 attorneys	28%
Private practice 11-25 attorneys	15%
Private practice 26-50 attorneys	8%
Private practice 51-100 attorneys	8%
Government/Public Interest	17%
Business/industry	15%
Judicial clerkships	5%
Academic	2%

visiting professors and other distinguished lecturers and visitors to campus.

Students
About 45% of the student body are women; 8%, minorities; 3%, African American; 3%, Asian American; and 2%, Hispanic. The majority of students come from Kentucky (70%). The average age of entering students is 24; age range is 21 to 54. About 5% drop out after the first year for academic or personal reasons; 95% remain to receive a law degree.

UNIVERSITY OF MAINE

School of Law

246 Deering Avenue
Portland, ME 04102

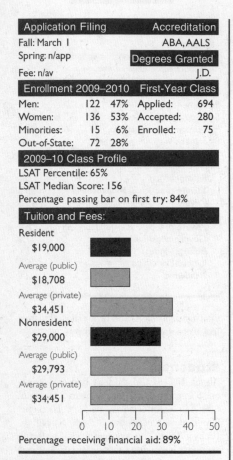

Application Filing	Accreditation
Fall: March 1	ABA, AALS
Spring: n/app	**Degrees Granted**
Fee: n/av	J.D.

Enrollment 2009–2010   First-Year Class

Men:	122	47%	Applied:	694
Women:	136	53%	Accepted:	280
Minorities:	15	6%	Enrolled:	75
Out-of-State:	72	28%		

2009–10 Class Profile

LSAT Percentile: 65%
LSAT Median Score: 156
Percentage passing bar on first try: 84%

Tuition and Fees:

Resident
$19,000

Average (public)
$18,708

Average (private)
$34,451

Nonresident
$29,000

Average (public)
$29,793

Average (private)
$34,451

0   10   20   30   40   50

Percentage receiving financial aid: 89%

ADMISSIONS

In the fall 2009 first-year class, 694 applied, 280 were accepted, and 75 enrolled. Figures in the above capsule and in this profile are approximate. Six transfers enrolled. The median LSAT percentile of the most recent first-year class was 65; the median GPA was 3.31 on a scale of 4.0. The lowest LSAT percentile accepted was 15; the highest was 92.

Requirements

Applicants must have a bachelor's degree and take the LSAT. The most important admission factors include academic achievement. No specific undergraduate courses are required. Candidates are not interviewed.

Procedure

Applicants should submit an application form, LSAT results, transcripts, TOEFL (for foreign educated applicants only), a nonrefundable application fee, and 1 letters of recommendation. Notification of

the admissions decision is beginning in December each year through April. The latest acceptable LSAT test date for fall entry is February. Check with the school for current application deadlines. The law school uses the LSDAS.

Special

The law school recruits minority and disadvantaged students through law school admissions forums, scholarship assistance, contacts with law school minority organizations, and mailings to minority candidates through Law Service's C.R.S. Requirements are not different for out-of-state students. Transfer students must have one year of credit, have attended an ABA-approved law school, and have superior academic credentials.

Costs

Tuition and fees for the 2009-2010 academic year are $19,000 for full-time in-state students and $29,000 for out-of-state students. On-campus room and board costs about $8000 annually; books and supplies run $3500.

Financial Aid

In a recent year, about 89% of current law students received some form of aid. The average annual amount of aid from all sources combined, including scholarships, loans, and work contracts, was $21,115; maximum, $31,235. Awards are based on need. Required financial statement is the FAFSA. Check with the school for current deadlines. Special funds for minority or disadvantaged students include 3 full-tuition scholarships available for each class. First-year students are notified about their financial aid application before or at the time a nonrefundable tuition deposit is due.

About the Law School

University of Maine School of Law was established in 1962 and is a public institution. The campus is in an urban area in Portland. The primary mission of the law school is to educate students to serve the public and private sectors with distinction; to contribute to the advancement of the law through scholarly and professional research and writing; and to engage in public services aimed at improving the legal system. Students have access to fed-

eral, state, county, city, and local agencies, courts, correctional facilities, law firms, and legal aid organizations in the Portland area. Portland is the major urban and legal center in the state. Facilities of special interest to law students are the Cumberland County Superior Court, the Maine Supreme Judicial Court, and the Federal District Court. Housing for students is available in university dorms, but most students prefer to find housing in and around Portland. All law school facilities are accessible to the physically disabled.

Calendar

The law school operates on a traditional semester basis. Courses for full-time students are offered days only and must be completed within 3 years. For part-time students, courses are offered days only and must be completed within 5 years. New full- and part-time students are admitted in the fall. There is a 7-week summer session. Transferable summer courses are offered.

Programs

Students may take relevant courses in other programs and apply credit toward the J.D.; the maximum number of credits be approved. The following joint degrees may be earned: J.D./M.A. (Juris Doctor/Master of Arts in public policy and management), J.D./M.B.A. (Juris Doctor/Master of Science in Business Administration), J.D./M.C.P (Juris Doctor/Master in Community Planning and Development), and J.D./M.S. (Juris Doctor/Master of Science in health policy and management).

Required

To earn the J.D., candidates must complete 90 total credits, of which 56 are for required courses. They must maintain a minimum GPA of 2.0 in the required courses. The following first-year courses are required of all students: Civil Procedure I and II, Constitutional Law I, Contracts I and II, Criminal Law, Legal Research and Writing I and II, Property, and Torts. Required upper-level courses consist of a perspectives course, an independent writing requirement, Constitutional Law II, and Professional Responsibility. The required orientation program for first-year students is 2 days. The first day includes mini-classes, then discussion with alumni on the same case, and small

Phone: 207-780-4341
Fax: 207-780-4239
E-mail: *mainelaw@usm.maine.edu*
Web: *mainelaw.maine.edu*

Contact

Director of Admissions, 207-780-4341 for general inquiries; Assistant Director, 207-780-5250 for financial aid information.

MAINE

group discussions with faculty; the second day is information on university services, student organizations, and a session on professional responsibility.

Electives

The School of Law offers an Integrated Clinical Education Program to third-year students and includes civil practice and criminal defense under the auspices of the Cumberland Legal Aid Clinic. This clinic includes the General Practice Clinic, Prisoner Assistance Clinic (civil matters), Criminal Law and Family practicum's. A transactional Intellectual Property Clinic will be available. All clinics are open to third-year students and range from 3 to 6 credits. Students can also gain academic credit for work at many non-profit and government agencies through an extensive externship program. Seminars in commercial law, consumer law, constitutional law, intellectual property law, and international law are open to second- and third-year students. The Frank M. Coffin Lecture on Law and Public Service is held annually, along with the Godfrey Distinguished Visiting Lecturer and the Deans Distinguished Lecture Series. The Student Bar Association and other student organizations also offer guest lectures. There is a 1-semester option at Dalhousie Law School in Halifax, Nova Scotia; the University of New Brunswick, Canada; University College, Galway, Ireland; University of Buckingham, England; Université du Maine, LeMans, France; or Cergy-Pontoise University in Paris, France. All first- year students can participate in the Academic Support Program through which students are exposed to basic skills necessary to study law effectively and to strategies that enable students to make the most of their academic efforts and to minimize stress. The most widely taken electives are Trial Practice, Business Associations, and Evidence.

Graduation Requirements

In order to graduate, candidates must have a GPA of 2.0, have completed the upper-division writing requirement, which may be fulfilled with *Law Review, Ocean and Coastal Law Journal*, Moot Court, or an independent writing project; and have taken Constitutional Law II, 1 course that places the law in a broader philosophic, historic, or comparative context, and a course in professional responsibility.

Organizations

Students edit the *Maine Law Review and Ocean and Coastal Law Journal*. The second-year Moot Court Board is chosen by internal competition. Board members compete in a number of regional, national, and international competitions, such as the National Moot Court Competition, Jessup International, and the Trilateral Moot Court competition with Canadian law schools. Other competitions include the National Mock Trial Competition. Student organizations include the Student Bar Association, Black Law Students Association, the Maine Association for Public Interest Law, Environmental Law Society, Maine Law and Technology Association, and the Lesbian, Gay and Bisexual Law Caucus. Local chapters of national associations include the National Lawyers Guild, International Law Society, and the Federalist Society.

Library

The law library contains 330,999 hardcopy volumes and 132,739 microform volume equivalents, and subscribes to 5691 serial publications. Such on-line databases and networks as LEXIS, LOIS, OCLC First Search, RLIN, and WESTLAW are available to law students for research. Special library collections include EU and U.S. government publications depository and Canadian and British Commonwealth law reports and statutes. The ratio of library volumes to faculty is 18,389 to 1 and to students is 1283 to 1. The ratio of seats in the library to students is 1 to 1.

Faculty

The law school has 18 full-time and 7 part-time faculty members, of whom 9 are women. About 30% of full-time faculty have a graduate law degree in addition to the J.D. The ratio of full-time students to full-time faculty in an average class is 40 to 1; in a clinic, 6 to 1. The law school has a regular program of bringing visiting professors and other distinguished lecturers and visitors to campus.

Students

About 53% of the student body are women; 6%, minorities; 2%, African American; 4%, Asian American; and 1%, Hispanic. The majority of students come from Maine (72%). The average age of entering students is 27; age range is 21 to

Placement

J.D.s awarded:	96
Services available through: a separate law school placement center	
Special features: personalized, individualized attention.	
Full-time job interviews:	n/av
Summer job interviews:	n/av
Placement by graduation:	n/av
Placement within 9 months:	90% of class
Average starting salary:	$39,000 to $52,000
Areas of placement:	
Private practice 2-10 attorneys	19%
Private practice 11-25 attorneys	9%
Private practice 26-50 attorneys	9%
Private practice 51-100 attorneys	9%
Business/industry	18%
Judicial clerkships	15%
Government	15%
Public interest	5%
Academic	1%

60. About 21% of students enter directly from undergraduate school, 14% have a graduate degree, and 82% have worked full-time prior to entering law school. About 3% drop out after the first year for academic or personal reasons; 97% remain to receive a law degree.

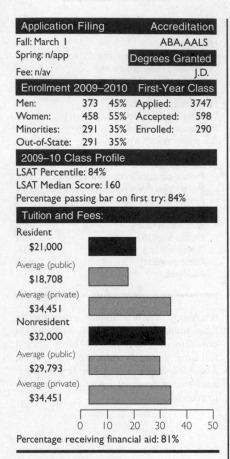

Application Filing			Accreditation
Fall: March 1			ABA, AALS
Spring: n/app			**Degrees Granted**
Fee: n/av			J.D.

Enrollment 2009–2010		First-Year Class	
Men:	373 45%	Applied:	3747
Women:	458 55%	Accepted:	598
Minorities:	291 35%	Enrolled:	290
Out-of-State:	291 35%		

2009–10 Class Profile

LSAT Percentile: 84%

LSAT Median Score: 160

Percentage passing bar on first try: 84%

Tuition and Fees:

Resident
$21,000

Average (public)
$18,708

Average (private)
$34,451

Nonresident
$32,000

Average (public)
$29,793

Average (private)
$34,451

0 10 20 30 40 50

Percentage receiving financial aid: 81%

ADMISSIONS

In the fall 2009 first-year class, 3747 applied, 598 were accepted, and 290 enrolled. Figures in the above capsule and in this profile are approximate. Twenty-nine transfers enrolled. The median LSAT percentile of the most recent first-year class was 84; the median GPA was 3.59 on a scale of 4.0. The lowest LSAT percentile accepted was 20; the highest was 99.

Requirements

Applicants must have a bachelor's degree and take the LSAT. Outstanding applicants at minimum age 23 with 3 years of college are considered. The most important admission factors include GPA, general background, and faculty recommendation; however, each factor's importance may vary from candidate to candidate. No specific undergraduate courses are required. Candidates are not interviewed.

Procedure

Applicants should submit an application form, LSAT results, transcripts, a personal statement, a nonrefundable application fee, and 2 letters of recommendation. Notification of the admissions decision

is December through April. The latest acceptable LSAT test date for fall entry is February. Check with the school for current application deadlines. The law school uses the LSDAS.

Special

The law school recruits minority and disadvantaged students by encouraging applications from African Americans and other students of color, and from disadvantaged persons who will enrich the law school and the profession. Requirements are not different for out-of-state students. Transfer students must have one year of credit, have attended an ABA-approved law school, and have competitive academic credentials.

Costs

Tuition and fees for the 2009-2010 academic year are $21,000 for full-time in-state students and $32,000 for out-of-state students. Tuition for part-time students is $16,000 in-state and $25,000 out-of-state. On-campus room and board costs about $21,000 annually; books and supplies run $3500.

Financial Aid

In a recent year, about 81% of current law students received some form of aid. The average annual amount of aid from all sources combined, including scholarships, loans, and work contracts, was $27,061; maximum, $55,621. Awards are based on need and merit. The average financial package is $48,891, based on need. There are a limited number of merit scholarships awarded through the admissions process. Required financial statement is the FAFSA. Check with the school for current application deadlines. Special funds for minority or disadvantaged students consist of grants that are available for students whose enrollment would add significantly to student diversity. First-year students are notified about their financial aid application at time of acceptance.

About the Law School

University of Maryland School of Law was established in 1816 and is a public institution. The 24-acre campus is in an urban area adjacent to a revitalized cultural and arts district. The primary mission of the law school is to contribute to the achievement of a more just society by educating outstanding lawyers, advancing understanding of law and legal institutions, and enhancing access to justice. The school is a leader in clinical education and public service law. Students have access to

federal, state, county, city, and local agencies, courts, correctional facilities, law firms, and legal aid organizations in the Baltimore area. The law school is within walking distance of local and federal courts. Facilities of special interest to law students include classrooms on each of its four floors and more than 400 study seats. State-of-the-art technology is integrated throughout with wired and wireless networks, smart podiums in the classrooms and video conferencing capabilities in all three courtrooms. The law library has 97 computer workstations and 424 wired network connections. Housing for students consists of campus apartments; board is not offered. The university's Residence Life Office assists in finding off-campus housing. All law school facilities are accessible to the physically disabled.

Calendar

The law school operates on a traditional semester basis. Courses for full-time students are offered day only for required courses; day and evening for electives and must be completed within 7 years. For part-time students, courses are offered both day and evening and must be completed within 7 years. New full- and part-time students are admitted in the fall. There is a 7-week summer session. Transferable summer courses are offered.

Programs

Students may take relevant courses in other programs and apply credit toward the J.D.; a maximum of 32 credits may be applied. The following joint degrees may be earned: J.D./M.A. (Juris Doctor/Master of Arts in criminal justice), J.D./M.B.A. (Juris Doctor/Master of Business Administration), J.D./M.S.W. (Juris Doctor/Master of Social Work), J.D./Ph.D. (Juris Doctor/Doctor of Philosophy in public policy), and J.D./Pharm. D. (Juris Doctor/Doctor of Pharmacy).

Required

To earn the J.D., candidates must complete 85 total credits, of which 34 to 35 are for required courses. They must maintain a minimum GPA of 2.0 in the required courses. The following first-year courses are required of all students: Civil Procedure, Constitutional Law: Governance, Contracts, Criminal Law, Legal Analysis, Writing and Research (LAWR I), Legal Analysis, Writing and Research (LAWR II), Property, and Torts. Required upper-level courses consist of Advanced Legal Research, Advanced Writing Requirement,

Contact

Michele Hayes, Director of Admissions, 410-706-3492 for general inquiries; Marilyn Heath, Student Financial Planning Coordinator 410-706-0873 for financial aid information.

Cardin Requirement, Constitutional Law: Individual Rights, and Legal Profession. All students must take clinical courses. The required orientation program for first-year students lasts 2 days. During that time, students receive instruction in case briefing, attend a sample class, are introduced to the web and technology-based law school systems, learn about the honor code, have lunch with faculty and deans, and meet with upper-class peer advisers.

Electives

The School of Law offers concentrations in corporate law, criminal law, environmental law, family law, intellectual property law, international law, juvenile law, labor law, litigation, securities law, tax law, health care law, public interest law, mediation, constitutional law, jurisprudence/legal theory, legislation/public policy, and human and civil rights. In addition, the Clinical Law Program offers 20 legal clinics that operate in a wide range of practice areas such as environmental law, disability law, family law, mediation, youth, education, healthcare, and community development. Approximately 55 seminars are offered. Externships are available in public agencies and nonprofit organizations for 1 to 13 credits. Externships are coordinated with classroom discussion and a writing requirement. Research may be undertaken through 4 legal journals, through independent research/writing under faculty supervision, by acting as research assistants for faculty, and in courses and seminars. Several annual lectures are sponsored by alumni gifts, student organizations, law school faculty/administration, and campus administration. Study abroad consists of an ABA-approved summer program in Aberdeen, Scotland, and semester-long foreign study or externship programs in Chile, China, Costa Rica, Germany, South Africa, Switzerland, and with the law reform commissions of a variety of commonwealth countries. The Academic Achievement Program enlists the assistance of upper-level students who, as teaching fellows, work directly with first-year students. The fellows lead seminars and work one-on-one with these students. In addition, the law school has an active Peer Advisor Program, where upper-level students provide additional support in this regard. First-year students are eligible to join any of the more than 30 student groups, which include the Asian/Pacific American Law Students Association, Black Law Students Association, Latino Law Students Association, and the LGBT

Law School Alliance. The most widely taken electives are Business, Environmental, and Health Law related courses.

Graduation Requirements

In order to graduate, candidates must have a GPA of 2.0, have completed the upper-division writing requirement, and meet the residency requirements of 6 semesters of attendance for full-time students, and 8 semesters for part-time students.

Organizations

The primary law review is the *Maryland Law Review*. Other law reviews include *The Journal of Health Care Law and Policy*, *The Journal Business and Technology*, and the *University of Maryland Journal Race, Religion, Gender and Class*. The student newspaper is *The Raven*. Moot court competitions include the Morris B. Myerowitz Competition, Jessup International Moot Court Competition, and Pace University National Environmental Law Moot Court Competition. Other competitions include Health Law Moot Court, Robert R. Merhige, Jr. National Environmental Negotiations Competition, American College of Trial Lawyers, and Association of Trial Lawyers of America. Law student organizations, local chapters of national associations, and campus organizations include the Maryland Environmental Law Society, Student Health Law Organization, American Constitution Society, Student Bar Association, Women's Bar Association (student chapter), Phi Alpha Delta, Criminal Law Association, International Law Society, and Business Law Society.

Library

The law library contains 353,820 hardcopy volumes and 141,718 microform volume equivalents, and subscribes to 3780 serial publications. Such on-line databases and networks as CALI, Infotrac, LegalTrac, LEXIS, LOIS, Mathew Bender, NEXIS, OCLC First Search, WESTLAW, Wilsonline Indexes, are available to law students for research. See *www.law.umaryland.edu/marshall/marshall_index.asp* for a list of other databases and networks. Special library collections include a partial federal government depository, African-Americans in the Law, and historical publications of the U.S. Civil Rights Commission. Recently, the library expanded and includes spacious reading rooms, group study rooms, and state-of-the-art technology. The ratio of library volumes to faculty is 6318 to 1 and to students is

Placement

J.D.s awarded:	254

Services available through: a separate law school placement center

Services: job fairs, on-line jobs/internship listing database

Special features: Career Development staff assists in developing job search strategies, facilitates year-round on-campus interviewing and other recruitment programs, and provides professional development workshops and seminars.

Full-time job interviews:	69 employers
Summer job interviews:	123 employers
Placement by graduation:	83% of class
Placement within 9 months:	98% of class
Average starting salary:	$61,498 to $150,000

Areas of placement:

Private practice 2-10 attorneys	12%
Private practice 11-25 attorneys	3%
Private practice 26-50 attorneys	4%
Private practice 51-100 attorneys	2%
Private practice 101-501+ attorneys	19%
Judicial clerkships	25%
Government	13%
Business/industry	10%
Public interest	5%
Academic	5%
Military	2%

426 to 1. The ratio of seats in the library to students is 1 to 1.

Faculty

The law school has 56 full-time and 99 part-time faculty members, of whom 65 are women. According to AAUP standards for Category I institutions, faculty salaries are average. About 25% of full-time faculty have a graduate law degree in addition to the J.D.; about 4% of part-time faculty have one. The ratio of full-time students to full-time faculty in an average class is 11 to 1; in a clinic, 8 to 1. The law school has a regular program of bringing visiting professors and other distinguished lecturers and visitors to campus. There is a chapter of the Order of the Coif.

Students

About 55% of the student body are women; 35%, minorities; 14%, African American; 13%, Asian American; 8%, Hispanic; and 1%, Native American. The majority of students come from Maryland (65%). The average age of entering students is 25; age range is 20 to 56. About 35% of students enter directly from undergraduate school, 20% have a graduate degree, and 65% have worked full-time prior to entering law school. About 1% drop out after the first year for academic or personal reasons; 94% remain to receive a law degree.

University of Maryland 499

UNIVERSITY OF MEMPHIS

Cecil C. Humphreys School of Law

1 North Front Street Memphis, TN 38103-2189

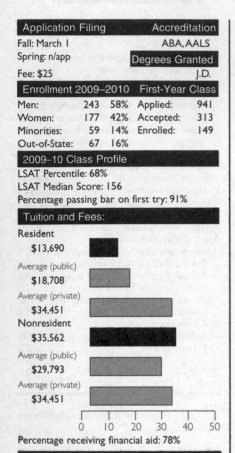

Application Filing		Accreditation
Fall: March 1		ABA, AALS
Spring: n/app		**Degrees Granted**
Fee: $25		J.D.

Enrollment 2009–2010			First-Year Class	
Men:	243	58%	Applied:	941
Women:	177	42%	Accepted:	313
Minorities:	59	14%	Enrolled:	149
Out-of-State:	67	16%		

2009–10 Class Profile

LSAT Percentile: 68%

LSAT Median Score: 156

Percentage passing bar on first try: 91%

Tuition and Fees:

Resident
$13,690

Average (public)
$18,708

Average (private)
$34,451

Nonresident
$35,562

Average (public)
$29,793

Average (private)
$34,451

0   10   20   30   40   50

Percentage receiving financial aid: 78%

ADMISSIONS

In the fall 2009 first-year class, 941 applied, 313 were accepted, and 149 enrolled. Three transfers enrolled. The median LSAT percentile of the most recent first-year class was 68; the median GPA was 3.37 on a scale of 4.0. The lowest LSAT percentile accepted was 23; the highest was 98.

Requirements

Applicants must have a bachelor's degree and take the LSAT. Minimum acceptable GPA is 2.0 on a scale of 4.0. The most important admission factors include academic achievement, LSAT results, and GPA. All files are reviewed, and all factors are evaluated on a subjective basis. No specific undergraduate courses are required. Candidates are not interviewed.

Procedure

The application deadline for fall entry is March 1. Applicants should submit an application form, LSAT results, a personal statement, a recent TOEFL score for foreign-educated international, students and a nonrefundable application fee of $25. Three letters of recommendation are encouraged but not required, and nonresident candidates must submit a Nonresident Addendum. Notification of the admissions decision is from December to May. The latest acceptable LSAT test date for fall entry is February. The law school uses the LSDAS.

Special

The law school recruits minority and disadvantaged students by means of representatives attending graduate and professional fairs and national LSAC forums and visiting HBCU institutions in the region. View books are sent to diversity candidates from Tennessee in LSAC's Candidate Referral Services (CRS) pool. An on-campus diversity workshop is held in February. Requirements are not different for out-of-state students. Transfer students must have 1 year of credit; criteria is based on prelaw school variables (LSAT and GPA) and class rank at ABA- and AALS-approved law schools.

Costs

Tuition and fees for the 2009-2010 academic year are $13,690 for full-time in-state students and $35,562 for out-of-state students. Tuition for part-time students is $11,837 in-state and $30,723 out-of-state. On-campus room and board costs about $8731 annually; books and supplies run $1700.

Financial Aid

About 78% of current law students receive some form of aid. The average annual amount of aid from all sources combined, including scholarships, loans, and work contracts, is $25,175; maximum, $55,986. Awards are based on need and merit. Required financial statement is the FAFSA. The aid application deadline for fall entry is April 1. Special funds for minority or disadvantaged students include the Law Memphis Access and Diversity Scholarship. First-year students are notified about their financial aid application at time of acceptance.

About the Law School

University of Memphis Cecil C. Humphreys School of Law was established in 1962 and is a private institution. The 1160-acre campus is in downtown Memphis. The primary mission of the law school is to provide an excellent academic program whose graduates have attained knowledge of legal concepts, systems, and ethics, and the ability to articulate, analyze, apply, and further develop that knowledge and skill in their future intellectual pursuits, including primarily membership in the legal profession. Students have access to federal, state, county, city, and local agencies, courts, correctional facilities, law firms, and legal aid organizations in the Memphis area. Other resources include the University of Memphis library. Housing for students consists of university-owned and managed apartment-style units on the main campus. All law school facilities are accessible to the physically disabled.

Calendar

The law school operates on a traditional semester basis. Courses for full-time students are offered days only with limited elective courses in the evening and must be completed within 6 years. For part-time students, courses are offered days only with limited elective courses in the evening and must be completed within 6 years. New full- and part-time students are admitted in the fall. There is an 8-week summer session. Transferable summer courses are offered.

Programs

The following joint degrees may be earned: J.D./M.B.A. (Juris Doctor/Master of Business Administration).

Required

To earn the J.D., candidates must complete 90 total credits, of which 57 to 60 are for required courses. The following first-year courses are required of all students: Civil Procedure I and II, Contracts I and II, Criminal Law, Legal Methods I and II, Property I and II, and Torts I and II. Required upper-level courses consist of Advanced Writing and Research, Business Organizations I, Constitutional Law, Criminal Procedure I, Descedents' Estates, Evidence, Income Tax, Professional Responsibility, and Secured Transactions. All students must satisfy an upper-level skills requirement, which could include a clinic. The required orientation program for first-year students consists of a 2-day program that takes

Contact

Office of Law Admissions, 901-678-5403 for general inquiries; Debra Ann Brown, Assistant Director, Student Financial Aid, 901-678-4825, direct line 901-678-3737 for financial aid information.

TENNESSEE

place immediately before the beginning of fall classes.

Electives

The Cecil C. Humphreys School of Law offers concentrations in corporate law, criminal law, entertainment law, family law, intellectual property law, juvenile law, labor law, litigation, tax law, torts and insurance, commercial law, and real estate law. In addition, clinics offered are Civil Litigation, Elder Law, Child and Family Litigation, and Small Business (worth 4 credit hours each) and are available to upper-class students as an elective. Seminar classes are available to second- or third-year students, and they are typically 2-credit courses. Many different seminar options are available. The seminar courses satisfy the upper-division research requirement. Externship credit is available with the U.S. Attorney Office, Bankruptcy Court, National Labor Relations Board, Public Defenders, state appellate, federal district court, and Memphis area legal services. Students can receive research credit for law review or seminars. An academic support program (ASP) for first-year students helps ease the transition to law school. Its 2 primary components are group presentations and individual tutorials for selected first-year courses. The Tennessee Institute for Pre-Law (TIP) is an alternative admission program for Tennessee residents and Mississippi and Arkansas border counties; candidates must meet diversity criteria. TIP is a 5-week summer program and is limited to 20 students. The most widely taken electives are Family Law, Commercial Paper, and Copyright.

Graduation Requirements

In order to graduate, candidates must have a GPA of 2.0 and have completed the upper-division writing requirement.

Organizations

The primary law review is *The University of Memphis Law Review*. Moot court competitions include Freshman Moot Court (first year) and Mock Trial—Advanced Moot Court (second and third year). Other competitions include Frederick Douglass Moot Court, National Moot Court, ABA National Appellate Advocacy Competition, Duberstein Moot Court Competitions, Wagner Moot Court, National Mock

Trial and Thurgood Marshall Mock Trial, and the Public Action Law Society. Law student organizations, local chapters of national associations, and campus organizations include the Student Bar Association, the Association of Women Attorneys, the Public Action Law Society. Phi Alpha Delta, the Federalist Society, the Black Law Students Association, Intellectual Property Law Society, and Sports and Entertainment Society.

Library

The law library contains 274,325 hardcopy volumes and 105,352 microform volume equivalents, and subscribes to 2327 serial publications. Such on-line databases and networks as CALI, Legal-Trac, LEXIS, Mathew Bender, NEXIS, OCLC First Search, WESTLAW, Wilsonline Indexes, CCH Internet Tax Network, Environmental Law Report, HeinOnline, and Tennessee Attorney's Memo are available to law students for research. Installation of a new library system includes a new on-line catalog. The ratio of library volumes to faculty is 11,927 to 1 and to students is 653 to 1. The ratio of seats in the library to students is 1 to 1.

Faculty

The law school has 23 full-time and 26 part time faculty members, of whom 17 are women. According to AAUP standards for Category I institutions, faculty salaries are well below average. About 43% of full-time faculty have a graduate law degree in addition to the J.D.; about 22% of part-time faculty have one. The ratio of full-time students to full-time faculty in an average class is 18 to 1; in a clinic, 8 to 1.

Students

About 42% of the student body are women; 14%, minorities; 10%, African American; 2%, Asian American; 2%, Hispanic; and 1%, Native American. The majority of students come from Tennessee (84%). The average age of entering students is 26; age range is 21 to 48. About 37% of students enter directly from undergraduate school, 10% have a graduate degree, and 61% have worked full-time prior to entering law school. About 2% to 3% drop out after the first year for academic or personal reasons; 96% to 97% remain to receive a law degree.

Placement

J.D.s awarded:	117

Services available through: a separate law school placement center

Services: workshops, seminars, and nontraditional legal career advice

Special features: membership in regional, national, and minority law placement consortiums.

Full-time job interviews:	9 employers
Summer job interviews:	22 employers
Placement by graduation:	45% of class
Placement within 9 months:	95% of class
Average starting salary:	$25,000 to $100,000

Areas of placement:

Private practice 2-10	39
Private practice 11/25 attorneys	6
Private practice 26-50 attorneys	6%
Private practice 51-100 attorneys	2%
Private practice 100-250 attorneys	5%
Solo practice	4%
Business/industry	11%
Government	9%
Judicial clerkships	5%
Public interest	4%
Academic	2%
Unknown size firm	4%

UNIVERSITY OF MIAMI

School of Law

P.O. Box 248087, 1311 Miller Drive
Coral Gables, FL 33124-8087

Application Filing	Accreditation
Fall: February 4	ABA, AALS
Spring: n/app	**Degrees Granted**
Fee: $60	J.D., LL.M., LL.M. in taxation, estate planning, real property development

Enrollment 2009–2010		First-Year Class	
Men:	787 57%	Applied:	4695
Women:	597 45%	Accepted:	2409
Minorities:	415 30%	Enrolled:	530
Out-of-State:	803 58%		

2009–10 Class Profile
LSAT Percentile: 75%
LSAT Median Score: 157
Percentage passing bar on first try: 84%

Tuition and Fees:

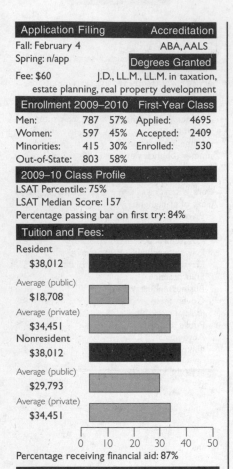

Resident
$38,012

Average (public)
$18,708

Average (private)
$34,451

Nonresident
$38,012

Average (public)
$29,793

Average (private)
$34,451

0   10   20   30   40   50

Percentage receiving financial aid: 87%

ADMISSIONS
In the fall 2009 first-year class, 4695 applied, 2409 were accepted, and 530 enrolled. Twenty-nine transfers enrolled. The median LSAT percentile of the most recent first-year class was 75; the median GPA was 3.46 on a scale of 4.0. The lowest LSAT percentile accepted was 25; the highest was 98.

Requirements
Applicants must have a bachelor's degree and take the LSAT. No specific undergraduate courses are required. Candidates are not interviewed.

Procedure
The application deadline for fall entry is February 4. Applicants should submit an application form, LSAT results, TOEFL for foreign students, a nonrefundable application fee of $60, and 2 letters of recommendation. Graduates from foreign institutions must submit transcript evaluations. All students must possess a bachelor's degree or its equivalent from a regionally accredited institution prior to the first day of classes. Notification of the admissions

decision is on a rolling basis. The latest acceptable LSAT test date for fall entry is June. The law school uses the LSDAS.

Special
The law school recruits minority and disadvantaged students by means of a committee reviewing all files, sending information to prelaw advisers at historically minority institutions, hosting diversity admissions fairs, and participating in recruiting events at historically black schools and locations at schools where minority population is strong; also, current minority students contact newly admitted minority students. Requirements are not different for out-of-state students. Transfer students must have one year of credit, have a minimum GPA of 3, have attended an ABA-approved law school, and have their LSAT and undergraduate performance reviewed.

Costs
Tuition and fees for the 2009-2010 academic year are $38,012 for all full-time students. Books and supplies run $1200.

Financial Aid
About 87% of current law students receive some form of aid. The average annual amount of aid from all sources combined, including scholarships, loans, and work contracts, is $26,926; maximum, $59,675. Awards are based on need and merit, but the majority of scholarships are merit-based. Required financial statement is the FAFSA. The aid application deadline for fall entry is February 1. Special funds for minority or disadvantaged students include need-based scholarships and merit scholarships, both institutional and donor, including the Colson Scholarship Fund, Florida Bar Minority Scholarships, and the Spellman and Baker McKenzie scholarships. First-year students are notified about their financial aid application at on a rolling basis as the files are complete.

About the Law School
University of Miami School of Law was established in 1926 and is a private institution. The 260-acre campus is in an urban area 7 miles south of Miami. The primary mission of the law school is to teach students the craft as well as the theory of law, develop the research and writing skills necessary to the legal profession, and expose students to other skills necessary to develop a deep intellectual founation for effective professional service, such as client counseling, fact investigation, and trial skills. Students have

access to federal, state, county, city, and local agencies, courts, correctional facilities, law firms, and legal aid organizations in the Coral Gables area. and the legal institutions and firms of Miami, Fort Lauderdale, West Palm Beach, and the Florida Keys. Facilities of special interest to law students include a broad variety of clinic and clerkship opportunities in Miami's vibrant legal and business communities, as well as numerous opportunities for practical community service experiences. Miami students also have access to the other libraries throughout the University of Miami academic community. Housing for students is limited on campus but is widely available off campus in the area, and roommate referral, apartment listings, and relocation guide are supplied to admitted students. All law school facilities are accessible to the physically disabled.

Calendar
The law school operates on a traditional semester basis. Courses for full-time students are offered both day and evening (evening courses offered after the first year only) and must be completed within 5 years. There is no part-time program. New students are admitted in the fall. There is an 8- to 9-week summer session. Transferable summer courses are offered.

Programs
In addition to the J.D., the law school offers the LL.M. and LL.M. in taxation, estate planning, real property development, ocean and coastal law, and international law. Students may take relevant courses in other programs and apply credit toward the J.D.; a maximum of 6 credits may be applied. The following joint degrees may be earned: J.D./LL.M. (Juris Doctor/Master of Laws in taxation, international law, ocean and coastal law, and property development), J.D./M.A. (Juris Doctor/Master of Marine Affairs), J.D./M.B.A. (Juris Doctor/Master of Business Administration), J.D./M.M. (Juris Doctor/Master of Music Affairs), and J.D./M.P.H. (Juris Doctor/Master of Public Health).

Required
To earn the J.D., candidates must complete 88 total credits, of which 72 are for required courses. They must maintain a minimum GPA of 2.0 in the required courses. The following first-year courses are required of all students: a first-year elective, Civil Procedure I, Constitutional Law I, Contracts, Criminal Procedure, Elements, Legal Writing and Research I and II, Property, and Torts. Required

Phone: 305-284-2523
Fax: 305-284-4400
E-mail: admissions@law.miami.edu
Web: law.miami.edu

Contact

Therese Lambert, Director of Student Recruiting, 305-284-6746 for general inquiries; Interim Director of Financial Aid, 305-284-3115 for financial aid information.

upper-level courses consist of 2 seminars/workshops, Professional Responsibility, skills course, and upper-level writing. The required orientation program for first-year students is a week-long formal program before classes begin. Students participate in panels and presentations, and lunches with faculty and current students.

Electives

The School of Law offers concentrations in corporate law, criminal law, entertainment law, environmental law, family law, international law, juvenile law, labor law, litigation, maritime law, securities law, sports law, tax law, and torts and insurance. In addition, a variety of clinics and hands-on legal training are offered through the Center for Ethics and Public Service, and various public interest programs, such as HOPE (Helping others through Pro Bono efforts), Street Law, and the Wrongful Convictions Project. The Children and Youth Law Clinic, the Health & Elder Clinic, and the Immigration Clinic are open to second- and third-year students. Seminars and workshops are typically 2 credits and limited to 20-25 students. Most seminars require some independent research and significant writing. During the fall and spring semesters of each year, more than 100 law firms, public interest organizations, and government agencies come to campus to interview students for summer internships. Second- and third-year students are also able to take part in individual research projects, worth 1-3 credits. Special lecture series bring distinguished judges, scholars, and practicing attorneys from around the world to campus. Summer-abroad programs include Ultimate China, LEAP (London, English countyside, Amsterdam, and Paris), Greece/Italy, and Middle Europe. An intensive short-term workshop is offered with law students from the University of Leipzig in Germany, and the University of Zurich in Switzerland. These competitive 3-credit programs, which meet in Miami in the winter and their respective European cities in the spring, focus on cutting-edge international and comparative law. All first-year students participate in the Legal Research and Writing program, a year-long program taught in small group settings. Additionally, the Academic Achievement Program offers a variety of programs such as the writing center, Dean's Fellows, and Exam Workshops. The Professional Opportunities Program for Black Students offers a 6-week internship in the chamber of federal, state, and county judges, the Florida

Attorney General's Office, the Miami-Dade State Atorney's Office, the Broward State Attorney's Office and the Miami-Dade County Public Defenders's Office. The John Kozak Minority Mentoring program and the Cuban American Bar Association Mentor program provide minority students with an opportunity to interact with community judges and attorneys. A select group of entering students is chosen to participate in the James Welden Johnson Institute. This 5-week summer fellowship program is designed to develop participant's legal, analytical, and writing skills. The institute is held prior to the beginning of fall classes and all financial aspects are covered by grants. The most widely taken electives are Litigation Skills and Clinical Program, Civil Procedure II, and Evidence.

Graduation Requirements

In order to graduate, candidates must have a GPA of 2.0, and have completed the upper-division writing requirement. Many offerings in the upper division require substantial papers.

Organizations

Student-edited publications include the *University of Miami Law Review; Inter-American Law Review; Business Law Review; International and Comparative Law Review; Psychology, Public Policy, and Law Journal*: the student newspaper *Res Ispa Loquitur*, the yearbook, *Amicus Curiae*, and *Tax Law Chronicle*. The Moot Court Board runs one of the nation's largest mock trial competitions, involving more than 200 experienced lawyers. This organization also sponsors several local, state, and regional moot court competitions, as well as negotiation and client counseling competitions. Other competitions include International Moot Court. Law student organizations, include Hispanic Law Students, Entertainment and Sports Law Society, and the Tax Law Society. Local chapters of national associations, include the ABA-Law Student Division, Association of Trial Lawyers of America, Black Law Students Association, and Phi Alpha Delta. Other campus organizations include Miami Law Woman and Society of Bar and Gavel.

Library

The law library contains 431,381 hardcopy volumes and 218,280 microform volume equivalents, and subscribes to 11,597 serial publications. Such on-line databases and networks as CALI, CIS Universe, Legal-Trac, LEXIS, LOIS, Mathew Bender, NEXIS, OCLC First Search, RLIN,

Placement

J.D.s awarded:	374

Services available through: a separate law school placement center, the university placement center, the graduate business school placement center, and reciprocal programs with other law schools.

Services: off-campus interview programs/job fairs; 9 practicing attorneys work in the Career Placement Center (6 full-time, 3 part-time)

Full-time job interviews:	50 employers
Summer job interviews:	80 employers
Placement by graduation:	74% of class
Placement within 9 months:	96% of class
Average starting salary:	$37,500 to $200,000

Areas of placement:

Private practice 2-10 attorneys	40%
Private practice 11-25 attorneys	11%
Private practice 26-50 attorneys	11%
Private practice 51-100 attorneys	5%
Government	10%
Business/industry	10%
Public interest	4%
Judicial clerkships	6%
Academic	1%
Unknown	2%

WESTLAW, Wilsonline Indexes, and the law school's home page - http://library.law.miami.edu are available to law students for research. Special library collections include Soia Mentschikoff papers and Everglades litigation files. Recently, the library became wireless. The ratio of library volumes to faculty is 5392 to 1 and to students is 311 to 1. The ratio of seats in the library to students is 1 to 2.

Faculty

The law school has 80 full-time and 104 part-time faculty members, of whom 64 are women. According to AAUP standards for Category I institutions, faculty salaries are average. About 31% of full-time faculty have a graduate law degree in addition to the J.D. The ratio of full-time students to full-time faculty in an average class is 17 to 1. There is a chapter of the Order of the Coif; 55 faculty and 974 graduates are members.

Students

About 45% of the student body are women; 30%, minorities; 7%, African American; 4%, Asian American; and 13%, Hispanic. The majority of students come from Florida (42%). The average age of entering students is 24; age range is 20 to 42. About 50% of students enter directly from undergraduate school and 50% have worked full-time prior to entering law school. About 2% drop out after the first year for academic or personal reasons.

University of Miami **503**

Law School

625 South State Street
Ann Arbor, MI 48109-1215

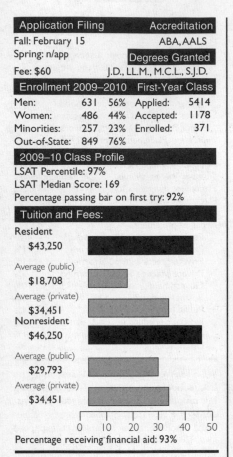

Application Filing		Accreditation
Fall: February 15		ABA, AALS
Spring: n/app		**Degrees Granted**
Fee: $60		J.D., LL.M., M.C.L., S.J.D.

Enrollment 2009–2010		First-Year Class	
Men:	631 56%	Applied:	5414
Women:	486 44%	Accepted:	1178
Minorities:	257 23%	Enrolled:	371
Out-of-State:	849 76%		

2009–10 Class Profile
LSAT Percentile: 97%
LSAT Median Score: 169
Percentage passing bar on first try: 92%

Tuition and Fees:

Resident
$43,250

Average (public)
$18,708

Average (private)
$34,451
Nonresident
$46,250

Average (public)
$29,793

Average (private)
$34,451

0 10 20 30 40 50

Percentage receiving financial aid: 93%

ADMISSIONS

In the fall 2009 first-year class, 5414 applied, 1178 were accepted, and 371 enrolled. Fifty-seven transfers enrolled. The median LSAT percentile of the most recent first-year class was 97; the median GPA was 3.7 on a scale of 4.0.

Requirements

Applicants must have a bachelor's degree and take the LSAT. No specific undergraduate courses are required. Candidates are not interviewed.

Procedure

The application deadline for fall entry is February 15. Applicants should submit an application form, LSAT results, transcripts, a personal statement, a non-refundable application fee of $60, and 1 letter of recommendation (although 3 are encouraged). Transcripts and LSAT results must be sent via LSDAS. There is an optional supplemental essay. Notification of the admissions decision is on a rolling basis from November. The latest acceptable LSAT test date for fall entry is December at the latest of the calendar

year prior to the year in which admission is sought. The law school uses the LSDAS.

Special

The law school recruits minority and disadvantaged students by reaching out to student populations that are likely to consist of minority or economically disadvantaged students in significant concentrations. Specific means of recruiting minority students include attending minority Law Days, writing to minority students who participate in the candidate referral service, and holding alumni receptions in various nationwide settings. The law school attempts to attract economically disadvantaged students by providing need-based financial aid packages, as well as some merit-based financial aid awards. Requirements are not different for out-of-state students. Transfer students must have one year of credit, have attended an ABA-approved law school, and typically must be in the top 5% to 10% of their first-year class.

Costs

Tuition and fees for the 2009-2010 academic year are $43,250 for full-time in-state students and $46,250 for out-of-state students. On-campus room and board costs about $11,386 annually; books and supplies run $1050.

Financial Aid

About 93% of current law students receive some form of aid. The average annual amount of aid from all sources combined, including scholarships, loans, and work contracts, is $47,662; maximum, $92,450. Awards are based on need and merit. Most aid is need-based, but a small number of merit-based grants are awarded each year. Required financial statement is the FAFSA. The aid application deadline for fall entry is rolling. First-year students are notified about their financial aid application 3 to 5 working days from the admission date or the middle of February, whichever is later.

About the Law School

University of Michigan Law School was established in 1859 and is a public institution. The 2860-acre campus is in a suburban area 45 miles west of Detroit. The primary mission of the law school is to bring human insight to the study of law and its institutions, drawing on the resources of the university and faculty. It seeks to share with its students a knowledge of

past and present forms and functions of law, and an engaged understanding of the law's evolution and future development. Students have access to federal, state, county, city, and local agencies, courts, correctional facilities, law firms, and legal aid organizations in the Ann Arbor area. Other resources come from the school's integration in an international university. Housing for students is available at the Lawyers Club; in university family housing; graduate dormitories; and other dormitories as resident advisers. Off-campus housing is also available. All law school facilities are accessible to the physically disabled.

Calendar

The law school operates on a traditional semester basis. Courses for full-time students are offered days only and must be completed within 5 years. There is no part-time program. New students are admitted in the fall and summer. There is a 11-week summer session. Transferable summer courses are not offered.

Programs

In addition to the J.D., the law school offers the LL.M., M.C.L., and S.J.D. Students may take relevant courses in other programs and apply credit toward the J.D.; a maximum of 12 credits may be applied. The following joint degrees may be earned: J.D./M.A. (Juris Doctor/Master of Arts in Japanese studies, Chinese Studies, Modern Middle Eastern and North African Studies, Russian and Eastern European Studies, and world politics), J.D./M.B.A. (Juris Doctor/Master of Business Administration), J.D./M.H.S.A. (Juris Doctor/Master of Health Services Administration), J.D./M.P.H. (Juris Doctor/Master of Public Health), J.D./M.P.P. (Juris Doctor/Master of Public Policy Studies), J.D./M.S. (Juris Doctor/Master of Science in natural resources), J.D./M.S.I. (Juris Doctor/Master of Science in Information), J.D./M.S.W. (Juris Doctor/Master of Social Work), J.D./M.U.P (Juris Doctor/Master of Urban Planning), and J.D./Ph.D. (Juris Doctor/Doctor of Philosophy in economics).

Required

To earn the J.D., candidates must complete 82 total credits, of which 32 are for required courses. They must maintain a minimum GPA of 2.0 in the required courses. The following first-year courses are required of all students: an elective, Civil Procedure, Contracts, Criminal Law,

Contact

Sarah C. Zearfoss, Assistant Dean, Director, 734-764-0537 for general inquiries; Katherine Gottschalk, Assistant Dean for Financial Aid, 734-764-5289 for financial aid information.

MICHIGAN

Introduction to Constitutional Law, Legal Practice I and II, Legal Practice Skills, Property, and Torts. Required upper-level courses consist of a course meeting the professional responsibility requirement, a course meeting the upper-level writing requirement, and Transnational Law. The required orientation program for first-year students consists of 2 days of presentations by deans, faculty, and upper-class students; tours; information about the school and Ann Arbor; and an introduction to the study of law. On the second day of orientation, new students, along with participating orientation leaders, administrators, and faculty are brought to various sites in the Ann Arbor and Detroit area to engage in a community service project. The orientation also includes a Commitment to Integrity Ceremony, during which new students are addressed by an esteemed judge or lawyer about issues related to ethics and professionalism and then pledge their commitment to comporting themselves professionally and with integrity during law school and throughout their careers.

Electives

The Law School offers concentrations in corporate law, criminal law, entertainment law, environmental law, family law, intellectual property law, international law, juvenile law, labor law, litigation, securities law, sports law, tax law, torts and insurance, civil rights, feminist legal theory, law and literature, and asylum and refugee law. In addition, upper-class students may take clinical and externship courses for up to 12 hours of credit. Students may elect a civil or criminal concentration. These clinics include Child Advocacy Law Clinic, Criminal Appellate Clinic, Environmental Law Clinic, Urban Communities Clinic, Mediation, Pediatric Advocacy, Low Income Taxpayer, International Transactions, Innocence, and Human Trafficking. Students must take at least 1 seminar in their second or third year; most recently, 74 seminars were offered. Students may spend a full semester on an externship and earn up to 12 hours of credit for the term. As part of the externship requirement, students produce a significant research paper under the supervision of a Michigan Law faculty member, on a subject related to the substantive field of the externship. Under the supervision of a school faculty member, students may pursue up to a total of 6 hours of independent research. The same variety that exists for the law school summer internships exist for pro bono legal work. Students do direct advocacy with a legal aid program, public defender, or a program focusing on one area, such as child advocacy. Among the law school's impressive partners in the effort are Human Rights Watch, an international NGO based in New York; the Mississippi Cente for Justice, a nonprofit public interest law firm dedicated to advancing economic and racial equity; the Center on Wrongful Convictions and the Innocence Project, from New York and Chicago; the Washington Lawyer's Committee for Civil Rights and Urban Affairs; and Michigan Law's own Environmental Law & Policy Program. Individual tutors are available to any students who request them. The most widely taken electives are Enterprise Organizations, Evidence, and Jurisdiction.

Graduation Requirements

In order to graduate, candidates must have a GPA of 2.0 and have completed the upper-division writing requirement.

Organizations

Students edit the *Michigan Law Review, Michigan Journal of International Law, University of Michigan Journal of Law Reform, Michigan Journal of Gender and Law, Michigan Journal of Race and Law, Michigan Telecommunications and Technology Law Review*, and the newspaper *Res Gestae*. Annual moot court competitions include the Henry M. Campbell Memorial, the Philip C. Jessup International Moot Court, and the Client Counseling Competition. Other competitions include the Sexual Orientation Moot Court, Child Advocacy Moot Court Competition, and National Environmental Moot Court. Law student organizations include the Black Law Student Association, Federalist Society, and Outlaws. There are local chapters of Phi Alpha Delta, Phi Delta Phi, ABA-Law Student Division, American Constitution Society, and American Civil Liberties Union.

Library

The law library contains 1,002,273 hardcopy volumes and 1,673,989 microform volume equivalents, and subscribes to 6026 serial publications. Such on-line databases and networks as CALI, CIS Universe, DIALOG, Infotrac, Legal-Trac, LEXIS, LOIS, Mathew Bender, NEXIS, OCLC First Search, WESTLAW, and Wilsonline Indexes are available to law students for research. Special library collections include a depository for U.S. and European Union documents, all documents from U.N. and other supra-national authorities, as well as U.S. state and federal material. There are also extensive special collections in the fields of Roman law, canon law, comparative law, indigenous nations, trials, biography, and legal bibliography. Recently, the library added a rare book room with customized reading space and a new stack area. The ratio of library volumes to faculty is 11,520 to 1 and to students is 897 to 1. The ratio of seats in the library to students is 1 to 1.

Faculty

The law school has 87 full-time and 33 part-time faculty members, of whom 38 are women. According to AAUP standards for Category I institutions, faculty salaries are well below average. About 43% of full-time faculty have a graduate law degree in addition to the J.D. The ratio of full-time students to full-time faculty in an average class is 11 to 1; in a clinic, 6 to 1. The law school has a regular program of bringing visiting professors and other distinguished lecturers and visitors to campus. There is a chapter of the Order of the Coif.

Students

About 44% of the student body are women; 23%, minorities; 5%, African American; 12%, Asian American; 4%, Hispanic; 2%, Native American; and 3%, Foreign National. The majority of students come from the Midwest (41%). The average age of entering students is 24; age range is 21 to 63.

UNIVERSITY OF MINNESOTA

Law School

229 19th Avenue S.
Minneapolis, MN 55455

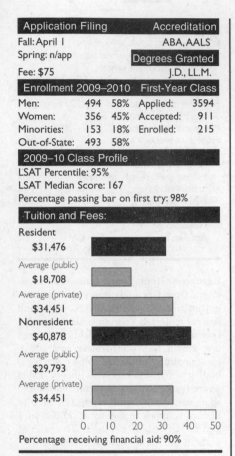

Application Filing		Accreditation	
Fall: April 1		ABA, AALS	
Spring: n/app		**Degrees Granted**	
Fee: $75		J.D., LL.M.	
Enrollment 2009–2010		**First-Year Class**	
Men:	494 58%	Applied:	3594
Women:	356 45%	Accepted:	911
Minorities:	153 18%	Enrolled:	215
Out-of-State:	493 58%		

2009–10 Class Profile
LSAT Percentile: 95%
LSAT Median Score: 167
Percentage passing bar on first try: 98%

Tuition and Fees:

Resident
$31,476

Average (public)
$18,708

Average (private)
$34,451

Nonresident
$40,878

Average (public)
$29,793

Average (private)
$34,451

0 10 20 30 40 50

Percentage receiving financial aid: 90%

ADMISSIONS
In the fall 2009 first-year class, 3594 applied, 911 were accepted, and 215 enrolled. Forty-one transfers enrolled. The median LSAT percentile of the most recent first-year class was 95; the median GPA was 3.64 on a scale of 4.0.

Requirements
Applicants must have a bachelor's degree and take the LSAT. The admissions committee takes all factors into consideration. No specific undergraduate courses are required. Candidates are not interviewed.

Procedure
The application deadline for fall entry is April 1. Applicants should submit an application form, LSAT results, transcripts, a personal statement, a nonrefundable application fee of $75, and 2 letters of recommendation. Notification of the admissions decision is on a rolling basis. The latest acceptable LSAT test date for fall entry is February. The law school uses the LSDAS.

Special
The law school recruits minority and disadvantaged students by means of national recruitment, CLEO, the Candidate Referral Service, the Legal Education Awareness Program, and an annual summer LSAT prep course hosted by the law school. Requirements are not different for out-of-state students. Transfer students must have one year of credit, have attended an ABA-approved law school, meet credentials to be admitted as a first-year law student, and exhibit good standing with quality work at a comparable law school.

Costs
Tuition and fees for the 2009-2010 academic year are $31,476 for full-time in-state students and $40,878 for out-of-state students. Books and supplies run $1666.

Financial Aid
More than 90% of current law students receive some form of aid. The average annual amount of aid from all sources combined, including scholarships, loans, and work contracts, total up to the cost of attendance. Awards are based on need and merit, along with . Required financial statements are the FAFSA and . The aid application deadline for fall entry is April 1. Special funds for minority or disadvantaged students are available. Student receive notice of their estimated financial aid and total cost of attendance upon admission and final notification in June.

About the Law School
University of Minnesota Law School was established in 1888 and is a public institution. The 446-acre campus is in an urban area in Minneapolis. The primary mission of the law school is to provide high quality legal education by educating men and women in the law principally through instruction leading to a J.D. degree and through other high quality programs, by contributing to knowledge of the legal order through the publication and other dissemination of scholarship, and by providing discipline-related public service. Students have access to federal, state, county, city, and local agencies, courts, correctional facilities, law firms, and legal aid organizations in the Minneapolis area. Facilities of special interest to law students consist of the clinic law office, 2 courtrooms, 24-hour library access, a Career and Professional Development Center, a bookstore, group study rooms, student publication and organization offices, café, and multiple lounge areas with an adjoining outdoor plaza. Housing for students is plentiful. Apartments, efficiencies, and housing near campus are available. All law school facilities are accessible to the physically disabled.

Calendar
The law school operates on a traditional semester basis. Courses for full-time students are offered days only and must be completed within 5 years. There is no part-time program. New students are admitted in the fall. There is an 8-week summer session. Transferable summer courses are offered.

Programs
In addition to the J.D., the law school offers the LL.M. Students may take relevant courses in other programs and apply credit toward the J.D.; a maximum of 6 credits may be applied. The following joint degrees may be earned: J.D./M.A. (Juris Doctor/Master of Arts), J.D./M.B.A (Juris Doctor/Master of Business Administration), J.D./M.B.S (Juris Doctor/Master of Biological Science), J.D./M.B.T. (Juris Doctor/Master of Business Tax), J.D./M.D. (Juris Doctor/Doctor of Medicine), J.D./M. Ed. (Juris Doctor/Master of Education), J.D./M.P.A. (Juris Doctor/Master of Public Affairs), J.D./M.P.H. (Juris Doctor/Master of Public Health), J.D./M.P.P. (Juris Doctor/Master of Public Policy), J.D./M.S. (Juris Doctor/Master of Science), J.D./M.U.R.P. (Juris Doctor/Master of Urban Regional Planning), and J.D./Ph.D. (Juris Doctor/Doctor of Philosophy).

Required
To earn the J.D., candidates must complete 88 total credits, of which 33 are for required courses. They must maintain a minimum GPA of 2.0 in the required courses. The following first-year courses are required of all students: Civil Procedure, Constitutional Law, Contracts, Criminal Law, Legal Research and Writing, Property, Statutory Interpretation, and Torts. Required upper-level courses consist of Professional Responsibility. Clinical courses are not required, but they are popular, with a 50% participation rate. The required orientation program

Phone: 612-625-3487
Fax: 612-626-1874
E-mail: jdadmissions@umn.edu
Web: www.law.umn.edu

Contact

Nick Wallace, Director of Admissions, 612-625-3487 for general inquiries; Office of Admissions, 612-625-3487 for financial aid information.

MINNESOTA

for first-year students consists of 2½ days in which the entering class is introduced to each other and the law school faculty and staff.

Electives

Students must take 12 credits in their area of concentration. The Law School offers concentrations in international law, labor law, litigation, health law, bioethics, human rights, labor and employment, and business law. In addition, second-and third-year students may enroll in 18 separate clinics in such areas as bankruptcy, child advocacy, and civil practice. Through these clinics, students receive academic credit while also providing more than 18,000 hours of pro bono legal assistance to low income individuals in the Twin Cities each year. More than 60 seminars, averaging 2 credits each, are available each year to upper-level students. The law school houses 10 research institutes: Human Rights Center, Institute on Race and Poverty, Kommerstad Center for Business Law and Entrepreneurship, Minnesota Center for Legal Studies, Institute for Law and Rationality, Institute for Law and Politics, Institute for Law and Economics, Institute for Crime and Public Policy, Institute on Intellectual Property, and Consortium on Law and Values in Health, Environment and Life Sciences. The Judicial Externship Program places students with local, federal, and state court judges. There is a variety of endowed lecture programs that bring special speakers to the law school each year. In addition, the Minnesota Supreme Court and the U.S. Court of Appeals for the Eighth Circuit preside over special hearings at the law school each year. Study abroad is available in France, Sweden, Germany, Ireland, the Netherlands, Uruguay, Italy, and Spain. A structured study group program is available to all first-year students. Student organizations include American Indian Law Student Association, Asian American Law Student Association, Black Law Students Association, Latino Law Students Alliance, and LAMBDA Law Students Association. The most widely taken electives are Business/Corporations, Tax, and Evidence.

Graduation Requirements

In order to graduate, candidates must have a GPA of 2.0 and have completed the upper-division writing requirement.

Organizations

Students edit the *Minnesota Law Review*, *Law and Inequality: A Journal of Theory and Practice*, *Minnesota Journal of Global Trade*, and the *Minnesota Intellectual Property Review*. Moot court competitions include Jessup International Law, Giles S. Rich Intellectual Property Moot Court, and the William McGee Civil Rights Moot Court. Other competitions include National Moot Court, Wagner Labor Law Moot Court, Environmental Law Moot Court, ABA Moot Court, and Maynard Pirsig Moot Court. Law student organizations, local chapters of national associations, and campus organizations include Law Council, Black Law Students Association, Student Intellectual Property Law Association, the ABA, National Lawyers Guild, and Federalist Society.

Library

The law library contains 1,083,918 hardcopy volumes and 366,973 microform volume equivalents, and subscribes to 11,015 serial publications. Such on-line databases and networks as CALI; CIS Universe, DIALOG; Infotrac, Legal-Trac, LEXIS; LOIS; NEXIS; OCLC First Search; RLIN; WESTLAW; Wilsonline Indexes; ALEPH, an on-line library catalog of University of Minnesota libraries; and Legi-Slate are available to law students for research. Special library collections include a U.S. documents depository as well as collections on the United Nations, European Community, and human rights; American Indian Law collection; Rare Books collection (especially early English and American law), Canon Law; and papers of Clarence Darrow. Recently, the library dedicated space for legal fiction collection, purchased new chairs for library reading room, and upgraded timed lights in library stacks. The ratio of library volumes to faculty is 16,423 to 1 and to students is 1275 to 1. The ratio of seats in the library to students is 1 to 1.

Faculty

The law school has 66 full-time and 121 part-time faculty members, of whom 87 are women. According to AAUP standards for Category I institutions, faculty salaries are average. About 42% of full-time faculty have a graduate law degree in addition to the J.D. The ratio of full-time students to full-time faculty in an average class is 11 to 1; in a clinic, 7 to 1. The law

Placement

J.D.s awarded:	255
Services available through: a separate law school placement center	
Special features: extensive career programming, an alumni networking program for students, and listings of employers by type, size, and city.	
Full-time job interviews:	405 employers
Summer job interviews:	405 employers
Placement by graduation:	87% of class
Placement within 9 months:	98% of class
Average starting salary:	$30,000 to $160,000
Areas of placement:	
Judicial clerkships	17%
Government	9%
Business/industry	6%
Public interest	4%
Military	2%
Private practice	60%

school has a regular program of bringing visiting professors and other distinguished lecturers and visitors to campus. There is a chapter of the Order of the Coif; 11 faculty are members.

Students

About 45% of the student body are women; 18%, minorities; 5%, African American; 7%, Asian American; 4%, Hispanic; and 1%, Native American. The majority of students come from Minnesota (42%). The average age of entering students is 25; age range is 21 to 41. About 89% of students enter directly from undergraduate school and 11% have a graduate degree. About 4% drop out after the first year for academic or personal reasons; 99% remain to receive a law degree.

L.Q.C. Lamar Hall

P.O. Box 1848 Lamar Law Center
University, MS 38677

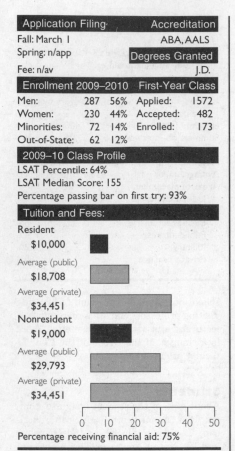

Application Filing	Accreditation
Fall: March 1	ABA, AALS
Spring: n/app	
	Degrees Granted
Fee: n/av	J.D.

Enrollment 2009–2010			First-Year Class	
Men:	287	56%	Applied:	1572
Women:	230	44%	Accepted:	482
Minorities:	72	14%	Enrolled:	173
Out-of-State:	62	12%		

2009–10 Class Profile
LSAT Percentile: 64%
LSAT Median Score: 155
Percentage passing bar on first try: 93%

Tuition and Fees:

Resident
$10,000

Average (public)
$18,708

Average (private)
$34,451

Nonresident
$19,000

Average (public)
$29,793

Average (private)
$34,451

0 10 20 30 40 50

Percentage receiving financial aid: 75%

ADMISSIONS

In the fall 2009 first-year class, 1572 applied, 482 were accepted, and 173 enrolled. Figures in the above capsule and in this profile are approximate. The median LSAT percentile of the most recent first-year class was 64; the median GPA was 3.59 on a scale of 4.0. The lowest LSAT percentile accepted was 15; the highest was 99.

Requirements
Applicants must have a bachelor's degree and take the LSAT. The most important admission factors include state or country of residence, LSAT results, and GPA. No specific undergraduate courses are required. Candidates are not interviewed.

Procedure
Applicants should submit an application form, LSAT results, transcripts, a personal statement, TOEFL for non-U.S. citizens whose native language is not English, a nonrefundable application fee,

and 2 letters of recommendation. Notification of the admissions decision is no later than April 15. The latest acceptable LSAT test date for fall entry is December. Check with the school for current application deadlines. The law school uses the LSDAS.

Special
The law school recruits minority and disadvantaged students by means of an extensive recruiting program aimed at historically black colleges and universities in Mississippi and in other states as well as participation in Law School Forums. Requirements are different for out-of-state students in that slightly higher credentials are required, and the percentage of nonresidents admitted is limited. Transfer students must have one year of credit and the law school from which the transfer is made must be both ABA and AALS accredited.

Costs

Tuition and fees for the 2009-2010 academic year are $10,000 for full-time in-state students and $19,000 for out-of-state students. Books and supplies run $1600.

Financial Aid

In a recent year, about 75% of current law students received some form of aid. The average annual amount of aid from all sources combined, including scholarships, loans, and work contracts, was $10,000; maximum, $18,500. Awards are based on need and merit. Required financial statements are the CSS Profile and the FAFSA. Check with the school for current application deadlines. Special funds for minority or disadvantaged students include tuition grants; some grants, based on both merit and need, exceed tuition. First-year students are notified about their financial aid application at time of acceptance.

About the Law School

University of Mississippi L.Q.C. Lamar Hall was established in 1854 and is a public institution. The 1900-acre campus is in a small town 80 miles southeast of Memphis, Tennessee. The primary mission of the law school is to provide a quality legal education that prepares graduates for the practice of law in the United States and for entry into government and public service or any profession in which

a legal education is a helpful or necessary background. Students have access to federal, state, county, city, and local agencies, courts, correctional facilities, law firms, and legal aid organizations in the University area. Housing for students is primarily off campus and is described as adequate and reasonably priced. All law school facilities are accessible to the physically disabled.

Calendar

The law school operates on a traditional semester basis. Courses for full-time students are offered days only. For part-time students, courses are offered and There is no part-time program. New students are admitted in the fall and summer. There is an 8-week summer session. Transferable summer courses are offered.

Programs

Students may take relevant courses in other programs and apply credit toward the J.D.; a maximum of 6 credits may be applied. The following joint degrees may be earned: J.D./M.A. (Juris Doctor/Master of Arts in taxation and in accounting) and J.D./M.B.A. (Juris Doctor/Master of Business Administration).

Required
To earn the J.D., candidates must complete 90 total credits, of which 36 to 37 are for required courses. The following first-year courses are required of all students: Civil Procedure I, Constitutional Law, Contracts, Criminal Law, Legal Research and Writing I and II, Property, and Torts. Required upper-level courses consist of Legal Profession and a skills/writing course. The required orientation program for first-year students is a 2-day program incorporating an introduction to the study of law, professionalism, analytical and case briefing skills, and exam-taking skills.

Electives
The L.Q.C. Lamar Hall offers concentrations in corporate law, criminal law, environmental law, family law, international law, juvenile law, labor law, litigation, tax law, and remote sensing and space law. In addition, the Civil Law Clinic, worth 4 credit hours, provides legal referral and assistance to indigent clients;

Phone: 662-915-6910
Fax: 662-915-1289
E-mail: *bvinson@olemiss.edu*
Web: *www.law.olemiss.edu*

Contact

Barbara Vinson/Director, Law Admissions, 662-915-6910 for general inquiries; Laura Diven-Brown, Director of Financial Aid, (662) 915-5633 for financial aid information.

MISSISSIPPI

also offered are the Criminal Appeals Clinic (4 hours credit), and Prosecutorial Externship (4 hours credit). Several seminars, including Constitutional Law, Bankruptcy Reorganization, and Family Law are offered. Public Service Internships, awarding up to 6 hours of pass/fail credit, are offered to senior students with more than 60 hours, a GPA of 2.2, and the permission of the Director. Law students work with judges, prosecuting attorneys, and public defenders under the Student Limited Practice Act. The Mississippi Law Research Institute, operated as an auxiliary program, offers students the opportunity to perform legal research. Students receive wages for their work but no law school credit. Field work opportunities are available. Special lectures include the Dunbar Lectures in Philosophy and the Law, the Currie lectures, which relate law, religion, and the behavioral sciences, and the McClure Memorial Lectures in Law. Upper-class students may take 6 hours in the study-abroad program in Cambridge, England, where various courses are offered. All first-year students may take advantage of a tutorial program in which upper-class students serve as teaching assistants. The program is under the direction of the Legal Writing Director. Minority programs consist of the Minority Tuition Scholarship Program and those offered through the Black Law Students Association (BLSA). There are various active special interest organizations. The most widely taken electives are Wills and Estates, Mississippi Civil Practice, and Corporations.

Graduation Requirements
In order to graduate, candidates must have a GPA of 2.0 and have completed the upper-division writing requirement.

Organizations

Student-edited publications include the *Mississippi Law Journal, Journal of Space Law, Mississippi Review of First Impressions*, and *The Advocate*, the School of Law yearbook. Moot court competitions include the Steen-Reynolds Competition in the fall semester and trial competitions and appellate competitions each semester. Other competitions include the National Moot Court, Douglass Moot Court, Student Trial, Craven Moot Court, Heidelberg, Woodliff Oral Advocacy, and Jessup International Law. Law student organiza-

tions, local chapters of national associations, and campus organizations include the Gorove Society of International Law, Law School Student Body Association, student divisions of ABA, Delta Theta Phi, and Phi Delta Phi, and other organizations such as Law Association for Women, Black Law Students Association, Environmental Law Society, and the American Constitution Society.

Library

The law library contains 336,487 hardcopy volumes and 172,860 microform volume equivalents, and subscribes to 2017 serial publications. Such on-line databases and networks as CALI, CIS Universe, DIALOG, Infotrac, Legal-Trac, LEXIS, LOIS, Mathew Bender, NEXIS, OCLC First Search, WESTLAW, mslawyer. com, HeinOnline, BNA Core Plus, CCH Business, Congressional Search, Disclosure, EBSCO host, IndexMaster, JSTOR, Social Science Research, and UM Online Database are available to law students for research. Special library collections include a depository of federal documents and a space law collection. The ratio of library volumes to faculty is 12,942 to 1 and to students is 651 to 1.

Faculty

The law school has 26 full-time and 16 part-time faculty members, of whom 15 are women. According to AAUP standards for Category I institutions, faculty salaries are well below average. About 12% of full-time faculty have a graduate law degree in addition to the J.D.; about 17% of part-time faculty have one. The ratio of full-time students to full-time faculty in an average class is 15 to 1; in a clinic, 7 to 1. The law school has a regular program of bringing visiting professors and other distinguished lecturers and visitors to campus. There is a chapter of the Order of the Coif; 9 faculty are members.

Students

About 44% of the student body are women; 14%, minorities; 11%, African American; 1%, Asian American; 1%, Hispanic; 1%, Native American; and 1%, multiracial. The majority of students come from Mississippi (88%). The average age of entering students is 23; age range is 21 to 44. About 75% of students enter directly from undergraduate school, 5% have a

Placement

J.D.s awarded:	153
Services available through: a separate law school placement center	
Services: a course in general practice offers insight into establishing a solo practice.	
Special features: personalized service based on the small student body.	
Full-time job interviews:	18 employers
Summer job interviews:	39 employers
Placement by graduation:	66% of class
Placement within 9 months:	93% of class
Average starting salary:	$28,000 to $100,000
Areas of placement:	
Private practice 2-10 attorneys	28%
Private practice 11-25 attorneys	5%
Private practice 26-50 attorneys	7%
Private practice 51-100 attorneys	8%
Private practice 101-250 attorneys	
4%; Private	11%
Judicial clerkships	18%
Government	10%
Business/industry	6%
Public interest	4%
Military	2%
Academic	2%

graduate degree, and 25% have worked full-time prior to entering law school. About 2% drop out after the first year for academic or personal reasons; 97% remain to receive a law degree.

School of Law

103 Hulston Hall
Columbia, MO 65211

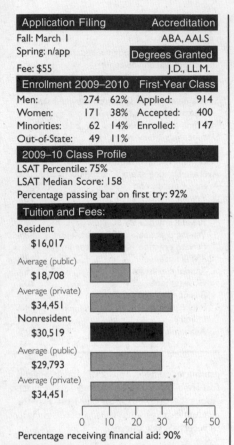

Application Filing		Accreditation	
Fall: March 1		ABA, AALS	
Spring: n/app		**Degrees Granted**	
Fee: $55		J.D., LL.M.	

Enrollment 2009–2010			First-Year Class	
Men:	274	62%	Applied:	914
Women:	171	38%	Accepted:	400
Minorities:	62	14%	Enrolled:	147
Out-of-State:	49	11%		

2009–10 Class Profile
LSAT Percentile: 75%
LSAT Median Score: 158
Percentage passing bar on first try: 92%

Tuition and Fees:

Resident
$16,017

Average (public)
$18,708

Average (private)
$34,451

Nonresident
$30,519

Average (public)
$29,793

Average (private)
$34,451

0   10   20   30   40   50

Percentage receiving financial aid: 90%

ADMISSIONS

In the fall 2009 first-year class, 914 applied, 400 were accepted, and 147 enrolled. Twenty-three transfers enrolled. The median LSAT percentile of the most recent first-year class was 75; the median GPA was 3.47 on a scale of 4.0.

Requirements
Applicants must have a bachelor's degree and take the LSAT. Minimum acceptable LSAT percentile is 27. The most important admission factors include LSAT results, GPA, and academic achievement. No specific undergraduate courses are required. Candidates are not interviewed.

Procedure
The application deadline for fall entry is March 1. Applicants should submit an application form, LSAT results, transcripts, a personal statement, a nonrefundable application fee of $55, and 2 letters of recommendation. For nonscholarship recipients, a first deposit of $250 is due on April 9; the second deposit of

$250 is due on May 7. For scholarship recipients, the full $500 deposit is due on April 9. The deposits are credited toward tuition. Notification of the admissions decision is on a rolling basis from October through April 10. The latest acceptable LSAT test date for fall entry is June. The law school uses the LSDAS.

Special
The law school recruits minority and disadvantaged students by attending LSAC forums, as well as graduate and career fairs at schools, including historically black colleges and universities. Requirements are not different for out-of-state students. Transfer students must have one year of credit, have attended an ABA-approved law school, and have a B average or better in their first-year law school classes.

Costs

Tuition and fees for the 2009-2010 academic year are $16,017 for full-time in-state students and $30,519 for out-of-state students. On-campus room and board costs about $8590 annually; books and supplies run $1550.

Financial Aid

About 90% of current law students receive some form of aid. The average annual amount of aid from all sources combined, including scholarships, loans, and work contracts, is $25,690; maximum, $41,000. Awards are based on need and merit. Required financial statement is the FAFSA. The aid application deadline for fall entry is March 1. Special funds for minority or disadvantaged students include need- and merit-based law school scholarships, ranging from $500 to full tuition. First-year students are notified about their financial aid application at time of acceptance, and will receive the award letter 6 to 8 weeks after completing the FAFSA.

About the Law School

University of Missouri-Columbia School of Law was established in 1872 and is a public institution. The 1348-acre campus is in a suburban area 125 miles west of St. Louis. The primary mission of the law school is to educate students about the fundamentals of legal reasoning and criti-

cal thinking, including the analysis and synthesis of court opinions, preparation and argument of cases, and the resolution of client problems and ethical issues that attorneys must face. Students have access to federal, state, county, city, and local agencies, courts, correctional facilities, law firms, and legal aid organizations in the Columbia area. Housing for students is available in on- and off-campus apartments and dormitories. All law school facilities are accessible to the physically disabled.

Calendar

The law school operates on a traditional semester basis. Courses for full-time students are offered days only. There is no part-time program. New students are admitted in the fall. There is a 7-week summer session. Transferable summer courses are offered.

Programs

In addition to the J.D., the law school offers the LL.M. Students may take relevant courses in other programs and apply credit toward the J.D.; a maximum of 3 to 6 credits may be applied. The following joint degrees may be earned: J.D./M.A. (Juris Doctor/Master of Arts in economics, journalism, and educational leadership and policy analysis), J.D./M.B.A. (Juris Doctor/Master of Business Administration), J.D./M.H.A. (Juris Doctor/Master of Health Administration), J.D./M.L.S. (Juris Doctor/Master of Library & Information Science), J.D./M.P.A. (Juris Doctor/Master of Public Affairs), J.D./M.S. (Juris Doctor/Master of Science in consumer and family), J.D./Ph.D. (Juris Doctor/Doctor of journalism, and J.D./M.A. or M.S. (Juris Doctor/Master of Arts or Master of Science in human development and family studies).

Required
To earn the J.D., candidates must complete 89 total credits, of which 45 are for required courses. They must maintain a minimum grade average of 70 in the required courses. The following first-year courses are required of all students: Advocacy and Research, Civil Procedure I and II, Contracts I and II, Criminal Law, Lawyering, Legal Research and Writing, Property, and Torts. Required upper-level courses consist of completion of a writing

Phone: 573-882-6042
888-685-2948
Fax: 573-882-9625
E-mail: *heckm@missouri.edu*
Web: *www.law.missouri.edu*

Contact

Michelle Heck, Admissions Representative, 573-882-6042 or 888-MULAW4U (685-2948) for general inquiries; Jeff Turnbull, Financial Aid Adviser, 573-882-1383 for financial aid information.

requirement, Constitutional Law, Criminal Procedure, Evidence, and Professional Responsibility. The required orientation program for first-year students is a 3 day program consisting of meetings with administration, faculty, and student organizations; learning rules and regulations; and learning to brief a case.

Electives

The School of Law offers concentrations in corporate law, criminal law, environmental law, family law, intellectual property law, international law, labor law, litigation, securities law, tax law, trial law, and alternative dispute resolution. In addition, the school offers a criminal clinic, a domestic violence clinic, a legislative clinic, a mediation clinic, and an Innocence Clinic. Internship programs are available to upper-level students who wish to experience the practice of civil and criminal law in various state and federal agencies; 3 credit hours are offered. Communication Law, Criminal Law, and Environmental Law seminars are open to upper-level students. Upper-level students may perform independent research for a faculty member and earn up to 3 credit hours. The main lecture series at the law school is the Nelson Lecture, in which noted national legal scholars deliver a major address. There are also annual lectures in dispute resolution and dispute resolution brown-bag lunches. The Professional Perspectives requirement is mandatory for all students. It is designed to enrich the law school experience. The School of Law participates in the London Law Consortium. A semester in the Bloomsbury district of London, in the winter semester, is available to second- and third-year law students in good standing. A summerabroad program in Capetown, South Africa, at the University of Western Cape is also offered. The school has a full-time academic counselor available to assist students with academic concerns. Remedial programs include Legal Reasoning. Scholarship funds are available; the law school is a supporting institution in CLEO and participates in the ABA-legal opportunity scholarship program. The most widely taken electives are Trial Practice, Family Law, and Secured Transactions.

Graduation Requirements

In order to graduate, candidates must have a grade average of 77.5 and have completed the upper-division writing requirement.

Organizations

Students edit the *Missouri Law Review*, the *Environmental Law and Policy Review*, and the *Journal of Dispute Resolution*. Moot court competitions include the Midwest Moot Court Competition, National Moot Court, and the ABA Moot Court. Other competitions are the Negotiation, Arbitration, Trial, Client Counseling, and First Year Moot Court. Student organizations, local chapters of national associations, and campus organizations include the Board of Advocates, the Student Bar Association, the Women's Law Association, Black Law Students Association, Non-Traditional Law Student Association, Intellectual Property and Entertainment Law, Phi Alpha Delta, the ABA-Law School Division, and the Association of Trial Lawyers of America.

Library

The law library contains 401,578 hardcopy volumes and 124,907 microform volume equivalents, and subscribes to 1755 serial publications. Such on-line databases and networks as CALI, DIALOG, LegalTrac, LEXIS, LOIS, OCLC First Search, WESTLAW, and Merlin are available to law students for research. Special library collections include U.S. and Missouri state documents and a 19 century criminal trial collection. Recently, the library added more carrel seating and the latest computer software. The ratio of library volumes to faculty is 18,254 to 1 and to students is 902 to 1. The ratio of seats in the library to students is 1 to 1.

Faculty

The law school has 22 full-time and 13 part-time faculty members, of whom 10 are women. According to AAUP standards for Category I institutions, faculty salaries are below average. The ratio of full-time students to full-time faculty in an average class is 18 to 1; in a clinic, 8 to 1. The law school has a regular program of bringing visiting professors and other distinguished lecturers and visitors to campus. There is a chapter of the Order of the Coif; 35 faculty and 15 graduates per year are members.

Placement

J.D.s awarded:	151

Services available through: a separate law school placement center, the university placement center, and Business and Public Administration Career Services

Services: access to electronic and hard-copy resume databases; counseling on professional development and career growth; and programming on law and lifestyles

Special features: individual counseling for each student, an active and successful judicial clerkship committee, and active alumni support

Full-time job interviews:	16 employers
Summer job interviews:	46 employers
Placement by graduation:	51% of class
Placement within 9 months:	88% of class
Average starting salary:	$30,000 to $160,000
Areas of placement:	
Private practice 2-10 attorneys	15%
Private practice 11-25 attorneys	6%
Private practice 26-50 attorneys	1%
Private practice 51-100 attorneys	3%
Private practice 100+ attorneys	30%
Government	14%
Judicial clerkships	13%
Business/industry	12%
Public interest	5%
Academic	2%

Students

About 38% of the student body are women; 14%, minorities; 7%, African American; 4%, Asian American; 2%, Hispanic; and 1%, Native American. The majority of students come from Missouri (89%). The average age of entering students is 25; age range is 21 to 37. About 75% of students enter directly from undergraduate school, 10% have a graduate degree, and 25% have worked full-time prior to entering law school. About 3% drop out after the first year for academic or personal reasons; 97% remain to receive a law degree.

School of Law

500 East 52nd Street
Kansas City, MO 64110-2499

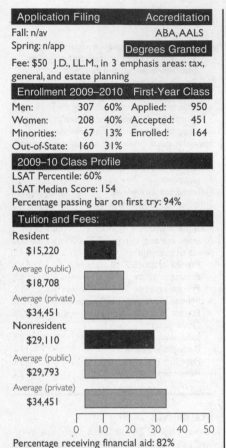

Application Filing	Accreditation
Fall: n/av	ABA, AALS
Spring: n/app	

Degrees Granted

Fee: $50 J.D., LL.M., in 3 emphasis areas: tax, general, and estate planning

Enrollment 2009–2010		First-Year Class	
Men:	307 60%	Applied:	950
Women:	208 40%	Accepted:	451
Minorities:	67 13%	Enrolled:	164
Out-of-State:	160 31%		

2009–10 Class Profile

LSAT Percentile: 60%

LSAT Median Score: 154

Percentage passing bar on first try: 94%

Tuition and Fees:

Resident
$15,220

Average (public)
$18,708

Average (private)
$34,451

Nonresident
$29,110

Average (public)
$29,793

Average (private)
$34,451

0 10 20 30 40 50

Percentage receiving financial aid: 82%

ADMISSIONS

In the fall 2009 first-year class, 950 applied, 451 were accepted, and 164 enrolled. Eleven transfers enrolled. The median LSAT percentile of the most recent first-year class was 60; the median GPA was 3.3 on a scale of 4.0. The lowest LSAT percentile accepted was 17; the highest was 96.

Requirements

Applicants must take the LSAT. Minimum acceptable GPA is 2.0 on a scale of 4.0. The most important admission factors include LSAT results, GPA, and academic achievement. No specific undergraduate courses are required. Candidates are interviewed.

Procedure

Applicants should submit an application form, LSAT results, transcripts, a personal statement, a nonrefundable application fee of $50, 2 letters of recommendation, and a $200 seat deposit. Notification of the admissions decision is on a rolling basis. The latest acceptable LSAT test date for fall entry is June. The law school uses the LSDAS.

Special

The law school recruits minority and disadvantaged students by means of minority recruitment, forums, personal letters, and telephone calls to potential applicants. Requirements are not different for out-of-state students. Transfer students must have 1 year of credit, have a minimum GPA of 2.3, and have attended an ABA-approved law school. Had the student not been admissible when applying for initial admission to the school, then a minimum GPA of 3.0 is required.

Costs

Tuition and fees for the 2009-2010 academic year are $15,220 for full-time in-state students and $29,110 for out-of-state students. Tuition for part-time students is $9230 in-state and $17,600 out-of-state. On-campus room and board costs about $10,467 annually; books and supplies run $4474.

Financial Aid

About 82% of current law students receive some form of aid. The average annual amount of aid from all sources combined, including scholarships, loans, and work contracts, is $30,449; maximum, $63,959. Awards are based on need and merit. Required financial statement is the FAFSA. Special funds for minority or disadvantaged students include scholarships and out-of-state tuition waivers. First-year students are notified about their financial aid application at time of acceptance.

About the Law School

University of Missouri-Kansas City School of Law was established in 1895 and is a public institution. The 93-acre campus is in an urban area in Kansas City. The primary mission of the law school is to prepare men and women for the general practice of law and for policy-forming functions in government, business, and organization community life, while providing a sound curriculum that offers a rigorous learning experience for students to obtain knowledge and skills in breadth and depth in an urban law school with a small liberal arts feel. Students have access to federal, state, county, city, and local agencies, courts, correctional facilities, law firms, and legal aid organizations in the Kansas City area. Clerkship opportunities are available in the numerous nearby law firms and government agencies. Facilities of special interest to law students include "virtual office" suites shared by faculty and students, designed to foster the exchange of ideas and promote collegiality between faculty and students. The school has more than 121,000 square feet of space, including the E.E. "Tom" Thompson Courtroom, which is equipped with audiovisual equipment, used to augment the advocacy training program of the school. Digital classrooms with wireless computer access enhance the learning experience for students. In addition, students have a spacious commons area, including an outdoor courtyard and a vending area. The Leon E. Bloch Law Library is a modern facility that combines the traditions of print with electronic media. Housing for students is limited on campus, while a large selection of housing is available off campus from private owners. About 95% of the law school facilities are accessible to the physically disabled.

Calendar

The law school operates on a traditional semester basis. Courses for full-time students are offered both day and evening and with most courses being offered during the day and must be completed within 5 years. For part-time students, courses are offered both day and evening with most courses being offered during the day and must be completed within 5 years. New full- and part-time students are admitted in the fall. There is a 7-week summer session. Transferable summer courses are offered.

Programs

In addition to the J.D., the law school offers the LL.M. in 3 emphasis areas: tax, general, and estate planning. Students may take relevant courses in other programs and apply credit toward the J.D.; a maximum of 10 credits may be applied. The following joint degrees may be earned: J.D./M.B.A. (Juris Doctor/Master of Business Administration) and J.D./M.P.A (Juris Doctor/Master of Public Administration).

Required

To earn the J.D., candidates must complete 91 total credits, of which 54 are for

Phone: 816-235-1644
Fax: 816-235-5276
E-mail: brooks@umkc.edu
Web: law.umkc.edu

Contact

Debbie Brooks, Associate Dean, 816-235-1672 for general inquiries; Linda Lawrence, Financial Aid Coordinator, 816-235-1236 for financial aid information.

MISSOURI

required courses. They must maintain a minimum GPA of 2.0 in the required courses. The following first-year courses are required of all students: Civil Procedure I, Constitutional Law, Contracts I and II, Criminal Law, Introduction to Law I and II, Property I and II, and Torts. Required upper-level courses consist of an advanced Torts course requirement, Business Organizations, Civil Procedure II, Criminal Procedure I, Evidence, Federal Taxation, Jurisprudence course requirement, Professional Responsibility, Research and Writing requirement, and U.C.C. course requirement. All students must take clinical courses. The required orientation program for first-year students is a 2-day program that introduces students to all aspects of law school, legal study, and registration and rules and includes discussion groups and lunch with faculty, and members of the local judiciary and bar.

Electives

Students must take 15 credits in their area of concentration. The School of Law offers concentrations in family law, international law, litigation, tax law, and business and entrepreneurial law; urban, land use, and environmental law; and estates and trust planning. In addition, in-house clinics from 2 to 6 credit hours include Child and Family Services, Tax, and Entrepreneurial Law and Practice. Seminars for 2 or 3 credit hours include Civil Rights Litigation, Gender and Justice, and Famous Trials. Internships from 2 to 6 credit hours include legal aid, public defender trial, and prosecutor and sports law. Research is conducted as part of the research and writing requirement for all students. Introduction to Law and Legal Processes, for 5 hours, requires all students to engage in research, case analysis, and synthesis, and Advanced Legal Writing, a 3-credit-hour course for upper-level students, focuses on drafting seminars in corporate law and litigation. Credit may be given for independent study/research projects conducted under faculty supervision, and which may include empirical studies/data gathering. The Cohen, Gage, and Smith Lecture Series bring national speakers to the Law School. Study abroad is possible in China, Ireland, and Wales. Structured study groups are offered in 1 substantive course in each first-year section. Trained upper-level study leaders model effective learning strategies and

assist in writing/synthesis skills. An academic enrichment program, focusing on analytical, organization, and exam-writing skills, also is offered. The Black Law Students Association, APILSA, and the National Hispanic Bar Association work closely with the Law School in offering educational and cultural programs that enhance cultural diversity and sensitivity. The Law School has more than 20 student groups in all interest areas that sponsor programs on a regular basis. The most widely taken electives are Family Law, Trial and Appellate Advocacy, Estates and Trusts, and Constitutional Law II.

Graduation Requirements

In order to graduate, candidates must have a GPA of 2.0, have completed the upper-division writing requirement, and the jurisprudential requirement, the advanced torts requirement, and the professional skills requirement.

Organizations

Students edit the *UMKC Law Review, Urban Lawyer*, and the *Journal of the American Academy of Matrimonial Lawyers*. Annual moot court competitions include the National Moot Court, Jessup International Law, and the National Appellate Advocacy Competition. Other competitions include the National Trial, Duberstein Bankruptcy Moot Court, Environmental Law, Frederick Douglass Moot Court, American Association for Justice Mock Trial, Client Counseling, and ABA Negotiation. Law student organizations include Public Interest Law Association, Business and Tax Society, and Environmental Law Society. Local chapters of national associations include Phi Alpha Delta, Theta Phi, Phi Delta Phi, and the Federalist Society.

Library

The law library contains 224,325 hardcopy volumes and 124,033 microform volume equivalents, and subscribes to 1889 serial publications. Such on-line databases and networks as CALI, CIS Universe, DIALOG, Infotrac, Legal-Trac, LEXIS, Mathew Bender, NEXIS, OCLC First Search, WESTLAW, Wilsonline Indexes, and OCLC Merlin, the library catalog of the 4 University of Missouri campuses, and INNOPAC for serials control and budgeting are available to law students for research. Special library collections

Placement

J.D.s awarded:	155
Services available through: a separate law school placement center	
Services: career services, e-job bulletins, and the career services library	
Special features: support and resources for students interested in solo and small firm practice	
Full-time job interviews:	5 employers
Summer job interviews:	29 employers
Placement by graduation:	44% of class
Placement within 9 months:	56% of class
Average starting salary:	$30,000 to $115,000
Areas of placement:	
Private practice 2-10 attorneys	22%
Private practice 11-25 attorneys	4%
Private practice 26-50 attorneys	2%
Government	16%
Judicial clerkships	11%
Military	8%
Business/industry	6%
Public interest	5%
Academic	1%

include a depository for federal, Missouri, and Kansas documents, an urban law collection, and a tax law concentration. Recently, the library added a reading room area, and 3 study group rooms. The ratio of library volumes to faculty is 6798 to 1 and to students is 436 to 1. The ratio of seats in the library to students is 1 to 1.

Faculty

The law school has 33 full-time and 41 part-time faculty members, of whom 22 are women. According to AAUP standards for Category I institutions, faculty salaries are well below average. The ratio of full-time students to full-time faculty in an average class is 14 to 1. The law school has a regular program of bringing visiting professors and other distinguished lecturers and visitors to campus.

Students

About 40% of the student body are women; 13%, minorities; 6%, African American; 3%, Asian American; 3%, Hispanic; 1%, Native American; and 1%, foreign national. The majority of students come from the Midwest (92%). The average age of entering students is 25; age range is 21 to 49. About 8% of students have a graduate degree. About 13% drop out after the first year for academic or personal reasons; 77% remain to receive a law degree.

School of Law

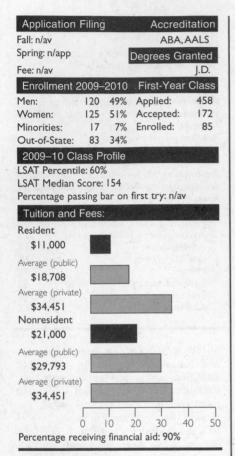

Application Filing	Accreditation
Fall: n/av	ABA, AALS
Spring: n/app	Degrees Granted
Fee: n/av	J.D.

Enrollment 2009–2010		First-Year Class	
Men:	120 49%	Applied:	458
Women:	125 51%	Accepted:	172
Minorities:	17 7%	Enrolled:	85
Out-of-State:	83 34%		

2009–10 Class Profile
LSAT Percentile: 60%
LSAT Median Score: 154
Percentage passing bar on first try: n/av

Tuition and Fees:

Resident
$11,000

Average (public)
$18,708

Average (private)
$34,451

Nonresident
$21,000

Average (public)
$29,793

Average (private)
$34,451

0   10   20   30   40   50

Percentage receiving financial aid: 90%

ADMISSIONS

In the fall 2009 first-year class, 458 applied, 172 were accepted, and 85 enrolled. Figures in the above capsule and in this profile are approximate. One transfer enrolled. The median LSAT percentile of the most recent first-year class was 60; the median GPA was 3.41 on a scale of 4.0. The lowest LSAT percentile accepted was 9; the highest was 95.

Requirements
Applicants must have a bachelor's degree and take the LSAT. The most important admission factors include LSAT results, life experience, and academic achievement. No specific undergraduate courses are required. Candidates are not interviewed.

Procedure
Applicants should submit an application form, LSAT results, transcripts, TOEFL for foreign applicants, a nonrefundable application fee, 3 letters of recommenda-

tion, and personal statements. Notification of the admissions decision is from October to April. Check with the school for current appication deadlines. The law school uses the LSDAS.

Special
The law school recruits minority and disadvantaged students by means of special recruiting efforts aimed at Native American and other minority students. Requirements are not different for out-of-state students. Transfer students must have one year of credit.

Costs

Tuition and fees for the 2009-2010 academic year are $11,000 for full-time in-state students and $21,000 for out-of-state students. On-campus room and board costs about $10,000 annually; books and supplies run $1100.

Financial Aid

In a recent year, about 90% of current law students received some form of aid. The average annual amount of aid from all sources combined, including scholarships, loans, and work contracts, was $14,254; maximum, $18,500. Awards are based on need and merit. Required financial statement is the FAFSA. Check with the school for current application deadlines. Special funds for minority or disadvantaged students include Native American fee waivers and scholarships. First-year students are notified about their financial aid application at a time determined by the University Financial Aid Office.

About the Law School

University of Montana School of Law was established in 1911 and is a public institution. The campus is in the small town of Missoula, Montana. The primary mission of the law school is to teach a competency-based curriculum. Legal writing, trial practice, and clinical programs require students to demonstrate their abilities to apply highly technical legal knowledge to practical situations. Students have access to federal, state, county, city, and local agencies, courts, correctional facilities, law firms, and legal aid organizations in the Missoula area. Students in clinics benefit from natural resource groups and Native American tribal courts and govern-

ments. Facilities of special interest to law students include a computerized courtroom facility and first-year moot "law firms." Housing for students is available for students in university housing; apartments and houses are available for rent in the community. All law school facilities are accessible to the physically disabled.

Calendar

The law school operates on a traditional semester basis. Courses for full-time students are offered days only and must be completed within 3 years. There is no part-time program. New students are admitted in the fall. There is a 6-week summer session. Transferable summer courses are offered.

Programs

Students may take relevant courses in other programs and apply credit toward the J.D. The following joint degrees may be earned: J.D./M.B.A. (Juris Doctor/Master of Business Administration), J.D./M.P.A. (Juris Doctor/Master of Public Administration), and J.D./M.S. (Juris Doctor/Master of Science in environmental studies).

Required
To earn the J.D., candidates must complete 90 total credits, of which 56 are for required courses. They must maintain a minimum GPA of 2.0 in the required courses. The following first-year courses are required of all students: Civil Procedure I and II, Contracts I and II, Criminal Law and Procedure I and II, Legal Research and Analysis, Legal Writing I, Pre-Trial Advocacy I and II, and Torts I and II. Required upper-level courses consist of an advanced writing component, Business Organizations, Business Transactions, clinical training, Constitutional Law, Evidence, Federal Tax, Professional Responsibility, Property I and II, and Trial Practice. All students must take clinical courses. The required orientation program for first-year students is 7 days and includes concepts of jurisprudence, the role of lawyers in society, legal history, and other topics.

Electives
The School of Law offers concentrations in corporate law, criminal law, environmental law, family law, labor law, litigation,

Phone: 406-243-2698
Fax: 406-243-2576
E-mail: *heidi.fanslow@umontana.edu*
Web: *http://www.umt.edu/law*

Contact
Heidi Fanslow, Director of Admissions, 406-243-2698 for general inquiries; Connie Bowman, 406-243-5524 for financial aid information.

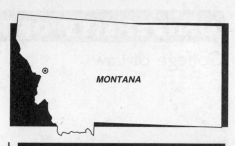

MONTANA

tax law, torts and insurance, and Indian law. In addition, clinics, field work, and internships include the Criminal Defense Clinic, Montana Legal Services, and Natural Resource Clinic for 1 to 4 credit hours for third-year students. Seminars include Contemporary Problems in Constitutional Law, Problems in Estate Planning, and Problems in Indian Law Regulation for 2 credit hours each, open to second- and third-year students. Independent study programs designed by law students and professors for 1 to 2 credit hours for third-year students and periodic law reform projects for second- and third-year students, for no credit hours, are available. Special lectures include the Blankenbaker Lecture in Ethics and the Judge William B. Jones and Judge Edward A. Tamm Judicial Lecture Series. Tutorial programs include the Academic Assistance Program. Minority programs are sponsored by the Native American Law Students Association. Periodic programs are offered by the Federalist Society, Women's Law Caucus, Phi Delta Phi, Student Bar Association, and 8 other student groups. The most widely taken electives are Family Law, Environmental Law, and Real Estate Transactions.

Graduation Requirements
In order to graduate, candidates must have a GPA of 2.0 and have completed the upper-division writing requirement.

Organizations
Students edit the *Montana Law Review* and the *Public Land and Resource Law Review*. Moot court competitions include National Moot Court Team, NALSA Moot Court Team, Pace Environmental Moot Court Team, and International Law Moot Court Team (Jessup). Other competitions include ATLA Trial Team, ABA Negotiations Team, and ABA Client Counseling Team. Student organizations include the Student Bar Association, Phi Delta Phi, and Women's Law Caucus. Local chapters of national organizations include American Trial Lawyers and ACLU.

Library
The law library contains 123,661 hardcopy volumes and 134,480 microform volume equivalents, and subscribes to 1250 serial publications. Such on-line databases and networks as LEXIS, OCLC First

Search, WESTLAW, Wilsonline Indexes, MontLaw, HeinOnline, and Law Library microfiche Consortium are available to law students for research. Recently, the library was made completely wireless, added an IT Department, 2 full-time employess, electronic reserver, and video conferencing. The ratio of library volumes to faculty is 5620 to 1 and to students is 522 to 1. The ratio of seats in the library to students is 1 to 2.

Faculty
The law school has 22 full-time and 21 part-time faculty members, of whom 14 are women. According to AAUP standards for Category I institutions, faculty salaries are well below average. About 43% of full-time faculty have a graduate law degree in addition to the J.D.; about 27% of part-time faculty have one. The ratio of full-time students to full-time faculty in an average class is 19 to 1; in a clinic, 10 to 1. The law school has a regular program of bringing visiting professors and other distinguished lecturers and visitors to campus.

Students
About 51% of the student body are women; 7%, minorities; 1%, Asian American; and 5%, Native American. The majority of students come from Montana (66%). The average age of entering students is 27; age range is 21 to 54. About 22% of students enter directly from undergraduate school, 5% have a graduate degree, and 60% have worked full-time prior to entering law school.

Placement

J.D.s awarded:	n/av
Services available through: a separate law school placement center	
Special features: semiannual on-campus recruitment conferences.	
Full-time job interviews:	40 employers
Summer job interviews:	n/av
Placement by graduation:	n/av
Placement within 9 months:	90% of class
Average starting salary:	$33,750
Areas of placement:	
Private practice 2-10 attorneys	39%
Judicial clerkships	24%
Government	10%
Business/industry	9%
Advanced Degree Program	14%
Unknown	3%
Academic	1%

UNIVERSITY OF NEBRASKA-LINCOLN

College of Law

P.O. Box 830902
Lincoln, NE 68583-0902

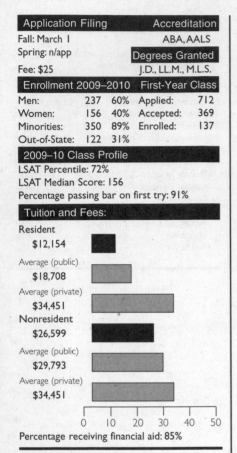

Application Filing	Accreditation
Fall: March I	ABA, AALS
Spring: n/app	**Degrees Granted**
Fee: $25	J.D., LL.M., M.L.S.

Enrollment 2009–2010		First-Year Class	
Men:	237 60%	Applied:	712
Women:	156 40%	Accepted:	369
Minorities:	350 89%	Enrolled:	137
Out-of-State:	122 31%		

2009–10 Class Profile
LSAT Percentile: 72%
LSAT Median Score: 156
Percentage passing bar on first try: 91%

Tuition and Fees:

Resident
$12,154

Average (public)
$18,708

Average (private)
$34,451

Nonresident
$26,599

Average (public)
$29,793

Average (private)
$34,451

0   10   20   30   40   50

Percentage receiving financial aid: 85%

ADMISSIONS

In the fall 2009 first-year class, 712 applied, 369 were accepted, and 137 enrolled. Three transfers enrolled. The median LSAT percentile of the most recent first-year class was 72; the median GPA was 3.55 on a scale of 4.0. The lowest LSAT percentile accepted was 44; the highest was 98.

Requirements
Applicants must have a bachelor's degree (unless they are applying under the 3/3 combined program) and take the LSAT. The most important admission factors include LSAT results, GPA, and academic achievement. No specific undergraduate courses are required. Candidates are not interviewed.

Procedure
The application deadline for fall entry is March 1. Applicants should submit an application form, LSAT results, transcripts, a personal statement, a nonre-

fundable application fee of $25, and 2 recommended letters of recommendation. Notification of the admissions decision is on a rolling basis after January 1. The latest acceptable LSAT test date for fall entry is February. The law school uses the LSDAS.

Special
The law school recruits minority and disadvantaged students by sponsoring and attending events to promote the College of Law. Requirements are not different for out-of-state students. Transfer students must have one year of credit, have attended an ABA-approved law school, and must be in good standing at the end of a full year of study and eligible to continue at their current law school. Other requirements may apply.

Costs

Tuition and fees for the 2009-2010 academic year are $12,154 for full-time in-state students and $26,599 for out-of-state students. On-campus room and board costs about $8430 annually; books and supplies run $1340.

Financial Aid

About 85% of current law students receive some form of aid. The average annual amount of aid from all sources combined, including scholarships, loans, and work contracts, is $18,027; maximum, $22,000. Awards are based on need and merit. Required financial statements are the FAFSA and institutional need-based grant form. The aid application deadline for fall entry is May 1. Special funds for minority or disadvantaged students include college funds for need-based grants and opportunity scholarships. First-year students are notified about their financial aid application from January to April for scholarships and grants and March through August for loans.

About the Law School

University of Nebraska-Lincoln College of Law was established in 1888 and is a public institution. The 339-acre campus is in a suburban area on the east campus of the University of Nebraska. The primary mission of the law school is to provide an excellent, affordable legal education with a balance between legal theory and

professional skills in the atmosphere of a small law school. Students have access to federal, state, county, city, and local agencies, courts, correctional facilities, law firms, and legal aid organizations in the Lincoln area. As Lincoln is the state capital, the legislature, the State Supreme Court, and the Court of Appeals are nearby. Facilities of special interest to law students include 3 clinical programs: the civil clinic and immigration clinics are located at the college, providing civil legal services and immigration assistance to low income clients. The other clinic is located within the Lancaster County Attorney's Office, permitting third-year students to prosecute misdemeanor and some felony cases. The federal and state appellate courts frequently hear cases at the college. The Shermon S. Welpton, Jr. courtroom is used for actual trials as well as practical skills training. Housing for students is available as on-campus graduate housing-on-campus family housing, and off-campus apartments and homes. All law school facilities are accessible to the physically disabled.

Calendar

The law school operates on a traditional semester basis. Courses for full-time students are offered days only and must be completed within 2 1/2 to 3 years. There is no part-time program. New students are admitted in the fall. There are 2-5-week summer sessions. Transferable summer courses are offered.

Programs

In addition to the J.D., the law school offers the M.L.S. (Master of Legal Studies) and LL.M. in Space and Telecommunications Law. Students may take relevant courses in other programs and apply credit toward the J.D.; a maximum of 6 nonlaw graduate credit credits in non-joint degree programs may be applied. The following joint degrees may be earned: J.D./M.A. (Juris Doctor/Master of Arts in psychology, economics, political science, journalism), J.D./M.B.A. (Juris Doctor/Master of Business Administration), J.D./M.C.R.P. (Juris Doctor/Master of Community and Regional Planning), J.D./M.P.A. (Juris Doctor/Master of Professional Accountancy), and J.D./Ph.D (Juris Doctor/Doctor of Philosophy in psychology or education).

Phone: 402-472-2161
Fax: 402-472-5185
E-mail: *lawadm@unl.edu*
Web: *http://law.unl.edu*

Contact
Glenda J. Pierce, Associate Dean, 402-472-2161 for general inquiries and financial aid information.

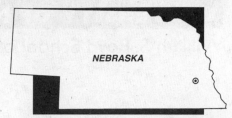

NEBRASKA

Required

To earn the J.D., candidates must complete 93 total credits, of which 45 are for required courses. They must maintain a minimum GPA of 4.0 (average) in the required courses. The following first-year courses are required of all students: Civil Procedure, Contracts, Criminal Law, Legal Research and Writing, Property, and Torts. Required upper-level courses consist of a professional skills course, a seminar with substantial writing requirements, Constitutional Law I, and Legal Profession. The required orientation program for first-year students is 2 days prior to the beginning of the fall semester. Students listen to speakers, tour the college, meet faculty and upper-level students, and attend a legal writing class. Students also participate in an orientation on professionalism and ethics with judges and attorneys.

Electives

Students must take 15 or more credits depending on their area of concentration. The College of Law offers concentrations in corporate law, criminal law, entertainment law, environmental law, family law, international law, juvenile law, labor law, litigation, securities law, sports law, tax law, torts and insurance. However, students may design an individualized program of concentrated study in virtually any area. In addition, students who have obtained senior standing are eligible to take either a 6-credit hour civil or criminal clinic, 4-credit hour civil clinic, or 6-credit hour immigration clinic. Second- or third-year students must take a 3-credit-hour seminar with a substantial writing requirement. Externships are available for 1 to 3 credit hours. A 1 to 3-credit-hour research program in a selected field under the supervision of a faculty member is available to any upper-level student. Students may take a maximum of 6 credit hours. With the approval of a sponsoring faculty member, students may register for 1 to 3 credit hours of externship credit to be earned in a field placement program. Each exterhsip shall involve at least 40 credit hours of field experience for every credit hour earned. Special lecture series include many national and international speakers for no credit. The Academic Resource Program offers a non-credit skills class for first-year students to assist in developing such skills as note taking,

case briefing, and exam taking. The most widely taken electives are Corporations, Evidence, and Wills and Trusts.

Graduation Requirements

In order to graduate, candidates must have a GPA of 4.0 on a scale of 9.0, have completed the upper-division writing requirement, and have taken a Legal Professional Responsibility course, Constitutional Law I, and a Professional Skills course, and have completed 93 credit hours.

Organizations
Students edit the *Nebraska Law Review* and an on-line Nebraska Law Review Bulletin. Moot court competitions include the Fall Grether Moot Court Competition for second-year students, Allen Moot Court Competition, and the Animal Law Competition. Other competitions include Client Counseling and National Trial. Student organizations include the Student Bar Association, Women's Law Caucus, and Community Legal Education Project. Delta Theta Phi, ABA-Law Student Division, and Phi Alpha Delta have local chapters. Other organizations include the Multi-Cultural Legal Society, Environmental and Agriculture Law Society, and Equal Justice Society.

Library
The law library contains 243,206 hardcopy volumes and 175,351 microform volume equivalents, and subscribes to 2571 serial publications. Such on-line databases and networks as CALI, CIS Universe, DIALOG, Infotrac, Legal-Trac, LEXIS, Mathew Bender, NEXIS, OCLC First Search, WESTLAW, Wilsonline Indexes, and Expanded Academic Index Full Text are available to law students for research. Special library collections include a selected federal government depository and the Great Plains Tax Library. Recently, the library completed a $9 million renovation and addition to the library. The ratio of library volumes to faculty is 6756 to 1 and to students is 619 to 1. The ratio of seats in the library to students is 1 to 1.

Faculty
The law school has 36 full-time and 23 part-time faculty members, of whom 19 are women. According to AAUP standards for Category I institutions, faculty salaries

Placement

J.D.s awarded:	134
Services available through: a separate law school placement center	
Special features: video conferencing capabilities, free newly renovated interview facilities.	
Full-time job interviews:	28 employers
Summer job interviews:	35 employers
Placement by graduation:	n/av
Placement within 9 months:	93% of class
Average starting salary:	$24,000 to $115,000
Areas of placement:	
Private Practice	41%
Government	23%
Business/industry	15%
Judicial clerkships	11%
Public interest	4%
Academic	4%
Military	3%

are below average. About 21% of full-time faculty have a graduate law degree in addition to the J.D. The ratio of full-time students to full-time faculty in an average class is 20 to 1; in a clinic, 12 to 1. The law school has a regular program of bringing visiting professors and other distinguished lecturers and visitors to campus. There is a chapter of the Order of the Coif; 10 faculty and 699 graduates are members.

Students
About 40% of the student body are women; 89%, minorities; 3%, African American; 2%, Asian American; 2%, Hispanic; and 1%, Native American. The majority of students come from the Midwest (82%). The average age of entering students is 24; age range is 20 to 41. About 55% of students enter directly from undergraduate school, 6% have a graduate degree, and 43% have worked full-time prior to entering law school. About 6% drop out after the first year for academic or personal reasons; 94% remain to receive a law degree.

William S. Boyd School of Law

4505 Maryland Parkway, Box 451003
Las Vegas, NV 89154-1003

Application Filing		Accreditation	
Fall: March 15		ABA, AALS	
Spring: n/app		**Degrees Granted**	
Fee: $50			J.D.

Enrollment 2009–2010		First-Year Class	
Men:	261 53%	Applied:	1737
Women:	227 47%	Accepted:	384
Minorities:	142 29%	Enrolled:	158
Out-of-State:	102 21%		

2009–10 Class Profile
LSAT Percentile: n/av
LSAT Median Score: 158
Percentage passing bar on first try: 85%

Tuition and Fees:

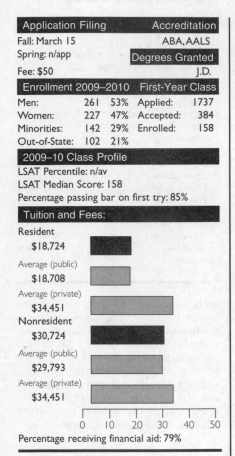

Resident
$18,724

Average (public)
$18,708

Average (private)
$34,451

Nonresident
$30,724

Average (public)
$29,793

Average (private)
$34,451

0   10   20   30   40   50

Percentage receiving financial aid: 79%

ADMISSIONS
In the fall 2009 first-year class, 1737 applied, 384 were accepted, and 158 enrolled. Nineteen transfers enrolled. The median GPA of the most recent first-year class was 3.48.

Requirements
Applicants must have a bachelor's degree and take the LSAT. No specific undergraduate courses are required. Candidates are not interviewed.

Procedure
The application deadline for fall entry is March 15. Applicants should submit an application form, LSAT results, transcripts, a personal statement, a nonrefundable application fee of $50, 1 letter of recommendation, and a résumé. Notification of the admissions decision is generally April. The latest acceptable LSAT test date for fall entry is February. The law school uses the LSDAS.

Special
The law school recruits minority and disadvantaged students through outreach to various individuals and community organizations to generate a large and diverse applicant pool. Requirements are not different for out-of-state students. Transfer students must have one year of credit, have attended an ABA-approved law school, and have admissions committee review.

Costs
Tuition and fees for the 2009-2010 academic year are $18,724 for full-time in-state students and $30,724 for out-of-state students. Books and supplies run $1700.

Financial Aid
About 79% of current law students receive some form of aid. The maximum annual amount of aid from all sources combined, including scholarships, loans, and work contracts, is $34,860. Awards are based on need and merit. Required financial statement is the FAFSA. The aid application deadline for fall entry is February 1. First-year students are notified about their financial aid application at on a rolling basis.

About the Law School
University of Nevada, Las Vegas William S. Boyd School of Law was established in 1998 and is a public institution. The 335-acre campus is in an urban area in one of the fastest growing metropolitan areas. The primary mission of the law school is to serve the State of Nevada and the national international legal and academic communities through an innovative educational program that will train ethical and effective lawyers and leaders, and to stress community service and excellent scholarship. Students have access to federal, state, county, city, and local agencies, courts, correctional facilities, law firms, and legal aid organizations in the Las Vegas area. Facilities of special interest to law students include the Thomas and Mack Moot Court Facility that supports the school's trial advocacy, Kids' Court, and appellate advocacy programs and provides a venue for judicial proceedings by state and federal courts, including the Nevada Supreme Court and the U.S. Court of Appeals for the Ninth Circuit. Housing for students is not available on

campus, but is abundantly available off campus. All law school facilities are accessible to the physically disabled.

Calendar
The law school operates on a traditional semester basis. Courses for full-time students are offered both day and evening and must be completed within 5 years. For part-time students, courses are offered both day and evening and must be completed within 6 years. New full- and part-time students are admitted in the fall. There is a 10-week summer session. Transferable summer courses are offered.

Programs
Students may take relevant courses in other programs and apply credit toward the J.D.; a maximum of 6 credits may be applied. The following joint degrees may be earned: J.D./M.B.A. (Juris Doctor/Master of Business Administration), J.D./M.S.W. (Juris Doctor/Master of Social Work), and J.D./PH.D (Juris Doctor/Doctor of Philosophy in education).

Required
To earn the J.D., candidates must complete 89 total credits, of which 41 are for required courses. The following first-year courses are required of all students: Civil Procedure/Alternative Dispute Resolution I and II, Constitutional Law I, Contracts I, Criminal Law I, Introduction to Law, Lawyering Process I and II, Property I and II, and Torts. Required upper-level courses consist of Constitutional Law II, Lawyering Process III, and Professional Responsibility. The required orientation program for first-year students is introduction to Law, a 1-week course.

Electives
The Capital Defense Clinic, Child Welfare Clinic, and Immigration Clinic, worth 1 to 6 credits each, afford students the opportunity to represent clients in real-life settings, under faculty supervision. Each clinic also has a classroom component. In the Child Welfare Clinic, students represent children, parents, or guardians in child protection, termination of parental rights, guardianship, and related matters that involve contested trials, administrative advocacy and sometimes cutting edge legal issues. In the Juvenile Justice

Phone: 702-895-2440
Fax: 702-895-2414
E-mail: request@law.unlv.edu
Web: www.law.unlv.edu

Contact

Nathan Neely, Director of Admissions and Financial Aid, 702-895-2440 for general inquiries; Christopher Kypunos, Associate Director, 702-895-3424 for financial aid information.

NEVADA

Clinic, students represent children who have been charged in juvenile delinquency proceedings. In the Capital Defense Clinic, students represent defendants in Nevada death penalty cases, focusing primarily on preparing mitigating evidence and argument, the legal case for a sentence less than death. In the Immigration Clinic, students represent clients in a variety of matters involving immigration and immigrant rights. In the Education Clinic, students represent children and parents in education matters in the Clark County School System, such as special education, suspension, expulsion, and English as a Second Language. In the Criminal Appellate Clinic, students represent young convicted criminal defendants in state post-conviction appellate proceedings. Seminars include Bill of Rights in Law and History, Education Law and Policy, Natural Resources Field Seminar, Domestic Violence, Advanced Intellectual Practice, Death Penalty, and Gaming Policy Law. Government and Public Interest Externship, worth 1 to 12 credits; Judicial Externship, worth 3 to 6 credits; and Legislative Externship, worth 1 to 12 credits are also offered. Research programs include Directed Readings, where students earn credit for completing readings under the supervision and approval of a faculty member for 1 credit, or Directed Research, where they research and write about a legal topic of their choice under faculty supervision, for 1 to 3 credits. The law school provides an Academic Success Program, a comprehensive network of presentations, activities, tutorials, and workshops designed to stimulate learning and amplify the classroom experience. This program, which supplements the required curriculum, supervises the Center for Academic Success and Enrichment, a student-operated mentoring, advising, and tutoring program. The most widely taken electives are Evidence; Criminal Procedure; and Wills, Trusts, and Estates.

Graduation Requirements

In order to graduate, candidates must have a GPA of 2.0, have completed the upper-division writing requirement, and have completed community service and writing requirements.

Organizations

Students edit the *Nevada Law Journal.* Moot Court Competitions include the ABA-LSD National Appellate Advocacy, Jessup International Law Moot Court Competition, and Bar Association of the City of New York National Moot Court Competition. Other competitions include the ABA-LSD Negotiation Competition, Clark County Client Counseling Competition, and Clark County Moot Court Competition. Law student organizations include the American Constitution Society, Federalist Society, and Phi Alpha Delta. Local chapters of national associations include the Student Bar Association, Minority Law Students Association, and Public Interest Law Association. Other organizations include the Environmental Law Society, Sports and Entertainment Law Association and Organizations of Woman Law Students.

Library

The law library contains 330,808 hardcopy volumes and 198,454 microform volume equivalents, and subscribes to 3870 serial publications. Such on-line databases and networks as CALI, Infotrac, Legal-Trac, LEXIS, LOIS, Mathew Bender, NEXIS, OCLC First Search, and WESTLAW are available to law students for research. The ratio of library volumes to faculty is 4411 to 1 and to students is 678 to 1. The ratio of seats in the library to students is 1 to 1.

Faculty

The law school has 52 full-time and 23 part-time faculty members, of whom 32 are women. According to AAUP standards for Category I institutions, faculty salaries are average. About 19% of full-time faculty have a graduate law degree in addition to the J.D. The ratio of full-time students to full-time faculty in an average class is 14 to 1; in a clinic, 8 to 1. The law school has a regular program of bringing visiting professors and other distinguished lecturers and visitors to campus.

Students

About 47% of the student body are women; 29%, minorities; 6%, African American; 11%, Asian American; 10%, Hispanic; and 2%, Native American. The majority of students come from Nevada (79%). The average age of entering students is 27; age range is 21 to 73.

Placement

J.D.s awarded:	145

Services available through: a separate law school placement center

Services: Utilizes web-based recruiting and placement software program accessible 24 hours a day to students and employers; maintains Career Services Library and Resource Center; maintains judicial clerkship resource manual pertaining to hiring practices of the Nevada and federal judiciary.

Full-time job interviews:	8 employers
Summer job interviews:	35 employers
Placement by graduation:	78% of class
Placement within 9 months:	94% of class
Average starting salary:	$56,000 to $87,500

Areas of placement:

Private practice 2-25 attorneys	33%
Private practice 26-100 attorneys	6%
Private practice 100+attorneys	3%
Private practice 51-100 attorneys	13%
Private practice solo	2%
Judicial clerkships	16%
Business/industry	12%
Government	8%
Public interest	4%
Military	2%
Academic	2%

UNIVERSITY OF NEW MEXICO

School of Law

MSC11-6070, 1
University of New Mexico
Albuquerque, NM 87131-0001

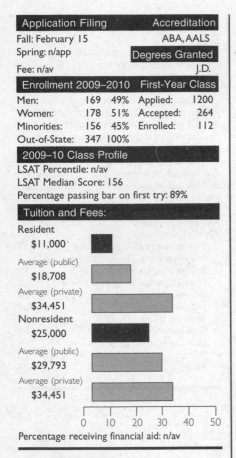

Application Filing		Accreditation
Fall: February 15		ABA, AALS
Spring: n/app		**Degrees Granted**
Fee: n/av		J.D.

Enrollment 2009–2010		First-Year Class	
Men:	169 49%	Applied:	1200
Women:	178 51%	Accepted:	264
Minorities:	156 45%	Enrolled:	112
Out-of-State:	347 100%		

2009–10 Class Profile
LSAT Percentile: n/av
LSAT Median Score: 156
Percentage passing bar on first try: 89%

Tuition and Fees:

Resident
$11,000

Average (public)
$18,708

Average (private)
$34,451

Nonresident
$25,000

Average (public)
$29,793

Average (private)
$34,451

0 10 20 30 40 50

Percentage receiving financial aid: n/av

ADMISSIONS
In the fall 2009 first-year class, 1200 applied, 264 were accepted, and 112 enrolled. Figures in the above capsule and in this profile are approximate. Six transfers enrolled. The median GPA of the most recent first-year class was 3.36.

Requirements
Applicants must have a bachelor's degree and take the LSAT. No specific undergraduate courses are required. Candidates are not interviewed.

Procedure
Applicants should submit an application form, a personal statement, a nonrefundable application fee, 1 letter of recommendation, LSDAS report, and a resumé. Notification of the admissions decision is on a rolling basis. The latest acceptable LSAT test date for fall entry is December (preferred). Check with the school for current application deadlines. The law school uses the LSDAS.

Special
Requirements are not different for out-of-state students. Transfer students must have one year of credit, have attended an ABA-approved law school, and have a letter from the dean of the previously attended school. The applicant must be in good academic standing.

Costs
Tuition and fees for the 2009-2010 academic year are $11,000 for full-time in-state students and $25,000 for out-of-state students. On-campus room and board costs about $7000 annually; books and supplies run $1100.

Financial Aid
Awards are based on need and merit. Required financial statements are the FAFSA and Need Access. Check with the school for current application deadlines. Special funds for minority or disadvantaged students include graduate fellowships, available through the Office of Graduate Studies. First-year students are notified about their financial aid application after acceptance.

About the Law School
University of New Mexico School of Law was established in 1947 and is a public institution. The 600-acre campus is in an urban area in the city of Albuquerque. The primary mission of the law school is to offer a legal education that combines training in legal doctrine, theory, and policy with the development of practical lawyering skills. Emphasis is placed on student-faculty interaction. Students have access to federal, state, county, city, and local agencies, courts, correctional facilities, law firms, and legal aid organizations in the Albuquerque area. Facilities of special interest to law students is Bratton Hall, which, in addition to housing the classrooms, seminar rooms, and faculty, staff, and student organization offices, is home to the Utton Transboundary Resources Center, the American Indian Law Center, and the Law Practice Clinic. Housing for students consists of off-campus rental homes and apartments, where most students live, and 200 student family apartments. The university helps with finding housing. All law school facilities are accessible to the physically disabled.

Calendar
The law school operates on a traditional semester basis. Courses for full-time students are offered days only and must be completed within 3 years. There is no part-time program. However, UNM offers a flexible time prgram, in which students may take fewer credit hours per semester. Courses are offered in the day only and must be completed within 5 years. New full- and part-time students are admitted in the fall. There is a 10 maximum-week summer session. Transferable summer courses are not offered.

Programs
Students may take relevant courses in other programs and apply credit toward the J.D.; a maximum of 6 to 9 credits may be applied. The following joint degrees may be earned: J.D./M.A. (Juris Doctor/Master of Arts in water resources), J.D./M.A., M.S., or Ph.D. (all degrees are available in various academic fields), J.D./M.A.L.A.S. (Juris Doctor/Master of Arts in Latin American Studies), J.D./M.B.A. (Juris Doctor/Master of Business Administration), and J.D./M.P.A. (Juris Doctor/Master of Public Administration).

Required
To earn the J.D., candidates must complete 86 total credits, of which 41 are for required courses. They must maintain a minimum GPA of 2.0 in the required courses. The following first-year courses are required of all students: Advocacy, Civil Procedure I, Constitutional Law, Contracts I, Criminal Law, Historical Introduction to Law, Legal Reasoning, Research and Writing, Practicum, Property I, and Torts. Required upper-level courses consist of 6 hours of clinical courses and a course in Professional Responsibility. All students must take clinical courses. The required orientation program for first-year students lasts 2 days.

Electives
The School of Law offers concentrations in Indian law and natural resources, and environmental law certificate programs are offered. In addition, UNM's Clinical Law Program is a requirement for the J.D. degree. Students, supervised by faculty members, may counsel and advise clients and appear in state, federal, and tribal courts in New Mexico. Judicial and law

520 Guide To Law Schools

Phone: 505-277-0958
Fax: 505-277-9958
E-mail: *witherington@law.unm.edu*
Web: *http://lawschool.unm.edu*

Contact

Rebecca Witherington, Admissions and Recruitment, 505-277-1030 for general inquiries; Susan Mitchell, Assistant Dean for Admissions and Financial Aid, 505-277-0959 for financial aid information.

NEW MEXICO

office externships are available. Individual research, worth from 1 to 3 credits, is available under faculty direction. There is also an Advanced Legal Research elective. Summer-abroad programs are available through the Guanajuato Summer Law Institute. Exchange programs are offered with schools in Mexico, Canada, and Australia. Students may visit at ABA-approval programs throughout the world. Tutorials are available for each substantive course to first-year students.

Graduation Requirements

In order to graduate, candidates must have a GPA of 2.0, have completed the upper-division writing requirement, and have at least 3 full academic years in residence. An ethics course must be taken.

Organizations

The primary law review is the *New Mexico Law Review*, which is published 3 times a year. Students also edit the *Natural Resources Journal and Tribal Law Journal*. Moot court teams attend the Native American Law Student Association, Hispanic, and National Moot Court competitions. Other competitions include the Jessup Moot Court Competition and Health Law Moot Court Competition. Law student organizations include the Student Bar Association, Environmental Law Society, International Law Students Association, Mexican American Law Students Association, Black Law Students Association, and Native American Law Students Association. There are campus chapters of Phi Alpha Delta, Phi Delta Phi, and Association of Trial Lawyers of America/New Mexico.

Library

The law library contains 433,064 hardcopy volumes and 39,325 microform volume equivalents, and subscribes to 3295 serial publications. Such on-line databases and networks as CALI, CIS Universe, Infotrac, Legal-Trac, LEXIS, LOIS, NEXIS, OCLC First Search, WESTLAW, Wilsonline Indexes, are available to law students for research. For a complete list, see http://lawschool.unm.edu/lawlib/databases. Special library collections include a selective federal and New Mexico government document depository, an extensive collection of New Mexico appellate briefs and records, American Indian law,

Mexican and Latin American law, land-grant law, and Water Policy Collection. Recently, the library installed a wireless network and new chairs throughout the library, new carpeting and circulation desk, new TV/VCR/DVD in the library study rooms, new furniture in student study rooms, more than 30 pieces of art , an elevator, and a library classroom. A special needs computer and adaptive software as well as 9 public PCs are available. A seminar and archival reading room opened. The ratio of library volumes to faculty is 11,704 to 1 and to students is 1248 to 1. The ratio of seats in the library to students is 1 to 1.

Faculty

The law school has 37 full-time and 20 part-time faculty members, of whom 25 are women. According to AAUP standards for Category 1 institutions, faculty salaries are well below average. About 24% of full-time faculty have a graduate law degree in addition to the J.D. The ratio of full-time students to full-time faculty in an average class is 10 to 1; in a clinic, 8 to 1. The law school has a regular program of bringing visiting professors and other distinguished lecturers and visitors to campus. There is a chapter of the Order of the Coif.

Students

About 51% of the student body are women; 45%, minorities; 3%, African American; 2%, Asian American; 29%, Hispanic; and 10%, Native American. The average age of entering students is 28; age range is 21 to 50.

Placement

J.D.s awarded:	105
Services available through: a separate law school placement center and the university placement center	
Services: various career fairs, externships, computer resources, practice area programs, mock interviews, support for students with disabilities, academic counseling from 2 full time attorney-counselors, mentorship, and judicial clerkship programs	
Special features: .	
Full-time job interviews:	21 employers
Summer job interviews:	20 employers
Placement by graduation:	58% of class
Placement within 9 months:	96% of class
Average starting salary:	$12,000 to $120,000
Areas of placement:	
Private practice 2-10 attorneys	29%
Private practice 11-25 attorneys	5%
Private practice 26-50 attorneys	5%
Private practice 51-100 attorneys	6%
Private practice 101-250 attorneys	1%
Government	17%
Public interest	12%
Judicial clerkships	9%
Business/industry	6%
Military	5%
Academic	5%

School of Law

Campus Box 3380,
Van Hecke-Wettach Hall
Chapel Hill, NC 27599-3380

Application Filing		Accreditation
Fall: February 1		ABA, AALS
Spring: n/app		Degrees Granted
Fee: n/av		J.D.
Enrollment 2009–2010		First-Year Class
Men:	337 48%	Applied: 3286
Women:	362 52%	Accepted: 609
Minorities:	168 24%	Enrolled: 241
Out-of-State:	175 25%	

2009–10 Class Profile
LSAT Percentile: 83%
LSAT Median Score: 161
Percentage passing bar on first try: 87%

Tuition and Fees:

Resident
$14,000

Average (public)
$18,708

Average (private)
$34,451

Nonresident
$26,000

Average (public)
$29,793

Average (private)
$34,451

0 10 20 30 40 50

Percentage receiving financial aid: 80%

ADMISSIONS

In the fall 2009 first-year class, 3286 applied, 609 were accepted, and 241 enrolled. Seven transfers enrolled. Figures in the above capsule and in this profile are approxiamate. The median LSAT percentile of the most recent first-year class was 83; the median GPA was 3.65 on a scale of 4.0. The lowest LSAT percentile accepted was 36; the highest was 99.

Requirements
Applicants must have a bachelor's degree and take the LSAT. The most important admission factors include academic achievement and LSAT results. No specific undergraduate courses are required. Candidates are not interviewed.

Procedure
Applicants should submit an application form, LSAT results, transcripts, a personal statement, a nonrefundable fee, 2 letters of recommendation, and a resume. Notification of the admissions decision is on a rolling basis from January. The latest acceptable LSAT test date for fall entry is February. Check with the school for current application deadlines. The law school uses the LSDAS.

Special
The law school recruits minority and disadvantaged students by means of the Candidate Referral Service, a special open house for minority students, LSAC forums, visits to HBCUs, HSIs, and other colleges and universities with significant minority populations. Requirements are not different for out-of-state students. Transfer students must have one year of credit, have attended an ABA-approved law school, and have a superior academic performance, have been originally admissible to UNC School of Law.

Costs

Tuition and fees for the 2009-2010 academic year are $14,000 for full-time in-state students and $26,000 for out-of-state students. On-campus room and board costs about $13,000 annually; books and supplies run $1500.

Financial Aid

In a recent year about 80% of current law students received some form of aid. Awards are based on need and merit. Required financial statement is the FAFSA. Check with the school for current financial deadlines. Special funds for minority or disadvantaged students consist of endowed scholarships. First-year students are notified about their financial aid application at time of enrollment from January through May.

About the Law School

University of North Carolina at Chapel Hill School of Law was established in 1845 and is a public institution. The 700-acre campus is in a small town 23 miles northwest of Raleigh. The primary mission of the law school is to educate future practitioners and leaders of the bench and bar. Students have access to federal, state, county, city, and local agencies, courts, correctional facilities, law firms, and legal aid organizations in the Chapel Hill area. Housing for students is available in the residence hall for graduate and professional students located near the law school; there are also many apartments in the area. About 95% of the law school facilities are accessible to the physically disabled.

Calendar

The law school operates on a traditional semester basis. Courses for full-time students are offered days only and must be completed within 5 years. There is no part-time program. New students are admitted in the fall. There is a 6-week summer session. Transferable summer courses are not offered.

Programs

Students may take relevant courses in other programs and apply credit toward the J.D.; a maximum of 3 credits may be applied. The following joint degrees may be earned: J.D./M.A.M.C. (Juris Doctor/ Master of Arts in Mass Communication), J.D./M.A.S.A. (Juris Doctor/Master of Arts in sports administration), J.D./M.B.A. (Juris Doctor/Master of Business Administration), J.D./M.P.A. (Juris Doctor/Master of Public Administration), J.D./M.P.H. (Juris Doctor/Master of Public Health), J.D./M.P.P.S. (Juris Doctor/Master of Public Policy), J.D./M.R.P. (Juris Doctor/Master of Regional Planning), J.D./ M.S.I.S. (Juris Doctor/Master of Science in information science), J.D./M.S.L.S. (Juris Doctor/Master of Science in library science), and J.D./M.S.W. (Juris Doctor/Master of Social Work).

Required
To earn the J.D., candidates must complete 86 total credits, of which 33 are for required courses. The following first-year courses are required of all students: Civil Procedure, Constitutional Law, Contracts, Criminal Law, Property, Research and Writing, and Torts. Required upper-level courses consist of Professional Responsibility, rigorous writing, and a third-year seminar. The required orientation program for first-year students is 2 1/2 days and includes an introduction to case study method and briefing and social activities.

Electives
The School of Law offers concentrations in corporate law, criminal law, environmental law, family law, international law, juvenile law, labor law, litigation, securities law, and tax law. In addition, third-year students may participate in the Criminal

Phone: 919-962-5109
Fax: 919-843-7939
E-mail: law_admission@unc.edu
Web: http://www.law.unc.edu

Contact
Admissions Office, 919-962-5109 for general inquiries; 919-962-8396, for financial aid information.

NORTH CAROLINA

Law Clinic, Immigration/Human Rights Clinic, Civil Legal Assistance Clinic, and Community Development Law Clinic. Students may also participate in the Policy Clinic- Gender and Human Rights. Domestic Violence Law is a prerequisite. There are approximately 40 seminars offered to upper-level students for 3 credit hours; preference is given to third-year students, then second-year students. Research may be undertaken for no more than 3 credit hours and only with faculty permission. The law school has an externship program for third-year students. Students are placed by the school and also take a required class. Students may study in Lyon, France; Nijmegen, The Netherlands; Glasgow, Scotland; Mexico City, Mexico; or Manchester, England during the spring semester of the second or third year for 12 credit hours. Courses focus on international law. There are summer study abroad programs in Sydney, Australia and Augsburg, Germany. The LEAP program is a first-year academic support program for a select group of entering students. The most widely taken electives are Business Associations, Trusts and Estates, and Evidence.

Graduation Requirements
In order to graduate, candidates must have a GPA of 2.25, have completed the upper-division writing requirement, and have completed the second-year writing class, and the seminar requirement in the third year.

Organizations
Students edit the *North Carolina Law Review, North Carolina Journal of International Law and Commercial Regulation, Journal of Online Technology, Banking Law Journal*, and *First Amendment Law Journal*. The Holderness Moot Court Bench consists of the negotiations team, client counseling team, invitational team, national team, constitutional team, and international team, and sponsors the annual Craven Moot Court competition. Other competitions include American Jurisprudence Award, Block Improvement, Burkan Memorial, Millard S. Breckenridge, Judge Heriot Clarkson, Chief Justice Walter Clark, Albert Coates, Investors Title Insurance, William T. Jayner, James William Morrow III, U.S. Law Week, and West Publishing Company. Law student organiza-

tions include Domestic Violence Advocacy Project, Environmental Law Project, and the Christian Society. Local chapters of national associations include American Civil Liberties Union, Black Law Students Association, and Federalist Society. Campus clubs and other organizations include Hispanic/Latino Law Students Association, LAMBDA Law Students Association, and Trial Law Academy.

Library
The law library contains 527,954 hardcopy volumes and 32,207 microform volume equivalents, and subscribes to 5600 serial publications. Such on-line databases and networks as LEXIS, LOIS, NEXIS, and WESTLAW are available to law students for research. Special library collections include Anglo-American legal materials. The ratio of library volumes to faculty is 11,999 to 1 and to students is 755 to 1.

Faculty
The law school has 44 full-time and 61 part-time faculty members, of whom 41 are women. According to AAUP standards for Category I institutions, faculty salaries are average. The ratio of full-time students to full-time faculty in an average class is 16 to 1; in a clinic, 12 to 1. The law school has a regular program of bringing visiting professors and other distinguished lecturers and visitors to campus. There is a chapter of the Order of the Coif; 40 faculty are members.

Students
About 52% of the student body are women; 24%, minorities; 7%, African American; 7%, Asian American; 5%, Hispanic; 2%, Native American; and 13%, other ethnicity or ethnicity unknown (includes biracial). The majority of students come from North Carolina (75%). The average age of entering students is 23; age range is 21 to 53. About 44% of students enter directly from undergraduate school and 12% have a graduate degree. About 3% drop out after the first year for academic or personal reasons; 95% remain to receive a law degree.

Placement

J.D.s awarded:	236
Services available through: a separate law school placement center and the university placement center	
Full-time job interviews:	63 employers
Summer job interviews:	141 employers
Placement by graduation:	63% of class
Placement within 9 months:	89% of class
Average starting salary:	$34,000 to $145,000
Areas of placement:	
Private practice 2-10 attorneys	15%
Private practice 11-25 attorneys	3%
Private practice 26-50 attorneys	4%
Private practice 51-100 attorneys	5%
Private practice 101+ attorneys or firm size	30%
Judicial clerkships	13%
Government	12%
Public interest	9%
Business/industry	5%
Academic	2%
Military	1%

UNIVERSITY OF NORTH DAKOTA

School of Law

Box 9003
Grand Forks, ND 58202

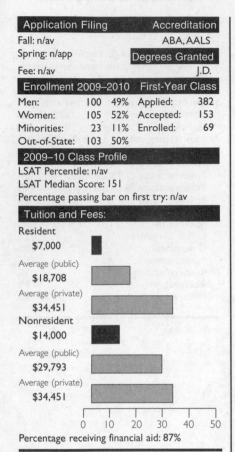

Application Filing

Fall: n/av
Spring: n/app
Fee: n/av

Accreditation

ABA, AALS

Degrees Granted

J.D.

Enrollment 2009–2010   First-Year Class

Men:	100	49%	Applied:	382
Women:	105	52%	Accepted:	153
Minorities:	23	11%	Enrolled:	69
Out-of-State:	103	50%		

2009–10 Class Profile

LSAT Percentile: n/av
LSAT Median Score: 151
Percentage passing bar on first try: n/av

Tuition and Fees:

Resident
$7,000

Average (public)
$18,708

Average (private)
$34,451

Nonresident
$14,000

Average (public)
$29,793

Average (private)
$34,451

Percentage receiving financial aid: 87%

ADMISSIONS

In the fall 2009 first-year class, 382 applied, 153 were accepted, and 69 enrolled. Figures in the above capsule and in this profile are approximate. Three transfers enrolled in a recent year. The median GPA of the most recent first-year class was 3.57.

Requirements

Applicants must have a bachelor's degree and take the LSAT. The most important admission factors include academic achievement, GPA, and LSAT results. No specific undergraduate courses are required. Candidates are not interviewed.

Procedure

Applicants should submit an application form a nonrefundable application fee, and 2 letters of recommendation. Notification of the admissions decision is on a rolling basis. The latest acceptable LSAT test date for fall entry is that which ensures the score is received by the application

deadlines. Check with the school for current application deadlines. The law school uses the LSDAS.

Special

The law school recruits minority and disadvantaged students as part of the school's philosophy of promoting diversity in the student body. Requirements are different for out-of-state students in that preference is given to qualified state residents, depending on the number of applications received. Transfer students must have a minimum GPA of 2.0 and have attended an ABA-approved law school; generally, no more than 2 semesters of course work are eligible for transfer.

Costs

Tuition and fees for the 2009-2010 academic year are $7000 for full-time in-state students and $14,000 for out-of-state students. On-campus room and board costs about $10,000 annually; books and supplies run $1000.

Financial Aid

In a recent year about 87% of current law students received some form of aid. The average annual amount of aid from all sources combined, including scholarships, loans, and work contracts, was $16,500; maximum, $37,800. Awards are based on need and merit. Required financial statement is the FAFSA. Check with the school for current application deadlines. Special funds for minority or disadvantaged students include Cultural Diversity Tuition Waivers. First-year students are notified about their financial aid application at time of acceptance.

About the Law School

University of North Dakota School of Law was established in 1899 and is a public institution. The campus is in a small town 320 miles northwest of Minneapolis-St. Paul, Minnesota. The primary mission of the law school is to provide education and training in legal analysis and the application of legal principles leading to professional competence. Students have access to federal, state, county, city, and local agencies, courts, correctional facilities, law firms, and legal aid organizations in the Grand Forks area. Housing for students is in residence halls, single-student

apartments, family housing apartments, and a trailer court, all adjacent to the campus. About 95% of the law school facilities are accessible to the physically disabled.

Calendar

The law school operates on a traditional semester basis. Courses for full-time students are offered days only and must be completed within 5 years. There is no part-time program. New students are admitted in the fall. There is a 6-week summer session. Transferable summer courses are offered.

Programs

Students may take relevant courses in other programs and apply credit toward the J.D.; a maximum of 6 credits may be applied. The following joint degree may be earned: J.D/M.P.A. (Juris Doctor/Master of Public Administration).

Required

To earn the J.D., candidates must complete 90 total credits, of which 34 are for required courses. They must maintain a minimum GPA of 2.0 in the required courses. The following first-year courses are required of all students: Brief Writing and Appellate Advocacy, Civil Procedure, Constitutional Law I and II, Contracts I and II, Criminal Law, Legal Process, Property I and II, and Torts I and II. Required upper-level courses consist of Professional Responsibility. The required orientation program for first-year students lasts 1 week.

Electives

Clinics, conducted under the supervision of the Director of Legal Aid and other clinical instructors, include a Civil Litigation Project and a Civil Rights Project. Internships are available with the North Dakota District Court, North Dakota Legislative Assembly, Grand Forks County States Attorney, and the Office of the Staff Judge Advocate at the Grand Forks Air Force Base. Various supervised research projects are available through the Special Projects Committee. Also, Central Legal Research employs second- and third-year students to work on current legal research questions. The Rocky Mountain Mineral Law Foundation, through grants, scholarships, seminars, and publications, promotes

Contact

Admissions and Records Associate, 701-777-2260 for general inquiries; Mark Brickson, Director of Career Services, 701-777-2269 for financial aid information.

NORTH DAKOTA

research in natural resources law. The Fode Lecture is a special lecture series. Students may receive credit for summer law study at the University of Oslo, Norway. The Canadian-American Law Institute encourages interchange among law students and faculty from North Dakota and several Canadian provinces. The most widely taken electives are bar courses, skills courses, and trial advocacy.

Graduation Requirements

In order to graduate, candidates must have a GPA of 2.0, have completed the upper-division writing requirement, and have completed Legal Process, Brief Writing, and Professional Responsibility, have completed 2 significant writing projects, and have completed the residency requirements of the last 4 semesters of study at the school.

Organizations

Students edit the *North Dakota Law Review* and the student newspaper, *Rhadamanthus*. The North Dakota Agricultural Law Institute serves the state's agricultural industry by publishing bulletins related to agriculture. Members of the Moot Court Association participate in an appellate moot court intraschool competition. During the past few years, members have also participated in the National Moot Court Competition, the Tulane Sports Law Competition, and various regional competitions. Student organizations, local chapters of national associations, and campus organizations include the Student Bar Association, Native American Law Students Association, Christian Law Students Society, Public Interest Law Students Association, Student Trial Lawyers Association, Law Women's Caucus, Phi Alpha Delta, Phi Delta Phi, and Order of the Coif.

Library

The law library contains 251,320 hardcopy volumes and 129,554 microform volume equivalents, and subscribes to 2710 serial publications. Such on-line databases and networks as DIALOG, LEXIS, WESTLAW, OCLC, ODIN, Internet, CALI, and Legal-Trac are available to law students for research. Special library collections include a good Canadian collection, partial U.S. government documents depository, and a Norwegian law collection. Recently,

the library added a computer laboratory and walk-up computer information kiosks. The ratio of library volumes to faculty is 22,847 to 1 and to students is 1257 to 1. The ratio of seats in the library to students is 1 to 1.

Faculty

The law school has 11 full-time and 16 part-time faculty members, of whom 13 are women. According to AAUP standards for Category I institutions, faculty salaries are well below average. About 36% of full-time faculty have a graduate law degree in addition to the J.D. There is a chapter of the Order of the Coif.

Students

About 52% of the student body are women; 11%, minorities; 1%, African American; 1%, Asian American; 2%, Hispanic; and 7%, Native American. The majority of students come from North Dakota (50%). The average age of entering students is 26; age range is 21 to 48. About 6% drop out after the first year for academic or personal reasons.

Placement

J.D.s awarded:	n/av
Services available through: a separate law school placement center	
Services: job board, on which full- and part-time positions are listed	
Special features: a job-seeking resource and reference library, files on individual firms or organizations, and files on job bulletins from over 80 other law schools around the nation. Internet, legal, and job-seeking sites are bookmarked from the school's web page.	
Full-time job interviews:	6 employers
Summer job interviews:	10 employers
Placement by graduation:	60% of class
Placement within 9 months:	91% of class
Average starting salary:	$24,000 to $90,000
Areas of placement:	
Private practice 2-10 attorneys	34%
Private practice 11-25 attorneys	7%
Private practice 26-50 attorneys	2%
Private practice 51-100 attorneys	9%
Judicial clerkships	15%
Government	14%
Public interest	8%
Business/industry	7%
Military	3%
Sole practitioner	1%

Notre Dame Law School

P.O. Box 780
Notre Dame, IN 46556-0780

Application Filing			Accreditation
Fall: March 15			ABA, AALS
Spring: n/app			**Degrees Granted**
Fee: $60			J.D., LL.M., S.J.D.

Enrollment 2009–2010			First-Year Class	
Men:	317	58%	Applied:	3178
Women:	231	42%	Accepted:	810
Minorities:	126	23%	Enrolled:	186
Out-of-State:	n/av			

2009–10 Class Profile
LSAT Percentile: n/av
LSAT Median Score: 166
Percentage passing bar on first try: n/av

Tuition and Fees:

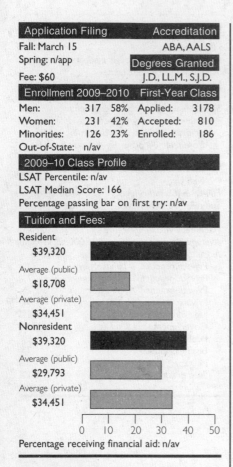

Resident
$39,320

Average (public)
$18,708

Average (private)
$34,451

Nonresident
$39,320

Average (public)
$29,793

Average (private)
$34,451

0   10   20   30   40   50

Percentage receiving financial aid: n/av

ADMISSIONS

In the fall 2009 first-year class, 3178 applied, 810 were accepted, and 186 enrolled. Thirteen transfers enrolled. The median GPA of the most recent first-year class was 3.6.

Requirements
Applicants must have a bachelor's degree and take the LSAT. The most important admissions factors are personal statement, grade trends, and service. No specific undergraduate courses are required. Candidates are not interviewed.

Procedure
The application deadline for fall entry is March 15. Applicants should submit an application form, LSAT results, transcripts, a personal statement, a nonrefundable application fee of $60, 2 letters of recommendation, and and optional Essay. Notification of the admissions decision is on a rolling basis. The latest acceptable LSAT test date for fall entry is February. The law school uses the LSDAS.

Special
The law school recruits minority and disadvantaged students through admissions representatives attendance at LSAC forums and university law days across the country. Requirements are not different for out-of-state students. Transfer students must have 1 year of credit and have attended an ABA-approved law school.

Costs

Tuition and fees for the 2009-2010 academic year are $39,320 for all full-time students. On-campus room and board costs about $8500 annually; books and supplies run $1400.

Financial Aid

Awards are based on need and merit. Required financial statement is the FAFSA. The aid application deadline for fall entry is February 15. Special funds for minority or disadvantaged students include special grants. First-year students are notified about their financial aid application at as soon as possible after acceptance and after financial documents are received.

About the Law School

University of Notre Dame Law School was established in 1869 and is a private institution. The 1250-acre campus is in a small town just north of South Bend. The primary mission of the law school is to educate a different kind of lawyer through the integration of faith and reason. The law school's goal is that the "Notre Dame Lawyer" should exemplify the legal profession at its best. Students have access to federal, state, county, city, and local agencies, courts, correctional facilities, law firms, and legal aid organizations in the Notre Dame area. Students also have access to the courts and legal aid clinics of South Bend, Chicago and Michigan. Housing for students is available as on-campus apartments for single and married students. Townhouses also are available for graduate and law students. The University assists in finding off-campus housing.

Calendar

The law school operates on a traditional semester basis. Courses for full-time students are offered both day and evening; most courses are offered during the day and must be completed within 5 years. There is no part-time program. New students are admitted in the fall. There is a 6- in Lond-week summer session in London. Transferable summer courses are offered.

Programs

In addition to the J.D., the law school offers the LL.M. and S.J.D. Students may take relevant courses in other programs and apply credit toward the J.D.; a maximum of 9 credits may be applied. The following joint degrees may be earned: J.B./M.B.A. (Juris Doctor/Master of Business Administration), J.D./M.A. (Juris Doctor/Master of Arts in English and other programs), and J.D./M.S. (Juris Doctor/Master of Science in Engineering).

Required
To earn the J.D., candidates must complete 90 total credits, of which 42 are for required courses. They must maintain a minimum GPA of 2.0 in the required courses. The following first-year courses are required of all students: Civil Procedure, Constitutional Law, Contracts, Criminal Law, Ethics I, Legal Research, Legal Research I and II, Moot Court, Legal Writing, Property, and Torts. Required upper-level courses consist of Business Associations, Ethics II, Federal Income Taxation, and Jurisprudence. The required orientation program for first-year students is 2 days in length.

Electives
Clinical training is available through Legal Aid, Appellate Advocacy, Criminal Practice, Public Interest Practice, and Trial Advocacy programs. Special seminars are offered in a variety of areas. Internships are available through the Public Defender and Prosecutor's offices. The law school as well as other academic departments offer an array of programs. A study-abroad program allows students to take their second year or a summer session at the law school's London campus. Tutorial programs are tailored to meet the needs of individual students. Diversity groups are actively involved in the law school and at the regional and national levels. The most widely taken electives are International Law, Trial Advocacy, and Legal Aid Clinic.

Phone: 574-631-6626
Fax: 574-631-5474
E-mail: lawadmit@nd.edu
Web: www.law.nd.edu

Contact

Melissa Fruscione, Acting Director of Admissions, 574-631-6626 for financial aid information.

INDIANA

Graduation Requirements

In order to graduate, candidates must have a GPA of 2.0 and have completed the upper-division writing requirement.

Organizations

Students edit the *Notre Dame Law Review*, published 5 times a year. Other publications include *Journal of Legislation, Journal of College and University Law*, and the *Journal of Law, Ethics, and Public Policy*. Moot court competitions include the National, Regional, and Seventh Circuit Moot Court Competitions and the Jessup Moot Court Competition. Other competitions include the National Trial Competition and Client Counseling. Law student organizations, local chapters of national associations, and campus organizations include Phi Alpha Delta, Business Law Forum, Environmental Law Society, Black Law Students of Notre Dame, Hispanic Law Students Association, Asian Law Students Association, Native American Law Students Association, Federalist Society, Public Interest Law Forum, and Women's Law Forum.

Library

The law library contains 356,733 hardcopy volumes and 315,657 microform volume equivalents. Such on-line databases and networks as CALI, CIS Universe, Infotrac, Legal-Trac, LEXIS, LOIS, Mathew Bender, NEXIS, OCLC First Search, RLIN, WESTLAW, and Wilsonline Indexes are available to law students for research. The law school is a member of the Federal Depository Library System. The law school has several archival sets of personal papers and a collection of approximately 800 rare book volumes. Recently, the library implemented an electronic resources management system. The ratio of library volumes to faculty is 6731 to 1 and to students is 650 to 1.

Faculty

The law school has 53 full-time and 43 part-time faculty members, of whom 33 are women. According to AAUP standards for Category I institutions, faculty salaries are above average. The ratio of full-time students to full-time faculty in an average class is 25 to 1; in a clinic, 6 to 1. The law school has a regular program of bringing visiting professors and other distinguished lecturers and visitors to campus.

Students

About 42% of the student body are women; 23%, minorities; 5%, African American; 8%, Asian American; 9%, Hispanic; and 1%, Native American. The average age of entering students is 24; age range is 20 to 42. About 1% drop out after the first year for academic or personal reasons; 99% remain to receive a law degree.

Placement

J.D.s awarded:	n/av
Services available through: a separate law school placement center	
Services: conducting seminars and surveys, maintaining a library, and networking through a national alumni network	
Special features: summer funded fellowships for work in the public sector	
Full-time job interviews:	n/av
Summer job interviews:	n/av
Placement by graduation:	90% of class
Placement within 9 months:	99% of class
Average starting salary:	n/av
Areas of placement:	
Private practice 2-100+ attorneys	61%
Judicial clerkships	14%
Government	12%
Public interest	7%
Business/industry	6%
Academic	1%

UNIVERSITY OF OKLAHOMA

College of Law

Andrew M. Coats Hall,
300 Timberdell Road
Norman, OK 73019

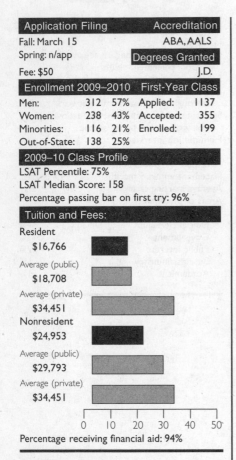

Application Filing			Accreditation
Fall: March 15			ABA, AALS
Spring: n/app			Degrees Granted
Fee: $50			J.D.

Enrollment 2009–2010		First-Year Class	
Men:	312 57%	Applied:	1137
Women:	238 43%	Accepted:	355
Minorities:	116 21%	Enrolled:	199
Out-of-State:	138 25%		

2009–10 Class Profile
LSAT Percentile: 75%
LSAT Median Score: 158
Percentage passing bar on first try: 96%

Tuition and Fees:

Resident
$16,766

Average (public)
$18,708

Average (private)
$34,451

Nonresident
$24,953

Average (public)
$29,793

Average (private)
$34,451

0   10   20   30   40   50

Percentage receiving financial aid: 94%

ADMISSIONS

In the fall 2009 first-year class, 1137 applied, 355 were accepted, and 199 enrolled. Twenty-one transfers enrolled. The median LSAT percentile of the most recent first-year class was 75; the median GPA was 3.51 on a scale of 4.0. The lowest LSAT percentile accepted was 49; the highest was 98.

Requirements
Applicants must have a bachelor's degree and take the LSAT. The most important admission factors include GPA, LSAT results, and character, personality. No specific undergraduate courses are required. Candidates are not interviewed.

Procedure
The application deadline for fall entry is March 15. Applicants should submit an application form, LSAT results, transcripts, a nonrefundable application fee of $50, and 2 letters of recommendations. Notification of the admissions decision is 2 to 6 weeks after packet completion. The

latest acceptable LSAT test date for fall entry is February. The law school uses the LSDAS.

Special
The law school recruits minority and disadvantaged students through prelaw fairs and career days at undergraduate institutions and through personal correspondence and contacts, LSAC Forums, and CRS searches. Requirements are not different for out-of-state students. Transfer students must have one year of credit and have attended an ABA-approved law school.

Costs

Tuition and fees for the 2009-2010 academic year are $16,766 for full-time in-state students and $24,953 for out-of-state students. On-campus room and board costs about $15,439 annually; books and supplies run $4235.

Financial Aid

About 94% of current law students receive some form of aid. The average annual amount of aid from all sources combined, including scholarships, loans, and work contracts, is $22,700; maximum, $23,300. Awards are based on need. Required financial statement is the FAFSA. The aid application deadline for fall entry is March 1. Special funds for minority or disadvantaged students include money that several donors have embarked for ethnic scholarships. First-year students are notified about their financial aid application at time of acceptance.

About the Law School

University of Oklahoma College of Law was established in 1909 and is a public institution. The 3905-acre campus is in a small town 20 miles south of Oklahoma City. The primary mission of the law school is to prepare qualified students to practice law or to use the law in their disciplines, to enable law graduates to remain qualified, and to promote further understanding of law and legal institutions. Students have access to federal, state, county, city, and local agencies, courts, correctional facilities, law firms, and legal aid organizations in the Norman area. Facilities of special interest to law students include three state-of-the-art courtrooms, largest law library in

the state, and a world class physical fitness center. Housing for students includes dormitories, off-campus apartments, and university owned apartments for graduate and law students. All law school facilities are accessible to the physically disabled.

Calendar

The law school operates on a traditional semester basis. Courses for full-time students are offered days only and must be completed within 7 years. There is no part-time program. New students are admitted in the fall. There is an 8-week summer session. Transferable summer courses are offered.

Programs

The following joint degrees may be earned: J.D./M.B.A. (Juris Doctor/Master of Business Administration) and J.D./M.P.H. (Juris Doctor/Master of Public Health).

Required
To earn the J.D., candidates must complete 90 total credits, of which 41 are for required courses. They must maintain a minimum GPA of 4.0 in the required courses. The following first-year courses are required of all students: Civil Procedure I; Civil Procedure II, Constitutional Law, Contracts, Criminal Law, Legal Research & Writing I; Legal Research and Writing II, Property, and Torts I and II. Required upper-level courses consist of a graduation writing requirement, Criminal Procedure I, Evidence, and Professional Responsibility. No clinical courses are required, but many students participate in an extremely strong clinical program. The required orientation program for first-year students is a 1-day orientation that provides a basic introduction to legal study and the OU Law Center.

Electives
The College of Law offers concentrations in corporate law, criminal law, environmental law, family law, international law, labor law, litigation, media law, securities law, sports law, tax law, torts and insurance, oil and gas, and Native American. In addition, the Civil Clinic, Criminal Defense Clinic, and International Human Rights Clinic are available for 3 hours per semester. All students who have completed their first year of law studies

Phone: 405-325-4728
Fax: 405-325-0502
E-mail: rlucas@ou.edu
Web: www.law.ou.edu

Contact

Becky Lucas, Administrative Assistant to Associate Dean, 405-325-4702 for general inquiries; University of Oklahoma-Main Office, 405-325-4521 for financial aid information.

OKLAHOMA
◉

may take seminars. Each semester several are offered for 2 credit hours each. There is no limit, though students generally take no more than 2 or 3. A federal Indian Law internship is available for 12 credit hours. Second- and third-year students may be research assistants for law professors for no credit while receiving an hourly wage. Field work includes Issues in Professionalism and Extern Placement. Strong enrichment programs include the Henry Lecture Series and the Chair Professorship Series. A summer program is available at Brasenose College, Oxford University, Oxford, England. In addition, students have the opportunity to study abroad for a semester or full academic year after they have completed at least the first year of law studies and are in good academic standing. Students can create individual study programs at foreign law schools, and if approved by the College of Law and the American Bar Association, they can receive up to 30 hours of credit. Such study programs are particularly relevant to students who have an interest in international law or international business. A mandatory mentoring program for incoming students, given by upper class members, is provided to ease their integration into the law school environment. The Early Admission Program (EAP) of 15 to 20 students is a special admissions program designed to provide a small class environment, mentoring, and head start for students prior to joining the regular fall class. Minority law student organizations provide extremely strong minority support programs to include retention, community activities, and graduation placement. The most widely taken electives are Corporations, Commercial Law, and Wills and Trusts.

Graduation Requirements

In order to graduate, candidates must have a GPA of 4.0 and have completed the upper-division writing requirement.

Organizations

Students edit the *Oklahoma Law Review, American Indian Law Review,* and *Oklahoma Journal of Law and Technology.* Moot court competitions include the National Moot Court, ABA NAAC, Jessup International, and 15 others. The College of Law has mandatory first-year moot court competitions and voluntary upper-class moot court competitions. Law

student organizations, local chapters of national associations, and campus organizations include BLSA, OAWL, Federalist Society, Student Bar Association, Phi Alpha Delta, Phi Delta Phi, J Ruben Clark Society, and student components of ABA and OBA.

Library

The law library contains 364,449 hardcopy volumes and 81,119 microform volume equivalents, and subscribes to 4389 serial publications. Such on-line databases and networks as CALI, CIS Universe, DIALOG, Dow-Jones, Infotrac, Legal-Trac, LEXIS, LOIS, Mathew Bender, NEXIS, OCLC First Search, and WESTLAW are available to law students for research. Special library collections include the Native Peoples Collection, GPO Depository, and Oil and Gas Law Collection. Recently, the library added new multimedia study rooms, and enhanced on-line resources. The ratio of library volumes to faculty is 9345 to 1 and to students is 663 to 1. The ratio of seats in the library to students is 1 to 1.

Faculty

The law school has 39 full-time and 29 part-time faculty members, of whom 22 are women. According to AAUP standards for Category I institutions, faculty salaries are well below average. About 18% of full-time faculty have a graduate law degree in addition to the J.D. The ratio of full-time students to full-time faculty in an average class is 16 to 1; in a clinic, 10 to 1. The law school has a regular program of bringing visiting professors and other distinguished lecturers and visitors to campus. There is a chapter of the Order of the Coif; 36 faculty and 1282 graduates are members.

Students

About 43% of the student body are women; 21%, minorities; 5%, African American; 5%, Asian American; 4%, Hispanic; and 9%, Native American. The majority of students come from Oklahoma (75%). The average age of entering students is 24; age range is 20 to 57. About 75% of students enter directly from undergraduate school, 5% have a graduate degree, and 25% have worked full-time prior to entering law school. About 2% drop out after the first year for academic or personal reasons; 98% remain to receive a law degree.

Placement

J.D.s awarded:	165

Services available through: a separate law school placement center

Special features: personal student counseling, on-campus seminars, mentoring by alumni, professional development workshops, and career development workshops.

Full-time job interviews:	18 employers
Summer job interviews:	58 employers
Placement by graduation:	55% of class
Placement within 9 months:	95% of class
Average starting salary:	$30,000 to $175,000

Areas of placement:

Private practice 2-10 attorneys	29%
Private practice 11-25 attorneys	10%
Private practice 26-50 attorneys	4%
Private practice 51-100 attorneys	2%
Private Practice - solo and 100+ attorneys	12%
Government	18%
Business/industry	15%
Judicial clerkships	3%
Academic	3%
Public interest	2%
Military	2%

School of Law, William W. Knight Law Center

1221 University of Oregon
Eugene, OR 97403-1221

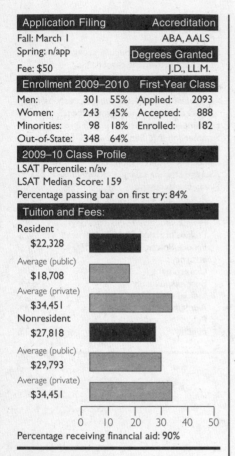

Application Filing	Accreditation
Fall: March 1	ABA, AALS
Spring: n/app	**Degrees Granted**
Fee: $50	J.D., LL.M.

Enrollment 2009–2010		First-Year Class	
Men:	301 55%	Applied:	2093
Women:	243 45%	Accepted:	888
Minorities:	98 18%	Enrolled:	182
Out-of-State:	348 64%		

2009–10 Class Profile
LSAT Percentile: n/av
LSAT Median Score: 159
Percentage passing bar on first try: 84%

Tuition and Fees:

Resident
$22,328

Average (public)
$18,708

Average (private)
$34,451

Nonresident
$27,818

Average (public)
$29,793

Average (private)
$34,451

0 10 20 30 40 50

Percentage receiving financial aid: 90%

ADMISSIONS

In the fall 2009 first-year class, 2093 applied, 888 were accepted, and 182 enrolled. Seventeen transfers enrolled. The median GPA of the most recent first-year class was 3.34.

Requirements
Applicants must have a bachelor's degree and take the LSAT. No specific undergraduate courses are required.

Procedure
The application deadline for fall entry is March 1. Applicants should submit an application form, LSAT results, transcripts, a personal statement, TOEFL if international, a nonrefundable application fee of $50, 2 letters of recommendation, and arésumé. Notification of the admissions decision is January through May. The latest acceptable LSAT test date for fall entry is February. The law school uses the LSDAS.

Special
The law school recruits minority and disadvantaged students in a variety of ways, in accordance with the law schools diversity plan. Requirements are not different for out-of-state students. Transfer students must have one year of credit and have attended an ABA-approved law school. The Admissions Committee considers each application on an individual basis.

Costs

Tuition and fees for the 2009-2010 academic year are $22,328 for full-time in-state students and $27,818 for out-of-state students.

Financial Aid

About 90% of current law students receive some form of aid. Awards are based on need and merit. Required financial statement is the FAFSA. Special funds are available for minority or disadvantaged students. Check the website for additional scholarship information. First-year students are notified about their financial aid application soon after acceptance.

About the Law School

University of Oregon School of Law, William W. Knight Law Center was established in 1884 and is a public institution. The 295-acre campus is in a small town of Eugene, Oregon. The primary mission of the law school is to offer a rigorous legal education with a curriculum that balances basic intellectual and analytical skills for the practice of law; an introduction to advanced and frontier areas of law; knowledge of the persistent values of law; and opportunities to develop hands-on legal skills. Students have access to federal, state, county, city, and local agencies, courts, correctional facilities, law firms, and legal aid organizations in the Eugene area. The law school is aggressive in its commitment to nationwide networks that provide both summer and permanent employment. Housing for students is available in Eugene and the surrounding area. Law students are also eligible for special graduate student housing. All law school facilities are accessible to the physically disabled.

Calendar

The law school operates on a traditional semester basis. Courses for full-time students are offered both day and evening and must be completed within 3 years. There is no part-time program. New students are admitted in the fall. There is an 8-week summer session. Transferable summer courses are offered.

Programs

In addition to the J.D., the law school offers the LL.M. Students may take relevant courses in other programs and apply credit toward the J.D.; a maximum of 5 semester credits may be applied. The following joint degrees may be earned: J.D./ M.B.A. (Juris Doctor/Master of Business Administration), J.D./M.S. (Juris Doctor/ Master of Science in international studies), J.D./M.S. or M.A. (Juris Doctor/Master of Science or Master of Arts in environmental studies), and J.D./M.SorM.A. (CRES/Master of Science or Master of Arts in conflict and Dispute Resolution).

Required
To earn the J.D., candidates must complete 85 total credits, of which 36 are for required courses. They must maintain a minimum GPA of 2.0 in the required courses. The following first-year courses are required of all students: Civil Procedure, Constitutional Law I, Contracts, Criminal Law, Legal Research and Writing, Property, and Torts. Required upper-level courses consist of a law school writing requirement, a law school skills requirement Constitutional Law II, and Legal Profession. Students are encouraged to participate in 1 of 7 clinics and/ or skills training courses. The required orientation program for first-year students consists of a 3-day orientation and registration before the first day of classes. Orientation includes a convocation, small group sessions, peer advising sessions, a library tour, and an all-school picnic. Peer and faculty advising continues throughout the J.D. program.

Electives
The School of Law, William W. Knight Law Center, offers concentrations in corporate law, criminal law, environmental law, family law, intellectual property law,

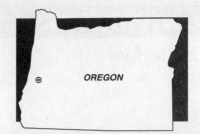

OREGON

Phone: 541-346-3846
800-825-6687
Fax: 541-346-3984
E-mail: *admissions@law.uoregon.edu*
Web: *www.law.uoregon.edu*

Contact
Law School Office Admissions, 541-346-3846 for general inquiries; Office of Financial Aid, 1-800-760-6953 for financial aid information.

international law, juvenile law, labor law, litigation, maritime law, securities law, tax law, torts and insurance, sustainable business law, ocean and coastal law, estate planning, public interest public service law, Oregon Child Advocacy Project, and appropriate dispute resolution/conflict resolution. In addition, a variety of clinics are offered that include the Civil Practice Clinic, Criminal Defense Clinic, Criminal Prosecution Clinic, Domestic Violence Clinic, Environmental Law Clinic, Mediation Clinic, and the Small Business Clinic. A variety of seminars are offered. Students have excellent opportunities for internships including the Federal Bankruptcy Court Internship, judicial internships, and the Legislative Issues Workshop. Faculty-supervised research may be done for school credit or for pay. Each year, the law school hosts symposia and lectures through the many programs, including the Wayne Morse Center for Law and Politics, Bowerman Center for Environmental Law, and the Center for Law and Entrepreneurship. A reciprocal student-abroad exchange has been established with the University of Adelaide in Australia. The Academic Choice for Excellence Program (ACE) is offered to all first-year students and addresses the needs of nontraditional law students. It provides tutorial assistance during the academic year. Law students are active in six multicultural organizations including the Minority Law Students Association (MLSA), and the Oregon State Bar Affirmative Action Program, which offers financial assistance through scholarships and loans. Additionally, the law school offers placement assistance and scholarships to ethnic minority students.

Graduation Requirements
In order to graduate, candidates must have a GPA of 2.0 and have completed the upper-division writing requirement.

Organizations
Students edit the *Oregon Law Review*, the *Journal of Environmental Law*, and the *Oregon Review of International Law*. Other publications include the *Western Environmental Law Update*. Students compete in the Client Counseling Competition, Mock Trial Competition, and the Environmental Moot Court Competition. Other competitions include the National Corporate Law Moot Court Competition and the

Technology Entrepreneurship Program (TEP). Student organizations include the Women's Law Forum, Outlaws (LGBT), and Land Air Water (LAW). Local chapters of national associations include the Black Law Student Association, Phi Alpha Delta, and the American Constitution Society for Law and Policy. Campus clubs and organizations include Streetlaw, Run Club, and the Legal Ballers Association.

Library
The law library contains 205,324 hardcopy volumes and 185,420 microform volume equivalents, and subscribes to 1055 serial publications. Such on-line databases and networks as CALI, CIS Universe, DIALOG, Infotrac, Legal-Trac, LEXIS, LOIS, Mathew Bender, NEXIS, OCLC First Search, WESTLAW, Wilsonline Indexes, Internet, HeinOnline, BNA All, MOML, LLMC, casemaker, SSRN, ECCO, Oxdord, Serial Set, CCH Tax and Business, RIA, and ELR are available to law students for research. Special library collections include an Ocean and Coastal Law Library, a rare book collection, an Indian Law and culture collection, a labor and employment collection, and a sustainable business collection. Recently, the library took on initiative to catalog all electronic files, law learning commons, new furniture and technology. The ratio of library volumes to faculty is 6222 to 1 and to students is 377 to 1. The ratio of seats in the library to students is 1 to 2.

Faculty
The law school has 33 full-time and 51 part-time faculty members, of whom 42 are women. According to AAUP standards for Category I institutions, faculty salaries are well below average. About 27% of full-time faculty have a graduate law degree in addition to the J.D.; about 6% of part-time faculty have one. The ratio of full-time students to full-time faculty in an average class is 34 to 1; in a clinic, 8 to 1. The law school has a regular program of bringing visiting professors and other distinguished lecturers and visitors to campus. There is a chapter of the Order of the Coif; 28 faculty and 618 graduates are members.

Students
About 45% of the student body are women; 18%, minorities; 3%, African American; 10%, Asian American; 4%, Hispanic;

Placement
J.D.s awarded:	178

Services available through: a separate law school placement center
Services: a Career Services Library with more than 500 references, and information on fellowships, graduate and summer writing programs, and writing competitions.
Special features: on-line job postings and bi-weekly newsletter for students; bi-monthly bulletin for alumni.

Full-time job interviews:	15 employers
Summer job interviews:	42 employers
Placement by graduation:	58% of class
Placement within 9 months:	90% of class
Average starting salary:	$24,000 to $120,000

Areas of placement:
Privte law firms of all sizes	45%
Government	16%
Judicial clerkships	14%
Business/industry	11%
Public interest	11%
Academic	4%
Military	1%

2%, Native American; and 1%, foreign nationals. The majority of students come from Oregon (36%). The average age of entering students is 26; age range is 21 to 56. About 8% of students have a graduate degree. About 1% drop out after the first year for academic or personal reasons; 99% remain to receive a law degree.

UNIVERSITY OF PENNSYLVANIA

Law School

3400 Chestnut Street
Philadelphia, PA 19104-6204

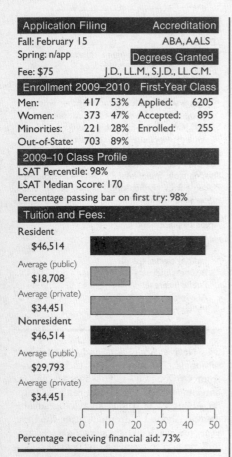

Application Filing		Accreditation
Fall: February 15		ABA, AALS
Spring: n/app		
		Degrees Granted
Fee: $75		J.D., LL.M., S.J.D., LL.C.M.

Enrollment 2009–2010   First-Year Class

Men:	417	53%	Applied:	6205
Women:	373	47%	Accepted:	895
Minorities:	221	28%	Enrolled:	255
Out-of-State:	703	89%		

2009–10 Class Profile

LSAT Percentile: 98%
LSAT Median Score: 170
Percentage passing bar on first try: 98%

Tuition and Fees:

Resident
$46,514

Average (public)
$18,708

Average (private)
$34,451

Nonresident
$46,514

Average (public)
$29,793

Average (private)
$34,451

0   10   20   30   40   50

Percentage receiving financial aid: 73%

ADMISSIONS

In the fall 2009 first-year class, 6205 applied, 895 were accepted, and 255 enrolled. Thirty transfers enrolled. The median LSAT percentile of the most recent first-year class was 98; the median GPA was 3.82 on a scale of 4.0. The lowest LSAT percentile accepted was 50; the highest was 99.

Requirements
Applicants must have a bachelor's degree and take the LSAT. No specific undergraduate courses are required. Candidates are not interviewed.

Procedure
The application deadline for fall entry is February 15. Applicants should submit an application form, LSAT results, transcripts, a personal statement, a nonrefundable application fee of $75, 2 letters of recommendation, and resume. Notification of the admissions decision is on a rolling basis. The latest acceptable LSAT

test date for fall entry is December. The law school uses the LSDAS.

Special
The law school recruits minority and disadvantaged students through a diversity brochure, diversity page on the website with student contracts, and targeted college units. Requirements are not different for out-of-state students. Transfer students must have 1 year of credit, have attended an ABA and AALS approved law school, and have completed a full-time first year curriculum.

Costs

Tuition and fees for the 2009-2010 academic year are $46,514 for all full-time students. On-campus room and board costs about $12,654 annually; books and supplies run $1225.

Financial Aid

About 73% of current law students receive some form of aid. The average annual amount of aid from all sources combined, including scholarships, loans, and work contracts, is $60,073; maximum, $65,610. Awards are based on need and merit. Required financial statements are the FAFSA and the institution's financial aid form. The aid application deadline for fall entry is March 1. First-year students are notified about their financial aid application shortly after acceptance.

About the Law School

University of Pennsylvania Law School was established in 1790 and is a private institution. The 260-acre campus is in an urban area 2 miles from central Philadelphia. The primary mission of the law school is based on a cross-disciplinary perspective that pervades the curriculum. Students graduate prepared to become leaders in the profession and society. Students have access to federal, state, county, city, and local agencies, courts, correctional facilities, law firms, and legal aid organizations in the Philadelphia area. The Pennsylvania Supreme Court is in Philadelphia. The federal courthouse headquarters the U.S. District Court for the Eastern District of Pennsylvania, and the Court of Appeals for the Third Circuit. Facilities of special interest to law students include the National Constitution

Center. Housing for students is available on and off campus with the majority of law students living in off-campus housing. The university also offers graduate housing 1 block from the law school. About 95% of the law school facilities are accessible to the physically disabled.

Calendar

The law school operates on a traditional semester basis. Courses for full-time students are offered both day and evening and must be completed within 3 years. There is no part-time program. New students are admitted in the fall. There is no summer session. Transferable summer courses are not offered.

Programs

In addition to the J.D., the law school offers the LL.M., S.J.D., and LL.C.M. Students may take relevant courses in other programs and apply credit toward the J.D.; a maximum of 12 credits may be applied. The following joint degrees may be earned: J.D./A.M. (Juris Doctor/Master of Arts in Islamic Studies, International), J.D./M. Bioethics (Juris Doctor/Master of Bioethics), J.D./M.A. (Juris Doctor/Master of Global Business Law), J.D./M.A./M.S. (Juris Doctor/Master of Criminology), J.D./M.B.A. (Juris Doctor/Master of Business Administration), J.D./M.C.P. (Juris Doctor/Master of City Planning), J.D./M.E.S. (Juris Doctor/Master of Environmental Studies), J.D./M.G.A. (Juris Doctor/Master of Government Administration), J.D./M.P.H. (Juris Doctor/Master of Public Health), J.D./M.S. (Juris Doctor/Master of Arts in Islamic Studies, International), J.D./M.S.Ed (Juris Doctor/Master of Education Policy or Higher Education), J.D./M.S.P. (Juris Doctor/Master of Social Policy), J.D./M.S.S.P. (Juris Doctor/Master of Social Policy and Practice), J.D./M.S.W. (Juris Doctor/Master of Social Work), J.D./Ph.D. (Juris Doctor/Doctor of Philosophy), and J.D.Ph.D. (Juris Doctor/Doctor of American Legal History).

Required
To earn the J.D., candidates must complete 89 total credits, of which 28 are for required courses. The following first-year courses are required of all students: Civil Procedure, Constitutional Law, Contracts, Criminal Law, Legal Writing, Property, and Torts. Required upper-level courses

Phone: 215-898-7400
Fax: 215-898-9606
E-mail: admissions@law.upenn.edu
Web: www.law.upenn.edu

Contact

Renee Post, Associate Dean for Admissions, 215-898-7400 for general inquiries; Anthony Henry, Director, 215-898-7400 for financial aid information.

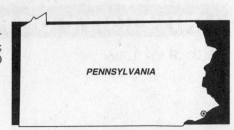

PENNSYLVANIA

consist of Professional Responsibility. The required orientation program for first-year students lasts 2 days.

Electives

The Law School offers concentrations in corporate law, criminal law, environmental law, family law, intellectual property law, international law, juvenile law, labor law, litigation, media law, securities law, tax law, torts and insurance, regulation of business, property and land development, perspectives on the law, law and the health services, constitutional law, courts and administration of justice, commercial law, urban and public interest law, and clinical, professional responsibility, as well as co-curricular courses. In addition, clinics and extern programs are available for credit in law-related agencies outside of the school. The clinical program includes courses in litigation, civil practice, interdisciplinary child advocacy, public interest, entrepreneurship, legislative process, transnational issues, meditation, and criminal defense. Seminars are available to second- and third-year students. First-year students enroll in 2 electives in regulatory/administrative law and 1 in perspectives. Each year a substantial number of students are employed as research assistants for faculty members. The school requires that all students complete 70 hours of service in public interest (pro bono). Penn Law has a partnership with the National Constitution Center that involves multiple events and lectures. Penn Law has programs in Hamburg, Germany; Tokyo, Japan; Beijing, China; Paris, France; Barcelona, Spain; Tel Aviv, Israel; a joint degree with Wharton's Lauder Institute that involves study abroad, and Penn Law's Global Research seminar. A wide range of minority organizations host conferences and social events. Upper-level students provide mentoring. Student groups reflect the interests of students. The most widely taken electives are Corporations, Evidence, and Federal Income Tax.

Graduation Requirements

In order to graduate, candidates must have completed the upper-division writing requirement .

Organizations

Students edit the *University of Pennsylvania Law Review*, the *University of Pennsylvania Journal of Business and Employment Law*, the *University of Pennsylvania Journal of Constitutional Law*, *University of Pennsylvania Journal of International Law, Journal of Law and Social Change*, and 2 student self-published journals, *East Asia Law Review* and *Journal of Animal Law and Ethics*.The student Moot Court Board, made up of third-year students, administers the Moot Court Program, which holds a voluntary intramural competition for the Edwin R. Keedy Trophy. The school also participates in several competitions sponsored by bar associations or other law schools, including the Jessup International Moot Court Competition, the Frederick Douglass Moot Court Competition, and others. Penn Law has more than 50 student organizations with a broad spectrum of interests, including academic, recreational, and areas of diversity.

Library

The law library contains 879,269 hardcopy volumes and 129,458 microform volume equivalents, and subscribes to 1433 serial publications. Such on-line databases and networks as CALI, CIS Universe, Infotrac, Legal-Trac, LEXIS, LOIS, NEXIS, OCLC First Search, WESTLAW, and Wilsonline Indexes are available to law students for research. Special library collections include foreign, international, and rare book collections, archives of the American Law Institute and the National Conference of Commissioners on Uniform State Laws, and the papers of Judge Bazelon and Bernard G. Segal. The ratio of library volumes to faculty is 11,882 to 1 and to students is 1112 to 1. The ratio of seats in the library to students is 1 to 2.

Faculty

The law school has 74 full-time and 82 part-time faculty members, of whom 37 are women. According to AAUP standards for Category I institutions, faculty salaries are well above average. About 72% of full-time faculty have a graduate law degree in addition to the J.D. The ratio of full-time students to full-time faculty in an average class is 11 to 1; in a clinic, 7 to 1. The law school has a regular program of bringing visiting professors and other distinguished lecturers and visitors to campus. There is a chapter of the Order of the Coif; 26 graduates are members.

Placement

J.D.s awarded:	258

Services available through: a separate law school placement center

Services: The placement library contains material on a wide variety of subjects and includes all major legal press. Many resources, including job postings, are available for students and alumni on-line.

Special features: Students work individually with counselors on their career searches. The office holds panel discussions and small-group meetings during the year to explore the practice of law and career opportunities. Additionally, first-year students work in small groups on issues such as resume writing and career opportunities.

Full-time job interviews:	300 employers
Summer job interviews:	340 employers
Placement by graduation:	97% of class
Placement within 9 months:	100% of class
Average starting salary:	$45,500 to $160,000
Areas of placement:	
private practice	76%
Judicial clerkships	16%
Business/industry	4%
Public interest	3%

Students

About 47% of the student body are women; 28%, minorities; 7%, African American; 14%, Asian American; and 7%, Hispanic. The majority of students come from the Northeast (48%). The average age of entering students is 24. About 29% of students enter directly from undergraduate school, 10% have a graduate degree, and 71% have worked full-time prior to entering law school. About 1% drop out after the first year for academic or personal reasons; 99% remain to receive a law degree.

University of Pennsylvania   **533**

School of Law

3900 Forbes Avenue
Pittsburgh, PA 15260

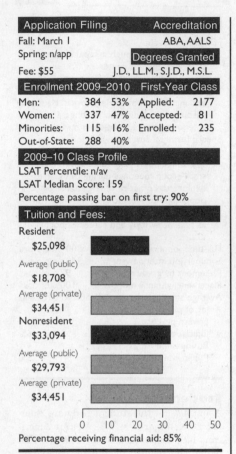

Application Filing	Accreditation
Fall: March 1	ABA, AALS
Spring: n/app	Degrees Granted
Fee: $55	J.D., LL.M., S.J.D., M.S.L.

Enrollment 2009–2010		First-Year Class	
Men:	384 53%	Applied:	2177
Women:	337 47%	Accepted:	811
Minorities:	115 16%	Enrolled:	235
Out-of-State:	288 40%		

2009–10 Class Profile
LSAT Percentile: n/av
LSAT Median Score: 159
Percentage passing bar on first try: 90%

Tuition and Fees:

Resident
$25,098

Average (public)
$18,708

Average (private)
$34,451

Nonresident
$33,094

Average (public)
$29,793

Average (private)
$34,451

0   10   20   30   40   50

Percentage receiving financial aid: 85%

ADMISSIONS

In the fall 2009 first-year class, 2177 applied, 811 were accepted, and 235 enrolled. Ten transfers enrolled. The median GPA of the most recent first-year class was 3.4. The highest LSAT percentile was 99.

Requirements
Applicants must have a bachelor's degree and take the LSAT. The most important admission factors include LSAT results, GPA, and academic achievement. No specific undergraduate courses are required. Candidates are not interviewed.

Procedure
The application deadline for fall entry is March 1. Applicants should submit an application form, LSAT results, transcripts, a nonrefundable application fee of $55, and 3 suggested letters of recommendation. Notification of the admissions decision is on a rolling basis. The latest acceptable LSAT test date for fall entry is February. The law school uses the LSDAS.

Special
The law school recruits minority and disadvantaged students by means of in-house programs, visits to minority institutions, e-mail, phone solicitation, and the Candidate Referral Service. Requirements are not different for out-of-state students. Transfer students must have one year of credit, have attended an ABA-approved law school, and must have maintained a "B" average or be in the top 25% of their class.

Costs

Tuition and fees for the 2009-2010 academic year are $25,098 for full-time in-state students and $33,094 for out-of-state students. On-campus room and board costs about $15,690 annually; books and supplies run $1500.

Financial Aid

About 85% of current law students receive some form of aid. Awards are based on need and merit. Required financial statement is the FAFSA. The aid application deadline for fall entry is April 1. Special funds for minority or disadvantaged students include scholarships provided by the school and the university. First-year students are notified about their financial aid application at time of acceptance.

About the Law School

University of Pittsburgh School of Law was established in 1895 and is a public institution. The 132-acre campus is in an urban area 3 miles from downtown Pittsburgh. The primary mission of the law school is to provide education, research, and public service. Students have access to federal, state, county, city, and local agencies, courts, correctional facilities, law firms, and legal aid organizations in the Pittsburgh area. They also have access to the county law library. Facilities of special interest to law students are the law library, classrooms, seminar rooms, courtroom complex, student lounge, student activities offices, meeting rooms, administrative offices, and computer laboratories and kiosks. Housing for students is in rental apartments that cost $500 to $600 and are available within 1 to 3 miles of the law school. On-campus housing is not available. All law school facilities are accessible to the physically disabled.

Calendar

The law school operates on a traditional semester basis. Courses for full-time students are offered days only and must be completed within 3 years. For part-time students (flex-time students), courses are offered days only and must be completed within 5 years. New full- and part-time students are admitted in the fall. There is no summer session. Transferable summer courses are not offered.

Programs

In addition to the J.D., the law school offers the LL.M., S.J.D., and M.S.L. Students may take relevant courses in other programs and apply credit toward the J.D.; a maximum of 6 credits may be applied. The following joint degrees may be earned: J.D./M.A. (Juris Doctor/Master of Arts in bioethics), J.D./M.B.A. (Juris Doctor/ Master of Business Administration), J.D./M.P.A. (Juris Doctor/ Master of Public Administration), J.D./M.P.H. (Juris Doctor/ Master of Public Health), J.D./M.P.I.A. (Juris Doctor/ Master of Public and International Affairs), J.D./M.S. (Juris Doctor/ Master of Science in law and public management), and J.D./M.S.W. (Juris Doctor/Master of Social Work).

Required
To earn the J.D., candidates must complete 88 total credits, of which 34 are for required courses. They must maintain a minimum GPA of 2.0 in the required courses. The following first-year courses are required of all students: Constitutional Law, Contracts, Criminal Law, Criminal Procedure, Legal Analysis and Writing, Legal Process and Civil Procedure, Property, and Torts. Required upper-level courses consist of 2 upper-level writing requirements, a course relating to international or comparative law, a legal research course, and Legal Profession. The required orientation program for first-year students is conducted over a 2-day period including a formal program, diversity training, discussion groups, family and friends orientation, lunch, and a student activities fair.

Electives
The School of Law offers concentrations in corporate law, criminal law, environmental law, family law, intellectual property law, international law, litiga-

Phone: 412-648-1413
Fax: 412-648-1318
E-mail: Mccall@law.pitt.edu
Web: www.pitt.law.edu

Contact

Charmaine C. McCall, Assistant Dean for Admission, 412-648-1413 for general inquiries; Meme Jeffries, Director of Financial Aid, 412-648-1415 for financial aid information.

PENNSYLVANIA

tion, tax law, torts and insurance, and health law. In addition, clinical offerings consist of the Tax Clinic, Family Law Clinic, Environmental Law Clinic, and Civil Practice Clinic, which includes Health Law and Elder Law. Second- and third-year students may receive 3 credits for a variety of seminars, which can satisfy the upper-level writing requirement. Externship opportunities are available with 62 federal and state judges, 34 other judges throughout Pennsylvania, and 34 judges in other states. Students are also placed in 91 Pennsylvania and federal agencies and out-of-state agencies; including Legal Aid Societies, the Urban Redevelopment Authority, U.S. Attorneys, neighborhood legal services, public defenders, the National Labor Relations Board, hospitals, and housing authorities. Students can earn a full-semester's credits by completing a semester-long externship in Washington, D.C. The school sponsors annual lectures in the fields of health law disability law, intellectual property law, ethics, law and social work, and lawering for social change. The school is a sponsor of a summer study program in Zagreb, Croatia. The Center for International Legal Education will work individually with students interested in studying abroad at any location. A Law at Sea program, in which each student is required to take 7 credits of law school courses, is also available. The Law School invites minority and other students to participate in the Mellon Legal Writing Program, which is designed to provide additional academic and social support for students confronting special challenges. The Law School has been co-sponsor of the CLEO (The Council for Legal Educational Opportunity) Institute. The Law School hosted the Institute in 1993, 1995, 1998, 2000, 2002, 2005, 2007 and 2009. Student organizations sponsor programs reflecting the interests of the group, such as Sports and Entertainment Law, International Law, Environmental Law, Health Law, Business Law, and Family Law. The most widely taken electives are Federal Income Tax, Corporations, and Evidence.

Graduation Requirements

In order to graduate, candidates must have a GPA of 2.0, have completed the upper-division writing requirement, a Legal Profession Ethics course, a course relating to international or comparative law, and a legal research course.

Organizations

Students edit the *University of Pittsburgh Law Review*, *University of Pittsburgh Journal of Law and Commerce*, *Pittsburgh Journal of Technology*, the *Pittsburgh Tax Review* and the *Pittsburgh Journal of Environmental* and *Public Health Law*. Moot court competitions include the Murray S. Love Trial Moot Court Competition, the National Health Law Moot Court Competition, and the BMI/Cardoza Entertainment Law Moot Court Competition. Law student organizations include The Pitt Legal Income Sharing Foundation, Hispanic Law Society, and Pitt Law Women's Association. There are local chapters of the Black Law Student's Association, International Law Society, and Phi Alpha Delta.

Library

The law library contains 470,958 hardcopy volumes and 204,232 microform volume equivalents, and subscribes to 4035 serial publications. Such on-line databases and networks as CALI, CIS Universe, DIALOG, Dow-Jones, Infotrac, Legal-Trac, LEXIS, Mathew Bender, NEXIS, OCLC First Search, WESTLAW, Wilsonline Indexes, and more than 300 separate databases available through the University of Pittsburgh Digital Library are available to law students for research. Special library collections include international law, tax and labor law, health law, and a selective federal depository. The library remodeled in 2004 to include wireless network access, updated seating, computer laboratories, and a llounge area. The ratio of library volumes to faculty is 8525 to 1 and to students is 664 to 1. The ratio of seats in the library to students is 1 to 2.

Faculty

The law school has 54 full-time and 97 part-time faculty members, of whom 51 are women. According to AAUP standards for Category I institutions, faculty salaries are below average. About 24% of full-time faculty have a graduate law degree in addition to the J.D. The ratio of full-time students to full-time faculty in an average class is 13 to 1; in a clinic, 8 to 1. The law school has a regular program of bringing visiting professors and other distinguished lecturers and visitors to campus. There is a chapter of the Order of the Coif; 8 faculty are members.

Placement

J.D.s awarded:	230

Services available through: a separate law school placement center

Services: training in computerized job searching, workshops, publication of a weekly student newsletter, on-line student and alumni job posting site, videotaped interviews, and participation in minority and other specialized job fairs

Special features: an emphasis on exploring career options and long-range career planning and developing and refining job procurement and retention skills. The professional staff consists of an Assistant Dean, a Director of Employer Relations and a Director of Career Services and Public Interest Initiatives, all of whom remain active in state and local bar associations and bring an array of legal practice experience to their work.

Full-time job interviews:	36 employers
Summer job interviews:	67 employers
Placement by graduation:	72% of class
Placement within 9 months:	94% of class
Average starting salary:	$40,000 to $145,000

Areas of placement:

Private practice 2-10 attorneys	22%
Private practice 11-25 attorneys	4%
Private practice 26-50 attorneys	2%
Private practice 51-100 attorneys	4%
firms with 101+ attorneys	28%
Business/industry	17%
Government	10%
Judicial clerkships	7%
Public interest	4%
Military	2%
Academic	1%

Students

About 47% of the student body are women; 16%, minorities; 7%, African American; 6%, Asian American; 3%, Hispanic; and fewer than 1%, Native American. The majority of students come from Pennsylvania (60%). The average age of entering students is 24; age range is 20 to 59. About 46% of students enter directly from undergraduate school and 7% have a graduate degree. About 1% drop out after the first year for academic or personal reasons.

UNIVERSITY OF PUERTO RICO

School of Law

P.O. Box 23349, UPR Station
Rio Piedras, PR 00931-3349

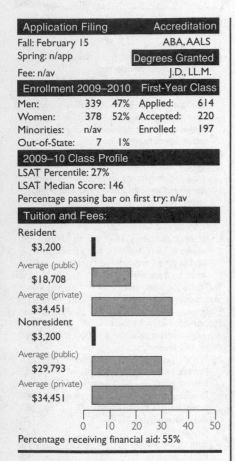

Application Filing	Accreditation
Fall: February 15	ABA, AALS
Spring: n/app	Degrees Granted
Fee: n/av	J.D., LL.M.

Enrollment 2009–2010			First-Year Class	
Men:	339	47%	Applied:	614
Women:	378	52%	Accepted:	220
Minorities:	n/av		Enrolled:	197
Out-of-State:	7	1%		

2009–10 Class Profile

LSAT Percentile: 27%
LSAT Median Score: 146
Percentage passing bar on first try: n/av

Tuition and Fees:

Resident
$3,200

Average (public)
$18,708

Average (private)
$34,451

Nonresident
$3,200

Average (public)
$29,793

Average (private)
$34,451

0   10   20   30   40   50

Percentage receiving financial aid: 55%

ADMISSIONS

In the fall 2009 first-year class, 614 applied, 220 were accepted, and 197 enrolled. Figures in the above capsule and in this profile are approximate. Twelve transfers enrolled. The median LSAT percentile of the most recent first-year class was 27; the median GPA was 3.64 on a scale of 4.0. The lowest LSAT percentile accepted was 2; the highest was 89.

Requirements
Applicants must have a bachelor's degree and take the LSAT. No specific undergraduate courses are required. Candidates are not interviewed.

Procedure
Applicants should submit an application form, LSAT results, transcripts, EXADEP, and a nonrefundable fee. Accepted students must pay a $45 seat deposit (credited toward tuition). Notification of the admissions decision is April and May. The latest acceptable LSAT test date for fall

entry is February. Check with the school for current application deadlines. The law school uses the LSDAS.

Special
Requirements are not different for out-of-state students. Transfer students must have a minimum GPA of 3.3, have attended an ABA-approved law school, and have 12 credits approved.

Costs

Tuition and fees for the 2009-2010 academic year are $3200 for all full-time students. Tuition for part-time students is $1600 in-state. On-campus room and board costs about $4200 annually; books and supplies run $2600.

Financial Aid

In a recent year, about 55% of current law students received some form of aid. The average annual amount of aid from all sources combined, including scholarships, loans, and work contracts, was $8500; maximum, $9864. Awards are based on need and merit. Required financial statement is the FAFSA. Check with the school for current application deadlines. First-year students are notified about their financial aid application at time of acceptance.

About the Law School

University of Puerto Rico School of Law was established in 1913 and is a public institution. The 5-acre campus is in an urban area in metropolitan San Juan. The primary mission of the law school is to train competent lawyers and jurists with a strong sense of professional, ethical, and social responsibility. Students have access to federal, state, county, city, and local agencies, courts, correctional facilities, law firms, and legal aid organizations in the Rio Piedras area. Housing for students is available in dormitories on campus. About 95% of the law school facilities are accessible to the physically disabled.

Calendar

The law school operates on a traditional semester basis. Courses for full-time students are offered both day and evening and must be completed within 6 semesters. For part-time students, courses are

offered both day and evening and must be completed within 8 semesters. New full- and part-time students are admitted in the fall. There is a 6-week summer session. Transferable summer courses are not offered.

Programs

In addition to the J.D., the law school offers the LL.M. Students may take relevant courses in other programs and apply credit toward the J.D.; a maximum of 6 credits may be applied. The following joint degrees may be earned: J.D./Lic. en Derecho (dual degree program with the University of Barcelo), J.D./M.B.A. (Juris Doctor/Master of Business Administration), J.D./M.D. (Juris Doctor/Doctor of Medicine), and J.D./M.P.P. (Juris Doctor/Master of Public Policy).

Required
To earn the J.D., candidates must complete 92 total credits, of which 46 are for required courses. They must maintain a minimum GPA of 2.0 in the required courses. The following first-year courses are required of all students: Civil Procedure, Constitutional Law, Criminal Law, Family Law, Introduction to Law, Legal Research, Obligations and Contracts Law, Problems in International Law, Property, and Torts. Required upper-level courses consist of Business Associations and Corporations, Evidence, Legal Aid Clinic I and II, and Theory of Law. All students must take clinical courses. The required orientation program for first-year students lasts 1 week and includes information on financial aid, required courses, exchange programs, methods of study, and a brief introduction to law school.

Electives
All students are required to take clinics on civil, criminal, or federal law, worth 6 credits, and 2 2-credit seminars. During the summer an elective legal practice workshop is offered; it is worth 2 credits. Legal research in urban planning, housing, poverty, and related subjects is encouraged in a number of courses. There is a summer course in Barcelona, worth up to 6 credits, that is open to all students in good standing. There is also a double-degree program with the University of Barcelona and an exchange program with the University of Chile Law School; Uni-

Phone: 787-999-9551
Fax: 787-999-9564
E-mail: *arosario-lebron@law.upr.edu*

PUERTO RICO

Contact
Director of Admissions, 787-999-9551 or 787-999-9563 for general inquiries; Michael Ayala, 787-999-9557 or 787-999-9563 for financial aid information.

versity of Ottawa, Canada; University of Palermo, Argentina; University of Arizona, USA; University of Connecticut, USA; and University of Antwerp, Belgium. The most widely taken electives are Bankruptcy, Taxation, and Criminology.

Graduation Requirements
In order to graduate, candidates must have a GPA of 2.0 and have completed the upper-division writing requirement.

Organizations
Students edit the *University of Puerto Rico Law Review* and the newspaper *El Nuevo Jurista*. Moot court competitions include the Annual Pace University School of Law National Environmental, NACDL Katty Bennet Criminal Trial, and Philip C. Jessup International. Another competition is the Miguel Velazquez Annual Debate. Law student organizations include the Student Council, Derecho Pa Vieques, Phi Alpha Delta fraternity, National Association of Law Students and ABA-Law Student Division. Student representatives chosen by the student council serve on all law school committees, except the personnel committee.

Library
The law library contains 283,745 hardcopy volumes and 172,059 microform volume equivalents, and subscribes to 5159 serial publications. Such on-line databases and networks as CALI, DIALOG, Infotrac, Legal-Trac, LEXIS, Mathew Bender, NEXIS, WESTLAW, Wilsonline Indexes, West Law Spain, Hein Online, Index to Foreign Legal Periodicals, RIA Checkpoint, LexisNexis Argentina, Microjuris, JTS Online, Consulta Legislativa, and EL Nuevo Dia are available to law students for research. Special library collections include extensive collections of Puerto Rico, Spain, Caribbean, Latin American and comparative and international law, a U.S. GPO government depository, Specialized European Communities Documentation Centre, and documents collection of former judges of the Supreme Court of Puerto Rico. Recently, the library installed wireless network access, upgraded the computer laboratory and the computer training room, and added an electronic reserve collection. The ratio of library volumes to faculty is 9458 to 1 and to stu-

dents is 396 to 1. The ratio of seats in the library to students is 1 to 1.

Faculty
The law school has 30 full-time and 66 part-time faculty members, of whom 36 are women. About 73% of full-time faculty have a graduate law degree in addition to the J.D.; about 40% of part-time faculty have one. The ratio of full-time students to full-time faculty in an average class is 15 to 1; in a clinic, 13 to 1. The law school has a regular program of bringing visiting professors and other distinguished lecturers and visitors to campus.

Students
About 52% of the student body are women; 12%, Hispanic; and 84%, Puerto Rican. The majority of students come from Puerto Rico (99%). The average age of entering students is 24; age range is 20 to 54. About 81% of students enter directly from undergraduate school and 19% have a graduate degree. About 5% drop out after the first year for academic or personal reasons; 95% remain to receive a law degree.

Placement	
J.D.s awarded:	174
Services available through: a separate law school placement center	
Special features: annual job fair.	
Full-time job interviews:	n/av
Summer job interviews:	n/av
Placement by graduation:	n/av
Placement within 9 months:	81% of class
Average starting salary:	$24,000 to $50,999
Areas of placement:	
Private practice 2-10 attorneys	15%
Private practice 11-25 attorneys	3%
Private practice 26-50 attorneys	22%
Business/industry	20%
Judicial clerkships	18%
Government	17%
Academic	5%

School of Law

28 Westhampton Way
Richmond, VA 23173

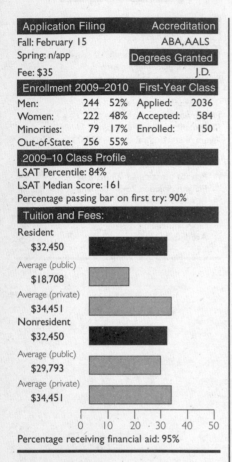

Application Filing		Accreditation
Fall: February 15		ABA, AALS
Spring: n/app		Degrees Granted
Fee: $35		J.D.

Enrollment 2009–2010		First-Year Class	
Men:	244 52%	Applied:	2036
Women:	222 48%	Accepted:	584
Minorities:	79 17%	Enrolled:	150
Out-of-State:	256 55%		

2009–10 Class Profile
LSAT Percentile: 84%
LSAT Median Score: 161
Percentage passing bar on first try: 90%

Tuition and Fees:

Resident
$32,450

Average (public)
$18,708

Average (private)
$34,451

Nonresident
$32,450

Average (public)
$29,793

Average (private)
$34,451

0 10 20 30 40 50

Percentage receiving financial aid: 95%

ADMISSIONS
In the fall 2009 first-year class, 2036 applied, 584 were accepted, and 150 enrolled. Nineteen transfers enrolled. The median LSAT percentile of the most recent first-year class was 84; the median GPA was 3.18 on a scale of 4.0. The lowest LSAT percentile accepted was 44; the highest was 99.

Requirements
Applicants must have a bachelor's degree and take the LSAT. The most important admission factors include academic achievement, LSAT results, and general background. No specific undergraduate courses are required. Candidates are not interviewed.

Procedure
The application deadline for fall entry is February 15. Applicants should submit an application form, LSAT results, transcripts, a personal statement, a nonrefundable application fee of $35, and 2 letters of recommendation. Notification of the admissions decision is by May 1. The latest acceptable LSAT test date for fall entry is February. The law school uses the LSDAS.

Special
The law school recruits minority and disadvantaged students by attending minority law forums, being a Council for Legal Education Opportunity (CLEO) sponsor, being a CLEO Regional Summer Institute site, visiting historically black colleges and universities, and offering scholarships. Requirements are not different for out-of-state students. Transfer students must have 1 year of credit, have attended an ABA-approved law school, and must be in good standing at an ABA-approved law school.

Costs
Tuition and fees for the 2009-2010 academic year are $32,450 for all full-time students. On-campus room and board costs about $10,530 annually; books and supplies run $1300.

Financial Aid
About 95% of current law students receive some form of aid. The average annual amount of aid from all sources combined, including scholarships, loans, and work contracts, is $34,240; maximum, $44,280. Awards are based on need and merit. All admitted students must file the FAFSA by February 15. Required financial statement is the FAFSA. The aid application deadline for fall entry is March 1. Special funds for minority or disadvantaged students consist of scholarships. First-year students are notified about their financial aid application by April 10.

About the Law School
University of Richmond School of Law was established in 1870 and is a private institution. The 350-acre campus is in a suburban area 2 miles west of Richmond. The primary mission of the law school is to train its graduates to practice law. Its relatively small size helps fashion a close and open relationship between students and faculty. Students have access to federal, state, county, city, and local agencies, courts, correctional facilities, law firms, and legal aid organizations in the Richmond area. Facilities of special interest to law students include the law library with a legal research and writing computer laboratory, and individualized study carrels that are electronically networked via students' personal computers to the Legal Information Center, a schoolwide computer system that gives instant access to the electronic age in law. Housing for students is available in a law dormitory with single rooms. Attractively priced apartments are available very close to the campus. All law school facilities are accessible to the physically disabled.

Calendar
The law school operates on a traditional semester basis. Courses for full-time students are offered days only and must be completed within 5 years. For part-time students, courses are offered days only and must be completed within 5 years. New full- and part-time students are admitted in the fall and summer. There is a 3- and 8-week summer session. Transferable summer courses are offered.

Programs
Students may take relevant courses in other programs and apply credit toward the J.D.; a maximum of 9 credits may be applied. The following joint degrees may be earned: J.D./M.B.A. (Juris Doctor/Master of Business Administration), J.D./M.H.A. (Juris Doctor/Master of Health Administration with Medical College of Virginia), J.D./M.P.A. (Juris Doctor/Master of Public Administration with Virginia Common Wealth), J.D./M.S.W. (Juris Doctor/Master of Social Work with Virginia Commonwealth), and J.D./M.U.R.P. (Juris Doctor/Master of Urban and Regional Planning with Virginia Common Wealth).

Required
To earn the J.D., candidates must complete 86 total credits, of which 35 are for required courses. The following first-year courses are required of all students: Civil Procedure, Constitutional Law, Contracts, Criminal Law, Environmental Law, Lawyering Skills I and II, Property, and Torts. Required upper-level courses consist of Professional Responsibility, upper-level Lawyering Skills III and IV, and upper-level writing requirements. The required orientation program for first-year stu-

Phone: 804-289-8189
Fax: 804-287-6516
E-mail: *lawadmissions@richmond.edu*
Web: *law.richmond.edu*

Contact

Michelle L. Rahman, Associate Dean, 804-289-8189 for general inquiries; C. Deffenbaugh, Director of Financial Aid, 804-289-8438 for financial aid information.

dents lasts 3 days and includes network and computer training and an introduction to lawyering skills as well as the law school administration, faculty, staff, student organizations, and law student advisers.

Electives

The School of Law offers concentrations in environmental law, family law, intellectual property law, torts and insurance, and Intellectual Property Certification, Environmental Law Certification, Family Law Certification. In addition, third-year students may participate in either the outplacement clinic or the school's in-house Children's Law Center, with Youth Advocacy and Mental Disabilities clinics. The outplacement clinic allows students to work in various legal offices in the community and is complemented by a classroom component. The clinical programs, supervised by a staff attorney, allow students to represent clients in business, civil, criminal, and judicial matters. Students may also participate in the D.C. Summer Environmental Internship Program in Washington, D.C. Credit varies for these programs. Special lecture series include the Allen Chair Lecture, Emroch Lecture, Austin Owen Lecture, and Legal Forum. There is a study-abroad option. Students may study international law for 5 weeks at Emmanuel College in Cambridge, England, or for a semester at any one of 9 foreign universities with which the law school has an exchange program. There is an academic support program for all students.

Graduation Requirements

In order to graduate, candidates must have a GPA of 2.2 and have completed the upper-division writing requirement.

Organizations

Students edit the *University of Richmond Law Review, Journal of Law and Technology* (on-line) *Perspectives on Law and the Public Interest, Journal of International Law and Business, Journal of Law and Public Interest*, and the newspaper *Juris Publici*. Moot court teams attend the Appellate Advocacy Moot Court Competition in the fall and the Motions and Interscholastic Motions Competition in the spring as well as the Judge John R. Brown Admiralty Moot Court Competi-

tion. There are intramural competitions in both client counseling and negotiations. The winning teams enter respective ABA competitions. Annually, the National Environmental Negotiation Competition is entered. The school has hosted the ABA regional competition. Law student organizations include the Student Bar Association, Client Counseling and Negotiation Board, American Constitution Society, and Federalist Society for Law and Public Policy Studies. There are local chapters of ABA-Student Division, the Black Law Students Association, and Phi Alpha Delta. Additionally, there are intramural sports, including soccer and softball.

Library

The law library contains 407,871 hardcopy volumes and 194,283 microform volume equivalents, and subscribes to 4619 serial publications. Such on-line databases and networks as CALI, CIS Universe, DIALOG, Infotrac, Legal-Trac, LEXIS, LOIS, NEXIS, OCLC First Search, WESTLAW, Wilsonline Indexes, HeinOnline, Michie's Virginia Law on Disc, BNA (online), West Pac, RIA Checkpoint, Making of Modern Law, LLMC-Digital, and CCH Business and Finance Research Network are available to law students for research. Special library collections include a U.S. government documents depository, Robert R. Merhige, Jr. judicial papers, Tokyo war crimes tribunal, Blackwell N. Shelley bankruptcy opinions, and Virginia Supreme Court records and briefs digital collection. Recently, the library added 9 group study tables with seating for 48. The ratio of library volumes to faculty is 8497 to 1 and to students is 875 to 1. The ratio of seats in the library to students is 1 to 1.

Faculty

The law school has 48 full-time and 74 part-time faculty members, of whom 43 are women. According to AAUP standards for Category IIB institutions, faculty salaries are above average. About 47% of full-time faculty have a graduate law degree in addition to the J.D. The ratio of full-time students to full-time faculty in an average class is 15 to 1; in a clinic, 6 to 1. The law school has a regular program of bringing visiting professors and other distinguished lecturers and visitors to campus.

Placement

J.D.s awarded:	163

Services available through: a separate law school placement center and the university placement center

Services: programs on law practice areas, minority job and career fairs, specialty fairs, and job search programs with national speakers and specialty career fairs

Special features: individual attention available to all students with 4 professional staff members in career services office.

Full-time job interviews:	15 employers
Summer job interviews:	44 employers
Placement by graduation:	69% of class
Placement within 9 months:	88% of class
Average starting salary:	$40,000 to $165,000

Areas of placement:

Private practice 2-10 attorneys	11%
Private practice 11-25 attorneys	9%
Private practice 26-50 attorneys	4%
Private practice 51-100 attorneys	2%
Private practice 100+ attorneys 21%,	
Contract and	25%
Government	20%
Judicial clerkships	18%
Business/industry	8%
Public interest	3%
Military	2%
Academic	1%

Students

About 48% of the student body are women; 17%, minorities; 9%, African American; 6%, Asian American; 1%, Hispanic; and 1%, Native American. The majority of students come from out of state (55%). The average age of entering students is 24; age range is 20 to 50. About 46% of students enter directly from undergraduate school, 10% have a graduate degree, and 54% have worked full-time prior to entering law school. About 1% drop out after the first year for academic or personal reasons; 99% remain to receive a law degree.

UNIVERSITY OF SAINT THOMAS

School of Law

1000 LaSalle Ave.
Minneapolis, MN 55403

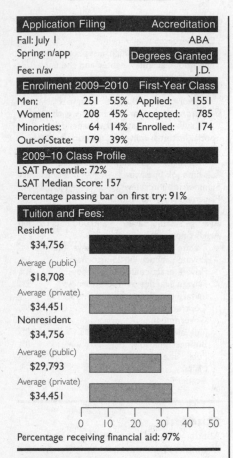

Application Filing	Accreditation
Fall: July 1	ABA
Spring: n/app	**Degrees Granted**
Fee: n/av	J.D.

Enrollment 2009–2010		First-Year Class	
Men:	251 55%	Applied:	1551
Women:	208 45%	Accepted:	785
Minorities:	64 14%	Enrolled:	174
Out-of-State:	179 39%		

2009–10 Class Profile
LSAT Percentile: 72%
LSAT Median Score: 157
Percentage passing bar on first try: 91%

Tuition and Fees:

Resident
$34,756

Average (public)
$18,708

Average (private)
$34,451

Nonresident
$34,756

Average (public)
$29,793

Average (private)
$34,451

0 10 20 30 40 50

Percentage receiving financial aid: 97%

ADMISSIONS

In the fall 2009 first-year class, 1551 applied, 785 were accepted, and 174 enrolled. Five transfers enrolled. The median LSAT percentile of the most recent first-year class was 72; the median GPA was 3.44 on a scale of 4.0. The lowest LSAT percentile accepted was 33; the highest was 99.

Requirements
Applicants must have a bachelor's degree and take the LSAT. The most important admission factors include academic achievement, motivations, general background, and whether the applicant is suited to the mission of the school. No specific undergraduate courses are required. Candidates are not interviewed.

Procedure
The application deadline for fall entry is July 1. Applicants should submit an application form, LSAT results, transcripts, a personal statement, and 2 letters of rec-

ommendation. Notification of the admissions decision is on a rolling basis. The latest acceptable LSAT test date for fall entry is June. The law school uses the LSDAS.

Special
The law school recruits minority and disadvantaged students through campus visits, advertising, direct mailings, participation in minority recruitment events, and a scholarship program. Requirements are not different for out-of-state students. Transfer students must have one year of credit and have attended an ABA-approved law school.

Costs

Tuition and fees for the 2009-2010 academic year are $34,756 for all full-time students. Books and supplies run $1550.

Financial Aid

About 97% of current law students receive some form of aid. The average annual amount of aid from all sources combined, including scholarships, loans, and work contracts, is $43,798; maximum, $55,636. Awards are based on need and merit. Required financial statement is the FAFSA. The aid application deadline for fall entry is July 1. Special funds for minority or disadvantaged students include the Ciresi scholarship. First-year students are notified about their financial aid application at time of acceptance.

About the Law School

University of Saint Thomas School of Law was established in 2001 and is a private institution. The 53-acre campus is in an urban area in downtown Minneapolis. The primary mission of the law school is to integrate faith and reason in the search for truth through a focus on morality and social justice. To implement this mission, each member of the law school community is dedicated to promoting excellence in professional preparation, knowledge creation and societal reform, and service and community. Students have access to federal, state, county, city, and local agencies, courts, correctional facilities, law firms, and legal aid organizations in the Minneapolis area. Students have access to in-house corporate legal staff, and there are mentors for each student. Facilities

of special interest to law students include the four-story atrium moot court room and chapel, modern technology throughout the building, and the library's strong electronic collection. There is no on-campus housing, but students live throughout the Twin Cities. The school offers assistance in finding housing. All law school facilities are accessible to the physically disabled.

Calendar

The law school operates on a traditional semester basis. Courses for full-time students are offered both day and evening and must be completed within 4 years. There is no part-time program. New students are admitted in the fall. There is a 7-week summer session. Transferable summer courses are offered.

Programs

Students may take relevant courses in other programs and apply credit toward the J.D.; a maximum of 6 credits may be applied. The following joint degrees may be earned: J.D./M.A. Prof. Psych. (Juris Doctor/Master of Arts in professional psychology), J.D./M.A.C.S. (Juris Doctor/Master of Arts in Catholic studies), J.D./M.A.Ed. (Juris Doctor/Master of Arts in educational leadership), J.D./M.B.A. (Juris Doctor/Master of Business Administration), and J.D./M.S.W. (Juris Doctor/Master of Social Work).

Required
To earn the J.D., candidates must complete 88 total credits, of which 46 are for required courses. They must maintain a minimum GPA of 2.0 in the required courses. The following first-year courses are required of all students: Civil Procedure I, Constitutional Law, Contracts, Criminal Law, Foundations of Justice, Lawyering Skills I and II, Property, and Torts. Required upper-level courses consist of Business Associations, Evidence, Lawyering Skills III, Mentor Externship, Professional Responsibility, and Public Service Requirement. The required orientation program for first-year students is "First Week", five days including a non-credit academic success course, a 1-credit Foundation of Justice course, and a variety of optional social, service, and informational programs.

Phone: 651-962-4895
800-328-6819
Fax: 651-962-4876
E-mail: *lawschool@stthomas.edu*
Web: *www.stthomas.edu/lawschool*

Contact

Director of Admissions, 651-962-4895 for general inquiries; Chad Nosbusch, 651-962-4051 for financial aid information.

MINNESOTA

Electives

Clinics include Immigration Law (6 credits), Community Justice Project (6 credits), and Elder Law (6 credits) (upper level). Seminars include Ethical Leadership in Corporate Practice (3 credits), Catholic Social Thought (2 credits), and Critical Perspectives on the Law: Race (2 credits). There is a Mentor Externship Program (2 credits) that combines mentor directed fieldwork with a contemporaneous faculty-led seminar (upper level). Supervised research and writing (1 to 2 credits) is available and Law Journal (1 to 2 credits). Field work includes District Court Judicial Externship (3 credits) and Business Law Externship (2 credits). Special lecture series include the Law Journal symposia (2 per year). The school accepts credit from ABA-approved study abroad programs and co-sponsors a summer program in Rome. Tutorial/remedial programs include a non-credit academic achievement program, study skills, advising, and a 2-credit bar skills course. There is a law firm-sponsored minority scholarship/mentor program; the Ciresi scholarship for minority students; and the Minnesota Minority Clerkship Program in which UST students can participate. The family law student group partners with law firms and agencies to assist in adoptions. The most widely taken electives are Wills, Estates, and Trusts; Employment Law; and Criminal Procedure.

Graduation Requirements

In order to graduate, candidates must have a GPA of 2.0, have completed the upper-division writing requirement, and public service (50 hours), and the Mentor Externship Program.

Organizations

Students edit the *University of St. Thomas Law Journal, Fides es Iustitia*, the student newspaper *Tommie Law News*, and the student organization published *Journal of Law and Public policy*. Moot court competitions include the National Advocacy competition, Giles Sutherland Rich Memorial Moot Court competition, and Philip C. Jessup International Law Moot Court Competition. Other competitions include ABA Negotiation Competition and AAJ Trial Advocacy Competition. Law student organizations include the Christian Legal Society, American Constitution Society, and Minnesota Justice Foundation. Local chapters of national associations

are the Black Law Students Association, the Federalist Society, and Phi Alpha Delta legal fraternity. Other clubs include Environmental Law Society, Business and Corporate Law Society, and Criminal Law Society.

Library

The law library contains 207,979 hardcopy volumes and 881,232 microform volume equivalents, and subscribes to 699 serial publications. Such on-line databases and networks as CALI, CIS Universe, Infotrac, Legal-Trac, LEXIS, LOIS, NEXIS, OCLC First Search, WESTLAW, Wilsonline Indexes, Hein Online, BNA Services, CCH Business and Finance Library, Digital Serial Set, RIA Checkpoint, Legal Scholarship Network, and United Nations Treaty Collection are available to law students for research. Recently, the library added several significant databases, including historical components of Lexis/Nexis Congressional. The ratio of library volumes to faculty is 5777 to 1 and to students is 453 to 1. The ratio of seats in the library to students is 1 to 1.

Faculty

The law school has 36 full-time and 61 part-time faculty members, of whom 38 are women. According to AAUP standards for Category I institutions, faculty salaries are well below average. About 21% of full-time faculty have a graduate law degree in addition to the J.D.; about 8% of part-time faculty have one. The ratio of full-time students to full-time faculty in an average class is 17 to 1; in a clinic, 7 to 1. The law school has a regular program of bringing visiting professors and other distinguished lecturers and visitors to campus.

Students

About 45% of the student body are women; 14%, minorities; 4%, African American; 6%, Asian American; 3%, Hispanic; 1%, Native American; and 11%, unknown race/ethnicity. The majority of students come from Minnesota (61%). The average age of entering students is 25; age range is 20 to 55. About 36% of students enter directly from undergraduate school, 5% have a graduate degree, and 64% have worked full-time prior to entering law school. About 3% drop out after the first year for academic or personal reasons; 96% remain to receive a law degree.

Placement

J.D.s awarded:	145
Services available through: a separate law school placement center	
Services: mock interviews; counseling on other application material preparation	
Full-time job interviews:	5 employers
Summer job interviews:	34 employers
Placement by graduation:	n/av
Placement within 9 months:	87% of class
Average starting salary:	n/av
Areas of placement:	
Private practice 2-10 attorneys	20%
Private practice 11-25 attorneys	4%
Private practice 26-50 attorneys	3%
Private practice 51-100 attorneys	3%
Business/industry	21%
8% in larger firms (private practice);	
5% in solo;	15%
Judicial clerkships	14%
Government	10%
Public interest	6%
Military	2%
Academic	2%

University of Saint Thomas **541**

School of Law

5998 Alcala Park
San Diego, CA 92110

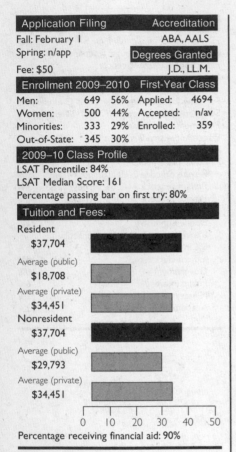

Application Filing		Accreditation	
Fall: February 1		ABA, AALS	
Spring: n/app		Degrees Granted	
Fee: $50		J.D., LL.M.	

Enrollment 2009–2010			First-Year Class	
Men:	649	56%	Applied:	4694
Women:	500	44%	Accepted:	n/av
Minorities:	333	29%	Enrolled:	359
Out-of-State:	345	30%		

2009–10 Class Profile
LSAT Percentile: 84%
LSAT Median Score: 161
Percentage passing bar on first try: 80%

Tuition and Fees:

Resident
$37,704

Average (public)
$18,708

Average (private)
$34,451

Nonresident
$37,704

Average (public)
$29,793

Average (private)
$34,451

0 10 20 30 40 50

Percentage receiving financial aid: 90%

ADMISSIONS

In a recent year, 4694 applied and 359 enrolled. The median LSAT percentile of the most recent first-year class was 84; the median GPA was 3.28 on a scale of 4.0. Figures in the above capsule and in this profile are approximate.

Requirements

Applicants must have a bachelor's degree and take the LSAT. The most important admission factors include academic achievement, GPA, and LSAT results. No specific undergraduate courses are required. Candidates are not interviewed.

Procedure

Applicants should submit an application form, LSAT results, transcripts, a personal statement, and a nonrefundable application fee of $50. Notification of the admissions decision is January through mid-April. The latest acceptable LSAT test date for fall entry is February (day program) and June (evening program). The law school uses the LSDAS. Check with the school for current application deadlines.

Special

The law school recruits minority and disadvantaged students by welcoming and respecting those whose lives are formed by different traditions, recognizing that diversity of viewpoint, background, and experience (including race, ethnicity, cultural diversity, gender, religion, age, socioeconomic status, and disability) among its student body is essential to the full and informed exchange of ideas and to the quality of legal education it seeks to provide. Requirements are not different for out-of-state students. Transfer students must have one year of credit, have attended an ABA-approved law school, and should have a rank in the top quintile of the first-year class.

Costs

Tuition and fees for the 2009-2010 academic year are approximately $37,704 for all full-time students. Tuition for part-time students is approximately $26,804 per year. On-campus room and board costs about $18,440 annually; books and supplies run about $956.

Financial Aid

In a recent year, about 90% of current law students received some form of aid. The average annual amount of aid from all sources combined, including scholarships, loans, and work contracts, is approximately $38,000; maximum, $57,100. Awards are based on need and merit. Required financial statements are the FAFSA and institutional application for accepted students. Check with the school for current application deadlines. Special funds for minority or disadvantaged students include need-based, full- and partial-tuition scholarships available to entering students. These scholarships are based on the applicant's academic promise, financial need, potential for service to the community, and contribution of diversity to the student body. First-year students are notified about their financial aid application at time of acceptance.

About the Law School

University of San Diego School of Law was established in 1954 and is a private institution. The 180-acre campus is in an urban area 5 miles north of downtown San Diego. The primary mission of the law school is to foster an environment of stimulating and rigorous intellectual exchange between teacher and student in which teaching and learning engage the full attention of faculty and students while maintaining concern for the broader personal and moral development of the law student. Students have access to federal, state, county, city, and local agencies, courts, correctional facilities, law firms, and legal aid organizations in the San Diego area. Facilities of special interest to law students . Housing for students is available in safe and affordable accommodations near campus. The Admissions Office maintains a listing of students seeking roommates and other resources. About 90% of the law school facilities are accessible to the physically disabled.

Calendar

The law school operates on a traditional semester basis. Courses for full-time students are offered days only and must be completed within 5 years. For part-time students, courses are offered evenings only and must be completed within 5 years. New full- and part-time students are admitted in the fall. There is an 8-week summer session. Transferable summer courses are offered.

Programs

In addition to the J.D., the law school offers the LL.M. Students may take relevant courses in other programs and apply credit toward the J.D.; a maximum of 6 credits may be applied. The following joint degrees may be earned: J.D./I.M.B.A. (Juris Doctor/International Master of Business Administration), J.D./M.A. (Juris Doctor/Master of Arts in International Relations), and J.D./M.B.A. (Juris Doctor/Master of Business Administration).

Required

To earn the J.D., candidates must complete 85 total credits, of which 35 are for required courses. They must maintain a minimum GPA of 2.0 in the required courses. The following first-year courses are required of all students: Civil Procedure, Constitutional Law, Contracts, Criminal Law, Lawyering Skills I, Prop-

Phone: 619-260-4528
800-248-4873
Fax: 619-260-2218
E-mail: jdinfo@sandiego.edu
Web: law.sandiego.edu

Contact

Assistant Dean of Admissions and Financial Aid, 619-260-4528 for general inquiries, and financial aid information.

erty, and Torts. Required upper-level courses consist of Professional Responsibility and Tax I. The required orientation program for first-year students is offered to incoming students, who attend a mandatory 2-day orientation. Many topics are presented for discussion including Socratic method, time management, and how to study for law school exams.

Electives

The School of Law offers concentrations in corporate law, criminal law, environmental law, family law, international law, labor law, litigation, tax law, torts and insurance, and public interest/children's advocacy. In addition, students may enroll for up to 10 credits of clinical field work. They represent clients in consumer, housing, family, and administrative matters. Several seminar courses are offered each semester. Internships are available in-house through the Clinical Education Program, as well as with local agencies, government offices, and law firms in a variety of areas. Research programs are available at the Center for Public Interest Law, Patient Advocacy Program, and the Children's Advocacy Institute. Special lecture series include the Nathanson Series and the Seigan Series. The Institute on International and Comparative Law sponsors the Summer Law Study Programs in England, France, Ireland, Italy, and Spain. Internships for credit are available in England France. The Academic Support Program provides special services to students. A faculty member provides academic counseling and sets up study groups for each class. Minority programs include a Multicultural Law Day. Pro Bono Legal Advocates promote diversity in the bar and donate students' talent and time to clients who cannot afford a lawyer. The most widely taken electives are courses relevant to international law, environmental law, and corporate law.

Graduation Requirements

In order to graduate, candidates must have a GPA of 2.0 and have completed the upper-division writing requirement.

Organizations

Students edit the *San Diego Law Review*, the *San Diego International Law Journal*, the newspaper *Motions*, the *Journal of Contemporary Legal Issues*, and *Legal*

Theory. Moot court competitions include the Alumni Tort, Annual USD National Criminal Procedure Competition, and Jessup International Law. Other competitions include Advanced Trial Advocacy, Mock Trial, and Thomas More Constitutional Law. Student organizations, local chapters of national associations, and campus organizations include American Trial Lawyers Association, Pro Bono Legal Advocates, Women's Law Caucus, Student Bar Association, Environmental Law Society, International Law Society, Phi Delta Phi, and Phi Alpha Delta.

Library

The law library contains 529,802 hardcopy volumes and 226,282 microform volume equivalents, and subscribes to 6250 serial publications. Such on-line databases and networks as CALI, CIS Universe, DIALOG, Dow-Jones, Infotrac, Legal-Trac, LEXIS, LOIS, Matthew Bender, NEXIS, OCLC First Search, RLIN, WESTLAW, and CCH, RIA, HeinOnline, LLMC, and Index Master are available to law students for research. Special library collections include state and federal depositories, tax collection, and California collection. Recently, the library installed a new computer instructional laboratory that provides state-of-the-art access to legal research tools, the internet, and law office technology. It also participates in a consortium of San Diego libraries. The ratio of library volumes to faculty is 9461 to 1 and to students is 461 to 1. The ratio of seats in the library to students is 1 to 2.

Faculty

The law school has 56 full-time and 39 part-time faculty members, of whom 23 are women. According to AAUP standards for Category 1 institutions, faculty salaries are average. The ratio of full-time students to full-time faculty in an average class is 18 to 1. The law school has a regular program of bringing visiting professors and other distinguished lecturers and visitors to campus. There is a chapter of the Order of the Coif.

Students

About 44% of the student body are women; 29%, minorities; 3%, African American; 15%, Asian American; 10%, Hispanic; 1%, Native American; and 1%, foreign nationals. The majority of students come

Placement	
J.D.s awarded:	333
Services available through: a separate law school placement center	
Special features: panel discussions sponsored by the Alumni Association that focus on law practice, alternative careers, and law clerk training.	
Full-time job interviews:	n/av
Summer job interviews:	n/av
Placement by graduation:	n/av
Placement within 9 months:	97% of class
Average starting salary:	$35,000 to $160,000
Areas of placement:	
Private practice 2-10 attorneys	38%
Private practice 11-25 attorneys	14%
Private practice 26-50 attorneys	10%
Private practice 51-100 attorneys	11%
Business/industry	17%
Government	13%
Public interest	5%
Judicial clerkships	2%
Academic	2%
Military	1%

from California (70%). The average age of entering students is 24; age range is 21 to 52. About 8% of students have a graduate degree. About 2% drop out after the first year for academic or personal reasons; 85% remain to receive a law degree.

UNIVERSITY OF SAN FRANCISCO

School of Law

2130 Fulton Street
San Francisco, CA 94117-1080

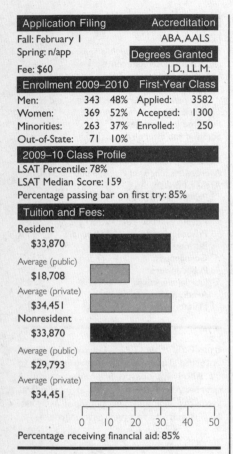

Application Filing		Accreditation	
Fall: February 1		ABA, AALS	
Spring: n/app		Degrees Granted	
Fee: $60		J.D., LL.M.	

Enrollment 2009–2010			First-Year Class	
Men:	343	48%	Applied:	3582
Women:	369	52%	Accepted:	1300
Minorities:	263	37%	Enrolled:	250
Out-of-State:	71	10%		

2009–10 Class Profile
LSAT Percentile: 78%
LSAT Median Score: 159
Percentage passing bar on first try: 85%

Tuition and Fees:

Resident
$33,870

Average (public)
$18,708

Average (private)
$34,451

Nonresident
$33,870

Average (public)
$29,793

Average (private)
$34,451

0   10   20   30   40   50

Percentage receiving financial aid: 85%

ADMISSIONS

In a recent year, 3582 applied, 1300 were accepted, and 250 enrolled. Three transfers enrolled. The median LSAT percentile of the most recent first-year class was 78; the median GPA was 3.28 on a scale of 4.0. The lowest LSAT percentile accepted was 15; the highest was 96. Figures in the above capsule and in this profile are approximate.

Requirements
Applicants must have a bachelor's degree and take the LSAT. The most important admission factors include academic achievement, minority status, and motivations. No specific undergraduate courses are required. Candidates are not interviewed.

Procedure
Applicants should submit an application form, LSAT results, transcripts, a personal statement, a nonrefundable application fee of $60, 2 letters of recommendation, and optional diversity statement. Notifi-

cation of the admissions decision is on a rolling basis. The latest acceptable LSAT test date for fall entry is December full-time, February part-time. The law school uses the LSDAS. Check with the school for current application deadlines.

Special
The law school recruits minority and disadvantaged students by actively recruiting and targeting colleges with large populations of students of color. Requirements are not different for out-of-state students. Transfer students must have one year of credit, have attended an ABA-approved law school, and deadline for transfer is June 26.

Costs

Tuition and fees for the 2009-2010 academic year are approximately $33,870 for all full-time students. Tuition for part-time students is approximately $24,245 per year. On-campus room and board costs about $14,000 annually; books and supplies run about $950.

Financial Aid

In a recent year, about 85% of current law students received some form of aid. The maximum annual amount of aid from all sources combined, including scholarships, loans, and work contracts, was approximately $52,980. Awards are based on need and merit. Required financial statement is the FAFSA. Check with the school for current application deadline.Special funds for minority or disadvantaged students include the Academic Support Program, which provides two grants that vary in amounts up to $3500, based on need. First-year students are notified about their financial aid application at time of acceptance.

About the Law School

University of San Francisco School of Law was established in 1912 and is a private institution. The 55-acre campus is in an urban area in the center of San Francisco, adjacent to Golden. The primary mission of the law school is to educate students to be skilled lawyers with a social conscience and a global perspective, emphasizing analytical ability and other fundamental skills, along with full awareness of special obligations to society. Students

have access to federal, state, county, city, and local agencies, courts, correctional facilities, law firms, and legal aid organizations in the San Francisco area. Facilities of special interest to law students include Kendrick Hall and the Dorraine Zief Library. In Kendrick Hall the classrooms include power and data connections at every seat, and state-of-the-art equipment throughout the building. Housing for students limited on campus; listings of off-campus accommodations are also available. All law school facilities are accessible to the physically disabled.

Calendar

The law school operates on a traditional semester basis. Courses for full-time students are offered and required courses are offered during the day, and must be completed within 5 years. For part-time students, courses are offered and mostly evenings and occasional weekend day and must be completed within 5 years. New full- and part-time students are admitted in the fall. There is a 7-week summer session. Transferable summer courses are offered.

Programs

In addition to the J.D., the law school offers the LL.M. The following joint degrees may be earned: J.D./M.B.A. (Juris Doctor/ Master of Business Administration).

Required
To earn the J.D., candidates must complete 86 total credits, of which 48 are for required courses. They must maintain a minimum GPA of 2.0 in the required courses. The following first-year courses are required of all students: Civil Procedure I and II, Contracts I and II, Criminal Law (second-year part time), Criminal Procedure (second-year part time), Legal Research, Writing, and Analysis I and II, Moot Court (second-year part time), Property, and Torts I and II. Required upper-level courses consist of a research and writing requirement, Constitutional Law I and II, Evidence, and Legal Ethics and the Practice of Law. The required orientation program for first-year students is a week long orientation program. An introduction course provides essential initiation to first-year courses.

Phone: 415-422-6586
Fax: 415-422-5442
E-mail: *lawadmissions@usfca.edu*
Web: *usfca.edu/law*

Contact

Director of Admissions, 415-422-6586 for general inquiries; Office of Financial Aid, 415-422-6210 for financial aid information.

CALIFORNIA

Placement

J.D.s awarded:	207
Services available through: a separate law school placement center	
Services: career seminars, on-campus interviewing, skills workshops, guest speakers, alumni panels	
Special features: Public Interest Law Program.	
Full-time job interviews:	21 employers
Summer job interviews:	47 employers
Placement by graduation:	n/av
Placement within 9 months:	92% of class
Average starting salary:	$38,000 to $135,000
Areas of placement:	
Private practice 2-10 attorneys	42%
Private practice 11-25 attorneys	8%
Private practice 26-50 attorneys	6%
Private practice 51-100 attorneys	8%
Private practice 101 to 501+ attorneys, and self-e	21%
Public interest	14%
Government	12%
Business/industry	12%
Judicial clerkships	4%

Electives

Students must take 15 credits in their area of concentration. The School of Law offers concentrations in corporate law, criminal law, environmental law, family law, international law, juvenile law, labor law, litigation, maritime law, securities law, tax law, torts and insurance, and intellectual property (including entertainment, sports, and media law). In addition, Clinical programs include International Human Rights Clinic (3 units), Criminal and Juvenile Justice Clinic (6 units), and the Child Advocacy Clinic (6 units). Seminars are offered in many subjects including International Business and Civil Dispute Resolution (3 units), Murder, A Study of Deadly Human Violence (3 units), and Legal Ethics and the Practice of Law (3 units). The Clinical Internship and Judicial Externship programs give students the opportunity to earn academic credit while working in legal agencies (3 to 6 units) or with federal and state judges (3 to 12 units) throughout the San Francisco Bay Area. Students may earn 1 to 2 units of credit working on a directed research project, under the supervision of a full-time faculty member. Special lecture series includes the McCarthy Institute, and the annual symposia of the USF Law Review, the Intellectual Property and Law Bulletin, the Journal of Law and Social Challenges, and the Center for Law and Global Justice. USF offers three summer abroad study opportunities in Dublin, Prague, and Budapest. Additional opportunities are offered in Brazil, Spain, and Cambodia. Academic support is available to select incoming students for the first semester based on admission criteria. All first year students are eligible for academic support, as needed, after the first semester or when referred by a faculty member. The Academic Support Program (ASP) was created to assist students of diverse backgrounds in succeeding in law school. Special interest groups include the Intellectual Property/Cyberlaw Certificate, International and Comparative Law Certificate, and Business Law Certificate. The most widely taken electives are Corporations, Wills and Trusts, and Remedies.

Graduation Requirements

In order to graduate, candidates must have a GPA of 2.0, have completed the upper-division writing requirement, and effective Spring 2010 graduating, 2.30 GPA.

Organizations

Students edit the *University of San Francisco Law Review* and the *University of San Francisco Maritime Law Journal*, 1 of only 2 maritime law reviews published in the United States. Student members of the Intellectual Property Law Association publish the *Intellectual Property Law Bulletin*. *The Forum* is the student newspaper. Students participate in the National Moot Court Competition, National Appellate Advocacy Competition, and Phillip C. Jessup International Law Competition. Other competitions include the Saul Lefkowitz Moot Court Competition, State Bar of California Environmental Negotiations Competition, San Francisco Trial Lawyers Association Mock Trial Competition, Judge John R. Brown Admiralty Moot Court Competition, Giles Sutherland Rich Memorial Moot Court Competition, and Roger J. Traynor California Moot Court Competition. Law student organizations, local chapters of national associations, and campus organizations include the Public Interest Law Foundation, the Sports and Entertainment Law Association, the International Law Society, the National Lawyers Guild, St. Thomas More Society, the Equal Justice Society, Pride Law Association, the Federalist Society, and the Law in Motion Service Program.

Library

The law library contains 136,407 hardcopy volumes and 216,954 microform volume equivalents, and subscribes to 1957 serial publications. Such on-line databases and networks as CALI, CIS Universe, Infotrac, Legal-Trac, LEXIS, LOIS, NEXIS, OCLC First Search, WESTLAW, Wilsonline Indexes, and Innovative OPAC; Internet legal resources. BNA, LLMC, Ind Law, Readex OPAC, Hein Online are available to law students for research. Special library collections include California and federal government documents depository collections. The ratio of library volumes to faculty is 4704 to 1 and to students is 192 to 1. The ratio of seats in the library to students is 1 to 2.

Faculty

The law school has 29 full-time and 64 part-time faculty members, of whom 30 are women. According to AAUP standards for Category I institutions, faculty salaries are above average. About 15% of full-time faculty have a graduate law degree in addition to the J.D.; about 5% of part-time faculty have one. The ratio of full-time students to full-time faculty in an average class is 49 to 1; in a clinic, 8 to 1. The law school has a regular program of bringing visiting professors and other distinguished lecturers and visitors to campus.

Students

About 52% of the student body are women; 37%, minorities; 7%, African American; 18%, Asian American; 10%, Hispanic; 1%, Native American; and 4%, multiethnic. The majority of students come from California (90%). The average age of entering students is 26; age range is 19 to 46. About 19% of students enter directly from undergraduate school and 5% have a graduate degree. About 9% drop out after the first year for academic or personal reasons; 90% remain to receive a law degree.

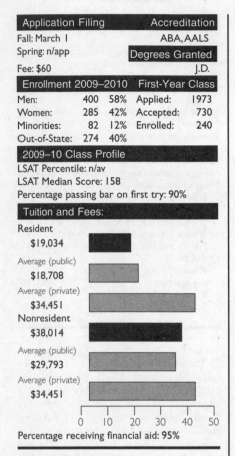

Application Filing		Accreditation
Fall: March 1		ABA, AALS
Spring: n/app		**Degrees Granted**
Fee: $60		J.D.

Enrollment 2009–2010			First-Year Class	
Men:	400	58%	Applied:	1973
Women:	285	42%	Accepted:	730
Minorities:	82	12%	Enrolled:	240
Out-of-State:	274	40%		

2009–10 Class Profile

LSAT Percentile: n/av
LSAT Median Score: 158
Percentage passing bar on first try: 90%

Tuition and Fees:

Resident
$19,034

Average (public)
$18,708

Average (private)
$34,451

Nonresident
$38,014

Average (public)
$29,793

Average (private)
$34,451

0   10   20   30   40   50

Percentage receiving financial aid: 95%

ADMISSIONS

In the fall 2009 first-year class, 1973 applied, 730 were accepted, and 240 enrolled. Twenty-one transfers enrolled. The median GPA of the most recent first-year class was 3.46. The highest LSAT percentile was 99.

Requirements
Applicants must have a bachelor's degree and take the LSAT. All admission factors are important in varying degrees for each applicant. No specific undergraduate courses are required.

Procedure
The application deadline for fall entry is March 1. Applicants should submit an application form, LSAT results, transcripts, a personal statement, a nonrefundable application fee of $60, 2 letters of recommendation, use of the LSDAS, a personal statement, and a resume. Notification of the admissions decision is from mid-December to May. The latest acceptable LSAT test date for fall entry is February. The law school uses the LSDAS.

Special
The law school recruits minority and disadvantaged students through campus visits and a minority recruitment day that is held on campus in the fall; students are invited to attend. Requirements are not different for out-of-state students. Transfer students must have one year of credit, have attended an ABA-approved law school, and be in good standing, be eligible to return to their current law school.

Costs
Tuition and fees for the 2009-2010 academic year are $19,034 for full-time in-state students and $38,014 for out-of-state students. Books and supplies run $1000.

Financial Aid
About 95% of current law students receive some form of aid. Awards are based on need and merit. Required financial statements are the FAFSA and the School of Law scholarship application. The aid application deadline for fall entry is March 1. First-year students are notified about their financial aid application at time of acceptance on or before May 1.

About the Law School
University of South Carolina School of Law was established in 1867 and is a public institution. The campus is in an urban area in downtown Columbia, South Carolina. The primary mission of the law school is to develop professional competence and responsibility. The school seeks to qualify its graduates for the highest opportunities in professional legal services and to instill a sense of perspective about what the law is capable of doing for the good of society. Students have access to federal, state, county, city, and local agencies, courts, correctional facilities, law firms, and legal aid organizations in the Columbia area. The U.S. Department of Justice's Legal Education Program has moved from Washington, D.C. to Columbia and is affiliated with the law school. Facilities of special interest to law students are the 2 courtrooms in the school. One is designed as a moot court room, and the other is an actual courtroom periodically used by the state court system. There is also a computer laboratory for student use. Housing for students is available in numerous apartments within commuting distance of the school. The university has apartments for married students near the campus. All law school facilities are accessible to the physically disabled.

Calendar
The law school operates on a traditional semester basis. Courses for full-time students are offered days only and must be completed within 3 years. There is no part-time program. New students are admitted in the fall. There is an 8-week summer session. Transferable summer courses are offered.

Programs
Students may take relevant courses in other programs and apply credit toward the J.D.; a maximum of 9 hours credits may be applied. The following joint degrees may be earned: J.D./H.R.M. (Juris Doctor/Master of Human Resource Management), J.D./I.M.B.A. (Juris Doctor/Master of International Business Administration), J.D./M.A. (Juris Doctor/Master of Arts in Criminal Justice), J.D./M.A.E. (Juris Doctor/Master of Arts in Economics), J.D./M. Acc. (Juris Doctor/Master of Accountancy), J.D./M.E.E.R.M. (Juris Doctor/Master of Earth and Environmental Resources), J.D./M.E.S. (Juris Doctor/Master of Environmental Science), J.D./M.H.A. (Juris Doctor/Master of Health Administration), J.D./M.P.A. (Juris Doctor/Master of Public Administration), and J.D./M.S.W. (Juris Doctor/Master of Social Work).

Required
To earn the J.D., candidates must complete 90 total credits, of which 46 are for required courses. They must maintain a minimum GPA of 2.0 in the required courses. The following first-year courses are required of all students: Legal Research, Civil Procedure I, Constitutional Law I, Contracts I and II, Criminal Law, Legal Writing I and II, Property I and II, and Torts I and II. Required upper-level courses consist of a perspective course, a professional skills course, a writing requirement, Civil Procedure II, Constitutional Law II, Criminal Procedure, and Professional Responsibility. The required orientation program for first-year students is 2 days before the start of classes.

Phone: 803-777-6605
Fax: 803-777-7751
E-mail: usclaw@law.sc.edu
Web: www.law.sc.edu

Contact

Director of Admissions, 803-777-6605 for general inquiries; Director of Admissions, 803-777-6605 for financial aid information.

SOUTH CAROLINA

Accepted students are also invited to a reception in the spring prior to the start of the first fall semester.

Electives

The School of Law offers concentrations in corporate law, environmental law, international law, litigation, tax law, torts and insurance, business law, commercial law and bankruptcy, probate and estate planning, and real estate. In addition, there are several types of clinics, usually for 3 credits hours. Clinics include Consumer Bankruptcy, Criminal Practice, Environmental Law, Federal Litigation, and Non-Profit Organizations. Students gain closely supervised training experience in the representation of clients. A number of seminars are offered each semester. All have limited enrollment, require a paper to be written, and are for 3 credit hours. In the area of research programs, students may take the course Supervised Legal Research for 2 credit hours. It is independent study performed under the supervision of a faculty member and requires a research paper. Many upper-level students clerk for law firms with state or federal government agencies, or with judges or the legislature, during the school year. A special lecture series is open to all students. Study abroad is offered the May semester in London. First-year students are offered a tutorial program. A minority peer assistance tutorial program is also available. Special interest group programs include the Pro Bono Program, which provides opportunities for volunteer law students to obtain practical legal training. The most widely taken electives are litigation, business, and commercial law.

Graduation Requirements

In order to graduate, candidates must have a GPA of 2.0 and have completed the upper-division writing requirement.

Organizations

The primary law review is the *South Carolina Law Review*; the other law reviews are *ABA Real Property, Probate, and Trust Journal, The Southeastern Environmental Law Journal, Law Education Journal, and Journal of International Law and Business*. The school sponsors teams in the National, International, American Bar Association, and Labor Law Moot Court competitions as well as the National Trial competitions. It also competes in the J. Woodrow Lewis Intramural Moot Court competition in appellate advocacy. Law student organizations, local chapters of national associations, and campus organizations include the Student Bar Association, Black Law Students Association, Women in Law, Phi Alpha Delta, Phi Delta Phi, Society of International Law, Wig and Robe, Federalist Society. American Constitution Society, Environmental Law Society, Public Interest Law Society, and Veterans in Law.

Library

The law library contains 500,000 hardcopy volumes and 2718 microform volume equivalents, and subscribes to 972 serial publications. Such on-line databases and networks as DIALOG, LEXIS, LOIS, NEXIS, SSRN, and WESTLAW are available to law students for research. Special library collections include a South Carolina legal history collection and a selective GPO depository. Recently, the library added 2 electronic classrooms. The ratio of library volumes to faculty is 13,158 to 1 and to students is 730 to 1. The ratio of seats in the library to students is 1 to 1.

Faculty

The law school has 31 full-time and 21 part-time faculty members, of whom 21 are women. According to AAUP standards for Category I institutions, faculty salaries are well below average. About 55% of full-time faculty have a graduate law degree in addition to the J.D. The ratio of full-time students to full-time faculty in an average class is 42 to 1; in a clinic, 12 to 1. The law school has a regular program of bringing visiting professors and other distinguished lecturers and visitors to campus. There is a chapter of the Order of the Coif; 19 faculty and 281 graduates are members.

Students

About 42% of the student body are women; 12%, minorities; 9%, African American; 2%, Asian American; and 1%, Hispanic. The majority of students come from South Carolina (60%). The average age of entering students is 24; age range is 20 to 50. About 33% of students enter directly from undergraduate school, 8% have a graduate degree, and 45% have worked full-time prior to entering law school.

Placement

J.D.s awarded:	218
Services available through: a separate law school placement center	
Services: eAttorney/OCI	
Special features: free job opportunities postings on the web site, eAttorney job listings and searchable web site of legal employers; reciprocity with other law schools	
Full-time job interviews:	31 employers
Summer job interviews:	46 employers
Placement by graduation:	60% of class
Placement within 9 months:	95% of class
Average starting salary:	$34,000 to $160,000
Areas of placement:	
Private practice 2-10 attorneys	19%
Private practice 11-25 attorneys	10%
Private practice 26-50 attorneys	5%
Private practice 51-100 attorneys	3%
Private practice 100+ attorneys	13%
Judicial clerkships	15%
Government	11%
Business/industry	9%
Public interest	7%
Military	1%
Academic	1%

About 3% drop out after the first year for academic or personal reasons; 97% remain to receive a law degree.

School of Law

414 East Clark Street
Vermillion, SD 57069-2390

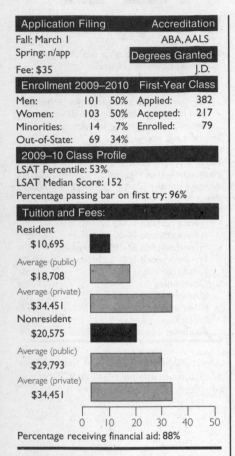

Application Filing		Accreditation	
Fall: March 1		ABA, AALS	
Spring: n/app		**Degrees Granted**	
Fee: $35			J.D.
Enrollment 2009–2010		**First-Year Class**	
Men:	101 50%	Applied:	382
Women:	103 50%	Accepted:	217
Minorities:	14 7%	Enrolled:	79
Out-of-State:	69 34%		

2009–10 Class Profile
LSAT Percentile: 53%
LSAT Median Score: 152
Percentage passing bar on first try: 96%

Tuition and Fees:

Resident
$10,695

Average (public)
$18,708

Average (private)
$34,451

Nonresident
$20,575

Average (public)
$29,793

Average (private)
$34,451

0   10   20   30   40   50

Percentage receiving financial aid: 88%

ADMISSIONS

In the fall 2009 first-year class, 382 applied, 217 were accepted, and 79 enrolled. Three transfers enrolled. The median LSAT percentile of the most recent first-year class was 53; the median GPA was 3.44 on a scale of 4.0. The lowest LSAT percentile accepted was 8; the highest was 84.

Requirements
Applicants must have a bachelor's degree and take the LSAT. The most important admission factors include GPA, LSAT results, and character, personality. No specific undergraduate courses are required. Candidates are not interviewed.

Procedure
The application deadline for fall entry is March 1. Applicants should submit an application form, LSAT and transcripts, a nonrefundable application fee of $35, 2 letters of recommendation, a personal statement, and the LSDAS report. Notification of the admissions decision is on a rolling basis. The latest acceptable LSAT test date for fall entry is February. The law school uses the LSDAS.

Special
The law school recruits minority and disadvantaged students by mail solicitation and meeting in person with prospects. Requirements are not different for out-of-state students. Transfer students must have 1 year of credit, have attended an ABA-approved law school, and be in good standing at their present law school.

Costs

Tuition and fees for the 2009-2010 academic year are $10,695 for full-time in-state students and $20,575 for out-of-state students. On-campus room and board costs about $5716 annually; books and supplies run $1400.

Financial Aid

About 88% of current law students receive some form of aid. The average annual amount of aid from all sources combined, including scholarships, loans, and work contracts, is $21,300; maximum, $32,000. Awards are based on need and merit. Required financial statement is the FAFSA. First-year students are notified about their financial aid application at time of acceptance.

About the Law School

University of South Dakota School of Law was established in 1901 and is a public institution. The 216-acre campus is in a small town 50 miles south of Sioux Falls. The primary mission of the law school is to prepare students for the practice of law and to train professionally competent graduates capable of achieving their career goals and serving their profession. Students have access to federal, state, county, city, and local agencies, courts, correctional facilities, law firms, and legal aid organizations in the Vermillion area. Facilities of special interest to law students . Housing for students is described as adequate. All law school facilities are accessible to the physically disabled.

Calendar

The law school operates on a traditional semester basis. Courses for full-time students are offered days only and must be completed within 6 semesters. For part-time students, courses are offered days only and must be completed within 10 semesters. New full- and part-time students are admitted in the fall. There is no summer session. Transferable summer courses are not offered.

Programs

Students may take relevant courses in other programs and apply credit toward the J.D.; a maximum of 9 credits may be applied. The following joint degrees may be earned: J.D./M.A. (Juris Doctor/Master of Arts in English, history, psychology,), J.D./M.B.A. (Juris Doctor/Master of Business Administration), J.D./M.P.A. (Juris Doctor/Master of Public Administration), J.D./M.P.Acc. (Juris Doctor/Master of Professional Accountancy), and J.D./M.S.A.S. (Juris Doctor/Master of Science in Administrative Studies).

Required
To earn the J.D., candidates must complete 90 total credits, of which 46 are for required courses. They must maintain a minimum GPA of 70.0 in the required courses. The following first-year courses are required of all students: Civil Procedure, Contracts, Criminal Law, Criminal Procedure, Fundamental Legal Skills, Property, and Torts. Required upper-level courses consist of a Skills course (Trial Techniques; ADR; Legislation; Negotiation, code course (Commercial Law, Secured Transactions, or Federal , Constitutional Law, Evidence, and Legal Profession. The required orientation program for first-year students lasts 5 days.

Electives
The School of Law offers concentrations in environmental law and Indian law. In addition, research programs, amounting to 1 or 2 hours of credit, are available for second- and third-year students. Externships are available for third-year students, and a federal judicial externship is available for second-year students. The most widely taken electives are Family Law, Commercial Law, and Trusts/Wills.

Phone: 605-677-5443
Fax: 605-677-5417
E-mail: *law.school@usd.edu*
Web: *www.usd.edu/law*

Contact

Jean Henriques, Admission Officer/Registrar, 605-677-5443 for general inquiries; University Financial Aid Office, 605-677-5446 for financial aid information.

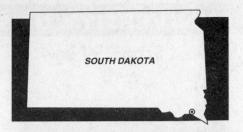

SOUTH DAKOTA

Graduation Requirements

In order to graduate, candidates must have a GPA of 70.0, have completed the upper-division writing requirement.

Organizations

The primary law review is the *South Dakota Law Review*. Other publications include the *Sustainable Development Law Journal*. Moot court competitions are the New York Bar, ABA, and Southern Illinois University Health Law Tournament. Other competitions include ABA-LSD Competitions (Negotiations, Client Counseling, Mediation) and the Robert R. Merhige, Jr. National Negotiation Competition. Law student organizations, local chapters of national associations, and campus organizations include Native American Law Students Association, Black Law Students Association, Federalist Society, Women in Law, R.D. Hurd Pro Bono Society, and Student Bar Association.

Library

The law library contains 213,077 hard-copy volumes and 46,922 microform volume equivalents, and subscribes to 280 serial publications. Such on-line databases and networks as CALI, CIS Universe, Infotrac, Legal-Trac, LEXIS, NEXIS, OCLC First Search, WESTLAW, and BNA resources, RIA Tax resources, and Hein Online are available to law students for research. Special library collections include a government documents depository collection, which is an extension of the main university library's collection. Other collections include reference, reserve, Indian law, and professional responsibility. Recently, the library became wireless. The ratio of library volumes to faculty is 14,205 to 1 and to students is 1044 to 1. The ratio of seats in the library to students is 1 to 1.

Faculty

The law school has 15 full-time faculty members, of whom 5 are women. According to AAUP standards for Category 1 institutions, faculty salaries are well below average. About 37% of full-time faculty have a graduate law degree in addition to the J.D. The law school has a regular program of bringing visiting professors and other distinguished lecturers and visitors to campus.

Students

About 50% of the student body are women; 7%, minorities; 1%, African American; 1%, Asian American; 1%, Hispanic; and 4%, Native American. The majority of students come from South Dakota (66%). The average age of entering students is 26; age range is 22 to 40. About 47% of students enter directly from undergraduate school and 4% have a graduate degree. About 3% drop out after the first year for academic or personal reasons; 97% remain to receive a law degree.

Placement

J.D.s awarded:	84
Services available through: a separate law school placement center and the university placement center	
Special features: alumni network, the Weekly Career Services and Alumni Newsletter	
Full-time job interviews:	18 employers
Summer job interviews:	24 employers
Placement by graduation:	63% of class
Placement within 9 months:	96% of class
Average starting salary:	$41,271 to $55,000
Areas of placement:	
Private practice 2-10 attorneys	22%
Private practice 11-25 attorneys	6%
Private practice 26-50 attorneys	4%
Government	22%
Judicial clerkships	18%
Business/industry	14%
Public interest	8%
Academic	4%

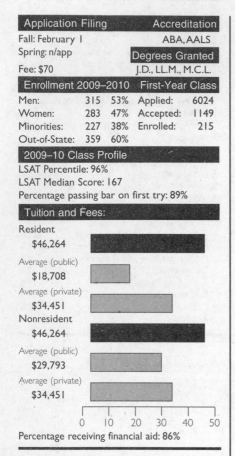

Application Filing		Accreditation	
Fall: February 1		ABA, AALS	
Spring: n/app		**Degrees Granted**	
Fee: $70		J.D., LL.M., M.C.L.	
Enrollment 2009–2010		**First-Year Class**	
Men:	315 53%	Applied:	6024
Women:	283 47%	Accepted:	1149
Minorities:	227 38%	Enrolled:	215
Out-of-State:	359 60%		

2009–10 Class Profile
LSAT Percentile: 96%
LSAT Median Score: 167
Percentage passing bar on first try: 89%

Tuition and Fees:

Resident
$46,264

Average (public)
$18,708

Average (private)
$34,451

Nonresident
$46,264

Average (public)
$29,793

Average (private)
$34,451

0 10 20 30 40 50

Percentage receiving financial aid: 86%

ADMISSIONS
In the fall 2009 first-year class, 6024 applied, 1149 were accepted, and 215 enrolled. Four transfers enrolled. The median LSAT percentile of the most recent first-year class was 96; the median GPA was 3.6 on a scale of 4.0.

Requirements
Applicants must have a bachelor's degree and take the LSAT. No specific undergraduate courses are required. Candidates are not interviewed.

Procedure
The application deadline for fall entry is February 1. Applicants should submit an application form, LSAT results, transcripts, a personal statement, a nonrefundable application fee of $70, and 2 letters of recommendation. Notification of the admissions decision is in the spring. The latest acceptable LSAT test date for fall entry is December. The law school uses the LSDAS.

Special
The law school recruits minority and disadvantaged students by means of mail outreach campaigns, school visits, and minority receptions; the minority student organizations also help recruit and retain qualified candidates. Requirements are not different for out-of-state students. Transfer students must have 1 year of credit, have attended an ABA-approved law school, and be in the top 20% of their first-year class.

Costs
Tuition and fees for the 2009-2010 academic year are $46,264 for all full-time students. On-campus room and board costs about $15,842 annually; books and supplies run $1664.

Financial Aid
About 86% of current law students receive some form of aid. The average annual amount of aid from all sources combined, including scholarships, loans, and work contracts, is $47,610; maximum, $64,290. Awards are based on need and merit. Required financial statements are the FAFSA and the law school financial aid application. The aid application deadline for fall entry is March 1. Special funds for minority or disadvantaged students consist of scholarships that are used in part to assist disadvantaged and minority students. First-year students are notified about their financial aid application at time of acceptance.

About the Law School
University of Southern California Gould School of Law was established in 1900 and is a private institution. The 226-acre campus is in an urban area 3½ miles south of downtown Los Angeles. The primary mission of the law school is to offer an innovative and interdisciplinary program focusing on the law as an expression of social values and as an instrument for implementing social goals. Students have access to federal, state, county, city, and local agencies, courts, correctional facilities, law firms, and legal aid organizations in the Los Angeles area. Facilities of special interest to law students include a computer laboratory, multimedia classrooms, large and high-tech library facilities, a spacious student cafe and lounge, and clinical law offices. The USC campus features a 24-hour library, fitness center,

specialty libraries, theaters, and restaurants. Housing for students consists of an on-campus apartment house designated for law students. All law school facilities are accessible to the physically disabled.

Calendar
The law school operates on a traditional semester basis. Courses for full-time students are offered days only and must be completed within 4 years. There is no part-time program. New students are admitted in the fall. There is no summer session. Transferable summer courses are not offered.

Programs
In addition to the J.D., the law school offers the LL.M. and M.C.L. Students may take relevant courses in other programs and apply credit toward the J.D.; a maximum of 12 credits may be applied. The following joint degrees may be earned: J.D./LL.M. (Juris Doctor/Master of Laws (London School of Economics)), J.D./M.A. (Juris Doctor/Master of Arts in economics, international), J.D./M.A.P. (Juris Doctor/Master of Philosophy), J.D./M.B.A. (Juris Doctor/Master of Business Administration), J.D./M.B.T. (Juris Doctor/Master of Business Taxation), J.D./M.C.M. (Juris Doctor/Master of Arts in communications management), J.D./M.P.A. (Juris Doctor/Master of Public Administration), J.D./M.P.P. (Juris Doctor/Master of Public Policy), J.D./M.R.E.D. (Juris Doctor/Master of Real Estate Development), J.D./M.S. (Juris Doctor/Master of Science in gerontology), J.D./M.S.W. (Juris Doctor/Master of Social Work), J.D./Ph.D. (Juris Doctor/Doctor of Philosophy in social science), and J.D./Pharm.D. (Juris Doctor/Doctor of Pharmacy).

Required
To earn the J.D., candidates must complete 88 total credits, of which 33 are for required courses. They must maintain a minimum GPA of 2.6 in the required courses. The following first-year courses are required of all students: Civil Procedure, Constitutional Law, Contracts, Criminal Law, Law Language and Ethics, Legal Profession, Legal Research, writing and advocacy, Property, and Torts I. Required upper-level courses consist of a writing requirement. The required orientation program for first-year students is a 2-day program that includes a

Phone: 213-740-2523
E-mail: *admissions@law.usc.edu*
Web: *www.law.usc.edu*

Contact

Chloe Reid, Associate Dean for Admissions, 213-740-2523 for general inquiries; Mary Bingham, Director of Financial Aid, 213-740-6314 for financial aid information.

welcoming address, luncheon, financial aid counseling, meetings with second-year advisers assigned to incoming students, and a barbecue. A student-run mentor program for first-year students has year-round activities.

Electives

The Gould School of Law offers concentrations in corporate law, criminal law, entertainment law, environmental law, family law, intellectual property law, international law, juvenile law, labor law, litigation, media law, securities law, sports law, tax law, torts and insurance, public interest, constitutional law, and civil rights. In addition, in-house and simulated clinics are available for upper-level students. In-house clinics include the Post-Conviction Justice project, Children's Legal Issues Clinic, Employer Legal Advice Clinic, Intellectual Property Clinic, the Immigration Clinic, and the Small Business Clinic. Seminars, available to upper-level students, are offered on many topics and facilitate intensive discussions in small groups. Internships, worth up to 4 credits, are available to upper-level students with government or public interest non-profit organizations. Judicial externships allow students to clerk for a state or federal judge. The law school co-sponsors the Pacific Center for Health Policy and Ethics research program; Center for Communications Law and Policy; Center for the Study of Law and Politics; the Initiative and Referendum Institute; Center for Law, History and Culture; Center for Law, Economics and Organization; and Center for Law and Philosophy. Multiple opportunities for hands-on experience are available through clinical programs, internships and externships, and public interest placements. Special lecture series include the annual Roth lecture, faculty workshops, and workshops sponsored by centers. The law school sponsors a semester exchange program with the University of Hong Kong and a dual degree program with the London School of Economics. Credit may be given for work done in other accredited law schools' study-abroad programs. Tutorials are arranged on a case-by-case basis. The school also offers a 5-part workshop on studying. An exam-taking skills course is offered to first-year students in the spring and upper-division students in the fall. Minority student organizations and minority alumni associations collaborate on a range of social and educational programs as well as networking opportunities. Stu-

dent-run organizations geared at specific areas of the legal profession include the Entertainment Law Society, International Law Society, Corporate Law Society, and Public Interest Law Foundation. The most widely taken electives are Evidence, Business Organizations, and Tax.

Graduation Requirements

In order to graduate, candidates must have completed the upper-division writing requirement.

Organizations

Students edit the *Southern California Law Review, Southern California Interdisciplinary Law Journal, Southern California Review of Law and Social Justice*, and *USC Law Magazine*, a semiannual alumni magazine, and *Deliberations*, a biannual, 12-page newsletter. All first-year students participate a in moot court competition; the 40 best advocates are selected to compete in their second year, in the Hale Moot Court Honors Program. In addition, the best advocates from the Hale Moot Court Competition participate in a numerous national competitions. Law student organizations, local chapters of national associations, and campus organizations include Women's Law Association, Phi Alpha Delta, Phi Delta Phi, La Raza Law Students Association, Public Interest Law Foundation, Entertainment Law Society, Street Law, and Order of the Coif.

Library

The law library contains 429,267 hardcopy volumes and 106,285 microform volume equivalents. Such on-line databases and networks as CALI, CIS Universe, Infotrac, Legal-Trac, LEXIS, LOIS, Mathew Bender, NEXIS, OCLC First Search, WESTLAW, and Wilsonline Indexes are available to law students for research. Special library collections include a selected depository. Among the important holdings are health law/bioethics, law and economics, law and philosophy, law and social sciences, taxation, preventive law, and historic documents concerning President Lincoln. Recently, the library increased group study areas and multimedia technology, enhanced computer access, and constructed computer training locations. A wireless network was also installed. The ratio of library volumes to faculty is 8585 to 1 and to students is 718 to 1. The ratio of seats in the library to students is 1 to 3.

CALIFORNIA

Placement

J.D.s awarded:	193

Services available through: a separate law school placement center

Services: lists of public interest contacts, counseling, a major on-campus placement program, videotaped practice interviews, 1-to-1 mentor program with graduates for first-year students in the second semester

Special features: 1-on-1 counseling session for each first-year student; the Career Services Office's *Guide to Public Interest Law* for its students/graduates; Alumni-Student Mock Interview Program.

Full-time job interviews:	57 employers
Summer job interviews:	181 employers
Placement by graduation:	90% of class
Placement within 9 months:	96% of class

Average starting salary: $135,000 to $165,000

Areas of placement:

Private practice 2-10 attorneys	9%
Private practice 11-25 attorneys	4%
Private practice 26-50 attorneys	4%
Private practice 51-100 attorneys	3%
Private practice 100+ attorneys/solo	49%
Unknown	50%
Business/industry	9%
Government	8%
Judicial clerkships	7%
Public interest	3%
Academic	2%

Faculty

The law school has 50 full-time and 105 part-time faculty members, of whom 56 are women. According to AAUP standards for Category I institutions, faculty salaries are above average. About 44% of full-time faculty have a graduate law degree in addition to the J.D. The ratio of full-time students to full-time faculty in an average class is 12 to 1; in a clinic, 5 to 1. The law school has a regular program of bringing visiting professors and other distinguished lecturers and visitors to campus. There is a chapter of the Order of the Coif; 10 faculty are members.

Students

About 47% of the student body are women; 38%, minorities; 9%, African American; 17%, Asian American; 11%, Hispanic; and 1%, Native American. The majority of students come from California (40%). The average age of entering students is 23; age range is 18 to 40. About 55% of students enter directly from undergraduate school, 8% have a graduate degree, and 35% have worked full-time prior to entering law school. About 1% drop out after the first year for academic or personal reasons; 99% remain to receive a law degree.

University of Southern California **551**

UNIVERSITY OF TENNESSEE

College of Law

1505 W. Cumberland Avenue
Knoxville, TN 37996-1810

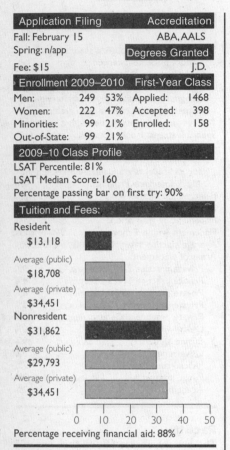

Application Filing		Accreditation
Fall: February 15		ABA, AALS
Spring: n/app		**Degrees Granted**
Fee: $15		J.D.

Enrollment 2009–2010		First-Year Class	
Men:	249 53%	Applied:	1468
Women:	222 47%	Accepted:	398
Minorities:	99 21%	Enrolled:	158
Out-of-State:	99 21%		

2009–10 Class Profile
LSAT Percentile: 81%
LSAT Median Score: 160
Percentage passing bar on first try: 90%

Tuition and Fees:

Resident
$13,118

Average (public)
$18,708

Average (private)
$34,451

Nonresident
$31,862

Average (public)
$29,793

Average (private)
$34,451

0 10 20 30 40 50

Percentage receiving financial aid: 88%

ADMISSIONS
In the fall 2009 first-year class, 1468 applied, 398 were accepted, and 158 enrolled. Two transfers enrolled. The median LSAT percentile of the most recent first-year class was 81; the median GPA was 3.55 on a scale of 4.0. The lowest LSAT percentile accepted was 26; the highest was 98.

Requirements
Applicants must have a bachelor's degree and take the LSAT. Admission factors are not ranked; all factors are considered. No specific undergraduate courses are required. Candidates are not interviewed.

Procedure
The application deadline for fall entry is February 15. Applicants should submit an application form, LSAT results, transcripts, a personal statement, a nonrefundable application fee of $15, 2 letters of recommendation, a personal statement, and an essay. Notification of the admis-

sions decision varies. The latest acceptable LSAT test date for fall entry is February. The law school uses the LSDAS.

Special
The law school recruits minority and disadvantaged students through on-campus visits, LSAC forums, on-campus workshops, Tennessee Pre-Law Day (each spring), and LSAC CRS Service. Requirements are not different for out-of-state students. Transfer students must have one year of credit, have a minimum GPA of 2.0, and have attended an ABA-approved law school. Transfer admission is competitive and contingent on available seats.

Costs
Tuition and fees for the 2009-2010 academic year are $13,118 for full-time in-state students and $31,862 for out-of-state students. On-campus room and board costs about $10,060 annually; books and supplies run $1606.

Financial Aid
About 88% of current law students receive some form of aid. The average annual amount of aid from all sources combined, including scholarships, loans, and work contracts, is $22,499; maximum, $30,510 (in) and $49,254 (out). Awards are based on need and merit. Required financial statement is the FAFSA. The aid application deadline for fall entry is March 1. Special funds for minority or disadvantaged students consist of scholarships that are awarded on the basis of demonstrated financial need and merit. First-year students are notified about their financial aid application usually in January.

About the Law School
University of Tennessee College of Law was established in 1890 and is a public institution. The 417-acre campus is in an urban area in Knoxville, Tennessee, in the heart of the university. The primary mission of the law school is to be a preeminent state-supported law school where faculty, staff, and students devoted to teaching, scholarship, and service thrive. Students have access to federal, state, county, city, and local agencies, courts, correctional facilities, law firms, and legal aid organizations in the Knoxville area. The College of Law is located approximately 1 mile

from downtown Knoxville law offices and the courts. Facilities of special interest to law students include a law center, which houses civil and criminal clinics, a mediation program, the center for entrepreneurial law, classrooms, law library, and faculty administrative offices. Housing for students consists of several off-campus university apartment complexes, available to law students. Several apartment complexes are located within a 5-mile radius of the campus. All law school facilities are accessible to the physically disabled.

Calendar
The law school operates on a traditional semester basis. Courses for full-time students are offered days only and must be completed within 5 years. There is no part-time program. New students are admitted in the fall. There is a 7-week summer session. Transferable summer courses are offered.

Programs
Students may take relevant courses in other programs and apply credit toward the J.D.; a maximum of 6 credits may be applied. The following joint degrees may be earned: J.D./M.B.A. (Juris Doctor/ Master of Business Administration) and J.D./M.P.A. (Juris Doctor/Master of Public Administration).

Required
To earn the J.D., candidates must complete 89 total credits, of which 38 are for required courses. They must maintain a minimum GPA of 2.0 in the required courses. The following first-year courses are required of all students: Civil Procedure I and II, Contracts I and II, Criminal Law, Legal Process I and II, Property, and Torts I and II. Required upper-level courses consist of a perspective course, a planning and drafting course, an expository writing course, Constitutional Law I, and Legal Profession. The required orientation program for first-year students begins with orientation, offers 3½days of mini courses in Civil Litigation Process and Case Analysis and Briefing, and concludes with one regular class meeting in Criminal Law, Contracts, and Torts.

Phone: 865-974-4131
Fax: 865-974-1572
E-mail: lawadmit@utk.edu
Web: www.law.utk.edu

Contact

Carolyn Dossett, Senior Admission Specialist, 865-974-4131 for general inquiries; Janet Hatcher, Admissions and Financial Aid Advisor, 865-974-4131 for financial aid information.

TENNESSEE

Electives

The College of Law offers concentrations in corporate law, business transactions, and advocacy and dispute resolution. In addition, clinics include Advocacy (6 credit hours), Prosecutional Externship (6 credit hours), Business Clinic (6 credit hours), Public Defender (6 credit hours), Judicial Externship (4 credit hours), Domestic Violence Clinic (3 credit hours), Wills Clinic (3 credit hours), and Mediation Clinic (3 credit hours). The Mediation Clinic is open to all upper-division students.Several special topic seminars are available for 2 hours credit. The Prosecutorial Externship, and Public Defender Externship are open to third-year students. Field work is available through "for-credit" externships. Special lecture series include the Alumni Distinguished Lecture in Jurisprudence, the Charles Henderson Miller Lecture in Professional Responsibility, and the Speaker Series, which hosts nationally known speakers. Any student may study abroad through ABA-approved summer abroad programs. A maximum of 8 credit hours may be transferred. Students with a first-semester average below 2.0 are invited to participate, in the second semester, in tutorials in Contracts, Civil Procedure, and Torts. First-year students attend Law School Success Skills seminars on topics such as Managing Time and Energy in Law School; Outlining; sample exams in Civil Procedure, Torts, and Contracts; and Final Exams. The most widely taken electives are Commercial Law, Trial Practice, and Evidence.

Graduation Requirements

In order to graduate, candidates must have a GPA of 2.0, have completed the upper-division writing requirement, expository writing, the perspective requirement, and the planning and drafting requirement.

Organizations

Students edit the *Tennessee Law Review*, *Journal of Law and Policy*, and *Transactions: Tennessee Journal of Business Law*. Moot court competitions include the National Moot Court, National Trial, and Jerome Prince Evidence. Other competitions include the Jenkins Trial Advocates Prize Moot Court, Intellectual Property, Labor Law, and Jessup International Law. Law student organizations, local chapters of national associations, and campus organizations include the Student Bar Association, Christian Legal Society, Speaker Series, the American Bar Associations-Law Student Division, Association of Trial Lawyers of America-Student Chapter, Hamilton Barrett Chapter of the American Inns of Court, the Black Law Students Association, Phi Delta Phi, and Tennessee Innocence Project.

Library

The law library contains 590,896 hardcopy volumes and 46,903 microform volume equivalents, and subscribes to 1025 serial publications. Such on-line databases and networks as CALI, CIS Universe, DIALOG, Dow-Jones, Infotrac, Legal-Trac, LEXIS, LOIS, Mathew Bender, NEXIS, OCLC First Search, RLIN, WESTLAW, Wilsonline Indexes, CCH, Business and Finance Internet Library, CCH Health and human resources internet library, Historical Documents, Curent Indexes to Legal Periodicals, Hein Online,Treaties and other International Agreements Online, LexisNexis, PAGER, LOIS, Hein Online, RIA Checkpoint, Westkaw, Legal scholarship network, aReaders guide to periodical literature, and the making of modern law are available to law students for research. Special library collections include several federal documents depositories, Tennessee Collection, and selected Braille Collection. Recently, the library painted and installed new carpet in heavily used areas. The ratio of library volumes to faculty is 21,103 to 1 and to students is 1255 to 1. The ratio of seats in the library to students is 1 to 1.

Faculty

The law school has 28 full-time and 41 part-time faculty members, of whom 23 are women. According to AAUP standards for Category 1 institutions, faculty salaries are well below average. About 21% of full-time faculty have a graduate law degree in addition to the J.D. The ratio of full-time students to full-time faculty in an average class is 13 to 1; in a clinic, 8 to 1. The law school has a regular program of bringing visiting professors and other distinguished lecturers and visitors to campus. There is a chapter of the Order of the Coif.

Students

About 47% of the student body are women; 21%, minorities; 12%, African American; 4%, Asian American; 2%, Hispanic; 1%, Native American; 1% Foreign National. The majority of students come from Tennessee (79%). The average age of entering students is 23; age range is 20 to 49. About 42% of students enter directly from undergraduate school, 6% have a graduate degree, and 52% have worked full-time prior to entering law school. About 2% drop out after the first year for academic or personal reasons; 98% remain to receive a law degree.

Placement

J.D.s awarded:	143

Services available through: a separate law school placement center and law students also may use the UTK placement center.

Services: off-campus recruiting events, the Southeastern Minority Job Fair, the Southeastern Law Placement Consortium, Patent Law Interview Program, Nashville Bar Association Minority Clerkship Program, Mid-Atlantic Legal Recruiting Conference, the Equal Justice Works Career Fair, Spring Southeastern Legal Hiring Conference, Southeastern Intellectual Property Job Fair

Special features: individual advising sessions, small-group orientations; a resource library with more than 1000 employer files, books, and videotapes; a booklet series of alumni career narratives; a web-based information system; Career Center Student Handbook.

Full-time job interviews:	6 employers
Summer job interviews:	51 employers
Placement by graduation:	74% of class
Placement within 9 months:	97% of class
Average starting salary:	$40,000 to $145,000

Areas of placement:

Private practice 2-10 attorneys	29%
Private practice 11-25 attorneys	5%
Private practice 26-50 attorneys	3%
Private practice 51-100 attorneys	22%
Government	14%
Judicial clerkships	13%
Business/industry	6%
Public interest	4%
Military	2%
Academic	2%

School of Law

727 East Dean Keeton Street
Austin, TX 78705

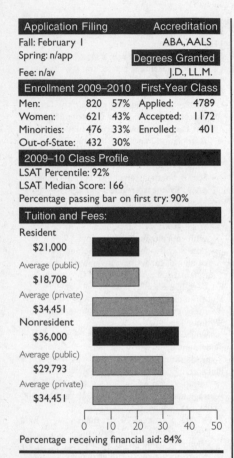

Application Filing	Accreditation
Fall: February 1	ABA, AALS
Spring: n/app	Degrees Granted
Fee: n/av	J.D., LL.M.

Enrollment 2009–2010		First-Year Class	
Men:	820 57%	Applied:	4789
Women:	621 43%	Accepted:	1172
Minorities:	476 33%	Enrolled:	401
Out-of-State:	432 30%		

2009–10 Class Profile
LSAT Percentile: 92%
LSAT Median Score: 166
Percentage passing bar on first try: 90%

Tuition and Fees:

Resident
$21,000

Average (public)
$18,708

Average (private)
$34,451

Nonresident
$36,000

Average (public)
$29,793

Average (private)
$34,451

0 10 20 30 40 50

Percentage receiving financial aid: 84%

ADMISSIONS

In the fall 2009 first-year class, 4789 applied, 1172 were accepted, and 401 enrolled. Figures in the above capsule and in this profile are approximate. Nineteen transfers enrolled. The median LSAT percentile of the most recent first-year class was 92; the median GPA was 3.6 on a scale of 4.0. The lowest LSAT percentile accepted was 35; the highest was 100.

Requirements
Applicants must have a bachelor's degree and take the LSAT. There is a comprehensive review of all credentials. Minimum acceptable GPA is 2.2 on a scale of 4.0. No specific undergraduate courses are required. Candidates are interviewed.

Procedure
The application deadline for fall entry is February 1. Applicants should submit an application form, a personal statement, a nonrefundable application fee, and registration with LSDAS, and a resumé. Notification of the admissions decision is December to April. The latest acceptable LSAT test date for fall entry is December. Check with the school for current application deadlines. The law school uses the LSDAS.

Special
The law school recruits minority and disadvantaged students through campus visits and law forums, and special mailings and phone calls. Requirements are different for out-of-state students in that Texas' state legislature limits nonresident enrollment to 35% of the entering class. Transfer students must have one year of credit, have a minimum GPA of 2.2, have attended an ABA-approved law school, demonstrate good cause for the transfer, and have a strong academic record prior to and during law school.

Costs

Tuition and fees for the 2009-2010 academic year are $21,000 for full-time in-state students and $36,000 for out-of-state students. On-campus room and board costs about $9000 annually; books and supplies run $4000.

Financial Aid

In a recent year, about 84% of current law students received some form of aid. The average annual amount of aid from all sources combined, including scholarships, loans, and work contracts, was $28,214; maximum, $34,268. Awards are based on need and merit. Required financial statement is the FAFSA. First-year students are notified about their financial aid application at time of acceptance. Financial aid notifications are sent either electronically or by mail. Students can check the status of their financial aid on-line through a secured I.D. process. Check with the school for current financial deadlines.

About the Law School

University of Texas at Austin School of Law was established in 1883 and is a public institution. The 350-acre campus is in an urban area within Austin. The primary mission of the law school is to educate students for the practice of law by advancing knowledge of the law as an institution to effect social change. Students have access to federal, state, county, city, and local agencies, courts, correctional facilities, law firms, and legal aid organizations in the Austin area. Facilities of special interest to law students include Townes Hall and Tarlton Law Library, which is housed in the Joseph D. Jamail Center for Legal Research, 2 connected buildings that house the law library, classrooms, seminar rooms, student organization areas, and other support facilities. Housing for students is available but few students select on-campus housing. All law school facilities are accessible to the physically disabled.

Calendar

The law school operates on a traditional semester basis. Courses for full-time students are offered days only and must be completed within five years. There is no part-time program. New students are admitted in the fall. There is a 10 1/2 -week summer session. Transferable summer courses are offered.

Programs

In addition to the J.D., the law school offers the LL.M. Students may take relevant courses in other programs and apply credit toward the J.D.; a maximum of 12 credits may be applied. The following joint degrees may be earned: J.D./M.A. (Juris Doctor/Master of Arts in Latin American, Middle Eastern, or Russian Euroasian studies), J.D./M.B.A. (Juris Doctor/Master of Business Administration), J.D./M.P.A. (Juris Doctor/Master of Public Affairs), J.D./M.S. (Juris Doctor/Master of Science in community and regional planning), and J.D./Ph.D. (Juris Doctor/Doctor of Philosophy in government, or philosophy).

Required
To earn the J.D., candidates must complete 86 total credits, of which 38 are for required courses. They must maintain a minimum GPA of 1.9 in the required courses. The following first-year courses are required of all students: Civil Procedure, Constitutional Law I, Contracts, Criminal Law, Legal Research and Legal Writing, Property, and Torts. Required upper-level courses consist of a writing seminar, Constitutional Law II, and Professional Responsibility. The required orientation program for first-year students is a 2-day program that familiarizes them with the physical facilities, rules, and procedures of the law school and the university. Students attend a general welcome and social event.

Phone: 512-232-1200
Fax: 512-471-2765
E-mail: *admissions@law.utexas.edu*
Web: *www.utexas.edu/law*

Contact

Samuel Riley, Director for Admissions Programs, 512-232-1200 for general inquiries; Linda Alba, Financial Aid Counselor, 512-232-1130 for financial aid information.

Electives

The School of Law offers concentrations in corporate law, criminal law, entertainment law, family law, international law, juvenile law, labor law, litigation, maritime law, media law, securities law, tax law, torts and insurance, natural resources law, civil liberties, commercial law, and intellectual property law. In addition, clinics are offered in Capital Punishment, Children's Rights, and Criminal Defense; students must have completed half of their degree, 43 hours; credit ranges from 4 to 6 hours. Examples of 3 seminars are: Supreme Court litigation, Entertainment Law, and Class Action. A seminar is for upper-division students and is worth 3 credits. Judicial internships are available with the Texas Supreme Court, the Texas Court of Criminal Appeals, and the Texas Court of Appeals through which a small number of students earn law school credit, 4 to 5 hours, for work done under the supervision of an individual justice. Empirical legal research projects sponsored and directly supervised by a faculty member are available. An advanced student may also conduct individual research projects. The school has a semester-long exchange program with Queen Mary College and Westfield College, which are both colleges of the University of London. Up to 30 upper-class students enroll for 4 approved courses in international or comparative law. Students can create their own study abroad program as well. Students on scholastic probation and second-semester first-year students at risk of being placed on scholastic probation are assigned tutors. There are student organizations focusing on almost any area of the law. The most widely taken electives are Wills and Estates, Business Associations, and Federal Income Tax.

Graduation Requirements

In order to graduate, candidates must have a GPA of 1.9, have completed the upper-division writing requirement, and 86 credit hours, of which 38 are required courses.

Organizations

Students edit the *Texas Law Review, Texas International Law Journal, American Journal of Criminal Law, The Review of Litigation, Texas Forum on Civil Liberties and Civil Rights, Texas Environmental Law Journal, Texas Intellectual Property Law Journal, Texas Journal of Women and the Law, Texas Hispanic Journal of Law and Policy, Texas Review of Law and Politics, Texas Review of Entertainment and Sports Law,* and *Texas Oil and Gas Journal.* The Board of Advocates directs a range of moot court, mock trial, and client counseling contests, both interscholastic and intrascholastic. Law student organizations, local chapters of national associations, and campus organizations include the Student Bar Association, Thurgood Marshall Legal Society, Chicano/Hispanic Law Students Association, Public Interest Law Association, Board of Advocates, and Assault and Flattery.

Library

The law library contains 1,046,921 hardcopy volumes and 350,983 microform volume equivalents, and subscribes to 8322 serial publications. Such on-line databases and networks as CALI, CIS Universe, DIALOG, Dow-Jones, Infotrac, Legal-Trac, LEXIS, LOIS, Mathew Bender, NEXIS, OCLC First Search, RLIN, WESTLAW, and Wilsonline Indexes are available to law students for research. Special library collections include an extensive collection of foreign law (Western Europe, Latin America), papers of Tom C. Clark, Associate Justice of the U.S. Supreme Court, ABA Gavel Committee Award Entries, EU depository, law in popular culture, U.S. Supreme Court briefs, and Canadian Government Document Depository. The papers of Associate Supreme Court Justice Tom C. Clark related to the civil liberties and civil rights cases considered by the Court durning his tenure were digitized and added to The University of Texas web site. Recently, the library added web access to its collection through TALLONS (Tartlton Law Library Online System), and to the resources of the other UT libraries and the Harry Ransom Humanities Research Center through UTCAT. The Law Library's Computer Learning Center (CLC) provides a networked environment for research, e-mail, and word processing applications with laser-printed output. The CLC has doubled in size, with more than 100 networked PCs now available for student use. Wireless network access is available throughout the library. The ratio of library volumes to faculty is 12,034 to 1 and to students is 727 to 1. The ratio of seats in the library to students is 1 to 1.

Placement

J.D.s awarded:	420

Services available through: a separate law school placement center

Services: Mentor Program/Directory, Judicial Clerkship Program, approximately 60 student programs/workshops per year

Special features: Founding member of PSLawNet.org; use of Simplicity; host of largest public service job fair for law students in Texas (Public Service Career Day).

Full-time job interviews:	174 employers
Summer job interviews:	466 employers
Placement by graduation:	95% of class
Placement within 9 months:	99% of class
Average starting salary:	$37,333 to $118,519

Areas of placement:

Private practice 2-10 attorneys	6%
Private practice 11-25 attorneys	4%
Private practice 26-50 attorneys	5%
Private practice 51-100 attorneys	3%
Private practice 100+ attorneys/solo practice	44%
Judicial clerkships	13%
Government	10%
Business/industry	7%
Public interest	5%
Military	2%
Academic	1%

Faculty

The law school has 87 full-time and 93 part-time faculty members, of whom 62 are women. According to AAUP standards for Category I institutions, faculty salaries are average. About 19% of full-time faculty have a graduate law degree in addition to the J.D.; about 5% of part-time faculty have one. The ratio of full-time students to full-time faculty in an average class is 14 to 1; in a clinic, 8 to 1. The law school has a regular program of bringing visiting professors and other distinguished lecturers and visitors to campus. There is a chapter of the Order of the Coif; 58 graduates are members.

Students

About 43% of the student body are women; 33%, minorities; 6%, African American; 7%, Asian American; 17%, Hispanic; and 3%, other minority. The majority of students come from Texas (70%). The average age of entering students is 24; age range is 18 to 49. About 1% drop out after the first year for academic or personal reasons; 99% remain to receive a law degree.

David A. Clarke School of Law

4200 Connecticut Avenue, N.W.
Washington, DC 20008

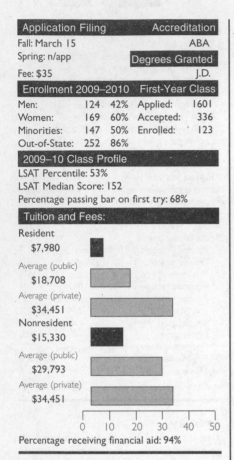

Application Filing	Accreditation
Fall: March 15	ABA
Spring: n/app	**Degrees Granted**
Fee: $35	J.D.

Enrollment 2009–2010		First-Year Class	
Men:	124 42%	Applied:	1601
Women:	169 60%	Accepted:	336
Minorities:	147 50%	Enrolled:	123
Out-of-State:	252 86%		

2009–10 Class Profile
LSAT Percentile: 53%
LSAT Median Score: 152
Percentage passing bar on first try: 68%

Tuition and Fees:

Resident
$7,980

Average (public)
$18,708

Average (private)
$34,451

Nonresident
$15,330

Average (public)
$29,793

Average (private)
$34,451

0 10 20 30 40 50

Percentage receiving financial aid: 94%

ADMISSIONS

In the fall 2009 first-year class, 1601 applied, 336 were accepted, and 123 enrolled. Three transfers enrolled. The median LSAT percentile of the most recent first-year class was 53; the median GPA was 3.0 on a scale of 4.0. The lowest LSAT percentile accepted was 23; the highest was 88.

Requirements
Applicants must have a bachelor's degree and take the LSAT. The most important admission factors include general background, GPA, and LSAT results. No specific undergraduate courses are required. Candidates are interviewed.

Procedure
The application deadline for fall entry is March 15. Applicants should submit an application form, LSAT results, transcripts, a personal statement, a nonrefundable application fee of $35, 2 letters of recommendation, and a supplemen-

tal essay. Notification of the admissions decision is on a rolling basis. The latest acceptable LSAT test date for fall entry is February. The law school uses the LSDAS.

Special
The law school recruits minority and disadvantaged students by direct mail recruitment campaigns, such as LSAC Candidate Referral Service; through visits to historically black and minority serving institutions; by maintaining contact with local community groups and organizations; holding Law Day and Open House programs; LSAC-sponsored minority program; and through advertising in school papers and local government periodicals. Requirements are not different for out-of-state students. Transfer students must have one year of credit, have a minimum GPA of 2.0, have attended an ABA-approved law school, and good/satisfactory academic status. Preadmissions courses consist of a 4 to 6 week summer conditional admission program offering courses in Legal Writing and Reasoning, Torts, and another substantive course.

Costs

Tuition and fees for the 2009-2010 academic year are $7980 for full-time in-state students and $15,330 for out-of-state students. Tuition for part-time students is $5880 in-state and $11,130 out-of-state. Books and supplies run $2000.

Financial Aid

About 94% of current law students receive some form of aid. The average annual amount of aid from all sources combined, including scholarships, loans, and work contracts, is $36,792; maximum, $47,799. Awards are based on need and merit. Students may apply for non-need-based alternative loans with eligibility based on credit worthiness. Required financial statements are the FAFSA and NEED ACCESS required for institutional scholarships. The aid application deadline for fall entry is March 31. Special funds for minority or disadvantaged students are available through need-based named scholarships donated to the law school's scholarship fund for minority student awards. First-year students are notified about their financial aid application at time of acceptance.

About the Law School

University of the District of Columbia David A. Clarke School of Law was established in 1987 and is a public institution. The campus is in an urban area of upper Northwest Washington, D.C. The primary mission of the law school is to represent the legal needs of low-income persons, particularly those who reside in the District of Columbia, while recruiting, enrolling, and training persons from racial, ethnic, or other population groups that have been traditionally underrepresented at the Bar. Students have access to federal, state, county, city, and local agencies, courts, correctional facilities, law firms, and legal aid organizations in the Washington area. Other resources include the Supreme Court, Capitol Hill, Library of Congress, and public interest groups and organizations. Facilities of special interest to law students include local and federal government offices, courts and administrative agencies, public interest organizations, and Capitol Hill. There is no on-campus housing. The School of Law assists incoming students with locating housing in the Washington, D.C. metropolitan area. All law school facilities are accessible to the physically disabled.

Calendar

The law school operates on a traditional semester basis. Courses for full-time students are offered both day and evening and must be completed within 5 years. For part-time students, courses are offered evenings only and must be completed within 5 years. New full- and part-time students are admitted in the fall. There is an 8- to 10-week summer session. Transferable summer courses are offered.

Programs

Required
To earn the J.D., candidates must complete 90 total credits, of which 75 are for required courses. They must maintain a minimum GPA of 2.0 in the required courses. The following first-year courses are required of all students: Civil Procedure I and II, Contracts I and II, Criminal Law, Criminal Procedure, Law and Justice, Lawyering Process I and II, and Torts I and II. Required upper-level courses consist of Clinic I and II, Constitutional Law I

Phone: 202-274-7341
Fax: 202-274-5583
E-mail: vcanty@udc.edu; lawadmission@udc.edu
Web: www.law.udc.edu

Contact

Vivian W. Canty, Assistant Dean of Admission, 202-274-7341 for general inquiries; Nailah Williams, Financial Aid Director, 202-274-7337 for financial aid information.

and II, Evidence, Moot Court, Professional Responsibility, and Property I and II. All students must take clinical courses. The required orientation program for first-year students begins in early to mid-August and lasts approximately 2 weeks. Students take two courses: Lawyering Process I and Law and Justice. There are other enrichment activities, such as student and faculty presentations, tours of the Supreme and D.C. Superior Courts, and a Dean's reception.

Electives

Students must take 14 credits in their area of concentration. The David A. Clarke School of Law offers concentrations in public interest law. In addition, 8 clinics are offered for 7 credits each in topics such as Small Business and Community Development, Government Accountability Project, Low-Income Tax, and Immigration Law. Seminars are offered each semester. A 2-credit internship seminar is required of all students who do an internship. Internships with government or nonprofit agencies, for 4 or 10 credits, are offered for advanced students who have completed 14 credits of clinic and are in good standing. Students may be selected to be research assistants on faculty research projects. The clinics involve students in various forms of field work. In addition, the internship program provides full-time field work. Special lecture series include the Dean's Lecture Series. The Career Services Office and student organizations also plan guest speakers' visits and programs. Students may participate in study abroad programs sponsored by other law schools. The Academic Success Program provides small group and individual tutorials for students during the 3 years of law school. The Program requires students to examine the analytic processes needed to solve legal problems. It also provides counseling and tutoring for students whose GPA falls below 2.0. This program also sponsors workshops on time management, test-taking, and self-regulated learning. The most widely taken electives are Race and The Law, Business Organizations I, and Uniform Commercial Code.

Graduation Requirements

In order to graduate, candidates must have a GPA of 2.0 and have completed the upper-division writing requirement.

Organizations

Students edit *The District of Columbia Law Review* and *The Advocate*, Law student organizations, local chapters of national associations, and campus organizations include the UDC-DCSL Student Bar Association, Women's Law Society, Black Law Students Association, Negotiatiion Team Competition, Client Counseling, Oral Advocacy Team, Phi Alpha Delta, National Lawyers Guild, National Association of Public Interest Law, Sports and Entertainment Student Lawyers Association, Latino/a Law Students Association, and Gay and Lesbian Outlaw Student Association.

Library

The law library contains 257,000 hardcopy volumes and 114,989 microform volume equivalents, and subscribes to 1585 serial publications. Such on-line databases and networks as CALI, Infotrac, Legal-Trac, LEXIS, Mathew Bender, NEXIS, OCLC First Search, WESTLAW, Wilsonline Indexes, BNA, and the Internet are available to law students for research. Special library collections include District of Columbia law and clinical legal practice materials. Recently, the library has had new computers installed and new furniture has been placed in the Clinic Library. The ratio of library volumes to faculty is 12,850 to 1 and to students is 877 to 1. The ratio of seats in the library to students is 1 to 1.

Faculty

The law school has 20 full-time and 17 part-time faculty members, of whom 17 are women. According to AAUP standards for Category IIA institutions, faculty salaries are above average. About 10% of full-time faculty have a graduate law degree in addition to the J.D.; about 22% of part-time faculty have one. The ratio of full-time students to full-time faculty in an average class is 11 to 1; in a clinic, 8 to 1. The law school has a regular program of bringing visiting professors and other distinguished lecturers and visitors to campus.

Students

About 60% of the student body are women; 50%, minorities; 29%, African American; 8%, Asian American; 11%, Hispanic;

Placement

J.D.s awarded:	67

Services available through: a separate law school placement center

Services: lists of judicial clerkships, fellowships, and writing competitions. In keeping with the school's mission, emphasis is placed on public sector careers.

Special features: personalized career counseling; guaranteed summer stipend for all qualifying first year students doing full time public interest work

Full-time job interviews:	7 employers
Summer job interviews:	40 employers
Placement by graduation:	n/av
Placement within 9 months:	85% of class
Average starting salary:	$37,000 to $66,000

Areas of placement:

Private practice 2-10 attorneys	29%
Government	21%
Business/industry	17%
Public interest	14%
Judicial clerkships	10%
Academic	5%
Public Service/unknown	4%

1%, Native American; and 1%, foreign nationals. The majority of students come from the South (46%). The average age of entering students is 28; age range is 20 to 63. About 37% of students enter directly from undergraduate school, 12% have a graduate degree, and 45% have worked full-time prior to entering law school. About 5% drop out after the first year for academic or personal reasons; 91% remain to receive a law degree.

UNIVERSITY OF THE PACIFIC

McGeorge School of Law

3200 Fifth Avenue
Sacramento, CA 95817

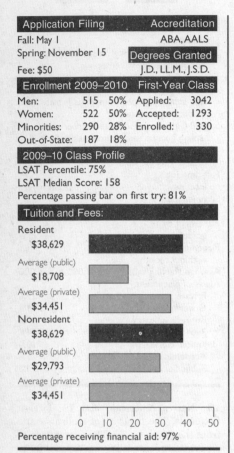

Application Filing		Accreditation
Fall: May 1		ABA, AALS
Spring: November 15		Degrees Granted
Fee: $50		J.D., LL.M., J.S.D.

Enrollment 2009–2010			First-Year Class	
Men:	515	50%	Applied:	3042
Women:	522	50%	Accepted:	1293
Minorities:	290	28%	Enrolled:	330
Out-of-State:	187	18%		

2009–10 Class Profile
LSAT Percentile: 75%
LSAT Median Score: 158
Percentage passing bar on first try: 81%

Tuition and Fees:

Resident
$38,629

Average (public)
$18,708

Average (private)
$34,451

Nonresident
$38,629

Average (public)
$29,793

Average (private)
$34,451

Percentage receiving financial aid: 97%

ADMISSIONS

In the fall 2009 first-year class, 3042 applied, 1293 were accepted, and 330 enrolled. Nine transfers enrolled. The median LSAT percentile of the most recent first-year class was 75; the median GPA was 3.4 on a scale of 4.3. The lowest LSAT percentile accepted was 44; the highest was 99.

Requirements
Applicants must have a bachelor's degree and take the LSAT. The most important admission factors include academic achievement, LSAT results, and general background. No specific undergraduate courses are required. Candidates are not interviewed.

Procedure
The application deadline for fall entry is May 1. Applicants should submit an application form, LSAT results, transcripts, a personal statement, a nonrefundable application fee of $50, and optional (3 are suggested) letters of recommendation.

Notification of the admissions decision is begins in January. The latest acceptable LSAT test date for fall entry is February; June if space is available. The law school uses the LSDAS.

Special
The law school recruits minority and disadvantaged students recruiting events, publications, letters, contacts with McGeorge students, and scholarship and grant programs. Requirements are not different for out-of-state students. Transfer students must have 1 year of credit and acceptance of transfer students is dependent upon space availability; preference is given to students with compelling reasons to request transfer.

Costs

Tuition and fees for the 2009-2010 academic year are $38,629 for all full-time students. Tuition for part-time students is $25,705 per year. On-campus room and board costs about $9738 annually; books and supplies run $1600.

Financial Aid

About 97% of current law students receive some form of aid. The average annual amount of aid from all sources combined, including scholarships, loans, and work contracts, is $47,237; maximum, $61,687. Awards are based on need and merit. Required financial statement is the FAFSA. The aid application deadline for fall entry is open. Diversity factors are considered in the award of scholarships and grants. First-year students are notified about their financial aid application at time of acceptance, assuming a completed application is on file.

About the Law School

University of the Pacific McGeorge School of Law was established in 1924 and is a private institution. The 13-acre campus is in a suburban area in Sacramento. The primary mission of the law school is to educate practice-ready graduates, able to represent clients skillfully and ethically, through a rigorous curriculum that unifies classroom study with development of professional skills. Students have access to federal, state, county, city, and local agencies, courts, correctional facilities, law firms, and legal aid organizations in the Sacramento area. Other resources

include state capital internships and campus administrative justice offices. Facilities of special interest to law students include the trial courtroom, the LawLab equipped with computer technology, the "live-client" clinical facilities, the student center with food service, the library with ample study and computer areas, and recreational facilities. Housing for students consists of 158 on-campus apartments; housing off campus is readily available in the Sacramento area at a reasonable cost. About 95% of the law school facilities are accessible to the physically disabled.

Calendar

The law school operates on a traditional semester basis. Courses for full-time students are offered both day and evening and must be completed within 4 years. For part-time students, courses are offered both day and evening and must be completed within 5 years. New full- and part-time students are admitted in the fall. There is a 7 1/2-week summer session. Transferable summer courses are offered.

Programs

In addition to the J.D., the law school offers the LL.M. and J.S.D. Students may take relevant courses in other programs and apply credit toward the J.D.; a maximum of 30 from an ABA law school credits may be applied. The following joint degrees may be earned: J.D./M.A. or M.S. (Juris Doctor/Master of Arts or Master of Science), J.D./M.B.A. (Juris Doctor/Master of Business Administration), and J.D./M.P.P.A. (Juris Doctor/Master of Public Policy and Administration).

Required
To earn the J.D., candidates must complete 88 total credits, of which 59 are for required courses. They must maintain a minimum GPA of 2.3 in the required courses. The following first-year courses are required of all students: Civil Procedure, Contracts, Criminal Law, Legal Process, Property, and Torts. Required upper-level courses consist of Appellate and International Advocacy, Business Associations, Community Property, Constitutional Law, Criminal Procedure, Evidence, Professional Responsibility, Remedies, and Wills and Trusts. The required orientation program for first-year students is a 3-day program at the beginning of the year that includes orientation

Guide To Law Schools

Phone: 916-739-7105
Fax: 916-739-7301
E-mail: mcgeorge@pacific.edu
Web: www.mcgeorge.edu

Contact

Mathiew H. Le, Associate Director of Admissions, 916-739-7105 for general inquiries; Joe Pinkas, Director of Financial Aid, 916-739-7158 for financial aid information.

classes, small group sessions, and social activities. First-year faculty provide special feedback programs, including practice examinations, throughout the first year.

Electives

Students must take 14 to 16 credits in their area of concentration. The McGeorge School of Law offers concentrations in corporate law, criminal law, environmental law, family law, intellectual property law, international law, juvenile law, litigation, tax law, torts and insurance, public law, and policy, and advocacy. In addition, on-campus clinics include Community Legal Services, which provides legal services for those not otherwise able to afford them; it is available to advanced students, carries a 2-semester commitment, and is worth 6 credits. Other campus-based clinics available to advanced students for 2 or 3 credits each semester are Administrative Adjudication Clinic, Parole Representation Clinic; Immigration Clinic, Bankruptcy Clinic, Business and Community Development Clinic, Civil Practice Clinic, Victims' Rights Clinic, and Legislative Process, Strategy and Ethics Clinic. A number of elective courses are in a seminar format with limited enrollment. Of particular interest are Advanced Intellectual Property; Negotiations and Settlement; California Law Revision; Reorganization, Recapitalization and Insolvency; and International Water Resources Law. More than 80 off-campus internships are available in nonprofit and local, state, and federal governmental offices and agencies. Internships are available to advanced students and are worth 2 or 3 credits per semester. Directed research, available as an elective for advanced students, is offered for 1 or 2 credits. Individual professors also have student research assistants. Additionally, the Research Pool undertakes research projects for practitioners. Lecture series such as the Distinguished Speaker's Series, Hefner Memorial Lecture Series, and Lou Ashe Symposium bring outstanding guest speakers to campus. The Institute on International Legal Studies includes a 3-week program in Salzburg, Austria, in cooperation with the University of Salzburg. International and comparative law courses are offered in public and commercial law fields. For more than a decade, Anthony M. Kennedy, Associate Justice of the U.S. Supreme Court, has co-taught "Fundamental Rights in

Europe and the U.S." McGeorge also has a Summer Institute in Suzhou, China, with courses and cultural visits in Chinese courts. Tutorial programs include the Skills Hour Program and the Practice Examination Program offered in the fall of the student's first year. A voluntary Minority Support Program provides a peer support and networking system as well as special orientation sessions, student-led discussion groups, and course review sessions. The most widely taken electives are Trial Advocacy, clinical offerings, and business courses.

Graduation Requirements

In order to graduate, candidates must have a GPA of 2.33 and have completed the upper-division writing requirement.

Organizations

Students edit the *McGeorge Law Review* and the *Pacific McGeorge Global Business and Development Law Journal*. McGeorge teams compete in the National and ABA Moot Court competitions and the Philip Jessup International Moot Court Competition. Other competitions include Willem C. Viz International Commercial Arbitration in Vienna, San Diego Defense Lawyers, William Daniel Mock Trial, San Diego Consumer Attorneys Mock Trial, Michigan State Competition, ABA Texas Young Lawyers National Trial Competition Nationals, ATLA National Student Advocacy Competition Nationals, ABA Client Counseling, and ABA Negotiation. Law student organizations include the Student Bar Association, Public Legal Services Society, and Government Affairs Student Association. There are local chapters of ABA-Law Student Division, and Phi Alpha Delta fraternity. Campus clubs and other organizations include Entertainment Law Society, Women's Caucus, and International Law Society.

Library

The law library contains 509,762 hardcopy volumes and 294,936 microform volume equivalents, and subscribes to 4503 serial publications. Such on-line databases and networks as CALI, CIS Universe, Legal-Trac, LEXIS, Mathew Bender, NEXIS, OCLC First Search, RLIN, WESTLAW, CCH, and BNA are available to law students for research. Special library collections include California legal materials,

CALIFORNIA

Placement

J.D.s awarded:	258
Services available through: a separate law school placement center	
Special features: practice interview program; alumni network program; first-year Career Development orientation program	
Full-time job interviews:	58 employers
Summer job interviews:	n/av
Placement by graduation:	50% of class
Placement within 9 months:	98% of class
Average starting salary:	$25,000 to $135,000
Areas of placement:	
Private practice 2-10 attorneys	50%
Government	25%
Public interest	9%
Business/industry	8%
Academic	3%
Judicial clerkships	2%

California and U.S. documents depository, tax, international law, and water, and natural resources. Recently, the library renovated prublic services, added a computer lab, and a student study. The ratio of library volumes to faculty is 9268 to 1 and to students is 492 to 1. The ratio of seats in the library to students is 1 to 1.

Faculty

The law school has 55 full-time and 57 part-time faculty members, of whom 42 are women. According to AAUP standards for Category IIA institutions, faculty salaries are above average. About 30% of full-time faculty have a graduate law degree in addition to the J.D.; about 11% of part-time faculty have one. The ratio of full-time students to full-time faculty in an average class is 16 to 1; in a clinic, 10 to 1. The law school has a regular program of bringing visiting professors and other distinguished lecturers and visitors to campus. There is a chapter of the Order of the Coif; 31 faculty and 712 graduates are members.

Students

About 50% of the student body are women; 28%, minorities; 3%, African American; 13%, Asian American; 9%, Hispanic; and 3%, Native American. The majority of students come from California (82%). The average age of entering students is 25; age range is 21 to 53. About 76% of students enter directly from undergraduate school and 2% have a graduate degree. About 14% drop out after the first year for academic or personal reasons.

UNIVERSITY OF TOLEDO

College of Law

2801 West Bancroft Street
Toledo, OH 43606-3390

Application Filing	Accreditation
Fall: July 1	ABA, AALS
Spring: n/app	**Degrees Granted**
Fee: n/av	J.D.

Enrollment 2009–2010		First-Year Class	
Men:	296 60%	Applied:	869
Women:	198 40%	Accepted:	522
Minorities:	49 10%	Enrolled:	182
Out-of-State:	148 30%		

2009–10 Class Profile
LSAT Percentile: 64%
LSAT Median Score: 155
Percentage passing bar on first try: 89%

Tuition and Fees:

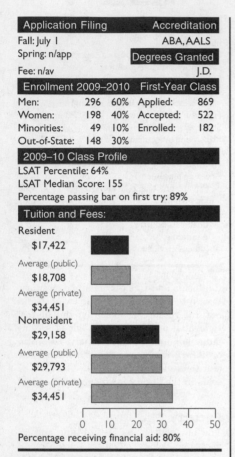

Resident
$17,422

Average (public)
$18,708

Average (private)
$34,451

Nonresident
$29,158

Average (public)
$29,793

Average (private)
$34,451

Percentage receiving financial aid: 80%

ADMISSIONS
In the fall 2009 first-year class, 869 applied, 522 were accepted, and 182 enrolled. Four transfers enrolled. The median LSAT percentile of the most recent first-year class was 64; the median GPA was 3.35 on a scale of 4.0. The lowest LSAT percentile accepted was 44; the highest was 97.

Requirements
Applicants must have a bachelor's degree and take the LSAT. Minimum acceptable LSAT percentile is 40 and minimum acceptable GPA is 2.0 on a scale of 4.0. The most important admission factors include LSAT results, GPA, and undergraduate curriculum. No specific undergraduate courses are required. Candidates are not interviewed.

Procedure
The application deadline for fall entry is July 1. Applicants should submit an application form, LSAT results, transcripts, and 2 letters of recommendation. They should indicate preference for full-

or part-time study. Accepted applicants must submit a $75 nonrefundable deposit, which is credited toward tuition. Notification of the admissions decision is on a rolling basis. The latest acceptable LSAT test date for fall entry is June. The law school uses the LSDAS.

Special
The law school recruits minority and disadvantaged students through Minority Preview Day, Minority Law Days, mailings, e-mails and law forums. Requirements are not different for out-of-state students. Transfer students must have attended an ABA-approved law school and be in good standing at the previous school.

Costs
Tuition and fees for the 2009-2010 academic year are $17,422 for full-time in-state students and $29,158 for out-of-state students. Tuition for part-time students is $13,066 in-state and $21,868 out-of-state. Books and supplies run $1154.

Financial Aid
About 80% of current law students receive some form of aid. The average annual amount of aid from all sources combined, including scholarships, loans, and work contracts, is $30,257; maximum, $60,962. Awards are based on need and merit. Required financial statement is the FAFSA. The aid application deadline for fall entry is July 1. First-year students are notified about their financial aid application at time of acceptance.

About the Law School
University of Toledo College of Law was established in 1906 and is a public institution. The 210-acre campus is in a suburban area west of downtown Toledo, adjacent to Ottawa Hills. The primary mission of the law school is to create a diverse intellectual environment that prepares students to engage in the legal practice of their choice, enhances the college's national and regional reputation for academic excellence, fosters a spirit of community, individual attention, and professional values, and encourages participation in the life of the university, region, and state. Students have access to federal, state, county, city, and local agencies, courts, correctional facilities,

law firms, and legal aid organizations in the Toledo area. Students are placed in prosecutor offices and public interest offices throughout the U.S. Facilities of special interest to law students include a state-of-the-art moot courtroom, which is available for trial practice and appellate advocacy programs, renovated classrooms, and the wireless Web. Housing for students consists of living accommodations located near the campus. The university assists students in finding housing. All law school facilities are accessible to the physically disabled.

Calendar
The law school operates on a traditional semester basis. Courses for full-time students are offered both day and evening and Saturday and must be completed within 5 years (suggested). For part-time students, courses are offered both day and evening and Saturday and must be completed within 6 years (suggested). New full- and part-time students are admitted in the fall. There is a 9-week summer session. Transferable summer courses are offered.

Programs
Students may take relevant courses in other programs and apply credit toward the J.D.; a maximum of 6 credits may be applied. The following joint degrees may be earned: J.D./M.A.C.J. (Juris Doctor/Master of Arts in Criminal Justice), J.D./M.B.A. (Juris Doctor/Master of Business Administration), J.D./M.P.A. (Juris Doctor/Master of Public Administration), and J.D./M.S.E. (Juris Doctor/Master of Science in Engineering).

Required
To earn the J.D., candidates must complete 89 total credits, of which 42 are for required courses. They must maintain a minimum GPA of 2.0 in the required courses. The following first-year courses are required of all students: Civil Procedure I and II, Constitutional Law I, Contracts I and II, Criminal Law, Legal Research, Writing, and Appellate Advocacy I and II, Property I and II, and Torts. Required upper-level courses consist of Constitutional Law II, Evidence, and Legal Ethics and Professional Responsibility. The required orientation program for first-year students lasts 2 days.

Phone: 419-530-4131
Fax: 419-530-4345
E-mail: law.utoledo.edu
Web: www.utlaw.edu

Contact
Lindsey Riesen, Assistant Director of Law, 419-530-4131 for general inquiries; Beth Solo, Assistant Director, Law Financial, 419-530-7929 for financial aid information.

OHIO

Electives
Students must take 14-16 credits in their area of concentration. The College of Law offers concentrations in criminal law, environmental law, intellectual property law, international law, and labor law. In addition, clinical programs include the College of Law Legal Clinic, Criminal Law Practice programs, the Domestic Violence Clinic, and the Dispute Resolution Clinic. These are offered to all upper-level writing experiences for 2 to 6 hours of credit. Upper-level units are required for graduation; offered to all upper-class students for 1 or 2 credits. Internships are available anywhere in the U.S. through the Criminal Law Practice programs and the Public Service Externship Program. Individual research programs allow students to develop their own research projects, which are pursued in consultation with a faculty adviser. The Cannon Lecture Series and the Stranahan National Issues Forum have hosted individuals of national prominence who provide the college and general public with timely discussions of legal and policy issues. Teaching assistants and tutors are available. The most widely taken electives are Criminal Procedure, Business Associations, and Federal Taxation.

Graduation Requirements
In order to graduate, candidates must have a GPA of 2.0 and have completed the upper-division writing requirement.

Organizations
Students edit the *University of Toledo Law Review* and the student/newspaper, *No Holds Bar Review*. The Moot Court program helps build skills in the arts of brief writing and oral advocacy through participation in national and intra-school competitions, such as the Charles W. Faroff Intra-School Competition. Competitions are managed by a student Moot Court Board. Other competitions include Family Law, Constitutional Law, and Jessup International Law. Law student organizations, local chapters of national associations, and campus organizations include Student Bar Association, BLSA, Health Law Association, American Constitution Society, Federalist Society, HLSA, Delta Theta Phi, Phi Alpha Delta, Inns of Court, Environmental Law, Public Interest Law Association, Women Law Students Asso-

ciation, and Labor and Employment Law Association.

Library
The law library contains 360,833 hardcopy volumes and 137,340 microform volume equivalents, and subscribes to 3371 serial publications. Such on-line databases and networks as CALI, CIS Universe, Legal-Trac, LEXIS, NEXIS, WESTLAW, Wilsonline Indexes, Ohio Capital Connection, CCH, and BNA are available to law students for research. Special library collections include significant holdings of primary materials for the United Kingdom, Canada, Australia, and New Zealand, and primary and secondary materials for studying international law. The library is a federal depository. Recently, the library modernized circulation, reference, and library entrance areas. The ratio of library volumes to faculty is 11,639 to 1 and to students is 730 to 1. The ratio of seats in the library to students is 1 to 1.

Faculty
The law school has 31 full-time and 18 part-time faculty members, of whom 18 are women. According to AAUP standards for Category I institutions, faculty salaries are well below average. About 20% of full-time faculty have a graduate law degree in addition to the J.D.; about 1% of part-time faculty have one. The ratio of full-time students to full-time faculty in an average class is 13 to 1; in a clinic, 5 to 1. The law school has a regular program of bringing visiting professors and other distinguished lecturers and visitors to campus. There is a chapter of the Order of the Coif; 40 faculty and 469 graduates are members.

Students
About 40% of the student body are women; 10%, minorities; 4%, African American; 4%, Asian American; and 3%, Hispanic. The majority of students come from Ohio (70%). The average age of entering students is 26; age range is 21 to 52. About 46% of students enter directly from undergraduate school and 8% have a graduate degree. About 8% drop out after the first year for academic or personal reasons; 92% remain to receive a law degree.

Placement

J.D.s awarded:	154

Services available through: a separate law school placement center

Services: arrange interviews using video conferencing equipment, organize mentor program, arrange for reciprocity with other law schools, and coordinate job fairs

Special features: the O.P.D. Resource Library, the O.P.D. Student Handbook, mentor program for first-year students, alumni on-line network for all students..

Full-time job interviews:	39 employers
Summer job interviews:	39 employers
Placement by graduation:	77% of class
Placement within 9 months:	95% of class
Average starting salary:	$32,000 to $100,000

Areas of placement:

Private practice 2-10 attorneys	23%
Private practice 11-25 attorneys	3%
Private practice 26-50 attorneys	5%
Private practice 51-100+ attorneys	2%
Private practice 100+ attorneys/ Unknown	11%
Business/industry	13%
Unknown, self employed	11%
Public interest	8%
Academic	5%
Judicial clerkships	4%
Military	3%
Government	22%

College of Law

3120 East Fourth Place
Tulsa, OK 74104-2499

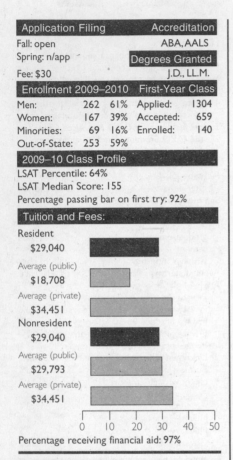

Application Filing	Accreditation
Fall: open	ABA, AALS
Spring: n/app	Degrees Granted
Fee: $30	J.D., LL.M.

Enrollment 2009–2010		First-Year Class	
Men:	262 61%	Applied:	1304
Women:	167 39%	Accepted:	659
Minorities:	69 16%	Enrolled:	140
Out-of-State:	253 59%		

2009–10 Class Profile
LSAT Percentile: 64%
LSAT Median Score: 155
Percentage passing bar on first try: 92%

Tuition and Fees:

Resident
$29,040

Average (public)
$18,708

Average (private)
$34,451

Nonresident
$29,040

Average (public)
$29,793

Average (private)
$34,451

0 10 20 30 40 50

Percentage receiving financial aid: 97%

ADMISSIONS

In the fall 2009 first-year class, 1304 applied, 659 were accepted, and 140 enrolled. Three transfers enrolled. The median LSAT percentile of the most recent first-year class was 64; the median GPA was 3.22 on a scale of 4.0. The lowest LSAT percentile accepted was 41; the highest was 92.

Requirements
Applicants must have a bachelor's degree and take the LSAT. The most important admission factors include LSAT results, GPA, and undergraduate curriculum. No specific undergraduate courses are required. Candidates are not interviewed.

Procedure
The application deadline for fall entry is open. Applicants should submit an application form, LSAT results, transcripts, a personal statement, a nonrefundable application fee of $30, and 2 letters of recommendation. The application fee is waived if students apply at *www.law. utulsa.edu/law*. Notification of the admissions decision is on an ongoing basis. The latest acceptable LSAT test date for fall entry is June. The law school uses the LSDAS.

Special
The law school recruits minority and disadvantaged students through CLEO, PLSI, an academic success program in summer, and recruitment at minority schools. Requirements are not different for out-of-state students. Transfer students must have 1 year of credit, have a minimum GPA of 2.6, and have attended an ABA-approved law school.

Costs

On-campus room and board costs about $8644 annually; books and supplies run $1500.

Financial Aid

About 97% of current law students receive some form of aid. The average annual amount of aid from all sources combined, including scholarships, loans, and work contracts, is $36,096; maximum, $67,684. Awards are based on need and merit. Required financial statement is the FAFSA. The aid application deadline for fall entry is open. Special funds for minority or disadvantaged students include scholarship awards. First-year students are notified about their financial aid application at time of acceptance.

About the Law School

University of Tulsa College of Law was established in 1923 and is a private institution. The 207-acre campus is in a suburban area 3 miles east of downtown Tulsa. The primary mission of the law school is to prepare students from diverse backgrounds to excel in the legal profession through an intellectually rigorous program that promotes the core values of excellence in scholarship, dedication to free inquiry, integrity of charter, professionalism, and commitment to humanity. Students have access to federal, state, county, city, and local agencies, courts, correctional facilities, law firms, and legal aid organizations in the Tulsa area. Tribal courts and agencies are also accessible. Facilities of special interest to law students include Collins Fitness Center, Mabee Legal Information Center, and Boesche Legal Clinic. Housing for students is available in university apartments. Accommodations are available in nonuniversity facilities at a reasonable cost. All law school facilities are accessible to the physically disabled.

Calendar

The law school operates on a traditional semester basis. Courses for full-time students are offered both day and evening and must be completed within 7 years. For part-time students, courses are offered both day and evening and Part-time students must have flexibility to attend classes during the day, and must be completed within 7 years. New full- and part-time students are admitted in the fall. There is a 4-, 6-, 12-week summer session. Transferable summer courses are offered.

Programs

In addition to the J.D., the law school offers the LL.M. Students may take relevant courses in other programs and apply credit toward the J.D.; a maximum of 6 credits may be applied. The following joint degrees may be earned: J.D./M.A. (Juris Doctor/Master of Arts in anthropology, history, psycholoy, English, industrial, and organizational), J.D./M.B.A. (Juris Doctor/Master of Business Administration), J.D./M.S. (Juris Doctor/Master of Science in biological science,geosciences, and computer science), J.D./M.S.F. (Juris Doctor/Master of Finance), and J.D./M. TAX (Juris Doctor/ Master of Taxation).

Required
To earn the J.D., candidates must complete 88 total credits, of which 50 to 53 are for required courses. They must maintain a minimum GPA of 2.0 in the required courses. The following first-year courses are required of all students: Civil Procedure I, Civil Procedure ll, Constitutional Law I, Contracts, Criminal Law and Administration, Legal Reasoning Analysis and Writing I and II, Legal Research, Property, and Torts. Required upper-level courses consist of Civil Procedure II, Constitutional Law II, Evidence, Perspective, Professional Responsibility, and Transnational. The required orientation program for first-year students starts 1 week before the beginning of other courses.

Phone: 918-631-2406
Fax: 918-631-3630
E-mail: april-fox@utulsa.edu
Web: www.law.utulsa.edu

Contact

April Fox, Dean of Admissions, 918-631-2709 for general inquiries; Kristi Emerson, Assistant Director of Financial Aid, 918-631-3325 for financial aid information.

Electives

The College of Law offers concentrations in environmental law, international law, Indian law, health law, entrepreneurial law, public policy, and energy law. In addition, clinics include Immigrant Rights Project, and the Social Enterprise and Economic Development (SEED) Law Project. At the University of Tulsa Boesche Legal Clinic, students represent under-served clients in a variety of civil cases. All students are supervised by a faculty member, and credit is offered. Numerous seminars are offered and have a limited enrollment. Through the college's Legal Internship Program, students may obtain practical experience gained under the supervision of practicing attorneys and the college. The Judicial Internships program offers students supervised educational experience in the Oklahoma District Court, Oklahoma Court of Appeals, U.S. District Court, U.S. Magistrate's Office, U.S. Bankruptcy Court, and the Muskogee Creek Nation Tribal Courts. Externships and internships with certificates are offered in Health Law and Indian Law. Qualified students may pursue independent study in specific areas of the law under the supervision of law professors. Through the In-Residence Program, students meet and talk with scholars, alumni, practitioners, and judges in classes and lectures. Special lecture series include the Legal Scholarship Symposium, Supreme Court Review, Buck Franklin Lecture, the Hager Lecture. Summer institutes in law are offered in Ireland, Switzerland, China, and Argentina. Students also have the opportunity to study abroad in London for a semester. A first-year workshop focuses on study and exam skills and a third-year bar exam preparation program is available. Minority programs include Black Law Students Association, Hispanic Law Students Association, Native American Law Students Association, Alumni Diversity Committee, College of Law Diversity Committee, and Tulsa Minority Networking Task Force. Special interest groups include the Comparative and International Law Center, Native American Law Center, and Sustainable Energy and Resources Law Program. The most widely taken electives are Basic Corporate Law, Decendants' Estates and Trusts, and Selling and Leasing of Goods.

Graduation Requirements

In order to graduate, candidates must have a GPA of 2.0 and have completed the upper-division writing requirement.

Organizations

Students edit the Tulsa Law Review; Energy Law Journal; Year in Review, published jointly with the ABA section of Environment, Energy and Resources (SEER); and the newspaper Dicta. The TU Law Board of Advocates sponsors 7 moot court competitions, including the first-year Client Counseling, Client Counseling (regional and national), and ABA Negotiation (regional and national). Other competitions include Native American Law and Health Law Competitions. Law student organizations, local chapters of national associations, and campus organizations include Native American Law Student Assocaition, Black Law Student Association, Hispanic Law Students Association, ABA-Law Student Division, Delta Theta Phi, Phi Alpha Delta, and Phi Delta Phi.

Library

The law library contains 410,962 hardcopy volumes and 1,066,843 microform volume equivalents, and subscribes to 3769 serial publications. Such on-line databases and networks as CALI, CIS Universe, DIALOG, Infotrac, Legal-Trac, LEXIS, Mathew Bender, NEXIS, OCLC First Search, and WESTLAW are available to law students for research. Special library collections include literature and information on energy, environmental law, Indian law, and international law. Recently, the library received upgraded software for virtual reference. The ratio of library volumes to faculty is 14,171 to 1 and to students is 958 to 1. The ratio of seats in the library to students is 1 to 1.

Faculty

The law school has 29 full-time and 28 part-time faculty members, of whom 19 are women. According to AAUP standards for Category IIA institutions, faculty salaries are above average. About 35% of full-time faculty have a graduate law degree in addition to the J.D.; about 22% of part-time faculty have one. The ratio of full-time students to full-time faculty in an average class is 12 to 1; in a clinic, 8 to 1. The law school has a regular program of bringing visiting professors and other distinguished lecturers and visitors to campus.

OKLAHOMA

Placement

J.D.s awarded:	167

Services available through: a separate law school placement center, the university placement center, and reciprocity services with other law schools
Services: seminars and panel presentations on various aspects of law practice and career options.

Special features:	n/av
Full-time job interviews:	9 employers
Summer job interviews:	20 employers
Placement by graduation:	n/av
Placement within 9 months:	93% of class
Average starting salary:	$50,794

Areas of placement:

Private practice 2-10 attorneys	33%
Private practice 11-25 attorneys	13%
Private practice 26-50 attorneys	2%
Private practice 51-100 attorneys	3%
Business/industry	21%
Government	10%
Firms larger than 100 and solo practitioners	8%
Public interest	5%
Academic	3%
Judicial clerkships	1%
Military	1%

Students

About 39% of the student body are women; 16%, minorities; 1%, African American; 3%, Asian American; 3%, Hispanic; 9%, Native American; and 1%, foreign nationals. The majority of students come from Oklahoma (41%). The average age of entering students is 28; age range is 20 to 57. About 40% of students enter directly from undergraduate school, 14% have a graduate degree, and 48% have worked full-time prior to entering law school. About 2% drop out after the first year for academic or personal reasons; 91% remain to receive a law degree.

UNIVERSITY OF UTAH

S.J. Quinney College of Law

332 South 1400 East Room 101
Salt Lake City, UT 84112

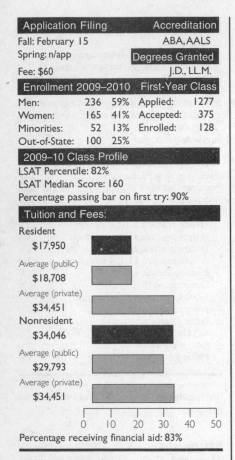

Application Filing		Accreditation
Fall: February 15		ABA, AALS
Spring: n/app		Degrees Granted
Fee: $60		J.D., LL.M.

Enrollment 2009–2010		First-Year Class	
Men:	236 59%	Applied:	1277
Women:	165 41%	Accepted:	375
Minorities:	52 13%	Enrolled:	128
Out-of-State:	100 25%		

2009–10 Class Profile
LSAT Percentile: 82%
LSAT Median Score: 160
Percentage passing bar on first try: 90%

Tuition and Fees:

Resident
$17,950

Average (public)
$18,708

Average (private)
$34,451

Nonresident
$34,046

Average (public)
$29,793

Average (private)
$34,451

0 10 20 30 40 50

Percentage receiving financial aid: 83%

ADMISSIONS

In the fall 2009 first-year class, 1277 applied, 375 were accepted, and 128 enrolled. Thirty-nine transfers enrolled. The median LSAT percentile of the most recent first-year class was 82; the median GPA was 3.6 on a scale of 4.0. The lowest LSAT percentile accepted was 17; the highest was 99.

Requirements

Applicants must have a bachelor's degree and take the LSAT. The most important admission factors include academic achievement, general background, and writing ability. No specific undergraduate courses are required. Candidates are not interviewed.

Procedure

The application deadline for fall entry is February 15. Applicants should submit an application form, LSAT results, transcripts, a personal statement, a nonrefundable application fee of $60, 1 letter of recommendation, and a resume. Noti-

fication of the admissions decision is from February on. The latest acceptable LSAT test date for fall entry is February. The law school uses the LSDAS.

Special

The law school recruits minority and disadvantaged students through extensive mailing to prospective applicants located through the Candidate Referral Service of LSAC and through special targeted recruitment programs. Council on Legal Opportunity fellows and Pre-Law Summer Institute fellows are recruited. Requirements are not different for out-of-state students. Transfer students must have one year of credit, have attended an ABA-approved law school, and be in the top 30% of the first-year class.

Costs

Tuition and fees for the 2009-2010 academic year are $17,950 for full-time in-state students and $34,046 for out-of-state students. On-campus room and board costs about $9360 annually; books and supplies run $1916.

Financial Aid

About 83% of current law students receive some form of aid. The average annual amount of aid from all sources combined, including scholarships, loans, and work contracts, is $20,450; maximum, $53,300. Awards are based on need and merit. Required financial statements are the FAFSA and College of Law need-based scholarship application. The aid application deadline for fall entry is April 1. Special funds for minority or disadvantaged students include need and merit scholarships, stipend for a summer intern program, and CLEO fellowships. First-year students are notified about their financial aid application at time of acceptance.

About the Law School

University of Utah S.J. Quinney College of Law was established in 1913 and is a public institution. The 1535-acre campus is in an urban area 1 1/2 miles east of downtown Salt Lake City. The primary mission of the law school is to achieve academic excellence in the professional education of lawyers, to advance knowledge through the dissemination of high-quality legal scholarship, and to perform public service to the University, the State of Utah, the nation, and the global community.

Students have access to federal, state, county, city, and local agencies, courts, correctional facilities, law firms, and legal aid organizations in the Salt Lake City area. Students have access to Salt Lake City, which is the state capital and county seat. Facilities of special interest to law students include the library, which features individual study carrels with wireless connections to laptop computers and extensive computing and on-line facilities. Housing for students is abundant and affordable on and off campus in safe neighborhoods within walking distance of campus. All law school facilities are accessible to the physically disabled.

Calendar

The law school operates on a traditional semester basis. Courses for full-time students are offered days only and must be completed within 6 semesters. There is no part-time program. New students are admitted in the fall. There is a 6-12-week summer session. Transferable summer courses are offered.

Programs

In addition to the J.D., the law school offers the LL.M. Students may take relevant courses in other programs and apply credit toward the J.D.; a maximum of 12 credits may be applied. The following joint degrees may be earned: J.D./M.B.A. (Juris Doctor/Master of Business Administration), J.D./M.P.A. (Juris Doctor/Master of Public Administration), and J.D./M.P.P (Juris Doctor/Master of Public Policy).

Required

To earn the J.D., candidates must complete 88 total credits, of which 40 are for required courses. They must maintain a minimum GPA of 2.5 in the required courses. The following first-year courses are required of all students: Civil Procedure, Constitutional Law, Contracts, Criminal Law, Legal Writing and Research, Property, and Torts. Required upper-level courses consist of Advanced Constitutional Law, Professional Ethics, and seminar. Students are not required to take clinical courses; however they are strongly encouraged to participate. The required orientation program for first-year students is a 4-day course before classes begin to help students understand the role of law, the tasks of a lawyer, and the method of legal education and study.

Phone: 801-581-7479
800-444-8638 ext. 1-7479
Fax: 801-581-6897
E-mail: *aguilarr@law.utah.edu*
Web: *www.law.utah.edu*

Contact

Reyes Aguilar, Associate Dean, 801-581-7479 for general inquiries; Law School Financial Aid Counselor, 801-581-6211 for financial aid information.

UTAH

Electives

The S.J. Quinney College of Law offers concentrations in corporate law, criminal law, environmental law, family law, intellectual property law, international law, juvenile law, litigation, and natural resources, public lands and energy, and constitutional law. In addition, live and simulation component clinics are offered for 2 to 4 credit hours. Clinics may be criminal, in which students work at the offices of the county attorney, U.S. Attorney, federal defender, or Salt Lake legal defenders; civil, in which students represent actual clients from a public-interest law firm; or judicial, in which students act as law clerks to state and federal judges. There are also placements in environmental law, health law, legislative and mediation program locations. In seminars, students perform closely supervised research, analysis, and writing, covering a wide array of topics. Students may spend a semester as full-time clerks in the judicial extern program as part of the judicial clinic. Numerous opportunities exist for students to be paid as research assistants for faculty, or to undertake directed research for credit or advanced legal research courses. Field placements with a public interest law office, Utah Legal Services, Legal Aid Society of Salt Lake, Legal Center for People with Disabilities, Catholic Community Services, and the ACLU are part of the clinical program. Special lecture series include the Leary Lecture, Fordham Debate, Distinguished Jurist in Residence, Law Review Symposium, the Natural Resources Law Forum, and the annual Wallace Stegner Symposium. Study abroad is possible for upper-level students in the London Law Consortium, a 1-semester, ABA-approved program. The academic support program is available for eligible students and includes a legal process tutorial course, organized study groups, and academic counseling. The college sponsors a summer intern program, funded with private donations, for minority students. Selected students intern with major Salt Lake City law firms for 10 weeks following the completion of their first year and receive a $3000 stipend. The college has hosted and regularly recruits participants from the Council on Legal Education Opportunity Summer Institute, and the Pre-Law Summer Institute. Special interest groups include the Utah Criminial Justice Center and the Global Justice Project.

The most widely taken electives are Evidence, Criminal Procedure, and Business Organization.

Graduation Requirements

In order to graduate, candidates must have a GPA of 2.5 and have completed the upper-division writing requirement.

Organizations

Students edit the *Utah Law Review, Journal of Law and Family Studies, Journal of Land Resources and Environmental Law,* and the newspaper, *Utah Law Forum.* Moot court competitions include the Annual National Moot Court, Pace University Environmental Law Moot Court, and Giles Rich Moot Court Competition. In addition, several writing and research competitions are offered in connection with scholarships and awards. Law student organizations include the Natural Resources Law Forum, Women's Law Caucus, and Minority Law Caucus. Local chapters of the Native American Law Student Association, Federalist Society, and American Constitution Society are represented on campus. Campus organizations include Phi Alpha Delta, Phi Delta Phi, and the International Law Society.

Library

The law library contains 340,000 hardcopy volumes and 103,000 microform volume equivalents, and subscribes to 4500 serial publications. Such on-line databases and networks as CALI, DIALOG, LEXIS, NEXIS, and WESTLAW are available to law students for research. Special library collections include environmental and natural resources law, Utah/Western United States law, tax and commercial law, U.S. government document depository, energy and public utilities regulation, and labor and employment law. Recently, the library expanded the reference room to provide additional workstations for access to legal research databases, added shelving, and attached network nodes to study carrels. The ratio of library volumes to faculty is 8095 to 1 and to students is 839 to 1. The ratio of seats in the library to students is 1 to 1.

Faculty

The law school has 42 full-time and 72 part-time faculty members, of whom 32

Placement

J.D.s awarded:	131

Services available through: a separate law school placement center
Services: pro bono initiative
Special features: Computer-maintained records of current and former students may be transmitted to prospective employers to facilitate both on- and off-campus recruiting. The Legal Career Services Office offers personal counseling, maintains a resource library, and sponsors seminars to aid students in their self-directed job search.

Full-time job interviews:	25 employers
Summer job interviews:	61 employers
Placement by graduation:	91% of class
Placement within 9 months:	98% of class
Average starting salary:	$25,000 to $215,000

Areas of placement:
Private practice 2-25 attorneys	33%
Private practice 26-100 attorneys	7%
Private practice 101+ attorneys	13%
Private practice solo	5%
Private practice, size unknown	2%
Government	13%
Judicial clerkships	10%
Business/industry	7%
Public interest	5%
Academic	3%
Military	2%

are women. According to AAUP standards for Category I institutions, faculty salaries are below average. About 36% of full-time faculty have a graduate law degree in addition to the J.D. The ratio of full-time students to full-time faculty in an average class is 27 to 1; in a clinic, 9 to 1. The law school has a regular program of bringing visiting professors and other distinguished lecturers and visitors to campus. There is a chapter of the Order of the Coif; 17 faculty and 10% of graduates are members.

Students

About 41% of the student body are women; 13%, minorities; 2%, African American; 3%, Asian American; 6%, Hispanic; and 2%, Native American. The majority of students come from the West (85%). The average age of entering students is 28; age range is 20 to 49. About 45% of students enter directly from undergraduate school, 16% have a graduate degree, and 55% have worked full-time prior to entering law school. About 2% drop out after the first year for academic or personal reasons; 97% remain to receive a law degree.

School of Law

580 Massie Road
Charlottesville, VA 22903-1738

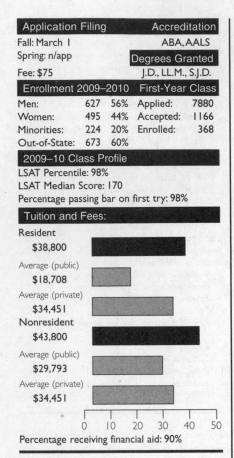

Application Filing		Accreditation
Fall: March 1		ABA, AALS
Spring: n/app		Degrees Granted
Fee: $75		J.D., LL.M., S.J.D.

Enrollment 2009–2010			First-Year Class	
Men:	627	56%	Applied:	7880
Women:	495	44%	Accepted:	1166
Minorities:	224	20%	Enrolled:	368
Out-of-State:	673	60%		

2009–10 Class Profile

LSAT Percentile: 98%
LSAT Median Score: 170
Percentage passing bar on first try: 98%

Tuition and Fees:

Resident
$38,800

Average (public)
$18,708

Average (private)
$34,451

Nonresident
$43,800

Average (public)
$29,793

Average (private)
$34,451

0   10   20   30   40   50

Percentage receiving financial aid: 90%

ADMISSIONS

In the fall 2009 first-year class, 7880 applied, 1166 were accepted, and 368 enrolled. Thirteen transfers enrolled. The median LSAT percentile of the most recent first-year class was 98; the median GPA was 3.85 on a scale of 4.0. The lowest LSAT percentile accepted was 48; the highest was 100.

Requirements

Applicants must have a bachelor's degree and take the LSAT. The admission process is highly individualized and considers a variety of factors. No specific undergraduate courses are required. Candidates are not interviewed.

Procedure

The application deadline for fall entry is March 1. Applicants should submit an application form, LSAT results, transcripts, a personal statement, a nonrefundable application fee of $75, and 2 letters of recommendation. Notification of the admissions decision is by April 15. The latest acceptable LSAT test date for fall entry is February. The law school uses the LSDAS.

Special

The law school recruits minority and disadvantaged students through the Candidate Referral Service, Law Days, and student initiated outreach. Requirements are not different for out-of-state students. Transfer students must have 1 year of credit.

Costs

Tuition and fees for the 2009-2010 academic year are $38,800 for full-time in-state students and $43,800 for out-of-state students. On-campus room and board costs about $14,050 annually; books and supplies run $5150.

Financial Aid

About 90% of current law students receive some form of aid. The average annual amount of aid from all sources combined, including scholarships, loans, and work contracts, is $46,053. Awards are based on need and merit. Required financial statements are the FAFSA and institutional forms. The aid application deadline for fall entry is March 1. First-year students are notified about their financial aid application January 1.

About the Law School

University of Virginia School of Law was established in 1819 and is a public institution. The 1135-acre campus is in a suburban area 115 miles southwest of Washington D.C. and 70 miles west of Richmond. The primary mission of the law school is to help build a new dedication in society to the classical roles and skills of lawyering and to foster an intellectual environment rich in the transmission of traditional values and character as well as immersed in new and creative legal thinking, analysis, and research. Students have access to federal, state, county, city, and local agencies, courts, correctional facilities, law firms, and legal aid organizations in the Charlottesville area. The Public Service Center and numerous student organizations offer pro bono opportunities and other practice situations. Facilities of special interest to law students include an extensive library, modern classrooms, moot court rooms, student organization offices, lounges, coffee facilities, and outdoor gardens and recreational areas. Housing for students is available in university housing for both single and married students; the Off-Grounds Housing Office also helps students find off-campus accommodations. All law school facilities are accessible to the physically disabled.

Calendar

The law school operates on a traditional semester basis. Courses for full-time students are offered days only and must be completed within a time set on a case-by-case basis. There is no part-time program. New students are admitted in the fall. There is no summer session. Transferable summer courses are not offered.

Programs

In addition to the J.D., the law school offers the LL.M. and S.J.D. Students may take relevant courses in other programs and apply credit toward the J.D.; a maximum of 12 credits may be applied. The following joint degrees may be earned: J.D./M.A. (Juris Doctor/Master of Arts in 8 areas), J.D./M.B.A. (Juris Doctor/Master of Business Administration), J.D./M.P.A. (Juris Doctor/Master of Public Affairs), J.D./M.P.H. (Juris Doctor/Master of Public Health), J.D./M.S. (Juris Doctor/Master of Science in Accounting), and J.D./M.U.E.P. (Juris Doctor/Master of Urban and Environmental Planning).

Required

To earn the J.D., candidates must complete 86 total credits, of which 29 are for required courses. They must maintain a minimum GPA of 2.3 in the required courses. The following first-year courses are required of all students: Civil Procedure, Constitutional Law, Contracts, Criminal Law, Legal Research and Writing, Property, and Torts. Required upper-level courses consist of a professional ethics course and a professional skills course. The required orientation program for first-year students is 2 days.

Electives

The School of Law offers concentrations in corporate law, criminal law, environmental law, family law, intellectual prop-

Phone: 434-924-7351
Fax: 434-982-2128
E-mail: lawadmit@virginia.edu
Web: www.law.virginia.edu

Contact

Jason Trvjilo, Senior Assistant Dean for Admission, 434-924-7351 for general inquiries; Jennifer Hulvey, Director of Financial Aid, 434-924-7805 for financial aid information.

erty law, international law, juvenile law, labor law, litigation, media law, securities law, tax law, business organizations and finance, commercial, constitutional, health, human rights and civil liberties, legal history, jurisprudence, comparative law, race and law, and public policy and regulation. In addition, clinical offerings include employment, environmental law and conservation, human rights, patents, criminal practice, housing environment, child advocacy, and others. More than 175 seminar offerings are available each year, two-thirds taught by full-time faculty. A special program of seminars in ethical values is also offered. Students may work with local judges in the surrounding jurisdictions, in commonwealth attorneys' offices, and with public defenders. Students may also work with individual faculty on independent research projects and assist faculty in research and publication projects. There are numerous special lecture series held throughout the year, including the Contemporary Legal Thought series. Study abroad programs are available at University of Auckland, New Zealand; Tel Aviv University, Israel; Bucerius Law School, Hamburg, Germany; University of Nottingham, England; Melbourne Law School, Australia; and Waseda Law School, Japan. Students may also gain experience through the University of Virginia's Legal Assistance Society, the Post-Conviction Assistance Project, the John M. Olin Program in Law and Economics, the Center for Oceans Law and Policy, the Institute of Law Psychiatry, and Public Policy, the Center for Environmental Studies, the Center for National Security Law, and the Human Rights Study Project. The most widely taken electives are Corporations, Evidence, and Federal Income Tax I.

Graduation Requirements
In order to graduate, candidates must have a GPA of 2.3 and, have completed the upper-division writing requirement, a professional ethics course, and a professional skills course.

Organizations

Students edit the *Virginia Law Review, Virginia Tax Review, Virginia Environmental Law Journal, Virginia Journal of International Law*, and the *Journal of Law and Politics, Virginia Journal of Social Policy and the Law, Virginia Journal of*

Law and Technology, Virginia Sports, and *Entertainment Law Journal, Virginia Law and Business Review*, and the newspaper *Virginia Law Weekly*. Students participate in in-house, intramural, and national competitions. More than 100 teams enter in the William Minor Lile Moot Court Competition. Law student organizations, local chapters of national associations, and campus organizations include the Federalist Society, American Constitution Society, Black Law Students Association, Phi Alpha Delta, Student Legal Forum, Public Interest Law Association, Environmental Law Forum, and John Basset Moore.

Library

The law library contains 876,458 hardcopy volumes and 275,048 microform volume equivalents, and subscribes to 5046 serial publications. Such on-line databases and networks as CALI, CIS Universe, Dow-Jones, Infotrac, Legal-Trac, LEXIS, LOIS, NEXIS, OCLC First Search, RLIN, WESTLAW, Wilsonline Indexes, CCH, HeinOnline, Justis, LLMC Digital, RIA, SSRN, and PACER are available to law students for research. Special library collections include Oceans Law Collection. The ratio of library volumes to faculty is 11,532 to 1 and to students is 781 to 1. The ratio of seats in the library to students is 1 to 1.

Faculty

The law school has 76 full-time and 94 part-time faculty members, of whom 41 are women. According to AAUP standards for Category I institutions, faculty salaries are above average. The ratio of full-time students to full-time faculty in an average class is 13 to 1. The law school has a regular program of bringing visiting professors and other distinguished lecturers and visitors to campus. There is a chapter of the Order of the Coif.

Students

About 44% of the student body are women; 20%, minorities; 5%, African American; 8%, Asian American; 5%, Hispanic; and 1%, Native American. The majority of students come from Virginia (40%). The average age of entering students is 24; age range is 18 to 45. About 38% of students enter directly from undergraduate school, 12% have a graduate degree, and 60%

Placement

J.D.s awarded:	403

Services available through: a separate law school placement center

Special features: computer network-based information on law firms and other employment opportunities, on-line interview sign-ups, and an extensive public service opportunities database. There is also an active and extensive national alumni network

Full-time job interviews:	214 employers
Summer job interviews:	865 employers
Placement by graduation:	96% of class
Placement within 9 months:	99% of class
Average starting salary:	$27,000 to $180,000

Areas of placement:

Private practice - size unknown	70%
Judicial clerkships	14%
Government	4%
Public interest	4%
Business/industry	1%

have worked full-time prior to entering law school. About 1% drop out after the first year for academic or personal reasons; 99% remain to receive a law degree.

University of Virginia **567**

UNIVERSITY OF WASHINGTON

School of Law

Box 353020
Seattle, WA 98195-3020

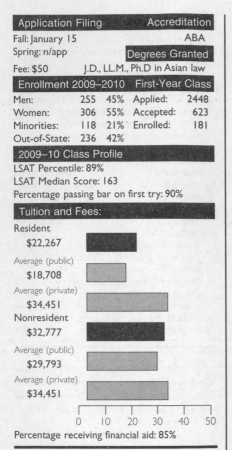

Application Filing		Accreditation	
Fall: January 15			ABA
Spring: n/app		Degrees Granted	
Fee: $50		J.D., LL.M., Ph.D in Asian law	

Enrollment 2009–2010		First-Year Class	
Men:	255 45%	Applied:	2448
Women:	306 55%	Accepted:	623
Minorities:	118 21%	Enrolled:	181
Out-of-State:	236 42%		

2009–10 Class Profile
LSAT Percentile: 89%
LSAT Median Score: 163
Percentage passing bar on first try: 90%

Tuition and Fees:

Resident
$22,267

Average (public)
$18,708

Average (private)
$34,451

Nonresident
$32,777

Average (public)
$29,793

Average (private)
$34,451

0 10 20 30 40 50

Percentage receiving financial aid: 85%

ADMISSIONS

In the fall 2009 first-year class, 2448 applied, 623 were accepted, and 181 enrolled. Five transfers enrolled. The median LSAT percentile of the most recent first-year class was 89; the median GPA was 3.66 on a scale of 4.0. The lowest LSAT percentile accepted was 49; the highest was 99.

Requirements
Applicants must have a bachelor's degree and take the LSAT. The most important admission factors include LSAT results, GPA, and academic achievement. No specific undergraduate courses are required. Candidates are not interviewed.

Procedure
The application deadline for fall entry is January 15. Applicants should submit an application form, LSAT results, transcripts, a personal statement, a nonrefundable application fee of $50, 2 optional letters of recommendation, a dean's cer-

tificate, and a resume. Notification of the admissions decision is April 1. The latest acceptable LSAT test date for fall entry is December. The law school uses the LSDAS.

Special
The law school recruits minority and disadvantaged students through West Coast law fairs, Washington undergraduate schools, law forums, and personal referrals. Requirements are not different for out-of-state students. Transfer students must have 1 year of credit, have attended an ABA-approved law school, and have attended AALS-member law school.

Costs

Tuition and fees for the 2009-2010 academic year are $22,267 for full-time in-state students and $32,777 for out-of-state students. On-campus room and board costs about $12,876 annually; books and supplies run $1206.

Financial Aid

About 85% of current law students receive some form of aid. The average annual amount of aid from all sources combined, including scholarships, loans, and work contracts, is $30,000. Awards are based on need. Required financial statement is the FAFSA. The aid application deadline for fall entry is February 28. Special funds for minority or disadvantaged students include scholarships that are available from the school's privately donated scholarship funds. Scholarships are awarded based on demonstrated financial need. First-year students are notified about their financial aid application in late spring for on-time applicants who have been admitted.

About the Law School

University of Washington School of Law was established in 1899 and is a public institution. The 20-acre campus is in an urban area 3 miles from downtown Seattle. The primary mission of the law school is a commitment to excellence in teaching, scholarship, and public service. Students have access to federal, state, county, city, and local agencies, courts, correctional facilities, law firms, and legal aid organizations in the Seattle area. Facilities of special interest to law students include a

well-stocked law library. Housing for students is available for single and married students to a limited degree in university housing; the Student Housing Affairs Office maintains listings of off-campus accommodations. All law school facilities are accessible to the physically disabled.

Calendar

The law school operates on a quarter basis. Courses for full-time students are offered days only and must be completed within 3 years. There is no part-time program. New students are admitted in the fall. There is a 2- 4-week summer session. Transferable summer courses are offered.

Programs

In addition to the J.D., the law school offers the LL.M. and Ph.D in Asian law. Students may take relevant courses in other programs and apply credit toward the J.D.; a maximum of 15 quarter credits credits may be applied. The following joint degrees may be earned: (Joint degree programs can be set up with 90 other graduate programs at the school).

Required
To earn the J.D., candidates must complete 135 quarters total credits, of which 49 are for required courses. The following first-year courses are required of all students: Basic Legal Skills, Civil Procedure, Constitutional Law, Contracts, Criminal Law, Property, and Torts. Required upper-level courses consist of 60 hours of pro bono legal work, Advanced Writing, and Professional Responsibility. The required orientation program for first-year students is 8 days (4 days per week for 2 weeks prior to first regular class day).

Electives
The School of Law offers concentrations in environmental law, intellectual property law, international law, and Asian law, alternative dispute resolution, public service , and health law. In addition, clinics open to second- and third-year students for 7 or 8 credits are available in mediation, child advocacy, unemployment, criminal law, low-income taxpayer, immigration, refugee and immigrant advocacy law, and Indian law. Seminars earning 3 to 6 credits and internships worth 1 to 15

Phone: 206-543-4078
Fax: 206-543-5671
E-mail: *lawadm@u.washington.edu*
Web: *www.law.washington.edu*

Contact
Norma Rodriguez, Director of Admissions, 206-543-4078 for general inquiries; Arlo Hammontree, Financial Aid Coordinator, 206-543-4552 for financial aid information.

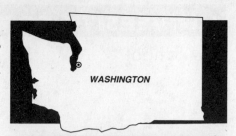

WASHINGTON

credits are also open to second- and third-year students. Also available are independent research programs earning 1 to 6 credits. Several study-abroad programs are coordinated by the law school, and students are eligible to pursue any ABA-approved study-abroad program. The law school offers peer tutoring through the Academic Support Program. The most widely taken electives are Trial Advocacy, Payment Systems, and Evidence.

Graduation Requirements
In order to graduate, candidates must have completed the upper-division writing requirement and 9 quarters in residence.

Organizations
Students edit the *Washington Law Review*, *Pacific Rim and Policy Journal*, and the *Shidler Journal of Law, Commerce, and Technology*. Moot court competitions include the Jessup and International Jessup. Law student organizations include the Student Bar Association, Women's Law Caucus, and Minority Law Students Association. Other organizations include International Law Society, Innocence Project Northwest, and Public Interest Law Association. Local chapters of national associations include the ABA Law Student Division, ACLU, and Federalist Society.

Library
The law library contains 617,260 hardcopy volumes and 187,870 microform volume equivalents, and subscribes to 950 serial publications. Such on-line databases and networks as LEXIS, WESTLAW, full Internet access; UW Information Navigator, and CD Law are available to law students for research. Special library collections include Japanese and other East Asian law materials. The library has been designated as a depository for U.S. government documents. The ratio of library volumes to faculty is 13,418 to 1 and to students is 1100 to 1. The ratio of seats in the library to students is 1 to 2.

Faculty
The law school has 46 full-time and 46 part-time faculty members, of whom 35 are women. According to AAUP standards for Category I institutions, faculty salaries are average. About 25% of full-time facul-

ty have a graduate law degree in addition to the J.D. The ratio of full-time students to full-time faculty in an average class is 11 to 1. The law school has a regular program of bringing visiting professors and other distinguished lecturers and visitors to campus. There is a chapter of the Order of the Coif; 100 faculty and 19 graduates are members.

Students
About 55% of the student body are women; 21%, minorities; 2%, African American; 12%, Asian American; 4%, Hispanic; and 2%, Native American. The majority of students come from Washington (58%). The average age of entering students is 26; age range is 21 to 45. About 20% of students enter directly from undergraduate school, 20% have a graduate degree, and 70% have worked full-time prior to entering law school. About 2% drop out after the first year for academic or personal reasons; 98% remain to receive a law degree.

Placement

J.D.s awarded:	177
Services available through: a separate law school placement center	
Special features: first-year student job workshops, first-year student mock interview program, and other career programs throughout the school year	
Full-time job interviews:	9 employers
Summer job interviews:	51 employers
Placement by graduation:	87% of class
Placement within 9 months:	98% of class
Average starting salary:	$48,150 to $119,298
Areas of placement:	
Private practice 2-10 attorneys	9%
Private practice 11-25 attorneys	2%
Private practice 26-50 attorneys	7%
Private practice 51-100 attorneys	2%
Judicial clerkships	16%
Government	13%
Business/industry	8%
Public Interest	7%
32% Private practice, graduate programs	3%
Academic	1%

UNIVERSITY OF WISCONSIN

Law School

975 Bascom Mall
Madison, WI 53706

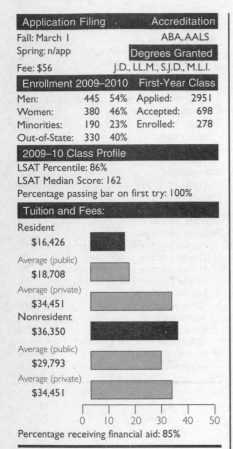

Application Filing	Accreditation
Fall: March 1	ABA, AALS
Spring: n/app	**Degrees Granted**
Fee: $56	J.D., LL.M., S.J.D., M.L.I.

Enrollment 2009–2010		First-Year Class	
Men:	445 54%	Applied:	2951
Women:	380 46%	Accepted:	698
Minorities:	190 23%	Enrolled:	278
Out-of-State:	330 40%		

2009–10 Class Profile
LSAT Percentile: 86%
LSAT Median Score: 162
Percentage passing bar on first try: 100%

Tuition and Fees:

Resident
$16,426

Average (public)
$18,708

Average (private)
$34,451

Nonresident
$36,350

Average (public)
$29,793

Average (private)
$34,451

0 10 20 30 40 50

Percentage receiving financial aid: 85%

ADMISSIONS

In the fall 2009 first-year class, 2951 applied, 698 were accepted, and 278 enrolled. Forty-four transfers enrolled. The median LSAT percentile of the most recent first-year class was 86; the median GPA was 3.6 on a scale of 4.0.

Requirements

Applicants must have a bachelor's degree and take the LSAT. The most important admission factors include LSAT results, GPA, and state or country of residence. No specific undergraduate courses are required. Candidates are not interviewed.

Procedure

The application deadline for fall entry is March 1. Applicants should submit an application form, LSAT results, transcripts, a personal statement, a nonrefundable application fee of $56, 2 letters of recommendation, and resume. Notification of the admissions decision is and rolling basis. The latest acceptable LSAT test date for fall entry is February. The law school uses the LSDAS.

Special

The law school recruits minority and disadvantaged students through mailings, law school and graduate school days, minority career fairs, and a network of alumni and current students. Requirements are not different for out-of-state students. Transfer students must have one year of credit, have attended an ABA-approved law school, and due to enrollment pressures, are accepted primarily on the basis of class rank in the transferring law school, or, if class rank is unavailable, on the basis of other evidence of academic performance.

Costs

Tuition and fees for the 2009-2010 academic year are $16,426 for full-time in-state students and $36,350 for out-of-state students. On-campus room and board costs about $8740 annually; books and supplies run $2250.

Financial Aid

About 85% of current law students receive some form of aid. The average annual amount of aid from all sources combined, including scholarships, loans, and work contracts, is $29,331. Awards are based on need and merit. Required financial statements are the FAFSA and student tax form. The aid application deadline for fall entry is March 1. Special funds for minority or disadvantaged students include need- and merit-based scholarships with criteria preference for students from disadvantaged backgrounds. Notification about financial application for frst-year students varies.

About the Law School

University of Wisconsin Law School was established in 1868 and is a public institution. The 933-acre campus is in an urban area In the middle of one of the world's leading research universities. The primary mission of the law school is to focus on helping its students understand how law both affects and is affected by every other institutional force in society. The law school pioneered the belief that law must be studied in action as it relates to society, and not in isolation. Students have access to federal, state, county, city, and local agencies, courts, correctional facilities, law firms, and legal aid organizations in the Madison area. All of the resources of the University of Wisconsin, including educational, cultural, and social opportunities, are available to law students. Facilities of special interest to law students include the State Capitol, State Supreme Court, Federal District Court, and County Court located in Madison, less than 1 mile from the law school. Housing for students is in university graduate student housing; however, most students live in private rental property close to campus. All law school facilities are accessible to the physically disabled.

Calendar

The law school operates on a traditional semester basis. Courses for full-time students and part-time students are offered both day and evening and must be completed within 6 years. New full- and part-time students are admitted in the fall. There is a 13-week summer session. Transferable summer courses are offered.

Programs

In addition to the J.D., the law school offers the LL.M., S.J.D., and M.L.I. (Master of Arts or Master of Science in Legal Institutions. Students may take relevant courses in other programs and apply credit toward the J.D.; a maximum of 6 credits may be applied. The following joint degrees may be earned: Law and Business, Law and Environmental Studies, Law and Latin American and Iberian Studies, Law and Library and Information Services, Law and Philosophy (Ph.D. level only), Law and Political Science, Law and Public Affairs, and Law and Sociology (Ph.D.) and Rural Sociology.

Required

To earn the J.D., candidates must complete 90 total credits, of which 40 to 45 are for required courses. They must maintain a minimum GPA of 2.0 in the required courses. The following first-year courses are required of all students: Civil Procedure I, Contracts I, Criminal Procedure, Introduction to Substantive Criminal Law, Legal Research and Writing, Property, and Torts I. Required upper-level courses consist of Civil Procedure II, Constitutional Law I, Contract II, Evi-

Phone: 608-262-5914
Fax: 608-263-3191
E-mail: admissions@law.wisc.edu
Web: www.law.wisc.edu

Contact
Michael A. Hall, Assistant Dean, Admissions, 608-262-5914 for general inquiries; Michael A. Hall, Assistant Dean, 608-262-1815 for financial aid information.

WISCONSIN

dence, International Law, Legal Process, Professional Responsibility, and Trust and Estates. An extensive selection of clinical courses is available for students who wish to participate.The required orientation program for first-year students is a 2-day program that includes a check-in with the Admissions Office staff, study skills workshop, first-year convocation, informal gatherings, and student photos.

Electives

The Law School offers concentrations in corporate law, criminal law, environmental law, family law, intellectual property law, international law, labor law, litigation, securities law, sports law, tax law, torts and insurance, and public interest law, and estate planning. See www.law.wisc.edu/academics/clinics/index.htm for a list of clinics offered. Numerous seminars are available. Hands on judicial interships are available with Wisconsin Supreme Court, Wisconsin Court of Appeals, Federal District Court, and various county circuit courts. Directed reading and research is available to all second- and third-year students to focus on a specific area of research under a professor's guidence. Field work includes such programs as Midwest Enviornmental Advocates and the Center for Patient Partnerships, among others. Tutorial programs and special interest group programs, including the Fairchild Lecture Series, the Robert W. Kastenmeier Lecture, and various student group lectures are offered. Study abroad is possible through the Germany, Holland, Italy, Chile, Peru, South Africa, United Kingdom, Brazil, France, and Asia programs. An individualized instruction service offering writing assistance, workshops on study skills, test taking, time management, research papers, and other topics is available to all students. The Legal Education Opportunities Program is available for students of color. There are more than 30 special interest group programs, with more being created each year. The most widely taken electives are Business Organizations, Tax, and Administrative Law.

Graduation Requirements

In order to graduate, candidates must have a GPA of 2.0 and have completed the upper-division writing requirement.

Organizations
Students edit the *Wisconsin Law Review, Wisconsin International Law Journal, Wisconsin Journal of Law*, and *Gender & Society*, Moot court competitions include Evan A. Evans Constitutional Law Competition, Philip C. Jessup International Law Moot Court Competition, and Saul Lefkowitz IP Moot Court. Law student organizations, inclued Intellectual Property Students Association Business and Tax Law Association, and Asian Pacific American/South Asian Law Students Association. Local chapters of national associations include, American Constitution Society, Federalist Society, and National Lawyers Guild. Campus organizations include Black Law Student Association, Indigenous Law Students Association, and Latino Law Students Association.

Library
The law library contains 449,048 hardcopy volumes and 168,407 microform volume equivalents, and subscribes to 6608 serial publications. Such on-line databases and networks as CIS Universe, DIALOG, Legal-Trac, LEXIS, LOIS, NEXIS, OCLC First Search, WESTLAW, and Wilsonline Indexes are available to law students for research. Special library collections include criminal justice, foreign and international law materials, and a federal depository. Recently, the library expanded and redesigned, and added staff and additional resources to the student computer laboratory. The ratio of library volumes to faculty is 4119 to 1 and to students is 567 to 1. The ratio of seats in the library to students is 1 to 1.

Faculty
The law school has 50 full-time and 59 part-time faculty members, of whom 50 are women. According to AAUP standards for Category I institutions, faculty salaries are average. The ratio of full-time students to full-time faculty in an average class is 13 to 1; in a clinic, 6 to 1. The law school has a regular program of bringing visiting professors and other distinguished lecturers and visitors to campus. There is a chapter of the Order of the Coif.

Students
About 46% of the student body are women; 23%, minorities; 7%, African American; 10%, Asian American; 6%, Hispanic;

Placement

J.D.s awarded:	257

Services available through: a separate law school placement center and workshops on careers in various areas of the law, including nontraditional careers

Services: information on diversity and opportunities, organizing employer visits; off-campus recruiting fairs, and participation in other national job fairs.

Special features: mentoring and tag-along program in cooperation with the State Bar of Wisconsin, a pro bono project matching students with practitioners, and set up mock interviews with practitioners.

Full-time job interviews:	29 employers
Summer job interviews:	102 employers
Placement by graduation:	75% of class
Placement within 9 months:	96% of class
Average starting salary:	$42,250 to $120,033

Areas of placement:

Solo practice/Private practice in firms over 101	28%
Private practice 2-10 attorneys	17%
Private practice 11-25 attorneys	6%
Private practice 26-50 attorneys	2%
Private practice 51-100 attorneys	3%
Government	12%
Business/industry	12%
Public interest	7%
Judicial clerkships	6%
Military	2%
Academic	2%

2%, Native American; and 1%, Middle Eastern. The majority of students come from Wisconsin (60%). The average age of entering students is 25; age range is 21 to 46. About 36% of students enter directly from undergraduate school and 10% have a graduate degree.

College of Law

Dept. 3035,
1000 East University Avenue
Laramie, WY 82071

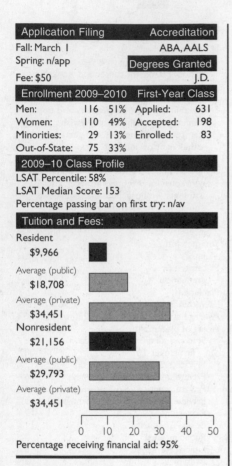

Application Filing		Accreditation	
Fall: March 1		ABA, AALS	
Spring: n/app		Degrees Granted	
Fee: $50		J.D.	
Enrollment 2009–2010		First-Year Class	
Men:	116 51%	Applied:	631
Women:	110 49%	Accepted:	198
Minorities:	29 13%	Enrolled:	83
Out-of-State:	75 33%		

2009–10 Class Profile
LSAT Percentile: 58%
LSAT Median Score: 153
Percentage passing bar on first try: n/av

Tuition and Fees:

Resident
$9,966

Average (public)
$18,708

Average (private)
$34,451

Nonresident
$21,156

Average (public)
$29,793

Average (private)
$34,451

0 10 20 30 40 50

Percentage receiving financial aid: 95%

ADMISSIONS

In the fall 2009 first-year class, 631 applied, 198 were accepted, and 83 enrolled. Five transfers enrolled. The median LSAT percentile of the most recent first-year class was 58; the median GPA was 3.41 on a scale of 4.0. The lowest LSAT percentile accepted was 13; the highest was 89.

Requirements
Applicants must have a bachelor's degree and take the LSAT. The most important admission factors include academic achievement, GPA, and LSAT results. No specific undergraduate courses are required. Candidates are not interviewed.

Procedure
The application deadline for fall entry is March 1. Applicants should submit an application form, LSAT results, transcripts, a personal statement, TOEFL, if applicable, a nonrefundable application fee of $50, and up to 3 letters of recommendation. Notification of the admissions decision is on a rolling basis, beginning in December. The latest acceptable LSAT test date for fall entry is February. The law school uses the LSDAS.

Special
The law school recruits minority and disadvantaged students by soliciting applications, hosting a law day session for minority undergraduate students at the university, attending LSAC forums and regional recruiting events focused on minority students, and multicultural events. Requirements are not different for out-of-state students. Transfer students must have one year of credit, have a minimum GPA of 2.0 have attended an ABA-approved law school, and have evidence of academic distinction.

Costs

Tuition and fees for the 2009-2010 academic year are $9966 for full-time in-state students and $21,156 for out-of-state students. On-campus room and board costs about $10,030 annually; books and supplies run $2200.

Financial Aid

About 95% of current law students receive some form of aid. The average annual amount of aid from all sources combined, including scholarships, loans, and work contracts, is $19,679; maximum, $29,967. Awards are based on need and merit. Required financial statement is the FAFSA. The aid application deadline for fall entry is March 1. Special funds for minority or disadvantaged students consist of minority graduate assistantships offered on a competitive basis. First-year students are notified about their financial aid application at time of acceptance.

About the Law School

University of Wyoming College of Law was established in 1920 and is a public institution. The 785-acre campus is in a small town in Laramie, Wyoming, 45 miles from Cheyenne, the Wyoming state capital, and 2 hours from Denver, Colorado. The primary mission of the law school is to provide students with the knowledge and training necessary to meet the responsibilities of the profession; students must secure a broad and basic knowledge of legal principles, understand the social and economic factors underlying these principles, and learn to judge the effectiveness of these principles in solving client and societal problems. Students have access to federal, state, county, city, and local agencies, courts, correctional facilities, law firms, and legal aid organizations in the Laramie area. Facilities of special interest to law students the state capital (Cheyenne). Students are actively involved in legislative, governmental, and judicial events and activities. Housing for students is available in a university residence hall for single students. Graduate and professional students are housed separately from undergraduates. The university also maintains 2-bedroom furnished apartments for married students. An ample supply of apartments and rental properties is available throughout the community. About 98% of the law school facilities are accessible to the physically disabled.

Calendar

The law school operates on a traditional semester basis. Courses for full-time students are offered days only and must be completed within 3 years. There is no part-time program. New students are admitted in the fall. There is no summer session. Transferable summer courses are not offered. Credits from ABA-approved study-abroad and summer programs can be applied toward graduation.

Programs

Students may take relevant courses in other programs and apply credit toward the J.D.; a maximum of 6 credits may be applied. The following joint degrees may be earned: J.D./M.A. in ENR (Juris Doctor/Master of Environment and Natural Resources), J.D./M.B.A. (Juris Doctor/Master of Business Administration), and J.D./M.P.A. (Juris Doctor/Master of Public Administration).

Required
To earn the J.D., candidates must complete 89 total credits, of which 37 are for required courses. They must maintain a minimum GPA of 2.0 in the required courses. The following first-year courses are required of all students: Appellate Advocacy, Civil Procedure I, Constitutional Law I, Contracts I and II, Criminal Law, Introduction to Law, Legal Writing

WYOMING

Phone: 307-766-6416
Fax: 307-766-6417
E-mail: *dburke@uwyo.edu*
Web: *uwyo.edu/law*

Contact

N. Denise Burke, Assistant Dean, 307-766-6416 for general inquiries; Office of Student Financial Aid, 307-766-2116 for financial aid information.

and Research, Property I and II, and Torts I and II. Required upper-level courses consist of an advanced writing requirement, Civil Procedure II, Constitutional Law II, Evidence, one skills course (selected from 10 offerings), and Professional Responsibility. The required orientation program for first-year students is a 3-day program including lectures on legal analysis, legal reasoning, the study of law, and case briefing sessions.

Electives

The College of Law offers concentrations in corporate law, criminal law, environmental law, family law, international law, litigation, and tax law. In addition, Defender Aid, Legal Services, Prosecution Assistance, and Domestic Violence programs are available to third-year students; 1 clinic per semester may be taken for 3 credit hours. To graduate, the advanced writing and skills requirements must be fulfilled; a variety of seminars that meet these requirements are offered for credits. Seminars are offered in Health Law, Education Law, Federal Water Rights, White Collar Crime, and Energy Law and Policy. Second- and third-year students may participate in the externship program for 2 to 3 credit hours per semester. Externs are placed with the Wyoming Attorney General's Office, Wyoming Supreme Court, the U.S. District Court, State Department of Revenue and Taxation, Wyoming state courts, U.S. Attorney's Office, state and federal public defender, and various state agencies, including Environmental Quality, Guardian ad Litem, and nonprofits such as ACLU, Biodiversity Alliance, Innocence Project, and Western Resource Advocates. Individualized tutoring is available through the Academic Support Program. Minority enrichment programs and lectures are also available through the Academic Support Program. A retention program is offered each spring to first-year students who have GPAs near or below 2.0 after the first semester. The most widely taken electives are Business Organizations, Family Law, and Trusts and Estates.

Graduation Requirements

In order to graduate, candidates must have a GPA of 2.0, have completed the upper-division writing requirement, and 1 skills course.

Organizations

Students edit the *Wyoming Law Review*. Moot court competitions include the National Moot Court, National Environmental Law Moot Court at Pace University, and Natural Resources Law Moot Court at the University of Denver. Other competitions include the National Client Counseling, the ATLA Student Trial Advocacy, and locally sponsored moot court and trial competitions. Law student organizations include the Potter Law Club, Natural Resources Law Forum, Women's Law Forum, Public Interest Law Forum, Sports Law Club, Students for Equal Justice, International Law Club, and J. Reuben Clark Law Society. There are local chapters of Phi Alpha Delta, Phi Delta Phi, and Delta Theta Phi. Campus clubs and other organizations include the Multicultural Students Organization, Associated Students of the University of Wyoming, and GLTB Organization.

Library

The law library contains 322,174 hardcopy volumes and 152,066 microform volume equivalents, and subscribes to 825 serial publications. Such on-line databases and networks as CALI, CIS Universe, Infotrac, Legal-Trac, LEXIS, LOIS, NEXIS, OCLC First Search, WESTLAW, Wilsonline Indexes, HeinOnline, LLMC Digital, VersusLaw, Making of Modern Law, JSTOR, Legal Periodicals Retrospective, Foreign and International Law, U.N. Treaty Collection, U.S. Supreme Court Records and Briefs, CCH Tax Network, ELR, and BNA Libraries are available to law students for research. Special library collections include a selective government depository and a Roman law collection. Recently, the library installed a wireless network. The ratio of library volumes to faculty is 14,008 to 1 and to students is 1426 to 1. The ratio of seats in the library to students is 1 to 1.

Faculty

The law school has 23 full-time and 10 part-time faculty members, of whom 15 are women. According to AAUP standards for Category I institutions, faculty salaries are well below average. About 10% of full-time faculty have a graduate law degree in addition to the J.D. The ratio of full-time students to full-time faculty in an average class is 12 to 1; in a clinic, 8 to 1. The law

Placement

J.D.s awarded:	71

Services available through: a separate law school placement center and the university placement center

Services: individual career counseling

Special features: on-line job database, on-campus interviews, on-campus job fairs, regional recruiting events, and access to subscription services.

Full-time job interviews:	4 employers
Summer job interviews:	13 employers
Placement by graduation:	55% of class
Placement within 9 months:	83% of class
Average starting salary:	$30,000 to $120,000

Areas of placement:

Private practice 2-10 attorneys	32%
Private practice 26-50 attorneys	2%
Private practice 251-500 attorneys	4%
Private practice, solo	2%
Private practic, unknown size	2%
Business/industry	15%
Judicial clerkships	14%
Government	12%
Public interest	7%
Military	5%
Academic	2%

school has a regular program of bringing visiting professors and other distinguished lecturers and visitors to campus. There is a chapter of the Order of the Coif; 15 faculty and 215 graduates are members.

Students

About 49% of the student body are women; 13%, minorities; 1%, African American; 3%, Asian American; 2%, Hispanic; 1%, Native American; and 11%, self-identified with LSDAS or on application as "Other." The majority of students come from the West (91%). The average age of entering students is 26; age range is 21 to 56. About 33% of students enter directly from undergraduate school and 11% have a graduate degree. About 2% drop out after the first year for academic or personal reasons; 93% remain to receive a law degree.

School of Law

Wesemann Hall,
656 S. Greenwich Street
Valparaiso, IN 46383-6493

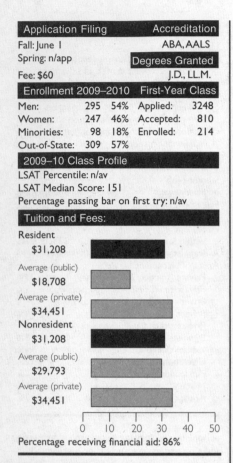

Application Filing		Accreditation	
Fall: June 1		ABA, AALS	
Spring: n/app		**Degrees Granted**	
Fee: $60		J.D., LL.M.	
Enrollment 2009–2010		**First-Year Class**	
Men:	295 54%	Applied:	3248
Women:	247 46%	Accepted:	810
Minorities:	98 18%	Enrolled:	214
Out-of-State:	309 57%		

2009–10 Class Profile
LSAT Percentile: n/av
LSAT Median Score: 151
Percentage passing bar on first try: n/av

Tuition and Fees:

Resident
$31,208

Average (public)
$18,708

Average (private)
$34,451

Nonresident
$31,208

Average (public)
$29,793

Average (private)
$34,451

0 10 20 30 40 50

Percentage receiving financial aid: 86%

ADMISSIONS

In a recent first-year class, 3248 applied, 810 were accepted, and 214 enrolled. Four transfers enrolled. The median GPA of the most recent first-year class was 3.47. Figures in the above capsule and in this profile are approximate.

Requirements
Applicants must have a bachelor's degree and take the LSAT. The most important admission factors include academic achievement, general background, and LSAT results. No specific undergraduate courses are required. Candidates are not interviewed.

Procedure
Applicants should submit an application form, LSAT results, transcripts, a personal statement, the TOEFL (international applicants), a nonrefundable application fee of $60, and 2 letters of recommendation. Notification of the admissions decision is on a rolling basis. The latest

acceptable LSAT test date for fall entry is February. The law school uses the LSDAS. Check with the school for the current application deadline.

Special
The law school recruits minority and disadvantaged students through recruitment mailings and relationship building. Requirements are not different for out-of-state students. Transfer students must have one year of credit, have a minimum GPA of 2, have attended an ABA-approved law school, and have their application reviewed by the admissions committee.

Costs

Tuition and fees for the 2009-2010 academic year are approximately $31,208 for all full-time students. Books and supplies run approximately $1200.

Financial Aid

In a recent year, about 86% of current law students received some form of aid. The average annual amount of aid from all sources combined, including scholarships, loans, and work contracts, was approximately $20,500; maximum, $42,318. Awards are based on need and merit. Required financial statements are the FAFSA. First-year students are notified about their financial aid application at time of acceptance. Check with the school for current application deadline.

About the Law School

Valparaiso University School of Law was established in 1879 and is a private institution. The 310-acre campus is in a suburban area 55 miles southeast of Chicago in northwest Indiana. The primary mission of the law school is to foster a learning environment; to maintain a community of teacher-scholars committed to excellence in legal research and publication that will shape the development of the law; and to embody an interaction between demands of the law and the Lutheran heritage of Valparaiso University. Students have access to federal, state, county, city, and local agencies, courts, correctional facilities, law firms, and legal aid organizations in the Valparaiso area. Valparaiso is the county seat of Porter County. Students also have access to charitable and community organizations for volunteer/pro bono

work in Porter and Lake counties, Indiana, and Cook County, Illinois (Chicago). Facilities of special interest to law students are Wesemann Hall, which houses classrooms, a courtroom, and an administrative complex, and Heritage Hall, which is listed on the National Register of Historic Places, housing the law clinic. Housing for students includes limited on-campus apartments; local apartments and large apartment complexes; and modest lakeside summer homes and cottages available for rent. The Admissions Office provides assistance in locating housing. About 75% of the law school facilities are accessible to the physically disabled.

Calendar

The law school operates on a traditional semester basis. Courses for full-time and part-time students are offered both day and evening and most courses are day and must be completed within 7 years. New full- and part-time students are admitted in the fall. There is an 8-week summer session. Transferable summer courses are offered.

Programs

In addition to the J.D., the law school offers the LL.M. The following joint degrees may be earned: J.D./M.A. (Juris Doctor/Master of Arts in psychology and clinical mental health counseling), J.D./M.A.C.S. (Juris Doctor/Master of Arts in Chinese Studies), J.D./M.A.L.S. (Juris Doctor/Master of Arts in Liberal Studies), J.D./M.B.A. (Juris Doctor/Master of Business Administration), J.D./M.S.I.C.P. (Juris Doctor/Master of International Commerce and Policy), and J.D./M.S.S.A. (Juris Doctor/Master of Science in Sports Administration).

Required
To earn the J.D., candidates must complete 90 total credits, of which 57 are for required courses. They must maintain a minimum GPA of 2.0 in the required courses. The following first-year courses are required of all students: Civil Procedure, Constitutional Law I, Contracts, Criminal Law, Legal Research, Legal Writing, Property, and Torts. Required upper-level courses consist of 1 of 3 administrative courses, 1 of 3 code courses, 1 of 3 property courses, 1 of 4 advanced writing courses, a seminar, and 1 of 5 perspective courses, Business Associations, Constitu-

Phone: 219-465-7821
888-VALPOLAW (825-7652)
Fax: 219-465-7808
E-mail: law.admissions@valpo.edu
Web: www.valpo.edu/law

Contact

Director of Admissions, 219-465-7829 for general inquiries; Financial Aid, 219-465-7818 for financial aid information.

INDIANA

tional Law II, Evidence, and Legal Profession. Third-year (and some second-year) law students in Indiana are permitted to represent clients in court, under supervision. The law clinic is available to third-year students and handles civil, criminal, tax, sports law, juvenile, and mediation law matters. The required orientation program for first-year students is 2 or 3 days preceding the start of the fall semester. Formal registration and meetings with current students, deans, and faculty advisers are included.

Electives

In addition, Clinics are available to third-year students for 2 or 3 credits a semester for a maximum of 12 credit hours. A seminar is required of all third-year students not on the *Law Review*, and a substantial paper is required. Second- and third-year students may also participate in up to 9 credit hours of an extern program. The law school supports 72 externship programs. Students may assist faculty with current representation or in research assistantships in which they work one-on-one with a professor in his or her area of current interest and research. No credit is given for the 20 hours of pro bono public service. Special lecture series include the Monsanto Annual Lecture on Tort Law Reform, the annual Seegers Lecture Series, the Distinguished Visitors Program, and the annual Tabor Institute on Legal Ethics. There is a summer study-abroad program in Cambridge, England. There is also a voluntary Academic Success Program; no credit is given and participation is by invitation only. Other tutorials are led by first-year faculty with student tutors available for individual consultation. The Hispanic Law Students Association, Black Law Students Association, and Multicultural Law Students Association sponsor minority programming. Special interest group programs include the Intellectual Property Association, Health Law Association, Sports and Entertainment Law Association, Coalition for Choice, Jus Vitae, Equal Justice Alliance, Third World Legal Studies, International Law, Pastoral Ministry, ATLA, and ABA/LSD. The most widely taken electives are Trusts and Estates, Federal Income Tax, and business and commercial law courses.

Graduation Requirements

In order to graduate, candidates must have a GPA of 2.0, have completed the upper-division writing requirement, and have completed the pro bono service requirement of 20 hours, for which there is no grade or credit.

Organizations

Students edit the *Valparaiso University Law Review*. The student newspaper is *The Forum*. Annually, moot court teams are sent to the Environmental Moot Court held at Pace University, the Giles Sutherland Rich Moot Court (1995 National Champions), and the Jessup International Moot Court. Other annual competitions are the Negotiations, the National Mock Trial, Association of Trial Lawyers of America, and Client Counseling. Law student organizations include Midwest Environmental Law Caucus and Christian Legal Society. Local chapters of national associations include Delta Theta Phi, Phi Alpha Delta, and Phi Delta Phi. Other groups include Just Democracy and Law Spouses Association.

Library

The law library contains 332,337 hardcopy volumes and 936,822 microform volume equivalents, and subscribes to 2371 serial publications. Such on-line databases and networks as CALI, CIS Universe, DIALOG, Infotrac, Legal-Trac, LEXIS, NEXIS, OCLC First Search, WESTLAW, and Wilsonline Indexes are available to law students for research. Special library collections include a selected U.S. Government Printing Office Depository, a Readex United Nations basic law library collection, and briefs from the Indiana Supreme Court and Indiana Court of Appeals. The ratio of library volumes to faculty is 8982 to 1 and to students is 613 to 1. The ratio of seats in the library to students is 1 to 2.

Faculty

The law school has 37 full-time and 40 part-time faculty members, of whom 27 are women. According to AAUP standards for Category IIA institutions, faculty salaries are average. About 23% of full-time faculty have a graduate law degree in addition to the J.D. The law school has a regular program of bringing visiting professors and other distinguished lecturers and visitors to campus.

Placement

J.D.s awarded:	150

Services available through: a separate law school placement center

Services: annually participate in job fairs, write articles for students, and hold numerous seminars and workshops. Focus on personalized counseling through meeting with 1 of 3 professional counselors. Host professional Career Day where alumni and practitioners in a wide variety of legal practice areas come to the school to provide 1-on-1 counseling to students.

Special features: member of NACD and Chicago Area Law School Consortium; Administer Loan Repayment Assistance Program and Public Interest Scholarship.

Full-time job interviews:	16 employers
Summer job interviews:	33 employers
Placement by graduation:	39% of class
Placement within 9 months:	88% of class
Average starting salary:	$35,000 to $140,000
Areas of placement:	
Law firms, all sizes	56%
Government	16%
Business/industry	14%
Judicial clerkships	7%
Public interest	4%
Academic	1%

Students

In a recent year, about 46% of the student body are women; 18%, minorities; 5%, African American; 2%, Asian American; 5%, Hispanic; and 6%, international and multiracial. The majority of students come from Indiana (43%). The average age of entering students is 25; age range is 20 to 55. About 56% of students enter directly from undergraduate school and 8% have a graduate degree. About 15% drop out after the first year for academic or personal reasons; 86% remain to receive a law degree.

131 21st Avenue South
Nashville, TN 37203

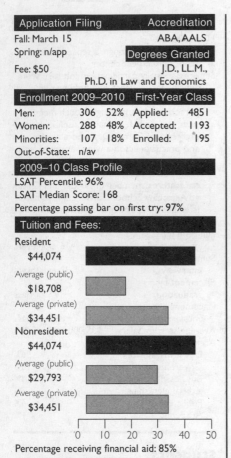

Application Filing	Accreditation
Fall: March 15	ABA, AALS
Spring: n/app	**Degrees Granted**
Fee: $50	J.D., LL.M.,
	Ph.D. in Law and Economics

Enrollment 2009–2010		First-Year Class	
Men:	306 52%	Applied:	4851
Women:	288 48%	Accepted:	1193
Minorities:	107 18%	Enrolled:	195
Out-of-State:	n/av		

2009–10 Class Profile
LSAT Percentile: 96%
LSAT Median Score: 168
Percentage passing bar on first try: 97%

Tuition and Fees:

Resident
$44,074

Average (public)
$18,708

Average (private)
$34,451

Nonresident
$44,074

Average (public)
$29,793

Average (private)
$34,451

0   10   20   30   40   50

Percentage receiving financial aid: 85%

ADMISSIONS
In the fall 2009 first-year class, 4851 applied, 1193 were accepted, and 195 enrolled. Twenty-eight transfers enrolled. The median LSAT percentile of the most recent first-year class was 96; the median GPA was 3.71 on a scale of 4.0.

Requirements
Applicants must have a bachelor's degree and take the LSAT. No specific undergraduate courses are required. Candidates are interviewed.

Procedure
The application deadline for fall entry is March 15. Applicants should submit an application form, LSAT results, transcripts, a personal statement, TOEFL if foreign applicant, a nonrefundable application fee of $50, and 2 (mimimum) letters of recommendation. Notification of the admissions decision is on a rolling basis. The latest acceptable LSAT test date for

fall entry is February. The law school uses the LSDAS.

Special
The law school recruits minority and disadvantaged students by means of on-campus recruiting, general mailings, consortium recruiting events, and LSAC Forums. Requirements are not different for out-of-state students. Transfer students must have one year of credit and have attended an ABA-approved law school. Applicant's reasons for relocating to Nashville and for studying at Vanderbilt are considered. There is also an interview requirement.

Costs
Tuition and fees for the 2009-2010 academic year are $44,074 for all full-time students. Books and supplies run $1720.

Financial Aid
About 85% of current law students receive some form of aid. The maximum annual amount of aid from all sources combined, including scholarships, loans, and work contracts, is $66,022. Awards are based on need and merit. Required financial statements are the FAFSA and Need Access. The aid application deadline for fall entry is February 15. First-year students are notified about their financial aid application after acceptance.

About the Law School
Vanderbilt University Law School was established in 1874 and is a private institution. The 330-acre campus is in an urban area 1.5 miles west of downtown Nashville. The primary mission of the law school is to educate effective lawyers in a wide range of professional areas. Students have access to federal, state, county, city, and local agencies, courts, correctional facilities, law firms, and legal aid organizations in the Nashville area. Law School facilities of special interest to law students include a courtyard with adjacent café, comfortable lounges, high-tech classrooms and trial courtroom, wireless connectivity, and access to many electronic resources for legal research. Housing for students includes a variety of options near the campus. All law school facilities are accessible to the physically disabled.

Calendar
The law school operates on a traditional semester basis. Courses for full-time students are offered days only and must be completed within 3 years. There is no part-time program. New students are admitted in the fall. There is no summer session. Transferable summer courses are not offered.

Programs
In addition to the J.D., the law school offers the LL.M. and Ph.D. in Law and Economics. Students may take relevant courses in other programs and apply credit toward the J.D.; a maximum of 6 credits may be applied. The following joint degrees may be earned: J.D./D.I.V. (Juris Doctor/Master of Divinity), J.D./M.A. (Juris Doctor/Master of Arts), J.D./M.B.A. (Juris Doctor/Master of Business Administration), J.D./M.D. (Juris Doctor/Doctor of Medicine), J.D./M.P.P (Juris Doctor/Master of Public Policy), J.D./M.T.S. (Juris Doctor/Master of Theological Studies), J.D./Ph.D. (Juris Doctor/Doctor of Philosophy), and LL.M./M.A. (Master of Laws/Master of Arts in Latin American studies).

Required
To earn the J.D., candidates must complete 88 total credits, of which 38 are for required courses. They must maintain a minimum GPA of 2.0 in the required courses. The following first-year courses are required of all students: Civil Procedure, Constitutional Law, Contracts, Criminal Law, Legal Research and Writing I and II, Life of the Law, Property, Regulatory State, and Torts. Required upper-level courses consist of Professional Responsibility, seminar, and skills requirement. The required orientation program for first-year students consists of a comprehensive 5-day orientation including a 1-credit course surveying the U.S. legal system and legal education.

Electives
The Law School offers concentrations in corporate law, criminal law, entertainment law, environmental law, family law, intellectual property law, international law, juvenile law, labor law, litigation, media law, securities law, sports law, tax law, torts and insurance, and law and social behavior. In addition, clinic offerings include business law, child

Phone: 615-322-6452
Fax: 615-322-1531
E-mail: *admissions@law.vanderbilt.edu*
Web: *law.vanderbilt.edu*

Contact

G. Todd Morton, Assistant Dean and Dean of Admissions, 615-322-6452 for general inquiries; Richelle Acker, Associate Director of Admissions, 615-322-6452 for financial aid information.

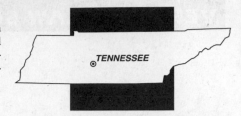

and family law, civil practice, criminal practice, domestic violence, intellectual property and the arts, international law practice, and juvenile practice. Students may also pursue externships that provide valuable experience while gaining academic credit. In 2009-2010, 18 seminars were offered to second- and third-year students. Research programs consist of faculty research assistantships. Students can gain valuable professional experience in nonprofits, government agencies, and other organizations around the world supported by various stipend opportunities, including the Legal Aid Society and Public Interest Stipend Fund. Students gain experience and academic credits through individual externship placements. An array of speakers, academic conferences, and symposia are held each year, including student-initiated events funded by the Hyatt Student Activities Fund. Students may participate in summer study-abroad programs sponsored by ABA-accredited law schools. Vanderbilt offers a "Summer in Venice" study-abroad program. Special writing assistance is available for first-year students who need tutoring. Legal writing workshops are offered for second- and third year students. A bar preparation seminar is offered for third-year students. Minority programs include the Asian-Pacific American Law Student Association (APLA), Black Law Students Association (BLSA), and South Asian Law Students Association. Special interest groups include OutLaw, Jewish Law Students Association (JLSA), Environmental Law Society, and Law Students for Veterans Affairs.

Graduation Requirements

In order to graduate, candidates must have a GPA of 2.0 and have completed the upper-division writing requirement.

Organizations

Students edit the *Vanderbilt Law Review, Journal of Transnational Law, Vanderbilt Journal of Entertainment* and *Technology Law, Journal of Risk and Uncertainty, The Environmental Law & Policy Annual Review,* and *Health Law & Public Policy Forum.* Moot court competitions include the First Amendment Moot Court Competition, VULS Mock Trial, and VULS Intramural Appellate Advocacy Competititon. Law student organizations include the Vanderbilt Bar Association, Environmen-

tal Law Society, and Law and Business Society. There are almost 50 different organizations active in the law school. There are local chapters of BLSA, Street Law, La Alianza, and Phi Alpha Delta.

Library

The law library contains 480,079 hardcopy volumes and 740,667 microform volume equivalents, and subscribes to 1114 serial publications. Such on-line databases and networks as CALI, CIS Universe, DIALOG, Infotrac, Legal-Trac, LEXIS, Mathew Bender, NEXIS, OCLC First Search, WESTLAW, and Wilsonline Indexes are available to law students for research. Special library collections include Stumpf Collection (Jurisprudence and Bioethics). Recently, the library acquired additional tables and seating and installation of more power outlets. The ratio of library volumes to faculty is 10,002 to 1 and to students is 813 to 1. The ratio of seats in the library to students is 1 to 2.

Faculty

The law school has 48 full-time and 75 part-time faculty members, of whom 42 are women. According to AAUP standards for Category I institutions, faculty salaries are above average. About 13% of full-time faculty have a graduate law degree in addition to the J.D. The ratio of full-time students to full-time faculty in an average class is 20 to 1; in a clinic, 7 to 1. The law school has a regular program of bringing visiting professors and other distinguished lecturers and visitors to campus. There is a chapter of the Order of the Coif, the top 10% of graduates are members.

Students

About 48% of the student body are women; 18%, minorities; 9%, African American; 4%, Asian American; 4%, Hispanic; 1%, Native American; and 2%, foreign nationals. The average age of entering students is 23; age range is 19 to 40. About 40% of students enter directly from undergraduate school, 7% have a graduate degree, and 60% have worked full-time prior to entering law school. Fewer than 1% drop out after the first year for academic or personal reasons; 99% remain to receive a law degree.

Placement	
J.D.s awarded:	189
Services available through: a separate law school placement center	
Special features: etiquette dinner, mock interview program, public service initiative, and speakers series.	
Full-time job interviews:	597 employers
Summer job interviews:	597 employers
Placement by graduation:	95% of class
Placement within 9 months:	99% of class
Average starting salary:	$52,000 to $165,000
Areas of placement:	
Private practice 2-10 attorneys	4%
Private practice 11-25 attorneys	5%
Private practice 26-50 attorneys	2%
Private practice 51-100 attorneys	3%
Private practice 101+ attorneys	59%
Judicial clerkships	15%
Government	6%
Business/industry	3%
Public interest	3%

VERMONT LAW SCHOOL

P.O. Box 96, Chelsea Street
South Royalton, VT 05068-0096

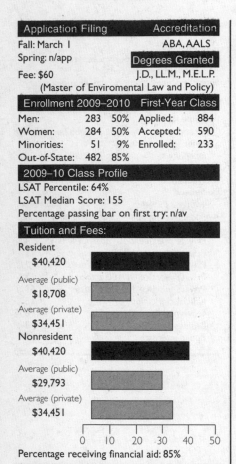

Application Filing		Accreditation
Fall: March 1		ABA, AALS
Spring: n/app		
Fee: $60		J.D., LL.M., M.E.L.P.
		Degrees Granted
(Master of Enviromental Law and Policy)		

Enrollment 2009–2010		First-Year Class	
Men:	283 50%	Applied:	884
Women:	284 50%	Accepted:	590
Minorities:	51 9%	Enrolled:	233
Out-of-State:	482 85%		

2009–10 Class Profile
LSAT Percentile: 64%
LSAT Median Score: 155
Percentage passing bar on first try: n/av

Tuition and Fees:

Resident
$40,420

Average (public)
$18,708

Average (private)
$34,451

Nonresident
$40,420

Average (public)
$29,793

Average (private)
$34,451

0   10   20   30   40   50

Percentage receiving financial aid: 85%

ADMISSIONS

In the fall 2009 first-year class, 884 applied, 590 were accepted, and 233 enrolled. 1 transfer enrolled. The median LSAT percentile of the most recent first-year class was 64; the median GPA was 3.32 on a scale of 4.0. The highest LSAT percentile was 98.

Requirements

Applicants must have a bachelor's degree and take the LSAT. The most important admission factors include academic achievement, character, personality, LSAT results and 2 essay statements. No specific undergraduate courses are required. Candidates are interviewed.

Procedure

The application deadline for fall entry is March 1. Applicants should submit an application form, a personal statement, a nonrefundable application fee of $60, 2 letters of recommendation, and 2 essay questions. Notification of the admissions decision is on a rolling basis. The latest acceptable LSAT test date for fall entry is February. The law school uses the LSDAS.

Special

The law school recruits minority and disadvantaged students through the Council on Legal Education Opportunity (CLEO) program, direct mail through the Candidate Referral Service (CRS), participation in college minority student events and a diversity scholarship program. Requirements are not different for out-of-state students. Transfer students must be in good academic standing and eligible to return to the school from which they are transferring.

Costs

Tuition and fees for the 2009-2010 academic year are $40,420 for all full-time students. Books and supplies run $1500.

Financial Aid

About 85% of current law students receive some form of aid. The average annual amount of aid from all sources combined, including scholarships, loans, and work contracts, is $34,000; maximum, $61,480. Awards are based on need and merit. Required financial statement is the FAFSA. The aid application deadline for fall entry is March 1. Special funds for minority or disadvantaged students include the Debevoise Family Scholarship Fund, which provides grants to qualified diverse applicants from traditionally underrepresented groups with demonstrated financial need. First-year students are notified about their financial aid application at as early as possible after acceptance (usually late March). Merit awards are included in the packet with the acceptance letter.

About the Law School

Vermont Law School was established in 1972 and is independent. The 13-acre campus is in a small town 70 miles southeast of Burlington. The primary mission of the law school is to provide a thorough understanding of the nature and function of law in society and to equip graduates to serve their communities in positions of leadership and responsibility. The school believes lawyers should be liberally educated, ethical, competent, and committed to improving the law and its administration. Students have access to federal, state, county, city, and local agencies, courts, correctional facilities, law firms, and legal aid organizations in the South Royalton area. The South Royalton Legal Clinic is located on campus. Facilities of special interest to law students include a modern library constructed in 1991 and a new classroom building constructed in 1998. Nearby Hanover, New Hampshire, home of Dartmouth College, is a source of student cultural and social life. Child care is available on campus. Housing for students is available in private houses, apartments, or rooms in the community or nearby towns. Rental units are plentiful; the law school provides students a listing. About 75% of the law school facilities are accessible to the physically disabled.

Calendar

The law school operates on a traditional semester basis. Courses for full-time students are offered days only and must be completed within 4 years. There is no part-time program. New students are admitted in the fall. There is an 8-week summer session. Transferable summer courses are offered.

Programs

In addition to the J.D., the law school offers the LL.M. and M.E.L.P. (Master of Enviromental Law and Policy). Students may take relevant courses in other programs and apply credit toward the J.D.; a maximum of 9 credits may be applied. The following joint degrees may be earned: J.D./M.E.L.P. (Juris Doctor/Master of Environmental Law and Policy).

Required

To earn the J.D., candidates must complete 87 total credits, of which 52 are for required courses. They must maintain a minimum GPA of 2.20 in the required courses. The following first-year courses are required of all students: Civil Procedure I and II, Constitutional Law I and II, Contracts, Criminal Law, Legal Reasoning, Writing, and Research, Property, and Torts. Required upper-level courses consist of 1 perspective elective, 1 skills or clinical elective, advanced writing project, Appellate Advocacy, and Legal Profession. All students must take clinical courses. The required orientation program for

Phone: 802-831-1239
888-277-5985
Fax: 802-831-1174
E-mail: *admiss@vermontlaw.edu*
Web: *www.vermontlaw.edu*

Contact
Kathy Hartman, Assoc. Dean for Enrollment Mgmt, 802-831-1232 or 888-277-5985 for general inquiries; David Myette, Director of Financial Aid, 802-831-1235 or 888-277-5985 for financial aid information.

first-year students is 5 days of lectures and workshops on the legal process, court systems, and sources of law, and the analysis and briefing of cases. It also includes an orientation to the law library, its resources and support systems, and meetings with faculty advisers.

Electives
The Vermont Law School offers concentrations in corporate law, criminal law, environmental law, family law, international law, labor law, and general practice; alternative dispute resolution; land use and real estate; and traditionally disadvantaged groups. In addition, clinics are open to second- and third-year students, but enrollment is limited. Clinics are Semester in Practice for 13 credits, Legislation Clinic for 6 credits, Environmental Semester in Washington, D.C. for 13 credits, Environmental and Natural Resources Law Clinic for 4 credits, and South Royalton Legal Clinic for 6 or 13 credits. About 20 seminars are offered annually on various topics to second- and third-year students for 2 or 3 credits each. Faculty-supervised internships are open to second- and third-year students. Credit varies and placement can be in a variety of legal settings, including private practice, government, nonprofit agencies, the judiciary, and businesses. Faculty-supervised research programs are open to second- and third-year students and culminate in a major piece of legal writing. Special lecture series include the Waterman Lectures and other lectures arranged by faculty and student organizations. There is an exchange program with McGill University, Faculty of Law in Montreal, University of Paris (France), and University of Trento (Italy). Tutorial programs and the Program for Academic Success are offered. Workshops on topics such as time and stress management, case briefing, and exam taking are held. Minority programs are offered through the Coalition for Diversity, BALSA, APALSA, NLALSA, Native American Law Society, and the Office of the Dean of Student Services and Diversity. Special interest group programs are offered through the Alliance, Animal Law League, Environmental Law Society, and other groups. The most widely taken electives are Environmental Law, Corporations, and Estates.

Graduation Requirements
In order to graduate, candidates must have a GPA of 2.2, and have completed the upper-division writing requirement, Legal Profession course, 1 perspective elective, and 1 skills elective.

Organizations
Students edit the *Vermont Law Review*, the *Environmental Law Journal*, a literary journal *Hearsay*, and the newspaper, *The Forum*. Moot court competitions include the annual Thomas M. Debevoise Moot Court, with finals argued before the Vermont Supreme Court, the annual Douglas M. Costle Environmental Moot Court, and various regional and national moot court competitions. Student organizations include the Jewish Students Group, Guardians ad Litem, and Coalition for Diversity. There are local chapters of Amnesty International, Association of Trial Lawyers of America, and Equal Justice Foundation. Campus clubs include the Barrister Bookshop, Law Partners, and Chamber Music Group.

Library
The law library contains 254,127 hardcopy volumes and 122,219 microform volume equivalents, and subscribes to 1856 serial publications. Such on-line databases and networks as CALI, CIS Universe, DIALOG, Infotrac, Legal-Trac, LEXIS, LOIS, NEXIS, OCLC First Search, WESTLAW, ECONET, and EPIC are available to law students for research. Special library collections include environmental law, historic preservation, and alternative dispute resolution. The ratio of library volumes to faculty is 4307 to 1 and to students is 448 to 1. The ratio of seats in the library to students is 1 to 5.

Faculty
The law school has 59 full-time and 14 part-time faculty members, of whom 32 are women. About 20% of full-time faculty have a graduate law degree in addition to the J.D.; about 15% of part-time faculty have one. The ratio of full-time students to full-time faculty in an average class is 10 to 1; in a clinic, 6 to 1. The law school has a regular program of bringing visiting professors and other distinguished lecturers and visitors to campus.

Placement

J.D.s awarded:	191

Services available through: a separate law school placement center

Services: travel stipend for interview

Special features: Letters of application are prepared for students from an employer database, leading to computerized matching of student interests and employers. Services are characterized by individual attention, with particularly strong public interest and environmental employer listings.

Full-time job interviews:	17 employers
Summer job interviews:	35 employers
Placement by graduation:	66% of class
Placement within 9 months:	96% of class
Average starting salary:	$30,000 to $160,000

Areas of placement:

Private practice 2-10 attorneys	15%
Private practice 11-25 attorneys	6%
Private practice 26-50 attorneys	4%
Private practice 51-100 attorneys	4%
Private practice 100+ attorneys	6%
Business/industry	19%
Judicial clerkships	15%
Government	15%
Public interest	15%
Military	1%
Academic	1%

Students
About 50% of the student body are women; 9%, minorities; 3%, African American; 3%, Asian American; and 3%, Hispanic. The majority of students come from the Northeast (50%). The average age of entering students is 26; age range is 22 to 51. About 24% of students enter directly from undergraduate school, 15% have a graduate degree, and 75% have worked full-time prior to entering law school. About 8% drop out after the first year for academic or personal reasons; 92% remain to receive a law degree.

VILLANOVA UNIVERSITY

School of Law

299 N. Spring Mill Road
Villanova, PA 19085

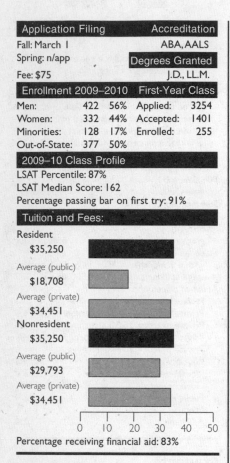

Application Filing		Accreditation
Fall: March 1		ABA, AALS
Spring: n/app		**Degrees Granted**
Fee: $75		J.D., LL.M.

Enrollment 2009–2010			First-Year Class	
Men:	422	56%	Applied:	3254
Women:	332	44%	Accepted:	1401
Minorities:	128	17%	Enrolled:	255
Out-of-State:	377	50%		

2009–10 Class Profile
LSAT Percentile: 87%
LSAT Median Score: 162
Percentage passing bar on first try: 91%

Tuition and Fees:

Resident
$35,250

Average (public)
$18,708

Average (private)
$34,451

Nonresident
$35,250

Average (public)
$29,793

Average (private)
$34,451

0 10 20 30 40 50

Percentage receiving financial aid: 83%

ADMISSIONS

In the fall 2009 first-year class, 3254 applied, 1401 were accepted, and 255 enrolled. Nine transfers enrolled. The median LSAT percentile of the most recent first-year class was 87; the median GPA was 3.44 on a scale of 4.0. The lowest LSAT percentile accepted was 53; the highest was 99.

Requirements
Applicants must have a bachelor's degree and take the LSAT. The most important admission factors include GPA, LSAT results, and letter of recommendation. No specific undergraduate courses are required. Candidates are not interviewed.

Procedure
The application deadline for fall entry is March 1. Applicants should submit an application form, LSAT results, transcripts, a personal statement, a nonrefundable application fee of $75, and 2 or 3 letters of recommendation. Deposits are required of students after acceptance.

Notification of the admissions decision is on a rolling basis beginning in December. The latest acceptable LSAT test date for fall entry is February. The law school uses the LSDAS.

Special
The law school recruits minority and disadvantaged students at LSAC forums, through outreach programs offered by various minority student groups on campus through the Deirdre Bailey Leadership Scholarships, and by targeted mailings and targeted college visits. Requirements are not different for out-of-state students. Transfer students must have 1 year of credit and have attended an ABA-approved law school.

Costs

Tuition and fees for the 2009-2010 academic year are $35,250 for all full-time students. Books and supplies run $1400.

Financial Aid

About 83% of current law students receive some form of aid. The average annual amount of aid from all sources combined, including scholarships, loans, and work contracts, is $43,569; maximum, $79,631. Awards are based on need and merit. Required financial statement is the FAFSA. The priority aid application deadline for fall entry is March 1. Special funds for minority or disadvantaged students include Deidre Bailey Scholarships. First-year students are notified about their financial aid application at time of acceptance.

About the Law School

Villanova University School of Law was established in 1953 and is a private institution. The 250-acre campus is in a suburban area 15 miles west of Philadelphia. The primary mission of the law school is to provide the opportunity for students to develop an understanding of Anglo-American law in the common-law tradition, a knowledge of federal and state statutory and administrative developments, and the analytical and practice skills required by the modern lawyer and to do so in a community with a strong sense of ethics and values. The curriculum is broad-based, especially in the profession's obligation to the poor, and responsive to the needs of

modern law practice. Students have access to federal, state, county, city, and local agencies, courts, correctional facilities, law firms, and legal aid organizations in the Villanova area. They also have access to the numerous colleges and universities in the Philadelphia area. Facilities of special interest to law students include a new building, operational since July 2009, with state-of-the-art technology, including wireless network access and instructional technology available in every classroom, along with a computer lab containing 25 workstations. The new law school building also houses a spacious library with many comfortable and inviting workspaces for student use. Housing for students is in off-campus apartments and other facilities. On-campus housing is not available. The university's Director of Residence Life and the law school's admissions office assist students in finding housing. About 98% of the law school facilities are accessible to the physically disabled.

Calendar

The law school operates on a traditional semester basis. The majority of courses are offered during the day and must be completed within 3 years. There is no part-time program. New students are admitted in the fall. There is no summer session. Transferable summer courses are not offered.

Programs

In addition to the J.D., the law school offers the LL.M. The following joint degrees may be earned: J.D./LL.M. (Juris Doctor/Master of Law in Taxation) and J.D./M.B.A. (Juris Doctor/Master of Business Administration).

Required
To earn the J.D., candidates must complete 88 total credits, of which 44 are for required courses. The following first-year courses are required of all students: Civil Procedure I and II, Constitutional Law 1, Contracts I and II, Criminal Law, Legal Research, Legal Writing, Analysis, and Oral Advocacy, 1L Elective, Property, and Torts. Required upper-level courses consist of a practical skills writing course, a research paper course, Appellate Advocacy, Constitutional Law, and Legal Profession. A wide variety of clinics, practicums, and externships is available. Students

Phone: 610-519-7010
Fax: 610-519-6291
E-mail: *admissions@law.villanova.edu*
Web: *http://www.law.villanova.edu*

Contact

Assistant Dean for Admissions, 610-519-7010 for general inquiries; Wendy C. Barron, Assst. Dean for Financial Aid, 610-519-7015 for financial aid information.

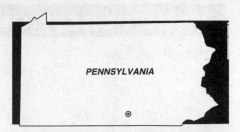

PENNSYLVANIA

are encouraged, but not required, to take advantage of these opportunities. The required orientation program for first-year students is a 2 1/2 day course.

Electives

The law school does not have concentrations but suggests curricula for a broad range of specialties. In addition, clinics, open to second- and third- year students, include Farm Workers Legal Aid (6 credits), Federal Tax (4 credits), Civil Justice (6 credits), Asylum, Refugee, and Emigrant Services (8 credits), and Advance Advocacy (2-4 credits). Seminars, also open to second- and third- year students, give students 2 credits of intensive learning, research, and writing, working closely with a faculty member. Internships/externships include the U.S. Attorney's Office (Philadelphia, Delaware), EPA, IRS, NLRB, various District Attorneys' and judges' offices, University Counsel's Office, Legal Aid, the U.S. Department of Justice (Antitrust Division), Volunteer Lawyers for the Arts, in-house counsel and defenders. Research assistantships are available. Two practicums are offered: a Capital Defense Practicum, in which students work representing death row inmates, and a Mediation Practicum, in which students are trained for and then handle mediations for the courts and public interest agencies. Special lecture series include Donald A. Giannella Memorial Lecture, Law Review Symposium, Environmental Law Symposium, Sports and Entertainment Law Symposium, Law and Psychology lecture series, BLSA Symposium, Symposium on Law and Catholic Thought, and Martin Luther King lectures. Villanova offers a summer program in Rome, Italy. The school also accepts up to 6 credits from an accredited American Law summer program abroad, provided it meets the standards of the school. Academic support is provided after the first semester to students at risk and to upper level students with identified learning issues or who are at risk of failing the bar exam. In support of its minority students and diversity, an active Minority Alumni Society, a minority mentoring program, several affinity groups including BLSA, LALSA, and APALSA, and a joint student/faculty/staff committee charged with fostering inclusiveness are available. The most widely taken electives are Corporations, Evidence, and Trial Practice.

Graduation Requirements

In order to graduate, candidates must have a GPA of 2.0 and have completed the upper-division writing requirement, and Constitutional Law I and II, and upper level Appellate Advocacy and Legal Professional. The upper-division writing requirement consists of a research paper course and a practical writing course.

Organizations

Law students publish the *Villanova Law Review, Villanova Environmental Law Journal*, and *Villanova Sports and Entertainment Law Journal*. Law students edit, with the faculty, the *Journal of Catholic Social Thought* and the *Journal of Law and Investment Management, Women's Law Forum* (online), and the *Villanova International Law Quarterly Newsletter*. Students contribute to *The Gavel Gazette*, the school's weekly newsletter. Annually, the school sponsors the Reimel Moot Court Competition and students participate in numerous outside moot court competitions, including Jessup Law and Benton. Other competitions include the ABA Client Interviewing and Counseling Competition and Trial Practice. Competition is offered by students in the for-credit trial competition courses. Law student organizations, local chapters of national associations, and campus organizations include Women's Law Caucus, Public Interest Fellowship Program, OUTlaw, Student Bar Association, Black Law Students Association (BLSA), Latin American Law Students Association (LALSA), Phi Delta Phi, the Justinian Society, and the Federalist Society.

Library

The law library contains 345,482 hardcopy volumes and 1,150,098 microform volume equivalents, and subscribes to 981 serial publications. Such on-line databases and networks as CIS Universe, DIALOG, Infotrac, Legal-Trac, LEXIS, LOIS, NEXIS, OCLC First Search, WESTLAW, CCH Tax Library, RIA Checkpoint, Social Science Research network, HeinOnLine, TRAC, BNA Tax Management Library, PA Law Library, and UN Treaty Collection are available to law students for research. The ratio of library volumes to faculty is 7677 to 1 and to students is 458 to 1. The ratio of seats in the library to students is 1 to 2.

Placement

J.D.s awarded:	235

Services available through: a separate law school placement center
Services: career seminars and job fairs, a career development and research library, alumni networking opportunities
Special features: 3 attorney-advisers on staff, consortium interview programs, public interest job fairs, state-of-the-art technology, various minority job fairs, and geographic location job fairs

Full-time job interviews:	100 employers
Summer job interviews:	100 employers
Placement by graduation:	68% of class
Placement within 9 months:	95% of class
Average starting salary:	$28,000 to $145,000

Areas of placement:

Private practice 2-10 attorneys	11%
Private practice 11-25 attorneys	6%
Private practice 26-50 attorneys	8%
Private practice 51-100 attorneys	4%
Private practice 101+ attorneys	26%
Business/industry	17%
Judicial clerkships	15%
Public interest	6%
Government	4%
Military	2%

Faculty

The law school has 45 full-time and 65 part-time faculty members, of whom 34 are women. According to AAUP standards for Category IIA institutions, faculty salaries are above average. About 29% of full-time faculty have a graduate law degree in addition to the J.D. The ratio of full-time students to full-time faculty in an average class is 17 to 1; in a clinic, 7 to 1. The law school has a regular program of bringing visiting professors and other distinguished lecturers and visitors to campus. There is a chapter of the Order of the Coif; 35 faculty and 821 graduates are members.

Students

About 44% of the student body are women; 17%, minorities; 2%, African American; 9%, Asian American; 6%, Hispanic; and 1%, Native American. The majority of students come from the Northeast (80%). The average age of entering students is 23; age range is 21 to 45. About 48% of students enter directly from undergraduate school, 7% have a graduate degree, and 52% have worked full-time prior to entering law school. About 1% drop out after the first year for academic or personal reasons; 99% remain to receive a law degree.

WAKE FOREST UNIVERSITY

School of Law

P.O. Box 7206, Reynolda Station
Winston-Salem, NC 27109

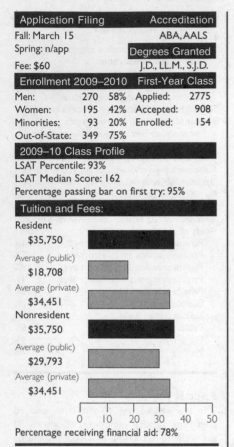

Application Filing	Accreditation
Fall: March 15	ABA, AALS
Spring: n/app	**Degrees Granted**
Fee: $60	J.D., LL.M., S.J.D.

Enrollment 2009–2010		First-Year Class	
Men:	270 58%	Applied:	2775
Women:	195 42%	Accepted:	908
Minorities:	93 20%	Enrolled:	154
Out-of-State:	349 75%		

2009–10 Class Profile
LSAT Percentile: 93%
LSAT Median Score: 162
Percentage passing bar on first try: 95%

Tuition and Fees:

Resident
$35,750

Average (public)
$18,708

Average (private)
$34,451

Nonresident
$35,750

Average (public)
$29,793

Average (private)
$34,451

0   10   20   30   40   50

Percentage receiving financial aid: 78%

ADMISSIONS

In the fall 2009 first-year class, 2775 applied, 908 were accepted, and 154 enrolled. Fourteen transfers enrolled. The median LSAT percentile of the most recent first-year class was 93; the median GPA was 3.6 on a scale of 4.0. The lowest LSAT percentile accepted was 40; the highest was 98.

Requirements
Applicants must have a bachelor's degree and take the LSAT. The most important admission factors include academic achievement, GPA, and LSAT results. A combination of the GPA and LSAT results is used. No specific undergraduate courses are required. Candidates are interviewed.

Procedure
The application deadline for fall entry is March 15. Applicants should submit an application form, LSAT results, transcripts, a personal statement, a nonrefundable application fee of $60, 2 letters of recommendation, through LSAC. A dean's certification is required prior to matriculation. Notification of the admissions decision is on a rolling basis. The latest acceptable LSAT test date for fall entry is February. The law school uses the LSDAS.

Special
The law school recruits minority and disadvantaged students through collaboration with the Black Law Students Association (BLSA), and Latino and Pan Asian organizations who call accepted minority candidates to discuss the school and answer questions. These groups and the school sponsor a minority recruitment day where students visit the campus, meet with enrolled students, and attend a mock class and a moot court presentation. Also, the Career Services Office works with major law firms in the state to place minority candidates for summer employment and to expedite consideration of minority applicants. Requirements are not different for out-of-state students. Transfer students must have one year of credit, have attended an ABA-approved law school, and have a letter of good standing from the dean of the law school and an official transcript of first-year grades.

Costs

Tuition and fees for the 2009-2010 academic year are $35,750 for all full-time students. Books and supplies run $1000.

Financial Aid

About 78% of current law students receive some form of aid. The maximum annual amount of aid from all sources combined, including scholarships, loans, and work contracts, is $35,450. Awards are based on need and merit. Required financial statement is the FAFSA. The aid application deadline for fall entry is May 1. Special funds for minority or disadvantaged students include full-tuition scholarships that are awarded in each entering class and for which all candidates are eligible. First-year students are notified about their financial aid application at time of acceptance or early February.

About the Law School

Wake Forest University School of Law was established in 1894 and is a private institution. The 340-acre campus is in an urban area 3 miles north of Winston-Salem. The primary mission of the law school is to graduate students eligible and qualified to practice law. Students have access to federal, state, county, city, and local agencies, courts, correctional facilities, law firms, and legal aid organizations in the Winston-Salem area. Clinical placements are with the district attorney, U.S. attorney, Legal Aid, private practitioners, U.S. bankruptcy judge, and public defender. Housing for students is available in approximately 6000 apartment units that are within a 2 1/2 mile radius of the campus. All law school facilities are accessible to the physically disabled.

Calendar

The law school operates on a traditional semester basis. Courses for full-time students are offered days only and must be completed within 3 years. There is no part-time program. New students are admitted in the fall. There are two 5-week summer sessions. Transferable summer courses are offered.

Programs

In addition to the J.D., the law school offers the LL.M. in American Law (for foreign law school graduates) and S.J.D. Students may take relevant courses in other programs and apply credit toward the J.D.; a maximum of 7 credits may be applied. The following joint degrees may be earned: J.D./M.A. (Juris Doctor/Master of Arts in bioethics and in religion) and J.D./M.D.V. (Juris Doctor/Master of Divinity).

Required
To earn the J.D., candidates must complete 89 total credits, of which 41 are for required courses. They must maintain a minimum grade average of 73 on a scale of 100 in the required courses. The following first-year courses are required of all students: Civil Procedure I and II, Constitutional Law I, Contracts I and II, Criminal Law I, Legal Research and Writing I and II, Property, and Torts. Required upper-level courses consist of Constitutional Law II, Evidence, Legal Writing III, plus 1 substantial writing project, Legislation and Administrative Law, and Professional Responsibility. All students may take clinics in addition to the skill courses. The required orientation program

Phone: 336-758-5437
Fax: 336-758-4632
E-mail: admissions@law.wfu.edu
Web: law.wfu.edu

Contact
Melanie E. Nutt, Admissions Director, 336-758-5437 for general inquiries and financial aid information.

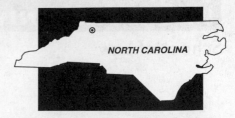

NORTH CAROLINA

for first-year students is a 1-week program before the beginning of classes devoted to the basics of legal research and writing.

Electives
The School of Law offers concentrations in corporate law, family law, international law, labor law, litigation, securities law, tax law, torts and insurance, and clinical law. In addition, clinics include the Appellate Advocacy Clinic, which represents low-income clients in all sorts of appeals, both civil and criminal; the Community Law & Business Clinic, available to law and graduate business students; the Elder Law Clinic, created by the School of Law and Wake Forest's School of Medicine; the Innocence & Justice Clinic, which gives students the opportunity to review and investigate all types of innocence claims and pursue litigation when appropriate; and the Litigation Clinic. The Constitutional Lecture Series is an annual program featuring an address by a nationally prominent figure in the field of constitutional law. Three 5-week summer programs are offered, one in London, England; one in Vienna, Austria; and the other in Venice, Italy. Enrollment is open to all students depending on availability. A tutorial program is offered to first-year students through the Dean's Office. The most widely taken electives are Federal Tax, Decedents' Estates, and Business Organizations.

Graduation Requirements
In order to graduate, candidates must have a grade average of 73, have completed the upper-division writing requirement, and have written a paper or a brief to the satisfaction of the instructor in a course approved by the faculty.

Organizations
Students edit the *Wake Forest Law Review*, the On-Line Intellectual Property Journal, the student newspaper *The Hearsay*, and *The Jurist*, an alumni magazine published in the spring and fall of each year. Moot court competitions include the Marshall Competition in Chicago, National Moot Court Competition, and Jessup International Moot Court Competition. Student organizations include ABA-Law Student Division, Environmental Law Society, and the BLSA/Latino/Pan-Asian

Associations. There is a local chapter of the Inns of Court.

Library
The law library contains 419,496 hardcopy volumes. Such on-line databases and networks as CALI, Dow-Jones, Infotrac, Legal-Trac, LEXIS, Matthew Bender, NEXIS, OCLC First Search, and WESTLAW are available to law students for research. Special library collections include a U.S. government documents depository. Recently, the library moved to a 43,000-square-foot facility, the Worrell Professional Center. It contains 438 student carrels and employs a wireless network. The ratio of library volumes to faculty is 10,756 to 1 and to students is 902 to 1. The ratio of seats in the library to students is 1 to 1.

Faculty
The law school has 39 full-time and 18 part-time faculty members, of whom 19 are women. According to AAUP standards for Category IIA institutions, faculty salaries are well above average. The ratio of full-time students to full-time faculty in an average class is 10 to 1; in a clinic, 10 to 1. The law school has a regular program of bringing visiting professors and other distinguished lecturers and visitors to campus. There is a chapter of the Order of the Coif.

Students
About 42% of the student body are women; 20%, minorities; 8%, African American; 2%, Asian American; and 2%, Hispanic. The majority of students come from the Northeast (30%) and South (30%). The average age of entering students is 24; age range is 20 to 47. About 50% of students enter directly from undergraduate school, 50% have a graduate degree, and 50% have worked full-time prior to entering law school. About 3% drop out after the first year for academic or personal reasons; 94% remain to receive a law degree.

Placement

J.D.s awarded:	152
Services available through: a separate law school placement center	
Special features: The Career Services Office sponsors an Employment Fair that targets small North Carolina legal employers, the Southeastern Minority Job Fair, regional job fairs in Chicago, New York, Washington D.C., Texas, and Southern California.	
Full-time job interviews:	n/av
Summer job interviews:	n/av
Placement by graduation:	n/av
Placement within 9 months:	96% of class
Average starting salary:	$73,000 to $145,000
Areas of placement:	
Private practice 2-100	70%
Judicial clerkships	9%
Government	9%
Business/industry	6%
Academic	4%
Unknown	3%

School of Law

1700 College
Topeka, KS 66621

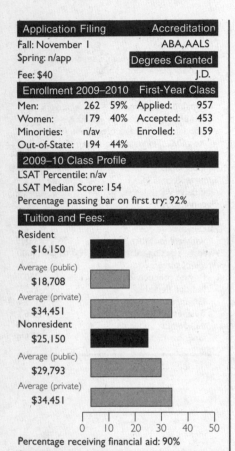

Application Filing	Accreditation
Fall: November 1	ABA, AALS
Spring: n/app	**Degrees Granted**
Fee: $40	J.D.

Enrollment 2009–2010		First-Year Class	
Men:	262 59%	Applied:	957
Women:	179 40%	Accepted:	453
Minorities:	n/av	Enrolled:	159
Out-of-State:	194 44%		

2009–10 Class Profile
LSAT Percentile: n/av
LSAT Median Score: 154
Percentage passing bar on first try: 92%

Tuition and Fees:

Resident
$16,150

Average (public)
$18,708

Average (private)
$34,451

Nonresident
$25,150

Average (public)
$29,793

Average (private)
$34,451

0 10 20 30 40 50

Percentage receiving financial aid: 90%

ADMISSIONS

In the fall 2009 first-year class, 957 applied, 453 were accepted, and 159 enrolled. Seven transfers enrolled. The median GPA of the most recent first-year class was 3.31.

Requirements

Applicants must have a bachelor's degree and take the LSAT. Credential evaluation is required for most foreign bachelor's degrees. The most important admission factors include LSAT results, GPA, and academic achievement. No specific undergraduate courses are required. Candidates are not interviewed.

Procedure

The application deadline for fall entry is November 1. Applicants should submit an application form, LSAT results, transcripts, a nonrefundable application fee of $40, 1 required, 2 or 3 are recommended letters of recommendation, and a personal statement plus a credential evaluation if for a foreign bachelor's degree. Notification of the admissions decision is November to May. The latest acceptable LSAT test date for fall entry is February. The law school uses the LSDAS.

Special

The law school recruits minority and disadvantaged students through CRS mailings; CLEO; law school forums in Chicago, Atlanta, Dallas, Houston and accompanying workshops; law fairs at many colleges and universities; events in conjunction with BLSA, HALSA, AALSA, and NALSA; scholarships (merit and need); through efforts with HBCU and Hispanic colleges and universities, and events cosponsored with LSAC for diversity outreach. Requirements are not different for out-of-state students. Transfer students must have one semester of credit, have a minimum GPA of 2.5, have attended an ABA-approved law school, and present a copy of the LSDAS report, official undergraduate degree transcript, a letter of good standing from the dean of the law school, an official transcript of law school grades, law school class rank, and 1 letter of recommendation from a law school professor. Preadmissions courses consist of an academic support program orientation held immediately prior to enrollment for admitted students. There are no provisional-admit summer courses.

Costs

Tuition and fees for the 2009-2010 academic year are $16,150 for full-time in-state students and $25,150 for out-of-state students. On-campus room and board costs about $8942 annually; books and supplies run $2005.

Financial Aid

About 90% of current law students receive some form of aid. The average annual amount of aid from all sources combined, including scholarships, loans, and work contracts, is $28,016. Awards are based on need and merit, along with federal loans up to $20,500, which have no need or merit base. Factors that could increase the total award amount include number of dependents and other unusual expenses. All admitted applicants are automatically considered for academic scholarships. Required financial statement is the FAFSA. The aid application deadline for fall entry is June 1. Special funds for minority or disadvantaged students include need and academic scholarships. First-year students are notified about their financial aid application at time of acceptance. Students are encouraged to apply for loans at the time of application. Academic and need scholarships are usually awarded shortly after admission.

About the Law School

Washburn University School of Law was established in 1903 and is a public institution. The 160-acre campus is in an urban area 60 miles west of Kansas City. The primary mission of the law school is to provide a foundation in the theory, doctrine,

and practice of law with a strong emphasis on professionalism in an atmosphere of cooperation and congeniality. Students have access to federal, state, county, city, and local agencies, courts, correctional facilities, law firms, and legal aid organizations in the Topeka area. The law school is located in the capital city of Kansas, providing students direct access to clerkship, internship, and externship experiences. The Kansas Judicial Center, Capitol , and state office complex are located only minutes from the law school, providing students unique opportunities to meet and interact with key community and state leaders. Facilities of special interest to law students include a 4-story library, 2 computer laboratories, high-speed wireless network throughout the building, group study rooms, individual study carrels, and a special collections room. The state-of-the-art courtroom is regularly used for state administrative law hearings and occasional sittings by the Kansas Court of Appeals and the U.S. Tenth Circuit Court of Appeals. Housing for students is available on campus, but most students live in the many reasonably priced houses and apartments near the campus. About 90% of the law school facilities are accessible to the physically disabled.

Calendar

The law school operates on a traditional semester basis. Courses for full-time students are offered both day and evening and must be completed within 7 years. There is no part-time program. New students are admitted in the fall. There are 2 6-week summer sessions. Transferable summer courses are offered.

Programs

The following joint degrees may be earned: J.D./M.B.A. (Juris Doctor/Master of Business Administration) and J.D./M.S.W. (Juris Doctor/Master of Social Work).

Required

To earn the J.D., candidates must complete 90 total credits, of which 44 are for required courses. They must maintain a minimum GPA of 2.0 in the required courses. The following first-year courses are required of all students: Civil Procedure I, Constitutional Law I, Contracts I and II, Criminal Law, Criminal Procedure, Property, and Torts. Required upper-level courses consist of a skills course, a writing requirement, an oral presentation requirement, Constitutional Law II, Evidence, Perspectives on Law course--students choose from 27 listed, Professional Responsibility, and Secured Transactions. The required orientation program for first-year students is 1 week and contains an intensive academic component as well as administrative and social events.

Phone: 785-670-1185
800-WASHLAW
Fax: 785-670-1120
E-mail: *admissions@washburnlaw.edu*
Web: *http://washburnlaw.edu*

Contact

Karla Whitaker, Director of Admissions, 785-670-1706 or 800-WASHLAW (800-927-4529) for general inquiries; Janessa Akin, Scholarships, 800-927-4529 for financial aid information.

KANSAS

Placement

J.D.s awarded:	148
Services available through: a separate law school placement center	
Services: presentations and panel discussions by employers, alumni, and practitioners (e.g., U.S. Attorney's Office, Judicial Clerkships, alternative careers, diversity issues)	
Special features: coordinated meetings with all first-year students; on-campus interview and resume collection service	
Full-time job interviews:	16 employers
Summer job interviews:	39 employers
Placement by graduation:	n/av
Placement within 9 months:	97% of class
Average starting salary:	$38,000 to $105,000
Areas of placement:	
Private practice 2-10 attorneys	28%
Private practice 11-50attorneys	4%
Private practice 51-100 + attorneys	5%
Solo practice	3%
Unknown practice	2%
Government	21%
Business/industry	13%
Judicial clerkships	9%
Public interest	9%
Military	2%
Academic	1%

Electives

Students must take 12 hours credits in their area of concentration. The School of Law offers concentrations in corporate law, environmental law, family law, international law, litigation, tax law, torts and insurance, certificates in tax law, family law, natural resources law, advocacy, estate planning, transactional law, ilnternational, and comparative law. In addition, Law Clinic may be taken as a one-semester elective for 4 to 5 credit hours by students with 60 or more credit hours and upon completion of prerequisite courses. In-house, live client opportunities exist in the areas of Family Law, Juvenile Law, Civil Law, Criminal Defense, Native American, and Transactional Law. A Directed Clinical Internship is available by permission for 1 to 3 credit hours after successful completion of Law Clinic. Clinical Internship is available by permission for 1 to 3 credit hours after successful completion of Law Clinic. Second- or third-year students may take seminars for 2 to 3 credit hours in areas such as civil liberties, civil rights, constitutional litigation, family law, negotiation and settlement, and natural resources. Informal internships (part-time professional librarian positions) may be available in the law library for those with an MLS degree working toward a J.D. Research may be done as a student option through the Advanced Legal Research course for 2 credit hours or Directed Research for 1 to 3 credit hours. Students who have completed one year of study are eligible to enroll in the Externship Program. This program enables students to work outside of the law school for course credit. Students may apply 2 to 4 hours of extership course credit toward graduation. Placements are available in the Kansas Legislature, state agencies, the Kansas Judiciary, and in corporations. Special lecture series include the Foulson and Siefkin LLP Law Journal Lecture Series. A 65-credit-hour summer program, with various courses in comparative law, is conducted at the University of the West Indiles in Barbados each year. A full semester program is also available at Maastricht University in the Netherlands. Every first-year student participates in a small study group facilited by an upper-division student. Groups meet weekly to collaborate on understanding their first-year course, write practice exams, and egage in other law school success-related activies. All prospective bar takers are invited to participate in a variety of bar preparation and bar exam practice programs. At risk second- and third- year students receive one-on-one help from the academic success program director and from a faculty member chosen by the student. Minority programs include active chapters of Black (BLSA), Asian (AALSA), Hispanic (HALSA), and Native American (NALSA), law student

associations; supporting institution of CLEO program; Women's Legal Forum; and Gay/Straight Legal Alliance. Special interest group programs are offered at the Business Transactional Law Center, Children and Family Law Center, Center for Excellence in Advocacy, and Center for Law and Government. The most widely taken electives are Business Associations, Civil Procedure II, and Decedents' Estates.

Graduation Requirements

In order to graduate, candidates must have a GPA of 2.0, have completed the upper-division writing requirement, and have completed upper-level oral presentation.

Organizations

The primary law review is the *Washburn Law Journal*. Students also solicit articles for and edit *The ABA Family Law Quarterly*. Students participate in numerous moot court competitions each year, including the Evan A. Evans Constitutional Moot Court Competition; Herbert Wechsler National Criminal Law Moot Court Competition; and the John J. Gibbons National Criminal Procedure Moot Court Competition. Other competitions include the Pace Environmental Law Competition, Dominick Gabriella National Family Law Competition, and J. Buberstein Bankruptcy. Law student organizations, local chapters of national associations, and campus clubs and organizations include The Washburn Association of Public Interest Lawyers, J. Reuben Clark Law Society, American Bar Association-Student Division, Veterans Legal Association of Washburn, Washburn Tax Law Society, Equal Justice Works, Phi Alpha Delta and Phi Delta Phi legal fraternities, and Washburn Law Volunteer Society.

Library

The law library contains 395,673 hardcopy volumes and 179,562 microform volume equivalents, and subscribes to 4093 serial publications. Such on-line databases and networks as CALI, CIS Universe, DIALOG, Infotrac, Legal-Trac, LEXIS, LOIS, Mathew Bender, NEXIS, OCLC First Search, WESTLAW, Wilsonline Indexes, http://washlaw.edu, Hein Online, Pacer, Marcive, Index Master, Gale Ready Reference Shelf, Foreign Law Guide, UN Treaty Collect, Access UN, and CCH Internet Research Network, serials solution, BNA's Law School Professional Information Center, and Making of Modern Law are available to law students for research. Special library collections include U.S. documents, Kansas documents, U.S. Supreme Court autographs, and U.S. Serial Set (digital). Recently, the library added study group rooms,

enhanced Wash Law, enhanced wireless network, added Encore library catalog, and expanded electronic research resources. The ratio of library volumes to faculty is 11,990 to 1 and to students is 897 to 1. The ratio of seats in the library to students is 1 to 1.

Faculty

The law school has 33 full-time and 51 part-time faculty members, of whom 33 are women. According to AAUP standards for Category IIA institutions, faculty salaries are below average. About 30% of full-time faculty have a graduate law degree in addition to the J.D. The ratio of full-time students to full-time faculty in an average class is 13 to 1; in a clinic, 8 to 1. The law school has a regular program of bringing visiting professors and other distinguished lecturers and visitors to campus.

Students

About 40% of the student body are women; 4%, African American; 3%, Asian American; 5%, Hispanic; and 2%, Native American. The majority of students come from Kansas (56%). The average age of entering students is 25; age range is 20 to 55. About 47% of students enter directly from undergraduate school and 8% have a graduate degree. About 4% drop out after the first year for academic or personal reasons; 94% remain to receive a law degree.

School of Law

Lewis Hall
Lexington, VA 24450

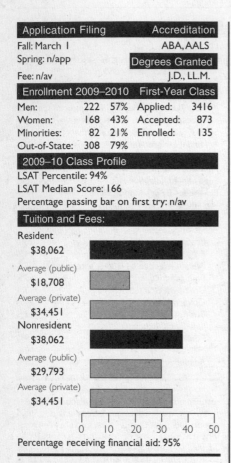

Application Filing		Accreditation	
Fall: March 1		ABA, AALS	
Spring: n/app		**Degrees Granted**	
Fee: n/av		J.D., LL.M.	
Enrollment 2009–2010		**First-Year Class**	
Men:	222 57%	Applied:	3416
Women:	168 43%	Accepted:	873
Minorities:	82 21%	Enrolled:	135
Out-of-State:	308 79%		

2009–10 Class Profile
LSAT Percentile: 94%
LSAT Median Score: 166
Percentage passing bar on first try: n/av

Tuition and Fees:

Resident
$38,062

Average (public)
$18,708

Average (private)
$34,451

Nonresident
$38,062

Average (public)
$29,793

Average (private)
$34,451

0 10 20 30 40 50

Percentage receiving financial aid: 95%

ADMISSIONS

In the fall 2009 first-year class, 3416 applied, 873 were accepted, and 135 enrolled. Eleven transfers enrolled. The median LSAT percentile of the most recent first-year class was 94; the median GPA was 3.53 on a scale of 4.0. The lowest LSAT percentile accepted was 44; the highest was 99.

Requirements

Applicants must have a bachelor's degree and take the LSAT. All factors of a candidate's background are considered important. No specific undergraduate courses are required. Candidates are interviewed.

Procedure

The application deadline for fall entry is March 1. Applicants should submit an application form, LSAT results, transcripts, and 2 letters of recommendation. Notification of the admissions decision is by April 1. The latest acceptable LSAT test date for fall entry is February. The law school uses the LSDAS.

Special

The law school recruits minority and disadvantaged students through regional law forums sponsored by LSDAS and college-sponsored forums, with interviews at institutions with a substantial proportion of minority students, and with direct mail. Requirements are not different for out-of-state students. Transfer students must have attended an ABA-approved law school.

Costs

Tuition and fees for the 2009-2010 academic year are $38,062 for all full-time students. On-campus room and board costs about $17,063 annually; books and supplies run $2000.

Financial Aid

About 95% of current law students receive some form of aid. The average annual amount of aid from all sources combined, including scholarships, loans, and work contracts, is $43,776; maximum, $57,102. Awards are based on need and merit. Required financial statement is the FAFSA. The aid application deadline for fall entry is February 15. First-year students are notified about their financial aid application at time of acceptance.

About the Law School

Washington and Lee University School of Law was established in 1849 and is a private institution. The 322-acre campus is in a small town 3 hours southwest of Washington, D.C. The primary mission of the law school is to provide a rigorous, writing-intensive, and personalized legal education to each student as preparation for the legal profession in an atmosphere of mutual respect, collegiality, and appreciation for each person's dignity, and to inculcate a sense of the responsibility placed on lawyers and the ethical obligations of law practice. Students have access to federal, state, county, city, and local agencies, courts, correctional facilities, law firms, and legal aid organizations in the Lexington area. Housing for students includes on-campus apartments adjacent to the law school building for single students, and private apartments, rooms, and houses in Lexington and the surrounding area. All law school facilities are accessible to the physically disabled.

Calendar

The law school operates on a traditional semester basis. Courses for full-time students are offered days only and must be completed within 6 semesters. There is no part-time program. New students are admitted in the fall. There is no summer session. Transferable summer courses are not offered.

Programs

In addition to the J.D., the law school offers the LL.M. The following joint degree may be earned: J.D./M.H.A. (Juris Doctor/Master of Health Administration).

Required

To earn the J.D., candidates must complete 85 total credits, of which 37 are for required courses. They must maintain a minimum GPA of 1.0 in the required courses. The following first-year courses are required of all students: American Public Law Process, Civil Procedure I and II, Contracts, Criminal Law, Legal Writing, Property, Torts, and Transnational Law. Required upper-level courses consist of Constitutional Law and Professional Responsibility. The required orientation program for first-year students is 3 days and includes social activities for the entire student body, introduction to the case method and case briefing techniques, introduction to legal research, an honor system orientation, and a university orientation.

Electives

Various clinics, open to second- and third-year students, provide direct service to miners seeking black lung benefits, to clients facing the death penalty, and to lower-income clients in the region. Credit ranges from 5 to 10 hours. Seminars, available to upper-level students, are worth 2 or 3 credits and are offered in a variety of areas. Upper-level students may perform internships with judges or prosecutors during the academic year for 5 to 10 graded credits or with government or nonprofit employers in the summer for 2 ungraded credits. Independent research projects may be undertaken by

Phone: 540-458-8503
Fax: 540-458-8586
E-mail: *lawadm@wlu.edu*
Web: *www.wlu.edu*

Contact

Andrea Hilton, Director of Admissions, 540-458-8503 for general inquiries; Cynthia Hintze, Assistant Director of Financial, 540-458-8032 for financial aid information.

VIRGINIA

second- or third-year students, for 1 to 2 ungraded credits. The Frances Lewis Law Center sponsors research fellowships for third-year students. Bain and Shepherd Fellowships provide stipends to support collaborative research projects between students and faculty. Special lecture series include the annual John Randolph Tucker Lecture and visiting lectures sponsored by the Frances Lewis Law Center and other law student organizations in areas of special interest to their members. The school offers no summer session but may accept credit for courses taken in programs offered by other ABA-approved law schools. The school offers exchange programs with Bucerius Law School in Hamburg, Germany; Trinity College Dublin in Dublin, Ireland; the University of Copenhagen in Denmark; and the University of Western Ontario in Ontario, Canada. Tutorials are offered to upperclass students in a variety of fields. The Academic Support Program offers a series of programs introducing the case method and legal analysis, and provides continuing academic support throughout the year. Special interest group programs include Women Law Students Organization, Black Law Students Association, Christian Legal Society, and Gay Law. The most widely taken electives are Federal Income Tax, Family Law, and Close Business Arrangements.

Graduation Requirements

In order to graduate, candidates must have a GPA of 2.0 and have completed the upper-division writing requirement.

Organizations

Students edit the *Washington and Lee Law Review, German Law Journal, Journal of Energy, Climate* and the *Environment, Journal of Civil Rights* and *Social Justice*, and the newspaper *Law News.* Moot court competitions include Robert J. Grey, Jr. Negotiation Competition, John W. Davis Moot Court, and Jessup International Law Moot Court. Other competitions include National Mock Trial, Client Counseling, Mediation, Negotiation, and Arbitration competitions. Law student organizations, local chapters of national associations, and campus organizations include American Constitution Society, Federalist Society, National Lawyers Guild, Environmental Law Society, Intellectual Property and Technology Law

Society, International Law Society, Public Interest Law Students Association, and Asian American Law Society.

Library

The law library contains 444,532 hardcopy volumes and 187,924 microform volume equivalents, and subscribes to 4086 serial publications. Such on-line databases and networks as CALI, CIS Universe, DIALOG, Dow-Jones, Infotrac, Legal-Trac, LEXIS, LOIS, Matthew Bender, NEXIS, OCLC First Search, RLIN, WESTLAW, Wilsonline Indexes, and CIS Serial Set are available to law students for research. Special library collections include the Bankruptcy Revision Act 1978 (committee papers), the John W. Davis Collection of Records and Briefs, the Impeachment of President Nixon (committee papers), and the Lewis F. Powell, Jr. Archives. The ratio of library volumes to faculty is 11,398 to 1 and to students is 1140 to 1. The ratio of seats in the library to students is 1 to 1.

Faculty

The law school has 39 full-time and 21 part-time faculty members, of whom 11 are women. According to AAUP standards for Category IIB institutions, faculty salaries are above average. About 27% of full-time faculty have a graduate law degree in addition to the J.D. The ratio of full-time students to full-time faculty in an average class is 10 to 1; in a clinic, 10 to 1. The law school has a regular program of bringing visiting professors and other distinguished lecturers and visitors to campus. There is a chapter of the Order of the Coif; 38 faculty and 348 graduates are members.

Students

About 43% of the student body are women; 21%, minorities; 9%, African American; 6%, Asian American; 4%, Hispanic; 2%, Native American; and 1%, multiracial. The majority of students come from the South (34%). The average age of entering students is 24; age range is 19 to 34. About 50% of students enter directly from undergraduate school, 4% have a graduate degree, and 55% have worked full-time prior to entering law school. About 1% drop out after the first year for academic or personal reasons; 99% remain to receive a law degree.

Placement

J.D.s awarded:	138

Services available through: a separate law school placement center

Services: advice on networking, and programs on specific practice areas, (e.g., corporate law, small firms, prosecution)

Special features: one-on-one work with students on resumes, cover letters, job search advice; preparation for practice program, mock interviews with alumni and faculty; interviews via videoconferencing; job fairs in New York, Chicago, Atlanta, Dallas, Boston, and Southern California

Full-time job interviews:	94 employers
Summer job interviews:	n/av
Placement by graduation:	83% of class
Placement within 9 months:	91% of class
Average starting salary:	$12,000 to $160,000

Areas of placement:

Private practice 2-10 attorneys	6%
Private practice 11-25 attorneys	3%
Private practice 26-50 attorneys	5%
Private practice 51-100 attorneys	6%
Private practice 101+ attorneys	37%
Judicial clerkships	20%
Government	9%
Business/industry	7%
Public interest	6%
Academic	1%

WASHINGTON UNIVERSITY IN ST. LOUIS

School of Law

Box 1120, One Brookings Drive
St. Louis, MO 63130

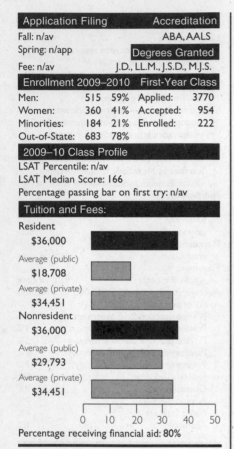

Application Filing		Accreditation	
Fall: n/av		ABA, AALS	
Spring: n/app		**Degrees Granted**	
Fee: n/av		J.D., LL.M., J.S.D., M.J.S.	

Enrollment 2009–2010		First-Year Class	
Men:	515	59%	Applied:	3770
Women:	360	41%	Accepted:	954
Minorities:	184	21%	Enrolled:	222
Out-of-State:	683	78%		

2009–10 Class Profile
LSAT Percentile: n/av
LSAT Median Score: 166
Percentage passing bar on first try: n/av

Tuition and Fees:

Resident
$36,000

Average (public)
$18,708

Average (private)
$34,451

Nonresident
$36,000

Average (public)
$29,793

Average (private)
$34,451

0 10 20 30 40 50

Percentage receiving financial aid: 80%

ADMISSIONS

In a recent year, 3770 applied, 954 were accepted, and 222 enrolled. Fifty-four transfers enrolled. The median GPA of the most recent first-year class was 3.6. The lowest LSAT percentile accepted was 50; the highest was 99. Figures in the above capsule and in this profile are approximate.

Requirements
Applicants must have a bachelor's degree and take the LSAT. Minimum acceptable GPA is 2.0 on a scale of 4.0. The most important admission factors include LSAT results, GPA, and academic achievement. No specific undergraduate courses are required. Candidates are not interviewed.

Procedure
Applicants should submit an application form, LSAT results, 2 letters are recommended, and a personal statement. Notification of the admissions decision is by April. The latest acceptable LSAT test

date for fall entry is February. The law school uses the LSDAS. Check with the school for application deadlines.

Special
The law school recruits minority and disadvantaged students by means of a minority admissions counselor, specific mailings, scholarship programs, and visitation programs. Requirements are not different for out-of-state students. Transfer students must have one year of credit and have attended an ABA-approved law school.

Costs

Tuition and fees for the 2009-2010 academic year are approximately $36,000 for all full-time students. Books and supplies run approximately $2000.

Financial Aid

In a recent year, about 80% of current law students received some form of aid. The average annual amount of aid from all sources combined, including scholarships, loans, and work contracts, was approximately $42,000; maximum, $51,000. Awards are based on merit along with Scholarships are based on merit; loans are based on need. Required financial statement is the FAFSA. Special funds for minority or disadvantaged students include the Farmer Scholarship and the Chancellor's Fellowship. First-year students are notified about their financial aid application at between the time of acceptance and enrollment. Check with the school for application deadline.

About the Law School

Washington University in St. Louis School of Law was established in 1867 and is a private institution. The 160-acre campus is in a suburban area in St. Louis. The primary mission of the law school is to provide an enduring foundation of legal education that is useful for whatever field of law is chosen. Students have access to federal, state, county, city, and local agencies, courts, correctional facilities, law firms, and legal aid organizations in the St. Louis area. Students have access to a congressional clinic and a federal administrative agency clinic in Washington, D.C. Facilities of special interest to law students include St. Louis-based national

and international corporations. Housing for students is available in surrounding neighborhoods; listings are available through an off-campus referral service. About 90% of the law school facilities are accessible to the physically disabled.

Calendar

The law school operates on a traditional semester basis. Courses for full-time students are offered days only. There is no part-time program. New students are admitted in the fall. There is a 5-week summer session. Transferable summer courses are offered.

Programs

In addition to the J.D., the law school offers the LL.M. and J.S.D., M.J.S. Students may take relevant courses in other programs and apply credit toward the J.D.; a maximum of 9 credits may be applied. The following joint degrees may be earned: J.D./M.A. (Juris Doctor/Master of Arts in East Asian studies, political s), J.D./M.B.A. (Juris Doctor/Master of Business Administration), J.D./M.H.A. (Juris Doctor/Master of Health Administration), J.D./M.S.W. (Juris Doctor/Master of Social Work), and J.D./Ph.D. (Juris Doctor/Doctor of political science).

Required
To earn the J.D., candidates must complete 85 total credits, of which 35 are for required courses. They must maintain a minimum GPA of 79.0 in the required courses. The following first-year courses are required of all students: Civil Procedure, Constitutional Law I, Contracts, Criminal Law, Legal Research and Writing, Property, and Torts. Required upper-level courses consist of 1 additional writing seminar and Professional Responsibility-Legal Profession. The required orientation program for first-year students runs for 5 days and focuses on academic, social, and administrative components of the school.

Electives
The School of Law offers concentrations in corporate law, criminal law, environmental law, family law, international law, labor law, litigation, securities law, tax law, torts and insurance, and transactional (planning and drafting) courses.

Phone: 314-935-4525
Fax: 314-935-8778
E-mail: *admiss@wulaw.wustl.edu*
Web: *law.wustl.edu*

Contact

Admissions Office, 314-935-4525 for general inquiries; Associate Director, 314-935-4605 for financial aid information.

In addition, clinics are offered for 3 to 10 credit hours, including Congressional Clinic in Washington, D.C.; Civil Justice Clinic, and Interdisciplinary Environmental Clinic. Seminars include White Collar Crime Seminar, Biomedical Research Law and Policy Seminar, and Racial Profiling Seminar. Students may participate in research programs after the first year. Field work is performed as part of the clinics; 9 clinics are offered. Special lectures include the Tyrrell Williams Memorial Lectures and the Public Interest Speakers Series. Students may study abroad in Germany, London, South Africa, Netherlands, and Singapore. Tutorial programs are available on an individual basis. The Black Law Students Association organizes student study groups and visiting minority speakers. The most widely taken electives are Evidence, Corporations, and Federal Income Tax.

Graduation Requirements

In order to graduate, candidates must have a GPA of 79.0, and have completed the upper-division writing requirement.

Organizations

Students edit *The Washington University Law Quarterly, Journal of Law and Policy*, and the *Global Studies Law Review*. The student newspaper is *The Devil's Advocate*. Moot court competitions include the Wiley Rutledge Moot Court program held in the fall and spring, Environmental Moot Court, and the Jessup International Law Moot Court. Other competitions include National Mock Trial, Intellectual Property Moot Court, National Client Counseling, Negotiation, and Intramural Client Counseling. Student organizations include the Student Bar Association, Environmental Law Society, and International Law Society. The Federalist Society, Phi Alpha Delta, and Phi Delta Phi have local chapters. There are numerous other campus organizations.

Library

The law library contains 660,000 hardcopy volumes and 1,389,966 microform volume equivalents, and subscribes to 6074 serial publications. Such on-line databases and networks as CALI, CIS Universe, DIALOG, Infotrac, Legal-Trac, LEXIS, LOIS, NEXIS, OCLC First Search, WEST-LAW, Wilsonline Indexes, and Index to Foreign Legal Periodicals, LawInfoChina, BNA Core Plus Package, 3 CCH Internet Research Network Libraries, Aspen Treatises Online, Oceana Constitutions of the World, more than 30 other legal information databases plus access to more than 100 interdisciplinary databases through the Olin Library System. are available to law students for research. Special library collections include a depository for Federal and Missouri government documents, and Chinese and Japanese law collections. Recently, the library added Web-based subscriptions and wireless network access, and constructed additional group study room. The ratio of library volumes to faculty is 12,222 to 1 and to students is 761 to 1. The ratio of seats in the library to students is 1 to 1.

Faculty

The law school has 54 full-time and 107 part-time faculty members, of whom 56 are women. According to AAUP standards for Category I institutions, faculty salaries are above average. About 21% of full-time faculty have a graduate law degree in addition to the J.D.; about 17% of part-time faculty have one. The ratio of full-time students to full-time faculty in an average class is 14 to 1; in a clinic, 8 to 1. The law school has a regular program of bringing visiting professors and other distinguished lecturers and visitors to campus. There is a chapter of the Order of the Coif.

Students

About 41% of the student body are women; 21%, minorities; 10%, African American; 7%, Asian American; 2%, Hispanic; and 1%, Native American. The majority of students come from the Midwest (24%). The average age of entering students is 23; age range is 21 to 34. About 35% of students enter directly from undergraduate school, 11% have a graduate degree, and 52% have worked full-time prior to entering law school. About 6% drop out after the first year for academic or personal reasons; 93% remain to receive a law degree.

Placement

J.D.s awarded:	n/av
Services available through: a separate law school placement center	
Services: videoconferencing for individual interviews, networking receptions, extensive programming, job fairs	
Special features: personalized services of 4 professionals who experienced in the legal field.	
Full-time job interviews:	125 employers
Summer job interviews:	125 employers
Placement by graduation:	86% of class
Placement within 9 months:	99% of class
Average starting salary:	$30,000 to $125,000
Areas of placement:	
Private practice 2-10 attorneys	4%
Private practice 11-25 attorneys	8%
Private practice 26-50 attorneys	12%
Private practice 51-100 attorneys	9%
Private practice 100+ attorneys	30%
Government	16%
Judicial clerkships	9%
Business/industry	5%
Public interest	5%
Military	1%
Academic	1%

Law School

471 West Palmer Street
Detroit, MI 48202

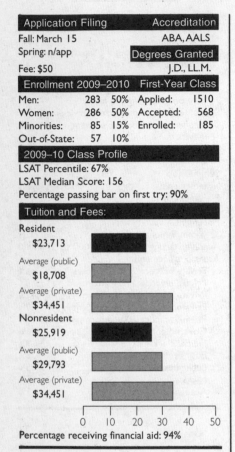

Application Filing			Accreditation	
Fall: March 15			ABA, AALS	
Spring: n/app			**Degrees Granted**	
Fee: $50			J.D., LL.M.	

Enrollment 2009–2010			First-Year Class	
Men:	283	50%	Applied:	1510
Women:	286	50%	Accepted:	568
Minorities:	85	15%	Enrolled:	185
Out-of-State:	57	10%		

2009–10 Class Profile
LSAT Percentile: 67%
LSAT Median Score: 156
Percentage passing bar on first try: 90%

Tuition and Fees:

Resident
$23,713

Average (public)
$18,708

Average (private)
$34,451

Nonresident
$25,919

Average (public)
$29,793

Average (private)
$34,451

0 10 20 30 40 50

Percentage receiving financial aid: 94%

ADMISSIONS

In the fall 2009 first-year class, 1510 applied, 568 were accepted, and 185 enrolled. Four transfers enrolled. The median LSAT percentile of the most recent first-year class was 67; the median GPA was 3.51 on a scale of 4.0. The lowest LSAT percentile accepted was 35; the highest was 95.

Requirements
Applicants must have a bachelor's degree and take the LSAT. The most important admission factors include LSAT results, GPA, and letter of recommendation. No specific undergraduate courses are required. Candidates are not interviewed.

Procedure
The application deadline for fall entry is March 15. Applicants should submit an application form, LSAT results, transcripts, a personal statement, a nonrefundable application fee of $50, and 2 letters of recommendation. Notification

of the admissions decision is on a rolling basis. The latest acceptable LSAT test date for fall entry is February. The law school uses the LSDAS.

Special
The law school recruits minority and disadvantaged students by hosting Diversity Law Day, recruiting at historically black colleges and universities and at Hispanic service institutions, and participating in the lSAC Discover Law Program. Requirements are not different for out-of-state students. Transfer students must have 1 year of credit, have attended an ABA-approved law school, have official transcripts sent from their current law school and their undergraduate institution, submit a letter of good standing from the dean, and submit a copy of the LSDAS report.

Costs

Tuition and fees for the 2009-2010 academic year are $23,713 for full-time in-state students and $25,919 for out-of-state students. Tuition for part-time students is $12,815 in-state and $13,992 out-of-state. On-campus room and board costs about $8170 annually; books and supplies run $1240.

Financial Aid

About 94% of current law students receive some form of aid. The average annual amount of aid from all sources combined, including scholarships, loans, and work contracts, is $30,110; maximum, $65,861. Awards are based on need and merit. Required financial statement is the FAFSA. The aid application deadline for fall entry is June 30. First-year students are notified about their financial aid application at the time of acceptance in most cases.

About the Law School

Wayne State University Law School was established in 1927 and is a public institution. The campus is in an urban area in Detroit. The primary mission of the law school is to promote excellence in teaching, and scholarly research, and provide service to the community, the bench, and the bar. Students have access to federal, state, county, city, and local agencies, courts, correctional facilities, law

firms, and legal aid organizations in the Detroit area. Facilities of special interest to law students consists of 3 connected buildings, which house classrooms, seminar rooms, a moot court room, the law library, offices for faculty and student groups, a student lounge, and a 250-seat auditorium that can be used as either a trial or appellate courtroom. Classrooms are set up for multimedia presentations, and a wireless Internet access is available throughout. The top floor of a residence hall is reserved for law students. Other housing is available on and nearby the campus and throughout the metropolitan area. All law school facilities are accessible to the physically disabled.

Calendar

The law school operates on a traditional semester basis. Courses for full-time students are offered both day and evening and must be completed within 5 years. For part-time students, courses are offered both day and evening and must be completed within 6 years. New full- and part-time students are admitted in the fall. There is a 6 1/2-week summer session. Transferable summer courses are offered.

Programs

In addition to the J.D., the law school offers the LL.M. Students may take relevant courses in other programs and apply credit toward the J.D.; a maximum of 16 credits may be applied. The following joint degrees may be earned: J.D./M.A. (Juris Doctor/Master of Arts in history, economics, political science, and dispute resolution) and J.D./M.B.A. (Juris Doctor/Master of Business Administration).

Required
To earn the J.D., candidates must complete 86 total credits, of which 35 are for required courses. They must maintain a minimum GPA of 2.0 in the required courses. The following first-year courses are required of all students: Civil Procedure A, Constitutional Law I, Contracts, Criminal Law, Legal Research and Writing, Property, The Regulatory State, and Torts. Required upper-level courses consist of Civil Procedure B and Professional Responsibility and the Legal Profession. The required orientation program for first-year students is a 3-day program introducing sources of law and the struc-

Phone: 313-577-3937
Fax: 313-993-8129
E-mail: emjackson@wayne.edu
Web: www.law.wayne.edu

Contact

Ericka M. Jackson, Assistant Dean of Admissions, 313-577-3937 for general inquiries; Karen Fulford, Assistant Director of Financial Aid, 313-577-5142 for financial aid information.

ture of the court system; the development of the law through the common law process; the relationship between statues and case law; reading, analyzing, and synthesizing case law; citation to provide authority and attribution; and professionalism.

Electives

In addition, The law school offers a concentration in commercial law. Clinical experience is offered through a range of clinics, including the Child Advocacy Clinic, Disablility Law Clinic, and the Criminal Appellate Practice Program. There are 20 to 25 seminars. Second- and third-year students may receive 1 to 3 credits through internships with distinguished judges and a variety of governmental and nonprofit agencies. Special lecture series include the I. Goodman Cohen Lecture in Trial Advocacy, Driker Forum for Excellence in the Law, Biennial Keith Lecture, and Bernard Gottfried Memorial Labor Law Symposium. There are summer exchange programs in England, and the Netherlands. The Intellectual Property Law Institute, a consortium with 2 local law schools, offers additional intellectual property courses to law students. The most widely taken electives are Evidence, Corporations, and Trusts and Estates.

Graduation Requirements

In order to graduate, candidates must have a GPA of 2.0 and have completed the upper-division writing requirement.

Organizations

Students edit the *The Wayne State Law Review*, *The Journal of Law in Society*, and the newspaper *The Advocate*. Moot court competitions include the New York City Bar National Moot Court, and Jessup International Moot Court Competitions. Law student organizations include Student Board of Governors, Black Law Students Association, and Sports and Entertainment Law Society. There are local chapters of national Lawyers Guild, the Federalist Society, and Phi Delta. Other organizations include the St. Thomas More Society, the Outlaws, and the Wayne Intellectual Property Student Association.

Library

The law library contains 627,452 hardcopy volumes and 224,071 microform volume equivalents, and subscribes to 5059 serial publications. Such on-line databases and networks as CALI, CIS Universe, DIALOG, Dow-Jones, Infotrac, Legal-Trac, LEXIS, Mathew Bender, NEXIS, OCLC First Search, WESTLAW, Wilsonline Indexes, Access UN, BNA, CCH Intelliconnect, CIAO, CQ Researcher, Ebrary, EISIL, HeinOnline, IBFD, JSTOR, LSN, LLMC Digital, MOML, PACER, and RIA Checkpoint are available to law students for research. Special library collections include a U.S. government document depository, Michigan Supreme Court records and briefs, Michigan Probate Court opinions, and Michigan Superfund Sites Collection. Recently, the library upgraded all computer lab computers, added a new network printer, and improved wireless connectivity. The ratio of library volumes to faculty is 14,592 to 1 and to students is 1103 to 1. The ratio of seats in the library to students is 1 to 6.

Faculty

The law school has 43 full-time and 24 part-time faculty members, of whom 23 are women. According to AAUP standards for Category 1 institutions, faculty salaries are below average. About 23% of full-time faculty have a graduate law degree in addition to the J.D.; about 7% of part-time faculty have one. The ratio of full-time students to full-time faculty in an average class is 26 to 1; in a clinic, 6 to 1. The law school has a regular program of bringing visiting professors and other distinguished lecturers and visitors to campus. There is a chapter of the Order of the Coif; 36 faculty and 700 graduates are members.

Students

About 50% of the student body are women; 15%, minorities; 8%, African American; 4%, Asian American; 2%, Hispanic; and 1%, Native American. The majority of students come from Michigan (90%). The average age of entering students is 25; age range is 20 to 46. About 46% of students enter directly from undergraduate school. About 4% drop out after the first year for academic or personal reasons; 96% remain to receive a law degree.

Placement

J.D.s awarded:	184
Services available through: a separate law school placement center	
Services: a full placement service that provides career counseling	
Special features: Students are offered free use of fax, photocopier, and telephone.	
Full-time job interviews:	63 employers
Summer job interviews:	63 employers
Placement by graduation:	n/av
Placement within 9 months:	88% of class
Average starting salary:	$24,000 to $125,000
Areas of placement:	
Private practice 2-10 attorneys	35%
Private practice 11-25 attorneys	7%
Private practice 26-50 attorneys	9%
Private practice 51-100 attorneys	3%
Business/industry	13%
101-250 Attorney firms	9%
Government	4%
Judicial clerkships	3%
Public interest	3%
Academic	2%

WEST VIRGINIA UNIVERSITY
College of Law

P.O. Box 6130
Morgantown, WV 26506

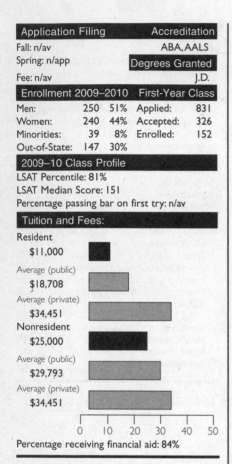

Application Filing	Accreditation
Fall: n/av	ABA, AALS
Spring: n/app	Degrees Granted
Fee: n/av	J.D.

Enrollment 2009–2010		First-Year Class	
Men:	250 51%	Applied:	831
Women:	240 44%	Accepted:	326
Minorities:	39 8%	Enrolled:	152
Out-of-State:	147 30%		

2009–10 Class Profile
LSAT Percentile: 81%
LSAT Median Score: 151
Percentage passing bar on first try: n/av

Tuition and Fees:

Resident
$11,000

Average (public)
$18,708

Average (private)
$34,451

Nonresident
$25,000

Average (public)
$29,793

Average (private)
$34,451

Percentage receiving financial aid: 84%

ADMISSIONS
In the fall 2009 first-year class, 831 applied, 326 were accepted, and 152 enrolled. Figures in the above capsule and in this profile are approximate. Ten transfers enrolled in a recent year. The median LSAT percentile of the most recent first-year class was 81; the median GPA was 3.51 on a scale of 4.0. The lowest LSAT percentile accepted was 9; the highest was 98.

Requirements
Applicants must have a bachelor's degree and take the LSAT. The most important admission factors include LSAT results, academic achievement, and GPA. No specific undergraduate courses are required. Candidates are not interviewed.

Procedure
Applicants should submit an application form, LSAT results, transcripts, (submitted by LSDAS), 3 letters of recommendation, and a personal statement.

Notification of the admissions decision is on a rolling basis. Check with the school for current application deadlines. The law school uses the LSDAS.

Special
The law school recruits minority and disadvantaged students through mailings, Minority Law Day, forums, and personal contacts from the school's Graduate Assistant for Minority Recruitment. Requirements are different for out-of-state students in that preference is given to West Virginia residents. Transfer students must have one year of credit, have a minimum GPA of 2.5, and have attended an ABA-approved law school.

Costs
Tuition and fees for the 2009-2010 academic year are $11,000 for full-time in-state students and $25,000 for out-of-state students. Books and supplies run $1100.

Financial Aid
In a recent year about 84% of current law students received some form of aid. The average annual amount of aid from all sources combined, including scholarships, loans, and work contracts, was $13,743; maximum, $23,291. Awards are based on need and merit. Required financial statement is the FAFSA. Check with the school for current application deadlines. The aid application deadline for fall entry is March 1. Special funds for minority or disadvantaged students include scholarships, and vocational-rehabilitation is offered to disabled and disadvantaged students. First-year students are notified about their financial aid application at the time of application.

About the Law School
West Virginia University College of Law was established in 1878 and is a public institution. The 1000-acre campus is in a small town 77 miles south of Pittsburgh, Pennsylvania. The primary mission of the law school is to prepare students for the practice of law and for public leadership through a curriculum that stresses basic legal principles, lawyering skills, and the responsibilities of the legal profession. Students have access to federal, state, county, city, and local agencies, courts, correctional facilities, law firms, and legal

aid organizations in the Morgantown area. Facilities of special interest to law students are the Leo Carlin Computer Laboratory; the Marlyn E. Lugar Courtroom, a combination courtroom-auditorium; a mini-courtroom; 3 conference-seminar rooms; 1 large courtroom; the law library; the Meredith Career Services Center with placement interview rooms; a student lounge; and a child-care cooperative. Housing for students is available for both single and married students. The university housing office helps students find off-campus housing. All law school facilities are accessible to the physically disabled.

Calendar
The law school operates on a traditional semester basis. Courses for full-time students are offered days only and must be completed within 6 years. For part-time students, courses are offered days only and must be completed within 6 years. New full- and part-time students are admitted in the fall. There is no summer session. Transferable summer courses are not offered.

Programs
The following joint degrees may be earned: J.D./M.B.A. (Juris Doctor/Master of Business Administration) and J.D./M.P.A. (Juris Doctor/Master of Public Administration).

Required
To earn the J.D., candidates must complete 91 total credits, of which 37 are for required courses. They must maintain a minimum GPA of 2.0 in the required courses. The following first-year courses are required of all students: Civil Procedure Jurisdiction, Civil Procedure Rules, Constitutional Law, Contracts I, Criminal Law, Legal Research and Writing I and II, Professional Responsibility, Property I, and Torts. Required upper-level courses consist of 2 perspective courses, a seminar, Appellate Advocacy, and Trial advocacy, clinic, business drafting, *or* a judicial externship. The required orientation program for first-year students is a 2-1/2-day program featuring large group discussion and mini classes covering introduction to legal analysis, legal writing, note taking, class participation, and law school exam taking; student panels on first-year life; and presentation about services avail-

Phone: 304-293-5304
Fax: 304-293-6891
E-mail: wvulaw.Admissions@mail.wvu.edu
Web: wvu.edu/~law/

Contact
Admissions Office, 304-293-5304 for general inquiries; Joanna Hastings, Financial Counselor, 304-293-5302 for financial aid information.

WEST VIRGINIA

able to law students including counseling, financial aid information, and a computer workshop for interested students. During the first semester there are 3 one hour programs: state bar license, class preparation and final exam taking. There is also a picnic with upper-class students and faculty, at which families are welcome.

Electives
Although the College of Law school has no concentrations, it has a full curriculum in all subjects except juvenile law and maritime law. In addition, approved upper-class students may earn 14 credit hours in a civil legal clinic. There is also an immigration clinic for 5 credit hours. The most widely taken electives are Business Organizations, Evidence, and Advanced Property.

Graduation Requirements
In order to graduate, candidates must have a GPA of 2.0, have completed the upper-division writing requirement, and must satisfactorily complete all first-year requirements, the seminar and the perspectives course requirements, and the capstone/practicum requirement.

Organizations
Students edit the *West Virginia Law Review*, the fourth oldest legal journal in the United States; the *Journal of College and University Law* in conjunction with the National Association of College and University Attorneys; and the newspaper *On-Point*. Moot court competitions include the Moot Court Board, Baker Cup Competition, held annually; Marlyn E. Lugar Trial Association Mock Trial Competition, held 4 times per year; and Gourley Cup Trial Competition. The College of Law sends 2-to 6-person teams to 5 outside appellate advocacy competitions and 2-to 5-person teams to several outside trial advocacy competitions. Law student organizations, local chapters of national associations, and campus clubs and organizations include the Black Law Students Association, Women's Law Caucus, Public Interest Advocates, Environmental Law Society, Labor and Employment Law Association, Student Bar Association, National Lawyers Guild, Energy Law Club, and Phi Delta Phi.

Library
The law library contains 347,393 hardcopy volumes and 550,200 microform volume equivalents, and subscribes to 1070 serial publications. Such on-line databases and networks as CALI, CIS Universe, Legal-Trac, LEXIS, LOIS, NEXIS, OCLC First Search, WESTLAW, and Wilsonline Indexes are available to law students for research. Special library collections include a rare book room. Recently, the library purchased 42 Dell Pentium 4 computers to replace all of the research work stations in the library. The ratio of library volumes to faculty is 18,284 to 1 and to students is 734 to 1. The ratio of seats in the library to students is 1 to 2.

Faculty
The law school has 19 full-time and 21 part-time faculty members, of whom 12 are women. According to AAUP standards for Category I institutions, faculty salaries are well below average. About 80% of full-time faculty have a graduate law degree in addition to the J.D. The ratio of full-time students to full-time faculty in an average class is 18 to 1; in a clinic, 10 to 1. The law school has a regular program of bringing visiting professors and other distinguished lecturers and visitors to campus. There is a chapter of the Order of the Coif; 4 faculty are members.

Students
About 44% of the student body are women; 8%, minorities; 5%, African American; 2%, Asian American; 1%, Hispanic; and 1%, Native American. The majority of students come from the Northeast (87%). The average age of entering students is 26; age range is 21 to 68. About 82% of students enter directly from undergraduate school, 8% have a graduate degree, and 6% have worked full-time prior to entering law school. About 1% drop out after the first year for academic or personal reasons; 99% remain to receive a law degree.

Placement

J.D.s awarded:	n/av
Services available through: a separate law school placement center and the university placement center	
Services: workshops on interviewing, resume writing, alternative jobs, working in a small firm, finding a judicial clerkship.	
Special features: The college has a close working relationship with the West Virginia State Bar.	
Full-time job interviews:	25 employers
Summer job interviews:	30 employers
Placement by graduation:	67% of class
Placement within 9 months:	88% of class
Average starting salary:	$45,000 to $110,000
Areas of placement:	
Private practice 2-10 attorneys	37%
Private practice 11-25 attorneys	14%
Private practice 26-50 attorneys	7%
Private practice 51-100 attorneys	10%
Judicial clerkships	18%
Government	8%
Business/industry	5%
Military	2%
Public interest	1%

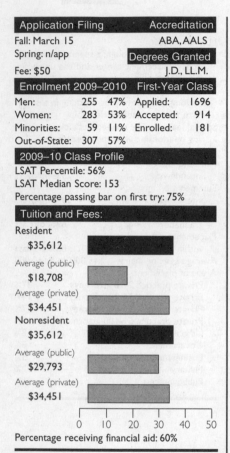

Application Filing		Accreditation	
Fall: March 15		ABA, AALS	
Spring: n/app		**Degrees Granted**	
Fee: $50		J.D., LL.M.	
Enrollment 2009–2010		**First-Year Class**	
Men:	255 47%	Applied:	1696
Women:	283 53%	Accepted:	914
Minorities:	59 11%	Enrolled:	181
Out-of-State:	307 57%		

2009–10 Class Profile

LSAT Percentile: 56%
LSAT Median Score: 153
Percentage passing bar on first try: 75%

Tuition and Fees:

Resident
$35,612

Average (public)
$18,708

Average (private)
$34,451

Nonresident
$35,612

Average (public)
$29,793

Average (private)
$34,451

Percentage receiving financial aid: 60%

ADMISSIONS

In the fall 2009 first-year class, 1696 applied, 914 were accepted, and 181 enrolled. One transfer enrolled. The median LSAT percentile of the most recent first-year class was 56; the median GPA was 3.23 on a scale of 4.0. The lowest LSAT percentile accepted was 33; the highest was 95.

Requirements

Applicants must have a bachelor's degree and take the LSAT. The most important admission factors include academic achievement, life experience, and character, personality. No specific undergraduate courses are required. Candidates are not interviewed.

Procedure

The application deadline for fall entry is March 15. Applicants should submit an application form, LSAT results, transcripts, a personal statement, a nonrefundable application fee of $50, 2 letters of recommendation, and resume. Notification of the admissions decision is on a rolling basis. The latest acceptable LSAT test date for fall entry is June. The law school uses the LSDAS.

Special

The law school recruits minority and disadvantaged students by means of Law Services forums, attendance at historically black college recruiting events, mailings through the Candidate Referral Service, and scholarships. Requirements are not different for out-of-state students. Transfer students must have 1 year of credit.

Costs

Tuition and fees for the 2009-2010 academic year are $35,612 for all full-time students. Tuition for part-time students is $26,328 per year. Books and supplies run $1528.

Financial Aid

About 60% of current law students receive some form of aid. The average annual amount of aid from all sources combined, including scholarships, loans, and work contracts, is $16,519; maximum, $34,378. Awards are based on need and merit. Required financial statements are the FAFSA, the college financial aid application, and tax returns with W2 statements for returning law students. The aid application deadline for fall entry is rolling. Special funds for minority or disadvantaged students include awards to students who have overcome educational, cultural, economic, or physical barriers to achieve success at the undergraduate level. First-year students are notified about their financial aid application at time of acceptance on a rolling basis.

About the Law School

Western New England College School of Law was established in 1919 and is a private institution. The 215-acre campus is in a suburban area 25 miles north of Hartford, 90 miles west of Boston. The primary mission of the law school is to provide a practical and effective legal education in a humane and supportive environment, in which faculty and students work together in a rigorous yet rewarding educational process. Students have access to federal, state, county, city, and local agencies, courts, correctional facilities, law firms, and legal aid organizations in the Springfield area. Students have opportunities to work for federal and state judges, government agencies, and public interest organizations arranged through the internship program, or by individual students. Facilities of special interest to law students include a 490,000-volume law library that contains computer laboratories exclusively for student use; a moot court room used for law trial simulation classes, moot court competitions, and semiannual visits by the Massachusetts appeals court; and the Healthful Living Center, a state-of-the-art athletic and recreation facility. Housing for students is available in Springfield, which offers a variety of housing. There is limited on-campus housing for law students. All law school facilities are accessible to the physically disabled.

Calendar

The law school operates on a traditional semester basis. Courses for full-time students are offered both day and evening and must be completed within 4 years. For part-time students, courses are offered both day and evening and must be completed within 5 years. New full- and part-time students are admitted in the fall. There is a 7-week summer session. Transferable summer courses are offered.

Programs

In addition to the J.D., the law school offers the LL.M. The following joint degrees may be earned: J.D./M.B.A. (Juris Doctor/Master of Business Administration), J.D./M.R.P. (Juris Doctor/Master of Regional Planning), and J.D./M.S.W. (Juris Doctor/Master of Social Work).

Required

To earn the J.D., candidates must complete 88 total credits, of which 46 are for required courses. They must maintain a minimum GPA of 70.0 in the required courses. The following first-year courses are required of all students: Civil Procedure, Constitutional Law, Contracts, Criminal Law, Lawyering Process, Property, and Torts. Required upper-level courses consist of Business Organizations, Evidence, Income Tax, Legal Profession, Practical Skills Elective, and Qualified Writing Elective. The required orientation program for first-year students is a 3-day

Phone: 413-782-1406
800-782-6665
Fax: 413-796-2067
E-mail: admissions@law.wnec.edu
Web: www.law.wnec.edu

Contact

Associate Dean for External Affairs, 413-782-1406 or 800-782-6665 for general inquiries; Sandra Belanger, Financial Aid Specialist, 413-796-2080 for financial aid information.

MASSACHUSETTS

program at which students meet faculty members, administrators, and representatives of various student organizations and attend Lawyering Process Orientation sessions.

Electives

The School of Law offers concentrations in corporate law, criminal law, international law, public interest law, real estate, and estate planning. Upper-level students may enroll in the Legal Services Clinic for 6 credits, Criminal Law Clinic for 6 credits, the Consumer Protection Clinic for 4 credits, the Small Business Clinic for 4 credits, and the Real Estate Practicum for 4 credits. There are a number of limited enrollment upper-level courses offered in a broad range of subject areas. Each is a 3-credit course designed to satisfy the upper-class writing requirement. Internships are available with, among others, the Massachusetts State Attorney, Connecticut State Attorney, Western Massachusetts Legal Services, Federal Judicial, U.S. Attorney, and the Internal Revenue Service's Regional Counsel Office. In independent study programs, a student may engage in advanced legal research for 2 to 3 credits, under the supervision of 2 faculty members. Special lecture series include the Clason Lecture Series, events at the Legislative Institute, and a speaker series sponsored by the Law and Business Center for Advanced Entrepreneurship. Students may take summer programs offered by other ABA-accredited law schools. Students may study in tutorials with a faculty member on a mutually agreed upon subject and earn 1 to 3 credits. Remedial programs consist of a Legal Education Assistance Program, which is voluntary and available to all students. The goal of the program is to provide additional assistance in legal research, writing, reasoning, and examination-taking skills. The Multi-Cultural Law Students Association (MCLSA) provides support and mentoring. Special interest group programs include the ABA Tax Challenge. The most widely taken electives are Criminal Procedure: Investigation, Trusts and Estates, and Trial Methods.

Graduation Requirements

In order to graduate, candidates must have a GPA of 70.0 and have completed the upper-division writing requirement.

Organizations

Students edit the *Western New England Law Review and Lex Brevis*, the student newspaper. Annually, teams are sent to the National Moot Court, Jessup Moot Court International Law Competition, and Frederick Douglass Moot Court Competition. Other competitions include the ABA National Trial Competition and the ABA National Negotiation Competition. Law student organizations, local chapters of national associations, and campus organizations include the Multi-Cultural Law Students Association, Women's Law Association, and OUTlaw (Gay/Lesbian/Bisexual/Straight Alliance). Local chapters of national associations include Phi Alpha Delta, ABA-Law Student Division, and Equal Justice Works. Other organizations include International Law Society, Environmental Law Coalition, and Federalist Society.

Library

The law library contains 362,091 hardcopy volumes and 227,772 microform volume equivalents, and subscribes to 882 serial publications. Such on-line databases and networks as CALI, CIS Universe, DIALOG, Infotrac, Legal-Trac, LEXIS, LOIS, NEXIS, OCLC First Search, WESTLAW, and Wilsonline Indexes are available to law students for research. Special library collections include a selective federal government document depository, publications of Massachusetts Continuing Legal Education, Inc., and a law and popular culture, print, video, and audio collection. Recently, the library was extensively renovated and expanded. The ratio of library volumes to faculty is 9528 to 1 and to students is 673 to 1. The ratio of seats in the library to students is 1 to 2.

Faculty

The law school has 38 full-time and 36 part-time faculty members, of whom 22 are women. According to AAUP standards for Category IIA institutions, faculty salaries are above average. About 18% of full-time faculty have a graduate law degree in addition to the J.D.; about 5% of part-time faculty have one. The ratio of full-time students to full-time faculty in an average class is 18 to 1; in a clinic, 8 to 1. The law school has a regular program of bringing visiting professors and other distinguished lecturers and visitors to campus.

Placement

J.D.s awarded:	163

Services available through: a separate law school placement center

Services: advice on judicial clerkships, fellowships, LL.M. programs, alternative careers, and practice in various areas of the law

Special features: networking functions, videotaped individual mock interviews, various panels and workshops presented on conducting a job search and on career options, a weekly Career Services newsletter containing part- and full-time job listings for students and alumni, articles of interest, and notices of writing competitions, summer study, study abroad, fellowships, clerkships, and internships. The school is an active member of 2 law school placement consortia, 1 state and 1 regional.

Full-time job interviews:	7 employers
Summer job interviews:	11 employers
Placement by graduation:	n/av
Placement within 9 months:	87% of class
Average starting salary:	$20,000 to $120,000

Areas of placement:

Private practice 2-10 attorneys	21%
Private practice 11-25 attorneys	9%
Business/industry	17%
Judicial clerkships	16%
Government	10%
Public interest	8%
Academic	2%

Students

About 53% of the student body are women; 11%, minorities; 3%, African American; 5%, Asian American; and 4%, Hispanic. The majority of students come from the Northeast (59%). The average age of entering students is 25; age range is 20 to 46. About 48% of students enter directly from undergraduate school and 2% have a graduate degree. About 9% drop out after the first year for academic or personal reasons; 91% remain to receive a law degree.

WESTERN STATE UNIVERSITY

College of Law

1111 North State College Blvd
Fullerton, CA 92831

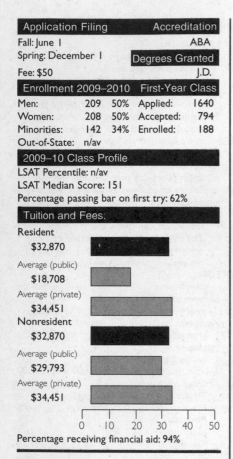

Application Filing		Accreditation
Fall: June 1		ABA
Spring: December 1		**Degrees Granted**
Fee: $50		J.D.

Enrollment 2009–2010			First-Year Class	
Men:	209	50%	Applied:	1640
Women:	208	50%	Accepted:	794
Minorities:	142	34%	Enrolled:	188
Out-of-State:	n/av			

2009–10 Class Profile
LSAT Percentile: n/av
LSAT Median Score: 151
Percentage passing bar on first try: 62%

Tuition and Fees:

Resident
$32,870

Average (public)
$18,708

Average (private)
$34,451

Nonresident
$32,870

Average (public)
$29,793

Average (private)
$34,451

0   10   20   30   40   50

Percentage receiving financial aid: 94%

ADMISSIONS
In the fall 2009 first-year class, 1640 applied, 794 were accepted, and 188 enrolled. Seven transfers enrolled. The median GPA of the most recent first-year class was 3.16.

Requirements
Applicants must have a bachelor's degree and take the LSAT. Minimum acceptable GPA is 2.3 on a scale of 4.0. The most important admission factors include LSAT results, GPA, and writing ability. No specific undergraduate courses are required. Candidates are interviewed.

Procedure
The application deadline for fall entry is June 1. Applicants should submit an application form, LSAT results, transcripts, a personal statement, a nonrefundable application fee of $50, and 2 letters of recommendation. Additional items are required for transfer and international applicants. Contact WSU for details. Noti-

fication of the admissions decision is 2 weeks after decision is made. The latest acceptable LSAT test date for fall entry is June. The law school uses the LSDAS.

Special
The law school recruits minority and disadvantaged students through diversity recruiting and scholarships. Requirements are not different for out-of-state students. Transfer students must have a minimum GPA of 2.3 and a letter of standing at an accredited law school.

Costs
Tuition and fees for the 2009-2010 academic year are $32,870 for all full-time students. Tuition for part-time students is $22,010 per year. Books and supplies run $1500.

Financial Aid
About 94% of current law students receive some form of aid. The average annual amount of aid from all sources combined, including scholarships, loans, and work contracts, is $34,775; maximum, $55,994. Awards are based on need and merit. Required financial statements are the FAFSA and an institutional application. The aid application deadline for fall entry is March 2. First-year students are notified about their financial aid application at time of acceptance.

About the Law School
Western State University College of Law was established in 1966 and is a private institution. The 4-acre campus is in a suburban area midway between Los Angeles and San Diego. The primary mission of the law school is to provide the highest quality legal education, based on an innovative program of studies designed to develop the tools of careful legal analysis and to foster a broad understanding of law, law practice, and legal theory. Students have access to federal, state, county, city, and local agencies, courts, correctional facilities, law firms, and legal aid organizations in the Fullerton area. Facilities of special interest to law students include county, state, city, and federal agencies, courts, correctional facilities, law firms, and legal aid organizations. Housing for students is widely available in a university environment adjacent to Western State and

California State University of Fullerton. About 98% of the law school facilities are accessible to the physically disabled.

Calendar
The law school operates on a traditional semester basis. Courses for full-time students are offered normally days only, with some electives offered in the evening, and must be completed within 5 years. For part-time students, courses are offered both day and evening and must be completed within 6 years. New full-time students are admitted in the fall; part-time, fall and spring. There is an 8-week summer session. Transferable summer courses are offered.

Programs

Required
To earn the J.D., candidates must complete 88 total credits, of which 72 are for required courses. They must maintain a minimum GPA of 2.0 in the required courses. The following first-year courses are required of all students: Civil Procedure I and II, Contracts I and II, Criminal Law, Criminial Procedure, Professional Skills I and II, and Torts I and II. Required upper-level courses consist of Advanced Professional Skills, Business Associations I and II, Community Property, Constitutional Law I and II, Estates, Evidence I and II, Federal Income Tax, Professional Responsibility, Property I and II, Remedies, and Sales. The required orientation program for first-year students is a 2 week program called Introduction to Legal Methods.

Electives
The College of Law offers concentrations in corporate law and criminal law. In addition, all students are eligible for Legal Clinic (5 credits) once prerequisites have been met. Research programs are available to all students for up to 3 credits. All students are eligible for externships (worth 5 to 8 credits) once prerequisites have been met. Study abroad is available to all students for a maximum of 6 credits. Non-credit tutorial and remedial programs are available to all students. There is a wide array of academic support programs available to all students.

Phone: 714-459-1101

800-978-4529

Fax: 714-441-1748

E-mail: adm@wsulaw.edu

Web: wsulaw.edu

Contact

Gloria Switzer, Assistant Dean of Admission, 714-459-1101 for general inquiries; Donna Espinoza, Director of Student Finance, 714-459-1120 for financial aid information.

Graduation Requirements

In order to graduate, candidates must have a GPA of 2.0, have completed the upper-division writing requirement, and an Advanced Professional Skills course for 6 credits and foundation law points.

Organizations

Students edit the *Western State University Law Review*. Moot Court competitions include the Roger J.Traynor California Moot Court Competition (sponsored by Witkin Institute), National Juvenile Law Moot Court Competition (Whitier Law School), and Herbert J. Wechsler National Criminal Law Moot Court Competition (SUNY Buffalo School of Law). Law student organizations, include Business Law Association, Criminal Law Association, Asian-Pacific Law Student Society, and Christian Legal Society. Local chapters of national associations include The Federalist Society, Black Law Students Association, and Christian Legal Society. Other campus organizations include Phi Alpha Delta, Student Bar Association, and Women's Law Associaiton. Phi Alpha Delta.

Library

The law library contains 208,080 hardcopy volumes and 99,070 microform volume equivalents, and subscribes to 2948 serial publications. Such on-line databases and networks as CALI, DIALOG, Infotrac, Legal-Trac, LEXIS, NEXIS, WESTLAW, Wilsonline Indexes, Hein Online, BNA, Intelliconnect, Foreign Law Grads, LexisNexis Congressional, and LLMC are available to law students for research. Recently, the library added $80.000 of online database available remotely. The ratio of library volumes to faculty is 9047 to 1 and to students is 536 to 1. The ratio of seats in the library to students is 1 to 1.

Faculty

The law school has 25 full-time and 23 part-time faculty members, of whom 17 are women. About 24% of full-time faculty have a graduate law degree in addition to the J.D. The ratio of full-time students to full-time faculty in an average class is 23 to 1, in a clinic, is 10 to 1. The law school has a regular program of bringing visiting professors and other distinguished lecturers and visitors to campus.

Students

About 50% of the student body are women; 34%, minorities; 4%, African American; 17%, Asian American; 6%, Hispanic; 1%, Native American; and 6%, Mexican-American. The average age of entering students is 26; age range is 21 to 62.

Placement

J.D.s awarded:	105
Services available through: a separate law school placement center	
Special features: public service program, externship program, on-line job listings, and alumni mentors.	
Full-time job interviews:	15 employers
Summer job interviews:	15 employers
Placement by graduation:	n/av
Placement within 9 months:	69% of class
Average starting salary:	$30,000 to $105,000
Areas of placement:	
Private practice 2-10 attorneys	46%
Private practice 11-25 attorneys	13%
Private practice 26-50 attorneys	3%
Private practice 51-100+ attorneys	13%
Solo practice	1%
Business/industry	13%
Government	6%
Academic	4%
Public interest	1%

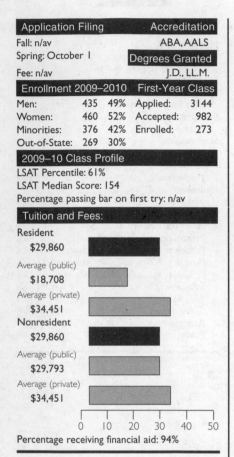

Application Filing		Accreditation	
Fall: n/av		ABA, AALS	
Spring: October 1		**Degrees Granted**	
Fee: n/av		J.D., LL.M.	
Enrollment 2009–2010		**First-Year Class**	
Men:	435 49%	Applied:	3144
Women:	460 52%	Accepted:	982
Minorities:	376 42%	Enrolled:	273
Out-of-State:	269 30%		

2009–10 Class Profile

LSAT Percentile: 61%
LSAT Median Score: 154
Percentage passing bar on first try: n/av

Tuition and Fees:

Resident
$29,860

Average (public)
$18,708

Average (private)
$34,451

Nonresident
$29,860

Average (public)
$29,793

Average (private)
$34,451

Percentage receiving financial aid: 94%

ADMISSIONS

In a recent year, 3144 applied, 982 were accepted, and 273 enrolled. Three transfers enrolled. The median LSAT percentile of the most recent first-year class was 61; the median GPA was 3.1 on a scale of 4.0. The lowest LSAT percentile accepted was 23; the highest was 85. Figures in the above capsule and in this profile are approximate.

Requirements

Applicants must have a bachelor's degree and take the LSAT. Minimum acceptable GPA is 2.0 on a scale of 4.0. The most important admission factors include academic achievement, GPA, and LSAT results. No specific undergraduate courses are required. Candidates are not interviewed.

Procedure

Applicants should submit an application form, LSAT results, transcripts, TOEFL, if English is not the primary language, 2 letters of recommendation, and a personal statement; if foreign, the applicant must have his/her foreign degree reviewed by an evaluation service approved by the school. Moreover, transcripts must be presented at matriculation. Notification of the admissions decision is as decisions are made. The latest acceptable LSAT test date for fall entry is June. The law school uses the LSDAS.

Special

The law school recruits minority and disadvantaged students by means of extensive fall recruiting, mass mailings targeted at minority groups, and diversity scholarships. Requirements are not different for out-of-state students. Transfer students must have one year of credit, have a minimum GPA of 3, and have attended an ABA-approved law school.

Costs

Tuition and fees for the 2009-2010 academic year are approximately $29,860 for all full-time students. Tuition for part-time students is approximately $19,500 per year. Books and supplies run $1008.

Financial Aid

In a recent year, about 94% of current law students received some form of aid. The average annual amount of aid from all sources combined, including scholarships, loans, and work contracts, was approximately $29,230; maximum, $53,202. Awards are based on need and merit. Required financial statement is the FAFSA. Special funds for minority or disadvantaged students include a limited number of diversity scholarships that are available. First-year students are notified about their financial aid application at time of acceptance. Check with the school for the current application deadlines.

About the Law School

Whittier College Whittier Law School was established in 1975 and is a private institution. The 15-acre campus is in a suburban area Costa Mesa, California. The primary mission of the law school is in the Quaker tradition of Whittier College, stressing concern for the individual student's intellectual and ethnic development. The Law School expresses this concern through a low student-to-faculty ratio, which allows for considerable interaction with students,

and by training socially and professionally responsible lawyers. Students have access to federal, state, county, city, and local agencies, courts, correctional facilities, law firms, and legal aid organizations in the Costa Mesa area. Facilities of special interest to law students include approximately 150 law firms that exist within a 5-mile radius of campus. Orange County courts provide abundant opportunities for externships, clerkships, and other associations for students. Substantial resources are also available in nearby Los Angeles. Housing for students is not available on campus but is available and affordable in surrounding areas. The Office of Student Advising and Career Counseling assists students seeking housing accommodations. All law school facilities are accessible to the physically disabled.

Calendar

The law school operates on a traditional semester basis. Courses for full-time students are offered both day and evening and must be completed within 5 years. For part-time students, courses are offered both day and evening and must be completed within 6 years. New full-time students are admitted in the fall and spring; part-time, fall. There is an 8-week summer session. Transferable summer courses are offered.

Programs

In addition to the J.D., the law school offers the LL.M. Students may take relevant courses in other programs and apply credit toward the J.D.; a maximum of 6 credits may be applied.

Required

To earn the J.D., candidates must complete 87 total credits, of which 40 are for required courses. They must maintain a minimum GPA of 77.0 in the required courses. The following first-year courses are required of all students: Civil Procedure I and II, Contracts I and II, Criminal Law, Legal Skills I and II, Real Property I and II, and Torts I and II. Required upper-level courses consist of Community Property, Constitutional Law I and II, Corporations, Criminal Procedure, Evidence, Professional Responsibility, Professional Responsibility Practicum, Remedies, and Wills and Trusts. Clinical students are required to take Legal Skills I and II

Phone: 714-444-4141, ext. 121
800-808-8188
Fax: 714-444-0250
E-mail: info@law.whittier.edu
Web: law.whittier.edu

Contact

Director of Admissions, 714-444-4141, ext. 123 for general inquiries; Director of Financial Aid, 714-444-4141, ext. 203, for financial aid information.

and Professional Skills I and II. The required orientation program for first-year students is a week-long program that includes introductions to and presentations by faculty, the administration, the library, financial aid office, and student organizations, plus a lecture entitled "How to Survive in Law School".

Electives

The Whittier Law School offers concentrations in environmental law, international law, and Center for Children's Rights, and intellectual property. In addition, 4 clinics are offered to upper division students for up to 4 units of credit. The Children's Rights Clinic offers 10 law students per semester the opportunity to provide pro bono legal assistance to children in selected cases on such matters as guardianship, custody, and adoption, under faculty supervision. The Special Education Clinic affords the same number of students the opportunity to assist special-needs children to request services from local school districts, in mediation sessions and administrative hearings. The Family Violence Clinic is designed to provide holistic legal services, combining the law with mental health, counseling, and other social services. Assistance is provided at several local shelter locations and up to 10 students can participate each term. The Legal Policy Clinic is a "clientless" clinic permitting students to advocate legal positions in the student's area of interest. Seminars are available including First Amendment, Advanced Torts, Natural Resources, Reproductive Technology, Information Privacy Seminar, and Adoption. Internships are permitted after the completion of the first year curriculum. Students can earn up to 6 units working the offices of county, state, city, and federal agencies and courts, such as the City Attorney's office, District Attorney's office, Department of Corporations and the public defender's office. Placements are also available with various public and private nonprofit legal entities. Student may take up to 3 units of independent study each semester with a full-time professor. Special lecture series include International Law, Health Law, and Center for Children's Fellow Program. Summer-abroad programs are offered in Israel, Spain, China, Amsterdam, and France. Exchange programs are available at University of Paris and University of Catabria and University of Seville in Spain.

Students are also permitted to enroll in ABA-approved study-abroad programs sponsored by other law schools for a maximum credit of 6 units. Each semester during the first year of law school, students are invited to attend extensive skills and exam writing workshops. The Academic Success Program is structured to meet the needs of individuals in mastering writing and other skills. Each semester during the first year of law school, students re required to attend weekly small group sessions and lectures on skills, including exam writing skills. The most widely taken electives are Criminal Procedure, Evidence, Wills and Trusts.

Graduation Requirements

In order to graduate, candidates must have a GPA of 77.0, have completed the upper-division writing requirement, and Students are required to take a 4-unit Professional Responsibility course, which includes a 1-unit writing skills component.

Organizations

Students edit the *Whittier Law Review*, the *Whittier Journal of Child and Family Advocacy*, and the student newspaper, *The Zealous Advocate*. Moot court teams are sent to the National Moot Court, National Criminal Procedure, and Jessup International Moot Court competitions, among others. The law schools also hosts the National Juvenile Law and Sonnenberg First Year Moot Court competitions. Law student organizations, local chapters of national associations, and campus organizations include the Alternative Dispute Resolution Group, Asian and Pacific Islander Law Students Association, Trial Advocacy Honors Board, Delta Theta Phi, Phi Alpha Delta, Phi Delta Phi, the Middle Eastern Law Students Organization, and Black Law Students and Women's Law Associations.

Library

The law library contains 421,678 hardcopy volumes and 133,552 microform volume equivalents, and subscribes to 3791 serial publications. Such on-line databases and networks as CALI, DIALOG, Infotrac, Legal-Trac, LEXIS, LOIS, Mathew Bender, NEXIS, RLIN, WESTLAW, Wilsonline Indexes, and JSTOR, HeinOnline, and New York Times are available to law students for research. Special library col-

Placement

J.D.s awarded:	n/av
Services available through: a separate law school placement center	
Services: a mentor program, mock interviews, informational programs, a comprehensive library of directories and other materials, on-line job postings; host Intellectual Property Associate Search	
Full-time job interviews:	10 employers
Summer job interviews:	20 employers
Placement by graduation:	61% of class
Placement within 9 months:	90% of class
Average starting salary:	$26,400 to $110,000
Areas of placement:	
Solo practice and private practice 100+ attorneys	3%
Private practice 2-10 attorneys	43%
Private practice 11-25 attorneys	3%
Private practice 26-50 attorneys	2%
Private practice 51-100 attorneys	2%
Business/industry	27%
Government	9%
Public interest	5%
Academic	5%
Military	1%

lections include a federal and a California state depository. The ratio of library volumes to faculty is 15,060 to 1 and to students is 475 to 1. The ratio of seats in the library to students is 1 to 43.

Faculty

The law school has 28 full-time and 41 part-time faculty members, of whom 29 are women. According to AAUP standards for Category IIB institutions, faculty salaries are above average. About 14% of full-time faculty have a graduate law degree in addition to the J.D.; about 5% of part-time faculty have one. The ratio of full-time students to full-time faculty in an average class is 22 to 1; in a clinic, 8 to 1. The law school has a regular program of bringing visiting professors and other distinguished lecturers and visitors to campus.

Students

About 52% of the student body are women; 42%, minorities; 5%, African American; 19%, Asian American; and 11%, Hispanic. The majority of students come from California (70%). The average age of entering students is 28; age range is 21 to 64. About 70% of students enter directly from undergraduate school. About 31% drop out after the first year for academic or personal reasons; 69% remain to receive a law degree.

WIDENER UNIVERSITY

Widener University School of Law

3800 Vartan Way, P.O. Box 69381
Harrisburg, PA 17106-9381

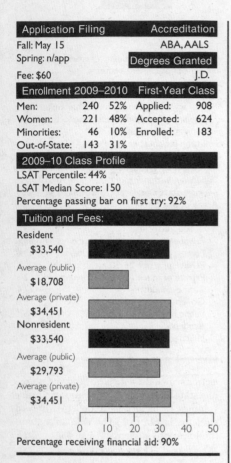

Application Filing	Accreditation
Fall: May 15	ABA, AALS
Spring: n/app	**Degrees Granted**
Fee: $60	J.D.

Enrollment 2009–2010		First-Year Class	
Men:	240 52%	Applied:	908
Women:	221 48%	Accepted:	624
Minorities:	46 10%	Enrolled:	183
Out-of-State:	143 31%		

2009–10 Class Profile
LSAT Percentile: 44%
LSAT Median Score: 150
Percentage passing bar on first try: 92%

Tuition and Fees:

Resident
$33,540

Average (public)
$18,708

Average (private)
$34,451

Nonresident
$33,540

Average (public)
$29,793

Average (private)
$34,451

0 10 20 30 40 50

Percentage receiving financial aid: 90%

ADMISSIONS

In the fall 2009 first-year class, 908 applied, 624 were accepted, and 183 enrolled. 1 transfer enrolled. The median LSAT percentile of the most recent first-year class was 44; the median GPA was 3.2 on a scale of 4.0. The lowest LSAT percentile accepted was 15; the highest was 81.

Requirements
Applicants must have a bachelor's degree and take the LSAT. The most important admission factors include LSAT results, GPA, and academic achievement. No specific undergraduate courses are required. Candidates are not interviewed.

Procedure
The application deadline for fall entry is May 15. Applicants should submit an application form, LSAT results, transcripts, a nonrefundable application fee of $60, strongly suggested, but not required letters of recommendation, and a personal

statement is highly encouraged. Notification of the admissions decision is on a rolling basis. The latest acceptable LSAT test date for fall entry is February. The law school uses the LSDAS.

Special
The law school recruits minority and disadvantaged students through programs sponsored by colleges and universities across the country. Additionally, applicants are encouraged to submit a personal statement detailing why they believe their admission would help to correct under representation of a particular minority or disadvantaged group in the legal profession. Requirements are not different for out-of-state students. Transfer students must have 1 year of credit, have attended an ABA-approved law school, and submit a certified transcript and letter of good standing, and be in the top third of their law school class.

Costs

Tuition and fees for the 2009-2010 academic year are $33,540 for all full-time students. Tuition for part-time students is $24,920 in-state and $24,620 out-of-state. Books and supplies run $1200.

Financial Aid

About 90% of current law students receive some form of aid. The average annual amount of aid from all sources combined, including scholarships, loans, and work contracts, is $37,585; maximum, $50,570. Awards are based on need and merit. A number of substantial scholarships are awarded to outstanding applicants and continuing students. Required financial statement is the FAFSA. The aid application deadline for fall entry is open. Special funds for minority or disadvantaged students include merit scholarships available to majority, minority and disadvantaged students, and deferred tuition. First-year students are notified about their financial aid application at time of acceptance.

About the Law School

Widener University Widener University School of Law was established in 1989 and is a private institution. The 25-acre campus is in a rural area 7 miles from the capital. The primary mission of the law school is to offer students a dynamic

environment from which to enter the legal profession; to encourage students to actively engage in the development of the law. Widener Law gives students a strong foundation in the fundamental theories and principles of law. Students have access to federal, state, county, city, and local agencies, courts, correctional facilities, law firms, and legal aid organizations in the Harrisburg area. In addition, students have access to numerous resources available at the university's main campus. Facilities of special interest to law students include extensive clinical and skills programs, moot court rooms, extensive law library, computer laboratory, lounge areas, and student dining center. Housing for students is available in several apartment complexes within walking distance of campus, including a modern apartment complex adjacent to campus. About 90% of the law school facilities are accessible to the physically disabled.

Calendar

The law school operates on a traditional semester basis. Courses for full-time students are offered days only and must be completed within 6 years. For part-time students, courses are offered both day and evening and must be completed within 6 years. New full- and part-time students are admitted in the fall. There is a 7-week summer session. Transferable summer courses are offered.

Programs

Students may take relevant courses in other programs and apply credit toward the J.D.; a maximum of 9 credits may be applied. The following joint degrees may be earned: J.D./M.S.L.S. (Juris Doctor/Master of Science in Library Science).

Required
To earn the J.D., candidates must complete 88 total credits, of which 66 are for required courses. They must maintain a minimum GPA of 2.0 in the required courses. The following first-year courses are required of all students: Civil Procedure I and II, Contracts I and II, Legal Methods I and II, Property I and II, and Torts I and II. Required upper-level courses consist of Administrative Law, Business Organizations, Constitutional Law, Criminal Law, Criminal Procedure, Evidence, Federal Income Tax, Professional Respon-

Phone: 717-541-3903
1-888-WIDENER
Fax: 717-541-3999
E-mail: law.admissions@law.widener.edu
Web: law.widener.edu

Contact

Director for Admissions, 717-541-3903 for general inquiries; Eleanor Kelly, Director of Financial Aid, 302-477-2273 for financial aid information.

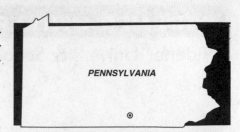

PENNSYLVANIA

sibility, Sales and Leases, Secured Transactions, Skills Requirement, Wills and Trusts, and Writing Requirement. The required orientation program for first-year students is a 1-week orientation that includes an introduction to law course and informational sessions on information technology, the legal information center, stress management, student organizations, meet the faculty, financial aid, and character and fitness to practice law.

Electives

Students must take 12 to 18 credits in their area of concentration. The Widener University School of Law offers concentrations in environmental law and Law and Government. In the Harrisburg Civil Law Clinic, students represent clients in a myriad of civil litigation areas. A variety of seminars is offered in specialized topic areas to upper-level students. Students may take part in extensive externship opportunities with legislative and state agencies, district attorneys, public defenders, legal aid societies, and state and local courts. All students must complete a major research paper in a seminar or directed research. Special lecture series are provided by the Law and Government Institute and the Career Development Office. Study-abroad programs are available at Macquarie University in Sydney, Australia, the University of Nairobi in Kenya, the University of Lausanne in Lausanne, Switzerland, the University of Venice, Italy, and the Southwest University of Political Science and Law in Chongging, China. Widener has an Academic Support Program that provides a comprehensive program focusing on basic examination skills, studying and outlining skills, and time management. An Intensive Legal Analysis course is offered for some first-year students. Specialized programs for minority students are provided through the Career Development Office, the Black Law Students Association, and the Minority Law Students Association. The most widely taken electives are Family Law, Sports Law, and Trial Advocacy.

Graduation Requirements

In order to graduate, candidates must have a GPA of 2.0, have completed the upper-division writing requirement, skills requirement, Professionalism Day, and Introduction to Law.

Organizations

Students edit the *Widener Law Journal,* and *Widener Journal of Law, Economics & Race.* Moot court competitions for students include the Burton Wexler First Amendment Competition, Jerome Prince Evidence Competition, and Jessup International Law Competition. Other competitions include the Buffalo Invitational Trial Advocacy Competition, National Trial Competition, Evan Gorley Trial Advocacy Competition, and the American Association for Justice Trial Advocacy Competition. Law student organizations include the Student Bar Association, Black Law Students Association, and Minority Law Students Association. There are local chapters of ATLA, Phi Alpha Delta, and the National Association of Public Interest Law. Campus clubs include St. Thomas More Society, Sports and Entertainment Law Society, and Criminal Law Society.

Library

The law library contains 258,433 hardcopy volumes and 332,319 microform volume equivalents, and subscribes to 6026 serial publications. Such on-line databases and networks as CALI, CIS Universe, Legal-Trac, LEXIS, LOIS, Mathew Bender, NEXIS, OCLC First Search, WESTLAW, Wilsonline Indexes, Full text sources Online, PROQUEST, UN Treaty Collection, Hein Online, CCH Research Network, and RIA Checkpoint, BNA All, constitutions of the countries of the world, JSTOR, world cat, LLMC Digital, EBSCO Host are available to law students for research. Special library collections include state and federal depository materials, U.S. Supreme Court records and briefs, CIS Congressional library, corporate law, law and government, health law collections. Recently, the library updated wireless connections throughout the library. The ratio of library volumes to faculty is 8614 to 1 and to students is 560 to 1. The ratio of seats in the library to students is 1 to 2.

Faculty

The law school has 30 full-time and 30 part-time faculty members, of whom 23 are women. According to AAUP standards for Category IIA institutions, faculty salaries are above average. About 30% of full-time faculty have a graduate law degree in addition to the J.D.; about 18%

Placement

J.D.s awarded:	106

Services available through: a separate law school placement center

Services: career resource library that includes books, directories, and periodicals, lists of area judges and firms.

Special features: Alumni-student mentor program; on-line job board; free faxing, photocopying, and telephone usage; videotaped mock interviews; career panels on various career options and professionalism programming; specialized for diverse students; and a weekly e-mail alumni employment newsletter. All professional staff possess J.D. degrees.

Full-time job interviews:	16 employers
Summer job interviews:	28 employers
Placement by graduation:	64% of class
Placement within 9 months:	97% of class
Average starting salary:	$35,000 to $135,000

Areas of placement:

Private practice 2-10 attorneys	30%
Private practice 11-25 attorneys	3%
Private practice 26-50 attorneys	3%
Government	21%
Business/industry	17%
Judicial clerkships	14%
Public interest	6%
firms with more than 100 attorneys	3%
Academic	2%
Military	1%

of part-time faculty have one. The ratio of full-time students to full-time faculty in an average class is 19 to 1; in a clinic, 10 to 1. The law school has a regular program of bringing visiting professors and other distinguished lecturers and visitors to campus.

Students

About 48% of the student body are women; 10%, minorities; 3%, African American; 2%, Asian American; and 2%, Hispanic. The majority of students come from the Northeast (93%). The average age of entering students is 23; age range is 21 to 51. About 35% of students enter directly from undergraduate school, 12% have a graduate degree, and 52% have worked full-time prior to entering law school. About 13% drop out after the first year for academic or personal reasons; 87% remain to receive a law degree.

WIDENER UNIVERSITY

Widener University School of Law

4601 Concord Pike, P.O. Box 7474
Wilmington, DE 19803-0474

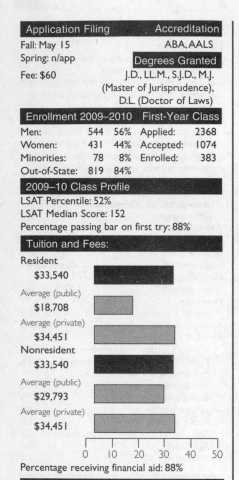

Application Filing	Accreditation
Fall: May 15	ABA, AALS
Spring: n/app	**Degrees Granted**
Fee: $60	J.D., LL.M., S.J.D., M.J.
	(Master of Jurisprudence),
	D.L. (Doctor of Laws)

Enrollment 2009–2010			First-Year Class	
Men:	544	56%	Applied:	2368
Women:	431	44%	Accepted:	1074
Minorities:	78	8%	Enrolled:	383
Out-of-State:	819	84%		

2009–10 Class Profile
LSAT Percentile: 52%
LSAT Median Score: 152
Percentage passing bar on first try: 88%

Tuition and Fees:

Resident
$33,540

Average (public)
$18,708

Average (private)
$34,451

Nonresident
$33,540

Average (public)
$29,793

Average (private)
$34,451

0 10 20 30 40 50

Percentage receiving financial aid: 88%

ADMISSIONS
In the fall 2009 first-year class, 2368 applied, 1074 were accepted, and 383 enrolled. 1 transfer enrolled. The median LSAT percentile of the most recent first-year class was 52; the median GPA was 3.12 on a scale of 4.0. The lowest LSAT percentile accepted was 15; the highest was 96.

Requirements
Applicants must have a bachelor's degree and take the LSAT. The most important admission factors include LSAT results, GPA, and academic achievement. No specific undergraduate courses are required. Candidates are not interviewed. A personal statement is highly recommended.

Procedure
The application deadline for fall entry is May 15. Applicants should submit an application form, LSAT results, transcripts, a nonrefundable application fee of $60, are letters of recommendation, and a personal statement is highly recommend-

ed. Notification of the admissions decision is on a rolling basis. The latest acceptable LSAT test date for fall entry is February. The law school uses the LSDAS.

Special
The law school recruits minority and disadvantaged students at programs sponsored by colleges and universities across the country. Additionally, the application encourages applicants to submit a personal statement. Applicants are instructed that the admissions committee may consider relevant such factors as a history of economic or educational disadvantage, cultural or language differences, disability, and whether they believe their admission would help to correct under representation of a particular minority or disadvantaged group in the legal profession. Requirements are not different for out-of-state students. Transfer students must have 1 year of credit, have attended an ABA-approved law school, and certified transcript and letter of good standing must be submitted. A maximum of 35 qualified credits will be accepted in transfer. Transfer candidates must be in the top-third of their law school class.

Costs
Tuition and fees for the 2009-2010 academic year are $33,540 for all full-time students. Tuition for part-time students is $24,620 per year. On-campus room and board costs about $4800 annually; books and supplies run $1200.

Financial Aid
About 88% of current law students receive some form of aid. The average annual amount of aid from all sources combined, including scholarships, loans, and work contracts, is $32,163; maximum, $50,570. Awards are based on merit. A number of substantial scholarships are awarded to outstanding applicants and continuing students. Required financial statement is the FAFSA. The aid application deadline for fall entry is open. Special funds for minority or disadvantaged students include merit scholarships available to majority, minority, and disadvantaged students. Deferred tuition loans are offered to students maintaining a satisfactory GPA. First-year students are notified about their financial aid application at time of acceptance.

About the Law School
Widener University Widener University School of Law was established in 1971 and is a private institution. The 40-acre campus is in a suburban area in Delaware,

3 miles from downtown Wilmington. The Law School, gives students a strong foundation in the fundamental theories and principles of law. Students have access to federal, state, county, city, and local agencies, courts, correctional facilities, law firms, and legal aid organizations in the Wilmington area. In addition, students have access to the numerous resources available at the university's main campus. Facilities of special interest to law students include extensive clinical and skills programs, moot court rooms, extensive law library, audiovisual centers, computer laboratory, student lounge areas, private study/conference rooms, recreational facilities, and student dining center. Housing for students consists of residence halls and townhouse apartments. Area apartments are widely available. All law school facilities are accessible to the physically disabled.

Calendar
The law school operates on a traditional semester basis. Courses for full-time students are offered days only and evening classes are offered on a space-available and must be completed within 6 years. For part-time students, courses are offered both day and evening and some elective courses are offered on Saturdays and must be completed within 6 years. New full- and part-time students are admitted in the fall. There is a 7-week summer session. Transferable summer courses are offered.

Programs
In addition to the J.D., the law school offers the LL.M., S.J.D., and M.J. (Master of Jurisprudence), D.L. (Doctor of Laws). Students may take relevant courses in other programs and apply credit toward the J.D.; a maximum of 9 credits may be applied. The following joint degrees may be earned: J.D./M.B.A. (Juris Doctor/Master of Business Administration), J.D./M.M.P. (Juris Doctor/Master of Marine Policy), J.D./M.P.H. (Juris Doctor/Master of Public Health), and J.D./Psy.D. (Juris Doctor/Doctor of Psychology in Law).

Required
To earn the J.D., candidates must complete 88 total credits, of which 57 are for required courses. They must maintain a minimum GPA of 2.0 in the required courses. The following first-year courses are required of all students: Civil Procedure, Constitutional Law I, Contracts, Criminal Law, Legal Methods I/Analysis, Legal Methods II/Advocacy, Property I and II, and Torts. Required upper-level courses consist of Administrative Law,

Phone: 302-477-2162
1-888-WIDENER
Fax: 302-477-2224
E-mail: law.admissions@law.widener.edu
Web: widener.edu/law/law.html

Contact

Assistant Dean for Admissions, 302-477-2162 for general inquiries; Eleanor Kelly, Director of Financial Aid, 302-477-2272 for financial aid information.

Business Organizations, Constitutional Law II, Criminal Procedure, Evidence, Federal Income Tax, Legal Methods III, Professional Responsibility, Sales and Leases, Skill Requirement, and Writing Requirement.

Electives
Students must take 12 - 18 credits in their area of concentration. The Widener University School of Law offers concentrations in corporate law, criminal law, environmental law, litigation, health law, and technology and law. In addition, clinics for up to 8 credits include Environmental Law, Family Law, Consumer Bankruptcy, Veterans Affairs, and Criminal Defense. Clinical education also includes a comprehensive trial advocacy training program. Seminars are offered in a variety of specialized areas, to all upper-level students. Students may take part in externships with legislative and state agencies, district attorneys, public defenders, legal aid societies, and state and local courts. All students must complete a major research paper or directed research project. The Law School's law journals, moot court, and trial advocacy programs, and the many institutes and organizations provide additional opportunities for scholarly research. Field work opportunities include the Wolcott Fellowship Program, which places students each academic year as part-time clerks for the Delaware Supreme Court. The Francis G. Pileggi Distinguished Lecture in Law is an annual lecture series featuring practitioners, judges, academicians, and distinguished experts in corporate law, held for the benefit of the Delaware bench and bar and Widener students. Study-abroad programs are offered at the University of Technology in Sydney, Australia, the University of Nairobi in Kenya, the University of Lausanne in Lausanne Switzerland, the University of Venice in Italy and the Southwest University of Political Science and Law in Chongqing, China. The content of the program varies by academic level. An intensive Legal Analysis course and an Advanced Analyticals course are also offered for some second-year students. Specialized programs for minority students are offered through the Career Development Office, the Black Law Students Association, and the Minority Law Students Association. The most widely taken electives are Wills and Trusts, Family Law, and Trial Advocacy.

Graduation Requirements
In order to graduate, candidates must have a GPA of 2.0, have completed the upper-division writing requirement, and

Skills Requirement, Professionalism Day, Introduction to Law.

Organizations

The primary law reviews are *Delaware Journal of Corporate Law* and *The Widener Law Review*. Other law reviews include the *Widener Journal of Law, Economics and Race*. The student newspaper is *The Law Forum*. The Health Institute publishes the *Newsletter of the Society of Health Care Attorneys*. The Moot Court Honor Society sponsors the G. Fred DiBona Competition and the Delaware-Harrisburg Moot Court Competition, and hosts the Ruby R. Vale Interschool Corporate Moot Court Competition. The Moe Levine Trial Advocacy Honor Society sponsors the Hugh B. Pearce Trial Competition. Law student organizations, local chapters of national associations, and campus organizations include the Student Bar Association, ADR Society, Black Law Students Association, ACLU, ATLA, Phi Delta Phi, Rugby Club, Women's Law Caucus, and Health Law Society.

Library

The law library contains 258,433 hardcopy volumes and 332,319 microform volume equivalents, and subscribes to 6026 serial publications. Such on-line databases and networks as CALI, CIS Universe, Legal-Trac, LEXIS, LOIS, Mathew Bender, NEXIS, OCLC First Search, WESTLAW, Wilsonline Indexes, Full text sources On-line, Proquest, UN Treaty Collection, HeinOnline, CCH Research Network, RIA Checkpoint, BNA All, Constitutions of the Countries of the World, JSTOR, WorldCat, EBSO, and LLMC Digital are available to law students for research. Special library collections include state and federal depository materials, U.S. Supreme Court records and briefs, CIS congressional library, corporate law, law and government, and health law collections. The ratio of library volumes to faculty is 4236 to 1 and to students is 265 to 1. The ratio of seats in the library to students is 1 to 3.

Faculty

The law school has 61 full-time and 68 part-time faculty members, of whom 50 are women. About 20% of full-time faculty have a graduate law degree in addition to the J.D.; about 18% of part-time faculty have one. The ratio of full-time students to full-time faculty in an average class is 10 to 1; in a clinic, 10 to 1. The law school has a regular program of bringing visiting professors and other distinguished lecturers and visitors to campus.

Placement

J.D.s awarded:	215
Services available through: a separate law school placement center	
Services: career resource library that includes books, directories, and periodicals, videotapes; lists of area judges and firms.	
Full-time job interviews:	16 employers
Summer job interviews:	28 employers
Placement by graduation:	72% of class
Placement within 9 months:	93% of class
Average starting salary:	$28,000 to $160,000
Areas of placement:	
Private practice 2-10 attorneys	24%
Private practice 11-25 attorneys	5%
Private practice 26-50 attorneys	2%
Private practice 51-100 attorneys	4%
Private practice 100+ attorneys	8%
Judicial clerkships	23%
Business/industry	21%
Government	7%
Public interest	3%
Academic	2%
Military	1%

Students

About 44% of the student body are women; 8%, minorities; 3%, African American; 4%, Asian American; and 1%, Hispanic. The majority of students come from the Northeast (96%). The average age of entering students is 24; age range is 20 to 68. About 38% of students enter directly from undergraduate school, 12% have a graduate degree, and 58% have worked full-time prior to entering law school. About 28% drop out after the first year for academic or personal reasons; 70% remain to receive a law degree.

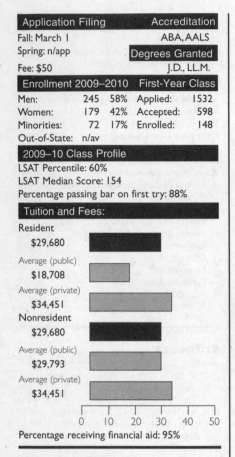

Application Filing		Accreditation	
Fall: March 1		ABA, AALS	
Spring: n/app		**Degrees Granted**	
Fee: $50		J.D., LL.M.	

Enrollment 2009–2010			First-Year Class	
Men:	245	58%	Applied:	1532
Women:	179	42%	Accepted:	598
Minorities:	72	17%	Enrolled:	148
Out-of-State:	n/av			

2009–10 Class Profile
LSAT Percentile: 60%
LSAT Median Score: 154
Percentage passing bar on first try: 88%

Tuition and Fees:

Resident
$29,680

Average (public)
$18,708

Average (private)
$34,451

Nonresident
$29,680

Average (public)
$29,793

Average (private)
$34,451

0 10 20 30 40 50

Percentage receiving financial aid: 95%

ADMISSIONS
In the fall 2009 first-year class, 1532 applied, 598 were accepted, and 148 enrolled. Two transfers enrolled. The median LSAT percentile of the most recent first-year class was 60; the median GPA was 3.22 on a scale of 4.0.

Requirements
Applicants must have a bachelor's degree and take the LSAT. The most important admission factors include LSAT results, GPA, and academic achievement. No specific undergraduate courses are required. Candidates are not interviewed.

Procedure
The application deadline for fall entry is March 1. Applicants should submit an application form, LSAT results, transcripts, a personal statement, a nonrefundable application fee of $50, 2 letters of recommendation, and a resume. Notification of the admissions decision is between January and May. The latest acceptable

LSAT test date for fall entry is February. The law school uses the LSDAS.

Special
The College of Law has a Coordinator for Multicultural Affairs whose principal responsibility is the recruitment and retention of students of color. Requirements are not different for out-of-state students. Transfer students must have attended an ABA-approved law school and be in good standing academically and eligible to return to their current law school.

Costs
Tuition and fees for the 2009-2010 academic year are $29,680 for all full-time students. Books and supplies run $1450.

Financial Aid
About 95% of current law students receive some form of aid. The average annual amount of aid from all sources combined, including scholarships, loans, and work contracts, is $38,713. Awards are based on need and merit. Required financial statement is the FAFSA. The aid application deadline for fall entry is March 1. First-year students are notified about their financial aid application approximately 2 weeks after acceptance.

About the Law School
Willamette University College of Law was established in 1883 and is a private institution. The 65-acre campus is in an urban area in Salem, the capital of Oregon, which is 45 miles south of Portland. The primary mission of the law school is to pursue academic and professional excellence in a supportive environment that maximizes a student's potential. Students have access to federal, state, county, city, and local agencies, courts, correctional facilities, law firms, and legal aid organizations in the Salem area. The college is within walking distance of several courts and their libraries and virtually all state agencies and departments. Housing for students is available in affordable apartments and houses located near the campus. All law school facilities are accessible to the physically disabled.

Calendar
The law school operates on a traditional semester basis. Courses for full-time stu-

dents are offered days only and must be completed within 3 years. There is no part-time program. New students are admitted in the fall. There is a 7-week summer session. Transferable summer courses are offered.

Programs
In addition to the J.D., the law school offers the LL.M. Students may take relevant courses in other programs and apply credit toward the J.D.; a maximum of 6 credits may be applied. The following joint degree may be earned: J.D./M.B.A. (Juris Doctor/Master of Business Administration).

Required
To earn the J.D., candidates must complete 90 total credits, of which 40 are for required courses. They must maintain a minimum GPA of 2.3 in the required courses. The following first-year courses are required of all students: Civil Procedure, Constitutional Law I, Contracts I and II, Criminal Law, Legal Research and Writing, Property, Torts and an elective course. Required upper-level courses consist of Constitutional Law II, Evidence, and Professional Responsibility. The required orientation program for first-year students lasts 3 days and consists of an introduction to the law program and to legal research and writing.

Electives
The College of Law offers concentrations in corporate law, criminal law, environmental law, family law, international law, labor law, litigation, tax law, torts and insurance, dispute resolution, law and government, commercial law, and estate planning. In the Civil Practice Clinic (worth 3 hours of credit), students represent clients in actual cases and transactions under the close supervision of faculty. Seminars (worth 2 hours of credit) are offered to second- and third-year students on such topics as First Amendment law, American Indian law, Global Sustainability, Human Rights, and Advanced Topics in Conflict Theory. Students receive academic credit while working in a close mentoring relationship with attorneys in the courts, the state legislature, state agencies, non-profits, and legal departments of private companies. All first-year students are required to take a yearlong legal research

Phone: 503-370-6282
Fax: 503-370-6087
E-mail: *law-admission@willamette.edu*
Web: *www.willamette.edu/wucl*

Contact
Carolyn Dennis, Director of Admissions, 503-370-6282 for general inquiries; Katy Wilson, Senior Financial Aid Counselor, 503-370-6273 for financial aid information.

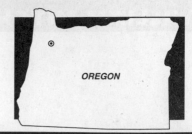

OREGON

and writing course. There is an Annual Lecture Series, Dispute Resolution Series, and Paulus Lecture Series. A Summer in China study program (worth 5 hours of credit) is offered to second- and third-year students. In addition, individual students, with ABA approval, may spend a semester at a leading new law school in Quito, Ecuador or Hamburg, Germany. Special student assistants are available for students in Legal Research and Writing. The College of Law has an active multicultural law student organization that, among other activities, sponsors a Martin Luther King event involving the community at large. The college offers simulation courses on negotiations, mediation, arbitration, interviewing and counseling, and trial practice. The most widely taken electives are various simulation courses and seminars.

Graduation Requirements
In order to graduate, candidates must have a GPA of 2.3 and have completed the upper-division writing requirement.

Organizations
Students edit the *Willamette Law Review, Willamette Journal of International Law & Dispute Resolution*, and the *Willamette Law Online* (a student run/edited on-line service providing case summaries and law updates). Students participate in a number of moot court competitions, including the National Appellate Competition, the International Law Competition, and the ATLA Trial Competition. Other moot court competitions students participate in include the Environmental Appellate Competition, Negotiation Competition, and Criminal Law Competition. Law student organizations include the Multi-Cultural Law Students Association, International Law Society, and Women's Law Caucus. There are local chapters of Phi Alpha Delta and Phi Delta Phi. Campus clubs and other organizations include the Public Interest Law Society, Environmental Law Society, and Willamette Lambda Legal Organization.

Library
The law library contains 299,123 hardcopy volumes and 156,790 microform volume equivalents, and subscribes to 3190 serial publications. Such on-line databases and networks as CALI, CIS Universe,

Legal-Trac, LEXIS, LOIS, Matthew Bender, NEXIS, OCLC First Search, WESTLAW, Wilsonline Indexes, and Summit are available to law students for research. Special library collections include a federal depository, Public International Law, and tax and labor collections. Recently, the library added a wireless network and developed a research web site. The ratio of library volumes to faculty is 8084 to 1 and to students is 705 to 1. The ratio of seats in the library to students is 1 to 1.

Faculty
The law school has 37 full-time and 22 part-time faculty members, of whom 18 are women. According to AAUP standards for Category IIA institutions, faculty salaries are above average. About 14% of full-time faculty have a graduate law degree in addition to the J.D.; about 9% of part-time faculty have one. The ratio of full-time students to full-time faculty in an average class is 13 to 1; in a clinic, 8 to 1. The law school has a regular program of bringing visiting professors and other distinguished lecturers and visitors to campus.

Students
About 42% of the student body are women; 17%, minorities; 2%, African American; 8%, Asian American; 6%, Hispanic; and 1%, Native American. The average age of entering students is 26; age range is 20 to 49. About 4% drop out after the first year for academic or personal reasons; 96% remain to receive a law degree.

Placement

J.D.s awarded:	130

Services available through: a separate law school placement center

Services: attorney-student extensive mentor program; public interest clerkship stipends; public interest loan repayment program for graduates; and a fellowship program for minority students through the Oregon State Bar

Special features: Career services web site includes a C.S. calendar, events, information, as well as job postings; coordinated effort for joint degree with Atkinson Graduate School of Management; and specialty law attorney panels and career workshops.

Full-time job interviews:	n/av
Summer job interviews:	n/av
Placement by graduation:	n/av
Placement within 9 months:	94% of class
Average starting salary:	$19,760 to $178,500

Areas of placement:

Private practice 2-10 attorneys	28%
Private practice 11-50attorneys	8%
Private practice 100+ attorneys or solo	14%
Business/industry	19%
Government	17%
Judicial clerkships	6%
Public interest	6%
Military	1%
Academic	1%

875 Summit Avenue
St. Paul, MN 55105-3076

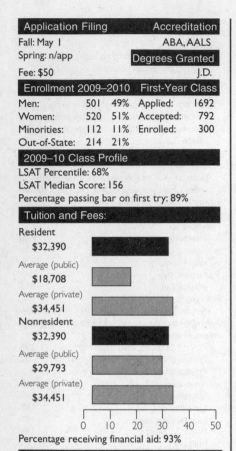

Application Filing		Accreditation	
Fall: May 1		ABA, AALS	
Spring: n/app		Degrees Granted	
Fee: $50			J.D.

Enrollment 2009–2010			First-Year Class	
Men:	501	49%	Applied:	1692
Women:	520	51%	Accepted:	792
Minorities:	112	11%	Enrolled:	300
Out-of-State:	214	21%		

2009–10 Class Profile
LSAT Percentile: 68%
LSAT Median Score: 156
Percentage passing bar on first try: 89%

Tuition and Fees:

Resident
$32,390

Average (public)
$18,708

Average (private)
$34,451

Nonresident
$32,390

Average (public)
$29,793

Average (private)
$34,451

0 10 20 30 40 50

Percentage receiving financial aid: 93%

ADMISSIONS
In the fall 2009 first-year class, 1692 applied, 792 were accepted, and 300 enrolled. One transfers enrolled. The median LSAT percentile of the most recent first-year class was 68; the median GPA was 3.4 on a scale of 4.0. The lowest LSAT percentile accepted was 24; the highest was 97.

Requirements
Applicants must have a bachelor's degree and take the LSAT. The most important admission factors include academic achievement, LSAT results, and life experience. No specific undergraduate courses are required. Candidates are not interviewed.

Procedure
The application deadline for fall entry is May 1. Applicants should submit an application form, LSAT results, transcripts, a personal statement, TOEFL if English is a second language, a nonrefundable applica-

tion fee of $50, 2 letters of recommendation, and a résumé. Notification of the admissions decision is on a rolling basis. The latest acceptable LSAT test date for fall entry is February. The law school uses the LSDAS.

Special
The law school recruits minority and disadvantaged students through a general policy of admissions that encourages diversity in the student body and on-campus visits. Requirements are not different for out-of-state students. Transfer students must have 1 year of credit, have a minimum GPA of 2, have attended an ABA-approved law school, and submit a letter of good standing from the dean of the previously attended school. 24 credits must by completed at William Mitchell. Preadmissions courses consist of the Summer Partnership in Law (SPIL) for college sophomores and juniors. Introduction to Legal Theory is also taught to students accepted for the fall term.

Costs
Tuition and fees for the 2009-2010 academic year are $32,390 for all full-time students. Tuition for part-time students is $23,450 per year. Books and supplies run $1550.

Financial Aid
About 93% of current law students receive some form of aid. The average annual amount of aid from all sources combined, including scholarships, loans, and work contracts, is $45,245; maximum, $49,790. Awards are based on need and merit. Required financial statement is the FAFSA. The aid application deadline for fall entry is March 15. Special funds for minority or disadvantaged students include many named scholarships. First-year students are notified about their financial aid application at time of acceptance.

About the Law School
William Mitchell College of Law was established in 1900 and is a private institution. The 7-acre campus is in an urban area in an urban residential area of St. Paul. The primary mission of the law school is to pioneer a demanding legal education so engaged with the profession that gradu-

ates have an enduring advantage as they meet the challenges of an increasingly complex world. Students have access to federal, state, county, city, and local agencies, courts, correctional facilities, law firms, and legal aid organizations in the St. Paul area. There are numerous corporations and nonprofit organizations in the Twin Cities metropolitan area providing opportunities and resources for students. Facilities of special interest to law students are the Warren E. Burger Library, high-tech classrooms, 4 high-tech courtrooms, student center with comfortable areas for individual and group study as well as socializing outside the classroom, and a wireless network, which has been expanded to include all classrooms and common areas. Housing for students is available in the neighborhood and elsewhere in Minneapolis-St. Paul. About 99% of the law school facilities are accessible to the physically disabled.

Calendar
The law school operates on a traditional semester basis. Courses for full-time students are offered both day and evening and must be completed within 6 years. For part-time students, courses are offered both day and evening and must be completed within 6 years. New full- and part-time students are admitted in the fall. There is a 7 week summer session. Transferable summer courses are offered.

Programs
Students may take relevant courses in other programs and apply credit toward the J.D.; a maximum of 9 credits may be applied. The following joint degrees may be earned: J.D./M.A.P.A. (Juris Doctor/Master of Arts in Public Administration), J.D./M.S (Juris Doctor/Master of Science in Community Health), and J.D./M.S. (Juris Doctor/Master of Science in Women's Studies).

Required
To earn the J.D., candidates must complete 86 total credits, of which 46 are for required courses. They must maintain a minimum GPA of 2.0 in the required courses. The following first-year courses are required of all students: Civil Procedure, Contracts, Property I and II, Torts I and II, and Writing and Representation: Advice and Persuasion. Required upper-

Phone: 651-290-6343
888-WMCL-LAW
Fax: 651-290-6414
E-mail: admissions@wmitchell.edu
Web: www.wmitchell.edu

Contact

Kendra Dane, Assistant Dean and Director, 651-290-6476 for general inquiries; Patty Harris, Director of Financial Aid, 651-290-6358 for financial aid information.

MINNESOTA

level courses consist of 2 statutory courses, a skills course, Advanced Research and Writing, Constitutional Law-Liberties, Constitutional Law-Powers, PLP - Perspectives on the Legal Profession, Professional Responsibility, and Writing and Representation: Advocacy. Clinical courses are offered, but not required. The required orientation program for first-year students lasts 2 days and covers an introduction to law school, tours, the first class, and writing and representation.

Electives

The William Mitchell College of Law offers concentrations in corporate law, criminal law, family law, intellectual property law, international law, labor law, litigation, tax law, torts and insurance, commercial, property, estates, government, and ADR. In addition, there are 11 clinics available including Civil Advocacy, Business Law, and Immigration Law. Seminars are available in several areas. Externships are also available. Independent research projects are available for 1 to 4 credits. Special lecture series include the Public Square Lecture Series and the National Security Forum. Study abroad consists of summer programs in London, Galway (U.K.) Malta, Chile, Turkey, and Czech Republic. Minority programs are provided by the Black Law Students Association, Jewish Law Students Association, Asian Law Students Association, Latino/a Law Students Association, and the Native American Law Students Association. The college also has an Office of Multicultural Affairs which, among other things, offers services and support to traditionally underrepresented populations. Special interest group programs are provided by the Student Intellectual Property Association, Christian Law Society, National Lawyers Guild, Minnesota Justice Foundation, Women Law Students Association, Health Law Society, Italian American Bar Association, Federalist Society, and Outlet. The most widely taken electives are Evidence, Business-Agency, Partnerships, and Limited Liability Companies and Family Law.

Graduation Requirements

In order to graduate, candidates must have a GPA of 2.0 and have completed the upper-division writing requirement.

Organizations

The primary law review is the *William Mitchell Law Review* and the student newspaper is the *Opinion*. Teams participate in the William E. McGee National Civil Rights Moot Court, New York City Bar/ACTL National Moot Court, and Philip C. Jessup International Moot Court. Other competitions include Cardozol BMI Moot Court Competition and Saul Lefkowitz Moot Court Competititon. Law student organizations, local chapters of national associations, and campus organizations include Association for International Law, Health Law Society, Women's Law Student Association, American Constitution Society, Federalist Society, Black Law Students Association, Delta Theta Phi, Hockey Club, and William Mitchell Families Organization.

Library

The law library contains 356,269 hardcopy volumes and 154,517 microform volume equivalents, and subscribes to 809 serial publications. Such on-line databases and networks as CALI, CIS Universe, Infotrac, Legal-Trac, LEXIS, LOIS, NEXIS, OCLC First Search, WESTLAW, Wilsonline Indexes, Worldcat, HeinOnline, RIA checkpoint, CCH Intelliconnect, EBSCO, Gale Collections, Access UN, BNA Online, Jstor, LexisNexis Congressional, and Readex Serial Set are available to law students for research. Special library collections include a selective federal depository library. Recently, the library assembled a computer lab for faculty to experiment with news teaching tools using latest software and high end comuter technology. The ratio of library volumes to faculty is 9896 to 1 and to students is 365 to 1. The ratio of seats in the library to students is 1 to 2.

Faculty

The law school has 36 full-time and 229 part-time faculty members, of whom 113 are women. About 11% of full-time faculty have a graduate law degree in addition to the J.D. The ratio of full-time students to full-time faculty in an average class is 20 to 1; in a clinic, 4 to 1. The law school has a regular program of bringing visiting professors and other distinguished lecturers and visitors to campus.

Placement

J.D.s awarded:	327

Services available through: a separate law school placement center and Career and Professional Development Office

Services: career programs, resource library, out-of-state job-search resources, on-line resources on the web site, on campus interviews, mock interviews, and student assessments.

Special features: career development staff members who provide legal experiences as well as career development experience.

Full-time job interviews:	10 employers
Summer job interviews:	43 employers
Placement by graduation:	n/av
Placement within 9 months:	97% of class
Average starting salary:	$20,000 to $200,000

Areas of placement:

Private practice 2-10 attorneys	25%
Private practice 11-25 attorneys	9%
Private practice 26-50 attorneys	3%
Private practice 51-100 attorneys	9%
Business/industry	24%
Judicial clerkships	10%
Self-employed/unknown	7%
Government	6%
Public interest	3%
Academic	1%

Students

About 51% of the student body are women; 11%, minorities; 2%, African American; 5%, Asian American; 2%, Hispanic; 1%, Native American; and 1%, other/non-white. The majority of students come from Minnesota (79%). The average age of entering students is 27; age range is 20 to 56. About 33% of students enter directly from undergraduate school and 8% have a graduate degree. About 11% drop out after the first year for academic or personal reasons; 89% remain to receive a law degree.

YALE UNIVERSITY

Yale Law School

P.O. Box 208329
New Haven, CT 06520-8329

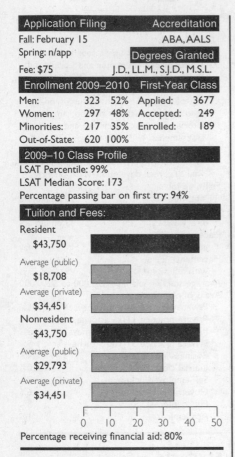

Application Filing	Accreditation
Fall: February 15	ABA, AALS
Spring: n/app	**Degrees Granted**
Fee: $75	J.D., LL.M., S.J.D., M.S.L.

Enrollment 2009–2010		First-Year Class	
Men:	323 52%	Applied:	3677
Women:	297 48%	Accepted:	249
Minorities:	217 35%	Enrolled:	189
Out-of-State:	620 100%		

2009–10 Class Profile
LSAT Percentile: 99%
LSAT Median Score: 173
Percentage passing bar on first try: 94%

Tuition and Fees:

Resident
$43,750

Average (public)
$18,708

Average (private)
$34,451

Nonresident
$43,750

Average (public)
$29,793

Average (private)
$34,451

0 10 20 30 40 50

Percentage receiving financial aid: 80%

ADMISSIONS

In a recent year, 3677 applied, 249 were accepted, and 189 enrolled. Twelve transfers enrolled. The median LSAT percentile of the most recent first-year class was 99; the median GPA was 3.91 on a scale of 4.0. The lowest LSAT percentile accepted was 80; the highest was 99. Figures in the above capsule and in this profile are approximate.

Requirements

Applicants must have a bachelor's degree and take the LSAT. No specific undergraduate courses are required. Candidates are not interviewed.

Procedure

Applicants should submit an application form, LSAT results, transcripts, a nonrefundable application fee of approximately $75, 2 letters of recommendation, and a 250-word essay. Notification of the admissions decision is on a rolling basis; most are. The latest acceptable LSAT test date

for fall entry is December. The law school uses the LSDAS. Check with the school for current application deadlines.

Special

The law school recruits minority and disadvantaged students by means of Candidate Referral Services through Law Services. Requirements are not different for out-of-state students. Transfer students must have one year of credit, have attended an ABA-approved law school, and have a weighted average of not less than B.

Costs

Tuition and fees for the 2009-2010 academic year are approximately $43,750 for all full-time students. Books and supplies run approximately $950.

Financial Aid

In a recent year, about 80% of current law students received some form of aid. The average annual amount of aid from all sources combined, including scholarships, loans, and work contracts, was approximately $27,000; maximum, $52,175. Awards are based on need. Required financial statements are the FAFSA and Need Access. First-year students are notified about their financial aid application at time of acceptance. Check with the school for the current application deadline.

About the Law School

Yale University Yale Law School was established in 1801 and is a private institution. The campus is in an urban area in New Haven on the block bounded by Grove, High,. The primary mission of the law school is to train lawyers and leaders in the public and private sectors, and to encourage research in the law. Students have access to federal, state, county, city, and local agencies, courts, correctional facilities, law firms, and legal aid organizations in the New Haven area. Facilities of special interest to law students include a renovated law library and computer facility; the Jerome W. Frank Legal Services Organization; the Orville H. Shell, Jr. Center for International Human Rights; the Center for the Study of Corporate Law and numerous endowed lecture programs that bring distinguished speakers from around the world. Housing for students includes off-campus housing, and some

family housing is available from the university. The university also has a housing office that assists students in locating housing.

Calendar

The law school operates on a traditional semester basis. Courses for full-time students are offered days only and must be completed within 6 terms. There is no part-time program. New students are admitted in the fall. There is no summer session. Transferable summer courses are not offered.

Programs

In addition to the J.D., the law school offers the LL.M., S.J.D., and M.S.L. Master of Studies in Law, including fellowships in law. Students may take relevant courses in other programs and apply credit toward the J.D.; a maximum of 12 credits may be applied. The following joint degrees may be earned: J.D./M.A. (Juris Doctor/Master of Arts), J.D./M.A.R. (Juris Doctor/Master of Arts in religion), J.D./M.B.A. (Juris Doctor/Master of Business Administration), J.D./M.D. (Juris Doctor/Doctor of Medicine), J.D./M.Div. (Juris Doctor/Master of Divinity), J.D./M.E.S. (Juris Doctor/Master of Environmental Studies), and J.D./Ph.D. (Juris Doctor/Doctor of Philosophy).

Required

To earn the J.D., candidates must complete 83 total credits, of which 21 are for required courses. The following first-year courses are required of all students: Constitutional Law, Contracts, Procedure, and Torts. Required upper-level courses consist of a supervised analytic writing paper and a substantial paper, Criminal Law and Administration, and Professional Responsibility Legal Ethics. The optional orientation program for first-year students consists of a weekend prior to registration at which life at the law school and in New Haven is discussed.

Electives

The Yale Law School offers concentrations in corporate law, criminal law, entertainment law, environmental law, family law, international law, juvenile law, labor law, litigation, media law, securities law, sports law, tax law, torts and insur-

Phone: 203-432-4995
E-mail: admissions.law@yale.edu
Web: www.law.yale.edu

Contact

Dean of Admissions, 203-432-4995 for general inquiries; Director of Financial Aid, 203-432-1688 for financial aid information.

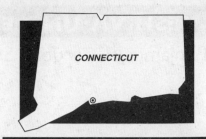

ance, and administrative law, constitutional law, comparative law, legal history, torts, criminal procedure, bankruptcy, law and economics, employment discrimination, property, health, antitrust, evidence, and international business. In addition, clinical opportunities are offered through many clinics including Community and Economic Development, Complex Federal Litigation, and the Allard K. Lowenstein International Human Rights Law Clinic. In addition to the many seminars offered during the fall and spring terms, students may submit proposals for research and legislative drafting seminars. Research programs and independent reading may be undertaken after the first term with faculty permissions. Numerous special lecture series are held annually, including the Timothy B. Atkeson Environmental Practitioner in Residence; the Cover Lecture in Law and Religion; the Ralph Gregory Elliot First Amendment Lecture; the Preiskel/Silverman Program on the Practicing Lawyer and the Public Interest; and the Robert L. Bernstein Lecture in International Human Rights. In the second term, students may begin participation in programs managed primarily by students under the supervision of a faculty adviser. These include the Capital Defense Project, the Domestic Violence Temporary Restraining Order Project, the Greenhaven Prison Project, Street Law, Thomas Swan Barristers' Union, Morris Tyler Moot Court of Appeals, and numerous reviews and journals.

Graduation Requirements

In order to graduate, candidates must have completed the upper-division writing requirement.

Organizations

Student-edited publications include the *Yale Law Journal, Yale Journal of International Law, Yale Journal of Law and Feminism, Yale Journal of Law and Humanities, Yale Journal on Regulation, Yale Human Rights and Development Law Journal, Yale Law and Policy Review*, and *Yale Journal of Health Policy, Law, and Ethics*. Moot court competitions include the Thurman Arnold Appellate Competition Prize, the Benjamin N. Cardozo Prize, and the John Fletcher Caskey prize. Other competitions or prizes include the Albom, Brody, Burkan Memorial, Cohen, Connecticut Attorneys'

Title Insurance Company, Cullen, Egger, Emerson, Gherini, Gruter, Jewell, Khosla, Lemkin, Massey, Miller, Munson, Olin, Parker, Peres, Porter, Robbins Memorial, Scharps, Townsend, Wang, and Wayland. Law student organizations include the Asia Law Forum, the Initiative for Public Interest Law at Yale, and the Yale Law and Technology Society. There are local chapters of the Black Law Students Association, the Federalist Society, and the American Constitution Society.

Library

The law library contains 874,393 hardcopy volumes and 40,781 microform volume equivalents, and subscribes to 11,267 serial publications. Such on-line databases and networks as CALI, CIS Universe, DIALOG, Dow-Jones, Infotrac, Legal-Trac, LEXIS, LOIS, Mathew Bender, NEXIS, OCLC First Search, RLIN, WESTLAW, Wilsonline Indexes, and ORBIS (Yale University catalog), MORRIS (Yale Law School catalog) are available to law students for research. Special library collections include a 200,000-volume foreign and international law collection and a rare book collection of 20,000 volumes. Recently, the library underwent a major renovation as part of a comprehensive, $90 million renovation of the Sterling Law Building. The ratio of library volumes to faculty is 13,051 to 1 and to students is 1410 to 1. The ratio of seats in the library to students is 1 to 2.

Faculty

The law school has 67 full-time and 42 part-time faculty members, of whom 27 are women. According to AAUP standards for Category I institutions, faculty salaries are well above average. The ratio of full-time students to full-time faculty in an average class is 8 to 1. The law school has a regular program of bringing visiting professors and other distinguished lecturers and visitors to campus.

Students

About 48% of the student body are women; 35%, minorities; 8%, African American; 18%, Asian American; 8%, Hispanic; and 5%, unknown/unreported. The majority of students come from foreign countries (4%). The average age of entering students is 25.

Placement

J.D.s awarded:	188
Services available through: a separate law school placement center	
Services: judicial clerkship counseling and programs, public interest counseling and programs, career counseling, publications, recruiting events, resource library	
Special features: a professional counseling staff, comprehensive individual career counseling, a program resource library, publications, and recruiting events..	
Full-time job interviews:	n/av
Summer job interviews:	n/av
Placement by graduation:	97% of class
Placement within 9 months:	97% of class
Average starting salary:	$30,000 to $160,000
Areas of placement:	
Private practice 2-10 attorneys	42%
Judicial clerkships	42%
Public interest	7%
Business/industry	4%
Academic	3%
Government	2%

Benjamin N. Cardozo School of Law

55 Fifth Avenue
New York, NY 10003

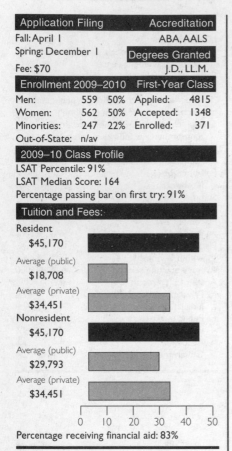

Application Filing	Accreditation
Fall: April 1	ABA, AALS
Spring: December 1	**Degrees Granted**
Fee: $70	J.D., LL.M.

Enrollment 2009–2010		First-Year Class	
Men:	559 50%	Applied:	4815
Women:	562 50%	Accepted:	1348
Minorities:	247 22%	Enrolled:	371
Out-of-State:	n/av		

2009–10 Class Profile
LSAT Percentile: 91%
LSAT Median Score: 164
Percentage passing bar on first try: 91%

Tuition and Fees:

Resident
$45,170

Average (public)
$18,708

Average (private)
$34,451

Nonresident
$45,170

Average (public)
$29,793

Average (private)
$34,451

0 10 20 30 40 50

Percentage receiving financial aid: 83%

ADMISSIONS

In the fall 2009 first-year class, 4815 applied, 1348 were accepted, and 371 enrolled. Fifty-one transfers enrolled. The median LSAT percentile of the most recent first-year class was 91; the median GPA was 3.52 on a scale of 4.0.

Requirements
Applicants must have a bachelor's degree and take the LSAT. The most important admission factors include academic achievement, LSAT results, and general background. No specific undergraduate courses are required. Candidates are not interviewed.

Procedure
The application deadline for fall entry is April 1. Applicants should submit an application form, LSAT results, transcripts, a personal statement, a nonrefundable application fee of $70, and 2 letters of recommendation. A resumé is also recommended. Notification of the admissions decision is on a rolling basis.

The latest acceptable LSAT test date for fall entry is February. The law school uses the LSDAS.

Special
The law school recruits minority and disadvantaged students by means of special mailings, attendance at law fairs and receptions, a brochure designed for minority applicants, and an on-campus visitation program. Requirements are not different for out-of-state students. Transfer students must have 1 year of credit and have attended an ABA-approved law school most of the emphasis in the admissions decision is placed on first-year performance.

Costs

Tuition and fees for the 2009-2010 academic year are $45,170 for all full-time students. On-campus room and board costs about $18,400 annually; books and supplies run $5971.

Financial Aid

About 83% of current law students receive some form of aid. The average annual amount of aid from all sources combined, including scholarships, loans, and work contracts, is $51,233; maximum, $69,541. Awards are based on need and merit. Required financial statements are the FAFSA and Need Access. The aid application deadline for fall entry is April 15. Special funds for minority or disadvantaged students are available. First-year students are notified about their financial aid application at time of acceptance.

About the Law School

Yeshiva University Benjamin N. Cardozo School of Law was established in 1976 and is a private institution. The campus is in an urban area in the heart of Greenwich Village in lower Manhattan. The primary mission of the law school is to enhance the student's understanding of the legal profession and of the ethical dilemmas and professional responsibilities for a lawyer in today's society. Students have access to federal, state, county, city, and local agencies, courts, correctional facilities, law firms, and legal aid organizations in the New York area. Students benefit from the school's proximity to city, state, and federal offices. Organizations within proximity of the law school include the New

York Stock Exchange, American Stock Exchange, the United Nations, and New York's many cultural institutions. Housing for students is available in a residence hall, which is located 1 block from the law school. The Admissions Office maintains apartment listings and circulates a roommate newsletter. All law school facilities are accessible to the physically disabled.

Calendar

The law school operates on a traditional semester basis. Courses for full-time students are offered days only and must be completed within 5 years. For part-time students, courses are offered days only and must be completed within 5 years. New full-time students are admitted in the fall and spring; part-time, summer. There is a 13-week summer session. Transferable summer courses are not offered.

Programs

In addition to the J.D., the law school offers the LL.M. Students may take relevant courses in other programs and apply credit toward the J.D.; a maximum of 2 credits may be applied. The following joint degrees may be earned: J.D./M.S.W (Juris Doctor/Master of Social Work).

Required
To earn the J.D., candidates must complete 84 total credits, of which 55 are for required courses. They must maintain a minimum GPA of 2.4 in the required courses. The following first-year courses are required of all students: Civil Procedure, Constitutional Law, Contracts, Criminal Law, Elements of the Law, Legal Writing I and II, Property, and Torts. Required upper-level courses consist of Advanced Legal Research, distribution requirements, Professional Responsibility, and upper-level writing requirement. The required orientation program for first-year students is held over 3 days and includes programs to introduce students to Cardozo and the legal profession as well as social gatherings.

Electives
Students must take 5 courses credits in their area of concentration. The Benjamin N. Cardozo School of Law offers concentrations in corporate law, criminal law, entertainment law, family law, intellectual property law, international law, litiga-

Phone: 212-790-0274
Fax: 212-790-0482
E-mail: *lawinfo@yu.edu*
Web: *www.cardozo.yu.edu/*

Contact

David G. Martinidez, Associate Dean, 212-790-0274 for general inquiries; Kahryn Tuman, Director of Student Finance, 212-790-0392 for financial aid information.

NEW YORK

tion, media law, tax law, communications law, commercial law, constitutional law and rights, property and real estate, and dispute resolution. Clinics, open to second- and third-year students, include the Innocence Project (4 credits per semester), Mediation Clinic (4 credits per semester), and Human Rights and Genocide Clinic (4 credits for one semester only). Special courses and seminars are offered in human rights and children, intellectual property and globalization, and multicultural dispute resolution. A wide variety of internships and externships is offered during the academic year including a full-time internship with the Manhattan District Attorney's Office. Research assistants are hired by professors. Students also have the option to conduct their own research under the supervision of a faculty member. Field work opportunities include the Alexander Fellows Program. Cardozo hosts numerous lectures including the Uri and Caroline Bauer Memorial Lecture, the Jacob Burns Institute for Advanced Legal Studies, and the Distinguished Lecture in Intellectual Property Law. Cardozo offers summer programs at Oxford in Comparative Corporate Governance and Mediation and Democratic Dialogue in Budapest. Cardozo students also have the opportunity to spend a semester in Hamburg, Germany; Budapest, Hungary; Tel Aviv, Israel; Amsterdam the Netherlands; Hong Kong; and Bilbao, Spain. Cardozo also offers short-term intensive programs abroad scheduled during winter breaks. Seminars in 2008-2009 were held in Japan, Rwanda, India, and China. Minority programs include activities of the Minority Law Student Association, and Outlaw. Panels and outside speakers are sponsored by such institutes as the Howard M. Squadron Program in Law, Media, and Society, the Samuel and Ronnie Heyman Center on Corporate Governance, the Kukin Program for Conflict Resolution, the Floersheimer Center for Constitutional Democracy, Cardozo Center for Public Service Law, and the Program in Family Law, Policy, and Bioethics. The most widely taken elective subjects are copyright, corporations, and evidence.

Graduation Requirements

In order to graduate, candidates must have a GPA of 2.4, completed the upper-division writing requirement, ompleted the Advanced Legal Research and Professional Responsibility courses, and fulfilled distribution requirements.

Organizations

Students edit the *Cardozo Law Review, Arts and Entertainment Law Journal, Cardozo Journal of Law and Gender, Cardozo Journal of International and Comparative Law, Cardozo Journal of Conflict Resolution, The Cardozo Public Law, Policy, and Ethics Journal, Law and Literature, New York Real Estate Reports*, and the newspaper *The Cardozo Dispatch*. Cardozo students compete in numerous moot court competitions including the Peperdine University School of Law National Entertainment and Law Moot Court Competition, the Appellate Lawyers Association Moot Court Competition, and the Wechler First Amendment Moot Court Competition at American University. Cardozo's Moot Court Honor Society hosts the national Cardozol BMI Entertainment and Communications Law Moot Court Competition and the Monrad G. Paulsen Intramural Moot Court Competition. Law student organizations, local chapters of national associations, and campus organizations include the Intellectual Property Law Society Public Interest Law Students Association, the Federalist Society, Minority Law Students Alliance, Cardozo Women Law Students Associations, and Outlaw.

Library

The law library contains 560,325 hardcopy volumes and 1,338,310 microform volume equivalents, and subscribes to 7989 serial publications. Such on-line databases and networks as CALI, Legal-Trac, LEXIS, NEXIS, OCLC First Search, WESTLAW, Wilsonline Indexes, Hein Online, BNA All Library, Index to Foreign Legal Periodicals, Legal Scholarship Network, LLMC Digital, Cambridge Journals Online, JSTOR, LEXIS NEXIS Congressional Research Digital Collection, CIAO, Leadership Directories Online, Intelliconnect, MDML, and ECCO are available to law students for research. Special library collections include the Louis and Ida Shlansky Family Foundation Library of Jewish and Israeli Law and U.S. government depository. The ratio of library volumes to faculty is 9830 to 1 and to students is 500 to 1. The ratio of seats in the library to students is 1 to 2.

Faculty

The law school has 57 full-time and 76 part-time faculty members, of whom 45 are women. According to AAUP standards

Placement

J.D.s awarded:	354

Services available through: a separate law school placement center

Services: The Career Services Office offers access to a national job database computerized databases for student and alumni use and on-line registration system for on-campus recruitment.

Special features: six full-time counselors provide comprehensive advice on interviewing and résumé writing. Career Services coordinates a myriad of programs including the Practice Area Symposium during which students learn about different areas of law, the Mentor/Mentee Program through which students are paired with alumni mentors, and the Public Sector Law Expo, which provides information about summer public sector opportunities.

Full-time job interviews:	41 employers
Summer job interviews:	122 employers
Placement by graduation:	75% of class
Placement within 9 months:	94% of class
Average starting salary:	$35,000 to $160,000

Areas of placement:

Private practice 2-10 attorneys	19%
Private practice 11-25 attorneys	10%
Private practice 26-50 attorneys	7%
Private practice 51-100 attorneys	7%
Private practice 101-500+ attorneys	58%
Business/industry	19%
Public interest	10%
Government	8%
Judicial clerkships	5%

for Category I institutions, faculty salaries are above average. About 16% of full-time faculty have a graduate law degree in addition to the J.D. The ratio of full-time students to full-time faculty in an average class is 16 to 1; in a clinic, 16 to 1. The law school has a regular program of bringing visiting professors and other distinguished lecturers and visitors to campus. There is a chapter of the Order of the Coif; 11 faculty and 476 graduates are members.

Students

About 50% of the student body are women; 22%, minorities; 5%, African American; 9%, Asian American; 6%, Hispanic; and 34%, race/ethnicity unknown. The average age of entering students is 24; age range is 20 to 46. About 36% of students enter directly from undergraduate school, 11% have a graduate degree, and 51% have worked full-time prior to entering law school. About 3% drop out after the first year for academic or personal reasons; 97% remain to receive a law degree.

CHAPTER 16

Law Schools Not Approved by the ABA

AN OVERVIEW

Although the vast majority of law school students attend institutions approved by the American Bar Association, a distinct minority attend schools that have not received ABA accreditation. Applicants frequently wonder whether it will make a difference if they attend a nonapproved school. The answer to this question requires an understanding of what it means for a law school to be accredited.

For nearly a century, the American Bar Association has developed educational standards for law schools, reviewed institutional adherence to those standards, and approved law schools that complied with the standards. The standards themselves have evolved out of the crucible of experience with input from legal educators, practitioners, and judges. The standards, while sometimes mystifying to those who do not understand legal education, represent well-reasoned statements of policy aimed at assuring that individuals who enter the practice of law undertake a rigorous curriculum in an intellectually demanding setting. Over the years the ABA approval process has established and maintained a basic set of standards for entry into the practice of law that is accepted by bar licensing authorities, practitioners, and the courts.

Recognizing the value of the accreditation process in upholding the quality of legal education and ultimately the legal profession, most states require candidates for the bar examination to have graduated from an ABA-approved law school. Some other states certify graduates of law schools located in the state but not approved by the ABA to sit for the bar exam in that state. It is virtually impossible for graduates of a nonapproved law school to take the bar outside the state where they attended law school.

The non-ABA schools generally fall into three groups: new schools seeking ABA approval, state-approved schools, and unapproved schools. New law schools seeking ABA accreditation must go through an initial review and provisional accreditation before becoming fully approved. During this period of several years the school undergoes strict scrutiny, and students who enroll run the risk that the institution may never meet ABA standards. In recent years, more than a few such schools have dissolved when they could not secure ABA approval. If this happens, students may lose all their law school credits, and, worse, find that they cannot take a bar examination anywhere. On the other hand, if the school gains ABA approval, the risk will turn out to have been worthwhile.

The differences between state-approved and unapproved schools may seem murky. In most states where graduates of non-ABA schools can take the bar, there are only one or two non-ABA schools. Whether these schools are accredited by a state accrediting agency or whether the graduates simply are certified by the bar examiners is probably immaterial to most students. In California, however, the distinction does have ramifications. Significantly, that state has the largest number of lawyers as well as the largest number of non-ABA schools. In California, the state approves law schools using a procedure similar to but different from the ABA. State-approved law schools are treated within the state much like ABA schools; outside California the graduates of these schools usually will be considered like graduates of any other non-ABA approved school. Schools in California that have not been approved by either the state or the ABA represent a separate group within that state, and graduates face additional restrictions on (but not prohibition from) bar admission.

Why would you choose to attend a non-ABA law school? The most common reason might be that you do not gain admission to an ABA school. There is definitely a pecking order among law schools from elite schools like Harvard or Yale down to the unapproved schools. Generally, the more prestigious the law school, the more competitive it will be, and, conversely, the lower the school's perceived ranking, the less stringent will be the admission standards. Legal educators frequently warn prelaw students to beware of law school rankings because they often are based on reputations decades old rather than the current state of legal education at the schools. Rankings also overlook distinctions among schools that make different schools the best choice for different students. In this sense you should evaluate the quality of education at an unapproved school the same way you would evaluate an approved school. The point here is that some students whose traditional qualifications (such as undergraduate GPA and LSAT percentile) will not get them into an approved school may be able to secure a seat at an unapproved one. Some candidates may decide not to attend law school at all if they are not accepted at an ABA school; others may want a law degree so much that they select one of the non-ABA institutions.

A second reason that some students give for attending an unapproved school is cost. Because they are not bound by ABA requirements, non-ABA schools frequently rely heavily on part-time instructors, who cost less than full-time professors. In addition, non-ABA schools may provide more spartan facilities (the library, for example). This bargain basement approach to education can mean tuition savings for students.

Those considering attending an unapproved law school should consider also the educational experience they will receive. Since many such schools provide a bare bones education, applicants should scrutinize the academic program of the school at least as carefully as they would that of an ABA-approved school. While many non-ABA schools have existed for many years and maintain sound local reputations, other schools have less than solid foundations.

A final consideration that anyone contemplating attending a non-ABA-approved law school should address involves the career opportunities available to graduates. Not only is the bar passage rate lower at some non-ABA schools, thereby limiting career opportunities, but also the placement patterns of the graduates may be significantly different. The bottom line is that anyone considering law school should carefully investigate and research all aspects of each potential school before applying.

PROFILES OF SELECTED LAW SCHOOLS

Brief profiles of selected law schools not approved by the ABA appear on the following pages. The pros and cons of such law schools are discussed above. Only schools responding to our request for current information are included here.

Each profile begins with the name of the law school, its address and phone and fax numbers, and e-mail and Web addresses if provided. The capsule of basic information about the law school presents the following information.

Application Filing Fall and spring application deadlines and the application fee are given.

Accreditation Any professional accreditation is noted. (See **Abbreviations and Degrees** on page v).

Degrees Granted Degrees are nearly always limited to the J.D.

Enrollment Enrollment breakdowns for 2009–2010 include men, women, minorities, and out-of-state students.

First-Year Class The applied, accepted, and enrolled figures refer to the number of students applying for the 2009–2010 entering class.

Class Profile This section includes the median LSAT percentile and the median LSAT score of freshmen in the 2009–2010 entering class, as well as the percentage of a recent graduating class that passed the bar on the first attempt.

Tuition and Fees Tuition and Fees figures given here are annual amounts, unless otherwise indicated. Because tuition charges change periodically, it is important to check with the school for current figures. This section also features the percentage of current students receiving financial aid.

Contact The person or position to whom inquiries should be directed is given, along with appropriate phone numbers.

AMERICAN COLLEGE OF LAW

3745 W. Chapman Avenue, #250
Orange, CA 92868

Phone: 714-772-9000
Fax: 714-634-3330
E-mail: americalaw@aclaw.com
Web: www.aclaw.com

Application Filing		Accreditation
Fall: August 30		no
Spring: January 20	**Degrees Granted**	
Fee: $25		J.D.

Enrollment 2009–2010			First-Year Class	
Men:	51	58%	Applied:	32
Women:	37	42%	Accepted:	24
Minorities:	62	70%	Enrolled:	24
Out-of-State:	9	10%		

2009–10 Class Profile
LSAT Percentile: 67%
LSAT Median Score: n/av
Percentage passing bar on first try: 22%

Tuition and Fees:

Resident
$400 (P/T) (PER CREDIT)

Average (public)
$18,708

Average (private)
$34,451

Nonresident
$400 (P/T) (PER CREDIT)

Average (public)
$29,793

Average (private)
$34,451

0 10 20 30 40 50
Percentage receiving financial aid: 80%

Contact
Waleed Akleh, Dean, 714-772-9000 for general inquiries; Waleed Akleh, Dean, 714-772-9000 for financial aid information.

HUMPHREYS COLLEGE

Laurence Drivon School of Law

6650 Inglewood
Stockton, CA 95207

Phone: 209-478-0800 ext. 5
Fax: 209-235-2889
E-mail: lawadmission@humphreys.edu
Web: www.humphreys.edu

Application Filing		Accreditation
Fall: July 1		no
Spring: n/app	**Degrees Granted**	
Fee: $35		J.D.

Enrollment 2009–2010			First-Year Class	
Men:	33	38%	Applied:	83
Women:	53	62%	Accepted:	41
Minorities:	20	23%	Enrolled:	29
Out-of-State:	0	0%		

2009–10 Class Profile
LSAT Percentile: 27%
LSAT Median Score: 145
Percentage passing bar on first try: 50%

Tuition and Fees:

Resident
$8,937 (P/T)

Average (public)
$18,708

Average (private)
$34,451

Nonresident
$8,937 (P/T)

Average (public)
$29,793

Average (private)
$34,451

0 10 20 30 40 50
Percentage receiving financial aid: 81%

Contact
Santa Lopez, Admissions Officer, 209-478-0800 for general inquiries; Judi Johnstone, 209-478-0800, ext. 3 for financial aid information.

LINCOLN LAW SCHOOL OF SACRAMENTO

3140 J Street
Sacramento, CA 95816

Phone: 916-446-1275
Fax: 916-446-5641
E-mail: info@lincolnlaw.edu
Web: www.lincolnlaw.edu

Application Filing		Accreditation
Fall: June 15		no
Spring: November 15	**Degrees Granted**	
Fee: $50		J.D.

Enrollment 2009–2010			First-Year Class	
Men:	115	48%	Applied:	140
Women:	125	52%	Accepted:	102
Minorities:	77	32%	Enrolled:	98
Out-of-State:	n/av			

2009–10 Class Profile
LSAT Percentile: 35%
LSAT Median Score: 148
Percentage passing bar on first try: 46%

Tuition and Fees:

Resident
$8,560 (P/T)

Average (public)
$18,708

Average (private)
$34,451

Nonresident
$8,560 (P/T)

Average (public)
$29,793

Average (private)
$34,451

0 10 20 30 40 50
Percentage receiving financial aid: n/av

Contact
Angelia Harlow, Registrar, 916-446-1275 for general inquiries; Melissa Fuller, Assistant Registrar, 916-446-1275 for financial aid information.

500 Federal Street
Andover, MA 01810

Phone: 978-681-0800
Fax: 978-681-6330
E-mail: pcolby@mslaw.edu
Web: www.mslaw.edu

Application Filing	Accreditation
Fall: July 30	AALS
Spring: January I	Degrees Granted
Fee: $40	J.D.

Enrollment 2009–2010		First-Year Class	
Men:	350 5%	Applied:	431
Women:	350 50%	Accepted:	328
Minorities:	175 25%	Enrolled:	260
Out-of-State:	140 20%		

2009–10 Class Profile

LSAT Percentile: n/av
LSAT Median Score: n/av
Percentage passing bar on first try: 65%

Tuition and Fees:

Resident
$15,240

Average (public)
$18,708

Average (private)
$34,451

Nonresident
$15,240

Average (public)
$29,793

Average (private)
$34,451

0 10 20 30 40 50
Percentage receiving financial aid: 70%

Contact
Director of Admissions, 978-681-0800 for general inquiries; Director of Financial Aid, 978-681-0800 for financial aid information.

---

100 Col. Durham Street
Seaside, CA 93955

Phone: 831-582-4000
Fax: 831-582-4095
E-mail: wlariviere@montereylaw.edu
Web: www.montereylaw.edu

Application Filing	Accreditation
Fall: May I	no
Spring: n/app	Degrees Granted
Fee: $75	J.D., M.L.S.

Enrollment 2009–2010		First-Year Class	
Men:	50 45%	Applied:	115
Women:	60 55%	Accepted:	50
Minorities:	41 37%	Enrolled:	36
Out-of-State:	4 5%		

2009–10 Class Profile

LSAT Percentile: 47%
LSAT Median Score: n/av
Percentage passing bar on first try: 37%

Tuition and Fees:

Resident
$600 (P/T) (per credit)

Average (public)
$18,708

Average (private)
$34,451

Nonresident
$600 (P/T) (per credit)

Average (public)
$29,793

Average (private)
$34,451

0 10 20 30 40 50
Percentage receiving financial aid: 30%

Contact
Wendy LaRiviere, Dean of Admissions and Placement, 831-582-4000 for general inquiries for financial aid information.

School of Law

50 Fell Street
San Francisco, CA 94102

Phone: (415) 241-1314
Fax: (415) 241-1353
E-mail: lawadmissions@newcollege.edu
Web: www.newcollege.edu

Application Filing	Accreditation
Fall: May I	no
Spring: n/app	Degrees Granted
Fee: $55	J.D.

Enrollment 2009–2010		First-Year Class	
Men:	107 54%	Applied:	200
Women:	93 50%	Accepted:	52
Minorities:	140 70%	Enrolled:	50
Out-of-State:	200 100%		

2009–10 Class Profile

LSAT Percentile: 20%
LSAT Median Score: 142
Percentage passing bar on first try: 33%

Tuition and Fees:

Resident
$12,756 (F/T)

Average (public)
$18,708

Average (private)
$34,451

Nonresident
$12,756 (F/T)

Average (public)
$29,793

Average (private)
$34,451

0 10 20 30 40 50
Percentage receiving financial aid: 89%

Contact
Assistant Dean, 415-241-1374 for general inquiries; 415-437-3442, for financial aid information.

SAN FRANCISCO LAW SCHOOL

20 Haight Street
San Francisco, CA 94102

Phone: 415-626-5550, ext.123
Fax: 415-626-5584
E-mail: admin@sfls.edu
Web: www.sfls.edu

Application Filing	Accreditation
Fall: June 15	no
Spring: n/app	Degrees Granted
Fee: $75	J.D.

Enrollment 2009–2010		First-Year Class	
Men:	62 52%	Applied:	82
Women:	58 48%	Accepted:	45
Minorities:	60 50%	Enrolled:	28
Out-of-State:	1 1%		

2009–10 Class Profile
LSAT Percentile: 33%
LSAT Median Score: 147
Percentage passing bar on first try: n/av

Tuition and Fees:
Resident
$5,000 (P/T)

Average (public)
$18,708

Average (private)
$34,451

Nonresident
$5,000 (P/T)

Average (public)
$29,793

Average (private)
$34,451

0 10 20 30 40 50
Percentage receiving financial aid: 40%

Contact
Registrar, 415-626-5550, ext. 123 for general inquiries; Jane Gamp, 415-626-5550, ext. 121 for financial aid information.

SANTA BARBARA AND VENTURA COLLEGES OF LAW

Santa Barbara College of Law

20 East Victoria Street
Santa Barbara, CA 93101

Phone: 805-966-0010
Fax: 805-966-7181
E-mail: admits@venturalaw.edu
Web: www.santabarbaralaw.edu

Application Filing	Accreditation
Fall: n/av	no
Spring: n/app	Degrees Granted
Fee: n/av	J.D., None

Enrollment 2009–2010		First-Year Class	
Men:	45 43%	Applied:	n/av
Women:	60 59%	Accepted:	n/av
Minorities:	17 16%	Enrolled:	n/av
Out-of-State:	0 0%		

2009–10 Class Profile
LSAT Percentile: 40%
LSAT Median Score: 149
Percentage passing bar on first try: 48%

Tuition and Fees:
Resident
$3,500 (P/T)

Average (public)
$18,708

Average (private)
$34,451

Nonresident
$3,500 (P/T)

Average (public)
$29,793

Average (private)
$34,451

0 10 20 30 40 50
Percentage receiving financial aid: n/av

Contact
Director of Admissions, 805-966-0010 ext.18 for general inquiries.

SOUTHERN NEW ENGLAND SCHOOL OF LAW

333 Faunce Corner Road
North Dartmouth, MA 02747

Phone: 508-998-9400
800-213-0060
Fax: 508-998-9561
E-mail: cvidal@snesl.edu
Web: www.snesl.edu

Application Filing	Accreditation
Fall: June 30	no
Spring: n/app	Degrees Granted
Fee: $50	J.D.

Enrollment 2009–2010		First-Year Class	
Men:	104 44%	Applied:	201
Women:	132 57%	Accepted:	174
Minorities:	80 34%	Enrolled:	73
Out-of-State:	219 93%		

2009–10 Class Profile
LSAT Percentile: n/av
LSAT Median Score: 142
Percentage passing bar on first try: 78%

Tuition and Fees:
Resident
$22,175 (F/T)

Average (public)
$18,708

Average (private)
$34,451

Nonresident
$22,175 (F/T)

Average (public)
$29,793

Average (private)
$34,451

0 10 20 30 40 50
Percentage receiving financial aid: 80%

Contact
Carol A. Vidal, Registrar, 508-998-9600 for general inquiries; Sandra Leger Silva, Director of Financial Aid, 508-998-9600, ext. 112 for financial aid information.

TRINITY INTERNATIONAL UNIVERSITY

Trinity Law School

2200 North Grand Avenue
Santa Ana, CA 92705

Phone: 714-796-7100
800-345-4748
Fax: 714-796-7190
E-mail: *tls@tiu.edu*
Web: *www.tiu.edu/law/*

Application Filing	Accreditation
Fall: May 1	no
Spring: December 1	Degrees Granted
Fee: $35	J.D.

Enrollment 2009–2010			First-Year Class	
Men:	67	49%	Applied:	160
Women:	70	51%	Accepted:	80
Minorities:	75	55%	Enrolled:	45
Out-of-State:	1	1%		

2009–10 Class Profile
LSAT Percentile: 37%
LSAT Median Score: 147
Percentage passing bar on first try: n/av

Tuition and Fees:

Resident
$8,700 (F/T)

Average (public)
$18,708

Average (private)
$34,451

Nonresident
$8,700 (F/T)

Average (public)
$29,793

Average (private)
$34,451

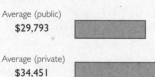

```
0    10    20    30    40    50
```
Percentage receiving financial aid: 78%

Contact
Admissions Office, 800 922-4748 or 714 796-7100 for general inquiries; Mike Peterson, 714-796-7120 for financial aid information.

UNIVERSITY OF NORTHERN CALIFORNIA

Lorenzo Patino School of Law

1012 J Street
Sacramento, CA 95814

Phone: (916) 441-4485
Fax: (916) 441-0175

Application Filing	Accreditation
Fall: n/av	no
Spring: n/app	Degrees Granted
Fee: n/av	J.D.

Enrollment 2009–2010			First-Year Class	
Men:	23	38%	Applied:	78
Women:	37		Accepted:	75
Minorities:	n/av		Enrolled:	75
Out-of-State:	60	100%		

2009–10 Class Profile
LSAT Percentile: n/av
LSAT Median Score: n/av
Percentage passing bar on first try: n/av

Tuition and Fees:

Resident
$1,875 (F/T)

Average (public)
$18,708

Average (private)
$34,451

Nonresident
$1,875 (F/T)

Average (public)
$29,793

Average (private)
$34,451

```
0    10    20    30    40    50
```
Percentage receiving financial aid: n/av

Contact
Registrar's Office, (916) 441-4485 for general inquiries.

UNIVERSITY OF WEST LOS ANGELES

School of Law

9920 S. LaCienega Blvd. #404
Inglewood, CA 90301-2902

Phone: 310-342-5210
Fax: 310-342-5295
E-mail: *tsmith@uwla.edu*
Web: *uwla.edu*

Application Filing	Accreditation
Fall: open	no
Spring: n/app	Degrees Granted
Fee: $55	J.D., n/a

Enrollment 2009–2010			First-Year Class	
Men:	126	49%	Applied:	217
Women:	133	51%	Accepted:	118
Minorities:	78	30%	Enrolled:	104
Out-of-State:	n/av			

2009–10 Class Profile
LSAT Percentile: 31%
LSAT Median Score: 150
Percentage passing bar on first try: 25%

Tuition and Fees:

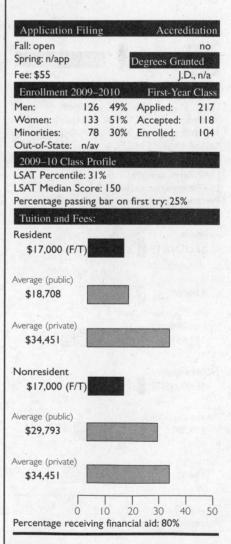

Resident
$17,000 (F/T)

Average (public)
$18,708

Average (private)
$34,451

Nonresident
$17,000 (F/T)

Average (public)
$29,793

Average (private)
$34,451

```
0    10    20    30    40    50
```
Percentage receiving financial aid: 80%

Contact
Associate Dean, 310-342-5210 for general inquiries; Danielle Reeves, Financial Administrator, 310-342-5268 for financial aid information.

WILLIAM HOWARD TAFT UNIVERSITY

3700 S. Susan Street
Santa Ana, CA 92704

Phone: (714) 850-4800
800-882-4555
Fax: (714) 708-2082
E-mail: *admissions@taftu.edu*
Web: *taftu.edu*

Application Filing	Accreditation
Fall: n/av	no
Spring: n/app	**Degrees Granted**
Fee: n/av	J.D., LL.M.

Enrollment 2009–2010			First-Year Class	
Men:	150	63%	Applied:	n/av
Women:	90	37%	Accepted:	n/av
Minorities:	82	34%	Enrolled:	n/av
Out-of-State:	144	60%		

2009–10 Class Profile
LSAT Percentile: n/av
LSAT Median Score: n/av
Percentage passing bar on first try: 50%

Tuition and Fees:

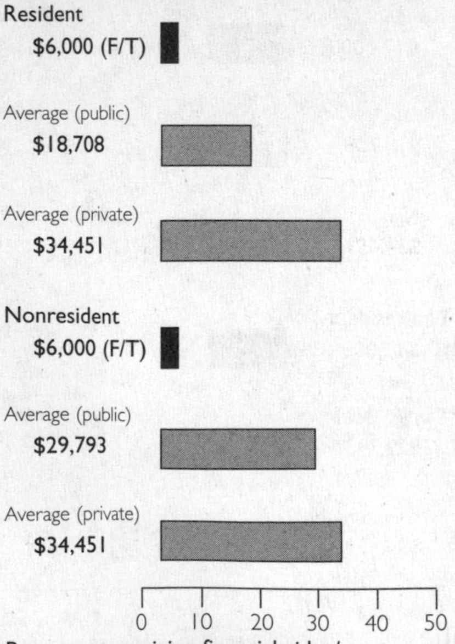

Resident
$6,000 (F/T)

Average (public)
$18,708

Average (private)
$34,451

Nonresident
$6,000 (F/T)

Average (public)
$29,793

Average (private)
$34,451

0   10   20   30   40   50

Percentage receiving financial aid: n/av

Contact
Director of Student Services, 714-850-4800 or 800-882-4555 for general inquiries; Tina Saxon, Financial Director, 800-882-4555 for financial aid information.

INDEX

Entries set in roman type are law schools approved by the American Bar Association.
Entries set in italic type are law schools not approved by the American Bar Association.